XHTML
Black Book

Steven Holzner

President and CEO *Keith Weiskamp*	**XHTML Black Book** © 2000 The Coriolis Group. All rights reserved.
Publisher *Steve Sayre*	This book may not be duplicated in any way without the express written consent of the publisher, except in the form of brief excerpts or quotations for the purposes of review. The information contained herein is for the personal use of the reader and may not be incorporated in any commercial programs, other books, databases, or any kind of software without written consent of the publisher. Making copies of this book or any portion for any purpose other than your own is a violation of United States copyright laws.
Acquisitions Editor *Charlotte Carpentier*	**Limits of Liability and Disclaimer of Warranty** The author and publisher of this book have used their best efforts in preparing the book and the programs contained in it. These efforts include the development, research, and testing of the theories and programs to determine their effectiveness. The author and publisher make no warranty of any kind, expressed or implied, with regard to these programs or the documentation contained in this book.
Marketing Specialist *Tracy Schofield*	
Project Editor *Dan Young*	The author and publisher shall not be liable in the event of incidental or consequential damages in connection with, or arising out of, the furnishing, performance, or use of the programs, associated instructions, and/or claims of productivity gains.
Technical Reviewer *Scott Duffy*	**Trademarks** Trademarked names appear throughout this book. Rather than list the names and entities that own the trademarks or insert a trademark symbol with each mention of the trademarked name, the publisher states that it is using the names for editorial purposes only and to the benefit of the trademark owner, with no intention of infringing upon that trademark.
Production Coordinator *Meg E. Turecek*	The Coriolis Group, LLC 14455 N. Hayden Road Suite 220 Scottsdale, Arizona 85260
Cover Designer *Jody Winkler*	(480) 483-0192 FAX (480) 483-0193 www.coriolis.com

Layout Designer
April Nielsen
	Library of Congress Cataloging-in-Publication Data
	Holzner, Steven.
	   XHTML black book / by Steven Holzner.
	      p. cm.
	   ISBN 1-57610-760-4
	   1. XHTML (Document markup language). I. Title.

CD-ROM Developer *Michelle McConnell*	QA76.76.H94 H65 2000 005.7'2--dc21 00-058995 CIP

Printed in the United States of America
10 9 8 7 6 5 4 3 2 1

The Coriolis Group, LLC • 14455 North Hayden Road, Suite 220 • Scottsdale, Arizona 85260

Dear Reader:

Coriolis Technology Press was founded to create a very elite group of books: the ones you keep closest to your machine. Sure, everyone would like to have the Library of Congress at arm's reach, but in the real world, you have to choose the books you rely on every day *very* carefully.

To win a place for our books on that coveted shelf beside your PC, we guarantee several important qualities in every book we publish. These qualities are:

- *Technical accuracy*—It's no good if it doesn't work. Every Coriolis Technology Press book is reviewed by technical experts in the topic field, and is sent through several editing and proofreading passes in order to create the piece of work you now hold in your hands.

- *Innovative editorial design*—We've put years of research and refinement into the ways we present information in our books. Our books' editorial approach is uniquely designed to reflect the way people learn new technologies and search for solutions to technology problems.

- *Practical focus*—We put only pertinent information into our books and avoid any fluff. Every fact included between these two covers must serve the mission of the book as a whole.

- *Accessibility*—The information in a book is worthless unless you can find it quickly when you need it. We put a lot of effort into our indexes, and heavily cross-reference our chapters, to make it easy for you to move right to the information you need.

Here at The Coriolis Group we have been publishing and packaging books, technical journals, and training materials since 1989. We're programmers and authors ourselves, and we take an ongoing active role in defining what we publish and how we publish it. We have put a lot of thought into our books; please write to us at **ctp@coriolis.com** and let us know what you think. We hope that you're happy with the book in your hands, and that in the future, when you reach for software development and networking information, you'll turn to one of our books first.

Keith Weiskamp
President and CEO

Jeff Duntemann
VP and Editorial Director

Look for these related books from The Coriolis Group:

Active Server Pages Solutions
By Al Williams, Kim Barber, Paul Newkirk

HTML Black Book
By Steven Holzner

Java Black Book
By Steven Holzner

XML Black Book
By Natanya Pitts-Moultis and Cheryl Kirk

Also recently published by Coriolis Technology Press:

Exchange 2000 Server Black Book
By Marcus Goncalves

Windows 2000 TCP/IP Black Book
By Ian McLean

Windows 2000 System Administrator's Black Book
By Stu Sjouwerman, Barry Shilmover, and James Michael Stewart

Windows 2000 Registry Little Black Book
By Nathan Wallace

Windows 2000 Security Little Black Book
By Ian McLean

Windows 2000 Professional Upgrade Little Black Book
By Nathan Wallace

To Nancy,
for more reasons than there are numbers to count.

About the Author

This is the 61st book written by **Steven Holzner**. His books have sold well over one million copies, and they have been translated into 16 languages. A former *PC Magazine* contributing editor, he is a graduate of MIT and earned his Ph.D. at Cornell University. He has been on the faculty at both universities.

He and Nancy travel extensively and spend time at their homes near Tanglewood, Massachusetts, in the Austrian Alps, and in a small, picturesque New England coastal town.

Acknowledgments

This book was exceptionally fortunate in having an outstanding team working on it. First, I'd like to thank the technical reviewer, Scott Duffy, for his microscopic attention to detail—very much appreciated. You did a great, conscientious job; thanks for your hard work and long hours. And the same to the project editor, Dan Young, who did a terrific job, also working long hours and with a great deal of dedication. Dan, I appreciate the work you put in and all your on-target comments.

Also, I'd like to thank Charlotte Carpentier, acquisitions editor, for her attentiveness and hard work; Meg E. Turecek, the production coordinator who kept things on track with good grace; Michelle McConnell, the CD-ROM developer, who jumped in with both feet and produced the CD-ROM; Rachel Anderson, the eagle-eyed proofreader; Caroline Parks, the accomplished indexer; April Nielsen, who designed the interior; and Jody Winkler, who designed the cover. Thanks to all: Great job!

—*Steven Holzner*

Contents at a Glance

Chapter 1	Essential XHTML	1
Chapter 2	Working with Text	65
Chapter 3	Arranging Text	139
Chapter 4	Working with Images	207
Chapter 5	Links and Lists	253
Chapter 6	Creating Tables	329
Chapter 7	Working with Frames	405
Chapter 8	Working with Multimedia	455
Chapter 9	Cascading Style Sheets	503
Chapter 10	Essential JavaScript	569
Chapter 11	Putting JavaScript to Work	637
Chapter 12	Creating XHTML Forms and XHTML Controls	693
Chapter 13	Dynamic XHTML: Changing Web Pages on the Fly	771
Chapter 14	Dynamic XHTML: Drag and Drop, Data Binding, and Behaviors	837
Chapter 15	XML and Extending XHTML	903
Chapter 16	Essential Java	971
Chapter 17	Creating Java Applets	1009
Chapter 18	Essential Perl	1059
Chapter 19	CGI Scripting with Perl	1109

Table of Contents

Introduction xxix

Chapter 1
Essential XHTML 1

In Depth
HTML   2
XML   10
XHTML   14
Is It True XHTML?   20
How XHTML Differs from HTML   21
Converting from HTML to XHTML Automatically   24
XHTML in Today's Browsers   26
Creating a Web Page   27
Installing a Web Page   29
Viewing a Web Page   32
Checking Your Web Page   33

Immediate Solutions
<?xml?>—Starting an XML Document   35
<!DOCTYPE>—Specifying a Document's Type   36
<html>—Creating the Document's Root Element   37
Creating the Structure of a Web Page: Head and Body   39
<head>—Creating a Web Page's Head   40
<title>—Giving a Web Page a Title   42
<meta>—Giving More Information about Your Web Page   43
</head>—Ending a Web Page's Head   46
<body>—Creating a Web Page's Body   47
Setting Web Page Colors   53
   Using Predefined Colors   54
   Creating Color Values   57
Adding Text to a Web Page   58
Basic Text Formatting   59
<!-->—Comments and Server Side Includes   60
</body>—Ending a Web Page's Body   64
</html>—Ending a Web Page   64

xi

Chapter 2
Working with Text 65

In Depth
Character Sets in XHTML 67
Formatting with XHTML Elements 69
Physical XHTML Styles 72
Logical XHTML Styles 72
Setting Fonts 76
Headings 76
Some Removed Tags 78

Immediate Solutions
Displaying Plain Text 79
<h1> Through <h6>—Creating Web Page Headings 80
<b>—Creating Bold Text 83
<i>—Creating Italic Text 84
<tt>—Creating "Teletype" Text 85
<u>—Underlining Text 87
<s> and <strike>—Striking Text Out 89
<big>—Creating Big Text 91
<small>—Creating Small Text 93
<sub>—Creating Subscripts 94
<sup>—Creating Superscripts 96
<em>—Emphasizing Text 98
<strong>—Strongly Emphasizing Text 99
<code>—Displaying Program Code 101
<samp>—Displaying Sample Program Output 102
<kbd>—Displaying Text the User is to Type 104
<var>—Displaying Program Variables and Arguments 105
<dfn>—Defining New Terms 106
<cite>—Creating a Citation 108
<abbr>—Displaying Abbreviations 109
<acronym>—Displaying Acronyms 110
<font>—Specifying a Font 111
Setting Font Size in Points 115
<basefont>—Setting the Base Font 116
<q>—Displaying Short Quotations 118
<blink>—Making Text Blink 119
<ins>—Displaying Inserted Text 120
<del>—Displaying Text as Deleted 122
<address>—Displaying an Address 124
<bdo>—Overriding the Bidirectional Character Algorithm 126
Displaying Special Characters: Character Entities 128

Chapter 3
Arranging Text 139

In Depth
Arranging Text   140
Using **<div>** and **<span>**   146
Using Layers   149
More Formatting Power   150
Preformatting Text   150

Immediate Solutions
Avoiding Plain Text Wrapping   153
**
**—Inserting Line Breaks   154
<nobr>—Avoiding Line Breaks   157
<wbr>—Allowing Word Breaks   159
<p>—Creating Paragraphs   160
<hr>—Creating Horizontal Rules   163
<center>—Centering Text   166
<blockquote>—Indenting Quotations   168
<pre>—Displaying Preformatted Text   170
<multicol>—Creating Columns   172
<spacer>—Controlling Horizontal and Vertical Spacing   174
<marquee>—Displaying Text in a Scrolling Marquee   176
<div>—Formatting Block Text   179
<span>—Formatting Inline Text   182
Formatting Text with Tables   184
<layer>—Arranging Text in Layers   193
<nolayer>—Handling Browsers That Don't Handle Layers   196
<ilayer>—Creating Inline Layers   197
  <ilayer>   197
Positioning Text with **<div>**   200
<ruby>, **<rbc>**, **<rtc>**, **<rb>**, **<rt>**, **<rp>**—Creating Ruby (Captioned) Text   201
  <ruby>   202
  <rbc>   203
  <rtc>   203
  <rb>   204
  <rt>   204
  <rp>   205

Chapter 4
Working with Images 207

In Depth
Images in Web Pages   208
Graphics File Formats   212

Graphics Programs and Resources   215
Using Clip Art   216
Graphics Color   216
Creating Images   218

Immediate Solutions

Creating Transparent GIF Images   220
Creating Interlaced GIF Images   221
Creating Animated GIF Images   223
Testing Your Images   224
<img>—Adding an Image to a Web Page   225
Displaying Alternate Text in Place of Images   229
Allocating Space for an Image   231
Adding Borders to Images   232
Adding Space around Images   234
Aligning Text and Images   235
   Vertically Aligning Text   236
   Horizontally Aligning Text   237
Avoiding Text Wrapping   239
Scaling Images to Different Sizes   241
Using the **lowsrc** Attribute for Image Previews   243
Setting Page Background Images   243
Using the <object> Tag to Insert Images   245
Using Images to Replace Missing Content   246
Tiling Images—Creating Image Mosaics   247
Creating Overlapping Images   250

Chapter 5
Links and Lists 253

In Depth

Creating Hyperlinks   255
All about URLs   263
Creating Image Maps   266
Creating Lists   269

Immediate Solutions

<a>—Creating a Hyperlink or Anchor   273
Setting Hyperlink Colors   276
Creating Graphical Hyperlinks   278
<base>—Setting the Base for Hyperlinks   279
<link>—Setting Link Information   281
Giving Hyperlinks Access Keys   284
Using Graphical Hyperlinks for Navigation   285
Creating Navigation Bars   286

Creating Anchors and Linking to Sections in a Page   288
Creating Clickable Footnotes   291
Emailing with Hyperlinks   292
Downloading Files with the HTTP and FTP Protocols   294
<map>—Creating Client-Side Image Maps   295
<area>—Creating Clickable Regions in Image Maps   296
Creating Client-Side Image Maps   299
Creating Server-Side Image Maps   301
Creating Image Maps with the **<object>** Element   305
Creating Combined Client-Side and Server-Side Image Maps   305
Creating Lists   307
<li>—Creating List Items   309
<ul>—Creating Unordered Lists   310
<ol>—Creating Ordered Lists   312
Creating Customized Unordered Lists   314
Creating Customized Ordered Lists   316
<dl>, **<dt>**, and **<dd>**—Creating Definition Lists   319
   <dl>   319
   <dt>   320
   <dd>   321
Nesting Lists   323
<dir> and **<menu>**—Deprecated Lists   325
   <dir>   325
   <menu>   325

Chapter 6
Creating Tables 329

In Depth
The Parts of a Table   330
Creating a Table   331
Adding a Border   334
Padding Your Cells   334
Widening the Cell Spacing   336
Aligning Your Data Horizontally   338
Aligning Your Data Vertically   338
Spanning Columns   340
Spanning Rows   342
Setting Colors   343

Immediate Solutions
<table>—Creating a Table   356
<tr>—Creating a Table Row   358
<th>—Creating Table Headings   360

<td>—Creating Table Data   363
<caption>—Creating a Table Caption   365
Setting Table Border Widths   367
Setting Cell Padding   369
Setting Cell Spacing   369
Setting Table and Column Widths   370
Setting Table Colors   372
Aligning Tables in Web Pages   374
Aligning Cell Text   375
Using Images in Tables   377
Nesting Tables   378
Spanning Multiple Columns   380
Spanning Multiple Rows   380
<colgroup> and <col>—Grouping and Formatting Columns   381
  <colgroup>   381
  <col>   382
  <colgroup>—Creating Column Groups   384
  Customizing Columns in Column Groups   386
<thead>, <tbody>, <tfoot>—Grouping and Formatting Rows   388
  <thead>   388
  <tbody>   389
  <tfoot>   390
  Creating Row Groups   391
  Configuring Row Group Borders   393
Formatting Text with Tables   396

Chapter 7
Working with Frames 405

In Depth
To Frame or Not to Frame   407
Creating Vertical Frames   408
What if the Browser Doesn't Do Frames?   412
Creating Horizontal Frames   414
Creating Horizontal and Vertical Frames   415
Named Frames   419
Opening New Browser Windows   422

Immediate Solutions
<frameset>—Creating Frames   425
<frame>—Creating Frames   427
Creating Vertical Frames   430
Creating Horizontal Frames   431
Creating Both Horizontal and Vertical Frames   432

Using Named Frames as Hyperlink Targets 434
Using Predefined Target Names 436
<noframes>—Handling Browsers That Don't Handle Frames 436
Opening New Browser Windows 438
Creating Borderless Frames 439
Creating Navigation Bars 441
Enabling and Disabling Scrolling 444
Stopping Frames from Being Resized 446
Setting Frame Border Thickness 446
Setting Frame Color 447
<iframe>—Creating Inline or Floating Frames 449
Creating Borderless Inline Frames 452

Chapter 8
Working with Multimedia 455

In Depth
Multimedia Sound 458
Multimedia Video 460
Multimedia 3D 461
Creating Your Own Multimedia 462
Connecting to External Multimedia Files 463
Creating Inline Sound 465
Creating Inline Video 467

Immediate Solutions
Creating Links to External Multimedia Files 470
What MIME Types Are Available? 471
<bgsound>—Adding Background Sounds 477
<embed>—Embedding Multimedia and Plug-Ins in a Web Page 479
<noembed>—Handling Browsers That Don't Handle Embedding 481
Creating Inline Sounds 482
<object> and <param>—Placing an Object into a Web Page 484
  <object> 484
  <param> 486
Creating Inline Video 494
Displaying Loading Images for Inline Video 496
Using Scrolling Marquees 498
Using Internet Explorer's Multimedia Controls 499

Chapter 9
Cascading Style Sheets 503

In Depth
What Are Style Sheets All About? 504
External Style Sheets 508

Embedded Style Sheets   511
Inline Styles   512
Creating Style Classes   514
Cascading Styles   516
Organizing Styles   517
Understanding Style Specifications   518

Immediate Solutions

Using External Style Sheets   522
<style>—Using Embedded Style Sheets   524
Using Inline Styles   525
Creating and Using Style Classes   527
Specifying Styles by Element ID   529
What Background and Color Properties Are Available?   530
   background   530
   background-attachment   530
   background-color   531
   background-image   531
   background-position   531
   background-repeat   532
   color   532
What Positioning and Block Properties Are Available?   533
   bottom, top, left, right   533
   direction   533
   display   533
   float   534
   position   534
   unicode-bidi   534
   z-index   535
What XHTML Element Box Properties Are Available?   535
   border   535
   border-top, border-right, border-bottom, border-left   536
   border-color   536
   border-top-color, border-right-color, border-bottom-color, border-left-color   536
   border-style   537
   border-top-style, border-right-style, border-bottom-style, border-left-style   537
   border-width   537
   border-top-width, border-right-width, border-bottom-width, border-left-width   538
   clear   538
   height, width   538
   margin   539
   margin-top, margin-right, margin-bottom, margin-left   539
   max-height, max-width   539

min-height 539
min-width 540
padding 540
padding-top, padding-right, padding-bottom, padding-left 540
What Font Properties Are Available? 541
font 541
font-family 541
font-size 542
font-stretch 542
font-style 542
font-variant 543
font-weight 543
What List Properties Are Available? 543
list-style 543
list-style-image 544
list-style-position 544
list-style-type 544
What Text Properties Are Available? 545
letter-spacing 545
line-height 545
text-align 546
text-decoration 546
text-indent 546
text-shadow 547
vertical-align 547
white-space 547
word-spacing 548
What Table Properties Are Available? 548
border-collapse 548
border-spacing 548
column-span, row-span 549
empty-cells 549
table-layout 549
What Visual Effects Properties Are Available? 550
clip 550
overflow 550
visibility 550
Using `<span>` to Apply Styles 551
Using `<div>` to Apply Styles 552
Applying Styles to Text: Bold, Italic, and Underlined 553
Applying Styles to Fonts: Font, Font Size, Font Weight, Font Style 554
Setting Colors and Backgrounds 558

Applying Styles to Margins, Indentations, and Alignments   561
Applying Styles to Hyperlinks   562
Applying Styles to Lists   563
Using Styles to Position Elements: Absolute Positioning   565
Using Styles to Position Elements: Relative Positioning   567

Chapter 10
Essential JavaScript 569

In Depth
What Is JavaScript?   570
The Main JavaScript Implementations   575
JavaScript Objects   577
Object Properties and Methods   578
JavaScript Events   579
JavaScript Programming   587

Immediate Solutions
<script>—Creating a Script   589
<noscript>—Handling Browsers that Don't Handle JavaScript   591
<server>—Running Server-Side JavaScript Scripts   593
Commenting Your JavaScript   594
Working with Data in JavaScript   594
Working with JavaScript Operators   597
Creating **if** Statements   600
Creating **if...else** Statements   602
Creating **switch** Statements   604
Creating **for** Loop Statements   605
Creating **while** Loop Statements   609
Creating **do...while** Loop Statements   610
Creating Functions   611
Passing Arguments to Functions   613
Creating JavaScript Objects   616
Using JavaScript **String** Objects   617
Creating Arrays with the **Array** Class   620
Handling Events in Browsers   623
Event Handling: Mouse Events   628

Chapter 11
Putting JavaScript to Work 637

In Depth
JavaScript Objects in Overview   638
The **document** Object   642
The **window** Object   649

The **location** Object   655
  The **history** Object   656

  Immediate Solutions

  Determining Browser Type in Code   658
  Creating a Self-Modifying Web Page   660
  Setting a Page's Background Color   665
  Reloading Images at Runtime   666
  Opening a New Browser Window   667
  Configuring and Writing to a New Window   672
  Creating Alert Dialog Boxes   675
  Creating Confirmation Dialog Boxes   676
  Creating Prompt Dialog Boxes   678
  Writing to the Browser's Status Bar   680
  Navigating with the **location** Object   681
  Navigating with the **history** Object   684
  Creating JavaScript URLs: Improving Image Maps   686
  Creating Cookies with JavaScript   688
   Creating a Cookie   688
   Retrieving a Cookie   689

Chapter 12
Creating XHTML Forms and XHTML Controls 693

  In Depth

  What's a Form?   694
  What Controls Are Available?   695
  Creating a Form and Adding XHTML Controls   697
  Submitting Data from Forms   703
  Using **<fieldset>**, **<legend>**, and **<label>**   706
  XForms   707

  Immediate Solutions

  <form>—Creating XHTML Forms   709
  <input type="button">—Creating Buttons   713
  <input type="checkbox">—Creating Checkboxes   716
  <input type="file">—Creating File Input for a Form   721
  <input type="hidden">—Creating Hidden Data   725
  <input type="image">—Creating Image Submit Buttons   728
  <input type="password">—Creating Password Controls   731
  <input type="radio">—Creating Radio Buttons   735
  <input type="reset">—Creating Reset Buttons   739
  <input type="submit">—Creating Submit Buttons   741
  <input type="text">—Creating Text Fields   745
  <textarea>—Creating Text Areas   748

Table of Contents

      <button>—Creating a Customizable Button   751
      <select>, <option>, and <optgroup>—Creating a Select Control   754
        <select>   754
        <option>   756
        <optgroup>   757
      <fieldset>, <legend>, and <label>—Grouping and Labeling Form Elements   761
        <fieldset>   761
        <legend>   762
        <label>   763
      <isindex>—Using an Index   766
      <keygen>—Processing Secure Transactions   767

Chapter 13
Dynamic XHTML: Changing Web Pages on the Fly 771

In Depth

    W3C and Dynamic HTML   773
    Dynamic HTML in Internet Explorer   773
    Dynamic HTML in Netscape Navigator   774
    Dynamic Styles: Setting Styles on the Fly   775
    Dynamic Content: Changing Web Pages on the Fly   776
    Creating **mouseover** Effects   781

Immediate Solutions

    Using Dynamic Styles   784
    Toggling Style Sheets On and Off   787
    Dynamic Content: **document.write**   791
    Dynamic Content: The **insertAdjacentHTML** and **insertAdjacentText** Methods   795
    Dynamic Content: The **innerText**, **outerText**, **innerHMTL**,
        and **outerHTML** Properties   797
    Dynamic Content: Using Text Ranges   800
    Dynamic Content: Using the **createElement** Method   802
    Dynamic Content: Creating Dynamic Tables   804
    Dynamic Content: Using Conditional Comments to Set Content on the Fly   807
    Creating Amazing **mouseover** Effects   808
    Positioning Elements by Using Styles   813
    Creating Animation   815
    Creating Animation with Layers   817
    Using Vector Markup Language (VML)   819
    Setting Element Visibility   821
    Printing Web Pages   824
    Using Dynamic Fonts   825
    Visual Effects: Filters   827
    Visual Effects: Transitions   831
    Visual Effects: Transitions Using Layers   835

Chapter 14
Dynamic XHTML: Drag and Drop, Data Binding, and Behaviors 837

In Depth
Dragging and Dropping   838
Data Binding   841
Internet Explorer Behaviors   846

Immediate Solutions
Dragging and Dropping   851
Dragging and Dropping Data   853
Dragging and Dropping by Using Layers   856
Using the MSHTML Data Source Control   859
Creating Tables with the MSHTML Control   865
Using the Tabular Data Control   867
Creating Tables with the TDC   871
Using the XML Data Source Control   873
Creating Tables with the XML Data Source Control   877
Using the RDS Control   879
Creating Tables with the RDS Control   885
Behaviors: Attaching to Events   887
Behaviors: Creating Properties   889
Behaviors: Creating Methods   895
Behaviors: Creating Events   897
Behaviors: Using Default Behaviors   898

Chapter 15
XML and Extending XHTML 903

In Depth
What Does XML Look Like?   904
Valid and Well-Formed XML Documents   909
XML Document Type Definitions   911
XML Schemas   914
XML in Internet Explorer 5   916
Extending XHTML   922

Immediate Solutions
Creating XML Documents   926
Creating XML Documents with DTDs   927
Specifying Attributes in DTDs   931
Creating XML Documents with Schemas   934
Accessing XML Data by Loading XML Documents   936
<xml>—Accessing XML Data with an XML Data Island   939
Getting Attribute Values from XML Elements   943

Table of Contents

Parsing XML Documents in Code   946
Parsing XML to Get Element Content   948
Parsing XML to Get Attribute Values   952
Handling Events while Loading XML Documents   956
Extending XHTML by Adding New Attributes   958
Extending XHTML 1.0 by Adding New Elements   959
Understanding XHTML 1.1 Modules   961
   Abstract Modules   962
   Module Implementations   962
Extending XHTML 1.1 by Adding New Elements   966
Customizing XHTML 1.1 by Removing Modules   967
Using XHTML with Other Namespaces   968

Chapter 16
Essential Java 971

In Depth
Writing Java Programs   974

Immediate Solutions
Getting and Installing the Java SDK   982
Writing Code: Creating Code Files   983
Writing Code: Creating an Application   983
   public class app   984
   public static void main(String[] args)   985
   System.out.println("Hello from Java!");   985
Compiling Code   986
Running Code   987
Basic Skills: Commenting Your Code   988
Basic Skills: Importing Java Packages and Classes   990
Creating Variables   993
Creating Arrays   995
Creating Strings   998
Using Operators   999
Using Conditional Statements: **if**, **if...else**, **switch**   1001
Using Loops: **for**, **while**, **do...while**   1002
Declaring and Creating Objects   1004

Chapter 17
Creating Java Applets 1009

In Depth
The Abstract Windowing Toolkit   1010
Creating Applets   1011
Running Applets   1013

Uploading Applets   1015
Controls in Applets   1017
Graphics in Applets   1018

Immediate Solutions

Creating Applets   1020
<applet>—Embedding Applets in Web Pages   1021
Handling Non-Java Browsers   1025
Using the **init**, **start**, **stop**, **destroy**, **paint**, and **update** Methods—
  and Setting Applet Color   1025
Using the Java Browser Plug-in   1027
Reading Parameters in Applets   1028
Using Java Consoles in Browsers   1029
Creating Text Fields   1030
Creating Buttons   1032
Handling Events   1033
Creating Labels   1038
Creating Checkboxes   1039
Creating Radio Buttons   1042
Using Fonts   1044
Handling Images   1047
Drawing Graphics   1049
  Using the Mouse   1053
  Drawing Lines   1055
  Drawing Ovals   1056
  Drawing Rectangles   1057
  Drawing Rounded Rectangles   1057
  Drawing Freehand   1058

Chapter 18
Essential Perl 1059

In Depth

Creating Perl Programs   1064
Handling Data in Perl   1065
Using Perl Modules   1071
Creating Objects   1072

Immediate Solutions

Writing Code: Creating Code Files   1073
Writing Code: Statements and Declarations   1074
Writing Code: Finding the Perl Interpreter   1074
  Finding Perl Explicitly   1074
  Finding Perl Implicitly   1075

Running Perl Code   1076
    If Your Script Can Find Perl   1076
    If You Want to Use Perl from the Command Line   1076
Basic Skills: Text Input and Output   1077
Basic Skills: Using the **print** Function   1077
Basic Skills: Commenting Your Code   1078
Basic Skills: Reading Typed Input   1079
Basic Skills: Using the Default Variable **$_**   1080
Basic Skills: Cleaning up Typed Input   1081
Basic Skills: Avoiding Immediate Script Closings in Windows   1082
Creating Scalar Variables   1084
Using Assignment Operators on Scalars   1085
Using Numbers in Scalar Variables   1086
Handling Truth Values in Perl   1087
Using Strings in Scalar Variables   1087
Using Variable Interpolation   1088
Defining a List   1089
Assigning Lists to Other Lists   1090
Joining a List into a String   1091
Creating Arrays   1092
Using Arrays   1094
Creating Hashes   1095
Using Hashes   1098
Using Perl Operators   1100
Using Relational (Comparison) Operators   1100
Using Equality Operators   1101
Using the **if** Statement   1102
Looping with the **for** Loop   1104
Looping with the **foreach** Loop   1106
Looping with the **while** Loop   1107
Using the **die** Statement   1108
Creating Objects   1108

Chapter 19
CGI Scripting with Perl 1109

In Depth
CGI Programming with CGI.pm   1111
Creating HTML Controls in cgi1.cgi   1117
Reading Data from HTML Controls in cgi2.cgi   1123

Immediate Solutions
Starting a Document   1128
Displaying Images   1128

Creating Headings   1129
Centering Elements   1130
Creating a Bulleted List   1130
Creating a Hyperlink   1131
Creating Horizontal Rules   1132
Creating a Form   1132
Working with Text Fields   1133
Reading Data from Controls   1134
Working with Text Areas   1135
Working with Checkboxes   1136
Working with Scrolling Lists   1137
Working with Radio Buttons   1139
Working with Password Fields   1140
Working with Pop-up Menus   1141
Working with Hidden Data Fields   1142
Creating Submit and Reset Buttons to Upload Data from an HTML Form   1143
Ending a Form   1144
Ending a Document   1145
Calling a CGI Script from an XHTML Page   1146

Index **1149**

Introduction

Welcome to the big book of Extensible Hypertext Markup Language (XHTML). This book is designed to be as comprehensive—and as accessible—as is possible for a single book on XHTML. In fact, this book is written to be the only Web development resource you'll need. Nearly everything is in here, ready for you to use.

You'll find coverage of every XHTML tag with at least one example showing how it works. I'll discuss not only all the official XHTML tags, but also all the additional tags supported by Microsoft Internet Explorer and Netscape Navigator. I'll also discuss how to extend XHTML by making up new tags.

That's just part of the story, of course—we'll put XHTML to work in depth, pushing the envelope as far as it can go. Writing Web pages with XHTML is not some ordinary and monotonous task: It inspires artistry, devotion, passion, exaltation, and eccentricity—not to mention exasperation and frustration. I'll try to be true to that spirit and capture as much of the excitement and fun of XHTML in this book as I can.

Besides covering every aspect of XHTML, this book adds the other up-to-date skills you can use to create modern Web pages. You'll get a detailed tour of the dynamic XHTML, JavaScript, Java, and XML languages and of Perl Common Gateway Interface (CGI) scripts. And we won't just gloss over the surface of those topics—you'll get a real working knowledge of them all. (We can't cover all those topics in as much detail as a dedicated book on each subject would. For that kind of depth, I recommend books like my *Java Black Book* [The Coriolis Group, ©2000] and my *Perl Black Book* [The Coriolis Group, ©1999].)

What's in This Book

This book is designed to give you as much of the whole XHTML story as one book can hold. We'll not only see the full XHTML syntax—from the most basic to the advanced XHTML tags—but also dig into every major way in which XHTML is used.

This book covers many real-world topics, including connecting XHTML to databases on Web servers and creating and using XHTML tables, lists, images, frames, image maps, and Java applets. We'll create Web pages that can send email, create and use cookies, redirect browsers, change themselves on the fly, react to the time of day, and so on. And each of these topics will be presented using examples showing how they work. That's one important aspect of this book—every important topic has an example, ready to be used. (You can find all the examples on the CD-ROM, along with free and powerful software.)

The material that you need to create dazzling Web pages is here. In addition to standard XHTML, I'll dig into dynamic XHTML, so our Web pages can come alive by responding to mouse movements, rewriting themselves as directed by the user, and binding to databases.

You'll also find JavaScript, which allows us to add code to Web pages, create cookies, add Web-page controls like text fields and checkboxes, and even add graphics animation. You'll learn how to determine which browser the user has, open new browser windows, display dialog boxes, and more.

I'll also take an in-depth look at using Java, showing you how to program in Java and how to embed the applets we create in Web pages. Using Java applets, we'll display images, radio buttons, buttons, and other items.

We'll also take a look at the language XHTML is written in, Extensible Markup Language (XML), which has been getting a great deal of attention these days. We'll learn how to use XML to format data in XML documents that you can read in and manipulate, and how to create XML data islands in Internet Explorer. Using XML, we'll see how to extend XHTML with new tags—after all, one of the attractions of XHTML is that it's *extensible*, and you use XML to extend it.

We'll also dig into Common Gateway Interface (CGI) programming—those Internet scripts that you can use to create Web pages dynamically. Using the Perl programming language, we'll learn how to write CGI scripts that reside on Web servers. I'll discuss how to create and use nearly all of the XHTML controls in Web pages: text fields, text areas, checkboxes, scrolling lists, radio buttons, password fields, popup menus, hidden data fields, and Submit and Reset buttons.

This book is divided into separate, easily accessible topics—nearly 500 of them. Some of the topics we'll cover include:

- Working with the full XHTML 1.0 and 1.1 syntax
- Extending XHTML with new tags
- Formatting text
- Creating transparent, interlaced, and animated GIF images
- Displaying alternate text in place of images
- Creating JavaScript code
- Creating self-modifying Web pages

- Creating and using buttons, checkboxes, hidden data, image controls, submit buttons, password controls, radio buttons, reset buttons, text fields, text areas, and select controls
- Creating graphics animation
- Using Vector Markup Language (VML)
- Creating Java applets
- Creating XML documents
- Handling events while loading XML documents
- Creating Perl Common Gateway Interface (CGI) scripts
- Using Perl variable interpolation
- Using Perl arrays and hashes
- Using Perl operators
- Creating Web pages from CGI scripts
- Using non-object-oriented CGI programming

In addition to the code examples, the accompanying CD-ROM contains a complete, searchable XHTML tag reference, xhtmlref.html. You can open this handy reference in your browser and search for any official XHTML, Internet Explorer, or Netscape Navigator tag. They're all listed, and all the details are there. You'll find all the details in the text as well, but the XHTML tag reference on the CD-ROM is already in browser-ready format.

Conventions Used in This Book

This book has several conventions that you should be aware of. For example, when a particular line of XHTML needs to be pointed out, I'll highlight it in this way:

```
<?xml version="1.0"?>
<!DOCTYPE html PUBLIC "-//W3C//DTD XHTML 1.0 Transitional//EN"
"http://www.w3.org/TR/xhtml1/DTD/xhtml1-transitional.dtd">
<html xmlns="http://www.w3.org/1999/xhtml" xml:lang="en" lang="en">
    <head>
        <title>
            Using The &lt;tt&gt; Tag
        </title>
    </head>

    <body>
        At this point, the program should display:
        <br />
```

```
        <tt>Warning! The CPU is on fire. Do you wish to quit?</tt>
    </body>
</html>
```

I'll also add tips and notes to the text like this:

TIP: *This is a tip. Tips provide added information, such as where to go on the Internet for certain resources or how the unexpected behavior of a particular XHTML tag can be used to your advantage.*

NOTE: *This is a note. Notes add information that you should be aware of, such as why it's not a good idea to use an XHTML tag in a certain way or when a certain browser doesn't actually do what you expect it should.*

Each XHTML tag has its own reference both in the text and in the complete XHTML tag reference, called xhtmlref.html, included on the CD-ROM. For example, here's what such a reference looks like for the **<tt>** tag:

<tt>—Creating "Teletype" Text

Purpose: Displays text in a monospace "teletype" font.

When used as HTML: Start tag/End tag: Required/Required

Supported: [1.0S, 1.0T, 1.0F, 1.1, 2, 3, 3.2, 4, IE1, IE2, IE3, IE4, IE5, NS1, NS2, NS3, NS4]

Attributes:

- **class**—Class of the element (used for rendering). [1.0S, 1.0T, 1.0F, 1.1, 3, 4, IE4, IE5, NS4]
- **dir**—Gives the direction of directionally neutral text (text that doesn't have an inherent direction in which you should read it). Possible values: **ltr**, left-to-right text or table; and **rtl**, right-to-left text or table. [1.0S, 1.0T, 1.0F, 1.1, 4, IE5]
- **id**—Unique alphanumeric identifier for the tag; use the ID to refer to the tag. [1.0S, 1.0T, 1.0F, 1.1, 3, 4, IE4, IE5, NS4]
- **lang**—Base language used for the tag. [1.0S, 1.0T, 1.0F, 1.1, 3, 4, IE4, IE5]
- **language**—Scripting language used for the tag. [IE4, IE5]
- **style**—Inline style indicating how to render the element. [1.0S, 1.0T, 1.0F, 1.1, 4, IE3, IE4, IE5, NS4]
- **title**—Holds additional information (as might be displayed in tool tips). [1.0S, 1.0T, 1.0F, 1.1, 3, 4, IE4, IE5]

- **xml:lang**—Holds the base language for the element when the document is interpreted as an XML document. [1.0S, 1.0T, 1.0F, 1.1]

XHTML events: onclick, ondblclick, onmousedown, onmouseup, onmouseover, onmousemove, onmouseout, onkeypress, onkeydown, onkeyup

Note in particular the expressions in square brackets: [1.0S, 1.0T, 1.0F, 1.1, 2, 3, 3.2, 4, IE1, IE2, IE3, IE4, IE5, NS1, NS2, NS3, NS4]. This key indicates where a particular item is supported. In this case, the expression indicates that the item is supported in the official XHTML 1.0 *Strict* Document Type Definition (DTD), the XHTML 1.0 *Transitional* DTD, the XHTML 1.0 *Frameset* DTD, and the XHTML 1.1 DTD (see Chapter 1 to learn what these mean), as well as the official specification for HTML 2, HTML 3, and HTML 4, the Microsoft Internet Explorer browser versions 1, 2, 3, 4, and 5, and the Netscape Navigator browser versions 1, 2, 3, and 4. Using these expressions, you can determine exactly which items are supported in what specifications and in which versions of the two major browsers, Microsoft Internet Explorer and Netscape Navigator. Here are the terms you'll find in square brackets, and what they mean:

- *1.0S*—Supported in the XHTML 1.0 Strict Document Type Definition (DTD)
- *1.0T*—Supported in the XHTML 1.0 Transitional DTD
- *1.0F*—Supported in the XHTML 1.0 Frameset DTD
- *1.1*—Supported in the XHTML 1.1 DTD
- *2*—Supported in HTML 2
- *3*—Supported in HTML 3
- *3.2*—Supported in HTML 3.2
- *4*—Supported in HTML 4
- *IEx*—Supported in Internet Explorer version x
- *NSx*—Supported in Netscape Navigator version x

Also note the line that says **"When used as HTML: Start tag/End tag:** Required/Required." As we'll see in Chapter 1, *start tags* begin XHTML elements, and *end tags* end them; in XHTML, you need both—but you don't necessarily need both in HTML. For each element, I'll give the HTML syntax as well as the XHTML syntax, indicating, for example, when end tags can be considered optional if the element is treated as HTML.

I'll list all the XHTML *events*—such as whether or not the tag can handle mouse clicks in code—that are supported by each tag. (For all the details on events, see Chapter 10.) It's important to remember that this list holds the *official* W3C events for each tag; browsers such as Internet Explorer and Netscape Navigator might not support all those events yet—or might support more events than are listed.

What You'll Need

To use this book and display Web pages on the Internet, you'll need a connection to an Internet Service Provider (ISP) and a way of installing your XHTML documents on that ISP's Web server. I address this in more detail in Chapter 1, and you can get more details from your ISP.

You'll need a way to create XHTML documents. Such documents are just plain text files filled with XHTML statements. To create an XHTML document, you should have either a dedicated XHTML editor or an editor program that can save files in plain text format. See Chapter 1 for more information.

You should also have the latest version of a good Web browser. In particular, this book was written using Microsoft Internet Explorer 5 and Netscape Communicator 4.7. You can find a list of Web browsers and where to get them in Chapter 1.

Other Resources

Throughout this book, I'll list many online resources for additional information. The following list contains the primary resources for XHTML development, including the official XHTML home pages of the World Wide Web Consortium (W3C), which is the organization that sets the XHTML standards:

- **www.w3.org/TR/xhtml1/**—The complete W3C recommendation for XHTML 1.0
- **www.w3.org/TR/xhtml11/**—The current W3C working draft for XHTML 1.1
- **www.w3.org/TR/xhtml-basic/**—The current W3C working draft for XHTML Basic
- **www.w3.org/TR/xhtml11/changes.html#a_changes**—The differences between XHTML 1.0 and 1.1
- **validator.w3.org/**—The W3C's HTML and XHTML validator, which can check the syntax of your XHTML pages
- **www.w3.org/TR/xhtml-modularization/**—The W3C's discussion of the modularization of XHTML
- **www.w3.org/TR/xhtml-building/**—The W3C's discussion on building XMHTML modules
- **www.w3.org/MarkUp/Forms/**—The W3C's discussion of the new version of XHTML forms called XForms
- **www.w3.org/2000/01/xhtml-pressrelease.html.en**—The W3C press release on XHTML
- **www.w3.org/MarkUp/**—The W3C's HTML home page

- **http://developer.netscape.com/docs/manuals/htmlguid/index.htm**—Netscape's HTML guide
- **http://msdn.microsoft.com/workshop/c-frame.htm#/workshop/author/default.asp**—Microsoft's HTML reference and help

Chapter 1 lists several XHTML resources. If you want to take a look at some online XHTML material in addition to this book, there are many sites on the Web (a casual Web search for "XHTML" turns up 7,984 pages). Here is a starter list:

- **www.site-builder.co.uk/xhtml.htm**—An XHTML tutorial
- **www.mozquito.org/news/index.html**—Links to many XHTML articles
- **webreview.com/wr/pub/1999/07/16/feature/index.html**—A good overview of XHTML

And that's all the introduction needed. Now it's time to get into XHTML, starting with Chapter 1.

Chapter 1
Essential XHTML

If you need an immediate solution to:	See page:
`<?xml?>`—Starting an XML Document	35
`<!DOCTYPE>`—Specifying a Document's Type	36
`<html>`—Creating the Document's Root Element	37
Creating the Structure of a Web Page: Head and Body	39
`<head>`—Creating a Web Page's Head	40
`<title>`—Giving a Web Page a Title	42
`<meta>`—Giving More Information about Your Web Page	43
`</head>`—Ending a Web Page's Head	46
`<body>`—Creating a Web Page's Body	47
Setting Web Page Colors	53
Adding Text to a Web Page	58
Basic Text Formatting	59
`<!-->`—Comments and Server Side Includes	60
`</body>`—Ending a Web Page's Body	64
`</html>`—Ending a Web Page	64

In Depth

Welcome to the big book of Extensible Hypertext Markup Language, XHTML. XHTML is the new language you write Web pages in, and if you want to create Web pages, you've come to the right place. This book is packed with all that you need.

Many people think writing Web pages is a difficult process—which is why many people don't do it—but the truth is that it's easy once you get the fundamentals down. The easiest way to see this is through examples, and this is an example-oriented book. We're not going to wade through chapters of obscure theory as many books do before getting to the heart of the matter—we'll start creating Web pages right away, putting XHTML to use. As we'll see, XHTML is the language you use to tell Web browsers how to display your Web page, and after you've mastered the basics, you'll soon be creating terrific Web pages.

XHTML builds on and extends Hypertext Markup Language (HTML), the current language of the Web. In fact, XHTML is a complete rewrite of HTML 4 in Extensible Markup Language (XML). The fact that XHTML is actually written in XML means that you can extend it—and that's what makes XHTML so popular. To see how this works, and to understand the genius behind XHTML, I'm going to look at HTML, then at XML, and then at how the synthesis of the two created XHTML.

HTML

HTML is the amazingly popular language that many people use to create Web pages. Because XHTML is a rewrite of HTML 4 in XML, it's worthwhile getting to know HTML before digging into XHTML.

Left to themselves, Web browsers would take the text and images in your Web page and wrap them up into what looks like a single paragraph without any line breaks. With HTML, a Web-page author acts much like an editor does, *marking up* a page to indicate its format, telling the Web browser where to begin a new line or how to align text or images, and more. In other words, HTML is all about specifying the structure and format of a Web page.

Who actually created HTML? All the languages we're talking about here—HTML, XML, and XHTML—are recommendations of an important body named the World Wide Web Consortium (W3C, **www.w3c.org**), and you'll see frequent references to W3C in this book. It's W3C that's responsible for the various versions of HTML—that's the group that sets the standards.

Here's an HTML example to get us started. This first Web page is a simple one, and we'll see it first in HTML, then in XHTML. This page displays the text "Web page number one!" in a Web browser's title bar and displays the text "Welcome to HTML!" in the Web browser window:

```
<HTML>
    <HEAD>
        <TITLE>
            Web page number one!
        </TITLE>
    </HEAD>

    <BODY>
        <H1>
            Welcome to HTML!
        </H1>
    </BODY>
</HTML>
```

The results of this HTML appear in Microsoft Internet Explorer in Figure 1.1.

The first thing to note is that all the HTML terms here, such as **<BODY>**, are enclosed in angle brackets, **<** and **>**, and such terms are called *tags*. For example, I use the **<HTML>** tag to indicate that this Web page is written in HTML. I enclose

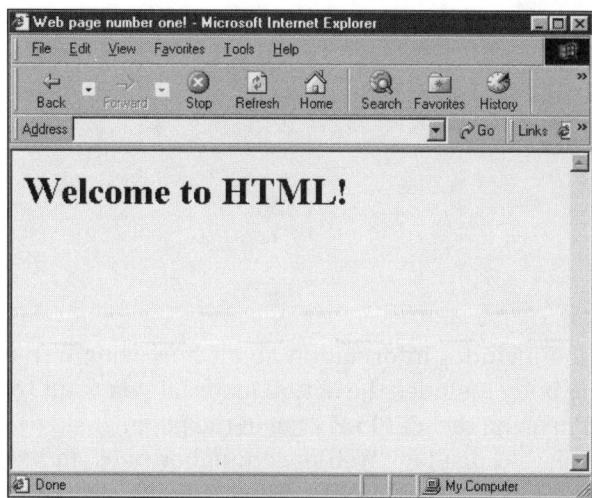

Figure 1.1   Our first Web page.

the entire document between the **<HTML>** *starting* or *opening tag* and the corresponding *ending* or *closing tag*, **</HTML>**. (In HTML, the closing tag is always the same as the opening tag, but with a **/** character). Notice the opening and closing tags in the following code:

```
<HTML>
    <HEAD>
        <TITLE>
            Web page number one!
        </TITLE>
    </HEAD>

    <BODY>
        <H1>
            Welcome to HTML!
        </H1>
    </BODY>
</HTML>
```

Collectively, a starting tag, an ending tag, and everything between them make up an HTML *element*. In this example, every element has both an opening and a closing tag. I'm creating the two necessary sections of a Web page—its head and its body—with the **<HEAD>** and **<BODY>** tags:

```
<HTML>
    <HEAD>
        <TITLE>
            Web page number one!
        </TITLE>
    </HEAD>

    <BODY>
        <H1>
            Welcome to HTML!
        </H1>
    </BODY>
</HTML>
```

As we'll see, the head section includes information about how your Web page should be displayed, and the body includes the actual material you want to display. In the previous code, I'm using the **<TITLE>** tag in the page's head to indicate that the Web browser should display "Web page number one!" in its title bar. And I'm using the **<H1>** tag in the page's body to indicate that the Web browser should display "Welcome to HTML!" in the actual page, using heading style number one (H1). This heading style creates big boldface type. You can see the result in Figure 1.1.

This example helps make HTML more concrete. As you can see, I've used the HTML tags **<HTML>**, **<HEAD>**, **<TITLE>**, **<BODY>**, and **<H1>** to structure and create this Web page. HTML is based on tags like **<HEAD>** and **<BODY>**. Tags like **<HEAD>** and **<BODY>** can enclose other tags, as you saw in the previous example, allowing you to create complex nested structures.

Note that the **<H1>** tag, which displays a heading (in big, bold type), needs a closing tag **</H1>** to enclose the text you want to set in that heading style as shown here:

```
<H1>
    Welcome to HTML!
</H1>
```

In contrast, the **<P>** tag, which starts a new paragraph of text (and skips some space between paragraphs), doesn't need a closing tag **</P>** in HTML. (It will in XHTML.) Even in HTML, you can use a closing tag if you want to, but if you just start a new paragraph with a new **<P>** tag, the browser will know what to do. For that reason, closing tags are *optional* for the **<P>** element in HTML, and you can omit them, as I do here:

```
<P>
    Here's a paragraph of text.
<P>
    Here's another paragraph!
```

In addition, some elements, such as the **<H1>** element, are designed to enclose some text, called *content*, between the opening and closing tags. Other elements, such as the **<META>** element, are called *empty elements*; they do not use opening and closing tags. Here's an example in which I set the name of a Web-page author to "Steve" by using a **<META>** element in HTML:

```
<HEAD>
    <TITLE>
        Web page number one!
        <META NAME="Author" CONTENT="Steve">
    </TITLE>
</HEAD>
```

In this example, note the terms **NAME** and **CONTENT**, which I set to the values **"Author"** and **"Steve"** respectively. These terms are called *attributes*, and they're another important part of working with tags in both HTML and XHTML.

Using Tag Attributes

Tags tell Web browsers how to format and organize your Web pages, but there's more potential here—you can customize the behavior of most tags by using attributes. An *attribute* is a keyword that you use in an opening tag to give more information to the Web browser. An attribute follows this format:

```
<TAGNAME ATTRIBUTE = VALUE>
```

In the following example, I use the **ALIGN** attribute of the **<H1>** tag and set it equal to **CENTER** to indicate that I want the text in this tag to appear centered on the Web page:

```
<HTML>
    <HEAD>
        <TITLE>
            Web page number one!
        </TITLE>
    </HEAD>

    <BODY>
        <H1 ALIGN = "CENTER">
            Welcome to HTML!
        </H1>
    </BODY>
</HTML>
```

The result appears in Figure 1.2, where, as you can see, the text has indeed been centered.

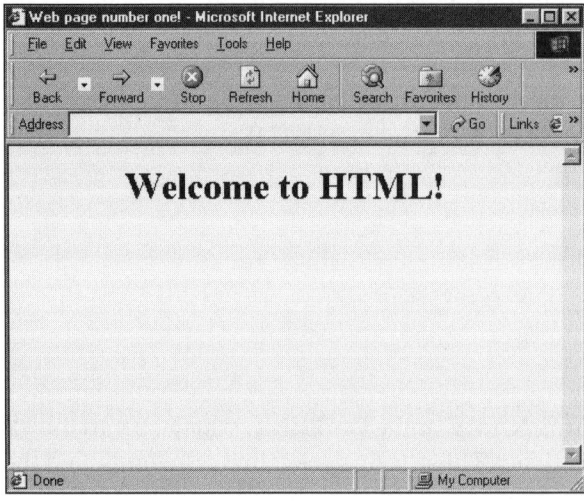

Figure 1.2 Using a tag attribute to center text.

You can have a number of attributes in the same opening tag, like this:

```
<TAGNAME ATTRIBUTE1 = VALUE1 ATTRIBUTE2 = VALUE2>
```

Now we have an idea of general HTML terminology. As I mentioned, XHTML is a rewrite of HTML 4, and it's worth taking a look at HTML 4 in more detail here. For example, there are actually three versions of HTML 4, and knowing that will be important to us when we use XHTML.

HTML 4

HTML 4 (the current version is actually HTML 4.01) replaced its predecessor, HTML 3., the successor to version 2. HTML 4 introduced substantial changes from HTML 3.2, and I'll discuss some of them here because they will be important to us.

Two big changes in HTML 4 were the addition of *IDs* and *event capturing* for nearly all elements. You can now specify an ID for just about every element by using the ID attribute, like this: **<H1 ID = HEADING1>**. In this case, I've named the **<H1>** heading **HEADING1**, so I can refer to it that way in code (using scripting languages such as JavaScript or VBScript). Event capturing is closely aligned with dynamic HTML (which I'll discuss in Chapters 16 and 17), and it lets your elements "come alive" in new ways. For example, if I use the **ONCLICK** attribute like this—**<H1 ONCLICK = HANDLE_CLICK>**—then when the user clicks on this H1 heading, the code I've created and named **HANDLE_CLICK** will be called. Using event capturing in this way, you can create special effects, such as highlighting hyperlinks when the mouse moves over them.

Perhaps the biggest change was the move from using tags to format text to using *style sheets*. Style sheets let you specify the formatting for elements in a Web page. For example, you can use the **<B>** tag to format text as bold and **<I>** to format it in italics, but with HTML 4 you can use style sheets to create these effects. (I'll cover style sheets in detail in Chapter 9.) However, because style sheets changed a cherished part of HTML, it's a safe bet that formatting tags like **<B>** and **<I>** will be around for some time. That's one of the reasons there are three versions of HTML 4 now.

In addition, the **<OBJECT>** element was expanded to include Java *applets* (discussed in Chapter 19) as well as just about any kind of external file you want to include in a Web page. In fact, **<OBJECT>** now seems intended to supersede the **<APPLET>** and **<EMBED>** tags and eventually even the **<IMG>** tag, which you currently use to embed images.

You can find the official HTML 4.01 specification, as of this writing, at **http://www.w3.org/TR/1999/PR-html40-19990824/**. This document will probably have been superseded by the time you read this book. You can always find the latest HTML 4 specification at **www.w3.org/TR/REC-html40/** (which currently points to the HTML 4.01 specification).

HTML 4 also introduced a number of new HTML tags. You can see these tags in Table 1.1.

Deprecated Features

It's difficult for W3C to make universal changes to HTML because many HTML authors are accustomed to the old ways. For that reason, W3C marks features it wants to eliminate from HTML as *deprecated*. When something is marked as deprecated, that means that it'll be removed from HTML in a future version. It's usually good practice to avoid deprecated tags, although common ones like **<CENTER>** will be around for a long time.

HTML 4, with its emphasis on style sheets, deprecated quite a lot of tags, including the **<CENTER>**, **<BASEFONT>**, **<FONT>**, **<STRIKE>** (also called **<S>**), and **<U>** tags. These tags all format text. W3C decided that such formatting should take place with style sheets instead.

Besides deprecating many formatting tags, W3C has deprecated a number of other tag attributes that determine appearance, such as the **ALINK**, **VLINK**, **BGCOLOR**, **COLOR**, and **LINK** attributes of the **<BODY>** tag. In addition, the following tags are now deprecated: **<APPLET>** (replaced by **<OBJECT>**); **<ISINDEX>** (which generates a text field that the user can type into and which has been replaced by the **<INPUT>** tag in forms); and **<DIR>** and **<MENU>** (which create vertical lists of items and duplicate the **<UL>** tag).

Table 1.1 New tags in HTML 4.

Tag	Does This
<ACRONYM>	Marks a group of letters that stand for something else.
<BUTTON>	Adds functionality to invoke scripts, calculate values, perform formatting, and more. A fully featured button for use in forms. Can be used for more than just a Submit or Reset button.
<COLGROUP>	Identifies a column in a table for easy formatting.
<FIELDSET>	Identifies sets of form elements as logical groups.
<LEGEND>	Provides groups of elements in forms.
<INS> and **<DEL>**	**<INS>** marks text as newly inserted with the date of insertion, and **<DEL>** marks text as deleted with the date of deletion.
<Q>	Used for inline quotes (like an inline version of **<BLOCKQUOTE>**).

Removed Features

Some features that were deprecated a long time ago were removed from HTML 4. These features include the **<XMP>**, **<PLAINTEXT>**, and **<LISTING>** tags, which let you display preformatted text. These have now been taken over by the **<PRE>** tag.

Three Versions of HTML 4

Although W3C sets the HTML standards, languages such as HTML and XHTML are substantially implemented in the Web browsers of vendors such as Microsoft and Netscape. And millions of people are using these languages on the Web. All of which means that it's hard for W3C to make quick changes in a language. The fact that HTML 4 included such large changes from previous versions meant that there were actually three versions of HTML 4 released: the strict, transitional, and frameset versions. Each of these versions has its own *Document Type Definition (DTD)*, and which DTD you use will make a difference in XHTML. Here's how these three DTDs differ:

- *The strict HTML 4 DTD*—The strict DTD does not support the elements and attributes that W3C considers deprecated. In other words, it excludes the presentation attributes and elements that W3C expects to phase out as support for style sheets matures.

- *The transitional HTML 4 DTD*—The transitional DTD still supports the elements and attributes that were deprecated in HTML 4. This is also called the "loose" DTD, and it's the most popular version of HTML 4.

- *The frameset HTML 4 DTD*—The frameset DTD is the one you use when you work with frames in a Web browser (as I'll do in Chapter 7). When you create a frame-based Web page, you replace the **<BODY>** element with a **<FRAMESET>** element, and you use the frameset DTD.

XHTML includes explicit support for each of these three DTDs, as we'll see in the section on XHTML.

HTML became wildly popular on the Internet, far beyond W3C's original expectations. As time went on and HTML came into use by major corporations—and became the backbone of the Web—people ran into limitations. Say, for example, that you want to display pages with complex mathematical formulas or musical notations. Or say that you want to store data in involved data structures for transmission across the Internet. Which HTML tags could you use? There aren't any—there simply isn't enough support in HTML for sophisticated uses such as those.

That is to say, because the Web became so widely used, HTML was no longer enough. Many people found that they wanted to create their own elements, like **<DATE>** or **<TIMEOFDAY>** or **<CHAPTER>** or **<DATARECORD>** or

<PRICE>. Simple formatting tags—like **<B>** for boldface or **<I>** for italics—just weren't enough any more. So how could you create your own tags?

There was already a very popular way of doing just that—XML. XML is the language you can use to structure data for the Web, and it allows you to create your own tags. When the W3C was casting around for a way to extend HTML, XML seemed like the logical solution. The thought was: why not rewrite *all* of HTML in XML, and then the user can use XML to extend that version of HTML? And that's how XHTML was born.

Because XHTML is written in XML, it's a good idea to understand some XML before you work with XHTML. In fact, because XHTML is written in XML, there will be some differences from HTML 4. I'll provide an overview of XML now so that you can understand how these differences work. (To extend XHTML with our own tags, we'll have to know more about XML later in the book, in Chapters 13 and 14.)

XML

As I said earlier, XML is the language you use to structure your data for the Web. Like HTML, XML is a recommendation of W3C, and you can find the W3C's recommendation for XML 1, the language XHTML is written in, at **www.w3.org/TR/REC-xml**.

How does XML let you structure your own data? By letting you create your own tags—and then specifying the grammar of those tags. To show how this works, here's an example in which I'll create an XML page that holds the purchasing records of several customers. To start an XML page, you begin with the XML *processing instruction* **<?xml version = "1.0"?>**, which tells the browser that this document is XML.

NOTE: *XML is very particular about syntax; everything in the processing instruction **<?xml version = "1.0"?>** must be lowercase.*

Here's the necessary first line of an XML document:

```
<?xml version = "1.0"?>
```

You can name your own tags in XML, and I'll do that here. The body of the XML document should be enclosed in one XML element, which I'll call **<DOCUMENT>**:

In Depth

```
<?xml version = "1.0"?><DOCUMENT>     .
        .
        .
</DOCUMENT>
```

Now I'll start storing purchasing data by customer. To do this, I'll create a new element, **<CUSTOMER>**, which goes inside the **<DOCUMENT>** element:

```
<?xml version = "1.0"?><DOCUMENT>    <CUSTOMER>    .
        .
        .
    </CUSTOMER>
</DOCUMENT>
```

I can also store the customer's name by creating a new **<NAME>** element, which itself has two elements inside it—**<LAST_NAME>** and **<FIRST_NAME>**:

```
<?xml version = "1.0"?><DOCUMENT>
    <CUSTOMER>
        <NAME>
            <LAST_NAME>Thomson</LAST_NAME>
            <FIRST_NAME>Susan</FIRST_NAME>
        </NAME>
            .
            .
            .
    </CUSTOMER>
</DOCUMENT>
```

I also store the date of the record in a **<DATE>** element. I store the actual customer orders in an **<ORDERS>** element, where I place all the items the customer bought:

```
<?xml version = "1.0"?>
<DOCUMENT>
    <CUSTOMER>
        <NAME>
            <LAST_NAME>Thomson</LAST_NAME>
            <FIRST_NAME>Susan</FIRST_NAME>
        </NAME>
        <DATE>September 1, 2001</DATE>
        <ORDERS>
            <ITEM>
```

```
                <PRODUCT>Video tape</PRODUCT>
                <NUMBER>5</NUMBER>
                <PRICE>$1.25</PRICE>
            </ITEM>
            <ITEM>
                <PRODUCT>Shovel</PRODUCT>
                <NUMBER>2</NUMBER>
                <PRICE>$4.98</PRICE>
            </ITEM>
        </ORDERS>
    </CUSTOMER>
        .
        .
        .
</DOCUMENT>
```

I can store the records of as many customers as I want to in this XML page; here's how I add a new customer's record:

```
<?xml version = "1.0"?><DOCUMENT>
    <CUSTOMER>
        <NAME>
            <LAST_NAME>Thomson</LAST_NAME>
            <FIRST_NAME>Susan</FIRST_NAME>
        </NAME>
        <DATE>September 1, 2001</DATE>
        <ORDERS>
            <ITEM>
                <PRODUCT>Video tape</PRODUCT>
                <NUMBER>5</NUMBER>
                <PRICE>$1.25</PRICE>
            </ITEM>
            <ITEM>
                <PRODUCT>Shovel</PRODUCT>
                <NUMBER>2</NUMBER>
                <PRICE>$4.98</PRICE>
            </ITEM>
        </ORDERS>
    </CUSTOMER>
    <CUSTOMER>
        <NAME>
            <LAST_NAME>Smithson</LAST_NAME>
            <FIRST_NAME>Nancy</FIRST_NAME>
        </NAME>
```

```
            <DATE>September 2, 2001</DATE>
            <ORDERS>
                <ITEM>
                    <PRODUCT>Ribbon</PRODUCT>
                    <NUMBER>12</NUMBER>
                    <PRICE>$2.95</PRICE>
                </ITEM>
                <ITEM>
                    <PRODUCT>Goldfish</PRODUCT>
                    <NUMBER>6</NUMBER>
                    <PRICE>$1.50</PRICE>
                </ITEM>
            </ORDERS>
        </CUSTOMER>
</DOCUMENT>
```

As you can see, XML provides you with a way of creating and structuring your data in a way that fits that data. You might be wondering how browsers deal with such free-form data—for example, how will a browser know how you want the **<CUSTOMER>** element displayed? This question points out a fundamental difference between XML and HTML: XML provides a way to structure your data, not to format it, as HTML does (although you can use Cascading Style Sheets, CSS, or the Extensible Stylesheet Language, XSL, to do just that, as we'll see in Chapter 9). HTML may indicate what text should be bold and what text italic, but XML has no such formatting built in.

What makes XML more important than just a page of text where you've created your own tags? With an XML page, you can include instructions on how to check the data structure to make sure it's valid—for example, checking that only **<PRICE>** and **<DESCRIPTION>** elements go inside **<DATARECORD>** elements. You can also make sure that the data is structured in a consistent way—for example, checking that data elements are nested properly and don't overlap by mistake. Making sure that the data in the Web page follows the rules you set up for it brings us to two new concepts: *valid* and *well-formed* XML documents. (Our XHTML documents will have to be both.)

Valid and Well-Formed XML Documents

An XML document is considered *valid* if there is a document type definition or an XML *schema* (we'll see schemas in Chapter 13) associated with it and if the document complies with the DTD or schema. (We'll discuss schemas in Chapter 13.) That's all there is to making a document valid. The DTD or schema describes the grammar for tags you've created—which tags can contain which other tags and which attributes. We'll see how to specify a DTD in the next section.

An XML document is considered *well-formed* if it meets the following conditions:

- It contains one or more elements.
- There is precisely one element—the *root* or *document* element—for which neither the start tag nor the end tag is inside any other element.
- All other tags nest within each other correctly.
- All elements used in the document are defined in XML, in the DTD, or in the XML schema.

TIP: Note in particular the requirement that the entire XML document be enclosed in one element: the root element. This fact will be important when we start working with the contents of XML documents in code because we'll start by getting access to the root element, and then we'll move to other elements as required. Look at the previous XML example, where the root element is **<DOCUMENT>**. Because XHTML is a rewrite of HTML in XML, the root element of XHTML pages is going to be **<html>**.

So how exactly do you specify a DTD? Where do you get a DTD, anyway? DTDs and more are addressed in the next section, where we start working on XHTML.

XHTML

We've gotten an overview of HTML and an overview of XML; now it's time to start working with the synthesis of the two—XHTML.

There are really two big advantages to XHTML. The first is that you can use it to create your own tags and thereby extend what was possible in HTML. The second is that you can already view XHTML pages in current Web browsers. Let's see an example to get us started.

This was the first page we saw in this chapter, and it's written in HTML:

```
<HTML>
    <HEAD>
        <TITLE>
            Web page number one!
        </TITLE>
    </HEAD>

    <BODY>
        <H1>
            Welcome to HTML!
        </H1>
    </BODY>
</HTML>
```

Here's the same page, written in XHTML:

```
<?xml version="1.0"?>
<!DOCTYPE html PUBLIC "-//W3C//DTD XHTML 1.0 Transitional//EN"
"http://www.w3.org/TR/xhtml1/DTD/xhtml1-transitional.dtd">
<html xmlns="http://www.w3.org/1999/xhtml" xml:lang="en" lang="en">
    <head>
        <title>
            Web page number one!
        </title>
    </head>

    <body>
        <h1>
            Welcome to XHTML!
        </h1>
    </body>
</html>
```

This document produces the same result you see in Figure 1.1 except that this document says "Welcome to XHTML!" instead, as you can see in Figure 1.3.

Right away, you'll notice a few differences in the code. One difference is that all tags and attributes (except the **<!DOCTYPE>** element) are in lowercase. That's the rule in XHTML—use lowercase for tags and attributes. (Unlike HTML, XML and therefore XHTML are case sensitive.) Another difference is the **<?xml?>** processing instruction that starts the document and marks the document as an XML document. (This processing instruction can be omitted, but W3C recommends that you use it.) This is the instruction:

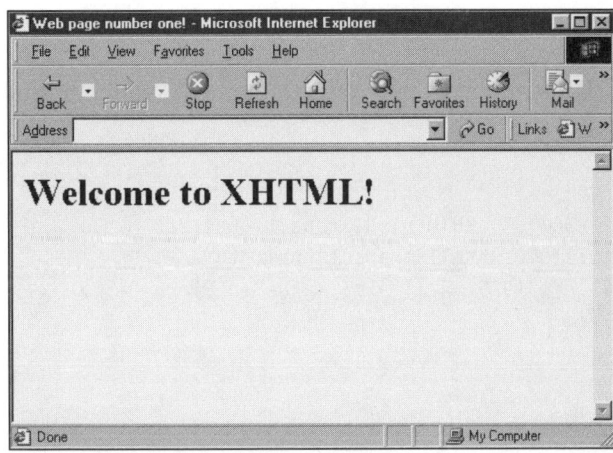

Figure 1.3   The first XHTML page.

```
<?xml version="1.0"?>
```
 .
 .
 .

Next comes the **<!DOCTYPE>** element. This element is written in all capitals, even though the following XHTML elements are not.

```
<?xml version="1.0"?>
<!DOCTYPE html PUBLIC "-//W3C//DTD XHTML 1.0 Transitional//EN"
 "http://www.w3.org/TR/xhtml1/DTD/xhtml1-transitional.dtd">
```
 .
 .
 .

This is where the XHTML page uses the **<!DOCTYPE>** element to specify the DTD to use. The first item in this element, **html**, indicates that the root element—that is, the element that contains all the others—will be **<html>**. The next item, **public**, indicates that the following identifier is the public name for the DTD. In this case, that identifier is "**-//W3C//DTD XHTML 1.0 Transitional//EN**", which is the XHTML 1 transitional DTD that corresponds to the HTML 4 transitional DTD. The **EN** part means that the DTD is written in English. The last item, "**http://www.w3.org/TR/xhtml1/DTD/xhtml1-transitional.dtd**", gives the URL of the DTD file. (We'll see how to create DTDs in Chapter 13.) W3C has provided DTDs for use with XHTML, and browsers can use those DTDs to check the syntax of an XHTML page. We'll see what DTDs you can use in XHTML, and where to get them, in a page or two.

TIP: *For more information on the **<!DOCTYPE>** element, see the "Immediate Solutions" section called "**<!DOCTYPE>**—Specifying a Document's Type."*

Following the **<!DOCTYPE>** element is the **<html>** element, which starts the actual XHTML code:

```
<?xml version="1.0"?>
<!DOCTYPE html PUBLIC "-//W3C//DTD XHTML 1.0 Transitional//EN"
 "http://www.w3.org/TR/xhtml1/DTD/xhtml1-transitional.dtd">
<html xmlns="http://www.w3.org/1999/xhtml" xml:lang="en" lang="en">
```
 .
 .
 .

The **<html>** element has three attributes: **xmlns**, **xml:lang**, and **lang**. The **xmlns** attribute names an XML *namespace*. I'll talk more about namespaces in Chapter 13, but here's the basic idea: because you can create your own tags in XML and XHTML, yours might conflict with someone else's, so you can define namespaces that keep such tags separate. The namespace for XHTML is **http://www.w3.org/1999/xhtml**, which means that the **xmlns** attribute should always be assigned this value. The next two attributes are optional; the **xml:lang** attribute is used when the document is treated as an XML document, and the **lang** attribute is used when the document is treated as an HTML document. In both cases, I'm indicating that the language of the document is English.

These three lines—the **<?xml?>**, **<!DOCTYPE>**, and **<html>** elements—might not be what you're used to if you're familiar with HTML, but it's easier than it might look. If you prefer, you can just use those lines as they appear here without having to know all the details of what they're actually doing. The rest of the XHTML that follows is very like the HTML of the first Web page we designed—the only difference is that the elements are written in lowercase:

```
<?xml version="1.0"?>
<!DOCTYPE html PUBLIC "-//W3C//DTD XHTML 1.0 Transitional//EN"
"http://www.w3.org/TR/xhtml1/DTD/xhtml1-transitional.dtd">
<html xmlns="http://www.w3.org/1999/xhtml" xml:lang="en" lang="en">
    <head>
        <title>
            Web page number one!
        </title>
    </head>

    <body>
        <h1>
            Welcome to XHTML!
        </h1>
    </body>
</html>
```

When a browser reads this XHTML page, the browser is supposed also to read the document type definition it finds at **http://www.w3.org/TR/xhtml1/DTD/xhtml1-transitional.dtd** and check the document against the syntax defined in that DTD. (In fact, there are no XHTML browsers yet, although we'll come close by using various other browsers.) In this way, the whole syntax of XHTML is contained in the DTD. What XHTML DTDs are available? That depends on what version of XHTML you are using.

XHTML Version 1

The first version of XHTML, version 1, is a simple rewrite of HTML 4 in XML. You can find the complete W3C recommendation for XHTML 1 at **www.w3.org/TR/xhtml1/**. As with HTML 4, XHTML 1 has three DTDs:

- *The strict XHTML 1 DTD*—The strict DTD is based on the strict HTML 4 DTD and does not support the elements and attributes that W3C considers deprecated in HTML 4. In other words, it excludes the presentation attributes and elements that W3C expects to phase out as support for style sheets matures.

- *The transitional XHTML 1 DTD*—The transitional DTD is based on the transitional HTML 4 DTD and still supports the elements and attributes that were deprecated in HTML 4. This is also called the "loose" DTD, and it's the most popular version of HTML 4.

- *The frameset XHTML 1 DTD*—The frameset DTD is based on the frameset HTML 4 DTD and is the one you use when you work with frames in a Web browser. When you create a frame-based Web page, you replace the **<BODY>** element with a **<FRAMESET>** element, and you use the frameset DTD.

To include these DTDs, here are the **<!DOCTYPE>** elements you can use in XHTML:

```
<!DOCTYPE html
    PUBLIC "-//W3C//DTD XHTML 1.0 Strict//EN"
    "http://www.w3.org/TR/xhtml1/DTD/xhtml1-strict.dtd">

<!DOCTYPE html
    PUBLIC "-//W3C//DTD XHTML 1.0 Transitional//EN"
    "http://www.w3.org/TR/xhtml1/DTD/xhtml1-transitional.dtd">

<!DOCTYPE html
    PUBLIC "-//W3C//DTD XHTML 1.0 Frameset//EN"
    "http://www.w3.org/TR/xhtml1/DTD/xhtml1-frameset.dtd">
```

For most examples in this book, I'll use the transitional DTD because that DTD most closely matches the coding that's on the Web today. However, for each tag and each attribute, I'll also indicate which DTDs support it.

Here's one thing to note: I'm giving the full URL of the various DTD files in these **<!DOCTYPE>** elements, which means that the browser has to fetch the full DTD file from the W3C before it can check your document. If everyone did that, W3C would be swamped as millions of browsers tried to read the same files. To prevent that, you can copy the DTD files from those URLs and place local copies on your Web site. For example, if you place the DTD files in a directory named DTD in your Web site, your **<!DOCTYPE>** elements might look more like this:

```
<!DOCTYPE html
    PUBLIC "-//W3C//DTD XHTML 1.0 Strict//EN"
    "DTD/xhtml1-strict.dtd">

<!DOCTYPE html
    PUBLIC "-//W3C//DTD XHTML 1.0 Transitional//EN"
    "DTD/xhtml1-transitional.dtd">

<!DOCTYPE html
    PUBLIC "-//W3C//DTD XHTML 1.0 Frameset//EN"
    "DTD/xhtml1-frameset.dtd">
```

You can even omit the **<!DOCTYPE>** element, but then your XHTML is not strictly-conforming XHTML. My guess for the longer term is that true XHTML browsers will have the XHTML DTDs built-in, and will be able to validate documents against them without having to fetch those DTDs at all

XHTML Version 1.1

The new version, XHTML version 1.1, is not yet an official recommendation of W3C. Instead, it's in working draft form, which means that it may still change before being accepted and released. You can find the current working draft of XHTML 1.1 at **www.w3.org/TR/xhtml11/**.

XHTML 1.1 is a strict form of XHTML that leaves behind many of the features that have been deprecated but that browsers support today. XHTML 1.1 omits all the deprecated features in HTML 4, for example, and removes a few more as well. XHTML 1 is the present version of XHTML because many people still use deprecated features, but XHTML 1.1 is the future. Because so many deprecated features are still in widespread use, this book is based primarily on XHTML 1, but it's also important for you to know what will and what won't work in XHTML 1.1. For each XHTML tag and attribute, I'm going to indicate whether it's supported by XHTML 1.1.

TIP: *To see the full list of differences between XHTML 1 and XHTML 1.1, see **www.w3.org/TR/xhtml11/changes.html#a_changes**. All the information is included in this book because for each element and attribute, I indicate whether or not XHTML 1.1 supports it.*

If you want to use XHTML 1.1, here's the **<!DOCTYPE>** element you can use:

```
<!DOCTYPE html PUBLIC "-//W3C//DTD XHTML 1.1//EN"
    "http://www.w3.org/TR/xhtml11/DTD/xhtml11.dtd">
```

XHTML 1.1 is written to be *modular*, which means that its DTD is made up of many other, smaller DTDs. I'll discuss this more in Chapter 15; for now, you need to know that the advantage of using modular DTDs is that you can omit those DTDs that you don't want to support, and you can even write your own modules to extend XHTML.

XHTML Basic

There is another form of XHTML, which is also in the working draft stage—XHTML Basic. XHTML Basic is designed for programs that do not support the full set of XHTML features—for example, Web clients such as mobile phones, PDAs, and pagers—because W3C is looking forward to the time when you can use phones to browse the Web. XHTML Basic is a very small subset of XHTML, reduced to a very minimum, and I'm not going to go into it in great depth here. You can find the current working draft for XHTML Basic at **www.w3.org/TR/xhtml-basic/**.

If you want to try out XML Basic, here's the **<!DOCTYPE>** element you can use:

```
<!DOCTYPE html PUBLIC "-//W3C//DTD XHTML Basic 1.0//EN"
    "http://www.w3.org/TR/xhtml-basic/xhtml-basic10.dtd">
```

XHTML Basic is part of an effort to tailor XHTML to special uses. One part of this effort is the idea of document profiles, now under development by W3C. A *document profile* specifies the syntax and semantics of a set of documents. The document profile specifies the facilities required to process documents of that type (which image formats can be used, levels of scripting, style sheet support, and so on). Using document profiles, devices can tell in advance if they can display a particular XHTML document.

Is It True XHTML?

The W3C has specific guidelines for what makes a document a true XHTML document. In particular:

- The document must be validated against one of the official W3C XHTML DTDs.
- The document's root element (the element that encloses all the others that follow) must be **<html>**.
- The root element must designate the XHTML namespace by using the **xmlns** attribute; this namespace should be **"http://www.w3.org/1999/xhtml"**.
- There must be a **<!DOCTYPE>** element before the root element.

As we've seen, you can look at XHTML documents in HTML browsers. However, XHTML is different from HTML, and I'll take a look at the differences now.

How XHTML Differs from HTML

XHTML documents differ from HTML documents in several ways, and I'll list them here. Some of them might not make sense right now, but as you proceed through the book, you can refer to this list.

XHTML Documents Must Be Well-Formed

Well-formedness was first introduced in XML. This means that all elements must either have closing tags or be written in a special form indicating that a closing tag is not needed (see "Ending Empty Elements," coming up), and that all the elements must nest. For example, this is illegal in XHTML:

```
<p>Here is a word in <i>italics.</p></i>
```

This is the correct way:

```
<p>Here is a word in <i>italics.</i></p>
```

Element and Attribute Names Must Be Lowercase

We've already seen this one: XHTML documents must use lowercase for all HTML element and attribute names. This is one of the biggest items that Web-page authors have to adjust to.

Non-Empty Elements Need End Tags

In HTML 4, some elements—such as the **<p>** (paragraph) element—could omit end tags. This omission is not permitted in XML-based XHTML. All elements—other than those that are empty, which means they have no content that would be placed between opening and closing tags—must have an end tag. Here's the wrong way:

```
<p>This is paragraph one.<p>This is paragraph two.
```

Here's the right way:

```
<p>This is paragraph one.</p><p>This is paragraph two.</p>
```

Attribute Values Must Always Be Quoted

In XHTML, you must quote all the values you assign to attributes, even those values that are numeric. (You didn't have to do this in HTML.) Here's the wrong way:

```
<h1 align = center>
```

And here's the right way:

```
<h1 align = "center">
```

> **TIP:** When you're saving a Web page using Internet Explorer 5's Web Page Complete option, you can remove the quotes from the attribute tags within that page. If you want to save an XHTML page in its original format, choose the option to save a page as HTML Only.

No Standalone Attributes

XML does not support *standalone attributes* (such support is also called *attribute minimization*). HTML has a number of attributes that you don't need to assign values to; that is, they can stand alone. (These attributes are: **compact**, **nowrap**, **ismap**, **declare**, **noshade**, **checked**, **disabled**, **readonly**, **multiple**, **selected**, **noresize**, and **defer**.) However, in XHTML, you must assign a value to all attributes you use.

For example, I'm creating a checkbox control and using the **checked** attribute to indicate that the checkbox should appear checked when first displayed. The following way is legal in HTML but not in XHTML:

```
<input type = checkbox checked>
```

Here's the right way, where I'm assigning a value to **checked**:

```
<input type = checkbox checked = "checked">
```

Ending Empty Elements

Empty elements are those that don't take any content. (When defining each element, I'll indicate empty elements with the comment "This element takes no content" in the "Purpose" part of the element's description.) Unlike HTML, in XHTML, empty elements either must have an end tag or must use a start tag that ends with **/>**. For example, the **<hr>** element, which creates a horizontal rule or line, is an empty element and can be used this way in HTML:

```
<hr>
```

Here's one way—using an end tag—to do this in XHTML:

```
<hr></hr>
```

You can also use the XML shortcut for a closing tag by placing **/>** in the start tag, like this (W3C recommends a space before the /):

`<hr />`

In fact, W3C recommends that you use the **<hr />** form instead of the **<hr></hr>** form because expressions like **</hr>** can cause problems or warnings in some browsers.

No HTML Exclusions in XHTML

HTML is written in Standard Generalized Markup Language (SGML), which is a language you use to create markup languages. Using SGML, the developers of HTML included several rules, called *exclusions*, that were impossible to add to XHTML, which is based on XML (a simpler version of SGML).

For example, the HTML 4 strict DTD forbids the nesting of an **<a>** element (used for hyperlinks) within another **<a>** element. It is not possible to indicate such prohibitions in XML. Note that even though these prohibitions cannot be defined in the DTD, certain elements, like the **<a>** element, should not be nested. Here's the full list of prohibitions:

- **<a>** cannot contain other **<a>** elements.
- **<pre>** cannot contain the **<img>**, **<object>**, **<big>**, **<small>**, **<sub>**, or **<sup>** elements.
- **<button>** cannot contain the **<input>**, **<select>**, **<textarea>**, **<label>**, **<button>**, **<form>**, **<fieldset>**, **<iframe>**, or **<isindex>** elements.
- **<label>** cannot contain other **<label>** elements.
- **<form>** cannot contain other **<form>** elements.

Using Elements with id and name Attributes

HTML 4 defined the **name** attribute for the elements **<a>**, **<applet>**, **<form>**, **<frame>**, **<iframe>**, **<img>**, and **<map>**. HTML 4 also introduced the **id** attribute.

XHTML documents must use the **id** attribute and not the **name** attribute, even on elements that have also had a **name** attribute. In fact, in XHTML 1, the **name** attribute of these elements is formally deprecated.

Using Ampersands in Attribute Values

When an attribute value contains an ampersand (&), the ampersand must be expressed as a character entity reference—that is, as **&**. (We'll see more about character entities in Chapter 2.) For example, here's the wrong way to assign a value to an attribute that has an ampersand in it:

```
<input type = "button" value = "Visit BL&T Railroad"></input>
```

Here's the right way:

```
<input type = "button" value = "Visit BL&amp;T Railroad"></input>
```

Converting from HTML to XHTML Automatically

This book is all about writing good XHTML, but if you have a number of HTML pages already, you may wish there was an easy way to translate them all to XHTML. In fact, there is, and it's a utility called Tidy, created by Dave Raggett. This utility is available for a wide variety of platforms, and you can download it for free from **www.w3.org/People/Raggett/tidy**. There's also a complete set of instructions on that page.

Here's an example: I'll use Tidy in Windows to convert a file from HTML to XHTML. In this case, I'll use the example HTML file we developed earlier, as saved in a file named index.html:

```
<HTML>
    <HEAD>
        <TITLE>
            Web page number one!
        </TITLE>
    </HEAD>

    <BODY>
        <H1>
            Welcome to HTML!
        </H1>
    </BODY>
</HTML>
```

After downloading Tidy, you run it at the command prompt, which in Windows means that you open a DOS window. Here are the command-line switches, or options, you can use with Tidy:

- **-config** *file*—Use the configuration file named *file*.
- **-indent** *or* **-i**—Indent element content.
- **-omit** *or* **-o**—Omit optional end tags.

- **-wrap 72**—Wrap text at column 72 (default is 68).
- **-upper** *or* **-u**—Force tags to uppercase (default is lowercase).
- **-clean** *or* **-c**—Replace font, nobr, & and center tags, by CSS (Cascading Style Sheets).
- **-raw**—Don't substitute entities for characters 128 to 255.
- **-ascii**—Use ASCII for output, Latin-1 for input.
- **-latin1**—Use Latin-1 for both input and output.
- **-utf8**—Use UTF-8 for both input and output.
- **-iso2022**—Use ISO2022 for both input and output.
- **-numeric** *or* **-n**—Output numeric rather than named entities.
- **-modify** *or* **-m**—Modify original files.
- **-errors** *or* **-e**—Show only error messages.
- **-quiet** *or* **-q**—Suppress non-essential output.
- **-f** *file*—Write errors to *file*.
- **-xml**—Use this when input is in XML.
- **-asxml**—Convert HTML to XML.
- **-slides**—Burst into slides on h2 elements.
- **-help**—List command-line options.
- **-version**—Show release date.

In the following example, I'll use three switches: **-m** to indicate that I want Tidy to modify the file I pass to it, which will be index.html; **-i** to indicate that I want it to indent the resulting XHTML elements (the default is no indentation); and **-config** to indicate that I want to use a configuration file named config.txt. Here's the example:

```
C:/>tidy -m -i -config config.txt index.html
```

By default, Tidy only cleans up HTML; it does not generate XHTML. To make it generate XHTML, you must include a configuration file—config.txt in my example. (The complete set of configuration file options is available on the Tidy Web site.) Here are the entire contents of config.txt:

```
output-xhtml: yes
add-xml-pi: yes
doctype: loose
```

In this case, I'm using **output-xhtml** to indicate that I want Tidy to create an XHTML document, using **add-xml-pi** to add the **<?xml?>** processing instruction, and using **doctype: loose** to indicate that I want to use the XHTML 1 transitional DTD. (If you don't specify the DTD you want to use, Tidy will make its best guess.) Here's how Tidy changes the HTML file index.html into an XHTML file:

```
<?xml version="1.0"?>
<!DOCTYPE html PUBLIC "-//W3C//DTD XHTML 1.0 Transitional//EN"
    "http://www.w3.org/TR/xhtml1/DTD/xhtml1-transitional.dtd">

<html xmlns="http://www.w3.org/1999/xhtml">
  <head>
    <meta name="generator" content="HTML Tidy, see www.w3.org" />

    <title>Web page number one!</title>
  </head>

  <body>
    <h1> Welcome to HTML!</h1>
  </body>
</html>
```

You can even teach Tidy about new XHTML tags that you've added. If you're ever stuck and want a quick way of translating HTML into XHTML, check out Tidy; it's fast, it's effective, and it's free.

XHTML in Today's Browsers

XHTML is designed to be displayed in modern browsers, and there are some considerations we should think about here. The browser giants today are Netscape Navigator and Microsoft Internet Explorer. Both of them deviate to some degree from the HTML standard as set by W3C, and even further from the XHTML standards. For example, there are quite a few tag attributes that W3C has defined as standard that neither Netscape Navigator nor Internet Explorer implement. And there are quite a few attributes—and even elements—that are not part of the HTML standards at all, but are implemented by one or the other of the big browsers. (Examples include the Netscape Navigator **<LAYER>** element and the Internet Explorer **<MARQUEE>** element.) Things differ by browser version—some attributes appear only in Internet Explorer 5, for example.

It's quite a zoo out there when you come to the actual implementation of XHTML in the various browsers, and that's one of the areas this book is designed to clarify. I'll list the attributes that are part of the XHTML standard, and I'll indicate which attributes are supported by what browser (and even which version of what browser).

There is no true XHTML browser yet, although both Microsoft and Netscape have indicated that they'll produce conforming browser versions. However, you can treat XHTML pages as HTML pages in the major browsers, and for nearly all purposes, there will be no problem.

On the other hand, you can't extend HTML just by creating new XHTML tags because those browsers won't understand them. (The major browsers will not read and use DTDs for documents they think are HTML documents.) You can, though, treat XHTML documents as XML documents (by giving them the extension .xml) in Internet Explorer, and you can use style sheets to indicate how you want your new XHTML elements to be displayed. We'll see how this works in Chapter 15.

The upshot is that we'll push the envelope in this book, seeing exactly how far we can go with XHTML in today's browsers. When true XHTML browsers appear, creating and using new elements in Web pages will be a simple process.

That's it for our overview of HTML, XML, and XHTML. Now I'm going to start talking about the mechanics of actually getting some XHTML into a Web page—and seeing the results.

Creating a Web Page

So how exactly do you create a Web page? We've already seen an example page like this:

```
<?xml version="1.0"?>
<!DOCTYPE html PUBLIC "-//W3C//DTD XHTML 1.0 Transitional//EN"
"http://www.w3.org/TR/xhtml1/DTD/xhtml1-transitional.dtd">
<html xmlns="http://www.w3.org/1999/xhtml" xml:lang="en" lang="en">
    <head>
        <title>
            Web page number one!
        </title>
    </head>

    <body>
        <h1>
            Welcome to HTML!
        </h1>
    </body>
</html>
```

So how exactly do you create an XHTML Web page and get it into a browser? All you have to do is enter the XHTML into a file and then open that file in your Web browser. To create that file, you can use common text editors such as Windows WordPad or Notepad if you save the page in text format. You can even use a word processor such as Microsoft Word, but you cannot save Web pages in .doc format (which includes many special formatting characters that Web browsers won't understand). Files must be saved in a text format from the Save As dialog box.

*TIP: Here's a test for Windows users—if you can view the Web-page content by using the **type** command in a DOS window and see the code without any funny-looking characters, you're doing OK. (The real test, of course, is how your browser displays the page.)*

The name you give the Web page doesn't matter as long as you give it the extension .html to indicate that it should be treated as the browser would treat an HTML document. Because MS-DOS used to recognize only three-letter extensions, you can also use the extension .htm and not have a problem with most browsers.

That's the process. Just enter the previous XHTML in a file and save the file in text format, giving it the extension .html.

You can also use tools called editors to help with the process. I'll take a look at some of these in the next section. (For this book, all you need is a simple text editor like Windows WordPad or Notepad, or vi or emacs in Unix.)

What XHTML Editors Are Available?

XHTML documents are actually XML documents, so you can often use commercially available XML tools to work on them. In particular, you can use many XML editors to edit and create XHTML pages. Here's a starter list of XML editors that are available:

- **www.xmlspy.com/**—XML Spy is a professional validating XML editor that provides three integrated views of XML, XHTML, XSL, RDF, 3DML, and DTD documents. This is the only XML editor I could find that explicitly mentions XHTML.

- **http:// xml.t2000.co.kr/**—Techno2000's CLIP! XML Editor 1.5 provides advanced and powerful XML document creation and editing. An evaluation version is also available.

- **http://xmlwriter.net/**—XMLwriter is a powerful XML Editor, designed to help Web authors and Web application programmers take advantage of the latest XML and XML-related technologies, such as XSL and XQL. XMLwriter provides users with an extensive range of XML functionality, such as validation of XML documents against a DTD or XML schema and the ability to convert XML to HTML by using XSL style sheets. Users can also combine CSS with XML for direct formatting of XML data.

- **www.softquad.com**—SoftQuad Software Inc.'s XMetal makes it easy to create XML documents. XMetal 1 uses an intuitive word processor–like interface to help professional XML document creators quickly become more productive. (Although XMetal is easy to learn, it isn't a visual document creation tool.)

- **www.morphon.com**—The Morphon XML Editor lets you easily create and modify XML documents, checks them for validity, and presents data in a user-friendly way.

- **www.vtopia.com/products/markup/index.html**—According to this site, this editor, Visual Markup, is the most comprehensive XML editor and development tool on the market. With features designed exclusively for software developers, Visual Markup is the ideal tool for integrating applications with XML technology. It offers many, many features.

So, after you've created a Web page, how do you install it on your Web site? I'll take a look at that in the next section.

Installing a Web Page

To install a Web page on the World Wide Web, you use an Internet Service Provider (ISP), such as America Online (AOL), CompuServe, or any one of thousands of local companies (including, increasingly, phone companies that let you connect through fiber optics). You can also use Web sites like GeoCities (**www.geocities.com**) that let you install Web pages free of charge. (There are hundreds of such sites now—just use a Web search engine to search for the phrase "free Web page," and be prepared for many matches; I got 53,113 matches.) The actual installation process depends on your ISP, but I'll go over the process in general here.

What's My URL?

ISPs have their own ways of storing Web pages, and only they will be able to tell you what your page's Web address, its URL, will be. For example, if your ISP is named "**starpowder.com**," your account's name is "steve," and your document is named one.html, then your Web page's URL when you install it may be **http://www.starpowder.com/steve/one.html**

Note the parts of this URL: it begins with **http**, indicating that we're using HTTP (Hypertext Transfer Protocol), which is what you use to look at Web pages in browsers. Next is the name of the ISP followed by the name of your account and then the name of the page, one.html. What your Web page's actual URL will be depends on the ISP; for example, it's common to place a tilde (**~**) before the account name, like this: **http://www.starpowder.com/~steve/one.html**. You might even end up with something like this: **http://www.starpowder.com/customers/steve/one.html**. This is something only your ISP can tell you, so make sure you ask.

Uploading a Web Page

How do you actually send your Web page to your ISP? This also depends on your ISP. Some ISPs (like GeoCities) let you use a browser-based interface that asks you for your account name and password and lets you indicate what file to upload. All you have to do is click on a button, and your Web page is uploaded to the ISP.

It's far more common, however, to use a File Transfer Protocol (FTP) program to send your Web page to your ISP. You'll need an FTP program for that, and often your ISP can provide you with one free of charge. FTP programs exist just for the purpose you want here—to send files across the Internet. In this case, you want to upload your Web page to your ISP. To do that, you need to ask your ISP what its FTP address is. Typically, it'll be much the same as its URL except with **ftp** instead of **http**, like this: **ftp.starpowder.com**. You also need to give your username and password to the FTP program so it knows where to place the Web page you're uploading. If you get stuck, ask the people at your ISP, who will have dealt with similar questions many times before.

There are dozens of FTP programs out there for you to choose from. For example, two good sources of shareware programs for Windows are TUCOWS (The Ultimate Collection of Winsock Software, **www.tucows.com**) and CWSApps (**http://cws.internet.com/index.html**). Here are the FTP programs available at CWSApps (there are reviews of each at the CWSApps site):

- 3D-FTP
- AbsoluteFTP
- Bullet Proof FTP
- CuteFTP
- FTP Explorer
- FTP Icon Connection
- GetRight
- John Junod's WS-FTP
- LeechFTP
- Rhino Software's FTP Voyager
- TransSoft's FTP Control
- WinTelnet and FTP Pro

Here's an example of using CuteFTP to connect to a site. When you start the program, CuteFTP's Site Manager dialog box appears, as shown in Figure 1.4. You click the Add Site button, and in the dialog box that opens, you enter the FTP address of your ISP (such as **ftp.starpowder.com**), your username (such as "steve"), and your password (such as "open sesame"). Click OK to close the dialog box and add this new site to the Site Manager. Then select the site with the mouse and click the Connect button.

This connects to your account on your ISP, shown in Figure 1.5. In the left window is your local directory. You use the drop-down list boxes at the top to move to the

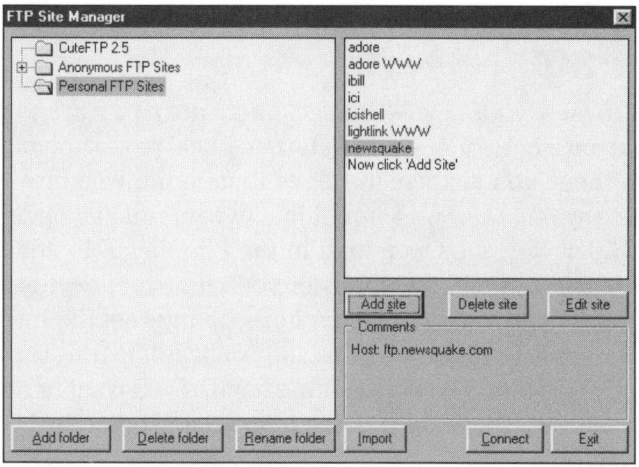

Figure 1.4   CuteFTP's Site Manager dialog box.

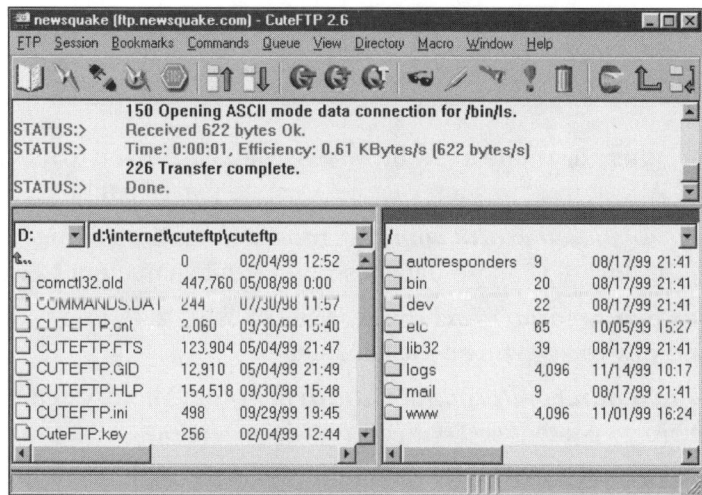

Figure 1.5   ISP account connection.

directory with your Web page, one.html. In the right window, there's a listing of your account on your ISP. To upload your Web page, all you have to do is to use the mouse to drag the one.html file from the left window to the right window, and the FTP program will do the rest. That's it—now your Web page is uploaded, installed on your ISP, and ready to view.

TIP: *The default Web page for your site should be called index.html (or index.htm) because Web browsers will look for a page with that name if no particular Web page is specified. For example, these refer to the same page:* **www.starpowder/steve/** *and* **www.starpowder/steve/index.html**. *Note that if your Web server uses Microsoft Internet Information Server (IIS), the default page is named default.htm.*

Viewing a Web Page

You use a Web browser to view your new Web page. There are two ways to view a Web page: locally and from a network like the Internet. Local pages are on your own computer. To open them, you just use the Open item in the Web browser's File menu. For example, say one.html was stored in c:\www. You can open that file directly in your browser with the Open item in the File menu. In addition, both Netscape Navigator and Internet Explorer let you enter the location of a Web page by typing it directly into a box (labeled Address in Internet Explorer, as you can see in Figure 1.3, and Location in Netscape Navigator). You can type **c:\www\one.html** directly into that box. On the other hand, if you want to open a Web page from the Internet, you just connect to the Internet and enter the URL of that page directly into that box.

TIP: *A great way to debug your Web pages is to work on them locally. Open them in your Web browser, and each time you change them, save the changes in your editor and reload the pages. (Use the Reload button in Netscape Navigator and the Refresh button in Internet Explorer.) This will save you from having to upload the page to your ISP each time you want to test a change.*

As you might expect, there are quite a few browsers available for you to use, and they all support XHTML, at least to some degree. Here's a partial list:

- *Alis Technology's Tango (**www.alis.com**)*—A browser that is good for handling Arabic, Devangari, Chinese, Japanese, and Kanji characters.
- *Amaya (**www.w3.org/Amaya/**)*—A browser used by W3C to test new HTML, and a good way to keep up on the latest features.
- *HotJava (**http://java.sun.com/products/hotjava/**)*—Sun Microsystems' browsers, which are well-integrated with current Java versions.
- *Lynx (**www.lynx.browser.org**)*—A text-based Web browser, popular in Unix shell accounts.

- *Microsoft Internet Explorer (**www.microsoft.com/ie/**)*—Microsoft's browser, now in Release 5. Internet Explorer is trying hard to become the king of browsers. Free and huge, it's become the choice of many. One of the two top browsers.
- *NCSA Mosaic (**www.ncsa.uiuc.edu/SDG/Software/Mosaic/**)*—One of the early and most popular browsers; development on it was stopped in 1997.
- *Netscape Navigator, part of the Netscape Communicator suite (**www.netscape.com**)*—The original big browser, now in competition with Internet Explorer. Navigator was the first one to come up with dynamic HTML and many other innovations. One of the two top browsers.
- *Opera (**www.operasoftware.com**)*—A small and innovative browser from Norway; Windows platform only.

Now that your Web page is up, how do you know it's proper XHTML? One way is to use an XHTML *validator*.

Checking Your Web Page

W3C has a special validator program that will tell you if your Web page is true XHTML. You can find this validator at **http://validator.w3.org/**. All you have to do is enter the URL of the Web page you want to check and click on the Validate This Page button. The W3C validator will check the page and give you a full report. Here's an example response:

```
Congratulations, this document validates as XHTML1.0 Transitional!
To show your readers that you have taken the care to create an
interoperable Web page, you may display this icon on any page that
validates. Here is the HTML you could use to add this icon to your
Web page:
  <p>
    <a href="http://validator.w3.org/check/referer"><img
        src="http://validator.w3.org/images/vxhtml10"
        alt="Valid XHTML 1.0!" height="31" width="88" /></a>
  </p>
```

The icon referred to in this output appears in Figure 1.6, and you can put such icons in your Web pages to indicate that they are true XHTML.

Figure 1.6   The W3C icon for validated XHTML.

You can often use HTML validators to check XHTML pages as well and, depending on the strictness of the validator, get useful information on how HTML browsers might view your page. (Sometimes, however, HTML validators will complain about things that browsers won't, such as the **<?xml?>** element or treating **/** as an "unknown attribute" of elements like **<hr />**.) Many such programs are free and exist on the Web; all you do is enter the URL of the page you want checked, and you'll get a full report. Here are some HTML validators available on the Web:

- *CAST's Bobby (**www.cast.org/bobby/**)*—A validator that lets you test for accessibility features as well as standard HTML.
- *CSE 3310 HTML Validator (**www.htmlvalidator.com**)*—A commercial validator used by thousands of users.
- *Neil Bower's Weblint (**www.cre.canon.co.uk/~neilb/weblint/**)*—An HTML validator, written in Perl, that operates online.
- *WebTechs Validation Service (**www.webtechs.com/html-val-svc/**)*—A validator that lets you check an entire page or just sections of HTML.

And that's it. We've taken a look at what XHTML is, where it comes from, how to use it to create Web pages, how to install and view those Web pages, and even how to check them. It's now time to get some hands-on experience in the "Immediate Solutions" section, beginning with how to start a Web page. Let's start writing some XHTML.

`<?xml?>`—Starting an XML Document

Purpose: Formally starts an XML document and indicates the version of XML used.

Supported: [1.0S, 1.0T, 1.0F, 1.1]

Attributes:

- **encoding**—Gives the character encoding set. The default is UTF-8 or UTF-16 (depends on the browser).

- **standalone**—Set this attribute to "Yes" if the document is complete by itself, or "No" if it imports other documents.

- **version**—This required attribute sets the XML version; for XHTML, that's 1.0.

The novice programmer says, "OK, I'm ready to start my XHTML document! Where do I begin?" "With the **`<?xml?>`** processing instruction," you say, in your capacity as Web Wizard. "**`<?xml?>`**?" the NP asks, "Never heard of it!"

Because XHTML documents are XML documents, you start them with the **`<?xml?>`** processing instruction, as we saw in the "In Depth" section of this chapter:

```
<?xml version="1.0"?>
<!DOCTYPE html PUBLIC "-//W3C//DTD XHTML 1.0 Transitional//EN"
   "http://www.w3.org/TR/xhtml1/DTD/xhtml1-transitional.dtd">
<html xmlns="http://www.w3.org/1999/xhtml" xml:lang="en" lang="en">
    <head>
        <title>
            Web page number one!
        </title>
    </head>

    <body>
        <h1>
            Welcome to XHTML!
        </h1>
    </body>
</html>
```

The **<?xml?>** processing instruction is not required. W3C strongly encourages you to use this processing instruction in all your documents, however, to indicate that the document is based on XML. In particular, you'll need that processing instruction when the character encoding of the document is something other than the default UTF-8 or UTF-16. However, XML processing instructions can be displayed in some browsers, which is a problem (neither Internet Explorer nor Netscape Navigator has this problem).

<!DOCTYPE>—Specifying a Document's Type

Purpose: Specifies a document's type. (This element and its attributes are all in capitals.)

When used as HTML: Start tag/End tag: Required/None

Supported: [1.0S, 1.0T, 1.0F, 1.1, 1, 2, 3, 3.2, 4]

Attributes: None

The novice programmer says, "OK, I'm ready to start adding text and images to my Web page!" "Not so fast," you say; "What about the **<!DOCTYPE>** tag?" "**<!DOCTYPE>**?" the NP asks, "Never heard of it!"

This is an important one; you need the **<!DOCTYPE>** element to indicate which XHTML DTD you want to use in your document; this DTD indicates which version of XHTML you want to use. Including this element is necessary to have a true XHTML document.

Here's how I used the **<!DOCTYPE>** element in the example developed in the "In Depth" section of this chapter:

```
<?xml version="1.0"?>
<!DOCTYPE html PUBLIC "-//W3C//DTD XHTML 1.0 Transitional//EN"
"http://www.w3.org/TR/xhtml1/DTD/xhtml1-transitional.dtd">
<html xmlns="http://www.w3.org/1999/xhtml" xml:lang="en" lang="en">
    <head>
        <title>
            Web page number one!
        </title>
    </head>

    <body>
        <h1>
```

```
        Welcome to XHTML!
    </h1>
  </body>
</html>
```

For the details—such as which XHTML DTDs are available, what those DTDs mean, and which **<!DOCTYPE>** element to use—see the section "XHTML" in the "In Depth" part of this chapter. We'll see how to create our own DTDs in Chapter 13. For the most part, I'll use the XHTML 1 transitional DTD in this book (as you see in the code example here). Throughout the book, when introducing elements and attributes, I'll indicate which ones are supported by which XHTML DTDs.

In practice, the major browsers ignore the **<!DOCTYPE>** tag for files with the extension .html because the browsers expect the document to be in HTML. (However, Internet Explorer will read it if the document is an XML document with the extension .xml.) That's a problem because if you're extending XHTML to create your own new elements, you do that in the DTD. If the browser doesn't read the DTD, it doesn't know about the new elements. That's one of the reasons a lot of XHTML authors can hardly wait for true XHTML browsers.

<html>—Creating the Document's Root Element

Purpose: The root element encloses all the following elements.

When used as HTML: Start tag/End tag: Optional/Optional

Supported: [1.0S, 1.0T, 1.0F, 1.1, 2, 3, 3.2, 4, IE1, IE2, IE3, IE4, IE5, NS1, NS2, NS3, NS4]

Attributes:

- **class**—Class of the element (used for rendering). [IE4, IE5]
- **dir**—Gives the direction of directionally neutral text (text that doesn't have an inherent direction in which you should read it). Possible values: **LTR**, left-to-right text or table; and **RTL**, right-to-left text or table. [1.0S, 1.0T. 1.0F, 1.1, 4, IE5]
- **id**—Unique alphanumeric identifier for the tag; you can use the ID to refer to the tag. [IE4, IE5]
- **lang**—Base language used for the tag. [1S, 1T, 1F, 4]
- **version**—Deprecated. Version of the language used. Version information is now stored in the **<!DOCTYPE>** tag. [1, 2, 3, 3.2]

- **xml:lang**—Holds the base language for the element when the document is interpreted as an XML document. [1.0S, 1.0T, 1.0F, 1.1]
- **xmlns**—Required in XHTML. This attribute should be set to "**http://www.w3.org/1999/xhtml**". [1.0S, 1.0T, 1.0F, 1.1, IE5]

XHTML events: None

"Say," asks the novice programmer, "I've heard that all XHTML elements must go into the document's root element. What's that?" "The **<html>** element," you say. "Ah," the NP replies, "tell me more."

The **<html>** element is the root element in XHTML pages, which means that it contains all the elements that follow it. The **<html>** element shows how XHTML rewrites HTML in XML—this element is the rewrite of the HTML **<HTML>** element in XML. As the root element of our XML-based documents, it could have any name, but to match HTML documents, W3C gave it the name **html**. Here's an example that we've already seen:

```
<?xml version="1.0"?>
<!DOCTYPE html PUBLIC "-//W3C//DTD XHTML 1.0 Transitional//EN"
 "http://www.w3.org/TR/xhtml1/DTD/xhtml1-transitional.dtd">
<html xmlns="http://www.w3.org/1999/xhtml" xml:lang="en" lang="en">
    <head>
        <title>
            Web page number one!
        </title>
    </head>

    <body>
        <h1>
            Welcome to XHTML!
        </h1>
    </body>
</html>
```

TIP: *The start and end tags for **<html>** are optional. However, that's not the case for a true XHTML document; you must have start and end tags for **<html>**.*

The one required attribute in **<html>** is the **xmlns** attribute—the XML namespace attribute—and it must be set to "**http://www.w3.org/1999/xhtml**" (see the "XHTML" section in the "In Depth" part of this chapter for more details). You can also use the **lang** and **xml:lang** attributes to change the language from the default English.

TIP: *You can find the possible settings for the **lang** and **xml:lang** attributes for languages other than English in the document RFC1766 (RFC stands for Request For Comments). You can find this document by searching the Internet.*

When you're specifying the language of an element (the default is English), use both the **lang** and **xml:lang** attributes (the value of the **xml:lang** attribute takes precedence in XHTML).

Creating the Structure of a Web Page: Head and Body

"Can you take a look at my Web page?" the novice programmer asks; "I think it's a doozy." "Hm," you say, "where's the head section? Where's the body?" "Do I need those?" the NP asks. You smile and say, "Pull up a chair."

XHTML documents have a certain structure, as defined in the XHTML DTD created by W3C. To be valid XHTML, a Web page must have an **<html>** element, and the **<html>** element can contain both a **<head>** element and a **<body>** element (except for Web pages that use the frameset DTD, where the **<html>** element can contain both a **<head>** element and a **<frameset>** element). The **<head>** element contains general information about the document, and the **<body>** element contains the contents of the document. The **<head>** element should contain a **<title>** element. The **<body>** element is not required to contain any other elements. Note the use of these elements in the following example:

```
<?xml version="1.0"?>
<!DOCTYPE html PUBLIC "-//W3C//DTD XHTML 1.0 Transitional//EN"
    "http://www.w3.org/TR/xhtml1/DTD/xhtml1-transitional.dtd">
<html xmlns="http://www.w3.org/1999/xhtml" xml:lang="en" lang="en">
    <head>
        <title>
            Web page number one!
        </title>
    </head>

    <body>
        <h1>
            Welcome to XHTML!
        </h1>
    </body>
</html>
```

Because Web pages are divided into head and body sections, I'll take a look at those sections in the remainder of this chapter.

<head>—Creating a Web Page's Head

Purpose: Contains the head of an XHTML document. Holds information about the document, such as its title.

When used as HTML: Start tag/End tag: Optional/Optional

Supported: [1.0S, 1.0T, 1.0F, 1.1, 2, 3, 3.2, 4, IE1, IE2, IE3, IE4, IE5, NS1, NS2, NS3, NS4]

Attributes:

- **class**—Class of the element (used for rendering). [IE4, IE5]
- **dir**—Gives the direction of directionally neutral text (text that doesn't have an inherent direction in which you should read it). Possible values: **LTR**, left-to-right text or table; and **RTL**, right-to-left text or table. [1.0S, 1.0T, 1.0F, 1.1, 4]
- **id**—Unique alphanumeric identifier for the tag; you can use the ID to refer to the tag. [IE4, IE5]
- **lang**—Base language used for the tag. [1.0S, 1.0T, 1.0F, 1.1, 4, IE4, IE5]
- **profile**—Gives the location of one or more white space–separated metadata profile URLs for the current document. Profiles can hold a great deal of information about the document. [1.0S, 1.0T, 1.0F, 1.1, 4]
- **xml:lang**—Holds the base language for the element when the document is interpreted as an XML document. [1.0S, 1.0T, 1.0F, 1.1]

XHTML events: None

The novice programmer wants to know, "What's so important about a Web page's head?" "Well," you say, "among other things, every Web page should have one. There are certain elements, like **<title>**, that can appear only in the page's head. Also, it's possible to request just a Web page's head, and search engines often do, so it's important to put lots of information in the head." "You've sold me," says the NP.

Each properly defined XHTML page should have a head, which you create with the **<head>** tag:

```
<?xml version="1.0"?>
<!DOCTYPE html PUBLIC "-//W3C//DTD XHTML 1.0 Transitional//EN"
    "http://www.w3.org/TR/xhtml1/DTD/xhtml1-transitional.dtd">
<html xmlns="http://www.w3.org/1999/xhtml" xml:lang="en" lang="en">
    <head>
        <title>
            Web page number one!
        </title>
    </head>
```

```
    <body>
        <h1>
            Welcome to XHTML!
        </h1>
    </body>
</html>
```

The head of a Web page holds information about the page, such as its title, keywords for search engines, a base address for URLs, and more.

In the **<head>** tag, you can use the standard attributes, such as **lang**, and one attribute particular to **<head>**: the **profile** attribute. This attribute can hold a list of URLs that contain metadata about the page that would be returned with the **<meta>** tag (coming up in a few pages). Metadata can include the page's author, copyright, description, and more. Note that although **profile** is part of the XHTML 1, XHTML 1.1, and HTML 4 specifications, neither Netscape Navigator nor Internet Explorer supports it yet.

Here are the elements that can appear in the head:

- **<base>**—Base URL for the document
- **<basefont>**—Base font for the document [IE]
- **<bgsound>**—Background sound [IE]
- **<isindex>**—Rudimentary input control
- **<link>**—Indicates a relationship between the document and another object
- **<meta>**—Header information
- **<nextid>**—Hint for the **name** value to use when creating a new hyperlink element [IE]
- **<noscript>**—Holds text that appears only if the browser does not support the **<script>** tag (some browsers might not display text from elements in the **<head>** element, so you might want to place **<noscript>** outside the **<head>** element)
- **<script>**—Holds programming script statements, such as JavaScript
- **<style>**—Includes style information for rendering
- **<title>**—The Web page's title, which appears in the Web browser

I'll cover the following tags throughout the book: working with **<bgsound>** in Chapter 8, **<isindex>** in Chapter 12, **<link>** and **<base>** in Chapter 5, **<style>** in Chapter 9, and **<script>** in Chapters 10 and 11. In this chapter, I'll look at the two important tags that can appear only in the head: **<title>** and **<meta>**. These two topics are discussed in the next two sections.

<title>—Giving a Web Page a Title

Purpose: Contains the title of the XHTML document. The title appears in the Web browser's title bar and is used by search engines to refer to the document. Each **<head>** element should include a **<title>** element.

When used as HTML: Start tag/End tag: Required/Required

Supported: [1.0S, 1.0T, 1.0F, 1.1, 2, 3, 3.2, 4, IE1, IE2, IE3, IE4, IE5, NS2, NS3, NS4]

Attributes:

- **class**—Class of the element (used for rendering). [NS4]
- **dir**—Gives the direction of directionally neutral text (text that doesn't have an inherent direction in which you should read it). Possible values: **LTR**, left-to-right text or table; and **RTL**, right-to-left text or table. [1.0S, 1.0T, 1.0F, 1.1]
- **id**—Unique alphanumeric identifier for the tag; you can use the ID to refer to the tag. [IE5, NS4]
- **lang**—Base language used for the tag. [1.0S, 1.0T, 1.0F, 1.1, 4, IE4, IE5, NS4]
- **style**—Inline style indicating how to render the element. [4, NS4]
- **xml:lang**—Holds the base language for the element when the document is interpreted as an XML document. [1.0S, 1.0T, 1.0F, 1.1]

XHTML events: None

"Hm," says the novice programmer, "Why does the HTML validator say: 'Error 34405: Missing **title** element' when I run it on my Web page?" You smile and say, "Probably because you didn't include a **<title>** element in the page's head. It's required for proper HTML pages, or for XHTML pages that want to be treated as such, and it must be in the head." "Well, that's it," the NP says, "No more HTML validators for me."

The **<title>** element indicates the document's title to the browsers. The W3C XHTML DTDs say "Exactly one title is required per document." Even though the W3C XHTML validator doesn't complain if you leave it out, you should put a **<title>** element in every document. The text in the **<title>** element is displayed in the browsers' title bars.

It's a good idea to keep the text in the title relatively short and to the point. Keep in mind that people may read the title out of context—as when it's displayed by a search engine—so try to establish a little context if you can. For example, rather than call your page "View 5," call it "The Austrian Alps At Sunset." You might also keep in mind that besides the list of keywords you embed in your Web page (see the following section), many search engines search a Web page's title first. So, if there are special keywords you want people to use to find your page, the title is one place to put them.

We've already seen an example **<title>** element at the beginning of this chapter:

```
<?xml version="1.0"?>
<!DOCTYPE html PUBLIC "-//W3C//DTD XHTML 1.0 Transitional//EN"
"http://www.w3.org/TR/xhtml1/DTD/xhtml1-transitional.dtd">
<html xmlns="http://www.w3.org/1999/xhtml" xml:lang="en" lang="en">
    <head>
        <title>
            Web page number one!
        </title>
    </head>

    <body>
        <h1>
            Welcome to XHTML!
        </h1>
    </body>
</html>
```

The result of this XHTML appears in Figure 1.3. Note that if you omit the title in a Web page, no browser (none that I know of, anyway) will react badly. In general, browsers are written to be very forgiving; however, I recommend that you do give all but the shortest pages a title because the title bar of the browser is a natural place for the user to check when they're looking at your pages.

TIP: *Some browsers will have problems if you use titles longer than 256 characters. In addition, some browsers may use the title as the page's file name if the user saves it. Be careful when defining multiple titles; Netscape Navigator will use the first one you've defined, for example, but earlier versions of Internet Explorer will use the last one.*

<meta>—Giving More Information about Your Web Page

Purpose: Includes metadata about your Web page. Metadata consists of keywords for search engines, refresh rates for client pull, and more. Metadata is passed as name/value pairs like this: **name="description"**, **value="Western view of the Alps"**, or **http-equiv="refresh" content="5"**. This element takes no content.

When used as HTML: Start tag/End tag: Required/Omitted.

Supported: [1.0S, 1.0T, 1.0F, 1.1, 2, 3, 3.2, 4, IE2, IE3, IE4, IE5, NS1, NS2, NS3, NS4]

Attributes:

- **content**—Required attribute giving the content of a name/value pair. The actual value you use depends on whether you're using the **name** attribute or the **http-equiv** attribute. [1.0S, 1.0T, 1.0F, 1.1, 2, 3, 3.2, 4, IE2, IE3, IE4, IE5, NS1, NS2, NS3, NS4]

- **dir**—Gives the direction of directionally neutral text (text that doesn't have an inherent direction in which you should read it). Possible values: **ltr**, left-to-right text or table; and **rtl**, right-to-left text or table. [1.0S, 1.0T, 1.0F, 1.1, 4]

- **id**—Unique alphanumeric identifier for the tag; you can use the ID to refer to the tag. [NS4]

- **http-equiv**—Connects the **content** attribute to an HTTP header field. If a browser asks for the page, the value of the **content** attribute will be passed to the browser as part of the HTTP header. [1.0S, 1.0T, 1.0F, 1.1, 2, 3, 3.2, 4, IE2, IE3, IE4, IE5, NS1, NS2, NS3, NS4]

- **lang**—Base language used for the tag. [1.0S, 1.0T, 1.0F, 1.1, 4, NS4]

- **name**—Connects the **content** attribute to a name, such as "Keywords." When a Web browser or other agent requests the data connected to the name, the value of the **content** attribute will be sent. [1.0S, 1.0T, 1.0F, 1.1, 2, 3, 3.2, 4, IE2, IE3, IE4, IE5, NS1, NS2, NS3, NS4]

- **scheme**—Specifies a predetermined format to be used to interpret the **content** attribute's value. [1.0S, 1.0T, 1.0F, 1.1, 4]

- **xml:lang**—Holds the base language for the element when the document is interpreted as an XML document. [1.0S, 1.0T, 1.0F, 1.1]

"I've finished my Web page," the novice programmer says, "but how do I get the search engines to notice it?" "Besides submitting the URL to the search engines," you say, "you should use the **<meta>** element to indicate the keywords that the search engines use to help people find your page."

The **<meta>** element, an empty element, lets you provide information about your page in two ways. First, the **<meta>** element connects values to names, such as **"Steve"** to **"Author"**; in this example, people who want to find out who the author of the page is can check the value corresponding to the **author** term. Second, by placing information in HTTP headers, you can determine the page's behavior. For example, you can tell the Web browser to refresh the page automatically every few seconds.

One very common use for the **<meta>** element is to include keywords that search engines will store to help people find your page. For example, if you wanted to connect the keywords "vacation," "Austria," and "sun" to your Web page, you would do that with a name/value pair by setting the **name** attribute to **"keywords"** and setting the **content** attribute to **"vacation, sun, Austria"**. (Because this is an empty element, I end it with **/>** as recommended by W3C.) Here's the code:

```
<meta name="keywords" content="vacation, sun, Austria" />
```

You can also specify the language for the tag, such as the following U.S. English, British English, and French versions:

```
<meta name="keywords" lang="en-us" content="vacation, sun, Austria" />
<meta name="keywords" lang="en" CONTENT="holiday, sun, Austria" />
<meta name="keywords" lang="fr" CONTENT="vacances, soleil, Austria" />
```

Here's a popular way to use the HTTP header, called *client pull*. In this case, you can instruct a browser to keep refreshing your page every few seconds by creating an HTTP REFRESH header with the **http-equiv** attribute. In the following code, I instruct the Web browser to refresh the page every five seconds:

```
<meta http-equiv="refresh" content="5" />
```

Another popular use for **<meta>** is to override the browser's caching system by using the **expires** value to give a time when the page expires (you've probably seen the warning "Page has expired" in your browser). Browsers must not cache the requested page beyond the date given. Here's an example:

```
<meta http-equiv="expires" content="date" />
```

You can also use the **<meta>** element in Internet Explorer 4 and later versions to allow special effects to occur while the page is loading or unloading. Here's how that works in general:

```
<meta http-equiv="[event]" content="Duration=[seconds],
transition=[transition]" />
```

In this case, *event* can be Page-Enter, Page-Exit, Site-Enter, or Site-Exit; *seconds* is the transition time in seconds, and *transition* is an integer from 0 to 23 that represents a transition effect.

You can also use **reply-to** to give an email address that users can reply to if they want to get in touch with you. Here's an example:

```
<meta http-equiv="reply-to" content="steve@starpowder.com" />
```

Many HTML editors use the **generator** value for **name** when giving the name of the editor that generated the code, like this:

```
<meta name="generator" content="SuperDuperHTMLEditorPro" />
```

The **<meta>** element should be used to include information about the page's author, a description of the page, and a copyright notice. Here's how that might look:

```
<?xml version="1.0"?>
<!DOCTYPE html PUBLIC "-//W3C//DTD XHTML 1.0 Transitional//EN"
"http://www.w3.org/TR/xhtml1/DTD/xhtml1-transitional.dtd">
<html xmlns="http://www.w3.org/1999/xhtml" xml:lang="en" lang="en">
    <head>
        <meta name="author" content="Steve" />
        <meta name="description" content="My Web Page" />
        <meta name="copyright" content="Copyright 2000 by Steve" />
        <title>
            Web page number one!
        </title>
    </head>

    <body>
        <h1>
            Welcome to XHTML!
        </h1>
    </body>
</html>
```

</head>—Ending a Web Page's Head

"Hey," says the novice programmer, "I've written my entire Web page, but nothing appears in my Web browser. Is it a bug? Here's the XHTML." "It's not a bug," you say, "you've just forgotten to end your **<head>** element, and because nothing in that element except the title is displayed in a Web browser, you end up with a blank page." "Oh," says the NP, "darn."

Don't forget to end your page's **<head>** element with the **</head>** tag:

```
<?xml version="1.0"?>
<!DOCTYPE html PUBLIC "-//W3C//DTD XHTML 1.0 Transitional//EN"
"http://www.w3.org/TR/xhtml1/DTD/xhtml1-transitional.dtd">
<html xmlns="http://www.w3.org/1999/xhtml" xml:lang="en" lang="en">
```

```
    <head>
        <title>
            Web page number one!
        </title>
    </head>

    <body>
        <h1>
            Welcome to XHTML!
        </h1>
    </body>
</html>
```

\<body\>—Creating a Web Page's Body

Purpose: Contains the body of the XHTML document. The body includes the content that will appear in the browser window. The entire content of the Web page is placed in the page's **\<body\>** element.

When used as HTML: Start tag/End tag: Optional/Optional

Supported: [1.0S, 1.0T, 1.1, 2, 3, 3.2, 4, IE1, IE2, IE3, IE4, IE5, NS1, NS2, NS3, NS4]

Attributes:

- **accesskey**—Keyboard shortcut key; a single character is used as the value of this attribute. The user can type a platform-dependent key (such as Alt) with the **accesskey** character to trigger the active field. Set to an alphanumeric character. [4, IE4, IE5]

- **alink**—Deprecated. Color of hyperlinks as they're being clicked. Set it to a color value or a predefined color name. [1.0T, 1.0F, 3.2, 4, IE4, IE5, NS1, NS2, NS3, NS4]

- **background**—Deprecated. The URL of a graphic file to be used in tiling the browser's background. [1.0T, 1.0F, 3, 3.2, 4, IE1, IE2, IE3, IE4, IE5, NS1, NS2, NS3, NS4]

- **bgcolor**—Deprecated. The color of the browser's background. Set it to one of the predefined colors or a color value. [1.0T, 1.0F, 3.2, 4, IE1, IE2, IE3, IE4, IE5, NS1, NS2, NS3, NS4]

- **bgproperties**—Indicates whether the background should scroll when the text does. If you set it to **fixed**, the only allowed value, the background will not scroll when the text does. [IE2, IE3, IE4, IE5]

- **bottommargin**—Specifies the bottom margin in pixels. [IE4, IE5]

- **class**—Class of the element (used for rendering). [1.0S, 1.0T, 1.0F, 1.1, 3, 4, IE4, IE5, NS4]
- **contenteditable**—Set to **true** if you want the content of the control to be editable. [IE5]
- **datafld**—Name of the column of the data source object that supplies the bound data. Set to alphanumeric characters. [IE4, IE5]
- **dataformatas**—Specifies if bound data is plain text or HTML. Set to **html**, **plaintext**, or **text**. [IE4, IE5]
- **datasrc**—Gives the URL or ID of the data source object supplying data bound to this element. W3C says this should be a URL, Internet Explorer says it should be a data source ID. [IE4, IE5]
- **dir**—Gives the direction of directionally neutral text (text that doesn't have an inherent direction in which you should read it). Possible values: **ltr**, left-to-right text or table; and **rtl**, right-to-left text or table. [1.0S, 1.0T, 1.0F, 1.1, 4, IE5]
- **id**—Unique alphanumeric identifier for the tag; you can use the ID to refer to the tag. [1.0S, 1.0T, 1.0F, 1.1, 3, 4, IE4, IE5, NS4]
- **lang**—Base language used for the tag. [1.0S, 1.0T, 1.0F, 1.1, 3, 4, IE4, IE5, NS4]
- **language**—Scripting language used for the tag. [IE4, IE5]
- **leftmargin**—Specifies the left margin in pixels. [IE2, IE3, IE4, IE5]
- **link**—Deprecated. Color of hyperlinks that have not been visited (identified by the browser). Set it to a color value or a predefined color name. [1.0T, 1.0F, 3.2, 4, IE1, IE2, IE3, IE4, IE5, NS1, NS2, NS3, NS4]
- **marginheight**—Gives the height of the top and bottom margins in pixels. [NS4]
- **marginwidth**—Gives the width of the left and right margins in pixels. [NS4]
- **nowrap**—Specifies if text wrapping is allowed or not. [IE4, IE5]
- **rightmargin**—Specifies the right margin in pixels. [IE4, IE5]
- **scroll**—Specifies whether a vertical scrollbar appears to the right of the document; can be **YES** (the default) or **NO**. [IE4, IE5]
- **style**—Inline style indicating how to render the element. [1.0S, 1.0T, 1.0F, 1.1, 4, IE3, IE4, IE5, NS4]
- **tabindex**—Sets the tab index of the element, which locates it in the tab order of the form, allowing the user to press the Tab key and navigate from element to element. Set to positive or negative integers. [4, IE4, IE5]
- **text**—Deprecated. Color of the text in the document. Set it to a color value or a predefined color. [1.0T, 1.0F, 3.2, 4, IE1, IE2, IE3, IE4, IE5, NS1, NS2, NS3, NS4]

- **title**—Holds additional information (as might be displayed in tool tips) for the element. [1.0S, 1.0T, 1.0F, 1.1, 3, 4, IE4, IE5]
- **topmargin**—Specifies the top margin in pixels. [IE2, IE3, IE4, IE5]
- **vlink**—Deprecated. Color of hyperlinks that have been visited (identified by the browser). Set it to a color value or a predefined color name. [1.0T, 1.0F, 3.2, 4, IE1, IE2, IE3, IE4, IE5, NS1, NS2, NS3, NS4]
- **xml:lang**—Holds the base language for the element when the document is interpreted as an XML document. [1.0S, 1.0T, 1.0F, 1.1]

XHTML events: onclick, ondblclick, onload, onmousedown, onmouseup, onmouseover, onmousemove, onmouseout, onkeypress, onkeydown, onkeyup, onunload

"What's so important about the **<body>** element?" the novice programmer asks; "Do I need to use it?" "Not if you don't want anything to appear in your Web page," you say. "Hey," the NP says, "I do!" "Then you should use the **<body>** element," you say.

The **<head>** element is where you place information about your page; the **<body>** element is where you place the content of the page (unless you're dividing the page into frames, in which case you use **<frameset>**). This is an important tag—and a big one, as you can see by its large number of attributes. Everything on your Web page—headings, text, images, multimedia elements, and animated graphics—goes into the **<body>** element.

We've already seen a rudimentary example where the content of a page is just an **<h1>** heading:

```
<?xml version="1.0"?>
<!DOCTYPE html PUBLIC "-//W3C//DTD XHTML 1.0 Transitional//EN"
"http://www.w3.org/TR/xhtml1/DTD/xhtml1-transitional.dtd">
<html xmlns="http://www.w3.org/1999/xhtml" xml:lang="en" lang="en">
    <head>
        <title>
            Web page number one!
        </title>
    </head>

    <body>
        <h1>
            Welcome to XHTML!
        </h1>
    </body>
</html>
```

Again, notice the great number of attributes available for this tag. Because it encloses the entire body of the document, this is a natural place to set attributes that affect the entire displayed content. For example, to add a left margin of 200 pixels to a page, you can use the Internet Explorer **leftmargin** attribute:

```
<?xml version="1.0"?>
<!DOCTYPE html PUBLIC "-//W3C//DTD XHTML 1.0 Transitional//EN"
"http://www.w3.org/TR/xhtml1/DTD/xhtml1-transitional.dtd">
<html xmlns="http://www.w3.org/1999/xhtml" xml:lang="en" lang="en">
    <head>
        <title>
            Web page number one!
        </title>
    </head>

    <body leftmargin = "200">
        <h1>
            Welcome to XHTML!
        </h1>
    </body>
</html>
```

The result appears in Figure 1.7.

The **leftmargin** attribute is specific to Internet Explorer. You can set margins in Netscape Navigator by using the attribute **marginwidth**. Here, I'm setting the horizontal margins to 200 pixels:

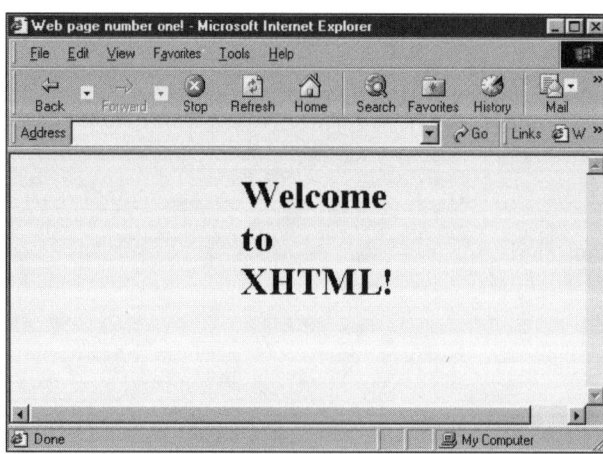

Figure 1.7 Setting margins in Internet Explorer.

```
<?xml version="1.0"?>
<!DOCTYPE html PUBLIC "-//W3C//DTD XHTML 1.0 Transitional//EN"
"http://www.w3.org/TR/xhtml1/DTD/xhtml1-transitional.dtd">
<html xmlns="http://www.w3.org/1999/xhtml" xml:lang="en" lang="en">
    <head>
        <title>
            Web page number one!
        </title>
    </head>

    <body marginwidth = "200">
        <h1>
            Welcome to XHTML!
        </h1>
    </body>
</html>
```

The results of this XHTML appear in Figure 1.8 (although strictly speaking, neither the **leftmargin** nor the **marginwidth** attributes are true XHTML).

If you've written HTML before, you may be startled to see that many cherished attributes (as of HTML 4) are now considered deprecated. Deprecated attributes include:

- **alink**—The color of links as they're clicked
- **background**—The URL of a background image to use to tile the browser's background
- **bgcolor**—The color of the browser's background
- **link**—The color of hyperlinks that have not been visited
- **text**—The color to use for the text in the page
- **vlink**—The color of hyperlinks that have been visited

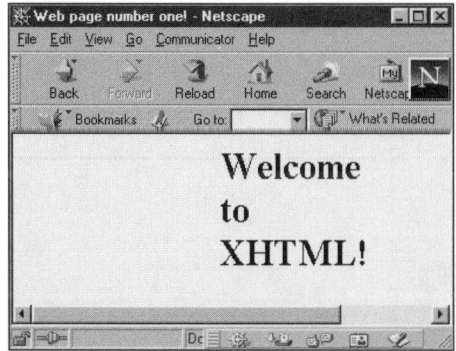

Figure 1.8   Setting margins in Netscape Navigator.

Instead of using these attributes, you're now supposed to use style sheets, which I'll discuss in Chapter 9.

In the following code, I set the background color of a page to white, its text color to black, the color of hyperlinks (created with the **<a>** tag) to red, the color of activated links to blue, and the color of visited links to green, all using attributes of the **<body>** element:

```
<?xml version="1.0"?>
<!DOCTYPE html PUBLIC "-//W3C//DTD XHTML 1.0 Transitional//EN"
"http://www.w3.org/TR/xhtml1/DTD/xhtml1-transitional.dtd">
<html xmlns="http://www.w3.org/1999/xhtml" xml:lang="en" lang="en">
    <head>
        <title>
            This is a Web page!
        </title>
    </head>

    <body bgcolor="white" text="black" link="red" alink="blue"
        vlink="green">
        Welcome to my page!
        If you don't like it, you can go to
        <a href="http://www.w3c.org">W3C</a>.
    </body>
</html>
```

This page, including the hyperlink to W3C (which appears in green because I've been to the W3C site before), is shown in Figure 1.9. As you can see, it works, but the fact is, it's not strict XHTML.

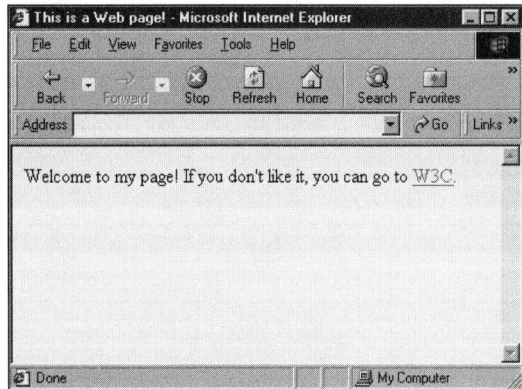

Figure 1.9   Using colors in a Web page.

To make the same page adhere to the XHTML strict standard, you'd use style sheets, as I'll do in Chapter 9. Here's how this page looks using a **<style>** element to set up the same colors:

```
<?xml version="1.0"?>
<!DOCTYPE html PUBLIC "-//W3C//DTD XHTML 1.0 Transitional//EN"
"http://www.w3.org/TR/xhtml1/DTD/xhtml1-transitional.dtd">
<html xmlns="http://www.w3.org/1999/xhtml" xml:lang="en" lang="en">
    <head>
        <title>
            This is a Web page!
        </title>
        <style type="text/css">
            body {background: white; color: black}
            a:link {color: red}
            a:visited {color: green}
            a:active {color: blue}
        </style>
    </head>

    <body>
        Welcome to my page!
        If you don't like it, you can go to
        <a href="http://www.w3c.org">W3C</a>.
    </body>
</html>
```

The result of this XHTML is shown in Figure 1.9. I've just used a style sheet instead of XHTML elements to specify colors. In fact, this brings up the question of just how do you specify colors in Web pages—to find out, see the following section.

TIP: *One nice effect in Internet Explorer is to turn off background scrolling, which you do by setting the **scroll** attribute to **no**. Only the content will scroll when the user manipulates the scrollbars. This gives the user the feeling that the content is being displayed on a glass sheet that moves up and down against a stationary background. To make this effect noticeable, of course, you have to provide background graphics using the **background** attribute. Also note that if you use the **background** attribute and the **bgcolor** attribute in the same page, the **bgcolor** attribute is ignored.*

Setting Web Page Colors

"Say," says the novice programmer, "I'm writing a page that shows the company's annual budget—how do you color text red?" "You can use color values or predefined colors," you say, "But what do you want red for?" "To show how far we're in the hole," the NP says. "Uh oh," you say.

Many XHTML elements and attributes let you specify colors. For example, you can set the **text** attribute of the **<body>** element to a specific color, which changes the color of the text in the document's body. To specify colors in Web pages, there are two ways that browsers will recognize: refer to predefined colors by name, or refer to colors by color values—also called RGB (Red, Green, Blue) triplets. I'll take a look at them both here.

NOTE: *It's still common for programmers to specify colors using elements and attributes, even though they have been deprecated. W3C encourages you to use style sheets instead.*

Using Predefined Colors

The W3C has added to HTML the names of 16 colors that browsers are supposed to recognize. They are listed in Table 1.2.

You can use these names directly when you want to specify a color, as in this example:

```
<?xml version="1.0"?>
<!DOCTYPE html PUBLIC "-//W3C//DTD XHTML 1.0 Transitional//EN"
    "http://www.w3.org/TR/xhtml1/DTD/xhtml1-transitional.dtd">
<html xmlns="http://www.w3.org/1999/xhtml" xml:lang="en" lang="en">
    <head>
        <title>
            Web page number one!
        </title>
    </head>

    <body text = "red">
        <h1>
            Welcome to XHTML!
        </h1>
    </body>
</html>
```

The result of this XHTML appears in Figure 1.10, and it works as intended.

Table 1.2 Colors recognized by browsers.

Aqua	Black	Blue	Fuchsia
Gray	Green	Lime	Maroon
Navy	Olive	Purple	Red
Silver	Teal	White	Yellow

Immediate Solutions

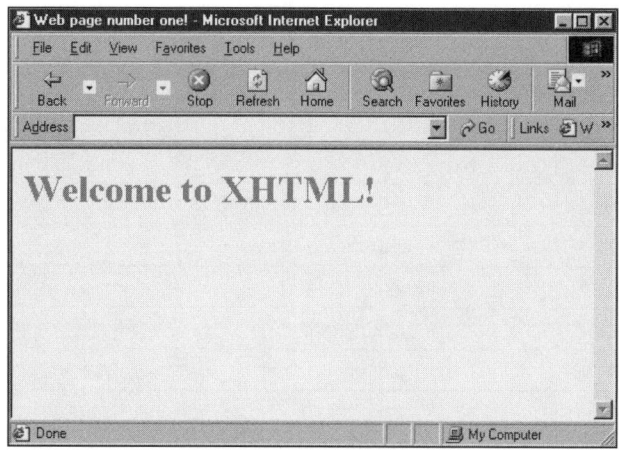

Figure 1.10   Using red text in a Web page.

As you know, the big browsers have a way of outpacing W3C. Both Internet Explorer and Netscape Navigator have defined additional colors. You'll find the predefined colors for Internet Explorer in Table 1.3 and the predefined colors for Netscape Navigator in Table 1.4.

Table 1.3   Predefined colors in Internet Explorer.

aliceblue	antiquewhite	aqua	aquamarine
azure	beige	bisque	black
blanchedalmond	blue	blueviolet	brown
burlywood	cadetblue	chartreuse	chocolate
coral	cornflowerblue	cornsilk	crimson
cyan	darkblue	darkcyan	darkgoldenrod
darkgray	darkkhaki	darkmagenta	darkolivegreen
darkorange	darkorchid	darkred	darksalmon
darkseagreen	darkslateblue	darkslategray	darkturquoise
darkviolet	deeppink	deepskyblue	dimgray
dodgerblue	firebrick	floralwhite	ghostwhite
gold	goldenrod	gray	green
greenyellow	honeydew	hotpink	indianred
indigo	ivory	khaki	lavender
lavenderblush	lawngreen	lemonchiffon	lightblue
lightcoral	lightcyan	lime	maroon
navy	olive	purple	red
silver	teal	white	yellow

Table 1.4 Predefined colors in Netscape Navigator.

aliceblue	antiquewhite	aqua	aquamarine
azure	beige	black	blanchedalmond
blue	blueviolet	brown	burlywood
cadetblue	chartreuse	chocolate	coral
cornflowerblue	cornsilk	crimson	cyan
darkblue	darkcyan	darkgoldenrod	darkgray
darkgreen	darkkhaki	darkmagenta	darkolivegreen
darkorange	darkorchid	darkred	darksalmon
darkseagreen	darkslateblue	darkslategray	darkturquoise
darkviolet	deeppink	deepskyblue	dimgray
dodgerblue	firebrick	floralwhite	forestgreen
fuchsia	gainsboro	ghostwhite	gold
goldenrod	gray	green	greenyellow
honeydew	hotpink	indianred	indigo
ivory	khaki	lavender	lavenderblush
lawngreen	lemonchiffon	lightblue	lightcoral
lightcyan	lightgoldenrodyellow	lightgreen	lightgray
lightpink	lightsalmon	lightseagreen	lightskyblue
lightslategray	lightsteelblue	lightyellow	lime
limegreen	linen	magenta	maroon
mediumaquamarine	mediumblue	mediumorchid	mediumpurple
mediumseagreen	mediumslateblue	mediumspringgreen	mediumturquoise
mediumvioletred	midnightblue	mintcream	mistyrose
moccasin	navajowhite	navy	oldlace
olive	olivedrab	orange	orangered
orchid	palegoldenrod	palegreen	paleturquoise
palevioletred	papayawhip	peachpuff	peru
pink	plum	powderblue	purple
red	rosybrown	royalblue	saddlebrown
salmon	sandybrown	seagreen	seashell
sienna	silver	skyblue	slateblue
slategray	snow	springgreen	steelblue
tan	teal	thistle	tomato
turquoise	violet	wheat	white
whitesmoke	yellow	yellowgreen	

Creating Color Values

You can also specify colors using color values. Color values are expressed as ***rrggbb***, where ***rr*** is the value you want to use for the red component of the color, ***gg*** specifies the green component, and ***bb*** specifies the blue component. Values range from 0 through 255 and are expressed as hexadecimal (Base16) two-digit numbers. The only trick here is getting used to using hexadecimal values ranging from **00** to ***ff*** (hexadecimal ***ff*** = 255 because hexadecimal digits range from 0 to 9 and then from a to f).

Here's an example. The color value for pure red is **ff0000** (you can use lowercase or uppercase letters as far as the browsers are concerned, so this is the same as **FF0000**). Although not required by many browsers, you indicate this number as hexadecimal by placing a number symbol (**#**, also called a sharp symbol) in front of it like this: **#ff0000**. So you would specify pure red to a browser as "**#ff0000**" (the quotes are necessary for all XHTML attribute values). Here's how the previous Web page would look using a color value instead of the predefined value **red**:

```
<?xml version="1.0"?>
<!DOCTYPE html PUBLIC "-//W3C//DTD XHTML 1.0 Transitional//EN"
"http://www.w3.org/TR/xhtml1/DTD/xhtml1-transitional.dtd">
<html xmlns="http://www.w3.org/1999/xhtml" xml:lang="en" lang="en">
    <head>
        <title>
            Web page number one!
        </title>
    </head>

    <body text = "#ff0000">
        <h1>
            Welcome to XHTML!
        </h1>
    </body>
</html>
```

Following is a list of the color values for each of the W3C predefined colors:

- Aqua = "**#00ffff**"
- Black = "**#000000**"
- Blue = "**#0000ff**"
- Fuchsia = "**#ff00ff**"
- Gray = "**#808080**"
- Green = "**#008000**"
- Lime = "**#00ff00**"

- Maroon = "**#800000**"
- Navy = "**#000080**"
- Olive = "**#808000**"
- Purple = "**#800080**"
- Red = "**#ff0000**"
- Silver = "**#c0c0c0**"
- Teal = "**#008080**"
- White = "**#ffffff**"
- Yellow = "**#ffff00**"

TIP: *How do you make sure that a color value appears as you want it to? The best way is to check it out in your browser. Another way is to find a color picker or color chooser online (just use a search engine to search for those terms); this utility often lets you use scrollbars to select the red, green, and blue settings for color values interactively.*

Adding Text to a Web Page

The novice programmer wants to know, "How do I add simple text to a Web page? What tag do I use?" You smile and say, "You don't use any tag at all. You just put the text right into the Web page." The NP asks, "Just like that? No tag?" "Just like that," you say.

I'll cover how to work with text in Chapter 2, but it's worthwhile getting the basics down now in this chapter on fundamentals. In its simplest form, it's easy to enter plain text into a Web page; you just place that text in the **<body>** element, like this:

```
<?xml version="1.0"?>
<!DOCTYPE html PUBLIC "-//W3C//DTD XHTML 1.0 Transitional//EN"
"http://www.w3.org/TR/xhtml1/DTD/xhtml1-transitional.dtd">
<html xmlns="http://www.w3.org/1999/xhtml" xml:lang="en" lang="en">
    <head>
        <title>
            Web page number one!
        </title>
    </head>

    <body>
        <h1>
```

```
            Welcome to XHTML!
        </h1>
            This is simple text that appears in this page.
    </body>
</html>
```

The result of this XHTML appears in Figure 1.11.

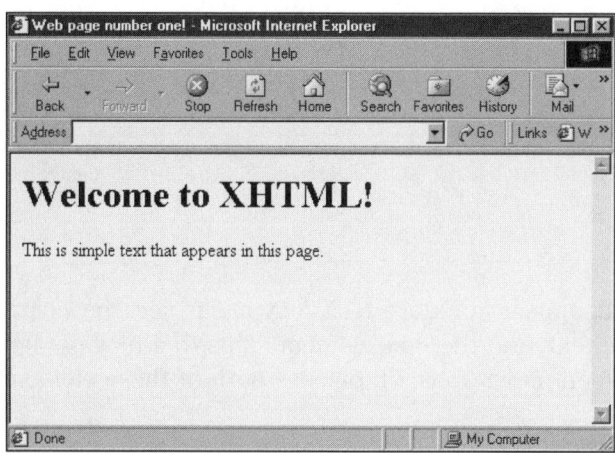

Figure 1.11   Displaying simple text in a page.

Basic Text Formatting

"Hey," says the novice programmer, "you said I could just enter text into a Web page, but when I try to skip to the next paragraph in the text, my browser just ignores it." "That's because browsers format what you type," you say, "so you have to use the **<p>** tag to start a new paragraph."

We'll see how to format text in Chapter 2, but again it's worth taking a quick look here to get some basic skills down. For example, to center text, you can use the **<center>** element. To start a new paragraph, you can use the **<p>** element. (Note that in XHTML, unlike HTML, the **<p>** tag needs a closing tag, **</p>**.) Here's an example:

```
<?xml version="1.0"?>
<!DOCTYPE html PUBLIC "-//W3C//DTD XHTML 1.0 Transitional//EN"
"http://www.w3.org/TR/xhtml1/DTD/xhtml1-transitional.dtd">
<html xmlns="http://www.w3.org/1999/xhtml" xml:lang="en" lang="en">
    <head>
        <title>
```

```
            Web page number one!
        </title>
    </head>

    <body>
        <h1>
            Welcome to XHTML!
        </h1>
        <center>
        This is simple text that appears in this page.
            <p>
                Here's a new paragraph!
            </p>
        </center>
    </body>
</html>
```

The results of this XHTML appear in Figure 1.12. As you can see, the **<center>** element has centered the text, and the **<p>** element skips to a new paragraph, leaving some space between paragraphs. I'll discuss both of these elements in more detail later.

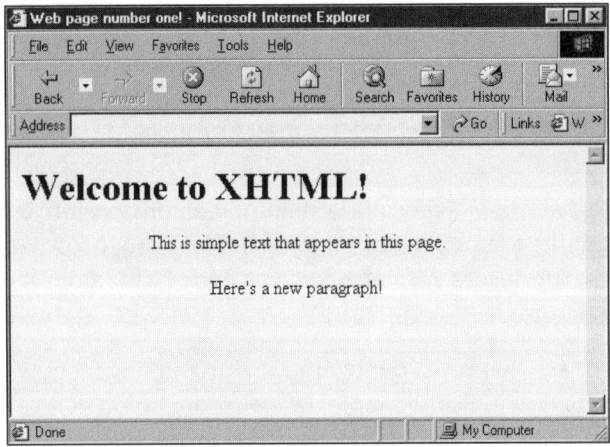

Figure 1.12 Displaying simple formatted text in a page.

<!-->—Comments and Server Side Includes

Purpose: Annotates a Web page with a comment in the XHTML. You can read the comment by looking at the XHTML, but it will not be displayed in the Web browser. This element takes no content.

When used as HTML: Start tag/End tag: Required/Omitted

Supported: [1.0S, 1.0T, 1.0F, 1.1, 2, 3, 3.2, 4, IE1, IE2, IE3, IE4, IE5, NS1, NS2, NS3, NS4]

Attributes: None

"There's one more basic skill you should have," you tell the novice programmer. "What's that?" the NP asks. "You should know how to comment a Web page by using the XHTML **comment** element."

Comments do not appear in the browser window. You use them to annotate a Web page so that you or someone else can tell what's going on in the code. You enclose an XHTML comment in the **<!--*comment*-->** tag, like this: **<!--This is a comment-->**. Here's an example where I've annotated this Web page with comments:

```
<?xml version="1.0"?>
<!DOCTYPE html PUBLIC "-//W3C//DTD XHTML 1.0 Transitional//EN"
"http://www.w3.org/TR/xhtml1/DTD/xhtml1-transitional.dtd">
<html xmlns="http://www.w3.org/1999/xhtml" xml:lang="en" lang="en">
    <!-- This is the head of the page-->
    <head>
        <!-- This title will appear in the browser's title bar-->
        <title>
            Web page number one!
        </title>
    </head>

    <!-- This is the body of the page-->
    <body>
        <h1>
            <!-- Here's an H1 element that makes up the body-->
            Welcome to XHTML!
        </h1>
    </body>
</html>
```

None of these comments will appear in the browser, but they'll all be in the XHTML, so you can take a look at them when you want. Because comments are in the XHTML, they'll be downloaded with the rest of the page. So if you have a lot of comments, bear in mind that they can affect download time.

Another use for the **<!-->** tag is to create *Server Side Includes*. You can use Server Side Includes to send commands to or get data from many Web servers. You embed Server Side Includes in XHTML pages, and you give those pages the extension .shtml, not .html. Table 1.5 lists of some of the popular Server Side includes.

Table 1.5 Popular Server Side Includes.

Server Side Include	Does This
`<!--#config errmsg="Uh oh"-->`	Sets the format for error messages
`<!--#config sizefmt="%d"-->`	Sets the format for displaying file sizes
`<!--#config timefmt="%s"-->`	Sets the format for displaying dates
`<!--#echo var="DATE_GMT" -->`	Echoes the Greenwich Mean Time (GMT) and date
`<!--#echo var="DATE_LOCAL" -->`	Echoes the local date and time
`<!--#echo var="DOCUMENT_NAME" -->`	Echoes the document's name
`<!--#echo var="DOCUMENT_URI" -->`	Echoes the document's virtual path and name
`<!--#echo var="LAST_MODIFIED" -->`	Echoes the date the document was last modified
`<!--#exec cgi="cgi/script.cgi"-->`	Executes a Common Gateway Interface (CGI) script
`<!--#exec cmd="shell command"-->`	Executes a shell command
`<!--#flastmod file="file.txt"-->`	Displays the time a file was last modified
`<!--#fsize file="file.txt"-->`	Displays the size of a file
`<!--#include file="file.txt"-->`	Displays a given file

I'll take a look at some Server Side Includes here by writing an example named ssi.shtml. In this case, I'll just display the values of various Server Side Include variables, such as the name of the document (ssi.shtml):

```
Document name: <!--#echo var="DOCUMENT_NAME" -->
```

Because the server I'll use is Unix-based, I'll also execute the Unix command **uptime** to find out how long the server has been up:

```
Up time: <!--#exec cmd="uptime" -->
```

Here's the full Web page, ssi.shtml:

```
<?xml version="1.0"?>
<!DOCTYPE html PUBLIC "-//W3C//DTD XHTML 1.0 Transitional//EN"
    "http://www.w3.org/TR/xhtml1/DTD/xhtml1-transitional.dtd">
<html xmlns="http://www.w3.org/1999/xhtml" xml:lang="en" lang="en">
    <head>
        <title>
            Server Side Includes
        </title>
    </head>

    <body>
        <center>
            <h1>
```

```
            Server Side Includes
        </h1>
    </center>
    <h3>
        <p>
            Document name: <!--#echo var="DOCUMENT_NAME" -->
        </p>
        <p>
            Document path: <!--#echo var="DOCUMENT_URI" -->
        </p>
        <p>
            Server name: <!--#echo var="SERVER_NAME" -->
        </p>
        <p>
            Local date: <!--#echo var="DATE_LOCAL" -->
        </p>
        <p>
            Up time: <!--#exec cmd="uptime" -->
        </p>
    </h3>
</body>
</html>
```

The results appear in Figure 1.13. As you can see, the server itself has filled in the values of the variables I want to display; it has also executed the **uptime** command, displaying how long the server has been up.

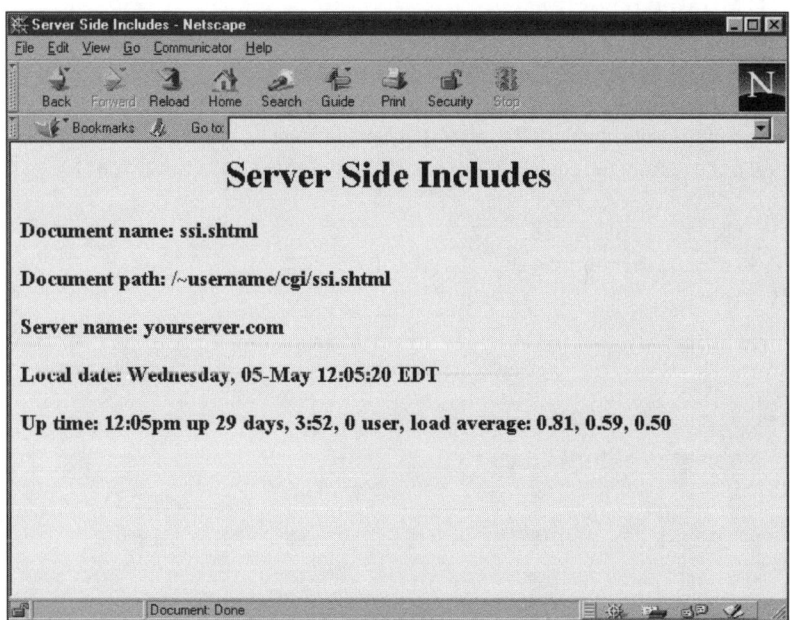

Figure 1.13   Using Server Side Includes.

</body>—Ending a Web Page's Body

To end the Web page's body, use the **</body>** tag:

```
<?xml version="1.0"?>
<!DOCTYPE html PUBLIC "-//W3C//DTD XHTML 1.0 Transitional//EN"
    "http://www.w3.org/TR/xhtml1/DTD/xhtml1-transitional.dtd">
<html xmlns="http://www.w3.org/1999/xhtml" xml:lang="en" lang="en">
    <head>
        <title>
            Web page number one!
        </title>
    </head>

    <body>
        <h1>
            Welcome to XHTML!
        </h1>
    </body>
</html>
```

</html>—Ending a Web Page

To end a Web page, use the closing **</html>** tag, which should always be the last tag in an XHTML Web page:

```
<?xml version="1.0"?>
<!DOCTYPE html PUBLIC "-//W3C//DTD XHTML 1.0 Transitional//EN"
    "http://www.w3.org/TR/xhtml1/DTD/xhtml1-transitional.dtd">
<html xmlns="http://www.w3.org/1999/xhtml" xml:lang="en" lang="en">
    <head>
        <title>
            Web page number one!
        </title>
    </head>

    <body>
        <h1>
            Welcome to XHTML!
        </h1>
    </body>
</html>
```

Chapter 2
Working with Text

If you need an immediate solution to:	See page:
Displaying Plain Text	79
`<h1>` through `<h6>`—Creating Web Page Headings	80
`<b>`—Creating Bold Text	83
`<i>`—Creating Italic Text	84
`<tt>`—Creating "Teletype" Text	85
`<u>`—Underlining Text	87
`<s>` and `<strike>`—Striking Text out	89
`<big>`—Creating Big Text	91
`<small>`—Creating Small Text	93
`<sub>`—Creating Subscripts	94
`<sup>`—Creating Superscripts	96
`<em>`—Emphasizing Text	98
`<strong>`—Strongly Emphasizing Text	99
`<code>`—Displaying Program Code	101
`<samp>`—Displaying Sample Program Output	102
`<kbd>`—Displaying Text the User is to Type	104
`<var>`—Displaying Program Variables and Arguments	105
`<dfn>`—Defining New Terms	106
`<cite>`—Creating a Citation	108
`<abbr>`–Displaying Abbreviations	109
`<acronym>`–Displaying Acronyms	110
`<font>`—Specifying a Font	111
Setting Font Size in Points	115
`<basefont>`—Setting the Base Font	116

(continued)

If you need an immediate solution to:	See page:
`<q>`—Displaying Short Quotations	118
`<blink>`—Making Text Blink	119
`<ins>`—Displaying Inserted Text	120
`<del>`—Displaying Text as Deleted	122
`<address>`—Displaying an Address	124
`<bdo>`—Overriding the Bidirectional Character Algorithm	126
Displaying Special Characters: Character Entities	128

In Depth

XHTML specializes in handling text, and we're going to take advantage of that in this chapter. The most basic element of Web pages in general does not consist of animated images, multimedia elements, Java applets, or ActiveX controls—it's text. And this is the chapter where we begin creating real Web pages that show what's possible when working with text in XHTML.

Originally, HTML could handle only text and not even simple images. So, throughout its history, HTML has had much opportunity to elaborate on how it works with text. There are dozens of HTML elements, and therefore XHTML elements, dedicated to this purpose. In this chapter, I'll look at how to set text styles in Web pages. I'll discuss everything from using bold, italics, and alternate fonts to creating headings and more. In Chapter 3, I'll discuss how to arrange text in a Web page by indenting it, spacing it vertically, and even overlapping it. Because creating Web pages has so much to do with displaying text, the material in both this chapter and Chapter 3 is essential information.

Character Sets in XHTML

Many different character sets are available on the Internet, and you can write your XHTML document in any of them (as long as your browser is familiar with it). To specify what character encoding you're using in the document, you use the **encoding** attribute of the **<?xml?>** processing instruction. The default, if you omit this attribute, is to use the Unicode UTF-8 eight-bit character set (or the UTF-16 sixteen-bit character set, depending on the browser you're using). You can specify the character encoding explicitly like this:

```
<?xml version="1.0" encoding="UTF-8"?>
<!DOCTYPE html PUBLIC "-//W3C//DTD XHTML 1.0 Transitional//EN"
    "http://www.w3.org/TR/xhtml1/DTD/xhtml1-transitional.dtd">
<html xmlns="http://www.w3.org/1999/xhtml" xml:lang="en" lang="en">
    <head>
        <title>
            Web page number one!
        </title>
    </head>
```

```
        <body>
            <h1>
                Welcome to XHTML!
            </h1>
        </body>
</html>
```

The character encoding you use can affect how the browser handles your text; for example, in Unicode, browsers are supposed to treat spaces, tabs, carriage returns, and line feeds all as "whitespace" characters, the same as a space. You can specify other character encodings, like Japanese, this way:

```
<?xml version="1.0" encoding="EUC-JP"?>
<!DOCTYPE html PUBLIC "-//W3C//DTD XHTML 1.0 Transitional//EN"
    "http://www.w3.org/TR/xhtml1/DTD/xhtml1-transitional.dtd">
<html xmlns="http://www.w3.org/1999/xhtml" xml:lang="en" lang="en">
    <head>
        <title>
            Web page number one!
        </title>
    </head>

    <body>
        <h1>
            Welcome to XHTML!
        </h1>
    </body>
</html>
```

W3C also recommends that you specify such encodings in a **<meta>** element with the **charset** attribute. (For details about the **<meta>** element, see Chapter 1.) Although this is not required, it can help some browsers and search engines to determine the language of your document. Here's an example of using the **<meta>** element with the **charset** attribute:

```
<?xml version="1.0" encoding="EUC-JP"?>
<!DOCTYPE html PUBLIC "-//W3C//DTD XHTML 1.0 Transitional//EN"
    "http://www.w3.org/TR/xhtml1/DTD/xhtml1-transitional.dtd">
<html xmlns="http://www.w3.org/1999/xhtml" xml:lang="en" lang="en">
    <head>
        <title>
            Web page number one!
        </title>
        <meta http-equiv="Content-type"
            content='text/html; charset="EUC-JP"' />
    </head>
```

```
        <body>
            <h1>
                Welcome to XHTML!
            </h1>
        </body>
</html>
```

HTML 4 has a number of significant changes concerning text formatting, and I'll provide an overview of them now.

Formatting with XHTML Elements

As we saw in the previous chapter, if you place just plain text in a Web page, Web browsers will simply treat it as a word processor would—displaying it in the current default font. To set the style of text for display in a Web page, you can use *text style tags*, such as **<i>** to make text italic and **<b>** to make text bold. The text between the opening **<i>** tag and the closing **</i>** tag will appear in italics in a Web page.

You can even *nest* text style tags. For example, within the text between the **<i>** and **</i>** tags, you can use the **<b>** and **</b>** tags; the text between those tags will be both italic *and* bold.

Here's an example showing how this works:

```
<?xml version="1.0"?>
<!DOCTYPE html PUBLIC "-//W3C//DTD XHTML 1.0 Transitional//EN"
"http://www.w3.org/TR/xhtml1/DTD/xhtml1-transitional.dtd">
<html xmlns="http://www.w3.org/1999/xhtml" xml:lang="en" lang="en">
    <head>
        <title>
            Using italics
        </title>
    </head>

    <body>
        <p>
            <i>Here is some text displayed in italics and
            <b>bold</b> too.</i>
        </p>
    </body>
</html>
```

The result of this XHTML appears in Figure 2.1.

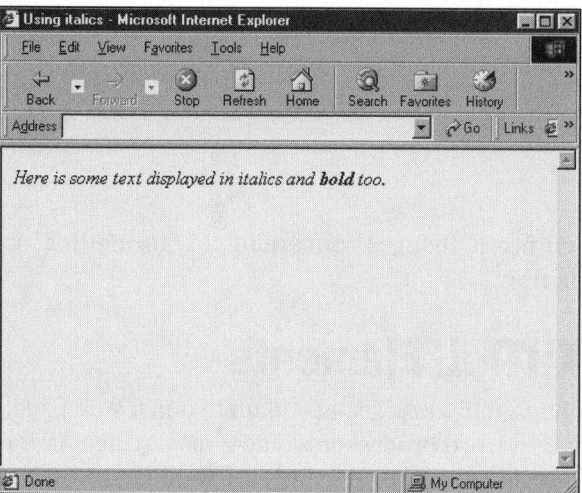

Figure 2.1   Using XHTML tags to format text as italic and bold.

As you see from this example, it was simple enough to set the style of text used in this page. However, this kind of direct formatting is somewhat rudimentary, and XHTML has advanced beyond it. Now you use style sheets instead of simple tags. Here's an example that reproduces the previous Web page. I'll set the style of the **<p>** tag to italics and use a **<span>** tag (covered in Chapter 3) to set the style of the word "bold" to bold. You might think that you could use the **font-style** style to set both italic and bold styles, but in fact you use **font-weight** to set the bold style.

```
<?xml version="1.0"?>
<!DOCTYPE html PUBLIC "-//W3C//DTD XHTML 1.0 Transitional//EN"
"http://www.w3.org/TR/xhtml1/DTD/xhtml1-transitional.dtd">
<html xmlns="http://www.w3.org/1999/xhtml" xml:lang="en" lang="en">
    <head>
        <title>
            Using italics
        </title>
    </head>

    <body>
        <p style="font-style: italic">
            Here is some text displayed in italics and
            <span style="font-weight: bold">bold</span> too.
        </p>
    </body>
</html>
```

This code produces the page you see in Figure 2.1. Actually, style sheets were not introduced to set the styles manually tag by tag as I've done here; rather, style sheets are intended to set the styles for whole documents and libraries of documents. The way this typically works is that you set the styles for entire tags all at once, as you see in the following example, where I'm making the **<p>** tag display italic text:

```
<?xml version="1.0"?>
<!DOCTYPE html PUBLIC "-//W3C//DTD XHTML 1.0 Transitional//EN"
 "http://www.w3.org/TR/xhtml1/DTD/xhtml1-transitional.dtd">
<html xmlns="http://www.w3.org/1999/xhtml" xml:lang="en" lang="en">
    <head>
        <title>
            Using italics
        </title>

        <style type="text/css">
            p {font-style: italic}
        </style>
    </head>

    <body>
        <p>
            Here is some text displayed in italics and
            <span style="font-weight: bold">bold</span> too.
        </p>
    </body>
</html>
```

There are a number of ways to apply styles to text. Some of them are quite sophisticated, and we'll cover them in Chapter 9. This new way is more complex than the old way, so even though the World Wide Web Consortium (W3C) now endorses the use of style sheets, you can be sure that the old way of doing things will be around for a long time.

Tags like **<i>** and **<b>** are called *physical styles* in XHTML; that is, they specify exactly how the browser should display text. In addition to physical styles, there are also *logical styles*, which leave the actual styling up to the browser. For example, one logical style is **<em>** for emphasized, and the interpretation of this tag is up to the browser. In practice, **<em>** is usually displayed as italics. I'll take a look at the physical styles first, then the logical styles.

Physical XHTML Styles

Here's a list of the original HTML physical style tags:

- **\<b\>**—Displays bold text.
- **\<i\>**—Displays italic text.
- **\<tt\>**—Displays "teletype" text, usually rendered in a monospace font (where each character has the same width).

HTML 3.2 added these physical styles:

- **\<big\>**—Displays text larger than usual.
- **\<small\>**—Displays text smaller than usual.
- **\<s\>** and **\<strike\>**—Displays struck-through text. These tags have been deprecated in HTML 4.
- **\<sub\>**—Displays a subscript.
- **\<sup\>**—Displays a superscript.
- **\<u\>**—Displays underlining. This tag has been deprecated in HTML 4.

TIP: *One reason the* **\<big\>** *and* **\<small\>** *elements were introduced was to allow people with disabilities to access the Web. Browsers can display text in a larger font, and even if you specify a text size that you think is large, that size may be smaller than what someone is used to reading. In such cases, it's better to use the* **\<big\>** *tag and leave the details up to the browser.*

You'll find all these elements in XHTML too. Physical styles were defined to let you format your text exactly, but there are also a number of tags—the logical style tags—that let you specify your intention and leave the details up to the browser.

Logical XHTML Styles

You use logical styles when you want to leave the formatting up to the browser. For example, when you want to emphasize text strongly, you can use the **\<strong\>** tag. Here's the list of the original logical HTML tags:

- **\<address\>**—Address
- **\<cite\>**—Citation or reference to another source
- **\<code\>**—Code (program listing) text
- **\<dfn\>**—Defining instance of the enclosed term
- **\<em\>**—Emphasized text
- **\<kbd\>**—Text the user should enter

- **<samp>**—Sample output (as from programs)
- **<strong>**—Strongly emphasized text
- **<var>**—Variable or programming term from code

HTML 4 added these logical tags:

- **<abbr>**—Abbreviation
- **<acronym>**—Acronym

TIP: *In fact, there is one more logical style,* ***<blockquote>****, which I'll deal with in Chapter 3. This style indents its text rather than just setting its style.*

XHTML supports these tags, too. In the preceding lists, you can see the beginnings of working with style sheets. The logical styles are one step up from the physical styles, like **<b>** and **<i>**, in that they leave the formatting up to the user environment. Because formatting is content-based, the logical styles include tags for all sorts of situations, such as defining a new term, displaying output from programs, requesting user input, and so on. Of course, using this method was naturally doomed to failure because no one can anticipate all the styles that will be needed in all documents. So the next step was to incorporate style sheets, which is the way things work today.

In fact, far from the rich formatting that W3C was hoping these logical styles would provide, they have been implemented in virtually all browsers only as simple italics, bold, and monospace fonts as you see in Table 2.1.

Table 2.1 How logical tags are rendered.

Tag	Rendered As
<abbr>	Italics or plain text
<acronym>	Italics or plain text
<address>	Italics
<cite>	Italics
<code>	Monospaced font
<dfn>	Italics or plain text
<em>	Italics
<kbd>	Bold or standard monospaced font
<samp>	Monospaced
<strong>	Bold
<var>	Italics

I'll put all these styles to work in one page. In the following example, I'm using the **
** element, which we'll see in the next chapter, to introduce a line break:

```
<?xml version="1.0"?>
<!DOCTYPE html PUBLIC "-//W3C//DTD XHTML 1.0 Transitional//EN"
"http://www.w3.org/TR/xhtml1/DTD/xhtml1-transitional.dtd">
<html xmlns="http://www.w3.org/1999/xhtml" xml:lang="en" lang="en">
    <head>
        <title>
            Using logical styles
        </title>
    </head>

    <body>
        <center>
            <h1>
                Using logical styles
            </h1>
        </center>
        <abbr>This is &lt;abbr&gt; style.</abbr>
        <br />
        <acronym>This is &lt;acronym&gt; style.</acronym>
        <br />
        <address>This is &lt;address&gt; style.</address>
        <br />
        <cite>This is &lt;cite&gt; style.</cite>
        <br />
        <code>This is &lt;code&gt; style.</code>
        <br />
        <dfn>This is &lt;dfn&gt; style.</dfn>
        <br />
        <em>This is &lt;em&gt; style.</em>
        <br />
        <kbd>This is &lt;kbd&gt; style.</kbd>
        <br />
        <samp>This is &lt;samp&gt; style.</samp>
        <br />
        <strong>This is &lt;strong&gt; style.</strong>
        <br />
        <var>This is &lt;var&gt; style.</var>
    </body>
</html>
```

The results of this page appear in Netscape Navigator in Figure 2.2 and in Internet Explorer in Figure 2.3. Note that the **<address>** style adds a line after itself. And because the **<abbr>** and **<acronym>** styles are too new to have been implemented in either browser yet, they are implemented in plain text.

NOTE: *The terms **<** and **>** in the previous code example are called* character entities *and are used to display the angle-bracket characters—**<** and **>** respectively—in a Web page. Because **<** and **>** are identified as part of XHTML tags by browsers, using character entities solves the problem of utilizing them in a Web page. You can use these codes, which begin with an ampersand (**&**) and end with a semicolon (**;**) to display characters that might have other meanings to the browser. You can also use character entities to display characters that you might not find on your keyboard, such as characters with accents or umlauts. At the end of this chapter, I'll list every character entity (and there are a lot of them) available in XHTML.*

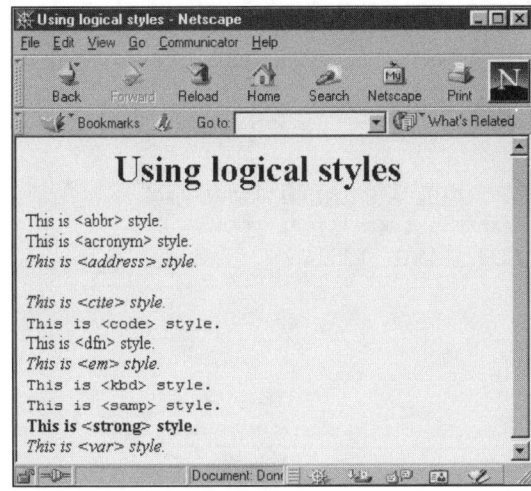

Figure 2.2   The logical styles in Netscape Navigator.

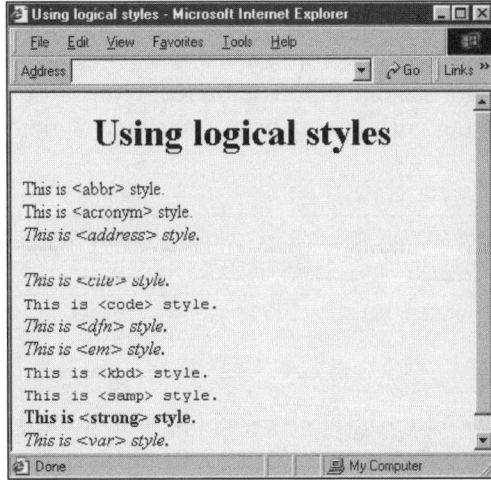

Figure 2.3   The logical styles in Internet Explorer.

TIP: *Note in particular how both the **<abbr>** and **<acronym>** elements are displayed in Netscape Navigator and Internet Explorer. Because they're not implemented in those browsers (except that in Internet Explorer 5, **<acronym>** elements are displayed as plain text, but the value of the **title** attribute is displayed in a tool tip), the browsers just ignore the tags and display the text as plain text. The fact that browsers ignore tags they don't understand will be important when we start working with scripts to manage other browsers that don't handle scripts.*

Setting Fonts

In addition to using the physical and logical tags to style text, you can use the **<font>** tag to set text color, typeface (such as Times New Roman, Arial, and so on), and size. With the new emphasis on style sheets, **<font>** has been deprecated in HTML 4, so it's not available in the XHTML 1.0 Strict or XHTML 1.1 DTDs, but it's still in common usage on the Internet. Here's an example showing how it works. In this case, I'll display text in Arial in blue:

```
<?xml version="1.0"?>
<!DOCTYPE html PUBLIC "-//W3C//DTD XHTML 1.0 Transitional//EN"
    "http://www.w3.org/TR/xhtml1/DTD/xhtml1-transitional.dtd">
<html xmlns="http://www.w3.org/1999/xhtml" xml:lang="en" lang="en">
    <head>
        <title>
            Using the &lt;font&gt; Tag
        </title>
    </head>

    <body>
        <font size="6" color="#0000ff" face="Arial">Here is some text!</font>
    </body>

</html>
```

The results of this code appear in Figure 2.4 in a large, blue Arial font. Note that you specify font size in the **<font>** tag with values from 1 through 7, not with point size directly.

TIP: *There is a way you can specify a font's size in points; in Netscape Navigator, you can use the **POINT-SIZE** attribute with the **<font>** tag. And you can use style sheets to do the same thing in Internet Explorer.*

Headings

The heading element tags are **<h1>**, **<h2>**, **<h3>**, **<h4>**, **<h5>**, and **<h6>**. These elements create the headlines in your Web pages by displaying bold text in a variety of sizes—**<h1>** being the largest. Here's an example of how these tags work:

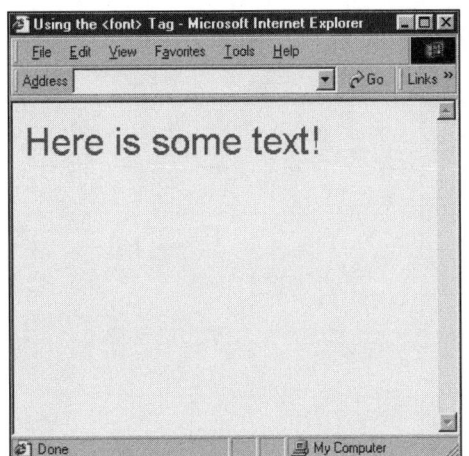

Figure 2.4 Using the **<font>** tag.

```
<?xml version="1.0"?>
<!DOCTYPE html PUBLIC "-//W3C//DTD XHTML 1.0 Transitional//EN"
    "http://www.w3.org/TR/xhtml1/DTD/xhtml1-transitional.dtd">
<html xmlns="http://www.w3.org/1999/xhtml" xml:lang="en" lang="en">
    <head>
        <title>
            Using the &lt;h1 - h6&gt; Tags
        </title>
    </head>

    <body>
        <center>
            <h1>Here is an &lt;h1&gt; heading</h1>
            <br />
            <h2>Here is an &lt;h2&gt; heading</h2>
            <br />
            <h3>Here is an &lt;h3&gt; heading</h3>
            <br />
            <h4>Here is an &lt;h4&gt; heading</h4>
            <br />
            <h5>Here is an &lt;h5&gt; heading</h5>
            <br />
            <h6>Here is an &lt;h6&gt; heading</h6>
        </center>
    </body>

</html>
```

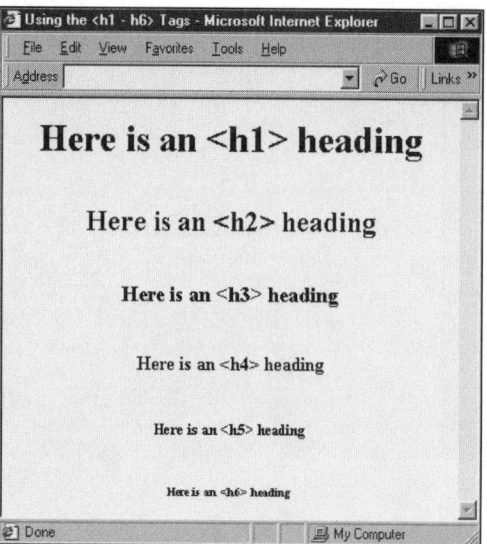

Figure 2.5 The heading tags, **<h1>** through **<h6>**.

You can see the results of this XHTML in Figure 2.5, which shows the relative sizes of all six heading tags, **<h1>** through **<h6>**.

Some Removed Tags

Over the years, some text style tags have gone from deprecated to *removed status*, which means that they're no longer supported in HTML 4 and so don't appear in XHTML. They still work in browsers, however. Here are the removed elements designated as obsolete by W3C:

- **<listing>**
- **<plaintext>**
- **<xmp>**

These three tags do essentially the same thing—display text "as is" without being interpreted by the browser. Instead of using these tags, you should now use the **<pre>** tag (preformatted text), which I'll cover in Chapter 3.

That's it, then—there's a lot of text handling coming up here, so I'll turn to the Immediate Solutions section now and start by explaining headings **<h1>** through **<h6>**.

TIP: In this chapter, you'll start seeing significant differences between the XHTML used in Internet Explorer and the XHTML used in Netscape Navigator. One way to handle these discrepancies is to check what browser the user has and adjust your XHTML accordingly. I'll show you how to do this when we start working with dynamic XHTML in Chapter 16.

Immediate Solutions

Displaying Plain Text

The novice programmer has a problem and says, "All I want to do is to display some plain text in a Web page, no formatting, nothing special. How do I do that?" "Easy," you reply, "just put the text directly into the Web page's body."

If you put plain text into a Web page's body, the Web browser will display it in its current default font, color, and font size. Web browsers will not, however, respect the line breaks you've added to the text (unless you use a special tag like **<pre>** for preformatted text, as we'll see in the next chapter), and they will wrap everything into a single paragraph. Here's an example:

```
<?xml version="1.0"?>
<!DOCTYPE html PUBLIC "-//W3C//DTD XHTML 1.0 Transitional//EN"
    "http://www.w3.org/TR/xhtml1/DTD/xhtml1-transitional.dtd">
<html xmlns="http://www.w3.org/1999/xhtml" xml:lang="en" lang="en">
    <head>
        <title>
            Using Plain Text
        </title>
    </head>

    <body>
        Hey what gives?
        This text is all supposed to be on different lines!
        But it looks like it's all been put in the same paragraph!
    </body>
</html>
```

The result appears in Figure 2.6, and as you can see, all the text has been wrapped into the same paragraph.

If you want to separate the text into paragraphs, you can use the tag **<p>** for paragraph, which we saw in Chapter 1. Each sentence will now begin on a new line:

```
<?xml version="1.0"?>
<!DOCTYPE html PUBLIC "-//W3C//DTD XHTML 1.0 Transitional//EN"
    "http://www.w3.org/TR/xhtml1/DTD/xhtml1-transitional.dtd">
<html xmlns="http://www.w3.org/1999/xhtml" xml:lang="en" lang="en">
```

```
<head>
    <title>
        Using Plain Text
    </title>
</head>

<body>
    Hey what gives?
    <p>
        This text is all supposed to be on different lines!
    </p>
    <p>
        But it looks like it's all been put in the same paragraph!
    </p>
</body>
</html>
```

For more about text formatting, see Chapter 3.

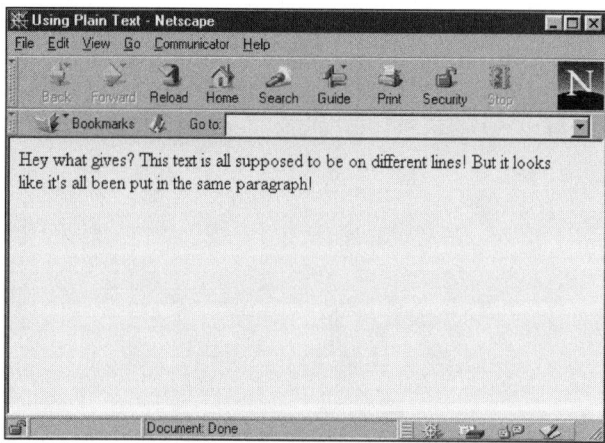

Figure 2.6   Displaying plain text.

\<h1\> through \<h6\>—Creating Web Page Headings

Purpose: Create headings in Web pages, using bold text and various sizes. **\<h1\>** creates the largest text, and **\<h6\>** the smallest.

When used as HTML: Start tag/End tag: Required/Required

Supported: [1.0S, 1.0T, 1.0F, 1.1, 2, 3, 3.2, 4, IE1, IE2, IE3, IE4, IE5, NS1, NS2, NS3, NS4]

Attributes:

- **align**—Specifies the alignment of text in the heading. Set to **left** (the default), **center**, **right**, or **justify**. [1.0T, 1.0F, 3, 3.2, 4, IE4, IE5, NS1, NS2, NS3, NS4]
- **class**—Class of the element (used for rendering). [1.0S, 1.0T, 1.0F, 1.1, 3, 4, IE4, IE5, NS4]
- **dir**—Gives the direction of directionally neutral text (text that doesn't have inherent direction in which you should read it). Possible values: **ltr**: left-to-right text or table and **rtl**: right-to-left text or table. [1.0S, 1.0T, 1.0F, 1.1, 4, IE5]
- **id**—Unique alphanumeric identifier for the tag, which you can use to refer to it. [1.0S, 1.0T, 1.0F, 1.1, 3, 4, IE4, IE5, NS4]
- **lang**—Base language used for the tag. [1.0S, 1.0T, 1.0F, 1.1, 3, 4, IE4, IE5]
- **language**—Scripting language used for the tag. [IE4, IE5]
- **style**—Inline style indicating how to render the element. [1.0S, 1.0T, 1.0F, 1.1, 4, IE4, IE5, NS4]
- **title**—Holds additional information (as might be displayed in tool tips) for the element. [1.0S, 1.0T, 1.0F, 1.1, 3, 4, IE4, IE5]
- **xml:lang**—Holds the base language for the element when the document is interpreted as an XML document. [1.0S, 1.0T, 1.0F, 1.1]

XHTML events: onclick, ondblclick, onmousedown, onmouseup, onmouseover, onmousemove, onmouseout, onkeypress, onkeydown, onkeyup

The Web-page style czar gives you a call and says, "About your new Web page—where's the style, the zing, the pizzazz?" You ask, "*Pizzazz*?" "Why doesn't the page reach out and grab me?" the Web-page style czar asks. "I'll add some headings," you say. The Web-page style czar says, "Great!"

Headings act much like headlines in newspapers. They present text in bold and often are larger than the text they appear above. There are six heading tags, all beloved by HTML programmers: **<h1>**, **<h2>**, **<h3>**, **<h4>**, **<h5>**, and **<h6>**. **<h1>** creates the largest text and **<h6>** the smallest, with a smooth progression between those levels.

Headings are not just about big bold text—they really act like headings by getting their own line in the Web page and starting a new paragraph. Even if you use a heading tag in the middle of other text, it'll get its own line in the page.

You can add other formatting in a heading by using different tags, such as the **<i>** tag to make all or part of the heading italic, or **<s>** to strike out all or part of the heading, and so on.

Here's an example:

```
<?xml version="1.0"?>
<!DOCTYPE html PUBLIC "-//W3C//DTD XHTML 1.0 Transitional//EN"
"http://www.w3.org/TR/xhtml1/DTD/xhtml1-transitional.dtd">
<html xmlns="http://www.w3.org/1999/xhtml" xml:lang="en" lang="en">
    <head>
        <title>
            Using the &lt;h1 - h6&gt; Tags
        </title>
    </head>

    <body>
        <center>
            <h1>Here is an &lt;h1&gt; heading</h1>
            <br />
            <h2>Here is an &lt;h2&gt; heading</h2>
            <br />
            <h3>Here is an &lt;h3&gt; heading</h3>
            <br />
            <h4>Here is an &lt;h4&gt; heading</h4>
            <br />
            <h5>Here is an &lt;h5&gt; heading</h5>
            <br />
            <h6>Here is an &lt;h6&gt; heading</h6>
        </center>
    </body>

</html>
```

The results of this XHTML appear in Figure 2.5, where you can see every heading XHTML supports. Headings are good tags, and I encourage you to use plenty of them. They help break up monotonous text and let the structure of your page stand out.

TIP: *Some people consider the skipping of heading levels to be bad practice. For example, you might have an **<h2>** heading followed by an **<h3>**, but not an **<h1>** heading followed by an **<h3>** because you'd skip the **<h2>** that way.*

\<b\>—Creating Bold Text

Purpose: Sets the text style to bold.

When used as HTML: Start tag/End tag: Required/Required

Supported: [1.0S, 1.0T, 1.0F, 1.1, 2, 3, 3.2, 4, IE1, IE2, IE3, IE4, IE5, NS1, NS2, NS3, NS4]

Attributes:

- **class**—Class of the element (used for rendering). [1.0S, 1.0T, 1.0F, 1.1, 3, 4, IE4, IE5, NS4]
- **dir**—Gives the direction of directionally neutral text (text that doesn't have inherent direction in which you should read it). Possible values: **ltr**: left-to-right text or table and **rtl**: right-to-left text or table. [1.0S, 1.0T, 1.0F, 1.1, 4, IE5]
- **id**—Unique alphanumeric identifier for the tag, which you can use to refer to it. [1.0S, 1.0T, 1.0F, 1.1, 3, 4, IE4, IE5, NS4]
- **lang**—Base language used for the tag. [1.0S, 1.0T, 1.0F, 1.1, 3, 4, IE4, IE5]
- **language**—Scripting language used for the tag. [IE4, IE5]
- **style**—Inline style indicating how to render the element. [1.0S, 1.0T, 1.0F, 1.1, 4, IE3, IE4, IE5, NS4]
- **title**—Holds additional information (as might be displayed in tool tips) for the element. [1.0S, 1.0T, 1.0F, 1.1, 3, 4, IE4, IE5]
- **xml:lang**—Holds the base language for the element when the document is interpreted as an XML document. [1.0S, 1.0T, 1.0F, 1.1]

XHTML events: onclick, ondblclick, onmousedown, onmouseup, onmouseover, onmousemove, onmouseout, onkeypress, onkeydown, onkeyup

"Hey," says the novice programmer, "I want some words to stand out in my page. Is there any way to do that?" "Well," you explain, "you can use the **\<b\>** tag to set those words in bold." "Swell!" says the NP and is gone like a shot.

The **\<b\>** element encloses text that you want to display in bold. You can use this tag together with other styles, like **\<i\>**, as we see in this next example, from the beginning of this chapter:

```
<?xml version="1.0"?>
<!DOCTYPE html PUBLIC "-//W3C//DTD XHTML 1.0 Transitional//EN"
 "http://www.w3.org/TR/xhtml1/DTD/xhtml1-transitional.dtd">
<html xmlns="http://www.w3.org/1999/xhtml" xml:lang="en" lang="en">
```

Chapter 2 Working with Text

```
<head>
    <title>
        Using italics
    </title>
</head>

<body>
    <p>
        <i>Here is some text displayed in italics and
        <b>bold</b> too.</i>
    </p>
</body>
</html>
```

The results of this XHTML appear in Figure 2.1. The **<b>** tag is a favorite among many programmers, and it's easy to use.

<i>—Creating Italic Text

Purpose: Displays text in italics.

When used as HTML: Start tag/End tag: Required/Required

Supported: [1.0S, 1.0T, 1.0F, 1.1, 2, 3, 3.2, 4, IE1, IE2, IE3, IE4, IE5, NS1, NS2, NS3, NS4]

Attributes:

- **class**—Class of the element (used for rendering). [1.0S, 1.0T, 1.0F, 1.1, 3, 4, IE4, IE5, NS4]
- **dir**—Gives the direction of directionally neutral text (text that doesn't have inherent direction in which you should read it). Possible values: **ltr**: left-to-right text or table and **rtl**: right-to-left text or table. [1.0S, 1.0T, 1.0F, 1.1, 4, IE5]
- **id**—Unique alphanumeric identifier for the tag, which you can use to refer to it. [1.0S, 1.0T, 1.0F, 1.1, 3, 4, IE4, IE5, NS4]
- **lang**—Base language used for the tag. [1.0S, 1.0T, 1.0F, 1.1, 3, 4, IE4, IE5]
- **language**—Scripting language used for the tag. [IE4, IE5]
- **style**—Inline style indicating how to render the element. [1.0S, 1.0T, 1.0F, 1.1, 4, IE3, IE4, IE5, NS4]
- **title**—Holds additional information (as might be displayed in tool tips) for the element. [1.0S, 1.0T, 1.0F, 1.1, 3, 4, IE4, IE5]

- **xml:lang**—Holds the base language for the element when the document is interpreted as an XML document. [1.0S, 1.0T, 1.0F, 1.1]

XHTML events: onclick, ondblclick, onmousedown, onmouseup, onmouseover, onmousemove, onmouseout, onkeypress, onkeydown, onkeyup

"That darn Johnson read my page about mountaineering," the novice programmer says, "and skipped over all the warnings. Now that darn Johnson is in the hospital and I'm talking to lawyers!" "Hm," you say, "Next time, why not set the warnings in italics with the **<i>** tag to emphasize them?"

You can use the **<i>** element to display italicized text. You can also combine this style with other styles, as we saw in the beginning of this chapter:

```
<?xml version="1.0"?>
<!DOCTYPE html PUBLIC "-//W3C//DTD XHTML 1.0 Transitional//EN"
"http://www.w3.org/TR/xhtml1/DTD/xhtml1-transitional.dtd">
<html xmlns="http://www.w3.org/1999/xhtml" xml:lang="en" lang="en">
    <head>
        <title>
            Using italics
        </title>
    </head>

    <body>
        <p>
            <i>Here is some text displayed in italics and
            <b>bold</b> too.</i>
        </p>
    </body>
</html>
```

The results of this XHTML appear in Figure 2.1. The **<i>** tag is another favorite among many programmers, and it's easy to use when you want to italicize text.

<tt>—Creating "Teletype" Text

Purpose: Displays text in a monospaced "teletype" font. Because it's a fixed-width font, it's effective for displaying program output and arranging text and numbers into columns.

When used as HTML: Start tag/End tag: Required/Required

Supported: [1.0S, 1.0T, 1.0F, 1.1, 2, 3, 3.2, 4, IE1, IE2, IE3, IE4, IE5, NS1, NS2, NS3, NS4]

Attributes:

- **class**—Class of the element (used for rendering). [1.0S, 1.0T, 1.0F, 1.1, 3, 4, IE4, IE5, NS4]
- **dir**—Gives the direction of directionally neutral text (text that doesn't have inherent direction in which you should read it). Possible values: **ltr**: left-to-right text or table and **rtl**: right-to-left text or table. [1.0S, 1.0T, 1.0F, 1.1, 4, IE5]
- **id**—Unique alphanumeric identifier for the tag, which you can use to refer to it. [1.0S, 1.0T, 1.0F, 1.1, 3, 4, IE4, IE5, NS4]
- **lang**—Base language used for the tag. [1.0S, 1.0T, 1.0F, 1.1, 3, 4, IE4, IE5]
- **language**—Scripting language used for the tag. [IE4, IE5]
- **style**—Inline style indicating how to render the element. [1.0S, 1.0T, 1.0F, 1.1, 4, IE3, IE4, IE5, NS4]
- **title**—Holds additional information (as might be displayed in tool tips) for the element. [1.0S, 1.0T, 1.0F, 1.1, 3, 4, IE4, IE5]
- **xml:lang**—Holds the base language for the element when the document is interpreted as an XML document. [1.0S, 1.0T, 1.0F, 1.1]

XHTML events: onclick, ondblclick, onmousedown, onmouseup, onmouseover, onmousemove, onmouseout, onkeypress, onkeydown, onkeyup

The big boss appears and says, "How's the training manual coming?" "Pretty well," you report, "I'm just getting to the part where I display the program output in a **<tt>** element." "What's that?" the BB asks. "Monospace font," you say.

Here's an example of using the **<tt>** tag to create a monospace font:

```
<?xml version="1.0"?>
<!DOCTYPE html PUBLIC "-//W3C//DTD XHTML 1.0 Transitional//EN"
    "http://www.w3.org/TR/xhtml1/DTD/xhtml1-transitional.dtd">
<html xmlns="http://www.w3.org/1999/xhtml" xml:lang="en" lang="en">
    <head>
        <title>
            Using the &lt;tt&gt; Tag
        </title>
    </head>
```

```
<body>
    At this point, the program should display:
    <br />
    <tt>Warning! The CPU is on fire. Do you wish to quit?</tt>
</body>
</html>
```

The result of this XHTML appears in Figure 2.7.

TIP: Although this tag is similar to the <pre> tag (as we'll see in Chapter 3), it is by no means identical. The <pre> tag displays text completely as is, whereas the <tt> tag ignores line breaks, for example.

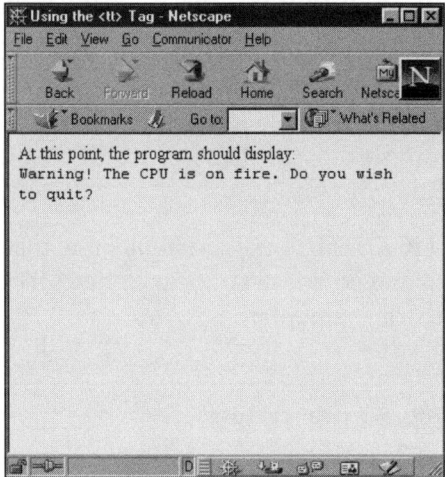

Figure 2.7   Using the <tt> tag.

<u>—Underlining Text

Purpose: Underlines text. Deprecated in HTML 4.

When used as HTML: Start tag/End tag: Required/Required

Supported: [1.0T, 1.0F, 3, 3.2, 4, IE1, IE2, IE3, IE4, IE5, NS3, NS4]

Attributes:

- **class**—Class of the element (used for rendering). [1.0T, 1.0F, 3, 4, IE4, IE5, NS4]
- **dir**—Gives the direction of directionally neutral text (text that doesn't have inherent direction in which you should read it). Possible values: **ltr**: left-to-right text or table and **rtl**: right-to-left text or table. [1.0T, 1.0F, 4, IE5]

- **id**—Unique alphanumeric identifier for the tag, which you can use to refer to it. [1.0T, 1.0F, 3, 4, IE4, IE5, NS4]
- **lang**—Base language used for the tag. [1.0T, 1.0F, 3, 4, IE4, IE5]
- **language**—Scripting language used for the tag. [IE4, IE5]
- **style**—Inline style indicating how to render the element. [1.0T, 1.0F, 4, IE3, IE4, IE5, NS4]
- **title**—Holds additional information (as might be displayed in tool tips) for the element. [1.0T, 1.0F, 3, 4, IE4, IE5]
- **xml:lang**—Holds the base language for the element when the document is interpreted as an XML document. [1.0T, 1.0F]

XHTML events: onclick, ondblclick, onmousedown, onmouseup, onmouseover, onmousemove, onmouseout, onkeypress, onkeydown, onkeyup

"I can create bold and italic text in Web pages," the novice programmer says, "but what about underlining?" "Well, you can use the **<u>** tag, but it's deprecated." "The **<u>** tag," the NP says; "thanks!" "Hm," you say.

You can use the **<u>** tag to underline text in XHTML, but you should note that this element has been deprecated in HTML 4 and so doesn't appear in the XHTML 1 Strict DTD, or the XHTML 1.1 DTD. Here's an example:

```
<?xml version="1.0"?>
<!DOCTYPE html PUBLIC "-//W3C//DTD XHTML 1.0 Transitional//EN"
"http://www.w3.org/TR/xhtml1/DTD/xhtml1-transitional.dtd">
<html xmlns="http://www.w3.org/1999/xhtml" xml:lang="en" lang="en">
    <head>
        <title>
            Using the &lt;u&gt; Tag
        </title>
    </head>

    <body>
        You can <u>underline</u> text with the &lt;u&gt; tag.
    </body>

</html>
```

The result of this XHTML appears in Figure 2.8.

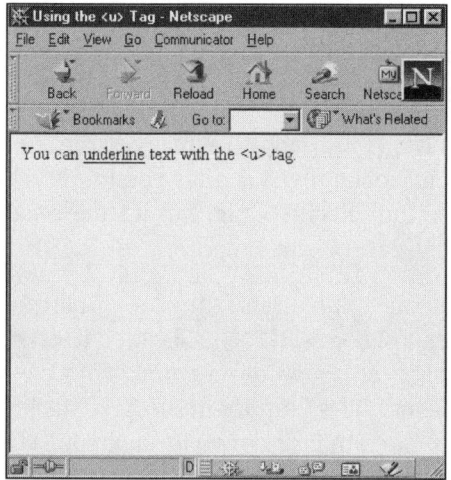

Figure 2.8   Using the <u> tag.

<s> and <strike>—Striking Text out

Purpose: Displays text in strikethrough style. Deprecated in HTML 4.

When used as HTML: Start tag/End tag: Required/Required

Supported: [1.0T, 1.0F, 3, 4, IE1, IE2, IE3, IE4, IE5, NS3, NS4]

Attributes:

- **class**—Class of the element (used for rendering). [1.0T, 1.0F, 3, 4, IE4, IE5, NS4]

- **dir**—Gives the direction of directionally neutral text (text that doesn't have inherent direction in which you should read it). Possible values: **ltr**: left-to-right text or table and **rtl**: right-to-left text or table. [1.0T, 1.0F, 4, IE5]

- **id**—Unique alphanumeric identifier for the tag, which you can use to refer to it. [1.0T, 1.0F, 3, 4, IE4, IE5, NS4]

- **lang**—Base language used for the tag. [1.0T, 1.0F, 3, 4, IE4, IE5]

- **language**—Scripting language used for the tag. [IE4, IE5]

- **style**—Inline style indicating how to render the element. [1.0T, 1.0F, 4, IE3, IE4, IE5, NS4]

- **title**—Holds additional information (as might be displayed in tool tips) for the element. [1.0T, 1.0F, 3, 4, IE4, IE5]

- **xml:lang**—Holds the base language for the element when the document is interpreted as an XML document. [1.0T, 1.0F]

XHTML events: onclick, ondblclick, onmousedown, onmouseup, onmouseover, onmousemove, onmouseout, onkeypress, onkeydown, onkeyup

The novice programmer appears and says, "I'm ready to write version 2 of my online manual, but I want to indicate what's been revised since version 1. Is there any way to do that?" "Well, you can use the **<strike>** tag, but it's deprecated." "The **<strike>** tag," the NP says; "thanks!" "Hm," you say.

The **<s>** and **<strike>** tags are used for the same effect: they let you strike out text. (HTML 2 used **<strike>**, HTML 3 called it **<s>**, HTML 3.2 called it **<strike>** again, and in HTML 4, both were available, although deprecated. They're available in XHTML 1 Transitional and Frameset DTDs, but not in the XHTML 1 Strict or XHTML 1.1 DTD.) Both tags are deprecated in favor of style sheets in HTML 4 and XHTML.

Here's a quick example of the **<strike>** tag at work:

```xhtml
<?xml version="1.0"?>
<!DOCTYPE html PUBLIC "-//W3C//DTD XHTML 1.0 Transitional//EN"
"http://www.w3.org/TR/xhtml1/DTD/xhtml1-transitional.dtd">
<html xmlns="http://www.w3.org/1999/xhtml" xml:lang="en" lang="en">
    <head>
        <title>
            Using the &lt;strike&gt; Tag
        </title>
    </head>

    <body>
        You <strike>ain't allowed to</strike> shouldn't use
        the &lt;strike&gt; tag, because it's deprecated.
    </body>

</html>
```

The result of this XHTML appears in Figure 2.9.

TIP: *Note that HTML 4 lists both **<s>** and **<strike>** (even though they're deprecated), and HTML 3.2 lists only **<strike>**. So, if you really want to use this tag instead of style sheets, it's best to use **<strike>**.*

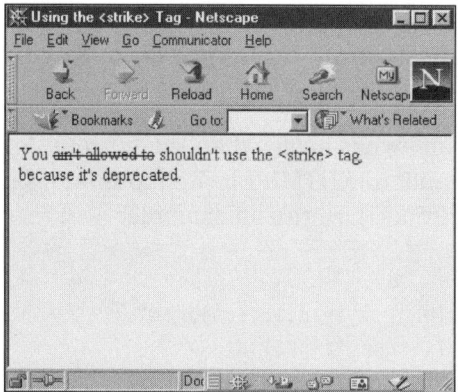

Figure 2.9 Using the <strike> tag.

<big>—Creating Big Text

Purpose: Renders text in a bigger font than the current default. Often used for emphasis.

When used as HTML: Start tag/End tag: Required/Required

Supported: [1.0S, 1.0T, 1.0F, 1.1, 3, 3.2, 4, IE3, IE4, IE5, NS2, NS3, NS4]

Attributes:

- **class**—Class of the element (used for rendering). [1.0S, 1.0T, 1.0F, 1.1, 3, 4, IE4, IE5, NS4]

- **dir**—Gives the direction of directionally neutral text (text that doesn't have inherent direction in which you should read it). Possible values: **ltr**: left-to-right text or table and **rtl**: right-to-left text or table. [1.0S, 1.0T, 1.0F, 1.1, 4, IE5]

- **id**—Unique alphanumeric identifier for the tag, which you can use to refer to it. [1.0S, 1.0T, 1.0F, 1.1, 3, 4, IE4, IE5, NS4]

- **lang**—Base language used for the tag. [1.0S, 1.0T, 1.0F, 1.1, 3, 4, IE4, IE5]

- **language**—Scripting language used for the tag. [IE4, IE5]

- **style**—Inline style indicating how to render the element. [1.0S, 1.0T, 1.0F, 1.1, 4, IE3, IE4, IE5, NS4]

- **title**—Holds additional information (as might be displayed in tool tips) for the element. [1.0S, 1.0T, 1.0F, 1.1, 3, 4, IE4, IE5]

- **xml:lang**—Holds the base language for the element when the document is interpreted as an XML document. [1.0S, 1.0T, 1.0F, 1.1]

XHTML events: onclick, ondblclick, onmousedown, onmouseup, onmouseover, onmousemove, onmouseout, onkeypress, onkeydown, onkeyup

You use the **<big>** tag to make text somewhat bigger than the current default (normally by one font size, using the standard XHTML 1 to 7 simple values mentioned in the In Depth section "Setting Fonts"). Here's an example:

```
<?xml version="1.0"?>
<!DOCTYPE html PUBLIC "-//W3C//DTD XHTML 1.0 Transitional//EN"
"http://www.w3.org/TR/xhtml1/DTD/xhtml1-transitional.dtd">
<html xmlns="http://www.w3.org/1999/xhtml" xml:lang="en" lang="en">
    <head>
        <title>
            Using the &lt;big&gt; and &lt;small&gt; Tags
        </title>
    </head>

    <body>
        Here's some text that's <big>big</big>.
        <p>
            And here's some text that's <small>small</small>.
        </p>
    </body>

</html>
```

The results of this XHTML appear in Figure 2.10.

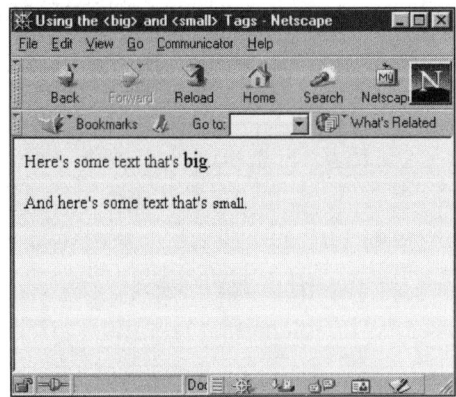

Figure 2.10   Using the **<big>** and **<small>** tags.

So why should you use **<big>** instead of, say, the **<font>** tag, which lets you specify the actual size of text? One reason is that browsers are now displaying text larger for visually impaired users, and if you specify a font size with **<font>**, the result might be smaller than the rest of the text. **<big>** is intended to mean "bigger than the default" text.

TIP: What does "big" really mean? In terms of the now deprecated **<font>** tag, the default font size for text is usually size 3, and browsers usually implement **<big>** as size 4 when compared to default text. You can also nest **<big>**.

<small>—Creating Small Text

Purpose: Renders text in a smaller font than the current default.

When used as HTML: Start tag/End tag: Required/Required

Supported: [1.0S, 1.0T, 1.0F, 1.1, 2, 3, 3.2, 4, IE1, IE2, IE3, IE4, IE5, NS2, NS3, NS4]

Attributes:

- **class**—Class of the element (used for rendering). [1.0S, 1.0T, 1.0F, 1.1, 3, 4, IE4, IE5, NS4]
- **dir**—Gives the direction of directionally neutral text (text that doesn't have inherent direction in which you should read it). Possible values: **ltr**: left-to-right text or table and **rtl**: right-to-left text or table. [1.0S, 1.0T, 1.0F, 1.1, 4, IE5]
- **id**—Unique alphanumeric identifier for the tag, which you can use to refer to it. [1.0S, 1.0T, 1.0F, 1.1, 3, 4, IE4, IE5, NS4]
- **lang**—Base language used for the tag. [1.0S, 1.0T, 1.0F, 1.1, 3, 4, IE4, IE5]
- **language**—Scripting language used for the tag. [IE4, IE5]
- **style**—Inline style indicating how to render the element. [1.0S, 1.0T, 1.0F, 1.1, 4, IE3, IE4, IE5, NS4]
- **title**—Holds additional information (as might be displayed in tool tips) for the element. [1.0S, 1.0T, 1.0F, 1.1, 3, 4, IE4, IE5]
- **xml:lang**—Holds the base language for the element when the document is interpreted as an XML document. [1.0S, 1.0T, 1.0F, 1.1]

XHTML events: onclick, ondblclick, onmousedown, onmouseup, onmouseover, onmousemove, onmouseout, onkeypress, onkeydown, onkeyup

You use the **<small>** tag to make text somewhat smaller than the current default (normally by one font size, using the standard XHTML 1 to 7 simple values mentioned in the In Depth section "Setting Fonts"). Here's an example:

```
<?xml version="1.0"?>
<!DOCTYPE html PUBLIC "-//W3C//DTD XHTML 1.0 Transitional//EN"
"http://www.w3.org/TR/xhtml1/DTD/xhtml1-transitional.dtd">
<html xmlns="http://www.w3.org/1999/xhtml" xml:lang="en" lang="en">
    <head>
        <title>
            Using the &lt;big&gt; and &lt;small&gt; Tags
        </title>
    </head>

    <body>
        Here's some text that's <big>big</big>.
        <p>
            And here's some text that's <small>small</small>.
        </p>
    </body>
</html>
```

The results of this XHTML appear in Figure 2.10.

So why should you use **<small>** instead of the **<font>** tag, which lets you specify the actual size of text? One reason is that browsers are now displaying larger text for visually impaired users, and if you specify a font size with **<font>**, the result might be a great deal smaller than the rest of the text. **<small>** is intended to mean "smaller than the default" text.

TIP: *What does "small" really mean? In terms of the now deprecated **<font>** tag, the default font size for text is usually size 3, and browsers usually implement **<small>** as size 2 when compared to default text. You can also nest this element.*

<sub>—Creating Subscripts

Purpose: Styles text as a subscript.

When used as HTML: Start tag/End tag: Required/Required

Supported: [1.0S, 1.0T, 1.0F, 1.1, 3, 3.2, 4, IE3, IE4, IE5, NS2, NS3, NS4]

Attributes:

- **class**—Class of the element (used for rendering). [1.0S, 1.0T, 1.0F, 1.1, 3, 4, IE4, IE5, NS4]
- **dir**—Gives the direction of directionally neutral text (text that doesn't have inherent direction in which you should read it). Possible values: **ltr**: left-to-right text or table or **rtl**: right-to-left text or table. [1.0S, 1.0T, 1.0F, 1.1, 4, IE5]
- **id**—Unique alphanumeric identifier for the tag, which you can use to refer to it. [1.0S, 1.0T, 1.0F, 1.1, 3, 4, IE4, IE5, NS4]
- **lang**—Base language used for the tag. [1.0S, 1.0T, 1.0F, 1.1, 3, 4, IE4, IE5]
- **language**—Scripting language used for the tag. [IE4, IE5]
- **style**—Inline style indicating how to render the element. [1.0S, 1.0T, 1.0F, 1.1, 4, IE3, IE4, IE5, NS4]
- **title**—Holds additional information (as might be displayed in tool tips) for the element. [1.0S, 1.0T, 1.0F, 1.1, 3, 4, IE4, IE5]
- **xml:lang**—Holds the base language for the element when the document is interpreted as an XML document. [1.0S, 1.0T, 1.0F, 1.1]

XHTML events: onclick, ondblclick, onmousedown, onmouseup, onmouseover, onmousemove, onmouseout, onkeypress, onkeydown, onkeyup

"I'm working on my new online novel," the novice programmer says, "but is there any way to display subscripts as in H_2SO_4?" "Sounds exciting," you say, "and you can indicate subscripts with the **<sub>** tag."

The **<sub>** tag lets you create subscripts in a Web page. Here's an example:

```
<?xml version="1.0"?>
<!DOCTYPE html PUBLIC "-//W3C//DTD XHTML 1.0 Transitional//EN"
"http://www.w3.org/TR/xhtml1/DTD/xhtml1-transitional.dtd">
<html xmlns="http://www.w3.org/1999/xhtml" xml:lang="en" lang="en">
    <head>
        <title>
            Using the &lt;sub&gt; and &lt;sup&gt; Tags
        </title>
    </head>

    <body>
        <p>
            "Don't drink that pure H<sub>2</sub>SO<sub>4</sub>, Jim,"
                I said.
            "It's not very good for you."
        </p>
```

```
<p>
    "Good point," Jim said,
    "I remember that from our previous adventure<sup>1</sup>."
</p>
<br />
<br />
<br />
<hr />
<sup>1</sup><i>The Astounding H<sub>2</sub>SO<sub>4</sub>
Adventure</i>, now available in paperback.
</body>

</html>
```

The results of this XHTML appear in Figure 2.11.

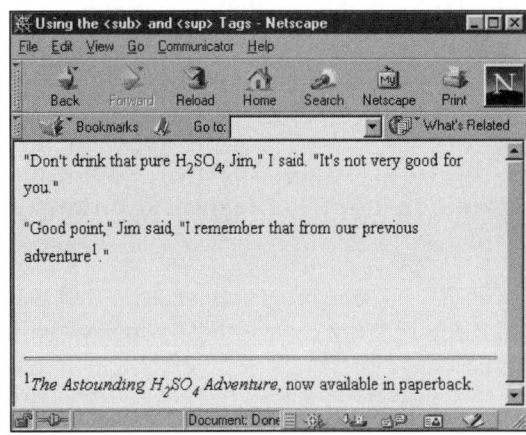

Figure 2.11   Using the <sub> and <sup> tags.

<sup>—Creating Superscripts

Purpose: Styles text as a superscript.

When used as HTML: Start tag/End tag: Required/Required

Supported: [1.0S, 1.0T, 1.0F, 1.1, 2, 3, 3.2, 4, IE1, IE2, IE3, IE4, IE5, NS2, NS3, NS4]

Attributes:

- **class**—Class of the element (used for rendering). [1.0S, 1.0T, 1.0F, 1.1, 3, 4, IE4, IE5, NS4]

- **dir**—Gives the direction of directionally neutral text (text that doesn't have inherent direction in which you should read it). Possible values: **ltr**: left-to-right text or table and **rtl**: right-to-left text or table. [1.0S, 1.0T, 1.0F, 1.1, 4, IE5]
- **id**—Unique alphanumeric identifier for the tag, which you can use to refer to it. [1.0S, 1.0T, 1.0F, 1.1, 3, 4, IE4, IE5, NS4]
- **lang**—Base language used for the tag. [1.0S, 1.0T, 1.0F, 1.1, 3, 4, IE4, IE5]
- **language**—Scripting language used for the tag. [IE4, IE5]
- **style**—Inline style indicating how to render the element. [1.0S, 1.0T, 1.0F, 1.1, 4, IE3, IE4, IE5, NS4]
- **title**—Holds additional information (as might be displayed in tool tips) for the element. [1.0S, 1.0T, 1.0F, 1.1, 3, 4, IE4, IE5]
- **xml:lang**—Holds the base language for the element when the document is interpreted as an XML document. [1.0S, 1.0T, 1.0F, 1.1]

XHTML events: onclick, ondblclick, onmousedown, onmouseup, onmouseover, onmousemove, onmouseout, onkeypress, onkeydown, onkeyup

The big boss appears and says nervously, "About this online annual report for the company—I want to explain to the stockholders why we lost so much money last quarter." "Do you really want to explain your trip to Las Vegas?" you ask. "Hm," says the BB, "maybe we should bury it a little. Let's add it in a footnote." "OK," you say, "I'll use the **<sup>** tag."

The **<sup>** tag lets you create superscripts in a Web page. Here's an example:

```
<?xml version="1.0"?>
<!DOCTYPE html PUBLIC "-//W3C//DTD XHTML 1.0 Transitional//EN"
"http://www.w3.org/TR/xhtml1/DTD/xhtml1-transitional.dtd">
<html xmlns="http://www.w3.org/1999/xhtml" xml:lang="en" lang="en">
    <head>
        <title>
            Using the &lt;sub&gt; and &lt;sup&gt; Tags
        </title>
    </head>

    <body>
        <p>
            "Don't drink that pure H<sub>2</sub>SO<sub>4</sub>, Jim,"
            I said.
            "It's not very good for you."
        </p>
```

```
        <p>
            "Good point," Jim said,
            "I remember that from our previous adventure<sup>1</sup>."
        </p>
        <br />
        <br />
        <br />
        <hr />
        <sup>1</sup><i>The Astounding H<sub>2</sub>SO<sub>4</sub>
        Adventure</i>, now available in paperback.
    </body>
</html>
```

The results of this XHTML appear in Figure 2.11.

TIP: *As with other XHTML tags, you can nest* **<sup>** *tags inside other tags. Nesting is useful if the explanatory text for footnotes is in some other document—in which case, you can make the superscript footnote numbers into hyperlinks to that document.*

<em>—Emphasizing Text

Purpose: Emphasizes text; usually rendered as italics.

When used as HTML: Start tag/End tag: Required/Required

Supported: [1.0S, 1.0T, 1.0F, 1.1, 2, 3, 3.2, 4, IE1, IE2, IE3, IE4, IE5, NS1, NS2, NS3, NS4]

Attributes:

- **class**—Class of the element (used for rendering). [1.0S, 1.0T, 1.0F, 1.1, 3, 4, IE4, IE5, NS4]
- **dir**—Gives the direction of directionally neutral text (text that doesn't have inherent direction in which you should read it). Possible values: **ltr**: left-to-right text or table and **rtl**: right-to-left text or table. [1.0S, 1.0T, 1.0F, 1.1, 4, IE5]
- **id**—Unique alphanumeric identifier for the tag, which you can use to refer to it. [1.0S, 1.0T, 1.0F, 1.1, 3, 4, IE4, IE5, NS4]
- **lang**—Base language used for the tag. [1.0S, 1.0T, 1.0F, 1.1, 3, 4, IE4, IE5]
- **language**—Scripting language used for the tag. [IE4, IE5]
- **style**—Inline style indicating how to render the element. [1.0S, 1.0T, 1.0F, 1.1, 4, IE3, IE4, IE5, NS4]

- **title**—Holds additional information (as might be displayed in tool tips) for the element. [1.0S, 1.0T, 1.0F, 1.1, 3, 4, IE4, IE5]
- **xml:lang**—Holds the base language for the element when the document is interpreted as an XML document. [1.0S, 1.0T, 1.0F, 1.1]

XHTML events: onclick, **ondblclick**, **onmousedown**, **onmouseup**, **onmouseover**, **onmousemove**, **onmouseout**, **onkeypress**, **onkeydown**, **onkeyup**

The **<em>** logical style emphasizes text. In practice, this element is usually rendered in italics. Here's an example showing how to use this tag:

```
<?xml version="1.0"?>
<!DOCTYPE html PUBLIC "-//W3C//DTD XHTML 1.0 Transitional//EN"
"http://www.w3.org/TR/xhtml1/DTD/xhtml1-transitional.dtd">
<html xmlns="http://www.w3.org/1999/xhtml" xml:lang="en" lang="en">
    <head>
        <title>
            Using logical styles
        </title>
    </head>

    <body>
        This is the <em>second</em> time it's happened.
    </body>
</html>
```

You can see this style in Netscape Navigator, shown in Figure 2.2, and in Internet Explorer, shown in Figure 2.3.

<strong>—Strongly Emphasizing Text

Purpose: Emphasizes text strongly; usually rendered in bold.

When used as HTML: Start tag/End tag: Required/Required

Supported: [1.0S, 1.0T, 1.0F, 1.1, 2, 3, 3.2, 4, IE1, IE2, IE3, IE4, IE5, NS1, NS2, NS3, NS4]

Attributes:

- **class**—Class of the element (used for rendering). [1.0S, 1.0T, 1.0F, 1.1, 3, 4, IE4, IE5, NS4]

- **dir**—Gives the direction of directionally neutral text (text that doesn't have inherent direction in which you should read it). Possible values: **ltr**: left-to-right text or table and **rtl**: right-to-left text or table. [1.0S, 1.0T, 1.0F, 1.1, 4, IE5]
- **id**—Unique alphanumeric identifier for the tag, which you can use to refer to it. [1.0S, 1.0T, 1.0F, 1.1, 3, 4, IE4, IE5, NS4]
- **lang**—Base language used for the tag. [1.0S, 1.0T, 1.0F, 1.1, 3, 4, IE4, IE5]
- **language**—Scripting language used for the tag. [IE4, IE5]
- **style**—Inline style indicating how to render the element. [1.0S, 1.0T, 1.0F, 1.1, 4, IE3, IE4, IE5, NS4]
- **title**—Holds additional information (as might be displayed in tool tips) for the element. [1.0S, 1.0T, 1.0F, 1.1, 3, 4, IE4, IE5]
- **xml:lang**—Holds the base language for the element when the document is interpreted as an XML document. [1.0S, 1.0T, 1.0F, 1.1]

XHTML events: onclick, ondblclick, onmousedown, onmouseup, onmouseover, onmousemove, onmouseout, onkeypress, onkeydown, onkeyup

You use **<strong>** when you want to strongly emphasize text. In practice, **<strong>** text is usually rendered as bold text. Here's an example showing how to use **<strong>**:

```
<?xml version="1.0"?>
<!DOCTYPE html PUBLIC "-//W3C//DTD XHTML 1.0 Transitional//EN"
"http://www.w3.org/TR/xhtml1/DTD/xhtml1-transitional.dtd">
<html xmlns="http://www.w3.org/1999/xhtml" xml:lang="en" lang="en">
    <head>
        <title>
            Using logical styles
        </title>
    </head>

    <body>
        <strong>Do not</strong> press the ejector seat button!
    </body>
</html>
```

You can see this style in Netscape Navigator, shown in Figure 2.2, and in Internet Explorer, shown in Figure 2.3.

<code>—Displaying Program Code

Purpose: Styles text as program code in a monospace (fixed-width) font.

When used as HTML: Start tag/End tag: Required/Required

Supported: [1.0S, 1.0T, 1.0F, 1.1, 2, 3, 3.2, 4, IE1, IE2, IE3, IE4, IE5, NS1, NS2, NS3, NS4]

Attributes:

- **class**—Class of the element (used for rendering). [1.0S, 1.0T, 1.0F, 1.1, 3, 4, IE4, IE5, NS4]

- **dir**—Gives the direction of directionally neutral text (text that doesn't have inherent direction in which you should read it). Possible values: **ltr**: left-to-right text or table and **rtl**: right-to-left text or table. [1.0S, 1.0T, 1.0F, 1.1, 4, IE5]

- **id**—Unique alphanumeric identifier for the tag, which you can use to refer to it. [1.0S, 1.0T, 1.0F, 1.1, 3, 4, IE4, IE5, NS4]

- **lang**—Base language used for the tag. [1.0S, 1.0T, 1.0F, 1.1, 3, 4, IE4, IE5]

- **language**—Scripting language used for the tag. [IE4, IE5]

- **style**—Inline style indicating how to render the element. [1.0S, 1.0T, 1.0F, 1.1, 4, IE3, IE4, IE5, NS4]

- **title**—Holds additional information (as might be displayed in tool tips) for the element. [1.0S, 1.0T, 1.0F, 1.1, 3, 4, IE4, IE5]

- **xml:lang**—Holds the base language for the element when the document is interpreted as an XML document. [1.0S, 1.0T, 1.0F, 1.1]

XHTML events: onclick, ondblclick, onmousedown, onmouseup, onmouseover, onmousemove, onmouseout, onkeypress, onkeydown, onkeyup

The **<code>** element styles text as program code. It is usually rendered in a monospace font where each character has equal width. Here's an example showing how to use **<code>**:

```
<?xml version="1.0"?>
<!DOCTYPE html PUBLIC "-//W3C//DTD XHTML 1.0 Transitional//EN"
"http://www.w3.org/TR/xhtml1/DTD/xhtml1-transitional.dtd">
<html xmlns="http://www.w3.org/1999/xhtml" xml:lang="en" lang="en">
    <head>
        <title>
            Using logical styles
        </title>
    </head>
```

```
        <body>
            You can try this Web page in your browser:
            <code>
                <br />
                    &lt;html&gt;
                <br />
                    &lt;head&gt;
                <br />
                    &lt;title&gt;
                <br />
                    This is my page.
                <br />
                    &lt;/title&gt;
                <br />
                    &lt;/head&gt;
                <br />
                    &lt;/html&gt;
            </code>
        </body>
</html>
```

You can see this style in Netscape Navigator, shown in Figure 2.2, and in Internet Explorer, shown in Figure 2.3.

TIP: *The* **<code>** *element is expressly for displaying code samples. If you just want to display monospace text, it's better to use the* **<tt>** *element because that's* **<tt>** *'s job. If the browser displays* **<code>** *elements in a different way from* **<tt>** *elements, the user can be confused if you use* **<code>** *for monospace text and not for code samples. Note that like* **<tt>**, **<code>** *ignores line breaks.*

<samp>—Displaying Sample Program Output

Purpose: Styles text as sample program output; usually rendered in a monospace font.

When used as HTML: Start tag/End tag: Required/Required

Supported: [1.0S, 1.0T, 1.0F, 1.1, 2, 3, 3.2, 4, IE1, IE2, IE3, IE4, IE5, NS1, NS2, NS3, NS4]

Attributes:

- **class**—Class of the element (used for rendering). [1.0S, 1.0T, 1.0F, 1.1, 3, 4, IE4, IE5, NS4]

- **dir**—Gives the direction of directionally neutral text (text that doesn't have inherent direction in which you should read it). Possible values: **ltr**: left-to-right text or table and **rtl**: right-to-left text or table. [1.0S, 1.0T, 1.0F, 1.1, 4, IE5]
- **id**—Unique alphanumeric identifier for the tag, which you can use to refer to it. [1.0S, 1.0T, 1.0F, 1.1, 3, 4, IE4, IE5, NS4]
- **lang**—Base language used for the tag. [1.0S, 1.0T, 1.0F, 1.1, 3, 4, IE4, IE5]
- **language**—Scripting language used for the tag. [IE4, IE5]
- **style**—Inline style indicating how to render the element. [1.0S, 1.0T, 1.0F, 1.1, 4, IE3, IE4, IE5, NS4]
- **title**—Holds additional information (as might be displayed in tool tips) for the element. [1.0S, 1.0T, 1.0F, 1.1, 3, 4, IE4, IE5]
- **xml:lang**—Holds the base language for the element when the document is interpreted as an XML document. [1.0S, 1.0T, 1.0F, 1.1]

XHTML events: onclick, ondblclick, onmousedown, onmouseup, onmouseover, onmousemove, onmouseout, onkeypress, onkeydown, onkeyup

You use the **<samp>** element to display program output or sample text. This element usually renders text in a monospace font; here's an example using **<samp>**:

```
<?xml version="1.0"?>
<!DOCTYPE html PUBLIC "-//W3C//DTD XHTML 1.0 Transitional//EN"
 "http://www.w3.org/TR/xhtml1/DTD/xhtml1-transitional.dtd">
<html xmlns="http://www.w3.org/1999/xhtml" xml:lang="en" lang="en">
    <head>
        <title>
            Using logical styles
        </title>
    </head>

    <body>
        At this point, the program displays:
        <samp>Sorry, wrong password!</samp>
    </body>
</html>
```

You can see this style in Netscape Navigator, shown in Figure 2.2, and in Internet Explorer, shown in Figure 2.3.

> **TIP:** The **<samp>** element is expressly for displaying sample text. If you just want to display monospace text, it's better to use the **<tt>** element because that's **<tt>**'s job. If the browser displays **<samp>** elements in a different way from **<tt>** elements, the user can be confused if you use **<samp>** for monospace text and not for sample text. Note that like **<tt>**, **<samp>** ignores line breaks.

<kbd>—Displaying Text the User is to Type

Purpose: Displays text that the user is supposed to type; usually rendered in a bold or standard monospace font.

When used as HTML: Start tag/End tag: Required/Required

Supported: [1.0S, 1.0T, 1.0F, 1.1, 2, 3, 3.2, 4, IE1, IE2, IE3, IE4, IE5, NS1, NS2, NS3, NS4]

Attributes:

- **class**—Class of the element (used for rendering). [1.0S, 1.0T, 1.0F, 1.1, 3, 4, IE4, IE5, NS4]

- **dir**—Gives the direction of directionally neutral text (text that doesn't have inherent direction in which you should read it). Possible values: **ltr**: left-to-right text or table and **rtl**: right-to-left text or table. [1.0S, 1.0T, 1.0F, 1.1, 4, IE5]

- **id**—Unique alphanumeric identifier for the tag, which you can use to refer to it. [1.0S, 1.0T, 1.0F, 1.1, 3, 4, IE4, IE5, NS4]

- **lang**—Base language used for the tag. [1.0S, 1.0T, 1.0F, 1.1, 3, 4, IE4, IE5]

- **language**—Scripting language used for the tag. [IE4, IE5]

- **style**—Inline style indicating how to render the element. [1.0S, 1.0T, 1.0F, 1.1, 4, IE3, IE4, IE5, NS4]

- **title**—Holds additional information (as might be displayed in tool tips) for the element. [1.0S, 1.0T, 1.0F, 1.1, 3, 4, IE4, IE5]

- **xml:lang**—Holds the base language for the element when the document is interpreted as an XML document. [1.0S, 1.0T, 1.0F, 1.1]

XHTML events: onclick, ondblclick, onmousedown, onmouseup, onmouseover, onmousemove, onmouseout, onkeypress, onkeydown, onkeyup

You use the **<kbd>** element to display text that you want the user to type (for example, when writing a training manual and you want to indicate what users should type into their computer). The text in this element is usually displayed in a bold or standard monospace font. Here's an example of using the **<kbd>** element:

```
<?xml version="1.0"?>
<!DOCTYPE html PUBLIC "-//W3C//DTD XHTML 1.0 Transitional//EN"
    "http://www.w3.org/TR/xhtml1/DTD/xhtml1-transitional.dtd">
<html xmlns="http://www.w3.org/1999/xhtml" xml:lang="en" lang="en">
    <head>
        <title>
            Using logical styles
        </title>
    </head>

    <body>
        Now type this: <kbd>Search all records</kbd>.
    </body>
</html>
```

You can see this style in Netscape Navigator, shown in Figure 2.2, and in Internet Explorer, shown in Figure 2.3.

<var>—Displaying Program Variables and Arguments

Purpose: Styles text as a program variable or argument; usually rendered in italics.

When used as HTML: Start tag/End tag: Required/Required

Supported: [1.0S, 1.0T, 1.0F, 1.1, 2, 3, 3.2, 4, IE1, IE2, IE3, IE4, IE5, NS1, NS2, NS3, NS4]

Attributes:

- **class**—Class of the element (used for rendering). [1.0S, 1.0T, 1.0F, 1.1, 3, 4, IE4, IE5, NS4]
- **dir**—Gives the direction of directionally neutral text (text that doesn't have inherent direction in which you should read it). Possible values: **ltr**: left-to-right text or table and **rtl**: right-to-left text or table. [1.0S, 1.0T, 1.0F, 1.1, 4, IE5]
- **id**—Unique alphanumeric identifier for the tag, which you can use to refer to it. [1.0S, 1.0T, 1.0F, 1.1, 3, 4, IE4, IE5, NS4]
- **lang**—Base language used for the tag. [1.0S, 1.0T, 1.0F, 1.1, 3, 4, IE4, IE5]

- **language**—Scripting language used for the tag. [IE4, IE5]
- **style**—Inline style indicating how to render the element. [1.0S, 1.0T, 1.0F, 1.1, 4, IE3, IE4, IE5, NS4]
- **title**—Holds additional information (as might be displayed in tool tips) for the element. [1.0S, 1.0T, 1.0F, 1.1, 3, 4, IE4, IE5]
- **xml:lang**—Holds the base language for the element when the document is interpreted as an XML document. [1.0S, 1.0T, 1.0F, 1.1]

XHTML events: onclick, ondblclick, onmousedown, onmouseup, onmouseover, onmousemove, onmouseout, onkeypress, onkeydown, onkeyup

Often, when you're writing technical material that involves programming, the convention is to highlight program variables or arguments within text to distinguish them from the standard text. You can use the **<var>** element to do this. This element usually displays its text in italics. Here's an example:

```
<?xml version="1.0"?>
<!DOCTYPE html PUBLIC "-//W3C//DTD XHTML 1.0 Transitional//EN"
"http://www.w3.org/TR/xhtml1/DTD/xhtml1-transitional.dtd">
<html xmlns="http://www.w3.org/1999/xhtml" xml:lang="en" lang="en">
    <head>
        <title>
            Using logical styles
        </title>
    </head>

    <body>
        The Perl <var>$input</var> argument will hold 5.
    </body>
</html>
```

You can see this style in Netscape Navigator, shown in Figure 2.2, and in Internet Explorer, shown in Figure 2.3.

<dfn>—Defining New Terms

Purpose: Styles text to indicate the first time a term is used—that is, to indicate that you're defining the term; usually rendered as italics.

When used as HTML: Start tag/End tag: Required/Required

Supported: [1.0S, 1.0T, 1.0F, 1.1, 3, 3.2, 4, IE1, IE2, IE3, IE4, IE5]

Attributes:

- **class**—Class of the element (used for rendering). [1.0S, 1.0T, 1.0F, 1.1, 3, 4, IE4, IE5]

- **dir**—Gives the direction of directionally neutral text (text that doesn't have inherent direction in which you should read it). Possible values: **ltr**: left-to-right text or table and **rtl**: right-to-left text or table. [1.0S, 1.0T, 1.0F, 1.1, 4, IE5]

- **id**—Unique alphanumeric identifier for the tag, which you can use to refer to it. [1.0S, 1.0T, 1.0F, 1.1, 3, 4, IE4, IE5]

- **lang**—Base language used for the tag. [1.0S, 1.0T, 1.0F, 1.1, 3, 4, IE4, IE5]

- **language**—Scripting language used for the tag. [IE4, IE5]

- **style**—Inline style indicating how to render the element. [1.0S, 1.0T, 1.0F, 1.1, 4, IE3, IE4, IE5]

- **title**—Holds additional information (as might be displayed in tool tips) for the element. [1.0S, 1.0T, 1.0F, 1.1, 3, 4, IE4, IE5]

- **xml:lang**—Holds the base language for the element when the document is interpreted as an XML document. [1.0S, 1.0T, 1.0F, 1.1]

XHTML events: onclick, ondblclick, onmousedown, onmouseup, onmouseover, onmousemove, onmouseout, onkeypress, onkeydown, onkeyup

You can use the **<dfn>** element when introducing a new term (that is, a definition). In practice, however, this element is usually just rendered in italics. Here's an example of using the **<dfn>** element:

```
<?xml version="1.0"?>
<!DOCTYPE html PUBLIC "-//W3C//DTD XHTML 1.0 Transitional//EN"
"http://www.w3.org/TR/xhtml1/DTD/xhtml1-transitional.dtd">
<html xmlns="http://www.w3.org/1999/xhtml" xml:lang="en" lang="en">
    <head>
        <title>
            Using logical styles
        </title>
    </head>

    <body>
        This is known as a <dfn>SNAFU.</dfn>
    </body>
</html>
```

You can see this style in Netscape Navigator, shown in Figure 2.2, and in Internet Explorer, shown in Figure 2.3.

\<cite\>—Creating a Citation

Purpose: Styles text as a citation; usually rendered in italics.

When used as HTML: Start tag/End tag: Required/Required

Supported: [1.0S, 1.0T, 1.0F, 1.1, 2, 3, 3.2, 4, IE1, IE2, IE3, IE4, IE5, NS1, NS2, NS3, NS4]

Attributes:

- **class**—Class of the element (used for rendering). [1.0S, 1.0T, 1.0F, 1.1, 3, 4, IE4, IE5, NS4]
- **dir**—Gives the direction of directionally neutral text (text that doesn't have inherent direction in which you should read it). Possible values: **ltr**: left-to-right text or table and **rtl**: right-to-left text or table. [1.0S, 1.0T, 1.0F, 1.1, 4, IE5]
- **id**—Unique alphanumeric identifier for the tag, which you can use to refer to it. [1.0S, 1.0T, 1.0F, 1.1, 3, 4, IE4, IE5, NS4]
- **lang**—Base language used for the tag. [1.0S, 1.0T, 1.0F, 1.1, 3, 4, IE4, IE5]
- **language**—Scripting language used for the tag. [IE4, IE5]
- **style**—Inline style indicating how to render the element. [1.0S, 1.0T, 1.0F, 1.1, 4, IE3, IE4, IE5, NS4]
- **title**—Holds additional information (as might be displayed in tool tips) for the element. [1.0S, 1.0T, 1.0F, 1.1, 3, 4, IE4, IE5]
- **xml:lang**—Holds the base language for the element when the document is interpreted as an XML document. [1.0S, 1.0T, 1.0F, 1.1]

XHTML events: onclick, ondblclick, onmousedown, onmouseup, onmouseover, onmousemove, onmouseout, onkeypress, onkeydown, onkeyup

You can use the **\<cite\>** element to indicate that certain text is a citation. Usually, this text is rendered in italics. Here's an example of using the **\<cite\>** element:

```
<?xml version="1.0"?>
<!DOCTYPE html PUBLIC "-//W3C//DTD XHTML 1.0 Transitional//EN"
    "http://www.w3.org/TR/xhtml1/DTD/xhtml1-transitional.dtd">
<html xmlns="http://www.w3.org/1999/xhtml" xml:lang="en" lang="en">
    <head>
        <title>
            Using logical styles
        </title>
    </head>
```

```
    <body>
        Yogi Berra said, <cite>I didn't really say everything I said</cite>.
        Or did he?
    </body>
</html>
```

You can see this style in Netscape Navigator, shown in Figure 2.2, and in Internet Explorer, shown in Figure 2.3.

<abbr>—Displaying Abbreviations

Purpose: Styles text as an abbreviation.

When used as HTML: Start tag/End tag: Required/Optional

Supported: [1.0S, 1.0T, 1.0F, 1.1, 4]

Attributes:

- **class**—Class of the element (used for rendering). [1.0S, 1.0T, 1.0F, 1.1, 4]
- **dir**—Gives the direction of directionally neutral text (text that doesn't have inherent direction in which you should read it). Possible values: **ltr**: left-to-right text or table and **rtl**: right-to-left text or table. [1.0S, 1.0T, 1.0F, 1.1, 4]
- **id**—Unique alphanumeric identifier for the tag, which you can use to refer to it. [1.0S, 1.0T, 1.0F, 1.1, 4]
- **lang**—Base language used for the tag. [1.0S, 1.0T, 1.0F, 1.1, 4]
- **style**—Inline style indicating how to render the element. [1.0S, 1.0T, 1.0F, 1.1, 4]
- **title**—Holds additional information (as might be displayed in tool tips) for the element. [1.0S, 1.0T, 1.0F, 1.1, 4]
- **xml:lang**—Holds the base language for the element when the document is interpreted as an XML document. [1.0S, 1.0T, 1.0F, 1.1]

XHTML events: onclick, ondblclick, onmousedown, onmouseup, onmouseover, onmousemove, onmouseout, onkeypress, onkeydown, onkeyup

You use the **<abbr>** element to indicate that a term is an abbreviation. This element is new in HTML 4 and has not been implemented by the major browsers yet, but will probably be implemented as italics or boldface. Here's an example:

```
<?xml version="1.0"?>
<!DOCTYPE html PUBLIC "-//W3C//DTD XHTML 1.0 Transitional//EN"
"http://www.w3.org/TR/xhtml1/DTD/xhtml1-transitional.dtd">
<html xmlns="http://www.w3.org/1999/xhtml" xml:lang="en" lang="en">
    <head>
        <title>
            Using logical styles
        </title>
    </head>

    <body>
        MIT is on Massachusetts Avenue, which people call
        <abbr title="Massachusetts Avenue">Mass Ave</abbr>.
    </body>
</html>
```

TIP: W3C suggests using the **title** attribute to hold the expanded version of the abbreviation.

<acronym>—Displaying Acronyms

Purpose: Used to display acronyms.

When used as HTML: Start tag/End tag: Required/Required

Supported: [1.0S, 1.0T, 1.0F, 1.1, 4, IE4, IE5]

Attributes:

- **class**—Class of the element (used for rendering). [1.0S, 1.0T, 1.0F, 1.1, 4, IE4, IE5]

- **dir**—Gives the direction of directionally neutral text (text that doesn't have inherent direction in which you should read it). Possible values: **ltr**: left-to-right text or table and **rtl**: right-to-left text or table. [1.0S, 1.0T, 1.0F, 1.1, 4, IE5]

- **id**—Unique alphanumeric identifier for the tag, which you can use to refer to it. [1.0S, 1.0T, 1.0F, 1.1, 4, IE4, IE5]

- **lang**—Base language used for the tag. [1.0S, 1.0T, 1.0F, 1.1, 4, IE4, IE5]

- **language**—Scripting language used for the tag. [IE4, IE5]

- **style**—Inline style indicating how to render the element. [1.0S, 1.0T, 1.0F, 1.1, 4, IE4, IE5]

- **title**—Holds additional information (as might be displayed in tool tips) for the element. [1.0S, 1.0T, 1.0F, 1.1, 4, IE4, IE5]

- **xml:lang**—Holds the base language for the element when the document is interpreted as an XML document. [1.0S, 1.0T, 1.0F, 1.1]

XHTML events: onclick, ondblclick, onmousedown, onmouseup, onmouseover, onmousemove, onmouseout, onkeypress, onkeydown, onkeyup

You use the **<acronym>** element to indicate that a term is an acronym. This element is new in HTML 4 and has only been implemented by Internet Explorer. Here's an example:

```
<?xml version="1.0"?>
<!DOCTYPE html PUBLIC "-//W3C//DTD XHTML 1.0 Transitional//EN"
"http://www.w3.org/TR/xhtml1/DTD/xhtml1-transitional.dtd">
<html xmlns="http://www.w3.org/1999/xhtml" xml:lang="en" lang="en">
    <head>
        <title>
            Using logical styles
        </title>
    </head>

    <body>
        XHTML is standardized by the
        <acronym title="World Wide Web Consortium">W3C</acronym>.
    </body>
</html>
```

TIP: W3C suggests using the **title** attribute to hold the expanded version of the acronym.

<font>—Specifying a Font

Purpose: Lets you select text size, color, and face. Deprecated in HTML 4.

When used as HTML: Start tag/End tag: Required/Required

Supported: [1.0T, 1.0F, 3.2, 4, IE1, IE2, IE3, IE4, IE5, NS1, NS2, NS3, NS4]

Attributes:

- **class**—Class of the element (used for rendering). [1.0T, 1.0F, 3, 4, IE4, IE5, NS4]
- **color**—Deprecated. Color of the text; set it to a color value or predefined color [1.0T, 1.0F, 3.2, 4, IE1, IE2, IE3, IE4, IE5, NS2, NS3, NS4]
- **dir**—Gives the direction of directionally neutral text (text that doesn't have inherent direction in which you should read it). Possible values: **ltr**: left-to-right text or table and **rtl**: right-to-left text or table. [1.0T, 1.0F, 4, IE5]
- **face**—Deprecated. The font face can be a list of names separated by commas. The browser will select the first font face from the list it can find in the system it's running on. [1.0T, 1.0F, 4, IE1, IE2, IE3, IE4, IE5, NS3, NS4]
- **id**—Unique alphanumeric identifier for the tag, which you can use to refer to it. [1.0T, 1.0F, 3, 4, IE4, IE5, NS4]
- **lang**—Base language used for the tag. [1.0T, 1.0F, 3, 4, IE4, IE5]
- **language**—Scripting language used for the tag. [IE4, IE5]
- **point-size**—Size of the text in points (1/72 of an inch). [NS4]
- **size**—Deprecated. Size of the text. Possible values range from 1 through 7. You can also specify sizes relative to the current base font (see the **<basefont>** tag) by placing a + or - in front of the **size** attribute's value. Relative values can range from –6 through +6. [1.0T, 1.0F, 3.2, 4, IE1, IE2, IE3, IE4, IE5, NS1, NS2, NS3, NS4]
- **style**—Inline style indicating how to render the element. [1.0T, 1.0F, 4, IE4, IE5, NS4]
- **title**—Holds additional information (as might be displayed in tool tips) for the element. [1.0T, 1.0F, 3, 4, IE4, IE5]
- **weight**—Sets the font weight from 100 to 900 (possible values are 100 up to 900 in steps of 100). [NS4]
- **xml:lang**—Holds the base language for the element when the document is interpreted as an XML document. [1.0T, 1.0F]

XHTML events: None.

The **<font>** tag is cherished by many HTML authors, but was deprecated in HTML 4 in favor of style sheets. That means you'll only find it in the XHTML 1.0 Transitional and Frameset DTDs. You use this tag to select a typeface, size, and color. Here's an example, displaying text in large blue Arial type:

```
<?xml version="1.0"?>
<!DOCTYPE html PUBLIC "-//W3C//DTD XHTML 1.0 Transitional//EN"
"http://www.w3.org/TR/xhtml1/DTD/xhtml1-transitional.dtd">
<html xmlns="http://www.w3.org/1999/xhtml" xml:lang="en" lang="en">
    <head>
        <title>
            Using the &lt;font&gt; Tag
        </title>
    </head>

    <body>
        <font size="6" color="#0000ff" face="Arial">Here is some text!</font>
    </body>

</html>
```

The results appear in Figure 2.4. You specify font sizes by using the values 1 through 7 or—if you've set the base font size with the **<basefont>** element—as relative values –6 through +6. If you're using Netscape Navigator, you can set the font size in points with the **point-size** attribute. In practice, font size 1 is about 6 points, font size 2 is about 12 points, and so on, but actual sizes vary by system. Here's an example showing the range of possible sizes:

```
<?xml version="1.0"?>
<!DOCTYPE html PUBLIC "-//W3C//DTD XHTML 1.0 Transitional//EN"
"http://www.w3.org/TR/xhtml1/DTD/xhtml1-transitional.dtd">
<html xmlns="http://www.w3.org/1999/xhtml" xml:lang="en" lang="en">
    <head>
        <title>
            Using the &lt;font&gt; Tag
        </title>
    </head>

    <body>
        <center>
            <h1>
                Using the &lt;font&gt; tag
            </h1>
            <font size="1">This is font size 1.</font>
            <br />
            <font size="2">This is font size 2.</font>
            <br />
            <font size="3">This is font size 3.</font>
            <br />
```

```
            <font size="4">This is font size 4.</font>
            <br />
            <font size="5">This is font size 5.</font>
            <br />
            <font size="6">This is font size 6.</font>
            <br />
            <font size="7">This is font size 7.</font>
        </center>
    </body>
</html>
```

The results of this XHTML appear in Figure 2.12.

Sometimes, the font you've specified might not be installed on the system the browser is running on. To anticipate any problems, you can specify a list of fonts to use, and the browser will select the first one that it can use. (Note that you specify font names containing multiple words by using single quotes.) Here's an example:

```
<font size="6" color="#0000ff" face="Arial, 'Courier New', 'Times New Roman'">Here is some text!</font>
```

TIP: *A popular use of* **<font>** *is to color text inline, as in this example:* **<font color="red">Warning!</font> You're about to delete all your files!**

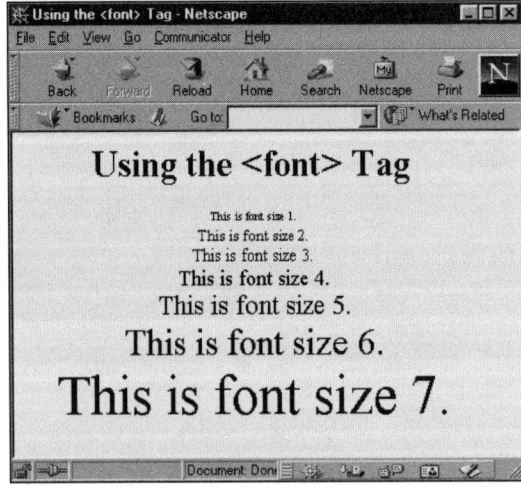

Figure 2.12 Using the **<font>** tag.

Setting Font Size in Points

The novice programmer says, "Jeez, what's all this about setting font sizes using values from 1 through 7 with the **<font>** tag? I'm used to using the point sizes you see in word processors." "OK," you say, "There is a way to do that." "Tell me all about it!" the NP cries.

In Netscape Navigator, you can set the font size in points (1/72 of an inch) by using the **point-size** attribute of the **<font>** tag. In this example, I'm setting the size of text to 50 points:

```
<?xml version="1.0"?>
<!DOCTYPE html PUBLIC "-//W3C//DTD XHTML 1.0 Transitional//EN"
    "http://www.w3.org/TR/xhtml1/DTD/xhtml1-transitional.dtd">
<html xmlns="http://www.w3.org/1999/xhtml" xml:lang="en" lang="en">
    <head>
        <title>
            Using the &lt;font&gt; Tag
        </title>
    </head>

    <body>
            <font point-size="50">
                Some big text.
            </font>
    </body>
</html>
```

Internet Explorer, on the other hand, does not support the **point-size** attribute, but you can do the same thing with style sheets. In this case, I'm setting the style of the **<p>** paragraph tag to use 50-point text (this code works only in Internet Explorer):

```
<?xml version="1.0"?>
<!DOCTYPE html PUBLIC "-//W3C//DTD XHTML 1.0 Transitional//EN"
    "http://www.w3.org/TR/xhtml1/DTD/xhtml1-transitional.dtd">
<html xmlns="http://www.w3.org/1999/xhtml" xml:lang="en" lang="en">
    <head>
        <title>
            Specific tag styling example
        </title>

        <style type="text/css">
            p {font-size = 50pt}
        </style>
    </head>
```

```
            <body>
                <p>
                    Some big text.
                </p>
            </body>
        </html>
```

<basefont>—Setting the Base Font

Purpose: Sets the base font. Relative font changes (created with the **<font>** element) are made with respect to the base font. Deprecated in HTML 4. This element takes no content.

When used as HTML: Start tag/End tag: Required/Omitted

Supported: [1.0T, 1.0F, 3.2, 4, IE1, IE2, IE3, IE4, IE5, NS1, NS2, NS3, NS4]

Attributes:

- **class**—Class of the element (used for rendering). [3, 4, IE4, IE5, NS4]
- **color**—Deprecated. Color of the default text; set it to a color value or predefined color. [1.0T, 1.0F, 4, IE1, IE2, IE3, IE4, IE5]
- **dir**—Gives the direction of directionally neutral text (text that doesn't have inherent direction in which you should read it). Possible values: **ltr**: left-to-right text or table and **rtl**: right-to-left text or table. [4, IE5]
- **face**—Deprecated. The font face of default text can be a comma-separated list of font names. The browser will select the first one it can find in the system it's running on. [1.0T, 1.0F, 4, IE1, IE2, IE3, IE4, IE5]
- **id**—Unique alphanumeric identifier for the tag, which you can use to refer to it. [1.0T, 1.0F, 3, 4, IE4, IE5, NS4]
- **lang**—Base language used for the tag. [3, 4]
- **size**—Deprecated. Size of default text. Possible values range from 1 through 7. [1.0T, 1.0F, 3.2, 4, IE1, IE2, IE3, IE4, IE5, NS1, NS2, NS3, NS4]
- **style**—Inline style indicating how to render the element. [4, NS4]
- **title**—Holds additional information (as might be displayed in tool tips) for the element. [3, 4, IE4, IE5]
- **xml:lang**—Holds the base language for the element when the document is interpreted as an XML document. [1.0T, 1.0F]

XHTML events: None

The **<basefont>** element sets the font for default text enclosed in the element and replaces the default font used by the browser. Possible values range from 1 through 7. You can use the **<font>** tag to specify relative sizes with respect to the base font.

NOTE: *The **<basefont>** tag is deprecated in HTML 4, so it appears only in the XHTML 1.0 Transitional and Frameset DTDs. Because the **<basefont>** tag will disappear from XHTML as of version 1.1, the use of style sheets is a better choice.*

In the following example, I'm setting the base font size to 4, then temporarily increasing that size to 6 for one word by using a **<font>** tag to add 2 to the base font size:

```
<?xml version="1.0"?>
<!DOCTYPE html PUBLIC "-//W3C//DTD XHTML 1.0 Transitional//EN"
"http://www.w3.org/TR/xhtml1/DTD/xhtml1-transitional.dtd">
<html xmlns="http://www.w3.org/1999/xhtml" xml:lang="en" lang="en">
    <head>
        <title>
            Using the &lt;basefont&gt; Tag
        </title>
    </head>

    <body>
        <center>
            <h1>
                Using the &lt;basefont&gt; tag
            </h1>
        </center>
        <basefont size = "4">
            Here's some <font size="+2">bigger</font> text.
        </basefont>
    </body>

</html>
```

The results appear in Figure 2.13. As you can see, the word I've increased in size is indeed bigger. Keep in mind that **<basefont>** is deprecated, which means it'll disappear from XHTML as of version 1.1 (and it's already gone in the XHTML 1.0 strict DTD). The use of style sheets is a better choice.

TIP: *Neither Internet Explorer nor Netscape Navigator apply the **basefont size** attribute value to heading levels. Internet Explorer, does, however, apply the **face** and **color** values to headings. (Netscape Navigator does not.)*

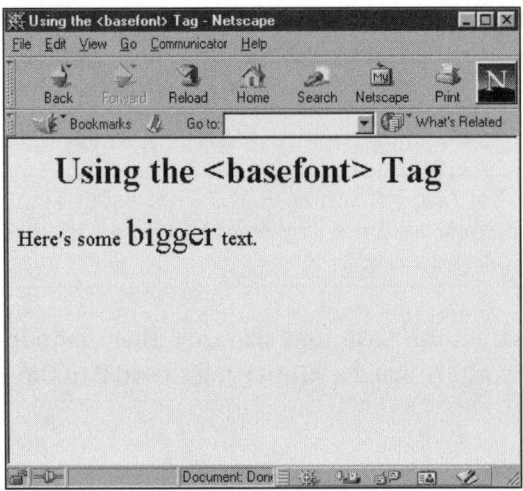

Figure 2.13   Using the **<basefont>** tag with the **<font>** tag.

<q>—Displaying Short Quotations

Purpose: Displays a short, inline quotation.

When used as HTML: Start tag/End tag: Required/Required

Supported: [1.0S, 1.0T, 1.0F, 1.1, 4, IE4, IE5]

Attributes:

- **cite**—Gives a citation for the quotation [1.0S, 1.0T, 1.0F, 1.1, 4]
- **class**—Class of the element (used for rendering). [4, IE4, IE5]
- **dir**—Gives the direction of directionally neutral text (text that doesn't have inherent direction in which you should read it). Possible values: **ltr**: left-to-right text or table and **rtl**: right-to-left text or table. [1.0S, 1.0T, 1.0F, 1.1, 4, IE5]
- **id**—Unique alphanumeric identifier for the tag, which you can use to refer to it. [1.0S, 1.0T, 1.0F, 1.1, 4, IE4, IE5]
- **lang**—Base language used for the tag. [1.0S, 1.0T, 1.0F, 1.1, 4, IE4, IE5]
- **language**—Scripting language used for the tag. [IE4, IE5]
- **style**—Inline style indicating how to render the element. [1.0S, 1.0T, 1.0F, 1.1, 4, IE4, IE5]
- **title**—Holds additional information (as might be displayed in tool tips) for the element. [1.0S, 1.0T, 1.0F, 1.1, 4, IE4, IE5]

- **xml:lang**—Holds the base language for the element when the document is interpreted as an XML document. [1.0S, 1.0T, 1.0F, 1.1]

XHTML events: onclick, ondblclick, onmousedown, onmouseup, onmouseover, onmousemove, onmouseout, onkeypress, onkeydown, onkeyup

The **<q>** tag is for inline quotations that do *not* include line breaks. It can be used on a word-by-word or character-by-character basis. The **<cite>** tag is used for longer quotations and **<q>** for shorter ones. Theoretically, the browser is supposed to add the right kind of locale-specific quotation marks around the quotation, but this element is too new for either Internet Explorer or Netscape Navigator to do anything but render it as plain text. Here's an example:

```
<?xml version="1.0"?>
<!DOCTYPE html PUBLIC "-//W3C//DTD XHTML 1.0 Transitional//EN"
"http://www.w3.org/TR/xhtml1/DTD/xhtml1-transitional.dtd">
<html xmlns="http://www.w3.org/1999/xhtml" xml:lang="en" lang="en">
    <head>
        <title>
            Using the &lt;q&gt; Tag
        </title>
    </head>

    <body>
        Yogi Berra said, <q>I didn't really say everything I said</q>.
        Or did he?
    </body>

</html>
```

<blink>—Making Text Blink

Purpose: Displays enclosed text as blinking on and off approximately once a second.

When used as HTML: Start tag/End tag: Required/Required

Supported: [NS1, NS2, NS3, NS4]

Attributes: None

"Hey look," the novice programmer says, "I can make my whole page blink." "Yes," you say, "that's quite an effect." The NP studies the blinking screen for a few moments and says, "Kind of annoying, isn't it?"

The **<blink>** element is a little notorious because the result, text that blinks on and off, can irritate people. Reading such text can be difficult and—if you're looking at other parts of the page—distracting. In fact, many people consider it a little juvenile, so you might want to consider this before using the **<blink>** tag. Netscape created this tag early on and still supports it; Internet Explorer now recognizes it but does not implement this tag. For instance, you can use the tag attributes, like **id** in Internet Explorer, but the text will not blink.

This element is not recognized in XHTML, but because you can use it in Netscape Navigator, here's an example (note that because of the **<blink>** element, this example is not true XHTML, although it passes the W3C XHTML validator):

```
<?xml version="1.0"?>
<!DOCTYPE html PUBLIC "-//W3C//DTD XHTML 1.0 Transitional//EN"
"http://www.w3.org/TR/xhtml1/DTD/xhtml1-transitional.dtd">
<html xmlns="http://www.w3.org/1999/xhtml" xml:lang="en" lang="en">
    <head>
        <title>
            Using the &lt;blink&gt; Tag
        </title>
    </head>

    <body>
        <blink>HAPPY NEW YEAR!!</blink>
    </body>

</html>
```

This is not to say that **<blink>** doesn't have its uses. Blinking the heading "Warning," for example, can be useful to draw attention.

TIP: Due, one imagines, to popular request, you can now disable blinking text in Netscape Navigator, but it's not easy and it can involve editing the Windows Registry. See the directions at **www.sightspecific.com/~mosh/WWW_FAQ/ noblink.html** for examples.

<ins>—Displaying Inserted Text

Purpose: Styles text as inserted text; used to track document changes. Rendered in Internet Explorer as underlined.

When used as HTML: Start tag/End tag: Required/Required

Supported: [1.0S, 1.0T, 1.0F, 1.1, 4, IE4, IE5]

Attributes:

- **cite**—Text that cites the reason for the insertion. [1.0S, 1.0T, 1.0F, 1.1, 4]
- **class**—Class of the element (used for rendering). [1.0S, 1.0T, 1.0F, 1.1, 4, IE4, IE5]
- **datetime**—Displays the date and time of the change. [1.0S, 1.0T, 1.0F, 1.1, 4]
- **dir**—Gives the direction of directionally neutral text (text that doesn't have inherent direction in which you should read it). Possible values: **ltr**: left-to-right text or table and **rtl**: right-to-left text or table. [1.0S, 1.0T, 1.0F, 1.1, 4, IE5]
- **id**—Unique alphanumeric identifier for the tag, which you can use to refer to it. [1.0S, 1.0T, 1.0F, 1.1, 4, IE4, IE5]
- **lang**—Base language used for the tag. [1.0S, 1.0T, 1.0F, 1.1, 4, IE4, IE5]
- **language**—Scripting language used for the tag. [IE4, IE5]
- **style**—Inline style indicating how to render the element. [1.0S, 1.0T, 1.0F, 1.1, 4, IE3, IE4, IE5]
- **title**—Holds additional information (as might be displayed in tool tips) for the element. [1.0S, 1.0T, 1.0F, 1.1, 4, IE4, IE5]
- **xml:lang**—Holds the base language for the element when the document is interpreted as an XML document. [1.0S, 1.0T, 1.0F, 1.1]

XHTML events: onclick, ondblclick, onmousedown, onmouseup, onmouseover, onmousemove, onmouseout, onkeypress, onkeydown, onkeyup

The novice programmer says, "It would be great if I could track changes in my online training manual by date and time." "Theoretically," you say, "you can use the **<ins>** tag to indicate what text has been inserted and when." "Great!" says the NP. "Except," you add, "that Internet Explorer is the only browser to implement **<ins>** so far, and it doesn't handle attributes like **datetime**, which stores the time of the change." "Great," sighs the NP.

Together with the **<del>** element, the **<ins>** element lets you track changes in the content of XHTML documents; **<ins>** indicates insertions, and **<del>** indicates deletions. Theoretically, you can record the time and date of the change with the **datetime** attribute, but browsers do not support this attribute yet. Here's the format to set dates and times: *YYYY-MM-DDThh:mm:ssTZD* (following the ISO8601 standard):

- *YYYY*—Four-digit year
- *MM*—Two-digit month (01 through 12)
- *DD*—Two-digit day of month (01 through 31)

- **hh**—Two-digit hour (00 through 23, no A.M./P.M. designation is used)
- **mm**—Two-digit minute (00 through 59)
- **ss**—Two-digit second (00 through 59)
- **TZD**—Time zone designator

The time zone designator is a simple **z** for Universal Coordinated Time (UTC, formerly Greenwich Mean Time) or is the number of hours and minutes that your time zone is ahead or behind UTC, like this: **+hh:mm** or **-hh:mm**. For example, because Mountain Standard Time (MST) is seven hours behind UTC, 6:00 P.M. September 2, 2000 is designated as: **2000-09-02T18:00:00-07:00**.

Currently only Internet Explorer implements **<ins>** by underlining the enclosed text, but it does not implement the **datetime** or **cite** attributes. Here's an example:

```
<?xml version="1.0"?>
<!DOCTYPE html PUBLIC "-//W3C//DTD XHTML 1.0 Transitional//EN"
"http://www.w3.org/TR/xhtml1/DTD/xhtml1-transitional.dtd">
<html xmlns="http://www.w3.org/1999/xhtml" xml:lang="en" lang="en">
    <head>
        <title>
            Using the &lt;ins&gt; Tag
        </title>
    </head>

    <body>
        Here is <ins datetime="2000-01-01T09:00:00-06:00"
        cite="Grammar correction">the</ins> page.
    </body>

</html>
```

<del>—Displaying Text as Deleted

Purpose: Marks text as deleted. Rendered as struck-through text in Internet Explorer.

When used as HTML: Start tag/End tag: Required/Required

Supported: [1.0S, 1.0T, 1.0F, 1.1, 4, IE4, IE5]

Attributes:

- **cite**—Text that cites the reason for the insertion. [1.0S, 1.0T, 1.0F, 1.1, 4]
- **class**—Class of the element (used for rendering). [1.0S, 1.0T, 1.0F, 1.1, 4, IE4, IE5]
- **datetime**—Displays the date and time of the change (for format, see the **datetime** entry in the **<ins>** section). [1.0S, 1.0T, 1.0F, 1.1, 4]
- **dir**—Gives the direction of directionally neutral text (text that doesn't have inherent direction in which you should read it). Possible values: **ltr**: left-to-right text or table and **rtl**: right-to-left text or table. [1.0S, 1.0T, 1.0F, 1.1, 4, IE5]
- **id**—Unique alphanumeric identifier for the tag, which you can use to refer to it. [1.0S, 1.0T, 1.0F, 1.1, 4, IE4, IE5]
- **lang**—Base language used for the tag. [1.0S, 1.0T, 1.0F, 1.1, 4, IE4, IE5]
- **language**—Scripting language used for the tag. [IE4, IE5]
- **style**—Inline style indicating how to render the element. [1.0S, 1.0T, 1.0F, 1.1, 4, IE4, IE5]
- **title**—Holds additional information (as might be displayed in tool tips) for the element. [1.0S, 1.0T, 1.0F, 1.1, 4, IE4, IE5]
- **xml:lang**—Holds the base language for the element when the document is interpreted as an XML document. [1.0S, 1.0T, 1.0F, 1.1]

XHTML events: onclick, ondblclick, onmousedown, onmouseup, onmouseover, onmousemove, onmouseout, onkeypress, onkeydown, onkeyup

Like the **<ins>** element, **<del>** lets you track changes in a document. The **<ins>** tag marks inserted text, and the **<del>** tag marks deleted text. Currently, the only browser that implements the **<del>** tag is Internet Explorer, and it renders the text in this element as struck through (much like the **<strike>** tag would). Note, however, that Internet Explorer does not yet implement the **datetime** attribute (which is the date and time of the deletion—for information on the format of this attribute's values, see the previous section "**<ins>**—Display Inserted Text")—nor the **cite** (reason for the deletion) attribute.

Here's an example showing how to use **<del>**:

```
<?xml version="1.0"?>
<!DOCTYPE html PUBLIC "-//W3C//DTD XHTML 1.0 Transitional//EN"
"http://www.w3.org/TR/xhtml1/DTD/xhtml1-transitional.dtd">
<html xmlns="http://www.w3.org/1999/xhtml" xml:lang="en" lang="en">
```

```
        <head>
            <title>
                Using the &lt;del&gt; Tag
            </title>
        </head>

        <body>
            Here is <del datetime="2000-01-01T09:00:00-06:00"
            cite="Grammar correction">the</del> the page.
        </body>

</html>
```

<address>—Displaying an Address

Purpose: Displays text styled as an address.

When used as HTML: Start tag/End tag: Required/Required

Supported: [1.0S, 1.0T, 1.0F, 1.1, 2, 3, 3.2, 4, IE1, IE2, IE3, IE4, IE5, NS1, NS2, NS3, NS4]

Attributes:

- **class**—Class of the element (used for rendering). [1.0S, 1.0T, 1.0F, 1.1, 3, 4, IE4, IE5, NS4]
- **dir**—Gives the direction of directionally neutral text (text that doesn't have inherent direction in which you should read it). Possible values: **ltr**: left-to-right text or table and **rtl**: right-to-left text or table. [1.0S, 1.0T, 1.0F, 1.1, 4, IE5]
- **id**—Unique alphanumeric identifier for the tag, which you can use to refer to it. [1.0S, 1.0T, 1.0F, 1.1, 3, 4, IE4, IE5, NS4]
- **lang**—Base language used for the tag. [1.0S, 1.0T, 1.0F, 1.1, 3, 4, IE4, IE5]
- **language**—Scripting language used for the tag. [IE4, IE5]
- **style**—Inline style indicating how to render the element. [1.0S, 1.0T, 1.0F, 1.1, 4, IE3, IE4, IE5, NS4]
- **title**—Holds additional information (as might be displayed in tool tips) for the element. [1.0S, 1.0T, 1.0F, 1.1, 3, 4, IE4, IE5]
- **xml:lang**—Holds the base language for the element when the document is interpreted as an XML document. [1.0S, 1.0T, 1.0F, 1.1]

XHTML events: onclick, ondblclick, onmousedown, onmouseup, onmouseover, onmousemove, onmouseout, onkeypress, onkeydown, onkeyup

You use the **<address>** element to indicate an address, or authorship, or a signature of some kind. This tag acts much like a **<p>** element, setting its text apart in its own paragraph. It also sets its text in italics in Netscape Navigator and Internet Explorer (I've heard reports that text is also indented in some other browsers). Here's an example in which I'm using a **mailto** hyperlink (covered in Chapter 5) to let people send email to a page's author:

```
<?xml version="1.0"?>
<!DOCTYPE html PUBLIC "-//W3C//DTD XHTML 1.0 Transitional//EN"
    "http://www.w3.org/TR/xhtml1/DTD/xhtml1-transitional.dtd">
<html xmlns="http://www.w3.org/1999/xhtml" xml:lang="en" lang="en">
    <head>
        <title>
            Using the &lt;address&gt; Tag
        </title>
    </head>

    <body>
        <center>
            <h1>
                Using the &lt;address&gt; tag
            </h1>
        </center>
        I take a firm stand and say: "<i>Maybe</i>"!
        Have comments on my opinion? Write to me!
        <address>
            <a href="MAILTO:author@starpowder.com">Arthur T. Author</a>
            <br />
            Negligible, Mass.
        </address>
        The opinions expressed are mine.
    </body>

</html>
```

The results of this code appear in Figure 2.14.

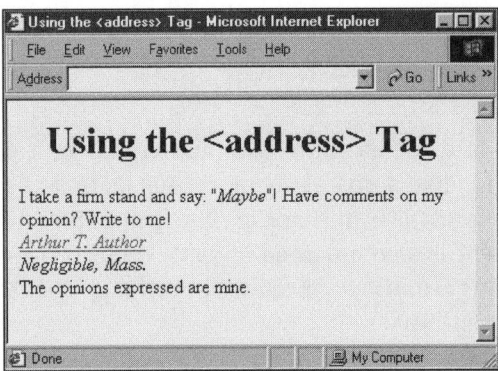

Figure 2.14   Using the **<address>** tag.

<bdo>—Overriding the Bidirectional Character Algorithm

Purpose: Overrides the direction in which text is to be read, so the browser can render text from different languages satisfactorily.

When used as HTML: Start tag/End tag: Required/Required

Supported: [1.0S, 1.0T, 1.0F, 1.1, 4, IE5]

Attributes:

- **class**—Class of the element (used for rendering). [1.0S, 1.0T, 1.0F, 1.1, 4, IE5]
- **dir**—This required attribute gives the direction of text. Possible values: **ltr**: left-to-right text or table and **rtl**: right-to-left text or table. [1.0S, 1.0T, 1.0F, 1.1, 4, IE5]
- **id**—Unique alphanumeric identifier for the tag, which you can use to refer to it. [1.0S, 1.0T, 1.0F, 1.1, 4, IE5]
- **lang**—Base language used for the tag. [1.0S, 1.0T, 1.0F, 1.1, 4, IE5]
- **language**—String indicating the language or character set used in the **<bdo>** element. Adheres to Request For Comment (RFC) 1766, which is available on the Internet. [1.0S, 1.0T, 1.0F, 1.1, 4, IE5]
- **style**—Inline style indicating how to render the element. [1.0S, 1.0T, 1.0F, 1.1, 4, IE5]
- **title**—Holds additional information (as might be displayed in tool tips) for the element. [1.0S, 1.0T, 1.0F, 1.1, 4, IE5]

- **xml:lang**—Holds the base language for the element when the document is interpreted as an XML document. [1.0S, 1.0T, 1.0F, 1.1]

XHTML events: onclick, ondblclick, onmousedown, onmouseup, onmouseover, onmousemove, onmouseout, onkeypress, onkeydown, onkeyup

"Hm," says the big boss, "as we open up the Arabic and Hebrew markets, we're running into some trouble because those languages are written and read right to left. The problem is that in documents that mix English and those languages, browsers have no idea how to render character combinations, such as some Unicode, correctly." "That's no problem," you say, "I can just use the **<bdo>** element to specify the direction of the text." "Great," says the BB, "you've earned a raise." "Really?" you ask. The BB replies, "No, not really."

Languages have an inherent directionality, left-to-right or right-to-left, but when you mix languages, it can be difficult to specify directionality. That's a problem when you're working with some special character combinations, such as those that make up symbol sets like Unicode. To fix this problem, you can use the **<bdo>** tag, which is implemented in HTML 4 and Internet Explorer 5. To specify text direction, you set the **dir** attribute to **rtl** (right-to-left) or **ltr** (left-to-right). You can also specify the language used in the **language** attribute, which is a string from the RFC 1766 standard (you can find this on the Internet at **http://info.internet.isi.edu/in-notes/rfc/files/rfc1766.txt**).

Here's an example in which I'll reverse the direction of one word:

```
<?xml version="1.0"?>
<!DOCTYPE html PUBLIC "-//W3C//DTD XHTML 1.0 Transitional//EN"
    "http://www.w3.org/TR/xhtml1/DTD/xhtml1-transitional.dtd">
<html xmlns="http://www.w3.org/1999/xhtml" xml:lang="en" lang="en">
    <head>
        <title>
            Using the &lt;bdo&gt; Tag
        </title>
    </head>

    <body>
        <center>
            <h1>
                Using the &lt;bdo&gt; tag
            </h1>
        </center>
        There's something <bdo dir="rtl">funny</bdo> going on here!
    </body>

</html>
```

The result appears in Internet Explorer in Figure 2.15, where the word "funny" has been reversed. Most people won't have a lot of use for this tag unless their text is in a language like Arabic, or they like reversing text.

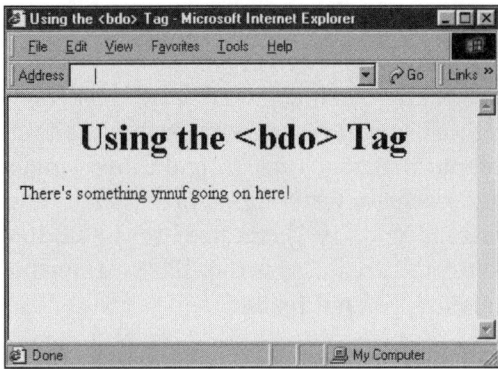

Figure 2.15   Using the **<bdo>** tag.

Displaying Special Characters: Character Entities

"I'm working on my online novel," the novice programmer says, "and I'm having some trouble—the word coöperation keeps coming out as cooperation, no double dots!" "That's an umlaut," you say, "and you can display it by using *character entities* in XHTML." "Terrific," the NP says, "now I can put the mysterious Monsieur Alphônsé back in the text." "Hm," you say.

You might want to display plenty of characters that don't appear on your keyboard—characters such as Greek letters; characters with umlauts and accent marks; various currency marks; math notations; and more. The W3C has added many of these as character entities to XHTML. The term *character entity* comes from SGML, which calls such codes *entities;* W3C calls them *character encodings*.

A character entity has this format: **&***name*;. Here, *name* is the name of the entity. You can also specify a character entity with its number, like this: **&#***number*;. For example, the character entity for ö is **ö** so you could place that character in your page like this:

```
<?xml version="1.0"?>
<!DOCTYPE html PUBLIC "-//W3C//DTD XHTML 1.0 Transitional//EN"
"http://www.w3.org/TR/xhtml1/DTD/xhtml1-transitional.dtd">
<html xmlns="http://www.w3.org/1999/xhtml" xml:lang="en" lang="en">
    <head>
```

```
        <title>
            Using Character Entities
        </title>
    </head>

    <body>
        <center>
            <h1>
                Using Character Entities
            </h1>
        </center>
        "Thanks for the co&ouml;peration," Jed said grimly to
        the trembling criminal.
    </body>
</html>
```

The result appears in Figure 2.16.

The **ö** entity's number is 246, so you can create the same result with this XHTML:

```
<?xml version="1.0"?>
<!DOCTYPE html PUBLIC "-//W3C//DTD XHTML 1.0 Transitional//EN"
"http://www.w3.org/TR/xhtml1/DTD/xhtml1-transitional.dtd">
<html xmlns="http://www.w3.org/1999/xhtml" xml:lang="en" lang="en">
    <head>
        <title>
            Using Character Entities
        </title>
    </head>

    <body>
        <center>
            <h1>
                Using Character Entities
            </h1>
        </center>
        "Thanks for the co&#246;peration," Jed said grimly to
        the trembling criminal.
    </body>
</html>
```

You may have seen Scandinavian, French, or German characters in Web pages, and now you know how it's done. The complete list of the character entities in HTML 4, and therefore XHTML, appears in Table 2.29, and although it's long, it's worth looking at the list to become familiar with it. When you want to display a

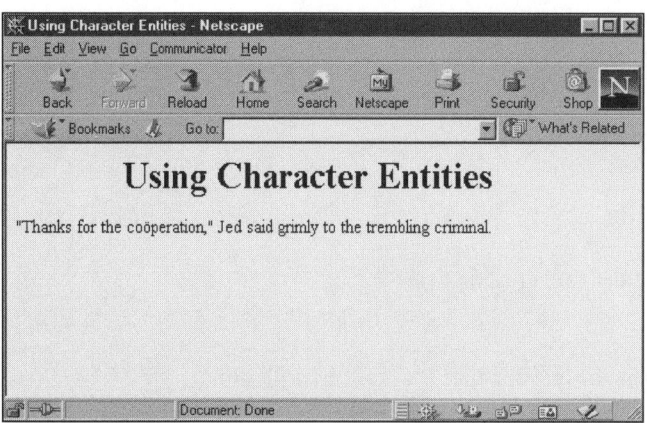

Figure 2.16   Using character entities.

special character and don't know how to do it, one of the first things you should consider is a character entity.

TIP: *In some cases, you can skip the final semicolon in a character entity, but I don't recommend it. The final semicolon is necessary if you want to embed a character entity in the middle of a word, for example, but not when the next character is a space. Because it's so easy to forget the semicolon if you start alternating between using them and not, I recommend that you always use it.*

Table 2.2   Character entities for HTML 4 (support varies by browser).

Entity	Numerical	Does This
Aacute	&#193;	Latin capital letter A with acute accent
aacute	&#225;	Latin small letter a with acute accent
Acirc	&#194;	Latin capital letter A with circumflex
acirc	&#226;	Latin small letter a with circumflex
acute	&#180;	Acute accent
AElig	&#198;	Latin capital letter AE
aelig	&#230;	Latin small letter ae
Agrave	&#192;	Latin capital letter A with grave
agrave	&#224;	Latin small letter a with grave
alefsym	&#8501;	Alef symbol = first transfinite cardinal
Alpha	&#913;	Greek capital letter alpha
alpha	&#945;	Greek small letter alpha
amp	&#38;	Ampersand

(continued)

Table 2.2 Character entities for HTML 4 (support varies by browser) *(continued)*.

Entity	Numerical	Does This
and	&#8743;	Logical and
ang	&#8736;	Angle
Aring	&#197;	Latin capital letter A with ring above
aring	&#229;	Latin small letter a with ring above
asymp	&#8776;	Almost equal to = asymptotic to
Atilde	&#195;	Latin capital letter A with tilde
atilde	&#227;	Latin small letter a with tilde
Auml	&#196;	Latin capital letter A with diæresis (umlaut)
auml	&#228;	Latin small letter a with diæresis (umlaut)
bdquo	&#8222;	Double low-9 quotation mark
Beta	&#914;	Greek capital letter beta
beta	&#946;	Greek small letter beta
brvbar	&#166;	Broken bar = broken vertical bar
bull	&#8226;	Bullet (black small circle)
cap	&#8745;	Intersection = cap
Ccedil	&#199;	Latin capital letter C with cedilla
ccedil	&#231;	Latin small letter c with cedilla
cedil	&#184;	Cedilla
cent	&#162;	Cent sign
Chi	&#935;	Greek capital letter chi
chi	&#967;	Greek small letter chi
circ	&#710;	Modifier letter circumflex accent
clubs	&#9827;	Black club suit = shamrock
cong	&#8773;	Approximately equal to
copy	&#169;	Copyright sign
crarr	&#8629;	Downward arrow with corner leftward
cup	&#8746;	Union = cup
curren	&#164;	Currency sign
dagger	&#8224;	Dagger
Dagger	&#8225;	Double dagger
darr	&#8595;	Downward arrow
dArr	&#8659;	Downward double arrow

(continued)

Table 2.2 Character entities for HTML 4 (support varies by browser) *(continued).*

Entity	Numerical	Does This
deg	&#176;	Degree sign
Delta	&#916;	Greek capital letter delta
delta	&#948;	Greek small letter delta
diams	&#9830;	Black diamond suit
divide	&#247;	Division sign
Eacute	&#201;	Latin capital letter E with acute accent
eacute	&#233;	Latin small letter e with acute accent
Ecirc	&#202;	Latin capital letter E with circumflex
ecirc	&#234;	Latin small letter e with circumflex
Egrave	&#200;	Latin capital letter E with grave accent
egrave	&#232;	Latin small letter e with grave accent
empty	&#8709;	Empty set = null set = diameter
emsp		Em space
ensp		En space
Epsilon	&#917;	Greek capital letter epsilon
epsilon	&#949;	Greek small letter epsilon
equiv	&#8801;	Identical to
Eta	&#919;	Greek capital letter eta
eta	&#951;	Greek small letter eta
ETH	&#208;	Latin capital letter eth
eth	&#240;	Latin small letter eth
Euml	&#203;	Latin capital letter E with diæresis (umlaut)
euml	&#235;	Latin small letter e with diæresis (umlaut)
euro	&#8364;	Euro sign
exist	&#8707;	There exists
fnof	&#402;	Latin small f with hook = function
forall	&#8704;	For all
frac12	&#189;	Vulgar fraction one half
frac14	&#188;	Vulgar fraction one quarter
frac34	&#190;	Vulgar fraction three quarters
frasl	&#8260;	Fraction slash
Gamma	&#915;	Greek capital letter gamma

(continued)

Table 2.2 Character entities for HTML 4 (support varies by browser) *(continued)*.

Entity	Numerical	Does This
gamma	&#947;	Greek small letter gamma
ge	&#8805;	Greater-than or equal to
gt	&#62;	Greater-than sign
harr	&#8596;	Left right arrow
hArr	&#8660;	Left right double arrow
hearts	&#9829;	Black heart suit = valentine
hellip	&#8230;	Horizontal ellipsis = three dot leader
Iacute	&#205;	Latin capital letter I with acute accent
iacute	&#237;	Latin small letter i with acute accent
Icirc	&#206;	Latin capital letter I with circumflex
icirc	&#238;	Latin small letter i with circumflex
iexcl	&#161;	Inverted exclamation mark
Igrave	&#204;	Latin capital letter I with grave accent
igrave	&#236;	Latin small letter i with grave accent
image	&#8465;	Blackletter capital I = imaginary part
infin	&#8734;	Infinity
int	&#8747;	Integral
Iota	&#921;	Greek capital letter iota
iota	&#953;	Greek small letter iota
iquest	&#191;	Inverted question mark
isin	&#8712;	Element of
Iuml	&#207;	Latin capital letter I with diæresis (umlaut)
iuml	&#239;	Latin small letter i with diæresis (umlaut)
Kappa	&#922;	Greek capital letter kappa
kappa	&#954;	Greek small letter kappa
Lambda	&#923;	Greek capital letter lambda
lambda	&#955;	Greek small letter lambda
lang	&#9001;	Left-pointing angle bracket = bra
laquo	&#171;	Left-pointing double angle quotation mark
larr	&#8592;	Leftward arrow
lArr	&#8656;	Leftward double arrow
lceil	&#8968;	Left ceiling = apl upstile

(continued)

Table 2.2 Character entities for HTML 4 (support varies by browser) *(continued)*.

Entity	Numerical	Does This
ldquo	&#8220;	Left double quotation mark
le	&#8804;	Less-than or equal to
lfloor	&#8970;	Left floor = apl downstile
lowast	&#8727;	Asterisk operator
loz	&#9674;	Lozenge
lrm	&#8206;	Left-to-right mark
lsaquo	&#8249;	Single left-pointing angle quotation mark
lsquo	&#8216;	Left single quotation mark
lt	&#60;	Less-than sign
macr	&#175;	Macron = spacing macron
mdash	&#8212;	Em dash
micro	&#181;	Micro sign
middot	&#183;	Middle dot
minus	&#8722;	Minus sign
Mu	&#924;	Greek capital letter mu
mu	&#956;	Greek small letter mu
nabla	&#8711;	Nabla = backward difference
nbsp		Nonbreaking space
ndash	&#8211;	En dash
ne	&#8800;	Not equal to
ni	&#8715;	Contains as member
not	&#172;	Not sign
notin	&#8713;	Not an element of
nsub	&#8836;	Not a subset of
Ntilde	&#209;	Latin capital letter N with tilde
ntilde	&#241;	Latin small letter n with tilde
Nu	&#925;	Greek capital letter nu
nu	&#957;	Greek small letter nu
Oacute	&#211;	Latin capital letter O with acute accent
oacute	&#243;	Latin small letter o with acute accent
Ocirc	&#212;	Latin capital letter O with circumflex
ocirc	&#244;	Latin small letter o with circumflex

(continued)

Table 2.2 Character entities for HTML 4 (support varies by browser) *(continued)*.

Entity	Numerical	Does This
OElig	&#338;	Latin capital ligature OE
oelig	&#339;	Latin small ligature oe
Ograve	&#210;	Latin capital letter O with grave accent
ograve	&#242;	Latin small letter o with grave accent
oline	&#8254;	Overline = spacing overscore
Omega	&#937;	Greek capital letter omega
omega	&#969;	Greek small letter omega
Omicron	&#927;	Greek capital letter omicron
omicron	&#959;	Greek small letter omicron
oplus	&#8853;	Circled plus = direct sum
or	&#8744;	Logical or = vee
ordf	&#170;	Feminine ordinal indicator
ordm	&#186;	Masculine ordinal indicator
Oslash	&#216;	Latin capital letter O with stroke
oslash	&#248;	Latin small letter o with stroke
Otilde	&#213;	Latin capital letter O with tilde
otilde	&#245;	Latin small letter o with tilde
otimes	&#8855;	Circled times = vector product
Ouml	&#214;	Latin capital letter O with diæresis (umlaut)
ouml	&#246;	Latin small letter o with diæresis (umlaut)
para	&#182;	Pilcrow sign
part	&#8706;	Partial differential
permil	&#8240;	Per mille sign
perp	&#8869;	Up tack = orthogonal to = perpendicular
Phi	&#934;	Greek capital letter phi
phi	&#966;	Greek small letter phi
Pi	&#928;	Greek capital letter pi
pi	&#960;	Greek small letter pi
piv	&#982;	Greek pi symbol
plusmn	&#177;	Plus-minus sign
pound	&#163;	Pound sign
prime	&#8242;	Prime = minutes = feet

(continued)

Table 2.2   Character entities for HTML 4 (support varies by browser) *(continued)*.

Entity	Numerical	Does This
Prime	&#8243;	Double prime = seconds = inches
prod	&#8719;	N-ary product = product sign
prop	&#8733;	Proportional to
Psi	&#936;	Greek capital letter psi
psi	&#968;	Greek small letter psi
quot	&#34;	Quotation mark = APL quote
radic	&#8730;	Square root = radical sign
rang	&#9002;	Right-pointing angle bracket = ket
raquo	&#187;	Right-pointing double angle quotation mark
rarr	&#8594;	Rightward arrow
rArr	&#8658;	Rightward double arrow
rceil	&#8969;	Right ceiling
rdquo	&#8221;	Right double quotation mark
real	&#8476;	Blackletter capital R = real part symbol
reg	&#174;	Registered sign
rfloor	&#8971;	Right floor
Rho	&#929;	Greek capital letter rho
rho	&#961;	Greek small letter rho
rlm	&#8207;	Right-to-left mark
rsaquo	&#8250;	Single right-pointing angle quotation mark
rsquo	&#8217;	Right single quotation mark
sbquo	&#8218;	Single low-9 quotation mark
Scaron	&#352;	Latin capital letter S with caron
scaron	&#353;	Latin small letter s with caron
sdot	&#8901;	Dot operator
sect	&#167;	Section sign
shy	&#173;	Soft hyphen
Sigma	&#931;	Greek capital letter sigma
sigma	&#963;	Greek small letter sigma
sigmaf	&#962;	Greek small letter final sigma
sim	&#8764;	Tilde operator
spades	&#9824;	Black spade suit

(continued)

Table 2.2 Character entities for HTML 4 (support varies by browser) *(continued)*.

Entity	Numerical	Does This
sub	&#8834;	Subset of
sube	&#8838;	Subset of or equal to
sum	&#8721;	N-ary summation
sup	&#8835;	Superset of
sup1	&#185;	Superscript one
sup2	&#178;	Superscript two
sup3	&#179;	Superscript three
supe	&#8839;	Superset of or equal to
szlig	&#223;	Latin small letter sharp s
Tau	&#932;	Greek capital letter tau
tau	&#964;	Greek small letter tau
there4	&#8756;	Therefore
Theta	&#920;	Greek capital letter theta
theta	&#952;	Greek small letter theta
thetasym	&#977;	Greek small letter theta symbol
thinsp		Thin space
THORN	&#222;	Latin capital letter thorn
thorn	&#254;	Latin small letter thorn
tilde	&#732;	Small tilde
times	&#215;	Multiplication sign
trade	&#8482;	Trademark sign
Uacute	&#218;	Latin capital letter U with acute accent
uacute	&#250;	Latin small letter u with acute accent
uarr	&#8593;	Upward arrow
uArr	&#8657;	Upward double arrow
Ucirc	&#219;	Latin capital letter U with circumflex
ucirc	&#251;	Latin small letter u with circumflex
Ugrave	&#217;	Latin capital letter U with grave accent
ugrave	&#249;	Latin small letter u with grave accent
uml	&#168;	Diæresis (umlaut)
upsih	&#978;	Greek upsilon with hook symbol
Upsilon	&#933;	Greek capital letter upsilon

(continued)

Table 2.2 Character entities for HTML 4 (support varies by browser) *(continued)*.

Entity	Numerical	Does This
upsilon	&#965;	Greek small letter upsilon
Uuml	&#220;	Latin capital letter U with diæresis (umlaut)
uuml	&#252;	Latin small letter u with diæresis (umlaut)
weierp	&#8472;	Script capital P = power set
Xi	&#926;	Greek capital letter xi
xi	&#958;	Greek small letter xi
Yacute	&#221;	Latin capital letter Y with acute accent
yacute	&#253;	Latin small letter y with acute accent
yen	&#165;	Yen sign = yuan sign
Yuml	&#376;	Latin capital letter Y with diæresis (umlaut)
yuml	&#255;	Latin small letter y with diæresis (umlaut)
Zeta	&#918;	Greek capital letter zeta
zeta	&#950;	Greek small letter zeta
zwj	&#8205;	Zero width joiner
zwnj	&#8204;	Zero width nonjoiner

Chapter 3
Arranging Text

If you need an immediate solution to:	See page:
Avoiding Plain Text Wrapping	153
` `—Inserting Line Breaks	154
`<nobr>`—Avoiding Line Breaks	157
`<wbr>`—Allowing Word Breaks	159
`<p>`—Creating Paragraphs	160
`<hr>`—Creating Horizontal Rules	163
`<center>`—Centering Text	166
`<blockquote>`—Indenting Quotations	168
`<pre>`—Displaying Preformatted Text	170
`<multicol>`—Creating Columns	172
`<spacer>`—Controlling Horizontal and Vertical Spacing	174
`<marquee>`—Displaying Text in a Scrolling Marquee	176
`<div>`—Formatting Block Text	179
`<span>`—Formatting Inline Text	182
Formatting Text with Tables	184
`<layer>`—Arranging Text in Layers	193
`<nolayer>`—Handling Browsers That Don't Handle Layers	196
`<ilayer>`—Creating Inline Layers	197
Positioning Text with `<div>`	200
`<ruby>`, `<rbc>`, `<rtc>`, `<rb>`, `<rt>`, `<rp>`—Creating Ruby (Captioned) Text	201

In Depth

The previous chapter was all about using XHTML to set text styles, and this chapter is all about the other aspect of working with text—arranging text on the page. In this chapter, we're going to start structuring what goes where in a Web page, which is vitally important to the success of your page. We'll use XHTML tags to arrange text into paragraphs and layers, add breaks and margins, set text alignment, create scrolling marquee-style text, overlap text, and more. This is where we actually start to structure Web pages visually.

Arranging Text

A great deal of designing Web pages is subjective—there's no firm set of rules. As with any visual art, it takes practice and a good feel for aesthetics. I'll talk about some of the subjective elements of Web page design throughout the book, but for now, it's worth noting that the subject matter of this chapter—how and where you place text in a page—has a lot to do with how well your Web page "works."

If we just stopped with the text handling discussed in Chapter 2, we'd be in trouble. That chapter was about text styles, not about arranging text in Web pages. If you didn't add any structure to the text, Web browsers would wrap all the text into a single paragraph, ignoring the line breaks you put in, unless you also added tags like **<p>** and **
**. Nothing makes a Web page more impenetrable than displaying a single long block of text.

When it comes to reading Web pages, people have notoriously short attention spans. The Back button is within easy reach of the mouse, and with all the multimedia elements flashing at them, people expect something that'll reach out and grab them. For that reason, it can be very important to arrange your text to avoid monolithic blocks. In fact, this is one of the skills that computer book authors are supposed to master, and it's time for a new heading now.

Using Headings to Structure Text

Headings do more than just break the text up and avoid massive blocks of unremitting words—headings also make the structure of your document evident at a glance. Just by observing the headings in your page, readers can follow the structure. Headings periodically remind readers what you're doing and where you're directing them.

Using headings is one way to make your document come alive to your readers, allowing them to see the structure and make a decision about reading it. Newspapers use headlines for the same effect. Another popular technique, used often in magazines, is to repeat pivotal sentences in blocks of larger type so the readers can view "outtakes" from the text and decide whether the topic interests them.

In general, if you want to catch the audience's attention, it's a good idea to break pages of text into a number of elements. In addition to applying headings, you can also use tips and notes of the kind you see in this book.

TIP: A hobby of mine is writing and designing advertising for computer book publishers because it's fun to pack as much as you can into just a few powerful sentences. It's become axiomatic in the advertising world that what attracts a reader's eye to an ad is not the elements of the ad itself, but the white space around the elements in the ad. The idea is that the eye naturally moves to the part of a page that is different—away from big blocks of text. However, this advertising technique has become overrated. But one fact is clear— overcrowded Web pages do turn readers off.

Using Paragraphs and Line Breaks

Besides making the structure of your document stand out with headings, you can also separate text with paragraphs and line breaks. It's best to avoid long paragraphs (unless you're a government agency and have a captive audience). Because the reader takes a mental breath at the end of each paragraph, similar to finishing a sentence when speaking, shorter paragraphs can help accelerate the reading pace.

The two XHTML tags you should use are **<p>** for paragraph and **
** for break. Some Web authors think these tags are more or less interchangeable, but they're very different. The **
** tag allows you to skip to the next line of text (within the same paragraph), and the **<p>** tag starts a new paragraph, which means that the browser will skip some additional vertical space. Here's an example showing both the **<p>** and **
** tags at work (note that **
** is an empty tag, so I end it with the XML shortcut, **/>**):

```
<?xml version="1.0"?>
<!DOCTYPE html PUBLIC "-//W3C//DTD XHTML 1.0 Transitional//EN"
    "http://www.w3.org/TR/xhtml1/DTD/xhtml1-transitional.dtd">
<html xmlns="http://www.w3.org/1999/xhtml" xml:lang="en" lang="en">
    <head>
        <title>
            Using the &lt;br&gt; and &lt;p&gt; tags
        </title>
    </head>
```

```
<body>
    <center>
        <h1>
            Using the &lt;br&gt; and &lt;p&gt; tags
        </h1>
    </center>
    Here's a line of text.
    <br />
    Using the &lt;br&gt; tag skips to the next line.
    <p>
        On the other hand, using the &lt;p&gt; tag
        starts a new paragraph.
    </p>
</body>
</html>
```

You can see the result in Figure 3.1. Note that the **
** tag simply made the browser skip to the next line, much like typing the Enter key in a word processor. The **<p>** tag made the browser skip some additional vertical space to start a new paragraph, much like typing the Enter key a second time.

The major difference between the **
** and **<p>** elements is that the **
** element is empty and the **<p>** element encloses text. Another difference is that you can use the **<p>** tag's **align** attribute to align the text in the paragraph—something you can't do with the **
** element. Here's an example of using the **align** attribute to center a paragraph:

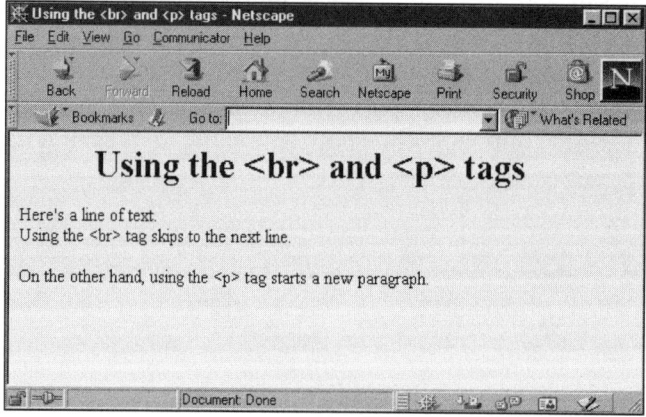

Figure 3.1 Using the **
** and **<p>** tags.

```
<?xml version="1.0"?>
<!DOCTYPE html PUBLIC "-//W3C//DTD XHTML 1.0 Transitional//EN"
"http://www.w3.org/TR/xhtml1/DTD/xhtml1-transitional.dtd">
<html xmlns="http://www.w3.org/1999/xhtml" xml:lang="en" lang="en">
    <head>
        <title>
            Using the &lt;br&gt; and &lt;p&gt; tags
        </title>
    </head>

    <body>
        <center>
            <h1>
                Using the &lt;br&gt; and &lt;p&gt; tags
            </h1>
        </center>
        Here's a line of text.
        <br />
        Using the &lt;br&gt; tag skips to the next line.
        <p align="center">
            On the other hand, using the &lt;p&gt; tag
            starts a new paragraph.
        </p>
    </body>
</html>
```

The results appear in Figure 3.2, where you can see that the text I've put into the paragraph is indeed centered. The **<p>** element does set the style for its enclosed text, so it differs substantially from the simple **
** tag.

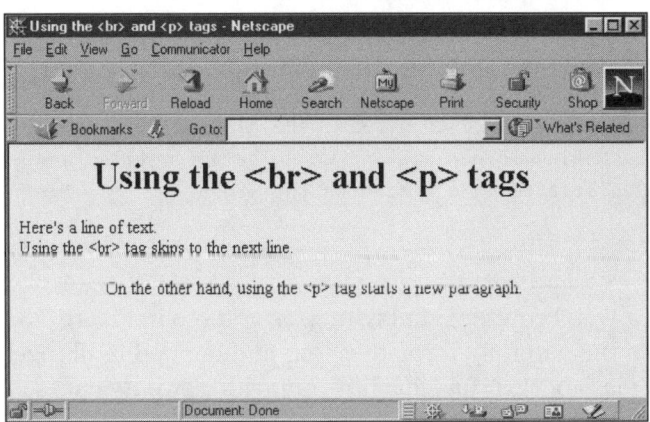

Figure 3.2 Using the **<p>** element to align text.

Aligning text, dividing text into paragraphs, and using other visual elements are a big part of what XHTML is all about and what it is designed to do. Here's an example showing the difference that arranging text in a Web page can make. The Web page doesn't look too bad here with the text arranged into paragraphs:

```
<?xml version="1.0"?>
<!DOCTYPE html PUBLIC "-//W3C//DTD XHTML 1.0 Transitional//EN"
"http://www.w3.org/TR/xhtml1/DTD/xhtml1-transitional.dtd">
<html xmlns="http://www.w3.org/1999/xhtml" xml:lang="en" lang="en">
    <head>
        <title>
            European Train Travel
        </title>
    </head>

    <body>
            So, you've decided to take the train in Europe!
            Congratulations, you're in for a great time. There are
            a few things you should know that will make
            things a lot easier.

            Many train stations are packed with crowds, especially
            in the summer, and you can save yourself a great deal of
            time waiting in lines that can last an hour or more by
            getting a complete train schedule, such as Thomas Cook's
            European Timetable. With a complete train schedule, you'll
            also become the most popular person in the youth hostel.

            In larger stations, you'll find a diagram showing where
            each wagon of the train will stop, so if you have a
            reservation for a specific wagon, you can wait in the right
            place with your luggage.

            Check the destination of the train, the class of the wagon, and
            whether it's a smoking or non-smoking wagon before getting on. This
            information is displayed on a plaque on the wagon.
    </body>
</html>
```

However, the result in a Web browser is uninviting, as you see in Figure 3.3. The Web browser has taken the carefully formatted text and lumped it all together. The result is one solid mass of text. Imagine how uninviting twenty pages of the same would be.

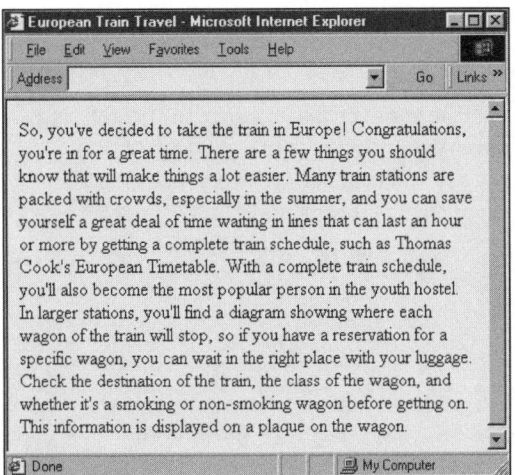

Figure 3.3 First attempt at a Web page.

Arranging the text and using headings, paragraphs, margins, alignments, and other visual elements, as we'll do in this chapter, is what text handling is all about, and what HTML was originally designed to do. Here's an example of using XHTML formatting tags to present the same text in a better way:

```
<?xml version="1.0"?>
<!DOCTYPE html PUBLIC "-//W3C//DTD XHTML 1.0 Transitional//EN"
"http://www.w3.org/TR/xhtml1/DTD/xhtml1-transitional.dtd">
<html xmlns="http://www.w3.org/1999/xhtml" xml:lang="en" lang="en">
    <head>
        <title>
            European Train Travel
        </title>
    </head>

    <body>
        <h1>
            European Train Travel
        </h1>
        So you've decided to take the train in Europe!
        Congratulations, you're in for a great time. There are
        a few things you should know that will make
        things a lot easier. Here's an overview:
        <ul>
            <li>Getting Train Times</li>
            <li>Getting On The Train</li>
            <li>Handling Security</li>
        </ul>
```

```
            <h2>
                Getting Train Times
            </h2>
            Many train stations are packed with crowds, especially in
            the summer, and you can save yourself a great deal of time
            waiting in lines that can last an hour or more by getting
            a complete train schedule, such as Thomas Cook's European
            Timetable.
            <p>
                <table bgcolor="#d0d0d0">
                    <tr>
                        <td>
                            TIP: With a complete train schedule, you'll
                            also become the most popular person in
                            the youth hostel.
                        </td>
                    </tr>
                </table>
            </p>
            <h2>
                Getting On The Train
            </h2>
            In larger stations, you'll find a diagram showing where
            each wagon of the train will stop so if you have a
            reservation for a specific wagon, you can wait in the right
            place with your luggage.
            <p>
                Check the destination of the train, the class of the wagon, and
                whether it's a smoking or non-smoking wagon before getting on.
                This information is displayed on a plaque on the wagon.
            </p>
        </body>
</html>
```

In this page, I've added headings to organize the text, and I've used a bulleted list, which we'll learn how to do in Chapter 5. I've also taken advantage of the fact that you can set the background color of cells in a table to create a plausible style for tips, as you see in Figure 3.4. The result is much more accessible than the page shown in Figure 3.3.

Using <div> and <span>

Two important formatting elements are the **<div>** and **<span>** elements. These elements are very useful when you're working with style sheets. Using **<div>** (which stands for division) and **<span>**, you can specify a range of text and style it as you want it.

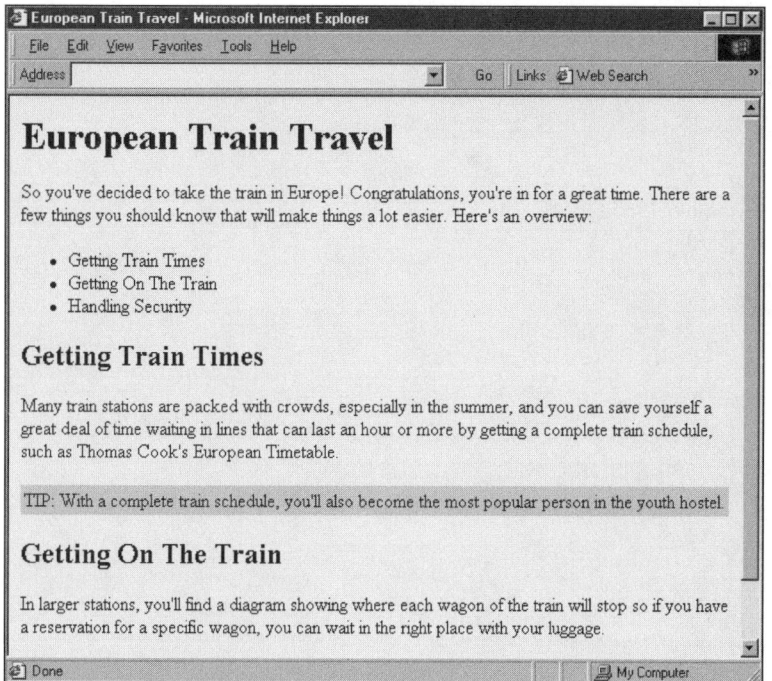

Figure 3.4   Improved Web page.

Earlier, I discussed using the **<p>** element to set the style for a paragraph of text, but you may not want to break your text into XHTML-style paragraphs. For that reason, XHTML includes tags, like **<div>** and **<span>**, that let you select the text you want to work with.

You normally use **<div>** to select a block of text and use **<span>** to select text inline. Here's an example of using the **<div>** tag with its **align** parameter to set the alignment of text without using the **<p>** tag:

```
<?xml version="1.0"?>
<!DOCTYPE html PUBLIC "-//W3C//DTD XHTML 1.0 Transitional//EN"
"http://www.w3.org/TR/xhtml1/DTD/xhtml1-transitional.dtd">
<html xmlns="http://www.w3.org/1999/xhtml" xml:lang="en" lang="en">
    <head>
        <title>
            Using the &lt;div&gt; tag
        </title>
    </head>

    <body>
        <center>
            <h1>
```

```
                    Using the &lt;div&gt; tag
                </h1>
            </center>
            <div align="left">
                Manager
                <br />
                SlowPoke Products, Inc.
                <br />
                Languid, TX
            </div>

            <p>
                Dear You:
                <div align="center" style="color: red; font-style: italic">
                    When are you going to ship my order?
                </div>
            </p>

            <div align="right">
                <p>
                    President
                    <br />
                    NeedItNow, Inc.
                    <br />
                    Speedy, CO
                </p>
            </div>
        </body>
</html>
```

The results appear in Figure 3.5. As you can see in the figure, I've aligned whole sections of text as I want them. The **<div>** tag really shines when you use styles with it. In the previous XHTML, I set the style of the middle **<div>** element to display its text in red italics. Using **<div>**, you can style whole blocks of text that even contain other XHTML elements. This gives you a flexible way of applying styles, as we'll see when working with style sheets in Chapter 9.

You can use the **<span>** tag to mark sections of text inline or text in the midst of other text. This lets you apply styles in a very precise way, like this:

```
<?xml version="1.0"?>
<!DOCTYPE html PUBLIC "-//W3C//DTD XHTML 1.0 Transitional//EN"
    "http://www.w3.org/TR/xhtml1/DTD/xhtml1-transitional.dtd">
<html xmlns="http://www.w3.org/1999/xhtml" xml:lang="en" lang="en">
```

In Depth

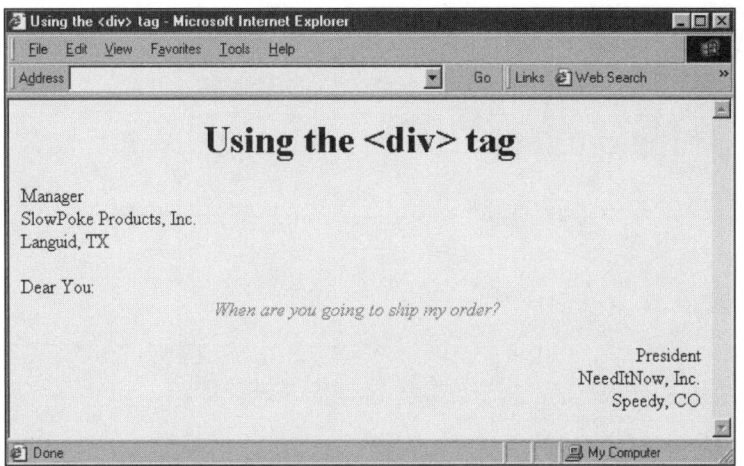

Figure 3.5 Using the **<div>** tag to enclose and align a range of text.

```
<head>
    <title>
        Using the &lt;span&gt; tag
    </title>
</head>

<body>
    <center>
        <h1>
            Using the &lt;span&gt; tag
        </h1>
    </center>
    This is <span style="font-style: italic">not</span> going to do!
</body>
</html>
```

The result of this XHTML appears in Figure 3.6. As you can see, working with **<div>** and **<span>** is one step up from using a simple **<p>** tag to enclose text. These two tags will become more important as we progress through the book. The possibilities of arranging text by using **<div>** and **<span>** are endless—in fact, we'll even display overlapping text with these elements.

Using Layers

One way of arranging text and other elements in Netscape Navigator (but not in Internet Explorer) is to use *layers*. You can divide the display into successive layers stacked one on top of the other, and you can move these layers.

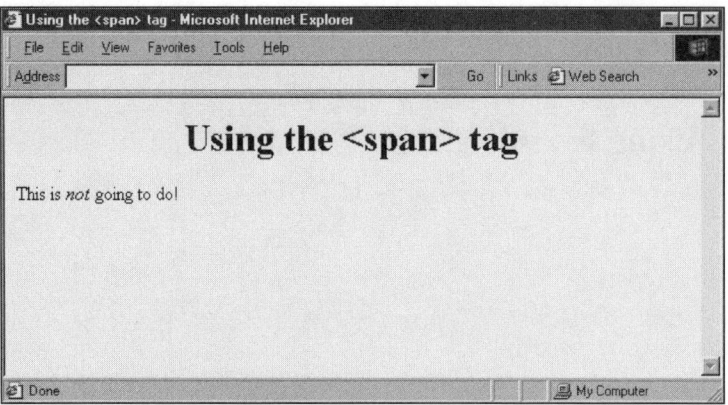

Figure 3.6   Using the `<span>` tag.

Because text in a layer is confined to that layer, you can arrange it on top of other layers. In fact, you can specify exactly where each layer is to be placed on the page, so you can use layers to create justified text, columns of text, and overlapping text.

Using layers is a powerful technique that we'll explore in a number of places in the book. In particular, layers are accessible to scripting and therefore have become an important part of dynamic XHTML.

More Formatting Power

In addition to the aforementioned XHTML elements, there are other ways you can structure your Web pages. For example, you can use visual elements, like *horizontal rules*, which are horizontal lines that you use to break text into sections; Internet Explorer marquees, which let you display text that scrolls across the page; *spacers* that let you set aside some horizontal and vertical space; multiple columns in Netscape Navigator; XHTML tables to structure text; and much more. Don't forget—a great deal of XHTML is about letting the Web browser know how you want to format a page. I'll start the guided tour of these elements and structures in the Immediate Solutions section.

Preformatting Text

Formatting and arranging text can be a frustrating process in XHTML, especially when you consider that different users have different screen resolutions (800×600 pixels, 1024×768, 1280×1024, and so on). Web browsers are going to make use of screen space in a variety of ways, possibly reducing your hard work to a hopeless hash.

Throughout the book, we'll see various ways of dealing with different screen sizes. For instance, you'll learn how to specify how much screen space certain elements should cover as a *percentage* of what's available. In the following code example, I'm creating a table that will cover 95 percent of the available display width in the browser:

```
<table noborder cellpadding = "4" width = "95%">
```

Even so, there are times when you'll be tempted to simply throw up your hands and ask why browsers can't just display your text *the way you've entered it*. In fact, they *can*. To display text exactly as entered in a Web page—line breaks and all—you can use the **<pre>** tag to tell the browser that the text is preformatted (by you or a word processor) and the browser should display the text as is.

In this example, I'm displaying a table that I've entered by hand, and I'm using the **<pre>** tag to preserve the formatting exactly as I've entered it:

```
<?xml version="1.0"?>
<!DOCTYPE html PUBLIC "-//W3C//DTD XHTML 1.0 Transitional//EN"
    "http://www.w3.org/TR/xhtml1/DTD/xhtml1-transitional.dtd">
<html xmlns="http://www.w3.org/1999/xhtml" xml:lang="en" lang="en">
    <head>
        <title>
            Using the &lt;pre&gt; tag
        </title>
    </head>

    <body>
        <center>
            <h1>
                Using the &lt;pre&gt; tag
            </h1>
        </center>
        <pre>
Name                    Email                   extension
---------------------------------------------------------
David                   david@starpowder.com    x4849
Sam                     sam@starpowder.com      x4850
Nancy                   nancy@starpowder.com    x4851
Jennifer                jennifer@starpowder.com x4852
Marty                   marty@starpowder.com    x4853
Frank                   frank@starpowder.com    x4854
        </pre>
    </body>
</html>
```

Chapter 3   Arranging Text

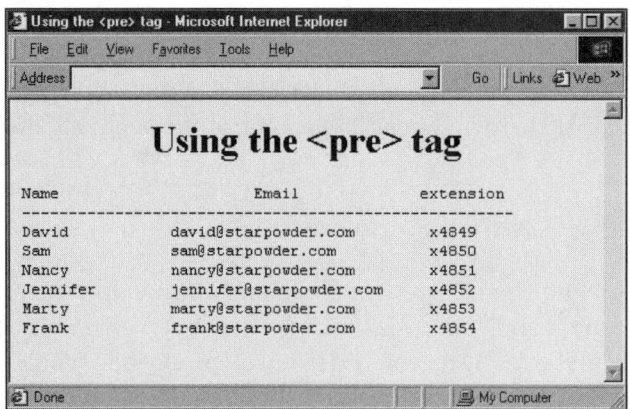

Figure 3.7   Using preformatted text.

The results of this XHTML appear in Figure 3.7.

The **<pre>** tag keeps you from blowing your stack when XHTML isn't cooperating, but keep in mind that using it is something of a cop-out. After all, HTML was invented to help arrange text, and XHTML is meant to provide you with that same capability. When you effectively turn browser formatting off, you're turning your back on a lot of power. Still, it's there if you need it.

That's it, then. There's a great deal of text presentation power coming up here, so I'm going to turn to the "Immediate Solutions" section now and start by looking at what happens if you *don't* arrange text the way you want it.

TIP: *In this chapter, you'll start seeing significant differences between the XHTML used in Internet Explorer and the XHTML used in Netscape Navigator. To handle these discrepancies, you can use dynamic XHTML to identify what browser the user has and adjust your XHTML accordingly. I'll show you how to do that when we start working with dynamic XHTML.*

Immediate Solutions

Avoiding Plain Text Wrapping

The novice programmer has a problem and says, "I'm writing this great page on train travel and have it all ready, but it appears in my browser all funny." "What do you mean?" you ask. "It's all wrapped up into one solid block," the NP says. You smile and reply, "Web browsers do that."

The first thing to know about arranging text in a Web page is that Web browsers are going to ignore the line breaks in your page's text (unless you've used a tag, like **<pre>**, to tell the browser that the page is already formatted). We saw an example of this example at the beginning of this chapter.

```
<?xml version="1.0"?>
<!DOCTYPE html PUBLIC "-//W3C//DTD XHTML 1.0 Transitional//EN"
    "http://www.w3.org/TR/xhtml1/DTD/xhtml1-transitional.dtd">
<html xmlns="http://www.w3.org/1999/xhtml" xml:lang="en" lang="en">
    <head>
        <title>
            European Train Travel
        </title>
    </head>

    <body>
            So, you've decided to take the train in Europe!
            Congratulations, you're in for a great time. There are
            a few things you should know that will make
            things a lot easier.

            Many train stations are packed with crowds, especially
            in the summer, and you can save yourself a great deal of
            time waiting in lines that can last an hour or more by
            getting a complete train schedule, such as Thomas Cook's
            European Timetable. With a complete train schedule, you'll
            also become the most popular person in the youth hostel.

            In larger stations, you'll find a diagram showing where
            each wagon of the train will stop, so if you have a
            reservation for a specific wagon, you can wait in the right
            place with your luggage.
```

```
                Check the destination of the train, the class of the wagon, and
            whether it's a smoking or non-smoking wagon before getting on. This
            information is displayed on a plaque on the wagon.
    </body>
</html>
```

In the previous code, the text is nicely set in paragraphs, but a Web browser treats line breaks in text as it would any other white space character, such as spaces—it reformats the text. You can see the sad result of this page in Figure 3.3. In fact, the Web browser even changes multiple spaces between words into single spaces, such as those used to indent the text.

So how do you tell a Web browser how to arrange the text the way you want it? That's the job of XHTML—just take a look at the following topics.

—Inserting Line Breaks

Purpose: Inserts a line break into a page. This tag does not contain any content.

When used as HTML: Start tag/End tag: Required/Omitted

Supported: [1.0S, 1.0T, 1.0F, 1.1, 2, 3, 3.2, 4, IE1, IE2, IE3, IE4, IE5, NS1, NS2, NS3, NS4]

Attributes:

- **class**—Class of the element (used for rendering). [1.0S, 1.0T, 1.0F, 1.1, 3, 4, IE4, IE5]

- **clear**—Used to move past-aligned images or other elements. Set to **none** (the default; just a normal break), **left** (breaks line and moves down until there is a clear left margin past the aligned element), **right** (breaks line and moves down until there is a clear right margin past the aligned element), or **all** (breaks line and moves down until both margins are clear of the aligned element). [1.0T, 1.0F, 3.2, 4, IE1, IE2, IE3, IE4, IE5, NS1, NS2, NS3, NS4]

- **id**—Unique alphanumeric identifier for the tag, which you can use to refer to it. [1.0S, 1.0T, 1.0F, 1.1, 3, 4, IE4, IE5]

- **style**—Inline style indicating how to render the element. [1.0S, 1.0T, 1.0F, 1.1, 4, IE4, IE5]

- **title**—Holds additional information (which might be displayed in tool tips) for the element. [1.0S, 1.0T, 1.0F, 1.1, 3, 4]

XHTML events: None.

The novice programmer wonders, "How do I add line breaks to text in a Web page? Browsers seem to treat the line breaks in the actual text as white space, just like space characters." "That's right," you confirm. "To tell the browser you want to skip to the next line, you use the **
** element."

The **
** element has one use, which is to move to the next line of text. It inserts a line break into your text, much like pressing the Enter key when you're working with a word processor. I'll review the example from the beginning of the chapter that used the **
** tag; note that because this element is empty that I use the XML ending shortcut, /> (you can use an explicit end tag, **</br>**, but W3C recommends the XML shortcut form for empty tags):

```
<?xml version="1.0"?>
<!DOCTYPE html PUBLIC "-//W3C//DTD XHTML 1.0 Transitional//EN"
 "http://www.w3.org/TR/xhtml1/DTD/xhtml1-transitional.dtd">
<html xmlns="http://www.w3.org/1999/xhtml" xml:lang="en" lang="en">
    <head>
        <title>
            Using the &lt;br&gt; and &lt;p&gt; tags
        </title>
    </head>

    <body>
        <center>
            <h1>
                Using the &lt;br&gt; and &lt;p&gt; tags
            </h1>
        </center>
        Here's a line of text.
        <br />
        Using the &lt;br&gt; tag skips to the next line.
        <p>
            On the other hand, using the &lt;p&gt; tag
            starts a new paragraph.
        </p>
    </body>
</html>
```

The results of this code appear in Figure 3.1. Using the **
** tag makes the Web browser move to the next line of text.

TIP: *Note that ideally, as with word processors, rather than insert line breaks directly into your text, you break the text up into paragraphs. In XHTML, you use the* ***<p>*** *tag and let the browser handle breaking the text into lines that match the browser-window width. That's the reason browsers format text as they do—to work smoothly with the display area available. The* ***
*** *tag is ideal for working with text, but it's also handy for working with other elements, like images, to specify that you want each element to be separated vertically.*

The **
** element is an empty element, which means that it doesn't take any content. Because this element is empty, you can use the XML ending shortcut, **/>**, with it. (You can use an explicit end tag, **</br>**, but W3C recommends the XML shortcut form for empty tags.)

Although the **
** tag doesn't take content, it does have attributes, and one attribute in particular is worth mentioning: **clear**. This attribute is available in the XHTML 1.0 Transitional and Frameset DTDs, but not the XHTML 1.0 Strict or XHTML 1.1 DTDs. (I'll take a closer look at this attribute in Chapter 4.) The **clear** attribute indicates how text should flow around images (and around other elements, too).

For example, if I align an image on the left of a page and then type text with line breaks, that text will all appear to the right of the image. However, if I use the line-break code **<br "clear=left">**, then the next line of text will appear *after* the image, where there's a clear left margin again. Here's an example:

```
<?xml version="1.0"?>
<!DOCTYPE html PUBLIC "-//W3C//DTD XHTML 1.0 Transitional//EN"
"http://www.w3.org/TR/xhtml1/DTD/xhtml1-transitional.dtd">
<html xmlns="http://www.w3.org/1999/xhtml" xml:lang="en" lang="en">
    <head>
        <title>
            Using the &lt;br&gt; tag
        </title>
    </head>

    <body>
        <center>
            <h1>
                Using the &lt;br&gt; tag
            </h1>
        </center>
        <img align="left" alt="An image" src="image.jpg" />
        Here's some text.
        <br />
        This text is still next to the image.
        <br />
        <br />
        <br />
        <br />
        <br />
        <br />
        <img align="left" alt="Another image" src="image.jpg" />
        Here is some new text.
        <br />
```

```
            Now I use the &lt;br clear="left" /&gt; tag.
        <br clear="left" />
        This next text starts when there's a clear left margin.
    </body>
</html>
```

You can see these results in Figure 3.8. Using **<br clear="left" />** makes the next line of text skip past the image to where there's a clear left margin again.

TIP: *In earlier versions of Netscape Navigator, the* **
** *tag skipped some additional vertical space, giving the impression of double spacing. That's been fixed in recent versions.*

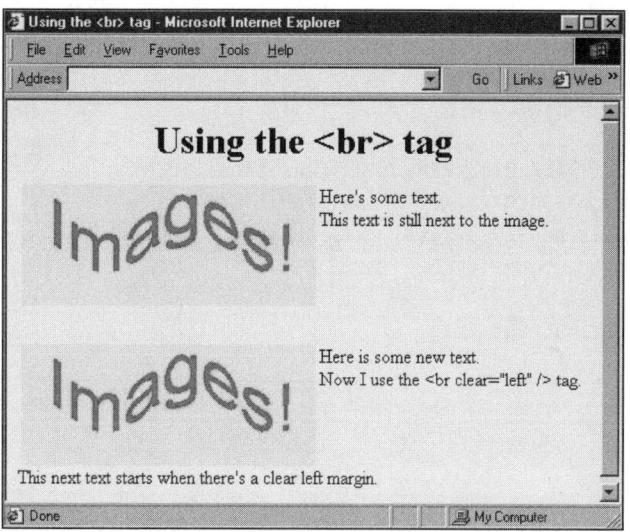

Figure 3.8 Using the **
 clear** attribute.

<nobr>—Avoiding Line Breaks

Purpose: Tells the browser to *not* break text into separate lines.

When used as HTML: Start tag/End tag: Required/Required

Supported: [IE1, IE2, IE3, IE4, IE5, NS1, NS2, NS3, NS4]

Attributes:

- **class**—Class of the element (used for rendering). [IE4, IE5]
- **dir**—Gives the direction of directionally neutral text (text that doesn't have inherent direction in which you should read it). Possible values: **ltr**: left-to-right text or table and **rtl**: right-to-left text or table. [IE5]

- **id**—Unique alphanumeric identifier for the tag, which you can use to refer to it. [IE4, IE5]
- **lang**—Base language used for the tag. [IE4, IE5]
- **language**—Scripting language used for the tag. [IE4, IE5]

XHTML Events: None.

Normally, Web browsers take text in a Web page and reformat it—adding line breaks to wrap text as needed—to fit the display area they have to work with. However, there's a way of effectively turning line wrap off. The **<nobr>** element is not part of the XHTML standard, but both Netscape Navigator and Internet Explorer implement it. This tag tells the browser not to introduce line breaks for the text you specify.

Here's an example:

```
<?xml version="1.0"?>
<!DOCTYPE html PUBLIC "-//W3C//DTD XHTML 1.0 Transitional//EN"
"http://www.w3.org/TR/xhtml1/DTD/xhtml1-transitional.dtd">
<html xmlns="http://www.w3.org/1999/xhtml" xml:lang="en" lang="en">
    <head>
        <title>
            Using the &lt;nobr&gt; tag
        </title>
    </head>

    <body>
        <center>
            <h1>
                Using the &lt;nobr&gt; tag
            </h1>
        </center>
        <nobr>
            Here's some text in a long line that may
            continue right off the edge of the Web browser's
            available display space.
        </nobr>
    </body>
</html>
```

As you can see in Figure 3.9, the result is that the text is displayed in one long line, even though that line extends beyond the browser's display area.

TIP: It's a good idea to use the **<nobr>** tag sparingly. Web browsers are designed to format text into the space they have available, and if you change the limits, the results may be unpredictable.

Immediate Solutions

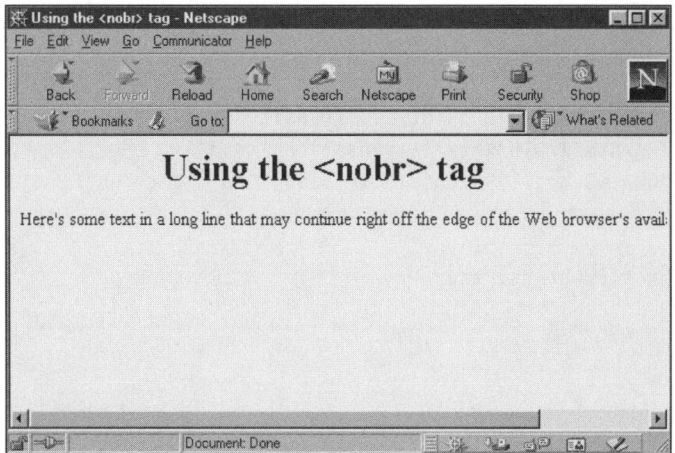

Figure 3.9   Using the **<nobr>** tag.

<wbr>—Allowing Word Breaks

Purpose: Indicates where word breaks are allowed. This element does not contain any content.

When used as HTML: Start tag/End tag: Required/Omitted

Supported: [IE1, IE2, IE3, IE4, IE5, NS1, NS2, NS3, NS4]

Attributes:

- **id**—Unique alphanumeric identifier for the tag, which you can use to refer to it. [IE4, IE5]

"Hm," says the novice programmer, "I've got a problem—I want to use the **<nobr>** element to avoid letting the browser break my poem into lines, but I also want to specify where breaks should go." "In that case," you explain, "you can use the **<wbr>** tag to show the browser exactly where line breaks should happen."

The **<wbr>** tag tells the browser where a word may be broken at the end of a line. This does not mean, however, that it *will* be broken (in fact, most browsers prefer to break lines on word boundaries, preserving whole words). If you use this tag inside a **<nobr>** element, it tells the browser just where line or word breaks should occur. This element is not a true XHTML element, but it's supported in Internet Explorer and Netscape Navigator.

Here's an example:

```
<?xml version="1.0"?>
<!DOCTYPE html PUBLIC "-//W3C//DTD XHTML 1.0 Transitional//EN"
"http://www.w3.org/TR/xhtml1/DTD/xhtml1-transitional.dtd">
<html xmlns="http://www.w3.org/1999/xhtml" xml:lang="en" lang="en">
    <head>
        <title>
            Using the &lt;wbr&gt; tag
        </title>
    </head>

    <body>
        <nobr>
            This is a really, really, really, really long amount of<wbr>
            text, and we only want to let it be broken in one place.
        </nobr>
    </body>
</html>
```

<p>—Creating Paragraphs

Purpose: Formats text into a paragraph and adds space before the paragraph.

When used as HTML: Start tag/End tag: Required/Optional

Supported: [1.0S, 1.0T, 1.0F, 1.1, 2, 3, 3.2, 4, IE1, IE2, IE3, IE4, IE5, NS1, NS2, NS3, NS4]

Attributes:

- **align**—Deprecated in HTML 4. Sets the alignment of the text in the paragraph; set to **left** (the default), **right**, **center**, or **justify**. [1.0T, 1.0F, 3, 3.2, 4, IE1, IE2, IE3, IE4, IE5, NS1, NS2, NS3, NS4]

- **class**—Class of the element (used for rendering). [1.0S, 1.0T, 1.0F, 1.1, 3, 4, IE4, IE5, NS4]

- **dir**—Gives the direction of directionally neutral text (text that doesn't have inherent direction in which you should read it). Possible values: **ltr**: left-to-right text or table and **rtl**: right-to-left text or table. [1.0S, 1.0T, 1.0F, 1.1, 4, IE5]

- **id**—Unique alphanumeric identifier for the tag, which you can use to refer to it. [1.0S, 1.0T, 1.0F, 1.1, 3, 4, IE4, IE5, NS4]

- **lang**—Base language used for the tag. [1.0S, 1.0T, 1.0F, 1.1, 3, 4, IE4, IE5, NS4]
- **language**—Scripting language used for the tag. [IE4, IE5]
- **style**—Inline style indicating how to render the element. [1.0S, 1.0T, 1.0F, 1.1, 4, IE3, IE4, IE5, NS4]
- **title**—Holds additional information (which might be displayed in tool tips) for the element. [1.0S, 1.0T, 1.0F, 1.1, 3, 4, IE4, IE5]
- **xml:lang**—Holds the base language for the element when the document is interpreted as an XML document. [1.0S, 1.0T, 1.0F, 1.1]

XHTML events: onclick, ondblclick, onmousedown, onmouseup, onmouseover, onmousemove, onmouseout, onkeypress, onkeydown, onkeyup

The **<p>** tag lets you organize your text into paragraphs. Paragraphs are relatively rudimentary formatting structures that just refer to blocks of text in which the browser inserts a little vertical space on top to separate them from other elements. Paragraphs in XHTML act much like the paragraphs in a word processor. The Web browser formats the text in a paragraph to fit the current page width. You don't have to format your text into paragraphs at all, of course, but doing so will aid readability.

I'll review an XHTML example of using the **<p>** tag from the beginning of this chapter:

```
<?xml version="1.0"?>
<!DOCTYPE html PUBLIC "-//W3C//DTD XHTML 1.0 Transitional//EN"
    "http://www.w3.org/TR/xhtml1/DTD/xhtml1-transitional.dtd">
<html xmlns="http://www.w3.org/1999/xhtml" xml:lang="en" lang="en">
    <head>
        <title>
            Using the &lt;br&gt; and &lt;p&gt; tags
        </title>
    </head>

    <body>
        <center>
            <h1>
                Using the &lt;br&gt; and &lt;p&gt; tags
            </h1>
        </center>
        Here's a line of text.
        <br />
        Using the &lt;br&gt; tag skips to the next line.
```

```
            <p>
                On the other hand, using the &lt;p&gt; tag
                starts a new paragraph.
            </p>
        </body>
</html>
```

You can see the results of this XHTML in Figure 3.1.

You can use the **<p>** tag's attributes, such as **align**, to work with the text enclosed in the element. For example, here's how I use the **align** attribute to center and right-align text:

```
<?xml version="1.0"?>
<!DOCTYPE html PUBLIC "-//W3C//DTD XHTML 1.0 Transitional//EN"
"http://www.w3.org/TR/xhtml1/DTD/xhtml1-transitional.dtd">
<html xmlns="http://www.w3.org/1999/xhtml" xml:lang="en" lang="en">
    <head>
        <title>
            Using the &lt;p&gt; tag
        </title>
    </head>

    <body>
        <center>
            <h1>
                Using the &lt;p&gt; tag
            </h1>
        </center>
        <p>
            Here's a standard paragraph. This text is left-aligned.
        </p>
        <p align="center">
            Here's a center-aligned paragraph.
        </p>
        <p align="right">
            Here's a right-aligned paragraph.
        </p>
    </body>
</html>
```

You can see the result of this XHTML in Figure 3.10.

NOTE: *The **align** attribute was deprecated in HTML 4 and so is not available in the XHTML 1.0 Strict DTD or the XHTML 1.1 DTD.*

Immediate Solutions

Figure 3.10   Aligning paragraph text.

<hr>—Creating Horizontal Rules

Purpose: Draws a horizontal line to separate or group elements vertically. This element contains no content.

When used as HTML: Start tag/End tag: Required/Omitted.

Supported: [1.0S, 1.0T, 1.0F, 1.1, 2, 3, 3.2, 4, IE1, IE2, IE3, IE4, IE5, NS1, NS2, NS3, NS4]

Attributes:

- **align**—Deprecated. Sets the alignment of the rule, set to **left**, **center** (the default), or **right**. Note that, if you want to set this attribute, you must also set the **width** attribute. [1.0T, 1.0F, 3.2, 4, IE1, IE2, IE3, IE4, IE5, NS1, NS2, NS3, NS4]

- **class**—Class of the element (used for rendering). [1.0S, 1.0T, 1.0F, 1.1, 3, 4, IE4, IE5]

- **color**—Sets the color of the rule. Set to a color value or predefined color. [IE3, IE4, IE5]

- **id**—Unique alphanumeric identifier for the tag, which you can use to refer to it. [1.0S, 1.0T, 1.0F, 1.1, 3, 4, IE4, IE5]

- **noshade**—Deprecated. Renders the rule as two-dimensional, not three-dimensional (the default), in appearance. [1.0T, 1.0F, 3.2, 4, IE1, IE2, IE3, IE4, IE5, NS1, NS2, NS3, NS4]

- **size**—Deprecated. Sets the vertical size of the horizontal rule in pixels. [1.0T, 1.0F, 3.2, 4, IE1, IE2, IE3, IE4, IE5, NS1, NS2, NS3, NS4]

- **style**—Inline style indicating how to render the element. [1.0S, 1.0T, 1.0F, 1.1, 4, IE3, IE4, IE5]
- **title**—Holds additional information (which might be displayed in tool tips) for the element. [1.0S, 1.0T, 1.0F, 1.1, 3, 4, IE4, IE5]
- **width**—Deprecated. Sets the horizontal width of the rule. Set to actual pixel count or a percentage. [1.0T, 1.0F, 3.2, 4, IE1, IE2, IE3, IE4, IE5, NS1, NS2, NS3, NS4]
- **xml:lang**—Holds the base language for the element when the document is interpreted as an XML document. [1.0S, 1.0T, 1.0F, 1.1]

XHTML events: onclick, ondblclick, onmousedown, onmouseup, onmouseover, onmousemove, onmouseout, onkeypress, onkeydown, onkeyup

Looking over the novice programmer's shoulder, you wonder, "What are you doing?" "Creating a horizontal-line graphic that I can use to divide a Web page's content," the novice programmer explains. "Uh huh," you say, "why don't you just use the **<hr>** element?" The NP asks, "The what?"

One easy way to break up a page or to group items together is to use horizontal rules (lines) created with the **<hr>** element. (It's an empty element, so use the XML shortcut **/>** to end it.) This element is especially useful in longer documents.

Following is an example showing a number of ways to display and align horizontal rules. Note that, as with most style attributes, these are officially deprecated in favor of style sheets. Note also that **noshade** is a standalone attribute; in XHTML, of course, you have to assign values to all attributes you use, so I'll assign it a value of "**noshade**". Here's the example:

```
<?xml version="1.0"?>
<!DOCTYPE html PUBLIC "-//W3C//DTD XHTML 1.0 Transitional//EN"
"http://www.w3.org/TR/xhtml1/DTD/xhtml1-transitional.dtd">
<html xmlns="http://www.w3.org/1999/xhtml" xml:lang="en" lang="en">
    <head>
        <title>
            Using the &lt;hr&gt; tag
        </title>
    </head>

    <body>
        <center>
            <h1>
                Using the &lt;hr&gt; tag
            </h1>
        </center>
```

```
        Here's what &lt;hr&gt; looks like:
        <hr />
        <br />
        Here's what &lt;hr align="left" width="80%"&gt; looks like:
        <hr align="left" width="80%" />
        <br />
        Here's what &lt;hr align="center" width="80%"&gt; looks like:
        <hr align="center" width="80%" />
        <br />
        Here's what &lt;hr align="right" width="80%"&gt; looks like:
        <hr align="right" width="80%" />
        <br />
        Here's what &lt;hr size="10"&gt; looks like:
        <hr align="center" size="10" />
        <br />
        Here's what &lt;hr size="10" noshade="noshade"&gt; looks like:
        <hr align="center" size="10" noshade="noshade" />
    </body>
</html>
```

You can see the results of this XHTML in Figure 3.11.

Two more quick notes: To use the **align** attribute, you must also use the **width** attribute; and using **<hr>** automatically adds a line break above and below the rule.

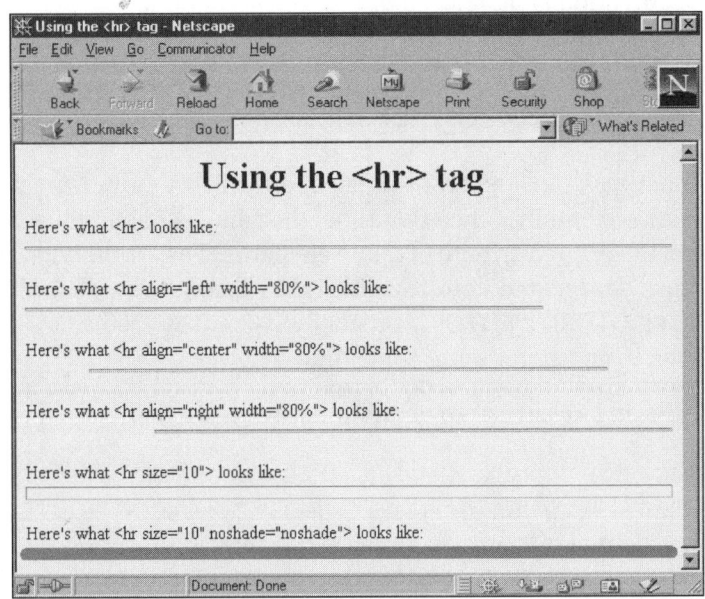

Figure 3.11   Using the **<hr>** element.

<center>—Centering Text

Purpose: Centers its enclosed text horizontally. Deprecated in HTML 4.

When used as HTML: Start tag/End tag: Required/Required

Supported: [1.0T, 1.0F, 3.2, 4, IE1, IE2, IE3, IE4, IE5, NS1, NS2, NS3, NS4]

Attributes:

- **class**—Class of the element (used for rendering). [1.0T, 1.0F, 4, IE4, IE5]
- **dir**—Gives the direction of directionally neutral text (text that doesn't have inherent direction in which you should read it). Possible values: **ltr**: left-to-right text or table and **rtl**: right-to-left text or table. [1.0T, 1.0F, 4, IE5]
- **id**—Unique alphanumeric identifier for the tag, which you can use to refer to it. [1.0T, 1.0F, 4, IE4, IE5]
- **lang**—Base language used for the tag. [1.0T, 1.0F, 4, IE4, IE5]
- **language**—Scripting language used for the tag. [IE4, IE5]
- **style**—Inline style indicating how to render the element. [1.0T, 1.0F, 4, IE3, IE4, IE5]
- **title**—Holds additional information (which might be displayed in tool tips) for the element. [1.0T, 1.0F, 4]
- **xml:lang**—Holds the base language for the element when the document is interpreted as an XML document. [1.0T, 1.0F]

XHTML events: onclick, ondblclick, onmousedown, onmouseup, onmouseover, onmousemove, onmouseout, onkeypress, onkeydown, onkeyup

The **<center>** element was introduced by Netscape to fill an early formatting need—centering text horizontally. Since that time, the same capability has been filled largely by using the **align** attribute of many elements. The World Wide Web Consortium (W3C) has deprecated **<center>** in HTML 4, so you won't find it in the XHTML 1.0 Strict or XHTML 1.1 DTDs. Nonetheless, **<center>** remains a cherished element and will be in use for quite some time.

Here's an example of using **<center>** to center multiline text:

```
<?xml version="1.0"?>
<!DOCTYPE html PUBLIC "-//W3C//DTD XHTML 1.0 Transitional//EN"
"http://www.w3.org/TR/xhtml1/DTD/xhtml1-transitional.dtd">
<html xmlns="http://www.w3.org/1999/xhtml" xml:lang="en" lang="en">
    <head>
```

```
            <title>
                Using the &lt;center&gt; tag
            </title>
        </head>

        <body>
            <center>
                <h1>
                    Using the &lt;center&gt; tag
                </h1>
            </center>
            <center>
                As you can see,
                <br />
                the &lt;center&gt; tag
                <br />
                can center multi-line text.
            </center>
        </body>
</html>
```

You can see the results of this XHTML in Figure 3.12.

Because **<center>** was introduced by Netscape and not by W3C, the interaction rules for this tag can be different in various browsers. For example, using **<center>** around a table centers the table in some browsers, but centers the text in each table cell in other browsers. It's best to test things out in as many browsers as you can.

TIP: *Now that the **<center>** tag is deprecated, what should you use to replace it? It turns out that the **<center>** element produces exactly the same effect as using the **<div>** element with the **align** attribute set to **center**. That's what W3C suggests you use.*

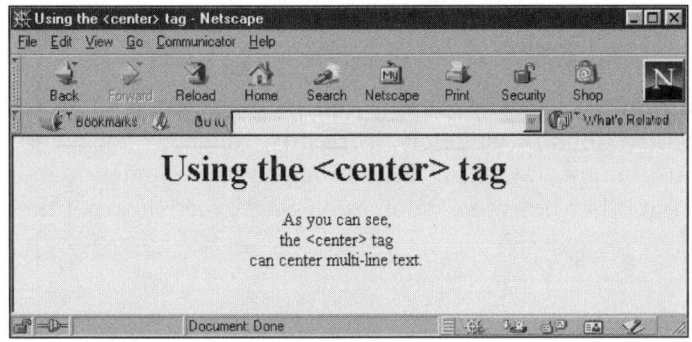

Figure 3.12   Using the **<center>** tag.

<blockquote>—Indenting Quotations

Purpose: Indents and styles text as a quotation. Use for longer, multiline quotations; otherwise, use **<q>**.

When used as HTML: Start tag/End tag: Required/Required

Supported: [1.0S, 1.0T, 1.0F, 1.1, 2, 3, 3.2, 4, IE1, IE2, IE3, IE4, IE5, NS1, NS2, NS3, NS4]

Attributes:

- **cite**—Indicates the source of the quotation. Set to text. [1.0S, 1.0T, 1.0F, 1.1, 4]
- **class**—Class of the element (used for rendering). [1.0S, 1.0T, 1.0F, 1.1, 3, 4, IE4, IE5, NS4]
- **dir**—Gives the direction of directionally neutral text (text that doesn't have inherent direction in which you should read it). Possible values: **ltr**: left-to-right text or table and **rtl**: right-to-left text or table. [1.0S, 1.0T, 1.0F, 1.1, 4, IE5]
- **id**—Unique alphanumeric identifier for the tag, which you can use to refer to it. [1.0S, 1.0T, 1.0F, 1.1, 3, 4, IE4, IE5, NS4]
- **lang**—Base language used for the tag. [1.0S, 1.0T, 1.0F, 1.1, 3, 4, IE4, IE5, NS4]
- **language**—Scripting language used for the tag. [IE4, IE5]
- **style**—Inline style indicating how to render the element. [1.0S, 1.0T, 1.0F, 1.1, 4, IE3, IE4, IE5, NS4]
- **title**—Holds additional information (which might be displayed in tool tips) for the element. [1.0S, 1.0T, 1.0F, 1.1, 3, 4, IE4, IE5]
- **xml:lang**—Holds the base language for the element when the document is interpreted as an XML document. [1.0S, 1.0T, 1.0F, 1.1]

XHTML events: onclick, ondblclick, onmousedown, onmouseup, onmouseover, onmousemove, onmouseout, onkeypress, onkeydown, onkeyup

You use the **<blockquote>** element to indent and set off longer quotations (for one-line quotations, use the **<q>** element). Currently, Netscape Navigator and Internet Explorer just indent the text in the **<blockquote>** element and set it in the default font, but other browsers, such as NCSA Mosaic, also set the text in bold.

Here's an example of using the **<blockquote>** element for a longer quotation:

```xml
<?xml version="1.0"?>
<!DOCTYPE html PUBLIC "-//W3C//DTD XHTML 1.0 Transitional//EN"
"http://www.w3.org/TR/xhtml1/DTD/xhtml1-transitional.dtd">
<html xmlns="http://www.w3.org/1999/xhtml" xml:lang="en" lang="en">
    <head>
        <title>
            Using the &lt;blockquote&gt; tag
        </title>
    </head>

    <body>
        <center>
            <h1>
                Using the &lt;blockquote&gt; tag
            </h1>
        </center>
        When it comes to block quotes, W3C says:
        <blockquote>
            We recommend that style sheet implementations provide
            a mechanism for inserting quotation marks before and
            after a quotation delimited by BLOCKQUOTE in a manner
            appropriate to the current language context and the
            degree of nesting of quotations.
            <p>
                However, as some authors have used BLOCKQUOTE merely
                as a mechanism to indent text, in order to preserve
                the intention of the authors, user agents should not
                insert quotation marks in the default style.
            </p>
        </blockquote>
    </body>
</html>
```

You can see the results of this XHTML in Figure 3.13. Although the **<blockquote>** tag can be useful, style sheets have become more powerful and allow you to style block quotes to your specification.

Figure 3.13   Using the **<blockquote>** tag.

<pre>—Displaying Preformatted Text

Purpose: Tells the browser that the enclosed text is already formatted and should not be reformatted.

When used as HTML: Start tag/End tag: Required/Required

Supported: [1.0S, 1.0T, 1.0F, 1.1, 2, 3, 3.2, 4, IE1, IE2, IE3, IE4, IE5, NS1, NS2, NS3, NS4]

Attributes:

- **class**—Class of the element (used for rendering). [1.0S, 1.0T, 1.0F, 1.1, 3, 4, IE4, IE5, NS4]
- **cols**—Indicates the number of columns to use for the text. [NS1, NS2, NS3, NS4]
- **dir**—Gives the direction of directionally neutral text (text that doesn't have inherent direction in which you should read it). Possible values: **ltr**: left-to-right text or table and **rtl**: right-to-left text or table. [1.0S, 1.0T, 1.0F, 1.1, 4, IE5]
- **id**—Unique alphanumeric identifier for the tag, which you can use to refer to it. [1.0S, 1.0T, 1.0F, 1.1, 3, 4, IE4, IE5, NS4]
- **lang**—Base language used for the tag. [1.0S, 1.0T, 1.0F, 1.1, 3, 4, IE4, IE5, NS4]
- **language**—Scripting language used for the tag. [IE4, IE5]

- **style**—Inline style indicating how to render the element. [1.0S, 1.0T, 1.0F, 1.1, 4, IE3, IE4, IE5, NS4]
- **title**—Holds additional information (which might be displayed in tool tips) for the element. [1.0S, 1.0T, 1.0F, 1.1, 3, 4, IE4, IE5]
- **width**—Sets the maximum number of characters per line, usually 40, 80, or 132. [1.0T, 1.0F, 2, 3, 3,2, 4]
- **wrap**—Indicates if the text should or should not wrap. [NS4]
- **xml:space**—A built-in attribute set to "preserve" in XHTML to indicate that the browser should preserve spacing. [1.0S, 1.0T, 1.0F, 1.1]
- **xml:lang**—Holds the base language for the element when the document is interpreted as an XML document. [1.0S, 1.0T, 1.0F, 1.1]

XHTML Events: onclick, ondblclick, onmousedown, onmouseup, onmouseover, onmousemove, onmouseout, onkeypress, onkeydown, onkeyup

The novice programmer enters screaming, "I can't get it to work!" "Get what to work, NP?" you inquire. "The company's annual report; there's just no way to do it in XHTML, it's too complex!" "Calm down, NP," you say soothingly, "you can always use the **<pre>** element." "Oh," says the NP.

To turn off the automatic formatting applied by Web browsers, you can use the **<pre>** element, which tells the browser that the enclosed text is already formatted and should not be interpreted or reformatted. This tag can be a good one if you're stuck in tangles of XHTML and want a quick, if somewhat crude, solution, because it tells the browser to display the text exactly as it is.

Here's an example that we saw in the beginning of this chapter, where I formatted a table for display:

```
<?xml version="1.0"?>
<!DOCTYPE html PUBLIC "-//W3C//DTD XHTML 1.0 Transitional//EN"
"http://www.w3.org/TR/xhtml1/DTD/xhtml1-transitional.dtd">
<html xmlns="http://www.w3.org/1999/xhtml" xml:lang="en" lang="en">
    <head>
        <title>
            Using the &lt;pre&gt; tag
        </title>
    </head>

    <body>
        <center>
            <h1>
                Using the &lt;pre&gt; tag
```

```
            </h1>
        </center>
        <pre>
Name                    Email                   extension
----------------------------------------------------------
David              david@starpowder.com         x4849
Sam                sam@starpowder.com           x4850
Nancy              nancy@starpowder.com         x4851
Jennifer           jennifer@starpowder.com      x4852
Marty              marty@starpowder.com         x4853
Frank              frank@starpowder.com         x4854
        </pre>
    </body>
</html>
```

The result appears in Figure 3.7. The text is displayed in the Web browser just as I've typed it. (Note that this includes spaces, so if you don't want your text to be indented, don't leave leading spaces on the line; remove them as I have done in this code sample.)

TIP: *In fact, you can use tags, like* **<b>** *and* **<i>**, *to style text inside a* **<pre>** *block and the browser will use them.* **<pre>** *is usually just used to preserve line breaks and indentation in the original text.*

NOTE: *The Active Bug list for the Microsoft XML Parser has an interesting entry in it listed as an active bug:* **Throw error when parsing XHTML DTD on the line "xml:space (preserve) #FIXED 'preserve'"**. *Microsoft is apparently having some trouble with the predefined* **xml:space** *attribute in the* **<pre>** *element. This error must be handled internally, however, because it doesn't cause any visible problem in the Internet Explorer.*

<multicol>—Creating Columns

Purpose: Breaks text into columns.

When used as HTML: Start tag/End tag: Required/Required

Supported: [NS3, NS4]

Attributes:

- **cols**—This required attribute indicates the number of columns you want to break the text into. Set it to a positive integer. [NS3, NS4]
- **gutter**—Sets the number of pixels between columns. Set to a positive integer; the default is 10. [NS3, NS4]

- **width**—Supposed to be the width of each column, actually seems to be the width of all columns plus gutters. The default value is 100 percent of the display width. [NS3, NS4]

The big boss says, "I want you to write the company newspaper. Here's the text." "OK," you say, "I can use the **<multicol>** tag to arrange it in columns, like a newspaper. What's this about how employees are happier if they leave all decisions to upper management?" "Completely true," says the BB, "as studies have shown."

The **<multicol>** tag is a Netscape-Navigator-only tag, and as such it's not part of official XHTML. However, it exists and can be quite useful. This element arranges its text into columns; you have control over the number of columns, the distance between the columns, and the total width of the result, but not much more. In particular, it's up to Netscape Navigator to determine how many lines of text each column will be. It seems to have a proclivity to keep the last column relatively empty and adds another line to each column when more text is added.

Here's an example of the **<multicol>** tag at work:

```
<?xml version="1.0"?>
<!DOCTYPE html PUBLIC "-//W3C//DTD XHTML 1.0 Transitional//EN"
 "http://www.w3.org/TR/xhtml1/DTD/xhtml1-transitional.dtd">
<html xmlns="http://www.w3.org/1999/xhtml" xml:lang="en" lang="en">
    <head>
        <title>
            Using the &lt;multicol&gt; tag
        </title>
    </head>

    <body>
        <h1 align="center">
            Using The &lt;multicol&gt; Tag
        </h1>
        <multicol cols="3" width="90%" gutter="10">
            This text is specifically distributed over
            three columns using the &lt;multicol&gt; tag.
            The &lt;multicol&gt; tag is useful when you
            want to get that "newspaper-like" look, much
            like you see in this case. It's a nice effect
            for some purposes, but not for everybody.
        </multicol>
    </body>
</html>
```

This XHTML arranges text into three columns, as you can see in Figure 3.14.

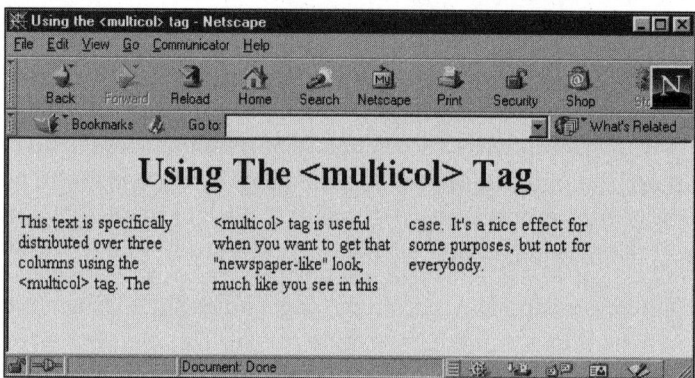

Figure 3.14 Using the **<multicol>** tag.

<spacer>—Controlling Horizontal and Vertical Spacing

Purpose: Gives you more control over horizontal and vertical spacing. This element does not contain any content.

When used as HTML: Start tag/End tag: Required/Omitted

Supported: [NS3, NS4]

Attributes:

- **align**—Sets alignment only when the **type** attribute is set to **block**. Possible values are: **left, right, top, texttop, middle, absmiddle, baseline, bottom,** and **absbottom**. [NS3, NS4]
- **height**—Sets the height in pixels of the spacer when the **type** attribute is set to **block**. [NS3, NS4]
- **size**—Sets the width or height in pixels of the spacer when the **type** attribute is set to **horizontal** or **vertical**. [NS3, NS4]
- **type**—Sets the type of the spacer. Required attribute. May be **horizontal, vertical,** or **block**. [NS3, NS4]
- **width**—Sets the width in pixels of the spacer when the **type** attribute is set to **block**. [NS3, NS4]

The novice programmer has a problem and says, "Jeez! Isn't there some way to space things the way I want them? I feel like putting in an invisible image of the same color as the background just so I can skip down exactly 100 pixels in my Web page before putting in some text." "There's an easy way to do that," you say; "just use the **<spacer>** element." The NP asks, "Why didn't someone think of this before?"

Web browsers move the elements of your page around to fit the available space. Netscape Navigator allows you to create a pseudo-element named a *spacer* that helps you set the amount of open space around the elements in your page. The **<spacer>** element is another of those Netscape-Navigator-specific elements that XHTML omits, but it exists and is useful.

Here's an example. In this case, I'm creating a spacer 100 pixels high and displaying a line of text right after it:

```
<?xml version="1.0"?>
<!DOCTYPE html PUBLIC "-//W3C//DTD XHTML 1.0 Transitional//EN"
    "http://www.w3.org/TR/xhtml1/DTD/xhtml1-transitional.dtd">
<html xmlns="http://www.w3.org/1999/xhtml" xml:lang="en" lang="en">
    <head>
        <title>
            Using the &lt;SPACER&gt; tag
        </title>
    </head>

    <body>
        <h1 align="center">
            Using The &lt;spacer&gt; Tag
        </h1>
            <spacer type="vertical" size="100" />
            There's an invisible spacer 100 pixels high above this text!
    </body>
</html>
```

The result of this XHTML appears in Figure 3.15.

NOTE: *Now that you can use styles to specify text position as well as formatting, it's a good idea to use style sheets instead of spacers.*

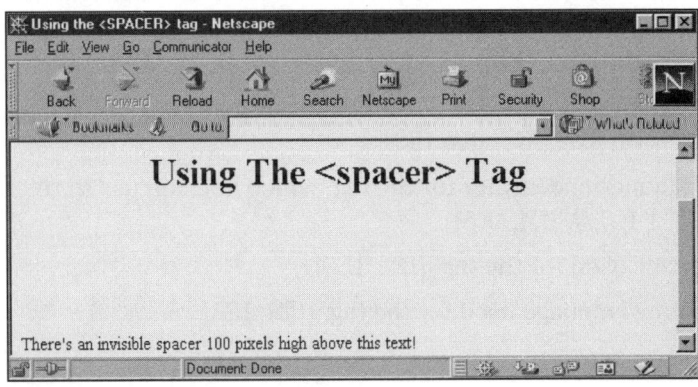

Figure 3.15   Using the **<spacer>** tag.

<marquee>—Displaying Text in a Scrolling Marquee

Purpose: Displays scrolling text in a "marquee" style.

When used as HTML: Start tag/End tag: Required/Required

Supported: [IE2, IE3, IE4, IE5]

Attributes:

- **behavior**—Sets how the text in the marquee should move. Can be: **scroll** (the default; text scrolls across the marquee), **slide** (text enters from one side and stops at the other side), or **alternate** (text seems to bounce from one side to the other). [IE2, IE3, IE4, IE5]

- **bgcolor**—Sets the background color for the marquee box. Set to a color value or a predefined color name. [IE2, IE3, IE4, IE5]

- **class**—Class of the element (used for rendering). [1.0S, 1.0T, 1.0F, 1.1, 3, 4, IE4, IE5]

- **datafld**—Name of the column of the data source object that supplies the bound data. Set to alphanumeric characters. [IE4, IE5]

- **dataformatas**—Specifies if bound data is plain text or HTML. Set to **html**, **plaintext**, or **text**. [IE4, IE5]

- **datasrc**—Gives the URL or ID of the data source object supplying data bound to this element. W3C says this should be a URL, Internet Explorer says it should be a data source ID. [IE4, IE5]

- **dir**—Gives the direction of directionally neutral text (text that doesn't have inherent direction in which you should read it). Possible values: **ltr**: left-to-right text or table and **rtl**: right-to-left text or table. [IE5]

- **direction**—Sets the direction the text should scroll. Can be: **left** (the default), **right**, **down**, or **up**. [IE2, IE3, IE4, IE5]

- **height**—Specifies the height of the marquee. The default is the height of the marquee's text. Set to a height in pixels or a percentage of the available display height. [IE2, IE3, IE4, IE5]

- **hspace**—Gives the left and right margins outside the marquee. Set to a pixel value (the default is 0). [IE2, IE3, IE4, IE5]

- **id**—Unique alphanumeric identifier for the tag, which you can use to refer to it. [1.0S, 1.0T, 1.0F, 1.1, 3, 4, IE4, IE5]

- **lang**—Base language used for the tag. [IE4, IE5]

- **language**—Scripting language used for the tag. [IE4, IE5]

- **loop**—Sets how many times you want the marquee to cycle. Set to a positive integer or −1 for continuous cycling. [IE2, IE3, IE4, IE5]
- **scrollamount**—Sets the horizontal space between each successive display of the text. Set to pixel values. [IE2, IE3, IE4, IE5]
- **scrolldelay**—Sets the number of milliseconds between each successive display of the text. Set to a positive integer millisecond value. [IE2, IE3, IE4, IE5]
- **style**—Inline style indicating how to render the element. [IE3, IE4, IE5]
- **title**—Holds additional information (which might be displayed in tool tips) for the element. [IE4, IE5]
- **truespeed**—Specifies that exact **scrolldelay** values should be used as given. If you don't use this attribute, values less than 59 are set to 60 milliseconds. Set to **true** or **false** (the default). [IE4, IE5]
- **vspace**—Sets the top and bottom spacing margins outside the marquee. Set to a positive pixel value. The default value is 0. [IE2, IE3, IE4, IE5]
- **width**—Sets the width of the marquee; the default value is 100 percent of the available display width. Set to positive integer pixel values or a percentage of the total display width. [IE2, IE3, IE4, IE5]

The novice programmer comes in frowning and says, "I've just got to get their attention." "Whose attention?" you ask. "Those mountaineering students who are reading my mountaineering page—I've got to get their attention about the safety warnings, they're dropping off mountains like flies." "Well," you suggest, "what about the **<marquee>** element?"

The **<marquee>** element is an Internet Explorer element, not an official XHTML element, that displays text in a moving banner (modeled after a moving movie marquee), which can scroll, slide, or bounce in a horizontal strip. It's up to you to set the size of the script in a marquee (similar to **<h1>** or **<h2>** headings). If you don't specify a font, the marquee will use the current default.

Scrolling text (**behavior="scroll"**) in the marquee does just that—scrolls left to right, top to bottom, or whatever you specify by setting the direction with the **direction** attribute. To make the text keep scrolling, you can set the **loop** attribute to a specific value, or you can set it to **infinite** to make it keep scrolling forever. Text that slides (**behavior="slide"**) enters from one side, slides to the other, and stays there. It does not repeat, no matter how you use the **loop** attribute. Text that bounces (**behavior="alternate"**) moves from one limit and then back to the other, such as left to right and then back. You can make it go on continuously with the **loop** attribute.

Here's an example showing various **<marquee>** options at work:

```xml
<?xml version="1.0"?>
<!DOCTYPE html PUBLIC "-//W3C//DTD XHTML 1.0 Transitional//EN"
"http://www.w3.org/TR/xhtml1/DTD/xhtml1-transitional.dtd">
<html xmlns="http://www.w3.org/1999/xhtml" xml:lang="en" lang="en">
    <head>
        <title>
            Using the &lt;marquee&gt; tag
        </title>
    </head>

    <body>
        <marquee align="top" loop="infinite" behavior="bounce"
            bgcolor="#00ff00" direction="right">
            <h2>
                Here's a marquee!
            </h2>
        </marquee>

        <center>
            <h1>
                Using Marquees
            </h1>
        </center>

        <marquee align="left" loop="infinite" behavior="scroll"
            bgcolor="#ff0000" height="40" width="300" direction="down">
            <h2>
                Here's another marquee!
            </h2>
        </marquee>

        <marquee align="top" loop="infinite" behavior="slide"
            bgcolor="#00ffff" width="100%" direction="right">
            <h2>
                And one more!
            </h2>
        </marquee>

    </body>
</html>
```

The results of this XHTML appear in Figure 3.16. (Of course, this figure, being static, can show the marquee colors but not the movement.)

Immediate Solutions

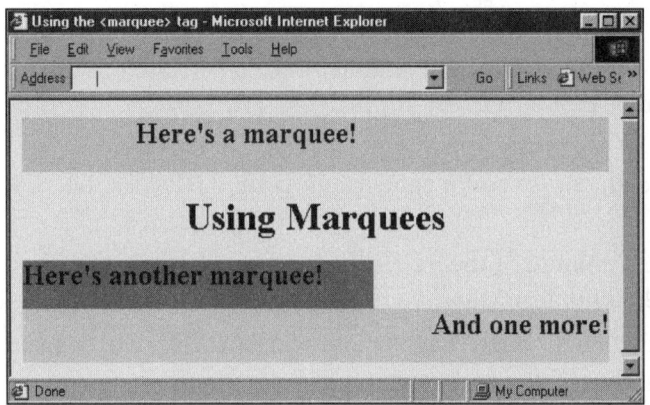

Figure 3.16   Using the **<marquee>** tag.

There's no denying the appeal of the **<marquee>** tag for getting attention, but because it's restricted to Internet Explorer, you should be careful when using it. In other browsers, the text in the marquee will simply appear static when displayed.

*NOTE: The **<marquee>** tag in Internet Explorer has changed as new versions of the browser have been introduced. For example, versions before Internet Explorer 4 won't understand the **up** and **down** directions for text.*

Note also that there's no easy way to be certain of the speed at which the text in the marquee will travel. You'll have to experiment with the **scrollamount** and **scrolldelay** attributes.

To create a marquee that will work in most browsers, you can use JavaScript instead.

*TIP: You can create a multiline marquee with a **<blockquote>** element. You shouldn't nest **<marquee>** elements. If you make the marquee large enough or use multiple marquees next to each other, you can create a striking effect in which the plain text in your Web page appears to be scrolling around by itself.*

<div>—Formatting Block Text

Purpose: Selects a block of text so you can apply styles.

When used as HTML: Start tag/End tag: Required/Required

Supported: [1.0S, 1.0T, 1.0F, 1.1, 3, 3.2, 4, IE3, IE4, IE5, NS2, NS3, NS4]

Attributes:

- **align**—Deprecated. Sets the horizontal alignment of the element in the page. Set to **left** (the default), **right**, **center**, or **justify**. [1.0T, 1.0F, 3, 3.2, 4, IE3, IE4, IE5, NS2, NS3, NS4]
- **class**—Class of the element (used for rendering). [1.0S, 1.0T, 1.0F, 1.1, 3, 4, IE4, IE5, NS4]
- **datafld**—Name of the column of the data source object that supplies the bound data. Set to alphanumeric characters. [IE4, IE5]
- **dataformatas**—Specifies if bound data is plain text or HTML. Set to **html**, **plaintext**, or **text**. [IE4, IE5]
- **datasrc**—Gives the URL or ID of the data source object supplying data bound to this element. W3C says this should be a URL, Internet Explorer says it should be a data source ID. [IE4, IE5]
- **dir**—Gives the direction of directionally neutral text (text that doesn't have inherent direction in which you should read it). Possible values: **ltr**: left-to-right text or table and **rtl**: right-to-left text or table. [1.0S, 1.0T, 1.0F, 1.1, 4, IE5]
- **id**—Unique alphanumeric identifier for the tag, which you can use to refer to it. [1.0S, 1.0T, 1.0F, 1.1, 3, 4, IE4, IE5, NS4]
- **lang**—Base language used for the tag. [1.0S, 1.0T, 1.0F, 1.1, 3, 4, IE4, IE5]
- **language**—Scripting language used for the tag. [IE4, IE5]
- **style**—Inline style indicating how to render the element. [1.0S, 1.0T, 1.0F, 1.1, 4, IE3, IE4, IE5, NS4]
- **title**—Holds additional information (which might be displayed in tool tips) for the element. [1.0S, 1.0T, 1.0F, 1.1, 3, 4, IE4, IE5]
- **xml:lang**—Holds the base language for the element when the document is interpreted as an XML document. [1.0S, 1.0T, 1.0F, 1.1]

XHTML events: onclick, ondblclick, onmousedown, onmouseup, onmouseover, onmousemove, onmouseout, onkeypress, onkeydown, onkeyup

The **<div>** tag provides you with an easy way to refer to a block of text. As discussed at the beginning of this chapter, you can use the **<p>** element to refer to a paragraph of text, but you might not want to divide your document into paragraphs (the kind that XHTML creates, anyway), so you can use the **<div>** element instead. Most Web browsers place a line break before and after **<div>** elements.

This element is very important when you're applying styles because you can mark specific blocks of text to apply styles to. (We'll discuss this more in Chapter 9.)

You can also use the attributes of this element to specify attributes of the enclosed text, as you can see in this example from the beginning of the chapter, where I use the **<div>** element to align text:

```
<?xml version="1.0"?>
<!DOCTYPE html PUBLIC "-//W3C//DTD XHTML 1.0 Transitional//EN"
"http://www.w3.org/TR/xhtml1/DTD/xhtml1-transitional.dtd">
<html xmlns="http://www.w3.org/1999/xhtml" xml:lang="en" lang="en">
    <head>
        <title>
            Using the &lt;div&gt; tag
        </title>
    </head>

    <body>
        <center>
            <h1>
                Using the &lt;div&gt; tag
            </h1>
        </center>
        <div align="left">
            Manager
            <br />
            SlowPoke Products, Inc.
            <br />
            Languid, TX
        </div>

        <p>
            Dear You:
            <div align="center" style="color: red; font-style: italic">
                When are you going to ship my order?
            </div>
        </p>

        <div align="right">
            <p>
                President
                <br />
                NeedItNow, Inc.
                <br />
                Speedy, CO
            </p>
        </div>
    </body>
</html>
```

You can see the results of this XHTML in Figure 3.5.

NOTE: Because the **align** attribute is deprecated in HTML 4, it's not available in the XHTML 1.0 Strict DTD or the XHTML 1.1 DTD. Therefore, if you have a style-sheet-enabled browser, you might want to switch to style sheets.

TIP: Now that the **<center>** tag is deprecated, you're supposed to use a **<div>** element with the **align** attribute set to center.

You can also position text with the **<div>** tag, even overlapping it. See the section "Positioning Text with **<div>**" near the end of this chapter. As you'll see in that section, you can use this element to restrict text to a specific rectangular region.

<span>—Formatting Inline Text

Purpose: Selects inline text to let you apply styles.

When used as HTML: Start tag/End tag: Required/Required

Supported: [1.0S, 1.0T, 1.0F, 1.1, 4, IE3, IE4, IE5, NS4]

Attributes:

- **class**—Class of the element (used for rendering). [1.0S, 1.0T, 1.0F, 1.1, 4, IE4, IE5, NS4]
- **datafld**—Name of the column of the data source object that supplies the bound data. Set to alphanumeric characters. [IE4, IE5]
- **dataformatas**—Specifies if bound data is plain text or HTML. Set to **html**, **plaintext**, or **text**. [IE4, IE5]
- **datasrc**—Gives the URL or ID of the data source object supplying data bound to this element. W3C says this should be a URL, Internet Explorer says it should be a data source ID. [IE4, IE5]
- **dir**—Gives the direction of directionally neutral text (text that doesn't have inherent direction in which you should read it). Possible values: **ltr**: left-to-right text or table and **rtl**: right-to-left text or table. [1.0S, 1.0T, 1.0F, 1.1, 4, IE5]
- **id**—Unique alphanumeric identifier for the tag, which you can use to refer to it. [1.0S, 1.0T, 1.0F, 1.1, 4, IE4, IE5, NS4]
- **lang**—Base language used for the tag. [1.0S, 1.0T, 1.0F, 1.1, 3, 4, IE4, IE5]
- **language**—Scripting language used for the tag. [IE4, IE5]

- **style**—Inline style indicating how to render the element. [1.0S, 1.0T, 1.0F, 1.1, 4, IE3, IE4, IE5, NS4]
- **title**—Holds additional information (which might be displayed in tool tips) for the element. [1.0S, 1.0T, 1.0F, 1.1, 4, IE4, IE5]
- **xml:lang**—Holds the base language for the element when the document is interpreted as an XML document. [1.0S, 1.0T, 1.0F, 1.1]

XHTML Events: onclick, ondblclick, onmousedown, onmouseup, onmouseover, onmousemove, onmouseout, onkeypress, onkeydown, onkeyup

When you don't have a well-delineated block of text to work with, you can use the **<span>** element to select and apply styles. You usually use **<span>** to apply styles inline—for example, in the middle of a sentence. (Remember: for blocks of text that can stand by themselves, use the **<div>** element; for words or sentences, use the **<span>** element.)

In this example, I'm using **<span>** to apply a style to a section of text, turning that text red:

```
<?xml version="1.0"?>
<!DOCTYPE html PUBLIC "-//W3C//DTD XHTML 1.0 Transitional//EN"
    "http://www.w3.org/TR/xhtml1/DTD/xhtml1-transitional.dtd">
<html xmlns="http://www.w3.org/1999/xhtml" xml:lang="en" lang="en">
    <head>
        <title>
            Using the &lt;span&gt; tag
        </title>
    </head>

    <body>
        <center>
            <h1>
                Using the &lt;span&gt; tag
            </h1>
        </center>
        <h2>
            Is my face <span class="redface" style="color: red">red</span>?
        </h2>
    </body>
</html>
```

You can see the results of this XHTML in Figure 3.17. The word "red" appears in red (although in black-and-white in the figure, of course).

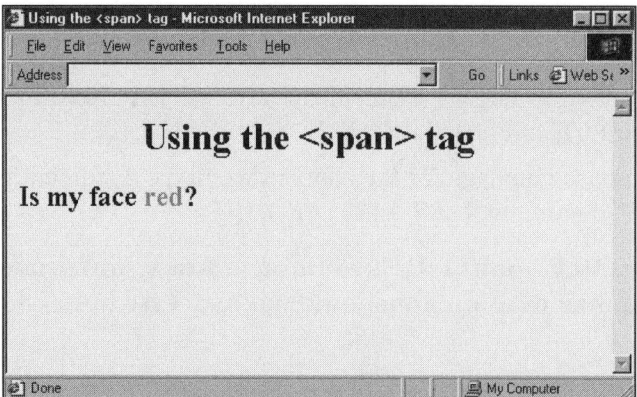

Figure 3.17   Using the **<span>** tag to format inline text.

TIP: *Now that the **<font>** element is deprecated, the **<span>** element provides a good substitute. Use inline styles to set the font attributes you want, such as I did for Figure 3.17.*

Formatting Text with Tables

The novice programmer enters, wailing, "I can't do it! I just can't format this text the way I want it!" "Calm down," you counsel; "have you tried using tables yet?" "Tables?" the NP asks.

One very powerful way to arrange text is with XHTML tables. Tables were introduced in Netscape Navigator 1.1, were implemented in Internet Explorer in version 2, and became standard in HTML 3. Using tables, you can create a grid of cells to display text and images. Early on, Web-page stylists realized that you could turn the border of a table off, making it invisible by using the **noborder** attribute; this gave them a way of arranging text into columns and rows on a Web page.

In fact, arranging text by using tables is a very common thing to do. And although you can now use the **<div>** element to do the same thing, even the big corporations still use the **<table>** element to arrange text in their Web sites, ensuring that early browsers can handle it. Using **<table>**, you can place text where you want it in a Web page, although it may take some work. (For more information on creating tables, see Chapter 6.)

As an example, say that I want to display a large number of hyperlinks in rows and columns. I can do that by using a table. I can even supply text as a caption, which I can spread over several columns by using the **colspan** attribute. Listing 3.1 shows how this looks—note how long the XHTML can get when you use tables for even relatively simple tasks.

Listing 3.1 Using the <table> element to arrange text.

```
<?xml version="1.0"?>
<!DOCTYPE html PUBLIC "-//W3C//DTD XHTML 1.0 Transitional//EN"
"http://www.w3.org/TR/xhtml1/DTD/xhtml1-transitional.dtd">
<html xmlns="http://www.w3.org/1999/xhtml" xml:lang="en" lang="en">
    <head>
        <title>
            Formatting text with the &lt;table&gt; tag
        </title>
    </head>

    <body>
        <center>
            <h1>
                Formatting text with the &lt;table&gt; tag
            </h1>
        </center>
        <table noborder = "noborder" cellpadding = "4" width = "95%">
            <tr>
                <th colspan = "4">
                    <h2>
                        Travel to these sites around the world
                    </h2>
                </th>
            </tr>
            <tr>
                <th colspan = "4">
                    Ever been to a site in Kenya? Russia? China?
                    You can travel to those countries now, because
                    each tour below is actually at a site in the
                    country it describes! <i>Bon Voyage...</i>
                </th>
            </tr>
            <tr align = "center">
                <td>
                    <a href = "http://www.secyt.gov.ar/arg/introi.html">
                        Argentina
                    </a>
                </td>
                <td>
                    <a href = "http://www.telstra.com.au/meta/australia.html">
                        Australia
                    </a>
                </td>
```

```
                <td>
                    <a href = "http://croco.atnet.at/tourism">
                        Austria
                    </a>
                </td>
                <td>
                    <a href =
                    "http://canada.gc.ca/canadiana/cdaind_e.html">
                        Canada
                    </a>
                </td>
            </tr>
            <tr align = "center">
                <td>
                    <a href =
                    "http://sunsite.dcc.uchile.cl/chile/chile.html">
                        Chile
                    </a>
                </td>
                <td>
                    <a href = "http://www.ihep.ac.cn/tour/china_tour.html">
                        China
                    </a>
                </td>
                <td>
                    <a href = "http://www.ciesin.ee/ESTCG/">
                        Estonia
                    </a>
                </td>
                <td>
                    <a href = "http://www.csc.fi/tiko/finland.html">
                        Finland
                    </a>
                </td>
            </tr>
            <tr align = "center">
                <td>
                    <a href = "http://www.iway.fr/internet-way/fr/france">
                        France
                    </a>
                </td>
                <td>
                    <a href =
                    "http://www.chemie.fu-berlin.de/adressen/brd.html">
                        Germany
                    </a>
                </td>
```

```
        <td>
            <a href =
            "http://www.culture.gr/2/21/maps/hellas.html">
                Greece
            </a>
        </td>
        <td>
            <a href = "http://www.arctic.is">
                Iceland
            </a>
        </td>
    </tr>
    <tr align = "center">
        <td>
            <a href = "http://slarti.ucd.ie/maps/ireland.html">
                Ireland
            </a>
        </td>
        <td>
            <a href = "http://ece.iisc.ernet.in/india.html">
                India
            </a>
        </td>
        <td>
            <a href = "http://www.travel.it">
                Italy
            </a>
        </td>
        <td>
            <a href = "http://www.recruit.co.jp/Jjapan">
                Japan
            </a>
        </td>
    </tr>
    <tr align = "center">
        <td>
            <a href = "http://www.arcc.or.ke">
                Kenya
            </a>
        </td>
        <td>
            <a href = "http://www.mty.itesm.mx/MexWeb/Info2/">
                Mexico
            </a>
        </td>
```

```
            <td>
                <a href = "http://www.govt.nz/nzinfo.html">
                    New Zealand
                </a>
            </td>
            <td>
                <a href = "http://info.fuw.edu.pl/pl/poland.html">
                    Poland
                </a>
            </td>
        </tr>
        <tr align = "center">
            <td>
                <a href = "http://indis.ici.ro/romania/romania.html">
                    Romania
                </a>
            </td>
            <td>
                <a href = "http://www.kiae.su/www/wtr">
                    Russia
                </a>
            </td>
            <td>
                <a href = "http://www.technet.sg">
                    Singapore
                </a>
            </td>
            <td>
                <a href =
                "http://osprey.unisa.ac.za/south-africa/home.html">
                    South Africa
                </a>
            </td>
        </tr>
        <tr align = "center">
            <td>
                <a href = "http://www.uji.es/spain_www.html">
                    Spain
                </a>
            </td>
            <td>
                <a href = "http://www.westnet.se/sweden">
                    Sweden
                </a>
            </td>
```

```
            <td>
                <a href = "http://heiwww.unige.ch/switzerland/">
                    Switzerland
                </a>
            </td>
            <td>
                <a href = "http://www.chiangmai.ac.th/thmap.html">
                    Thailand
                </a>
            </td>
        </tr>
        <tr align = "center">
            <td>
                <a href = "http://www.rada.kiev.ua/ukraine.htm">
                    Ukraine
                </a>
            </td>
            <td>
                <a href = "http://www.cs.ucl.ac.uk/misc/uk/intro">
                    United Kingdom
                </a>
            </td>
            <td>
                <a href = "http://www.zamnet.zm/zamnet/zntb.html">
                    Zambia
                </a>
            </td>
            <td>
                <a href = "http://cy.co.za/atg/stbroz.html">
                    Zimbabwe
                </a>
            </td>
        </tr>
    </table>
  </body>
</html>
```

The result of this XHTML appears in Figure 3.18. The hyperlinks appear neatly arranged in rows and columns. In addition, the explanatory text appears centered above it.

You can get more creative, of course, such as flanking an image with two columns of text. Here's a more advanced example that uses the **rowspan** attribute to create a nice effect:

Figure 3.18   Using a table to arrange hyperlinks in rows and columns.

```
<?xml version="1.0"?>
<!DOCTYPE html PUBLIC "-//W3C//DTD XHTML 1.0 Transitional//EN"
"http://www.w3.org/TR/xhtml1/DTD/xhtml1-transitional.dtd">
<html xmlns="http://www.w3.org/1999/xhtml" xml:lang="en" lang="en">
    <head>
        <title>
            Formatting text with the &lt;table&gt; tag
        </title>
    </head>

    <body>
        <center>
            <h1>
                Formatting text with the &lt;table&gt; tag
            </h1>
        </center>
        <table noborder = "noborder" cellpadding = "8" width = "90%">
            <tr align = "center">
                <th rowspan = "4">
```

```
                <h2>
                    High
                    <br />
                    culture
                    <br />
                    on
                    <br />
                    demand!
                </h2>
            </th>
            <td>
                Download
                <a href="darkness.zip">
                    Joseph Conrad's Heart of Darkness
                </a>
            </td>
        </tr>
        <tr align = "center">
            <td>
                Listen to some of
                <a href = "mozart1.mid">
                    Mozart's music
                </a>
            </td>
        </tr>
        <tr align = "center">
            <td>
                See a
                <a href="chaplin.html">
                    Charlie Chaplin movie
                </a>
            </td>
        </tr>
    </table>
</body>
</html>
```

The results of this XHTML appear in Figure 3.19. As you can see in the figure, you can use tables to format text in very powerful ways.

Another popular use of tables is to accentuate Web-page elements. Because you can set the background color of the cells in a table, you can surround text in colored boxes. I did this earlier in this chapter with this XHTML:

Chapter 3　Arranging Text

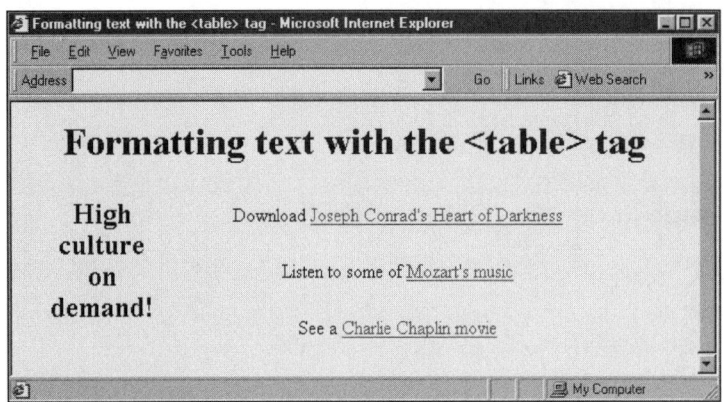

Figure 3.19　Using a table to format text.

```
<?xml version="1.0"?>
<!DOCTYPE html PUBLIC "-//W3C//DTD XHTML 1.0 Transitional//EN"
"http://www.w3.org/TR/xhtml1/DTD/xhtml1-transitional.dtd">
<html xmlns="http://www.w3.org/1999/xhtml" xml:lang="en" lang="en">
    <head>
        <title>
            European Train Travel
        </title>
    </head>

    <body>
        <h1>
            European Train Travel
        </h1>
        So you've decided to take the train in Europe!
        Congratulations, you're in for a great time. There are
        a few things you should know that will make
        things a lot easier. Here's an overview:
        <ul>
            <li>Getting Train Times</li>
            <li>Getting On The Train</li>
            <li>Handling Security</li>
        </ul>

        <h2>
            Getting Train Times
        </h2>
        Many train stations are packed with crowds, especially in
        the summer, and you can save yourself a great deal of time
        waiting in lines that can last an hour or more by getting
```

```
                a complete train schedule, such as Thomas Cook's European
                Timetable.
            <p>
                <table bgcolor="#d0d0d0">
                    <tr>
                        <td>
                            TIP: With a complete train schedule, you'll
                            also become the most popular person in
                            the youth hostel.
                        </td>
                    </tr>
                </table>
            </p>
            <h2>
                Getting On The Train
            </h2>
            In larger stations, you'll find a diagram showing where
            each wagon of the train will stop so if you have a
            reservation for a specific wagon, you can wait in the right
            place with your luggage.
            <p>
                Check the destination of the train, the class of the wagon, and
                whether it's a smoking or non-smoking wagon before getting on.
                This information is displayed on a plaque on the wagon.
            </p>
        </body>
</html>
```

You can see the results of this XHTML in Figure 3.4. Tables are good for many text formatting problems—especially when you get creative.

<layer>—Arranging Text in Layers

Purpose: Creates a layer with content that can overlap other layers.

When used as HTML: Start tag/End tag: Required/Required

Supported: [NS4]

Attributes:

- **above**—Gives the name of the layer that will occur directly above the current layer in the layer z-order (stacking order). Note that only one of these attributes: **z-index**, **above**, or **below**, can be used for a given layer. Set this attribute to an existing layer **id** value. [NS4]

- **background**—Indicates a background image to be tiled on the layer (the default for layers is that they are transparent). Set to the image's URL. [NS4]
- **below**—Gives the name of the layer that will occur directly below the current layer in the layer z-order (stacking order). Note that only one of these attributes: **z-index**, **above**, or **below**, can be used for a given layer. Set this attribute to an existing layer **id** value. [NS4]
- **bgcolor**—Gives the background color of the layer (the default for layers is that they are transparent). Set to a Red, Green, Blue (RGB) color value or a predefined color. [NS4]
- **clip**—Specifies the viewable area of the layer. Using this attribute, you can set the clipping area to values less than the width and height of the content of the layer. Set this attribute to a comma-separated list of integers specifying the pixel coordinates of the clipping rectangle (**clip="100, 100, 400, 400"** or **clip="400, 400"**, where the second form relies on the fact that the left and top settings default to 0). Note that the origin is at the top, left corner, and pixel values grow moving down and to the right. [NS4]
- **height**—Gives the height of the content of the layer and sets up a reference dimension for child layers. Set to positive pixel widths or a percentage of the container. [NS4]
- **id**—Unique alphanumeric identifier for the tag, which you can use to refer to it. [NS4]
- **left**—Gives the left location of the current layer relative to a parent layer if there is one, or the browser window otherwise. Set to an integer specifying screen position or a scripting expression. [NS4]
- **pagex**—Sets the absolute horizontal position of the left boundary of the current layer in relation to the document window. Set to a value giving screen position in pixels or an XHTML scripting expression. [NS4]
- **pagey**—Sets the absolute vertical position of the top boundary of the current layer in relation to the document window. Set to a value giving screen position in pixels or an XHTML scripting expression. [NS4]
- **src**—The URL of an XHTML document to be inserted in the layer (like using **iframe** in Internet Explorer). Set to a URL. [NS4]
- **top**—Gives the top location of the current layer relative to a parent layer if there is one, or the browser window otherwise. Set to an integer specifying screen position or a scripting expression. [NS4]
- **visibility**—Sets whether a layer is visible or not (by default, a layer has the same visibility as its parent layer). Set to: **show** (shows the layer), **hide** (hides the layer), or **inherit** (giving the layer the same visibility as its

parent). For top-level layers without a parent layer, **inherit** means the same as **show**. [NS4]

- **width**—Sets the width of the layer's content, controlling the layer's right margin for wrapping purposes. Set to positive pixel values. [NS4]
- **z-index**—Lets you specify the stacking order of a layer. Layers that have higher **z-index** values go above those with lower **z-index** values. **z-index** values that are positive stack layers above their parents, while negative ones stack them below their parents. Note that only one of these attributes: **z-index**, **above**, or **below**, can be used for a given layer. Set this attribute to an existing layer **id** value. [NS4]

The novice programmer has a problem and says, "All I want to do is display some text on top of other text. Why is that so hard?" You smile and say, "It's not so hard—just use the **<layer>** element." "Tell me all about it!" the NP says.

The **<layer>** element lets you create layers of content in Netscape Navigator. Each layer can hold text, images, and other content and can be stacked on top of other layers.

As you can see by the attribute list, this is an extensive element. I'll take a closer look at **<layer>** when working with dynamic XHTML in Chapters 16 and 17 because this element is the main method used by Netscape Navigator to implement dynamic XHTML. Layers are accessible from scripting languages such as JavaScript. Using a scripting language, you can move layers around as you like, giving the impression of animation.

I'll take a look at this tag now just to get us started. Here's an example showing how to add text to two layers, stacking one on top of the other by using the **left** and **top** attributes:

```
<?xml version="1.0"?>
<!DOCTYPE html PUBLIC "-//W3C//DTD XHTML 1.0 Transitional//EN"
    "http://www.w3.org/TR/xhtml1/DTD/xhtml1-transitional.dtd">
<html xmlns="http://www.w3.org/1999/xhtml" xml:lang="en" lang="en">
<head>
        <title>
            Working with layers
        </title>
    </head>

    <body>

        <h1 align="center">
            Working With Layers
        </h1>
```

```
          <layer name="layer1">
              <h1>This text is in layer 1.</h1>
          </layer>

          <layer name="layer2" left="50" top="80">
              <h1>This text is in layer 2.</h1>
          </layer>
    </body>
</html>
```

The result of this XHTML appears in Figure 3.20.

Unfortunately, Internet Explorer does not support the **<layer>** element, so before you use **<layer>** to arrange text, look at the **<div>** element in the section "Positioning Text with **<div>**" near the end of this chapter.

NOTE: *If you place <layer> tags in an XHTML form and draw controls in the layer, they will not be drawn in the browser. You must place the form in the layer as well.*

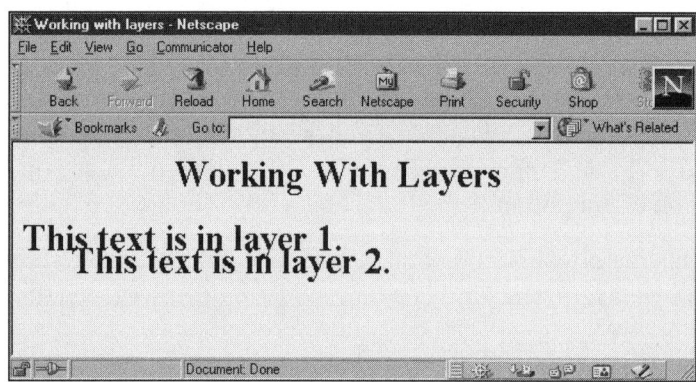

Figure 3.20 Creating overlapping text by using layers in Netscape Navigator.

<nolayer>—Handling Browsers That Don't Handle Layers

Purpose: Exposes text and/or XHTML in browsers that don't handle layers.

When used as HTML: Start tag/End tag: Required/Required

Supported: [NS4]

Attributes: None

To handle browsers that don't handle layers, you use the **<nolayer>** element. The text or XHTML in this element appears in browsers that don't support layers, and it is hidden in those that do. In fact, the **<nolayer>** element is a great place to put the XHTML for a version of your page that doesn't use layers.

Here's an example, displaying a message in browsers that don't support layers:

```
<layer src="coolstuff.html"></layer>
<nolayer>
    This page looks really great in browsers that support the
    &lt;layer&gt; element. Why not get such a browser today?
</nolayer>
```

<ilayer>—Creating Inline Layers

<ilayer>

Purpose: Creates a layer with content that can overlap other layers. An inline version of the **<layer>** tag.

When used as HTML: Start tag/End tag: Required/Required

Supported: [NS4]

Attributes:

- **above**—Gives the name of the layer that will occur directly above the current layer in the layer z-order (stacking order). Note that only one of these attributes: **z-index**, **above**, or **below**, can be used for a given layer. Set this attribute to an existing layer **id** value. [NS4]

- **background**—Indicates a background image to be tiled on the layer (the default for layers is that they are transparent). Set to the image's URL. [NS4]

- **below**—Gives the name of the layer that will occur directly below the current layer in the layer z-order (stacking order). Note that only one of these attributes: **z-index**, **above**, or **below** can be used for a given layer. Set this attribute to an existing layer **id** value. [NS4]

- **bgcolor**—Gives the background color of the layer (the default for layers is that they are transparent). Set to an RGB color value or a predefined color. [NS4]

- **clip**—Specifies the viewable area of the layer. Using this attribute, you can set the clipping area to values less than the width and height of the content of the layer. Set this attribute to a comma-separated list of integers specifying the pixel coordinates of the clipping rectangle (**clip="100, 100, 400, 400"** or

clip="400, 400", where the second form relies on the fact that the left and top settings default to 0). Note that the origin is at the top, left corner, and pixel values grow moving down and to the right. [NS4]

- **height**—Gives the height of the content of the layer and sets up a reference dimension for child layers. Set to positive pixel widths or a percentage of the container. [NS4]
- **id**—Unique alphanumeric identifier for the tag, which you can use to refer to it. [NS4]
- **left**—Gives the left location of the current layer relative to a parent layer if there is one, or the browser window otherwise. Set to an integer specifying the screen position or a scripting expression. [NS4]
- **pagex**—Sets the absolute horizontal position of the left boundary of the current layer in relation to the document window. Set to a value giving the screen position in pixels or an XHTML scripting expression. [NS4]
- **pagey**—Sets the absolute vertical position of the top boundary of the current layer in relation to the document window. Set to a value giving the screen position in pixels or an XHTML scripting expression. [NS4]
- **src**—The URL of an XHTML document to be inserted in the layer (like using **iframe** in Internet Explorer). Set to a URL. [NS4]
- **top**—Gives the top location of the current layer relative to a parent layer if there is one, or the browser window otherwise. Set to an integer specifying the screen position or a scripting expression. [NS4]
- **visibility**—Sets whether a layer is visible or not; by default, a layer has the same visibility as its parent layer. Set to: **SHOW** (shows the layer), **HIDE** (hides the layer), or **INHERIT** (giving the layer the same visibility as its parent). For top-level layers without a parent layer, **INHERIT** means the same as **SHOW**. [NS4]
- **width**—Sets the width of the layer's content, controlling the layer's right margin for wrapping purposes. Set to positive pixel values. [NS4]
- **z-index**—Lets you specify the stacking order of a layer. Layers that have higher **Z-index** values go above those with lower **z-index** values. **z-index** values that are positive stack layers above their parents, while negative ones stack them below their parents. Note that only one of these attributes: **z-index**, **above**, or **below**, can be used for a given layer. Set this attribute to an existing layer **id** value. Set this attribute to integer values. [NS4]

The **<ilayer>** element is to the **<layer>** element as the **<span>** tag is to the **<div>** element. It has much the same function, but rather than creating a standalone structure, the **<ilayer>** is supposed to be used inline (in the middle of other text).

The **<ilayer>** element lets you create layers inline, as in this example, where I'm creating a new layer inline to move some text up a little higher on the page:

```
<?xml version="1.0"?>
<!DOCTYPE html PUBLIC "-//W3C//DTD XHTML 1.0 Transitional//EN"
    "http://www.w3.org/TR/xhtml1/DTD/xhtml1-transitional.dtd">
<html xmlns="http://www.w3.org/1999/xhtml" xml:lang="en" lang="en">
    <head>
        <title>
            Working with layers
        </title>
    </head>

    <body>
        <h1 align="center">
            Working With Inline Layers
        </h1>

        <br />

        <h1>
            This text includes some that
            <ilayer name="layer1" left="5" top="-15">
            <i>pops up</i></ilayer>
            a little.
        </h1>
    </body>
</html>
```

You can see the results of this XHTML in Figure 3.21.

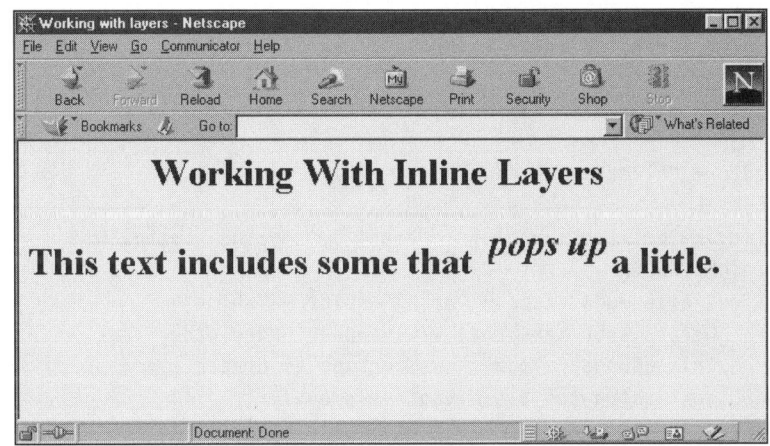

Figure 3.21 Using inline layers in Netscape Navigator.

Chapter 3   Arranging Text

There's a lot more to working with layers, and we'll dig into it later in Chapters 16 and 17. Meanwhile, the previous example showed you some of the possibilities. Unfortunately, Internet Explorer does not support the **<ilayer>** element, so before you use **<ilayer>** to arrange text, take a look at the **<div>** element in the next section, "Positioning Text with **<div>**."

NOTE: *If you place <ilayer> tags in an XHTML form and draw controls in the layer, they will not be drawn in the browser. You must place the form in the layer as well.*

Positioning Text with <div>

"Uh oh," worries the novice programmer, "I've got a problem. I want to overlap some text at a specific location in a Web page, so I can't use a table. On the other hand, the **<layer>** element will do the trick, but it works only in Netscape Navigator." "Well," you say in your capacity as XHTML guru, "you should use the **<div>** element instead."

You can use the **<div>** element's **style** attribute to set its position in a Web page. We'll discuss this more in Chapter 9, but because this chapter discusses positioning and arranging text, this tag deserves some mention here. Here's an example showing how it works and how it displays overlapping text:

```
<?xml version="1.0"?>
<!DOCTYPE html PUBLIC "-//W3C//DTD XHTML 1.0 Transitional//EN"
"http://www.w3.org/TR/xhtml1/DTD/xhtml1-transitional.dtd">
<html xmlns="http://www.w3.org/1999/xhtml" xml:lang="en" lang="en">
    <head>
        <title>
            Using The &lt;div&gt; Element To Overlap Text
        </title>
    </head>

    <body bgcolor= "black">
        <div style="position:absolute; left:100; top:30; width:250;
            height:280">
            <font size = "4" face = "Arial" color = "white">
                Here's some text that will appear under other text.
                This demonstration shows one way to create overlapping
                text using the &lt;div&gt; element.
            </font>
        </div>
```

```
            <div style="position:absolute; left:100; top:0; width:250;
                height:200">
                <font size = "7" face = "Verdana" color = "red">
                    <center>
                        Overlapping
                        Text!
                    </center>
                </font>
            </div>

    </body>
</html>
```

The result of this XHTML appears in Figure 3.22. As you can see, I've created overlapping text with the **<div>** element, which will work in both Netscape Navigator and Internet Explorer. To do so, I've used the **position**, **left**, **top**, **width**, and **height** styles.

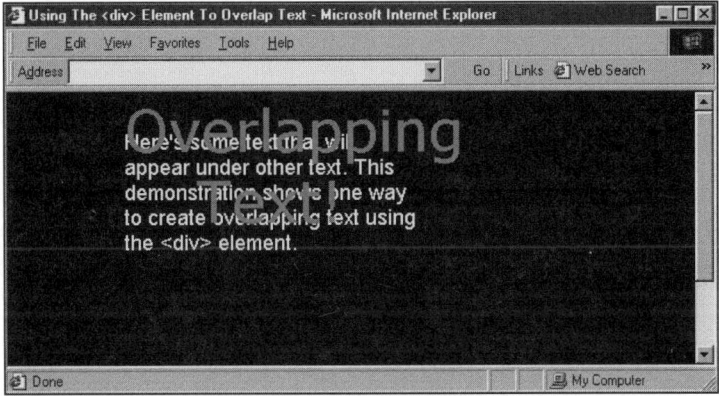

Figure 3.22   Using the **<div>** element to position text.

<ruby>, <rbc>, <rtc>, <rb>, <rt>, <rp>—Creating Ruby (Captioned) Text

There's one thing to point out here—by default, the ruby text is very small and nearly unreadable, so I'm using a larger font size for all the text. The result appears in Figure 3.23.

Following are details about the tags used to create the ruby base and ruby text elements.

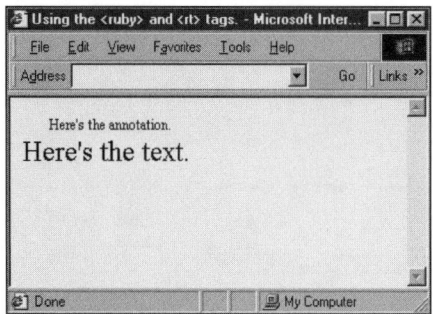

Figure 3.23   Creating ruby text.

<ruby>

Purpose: Creates a *ruby*, which is a set of text and a related annotation or caption.

When used as HTML: Start tag/End tag: Required/Required

Supported: [1.1, IE5]

Attributes:

- **class**—Class of the element (used for rendering). [1.1, IE5]
- **dir**—Gives the direction of directionally neutral text (text that doesn't have inherent direction in which you should read it). Possible values: **ltr**: left-to-right text or table and **rtl**: right-to-left text or table. [1.1, IE5]
- **id**—Unique alphanumeric identifier for the tag, which you can use to refer to it. [1.1, IE5]
- **lang**—Base language used for the tag. [1.1, IE5]
- **language**—Scripting language used for the tag. [IE5]
- **name**—Sets the name of the element. Set to alphanumeric text. [IE5]
- **style**—Inline style indicating how to render the element. [1.1, IE5]
- **title**—Holds additional information (which might be displayed in tool tips) for the element. [1.1, IE5]
- **xml:lang**—Holds the base language for the element when the document is interpreted as an XML document. [1.1]

XHTML events: onclick, ondblclick, onmousedown, onmouseup, onmouseover, onmousemove, onmouseout, onkeypress, onkeydown, onkeyup

<rbc>

Purpose: Contains **<rb>** elements, used in rubies that group items.

Supported: [1.1]

Attributes:

- **class**—Class of the element (used for rendering). [1.1]
- **dir**—Gives the direction of directionally neutral text (text that doesn't have inherent direction in which you should read it). Possible values: **ltr**: left-to-right text or table and **rtl**: right-to-left text or table. [1.1]
- **id**—Unique alphanumeric identifier for the tag, which you can use to refer to it. [1.1]
- **lang**—Base language used for the tag. [1.1]
- **style**—Inline style indicating how to render the element. [1.1]
- **title**—Holds additional information (which might be displayed in tool tips) for the element. [1.1]
- **xml:lang**—Holds the base language for the element when the document is interpreted as an XML document. [1.1]

XHTML events: onclick, ondblclick, onmousedown, onmouseup, onmouseover, onmousemove, onmouseout, onkeypress, onkeydown, onkeyup

<rtc>

Purpose: Container for **<rt>** elements.

Supported: [1.1]

Attributes:

- **class**—Class of the element (used for rendering). [1.1]
- **dir**—Gives the direction of directionally neutral text (text that doesn't have inherent direction in which you should read it). Possible values: **ltr**: left-to-right text or table and **rtl**: right-to-left text or table. [1.1]
- **id**—Unique alphanumeric identifier for the tag, which you can use to refer to it. [1.1]
- **lang**—Base language used for the tag. [1.1]
- **style**—Inline style indicating how to render the element. [1.1]
- **title**—Holds additional information (which might be displayed in tool tips) for the element. [1.1]

- **xml:lang**—Holds the base language for the element when the document is interpreted as an XML document. [1.1]

XHTML events: onclick, ondblclick, onmousedown, onmouseup, onmouseover, onmousemove, onmouseout, onkeypress, onkeydown, onkeyup

<rb>

Purpose: Container for the text of the ruby base. In a simple ruby, only one **<rb>** element can appear. In a group ruby, multiple **<rb>** elements can appear inside an **<rbc>** element, and each **<rb>** element can be connected to an **<rt>** element.

Supported: [1.1]

Attributes:

- **class**—Class of the element (used for rendering). [1.1]
- **dir**—Gives the direction of directionally neutral text (text that doesn't have inherent direction in which you should read it). Possible values: **ltr**: left-to-right text or table and **rtl**: right-to-left text or table. [1.1]
- **id**—Unique alphanumeric identifier for the tag, which you can use to refer to it. [1.1]
- **lang**—Base language used for the tag. [1.1]
- **style**—Inline style indicating how to render the element. [1.1]
- **title**—Holds additional information (which might be displayed in tool tips) for the element. [1.1]
- **xml:lang**—Holds the base language for the element when the document is interpreted as an XML document. [1.1]

XHTML events: onclick, ondblclick, onmousedown, onmouseup, onmouseover, onmousemove, onmouseout, onkeypress, onkeydown, onkeyup

<rt>

Purpose: Creates ruby text (the annotation or caption).

When used as HTML: Start tag/End tag: Required/Optional

Supported: [1.1, IE5]

Attributes:

- **class**—Class of the element (used for rendering). [1.1, IE5]

- **dir**—Gives the direction of directionally neutral text (text that doesn't have inherent direction in which you should read it). Possible values: **ltr**: left-to-right text or table and **rtl**: right-to-left text or table. [1.1, IE5]
- **id**—Unique alphanumeric identifier for the tag, which you can use to refer to it. [1.1, IE5]
- **lang**—Base language used for the tag. [1.1, IE5]
- **language**—Scripting language used for the tag. [IE5]
- **name**—Sets the name of the element. Set to alphanumeric text. [IE5]
- **style**—Inline style indicating how to render the element. [1.1, IE5]
- **title**—Holds additional information (which might be displayed in tool tips) for the element. [1.1, IE5]
- **xml:lang**—Holds the base language for the element when the document is interpreted as an XML document. [1.1]

XHTML events: onclick, ondblclick, onmousedown, onmouseup, onmouseover, onmousemove, onmouseout, onkeypress, onkeydown, onkeyup

<rp>

Purpose: Contains parenthesis characters in a simple ruby.

Supported: [1.1]

Attributes:

- **class**—Class of the element (used for rendering). [1.1]
- **dir**—Gives the direction of directionally neutral text (text that doesn't have inherent direction in which you should read it). Possible values: **ltr**: left-to-right text or table and **rtl**: right-to-left text or table. [1.1]
- **id**—Unique alphanumeric identifier for the tag, which you can use to refer to it. [1.1]
- **lang**—Base language used for the tag. [1.1]
- **style**—Inline style indicating how to render the element. [1.1]
- **title**—Holds additional information (which might be displayed in tool tips) for the element. [1.1]
- **xml:lang**—Holds the base language for the element when the document is interpreted as an XML document. [1.1]

XHTML events: onclick, ondblclick, onmousedown, onmouseup, onmouseover, onmousemove, onmouseout, onkeypress, onkeydown, onkeyup

Rubies, new in XHTML 1.1 and Internet Explorer 5, are content/caption text pairs. When you want to annotate text or add captions to text explaining that text, you can use rubies. Probably the most common use of rubies is to provide pronunciation guides to foreign language text.

The ruby base element, **<ruby>**, holds the main content text, and the ruby text itself, **<rt>**, holds the annotation or caption, which is displayed in a smaller font above the ruby base. Here's an example showing how to use these elements:

```
<?xml version="1.0"?>
<!DOCTYPE html PUBLIC "-//W3C//DTD XHTML 1.1//EN"
    "http://www.w3.org/TR/xhtml11/DTD/xhtml11.dtd">
<html xmlns="http://www.w3.org/1999/xhtml" xml:lang="en" lang="en">
    <head>
        <title>
            Using the &lt;ruby&gt; and &lt;rt&gt; tags.
        </title>
    </head>

    <body>
        <font size="5">
            <ruby>
                Here's the text.
                <rt>Here's the annotation.</rt>
            </ruby>
        </font>
    </body>
</html>
```

There's one thing to point out here—by default, the ruby text is very small and nearly unreadable, so I'm using a larger font size for all the text. The result appears in Figure 3.24.

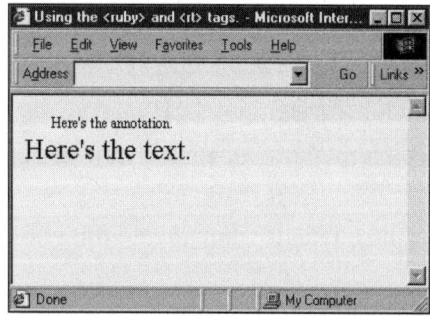

Figure 3.24   Creating ruby text.

Chapter 4

Working with Images

If you need an immediate solution to:	See page:
Creating Transparent GIF Images	220
Creating Interlaced GIF Images	221
Creating Animated GIF Images	223
Testing Your Images	224
`<img>`—Adding an Image to a Web Page	225
Displaying Alternate Text in Place of Images	229
Allocating Space for an Image	231
Adding Borders to Images	232
Adding Space around Images	234
Aligning Text and Images	235
Avoiding Text Wrapping	239
Scaling Images to Different Sizes	241
Using the **lowsrc** Attribute for Image Previews	243
Setting Page Background Images	243
Using the `<object>` Tag to Insert Images	245
Using Images to Replace Missing Content	246
Tiling Images—Creating Image Mosaics	247
Creating Overlapping Images	250

In Depth

This is our chapter on handling images, and as far as I am concerned, one could talk forever about images on the Web. There's so much material that it would easily fit into a book by itself. After all, how can you overestimate the power of graphics in Web pages?

In this chapter, we'll see how to put images in Web pages, how to display alternate text for browsers unable to display images, how to let the text in your page flow around images, what kind of images to use and when, how to put borders around images, how to overlap images, and more.

Images in Web Pages

Images are stored in files outside your Web pages, which means that you upload the files to your Web server separately from your Web pages. Using the **<img>** element, you can *point* to an image, and the Web browser will read that image from your server and place it directly into the page.

Following is an example showing how this works. I'm telling the Web browser that it will find the image I want to use at **www.starpowder.com/steve/image.gif**, that the image is 252 pixels wide and 115 pixels high, and that the text to display while the browser is loading the image or if the browser doesn't display images, is simply, "an image." Note that **<img>** is an empty tag, so I end it with **/>**. Here's the example:

```
<?xml version="1.0"?>
<!DOCTYPE html PUBLIC "-//W3C//DTD XHTML 1.0 Transitional//EN"
"http://www.w3.org/TR/xhtml1/DTD/xhtml1-transitional.dtd">
<html xmlns="http://www.w3.org/1999/xhtml" xml:lang="en" lang="en">
    <head>
        <title>
            Using the &lt;img&gt; tag.
        </title>
    </head>

    <body>
        <center>
            <h1>
                Working With Images
            </h1>
```

```
        </center>
        Here's an image:
        <img src="http://www.starpowder.com/steve/image.gif"
            width="252" height="115" alt="an image" />
    </body>
</html>
```

The result of this XHTML appears in Figure 4.1. As you can see, the image that I want to load, **www.starpowder.com/steve/image.gif**, appears in the Web page as planned. I've also included some text that appears on the same line as the image, but the result looks a little odd because the image is so much taller than the text. This is one of the issues I'll discuss at some length throughout the "Immediate Solutions" section—mixing text and graphics in a Web page.

TIP: *Something to bear in mind when you're working with images is that a URL like **www.starpowder.com/steve/image.gif** is a perfectly good URL (note that this is just an example; there's no actual image at this URL), and you can enter it directly into your browser to see the corresponding image. If for some reason your browser can't find an image in your Web page, you can enter its full URL directly to check on the location of the image.*

As we'll see in Chapter 5, you don't have to specify the full URL of an image to display it in your Web page; you can use a *relative URL*, which gives the location of the image file relative to the current page. If you've placed image.gif in the same directory as the Web page, you can just refer to the image file by name, like this:

```
<?xml version="1.0"?>
<!DOCTYPE html PUBLIC "-//W3C//DTD XHTML 1.0 Transitional//EN"
    "http://www.w3.org/TR/xhtml1/DTD/xhtml1-transitional.dtd">
<html xmlns="http://www.w3.org/1999/xhtml" xml:lang="en" lang="en">
    <head>
        <title>
            Using the &lt;img&gt; tag.
        </title>
    </head>

    <body>
        <center>
            <h1>
                Working With Images
            </h1>
        </center>
        Here's an image:
        <img src="image.gif" width="252" height="115" alt="an image" />
    </body>
</html>
```

Figure 4.1 Displaying an image in a Web page.

This XHTML works just as the previous example did and has the added advantage that the Web browser can use the same HTTP connection to get the image from a relative URL, saving you some time.

Internal vs. External Images

The image in Figure 4.1 is called an *inline image:* one that the browser (as opposed to a different application) displays as part of the Web page. Inline images must be in a format that the Web browser can handle, such as Graphics Interchange Format (GIF) or Joint Photographic Experts Group (JPEG) format, and for some browsers, Portable Network Graphics (PNG) format. (I'll discuss these formats in the next section.)

Image files can take many formats, such as PICT for the Macintosh, Tagged Image File Format (TIFF), XBM, and BMP. You may have illustration, paint, or page-layout applications that can display images in these formats. If your browser can find these programs (for example, if the applications are registered in Windows to handle specific file types), it can download images in these formats and start the appropriate image-displaying program.

To work with images stored in file formats that the browser doesn't handle, or to let users see very large graphic files if they want to, you can link to those image files. Doing so treats those files as *external images* as opposed to inline images. Here's an example in which I treat image.gif as an external image by linking to it with a type of hyperlink that we'll see how to create in Chapter 5:

```
<?xml version="1.0"?>
<!DOCTYPE html PUBLIC "-//W3C//DTD XHTML 1.0 Transitional//EN"
"http://www.w3.org/TR/xhtml1/DTD/xhtml1-transitional.dtd">
<html xmlns="http://www.w3.org/1999/xhtml" xml:lang="en" lang="en">
```

```
<head>
    <title>
        Using the &lt;img&gt; tag.
    </title>
</head>

<body>
    <center>
        <h1>
            Working With External Images
        </h1>
    </center>
    Here's an
    <a href="image.gif">image</a>.
</body>
</html>
```

This page appears in Figure 4.2. When the user clicks the hyperlink to the image, the image appears in the browser window, as you see in Figure 4.3.

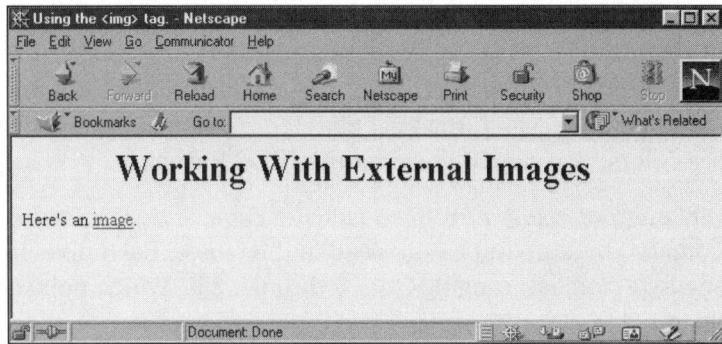

Figure 4.2   Displaying a link to an external image.

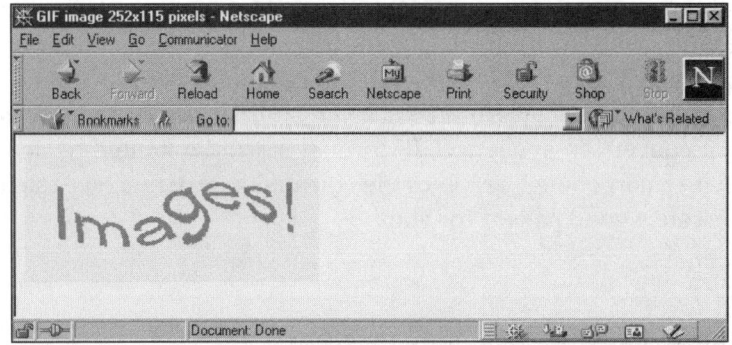

Figure 4.3   Displaying an external image.

As you start to work with graphics, you'll find it's an area with great depth—there's always something else to know. Broadly speaking, images are divided into two large categories: *bitmap* or *raster graphics* (which are often photographs, images composed in paint programs, or other types of continuous-tone images) and *vector graphics* (also called *line art*). As you can gather from its name, line art is drawn art, often containing high-resolution graphics and steep color gradients between elements. Of the two main graphic formats, GIF and JPEG, GIF is better for line art and JPEG is more suitable for photographic images.

Graphics File Formats

Although there are plenty of graphics file formats in existence, some of which I've already mentioned, like PICT, TIFF, XBM, BMP, JPEG, and GIF, you can't count on browsers knowing more than two standard formats—GIF and JPEG.

TIP: *Web servers and browsers know what kind of image file format you're using based on its file extension, such as .gif (for GIF files) and .jpg (for JPEG files). It's important to use the file extension for that reason. In fact, if you're working with a nonstandard file format, your Web server may not know how to handle it and try to convert it to text.*

GIF Format

GIF images were created by CompuServe and they are now stored in a format patented by Unisys. The GIF image format is limited to 256 colors, so if you want to work with more colors, you should consider the JPEG format.

GIF images use an *indexed color map* (also called a *color index*, *color lookup table* [CLUT], or *palette*) to store the colors used in the image. Each pixel in the image stores a one-byte number, ranging from 0 through 255, which points to a location in the palette.

The upshot is that, although you can store high-resolution images with the GIF format, you can use only 256 colors. Which of the 256 colors you use is up to you. If you have a good graphics software program, it will let you set the palette of colors yourself. When a GIF file is displayed, the image looks like it contains a lot more than 256 colors. What's really happening is that colors in the palette are *dithered*, which means that they are mixed using alternating pixels of various colors. When you convert an image to GIF format, it will be limited to the 256 colors. If you have a smart enough graphics file conversion program (see the next section), it can create a good palette for you.

TIP: *If you can use your software to reduce the number of colors in the image or if you start by drawing an image of only a few colors, then the palette can be smaller, and the resulting file can also be smaller. In general, it's a good idea to shoot for small palettes and small file sizes to make downloading the image easier and faster. Using color reduction techniques, you can create two-color images of full Web-page size that download faster than a small full-color image would. For example, look at the image in the Web page in Figure 4.1; it has few colors, so even stretched to a huge 1000×460 pixel size (larger than most Web pages), it's only 5K, which downloads in five or so seconds.*

In general, the GIF file format is a good choice for line-art graphics, graphics with few colors, and graphics that have a sharp gradation in color between elements.

There's one significant issue with the GIF format you should know about—it's patented by Unisys Corporation. Actually, Unisys has patented the Lempel Ziv Welch (LZW) data compression and decompression technology used to create and read GIF files. Software that creates or displays LZW-compressed GIF files should have a license from Unisys.

Because the GIF compression format is patented, it has had a dampening effect on developing software that uses GIF files. For example, if you write a program that's freeware (that is, freely available) but displays GIF files and you distribute it, Unisys requires that you license its technology. The licensing fees start at a rate of several thousand dollars and continue with fees (less than a dollar usually) for each copy of the software you distribute, even if your software is free. There's an ongoing debate about the patent; some people say that only the creation of GIF and other LZW files is patented, not reading and decompressing them. Although Internet Explorer has a license from Unisys, some other major browsers do not.

NOTE: *To find out more about the LZW patent and to get licensing information, see* **www.unisys.com**.

In any case, many people feel that they want to avoid the GIF format. Other formats are being explored, including the PNG format, which uses a different compression algorithm. The feeling among some developers is that the GIF format is slowly on the way out, although that remains to be seen.

TIP: *The PNG home page is* **www.cdrom.com/pub/png/png.html**. *To see a list of browsers that support the PNG format, see* **www.cdrom.com/pub/png/pngapbr.html**. *Currently, 48 browsers are listed, including Internet Explorer and Netscape Navigator.*

There are two GIF formats: GIF87, which is the standard format; and GIF89a, which supports image transparency and animation (called *animated GIFs*). Image transparency makes the background color clear so that images can appear in a variety of shapes.

In addition, GIF files can be *interlaced*, which means that they appear progressively in the Web browser as they are downloaded. While being downloaded, interlaced GIFs are displayed as full size but gradually improve in resolution. Many graphics programs let you store GIF images as interlaced. (I'll take a look at how the process works in the "Immediate Solutions" section "Creating Interlaced GIF Images.")

JPEG Format

JPEG (often abbreviated to JPG and used as the file extension) takes its name from the group that first created the format. Unlike GIF with its restricted format, you can create JPEG images using a virtually unlimited number of colors. The three popular formats use 256 colors (one byte per pixel, holding a color value from 0 through 255), 65,536 colors (two bytes per pixel), or 16,777,216 colors (three bytes per pixel).

Like GIF, JPEG files are stored as compressed. JPEG is a compression technology that can store images with various levels of perfection. Conversion software, such as LView Pro (**www.lview.com**), will let you set how perfectly an image is stored. Although there's less dithering with JPEG images than with GIF images, the JPEG compression format loses some precision in the image and has a tougher time dealing with sharp gradients in the image. On the other hand, JPEG image files are usually smaller for photographic images, which is what makes them so popular on Usenet, where they've just about replaced GIF files entirely.

In general, the JPEG format is a good choice for photographs that don't have sharp gradients and for images that have many colors, but not for line art or high-resolution graphics.

So which is the best format for a particular image, GIF or JPEG? It depends on your image and what you're shooting for. If you have a large image that you want to store in a small file, try JPEG, but you should also try using software that helps you convert the image to a small palette for use in GIF files. You can't tell which format will give you the smallest—and therefore the quickest—downloaded image file until you actually create the file. By putting in some hard work, I've been able to use such small palettes that huge images are packed into small files and downloaded in a snap. When you're using GIF files, use as few colors as you can get away with. The rule of thumb for 14.4K modems (although most are faster than that now) is that 1K of an image file downloads in one second, so it's best to keep your images smaller than 20K. It's also important to look at the resulting image. JPEG images that have lots of sharp gradients may be considerably distorted when uncompressed.

Wonder what graphics programs are out there to help you create images and convert them to various formats so you can find out which one is right for you? There are thousands of such programs, and I'll take a look at a few of them next.

Graphics Programs and Resources

There are so many graphics programs available that it's just about impossible to list them all. Some are free, some are shareware, some are expensive, and some are *very* expensive. Here's a starter list, beginning with what many Web designers consider the cream of the crop—Adobe Photoshop.

- *Adobe Photoshop and Illustrator (**www.adobe.com/prodindex/**)*—Use Photoshop for photographs and Illustrator for line art. These are top-of-the-line applications with seemingly endless capabilities.
- *Alchemy Mindworks' GIF Construction Set (**www.mindworkshop.com/alchemy/alchemy.html**)*—Lets you create animated GIFs as well as convert graphics formats and transparent GIFs.
- *Andreas Ley's GIFTrans (**ftp://ftp.rz.uni-karlsruhe.de/pub/net/www/tools/**)*—Makes transparent GIFs.
- *CorelDRAW! And PHOTO-PAINT (**www.corel.com**)*—Less expensive than Adobe and very powerful. Corel has been around a long time and is the choice of many Web designers.
- *DeBabelizer (**www.equil.com**)*—Lets you perform batch manipulations on many files at the same time, including finding the best palette automatically.
- *GIMP (**www.gimp.org**)*—Gnu Image Manipulation Program (GIMP) is a graphics editor and photo retouching program that works under Unix X Windows.
- *John Bradley's XV Image Viewer (**www.trilon.com/xv/**)*—Unix X Windows package. Multiple types of file conversions performed.
- *LView Pro (**www.lview.com**)*—Used for interchanging formats, creating transparent GIFs, and displaying files with multiple file formats.
- *Macromedia Freehand Graphics Studio (**www.macromedia.com**)*—Used for creating animated line art.
- *Paint Shop Pro (**www.jasc.com**)*—Used for hobby Web design.
- *SPG's ColorWorks: Web 3 (**www.spg-net.com**)*—Provides GIF animation optimization that can shrink animated GIFs by 50 percent, an image library browser, a Web graphics spider that downloads all the images from a site, and more.

Of course, to create images, you can also use software that comes with your operating system, such as Windows Paint (select Start|Programs|Accessories|Paint) in Windows. Paint can create images only in BMP (Windows bitmap) format, however, so you'll need a file-conversion program, like LView Pro, to convert your bitmaps to GIF or JPEG formats.

There are also online programs that let you create graphics online, such as CoolText.Com (**www.cooltext.com**). This service uses GIMP technology to let you create flashy text with a variety of special effects, such as starbursts and special textures.

In addition to these resources, you can also find free clip art on the Internet.

Using Clip Art

Many Web developers prefer not to have to create their own graphics—they get it ready-made from the Internet. Ready-made art is called *clip art*, and although it was originally popular to get snappy images for buttons and navigational aids in Web pages, clip-art images are getting more and more involved all the time.

NOTE: *Here's the requisite note on being careful about copyrights when you're downloading art from the Internet. If you download something from someone else's Web page and use it in your own page, that's likely to be copyright infringement—you're just asking for trouble. People can embed copyright notices inside graphics—it's very easy to do with animated GIFs, for example—so be careful about "borrowing" any art that may be copyrighted. Often a simple email to the Web page's creator can result in getting permission to use some graphics from the site; I've used this method a few times when I saw an outstanding piece of art that I wanted to use. Of course, on Web sites that advertise free, noncopyrighted clip art, you're all set.*

There's a great deal of free clip art available. A Web search engine turns up a mere 11,433 matches for the string "free clip art." Here's a short starter list:

- *Barry's Clip Art Server (**www.barrysclipart.com/index.html**)*—A huge collection of art, and the place I go to first. Also has animated GIFs.
- *iBAND Clip Art Mega Site (**www.iband.com/clip/clipart.html**)*—This site has many categories of art and is worth a look.
- *Wagon Train Animated GIFs (**http://dreamartists.com**)*—A collection of animated GIFs.
- *XOOM's Free Clip Art Library (**http://xoom.com/clips/website/**)*—A pretty good selection of art.

When you go to a site advertising free clip art, you'll see pages and pages of clip art. For instance, see Figure 4.4 to view a page from Barry's Clip Art Server.

TIP: *So how do you copy an image from a clip-art page to your own computer? If you're using Netscape Navigator or Internet Explorer on a PC, right-click the image and select Save Picture As in Internet Explorer or Save Image As in Netscape Navigator. If you're using a Macintosh, press the mouse button on the image you want to copy, and then select Save As.*

Graphics Color

Now that you're working with graphics programs, it's worthwhile knowing how to handle color in these programs. In Chapter 1, we saw the most common way of

In Depth

Figure 4.4   Finding clip art.

specifying colors directly—as color values, also called Red, Green, Blue (RGB) triplets.

Using RGB triplets, colors are expressed as **rrggbb**, where **rr** specifies the red component of the color, **gg** specifies the green component, and **bb** specifies the blue component. Color values range from 0 through 255 and are expressed as a hexadecimal (Base16) two-digit number. The only trick to utilizing RGB triplets is getting used to hexadecimal values, which range from 00 to *ff* (hexadecimal *ff* = 255 because hex digits range from 0 to 9 and then from a to f).

Here are some examples: the color value for pure red is **ff0000**, bright white is **ffffff**, black is **000000**, gray is **080808**, and yellow is **ffff00**. For more about RGB triplets, see Chapter 1.

The second way of specifying color is by using the Hue, Saturation, Brightness (HSB) method. This technique is modeled after the way you see color. *Hue* is the actual color, such as red or blue. Hue is specified with a color wheel that displays colors from 0 to 360 degrees. Red is at 0 and 360 degrees, yellow is at 120, blue is at 240, and so on.

Brightness indicates the intensity of the color. For example, even red can appear very dark without a lot of light shining on it. Brightness varies from 0 to 100.

Finally, *saturation* is the amount of color. The more the saturation, the more intense the color. Saturation values range from 0 to 100; lower values give you pastel-like colors, and higher values give you very strong colors.

Working with RGB values is far more common than using the HSB model, but you should know about both if you are going to work with graphics programs. In fact, most graphics programs that work with color let you specify color either way, so the final choice is up to you. It's a good idea to find out which one you feel more comfortable with.

Creating Images

There are thousands of programs available to create images, and some are very, very costly. However, if you're just starting out, it's a good idea to get at least a file converter, like LView Pro (**www.lview.com**), which is a program that also lets you create transparent and interlaced GIFs. You can use this kind of utility with an application you may already have, such as the Windows Paint program shown in Figure 4.5.

In Figure 4.5, the image I'm working with will be saved in the only format available, Windows BMP format. I can use a file converter to convert the file to GIF or JPEG format. Using LView Pro, open the BMP file, select Save As from the File menu, and save the file in the desired format. You can also customize the image's palette with the Retouch menu's Color Depth option. The image appears in LView Pro in Figure 4.6. Note that while the image is being converted to a GIF format, the dimensions of the image, 252×115 pixels, appear in LView Pro's title bar. This is handy information because you'll need these dimensions to use the image in a Web page.

Figure 4.5   Creating images.

In Depth

Figure 4.6 Opening an image in a file converter.

There are other ways of getting images, of course. You can also scan them in. Scanners are becoming cheaper and cheaper and are supporting higher resolutions. It's a good idea to use a high-resolution scan in a small image file to reduce download time, and then expand that image in your Web page (see the "Immediate Solutions" section "Scaling Images to Different Sizes").

After you've scanned the image, the scanner software might save the image in an unappealing format. For example, some scanners create multimegabyte BMP files. To convert the file, you can use a shareware program such as LView Pro. The program also allows you to save the file in another format, resize it, and change the shading to lighten or darken it as you like. You can even adjust the contrast. There's no end to the ways in which images can be manipulated.

Creating Transparent GIF Images

"Hey," says the novice programmer, "I've created some terrific icons I want to use as bullets in a bulleted list, but there's a problem—each bullet is supposed to be round, but my graphics program can only store rectangular images." "Ah," you say, "it's time for a transparent GIF." The NP asks, "It's time for *what*?"

One powerful aspect of the GIF format is that images can be *transparent*. What this means is that you select a background color to make the background transparent. When the image is displayed, the transparent background allows the underlying image to become visible.

For example, look at the image in Figure 4.1. As you can see, it has a rectangular shape. However, by making the background of the image transparent, I can make it appear as though the swirling text is alone on the page. I start by loading the image into LView Pro, shown in Figure 4.6. Then I select Options|Background Color to open the Select Color Palette Entry dialog box you see in Figure 4.7.

Using this dialog, I can select the color that I want to make transparent—the image background color. To do that, I click on the Dropper button and then move to the image itself. The mouse cursor changes to a medicine-dropper shape, and I

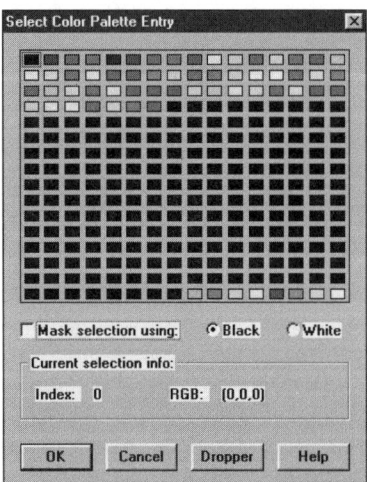

Figure 4.7 Selecting a color to make transparent.

just click anywhere on the background of the image. LView Pro makes that the background color. Finally, I save the new image, selecting GIF89a, the format that supports transparent GIFs, in the Save File As Type option in the Save Image As dialog box.

The results appear in Figure 4.8. As you can see in the figure, the background of the image is invisible, and the swirling text appears directly in the page.

TIP: *As you can imagine, using transparent GIFs is great when you want to use images that don't look rectangular, such as bullets in front of list items.*

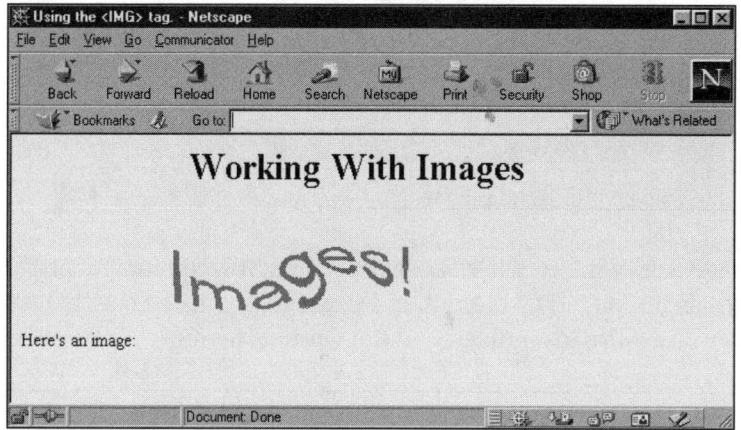

Figure 4.8   Displaying a transparent GIF file.

Creating Interlaced GIF Images

"Jeez," says the novice programmer, "images are great, but they take so long to download! I'm just sitting here watching a blank page in my browser." "Well," you say, "apart from using alternate text for images with the **alt** attribute, you can use interlaced GIFs to let the browser build the image progressively as it downloads more data." "Swell!" says the NP. "How does it work?"

Interlaced GIFs are written in such a way that the browser can display the whole image almost immediately in very low resolution, adding resolution as time goes on. For example, in Figure 4.9, I'm downloading the image as an interlaced GIF. We'll use this figure as an image map in Chapter 5. You can see that the text in the image is still rather crude at this early stage of the download, but as time goes on, it will get sharper. The idea here is that the user has something to look at instead of staring at a blank space while waiting for the image to finish downloading.

Chapter 4 Working with Images

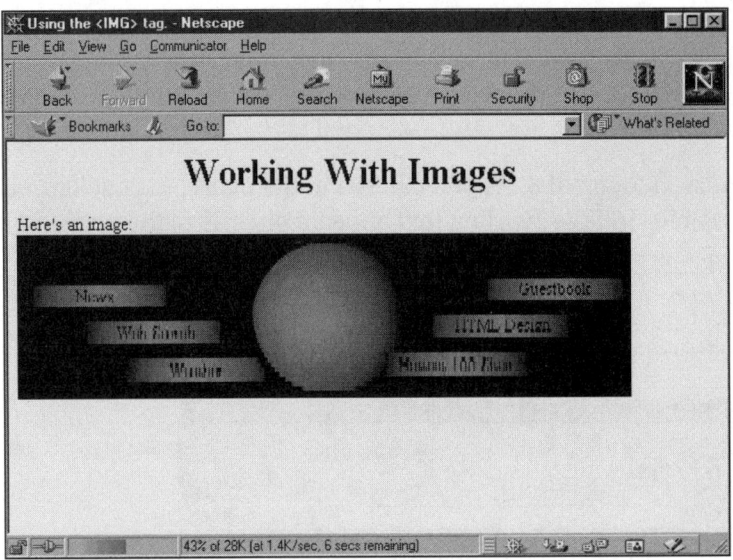

Figure 4.9   Downloading an interlaced GIF file.

How do you create an interlaced GIF? These days, most file-conversion programs store GIF images as interlaced by default. In Figure 4.10, you can see that it's the default setting in LView Pro, as indicated in the Options menu.

TIP: *You can't interlace JPEG images. However, a new format being developed, called progressive JPEGs, is similar. Programs such as Adobe Photoshop let you create progressive JPEG files.*

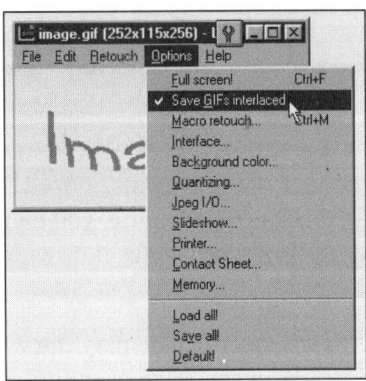

Figure 4.10   The LView Pro Options menu.

Creating Animated GIF Images

"Say," wonders the novice programmer, "what about creating animated images? Can I do that?" "Sure you can," you say, "provided you have the right software."

Animated GIF images have become very popular in Web pages. (Animated images are often used in those annoying banner ads.) There are a number of popular applications for creating animated GIF images; one application is Alchemy Mindworks' GIF Construction Set (**www.mindworkshop.com/alchemy/alchemy.html**).

You can see the GIF Construction Set at work in Figure 4.11. I'm creating a banner ad using the standard size for each image in the animation (468×60 pixels). As you can see in the figure, the animated GIF starts with a header announcing the format and size of the image. This header is automatically created when you create a new animated GIF, and the default size of the animated GIF is 640×480 pixels. Click on the Edit button to edit the header settings, and change it to the same size as the GIF files you're going to use in the animation (each of which must be exactly the same size, or some browsers will have problems). If you don't enter the image's correct size, the browser is going to allocate the wrong size for the image in the Web page.

After the header comes a **LOOP** command, which you can add by clicking the Insert button. By selecting the **LOOP** command and clicking on the Edit button, you can set the number of times the animation will execute. After the **LOOP** command, I've inserted a **CONTROL** command before each image; I edited this

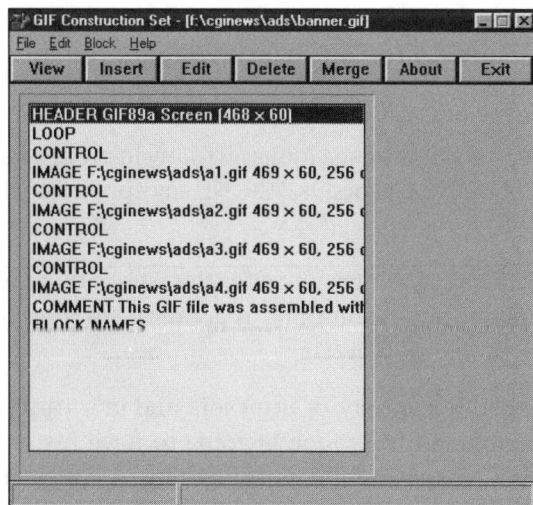

Figure 4.11   Using the GIF Construction Set to make an animated GIF.

command to set the delay for each image to 1/100 of a second. Following each delay is an **IMAGE** command added by clicking on the Insert button, which you use to load an image.

When you insert a new image, the GIF Construction Set asks you what palette to use, as you see in Figure 4.12. Although the default selection is Dither This Image To The Global Palette, I recommend that you use the Remap This Image To The Global Palette option because it produces the best results.

After you're done creating your **LOOP** and **CONTROL** statements, select File|Save As to save your new animated GIF image.

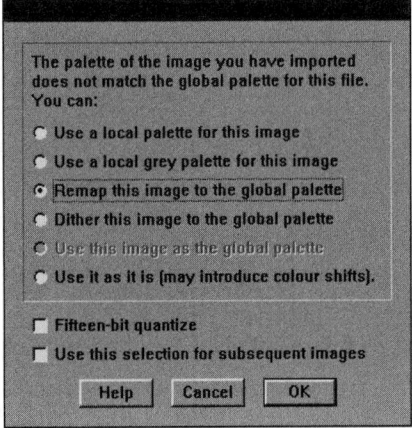

Figure 4.12 Setting a palette in the GIF Construction Set.

Testing Your Images

"Hey," says the novice programmer, "my new image looks all funny in my browser." "Kind of wide, isn't it?" you ask. "About 12,000 pixels," the NP says proudly. "Hm," you say.

One thing to bear in mind as you develop your graphics for the Web is that they'll be viewed in a variety of environments and resolutions. A good rule of thumb for image width is that it should be less than 600 pixels.

Ideally, you should test your images in a variety of browsers and in a variety of graphical environments. For example, not everyone is going to have his or her screen resolution set to 1,582×1,582 pixels, so this is something to consider. In addition, some people are still using screens that can display only 256 colors (or have set their screens to 256 colors in order to use programs that require it), so it's a good idea to take a look at your images after setting your screen to 256 colors.

Another consideration is download time—the general rule here is that 1K of image takes one second to download (although that's based on 14.4K modems, so downloads can actually be faster today). A file that's 50K can take 50 seconds to download, which is something to keep in mind because people who browse the Web can have very short attention spans. If your images are more than 20K, you might consider using *thumbnail images* instead. Thumbnails are smaller versions of an image—when clicked, they take the user to a larger version of the image on another page. You can use graphics programs to shrink an image, and there are dedicated applications that produce thumbnail images *en masse*.

Another way to reduce file size is to use palette reduction. If you can reduce the number of colors in an image, you can save a great deal of space. For example, because the image in the Web page in Figure 4.1 uses so few colors, I was able to enlarge it to a huge 1,000×460 pixels, but its image file was only 5K. Other images that size, using many colors, would be 100K or more. Smart software, like Adobe Photoshop, can help you with a number of palette reduction techniques.

<img>—Adding an Image to a Web Page

Purpose: Inserts an image into a Web page. This element does not contain any content.

When used as HTML: Start tag/End tag: Required/Omitted

Supported: [1.0S, 1.0T, 1.0F, 1.1, 2, 3, 3.2, 4, IE1, IE2, IE3, IE4, IE5, NS1, NS2, NS3, NS4]

Attributes:

- **align**—Sets the alignment of text, which follows the **img** reference relative to the image on the screen. You use **left** and **right** to indicate horizontal alignment of the image in the browser window, and the text that follows will wrap around the image. You use the other options to indicate vertical alignment of text relative to the image when the text is on the same line. Possible settings are: **left**, **right**, **top**, **texttop**, **middle** (you can also call this setting **center** in Internet Explorer and Netscape Navigator), **absmiddle**, **baseline**, **bottom**, and **absbottom**. [1.0T, 1.0F, 2, 3, 3.2, 4, IE1, IE2, IE3, IE4, IE5, NS1, NS2, NS3, NS4]

- **alt**—According to the World Wide Web Consortium (W3C), this attribute is required. You use this attribute to specify text to be displayed in place of an image for browsers that cannot handle graphics or have graphics disabled. Set this attribute to a string of valid alphanumeric characters. [1.0S, 1.0T, 1.0F, 1.1, 2, 3, 3.2, 4, IE1, IE2, IE3, IE4, IE5, NS1, NS2, NS3, NS4]

- **border**—Sets whether or not the image has a border, and if so, how thick the border is. If the image is not also a hyperlink, the border color is usually the color of the surrounding text. If the image is a hyperlink, the border color will be the default hyperlink color. Set to 0 for no border, or a positive integer pixel value. [1.0T, 1.0F, 3.2, 4, IE1, IE2, IE3, IE4, IE5, NS1, NS2, NS3, NS4]

- **class**—Class of the element (used for rendering). [1.0S, 1.0T, 1.0F, 1.1, 3, 4, IE4, IE5]

- **datafld**—Name of the column of the data source object that supplies the bound data. Set to alphanumeric characters. [IE4, IE5]

- **datasrc**—Gives the URL or ID of the data source object supplying data bound to this element. W3C says this should be a URL, Internet Explorer says it should be a data source ID. [IE4, IE5]

- **dir**—Gives the direction of directionally neutral text (text that doesn't have inherent direction in which you should read it). Possible values: **LTR**: left-to-right text or table, and **RTL**: right-to-left text or table. [IE5]

- **dynsrc**—Specifies the URL of an inline video. Set this attribute to a URL. [IE2, IE3, IE4, IE5]

- **height**—Indicates the height of the image. Can be omitted, but specifying a value here for the **HEIGHT** and for the **WIDTH** attribute can speed up the downloading of the image. Because the browser can draw a blank space for the image while it's being downloaded, the page elements will not move around. Set to pixel measurements. [1.0S, 1.0T, 1.0F, 1.1, 3, 3.2, 4, IE1, IE2, IE3, IE4, IE5, NS1, NS2, NS3, NS4]

- **hspace**—Sets the horizontal spacing (both left and right sides) around the image. Set to pixel measurements. [1.0T, 1.0F, 3.2, 4, IE1, IE2, IE3, IE4, IE5, NS1, NS2, NS3, NS4]

- **id**—A unique alphanumeric identifier for the tag, which you can use to refer to it. [1.0S, 1.0T, 1.0F, 1.1, 3, 4, IE4, IE5]

- **ismap**—Indicates that this image is to be used as an image map together with a map file. This attribute is a standalone attribute. The map file holds shape names and matching coordinate values that list corresponding URLs to navigate to. [1.0S, 1.0T, 1.0F, 1.1, 2, 3, 3.2, 4, IE1, IE2, IE3, IE4, IE5, NS1, NS2, NS3, NS4]

- **lang**—Base language used for the tag. [1.0S, 1.0T, 1.0F, 1.1, 3, 4, IE4, IE5]
- **language**—Scripting language used for the tag. [IE4, IE5]
- **longdesc**—Set to a longer description of the image. This attribute allows descriptive narrative with markup to be used for image descriptions. Set to a URL. [1.0S, 1.0T, 1.0F, 1.1, 4]
- **loop**—Sets the number of times a video will play. You use this attribute together with the **dynsrc** attribute. Set it to a positive integer, or –1 for a value of **infinite** (which makes the video loop forever). [IE2, IE3, IE4, IE5]
- **lowsrc**—Gives the URL of a low-resolution image, which should be downloaded before the higher resolution image given by the **src** attribute. The idea is to present some kind of image to user while the higher resolution image is downloading. The low-resolution image is displayed until the high-resolution image is fully downloaded. Set this attribute to a URL. [IE4, IE5, NS1, NS2, NS3, NS4]
- **name**—Gives a unique name to the image so you can reference it with scripting code. Set to valid alphanumeric characters. [IE4, IE5, NS3, NS4]
- **src**—This attribute is required. Specifies the URL of the actual image to display. Set to a URL. [1.0S, 1.0T, 1.0F, 1.1, 2, 3, 3.2, 4, IE1, IE2, IE3, IE4, IE5, NS1, NS2, NS3, NS4]
- **style**—Inline style indicating how to render the element. [1.0S, 1.0T, 1.0F, 1.1, 4, IE4, IE5]
- **title**—Holds additional information (which might be displayed in tool tips) for the element. [1.0S, 1.0T, 1.0F, 1.1, 3, 4, IE4, IE5]
- **usemap**—Gives the URL—usually inside the current document—of a client-side image map, and indicates that the image is to be used as an image map. Note that using **usemap** overrides any **<a>** element surrounding the **<img>** element. Set to a URL, or an anchor name internal to the file. [1.0S, 1.0T, 1.0F, 1.1, 3.2, 4, IE1, IE2, IE3, IE4, IE5, NS2, NS3, NS4]
- **vspace**—Sets the vertical spacing (both top and bottom sides) around the image. Set to pixel measurements. [1.0T, 1.0F, 3.2, 4, IE1, IE2, IE3, IE4, IE5, NS1, NS2, NS3, NS4]
- **width**—Indicates the width of the image. Can be omitted, but specifying a value for **width** here and for the image's **height** can speed up the downloading of the image. Because the browser can draw a blank space for the image while it's being downloaded, the page elements will not move around. Set to pixel measurements. [1.0S, 1.0T, 1.0F, 1.1, 3, 3.2, 4, IE1, IE2, IE3, IE4, IE5, NS1, NS2, NS3, NS4]
- **xml:lang**—Holds the base language for the element when the document is interpreted as an XML document. [1.0S, 1.0T, 1.0F, 1.1]

XHTML events: onclick, ondblclick, onmousedown, onmouseup, onmouseover, onmousemove, onmouseout, onkeypress, onkeydown, onkeyup

"I've got my super-duper image ready to go! Now how do I actually display an image in a Web page?" the novice programmer asks. "It's easy," you say, "Just use the **<img>** element."

You use the **<img>** element to insert images—as well as image maps and video clips—into Web pages. To use this element, you use the **src** attribute to supply the URL of the image you want to display, and you use the **alt** attribute to specify alternate text if the browser can't find the image or doesn't display images. W3C considers both of these attributes as required for the **<img>** element; interestingly, the **align** attribute is not deprecated in the **<img>** element as it is for virtually every other XHTML element that uses it. (The other element that still has an **align** attribute is the **<object>** element, see **<object>** And **<param>**—Placing An Object Into A Web Page" in Chapter 8; the **align** attribute is also not listed as deprecated in the **<applet>** element, but the **<applet>** element itself is deprecated, see "**<applet>**—Embedding Applets In Web Pages" in Chapter 16—although the XHTML 1.1 DTD actually supports **<applet>**.)

TIP: Most browsers also let you refer to the **<img>** element as **<image>**.

NOTE: As of version 4, the Netscape Navigator **<img>** element is supposed to take another attribute: **suppress**, which you set to values of **true** or **false**. When **suppress** is set to **true** (the default is **false**), the image-loading icon (which appears when the image is loading) is not supposed to appear, and the tool tip (which displays the image's alternate text when the mouse rests on the image) is also not supposed to appear. In practice, this attribute doesn't do anything.

Here's an example of using the **<img>** element, which we saw in the introduction to this chapter:

```
<?xml version="1.0"?>
<!DOCTYPE html PUBLIC "-//W3C//DTD XHTML 1.0 Transitional//EN"
"http://www.w3.org/TR/xhtml1/DTD/xhtml1-transitional.dtd">
<html xmlns="http://www.w3.org/1999/xhtml" xml:lang="en" lang="en">
    <head>
        <title>
            Using the &lt;img&gt; tag.
        </title>
    </head>

    <body>
        <center>
            <h1>
```

```
                Working With Images
            </h1>
        </center>
        Here's an image:
        <img src="http://www.starpowder.com/steve/image.gif"
            width="252" height="115" alt="an image" />
    </body>
</html>
```

You can see the result in Figure 4.1.

As you can see by the many attributes you can use with the **<img>** tag, there's a lot of depth to this element. I'll work through other uses of this element in the following sections.

***

TIP: *One thing to remember when you're working with images—browsers cache images. If you change an image and reload its page, you may see the old version of the image. However, you can see the updated image by clearing the browser's cache. To work with the cache in Netscape Navigator 4, select Edit|Preferences; in the Preferences dialog box, select Advanced and then Cache. (In Netscape Navigator 3, the Cache setting is in the Options menu.) In Internet Explorer, select Tools|Internet Options|General. If you're still having trouble, you should also know that some ISPs cache whole Web pages for quicker access, so if you change a page, including the images in it, you may still see the old page and images. One option in this case is to rename the page and the images. Ask your ISP for more details.*

***

NOTE: *Adobe Systems offers two HTML editing products: SiteMill and PageMill. If you use these products, you will find an additional attribute in your* **<img>** *elements. This attribute, used only by SiteMill and PageMill, is named* **naturalsizeflag***. This attribute indicates the size of the image in these editors.*

Displaying Alternate Text in Place of Images

"Huh," says the novice programmer, "I just ran my Web page through an HTML validator, and it said something about all my **<img>** elements needing a value for the **alt** attribute—surely that's some kind of bug?" "Nope," you say, "W3C lists the **alt** attribute as required for the **<img>** element." "That's interesting," the NP says, "What does **alt** do?"

The **alt** attribute lets you specify text that the browser can display before an image is displayed or, if the browser doesn't support graphics, instead of the image. As with the **src** attribute, W3C lists **alt** as a required attribute for the **<img>** element for proper HTML 4, and XHTML 1.0 and 1.1. It's worth providing text for the **alt** attribute in an **<img>** element because many people still use text-only browsers, such as Lynx in Unix.

Here's an example of using the **alt** attribute:

```
<?xml version="1.0"?>
<!DOCTYPE html PUBLIC "-//W3C//DTD XHTML 1.0 Transitional//EN"
"http://www.w3.org/TR/xhtml1/DTD/xhtml1-transitional.dtd">
<html xmlns="http://www.w3.org/1999/xhtml" xml:lang="en" lang="en">
    <head>
        <title>
            Using the &lt;img&gt; tag.
        </title>
    </head>

    <body>
        <center>
            <h1>
                Working With Images
            </h1>
        </center>
        Here's an image:
        <img src="http://www.starpowder.com/steve/image.gif"
             width="252" height="115" alt="a sunset view of the alps." />
    </body>
</html>
```

The result of this XHTML appears in Figure 4.13. In this case, Netscape Navigator can't find the file specified, so it indicates this fact by displaying a broken-image icon and the alternate text. The alternate text also appears before the image starts downloading.

The alternate text also appears in a tool tip, which is displayed when the user lets the mouse rest over the image. See Figure 4.14 for an example. As you can imagine, tool tips are useful for supplying captions for images.

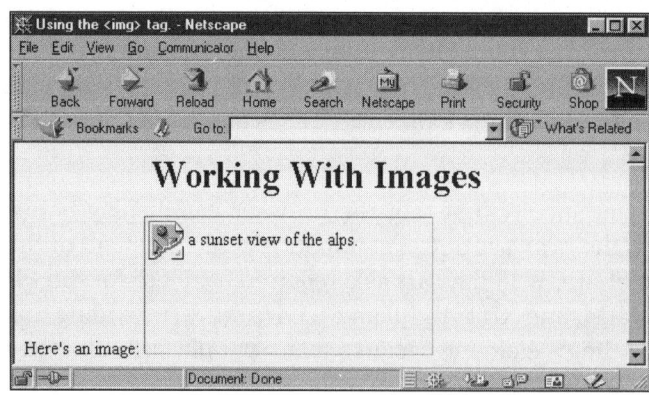

Figure 4.13 Using the **alt** attribute.

Immediate Solutions

Figure 4.14   Using the **alt** attribute as a tool tip.

Allocating Space for an Image

The novice programmer has a question. "What about the **width** and **height** attributes in the **<img>** element; do I need those?" "Actually," you say, "you don't need them, but there are several good reasons to use them."

The **width** and **height** attributes of the **<img>** element provide the width and height of the image in pixels. It's not necessary to supply values for these attributes, but it can be helpful. The following is an example from the beginning of this chapter:

```
<?xml version="1.0"?>
<!DOCTYPE html PUBLIC "-//W3C//DTD XHTML 1.0 Transitional//EN"
"http://www.w3.org/TR/xhtml1/DTD/xhtml1-transitional.dtd">
<html xmlns="http://www.w3.org/1999/xhtml" xml:lang="en" lang="en">
    <head>
        <title>
            Using the &lt;img&gt; tag.
        </title>
    </head>

    <body>
        <center>
            <h1>
                Working With Images
            </h1>
        </center>
```

```
            Here's an image:
                <img src="http://www.starpowder.com/steve/image.gif"
                    width="252" height="115" alt="a sunset view of the alps." />
        </body>
</html>
```

If you don't supply values for these attributes, your browser will still be able to load and display your images. However, if you do supply values for these attributes (be sure to provide a value for *each* attribute), the browser will display a box that is the same size as the image while the image loads, giving the impression that the image is loading faster than it actually does.

In addition, when the Web browser can allocate the correct size of the image as the image loads, it doesn't have to rearrange the other elements in the page when the image is finally downloaded. It can determine the correct size of the image from the image file itself. In other words, specifying a size for the image means that all the elements in your page won't have to move around to accommodate that image when its download is complete.

So how do you find the dimensions of an image? You can use a graphics program that displays the dimensions of the image in its title bar, or you can simply use your browser. In Netscape Navigator, select View|Document Info; in Internet Explorer, right-click on the image and select Properties from the menu.

TIP: *In Netscape Navigator 1 and Internet Explorer 3 (and later versions of both), you can specify the **height** and **width** values by using percentages of the screen area like this: **width="95%"**.*

NOTE: *If you set **height** and **width** to zero, strange things happen. In Netscape Navigator, the image appears with its normal, nonzero size. In Internet Explorer, the image becomes invisible.*

Adding Borders to Images

You can use the **<img>** element's **border** attribute to add borders to images. These borders are simple lines of various thickness, which you set by giving the **border** attribute a value in pixels. Normally, the color of the border is the same as the current default text color, but if you are using the image as a hyperlink, the border will be the same color as the current default hyperlink color (see Chapter 5 for more details). Note that the **border** attribute is not available in the XHTML 1.0 Strict and XHTML 1.1 DTDs.

Here's an example in which I set the border of an image to eight pixels:

```
<?xml version="1.0"?>
<!DOCTYPE html PUBLIC "-//W3C//DTD XHTML 1.0 Transitional//EN"
"http://www.w3.org/TR/xhtml1/DTD/xhtml1-transitional.dtd">
<html xmlns="http://www.w3.org/1999/xhtml" xml:lang="en" lang="en">
    <head>
        <title>
            Using the &lt;img&gt; tag.
        </title>
    </head>

    <body>
        <center>
            <h1>
                Working With Images
            </h1>
        </center>
        Here's an image with a border:
        <img src="flower1.jpg"
            width="85" height="129" alt="an image" border="8" />
    </body>
</html>
```

You can see the results of this XHTML in Figure 4.15, where a thick border appears around the image. Borders are useful for making images stand out from their surroundings—particularly when the image's background color is the same as the page's background color.

NOTE: *By using the setting **border=0**, you can remove the border around an image used as a hyperlink, but that's not a great idea because users rely on the border as a visual clue that the image is being treated as a hyperlink.*

Figure 4.15   Adding a border to an image.

Adding Space around Images

The novice programmer wants to know, "How can I set the spacing between images? There's usually a thin line of space between images, but that's not enough." "No problem at all," you say, "just use the **hspace** and **vspace** attributes."

You can set the horizontal spacing between images with the **hspace** attribute, and set the vertical spacing between images with the **vspace** attribute. You set these attributes to pixel values. Here's an example in which I'm setting the horizontal and vertical spacing between images to eight pixels:

```
<?xml version="1.0"?>
<!DOCTYPE html PUBLIC "-//W3C//DTD XHTML 1.0 Transitional//EN"
"http://www.w3.org/TR/xhtml1/DTD/xhtml1-transitional.dtd">
<html xmlns="http://www.w3.org/1999/xhtml" xml:lang="en" lang="en">
    <head>
        <title>
            Using the &lt;img&gt; tag.
        </title>
    </head>

    <body>
        <center>
            <h1>
                Setting Image Spacing
            </h1>
            <img src="flower1.jpg" alt="image 1"
                width="85" height="129" hspace="8" vspace="8" />
            <img src="flower1.jpg" alt="image 2"
                width="85" height="129" hspace="8" vspace="8" />
            <img src="flower1.jpg" alt="image 3"
                width="85" height="129" hspace="8" vspace="8" />
            <img src="flower1.jpg" alt="image 4"
                width="85" height="129" hspace="8" vspace="8" />
        </center>
    </body>
</html>
```

You can see the results of this XHTML in Figure 4.16.

NOTE: The **hspace** and **vspace** attributes are not available in the XHTML 1.0 Strict and XHTML 1.1 DTDs.

TIP: Want to get rid of all the space between images—even the space that appears there by default? See the "Immediate Solutions" section "Tiling Images—Creating Image Mosaics."

Immediate Solutions

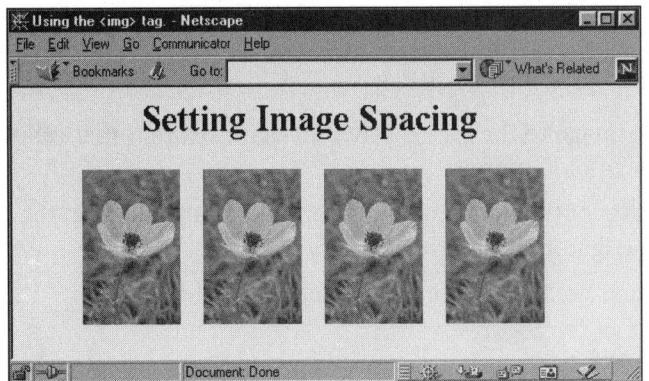

Figure 4.16　Using image spacing.

Aligning Text and Images

"OK," says the big boss, "I want you to write the company newsletter. It's supposed to have both images and text, just like a newspaper." "Fine," you say, "I can use the **<img>** element's **align** attribute."

You can use the **<img>** element's **align** attribute to align text and images. Unlike other elements' **align** attributes, the **<img>** element's **align** attribute is not deprecated in HTML 4. Note, however, that the **align** attribute is not available in the XHTML 1.0 Strict and XHTML 1.1 DTDs.

Here are the possible values for the **align** attribute:

- **absbottom**—Aligns the bottom of the image with the lowest item in the line of text, even if it's below the baseline of the text. (Netscape Navigator and Internet Explorer only.)

- **absmiddle**—Aligns the middle of the image with the middle of the largest item in the line of text. (Netscape Navigator and Internet Explorer only.)

- **baseline**—Aligns the bottom of the image with the baseline of the text (same as **bottom**, but a somewhat more descriptive term). (Netscape Navigator and Internet Explorer only.)

- **bottom**—Aligns the bottom of the image with the text baseline. This is the default.

- **left**—Positions the image to the current left margin; any text that follows flows around the image's right margin.

- **middle**—Aligns the vertical midline of the image with the baseline of the text. (You can also call this setting **center** in Internet Explorer and Netscape Navigator.)
- **right**—Positions the image to the current right margin; any text that follows flows around the image's left margin.
- **textop**—Aligns the top of the image with the top of the tallest text in the line of text. (Netscape Navigator and Internet Explorer only.)
- **top**—Positions the text next to the top of the image.

Vertically Aligning Text

To align text vertically, you can set the **align** attribute to settings such as **top**, **middle**, and **bottom**. Here's an example:

```
<?xml version="1.0"?>
<!DOCTYPE html PUBLIC "-//W3C//DTD XHTML 1.0 Transitional//EN"
    "http://www.w3.org/TR/xhtml1/DTD/xhtml1-transitional.dtd">
<html xmlns="http://www.w3.org/1999/xhtml" xml:lang="en" lang="en">
    <head>
        <title>
            Using the &lt;img&gt; tag.
        </title>
    </head>

    <body>
        <center>
            <h1>
                Aligning Text And Images
            </h1>
        </center>
        <img src="flower1.jpg" alt="image 1"
            width="85" height="129" align="top" />
        &lt;img src="flower1.jpg" alt="image 1"
            width="85" height="129" align="top" /&gt;
        <img src="flower1.jpg" alt="image 1"
            width="85" height="129" align="middle" />
        &lt;img src="flower1.jpg" alt="image 1"
            width="85" height="129" align="middle" /&gt;
        <img src="flower1.jpg" alt="image 1"
            width="85" height="129" align="bottom" />
        &lt;img src="flower1.jpg"
            width="85" height="129" align="bottom" /&gt;
    </body>
</html>
```

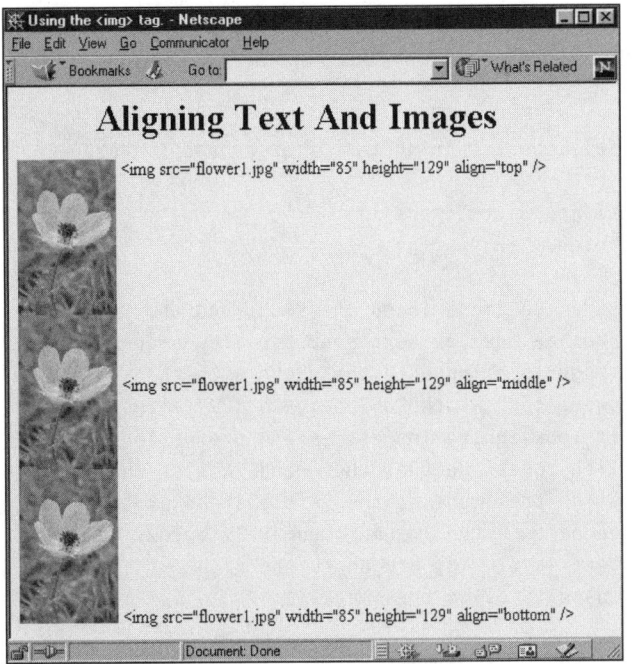

Figure 4.17 Setting vertical alignment.

The results of this XHTML appear in Figure 4.17, where you can see the three alignments at work.

Horizontally Aligning Text

You can also use the **align** attribute to set horizontal alignment. When you do, the text flows around the image. For example, if you align the image on the left, the text flows around to the right. Here's an example showing how this works:

```
<?xml version="1.0"?>
<!DOCTYPE html PUBLIC "-//W3C//DTD XHTML 1.0 Transitional//EN"
"http://www.w3.org/TR/xhtml1/DTD/xhtml1-transitional.dtd">
<html xmlns="http://www.w3.org/1999/xhtml" xml:lang="en" lang="en">
    <head>
        <title>
            Using the &lt;img&gt; tag.
        </title>
    </head>

    <body>
        <center>
```

```
            <h1>
                Aligning Text And Images
            </h1>
        </center>
        This example is all about letting text flow around images.

        <img src="flower1.jpg" alt="image 1"
            width="85" height="129" align="right" />

        Here's a case where the image is on the right and the text
        is on the left. Notice how the text seems to flow around
        the image. The image is aligned to the right with this XHTML:
        &lt;img src="flower1.jpg" width="85" height="129" align="right"
        /&gt;. The result looks quite impressive and professional, giving
        your page a stylish boost. On the other hand, notice what
        happens if you align the image to the left instead of to the
        right, as you see here in the image immediately below. In
        this case, the text is flowing around to the right of the image.
        Here, the XHTML used to align the image is:

        <img src="flower1.jpg" alt="image 1"
            width="85" height="129" align="left" />

        &lt;img src="flower1.jpg" width="85" height="129" align="left"
        /&gt; With this alignment, text continues on the right side of the
        image, wrapping around the image as needed. Using alignments
        like this makes it easy to present images and text together,
        much as you'd see in a newspaper. It's a nice effect that
        gives your pages some impact. Note that if the spacing is
        too tight for you, you can increase the &lt;img&gt; element's
        hspace and vspace settings.
    </body>
</html>
```

The results appear in Figure 4.18.

On the other hand, what if you want to stop text from wrapping around images? No problem—see the next section for the details.

Figure 4.18   Setting horizontal alignment.

Avoiding Text Wrapping

"I need more control," the novice programmer says, "I want to stop text from wrapping around images after a certain point. Can I do that?" "Actually," you say, "you can. Just use the **clear** attribute of the **
** element."

At times, you might want to stop filling in the text next to an aligned image and skip to a point beyond the image. You can't do that with a standard **
** or **<p>** element, but you can do it if you use the **clear** attribute for these tags. Here are the possible settings for this attribute:

- **left**—Move to a point past the image where the left margin is clear.
- **right**   Move to a point past the image where the right margin is clear.
- **all**—Move to a point past the image where both margins are clear.

The idea is that you use the **clear** attribute to indicate when text should start again—when the left margin is clear, the right margin, or both.

Here's an example. In this case, I stop text from wrapping around two images by using the **clear** attribute of the **
** element:

Chapter 4 Working with Images

```
<?xml version="1.0"?>
<!DOCTYPE html PUBLIC "-//W3C//DTD XHTML 1.0 Transitional//EN"
"http://www.w3.org/TR/xhtml1/DTD/xhtml1-transitional.dtd">
<html xmlns="http://www.w3.org/1999/xhtml" xml:lang="en" lang="en">
    <head>
        <title>
            Using the &lt;img&gt; tag.
        </title>
    </head>

    <body>
        <center>
            <h1>
                Aligning Text And Images
            </h1>
        </center>

        This example is all about letting text flow around images.

        <img src="flower1.jpg" alt="image 1"
            width="85" height="129" align="right" />

        Here's a case where the image is on the right and the text
        is on the left. Notice how the text seems to flow around
        the image. Now I use &lt;br clear="right" /&gt;,

        <br clear="right" />

        <img src="flower1.jpg" alt="image 2"
            width="85" height="129" align="left" />

        which skips to a point where the right margin is free
        again. Now the right margin is clear, but there's an
        image to the left. I can skip to a point where the left
        margin is clear again with &lt;br clear="right" /&gt;,

        <br clear="left" />

        which means that this text will continue after the image
        when the left margin is clear again.

    </body>
</html>
```

You can see the results of this XHTML in Figure 4.19.

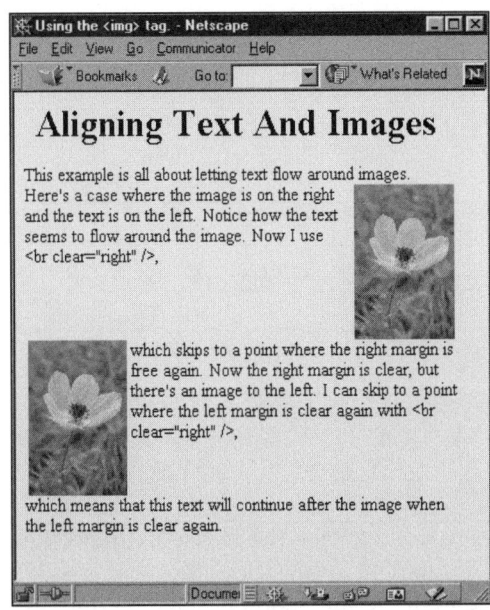

Figure 4.19 Using the <br> element's clear attribute.

Scaling Images to Different Sizes

When you use the **<img>** element's **width** and **height** attributes to set the size of an image, browsers use this size in preference to the image's actual size. For this reason, you can use these attributes to *scale* images, changing their size. In this example, I'm doubling the horizontal and vertical dimensions of an image with the **width** and **height** attributes:

```
<?xml version="1.0"?>
<!DOCTYPE html PUBLIC "-//W3C//DTD XHTML 1.0 Transitional//EN"
"http://www.w3.org/TR/xhtml1/DTD/xhtml1-transitional.dtd">
<html xmlns="http://www.w3.org/1999/xhtml" xml:lang="en" lang="en">
    <head>
        <title>
            Using the &lt;img&gt; tag.
        </title>
    </head>

    <body>
        <center>
            <h1>
                Scaling Images
```

```
            </h1>
        </center>
        here's an image (&lt;img src="image.gif"
            width="252" height="115" /&gt;):
        <br />
        <img src="image.gif"
            width="252" height="115" alt="An image" />
        <br />
        Doubled in both dimensions (&lt;img src="image.gif"
            width="504" height="230" /&gt;):
        <br />
        <img src="image.gif"
            width="504" height="230" alt="an image" />
    </body>
</html>
```

The results appear in Figure 4.20, where you can see the image in its normal and doubled sizes. This technique has one practical application: You can install high-resolution small images on your Web server so they'll download quickly, and then increase their size in the browser by using the **width** and **height** attributes. If your images are long on download time, you might want to consider using this method.

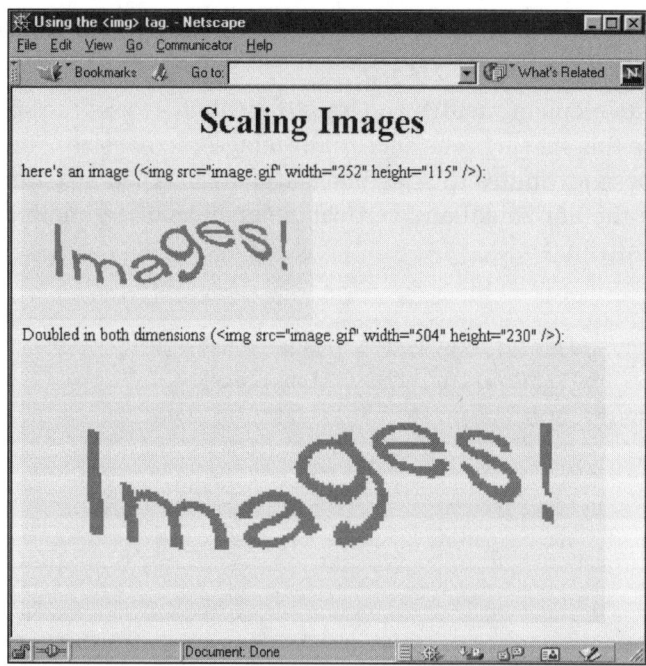

Figure 4.20 Scaling an image by doubling both dimensions.

Using the **lowsrc** Attribute for Image Previews

"Darn," says the novice programmer, "the high-resolution images in my page are still loading too slowly for users, who are moving on to other pages." "Well," you say, "what about using a low-resolution version of the image, which you can display with the **lowsrc** attribute, while the larger image is downloading? By the way, how big is the high-resolution image?" "It's 12,000×8,000 pixels," the NP says. You say, "Uh oh."

You can use **lowsrc** in browsers, like Netscape Navigator and Internet Explorer, to give the URL a fast-loading low-resolution version of an image. This attribute is not standard XHTML. When you use **lowsrc**, you specify a URL for both this attribute and the **src** attribute, which holds the URL for the larger, high-resolution image. Here's an example:

```
<img src="maximage.gif"
    lowsrc="minimage.gif"
    alt="a view of the alps."
    width="12000"
    height="8000"
/>
```

Setting Page Background Images

"Help!" the novice programmer cries. "What's wrong, NP?" you ask. "I want to use a cool background image that I found on the Internet for my Web page," the NP says, "but I have no clue how to do it!" "It's easy," you say, "just use the **background** attribute of the **<body>** element. By the way, NP, is that image copyrighted?" "Uh oh," says the NP.

You've undoubtedly seen Web pages with graphical backgrounds. Using such backgrounds is one of the most common and dazzling of Web-page effects. To add a background image to your Web page, you simply assign the URL of the image you want to use to the **background** attribute of the **<body>** element, like this:

```
<?xml version="1.0"?>
<!DOCTYPE html PUBLIC "-//W3C//DTD XHTML 1.0 Transitional//EN"
"http://www.w3.org/TR/xhtml1/DTD/xhtml1-transitional.dtd">
<html xmlns="http://www.w3.org/1999/xhtml" xml:lang="en" lang="en">
    <head>
        <title>
```

Chapter 4 Working with Images

```
            Using background images.
        </title>
    </head>

    <body background="flower.jpg">
        <center>
            <h1>
                Horticulture!
            </h1>
        </center>
        <br />
        <br />
        <br />
        <h2>
            Don't you just love horticulture? I know I do!
        </h2>
    </body>
</html>
```

The results of this XHTML appear in Figure 4.21, where as you can see, the browser has used the image I indicated to tile the background of the page.

There are thousands of free background images available on the Internet. For example, I just located 13,729 Web pages matching the search text "free backgrounds" in a Web search engine (and I've spent many hours among those pages in the past). Some of these backgrounds are very cool and contain textures and impressive designs—take a look! Just make sure they're really available (not copyrighted) before using them.

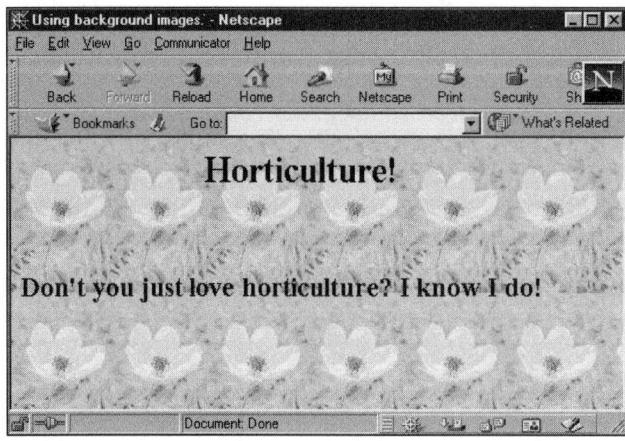

Figure 4.21   Giving a Web page a background image.

TIP: *In recent versions of Netscape Navigator and Internet Explorer, you can use animated GIFs as backgrounds. But be careful—the results can be very distracting, not to mention annoying.*

TIP: *Is your background image overwhelming your foreground text in your Web page? That's a common problem but one that's easy to fix. You can use a graphics program, such as LView Pro, to lighten the image to pastel colors that won't interfere with the foreground. To do that in LView Pro, for example, select Retouch|Gamma Corrections and slide the scrollbars to the right. You can also create stunning backgrounds—including effects such as making images appear to be engraved or etched—with graphics packages such as PhotoStudio 2000 (**www.arcsoft.com**).*

Using the <object> Tag to Insert Images

Originally, W3C had great plans for the **<object>** element, originally introduced by Microsoft and even meant to replace the Netscape **<applet>** element, among others. In fact, according to W3C, you're supposed to be able to use the **<object>** element in place of the **<img>** element. (We'll discuss the **<object>** element, which is a big one, in Chapter 8.)

In the following example, I'm specifying the image type as **image/gif** so the browser knows what kind of data it will be dealing with. **image/gif** is the GIF format's Multipurpose Internet Mail Extensions (MIME) type (for more on MIME types, see Chapter 8). Here's the example:

```
<?xml version="1.0"?>
<!DOCTYPE html PUBLIC "-//W3C//DTD XHTML 1.0 Transitional//EN"
"http://www.w3.org/TR/xhtml1/DTD/xhtml1-transitional.dtd">
<html xmlns="http://www.w3.org/1999/xhtml" xml:lang="en" lang="en">
    <head>
        <title>
            Using the &lt;object&gt; tag.
        </title>
    </head>

    <body>
        <center>
            <object src="flower1.gif" type="image/gif" standby="a flower">
            </object>
        </center>
    </body>
</html>
```

I'd like to show you how this would look in a browser, but unfortunately neither Netscape Navigator nor Internet Explorer implements this use of the **<object>** element. When they do, however, it'll be worth knowing about because you'll be able to handle PNG images smoothly even in browsers that don't handle that format. For instance, in this example, I'm giving the browser an alternate GIF image if it doesn't support PNG:

```
<?xml version="1.0"?>
<!DOCTYPE html PUBLIC "-//W3C//DTD XHTML 1.0 Transitional//EN"
"http://www.w3.org/TR/xhtml1/DTD/xhtml1-transitional.dtd">
<html xmlns="http://www.w3.org/1999/xhtml" xml:lang="en" lang="en">
    <head>
        <title>
            Using the &lt;object&gt; tag.
        </title>
    </head>

    <body>
        <center>
            <object src="flower1.png" type="image/png" standby="a flower">
                <object src="flower1.gif" type="image/gif"
                    standby="a flower">
                </object>
            </object>
        </center>
    </body>
</html>
```

However, it's not clear what the status of the **<object>** element is now, because it's not supported in XHTML 1.1, while the **<applet>** element is. We'll have to wait and see how the situation clarifies.

Using Images to Replace Missing Content

Sometimes, when you do something fancy, some browsers won't understand how to display your code. For example, say you have an image—created with a Java applet—in which the graphical letters in the message dance around. Now say that the Web page is loaded into a Web browser that doesn't understand Java—nothing will show up. By using the **<img>** element, you can present at least a static version of the message. Here's how: Just use the **<img>** element inside the **<applet>** or **<object>** element. For example:

```
<?xml version="1.0"?>
<!DOCTYPE html PUBLIC "-//W3C//DTD XHTML 1.0 Transitional//EN"
"http://www.w3.org/TR/xhtml1/DTD/xhtml1-transitional.dtd">
<html xmlns="http://www.w3.org/1999/xhtml" xml:lang="en" lang="en">
    <head>
        <title>
            Using the &lt;object&gt; tag.
        </title>
    </head>

    <body>

        <applet code="myterrificapplet.class"
            codebase="http://www.starpowder.com/steve" width="450"
                height="150">
            <param name="param1" value="ready" />
            <param name="param1" value="set" />
            <param name="param1" value="go" />
            <img alt="Image 1"
                src="staticappletimage.gif" />
        </applet>

    </body>
</html>
```

The browser that doesn't understand Java will ignore the **<applet>** and **<param>** elements (see "**<applet>**—Embedding Applets In Web Pages" in Chapter 16 and "**<object>** And **<param>**—Placing An Object Into A Web Page" in Chapter 8 for more on these elements) and only see the **<img>** element, which will display the static image you specified to replace the moving one.

Tiling Images—Creating Image Mosaics

You may have seen larger images broken up into pieces in Web pages. The individual pieces are downloaded separately and when they're all downloaded, the whole image is complete. One reason this is done is to increase download time. If you break a large image into four pieces, a browser can open four HTTP connections to the server instead of just one. When server connections are slow, using the tiling technique allows the browser to create multiple connections to the server, resulting in accelerated download time.

So how do you break an image into several pieces in a Web page and then put them together again? One way to do this is to simply put **<img>** elements right next to each other without any white space (including line breaks) between them.

This prevents the browser from adding spaces between the images. Here's an example:

```
<?xml version="1.0"?>
<!DOCTYPE html PUBLIC "-//W3C//DTD XHTML 1.0 Transitional//EN"
"http://www.w3.org/TR/xhtml1/DTD/xhtml1-transitional.dtd">
<html xmlns="http://www.w3.org/1999/xhtml" xml:lang="en" lang="en">
    <head>
        <title>
            Tiling images.
        </title>
    </head>

    <body>
        <center>
            <h1>
                Tiling Images
            </h1>
            <img src="flower1.jpg" width="85" height="129"
            border="0" alt="Image 1"/><img src="flower1.jpg"
            width="85" height="129" border="0" alt="Image 2"/>
            <img src="flower1.jpg" width="85" height="129"
            border="0" alt="Image 3"/><img src="flower1.jpg"
            width="85" height="129" border="0" alt="Image 4"/>
        </center>
    </body>
</html>
```

The results of this XHTML appear in Figure 4.22. All four copies of the same image are lined up right next to each other without any spacing between them.

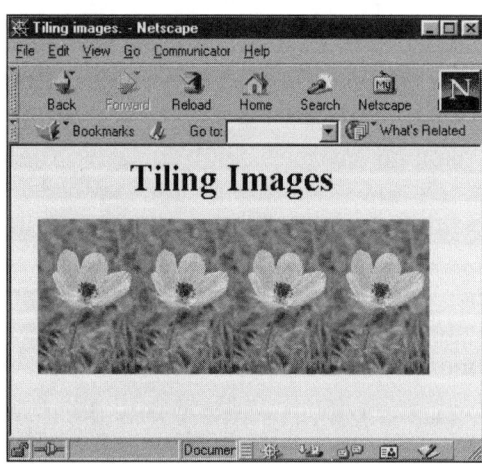

Figure 4.22   Tiling images in a row.

What if you wanted to arrange the images in some other way? That's commonly done with tables, which we'll discuss in depth in Chapter 6. Here's an example where I stack images on top of each other in a 2×2 pattern. Note that I turn off all the default table spacing by setting the **cellpadding**, **cellspacing**, and **border** attributes to 0:

```xml
<?xml version="1.0"?>
<!DOCTYPE html PUBLIC "-//W3C//DTD XHTML 1.0 Transitional//EN"
"http://www.w3.org/TR/xhtml1/DTD/xhtml1-transitional.dtd">
<html xmlns="http://www.w3.org/1999/xhtml" xml:lang="en" lang="en">
    <head>
        <title>
            Tiling images.
        </title>
    </head>

    <body>
        <center>
            <h1>
                Tiling Images
            </h1>
            <table cellpadding="0" cellspacing="0" border="0">
                <tr>
                    <td>
                        <img src="flower1.jpg" width="85" height="129"
                        border="0" alt="Image 1"/><img
                        src="flower1.jpg" width="85" height="129"
                        border="0" alt="Image 2"/></td></tr><tr><td>
                        <img src="flower1.jpg" width="85"
                        height="129" border="0" alt="Image 3"/><img
                        src="flower1.jpg" width="85" height="129"
                        border="0" alt="Image 4"/>

                    </td>
                </tr>
            </table>
        </center>
    </body>
</html>
```

The results of this XHTML appear in Figure 4.23.

Figure 4.23 Tiling images in a 2×2 pattern.

Creating Overlapping Images

One interesting effect using images is to overlap them in a Web page. You can do this with layers in Netscape Navigator. Here's an example:

```
<?xml version="1.0"?>
<!DOCTYPE html PUBLIC "-//W3C//DTD XHTML 1.0 Transitional//EN"
"http://www.w3.org/TR/xhtml1/DTD/xhtml1-transitional.dtd">
<html xmlns="http://www.w3.org/1999/xhtml" xml:lang="en" lang="en">
    <head>
        <title>
            Creating Overlapping Images With Layers
        </title>
    </head>

    <body>

        <h1 align="center">
            Creating Overlapping Images With Layers
        </h1>

        <layer name="layer1">
            <img src="flower1.jpg" width="85" height="129"
            alt="Image 1"/>
        </layer>
```

```
        <layer name="layer2" left="50" top="80">
            <img src="flower1.jpg" width="85" height="129"
        alt="Image 2"/>
        </layer>

        <layer name="layer3" left="100" top="100">
            <img src="flower1.jpg" width="85" height="129"
            alt="Image 3"/>
        </layer>

    </body>

</html>
```

The results of this XHTML appear in Figure 4.24. This technique works, but it's restricted to the only browser that supports layers—Netscape Navigator.

To overlap images with more general XHTML, use the **<div>** element. Here's a Web page that overlaps images by using **<div>**, which will work in both Netscape Navigator and Internet Explorer:

```
<?xml version="1.0"?>
<!DOCTYPE html PUBLIC "-//W3C//DTD XHTML 1.0 Transitional//EN"
"http://www.w3.org/TR/xhtml1/DTD/xhtml1-transitional.dtd">
<html xmlns="http://www.w3.org/1999/xhtml" xml:lang="en" lang="en">
    <head>
        <title>
            Using The &lt;div&gt; Element To Overlap Images
        </title>
    </head>

    <body>

        <h1 align="center">
            Creating Overlapping Images With &lt;div&gt;
        </h1>

        <div style="position:absolute; left:100; top:60;">
            <img src="flower1.jpg" width="85" height="129"
            alt="Image 1"/>
        </div>

        <div style="position:absolute; left:120; top:90;">
            <img src="flower1.jpg" width="85" height="129"
            alt="Image 2"/>
        </div>
```

```
            <div style="position:absolute; left:150; top:120;">
                <img src="flower1.jpg" width="85" height="129"
                alt="Image 3"/>
            </div>
        </body>
</html>
```

The results of this XHTML appear in Internet Explorer in Figure 4.25. As you can see, the copies of the same image appear in a cascade. Using the **<div>** element, you can arrange images as you like. I'll cover this element in greater depth when discussing styles in Chapter 9.

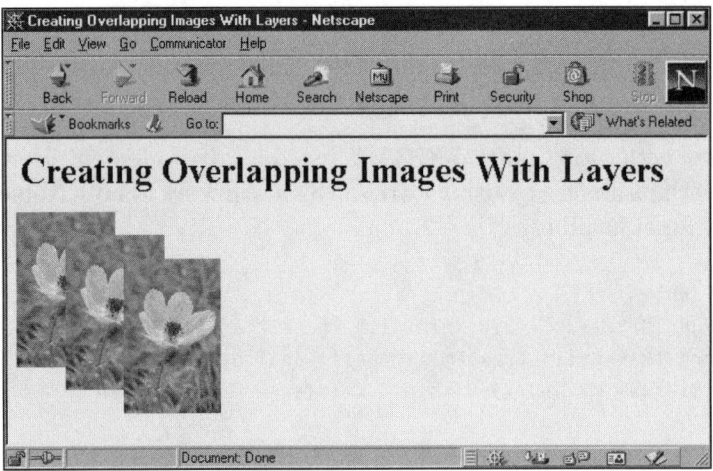

Figure 4.24   Overlapping images with layers.

Figure 4.25   Overlapping images with the **<div>** element.

Chapter 5

Links and Lists

If you need an immediate solution to:	See page:
`<a>`—Creating a Hyperlink or Anchor	273
Setting Hyperlink Colors	276
Creating Graphical Hyperlinks	278
`<base>`—Setting the Base for Hyperlinks	279
`<link>`—Setting Link Information	281
Giving Hyperlinks Access Keys	284
Using Graphical Hyperlinks for Navigation	285
Creating Navigation Bars	286
Creating Anchors and Linking to Sections in a Page	288
Creating Clickable Footnotes	291
Emailing with Hyperlinks	292
Downloading Files with the HTTP and FTP Protocols	294
`<map>`—Creating Client-Side Image Maps	295
`<area>`—Creating Clickable Regions in Image Maps	296
Creating Client-Side Image Maps	299
Creating Server-Side Image Maps	301
Creating Image Maps with the `<object>` Element	305
Creating Combined Client-Side and Server-Side Image Maps	305
Creating Lists	307
Nesting Lists	323
`<dir>` and `<menu>`—Deprecated Lists	325

In Depth

This chapter is about creating links and lists in XHTML. Both elements are integral to writing Web pages, but of the two, hyperlinks are by far the most popular. The World Wide Web thrives on hyperlinks. Imagine a Web without links, without browsers, without search engines that give you lists of hyperlinks to pages that match your search. What makes the Web a web? Hyperlinks.

Links connect the pages of the Web, letting the user navigate to a new page just by clicking on the link. Without links, the Web wouldn't work. Breaking long documents into multiple pages is made possible through hyperlinks, allowing you to navigate from section to section easily without waiting for everything to download at once. And without a mechanism like hyperlinks, it would be impossible to organize Web sites. Hyperlinks are what make the World Wide Web go round.

In the 1960s, Ted Nelson created hyperlinks and hypertext from the design of his famous Xanadu system. The idea was to create a new model of text to let users skip from place to place, and of course, the results are well-known to anyone who has even casually browsed the Web. Tired of where you are and want to take a look at something else? Just click on the link—usually set off from the surrounding text in color and underlined—and you're there.

There are a number of ways to work with hyperlinks, and I'll cover them in depth in this chapter. Standard hyperlinks are text based; the hyperlink is displayed as simple text. Graphical hyperlinks use images instead of text—click on the image and you navigate to the hyperlink's target. I'll also look at specialized uses of these two types of hyperlinks; these uses include making footnotes in hyperlinks for easy lookup and using graphical images, like arrows, specifically for navigation.

I'll also discuss how to create *image maps* in this chapter. Image maps are those images that you can click in various different places to make your browser navigate to a new location. Image maps provide an easy graphical way to navigate around a site and to other sites. They are becoming more and more popular, especially in larger sites.

The other types of XHTML elements I'll take a look at in this chapter are lists. You use these elements to display lists in a Web page, like this:

- Here's
- a
- list!

In this chapter, I'll also discuss lists. You can create all types of lists in XHTML, and lists let you save considerable space in Web pages. Space is always at a premium, and lists present material in a compact format. List possibilities include bulleted lists, numbered lists, nested lists, even lists that use Roman numerals.

The main topic of this chapter, however, is hyperlinks, so I'll start with those.

Creating Hyperlinks

You use the **<a>** element ("a" stands for "anchor") to create hyperlinks in XHTML. The most common form of hyperlink is undoubtedly the text hyperlink, where the hyperlink itself usually appears underlined and in a different color from the surrounding text to set it off from that text. I'll take a look at creating text hyperlinks first.

---

*TIP: According to the official HTML 4 specification, which XHTML is based on, nested links are illegal, so never use **<a>** tags inside **<a>** elements.*

Creating Text Hyperlinks

The standard form of a hyperlink element looks like this:

```
Find the answers at <a href="http://W3C.org">W3C</a>.
```

I'm using the **<a>** tag to set up a hyperlink, and I'm using the **href** attribute to set the target of the hyperlink to **http://W3C.org** (which is the home page for the World Wide Web Consortium). This is the URL that the browser will navigate to when the user clicks on the link. The text inside the **<a>** element will appear in the page's hyperlink style, which is underlined and usually in a different color from the surrounding text, like this:

```
Find the answers at W3C.
```

All the user has to do is to click the W3C hyperlink to be transported to the W3C Web site. Here's a full example, also linking to W3C:

```
<?xml version="1.0"?>
<!DOCTYPE html PUBLIC "-//W3C//DTD XHTML 1.0 Transitional//EN"
"http://www.w3.org/TR/xhtml1/DTD/xhtml1-transitional.dtd">
<html xmlns="http://www.w3.org/1999/xhtml" xml:lang="en" lang="en">
```

```
        <head>
            <title>
                Creating A Hyperlink
            </title>
        </head>

        <body>

            <center>

                <h1>
                    Creating A Hyperlink
                </h1>

                Here's a Web site to check out:
                    <a href="http://w3c.org">W3C</a>!
            </center>

        </body>
</html>
```

The results of this XHTML appear in Figure 5.1, where you can see the text hyperlink, ready to be clicked.

NOTE: *You might notice that I made the text of the hyperlink "W3C," not just "Click here" or "Here" or something like that. Web designers consider it better practice to make the hyperlink as descriptive as possible.*

Creating Graphical Hyperlinks

In addition to text, you can also use images as hyperlinks, adding a little pizzazz to your pages. Doing so is easy—just put an **<img>** element, instead of text, in the **<a>** element. Here's an example showing how this works:

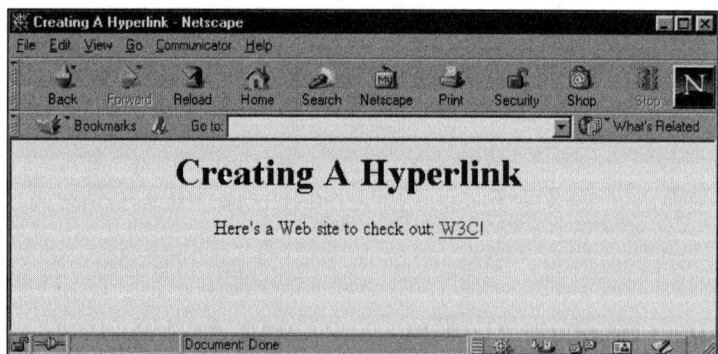

Figure 5.1 A text hyperlink.

```
<?xml version="1.0"?>
<!DOCTYPE html PUBLIC "-//W3C//DTD XHTML 1.0 Transitional//EN"
"http://www.w3.org/TR/xhtml1/DTD/xhtml1-transitional.dtd">
<html xmlns="http://www.w3.org/1999/xhtml" xml:lang="en" lang="en">
    <head>
        <title>
            Creating A Graphical Hyperlink
        </title>
    </head>

    <body>

        <center>

            <h1>
                Creating A Graphical Hyperlink
            </h1>

            <a href="http://w3c.org">
                <img width="277" height="114" src="clickme.gif"
                    alt="Click me to go to W3C!" />
            </a>
        </center>

    </body>
</html>
```

The results of this XHTML appear in Figure 5.2. When the user clicks the image in the figure, the browser navigates to the hyperlink's target, **http://W3C.org**. Note also that you should use the **<img>** element's **alt** attribute to add a tool tip to the hyperlink (in fact, **alt** is a required attribute for the **<img>** element); when the mouse rests over the hyperlink image, the tool tip appears, showing the hyperlink's target, as in Figure 5.2.

TIP: *Want to turn the border of a graphical hyperlink off or make it wider? Use the* **<img>** *element's* **border** *attribute:* **border=0** *turns off the border. This is probably not advisable for hyperlinks because seeing the border is how the user knows the image is a hyperlink.*

Linking to a Section of a Document

It's also possible to link to a section of a document instead of linking to the document as a whole. When you navigate to a document by using the document's URL, the browser opens the document and positions the top of the document at the top of the browser window. Say, however, that you've written a training manual with

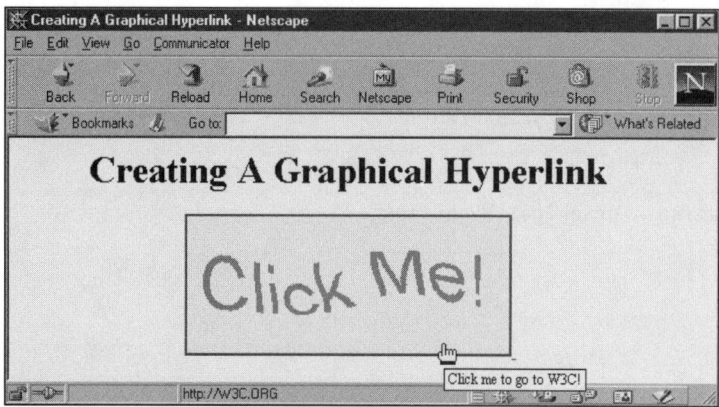

Figure 5.2 Creating a graphical hyperlink.

five individual topics in one page—how can you navigate to one of the topics, not just to the top of the page?

You can use *anchors*. Creating anchors is another valuable use of the **<a>** element. Anchors supply a name to a section of a page, so you can use the anchor's name to navigate to that section. Here's how you use the **<a>** element to create a named anchor:

```
<a id="SEASHORE">A guide to marine biology.</a>
```

In this example, note that I'm using the **id** attribute, not the **href** attribute, of the **<a>** element. In XHTML, you use the **id** attribute to establish an anchor. In many HTML browsers, the standard was to use the **name** attribute, but in XHTML, you are supposed to use **id**. That's a problem for some browsers—notably Netscape Navigator—that still use the **name** attribute to establish an anchor. To handle browsers like that, you can use the **name** attribute in addition to the **id** attribute, like this:

```
<a id="SEASHORE" name="SEASHORE">A guide to marine biology.</a>
```

However, XHTML 1.0 has deprecated the **name** attribute of the **<a>**, **<applet>**, **<form>**, **<frame>**, **<iframe>**, **<img>**, and **<map>** elements, and it will be removed from XHTML in subsequent versions. In particular, this attribute is still available in all three XHTML 1.0 DTDs but not in the XHTML 1.1 DTD.

Now that I've named the text in the anchor by using the name **"SEASHORE"**, I can refer to that anchor as **"#SEASHORE"** (the **#** is essential). For example, here's a hyperlink to that section from another place in the same document:

```
Want to learn more about the <a href="#SEASHORE">sea shore</a>?
```

When the user clicks on this hyperlink, the browser will place the **SEASHORE** anchor section at the top of the page.

Here's another example. In this case, the user can click on a hyperlink to move to the bottom of the page. Note that I'm using the **name** attribute in addition to the **id** attribute:

```
<?xml version="1.0"?>
<!DOCTYPE html PUBLIC "-//W3C//DTD XHTML 1.0 Transitional//EN"
    "http://www.w3.org/TR/xhtml1/DTD/xhtml1-transitional.dtd">
<html xmlns="http://www.w3.org/1999/xhtml" xml:lang="en" lang="en">
    <head>
        <title>
            Linking To A Section In A Page
        </title>
    </head>

    <body>

        <center>

            <h1>
                Linking To A Section In A Page
            </h1>

            Click here to go to the
            <a href="#BOTTOM">bottom</a>
            of the page.

            <br />
            <br />
            <br />
            <br />
            <br />
            <br />
            <br />
            <br />
            <br />
            <br />
            <br />
            <br />

            <hr />
```

```
            <a id="BOTTOM" name="BOTTOM">This is the bottom of the page.</a>
        </center>

    </body>
</html>
```

When the user clicks on the hyperlink, shown in Figure 5.3, the browser looks for the hyperlink's target—the anchor named **"BOTTOM"**—and navigates to that anchor. You can see the results in Figure 5.4.

TIP: *What if you're anchoring text that's in another element, such as a header? Consider this example:* **"<h1>What About Oil Painting?</h1>"**. *Should the* **<a>** *element be inside or outside of the header? Many browsers will function either way, but some will have problems unless you put the* **<a>** *tags inside the outer tags to make a well-defined anchor, like this:* **"<h1><a id="OILPAINTING">What About Oil Painting?</a></h1>"**.

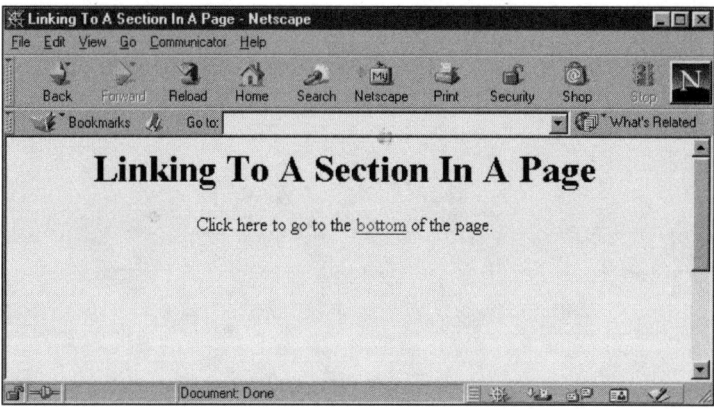

Figure 5.3 An anchored hyperlink.

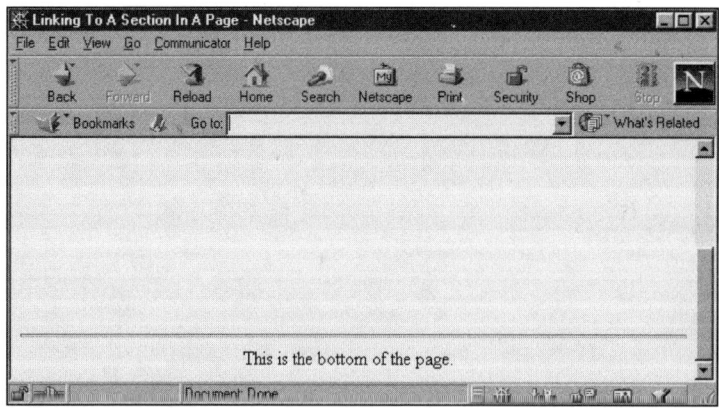

Figure 5.4 Navigating to an anchor.

The anchored section you link to doesn't need to be in the same document. You can link to a section inside another Web page as long as you add **#** and the anchor name to the end of the URL, like this: **www.starpowder.com/steve/ fishing.html#BAIT**. Here's an example where I link to the anchored section named **"BOTTOM"** in the page discussion.html:

```
<?xml version="1.0"?>
<!DOCTYPE html PUBLIC "-//W3C//DTD XHTML 1.0 Transitional//EN"
"http://www.w3.org/TR/xhtml1/DTD/xhtml1-transitional.dtd">
<html xmlns="http://www.w3.org/1999/xhtml" xml:lang="en" lang="en">
    <head>
        <title>
            Linking To A Section In Another Page
        </title>
    </head>

    <body>

        <center>

            <h1>
                Linking To A Section In Another Page
            </h1>

            Click here to go to the
            <a href="discussion.html#BOTTOM">bottom</a>
            of the <i>other</i> page.

        </center>

    </body>
</html>
```

When the user clicks on this hyperlink, the browser will open the page discussion.html and display the anchored section named **"BOTTOM"** at the top of the page.

Creating Navigational Aids with Hyperlinks

One popular use of hyperlinks is to make it easy to navigate around a Web site by using image buttons, like arrows. Here's an example that displays arrows to let the user navigate to the next or previous page in a series of pages, or to navigate to the home page just by clicking the appropriate image:

```xml
<?xml version="1.0"?>
<!DOCTYPE html PUBLIC "-//W3C//DTD XHTML 1.0 Transitional//EN"
"http://www.w3.org/TR/xhtml1/DTD/xhtml1-transitional.dtd">
<html xmlns="http://www.w3.org/1999/xhtml" xml:lang="en" lang="en">
    <head>
        <title>
            Creating Graphical Navigational Aids
        </title>
    </head>

    <body>

        <center>

            <h1>
                Creating Graphical Navigational Aids
            </h1>

            Want to get somewhere fast? Click a button below...

            <br />

            <a href="prev.html">
                <img width="172" height="117" src="left.gif"
                    alt="previous" border="0" />
            </a>

            <a href="index.html">
                <img width="161" height="105" src="home.gif"
                    alt="home" border="0" />
            </a>

            <a href="next.html">
                <img width="172" height="117" src="right.gif"
                    alt="next" border="0" />
            </a>

        </center>

    </body>
</html>
```

The results of this XHTML appear in Figure 5.5. As you can see in the figure, the user can click on any of the handy (if oversized, in this example) images to make navigation easier.

In Depth

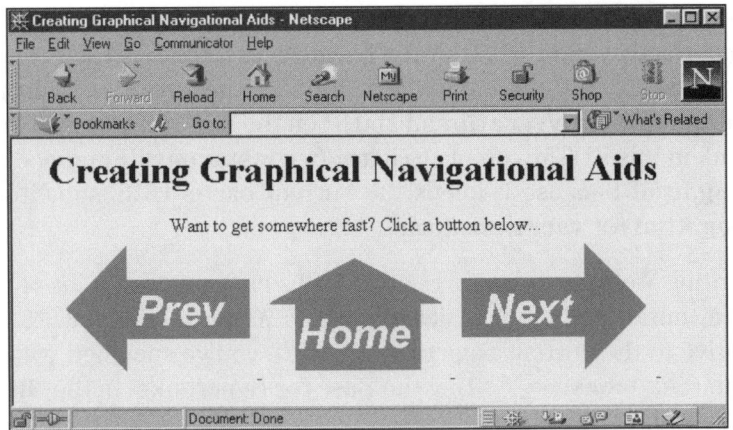

Figure 5.5 Using hyperlinks as navigational aids.

As you know, the target of a hyperlink is a URL, but browsers recognize many different types of URLs. It's essential that you know what URLs are, so I'll discuss creating URLs next.

All about URLs

URL stands for Uniform Resource Locator (not, as many people think, Universal Resource Locator). A URL is a Web address. Most people think of URLs as something like this: **http://www.starpowder.com/steve/superduperpage.html**, but there are many forms of URLs, including relative and absolute URLs. I'll take a look at these first.

TIP: Besides URL, there are some other abbreviations you might encounter when you're working with hyperlinks: URC (Uniform Resource Citation); URI (Uniform Resource Identifier); and URN (Uniform Resource Name).

NOTE: The case sensitivity of file names in URLs can be important. Some Web servers that run under Unix may have trouble finding the right file if you don't use the right case.

Relative and Absolute URLs

If I wrote something like this, **http://www.W3C.org**, you'd realize that I was referring to a specific URL:

```
<a href="http://W3C.org">
```

But what if I wrote this?

```
<a href="mountaineering.html">
```

In this example, I'm just giving a file name, mountaineering.html, as the URL—but it's a perfectly valid URL. It's valid because it's a *relative* URL, relative to the current page. If the current page visible in the browser is **http://www.starpowder.com/steve/vacations.html**, then the Web browser will know that the hyperlink in this XHTML points to **http://www.starpowder.com/steve/mountaineering.html** because it keeps the current page's URL, substituting **mountaineering.html** for **vacations.html**.

When you're writing Web pages, using relative URLs can save you a lot of time because they are shorter and often easier to specify. What's a relative URL relative to? It's relative to the current page or to the URL you've specified with the **<base>** element. (See "**<base>**—Setting the Base for Hyperlinks" in the "Immediate Solutions" section.)

Here are some examples of relative URLs:

- *bigtime.html*—Points to the page bigtime.html in the same directory on the Web server as the currently open page.

- *archives/bigtime.html*—Points to the page bigtime.html in the directory named **archives**, which is a subdirectory of the directory containing the current page.

- *archives/old/bigtime.html*—Points to the page bigtime.html in the directory named **old**, which is a subdirectory of the directory named **archives**, which is itself a subdirectory of the directory containing the current page.

- *../bigtime.html*—Points to bigtime.html in the directory *above* the directory containing the current page (".." refers to the directory above the current one).

- *../archives/bigtime.html*—Points to bigtime.html in the directory named **archives**, which is in the directory above the current directory.

Absolute URLs, on the other hand, do not rely on being relative to anything. They specify a page's full Web address, like this: **http://www.starpowder.com/steve/mountaineering.html**. All the information the browser needs to know is in the URL—the protocol to use (Hypertext Transfer Protocol [HTTP]), the domain name, the directory to search, and the name of the file to fetch. Here are some examples of absolute URLs:

- *http://www.starpowder.com/steve/bigtime.html*—Refers to the page bigtime.html in the **steve** directory of the **www.starpowder.com** domain.

- *http://www.w3.org/MarkUp/*—Refers to the page index.html (default.html under the Mircrosoft Internet Information Server) in the **MarkUp** directory in the **www.w3.org** domain.

TIP: *There's one good reason to use relative URLs instead of absolute URLs: If you move all your files en masse to a new directory in your Web server, all absolute links will become invalid (called* broken *links), but relative URLs will remain valid.*

Besides the standard characters you see in URLs, you might also see something like this from time to time:

```
http://www.starpowder.com/cgi/script.cgi?text=Now+is+the+time&color=blue
```

This kind of URL is used when your Web page sends data to the Web server after the user clicks on a Submit button. This data—which is tacked on to the end of the URL following a question mark (**?**)—consists of parameter pairs. In this example, the text parameter is being set to **Now is the time** (spaces are replaced with plus signs (**+**) by the browser), and the parameter named **color** is being set to blue. (We'll discuss this type of URL more when we're working with CGI scripts in Chapter 21.)

TIP: *What if your Web page is stored in a directory whose name has a space in it? Can you use a URL like* **http://www.starpowder.com/my cool pages/index.html** *in an* **<a>** *element? You can, but at the very least, you should enclose it in quotation marks—even then some browsers will have problems (such as Netscape 3 and earlier). It's best to use the URL escape code for a space, which is 20. The number 20 in hexadecimal is 32 in decimal, which is the ASCII (American Standard Code for Information Interchange) code for a space. For example,* **http://www.starpowder.com/my%20cool%20pages/index.html**.

You can open the file c:\html\bigtime.html on Windows systems by typing that path and file name directly into the browser, but there's another way of doing the same thing by using the file URL type, like this: **file://c:/html/bigtime.htm**. This tells the browser that the data you want to read is stored in a local file (so you don't need a forward slash at the very beginning of the URL). In fact, there are a number of URL types.

Types of URLs

Here is a list of the different types of protocols you can use to create URLs:

- *File*—File URLs; the address in the URL refers to a local file.
- *FTP*—File Transfer Protocol, the protocol for transporting files on the Internet. You can also specify an FTP username and password as part of the URL: **ftp://*username:password*@ftp.starpowder.com/steve/*filename***.
- *Gopher*—The Gopher protocol uses a Gopher server to find and get files.
- *HTTP*—Hypertext Transfer Protocol, the protocol you use with Web pages.
- *HTTPS*—Secure Hypertext Transfer Protocol, the protocol you use with secure Web pages.

- *Mailto*—An email URL; clicking this URL will open the user's email program so he or she can send email to the email address given in the URL.
- *News*—A Usenet URL pointing to a message on Usenet. You can use this kind of URL in two ways: **news:*groupname*** or **news:*messageID***. If your browser supports newsgroups, the first way will display all the posts in a Usenet group. The second way will display an individual message, which you must refer to by using a Usenet message ID.

Creating Image Maps

Using *image maps* is another powerful hyperlink technique that makes pages come alive. Image maps provide users with a graphical aid for navigation. For example, you might want to display an actual map of your site and let the user navigate to each location just by clicking in the right place on the map.

There are two kinds of image maps: server-side and client-side image maps. They differ in implementation details: server-side maps are processed on the Web server, and client-side image maps are processed in the Web browser.

Server-Side Image Maps

In the following example, I'll create a server-side image map by surrounding an **<img>** element with **<a>** tags, which are used to create hyperlinks. In this case, I'll point to a .map file that holds the image-map locations, so when the user clicks in a particular location, the server knows what to do. Here's the XHTML:

```
<?xml version="1.0"?>
<!DOCTYPE html PUBLIC "-//W3C//DTD XHTML 1.0 Transitional//EN"
"http://www.w3.org/TR/xhtml1/DTD/xhtml1-transitional.dtd">
<html xmlns="http://www.w3.org/1999/xhtml" xml:lang="en" lang="en">
    <head>
        <title>
            Using A Server Side Image Map
        </title>
    </head>

    <body bgcolor="black">
        <center>
            <a href="main.map">
                <img width="528" height="137" src="mainmenu.jpg"
                    border="0" alt="image map" ismap="ismap" />
            </a>
        </center>
    </body>
</html>
```

Note that I'm referring to a file named main.map on the server; that file connects clickable regions in the image with URLs that the browser will navigate to when those regions are clicked. Here's what's in main.map (we'll see how to create map files in "Immediate Solutions"):

```
default http://www.starpowder.com/steve/index.html#mainmenu
rect http://www.reuters.com 16,39 127,61
rect http://www.starpowder.com/steve/search.html 62,71 173,93
rect http://www.nnic.noaa.gov 98,104 209,126
rect http://www.starpowder.com/steve/gbook.htm 411,35 522,57
rect http://www.yahoo.com/guides_and_tutorials/ 360,67 471,89
rect http://www.web21.com/services/hot100/index.html 328,98 439,120
```

You can see the result in Figure 5.6. As you see in the figure, the image map is ready to be clicked, and when the user clicks one of the labels, the browser will navigate to the appropriate URL. Presenting a graphical navigation device like this is a terrific help for users and makes your site more attractive and accessible.

Client-Side Image Maps

In client-side image maps, all the work is done in the browser. You include the map information by using **<map>** and **<area>** elements. Following is an example that performs the same function as the example in the previous section. Note that like the **name** attribute in the **<a>** element, the **name** attribute of **<map>** is deprecated, and although it's still available in the three XHTML 1.0 DTDs, it's not available in the XHTML 1.1 DTD. To use browsers like Netscape Navigator that use **name**, not **id**, I'm giving **<map>** both an **id** and a **name** attribute here, just as I did for the **<a>** element (note that technically speaking, all **<area>** elements should also have an **alt** attribute). Here's the example:

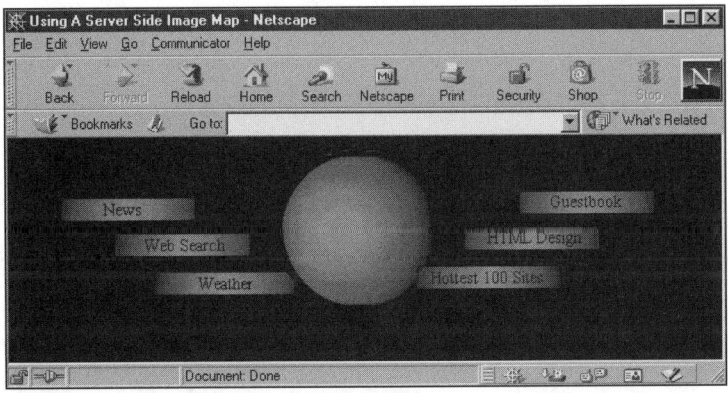

Figure 5.6   A server-side image map.

```xml
<?xml version="1.0"?>
<!DOCTYPE html PUBLIC "-//W3C//DTD XHTML 1.0 Transitional//EN"
"http://www.w3.org/TR/xhtml1/DTD/xhtml1-transitional.dtd">
<html xmlns="http://www.w3.org/1999/xhtml" xml:lang="en" lang="en">
    <head>
        <title>
            Using A Client Side Image Map
        </title>
    </head>

    <body bgcolor="black">

        <center>
            <img width="528" height="137" src="mainmenu.jpg"
                border="0" alt="image map" usemap="#imap" />
            <map id="imap" name="imap">
                <area shape="rect" coords="16,39 127,61"
                    href="http://www.reuters.com" />
                <area shape="rect" coords="62,71 173,93"
                    href="http://www.starpowder.com/steve/search.html" />
                <area shape="rect" coords="98,104 209,126"
                    href="http://www.nnic.noaa.gov" />
                <area shape="rect" coords="411,35 522,57"
                    href="http://www.starpowder.com/steve/gbook.htm" />
                <area shape="rect" coords="360,67 471,89"
                    href="http://www.yahoo.com/guides_and_tutorials/" />
                <area shape="rect" coords="328,98 439,120"
                    href="http://www.web21.com/services/hot100/index.html"
                />
                <area shape="default" href=
                    "http://www.starpowder.com/steve/index.html#mainmenu"
                />
            </map>
        </center>

    </body>
</html>
```

TIP: So what kind of image map should you use: server-side or client-side? The older server-side image maps are on their way out. Because they are processed on the server, information has to be sent back to the server and worked on there—which takes time. For a faster response, I recommend client-side image maps (if the user's browser supports them); they are also easier to create.

Creating image maps and getting the right coordinates for your link regions in the map can be a little difficult. A graphics tool such as LView Pro (**www.lview.com**) makes things easier by displaying the mouse's location in the title bar in pixel coordinates when you click on an image. Here are some dedicated image-map tools that can make the creation of these maps easier:

- *Imaptol*—A Unix tool, **www.sspitzer.org/imaptool/**.
- *LiveImage*—A Windows tool, **www.mediatec.com**.
- *Mapedit*—A Windows and Unix tool, **www.boutell.com/mapedit/**.
- *Web HotSpots*—A Windows tool, **www.concentric.net/~automata/hotspots.shtml**.

Creating Lists

Another popular XHTML topic is the creation of *lists*. Lists let you display information in a compact, tight format and are a useful asset to know about. There are three kinds of lists—unordered lists, ordered lists, and definition lists.

Unordered Lists

You can create *unordered lists* by using the **<ul>** element. Each item in the list gets its own element with the **<li>** (list item) tag. Here's an example showing how to create a bulleted list:

```
<?xml version="1.0"?>
<!DOCTYPE html PUBLIC "-//W3C//DTD XHTML 1.0 Transitional//EN"
"http://www.w3.org/TR/xhtml1/DTD/xhtml1-transitional.dtd">
<html xmlns="http://www.w3.org/1999/xhtml" xml:lang="en" lang="en">
    <head>
        <title>
            An Unordered List
        </title>
    </head>

    <body>

        <h1 align="center">
            Creating An Unordered List
        </h1>

        Here are some items to consider when buying a computer:
        <ul>
            <li>Speed</li>
```

```
            <li>Cost</li>
            <li>RAM</li>
            <li>Disk space</li>
            <li>CD ROM speed</li>
        </ul>

    </body>

</html>
```

The results appear in Figure 5.7, where you can see the bulleted list made from all the list items.

Ordered Lists

Whereas unordered lists display a bullet before each list item, *ordered lists* use a number (or lettering) system of some kind to indicate that the items are sequenced in some way. Here's an example that uses the **<ol>** (ordered list) element to create a simple numbered list:

```
<?xml version="1.0"?>
<!DOCTYPE html PUBLIC "-//W3C//DTD XHTML 1.0 Transitional//EN"
"http://www.w3.org/TR/xhtml1/DTD/xhtml1-transitional.dtd">
<html xmlns="http://www.w3.org/1999/xhtml" xml:lang="en" lang="en">
    <head>
        <title>
            An Ordered List
        </title>
    </head>

    <body>

        <h1 align="center">
            Creating An Ordered List
        </h1>

        Here are some items to consider when buying a computer:
        <ol>
            <li>Speed</li>
            <li>Cost</li>
            <li>RAM</li>
            <li>Disk space</li>
            <li>CD ROM speed</li>
        </ol>

    </body>

</html>
```

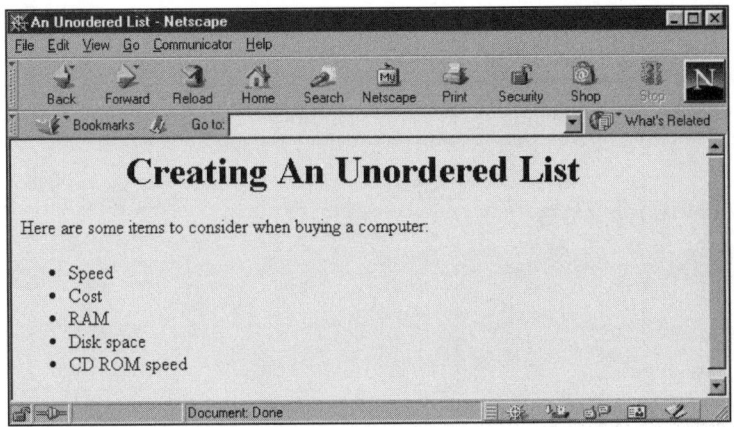

Figure 5.7   An unordered list.

The results of this XHTML appear in Figure 5.8. You can see that the listed items are numbered from one through five. There are other sequencing systems available—everything from letters to Roman numerals.

Definition Lists

There's a third type of list—*definition lists*. These lists include both terms and their definitions. You use the **<dl>** element to create these lists, use **<dt>** for terms, and use **<dd>** for the definition of each term. Here's an example:

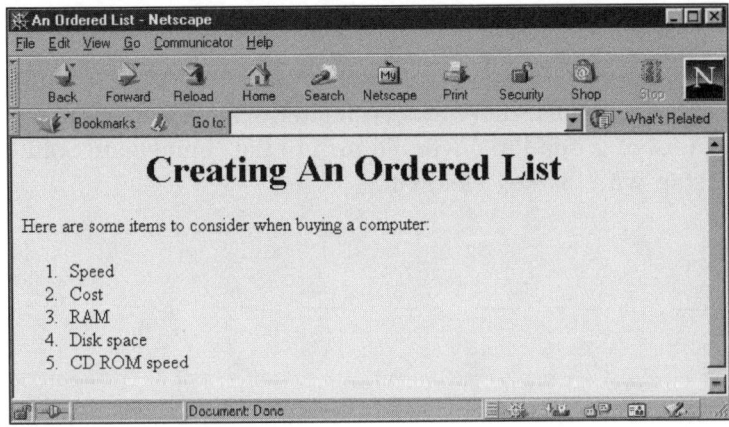

Figure 5.8   An ordered list.

```
<?xml version="1.0"?>
<!DOCTYPE html PUBLIC "-//W3C//DTD XHTML 1.0 Transitional//EN"
"http://www.w3.org/TR/xhtml1/DTD/xhtml1-transitional.dtd">
<html xmlns="http://www.w3.org/1999/xhtml" xml:lang="en" lang="en">
    <head>
        <title>
            A Definition List
        </title>
    </head>

    <body>

        <h1 align="center">
            Creating A Definition List
        </h1>

        Here are some items to consider when buying a computer:
        <dl>
            <dt>Speed</dt><dd>CPU speed in megahertz.</dd>
            <dt>Cost</dt><dd>Make sure to keep this down!</dd>
            <dt>RAM</dt><dd>Amount of memory in the computer.</dd>
            <dt>Disk space</dt><dd>Get plenty of gigabytes.</dd>
            <dt>CD ROM speed</dt><dd>Get at least 24X.</dd>
        </dl>

    </body>

</html>
```

We'll look more at definition lists later in this chapter. There's a lot more coming up, and we have a lot of ground to cover. I'll turn to the "Immediate Solutions" section now and start with the **<a>** element.

Immediate Solutions

<a>—Creating a Hyperlink or Anchor

Purpose: Creates a hyperlink (use the **href** attribute) or an anchor (use the **id** and/or the deprecated **name** attribute for browsers that need to use **name**).

When used as HTML: Start tag/End tag: Required/Required

Supported: [1.0S, 1.0T, 1.0F, 1.1, 2, 3, 3.2, 4, IE1, IE2, IE3, IE4, IE5, NS1, NS2, NS3, NS4]

Attributes:

- **accesskey**—Assigns a keyboard shortcut to the hyperlink; you usually use a platform-dependent key, like the Alt key in Windows, along with the shortcut to give the hyperlink the focus (when it has the focus, it receives keystrokes). Set to a single (case-insensitive) alphanumeric value. [1.0S, 1.0T, 1.0F, 4, IE4, IE5]

- **charset**—Specifies the character encoding of the target of the hyperlink. Set to a Request For Comments (RFC) 2045 language character set string (the default value is ISO-8859-1). [1.0S, 1.0T, 1.0F, 1.1, 4]

- **class**—Class of the element (used for rendering). [1.0S, 1.0T, 1.0F, 1.1, 3, 4, IE4, IE5]

- **coords**—Sets the coordinate values (in pixels) appropriate to the accompanying **shape** attribute to define a region of an image for image maps. Set up **shape** types and **coords** definitions as: **shape=rect coords=**"*left, top, right, bottom*"; **shape=circ coords=**"*centerx, centery, radius*"; **shape=poly coords=**"*x1, y1, x2, y2, ... , xn, yn*". [1.0S, 1.0T, 1.0F, 1.1, 4]

- **dir**—Gives the direction of directionally neutral text (text that doesn't have inherent direction in which you should read it). Possible values: **ltr**: left-to-right text or table and **rtl**: right-to-left text or table. [1.0S, 1.0T, 1.0F, 1.1, 4, IE5]

- **href**—Holds the target URL of the hyperlink. Either this attribute or the **id** attribute must be used. Set to a URL. [1.0S, 1.0T, 1.0F, 1.1, 2, 3, 3.2, 4, IE1, IE2, IE3, IE4, IE5, NS1, NS2, NS3, NS4]

- **hreflang**—Specifies the base language of the target indicated in the **href** attribute. Set to RFC 1766 values. [1.0S, 1.0T, 1.0F, 1.1, 4]

- **id**—A unique alphanumeric identifier for the tag, which you can use to create anchors that can be the target of hyperlinks. Either this attribute or the **href** attribute must be used. Set to a string of alphanumeric characters. [1.0S, 1.0T, 1.0F, 1.1, 3, 4, IE4, IE5]

- **lang**—Base language used for the tag. [1.0S, 1.0T, 1.0F, 1.1, 3, 4, IE4, IE5]

- **language**—Scripting language used for the tag. [IE4, IE5]

- **methods**—Can specify methods to be used in accessing the target. This attribute has disappeared from the HTML 3.2 recommendation. Set to names matching the protocol scheme of the URL in the **href** attribute. [2, 3, IE4, IE5]

- **name**—Available in the three XHTML 1.0 DTDs, but deprecated, not available in the XHTML 1.1 DTD (use **id** instead) Specifies an anchor name, the name you want to use when referring to the enclosed items (such as text, images, and so on) as the target of a hyperlink. Set to a string of alphanumeric characters. [1.0S, 1.0T, 1.0F, 2, 3, 3.2, 4, IE1, IE2, IE3, IE4, IE5, NS1, NS2, NS3, NS4]

- **rel**—Specifies the relationship described by the hyperlink. Set to a white space separated list of relationship names. See "**<link>**—Setting Link Information" in the Immediate Solutions section for more on the **rel** attribute. [1.0S, 1.0T, 1.0F, 1.1, 2, 3, 3.2, 4, IE3, IE4, IE5]

- **rev**—Essentially the same as the **rel** attribute, but the syntax works in the reverse direction. A link from A to B with **rel="x"** is the same relationship as a link from B to A with **rev="x"**. Set to a white space separated list of relationship names. [1.0S, 1.0T, 1.0F, 1.1, 2, 3, 3.2, 4, IE3, IE4, IE5]

- **shape**—Defines the type of region to be defined for mapping in the current **area** tag. Used with the **coords** attribute. Set to **rect** (the default), **circ**, **circle**, **POLY**, or **polygon**. [1.0S, 1.0T, 1.0F, 1.1, 3, 4]

- **style**—Inline style indicating how to render the element. [1.0S, 1.0T, 1.0F, 1.1, 4, IE3, IE4, IE5]

- **tabindex**—Sets the tab sequence of hyperlinks in the page (pressing the Tab key moves from one to the next hyperlink). Set to a positive or negative integer. [1.0S, 1.0T, 1.0F, 4, IE4, IE5]

- **target**—Indicates the named frame for the **href** hyperlink to jump to. Set to the name of a frame. [1.0T, 1.0F, 4, IE3, IE4, IE5, NS2, NS3, NS4]

- **title**—An advisory-only title for the target resource. The **title** attribute holds text that will be displayed in tool tips when the mouse rests over the hyperlink. Set to an alphanumeric string. [1.0S, 1.0T, 1.0F, 1.1, 2, 3, 3.2, 4, IE4, IE5]

- **type**—Specifies the Multipurpose Internet Mail Extensions (MIME) type of the target given in the **href** attribute. Set to an alphanumeric MIME type, like image/gif. [1.0S, 1.0T, 1.0F, 1.1, 4]

- **urn**—Designed to give a more persistent identifier for the **name** value of the hyperlink (but never implemented in the main browsers); has been removed from the HTML specification as of HTML 3.2. [2, 3, IE4, IE5]

- **xml:lang**—Holds the base language for the element when the document is interpreted as an XML document. [1.0S, 1.0T, 1.0F, 1.1]

XHTML events: onclick, ondblclick, onfocus, onblur, onmousedown, onmouseup, onmouseover, onmousemove, onmouseout, onkeypress, onkeydown, onkeyup

The big boss appears and says, "We need a hyperlink added to each of the company's Web pages." "OK," you say, "I'll use the **<a>** element. What's the hyperlink to?" "My own Web page," the BB says, "the one with the huge picture of me in it."

The **<a>** element is a big part of what makes XHTML work. This is the element you use to create hyperlinks and anchors. Here's an example that creates a hyperlink to the W3C Web site:

```
<?xml version="1.0"?>
<!DOCTYPE html PUBLIC "-//W3C//DTD XHTML 1.0 Transitional//EN"
    "http://www.w3.org/TR/xhtml1/DTD/xhtml1-transitional.dtd">
<html xmlns="http://www.w3.org/1999/xhtml" xml:lang="en" lang="en">
    <head>
        <title>
            Creating A Hyperlink
        </title>
    </head>

    <body>

        <center>

            <h1>
                Creating A Hyperlink
            </h1>

            Here's a Web site to check out:
            <a href="http://w3c.org">W3C</a>!
        </center>

    </body>
</html>
```

You can see the results of this XHTML in Figure 5.1. Note that I'm creating a hyperlink by assigning the target URL to the **href** attribute. The text in the **<a>**

element is what will appear as the hyperlink in the Web page. The hyperlink is usually underlined and in a different color from the surrounding text.

Another popular use of the **<a>** element is to create anchors. As discussed in the "In Depth" section of this chapter, you use anchors to label a section of a Web page as a hyperlink target. (For more information and examples, see "Creating Anchors and Linking to Sections in a Page," later in this chapter.)

As you can see by its number of attributes, the **<a>** element is an extensive one in XHTML. I'll take a more detailed look at it throughout the following sections.

Setting Hyperlink Colors

"Hey," says the novice programmer, "how do I set the color of a hyperlink? The default value seems to be blue—the same blue as the background of my page!" "There are two ways to do it," you say. "You can use attributes, like **alink**, **vlink**, and **link**, or you can use styles. Better get some coffee." "OK," says the NP and trots off.

The default color for hyperlinks in a page is blue. Hyperlinks that you've already visited are displayed in violet by default, and when you click on a hyperlink, it turns red when the mouse button is down, again by default. You can set these colors with the **<body>** element's **link**, **vlink** (visited link), and **alink** (active link) attributes.

Here's an example in which I set the color of hyperlinks to green, the color of visited hyperlinks to blue, and the color of active links to red:

```
<?xml version="1.0"?>
<!DOCTYPE html PUBLIC "-//W3C//DTD XHTML 1.0 Transitional//EN"
"http://www.w3.org/TR/xhtml1/DTD/xhtml1-transitional.dtd">
<html xmlns="http://www.w3.org/1999/xhtml" xml:lang="en" lang="en">
    <head>
        <title>
            Setting Hyperlink Colors
        </title>
    </head>

    <body link="green" vlink="blue" alink="red">

        <center>
```

```
        <h1>
            Setting Hyperlink Colors
        </h1>

        Here's a Web site to check out:
        <a href="http://W3C.ORG">W3C</a>!
    </center>

</body>
</html>
```

This works, but as with other style attributes, **alink**, **vlink**, and **link** have all been deprecated in HTML 4 in favor of style sheets. So how do you set those colors by using style sheets? We'll discuss style sheets in Chapter 9, but here's an example. I'll use the **<style>** element to reproduce the colors in the previous example and to add something new (supported only in Internet Explorer so far): a hover color set to yellow. A hover color is used when the mouse is over the hyperlink. Here's the code:

```
<?xml version="1.0"?>
<!DOCTYPE html PUBLIC "-//W3C//DTD XHTML 1.0 Transitional//EN"
"http://www.w3.org/TR/xhtml1/DTD/xhtml1-transitional.dtd">
<html xmlns="http://www.w3.org/1999/xhtml" xml:lang="en" lang="en">
    <head>
        <title>
            Setting Hyperlink Colors
        </title>

        <style type="text/css">

            a:link {color:green}
            a:visited {color:blue}
            a:hover {color:yellow}
            a:active {color:red}

        </style>
    </head>

    <body>

        <center>

            <h1>
                Setting Hyperlink Colors
            </h1>
```

```
            Click this hyperlink to go to
            <a href="http://w3c.org">W3C</a>!
        </center>

    </body>
</html>
```

Creating Graphical Hyperlinks

The Web page design czar is on the phone and says, "The hyperlinks in your page lack oomph." You ask, "*Oomph*?" "That's right," says the WPDC; "Can't you spice them up?" "Well," you say, "I can use images instead of text." "Great, do it *now*," says the WPDC and hangs up.

You can make images into hyperlinks by using an **<img>** element inside an **<a>** element. Doing this can spice up your Web pages considerably—especially if you have some powerful graphics. We saw an example of this in the "In Depth" section at the beginning of this chapter:

```
<?xml version="1.0"?>
<!DOCTYPE html PUBLIC "-//W3C//DTD XHTML 1.0 Transitional//EN"
    "http://www.w3.org/TR/xhtml1/DTD/xhtml1-transitional.dtd">
<html xmlns="http://www.w3.org/1999/xhtml" xml:lang="en" lang="en">
    <head>
        <title>
            Creating A Graphical Hyperlink
        </title>
    </head>

    <body>

        <center>

            <h1>
                Creating A Graphical Hyperlink
            </h1>

            <a href="http://w3c.org">
                <img width="277" height="114" src="clickme.gif"
                    alt="Click me to go to W3C!" />
            </a>
        </center>

    </body>
</html>
```

You can see the results of this XHTML in Figure 5.2. When the user clicks on this image, the browser will navigate to the hyperlink's target, **http://W3C.org**. Note that the text you use for the **alt** attribute of the **<img>** element appears as a tool tip when the mouse rests over the image, also shown in Figure 5.2.

*TIP: As noted in the "In Depth" section of this chapter, the border that appears around the image will use the same colors as the current text hyperlinks. You can regulate the thickness of the border with the <img> element's **border** attribute.*

The fact that you can use images as hyperlinks is significant because it allows you to use images for navigation. See "Using Graphical Hyperlinks for Navigation" in the Immediate Solutions section of this chapter for more information.

<base>—Setting the Base for Hyperlinks

Purpose: Sets the base URL for the hyperlinks in a page. Can be used only in the **<head>** section.

When used as HTML: Start tag/End tag: Required/Omitted. This element takes no content.

Supported: [1.0S, 1.0T, 1.0F, 2, 3, 3.2, 4, IE1, IE2, IE3, IE4, IE5, NS1, NS2, NS3, NS4]

Attributes:

- **href**—Holds the URL you want to use as the base URL of hyperlinks in the page. **href** is a required attribute. [1.0S, 1.0T, 1.0F, 2, 3, 3.2, 4, IE1, IE2, IE3, IE4, IE5, NS1, NS2, NS3, NS4]
- **target**—Gives the target frame for hyperlink targets to load to. [1.0T, 1.0F, 4, IE3, IE4, IE5, NS2, NS3, NS4]

XHTML events: None

"Jeez," says the novice programmer, "you try to do something just a little different, and nothing works." "What do you mean, NP?" you ask. "I have a page I want to use as an index to pages in another directory," the NP says, "and I keep getting fouled up when I have to put in the full URL of each of those pages." "Why didn't you just set the base URL with the **<base>** element?" you ask. "Because I never heard of it," the NP says, chagrined.

Relative hyperlinks are defined relative to the current page, unless you use the **<base>** element to specify a different base for hyperlinks. This element is available in the three XHTML 1.0 DTDs but not in the XHTML 1.1 DTD.

In the following example, I'm setting the base URL for a Web page to **http://www.starpowder.com/images/**. Now when I refer to a file with a relative URL—just the name of the file, clickme.gif—the browser will look for that file, using the full URL, **http://www.starpowder.com/images/clickme.gif**. Here's the code:

```
<?xml version="1.0"?>
<!DOCTYPE html PUBLIC "-//W3C//DTD XHTML 1.0 Transitional//EN"
"http://www.w3.org/TR/xhtml1/DTD/xhtml1-transitional.dtd">
<html xmlns="http://www.w3.org/1999/xhtml" xml:lang="en" lang="en">
    <head>
        <title>
            Creating A Graphical Hyperlink
        </title>

        <base href="http://www.starpowder.com/images" />

    </head>

    <body>

        <center>

            <h1>
                Creating A Graphical Hyperlink
            </h1>

            <a href="http://W3C.ORG">
                <img width="277" height="114" src="clickme.gif"
                    alt="Click me to go to W3C!" />
            </a>
        </center>

    </body>
</html>
```

Using the **<base>** element is a great idea if you have a lot of relative URLs in your pages, and the organization of your Web site has become complex.

<link>—Setting Link Information

Purpose: Specifies the relationship of other documents to the current one (such as specifying an external style sheet). The **<link>** element is used in the **<head>** section of a page. This element takes no content.

When used as HTML: Start tag/End tag: Required/Omitted

Supported: [1.0S, 1.0T, 1.0F, 1.1, 2, 3, 3.2, 4, IE3, IE4, IE5, NS4]

Attributes:

- **charset**—Specifies the character encoding of the target of the hyperlink. Set to an RFC 2045 language character set string (the default value is ISO-8859-1). [1.0S, 1.0T, 1.0F, 1.1, 4]
- **class**—Class of the element (used for rendering). [1.0S, 1.0T, 1.0F, 1.1, 2, 3, 4]
- **dir**—Gives the direction of directionally neutral text (text that doesn't have inherent direction in which you should read it). Possible values: **LTR**: left-to-right text or table and **RTL**: right-to-left text or table. [1.0S, 1.0T, 1.0F, 1.1, 4]
- **disabled**—Indicates that the relationship to other documents is initially disabled. [IE4]
- **href**—Holds the target URL of the resource. Either this attribute or the **id** attribute must be used. Set to a URL. [1.0S, 1.0T, 1.0F, 1.1, 2, 3, 3.2, 4, IE3, IE4, IE5]
- **hreflang**—Specifies the base language of the target indicated in the **href** attribute. Set to RFC 1766 values. [1.0S, 1.0T, 1.0F, 1.1, 4]
- **id**—A unique alphanumeric identifier for the tag, which you can use to refer to it. [1.0S, 1.0T, 1.0F, 1.1, 2, 3, 4, IE4, IE5]
- **lang**—Base language used for the tag. [1.0S, 1.0T, 1.0F, 1.1, 4]
- **media**—Indicates on what device the document will be rendered; possible values: **screen** (the default), **print**, **projection** (transparent projection devices), **braille**, **speech**, or **all** (style information should be used for all devices). [1.0S, 1.0T, 1.0F, 1.1, 4, IE4, IE5]
- **rel**—Specifies the relationship described by the hyperlink. Set to a white space separated list of relationship names. [1.0S, 1.0T, 1.0F, 1.1, 2, 3, 3.2, 4, IE4, IE5, NS4]
- **rev**—Essentially the same as the **REL** attribute, but the syntax works in the reverse direction. A link from A to B with **REL="X"** is the same relationship as a link from B to A with **REV="X"**. Set to a white-space separated list of relationship names. [1.0S, 1.0T, 1.0F, 1.1, 2, 3, 3.2, 4, IE4, IE5]

- **src**—Gives the link's source. [NS4]
- **style**—Inline style indicating how to render the element. [1.0S, 1.0T, 1.0F, 1.1, 4]
- **target**—Indicates the named frame for the **href** hyperlink to jump to. Set to the name of a frame. [1.0T, 1.0F, 4]
- **title**—Holds additional information (as might be displayed in tool tips) for the element. [1.0S, 1.0T, 1.0F, 1.1, 2, 3, 4, IE4, IE5]
- **type**—Specifies the MIME type of the target given in the **href** attribute. Set to an alphanumeric MIME type, like image/gif. [1.0S, 1.0T, 1.0F, 1.1, 4, NS4]
- **xml:lang**—Holds the base language for the element when the document is interpreted as an XML document. [1.0S, 1.0T, 1.0F, 1.1]

XHTML events: **onclick**, **ondblclick**, **onmousedown**, **onmouseup**, **onmouseover**, **onmousemove**, **onmouseout**, **onkeypress**, **onkeydown**, **onkeyup**

You use the **<link>** element to specify the relationship of the current page to other documents. The actual relationship is specified with the **rel** attribute, which can take these values:

- **rel=alternate** (Internet Explorer and XHTML, HTML 4 only)—Specifies an alternate resource.
- **rel=appendix** (Internet Explorer and XHTML, HTML 4 only)—Specifies an appendix.
- **rel=bookmark**—Provides links to entry points into a document (the **title** attribute may be used to label the bookmark).
- **rel=chapter** (Internet Explorer and XHTML, HTML 4 only)—Specifies a chapter.
- **rel=contents** (Internet Explorer and XHTML, HTML 4 only)—Specifies the contents section.
- **rel=copyright**—Specifies a copyright document for the current document.
- **rel=glossary**—Specifies a document providing a glossary of terms.
- **rel=help**—Specifies a document providing help.
- **rel=home**—Specifies a home page.
- **rel=index**—Specifies a document providing an index.
- **rel=next**—Specifies the next document.
- **rel=offline** (Internet Explorer only)—Specifies an offline resource.
- **rel=prev**—Specifies the previous document.

- **rel=section** (Internet Explorer and XHTML, HTML 4 only)—Specifies a section.
- **rel=shortcut icon** (Internet Explorer only)—Specifies a shortcut icon for the page; the icon will be used in the Internet Explorer Favorites folder.
- **rel=start** (Internet Explorer and XHTML, HTML 4 only)—Specifies the start of a resource.
- **rel=stylesheet**—Specifies an external style sheet.
- **rel=subsection** (Internet Explorer and XHTML, HTML 4 only)—Specifies a subsection.

Here's an example showing how to use an external style sheet (which we'll see more about in Chapter 9). Note that in Netscape Navigator, instead of using **href**, you use **src**, which is not available in true XHMTL. Here's the code:

```
<?xml version="1.0"?>
<!DOCTYPE html PUBLIC "-//W3C//DTD XHTML 1.0 Transitional//EN"
"http://www.w3.org/TR/xhtml1/DTD/xhtml1-transitional.dtd">
<html xmlns="http://www.w3.org/1999/xhtml" xml:lang="en" lang="en">
    <head>
        <title>
            Using An External Style Sheet
        </title>

        <link rel="stylesheet" href="style.css" />

    </head>

    <body>

        <center>

            <h1>
                Using An External Style Sheet
            </h1>

            <p>
                This page uses an external style sheet.
            </p>
        </center>

    </body>
</html>
```

Giving Hyperlinks Access Keys

In Internet Explorer, you can use the **<a>** element's **accesskey** attribute to assign an access key to the hyperlink to make it accessible from the keyboard. Note that although this attribute is available in the three XHTML 1.0 DTDs, it's been removed from the XHTML 1.1 DTD. Here's an example in which I assign the access key "I" to the Internet Explorer link and "N" to the Netscape Navigator link:

```xml
<?xml version="1.0"?>
<!DOCTYPE html PUBLIC "-//W3C//DTD XHTML 1.0 Transitional//EN"
"http://www.w3.org/TR/xhtml1/DTD/xhtml1-transitional.dtd">
<html xmlns="http://www.w3.org/1999/xhtml" xml:lang="en" lang="en">
    <head>
        <title>
            Using Hyperlink Access Keys
        </title>
    </head>

    <body>

        <center>

            <h1>
                Using Hyperlink Access Keys
            </h1>
            You might be interested in these two browsers:
            <p>
                <a href="http://www.microsoft.com/ie" accesskey="I">
                    Internet Explorer
                </a>
                <br />
                <a href="http://www.netscape.com" accesskey ="N">
                    Netscape Navigator
                </a>
            </p>
        </center>

    </body>
</html>
```

To activate the access key, the user presses a system-specific key and the access key at the same time. For example, in Windows, when the user presses Alt + I, the Internet Explorer hyperlink gets the focus (that is, it appears with a dotted box around it and receives keystrokes); pressing Enter at that point activates the hyperlink.

Using Graphical Hyperlinks for Navigation

The novice programmer wants to know, "Why can't I use the cute arrow buttons for navigation that other Web pages have?" "No reason at all," you say; "give it a whirl."

It's very common to use graphical symbols, like arrows and buttons, for navigation, and you can use them by making their images into hyperlinks. Here's an example showing how that works. I use arrow images to let users navigate to other pages, and I use the image of a house to let users navigate to the site's home page:

```xml
<?xml version="1.0"?>
<!DOCTYPE html PUBLIC "-//W3C//DTD XHTML 1.0 Transitional//EN"
    "http://www.w3.org/TR/xhtml1/DTD/xhtml1-transitional.dtd">
<html xmlns="http://www.w3.org/1999/xhtml" xml:lang="en" lang="en">
    <head>
        <title>
            Creating Graphical Navigational Aids
        </title>
    </head>

    <body>

        <center>

            <h1>
                Creating Graphical Navigational Aids
            </h1>

            Want to get somewhere fast? Click a button below...

            <br />

            <a href="prev.html">
                <img width="172" height="117" src="left.gif"
                    alt="previous"  border="0" />
            </a>

            <a href="index.html">
                <img width="161" height="105" src="home.gif"
                    alt="home"  border="0" />
            </a>
```

```
            <a href="next.html">
                <img width="172" height="117" src="right.gif"
                    alt="next"  border="0" />
            </a>
        </center>

    </body>
</html>
```

We first saw the previous example in the "In Depth" section of this chapter, and you can see the result of this XHTML in Figure 5.5.

Creating Navigation Bars

A popular use of hyperlinks is to create a *navigation bar*. Such bars display a number of small text or graphical hyperlinks that point to the other pages on the site so that users can navigate around the site. Navigation bars are extremely useful if you include them in all the pages in your site because they really open up your Web site to users, who can navigate anywhere from anywhere else. And these bars are unobtrusive, appearing at the bottom or top—or both—of your pages. You'll find that larger commercial Web sites almost invariably use navigation bars.

Navigation bars are usually created using tables to avoid letting the browser reposition the hyperlinks in them. Here's an example:

```
<?xml version="1.0"?>
<!DOCTYPE html PUBLIC "-//W3C//DTD XHTML 1.0 Transitional//EN"
"http://www.w3.org/TR/xhtml1/DTD/xhtml1-transitional.dtd">
<html xmlns="http://www.w3.org/1999/xhtml" xml:lang="en" lang="en">
    <head>
        <title>
            Creating Navigation Bars
        </title>
    </head>

    <body>

        <center>

            <h1>
                Creating Navigation Bars
            </h1>
```

```html
            Welcome to my page!

            <br />
            <br />
            <br />
            <br />
            <br />
            <br />
            <br />
            <br />

                    <table>
                        <tr>
                            <td>
                                <a href="http://www.starpowder.com">
                                    <img src="nav1.gif" vspace="1" hspace="1"
                                        alt = "Image 1" border="0" />
                                </a>
                            </td>
                            <td>
                                <a href="http://www.starpowder.com/tutorial.htm">
                                    <img src="nav2.gif" vspace="1" hspace="1"
                                        alt = "Image 2" border="0" />
                                </a>
                            </td>
                            <td>
                                <a href="http://www.starpowder.com/help.htm">
                                    <img src="nav3.gif" vspace="1" hspace="1"
                                        alt = "Image 3" border="0" />
                                </a>
                            </td>
                            <td>
                                <a href="http://www.starpowder.com/email.htm">
                                    <img src="nav4.gif" vspace="1" hspace="1"
                                        alt = "Image 4" border="0" />
                                </a>
                            </td>
                        </tr>
                    </table>
            </center>

        </body>
</html>
```

Figure 5.9   A navigation bar.

The results of this XHTML appear in Figure 5.9. As you can see in the figure, the navigation bar appears at the bottom of the page. Using that bar, the user can navigate to other locations on the site easily. Navigation bars are very useful and I highly recommend them for real Web sites.

Creating Anchors and Linking to Sections in a Page

"Darn," says the novice programmer, "this hyperlink stuff is no good." "Why?" you ask. "Well," the NP says, "my Web page is about 12,000 lines long, and when I send users there, they get impatient." "Why not send them to the exact section of the Web page instead of to the top of it?" The NP asks, "You can do that?"

You can use the **<a>** element with the **id** attribute to enclose a section of a Web page and create an *anchor*. When you create an anchor, you can make it the target of hyperlinks, allowing you to jump to a particular section of a Web page.

*TIP: Although you use the **href** attribute in **<a>** elements to create hyperlinks, and you use the **id** attribute to create anchors, you can actually use both of these attributes in the same **<a>** element.*

After naming an anchor, you can refer to it by adding a **#** symbol in front of the name and using it in the **href** attribute of a hyperlink. When the user clicks on that hyperlink, the browser will navigate to the anchor.

Following is an example that we saw in the "In Depth" section of this chapter, where I set up an anchor named **"bottom"** at the bottom of a page. This lets the user move there by clicking its hyperlink. Note that I'm using both an **id** attribute for proper XHTML and a **name** attribute for browsers (such as Netscape Navigator) that don't use the **id** attribute yet. Here's the code:

```
<?xml version="1.0"?>
<!DOCTYPE html PUBLIC "-//W3C//DTD XHTML 1.0 Transitional//EN"
"http://www.w3.org/TR/xhtml1/DTD/xhtml1-transitional.dtd">
<html xmlns="http://www.w3.org/1999/xhtml" xml:lang="en" lang="en">
    <head>
        <title>
            Linking To A Section In A Page
        </title>
    </head>

    <body>

        <center>

            <h1>
                Linking To A Section In A Page
            </h1>

            Click here to go to the
            <a href="#bottom">bottom</a>
            of the page.

            <br />
            <br />
            <br />
            <br />
            <br />
            <br />
            <br />
            <br />
            <br />
            <br />
            <br />
            <br />

            <hr />
```

```
            <a id="bottom" name="bottom">This is the bottom of the page.</a>
        </center>

    </body>
</html>
```

You can see the results of this XHTML in Figures 5.3 and 5.4.

The target anchor of a hyperlink doesn't have to be in the same document—you can link to an anchored section in another document as well. To do so, you include the URL of that page before the **#** and the anchor name in the hyperlink, like this: **href="http://www.starpowder.com/steve/mountains.html#alps"**.

Here's another example, from the "In Depth" section of this chapter, in which I'm linking to the **bottom** anchor in the previous page, but from another document:

```
<?xml version="1.0"?>
<!DOCTYPE html PUBLIC "-//W3C//DTD XHTML 1.0 Transitional//EN"
"http://www.w3.org/TR/xhtml1/DTD/xhtml1-transitional.dtd">
<html xmlns="http://www.w3.org/1999/xhtml" xml:lang="en" lang="en">
    <head>
        <title>
            Linking To A Section In Another Page
        </title>
    </head>

    <body>

        <center>

            <h1>
                Linking To A Section In Another Page
            </h1>

            Click here to go to the
            <a href="discussion.html#bottom">bottom</a>
            of the <i>other</i> page.

        </center>

    </body>
</html>
```

NOTE: *Browsers are supposed to be able to navigate to anchors, even if they do not enclose anything (that is, even if the* **<a>** *element is empty). However, some browsers have problems recognizing empty anchor elements.*

Creating Clickable Footnotes

If you use footnotes in your documents, then to make your pages more accessible, you can make those footnotes into hyperlinks—taking full advantage of what hypertext has to offer.

In this example, when the user clicks on footnote 1 (marking the University of Vienna), the browser navigates to the bottom of the page, where the footnote is expanded (into "Founded in 1365."):

```
<?xml version="1.0"?>
<!DOCTYPE html PUBLIC "-//W3C//DTD XHTML 1.0 Transitional//EN"
"http://www.w3.org/TR/xhtml1/DTD/xhtml1-transitional.dtd">
<html xmlns="http://www.w3.org/1999/xhtml" xml:lang="en" lang="en">
    <head>
        <title>
            Creating Hyperlink Footnotes
        </title>
    </head>

    <body>

        <center>

            <h1>
                Creating Hyperlink Footnotes
            </h1>

            Today, we visited the University of Vienna.
            <a href="#footnote"><sup>1</sup></a>.

            <br />
            <br />
            <br />
            <br />
            <br />
            <br />
            <br />
            <br />
            <br />
            <br />
            <br />
            <br />

            <hr />
```

```
           <a id="footnote">Founded in 1365.</a>
    </center>

  </body>
</html>
```

You can see the result of this XHTML in Figure 5.10.

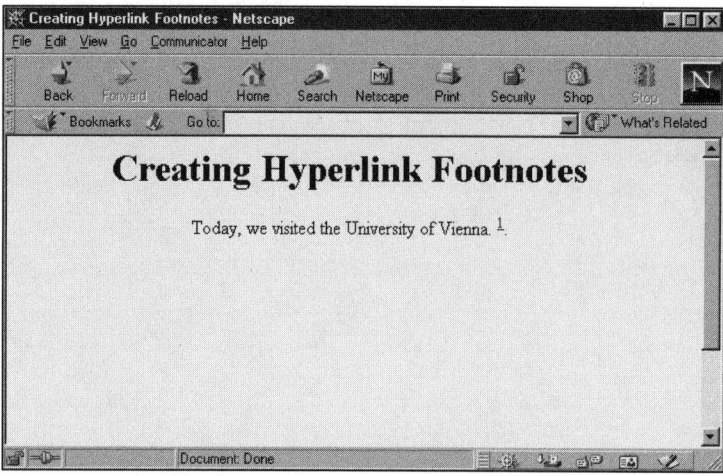

Figure 5.10   A hyperlink footnote.

Emailing with Hyperlinks

The novice programmer wants to know, "How can I get feedback from people who admire my Web page?" You smile and say, "You can include an email hyperlink, and when users click on it, their email programs will open with an empty message already addressed to you." "At last I can hear the applause!" the NP says.

You can use an email hyperlink to let users email you. When they click on the hyperlink, it opens their email programs and creates an empty message addressed to you. You create an email hyperlink by using the hyperlink protocol *mailto:* (see "Types of URLs" earlier in this chapter) followed by your email address. Here's an example showing how this works:

```
<?xml version="1.0"?>
<!DOCTYPE html PUBLIC "-//W3C//DTD XHTML 1.0 Transitional//EN"
  "http://www.w3.org/TR/xhtml1/DTD/xhtml1-transitional.dtd">
<html xmlns="http://www.w3.org/1999/xhtml" xml:lang="en" lang="en">
```

```
<head>
    <title>
        Creating A MAILTO Hyperlink
    </title>
</head>

<body>

    <center>

        <h1>
            Creating A MAILTO Hyperlink
        </h1>

        Want to contact me? Just
        <a href="mailto:steve@starpowder.com">email me
        </a>!
    </center>

</body>
</html>
```

You can see the result of this XHTML in Figure 5.11. When the user clicks the hyperlink, their email program opens and they can send email to you. As you can see, mailto: hyperlinks provide an easy way to get feedback from people who are viewing your Web page (easier than setting up CGI scripts, for example).

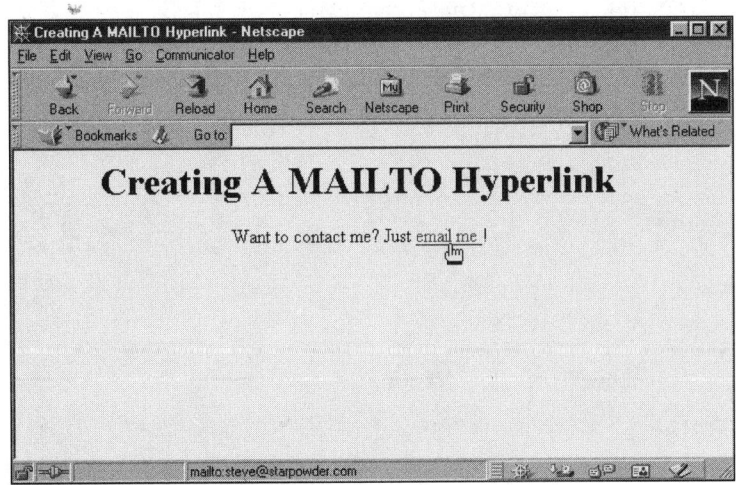

Figure 5.11 An email link.

Downloading Files with the HTTP and FTP Protocols

"I've got a Microsoft Word .doc file that I want to let people download," says the novice programmer. "Is there any way I can do it?" "Sure," you say, "just use a hyperlink to the file or use an FTP hyperlink." "How's that?" the NP asks.

Web browsers are capable of downloading files other than XHTML pages. If you specify a URL that corresponds to a text file, for example, the Web browser will download it using the standard HTTP protocol (which means that such files are valid hyperlink targets). If the browser thinks it can display the type of file you are downloading, it will; otherwise, it'll ask you if you want to run it, or where you want to save it on disk.

Although the HTTP protocol works for transferring files, using FTP is often faster. If you have access to an FTP server, you can upload your files there and provide FTP hyperlinks to them. An FTP hyperlink tells the Web browser to use the FTP protocol instead of HTTP. You can create an FTP hyperlink simply by starting it with FTP instead of HTTP, like this: **ftp://ftp.starpowder.com** (note that the FTP server name usually begins with **ftp**). You can also provide a username and password for the FTP server, if needed. For instance, here I'm referring to a specific file: **ftp://*username*:*password*@ftp.starpowder.com/steve/*filename***.

Here's an example of putting FTP hyperlinks to work:

```
<?xml version="1.0"?>
<!DOCTYPE html PUBLIC "-//W3C//DTD XHTML 1.0 Transitional//EN"
    "http://www.w3.org/TR/xhtml1/DTD/xhtml1-transitional.dtd">
<html xmlns="http://www.w3.org/1999/xhtml" xml:lang="en" lang="en">
    <head>
        <title>
            Creating An FTP Hyperlink
        </title>
    </head>

    <body>

        <center>

            <h1>
                Creating An FTP Hyperlink
            </h1>

            You can get the
            <a href =
                "ftp://username:password@ftp.starpowder.com/steve/list.txt">
```

```
            list of heroes</a> here!
        </center>

    </body>
</html>
```

<map>—Creating Client-Side Image Maps

Purpose: Creates an image-map specification and encloses **<area>** elements that define the shapes in the image map. Pass the name of this map to the **<img>** element's **usemap** attribute.

When used as HTML: Start tag/End tag: Required/Required

Supported: [1.0S, 1.0T, 1.0F, 1.1, 3.2, 4, IE1, IE2, IE3, IE4, IE5, NS2, NS3, NS4]

Attributes:

- **class**—Class of the element (used for rendering). [1.0S, 1.0T, 1.0F, 1.1, 4, IE4, IE5]

- **dir**—Gives the direction of directionally neutral text (text that doesn't have inherent direction in which you should read it). Possible values: **ltr**: left-to-right text or table and **rtl**: right-to-left text or table. [1.0S, 1.0T, 1.0F, 1.1, 4, IE5]

- **id**—Required. A unique alphanumeric identifier for the tag, which you can use to refer to it. Holds the id of the map for reference by other parts of the page.[1.0S, 1.0T, 1.0F, 1.1, 4, IE4, IE5]

- **lang**—Base language used for the tag. [1.0S, 1.0T, 1.0F, 1.1, 4, IE4, IE5]

- **language**—Scripting language used for the tag. [IE4, IE5]

- **name**—Used to hold the name of the map for reference by other parts of the page, now for backwards compatibility. See the **id** attribute instead. [1.0S, 1.0T, 1.0F, 3.2, 4, IE1, IE2, IE3, IE4, IE5, NS2, NS3, NS4]

- **style**—Inline style indicating how to render the element. [1.0S, 1.0T, 1.0F, 1.1, 4, IE4, IE5]

- **title**—Holds additional information (which might be displayed in tool tips) for the element. [1.0S, 1.0T, 1.0F, 1.1, 4, IE4, IE5]

- **xml:lang**—Holds the base language for the element when the document is interpreted as an XML document. [1.0S, 1.0T, 1.0F, 1.1]

XHTML events: onclick, ondblclick, onfocus, onblur, onmousedown, onmouseup, onmouseover, onmousemove, onmouseout, onkeypress, onkeydown, onkeyup

The big boss appears in a cloud of cigar smoke and says, "All our competitors have image maps on their Web sites for easier navigation. We need one like theirs, but better." "What do you mean by better?" you ask. "Bigger," says the BB and disappears.

Image maps present the user with an easy graphical way to use hyperlinks to navigate. All users have to do is click on a region in an image map—this region is called a *hotspot*—and the browser navigates to the corresponding URL.

There are two types of image maps—client-side and server-side. Client-side image maps run in the browser, and server-side image maps run in the server. You use the **<map>** element to create a client-side image map, which is defined in the Web page itself. To do that, you name the map with the **<map>** element's **id** attribute. (You can also use the **name** attribute at the same time for browsers, such as Netscape Navigator, that don't use **id** yet.) You also enclose **<area>** elements, which define the clickable regions in the image map, in the **<map>** element. Here's an example:

```
<map id="imap">
    <area shape=rect coords="16,39 127,61"
        alt = "Reuters" href="http://www.reuters.com" />
    <area shape=rect coords="62,71 173,93"
        alt = "Search"
        href="http://www.starpowder.com/steve/search.html" />
</map>
```

So how do you set up the **<area>** elements and tie the resulting map to an image? Take a look at the following two sections.

<area>—Creating Clickable Regions in Image Maps

Purpose: Specifies a clickable region in a client-side image map. Use this element in **<map>** elements. This element does not take any content.

When used as HTML: Start tag/End tag: Required/Omitted

Supported: [3.2, 4, IE1, IE2, IE3, IE4, IE5, NS2, NS3, NS4]

Attributes:

- **accesskey**—Assigns a keyboard shortcut to the hyperlink; you usually use a platform-dependent key, like the Alt key in Windows, along with the shortcut to give the hyperlink the focus. Set to a single (case-insensitive) alphanumeric value. [1.0S, 1.0T, 1.0F, 1.1, 4, IE4, IE5]
- **alt**—This required attribute holds alternate text for the region defined by the **<area>** element. [1.0S, 1.0T, 1.0F, 1.1, 3.2, 4, IE4, IE5]
- **class**—Class of the element (used for rendering). [1.0S, 1.0T, 1.0F, 1.1, 3, 4, IE4, IE5]
- **coords**—Specifies the actual coordinates for the clickable area. The coordinate system starts at the top-left corner of the image and coordinates get larger as you move down and to the right. Here are the **shape** types and **coords** definitions you can use: **shape=rect, coords="left, top, right, bottom"**; **shape=circle, coords="centerx, centery, radius"**; **shape=poly, coords="x1, y1, x2, y2, ... , xn, yn"**. [1.0S, 1.0T, 1.0F, 1.1, 3.2, 4, IE2, IE3, IE4, IE5, NS2, NS3, NS4]
- **dir**—Gives the direction of directionally neutral text (text that doesn't have inherent direction in which you should read it). Possible values: **ltr**: left-to-right text or table and **rtl**: right-to-left text or table. [1.0S, 1.0T, 1.0F, 1.1, 4, IE5]
- **href**—Holds the hyperlink target that the browser should navigate to when this clickable area is clicked. Set to a URL. [1.0S, 1.0T, 1.0F, 1.1, 3.2, 4, IE2, IE3, IE4, IE5, NS2, NS3, NS4]
- **id**—A unique alphanumeric identifier for the tag, which you can use to refer to it. [1.0S, 1.0T, 1.0F, 1.1, 3, 4, IE4, IE5]
- **lang**—Base language used for the tag. [1.0S, 1.0T, 1.0F, 1.1, 3, 4, IE4, IE5]
- **language**—Scripting language used for the tag. [IE4, IE5]
- **name**—Name used for the element. [NS4]
- **nohref**—Specifies that there is no hyperlink target for this **<area>** element. This is the default if you don't specify a hyperlink with the **href** attribute. This is a standalone attribute in HTML. [1.0S, 1.0T, 1.0F, 1.1, 3.2, 4, IE1, IE2, IE3, IE4, IE5, NS2, NS3, NS4]
- **shape**—Specifies the shape of the area. Use this attribute together with the **coords** attribute. Possible values: **rect** (the default, also **rectangle**), **circ** (also **circle**), **poly** (also **polygon**). [1.0S, 1.0T, 1.0F, 1.1, 3.2, 4, IE1, IE2, IE3, IE4, IE5, NS2, NS3, NS4]
- **style**—Inline style indicating how to render the element. [1.0S, 1.0T, 1.0F, 1.1, 4, IE4, IE5]

- **tabindex**—Sets the tab sequence of hyperlinks in the map (pressing the Tab key moves from one to the next hyperlink). Set to a positive or negative integer. [1.0S, 1.0T, 1.0F, 1.1, 4, IE4, IE5]
- **target**—Gives the name of a frame for the **href** hyperlink to jump to when clicked. [1.0T, 1.0F, 4, IE3, IE4, IE5, NS2, NS3, NS4]
- **title**—Holds additional information (which might be displayed in tool tips) for the element. [1.0S, 1.0T, 1.0F, 1.1, 3, 4, IE4, IE5]
- **xml:lang**—Holds the base language for the element when the document is interpreted as an XML document. [1.0S, 1.0T, 1.0F, 1.1]

XHTML events: onclick, ondblclick, onfocus, onblur, onmousedown, onmouseup, onmouseover, onmousemove, onmouseout, onkeypress, onkeydown, onkeyup

You use the **<area>** element to define clickable regions in image maps; **<area>** elements are enclosed in a **<map>** element. You can define three types of shapes in **<area>** elements—rectangles, circles, and polygons. You use the **shape** attribute to indicate the shape you want, use the **coords** attribute to set its coordinates, and use the **href** attribute to set the hyperlink target for the region. The coordinates for image maps start at (0, 0), at the upper-left corner, and increase as you move to the right and down. Coordinates are measured in pixels.

Here's how you define the three shapes you can use in client-side areas:

```
area shape="rect" alt = "Alt text"
coords="left, top, right, bottom" href="url1">
<area shape="circle" alt = "Alt text"
coords="centerx, centery, radius" href="url2">
<area shape="poly" alt = "Alt text"
coords="x1, y1, x2, y2, ... , xn, yn" href="url3">
```

And here's an example. Note that after defining a client-side image map with the **<map>** element, you pass its name to the **usemap** attribute of an **<img>** element:

```
<map id="imap">
    <area shape="rect" coords="0, 0, 100, 100" alt = "Alt text"
        href="http://www.w3c.org" />
    <area shape="circle" coords="200, 200, 50" alt = "Alt text"
        href="http://microsoft.com" />
    <area shape="poly" alt = "Alt text"
        coords="300, 300, 310, 320, 450, 473, 300, 300"
        href="http://www.netscape.com" />
</map>
```

An important point—there's a fourth "shape" you can use in image maps: **default**, which is the area not covered by any other **<area>** elements. When you set up a URL for **default**, that URL is used when the user clicks outside any clickable region.

Want to see a full client-side image map at work? Take a look at the next section.

NOTE: *The number of successive coordinates of polygons has no specific limits, but XHTML limits the values of attribute settings to 1,024 characters. Also, note that if the first and last coordinates of a polygon are not the same, then XHTML adds a final segment to close it.*

TIP: *You can specify an unlimited number of **<area>** regions in a client-side image map, and if two regions overlap, the one that was listed first should take precedence.*

Creating Client-Side Image Maps

The novice programmer asks, "So exactly how do I create a client-side image map? I know you use **<map>** and **<area>** elements." "Better pull up a chair," you say, "and we'll go through it."

You create client-side image maps by creating a **<map>** element to define the clickable regions in the map and then placing **<area>** elements, one per clickable region, in the **<map>** element. (See the sections "**<map>**—Creating Client-Side Image Maps" and "**<area>**—Creating Clickable Regions in Image Maps," earlier in this chapter.) You then assign the name of the **<map>** element to the **usemap** attribute of the **<img>** element; doing this inserts the actual image map into the Web page.

NOTE: *Netscape Navigator does not allow you to specify an external URL in the **usemap** attribute of the **<img>** element—you can only use internal anchors.*

In this example, I insert the image into the Web page with an **<img>** element, create a map named **imap** with the **<map>** element, define the regions in the map with **<area>** elements, and assign the name of the map—prefaced with a #—to the image with the **<img>** element's **usemap** attribute. Here's what it looks like (note that technically, all **<area>** elements should also have **alt** attributes):

```
<?xml version="1.0"?>
<!DOCTYPE html PUBLIC "-//W3C//DTD XHTML 1.0 Transitional//EN"
    "http://www.w3.org/TR/xhtml1/DTD/xhtml1-transitional.dtd">
<html xmlns="http://www.w3.org/1999/xhtml" xml:lang="en" lang="en">
```

```xhtml
        <head>
            <title>
                Using A Client Side Image Map
            </title>
        </head>

        <body bgcolor="black">

            <center>
                <img width="528" height="137" src="mainmenu.jpg"
                    border="0" alt="image map" usemap="#imap" />
                <map id="imap" name="imap">
                    <area shape="rect" coords="16,39 127,61"
                        href="http://www.reuters.com" />
                    <area shape="rect" coords="62,71 173,93"
                        href="http://www.starpowder.com/steve/search.html" />
                    <area shape="rect" coords="98,104 209,126"
                        href="http://www.nnic.noaa.gov" />
                    <area shape="rect" coords="411,35 522,57"
                        href="http://www.starpowder.com/steve/gbook.htm" />
                    <area shape="rect" coords="360,67 471,89"
                        href="http://www.yahoo.com/guides_and_tutorials/" />
                    <area shape="rect" coords="328,98 439,120"
                        href="http://www.web21.com/services/hot100/index.html"
                    />
                    <area shape="default" href=
                        "http://www.starpowder.com/steve/index.html#mainmenu"
                    />
                </map>
            </center>

        </body>
</html>
```

The results of this XHTML appear in Figure 5.12. As you can see, when the mouse rests over a clickable region in the image map, the URL of that region appears in the browser's status bar, and the **alt** text for the region appears as a tool tip next to the mouse cursor. When the user clicks a region, the browser navigates to the target URL.

Congratulations, you've just created an image map!

NOTE: *Some older browsers don't support client-side image maps, so you might want to create server-side image maps.*

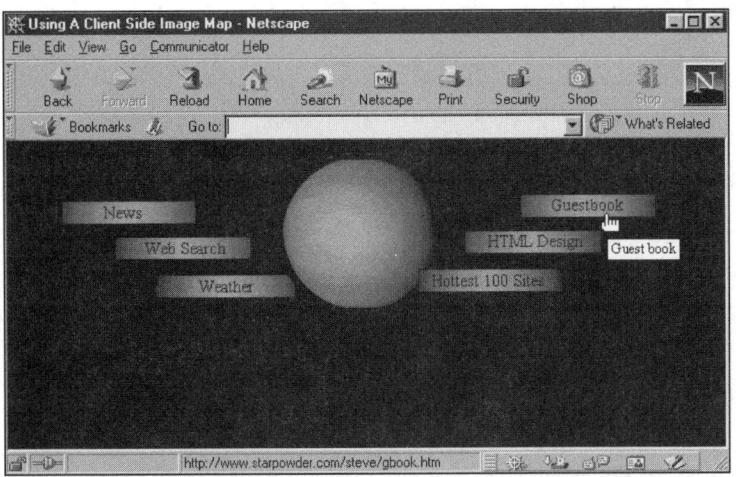

Figure 5.12 A client-side image map.

Creating Server-Side Image Maps

"Uh oh," says the novice programmer, "my favorite Web browser doesn't seem to support client-side image maps. Of course, my browser may be nonstandard." "What's it called?" you ask. "*SuperDuperWebProKing* 5.3, patch level 97," the NP says. "That does sound like a nonstandard browser," you say. "Maybe you should stick with server-side image maps."

Some older browsers don't support client-side image maps. In those cases, you should use server-side image maps, for which the work is done on the server. These maps work slowly, but they do work.

To create a server-side image map, you use the **ismap** standalone attribute of the **<img>** element (see Chapter 4). Surround the whole **<img>** element—which displays the map—in a hyperlink **<a>** element. The **<a>** element's **href** attribute gives the URL of the map file you want to use. The *map file* specifies the clickable regions in the image map, much as the **<map>** element does for client-side image maps. The map file is stored on your Web server.

As an example, I'll modify the client-side image map from the previous section into a server-side image map here. To do that, I'll create a map file, main.map, and store that on the server. I use the **ismap** attribute to connect the image to that map file. (Because you can't have standalone attributes in XHTML, I assign **ismap** the value **"ismap"**.) Note the use of the URL that's relative to the main.map file, which I'll store in the same directory as the main Web page:

```
<?xml version="1.0"?>
<!DOCTYPE html PUBLIC "-//W3C//DTD XHTML 1.0 Transitional//EN"
"http://www.w3.org/TR/xhtml1/DTD/xhtml1-transitional.dtd">
<html xmlns="http://www.w3.org/1999/xhtml" xml:lang="en" lang="en">
    <head>
        <title>
            Using A Server Side Image Map
        </title>
    </head>

    <body bgcolor="black">

        <center>
            <a href="main.map">
                <img width="528" height="137" src="mainmenu.jpg"
                    border="0" alt="image map" ismap="ismap" />
            </a>
        </center>

    </body>
</html>
```

There are two ways to create .map files—using the NCSA (National Center For Supercomputing Applications) format and the CERN (Conseil Européen pour la Recherche Nucléaire) format. Although the NCSA format is more widely used, the format your server uses is something you should determine.

Here's what the image-map file from the previous section looks like in NCSA format as stored in the main.map file (this follows the format of the **<area>** element):

```
default http://www.starpowder.com/steve/index.html#mainmenu
rect http://www.reuters.com 16,39 127,61
rect http://www.starpowder.com/steve/search.html 62,71 173,93
rect http://www.nnic.noaa.gov 98,104 209,126
rect http://www.starpowder.com/steve/gbook.htm 411,35 522,57
rect http://www.yahoo.com/guides_and_tutorials/ 360,67 471,89
rect http://www.web21.com/services/hot100/index.html 328,98 439,120
```

And here is the same map using the CERN format. Note that in this format (unlike the format used with the **<area>** element), you surround coordinate pairs in parentheses—the URL comes first, and you use **rectangle** instead of **rect**:

```
default http://www.starpowder.com/steve/index.html#mainmenu
rectangle (16,39) (127,61) http://www.reuters.com
rectangle (62,71) (173,93) http://www.starpowder.com/steve/search.html
```

```
rectangle (98,104) (209,126) http://www.nnic.noaa.gov
rectangle (411,35) (522,57) http://www.starpowder.com/steve/gbook.htm
rectangle (360,67) (471,89) http://www.yahoo.com/guides_and_tutorials/
rectangle (328,98) (439,120)
    http://www.web21.com/services/hot100/index.html
```

Here's the general format for NCSA image-map files:

```
default url
rect url x1, y1 x2, y2
circle url centerx, centery radius
poly url x1, y1 x2, y2 x3, y3 ... xn, yn
```

And here's the general format for CERN image-map files. In this format, you use a different spelling for each shape (**circ**, **rectangle**, and **polygon**), and as previously stated, you surround coordinate pairs with parentheses:

```
default url
rectangle (x1, y1) (x2, y2) url
circ (centerx, centery) radius url
polygon (x1, y1) (x2, y2) (x3, y3) ... (xn, yn) url
```

Many servers allow you to place the .map file where you want it (refer to the example at the beginning of this section, where I stored the .map file in the same directory as the Web page that displays the map). But sometimes you'll have to place the .map files in a special, reserved directory on your server (something you'll have to ask your ISP).

For example, the NCSA script that handles image maps is called *imagemap*, and you might have to store your map files in a directory called /cgi-bin/imagemap/ or /cgi-bin/imagemap/maps like this:

```
<?xml version="1.0"?>
<!DOCTYPE html PUBLIC "-//W3C//DTD XHTML 1.0 Transitional//EN"
"http://www.w3.org/TR/xhtml1/DTD/xhtml1-transitional.dtd">
<html xmlns="http://www.w3.org/1999/xhtml" xml:lang="en" lang="en">
    <head>
        <title>
            Using A Server Side Image Map
        </title>
    </head>

    <body bgcolor="black">
```

```
            <center>
                <a href="/cgi-bin/imagemap/main.map">
                    <img width="528" height="137" src="mainmenu.jpg"
                        border="0" alt="image map" ismap="ismap" />
                </a>
            </center>

        </body>
</html>
```

The script that handles CERN format scripts is called *htimage*, and if you have to place your map files in a special directory, it's typically called /cgi-bin/htimage:

```
<?xml version="1.0"?>
<!DOCTYPE html PUBLIC "-//W3C//DTD XHTML 1.0 Transitional//EN"
"http://www.w3.org/TR/xhtml1/DTD/xhtml1-transitional.dtd">
<html xmlns="http://www.w3.org/1999/xhtml" xml:lang="en" lang="en">
    <head>
        <title>
            Using A Server Side Image Map
        </title>
    </head>

    <body bgcolor="black">

        <center>
            <a href="/cgi-bin/htimage/main.map">
                <img width="528" height="137" src="mainmenu.jpg"
                    border="0" alt="image map" ismap="ismap" />
            </a>
        </center>

    </body>
</html>
```

The result of this server-side example looks just like the client-side image map you saw in Figure 5.12, except that all processing goes on in the server. For that reason, the browser will not display the URL of each clickable region as the mouse passes over it, nor will it display tool tips for each region.

So, when do you use client-side image maps and when do you use server-side image maps? It depends on the browser users have; to be safe, you can use *both*. See "Creating Combined Client-Side and Server-Side Image Maps," later in this chapter.

Creating Image Maps with the <object> Element

The W3C has stated that the **<object>** element should be able to support image maps—however, no browser does this yet. Here's an example showing how such an image map might be set up—note the **<area>** elements enclosed in the **<object>** element:

```
<object data="map.jpg">
    <area shape="rect" coords="0, 0, 100, 100" href="http://www.w3c.org">
    <area shape="circle" coords="200, 200, 50" href="http://microsoft.com">
    <area shape="poly" coords="300, 300, 310, 320, 450, 473, 300, 300"
        href="http://www.netscape.com">
</object>
```

However, this is pure conjecture, because XHTML does not allow **<area>** elements inside an **<object>** element yet. In fact, the **<object>** element has disappeared from the XHTML 1.1 specificiation.

Creating Combined Client-Side and Server-Side Image Maps

Client-side image maps are faster and more efficient than server-side maps (and can also display tool tips and target URLs), but some older browsers don't support client-side image maps. To accommodate older browsers, you can create Web pages that support both client-side and server-side image maps. In browsers that support client-side image maps, the client-side map will be used; otherwise, the server-side map will be used.

You do this by combining the client-side and server-side techniques:

- *For the client-side part*—You use the **usemap** attribute of the **<img>** element, and supply a **<map>** element with **<area>** elements.

- *For the server-side part*—You place the **<img>** element inside an **<a>** element that points to the server-side image .map file. You also use the **ismap** attribute in the **<img>** element.

That means you surround the **<img>** element that displays the image map in an **<a>** element that points to the server-side image .map file and use the **ismap** attribute in the **<img>** element. You also use the **usemap** attribute and supply a **<map>** element with **<area>** elements like this:

Chapter 5   Links and Lists

```xml
<?xml version="1.0"?>
<!DOCTYPE html PUBLIC "-//W3C//DTD XHTML 1.0 Transitional//EN"
"http://www.w3.org/TR/xhtml1/DTD/xhtml1-transitional.dtd">
<html xmlns="http://www.w3.org/1999/xhtml" xml:lang="en" lang="en">
    <head>
        <title>
            Using A Client Side And Server Side Image Map
        </title>
    </head>

    <body bgcolor="black">

        <center>
            <a href="main.map">
                <img width="528" height="137" src="mainmenu.jpg"
                    border="0" alt="image map" ismap="ismap"
                    usemap="#imap" />
            </a>
            <map id="imap" name="imap">
                <area shape="rect" coords="16,39 127,61"
                    href="http://www.reuters.com" alt="News" />
                <area shape="rect" coords="62,71 173,93"
                    href="http://www.starpowder.com/steve/search.html"
                    alt="Web search" />
                <area shape="rect" coords="98,104 209,126"
                    href="http://www.nnic.noaa.gov" alt="Weather" />
                <area shape="rect" coords="411,35 522,57"
                    href="http://www.starpowder.com/steve/gbook.htm"
                    alt="Guest book" />
                <area shape="rect" coords="360,67 471,89"
                    href="http://www.yahoo.com/guides_and_tutorials/"
                    alt="Create a Web page" />
                <area shape="rect" coords="328,98 439,120"
                    href="http://www.web21.com/services/hot100/index.html"
                    alt="Hottest 100 sites" />
                <area shape="default"
                    href=
                    "http://www.starpowder.com/steve/index.html#mainmenu"
                    alt="Image map" />
            </map>
        </center>

    </body>
</html>
```

Here's the main.map file (in NCSA format) as stored on the Web server:

```
default http://www.starpowder.com/steve/index.html#mainmenu
rect http://www.reuters.com 16,39 127,61
rect http://www.starpowder.com/steve/search.html 62,71 173,93
rect http://www.nnic.noaa.gov 98,104 209,126
rect http://www.starpowder.com/steve/gbook.htm 411,35 522,57
rect http://www.yahoo.com/Guides_and_Tutorials/ 360,67 471,89
rect http://www.web21.com/services/hot100/index.html 328,98 439,120
```

That's all it takes—now you're equipped to handle client-side and server-side image maps.

Creating Lists

The novice programmer appears and says, "How do I display a list in a Web page?" "There are plenty of ways," you say, "using ordered lists, unordered lists, customized lists, the old way, the new way—" "Hold it," the NP says, "I better get some coffee."

You use XHTML list elements to display lists in Web pages. The two broad categories for lists are unordered lists and ordered lists. (Both kinds of lists are indented.) Unordered lists display a bullet or other graphic in front of each list item, and ordered lists present the items in a numerical or alphabetical sequence.

Here's an example shown at the beginning of the chapter that creates an unordered list:

```
<?xml version="1.0"?>
<!DOCTYPE html PUBLIC "-//W3C//DTD XHTML 1.0 Transitional//EN"
"http://www.w3.org/TR/xhtml1/DTD/xhtml1-transitional.dtd">
<html xmlns="http://www.w3.org/1999/xhtml" xml:lang="en" lang="en">
    <head>
        <title>
            An Unordered List
        </title>
    </head>

    <body>

        <h1 align="center">
            Creating An Unordered List
        </h1>
```

```
            Here are some items to consider when buying a computer:
            <ul>
                <li>Speed</li>
                <li>Cost</li>
                <li>RAM</li>
                <li>Disk space</li>
                <li>CD ROM speed</li>
            </ul>

        </body>

</html>
```

Unordered lists display a simple bullet before each list item; ordered lists use a numbering (or lettering) system to indicate that the items are sequenced in some way. Here's an example that creates a simple numbered list:

```
<?xml version="1.0"?>
<!DOCTYPE html PUBLIC "-//W3C//DTD XHTML 1.0 Transitional//EN"
    "http://www.w3.org/TR/xhtml1/DTD/xhtml1-transitional.dtd">
<html xmlns="http://www.w3.org/1999/xhtml" xml:lang="en" lang="en">
    <head>
        <title>
            An Ordered List
        </title>
    </head>

    <body>

        <h1 align="center">
            Creating An Ordered List
        </h1>

        Here are some items to consider when buying a computer:
        <ol>
            <li>Speed</li>
            <li>Cost</li>
            <li>RAM</li>
            <li>Disk space</li>
            <li>CD ROM speed</li>
        </ol>

    </body>

</html>
```

To create ordered lists, you use the **<ol>** element, and to create unordered lists, you use the **<ul>** element. However, there's one element you use in common with these two tags—the **<li>** element, which creates a list item.

<li>—Creating List Items

Purpose: Creates a list item to use in ordered or unordered lists.

When used as HTML: Start tag/End tag: Required/Optional

Supported: [1.0S, 1.0T, 1.0F, 1.1, 2, 3, 3.2, 4, IE1, IE2, IE3, IE4, IE5, NS1, NS2, NS3, NS4]

Attributes:

- **class**—Class of the element (used for rendering). [1.0S, 1.0T, 1.0F, 1.1, 3, 4, IE4, IE5, NS4]
- **dir**—Gives the direction of directionally neutral text (text that doesn't have inherent direction in which you should read it). Possible values: **ltr**: left-to-right text or table and **rtl**: right-to-left text or table. [1.0S, 1.0T, 1.0F, 1.1, 4, IE5]
- **id**—A unique alphanumeric identifier for the tag, which you can use to refer to it. [1.0S, 1.0T, 1.0F, 1.1, 3, 4, IE4, IE5, NS4]
- **lang**—Base language used for the tag. [1.0S, 1.0T, 1.0F, 1.1, 3, 4, IE4, IE5, NS4]
- **language**—Scripting language used for the tag. [IE4, IE5]
- **style**—Inline style indicating how to render the element. [1.0S, 1.0T, 1.0F, 1.1, 4, IE3, IE4, IE5, NS4]
- **title**—Holds additional information (which might be displayed in tool tips) for the element. [1.0S, 1.0T, 1.0F, 1.1, 3, 4, IE4, IE5]
- **type**—Deprecated. Specifies the type of list item; for ordered lists, set to **A** (uppercase letters), **a** (lowercase letters), **I** (large roman numerals), **i** (small roman numerals), **1** (default numbering scheme); for unordered lists set to: **disc** (default solid bullet), **square** (solid square), or **circle** (hollow bullet). [1.0T, 1.0F, 2, 3, 3.2, 4, IE1, IE2, IE3, IE4, IE5, NS1, NS2, NS3, NS4]
- **value**—Deprecated. Specifies the number of the current list item, making it possible to create nonsequential lists. [1.0T, 1.0F, 3.2, 4, IE1, IE2, IE3, IE4, IE5, NS1, NS2, NS3, NS4]
- **xml:lang**—Holds the base language for the element when the document is interpreted as an XML document. [1.0S, 1.0T, 1.0F, 1.1]

XHTML events: onclick, ondblclick, onfocus, onblur, onmousedown, onmouseup, onmouseover, onmousemove, onmouseout, onkeypress, onkeydown, onkeyup

You use the **<li>** element to create a list item for use in ordered and unordered lists. Here's an example:

```
<?xml version="1.0"?>
<!DOCTYPE html PUBLIC "-//W3C//DTD XHTML 1.0 Transitional//EN"
"http://www.w3.org/TR/xhtml1/DTD/xhtml1-transitional.dtd">
<html xmlns="http://www.w3.org/1999/xhtml" xml:lang="en" lang="en">
    <head>
        <title>
            An Unordered List
        </title>
    </head>

    <body>

        <h1 align="center">
            Creating An Unordered List
        </h1>

        Here are some items to consider when buying a computer:
        <ul>
            <li>Speed</li>
            <li>Cost</li>
            <li>RAM</li>
            <li>Disk space</li>
            <li>CD ROM speed</li>
        </ul>
```

The results of this XHTML appear in Figure 5.7.

<ul>—Creating Unordered Lists

Purpose: Creates an unordered list. Surrounds **<li>** list items.

When used as HTML: Start tag/End tag: Required/Required

Supported: [1.0S, 1.0T, 1.0F, 1.1, 2, 3, 4, IE1, IE2, IE3, IE4, IE5, NS1, NS2, NS3, NS4]

Attributes:

- **class**—Class of the element (used for rendering). [1.0S, 1.0T, 1.0F, 1.1, 3, 4, IE4, IE5, NS4]
- **clear**—Used to move past aligned images or other elements. Set to **none** (the default; just a normal break), **left** (breaks line and moves down until there is a clear left margin past the aligned element), **right** (breaks line and moves down until there is a clear right margin past the aligned element), or **all** (breaks line and moves down until both margins are clear of the aligned element). [3]
- **compact**—Deprecated. Standalone attribute in HTML. This attribute should specifies that compact rendering should be used. [1.0T, 1.0F, 2, 3, 3.2, 4]
- **dir**—Gives the direction of directionally neutral text (text that doesn't have inherent direction in which you should read it). Possible values: **ltr**: left-to-right text or table and **rtl**: right-to-left text or table. [1.0S, 1.0T, 1.0F, 1.1, 4, IE5]
- **id**—A unique alphanumeric identifier for the tag, which you can use to refer to it. [1.0S, 1.0T, 1.0F, 1.1, 3, 4, IE4, IE5, NS4]
- **lang**—Base language used for the tag. [1.0S, 1.0T, 1.0F, 1.1, 3, 4, IE4, IE5, NS4]
- **language**—Scripting language used for the tag. [IE4, IE5]
- **style**—Inline style indicating how to render the element. [1.0S, 1.0T, 1.0F, 1.1, 4, IE3, IE4, IE5, NS4]
- **title**—Holds additional information (which might be displayed in tool tips) for the element. [1.0S, 1.0T, 1.0F, 1.1, 3, 4, IE4, IE5]
- **type**—Deprecated. Specifies the type of list item; for unordered lists set to: **disc** (default solid bullet), **square** (solid square), or **circle** (hollow bullet). Note that in Internet Explorer, you must set these values to lowercase. [1.0T, 1.0F, 2, 3, 3.2, 4, IE1, IE2, IE3, IE4, IE5, NS1, NS2, NS3, NS4]
- **xml:lang**—Holds the base language for the element when the document is interpreted as an XML document. [1.0S, 1.0T, 1.0F, 1.1]

XHTML events: onclick, ondblclick, onfocus, onblur, onmousedown, onmouseup, onmouseover, onmousemove, onmouseout, onkeypress, onkeydown, onkeyup

To create an unordered list, you place the list items, which are defined with the **<li>** element, inside the **<ul>** element. Here's an example, shown at the beginning of the chapter:

```
<?xml version="1.0"?>
<!DOCTYPE html PUBLIC "-//W3C//DTD XHTML 1.0 Transitional//EN"
 "http://www.w3.org/TR/xhtml1/DTD/xhtml1-transitional.dtd">
<html xmlns="http://www.w3.org/1999/xhtml" xml:lang="en" lang="en">
```

```
<head>
    <title>
        An Unordered List
    </title>
</head>

<body>

    <h1 align="center">
        Creating An Unordered List
    </h1>

    Here are some items to consider when buying a computer:
    <ul>
        <li>Speed</li>
        <li>Cost</li>
        <li>RAM</li>
        <li>Disk space</li>
        <li>CD ROM speed</li>
    </ul>

</body>

</html>
```

You can see the results of this XHTML in Figure 5.7. Note that you can also customize unordered lists—see "Creating Customized Unordered Lists," coming up in "Immediate Solutions."

<ol>—Creating Ordered Lists

Purpose: Creates an ordered list. You use this element to surround **<li>** list items.

When used as HTML: Start tag/End tag: Required/Required

Supported: [1.0S, 1.0T, 1.0F, 1.1, 2, 3, 3.2, 4, IE1, IE2, IE3, IE4, IE5, NS1, NS2, NS3, NS4]

Attributes:

- **class**—Class of the element (used for rendering). [1.0S, 1.0T, 1.0F, 1.1, 3, 4, IE4, IE5, NS4]

- **clear**—Used to move past aligned images or other elements. Set to **none** (the default; just a normal break), **left** (breaks line and moves down until there is a clear left margin past the aligned element), **right** (breaks line and moves down until there is a clear right margin past the aligned element), or **all** (breaks line and moves down until both margins are clear of the aligned element). [3]

- **compact**—Deprecated. Standalone attribute in HTML. This attribute specifies that compact rendering should be used. [1.0T, 1.0F, 2, 3, 3.2, 4]

- **dir**—Gives the direction of directionally neutral text (text that doesn't have inherent direction in which you should read it). Possible values: **ltr**: left-to-right text or table and **rtl**: right-to-left text or table. [1.0S, 1.0T, 1.0F, 1.1, 4, IE5]

- **id**—A unique alphanumeric identifier for the tag, which you can use to refer to it. [1.0S, 1.0T, 1.0F, 1.1, 3, 4, IE4, IE5, NS4]

- **lang**—Base language used for the tag. [1.0S, 1.0T, 1.0F, 1.1, 3, 4, IE4, IE5, NS4]

- **language**—Scripting language used for the tag. [IE4, IE5]

- **start**—Deprecated. Specifies the first number in the sequence if it's other than 1. [1.0T, 1.0F, 3.2, 4, IE1, IE2, IE3, IE4, IE5, NS1, NS2, NS3, NS4]

- **style**—Inline style indicating how to render the element. [1.0S, 1.0T, 1.0F, 1.1, 4, IE3, IE4, IE5, NS4]

- **title**—Holds additional information (which might be displayed in tool tips) for the element. [1.0S, 1.0T, 1.0F, 1.1, 3, 4, IE4, IE5]

- **type**—Deprecated. Specifies the type of list item; for ordered lists, set to **A** (uppercase letters), **a** (lowercase letters), **I** (large roman numerals), **i** (small roman numerals), **1** (default numbering scheme). [1.0T, 1.0F, 2, 3, 3.2, 4, IE1, IE2, IE3, IE4, IE5, NS1, NS2, NS3, NS4]

- **xml:lang**—Holds the base language for the element when the document is interpreted as an XML document. [1.0S, 1.0T, 1.0F, 1.1]

XHTML events: onclick, ondblclick, onfocus, onblur, onmousedown, onmouseup, onmouseover, onmousemove, onmouseout, onkeypress, onkeydown, onkeyup

You use the **<ol>** element to create ordered lists that display a list of items using ascending numbers or letters. It's easy to make these kinds of lists—just place the **<li>** list items inside an **<ol>** element, as we saw at the beginning of the chapter:

```
<?xml version="1.0"?>
<!DOCTYPE html PUBLIC "-//W3C//DTD XHTML 1.0 Transitional//EN"
"http://www.w3.org/TR/xhtml1/DTD/xhtml1-transitional.dtd">
<html xmlns="http://www.w3.org/1999/xhtml" xml:lang="en" lang="en">
```

```
        <head>
            <title>
                An Ordered List
            </title>
        </head>

        <body>

            <h1 align="center">
                Creating An Ordered List
            </h1>

            Here are some items to consider when buying a computer:
            <ol>
                <li>Speed</li>
                <li>Cost</li>
                <li>RAM</li>
                <li>Disk space</li>
                <li>CD ROM speed</li>
            </ol>

        </body>

</html>
```

The results of this XHTML appear in Figure 5.8. Note that you can also customize ordered lists—see "Creating Customized Ordered Lists," coming up in "Immediate Solutions."

Creating Customized Unordered Lists

You can customize unordered lists by setting the **type** attribute to one of three values—**disc** (the default), **square**, or **circle**—that set the type of bullet that appears before each list item. Here's an example that creates square bullets:

```
<?xml version="1.0"?>
<!DOCTYPE html PUBLIC "-//W3C//DTD XHTML 1.0 Transitional//EN"
"http://www.w3.org/TR/xhtml1/DTD/xhtml1-transitional.dtd">
<html xmlns="http://www.w3.org/1999/xhtml" xml:lang="en" lang="en">
    <head>
        <title>
            Customizing An Unordered List
        </title>
    </head>
```

```
            <body>

                <h1 align="center">
                    Customizing An Unordered List
                </h1>

                Here are some items to consider when buying a computer:
                <ul type="square">
                    <li>Speed</li>
                    <li>Cost</li>
                    <li>RAM</li>
                    <li>Disk space</li>
                    <li>CD ROM speed</li>
                </ul>

            </body>

</html>
```

The results of this XHTML appear in Figure 5.13, where you can see the square bullets.

Note, however, that the **type** attribute is deprecated in favor of style sheets. So how do you set the type of bullets the new way? We'll discuss style sheets in Chapter 9, but here's a sneak preview—you use the **list-style-type** attribute to set the style of list items. For unordered lists, you can set this style to **disc** (the default), **circle**, or **square**. Here's what the previous page looks like using style sheets:

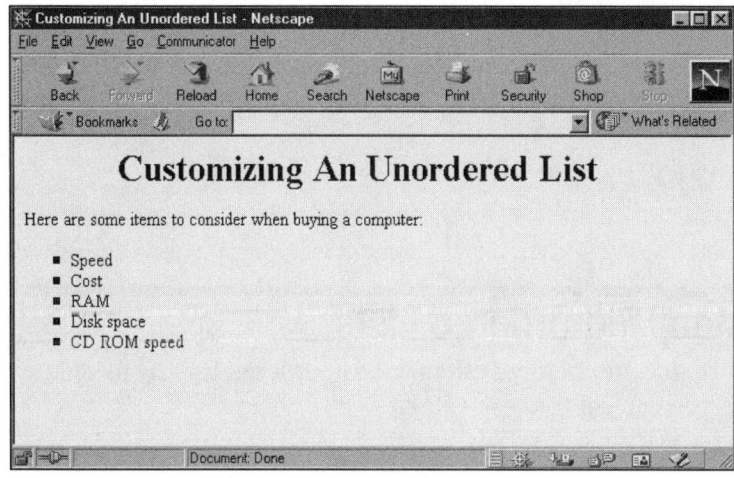

Figure 5.13 Customizing an unordered list.

```
<?xml version="1.0"?>
<!DOCTYPE html PUBLIC "-//W3C//DTD XHTML 1.0 Transitional//EN"
"http://www.w3.org/TR/xhtml1/DTD/xhtml1-transitional.dtd">
<html xmlns="http://www.w3.org/1999/xhtml" xml:lang="en" lang="en">
    <head>
        <title>
            Customizing An Unordered List
        </title>

        <style type="text/css">
            li {list-style-type: square}
        </style>
    </head>

    <body>

        <h1 align="center">
            Customizing An Unordered List
        </h1>

        Here are some items to consider when buying a computer:
        <ul>
            <li>Speed</li>
            <li>Cost</li>
            <li>RAM</li>
            <li>Disk space</li>
            <li>CD ROM speed</li>
        </ul>

    </body>

</html>
```

This XHTML gives you the same result you saw in Figure 5.13.

Creating Customized Ordered Lists

You can customize the numbering system used in ordered lists by using the **type** attribute, which you can set to these values:

- **1**—default numbering scheme (1, 2, 3...)
- **A**—uppercase letters (A, B, C...)
- **a**—lowercase letters (a, b, c...)

- **I**—large roman numerals (I, II, III...)
- **i**—small roman numerals (i, ii, iii...)

Here's an example showing how this works. I'll set the list order to A, B, C, and so on by setting the **type** attribute to "A":

```
<?xml version="1.0"?>
<!DOCTYPE html PUBLIC "-//W3C//DTD XHTML 1.0 Transitional//EN"
"http://www.w3.org/TR/xhtml1/DTD/xhtml1-transitional.dtd">
<html xmlns="http://www.w3.org/1999/xhtml" xml:lang="en" lang="en">
    <head>
        <title>
            Customizing An Ordered List
        </title>
    </head>

    <body>

        <h1 align="center">
            Customizing An Ordered List
        </h1>

        Here are some items to consider when buying a computer:
        <ol type="A">
            <li> speedSpeed</li>
            <li> costCost</li>
            <li> ramRAM</li>
            <li> disk Disk space </li>
            <li> cd romCD ROM speed</li>

        </ol>

    </body>

</html>
```

The results of this XHTML appear in Figure 5.14.

TIP: *To set the number of the first item in an ordered list, use the **start** attribute (note that **start** is deprecated in HTML 4).*

The **type** attribute is deprecated in HTML 4 in favor of style sheets. So how do you set the type of numbering system the new way? We'll discuss style sheets in Chapter 9, but here's a sneak preview—you use the **list-style-type** attribute to

Chapter 5   Links and Lists

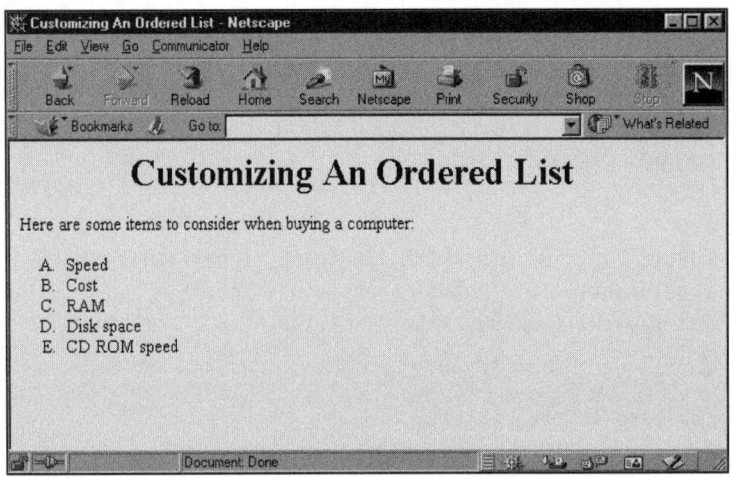

Figure 5.14   Customizing an ordered list.

set the style of list items. For ordered lists, set this style to **decimal** (the default), **lower-roman**, **upper-roman**, **lower-alpha**, or **none**. Here's what the previous page looks like using style sheets:

```
<?xml version="1.0"?>
<!DOCTYPE html PUBLIC "-//W3C//DTD XHTML 1.0 Transitional//EN"
"http://www.w3.org/TR/xhtml1/DTD/xhtml1-transitional.dtd">
<html xmlns="http://www.w3.org/1999/xhtml" xml:lang="en" lang="en">
    <head>
        <title>
            Customizing An Ordered List
        </title>

        <style type="text/css">
            li {list-style-type: upper-alpha}
        </style>
    </head>

    <body>

        <h1 align="center">
            Customizing An Ordered List
        </h1>

        Here are some items to consider when buying a computer:
        <ol>
            <li>Speed</li>
            <li>Cost</li>
```

```
            <li>RAM</li>
            <li>Disk space</li>
            <li>CD ROM speed</li>
        </ol>

    </body>

</html>
```

This XHTML gives you the same result you saw in Figure 5.14.

<dl>, <dt>, and <dd>—Creating Definition Lists

Definition lists organize terms and their definitions in pairs (although most browsers can handle these lists if you use terms and definitions separately). You create a definition list with the **<dl>** element. You create items in this list by using the **<dt>** element to define a term and the **<dd>** element to supply the term's definition. The definition usually appears indented under the term being defined. Of course, you don't have to use this list for definitions or glossaries only—you can use it for any list that should be annotated.

<dl>

Purpose: Creates a definition list. Embed **<dt>** and **<dd>** elements in a **<dl>** element.

When used as HTML: Start tag/End tag: Required/Required

Supported: [1.0S, 1.0T, 1.0F, 1.1, 2, 3, 3.2, 4, IE1, IE2, IE3, IE4, IE5, NS1, NS2, NS3, NS4]

Attributes:

- **class**—Class of the element (used for rendering). [1.0S, 1.0T, 1.0F, 1.1, 3, 4, IE4, IE5, NS4]
- **clear**—Used to move past aligned images or other elements. Set to **none** (the default; just a normal break), **left** (breaks line and moves down until there is a clear left margin past the aligned element), **right** (breaks line and moves down until there is a clear right margin past the aligned element), or **all** (breaks line and moves down until both margins are clear of the aligned element). [3]
- **compact**—Deprecated. Standalone attribute in HTML. This attribute specifies that compact rendering should be used. [1.0T, 1.0F, 2, 3, 3.2, 4, IE4, IE5, NS1, NS2, NS3, NS4]

- **dir**—Gives the direction of directionally neutral text (text that doesn't have inherent direction in which you should read it). Possible values: **ltr**: left-to-right text or table and **rtl**: right-to-left text or table. [1.0S, 1.0T, 1.0F, 1.1, 4, IE5]

- **id**—A unique alphanumeric identifier for the tag, which you can use to refer to it. [1.0S, 1.0T, 1.0F, 1.1, 3, 4, IE4, IE5, NS4]

- **lang**—Base language used for the tag. [1.0S, 1.0T, 1.0F, 1.1, 3, 4, IE4, IE5, NS4]

- **language**—Scripting language used for the tag. [IE4, IE5]

- **style**—Inline style indicating how to render the element. [1.0S, 1.0T, 1.0F, 1.1, 4, IE3, IE4, IE5, NS4]

- **title**—Holds additional information (which might be displayed in tool tips) for the element. [1.0S, 1.0T, 1.0F, 1.1, 3, 4, IE4, IE5]

- **xml:lang**—Holds the base language for the element when the document is interpreted as an XML document. [1.0S, 1.0T, 1.0F, 1.1]

XHTML events: onclick, ondblclick, onfocus, onblur, onmousedown, onmouseup, onmouseover, onmousemove, onmouseout, onkeypress, onkeydown, onkeyup

<dt>

Purpose: Specifies a definition term used in definition lists. Use inside a **<dl>** element, and pair with a **<dt>** element.

When used as HTML: Start tag/End tag: Required/Optional

Supported: [1.0S, 1.0T, 1.0F, 1.1, 2, 3, 3.2, 4, IE1, IE2, IE3, IE4, IE5, NS1, NS2, NS3, NS4]

Attributes:

- **class**—Class of the element (used for rendering). [1.0S, 1.0T, 1.0F, 1.1, 3, 4, IE4, IE5, NS4]

- **clear**—Used to move past aligned images or other elements. Set to **none** (the default; just a normal break), **left** (breaks line and moves down until there is a clear left margin past the aligned element), **right** (breaks line and moves down until there is a clear right margin past the aligned element), or **all** (breaks line and moves down until both margins are clear of the aligned element). [3]

- **dir**—Gives the direction of directionally neutral text (text that doesn't have inherent direction in which you should read it). Possible values: **ltr**: left-to-right text or table and **rtl**: right-to-left text or table. [1.0S, 1.0T, 1.0F, 1.1, 4, IE5]

- **id**—A unique alphanumeric identifier for the tag, which you can use to refer to it. [1.0S, 1.0T, 1.0F, 1.1, 3, 4, IE4, IE5, NS4]
- **lang**—Base language used for the tag. [1.0S, 1.0T, 1.0F, 1.1, 3, 4, IE4, IE5, NS4]
- **language**—Scripting language used for the tag. [IE4, IE5]
- **style**—Inline style indicating how to render the element. [1.0S, 1.0T, 1.0F, 1.1, 4, IE3, IE4, IE5, NS4]
- **title**—Holds additional information (which might be displayed in tool tips) for the element. [1.0S, 1.0T, 1.0F, 1.1, 3, 4, IE4, IE5]
- **xml:lang**—Holds the base language for the element when the document is interpreted as an XML document. [1.0S, 1.0T, 1.0F, 1.1]

XHTML events: onclick, ondblclick, onfocus, onblur, onmousedown, onmouseup, onmouseover, onmousemove, onmouseout, onkeypress, onkeydown, onkeyup

<dd>

Purpose: Specifies a definition description for use in definition lists. Use with **<dt>** elements inside a **<dl>** element.

When used as HTML: Start tag/End tag: Required/Optional

Supported: [1.0S, 1.0T, 1.0F, 1.1, 2, 3, 3.2, 4, IE1, IE2, IE3, IE4, IE5, NS1, NS2, NS3, NS4]

Attributes:

- **class**—Class of the element (used for rendering). [1.0S, 1.0T, 1.0F, 1.1, 3, 4, IE4, IE5, NS4]
- **clear**—Used to move past aligned images or other elements. Set to **none** (the default; just a normal break), **left** (breaks line and moves down until there is a clear left margin past the aligned element), **right** (breaks line and moves down until there is a clear right margin past the aligned element), or **all** (breaks line and moves down until both margins are clear of the aligned element). [3]
- **dir**—Gives the direction of directionally neutral text (text that doesn't have inherent direction in which you should read it). Possible values: **ltr**: left-to-right text or table and **rtl**: right-to-left text or table. [1.0S, 1.0T, 1.0F, 1.1, 4, IE5]
- **id**—A unique alphanumeric identifier for the tag, which you can use to refer to it. [1.0S, 1.0T, 1.0F, 1.1, 3, 4, IE4, IE5, NS4]
- **lang**—Base language used for the tag. [1.0S, 1.0T, 1.0F, 1.1, 3, 4, IE4, IE5, NS4]
- **language**—Scripting language used for the tag. [IE4, IE5]

- **style**—Inline style indicating how to render the element. [1.0S, 1.0T, 1.0F, 1.1, 4, IE3, IE4, IE5, NS4]
- **title**—Holds additional information (which might be displayed in tool tips) for the element. [1.0S, 1.0T, 1.0F, 1.1, 3, 4, IE4, IE5]
- **xml:lang**—Holds the base language for the element when the document is interpreted as an XML document. [1.0S, 1.0T, 1.0F, 1.1]

XHTML events: onclick, ondblclick, onfocus, onblur, onmousedown, onmouseup, onmouseover, onmousemove, onmouseout, onkeypress, onkeydown, onkeyup

Here's an example:

```
<?xml version="1.0"?>
<!DOCTYPE html PUBLIC "-//W3C//DTD XHTML 1.0 Transitional//EN"
"http://www.w3.org/TR/xhtml1/DTD/xhtml1-transitional.dtd">
<html xmlns="http://www.w3.org/1999/xhtml" xml:lang="en" lang="en">
    <head>
        <title>
            A Definition List
        </title>
    </head>

    <body>

        <h1 align="center">
            Creating A Definition List
        </h1>

        Here are some items to consider when buying a computer:
        <dl>
            <dt>Speed</dt><dd>CPU speed in MHz.</dd>
            <dt>Cost</dt><dd>Make sure to keep this down!</dd>
            <dt>RAM</dt><dd>Amount of memory in the computer.</dd>
            <dt>Disk space</dt><dd>Get plenty of gigabytes.</dd>
            <dt>CD ROM speed</dt><dd>Get at least 24X.</dd>
        </dl>

    </body>

</html>
```

You can see the results of this XHTML in Figure 5.15; each annotation is indented under the corresponding term.

TIP: *Some Web authors use the **<dl>** tag solely to create indentation in their Web pages.*

Immediate Solutions

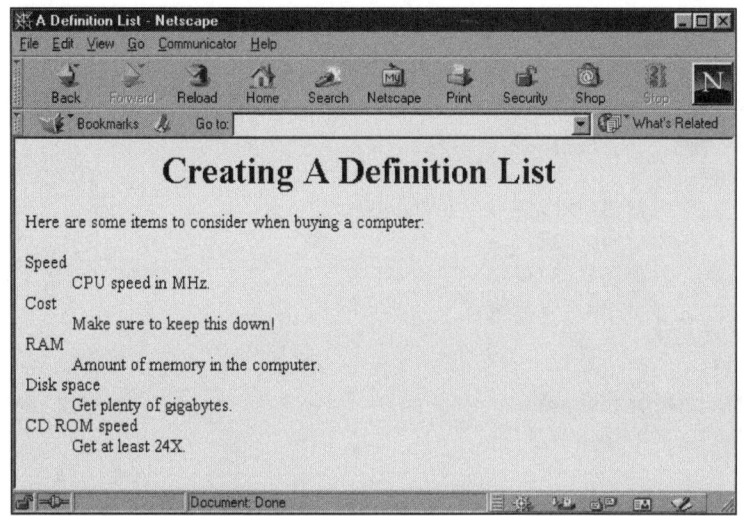

Figure 5.15   A definition list.

Nesting Lists

"Uh oh," the novice programmer says, "I need a list *inside* a list. Is there a fancy way to do that? Should I use a **<div>** element? Should I use dynamic XHTML? How about Java?" You smile and say, "How about straight XHTML? Nesting lists is no problem."

You can nest lists inside other lists in XHTML, and browsers will know what's going on. In fact, browsers will often provide a visual indication that the list is nested, such as using hollow bullets in a nested unordered list. Here's an example showing how that works:

```
<?xml version="1.0"?>
<!DOCTYPE html PUBLIC "-//W3C//DTD XHTML 1.0 Transitional//EN"
    "http://www.w3.org/TR/xhtml1/DTD/xhtml1-transitional.dtd">
<html xmlns="http://www.w3.org/1999/xhtml" xml:lang="en" lang="en">
    <head>
        <title>
            A Nested List
        </title>
    </head>

    <body>

        <h1 align="center">
            Creating A Nested List
        </h1>
```

323

```
            Here are some items to consider when buying a computer:
        <ul>
            <li>Speed</li>
            <li>Cost</li>
            <li>RAM - get one of these:
                <ul>
                    <li>32 MB</li>
                    <li>48 MB</li>
                    <li>64 MB</li>
                    <li>80 MB</li>
                </ul>
            </li>
            <li>Disk space</li>
            <li>CD ROM speed</li>
        </ul>

    </body>

</html>
```

The results of this XHTML appear in Figure 5.16. As you can see in the figure, one list is nested inside another, and the inner list does indeed have hollow bullets.

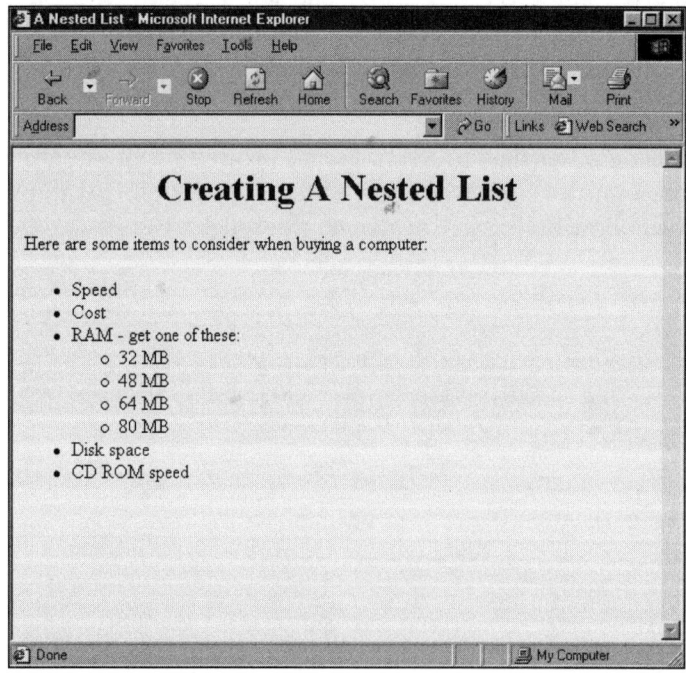

Figure 5.16 Nesting lists.

<dir> and <menu>—Deprecated Lists

<dir>

Purpose: Creates a directory list; usually displayed simply as an unordered list. Deprecated.

When used as HTML: Start tag/End tag: Required/Required

Supported: [1.0T, 1.0F, 2, 3, 3.2, 4, IE1, IE2, IE3, IE4, IE5, NS1, NS2, NS3, NS4]

Attributes:

- **class**—Class of the element (used for rendering). [1.0T, 1.0F, 4, IE4, IE5, NS4]
- **compact**—Deprecated. Standalone attribute in HTML. This attribute specifies that compact rendering should be used. [1.0T, 1.0F, 2, 3, 3.2, 4]
- **dir**—Gives the direction of directionally neutral text (text that doesn't have inherent direction in which you should read it). Possible values: **ltr**: left-to-right text or table and **rtl**: right-to-left text or table. [1.0T, 1.0F, IE4, IE5]
- **id**—A unique alphanumeric identifier for the tag, which you can use to refer to it. [1.0T, 1.0F, 4, IE4, IE5, NS4]
- **lang**—Base language used for the tag. [1.0T, 1.0F, 4, IE4, IE5, NS4]
- **language**—Scripting language used for the tag. [IE4, IE5]
- **style**—Inline style indicating how to render the element. [1.0T, 1.0F, 4, IE3, IE4, IE5, NS4]
- **title**—Holds additional information (which might be displayed in tool tips) for the element. [1.0T, 1.0F, 4, IE4, IE5]
- **xml:lang**—Holds the base language for the element when the document is interpreted as an XML document. [1.0T, 1.0F]

XHTML Events: onclick, ondblclick, onfocus, onblur, onmousedown, onmouseup, onmouseover, onmousemove, onmouseout, onkeypress, onkeydown, onkeyup

<menu>

Purpose: Creates a menu list; usually rendered as an unordered list. Deprecated.

When used as HTML: Start tag/End tag: Required/Required

Supported: [1.0T, 1.0F, 2, 3, 3.2, 4, IE1, IE2, IE3, IE4, IE5, NS1, NS2, NS3, NS4]

Attributes:

- **class**—Class of the element (used for rendering). [1.0T, 1.0F, 4, IE4, IE5, NS4]
- **compact**—Deprecated. Standalone attribute in HTML. This attribute specifies that compact rendering should be used. [1.0T, 1.0F, 2, 3, 3.2, 4]
- **dir**—Gives the direction of directionally neutral text (text that doesn't have inherent direction in which you should read it). Possible values: **ltr**: left-to-right text or table and **rtl**: right-to-left text or table. [1.0T, 1.0F, IE4, IE5]
- **id**—A unique alphanumeric identifier for the tag, which you can use to refer to it. [1.0T, 1.0F, 4, IE4, IE5, NS4]
- **lang**—Base language used for the tag. [1.0T, 1.0F, 4, IE4, IE5, NS4]
- **style**—Inline style indicating how to render the element. [1.0T, 1.0F, 4, IE3, IE4, IE5, NS4]
- **title**—Holds additional information (which might be displayed in tool tips) for the element. [1.0T, 1.0F, 4, IE4, IE5]
- **xml:lang**—Holds the base language for the element when the document is interpreted as an XML document. [1.0T, 1.0F]

XHTML events: onclick, ondblclick, onfocus, onblur, onmousedown, onmouseup, onmouseover, onmousemove, onmouseout, onkeypress, onkeydown, onkeyup

Both the **<dir>** and **<menu>** lists are deprecated. I'm including them here for completeness. In fact, most browsers just display these lists as unordered lists, although they were originally meant to handle short list items (about 20 characters) only. You use the **<li>** element to define list items.

Here's an example of using the **<menu>** element:

```
<?xml version="1.0"?>
<!DOCTYPE html PUBLIC "-//W3C//DTD XHTML 1.0 Transitional//EN"
"http://www.w3.org/TR/xhtml1/DTD/xhtml1-transitional.dtd">
<html xmlns="http://www.w3.org/1999/xhtml" xml:lang="en" lang="en">
    <head>
        <title>
            Creating A Menu List
        </title>
    </head>

    <body>

        <h1 align="center">
            Creating A Menu List
        </h1>
```

```
        Here are some items to consider when buying a computer:
        <menu>
            <li>Speed</li>
            <li>Cost</li>
            <li>RAM</li>
            <li>Disk space</li>
            <li>CD ROM speed</li>
        </menu>
    </body>
</html>
```

Most browsers will render this XHTML as a simple unordered list.

Chapter 6
Creating Tables

If you need an immediate solution to:	See page:
`<table>`—Creating a Table	356
`<tr>`—Creating a Table Row	358
`<th>`—Creating Table Headings	360
`<td>`—Creating Table Data	363
`<caption>`—Creating a Table Caption	365
Setting Table Border Widths	367
Setting Cell Padding	369
Setting Cell Spacing	369
Setting Table and Column Widths	370
Setting Table Colors	372
Aligning Tables in Web Pages	374
Aligning Cell Text	375
Using Images in Tables	377
Nesting Tables	378
Spanning Multiple Columns	380
Spanning Multiple Rows	380
`<colgroup>` and `<col>`—Grouping and Formatting Columns	381
`<thead>`, `<tbody>`, `<tfoot>`—Grouping and Formatting Rows	388
Formatting Text with Tables	396

In Depth

Tables are one of my favorite XHTML elements, and, after this chapter, I hope they'll be one of yours too. That's quite a claim because XHTML tables are the most complex standard XHTML elements that exist (currently, anyway). However, their usefulness far outweighs the inconvenience of creating them.

The popularity of tables has little to do with displaying data in tables; tables are popular with Web-page authors because tables let you arrange the elements of a Web page in such a way that the browser won't rearrange them. Often, it's good to let the browser do the rearranging, as when it reformats text to fit the available display area. However, there are many cases—often involving a series of images that should be next to each other (as in navigation bars) or text that should be formatted just so (as when you want some text to appear on the side of the page in annotations)—where you really want your text to be displayed just as you specify. Web-page authors frequently use tables to structure Web pages, and if you look at pages displayed by large corporations, you'll often find tables in them for just this reason.

The Parts of a Table

You can see a basic table in Figure 6.1. Above the table appears a *caption*, which you specify with the **<caption>** element. Below the caption and in the table itself

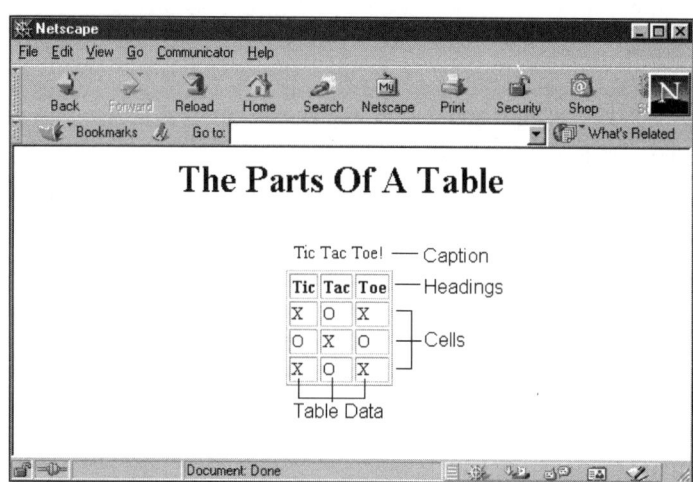

Figure 6.1   A basic table.

In Depth

appear *table headings*, one per column (although headings can span several columns). The rows and columns of the table are divided into *cells*, and each cell holds the actual *table data*, as you see in Figure 6.1.

Of course, this table is just a very basic one, but it shows the parts of a table. To see how to create a table like this, we have to dig into the XHTML.

Creating a Table

To create a table, you use the **<table>** element, which is the easy part. Then it's up to you to structure the table by using elements such as **<tr>** to create a *table row*, **<td>** to insert *data* into the table, and **<th>** to create *table headings*.

To make this clearer, I'll go through an example named tables.html, which you'll find on the CD-ROM as well as in Listing 6.1. In that Listing, you'll find several variations of how to work with tables, and I'll introduce them here. More advanced material will come later in the chapter.

I'll start by creating the table you see in Figure 6.2. The table in that figure is a simple one, without even a border. (The figures in this section also include the XHTML used to create the tables.)

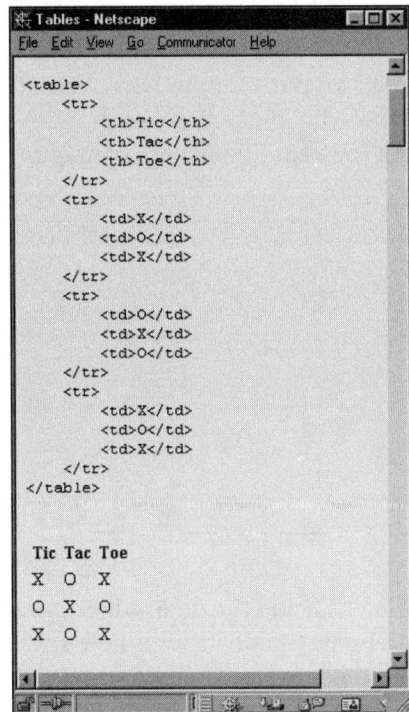

Figure 6.2 A borderless table.

To create this table, I begin with the **<table>** element:

```
<table>
    .
    .
    .
</table>
```

You build tables row by row by using the **<tr>** element inside the **<table>** element. Here's how I create the first (top) row of the table:

```
<table>
    <tr>
        .
        .
        .
    </tr>
    .
    .
    .
</table>
```

The top row of the table in Figure 6.2 holds headings for each column—Tic, Tac, and Toe. (Heading text is usually boldfaced and centered both vertically and horizontally.) Headings are optional in tables, but I've put them in here. You create headings with the **<th>** element. There are three headings here, each in its own column. Note that using three **<th>** elements (or **<td>**, table data elements) *defines* how many columns the row will have:

```
<table>
    <tr>
        <th>Tic</th>
        <th>Tac</th>
        <th>Toe</th>
    </tr>
    .
    .
    .
</table>
```

Now that I've created the first row with headings, I'll add the data, which consists of *X*s and *O*s. I do that by using the **<tr>** element to construct a new row and using the **<td>** element for the data that should go in each cell. (If you don't use **<th>** elements, the number of **<tr>** elements in a row defines the number of columns in the row.) Here's the code:

```
<table>
    <tr>
        <th>Tic</th>
        <th>Tac</th>
        <th>Toe</th>
    </tr>
    <tr>
        <td>X</td>
        <td>O</td>
        <td>X</td>
    </tr>
    .
    .
    .
</table>
```

Finally, I construct the last two rows in the same way:

```
<table>
    <tr>
        <th>Tic</th>
        <th>Tac</th>
        <th>Toe</th>
    </tr>
    <tr>
        <td>X</td>
        <td>O</td>
        <td>X</td>
    </tr>
    <tr>
        <td>O</td>
        <td>X</td>
        <td>O</td>
    </tr>
    <tr>
        <td>X</td>
        <td>O</td>
        <td>X</td>
    </tr>
</table>
```

And that's it—the table is done, and you can see it in Figure 6.2. It's interesting to note that tables have no border by default, indicating W3C's understanding that people often use tables to structure a page. However, you can easily add a border to a table.

Adding a Border

To add a border, all you have to do is to use the **<table>** element's **border** attribute. In HTML 2.0, you could use this attribute as a standalone attribute, and the browser would add a one-pixel border around the table and draw the internal lines that separate each cell. Since HTML 3.2, however, you're supposed to specify a value for the border attribute in pixels (**border="0"** would turn the border off), so I'll do that here by adding a border two pixels wide:

```
<table border="2">
    <tr>
        <th>Tic</th>
        <th>Tac</th>
        <th>Toe</th>
    </tr>
    <tr>
        <td>X</td>
        <td>O</td>
        <td>X</td>
    </tr>
    <tr>
        <td>O</td>
        <td>X</td>
        <td>O</td>
    </tr>
    <tr>
        <td>X</td>
        <td>O</td>
        <td>X</td>
    </tr>
</table>
```

The results of this XHTML appear in Figure 6.3.

Another option is to specify cell padding.

Padding Your Cells

To start tailoring your tables the way you want them, you can specify *cell padding*, which is the amount of space between the edges of the cell and the cell's contents. If your tables are looking too cramped, increasing cell padding is one way to go. Use the **cellspacing** attribute of the **<table>** element.

Here's an example showing what that looks like, where I'm increasing the cell padding to four pixels by assigning that value to the cell padding attribute:

In Depth

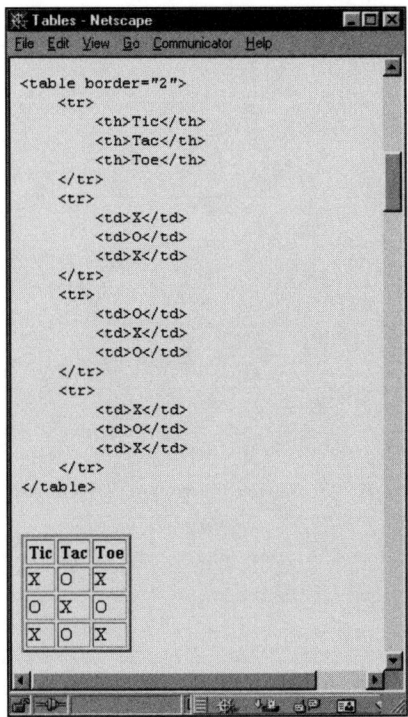

Figure 6.3   Adding a border to a table.

```
<table border="2" cellpadding = "4">
    <tr>
        <th>Tic</th>
        <th>Tac</th>
        <th>Toe</th>
    </tr>
    <tr>
        <td>X</td>
        <td>O</td>
        <td>X</td>
    </tr>
    <tr>
        <td>O</td>
        <td>X</td>
        <td>O</td>
    </tr>
    <tr>
        <td>X</td>
        <td>O</td>
        <td>X</td>
    </tr>
</table>
```

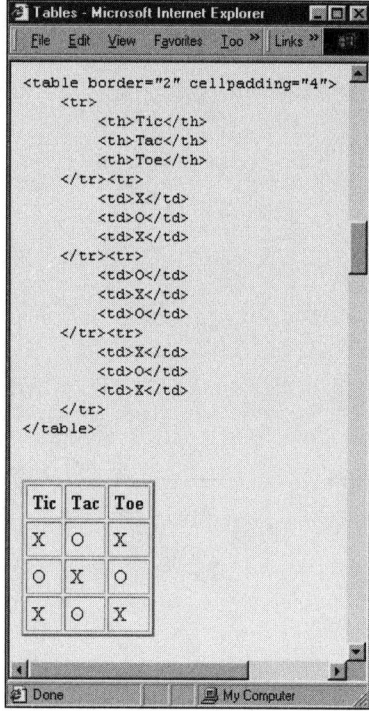

Figure 6.4   Increasing cell padding.

You can see the result in Figure 6.4, where the cells have widened somewhat from the previous version in Figure 6.3.

TIP: You can set cell padding to zero, but the cell walls actually touch the cell contents in that case—an effect that isn't so great.

Widening the Cell Spacing

Cell spacing might sound to you much like cell padding, but there's a difference. Cell padding sets the extra space used to separate cell walls from their contents, and cell spacing sets the space between cells. To set cell spacing, use the **cellspacing** attribute of the **<table>** element.

In the following example, I'll use the **cellspacing** attribute to set the cell spacing to four pixels:

```
<table border="2" cellspacing = "4">
    <tr>
        <th>Tic</th>
```

```
            <th>Tac</th>
            <th>Toe</th>
        </tr>
        <tr>
            <td>X</td>
            <td>O</td>
            <td>X</td>
        </tr>
        <tr>
            <td>O</td>
            <td>X</td>
            <td>O</td>
        </tr>
        <tr>
            <td>X</td>
            <td>O</td>
            <td>X</td>
        </tr>
</table>
```

You can see the results of this XHTML in Figure 6.5.

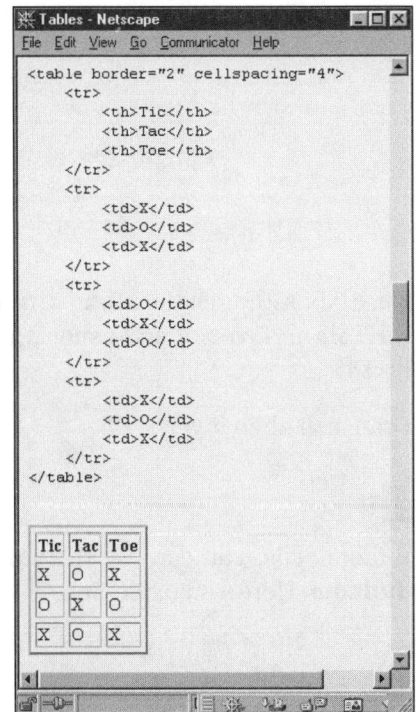

Figure 6.5 Setting cell spacing.

Aligning Your Data Horizontally

There are dozens of other options with tables, of course. One option is to align your data cell by cell by using the **align** attribute, which you set to **right**, **left**, or **center**. (The default for table data is to center the data vertically and left-align it.)

In the following example, I'm aligning data to the right, left, and center:

```
<table border="2" width="200">
    <tr>
        <th>Tic</th>
        <th>Tac</th>
        <th>Toe</th>
    </tr>
    <tr>
        <td align = "right">X</td>
        <td align = "left">O</td>
        <td align = "center">X</td>
    </tr>
    <tr>
        <td align = "right">O</td>
        <td align = "left">X</td>
        <td align = "center">O</td>
    </tr>
    <tr>
        <td align = "right">X</td>
        <td align = "left">O</td>
        <td align = "center">X</td>
    </tr>
</table>
```

You can see the results of this XHTML in Figure 6.6. Although the **align** attribute for the **<table>** element is deprecated in XHTML in favor of style sheets (see Chapter 9), it's not deprecated for **<th>** and **<td>**.

Besides aligning your text horizontally, you can also align it vertically.

Aligning Your Data Vertically

To set the vertical alignment of the data in table cells, you can use the **valign** attribute, which you set to **top**, **middle**, or **bottom**. Here's an example:

In Depth

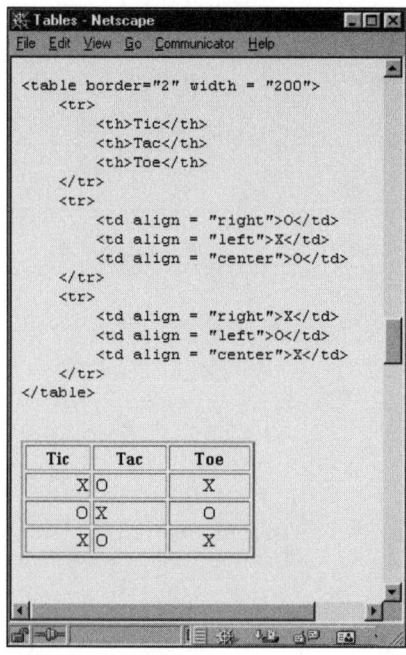

Figure 6.6   Aligning cell data horizontally.

```
<table border="2" height = "120">
    <tr>
        <th>Tic</th>
        <th>Tac</th>
        <th>Toe</th>
    </tr>
    <tr>
        <td valign = "top">X</td>
        <td valign = "middle">O</td>
        <td valign = "bottom">X</td>
    </tr>
    <tr>
        <td valign = "top">O</td>
        <td valign = "middle">X</td>
        <td valign = "bottom">O</td>
    </tr>
    <tr>
        <td valign = "top">X</td>
        <td valign = "middle">O</td>
        <td valign = "bottom">X</td>
    </tr>
</table>
```

Chapter 6 Creating Tables

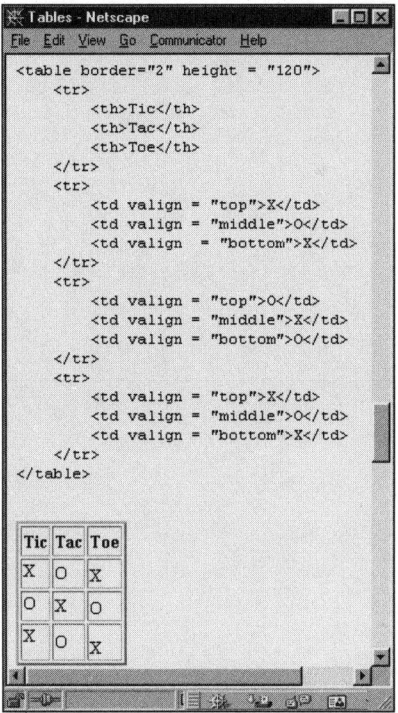

Figure 6.7 Aligning cell data vertically.

You can see the results of this XHTML in Figure 6.7.

***

TIP: *Although this example used the* **<td>** *element to align text cell by cell, you can use the* **valign** *attribute of the* **<tr>** *element to align the text vertically in whole rows.*

***

Spanning Columns

Of course, there's a great deal more that you can do with tables; for example, you can create cells and headings that *span* (stretch across) columns. To do that, use the **colspan** attribute of the **<th>** and **<td>** elements.

Following is an example to make this clearer. In this case, I'll change the headings so that I have only one heading that spans all three columns:

```
<table border="2">
    <tr>
        <th colspan="3"> TicTac Game</th>
```

```
        </tr>
        <tr>
            <td>X</td>
            <td>O</td>
            <td>X</td>
        </tr>
        <tr>
            <td>O</td>
            <td>X</td>
            <td>O</td>
        </tr>
        <tr>
            <td>X</td>
            <td>O</td>
            <td>X</td>
        </tr>
</table>
```

That's all it takes—now the headings span all three columns, as you see in Figure 6.8. Besides spanning columns, you can also span *rows*.

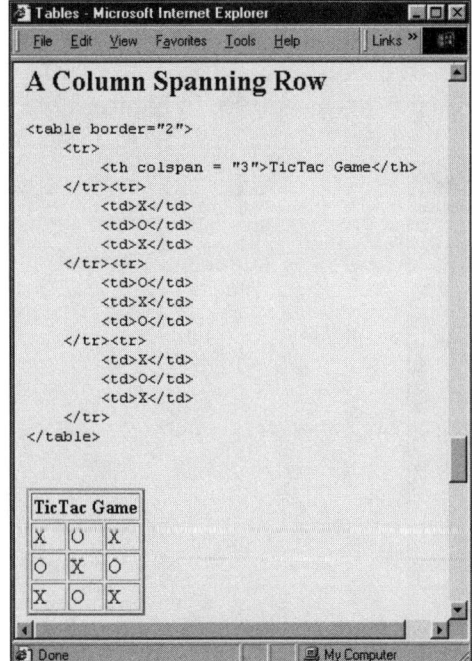

Figure 6.8 Spanning columns.

Spanning Rows

To span rows, you can use the **rowspan** attribute of the **<th>** and **<td>** elements. Here's an example showing how this looks; I use the **rowspan** attribute, like this:

```
<table border="2">
    <tr>
        <th rowspan = "3">TicTac<br />Game</th>
        <td>X</td>
        <td>O</td>
        <td>X</td>
    </tr>
    <tr>
        <td>O</td>
        <td>X</td>
        <td>O</td>
    </tr>
    <tr>
        <td>X</td>
        <td>O</td>
        <td>X</td>
    </tr>
</table>
```

Now the table headings will span all three rows, as you see in Figure 6.9.

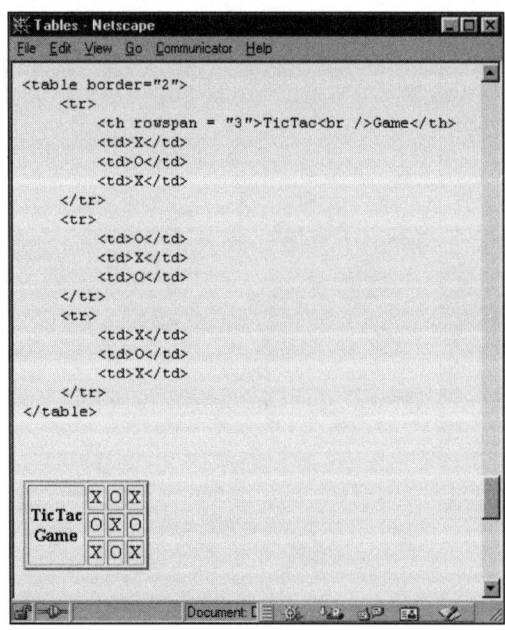

Figure 6.9   Spanning rows.

TIP: *Spanning rows and columns is a great way to format text in a Web page if you use a borderless table. (Although you can also use the **<div>** elements and style sheets to do the same thing, all browsers do not support styles sheets.)*

Setting Colors

To set colors in tables, you can use the **bgcolor** attributes of the **<table>**, **<tr>**, **<th>**, and **<td>** elements. (Note that these attributes have been deprecated in HTML 4.0 in favor of style sheets; later in this chapter, we'll see how to use style sheets to write the following example.) Here's an example where I'm coloring the cells of a table:

```
<table border="2">
    <tr>
        <th bgcolor = "#ff0000">Tic</th>
        <th bgcolor = "#ff0000">Tac</th>
        <th bgcolor = "#ff0000">Toe</th>
    </tr>
    <tr>
        <td bgcolor = "#ffffff">X</td>
        <td bgcolor = "#000000">
            <font color = "#ffffff">O</font>
        </td>
        <td bgcolor = "#ffffff">X</td>
    </tr>
    <tr>
        <td bgcolor = "#000000">
            <font color = "#ffffff">O</font>
        </td>
        <td bgcolor = "#ffffff">X</td>
        <td bgcolor = "#000000">
            <font color = "#ffffff">O</font>
        </td>
    </tr>
    <tr>
        <td bgcolor = "#ffffff">X</td>
        <td bgcolor = "#000000">
            <font color = "#ffffff">O</font>
        </td>
        <td bgcolor = "#ffffff">X</td>
    </tr>
</table>
```

The results of this XHTML, in glorious black and white, appear in Figure 6.10. (In fact, the headings should be red, and the table data is presented on a black-and-white checkerboard.)

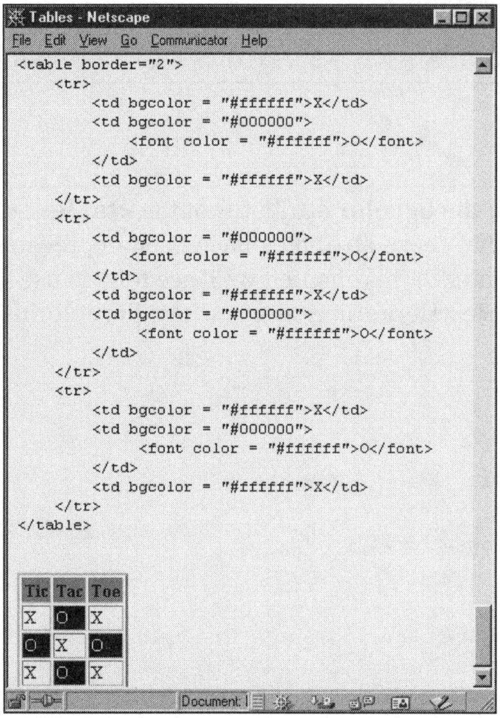

Chapter 6 Creating Tables

Figure 6.10 Coloring a table.

TIP: *You can also use the **background** attribute of the **<td>** element to set the background image used for a table.*

What we've been working with so far is called the *simple table model*. There's also a new *complex table model*. The complex table model introduces elements such as **<col>**, **<colgroup>**, **<thead>**, **<tbody>**, and **<tfoot>** to let you create column and row groups, a table foot, and a table head for your tables.

That's enough work with tables to get us started—now it's time to turn to the actual XHTML in the "Immediate Solutions." You can find the Web page for the examples tables in this chapter in Listing 6.1.

Listing 6.1 Tables.html displays different table types.

```
<?xml version="1.0"?>
<!DOCTYPE html PUBLIC "-//W3C//DTD XHTML 1.0 Transitional//EN"
"http://www.w3.org/tr/xhtml/DTD/xhtml1-transitional.dtd">
<html xmlns="http://www.w3.org/1999/xhtml" xml:lang="en" lang="en">
    <head>
        <title>
            Tables
        </title>
    </head>
```

```html
        <body>

            <center>
               <h1>
                    Creating Tables
               </h1>
            </center>

            <br />
            <h2>Borderless</h2>
            <pre>
&lt;table&gt;
    &lt;tr&gt;
        &lt;th&gt;Tic&lt;/th&gt;
        &lt;th&gt;Tac&lt;/th&gt;
        &lt;th&gt;Toe&lt;/th&gt;
    &lt;/tr&gt;
    &lt;tr&gt;
        &lt;td&gt;X&lt;/td&gt;
        &lt;td&gt;O&lt;/td&gt;
        &lt;td&gt;X&lt;/td&gt;
    &lt;/tr&gt;
    &lt;tr&gt;
        &lt;td&gt;O&lt;/td&gt;
        &lt;td&gt;X&lt;/td&gt;
        &lt;td&gt;O&lt;/td&gt;
    &lt;/tr&gt;
    &lt;tr&gt;
        &lt;td&gt;X&lt;/td&gt;
        &lt;td&gt;O&lt;/td&gt;
        &lt;td&gt;X&lt;/td&gt;
    &lt;/tr&gt;
&lt;/table&gt;
            </pre>

            <table>
                <tr>
                    <th>Tic</th>
                    <th>Tac</th>
                    <th>Toe</th>
                </tr>
                <tr>
                    <td>X</td>
                    <td>O</td>
                    <td>X</td>
                </tr>
```

```
            <tr>
                <td>O</td>
                <td>X</td>
                <td>O</td>
            </tr>
            <tr>
                <td>X</td>
                <td>O</td>
                <td>X</td>
            </tr>
        </table>


        <br />
        <br />
        <h2>Standard</h2>
        <pre>
&lt;table border="2"&gt;
    &lt;tr&gt;
        &lt;th&gt;Tic&lt;/th&gt;
        &lt;th&gt;Tac&lt;/th&gt;
        &lt;th&gt;Toe&lt;/th&gt;
    &lt;/tr&gt;
    &lt;tr&gt;
        &lt;td&gt;X&lt;/td&gt;
        &lt;td&gt;O&lt;/td&gt;
        &lt;td&gt;X&lt;/td&gt;
    &lt;/tr&gt;
    &lt;tr&gt;
        &lt;td&gt;O&lt;/td&gt;
        &lt;td&gt;X&lt;/td&gt;
        &lt;td&gt;O&lt;/td&gt;
    &lt;/tr&gt;
    &lt;tr&gt;
        &lt;td&gt;X&lt;/td&gt;
        &lt;td&gt;O&lt;/td&gt;
        &lt;td&gt;X&lt;/td&gt;
    &lt;/tr&gt;
&lt;/table&gt;
        </pre>

        <table border="2">
            <tr>
                <th>Tic</th>
                <th>Tac</th>
                <th>Toe</th>
```

```
            </tr>
            <tr>
                <td>X</td>
                <td>O</td>
                <td>X</td>
            </tr>
            <tr>
                <td>O</td>
                <td>X</td>
                <td>O</td>
            </tr>
            <tr>
                <td>X</td>
                <td>O</td>
                <td>X</td>
            </tr>
        </table>


        <br />
        <br />
        <h2>Cell Spacing</h2>

        <pre>
&lt;table border="2" cellspacing="4"&gt;
    &lt;tr&gt;
        &lt;th&gt;Tic&lt;/th&gt;
        &lt;th&gt;Tac&lt;/th&gt;
        &lt;th&gt;Toe&lt;/th&gt;
    &lt;/tr&gt;
    &lt;tr&gt;
        &lt;td&gt;X&lt;/td&gt;
        &lt;td&gt;O&lt;/td&gt;
        &lt;td&gt;X&lt;/td&gt;
    &lt;/tr&gt;
    &lt;tr&gt;
        &lt;td&gt;O&lt;/td&gt;
        &lt;td&gt;X&lt;/td&gt;
        &lt;td&gt;O&lt;/td&gt;
    &lt;/tr&gt;
    &lt;tr&gt;
        &lt;td&gt;X&lt;/td&gt;
        &lt;td&gt;O&lt;/td&gt;
        &lt;td&gt;X&lt;/td&gt;
    &lt;/tr&gt;
&lt;/table&gt;
        </pre>
```

```
            <table border="2" cellspacing = "4">
                <tr>
                    <th>Tic</th>
                    <th>Tac</th>
                    <th>Toe</th>
                </tr>
                <tr>
                    <td>X</td>
                    <td>O</td>
                    <td>X</td>
                </tr>
                <tr>
                    <td>O</td>
                    <td>X</td>
                    <td>O</td>
                </tr>
                <tr>
                    <td>X</td>
                    <td>O</td>
                    <td>X</td>
                </tr>
            </table>

            <br />
            <br />
            <h2>Wide border="2"</h2>

            <pre>
&lt;table border="2" cellspacing="4"&gt;
    &lt;tr&gt;
        &lt;th&gt;Tic&lt;/th&gt;
        &lt;th&gt;Tac&lt;/th&gt;
        &lt;th&gt;Toe&lt;/th&gt;
    &lt;/tr&gt;
    &lt;tr&gt;
        &lt;td&gt;X&lt;/td&gt;
        &lt;td&gt;O&lt;/td&gt;
        &lt;td&gt;X&lt;/td&gt;
    &lt;/tr&gt;
    &lt;tr&gt;
        &lt;td&gt;O&lt;/td&gt;
        &lt;td&gt;X&lt;/td&gt;
        &lt;td&gt;O&lt;/td&gt;
    &lt;/tr&gt;
    &lt;tr&gt;
```

In Depth

```
        <td>X</td>
        <td>O</td>
        <td>X</td>
    </tr>
</table>
```

```html
<table border="2" cellspacing = "4">
    <tr>
        <th>Tic</th>
        <th>Tac</th>
        <th>Toe</th>
    </tr>
    <tr>
        <td>X</td>
        <td>O</td>
        <td>X</td>
    </tr>
    <tr>
        <td>O</td>
        <td>X</td>
        <td>O</td>
    </tr>
    <tr>
        <td>X</td>
        <td>O</td>
        <td>X</td>
    </tr>
</table>

<br />
<br />
<h2>Data Aligned Right, Left, Center</h2>

<pre>
```
```
<table border="2" width = "200">
    <tr>
        <th>Tic</th>
        <th>Tac</th>
        <th>Toe</th>
    </tr>
    <tr>
        <td align = "right">O</td>
        <td align = "left">X</td>
        <td align = "center">O</td>
```

6. Creating Tables

349

```
            &lt;/tr&gt;
            &lt;tr&gt;
                &lt;td align = "right"&gt;X&lt;/td&gt;
                &lt;td align = "left"&gt;O&lt;/td&gt;
                &lt;td align = "center"&gt;X&lt;/td&gt;
            &lt;/tr&gt;
        &lt;/table&gt;
            </pre>

            <table border="2" width = "200">
                <tr>
                    <th>Tic</th>
                    <th>Tac</th>
                    <th>Toe</th>
                </tr>
                <tr>
                    <td align = "right">X</td>
                    <td align = "left">O</td>
                    <td align = "center">X</td>
                </tr>
                <tr>
                    <td align = "right">O</td>
                    <td align = "left">X</td>
                    <td align = "center">O</td>
                </tr>
                <tr>
                    <td align = "right">X</td>
                    <td align = "left">O</td>
                    <td align = "center">X</td>
                </tr>
            </table>


            <br />
            <br />
            <h2>Data Aligned Vertically</h2>

            <pre>
&lt;table border="2" height = "120"&gt;
    &lt;tr&gt;
        &lt;th&gt;Tic&lt;/th&gt;
        &lt;th&gt;Tac&lt;/th&gt;
        &lt;th&gt;Toe&lt;/th&gt;
    &lt;/tr&gt;
    &lt;tr&gt;
        &lt;td valign = "top"&gt;X&lt;/td&gt;
```

```
        &lt;td valign = "middle"&gt;O&lt;/td&gt;
        &lt;td valign  = "bottom"&gt;X&lt;/td&gt;
    &lt;/tr&gt;
    &lt;tr&gt;
        &lt;td valign = "top"&gt;O&lt;/td&gt;
        &lt;td valign = "middle"&gt;X&lt;/td&gt;
        &lt;td valign = "bottom"&gt;O&lt;/td&gt;
    &lt;/tr&gt;
    &lt;tr&gt;
        &lt;td valign = "top"&gt;X&lt;/td&gt;
        &lt;td valign = "middle"&gt;O&lt;/td&gt;
        &lt;td valign = "bottom"&gt;X&lt;/td&gt;
    &lt;/tr&gt;
&lt;/table&gt;
        </pre>

        <table border="2" height = "120">
            <tr>
                <th>Tic</th>
                <th>Tac</th>
                <th>Toe</th>
            </tr>
            <tr>
                <td valign = "top">X</td>
                <td valign = "middle">O</td>
                <td valign = "bottom">X</td>
            </tr>
            <tr>
                <td valign = "top">O</td>
                <td valign = "middle">X</td>
                <td valign = "bottom">O</td>
            </tr>
            <tr>
                <td valign = "top">X</td>
                <td valign = "middle">O</td>
                <td valign = "bottom">X</td>
            </tr>
        </table>


        <br />
        <br />
        <h2>A Column Spanning Row</h2>
        <pre>
&lt;table border="2"&gt;
    &lt;tr&gt;
```

Chapter 6 Creating Tables

```
            &lt;th colspan = "3"&gt;TicTac Game&lt;/th&gt;
        &lt;/tr&gt;
        &lt;tr&gt;
            &lt;td&gt;X&lt;/td&gt;
            &lt;td&gt;O&lt;/td&gt;
            &lt;td&gt;X&lt;/td&gt;
        &lt;/tr&gt;
        &lt;tr&gt;
            &lt;td&gt;O&lt;/td&gt;
            &lt;td&gt;X&lt;/td&gt;
            &lt;td&gt;O&lt;/td&gt;
        &lt;/tr&gt;
        &lt;tr&gt;
            &lt;td&gt;X&lt;/td&gt;
            &lt;td&gt;O&lt;/td&gt;
            &lt;td&gt;X&lt;/td&gt;
        &lt;/tr&gt;
    &lt;/table&gt;
        </pre>

        <table border="2">
            <tr>
                <th colspan="3"> TicTac Game</th>
            </tr>
            <tr>
                <td>X</td>
                <td>O</td>
                <td>X</td>
            </tr>
            <tr>
                <td>O</td>
                <td>X</td>
                <td>O</td>
            </tr>
            <tr>
                <td>X</td>
                <td>O</td>
                <td>X</td>
            </tr>
        </table>

        <br />
        <br />
        <h2>A Row Spanning Column</h2>
```

In Depth

```
            <pre>
&lt;table border="2"&gt;
    &lt;tr&gt;
        &lt;th rowspan = "3"&gt;TicTac&lt;br /&gt;Game&lt;/th&gt;
        &lt;td&gt;X&lt;/td&gt;
        &lt;td&gt;O&lt;/td&gt;
        &lt;td&gt;X&lt;/td&gt;
    &lt;/tr&gt;
    &lt;tr&gt;
        &lt;td&gt;O&lt;/td&gt;
        &lt;td&gt;X&lt;/td&gt;
        &lt;td&gt;O&lt;/td&gt;
    &lt;/tr&gt;
    &lt;tr&gt;
        &lt;td&gt;X&lt;/td&gt;
        &lt;td&gt;O&lt;/td&gt;
        &lt;td&gt;X&lt;/td&gt;
    &lt;/tr&gt;
&lt;/table&gt;
            </pre>

            <br />
            <table border="2">
                <tr>
                    <th rowspan = "3">TicTac<br />Game</th>
                    <td>X</td>
                    <td>O</td>
                    <td>X</td>
                </tr>
                <tr>
                    <td>O</td>
                    <td>X</td>
                    <td>O</td>
                </tr>
                <tr>
                    <td>X</td>
                    <td>O</td>
                    <td>X</td>
                </tr>
            </table>

            <br />
            <br />
            <h2>Color</h2>
```

```
<pre>
&lt;table border="2"&gt;
    &lt;tr&gt;
        &lt;td bgcolor = "#ffffff"&gt;X&lt;/td&gt;
        &lt;td bgcolor = "#000000"&gt;
            &lt;font color = "#ffffff"&gt;O&lt;/font&gt;
        &lt;/td&gt;
        &lt;td bgcolor = "#ffffff"&gt;X&lt;/td&gt;
    &lt;/tr&gt;
    &lt;tr&gt;
        &lt;td bgcolor = "#000000"&gt;
            &lt;font color = "#ffffff"&gt;O&lt;/font&gt;
        &lt;/td&gt;
        &lt;td bgcolor = "#ffffff"&gt;X&lt;/td&gt;
        &lt;td bgcolor = "#000000"&gt;
            &lt;font color = "#ffffff"&gt;O&lt;/font&gt;
        &lt;/td&gt;
    &lt;/tr&gt;
    &lt;tr&gt;
        &lt;td bgcolor = "#ffffff"&gt;X&lt;/td&gt;
        &lt;td bgcolor = "#000000"&gt;
            &lt;font color = "#ffffff"&gt;O&lt;/font&gt;
        &lt;/td&gt;
        &lt;td bgcolor = "#ffffff"&gt;X&lt;/td&gt;
    &lt;/tr&gt;
&lt;/table&gt;
</pre>

<table border="2">
    <tr>
        <th bgcolor = "#ff0000">Tic</th>
        <th bgcolor = "#ff0000">Tac</th>
        <th bgcolor = "#ff0000">Toe</th>
    </tr>
    <tr>
        <td bgcolor = "#ffffff">X</td>
        <td bgcolor = "#000000">
            <font color = "#ffffff">O</font>
        </td>
        <td bgcolor = "#ffffff">X</td>
    </tr>
    <tr>
        <td bgcolor = "#000000">
            <font color = "#ffffff">O</font>
        </td>
```

```
            <td bgcolor = "#ffffff">X</td>
            <td bgcolor = "#000000">
                <font color = "#ffffff">O</font>
            </td>
        </tr>
        <tr>
            <td bgcolor = "#ffffff">X</td>
            <td bgcolor = "#000000">
                <font color = "#ffffff">O</font>
            </td>
            <td bgcolor = "#ffffff">X</td>
        </tr>
    </table>

</body>

</html>
```

Immediate Solutions

<table>—Creating a Table

Purpose: Creates a table; encloses elements such as **<caption>**, **<tr>**, **<th>**, **<td>**, **<colspan>**, **<col>**, **<thead>**, **<tbody>**, and **<tfoot>**.

When used as HTML: Start tag/End tag: Required/Required

Supported: [1.0S, 1.0T, 1.0F, 1.1, 3, 3.2, 4, IE2, IE3, IE4, IE5, NS1, NS2, NS3, NS4]

Attributes:

- **align**—Specifies the horizontal alignment of the table in the browser window. Set to **left**, **center**, or **right**. Deprecated. [1.0T, 1.0F, 3, 3.2, 4, IE2, IE3, IE4, IE5, NS2, NS3, NS4]
- **background**—Specifies the URL of a background image to be used as a background for the table. All cell contents are displayed over this image. Note that if the image is smaller than the table, it is tiled to fit the table. Set to a URL. [IE3, IE4, IE5, NS4]
- **bgcolor**—Sets the background color of the table cells. You can override this attribute at the row and cell level. Set to a Red, Green, Blue (RGB) triplet color value or a predefined color name. Deprecated. [1.0T, 1.0F, 4, IE2, IE3, IE4, IE5, NS3, NS4]
- **border**—Sets the border width; set to a pixel width. If you set this attribute to 0, no border appears. Although this attribute used to be a standalone attribute in HTML 2, as of HTML 3.2, you should assign a number to it. [1.0T, 1.0F, 3, 3.2, 4, IE2, IE3, IE4, IE5, NS2, NS3, NS4]
- **bordercolor**—Sets the external border color for the entire table. Set to an RGB triplet color value or a predefined color name. [IE2, IE3, IE4, IE5]
- **cellpadding**—Sets the spacing between cell walls and cell contents. Set to a pixel size. [1.0S, 1.0T, 1.0F, 1.1, 3.2, 4, IE2, IE3, IE4, IE5, NS1, NS2, NS3, NS4]
- **cellspacing**—Gives the distance between cells (and therefore the width of the struts between cells). Set to pixel values. [1.0S, 1.0T, 1.0F, 1.1, 3.2, 4, IE2, IE3, IE4, IE5, NS1, NS2, NS3, NS4]
- **class**—Class of the element (used for rendering). [1.0S, 1.0T, 1.0F, 1.1, 3, 4, IE4, IE5]

- **cols**—Specifies the number of columns in the table. A Complex Table Model attribute. Set to a positive integer. [IE3, IE4, IE5, NS3, NS4]
- **datapagesize**—Sets the number of records displayed in a data bound repeated table. Set to a positive number. [IE4, IE5]
- **datasrc**—Gives the URL or ID of the data source object supplying data bound to this element. W3C says this should be a URL, Internet Explorer says it should be a data source ID. [IE4, IE5]
- **dir**—Gives the direction of directionally neutral text (text that doesn't have inherent direction in which you should read it). Possible values: **ltr**: left-to-right text or table and **rtl**: right-to-left text or table. [1.0S, 1.0T, 1.0F, 1.1, 4, IE5]
- **frame**—Specifies the outer border display of the table. A Complex Table Model attribute. Using this attribute coupled with the **rules** attribute yields much greater border display control than the older Simple Table Model. Possible values: **void** (no borders), **above** (border on top side only), **below** (border on bottom side only), **hsides** (horizontal borders only), **vsides** (vertical borders only), **lhs** (border on left side only), **rhs** (border on right side only), **box** (border on all four sides), **border** (the default, the same as **box**). [1.0S, 1.0T, 1.0F, 1.1, 4, IE3, IE4, IE5]
- **height**—Gives the height of the whole table, in pixels. [IE2, IE3, IE4, IE5, NS1, NS2, NS3, NS4]
- **hspace**—Sets the horizontal padding for the whole table, in pixels. [NS1, NS2, NS3, NS4]
- **id**—Unique alphanumeric identifier for the tag, which you can use to refer to it. [1.0S, 1.0T, 1.0F, 1.1, 3, 4, IE4, IE5]
- **lang**—Base language used for the tag. [1.0S, 1.0T, 1.0F, 1.1, 3, 4, IE4, IE5]
- **language**—Scripting language used for the tag. [IE4, IE5]
- **rules**—Sets the interior struts in a table. A Complex Table Model attribute. Set to: **none** (no interior struts are displayed), **groups** (horizontal struts displayed between table groups created with the **thead**, **tbody**, **tfoot**, and **colgroup** tags), **rows** (horizontal struts are displayed between all table rows), **cols** (vertical struts are displayed between all table columns), and **all** (struts displayed between all table cells). [1.0S, 1.0T, 1.0F, 1.1, 4, IE4, IE5]
- **style**—Inline style indicating how to render the element. [1.0S, 1.0T, 1.0F, 1.1, 4, IE3, IE4, IE5]
- **summary**—Sets accessibility information for nonvisual browsers. Set to a text string providing a summary of the table. [1.0S, 1.0T, 1.0F, 1.1, 4]
- **title**—Holds additional information (which might be displayed in tool tips) for the element. [1.0S, 1.0T, 1.0F, 1.1, 3, 4, IE4, IE5]

- **vspace**—Sets the vertical padding for the whole table, in pixels. [NS1, NS2, NS3, NS4]
- **width**—Sets the width of the table; set to a pixel value or a percentage of the display area (add a percent sign (%) to such values). [1.0S, 1.0T, 1.0F, 1.1, 3, 3.2, 4, IE2, IE3, IE4, IE5, NS1, NS2, NS3, NS4]
- **xml:lang**—Holds the base language for the element when the document is interpreted as an XML document. [1.0S, 1.0T, 1.0F, 1.1]

XHTML events: onclick, ondblclick, onfocus, onblur, onmousedown, onmouseup, onmouseover, onmousemove, onmouseout, onkeypress, onkeydown, onkeyup

The novice programmer appears and says, "I want to present my new Tic Tac Toe game in an XHTML table—where do I start?" You say, "Start with the **<table>** element." "Great," says the NP. "Here's my terminal—can you show me how?"

To create a table, you enclose everything in a **<table>** element, like this:

```
<table>
    .
    .
    .
</table>
```

That's all it takes to create a table. But this one is completely empty. So where do you go from here? Now you start building the rows in your table.

TIP: It's often a good idea to use the **summary** attribute to provide a summary of the table for non-visual browsers.

<tr>—Creating a Table Row

Purpose: Creates a row in a table; encloses **<th>** and **<td>** elements.

When used as HTML: Start tag/End tag: Required/Optional

Supported: [1.0S, 1.0T, 1.0F, 1.1, 3, 3.2, 4, IE2, IE3, IE4, IE5, NS1, NS2, NS3, NS4]

Attributes:

- **align**—Specifies the horizontal alignment of the text in this table row. Set to **left**, **center**, **right**, **justify**, or **char**. [1.0S, 1.0T, 1.0F, 1.1, 3, 3.2, 4, IE2, IE3, IE4, IE5, NS2, NS3, NS4]

- **bgcolor**—Sets the background color of the table cells. You can override this attribute at the row and cell level. Set to an RGB triplet color value or a predefined color name. Deprecated. [1.0T, 1.0F, 4, IE2, IE3, IE4, IE5, NS3, NS4]

- **bordercolor**—Sets the external border color for the row. Set to an RGB triplet color value or a predefined color name. [IE2, IE3, IE4, IE5]

- **char**—Specifies a character to align text on. Set to an alphanumeric character. [1.0S, 1.0T, 1.0F, 1.1, 4]

- **charoff**—Sets the alignment offset to the first character to align on, as set with **char**. [1.0S, 1.0T, 1.0F, 1.1, 4]

- **class**—Class of the element (used for rendering). [1.0S, 1.0T, 1.0F, 1.1, 3, 4, IE4, IE5]

- **dir**—Gives the direction of directionally neutral text (text that doesn't have inherent direction in which you should read it). Possible values: **ltr**: left-to-right text or table and **rtl**: right-to-left text or table. [1.0S, 1.0T, 1.0F, 1.1, 4, IE5]

- **id**—Unique alphanumeric identifier for the tag, which you can use to refer to it. [1.0S, 1.0T, 1.0F, 1.1, 3, 4, IE4, IE5]

- **lang**—Base language used for the tag. [1.0S, 1.0T, 1.0F, 1.1, 3, 4, IE4, IE5]

- **language**—Scripting language used for the tag. [IE4, IE5]

- **style**—Inline style indicating how to render the element. [1.0S, 1.0T, 1.0F, 1.1, 4, IE3, IE4, IE5]

- **title**—Holds additional information (which might be displayed in tool tips) for the element. [1.0S, 1.0T, 1.0F, 1.1, 3, 4, IE4, IE5]

- **valign**—Sets the vertical alignment of the data in this row. Set to **top**, **middle**, **bottom**, or **baseline**. [1.0S, 1.0T, 1.0F, 1.1, 3, 3.2, 4, IE2, IE3, IE4, IE5, NS1, NS2, NS3, NS4]

- **xml:lang**—Holds the base language for the element when the document is interpreted as an XML document. [1.0S, 1.0T, 1.0F, 1.1]

XHTML events: onclick, ondblclick, onfocus, onblur, onmousedown, onmouseup, onmouseover, onmousemove, onmouseout, onkeypress, onkeydown, onkeyup

"OK," says the novice programmer, "I've set up my table with the **<table>** element. What's next?" "Next," you say, "you create the rows with the **<tr>** element."

To create a row in a table, you use the **<tr>** element. The number of these elements that you use specifies the number of rows in your table. Here's how to create a row in a table:

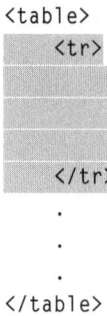

```
<table>
    <tr>
    .
    .
    .
    </tr>
    .
    .
    .
</table>
```

For each row in your table, there's a **<tr>** element; but how does the browser know how many columns you want to use? In the simple table model, the browser simply checks how many **<th>** or **<td>** elements you put into a row. **<th>** elements create table headings, and **<td>** elements create the table data that appears in the cells.

<th>—Creating Table Headings

Purpose: Creates a table heading; just like table data, but usually bold and centered vertically and horizontally.

When used as HTML: Start tag/End tag: Required/Optional

Supported: [1.0S, 1.0T, 1.0F, 1.1, 3, 3.2, 4, IE2, IE3, IE4, IE5, NS1, NS2, NS3, NS4]

Attributes:

- **abbr**—Specifies an abbreviated name for a header cell (the default abbreviation is the actual cell content). Set to alphanumeric characters. [1.0S, 1.0T, 1.0F, 1.1, 4]
- **align**—Sets the horizontal alignment of content in the table cell. Set to **left**, **center**, **right**, **justify**, or **char**. [1.0S, 1.0T, 1.0F, 1.1, 3, 3.2, 4, IE2, IE3, IE4, IE5, NS1, NS2, NS3, NS4]
- **axis**—Specifies a name for a cell and will usually only be applied to table heading cells, allowing the table to be mapped to a tree hierarchy. Set to alphanumeric characters. [1.0S, 1.0T, 1.0F, 1.1, 3, 4]
- **background**—Specifies the background image for the table cell. All cell contents are displayed over this image. If the image is smaller than the table cell, the image will be tiled. Set to an image's URL. [IE3, IE4, IE5]

- **bgcolor**—Sets the background color of the table cells. You can override this attribute at the row and cell level. Set to an RGB triplet color value or a predefined color name. Deprecated. [1.0T, 1.0F, 4, IE2, IE3, IE4, IE5, NS3, NS4]

- **bordercolor**—Sets the external border color for the cell. Set to an RGB triplet color value or a predefined color name. [IE2, IE3, IE4, IE5]

- **char**—Specifies a character to align text on. Set to an alphanumeric character. [1.0S, 1.0T, 1.0F, 1.1, 4]

- **charoff**—Sets the alignment offset to the first character to align on, as set with **char**. [1.0S, 1.0T, 1.0F, 1.1, 4]

- **class**—Class of the element (used for rendering). [1.0S, 1.0T, 1.0F, 1.1, 3, 4, IE4, IE5]

- **colspan**—Indicates how many cell columns of the table this cell should span. Set to a positive integer (the default is 1). [1.0S, 1.0T, 1.0F, 1.1, 3, 3.2, 4, IE2, IE3, IE4, IE5, NS1, NS2, NS3, NS4]

- **dir**—Gives the direction of directionally neutral text (text that doesn't have inherent direction in which you should read it). Possible values: **ltr**: left-to-right text or table and **rtl**: right-to-left text or table. [1.0S, 1.0T, 1.0F, 1.1, 4, IE5]

- **headers**—Gives the list of header cells that supply header information for the cell. Set to a space-separated list of table cell IDs. [1.0S, 1.0T, 1.0F, 1.1, 4]

- **height**—Sets the height of the cell (in general, also sets the height of the whole row). Set to pixel values. Deprecated. [1.0T, 1.0F, 3.2, 4, IE2, IE3, IE4, IE5, NS1, NS2, NS3, NS4]

- **id**—Unique alphanumeric identifier for the tag, which you can use to refer to it. [1.0S, 1.0T, 1.0F, 1.1, 3, 4, IE4, IE5]

- **lang**—Base language used for the tag. [1.0S, 1.0T, 1.0F, 1.1, 3, 4, IE4, IE5]

- **language**—Scripting language used for the tag. [IE4, IE5]

- **nowrap**—Specifies that data in the cell should not be wrapped by the browser, meaning the table cell will be made long enough to fit the contents without line breaks. Deprecated. [1.0T, 1.0F, 3, 3.2, 4, IE2, IE3, IE4, IE5, NS1, NS2, NS3, NS4]

- **rowspan**—Indicates how many rows of the table this cell should span. Set to a positive integer (the default is 1). [1.0S, 1.0T, 1.0F, 1.1, 3, 3.2, 4, IE2, IE3, IE4, IE5, NS1, NS2, NS3, NS4]

- **scope**—Specifies a set of data cells for which the header cell provides header information. Set to: **row** (cell provides header information for the rest of the row that contains it) or **col** (cell provides header information for the rest of the column), **rowgroup** (cell provides header information for the rest of the row group that contains it), or **colgroup** (cell provides header information for the rest of the column group that contains it). [1.0S, 1.0T, 1.0F, 1.1, 4]

- **style**—Inline style indicating how to render the element. [1.0S, 1.0T, 1.0F, 1.1, 4, IE4, IE5]

- **title**—Holds additional information (which might be displayed in tool tips) for the element. [1.0S, 1.0T, 1.0F, 1.1, 3, 4, IE4, IE5]

- **valign**—Sets the vertical alignment of the data in this cell. Set to **top**, **middle**, **bottom**, or **baseline**. [1.0S, 1.0T, 1.0F, 1.1, 3, 3.2, 4, IE2, IE3, IE4, IE5, NS1, NS2, NS3, NS4]

- **width**—Specifies the width of the cell. Set to a pixel width or a percentage of the display area (include a percent sign (%) after percentages). Deprecated. [1.0T, 1.0F, 3.2, 4, IE2, IE3, IE4, IE5, NS1, NS2, NS3, NS4]

- **xml:lang**—Holds the base language for the element when the document is interpreted as an XML document. [1.0S, 1.0T, 1.0F, 1.1]

XHTML events: onclick, ondblclick, onfocus, onblur, onmousedown, onmouseup, onmouseover, onmousemove, onmouseout, onkeypress, onkeydown, onkeyup

"Is it true," the novice programmer wants to know, "that you can use special table cells as table headers?" "Yes indeed," you say, "just use the **<th>** element." "Great," says the NP, sitting down; "tell me all about it."

The **<th>** element gives you an easy way to put a header on top of each column in a table (although you can also make headers span several columns). Here's an example in which I'm giving the three columns of a table the headings "Tic," "Tac," and "Toe":

```
<table>
    <tr>
        <th>Tic</th>
        <th>Tac</th>
        <th>Toe</th>
    </tr>
        .
        .
        .
</table>
```

You can see the results of this XHTML in Figure 6.3. The text in a table header is usually displayed in bold and centered vertically and horizontally.

<td>—Creating Table Data

Purpose: Specifies the data for a table cell. Used inside the **<tr>** element.

When used as HTML: Start tag/End tag: Required/Optional

Supported: [1.0S, 1.0T, 1.0F, 1.1, 3, 3.2, 4, IE1, IE2, IE3, IE4, IE5, NS1, NS2, NS3, NS4]

Attributes:

- **abbr**—Specifies an abbreviated name for a header cell (the default abbreviation is the actual cell content). Set to alphanumeric characters. [1.0S, 1.0T, 1.0F, 1.1, 4]

- **align**—Sets the horizontal alignment of content in the table cell. Set to **left**, **center**, **right**, **justify**, or **char**. [1.0S, 1.0T, 1.0F, 1.1, 3, 3.2, 4, IE2, IE3, IE4, IE5, NS1, NS2, NS3, NS4]

- **axis**—Specifies a name for a cell and will usually only be applied to table heading cells, allowing the table to be mapped to a tree hierarchy. Set to alphanumeric characters. [1.0S, 1.0T, 1.0F, 1.1, 3, 4]

- **background**—Specifies the background image for the table cell. All cell contents are displayed over this image. If the image is smaller than the table cell, the image will be tiled. Set to an image's URL. [IE3, IE4, IE5]

- **bgcolor**—Sets the background color of the table cells. You can override this attribute at the row and cell level. Set to an RGB triplet color value or a predefined color name. Deprecated. [1.0T, 1.0F, 4, IE2, IE3, IE4, IE5, NS3, NS4]

- **bordercolor**—Sets the external border color for the cell. Set to an RGB triplet color value or a predefined color name. [IE2, IE3, IE4, IE5]

- **char**—Specifies a character to align text on. Set to an alphanumeric character. [1.0S, 1.0T, 1.0F, 1.1, 4]

- **charoff**—Sets the alignment offset to the first character to align on, as set with **char**. [1.0S, 1.0T, 1.0F, 1.1, 4]

- **class**—Class of the element (used for rendering). [1.0S, 1.0T, 1.0F, 1.1, 3, 4, IE4, IE5]

- **colspan**—Indicates how many cell columns of the table this cell should span. Set to a positive integer (the default is 1). [1.0S, 1.0T, 1.0F, 1.1, 3, 3.2, 4, IE2, IE3, IE4, IE5, NS1, NS2, NS3, NS4]

- **dir**—Gives the direction of directionally neutral text (text that doesn't have inherent direction in which you should read it). Possible values: **ltr**: left-to-right text or table and **rtl**: right-to-left text or table. [1.0S, 1.0T, 1.0F, 1.1, 4, IE5]

- **headers**—Gives the list of header cells that supply header information for the cell. Set to a space-separated list of table cell IDs. [1.0S, 1.0T, 1.0F, 1.1, 4]
- **height**—Sets the height of the cell (in general, also sets the height of the whole row). Set to pixel values. Deprecated. [1.0T, 1.0F, 3.2, 4, IE2, IE3, IE4, IE5, NS1, NS2, NS3, NS4]
- **id**—Unique alphanumeric identifier for the tag, which you can use to refer to it. [1.0S, 1.0T, 1.0F, 1.1, 3, 4, IE4, IE5]
- **lang**—Base language used for the tag. [1.0S, 1.0T, 1.0F, 1.1, 3, 4, IE4, IE5]
- **language**—Scripting language used for the tag. [IE4, IE5]
- **nowrap**—Specifies that data in the cell should not be wrapped by the browser, meaning the table cell will be made long enough to fit the contents without line breaks. Deprecated. [1.0T, 1.0F, 3, 3.2, 4, IE2, IE3, IE4, IE5, NS1, NS2, NS3, NS4]
- **rowspan**—Indicates how many rows of the table this cell should span. Set to a positive integer (the default is 1). [1.0S, 1.0T, 1.0F, 1.1, 3, 3.2, 4, IE2, IE3, IE4, IE5, NS1, NS2, NS3, NS4]
- **scope**—Specifies a set of data cells for which the header cell provides header information. Set to: **row** (cell provides header information for the rest of the row that contains it) or **col** (cell provides header information for the rest of the column), **rowgroup** (cell provides header information for the rest of the row group that contains it), or **colgroup** (cell provides header information for the rest of the column group that contains it). [1.0S, 1.0T, 1.0F, 1.1, 4]
- **style**—Inline style indicating how to render the element. [1.0S, 1.0T, 1.0F, 1.1, 4, IE4, IE5]
- **title**—Holds additional information (which might be displayed in tool tips) for the element. [1.0S, 1.0T, 1.0F, 1.1, 3, 4, IE4, IE5]
- **valign**—Sets the vertical alignment of the data in this cell. Set to **top**, **middle**, **bottom**, or **baseline**. [1.0S, 1.0T, 1.0F, 1.1, 3, 3.2, 4, IE2, IE3, IE4, IE5, NS1, NS2, NS3, NS4]
- **width**—Specifies the width of the cell. Set to a pixel width or a percentage of the display area (include a percent sign (%) after percentages). Deprecated. [1.0T, 1.0F, 3.2, 4, IE2, IE3, IE4, IE5, NS1, NS2, NS3, NS4]
- **xml:lang**—Holds the base language for the element when the document is interpreted as an XML document. [1.0S, 1.0T, 1.0F, 1.1]

XHTML events: onclick, ondblclick, onfocus, onblur, onmousedown, onmouseup, onmouseover, onmousemove, onmouseout, onkeypress, onkeydown, onkeyup

"Now I know how to set up a table, how to add rows to it, and how to create a header for each column in a table," the novice programmer says, "but I still don't know how to add data to the table." "That's easy," you say; "just use the **<td>** element for the data for each cell, and enclose them all in a **<tr>** element." "Swell," says the NP, "I'll give it a try."

You use the **<td>** element to specify the data for the cells in a table. The browser knows how many columns to create in the table, depending on how many **<td>** or **<th>** elements you put into a row. Here's an example in which I'm adding data to the rows of a table by using **<td>** elements:

```
<table>
    <tr>
        <th>Tic</th>
        <th>Tac</th>
        <th>Toe</th>
    </tr>
    <tr>
        <td>X</td>
        <td>O</td>
        <td>X</td>
    </tr>
    <tr>
        <td>O</td>
        <td>X</td>
        <td>O</td>
    </tr>
    <tr>
        <td>X</td>
        <td>O</td>
        <td>X</td>
    </tr>
</table>
```

And that's it—the table is done, and you can see it in Figure 6.3.

You might take a moment to study the table in the previous example—when you have mastered the structure of that table, you will understand the simple table model.

<caption>—Creating a Table Caption

Purpose: Specifies the data for a table cell. Used inside the **<tr>** element.

When used as HTML: Start tag/End tag: Required/Required

Supported: [1.0S, 1.0T, 1.0F, 1.1, 3, 3.2, 4, IE1, IE2, IE3, IE4, IE5, NS1, NS2, NS3, NS4]

Attributes:

- **align**—Sets the alignment of the caption. Set to **top**, **bottom**, **left**, or **right**. Internet Explorer 2 also added setting **center**. Deprecated. [1.0T, 1.0F, 3, 3.2, 4, IE2, IE3, IE4, IE5, NS1, NS2, NS3, NS4]
- **class**—Class of the element (used for rendering). [1.0S, 1.0T, 1.0F, 1.1, 3, 4, IE4, IE5]
- **dir**—Gives the direction of directionally neutral text (text that doesn't have inherent direction in which you should read it). Possible values: **ltr**: left-to-right text or table and **rtl**: right-to-left text or table. [1.0S, 1.0T, 1.0F, 1.1, 4, IE5]
- **id**—Unique alphanumeric identifier for the tag, which you can use to refer to it. [1.0S, 1.0T, 1.0F, 1.1, 3, 4, IE4, IE5]
- **lang**—Base language used for the tag. [1.0S, 1.0T, 1.0F, 1.1, 3, 4, IE4, IE5]
- **language**—Scripting language used for the tag. [IE4, IE5]
- **style**—Inline style indicating how to render the element. [1.0S, 1.0T, 1.0F, 1.1, 4, IE3, IE4, IE5]
- **title**—Holds additional information (which might be displayed in tool tips) for the element. [1.0S, 1.0T, 1.0F, 1.1, 3, 4, IE4, IE5]
- **valign**—Sets the vertical alignment of the caption. Set to **top**, **middle**, **bottom**, or **baseline**. [IE2, IE3, IE4, IE5]
- **xml:lang**—Holds the base language for the element when the document is interpreted as an XML document. [1.0S, 1.0T, 1.0F, 1.1]

XHTML events: onclick, **ondblclick**, **onfocus**, **onblur**, **onmousedown**, **onmouseup**, **onmouseover**, **onmousemove**, **onmouseout**, **onkeypress**, **onkeydown**, **onkeyup**

You can give a table, as a whole, a caption by using the **<caption>** element. This element goes directly into the **<table>** element. Here's an example showing how this works:

```
<table>
    <caption>How About A Game?</caption>
    <tr>
        <th>Tic</th>
        <th>Tac</th>
        <th>Toe</th>
    </tr>
    <tr>
        <td>X</td>
        <td>O</td>
        <td>X</td>
```

```
        </tr>
        <tr>
            <td>O</td>
            <td>X</td>
            <td>O</td>
        </tr>
        <tr>
            <td>X</td>
            <td>O</td>
            <td>X</td>
        </tr>
    </tr>
</table>
```

You can see the results of this XHTML in Figure 6.11. Notice that the caption appears above the table. Although the **<caption>** element is useful, note that you can create the same effect with simple text or with headers such as **<h1>** or **<h2>**.

NOTE: *The **align** attribute is deprecated and so does not appear in the XHTML 1.0 Strict and XHTML 1.1 DTDs. To align the caption vertically in Internet Explorer, you use **valign**. The default alignment is centered at the top of the table.*

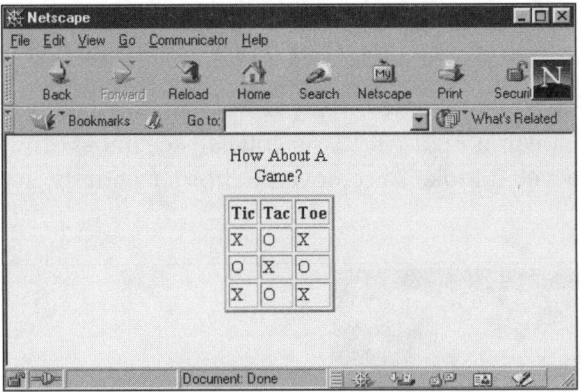

Figure 6.11   A table caption.

Setting Table Border Widths

You can set the width of table borders by using the **<table>** element's **border** attribute. Set this attribute to a positive integer (the number of pixels for the width). The default is 0.

In this example, I'm setting the border width of a table to 10 pixels:

```
<table border="10">
    <tr>
        <th>Tic</th>
        <th>Tac</th>
        <th>Toe</th>
    </tr>
    <tr>
        <td>X</td>
        <td>O</td>
        <td>X</td>
    </tr>
    <tr>
        <td>O</td>
        <td>X</td>
        <td>O</td>
    </tr>
    <tr>
        <td>X</td>
        <td>O</td>
        <td>X</td>
    </tr>
</table>
```

The results of this XHTML appear in Figure 6.12. As you can see, most browsers give wider table borders a beveled look. To remove the border entirely, set the border width to 0.

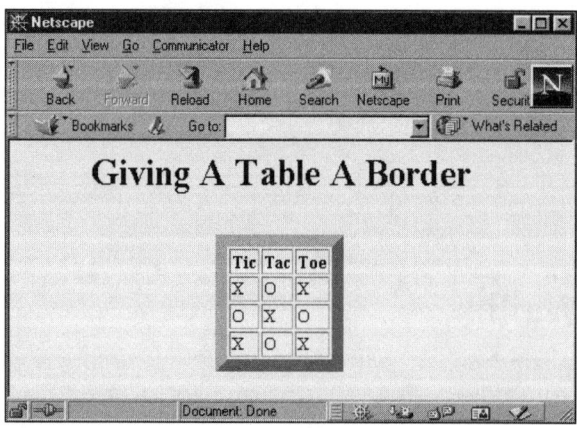

Figure 6.12   A table with a border.

Setting Cell Padding

"Your table looks too cramped," says the Web-page design czar. "Well," you say, "I could increase the cell padding." "Great," says the WPDC, "do that."

The cell padding is the amount of space in pixels between the walls of the cell and its content. Here's an example we saw at the beginning of this chapter, setting the cell padding to 4 pixels:

```
<table border="2" cellpadding = "4">
    <tr>
        <th>Tic</th>
        <th>Tac</th>
        <th>Toe</th>
    </tr>
    <tr>
        <td>X</td>
        <td>O</td>
        <td>X</td>
    </tr>
    <tr>
        <td>O</td>
        <td>X</td>
        <td>O</td>
    </tr>
    <tr>
        <td>X</td>
        <td>O</td>
        <td>X</td>
    </tr>
</table>
```

You can see the results in Figure 6.4. Note that if you set the cell padding to zero, the cell walls will actually touch the content of the cell. If you want to make your tables look less cramped, **cellpadding** is an attribute to keep in mind.

Setting Cell Spacing

The cell spacing of a table indicates the amount of space in pixels between each cell. You set the cell spacing with the **cellspacing** attribute. Here's an example, from the beginning of the chapter, showing how to set the cell spacing to 4 pixels:

```
<table border="2" cellspacing = "4">
    <tr>
        <th>Tic</th>
        <th>Tac</th>
        <th>Toe</th>
    </tr>
    <tr>
        <td>X</td>
        <td>O</td>
        <td>X</td>
    </tr>
    <tr>
        <td>O</td>
        <td>X</td>
        <td>O</td>
    </tr>
    <tr>
        <td>X</td>
        <td>O</td>
        <td>X</td>
    </tr>
</table>
```

You can see the results of this XHTML in Figure 6.5.

Setting Table and Column Widths

"Uh oh," says the novice programmer, "I'm in trouble now. I designed my new table to display all my data, but I just realized that other people will be using different screen resolutions, and my table might be too wide." "It's OK," you say, "just tie the width of the table to the width of the display area in the browser." The NP asks, "You can do that?"

You can specify the width of tables and columns by using the **width** attribute of the **<table>**, **<th>**, and **<tr>** elements. You can set this attribute to a pixel value; this can be a good idea if you have a table of graphics (such as a navigation bar). However, it's often better to set this attribute to a percentage instead. When you set the **<table>** element's **width** attribute to a percentage, the width is a percentage of the browser's display area; when you use this attribute with the **<th>** and **<tr>** elements, the width is a percentage of the table's width.

Immediate Solutions

In the following example, I'm setting the width of a table to 95 percent of the browser window's width, and I'm setting the width of the columns to 40, 35, and 25 percent of the total table width. Here's the code:

```
<table border="2" width="95%">
    <tr>
        <th width="40%">Tic</th>
        <th width="35%">Tac</th>
        <th width="25%">Toe</th>
    </tr>
    <tr>
        <td>X</td>
        <td>O</td>
        <td>X</td>
    </tr>
    <tr>
        <td>O</td>
        <td>X</td>
        <td>O</td>
    </tr>
    <tr>
        <td>X</td>
        <td>O</td>
        <td>X</td>
    </tr>
</table>
```

You can see the results of this XHTML in Figure 6.13. It's often a good idea to set the size of your tables yourself instead of letting the browser do it. And it's usually

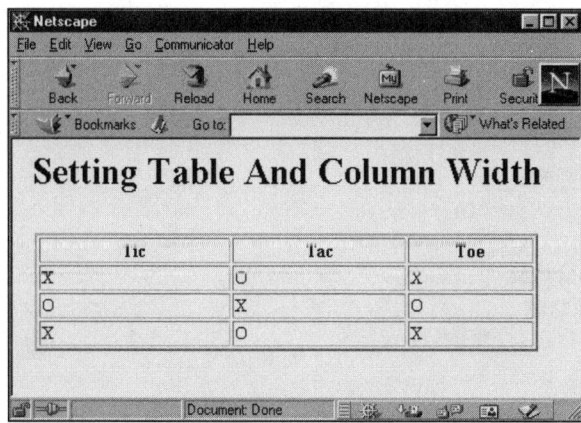

Figure 6.13 Setting table and column widths.

better to specify widths in terms of percentages, not absolute pixel measurements (unless you are displaying images or other fixed-width elements).

What happens if the percentages you give for the column widths don't add up to 100 percent? The browser will redistribute the columns, using the percentages you've given as relative widths for each column.

TIP: *If the text in a cell is too long, you can always add line breaks with the* **
** *element.*

Setting Table Colors

The Web-page design czar is back and says, "The table in your Web page is still too drab—you've got to punch it up." "Hm," you say, "I suppose I could add some color to it." "Now *there's* an idea," says the WPDC.

Using the example from the "In Depth" section of this chapter, we see the color elements of a table:

```
<table border="2">
    <tr>
        <th bgcolor = "ff0000">Tic</th>
        <th bgcolor = "ff0000">Tac</th>
        <th bgcolor = "ff0000">Toe</th>
    </tr>
    <tr>
        <td bgcolor = "#ffffff">X</td>
        <td bgcolor = "#000000">
            <font color = "#ffffff">O</font>
        </td>
        <td bgcolor = "#ffffff">X</td>
    </tr>
    <tr>
        <td bgcolor = "#000000">
            <font color = "#ffffff">O</font>
        </td>
        <td bgcolor = "#ffffff">X</td>
        <td bgcolor = "#000000">
            <font color = "#ffffff">O</font>
        </td>
    </tr>
    <tr>
```

```
        <td bgcolor = "#ffffff">X</td>
        <td bgcolor = "#000000">
            <font color = "#ffffff">O</font>
        </td>
        <td bgcolor = "#ffffff">X</td>
    </tr>
</table>
```

This example uses the **bgcolor** attribute to set the background color of cells and uses a **<font>** element to set the foreground (text) color. You can see the results of this XHTML in Figure 6.10. Note that you can also use the **bgcolor** attribute of the table as a whole to set the entire table's background color.

However, both **bgcolor** and the **<font>** element have been deprecated in favor of style sheets in HTML 4. So how do you set colors in tables now? We'll discuss style sheets in Chapter 9, but here's a sneak preview showing how to convert the XHTML in the previous example by using inline styles:

```
<table border="2">
    <tr>
        <th style="background-color: rgb(255, 0, 0)">Tic</th>
        <th style="background-color: rgb(255, 0, 0)">Tac</th>
        <th style="background-color: rgb(255, 0, 0)">Toe</th>
    </tr>
    <tr>
        <td style="background-color: rgb(255, 255, 255)">X</td>
        <td style="background-color: rgb(0, 0, 0); color:
            rgb(255, 255, 255)">
            O
        </td>
        <td style="background-color: rgb(255, 255, 255)">X</td>
    </tr>
    <tr>
        <td style="background-color: rgb(0, 0, 0); color:
            rgb(255, 255, 255)">
            O
        </td>
        <td style="background-color: rgb(255, 255, 255)">X</td>
        <td style="background-color: rgb(0, 0, 0); color:
            rgb(255, 255, 255)">
            O
        </td>
    </tr>
    <tr>
```

```
            <td style="background-color: rgb(255, 255, 255)">X</td>
            <td style="background-color: rgb(0, 0, 0); color:
                rgb(255, 255, 255)">
                O
            </td>
            <td style="background-color: rgb(255, 255, 255)">X</td>
        </tr>
</table>
```

TIP: You can also set the background image for tables and table cells by using the **background** attribute.

Aligning Tables in Web Pages

The big boss appears and says, "We need to add this table to the company newsletter. Can you make text flow around tables just as you can with images?" "Sure," you say, "no problem. As long as I get a little raise."

Using the **align** attribute of the **<table>** element, you can align the table in a Web page by setting this attribute to **right**, **left**, or **center**. In addition, text will flow around it just as it does with images. Here's an example:

```
<h1 align="center">Aligning Text And Tables</h1>
<table border="2" align="right">
    <tr>
        <th>Tic</th>
        <th>Tac</th>
        <th>Toe</th>
    </tr>
    <tr>
        <td>X</td>
        <td>O</td>
        <td>X</td>
    </tr>
    <tr>
        <td>O</td>
        <td>X</td>
        <td>O</td>
    </tr>
    <tr>
        <td>X</td>
        <td>O</td>
        <td>X</td>
```

```
        </tr>
    </table>
```
Here's an example in which I'm aligning text to the left of a table. In this case, the table holds a Tic Tac Toe game, as you can see. In fact, aligning text and tables works much as aligning text and images. This text will just keep flowing around the table until it skips to the line following the table, and then it will resume normally. Here's how that works; this line follows the table and so goes underneath it.

You can see the results of this XHTML in Figure 6.14.

NOTE: *Although the **align** attribute is deprecated in HTML 4 and therefore in XHTML, I can't show you a figure aligning a table with style sheets yet because neither Internet Explorer nor Netscape Navigator implements the table-alignment style properties yet. These properties are **margin-right** and **margin-left**. (To align a table at right, set **margin-right** to 0; to center a table, you set both **margin-right** and **margin-left** to **auto**.)*

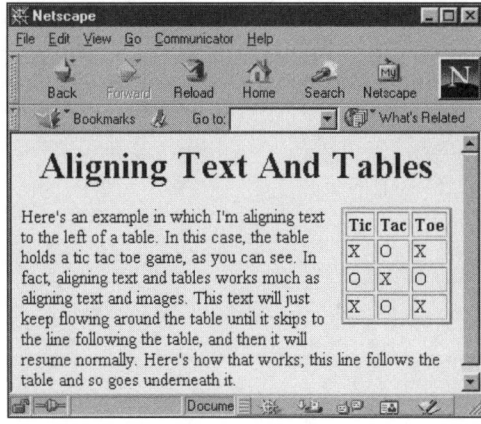

Figure 6.14   Aligning a table in a Web page.

Aligning Cell Text

You can align text in cells by using the **<tr>**, **<th>**, and **<td>** elements' **align** and **valign** attributes. (These are not deprecated in HTML 4 or XHTML, although the **align** attribute for other elements, such as the **<table>** element, is). We saw this example of horizontal alignment in the "In Depth" section of this chapter:

```
<table border="2" width="200">
    <tr>
        <th>Tic</th>
        <th>Tac</th>
        <th>Toe</th>
```

```
            </tr>
            <tr>
                <td align = "right">X</td>
                <td align = "left">0</td>
                <td align = "center">X</td>
            </tr>
            <tr>
                <td align = "right">0</td>
                <td align = "left">X</td>
                <td align = "center">0</td>
            </tr>
            <tr>
                <td align = "right">X</td>
                <td align = "left">0</td>
                <td align = "center">X</td>
            </tr>
        </table>
```

The results appear in Figure 6.6. You can also align text vertically by using the **valign** attribute, as we saw in the following example from the "In Depth" section of this chapter:

```
<table border="2" height = "120">
    <tr>
        <th>Tic</th>
        <th>Tac</th>
        <th>Toe</th>
    </tr>
    <tr>
        <td valign = "top">X</td>
        <td valign = "middle">0</td>
        <td valign = "bottom">X</td>
    </tr>
    <tr>
        <td valign = "top">0</td>
        <td valign = "middle">X</td>
        <td valign = "bottom">0</td>
    </tr>
    <tr>
        <td valign = "top">X</td>
        <td valign = "middle">0</td>
        <td valign = "bottom">X</td>
    </tr>
</table>
```

The results of this XHTML appear in Figure 6.7.

Using Images in Tables

"I want to display images in my tables," says the novice programmer. "Can I do that?" "Of course," you say; "just use **<img>** elements in the **<td>** elements." The NP asks, "Really? That easy?"

You can display all kinds of XHTML elements, including images, in tables. Just include the appropriate **<img>** elements in your table, as in this example (note that in the XHTML **<img>** element, an **alt** attribute is required technically, but I'm omitting it for clarity):

```
<table border="2">
    <tr>
        <th>Tic</th>
        <th>Tac</th>
        <th>Toe</th>
    </tr>
    <tr>
        <td><img src="x.gif" /></td>
        <td><img src="o.gif" /></td>
        <td><img src="x.gif" /></td>
    </tr>
    <tr>
        <td><img src="o.gif" /></td>
        <td><img src="x.gif" /></td>
        <td><img src="o.gif" /></td>
    </tr>
    <tr>
        <td><img src="x.gif" /></td>
        <td><img src="o.gif" /></td>
        <td><img src="x.gif" /></td>
    </tr>
</table>
```

The results of this XHTML appear in Figure 6.15. As you can see, I've replaced each X and O with an image of the same.

TIP: *One of the most common uses of tables in XHTML is to arrange images in Web pages exactly as you want them. For example, you might want to arrange figures next to explanatory text.*

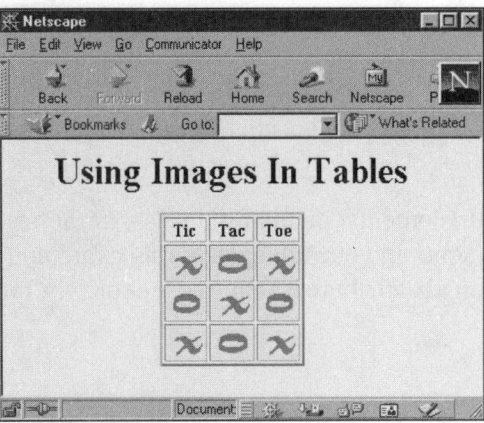

Figure 6.15   Using images in tables.

Nesting Tables

Can you nest tables inside tables? You certainly can. Here's an example in which I nest two tables into one:

```
<table border="2">
    <tr>
        <td>
            <table border="2">
                <tr>
                    <th>Tic</th>
                    <th>Tac</th>
                    <th>Toe</th>
                </tr>
                <tr>
                    <td>X</td>
                    <td>O</td>
                    <td>X</td>
                </tr>
                <tr>
                    <td>O</td>
                    <td>X</td>
                    <td>O</td>
                </tr>
                <tr>
                    <td>X</td>
                    <td>O</td>
                    <td>X</td>
                </tr>
```

```
                </table>
            </td>
            <td>
                <table border="2">
                    <tr>
                        <th>Tic</th>
                        <th>Tac</th>
                        <th>Toe</th>
                    </tr>
                    <tr>
                        <td>X</td>
                        <td>O</td>
                        <td>X</td>
                    </tr>
                    <tr>
                        <td>O</td>
                        <td>X</td>
                        <td>O</td>
                    </tr>
                    <tr>
                        <td>X</td>
                        <td>O</td>
                        <td>X</td>
                    </tr>
                </table>
            </td>
        </tr>
</table>
```

That's all it takes—the results appear in Figure 6.16. Because you can nest tables several levels deep, this capability lets you create very involved structures.

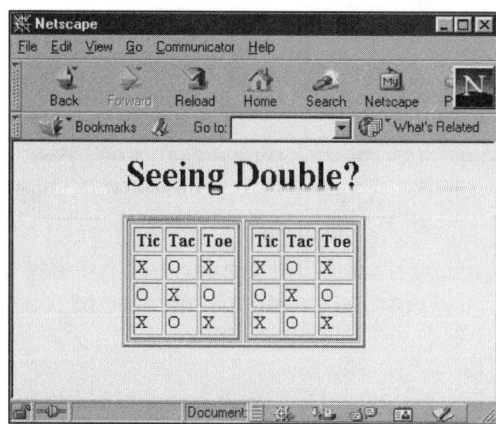

Figure 6.16   Nesting tables.

Spanning Multiple Columns

The novice programmer is back and says, "I have a problem. I'm using column headers, but I can't fit all I want to say into the heading on top of one column. Is there any way to *merge* columns together in a row?" "There sure is," you say; "you can use the **colspan** attribute."

You can use the **colspan** attribute in the **<th>** or **<td>** elements to indicate that the corresponding cell should span (that is, extend over) several columns. Here's an example we saw in the "In Depth" section of this chapter:

```
<table border="2">
    <tr>
        <th colspan="3"> TicTac Game</th>
    </tr>
    <tr>
        <td>X</td>
        <td>0</td>
        <td>X</td>
    </tr>
    <tr>
        <td>0</td>
        <td>X</td>
        <td>0</td>
    </tr>
    <tr>
        <td>X</td>
        <td>0</td>
        <td>X</td>
    </tr>
</table>
```

The results of this XHTML appear in Figure 6.8.

Spanning Multiple Rows

"OK," says the novice programmer, "here's the problem—I want to format text so that I can have sidebars, text that appears next to the regular text. No way to do that, huh?" "Sure there is," you say; "use **rowspan** to span a number of rows in a borderless table."

Just as **colspan** lets you span several columns, **rowspan** lets you span several rows. Here's an example that we saw in the "In Depth" section of this chapter, showing how this works:

```
<table border="2">
    <tr>
        <th rowspan = "3">TicTac<br />Game</th>
        <td>X</td>
        <td>O</td>
        <td>X</td>
    </tr>
    <tr>
        <td>O</td>
        <td>X</td>
        <td>O</td>
    </tr>
    <tr>
        <td>X</td>
        <td>O</td>
        <td>X</td>
    </tr>
</table>
```

You can see the results of this code in Figure 6.9.

<colgroup> and <col>—Grouping and Formatting Columns

<colgroup>

Purpose: Creates a column group, letting you format columns to your specifications.

When used as HTML: Start tag/End tag: Required/Optional

Supported: [1.0S, 1.0T, 1.0F, 1.1, 4, IE3, IE4, IE5]

Attributes:

- **align**—Specifies alignment of text in the column group. Set to **left**, **center**, **right**, **justify**, or **char**. [1.0S, 1.0T, 1.0F, 1.1, 4, IE4, IE5]
- **bgcolor**—Specifies the background color. Set to a color value. [IE4, IE5]
- **char**—Specifies a character to align text on. Set to an alphanumeric character. [1.0S, 1.0T, 1.0F, 1.1, 4]
- **charoff**—Sets the alignment offset to the first character to align on, as set with **char**. [1.0S, 1.0T, 1.0F, 1.1, 4]

- **class**—Class of the element (used for rendering). [1.0S, 1.0T, 1.0F, 1.1, 4, IE4, IE5]
- **dir**—Gives the direction of directionally neutral text (text that doesn't have inherent direction in which you should read it). Possible values: **ltr**: left-to-right text or table and **rtl**: right-to-left text or table. [1.0S, 1.0T, 1.0F, 1.1, 4, IE5]
- **id**—Unique alphanumeric identifier for the tag, which you can use to refer to it. [1.0S, 1.0T, 1.0F, 1.1, 4, IE4, IE5]
- **lang**—Base language used for the tag. [1.0S, 1.0T, 1.0F, 1.1, 4, IE4, IE5]
- **span**—Specifies the number of columns this column group includes (the default is 1). Set to positive integers. Note that this attribute is ignored if this element contains **<col>** elements. [1.0S, 1.0T, 1.0F, 1.1, 4, IE3, IE4, IE5]
- **style**—Inline style indicating how to render the element. [1.0S, 1.0T, 1.0F, 1.1, 4, IE4, IE5]
- **title**—Holds additional information (which might be displayed in tool tips) for the element. [1.0S, 1.0T, 1.0F, 1.1, 4, IE4, IE5]
- **valign**—Sets the vertical alignment of the text. Set to **top**, **middle**, **bottom**, or **baseline**. [1.0S, 1.0T, 1.0F, 1.1, 4, IE4, IE5]
- **width**—Sets the width of columns in the table. Set to a pixel measurement or percentage, or set to "0*" to make the browser display the column in the minimum appropriate width. [1.0S, 1.0T, 1.0F, 1.1, 4, IE3, IE4, IE5]
- **xml:lang**—Holds the base language for the element when the document is interpreted as an XML document. [1.0S, 1.0T, 1.0F, 1.1]

XHTML Events: onclick, **ondblclick**, **onfocus**, **onblur**, **onmousedown**, **onmouseup**, **onmouseover**, **onmousemove**, **onmouseout**, **onkeypress**, **onkeydown**, **onkeyup**

<col>

Purpose: Defines a column structure inside a **<colgroup>** element. Using this element is optional in **<colgroup>** elements. This element contains no content.

When used as HTML: Start tag/End tag: Required/Omitted

Supported: [1.0S, 1.0T, 1.0F, 1.1, 4, IE3, IE4, IE5]

Attributes:

- **align**—Specifies alignment of text in the column group. Set to **left**, **center**, **right**, **justify**, or **char**. [1.0S, 1.0T, 1.0F, 1.1, 4, IE4, IE5]
- **bgcolor**—Specifies the background color. Set to a color value. [IE4, IE5]

- **char**—Specifies a character to align text on. Set to an alphanumeric character. [1.0S, 1.0T, 1.0F, 1.1, 4]
- **charoff**—Sets the alignment offset to the first character to align on, as set with **char**. [1.0S, 1.0T, 1.0F, 1.1, 4]
- **class**—Class of the element (used for rendering). [1.0S, 1.0T, 1.0F, 1.1, 4, IE4, IE5]
- **dir**—Gives the direction of directionally neutral text (text that doesn't have inherent direction in which you should read it). Possible values: **ltr**: left-to-right text or table and **rtl**: right-to-left text or table. [1.0S, 1.0T, 1.0F, 1.1, 4, IE5]
- **id**—Unique alphanumeric identifier for the tag, which you can use to refer to it. [1.0S, 1.0T, 1.0F, 1.1, 4, IE4, IE5]
- **lang**—Base language used for the tag. [1.0S, 1.0T, 1.0F, 1.1, 4, IE4, IE5]
- **span**—Specifies the number of columns this column group includes (the default is 1). Set to positive integers. [1.0S, 1.0T, 1.0F, 1.1, 4, IE3, IE4, IE5]
- **style**—Inline style indicating how to render the element. [1.0S, 1.0T, 1.0F, 1.1, 4, IE4, IE5]
- **title**—Holds additional information (which might be displayed in tool tips) for the element. [1.0S, 1.0T, 1.0F, 1.1, 4, IE4, IE5]
- **valign**—Sets the vertical alignment of the text. Set to **top**, **middle**, **bottom**, or **baseline**. [1.0S, 1.0T, 1.0F, 1.1, 4, IE4, IE5]
- **width**—Sets the width of columns in the table. Set to a pixel measurement or percentage, or set to "0*" to make the browser display the column in the minimum appropriate width. [1.0S, 1.0T, 1.0F, 1.1, 4, IE3, IE4, IE5]
- **xml:lang**—Holds the base language for the element when the document is interpreted as an XML document. [1.0S, 1.0T, 1.0F, 1.1]

The novice programmer has a complaint. "You construct tables row by row," the NP says, "but that seems very row-centric. What if I want to make things stand out by column, not row?" "In that case," you say, "you can use the new <colgroup> and <col> elements."

You can group columns together and format them in groups by using the new **<colgroup>** and **<col>** elements introduced in HTML 4. However, these elements are supported only in Internet Explorer so far.

NOTE: *The new table model introduced in HTML 4—which uses the **<colgroup>**, **<col>**, **<thead>**, **<tbody>**, and **<tfoot>** elements—is called the complex table model. The other table tags, such as **<tr>** and **<td>**, are part of the simple table model.*

<colgroup>—Creating Column Groups

As an example of creating column groups, let's say that I want to display a table with three columns, and let's say that I want the first column to take up 40 percent of the width of the table and the next two columns to take up 30 percent each. Let's also say that I want to center the text in the last two columns. I can do that with the **<colgroup>** element, which is enclosed in the **<table>** element.

TIP: One nice aspect of using column groups is that the browser can load and display long tables incrementally.

To set up a column group consisting of only the first column in the table, and taking 40 percent of the width of the table, I can use this element:

```
<colgroup width="40%">
```

You can also set column width to a pixel value or to **"0*"**, which makes the browser allocate the minimum width needed for the column. If you use **"0*"**, however, the browser cannot display the table incrementally.

To create a column group of the next two columns, I use the **span** attribute and set it to two for the two columns. Then, to center the text in those columns, I use the **align** attribute:

```
<colgroup width="40%">
<colgroup span="2" width="30%" align="center">
```

Let's see this at work. Here are those two tags used in a real table:

```
<?xml version="1.0"?>
<!DOCTYPE html PUBLIC "-//W3C//DTD XHTML 1.0 Transitional//EN"
    "http://www.w3.org/tr/xhtml1/DTD/xhtml1-transitional.dtd">
<html xmlns="http://www.w3.org/1999/xhtml" xml:lang="en" lang="en">
    <head>
        <title>
            Creating Column Groups
        </title>
    </head>

    <body>
        <center>
            <h1>Creating Column Groups</h1>

            <table border="2" width="90%">
                <caption>Horses And Times</caption>
```

```
                <colgroup width="40%"></colgroup>
                <colgroup span="2" width="30%" align="center"></colgroup>
            <tr>
                <th>Horse</th>
                <th>Race</th>
                <th>Best Time</th>
            </tr>
            <tr>
                <td>Bluebell</td>
                <td>Foster Downs</td>
                <td>5:33</td>
            </tr>
            <tr>
                <td>Sea Breeze</td>
                <td>Harness Extra</td>
                <td>6:41</td>
            </tr>
            <tr>
                <td>No Way O'Shay</td>
                <td>Old Bowler</td>
                <td>9:29</td>
            </tr>
            </table>
        </center>
    </body>
</html>
```

You can see the results of this XHTML in Figure 6.17.

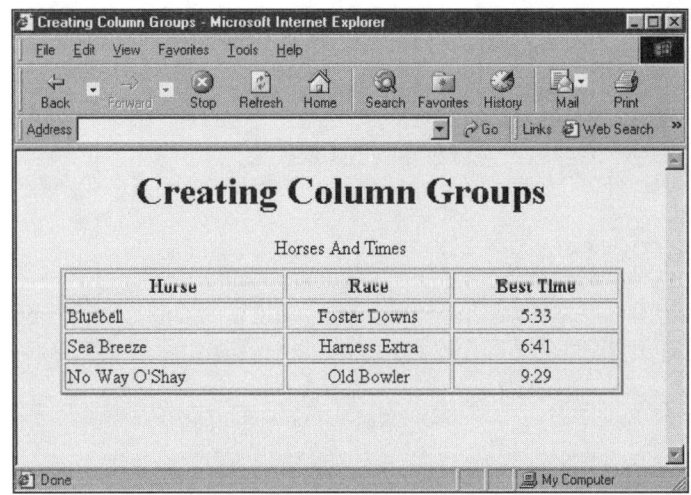

Figure 6.17   Formatting column groups with different widths.

Customizing Columns in Column Groups

You can use the **<col>** element to specify formatting for every column in a group if you include these elements inside a **<colgroup>** element. (If you do this, the **span** attribute of the **<colgroup>** element is ignored.)

The first **<col>** element in a **<colgroup>** element sets the formatting (using, for example, the **align** and **valign** attributes) and style (using the **style** attribute) for the first column. The next **<col>** element sets the formatting and style for the next column, and so on.

In this example, I'm setting the widths of two columns in a column group to different widths, 30 and 15 percent:

```xml
<?xml version="1.0"?>
<!DOCTYPE html PUBLIC "-//W3C//DTD XHTML 1.0 Transitional//EN"
"http://www.w3.org/tr/xhtml1/DTD/xhtml1-transitional.dtd">
<html xmlns="http://www.w3.org/1999/xhtml" xml:lang="en" lang="en">
    <head>
        <title>
            Creating Column Groups
        </title>
    </head>

    <body>
        <center>
            <h1>Creating Column Groups</h1>

            <table border="2" width="90%">
                <caption>Horses And Times</caption>
                <colgroup width="25%"></colgroup>
                <colgroup align="center">
                    <col span="2" width="30%" />
                    <col span="1" width="15%" />
                </colgroup>
                <tr>
                    <th>Horse</th>
                    <th>Race</th>
                    <th>Owner</th>
                    <th>Best Time</th>
                </tr>
                <tr>
```

```
                    <td>Bluebell</td>
                    <td>Foster Downs</td>
                    <td>Sad Sam</td>
                    <td>5:33</td>
                </tr>
                <tr>
                    <td>Sea Breeze</td>
                    <td>Harness Extra</td>
                    <td>Bright Bob</td>
                    <td>6:41</td>
                </tr>
                <tr>
                    <td>No Way O'Shay</td>
                    <td>Old Bowler</td>
                    <td>Funny Phil</td>
                    <td>9:29</td>
                </tr>
            </table>
        </center>
    </body>
</html>
```

The results of this XHTML appear in Figure 6.18, and you can see that the columns have indeed been formatted as specified. Note that besides working with column groups, you can also create row groups—see the next section for details.

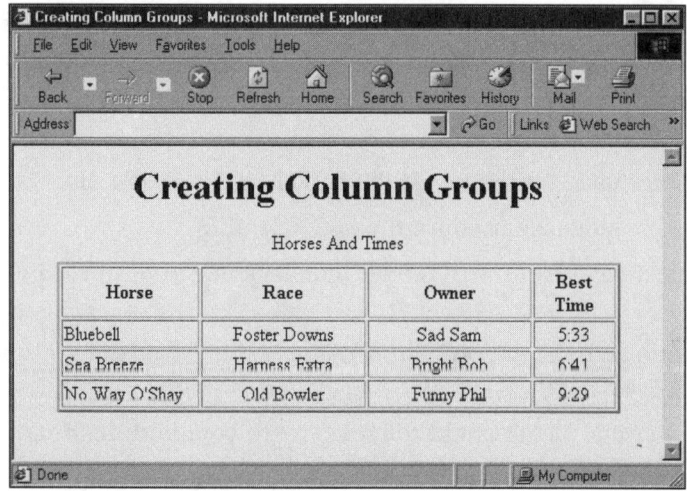

Figure 6.18   Using <col> elements.

<thead>, <tbody>, <tfoot>—Grouping and Formatting Rows

<thead>

Purpose: Creates a table head when you're grouping rows.

When used as HTML: Start tag/End tag: Required/Optional

Supported: [1.0S, 1.0T, 1.0F, 1.1, 4, IE3, IE4, IE5]

Attributes:

- **align**—Specifies alignment of text in the group. Set to **left**, **center**, **justify**, **char**, or **right**. [1.0S, 1.0T, 1.0F, 1.1, 4, IE4, IE5]
- **bgcolor**—Sets the background color for the group. Set to an RGB triplet color value or a predefined color. [IE4, IE5]
- **char**—Specifies a character on which to align text. Set to an alphanumeric character. [1.0S, 1.0T, 1.0F, 1.1, 4]
- **charoff**—Sets the alignment offset to the first character to align on, as set with **char**. [1.0S, 1.0T, 1.0F, 1.1, 4]
- **class**—Class of the element (used for rendering). [1.0S, 1.0T, 1.0F, 1.1, 4, IE4, IE5]
- **dir**—Gives the direction of directionally neutral text. Possible values: **ltr**, left-to-right text or table; and **rtl**, right-to-left text or table. [1.0S, 1.0T, 1.0F, 1.1, 4, IE5]
- **id**—Unique alphanumeric identifier for the tag; use the ID to refer to the tag. [1.0S, 1.0T, 1.0F, 1.1, 4, IE4, IE5]
- **lang**—Base language used for the tag. [1.0S, 1.0T, 1.0F, 1.1, 4, IE4, IE5]
- **language**—Scripting language used for the tag. [IE4, IE5]
- **style**—Inline style indicating how to render the element. [1.0S, 1.0T, 1.0F, 1.1, 4, IE4, IE5]
- **title**—Holds additional information (which might be displayed in tool tips). [1.0S, 1.0T, 1.0F, 1.1, 4, IE4, IE5]
- **valign**—Sets the vertical alignment of the text. Set to **top**, **middle**, **bottom**, or **baseline**. [1.0S, 1.0T, 1.0F, 1.1, 4, IE4, IE5]
- **xml:lang**—Holds the base language for the element when the document is interpreted as an XML document. [1.0S, 1.0T, 1.0F, 1.1]

XHTML events: onclick, ondblclick, onfocus, onblur, onmousedown, onmouseup, onmouseover, onmousemove, onmouseout, onkeypress, onkeydown, onkeyup

\<tbody\>

Purpose: Creates a table body when you're grouping rows. You can use multiple table bodies, each of which can be separated visually when you use the **frame** and **rules** attributes of the **\<table\>** element.

When used as HTML: Start tag/End tag: Optional/Optional

Supported: [1.0S, 1.0T, 1.0F, 1.1, 4, IE3, IE4, IE5]

Attributes:

- **align**—Specifies alignment of text in the group. Set to **left**, **center**, **justify**, **char**, or **right**. [1.0S, 1.0T, 1.0F, 1.1, 4, IE4, IE5]
- **bgcolor**—Sets the background color for the group. Set to an RGB triplet color value or a predefined color. [IE4, IE5]
- **char**—Specifies a character on which to align text. Set to an alphanumeric character. [1.0S, 1.0T, 1.0F, 1.1,4]
- **charoff**—Sets the alignment offset to the first character to align on, as set with **char**. [1.0S, 1.0T, 1.0F, 1.1, 4]
- **class**—Class of the element (used for rendering). [1.0S, 1.0T, 1.0F, 1.1, 4, IE4, IE5]
- **dir**—Gives the direction of directionally neutral text. Possible values: **ltr**, left-to-right text or table; and **rtl**, right-to-left text or table. [1.0S, 1.0T, 1.0F, 1.1, 4, IE5]
- **id**—Unique alphanumeric identifier for the tag; use the ID to refer to the tag. [1.0S, 1.0T, 1.0F, 1.1, 4, IE4, IE5]
- **lang**—Base language used for the tag. [1.0S, 1.0T, 1.0F, 1.1, 4, IE4, IE5]
- **language**—Scripting language used for the tag. [IE4, IE5]
- **style**—Inline style indicating how to render the element. [1.0S, 1.0T, 1.0F, 1.1, 4, IE4, IE5]
- **title**—Holds additional information (which might be displayed in tool tips). [1.0S, 1.0T, 1.0F, 1.1, 4, IE4, IE5]
- **valign**—Sets the vertical alignment of the text. Set to **top**, **middle**, **bottom**, or **baseline**. [1.0S, 1.0T, 1.0F, 1.1, 4, IE4, IE5]
- **xml:lang**—Holds the base language for the element when the document is interpreted as an XML document. [1.0S, 1.0T, 1.0F, 1.1]

XHTML events: onclick, ondblclick, onfocus, onblur, onmousedown, onmouseup, onmouseover, onmousemove, onmouseout, onkeypress, onkeydown, onkeyup

<tfoot>

Purpose: Creates a table foot when you're grouping rows.

When used as HTML: Start tag/End tag: Required/Optional

Supported: [1.0S, 1.0T, 1.0F, 1.1, 4, IE3, IE4, IE5]

Attributes:

- **align**—Specifies alignment of text in the group. Set to **left**, **center**, **justify**, **char**, or **right**. [1.0S, 1.0T, 1.0F, 1.1, 4, IE4, IE5]
- **bgcolor**—Sets the background color for the group. Set to an RGB triplet color value or a predefined color. [IE4, IE5]
- **char**—Specifies a character on which to align text. Set to an alphanumeric character. [1.0S, 1.0T, 1.0F, 1.1, 4]
- **charoff**—Sets the alignment offset to the first character to align on, as set with **char**. [1.0S, 1.0T, 1.0F, 1.1, 4]
- **class**—Class of the element (used for rendering). [1.0S, 1.0T, 1.0F, 1.1, 3, 4, IE4, IE5]
- **dir**—Gives the direction of directionally neutral text. Possible values: **ltr**, left-to-right text or table; and **rtl**, right-to-left text or table. [1.0S, 1.0T, 1.0F, 1.1, 4, IE5]
- **id**—Unique alphanumeric identifier for the tag; use the ID to refer to the tag. [1.0S, 1.0T, 1.0F, 1.1, 3, 4, IE4, IE5]
- **lang**—Base language used for the tag. [1.0S, 1.0T, 1.0F, 1.1, 3, 4, IE4, IE5]
- **language**—Scripting language used for the tag. [IE4, IE5]
- **style**—Inline style indicating how to render the element. [1.0S, 1.0T, 1.0F, 1.1, 4, IE4, IE5]
- **title**—Holds additional information (which might be displayed in tool tips). [1.0S, 1.0T, 1.0F, 1.1, 3, 4, IE4, IE5]
- **valign**—Sets the vertical alignment of the text. Set to **top**, **middle**, **bottom**, or **baseline**. [1.0S, 1.0T, 1.0F, 1.1, 4, IE4, IE5]
- **xml:lang**—Holds the base language for the element when the document is interpreted as an XML document. [1.0S, 1.0T, 1.0F, 1.1]

XHTML events: onclick, ondblclick, onfocus, onblur, onmousedown, onmouseup, onmouseover, onmousemove, onmouseout, onkeypress, onkeydown, onkeyup

The novice programmer wants to know, "I want to divide my table into groups of rows, setting each one off from the others. Is there any way to do that?" "Sure is," you say, "just create row groups." "Create what?" the NP wants to know.

You can use the **<thead>**, **<tbody>**, and **<tfoot>** elements to create row groups, just as you use the **<colgroup>** and **<col>** elements to create column groups. All of these elements were new in HTML 4 and so far are supported only by Internet Explorer.

NOTE: *The new table model—introduced in HTML 4—that uses the **<colgroup>**, **<col>**, **<thead>**, **<tbody>**, and **<tfoot>** elements is called the* complex table model. *Other table tags, such as **<tr>** and **<td>**, are part of the* simple table model.

Creating Row Groups

To create a row group, you use the **<thead>**, **<tbody>**, and **<tfoot>** elements. The **<thead>** element creates a head for the table; **<tbody>** creates the body of the table (you can create multiple table bodies, each of which will appear as a row group); and **<tfoot>** creates a table foot.

In the following example, I'll use **<thead>** to add a table head to a table. You place the head elements you want in the **<thead>** element, one to a column (unless you're spanning multiple columns). You can apply styles as well to the **<thead>** element, typically by placing the same elements that you would use in **<th>** elements in the **<thead>** element.

To create a table foot, use the **<tfoot>** element. This works just like **<thead>** but places its information at the bottom of the table.

If you use **<thead>** or **<tfoot>**, you must also use the **<tbody>** element. The **<tbody>** element is what defines a row group, and you can have as many **<tbody>** elements as you like.

Here's an example in which I create a table with a **<thead>** element, a **<tfoot>** element, and two **<tbody>** elements:

```
<?xml version="1.0"?>
<!DOCTYPE html PUBLIC "-//W3C//DTD XHTML 1.0 Transitional//EN"
"http://www.w3.org/tr/xhtml1/DTD/xhtml1-transitional.dtd">
<html xmlns="http://www.w3.org/1999/xhtml" xml:lang="en" lang="en">
    <head>
        <title>
            Creating Row Groups
        </title>
    </head>

    <body>
        <center>
            <h1>Creating Row Groups</h1>
```

```
<table border="2" width="90%" >
    <caption>Horses And Times</caption>
    <colgroup width="25%"></colgroup>
    <colgroup align="center">
        <col span="2" width="30%" />
        <col span="1" width="15%" />
    </colgroup>

    <thead>
        <tr>
            <th>Horse</th>
            <th>Race</th>
            <th>Owner</th>
            <th>Time</th>
        </tr>
    </thead>

    <tfoot>
        <tr>
            <th>Horse</th>
            <th>Race</th>
            <th>Owner</th>
            <th>Time</th>
        </tr>
    </tfoot>

    <tbody>
    <tr>
        <td>Bluebell</td>
        <td>Foster Downs</td>
        <td>Sad Sam</td>
        <td>5:33</td>
    </tr>
    <tr>
        <td>Sea Breeze</td>
        <td>Foster Downs</td>
        <td>Bright Bob</td>
        <td>6:41</td>
    </tr>
    </tbody>

    <tbody>
    <tr>
        <td>No Way O'Shay</td>
        <td>Old Bowler</td>
        <td>Funny Phil</td>
        <td>9:29</td>
```

```
                </tr>
                <tr>
                    <td>Crawler</td>
                    <td>Old Bowler</td>
                    <td>Maudlin Morton</td>
                    <td>12:23</td>
                </tr>
            </tbody>
        </table>
    </center>
</body>
</html>
```

The results of this XHTML appear in Figure 6.19. Although you can see the table head and foot in Figure 6.19, the fact that the rows are divided into two groups is not evident. To make it more evident, you can add borders to the row groups.

Configuring Row Group Borders

You can use the **frame** and **rules** attributes in the **<table>** element to specify the table's border display. Using the **frame** attribute with the **rules** attribute gives you much greater border control than does the older simple table model. Here are the possible values for **frame**:

- **void**—No borders
- **above**—Border on top only
- **below**—Border on bottom only

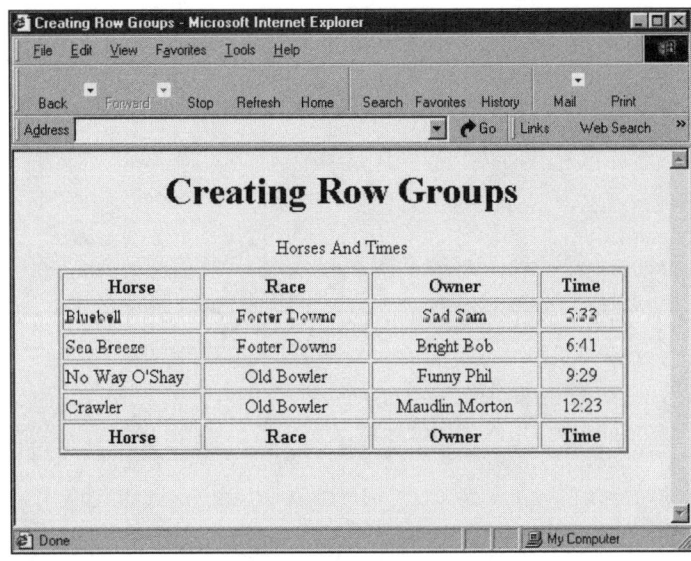

Figure 6.19 Adding table heads and feet.

- **hsides**—Horizontal borders only
- **vsides**—Vertical borders only
- **lhs**—Border on left side only
- **rhs**—Border on right side only
- **box**—Border on all four sides
- **border**—The default; the same as **box**

The **rules** attribute sets the style of the interior struts in a table. Here are the possible values:

- **none**—No interior struts are displayed.
- **groups**—Horizontal struts are displayed between table groups created with the **<thead>**, **<tbody>**, **<tfoot>**, and **<colgroup>** tags.
- **rows**—Horizontal struts are displayed between all table rows.
- **cols**—Vertical struts are displayed between all table columns.
- **all**—Struts are displayed between all table cells.

Here's an example that adds **frame** and **rules** to the previous table example:

```
<?xml version="1.0"?>
<!DOCTYPE html PUBLIC "-//W3C//DTD XHTML 1.0 Transitional//EN"
"http://www.w3.org/tr/xhtml1/DTD/xhtml1-transitional.dtd">
<html xmlns="http://www.w3.org/1999/xhtml" xml:lang="en" lang="en">
    <head>
        <title>
            Creating Row Groups
        </title>
    </head>

    <body>
        <center>
            <h1>Creating Row Groups</h1>

            <table border="2" width="90%" frame="hsides" rules="groups">
                <caption>Horses And Times</caption>
                <colgroup width="25%"></colgroup>
                <colgroup align="center">
                    <col span="2" width="30%" />
                    <col span="1" width="15%" />
                </colgroup>

                <thead>
                    <tr>
```

```
            <th>Horse</th>
            <th>Race</th>
            <th>Owner</th>
            <th>Time</th>
        </tr>
    </thead>

    <tfoot>
        <tr>
            <th>Horse</th>
            <th>Race</th>
            <th>Owner</th>
            <th>Time</th>
        </tr>
    </tfoot>

    <tbody>
    <tr>
        <td>Bluebell</td>
        <td>Foster Downs</td>
        <td>Sad Sam</td>
        <td>5:33</td>
    </tr>
    <tr>
        <td>Sea Breeze</td>
        <td>Foster Downs</td>
        <td>Bright Bob</td>
        <td>6:41</td>
    </tr>
    </tbody>

    <tbody>
    <tr>
        <td>No Way O'Shay</td>
        <td>Old Bowler</td>
        <td>Funny Phil</td>
        <td>9:29</td>
    </tr>
    <tr>
        <td>Crawler</td>
        <td>Old Bowler</td>
        <td>Maudlin Morton</td>
        <td>12:23</td>
    </tr>
    </tbody>
</table>
```

```
        </center>
    </body>
</html>
```

The results of this XHTML appear in Figure 6.20, where you can now see the borders introduced between row groups. As you can see, the complex table model gives you a lot of additional options when it comes to formatting tables.

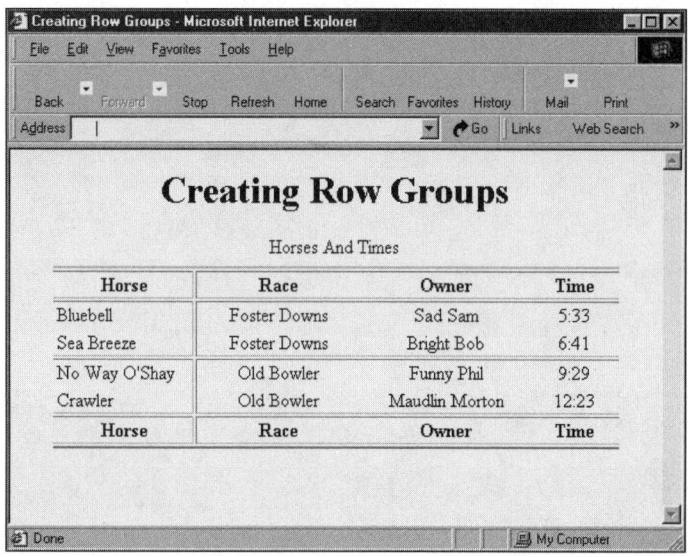

Figure 6.20 Formatting row groups.

Formatting Text with Tables

The novice programmer enters, screaming. "I can't do it! I just can't format this text the way I want it!" "Calm down," you say; "have you tried using tables yet?" "*Tables*?" the NP asks.

One very powerful way of arranging text is with XHTML tables. Using tables, you can create a grid of cells that can display text and images. Early on, Web-page stylists realized that you could turn the border of a table off, making it invisible; this, to their delight, gave them a way of arranging text into columns and rows on a Web page.

Arranging text by using XHTML tables is a very common thing to do. Here's an example we first saw in Chapter 3. Say that I want to display a large number of hyperlinks in rows and columns. I can do that by using a table, and I can even supply text as a caption, spreading the caption over several columns by using the **colspan** attribute. Here's how that looks:

```
<table noborder = "noborder" cellpadding = "4" width = "95%">
    <tr>
        <th colspan = "4">
            <h2>
                Travel to these sites around the world
            </h2>
        </th>
    </tr>
    <tr>
        <th colspan = "4">
            Ever been to a site in Kenya? Russia? China?
            You can travel to those countries now, because
            each tour below is actually at a site in the
            country it describes! <i>Bon Voyage...</i>
        </th>
    </tr>
    <tr align = "center">
        <td>
            <a href = "http://www.secyt.gov.ar/arg/introi.html">
                Argentina
            </a>
        </td>
        <td>
            <a href = "http://www.telstra.com.au/meta/australia.html">
                Australia
            </a>
        </td>
        <td>
            <a href = "http://croco.atnet.at/tourism">
                Austria
            </a>
        </td>
        <td>
            <a href = "http://canada.gc.ca/canadiana/cdaind_e.html">
                Canada
            </a>
        </td>
    </tr>
    <tr align = "center">
        <td>
            <a href = "http://sunsite.dcc.uchile.cl/chile/chile.html">
                Chile
            </a>
```

```
            </td>
            <td>
                <a href = "http://www.ihep.ac.cn/tour/china_tour.html">
                    China
                </a>
            </td>
            <td>
                <a href = "http://www.ciesin.ee/ESTCG/">
                    Estonia
                </a>
            </td>
            <td>
                <a href = "http://www.csc.fi/tiko/finland.html">
                    Finland
                </a>
            </td>
        </tr>
        <tr align = "center">
            <td>
                <a href = "http://www.iway.fr/internet-way/fr/france">
                    France
                </a>
            </td>
            <td>
                <a href = "http://www.chemie.fu-berlin.de/adressen/brd.html">
                    Germany
                </a>
            </td>
            <td>
                <a href = "http://www.culture.gr/2/21/maps/hellas.html">
                    Greece
                </a>
            </td>
            <td>
                <a href = "http://www.arctic.is">
                    Iceland
                </a>
            </td>
        </tr>
        <tr align = "center">
            <td>
                <a href = "http://slarti.ucd.ie/maps/ireland.html">
                    Ireland
                </a>
            </td>
            <td>
```

```
            <a href = "http://ece.iisc.ernet.in/india.html">
                India
            </a>
        </td>
        <td>
            <a href = "http://www.travel.it">
                Italy
            </a>
        </td>
        <td>
            <a href = "http://www.recruit.co.jp/Jjapan">
                Japan
            </a>
        </td>
    </tr>
    <tr align = "center">
        <td>
            <a href = "http://www.arcc.or.ke">
                Kenya
            </a>
        </td>
        <td>
            <a href = "http://www.mty.itesm.mx/MexWeb/Info2/">
                Mexico
            </a>
        </td>
        <td>
            <a href = "http://www.govt.nz/nzinfo.html">
                New Zealand
            </a>
        </td>
        <td>
            <a href = "http://info.fuw.edu.pl/pl/poland.html">
                Poland
            </a>
        </td>
    </tr>
    <tr align = "center">
        <td>
            <a href = "http://indis.ici.ro/romania/romania.html">
                Romania
            </a>
        </td>
        <td>
            <a href = "http://www.kiae.su/www/wtr">
                Russia
            </a>
```

```
            </td>
            <td>
                <a href = "http://www.technet.sg">
                    Singapore
                </a>
            </td>
            <td>
                <a href = "http://osprey.unisa.ac.za/south-africa/home.html">
                    South Africa
                </a>
            </td>
        </tr>
        <tr align = "center">
            <td>
                <a href = "http://www.uji.es/spain_www.html">
                    Spain
                </a>
            </td>
            <td>
                <a href = "http://www.westnet.se/sweden">
                    Sweden
                </a>
            </td>
            <td>
                <a href = "http://heiwww.unige.ch/switzerland/">
                    Switzerland
                </a>
            </td>
            <td>
                <a href = "http://www.chiangmai.ac.th/thmap.html">
                    Thailand
                </a>
            </td>
        </tr>
        <tr align = "center">
            <td>
                <a href = "http://www.rada.kiev.ua/ukraine.htm">
                    Ukraine
                </a>
            </td>
            <td>
                <a href = "http://www.cs.ucl.ac.uk/misc/uk/intro">
                    United Kingdom
                </a>
            </td>
            <td>
```

```
                <a href = "http://www.zamnet.zm/zamnet/zntb.html">
                    Zambia
                </a>
            </td>
            <td>
                <a href = "http://cy.co.za/atg/stbroz.html">
                    Zimbabwe
                </a>
            </td>
        </tr>
</table>
```

The result of this XHTML appears in Figure 6.21. As you can see, the hyperlinks appear neatly arranged in rows and columns. In addition, the explanatory text appears neatly centered above it.

You can get more creative, of course, such as flanking an image with two columns of text. Here's a more advanced example, also first introduced in Chapter 3, that uses the **rowspan** attribute to create a nice effect:

```
<table noborder = "noborder" cellpadding = "8" width = "90%">
    <tr align = "center">
        <th rowspan = "4">
```

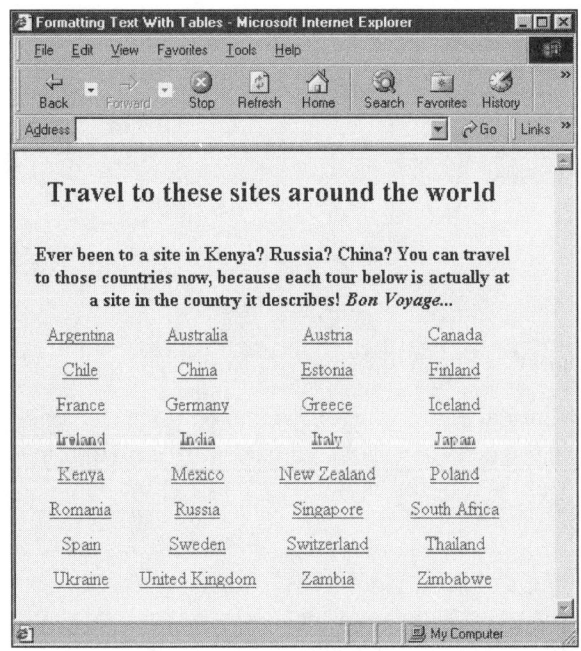

Figure 6.21 Formatting hyperlinks into rows and columns by using a table.

```
                <h2>
                    High
                    <br />
                    culture
                    <br />
                    on
                    <br />
                    demand!
                </h2>
            </th>
            <td>
                Download
                <a href="darkness.zip">
                    Joseph Conrad's Heart of Darkness
                </a>
            </td>
        </tr>
        <tr align = "center">
            <td>
                Listen to some of
                <a href = "mozart1.mid">
                    Mozart's music
                </a>
            </td>
        </tr>
        <tr align = "center">
            <td>
                See a
                <a href="chaplin.html">
                    Charlie Chaplin movie
                </a>
            </td>
        </tr>
</table>
```

The results of this XHTML appear in Figure 6.22.

Another popular use of tables is to accentuate Web-page elements. Because you can set the background color of the cells in a table, you can surround text in what appears to be colored boxes. Here's another example from Chapter 3:

```
<?xml version="1.0"?>
<!DOCTYPE html PUBLIC "-//W3C//DTD XHTML 1.0 Transitional//EN"
"http://www.w3.org/TR/xhtml1/DTD/xhtml1-transitional.dtd">
<html xmlns="http://www.w3.org/1999/xhtml" xml:lang="en" lang="en">
    <head>
        <title>
```

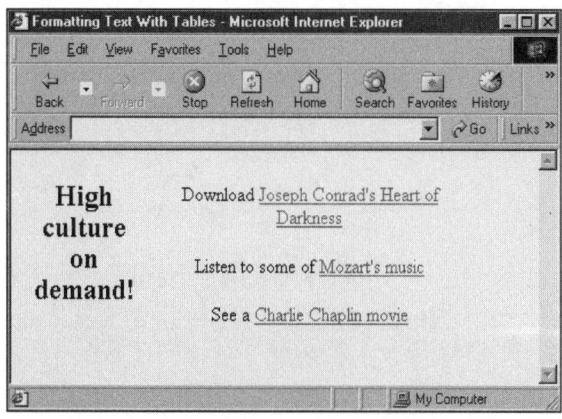

Figure 6.22 Formatting text as a table.

```
        European Train Travel
    </title>
</head>

<body>
    <h1>
        European Train Travel
    </h1>
    So you've decided to take the train in Europe!
    Congratulations, you're in for a great time. There are
    a few things you should know that will make
    things a lot easier. Here's an overview:
    <ul>
        <li>Getting Train Times</li>
        <li>Getting On The Train</li>
        <li>Handling Security</li>
    </ul>

    <h2>
        Getting Train Times
    </h2>
    Many train stations are packed with crowds, especially in
    the summer, and you can save yourself a great deal of time
    waiting in lines that can last an hour or more by getting
    a complete train schedule, such as Thomas Cook's European
    Timetable.
    <p>
        <table bgcolor="#d0d0d0">
            <tr>
                <td>
                    TIP: With a complete train schedule, you'll
                    also become the most popular person in
```

```
                                the youth hostel.
                        </td>
                    </tr>
                </table>
            </p>
            <h2>
                Getting On The Train
            </h2>
            In larger stations, you'll find a diagram showing where
            each wagon of the train will stop so if you have a
            reservation for a specific wagon, you can wait in the right
            place with your luggage.
            <p>
                Check the destination of the train, the class of the wagon, and
                whether it's a smoking or non-smoking wagon before getting on.
                This information is displayed on a plaque on the wagon.
            </p>
        </body>
</html>
```

You can see the results of this XHTML in Figure 6.23.

As you can see, tables are good for many text formatting problems—especially when you get creative.

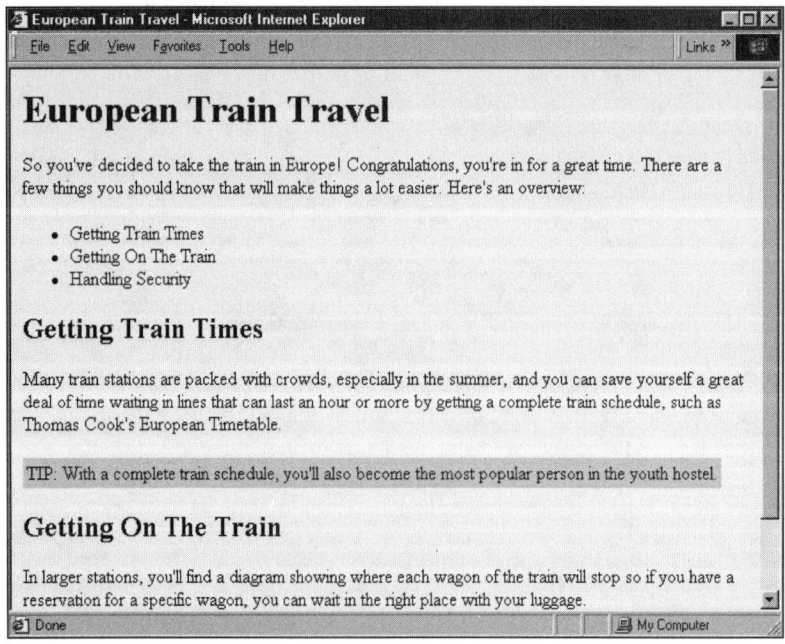

Figure 6.23   Emphasizing text by using a table.

Chapter 7

Working with Frames

If you need an immediate solution to:	See page:
<frameset>—Creating Frames	425
<frame>—Creating Frames	427
Creating Vertical Frames	430
Creating Horizontal Frames	431
Creating Both Horizontal and Vertical Frames	432
Using Named Frames as Hyperlink Targets	434
Using Predefined Target Names	436
<noframes>—Handling Browsers That Don't Handle Frames	436
Opening New Browser Windows	438
Creating Borderless Frames	439
Creating Navigation Bars	441
Enabling and Disabling Scrolling	444
Stopping Frames from Being Resized	446
Setting Frame Border Thickness	446
Setting Frame Color	447
<iframe>—Creating Inline or Floating Frames	449
Creating Borderless Inline Frames	452

In Depth

Frames are one of the most powerful aspects of XHTML programming, and many people have rigid opinions about them. In fact, many people hate them. But some people wouldn't create a Web site without them.

If you've browsed the Web, you know what frames are. They give you the ability to split a browser window into vertical or horizontal, or *both* vertical and horizontal, sections. You can load different pages into the various frames in the browser, creating a multipage display. With frames, you have a significant amount of added control over the browser's layout.

Frames were originally introduced in Netscape Navigator 2, and Internet Explorer added them in version 3. (Internet Explorer also added *inline frames*, which we'll see in the "Immediate Solutions" section "**<iframe>**—Creating Inline or Floating Frames.") However, many other browsers haven't added support for frames, or if they have, they've done so only recently because frames were not part of the HTML 3.2 specification. They are part of the HTML 4 specification, however (and so are inline frames), and therefore, they appear in XHTML as well.

One of the most common uses for frames is to give users an easy way to navigate around a site. For example, you can see two frames in action in Figure 7.1. The

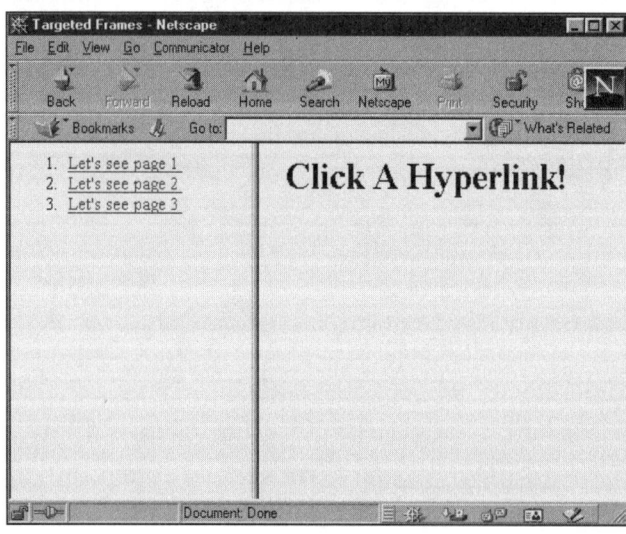

Figure 7.1   A vertical navigation bar.

frame on the left is acting as a vertical navigation bar, displaying a number of hyperlinks. When the user clicks a hyperlink, the corresponding page is loaded into the frame on the right. The navigation bar on the left remains visible, however, so the user can click other hyperlinks at will. Frames are customizable, so the user can use the mouse to resize the frames.

You can see another example in Figure 7.2. In this figure, I'm using the other common format for navigation bars in frames—making the navigation bar horizontal and placing it above the rest of the content in the browser window. In this case, I've also removed the borders from the page.

In this chapter, we'll discuss these techniques and everything you can do with frames in XHTML, including:

- Creating basic frames
- Handling browsers that don't handle frames
- Creating floating frames, which can appear in the center of the display, away from the edge of the browser window
- Opening a new browser window on demand

To Frame or Not to Frame

As a Web designer, you should keep one thing in mind—some people really do hate frames. If there are two topics that have significant disapproving populations among Web users, those topics are frames and cookies. I know users who refuse to look at pages that contain frames.

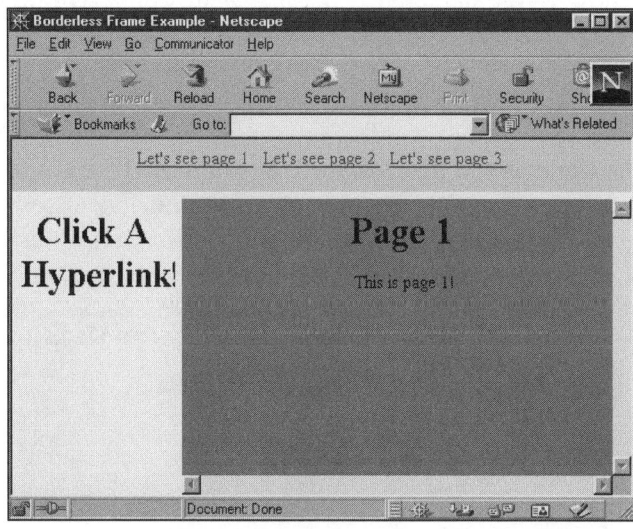

Figure 7.2 A horizontal navigation bar.

The most common reason for this animosity is that some users, out of choice or necessity, run their screens at a relatively low resolution; they find that carelessly designed frames either run off the page or display only small slices of what is supposed to be shown. Then again, some people just hate having their displays, where space is always at a premium, divided into smaller sections, making the screen too busy and hard to work with.

The best way to work with people who hate frames is to make sure you provide frameless alternatives. (To see how well your frames are received, track how many users use each page.) At the very least, you should check the appearance of your frames in various screen resolutions and with a variety browsers.

With that warning out of the way, I'll start digging into the XHTML now, beginning with creating vertical frames.

Creating Vertical Frames

How do you actually set up frames in a document? You use the **<frameset>** element to indicate how you want to configure the frames, and you use **<frame>** elements to create the actual frames. In a document that uses frames, the **<frameset>** element replaces the **<body>** element. That's a small problem in XHTML because the standard DTDs are set up so that the **<html>** element can contain only **<head>** and **<body>** elements, like this, in the XHTML 1.0 Strict DTD:

```
<!ELEMENT html (head, body)>
```

To use frames in a document, you should use the XHTML 1.0 *Frameset* DTD because that DTD sets up the **<html>** element to contain **<head>** and **<frameset>** elements:

```
<!ELEMENT html (head, frameset)>
```

The Frameset DTD is the same as the XHTML 1.0 Transitional DTD except that the Frameset DTD lets you use frames. This means that the elements introduced in this chapter—**<frame>**, **<frameset>**, **<iframe>**, and **<noframes>**—are *not* available in the XHTML 1.0 Strict DTD or the XHTML 1.1 DTD. In fact, only the **<iframe>** and **<noframes>** elements—not **<frame>** and **<frameset>**—are supported in the XHTML 1.0 Transitional DTD. The upshot is that I'll be using the XHTML 1.0 Frameset DTD for documents that contain frames:

```
<!DOCTYPE html PUBLIC "-//W3C//DTD XHTML 1.0 Frameset//EN"
"http://www.w3.org/TR/xhtml1/DTD/xhtml1-frameset.dtd">
```

In Depth

How to use frames is best seen in an example, so I'll create one now that divides the browser window into two vertical frames, with each frame taking up half of the available display area. To do that, I start by using the **<frameset>** element. From the frameset point of view, dividing the browser into two vertical frames means using the **<frameset>** element's **cols** attribute to create two columns. To indicate how many columns you want to create, you assign a comma-separated list of values, with the appropriate column widths, to the **cols** attribute. You can assign actual pixel values to **cols**, although it's usually not advisable when you're working with frames. In most cases, it is far better to assign percentages of the available display area to each column and let the browser set the columns to match the space it has to work with.

Here's how I create two-column frames, each of which takes 50 percent of the available horizontal display area:

```
<?xml version="1.0"?>
<!DOCTYPE html PUBLIC "-//W3C//DTD XHTML 1.0 Frameset//EN"
"http://www.w3.org/TR/xhtml1/DTD/xhtml1-frameset.dtd">
<html xmlns="http://www.w3.org/1999/xhtml" xml:lang="en" lang="en">
    <head>
        <title>
            Creating Frames
        </title>
    </head>

    <frameset cols = "50%, 50%">
        .
        .
        .
    </frameset>

</html>
```

When you're working with frames, it's usually not a good idea to specify actual pixel dimensions for frames. There is one technique that can help, though—you can use an asterisk (*) to represent the rest of the space available in the browser window. For example, **cols="145, *"** will create one column 145 pixels in width and assign the remaining horizontal width to the other column. In this way, if you really need to have a frame of a particular width or height (this happens most commonly when you're displaying images of fixed dimensions), you can do it and still let the browser arrange the other frame or frames as appropriate for the amount of space it has available. If you use more than one asterisk, the browser will give each asterisk-designated frame as much space as it can, dividing the space equally among those frames.

Now that I've set up the frameset for the page, it's time to set up the frames themselves with the **<frame>** element, which is an empty element. In this case, I'll load a page into each of these frames. You do that with the **<frame>** element's **src** attribute, as you can see in the following example. I'm loading frame1.htm into the frame on the left, and frame2.htm into the frame on the right. Note that you can set the **src** attribute to a full URL, not just a relative one as I've used here:

```
<?xml version="1.0"?>
<!DOCTYPE html PUBLIC "-//W3C//DTD XHTML 1.0 Frameset//EN"
"http://www.w3.org/TR/xhtml1/DTD/xhtml1-frameset.dtd">
<html xmlns="http://www.w3.org/1999/xhtml" xml:lang="en" lang="en">
    <head>
        <title>
            Creating Frames
        </title>
    </head>

    <frameset cols = "50%, 50%">
        <frame src="frame1.htm" />
        <frame src="frame2.htm" />
    </frameset>

</html>
```

We're going to need some pages to load into the frames, so I'll put together some pages that simply announce which page they are: page one, page two, or page three (using various colored backgrounds). Here's page one (these pages have **<body>** elements, so I'll use the XHTML 1.0 Transitional DTD here):

```
<?xml version="1.0"?>
<!DOCTYPE html PUBLIC "-//W3C//DTD XHTML 1.0 Transitional//EN"
"http://www.w3.org/tr/xhtml1/DTD/xhtml1-transitional.dtd">
<html xmlns="http://www.w3.org/1999/xhtml" xml:lang="en" lang="en">
    <head>
        <title>
            Page 1
        </title>
    </head>

    <body bgcolor="red">

        <center>
        <h1>
            Page 1
        </h1>
```

```
            This is page 1!
        </center>
    </body>

</html>
```

Here's page two:

```
<?xml version="1.0"?>
<!DOCTYPE html PUBLIC "-//W3C//DTD XHTML 1.0 Transitional//EN"
"http://www.w3.org/tr/xhtml1/DTD/xhtml1-transitional.dtd">
<html xmlns="http://www.w3.org/1999/xhtml" xml:lang="en" lang="en">
    <head>
        <title>
            Page 2
        </title>
    </head>

    <body bgcolor="yellow">

        <center>
        <h1>
            Page 2
        </h1>

            This is page 2!
        </center>
    </body>

</html>
```

And here's page three:

```
<?xml version="1.0"?>
<!DOCTYPE html PUBLIC "-//W3C//DTD XHTML 1.0 Transitional//EN"
"http://www.w3.org/tr/xhtml1/DTD/xhtml1-transitional.dtd">
<html xmlns="http://www.w3.org/1999/xhtml" xml:lang="en" lang="en">
    <head>
        <title>
            Page 3
        </title>
    </head>

    <body bgcolor="pink">
```

Chapter 7 Working with Frames

```
        <center>
        <h1>
            Page 3
        </h1>

            This is page 3!
        </center>
    </body>

</html>
```

You can see page one, which has a red background, in Figure 7.3. The other pages look the same except for the page number and color.

Now that the pages displayed in the frames are ready, we can take a look at the actual frames by loading the frameset page into the browser. In Figure 7.4, you can see two vertical frames, each displaying a page.

But what if the user's browser doesn't support frames? In that case, the user will see nothing because the browser will ignore the **<frameset>** and **<frame>** elements. However, there is a way around this, and we'll discuss the solution in the next section.

What if the Browser Doesn't Do Frames?

You might think that it would be hard to find a graphical browser that doesn't handle frames today, but that's not necessarily true. For example, Microsoft Word

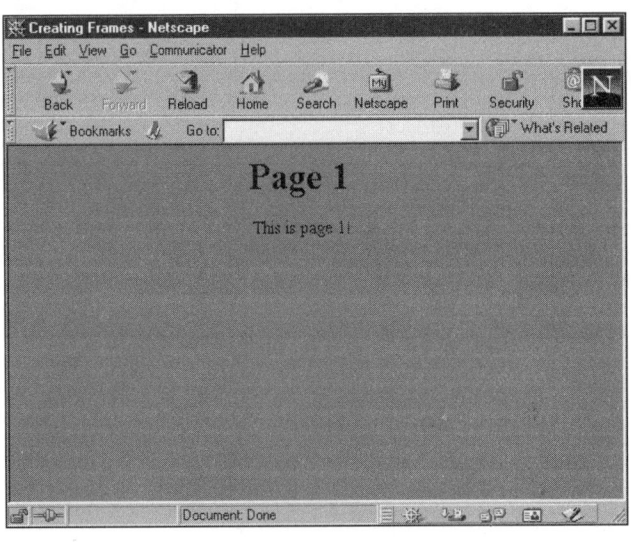

Figure 7.3 Page one to be loaded into frames.

In Depth

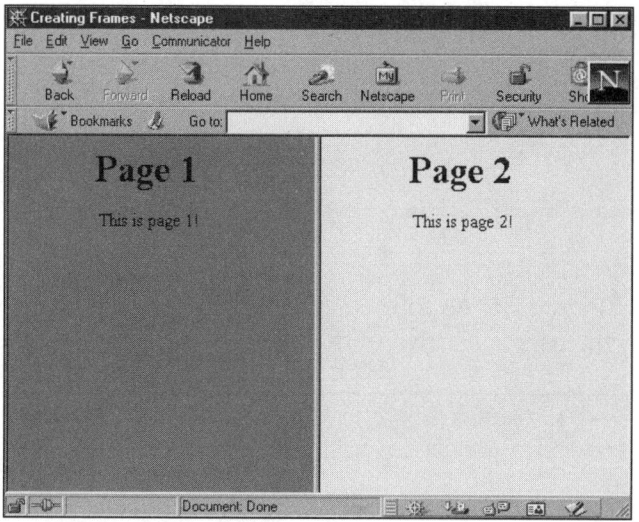

Figure 7.4 Vertical frames.

can now display XHTML documents—but it doesn't handle frames. How do you handle browsers that don't handle frames? You use the **<noframes>** element.

Browsers that handle frames ignore the <noframes> element; it's also ignored by browsers that don't handle frames, but in a different way. If a browser doesn't understand a tag, it'll just treat the tag's contents as plain text. Browsers that handle frames will ignore that text, so you can place text in the **<noframes>** element to indicate to users that they're missing something. In other words, you can use the **<noframes>** element in any kind of browser—those that handle frames and those that don't—and it'll do the right thing. Note that in the XHTML Frameset DTD, the **<noframes>** element goes inside the **<frameset>** element, and you're allowed only one **<noframes>** element per document. Here's an example:

```
<?xml version="1.0"?>
<!DOCTYPE html PUBLIC "-//W3C//DTD XHTML 1.0 Frameset//EN"
"http://www.w3.org/TR/xhtml1/DTD/xhtml1-frameset.dtd">
<html xmlns="http://www.w3.org/1999/xhtml" xml:lang="en" lang="en">
    <head>
        <title>
            Creating Frames
        </title>
    </head>

    <frameset cols = "50%, 50%">
        <noframes>
            <body>
```

```
                    Your browser does not support frames...
                </body>
        </noframes>
            <frame src="frame1.htm" />
            <frame src="frame2.htm" />
        </frameset>

</html>
```

You can see the result in Figure 7.5. As you see, Microsoft Word doesn't support frames in Web pages, so the user is notified of that fact.

TIP: It's good to include at least a hyperlink to the frameless version of your page in the text of the **<noframes>** element. In fact, you can include the entire frameless version of your page in the **<noframes>** element.

Creating Horizontal Frames

We've learned how to create vertical frames by using the **cols** attribute of the **<frameset>** element and how to create each frame with the **<frame>** element. What about creating horizontal frames?

As you might expect, there's another attribute of the **<frameset>** element we can use—**rows**. For example, converting the previous example to horizontal instead of vertical frames is easy. Here's what it looks like:

```
<?xml version="1.0"?>
<!DOCTYPE html PUBLIC "-//W3C//DTD XHTML 1.0 Frameset//EN"
 "http://www.w3.org/TR/xhtml1/DTD/xhtml1-frameset.dtd">
<html xmlns="http://www.w3.org/1999/xhtml" xml:lang="en" lang="en">
```

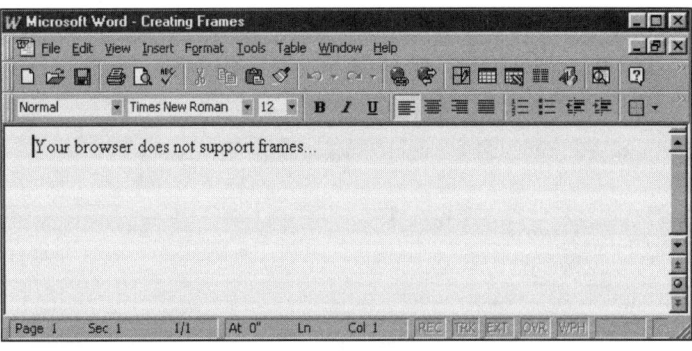

Figure 7.5   Handling browsers that don't handle frames.

In Depth

```
<head>
    <title>
        Creating Frames
    </title>
</head>

<frameset rows = "50%, 50%">
    <frame src="frame1.htm" />
    <frame src="frame2.htm" />
</frameset>

</html>
```

You can see the results of this XHTML in Figure 7.6, where there are now two horizontal frames instead of vertical frames.

We're on a roll—so how do we create horizontal *and* vertical frames in the same document? That's coming up in the next section.

Creating Horizontal and Vertical Frames

To create both horizontal and vertical frames in a document, you can use nested **<frameset>** elements. In one element, you set up the rows, and in the other element, you set up the columns. In this example, I'm using an outer **<frameset>** element to divide the display into two columns:

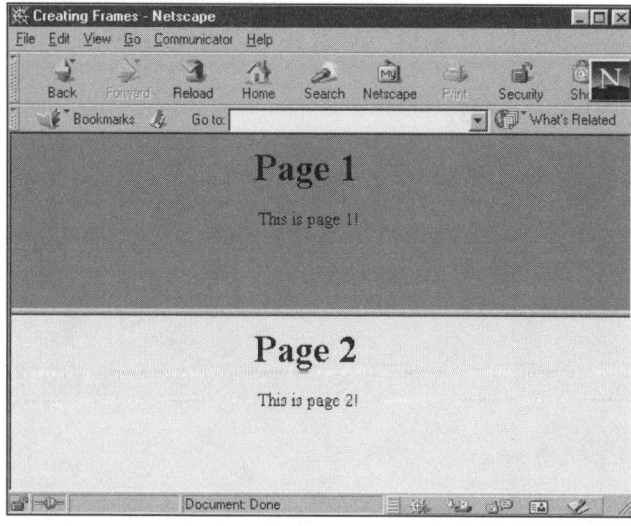

Figure 7.6   Horizontal frames.

```
<?xml version="1.0"?>
<!DOCTYPE html PUBLIC "-//W3C//DTD XHTML 1.0 Frameset//EN"
"http://www.w3.org/TR/xhtml1/DTD/xhtml1-frameset.dtd">
<html xmlns="http://www.w3.org/1999/xhtml" xml:lang="en" lang="en">
    <head>
        <title>Row And Column Frames</title>
    </head>

    <frameset cols = "50%, 50%">
        <noframes>
            <body>
                Your browser does not support frames...
            </body>
        </noframes>
            .
            .
            .
    </frameset>

</html>
```

Now I add two inner **<frameset>** elements to create three rows of various heights in each column:

```
<?xml version="1.0"?>
<!DOCTYPE html PUBLIC "-//W3C//DTD XHTML 1.0 Frameset//EN"
"http://www.w3.org/TR/xhtml1/DTD/xhtml1-frameset.dtd">
<html xmlns="http://www.w3.org/1999/xhtml" xml:lang="en" lang="en">
    <head>
        <title>Row And Column Frames</title>
    </head>

    <frameset cols = "50%, 50%">
        <noframes>
            <body>
                Your browser does not support frames...
            </body>
        </noframes>

        <frameset rows = "25%, 50%, 25%">
            <frame src="frame1.htm" />
            <frame src="frame2.htm" />
            <frame src="frame3.htm" />
        </frameset>
```

In Depth

```
    <frameset rows = "25%, 25%, 50%">
        <frame src="frame1.htm" />
        <frame src="frame2.htm" />
        <frame src="frame3.htm" />
    </frameset>
```
```
    </frameset>

</html>
```

You can see the result of this XHTML in Figure 7.7. As you can see, after you've created columns, you can break them up into rows with nested **<frameset>** elements. If you prefer, you can set up the rows first and then divide each row into columns.

You don't have to have the same number of rows in each column. In this example, I have no rows in the left frame and three in the right:

```
<?xml version="1.0"?>
<!DOCTYPE html PUBLIC "-//W3C//DTD XHTML 1.0 Frameset//EN"
"http://www.w3.org/TR/xhtml1/DTD/xhtml1-frameset.dtd">
<html xmlns="http://www.w3.org/1999/xhtml" xml:lang="en" lang="en">
    <head>
        <title>Row And Column Frames</title>
    </head>
```

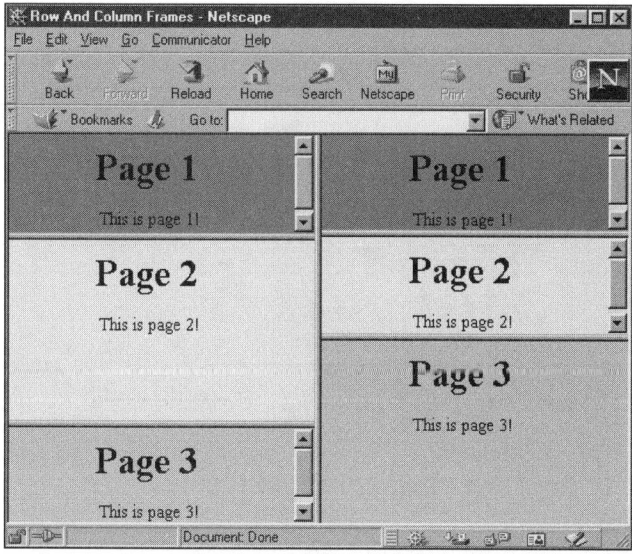

Figure 7.7   Horizontal and vertical frames.

Chapter 7   Working with Frames

```
<frameset cols = "30%, 70%">
    <noframes>
        <body>
            Your browser does not support frames...
        </body>
    </noframes>

    <frame src="frame1.htm" />

    <frameset rows = "25%, 25%, 50%">
        <frame src="frame1.htm" />
        <frame src="frame2.htm" />
        <frame src="frame3.htm" />
    </frameset>

</frameset>

</html>
```

You can see the results of this XHTML in Figure 7.8. Working with frames is a lot like working with tables—you have to experiment with the XHTML and frequently look at the results in your browser to get things just right.

TIP: *You can use the* **rows** *and* **cols** *attributes in the same* **<frameset>** *element—see "Creating Both Horizontal and Vertical Frames" in the "Immediate Solutions" section of this chapter.*

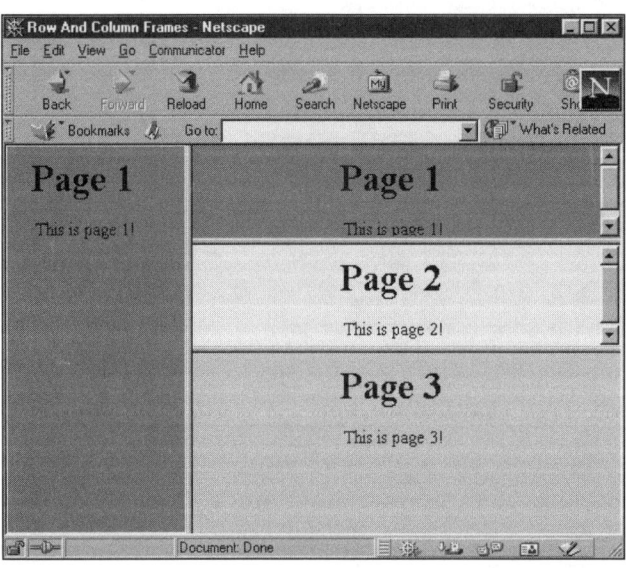

Figure 7.8   A new layout with horizontal and vertical frames.

Named Frames

One important aspect of working with frames is using *named frames*. When you use the **id** attribute to name a frame, you can use the name as a *target* to load new pages into (thus supporting the navigation bars I discussed in Chapter 5). Note that some browsers, like Netscape Navigator, don't yet support the **id** attribute for **<frame>** but still use the **name** attribute, so you can use both the **id** and **name** attributes for such browsers, even though **name** has been deprecated for frames.

In this example, I'm dividing the display into a vertical navigation bar and a display frame, and I'm naming that frame "display":

```
<?xml version="1.0"?>
<!DOCTYPE html PUBLIC "-//W3C//DTD XHTML 1.0 Frameset//EN"
"http://www.w3.org/TR/xhtml1/DTD/xhtml1-frameset.dtd">
<html xmlns="http://www.w3.org/1999/xhtml" xml:lang="en" lang="en">
    <head>
        <title>
            Targeted Frames
        </title>
    </head>

    <frameset cols = "40%, 60%">
        <frame src = "menu.htm" />
        <frame src = "default.htm" id = "display"
            name = "display" />
    </frameset>

</html>
```

In the navigation bar, I'll display a page named menu.htm, and in the display frame, I'll show a default welcoming page named default.htm. The navigation bar, menu.htm, has a list of hyperlinks to pages that, when clicked by the user, will appear in the display frame. How do we get those pages into the display frame when a hyperlink is clicked? All you have to do is use the **<a>** tag's **target** attribute to specify a frame to load those pages into, like this in menu.htm:

```
<?xml version="1.0"?>
<!DOCTYPE html PUBLIC "-//W3C//DTD XHTML 1.0 Transitional//EN"
"http://www.w3.org/tr/xhtml1/DTD/xhtml1-transitional.dtd">
<html xmlns="http://www.w3.org/1999/xhtml" xml:lang="en" lang="en">
    <head>
        <title>menu.htm</title>
    </head>
```

```
        <body>
            <ol>
                <li>
                    <a href = "frame1.htm" target = "display">
                    Let's see page 1
                    </a>
                </li>
                <li>
                    <a href = "frame2.htm" target = "display">
                    Let's see page 2
                    </a>
                </li>
                <li>
                    <a href = "frame3.htm" target = "display">
                    Let's see page 3
                    </a>
                </li>
            </ol>
        </body>
</html>
```

Before any of the linked-to pages are displayed, however, a default page, default.htm, is shown in the display frame. The default page looks like this:

```
<?xml version="1.0"?>
<!DOCTYPE html PUBLIC "-//W3C//DTD XHTML 1.0 Transitional//EN"
"http://www.w3.org/tr/xhtml1/DTD/xhtml1-transitional.dtd">
<html xmlns="http://www.w3.org/1999/xhtml" xml:lang="en" lang="en">
    <head>
        <title>
            Default Frame
        </title>
    </head>

    <body>

        <center>
        <h1>
            Click A Hyperlink!
        </h1>
        </center>
    </body>

</html>
```

You can see the results of this XHTML in Figure 7.9. As you see, the navigation bar, menu.htm, appears on the left, and the default display page, default.htm, appears on the right.

When the user clicks a hyperlink in the navigation bar, the appropriate page is loaded into the hyperlink's target frame, the display frame, as you see in Figure 7.10. And that's all there is to it.

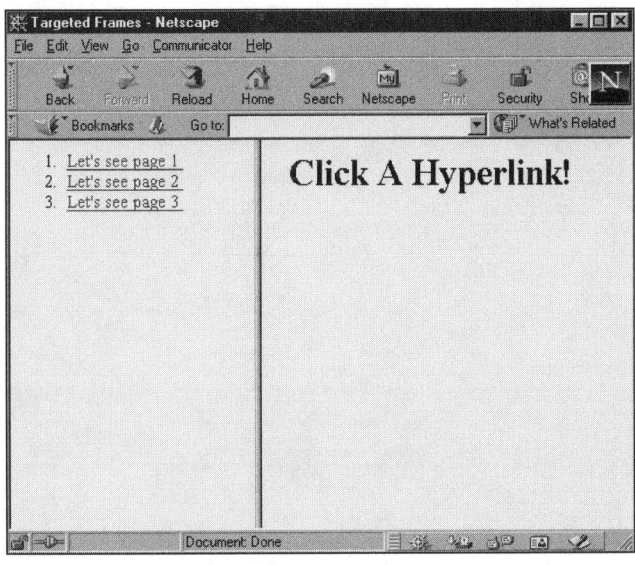

Figure 7.9   A vertical navigation bar.

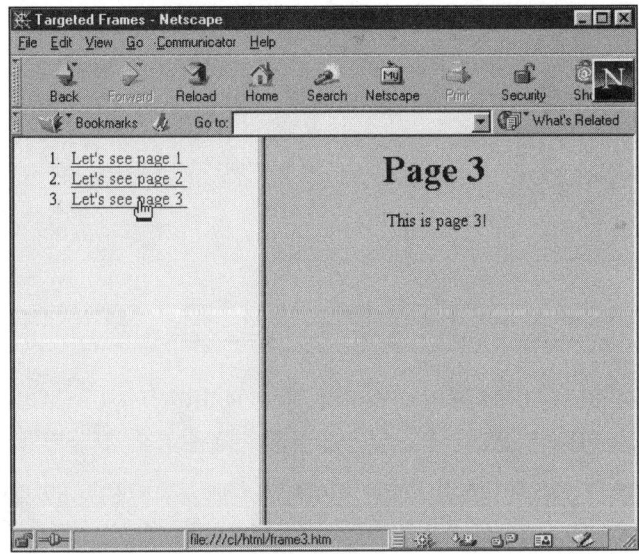

Figure 7.10   Using a navigation bar.

Opening New Browser Windows

What if, in the hyperlink, you specify the name of a target frame that doesn't exist? In that case, the browser will open a new window to display the linked-to page. This technique is useful if you want to link to a different site but don't want the user to leave your site.

In the following example, I'll let the user open a new browser window each time a hyperlink is clicked. To do that, I'll give the hyperlinks the targets of **"a"**, **"b"**, and **"c"**, which are *not* named frames in the document:

```
<?xml version="1.0"?>
<!DOCTYPE html PUBLIC "-//W3C//DTD XHTML 1.0 Transitional//EN"
"http://www.w3.org/tr/xhtml1/DTD/xhtml1-transitional.dtd">
<html xmlns="http://www.w3.org/1999/xhtml" xml:lang="en" lang="en">
    <head>
        <title>menu.htm</title>
    </head>

    <body>
        <ol>
            <li>
                <a href = "frame1.htm" target = "a">
                Let's see page 1
                </a>
            </li>
            <li>
                <a href = "frame2.htm" target = "b">
                Let's see page 2
                </a>
            </li>
            <li>
                <a href = "frame3.htm" target = "c">
                Let's see page 3
                </a>
            </li>
        </ol>
    </body>
</html>
```

Now when the user clicks one of the hyperlinks in the navigation bar, the browser will display the linked-to page in a new browser window, as you see in Figure 7.11.

It's worth noting that the browser will keep track of the name you've given the new display window. This feature allows you to use a navigation bar in one window to load pages into another window—if you always refer to that display

In Depth

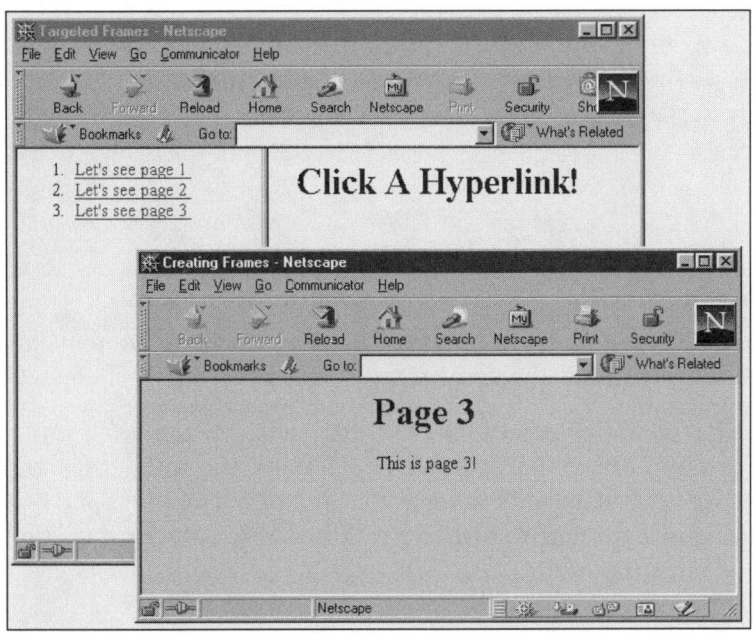

Figure 7.11 Opening a new browser window.

window with the same name. In the next example, I'm using the same name for the new display window in all hyperlinks. Now, each time the user clicks a hyperlink, the new page will be displayed in the same new browser window:

```
<?xml version="1.0"?>
<!DOCTYPE html PUBLIC "-//W3C//DTD XHTML 1.0 Transitional//EN"
"http://www.w3.org/tr/xhtml1/DTD/xhtml1-transitional.dtd">
<html xmlns="http://www.w3.org/1999/xhtml" xml:lang="en" lang="en">
    <head>
        <title>menu.htm</title>
    </head>

    <body>
    <ol>
        <li>
            <a href = "frame1.htm" target = "newwindow">
            Let's see page 1
            </a>
        </li>
        <li>
            <a href = "frame2.htm" target = "newwindow">
            Let's see page 2
            </a>
```

```
            </li>
            <li>
                <a href = "frame3.htm" target = "newwindow">
                Let's see page 3
                </a>
            </li>
        </ol>
    </body>
</html>
```

This technique allows you to use the original page as a table of contents and to open new pages as required in the new browser window.

All the information up to this point in the chapter has given us a good start with frames. We've created horizontal frames, vertical frames, and both horizontal and vertical frames. We've used named frames as the target for hyperlinks and opened new browser windows. It's time to turn to the "Immediate Solutions" section for more details and more topics.

Immediate Solutions

<frameset>—Creating Frames

Purpose: Structures a document by using frames. Replaces the **<body>** element and uses the **rows** and/or **cols** attribute to set up the frame. Use the **<frame>** element to specify the content and name of individual frames.

When used as HTML: Start tag/End tag: Required/Required

Supported: [1.0F, 4, IE3, IE4, IE5, NS2, NS3, NS4]

Attributes:

- **border**—Use this attribute in the outermost **frameset** tag to set the border thickness for all frames within the **frameset**. Set to positive integers indicating the pixel space between frames; set to 0 to set the **frameborder** to **no**. [IE4, IE5, NS3, NS4]

- **bordercolor**—Sets the color of the borders for all frames in the frameset. (Can be overridden in the **<frame>** tag for individual frames.) Set to an RGB triplet color value or a predefined color. [IE4, IE5, NS3, NS4]

- **class**—Class of the element (used for rendering). [1.0F, 4, IE4, IE5]

- **cols**—Sets the number of columns (vertical framed bands) in the frameset. Use commas to separate the values assigned to this attribute; each value represents the width of a column. The values you use should add up to the total display width available. Set to pixel values or percentages (include a percent sign [%] after the value), or use an asterisk (*) to specify that the browser should give the column or columns the remaining space. [1.0F, 4, IE3, IE4, IE5, NS2, NS3, NS4]

- **dir**—Gives the direction of directionally neutral text. Possible values: **ltr**, left-to-right text or table; and **rtl**, right-to-left text or table. [1.0F]

- **frameborder**—Specifies whether or not borders surround the frames in the **frameset**. (You can override this setting for individual frames with the **<frame>** element.) For Netscape Navigator, set to **yes** (the default) or **no**; for Internet Explorer lists, set to **1** (the default) or **0** (no border). [IE3, IE4, IE5, NS3, NS4]

- **framespacing**—Sets the pixel spacing between frames (you can override this setting for individual frames with the **<frame>** element). Set to positive integers. [IE3, IE4, IE5]

- **id**—Unique alphanumeric identifier for the tag; use the ID to refer to the tag. [1.0F, 4, IE4, IE5]
- **lang**—Base language used for the tag. [1.0F, IE4, IE5]
- **language**—Scripting language used for the tag. [IE4, IE5]
- **rows**—Sets the number of rows (horizontal framed bands) in the frameset. Use commas to separate the values assigned to this attribute; each value represents the height of a row. The values you use should add up to the total display height available. Set to pixel values or percentages (include a percent sign [%] after the value), or use an asterisk (*) to specify that the browser should give the row or rows the remaining space. [1.0F, 4, IE3, IE4, IE5, NS2, NS3, NS4]
- **style**—Inline style indicating how to render the element. [1.0F, 4]
- **title**—Holds additional information (which might be displayed in tool tips). [1.0F, 4, IE4, IE5]
- **xml:lang**—Holds the base language for the element when the document is interpreted as an XML document. [1.0F]

XHTML events: None

The novice programmer appears and says, "I want to create frames in my new Web pages, and I figure it'll be pretty easy. You start with the **<frame>** element, right?" "Sorry," you say, "you start with the **<frameset>** element."

As discussed in the "In Depth" section of this chapter, you use the **<frameset>** element and the XHTML Frameset DTD to format a page into frames. This element takes the place of the **<body>** element in documents that display frames. To create the frames themselves, you use the **<frame>** element (see the next section).

You can use the **rows** or **cols** attribute of the **<frameset>** element to divide the document into rows or columns. You specify the number of rows or columns by supplying their heights or widths in a comma-separated list. Following is an example from the beginning of the chapter. The example creates two columns—that is, two vertical frames—each of which take up half the available width. Note that I'm using the XHTML 1.0 Frameset DTD:

```
<?xml version="1.0"?>
<!DOCTYPE html PUBLIC "-//W3C//DTD XHTML 1.0 Frameset//EN"
"http://www.w3.org/TR/xhtml1/DTD/xhtml1-frameset.dtd">
<html xmlns="http://www.w3.org/1999/xhtml" xml:lang="en" lang="en">
    <head>
        <title>
```

```
                Creating Frames
        </title>
    </head>

    <frameset cols = "50%, 50%">
                    .
                    .
                    .
    </frameset>

</html>
```

You can assign pixel values to the **rows** and **cols** attributes, although it's not usually a good idea when you're working with frames. In most cases, it's better to assign percentages of the available display width to each column and let the browser set the column widths to match the space it has to work with.

You can use an asterisk (*) to represent the remaining available space. For example, **cols="180, *"** will create one column of 180 pixels in width and assign the remaining width to the other column. Using values allows you to have a frame of a specific width or height (for example, when you're displaying images of fixed dimensions) and still let the browser arrange the other frame or frames appropriately for the amount of space available. If you use more than one asterisk, you're telling the browser that it should divide the remaining space among all such frames.

TIP: *There is no limit to the number of <frameset> elements you can use in a document. In fact, you can load framed windows into frames. Keep in mind that too many frames will make your display surfaces too small to work with.*

As you see from the attributes listed for this tag, there are many options available—such as setting borders and border colors—when you're working with the **<frameset>** element. I'll take a look at more of these options in the coming sections.

<frame>—Creating Frames

Purpose: Creates a frame. Use inside the **<frameset>** element. This element contains no content.

When used as HTML: Start tag/End tag: Required/Omitted

Supported: [1.0F, 4, IE3, IE4, IE5, NS2, NS3, NS4]

Attributes:

- **bordercolor**—Sets the color used for the frame border. This setting overrides the color specified in the surrounding **<frameset>** element. Set to an RGB triplet color value or predefined color name. [IE4, IE5, NS3, NS4]

- **class**—Class of the element (used for rendering). [1.0F, 4, IE4, IE5]

- **datafld**—Name of the column of the data-source object that supplies the bound data. Set to alphanumeric characters. [IE4, IE5]

- **datasrc**—Gives the URL or ID of the data-source object supplying data bound to this element. The World Wide Web Consortium (W3C) says this should be a URL; IE says it should be a data-source ID. [IE4, IE5]

- **dir**—Gives the direction of directionally neutral text (text that doesn't have inherent direction in which you should read it). Possible values: **ltr**, left-to-right text or table; and **rtl**, right-to-left text or table. [1.0F]

- **frameborder**—Specifies whether or not borders surround the frame. For Netscape Navigator, set to **yes** (the default) or **no**; for Internet Explorer lists, set to **1** (the default) or **0** (no border). [1.0F, IE3, IE4, IE5, NS3, NS4]

- **id**—Unique alphanumeric identifier for the tag; use the ID to refer to the tag. [1.0F, 4, IE4, IE5]

- **lang**—Base language used for the tag. [1.0F, IE4, IE5]

- **language**—Scripting language used for the tag. [IE4, IE5]

- **longdesc**—Indicates the URL for a longer description of the frame contents. Set to a URL. [1.0F, 4]

- **marginheight**—Sets the size of the top and bottom margins used in the frame. Set to a pixel value. [1.0F, 4, IE3, IE4, IE5, NS2, NS3, NS4]

- **marginwidth**—Sets the size of the right and left margins used in the frame. Set to a pixel value. [1.0F, 4, IE3, IE4, IE5, NS2, NS3, NS4]

- **name**—Sets the name of the frame. You can use named frames as target destinations for **<a>**, **<area>**, **<base>**, and **<form>** elements. Set to a text string. [1.0F, 4, IE3, IE4, IE5, NS2, NS3, NS4]

- **noresize**—Indicates that the frame may not be resized. The default is that frames may be resized by dragging the border. [1.0F, 4, IE3, IE4, IE5, NS2, NS3, NS4]

- **scrolling**—Determines scrollbar action. Possible values: **auto** (the default; lets the browser decide when to display scrollbars), **yes** (always show a scrollbar), or **no** (never show a scrollbar). [1.0F, 4, IE3, IE4, IE5, NS2, NS3, NS4]

- **src**—Specifies the URL of the frame document. If you don't specify a URL, the frame will appear blank. Set to a URL. Required. [1.0F, 4, IE3, IE4, IE5, NS2, NS3, NS4]
- **style**—Inline style indicating how to render the element. [1.0F, 4]
- **title**—Holds additional information (which might be displayed in tool tips). [1.0F, 4, IE4, IE5]
- **xml:lang**—Holds the base language for the element when the document is interpreted as an XML document. [1.0F]

XHTML events: None

"OK," says the novice programmer, "I've created a **<frameset>** element—now I can use **<frame>** elements to actually create the frames I want, right?" "Exactly," you say, "one **<frame>** element to a frame, and you're all set."

You use the **<frame>** element inside a **<frameset>** element to create a frame. The **<frame>** element exists so you can specify the document that is displayed in a URL. In fact, you must specify a value for one attribute of this element—**src**, which holds the URL of the document the frame will display.

Here's an example from the beginning of this chapter, showing how to use the **<frame>** element to create two frames inside a frameset that renders them as vertical frames:

```
<?xml version="1.0"?>
<!DOCTYPE html PUBLIC "-//W3C//DTD XHTML 1.0 Frameset//EN"
 "http://www.w3.org/TR/xhtml1/DTD/xhtml1-frameset.dtd">
<html xmlns="http://www.w3.org/1999/xhtml" xml:lang="en" lang="en">
    <head>
        <title>
            Creating Frames
        </title>
    </head>

    <frameset cols = "50%, 50%">
        <frame src="frame1.htm" />
        <frame src="frame2.htm" />
    </frameset>

</html>
```

The result of this XHTML appears in Figure 7.4. As you can see in the list of attributes for this element, there are a lot of options here, too. I'll be exploring this element and **<frameset>** throughout the rest of the chapter.

Creating Vertical Frames

The big boss appears and says, "I want to divide our company Web page into two vertical frames, consolidating the content that's there now into one frame, and displaying something new in the other." "OK," you say; "I can use the **<frameset>** and **<frame>** tags for that. What's going to be in the new frame?" "A picture of me, of course," says the BB.

To divide a document into vertical frames, you use the **cols** attribute of the **<frameset>** element. You assign to this attribute a comma-separated list of values indicating the width of the columns you want to create. (Specify the values in pixel measurements, with percentages, or by using an asterisk to indicate that the frame or frames should be given the remaining available space.)

Here's an example from the beginning of this chapter. In this case, I'm creating two vertical frames:

```
<?xml version="1.0"?>
<!DOCTYPE html PUBLIC "-//W3C//DTD XHTML 1.0 Frameset//EN"
"http://www.w3.org/TR/xhtml1/DTD/xhtml1-frameset.dtd">
<html xmlns="http://www.w3.org/1999/xhtml" xml:lang="en" lang="en">
    <head>
        <title>
            Creating Frames
        </title>
    </head>

    <frameset cols = "50%, 50%">
        <frame src="frame1.htm" />
        <frame src="frame2.htm" />
    </frameset>

</html>
```

You can see the results of this XHTML in Figure 7.4. If I had wanted to create three columns with widths of 35, 35, and 30 percent, I could have done this:

```
<?xml version="1.0"?>
<!DOCTYPE html PUBLIC "-//W3C//DTD XHTML 1.0 Frameset//EN"
"http://www.w3.org/TR/xhtml1/DTD/xhtml1-frameset.dtd">
<html xmlns="http://www.w3.org/1999/xhtml" xml:lang="en" lang="en">
    <head>
        <title>
            Creating Frames
        </title>
    </head>
```

```
        <frameset cols = "35%, 35%, 30%">
            <frame src="frame1.htm" />
            <frame src="frame2.htm" />
            <frame src="frame3.htm" />
        </frameset>

</html>
```

Of course, these are pretty basic examples—the following sections discuss examples of greater complexity.

Creating Horizontal Frames

"No, no, no," the big boss says, "I've changed my mind. I don't want to divide the company Web page into two vertical frames; I want to create two *horizontal* frames." "Hm," you say; "looks like it's time to use the **rows** attribute."

When creating frame layouts, you use the **cols** attribute of the **<frameset>** element to create vertical frames, and you use the **rows** attribute to create horizontal frames. You assign to these attributes a comma-separated list of values indicating the width of the columns or the height of the rows you want to create. (Specify the values in pixel measurements, with percentages, or by using an asterisk to indicate that the frame or frames should be given the remaining space.)

Here's an example from the beginning of this chapter, where I'm creating two horizontal frames:

```
<?xml version="1.0"?>
<!DOCTYPE html PUBLIC "-//W3C//DTD XHTML 1.0 Frameset//EN"
"http://www.w3.org/TR/xhtml1/DTD/xhtml1-frameset.dtd">
<html xmlns="http://www.w3.org/1999/xhtml" xml:lang="en" lang="en">
    <head>
        <title>
            Creating Frames
        </title>
    </head>

    <frameset rows = "50%, 50%">
        <frame src="frame1.htm" />
        <frame src="frame2.htm" />
    </frameset>

</html>
```

You can see the results of this XHTML in Figure 7.6. If you wanted to divide the page into three rows, taking 35, 35, and 30 percent of the vertical display area, you could do this:

```
<?xml version="1.0"?>
<!DOCTYPE html PUBLIC "-//W3C//DTD XHTML 1.0 Frameset//EN"
"http://www.w3.org/TR/xhtml1/DTD/xhtml1-frameset.dtd">
<html xmlns="http://www.w3.org/1999/xhtml" xml:lang="en" lang="en">
    <head>
        <title>
            Creating Frames
        </title>
    </head>

    <frameset rows = "35%, 35%, 30%">
        <frame src="frame1.htm" />
        <frame src="frame2.htm" />
        <frame src="frame3.htm" />
    </frameset>

</html>
```

These are still pretty elementary examples. See the next section for information about how to create both rows and columns in the same document.

Creating Both Horizontal and Vertical Frames

"OK," says the big boss, "I've got it now. I want to break the company Web page into two columns, each with three rows." "You're sure that's what you want?" you ask. "Probably," says the BB.

You can nest **<frameset>** elements to create first columns, then rows—or rows, then columns—in a document. Here's an example from the beginning of this chapter. In this example, I'm creating two columns, each with three rows of different sizes:

```
<?xml version="1.0"?>
<!DOCTYPE html PUBLIC "-//W3C//DTD XHTML 1.0 Frameset//EN"
"http://www.w3.org/TR/xhtml1/DTD/xhtml1-frameset.dtd">
<html xmlns="http://www.w3.org/1999/xhtml" xml:lang="en" lang="en">
    <head>
        <title>Row And Column Frames</title>
    </head>
```

```
        <frameset cols = "50%, 50%">
            <noframes>
                <body>
                    Your browser does not support frames...
                </body>
            </noframes>
            <frameset rows = "25%, 50%, 25%">
                <frame src="frame1.htm" />
                <frame src="frame2.htm" />
                <frame src="frame3.htm" />
            </frameset>

            <frameset rows = "25%, 25%, 50%">
                <frame src="frame1.htm" />
                <frame src="frame2.htm" />
                <frame src="frame3.htm" />
            </frameset>

        </frameset>

</html>
```

The result of this XHTML appears in Figure 7.7.

You don't have to have the same number of rows in each column. Here's an example in which there is one row in the left frame and three in the right:

```
<?xml version="1.0"?>
<!DOCTYPE html PUBLIC "-//W3C//DTD XHTML 1.0 Frameset//EN"
"http://www.w3.org/TR/xhtml1/DTD/xhtml1-frameset.dtd">
<html xmlns="http://www.w3.org/1999/xhtml" xml:lang="en" lang="en">
    <head>
        <title>Row And Column Frames</title>
    </head>

    <frameset cols = "30%, 70%">
        <noframes>
            <body>
                Your browser does not support frames...
            </body>
        </noframes>

        <frame src="frame1.htm" />

        <frameset rows = "25%, 25%, 50%">
            <frame src="frame1.htm" />
```

```
            <frame src="frame2.htm" />
            <frame src="frame3.htm" />
        </frameset>

    </frameset>

</html>
```

The results of this XHTML appear in Figure 7.8.

TIP: *You can actually specify **rows** and **cols** in the same **frameset** element. If you do, the nested **frame** references are assigned sequentially to the **cols** and then to the **rows** specification.*

Using Named Frames as Hyperlink Targets

"Well," says the novice programmer proudly, "I've finished my novel. Now I want to use frames to display it. I'll provide hyperlinks to each chapter in one frame and provide the chapter itself in the other frame. Good idea, eh?" "Sounds good," you say, "but how will you display a chapter when the user clicks a hyperlink?" "Hm," says the NP.

As discussed in the "In Depth" section of this chapter, you can name frames, and when you do, you can use those names as the targets of hyperlinks in the **<a>**, **<area>**, **<base>**, and **<form>** elements.

Here's an example, from the beginning of this chapter, that appears in Figure 7.9. In this case, I'm creating a vertical navigation bar of hyperlinks in the left frame and displaying the documents they are linked to in the right frame. When the user clicks a hyperlink, the associated page is loaded into the browser in the frame on the right, as you see in Figure 7.10. The following code is what the XHTML for the main document looks like. Note that I'm setting up the vertical navigation bar, menu.htm, in the left frame and displaying a default introductory page, default.htm (see Figure 7.9), in the right frame—I'm naming that frame "display":

```
<?xml version="1.0"?>
<!DOCTYPE html PUBLIC "-//W3C//DTD XHTML 1.0 Frameset//EN"
"http://www.w3.org/TR/xhtml1/DTD/xhtml1-frameset.dtd">
<html xmlns="http://www.w3.org/1999/xhtml" xml:lang="en" lang="en">
    <head>
        <title>
            Targeted Frames
        </title>
    </head>
```

```
        <frameset cols = "40%, 60%">
            <frame src = "menu.htm" />
            <frame src = "default.htm" id = "display" name = "display" />
        </frameset>
</html>
```

The following XHTML is the menu.htm file, which includes the hyperlink for the navigation bar. Note that I'm assigning the **<a>** element's **target** attribute the name of the frame in which I want to display pages, like this:

```
<?xml version="1.0"?>
<!DOCTYPE html PUBLIC "-//W3C//DTD XHTML 1.0 Transitional//EN"
"http://www.w3.org/tr/xhtml1/DTD/xhtml1-transitional.dtd">
<html xmlns="http://www.w3.org/1999/xhtml" xml:lang="en" lang="en">
    <head>
        <title>menu.htm</title>
    </head>

    <body>
    <ol>
        <li>
            <a href = "frame1.htm" target = "display">
            Let's see page 1
            </a>
        </li>
        <li>
            <a href = "frame2.htm" target = "display">
            Let's see page 2
            </a>
        </li>
        <li>
            <a href = "frame3.htm" target = "display">
            Let's see page 3
            </a>
        </li>
    </ol>
    </body>
</html>
```

Because I've named a frame "display" and set up the hyperlinks to load into that frame, any pages that these hyperlinks load into the browser will be sent to that frame. In this way, you can create navigation bars easily, letting the user move around your site at will.

TIP: *A number of predefined target names are available. For instance, **_blank** opens a new, unnamed browser window. Take a look at the next section for more details.*

Using Predefined Target Names

There are several predefined target names that you can assign to the **target** attribute of the **<a>**, **<area>**, **<base>**, and **<form>** elements. The following list contains predefined target names and what they mean:

- **_blank**—Opens documents in a new, unnamed browser window.
- **_self**—Opens documents in the same window or frame.
- **_parent**—Opens documents in the **<frameset>** parent of the current document. (If there is no parent, **_self** is used.)
- **_top**—Replaces the current document when the linked-to document is opened. This is the same as **_self** except that **_top** replaces the entire top-level document, not just the current frame, if there is one.

TIP: When you want to replace the entire current document—for instance, when you're linking to another site—set **target="_top"**.

<noframes>—Handling Browsers That Don't Handle Frames

Purpose: Displays content in browsers that don't support frames.

When used as HTML: Start tag/End tag: Required/Required

Supported: [1.0T, 1.0F, 4, IE3, IE4, IE5, NS2, NS3, NS4]

Attributes:

- **class**—Class of the element (used for rendering). [1.0T, 1.0F, 4]
- **dir**—Gives the direction of directionally neutral text (text that doesn't have an inherent direction in which you should read it). Possible values: **ltr**, left-to-right text or table; and **rtl**, right-to-left text or table. [1.0T, 1.0F, 4]
- **id**—Unique alphanumeric identifier for the tag; use the ID to refer to the tag. [1.0T, 1.0F, 4, IE4, IE5]
- **lang**—Base language used for the tag. [1.0T, 1.0F]
- **style**—Inline style indicating how to render the element. [1.0T, 1.0F, 4]
- **title**—Holds additional information (which might be displayed in tool tips). [1.0T, 1.0F, 4]
- **xml:lang**—Holds the base language for the element when the document is interpreted as an XML document. [1.0T, 1.0F]

XHTML events: None

The novice programmer enters and says, "I'm using my favorite Web browser, SuperDuperWebProKing 5.3, patch level 97, which may be a little nonstandard, and I'm afraid it doesn't support frames. What the heck can I do?" "One thing you can do," you say, "is to include a **<noframes>** element. That's what you do when a browser can't handle frames." "Hm," says the NP, "tell me all about it."

Older browsers can't handle frames. Frames were introduced in Netscape Navigator 2 and were then implemented in Internet Explorer 3. You use the **<noframes>** element to handle them in older browsers; this element is supported in the XHTML 1.0 Transitional and Frameset DTDs. Browsers that handle frames will ignore the content of this element; browsers that don't handle frames will display the content directly. This means you can place a hyperlink to a frameless version of your page in the **<noframes>** element. In fact, you can include the entire XHTML of the frameless version of your page in the **<noframes>** element.

We saw this example in the beginning of this chapter:

```
<?xml version="1.0"?>
<!DOCTYPE html PUBLIC "-//W3C//DTD XHTML 1.0 Frameset//EN"
"http://www.w3.org/TR/xhtml1/DTD/xhtml1-frameset.dtd">
<html xmlns="http://www.w3.org/1999/xhtml" xml:lang="en" lang="en">
    <head>
        <title>
            Creating Frames
        </title>
    </head>

    <frameset cols = "50%, 50%">
        <noframes>
            <body>
                Your browser does not support frames...
            </body>
        </noframes>
        <frame src="frame1.htm" />
        <frame src="frame2.htm" />
    </frameset>

</html>
```

You can see the results of this XHTML in a browser that does not support frames—Microsoft Word, which can open rudimentary Web pages. See Figure 7.5.

Opening New Browser Windows

"Hey," the novice programmer says, "I just saw something cool. When I clicked a link, my browser opened a whole new, separate window and displayed the new page in it." "That's easy," you say; "you just set the hyperlink's **target** attribute to a new window name, one that doesn't match any named frame."

To open a new browser window when the user clicks a hyperlink, you can set the **target** attribute of the **<a>**, **<area>**, **<base>**, and **<form>** elements to the name you select for a new window.

Here's an example from the beginning of this chapter:

```
<?xml version="1.0"?>
<!DOCTYPE html PUBLIC "-//W3C//DTD XHTML 1.0 Transitional//EN"
"http://www.w3.org/tr/xhtml1/DTD/xhtml1-transitional.dtd">
<html xmlns="http://www.w3.org/1999/xhtml" xml:lang="en" lang="en">
    <head>
        <title>menu.htm</title>
    </head>

    <body>
    <ol>
        <li>
            <a href = "frame1.htm" target = "a">
            Let's see page 1
            </a>
        </li>
        <li>
            <a href = "frame2.htm" target = "b">
            Let's see page 2
            </a>
        </li>
        <li>
            <a href = "frame3.htm" target = "c">
            Let's see page 3
            </a>
        </li>
    </ol>
    </body>
</html>
```

In the previous example, I'm opening new, freestanding browser windows each time the user clicks a hyperlink; I do this by supplying different target names—"**a**", "**b**", and "**c**"—to each hyperlink. These target names do not correspond to any named frames in the document.

Note that the browser remembers the name you've given to the new browser window, so you can send all hyperlinked documents to the same new window by using the same target name, like this:

```
<?xml version="1.0"?>
<!DOCTYPE html PUBLIC "-//W3C//DTD XHTML 1.0 Transitional//EN"
"http://www.w3.org/tr/xhtml1/DTD/xhtml1-transitional.dtd">
<html xmlns="http://www.w3.org/1999/xhtml" xml:lang="en" lang="en">
    <head>
        <title>menu.htm</title>
    </head>

    <body>
    <ol>
        <li>
            <a href = "frame1.htm" target = "newwindow">
            Let's see page 1
            </a>
        </li>
        <li>
            <a href = "frame2.htm" target = "newwindow">
            Let's see page 2
            </a>
        </li>
        <li>
            <a href = "frame3.htm" target = "newwindow">
            Let's see page 3
            </a>
        </li>
    </ol>
    </body>
</html>
```

Creating Borderless Frames

"No, no, no," says the big boss, "we don't have the right look at all on the company Web site. Take a look at our competitor's Web site; their frames don't have any borders between them and they look a lot slicker." "Hm," you say, "I can remove the borders from our frames." "You're hired," says the BB. "I already work here," you say.

To remove the borders around frames, you can use the **frameborder** attribute of the **<frame>** and **<frameset>** elements and the **framespacing** attribute of the **<frameset>** element in Internet Explorer, or **border** in Netscape Navigator. To remove the borders around a frame, set the corresponding **<frame>** element's **frameborder** attribute to zero in Internet Explorer or **no** in Netscape Navigator; to remove the border around all frames, set the enclosing **<frameset>** element's **frameborder** and **framespacing** elements to zero.

Here's an example showing how to remove borders:

```xml
<?xml version="1.0"?>
<!DOCTYPE html PUBLIC "-//W3C//DTD XHTML 1.0 Frameset//EN"
"http://www.w3.org/TR/xhtml1/DTD/xhtml1-frameset.dtd">
<html xmlns="http://www.w3.org/1999/xhtml" xml:lang="en" lang="en">
    <head>
        <title>Borderless Frame Example</title>
    </head>

    <frameset rows = "110, *" frameborder = "0" framespacing = "0">
        <frame src = "frame1.htm" scrolling = "no" noresize = "noresize" />
        <frameset cols = "145, *">
            <frame id = "frame2" name = "frame2"
                src = "frame2.htm" scrolling = "no"
                noresize = "noresize" />
            <frame id = "frame3" name = "frame3"
                src = "frame3.htm" scrolling = "yes"
                noresize = "noresize" />
        </frameset>
    </frameset>
</html>
```

You can see the results of this XHTML in Figure 7.12; there are no borders between the frames. Note that I've used the **scrolling** attribute to set the scrolling behavior of the frames and used the **noresize** attribute to specify that the frames may not be resized.

TIP: *Netscape Navigator doesn't place frames right next to each other when this is requested, but instead leaves a thin white line between frames. You can fix this by setting **border** to **0** in the **<frameset>** element or by using a table instead of frames and setting **cellspacing** and **cellpadding** to **0**.*

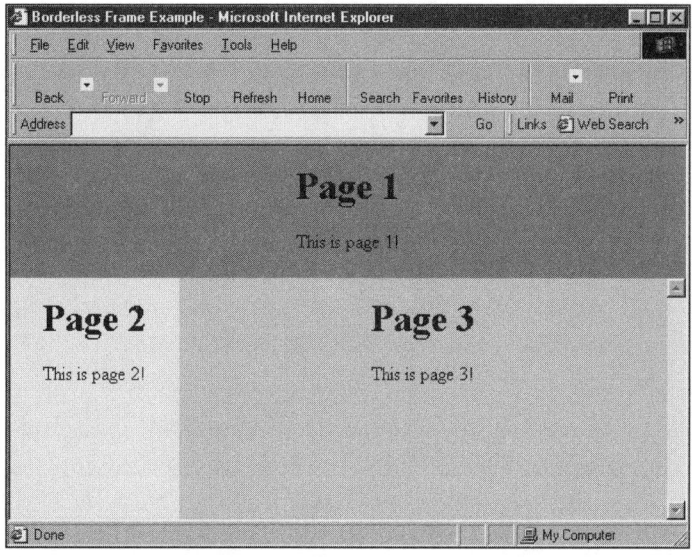

Figure 7.12 Borderless frames.

Creating Navigation Bars

The big boss is back and says, "We need navigation bars that will always stay visible to the users as they move through our site. I've been getting complaints that our site is too hard to use." "OK," you say; "what about creating a navigation bar using frames?" "Let's see it," the BB says, "and then I'll let you know."

Here's an example of using borderless named frames to create a horizontal navigation bar at the top of the browser's display area:

```
<?xml version="1.0"?>
<!DOCTYPE html PUBLIC "-//W3C//DTD XHTML 1.0 Frameset//EN"
"http://www.w3.org/TR/xhtml1/DTD/xhtml1-frameset.dtd">
<html xmlns="http://www.w3.org/1999/xhtml" xml:lang="en" lang="en">
    <head>
        <title>
            Borderless Frame Example
        </title>
    </head>

    <frameset rows = "50, *" frameborder = "0" framespacing = "0">

        <frame src = "menu.htm" scrolling = "no" noresize = "noresize" />
```

```
            <frameset cols = "165, *">

                <frame id = "frame2" name = "frame2" src = "default.htm"
                    scrolling = "no" noresize = "noresize" />
                <frame id = "display" name = "display" src = "frame3.htm"
                    scrolling = "yes" noresize = "noresize" />

            </frameset>

        </frameset>

</html>
```

And following is the page with the hyperlinks in it, menu.htm. (Note that I'm including nonbreaking spaces—whose character entities are ** **—to add spaces between the hyperlinks; see Chapter 2 for more on character entities.) Here's the code:

```
<?xml version="1.0"?>
<!DOCTYPE html PUBLIC "-//W3C//DTD XHTML 1.0 Transitional//EN"
    "http://www.w3.org/tr/xhtml1/DTD/xhtml1-transitional.dtd">
<html xmlns="http://www.w3.org/1999/xhtml" xml:lang="en" lang="en">
    <head>
        <title>menu.htm</title>
    </head>

    <body bgcolor="lightgreen">
        <center>
            <a href = "frame1.htm" target = "display">
                Let's see page 1
            </a>

             

            <a href = "frame2.htm" target = "display">
                Let's see page 2
            </a>

             

            <a href = "frame2.htm" target = "display">
                Let's see page 3
            </a>
        </center>
    </body>
</html>
```

You can see the results of this XHTML in Figure 7.13. (The figure shows the results in Internet Explorer; in Netscape Navigator, set **border** to **0** in the **<frameset>** element to get the same results.) The borderless navigation bar does indeed appear at the top of the browser window. When the user clicks a hyperlink, the browser loads the corresponding page into the display area under the navigation bar. Note that using images in your hyperlinks would improve the appearance of pages like this one.

Here's another example; this time, the navigation bar is on the left side:

```
<?xml version="1.0"?>
<!DOCTYPE html PUBLIC "-//W3C//DTD XHTML 1.0 Frameset//EN"
"http://www.w3.org/TR/xhtml1/DTD/xhtml1-frameset.dtd">
<html xmlns="http://www.w3.org/1999/xhtml" xml:lang="en" lang="en">
    <head>
        <title>
            Targeted Frames
        </title>
    </head>

    <frameset cols = "40%, 60%">
        <frame src = "menu.htm" />
        <frame src = "default.htm" id = "display" name = "display" />
    </frameset>
</html>
```

Here's the new version of menu.htm, the document I'm using to hold the hyperlinks:

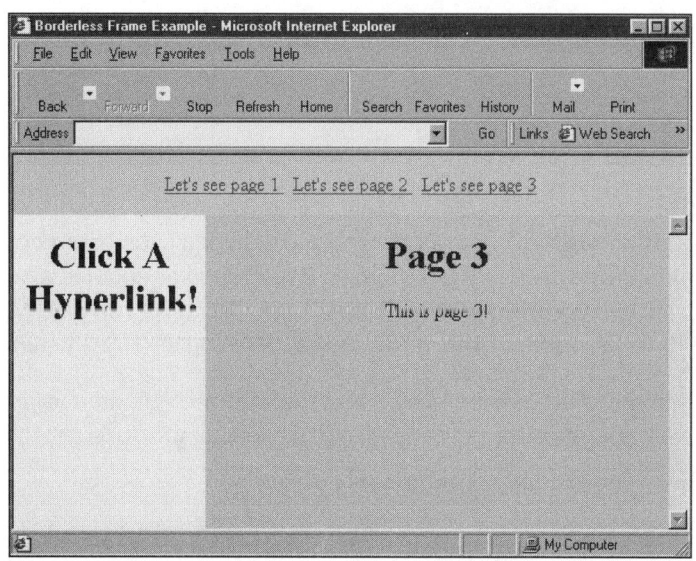

Figure 7.13   A borderless horizontal navigation bar.

```
<?xml version="1.0"?>
<!DOCTYPE html PUBLIC "-//W3C//DTD XHTML 1.0 Transitional//EN"
"http://www.w3.org/tr/xhtml1/DTD/xhtml1-transitional.dtd">
<html xmlns="http://www.w3.org/1999/xhtml" xml:lang="en" lang="en">
    <head>
        <title>menu.htm</title>
    </head>

    <body>
    <ol>
        <li>
            <a href = "frame1.htm" target = "display">
            Let's see page 1
            </a>
        </li>
        <li>
            <a href = "frame2.htm" target = "display">
            Let's see page 2
            </a>
        </li>
        <li>
            <a href = "frame3.htm" target = "display">
            Let's see page 3
            </a>
        </li>
    </ol>
    </body>
</html>
```

You can see the results of this XHTML in Figure 7.10.

Enabling and Disabling Scrolling

"Consistency, that's what we want," says the Web-page design czar. "Some of our frames have scrollbars, some don't." "That's because the browser decides whether or not there are scrollbars for frames, which it does by default," you say. "All of our frames should have scrollbars," the WPDC says. "See to it." "Hm," you say.

You can turn scrolling on or off in frames by using the **<frame>** element's **scrolling** attribute. The following list contains the possible settings for this attribute:

- **auto**—Lets the browser display scrollbars as needed.
- **no**—Never displays scrollbars.
- **yes**—Always displays scrollbars.

In this next example, I'm displaying scrollbars in two of the three frames, like this:

```
<?xml version="1.0"?>
<!DOCTYPE html PUBLIC "-//W3C//DTD XHTML 1.0 Frameset//EN"
"http://www.w3.org/TR/xhtml1/DTD/xhtml1-frameset.dtd">
<html xmlns="http://www.w3.org/1999/xhtml" xml:lang="en" lang="en">
    <head>
        <title>
            Borderless Frame Example
        </title>
    </head>

    <frameset rows = "80, *" frameborder = "0" framespacing = "0">

        <frame src = "frame1.htm" scrolling = "yes"
            noresize = "noresize" />

        <frameset cols = "200, *">
            <frame id = "frame2" name = "frame2" src = "frame2.htm"
                scrolling = "no" noresize = "noresize" />
            <frame id = "frame3" name = "frame3" src = "frame3.htm"
                scrolling = "yes" noresize = "noresize" />
        </frameset>

    </frameset>

</html>
```

You can see the results in Figure 7.14. (The figure shows results in Internet Explorer; to get the same results in Netscape Navigator, set **border** to "0" in the **<frameset>** element.)

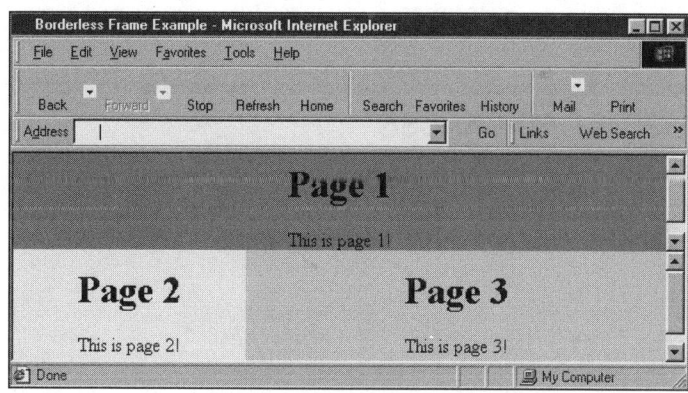

Figure 7.14   Frames with and without scrollbars.

Stopping Frames from Being Resized

By default, the user can resize frames in a browser just by dragging them with the mouse. You can, however, disable this feature by using the **noresize** attribute in the **<frame>** element. Following is an example from the previous section showing how this works. Note that because **noresize** is a standalone attribute, you must assign it some value in XHTML, and I assign it the value "**noresize**" here:

```
<?xml version="1.0"?>
<!DOCTYPE html PUBLIC "-//W3C//DTD XHTML 1.0 Frameset//EN"
"http://www.w3.org/TR/xhtml1/DTD/xhtml1-frameset.dtd">
<html xmlns="http://www.w3.org/1999/xhtml" xml:lang="en" lang="en">
    <head>
        <title>
            Borderless Frame Example
        </title>
    </head>

    <frameset rows = "110, *" frameborder = "0" framespacing = "0"
        border = "0">
        <frame src = "frame1.htm" scrolling = "no"
            noresize = "noresize" />
        <frameset cols = "145, *">
            <frame id = "frame2" name = "frame2" src = "frame2.htm"
                scrolling = "no" noresize = "noresize" />
            <frame id = "frame3" name = "frame3" src = "frame3.htm"
                scrolling = "yes" noresize = "noresize" />
        </frameset>
    </frameset>

</html>
```

Setting Frame Border Thickness

You can set the thickness of frame borders by using the **<frameset>** element's **framespacing** attribute in Internet Explorer. Here's an example in which I'm setting the thickness of the borders of frames to 10 pixels:

```
<?xml version="1.0"?>
<!DOCTYPE html PUBLIC "-//W3C//DTD XHTML 1.0 Frameset//EN"
"http://www.w3.org/TR/xhtml1/DTD/xhtml1-frameset.dtd">
<html xmlns="http://www.w3.org/1999/xhtml" xml:lang="en" lang="en">
    <head>
        <title>
```

```
        Border Example
    </title>
</head>

<frameset rows = "110, *" frameborder="1" framespacing="10">
    <frame src = "frame1.htm" scrolling = "no"
        noresize = "noresize" />
    <frameset cols = "145, *">
        <frame id = "frame2" name = "frame2" src = "frame2.htm"
            scrolling = "no" noresize = "noresize" />
        <frame id = "frame3" name = "frame3" src = "frame3.htm"
            scrolling = "yes" noresize = "noresize" />
    </frameset>
</frameset>

</html>
```

The results of this XHTML appear in Figure 7.15.

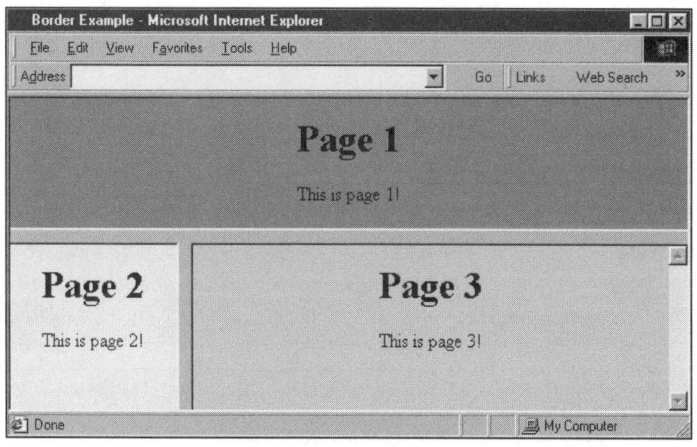

Figure 7.15   Frames with 10-pixel borders.

Setting Frame Color

You can set the color of frames by using the **<frameset>** and **<frame>** elements' **bordercolor** attribute. Here's an example in which I'm making the frame borders red:

```
<?xml version="1.0"?>
<!DOCTYPE html PUBLIC "-//W3C//DTD XHTML 1.0 Frameset//EN"
"http://www.w3.org/TR/xhtml1/DTD/xhtml1-frameset.dtd">
<html xmlns="http://www.w3.org/1999/xhtml" xml:lang="en" lang="en">
```

```
<head>
    <title>
        Border Example
    </title>
</head>

<frameset rows = "110, *" frameborder="1" bordercolor="red">

    <frame src = "frame1.htm" scrolling = "no"
        noresize = "noresize" />

    <frameset cols = "145, *">

        <frame id = "frame2" name = "frame2" src = "frame2.htm"
         scrolling = "no" noresize = "noresize" />
        <frame id = "frame3" name = "frame3" src = "frame3.htm"
         scrolling = "yes" noresize = "noresize" />

    </frameset>

</frameset>

</html>
```

The results of this XHTML appear in Figure 7.16.

NOTE: You can set the **bordercolor** attribute of both the **<frameset>** and **<frame>** elements. What if you set both and there's a conflict? Here's what happens: The attributes in the outermost element have the lowest precedence; attributes are overridden by attributes in nested **<frameset>** elements; and finally, attributes in the current **<frame>** element take precedence over attributes in the enclosing **<frameset>** element.

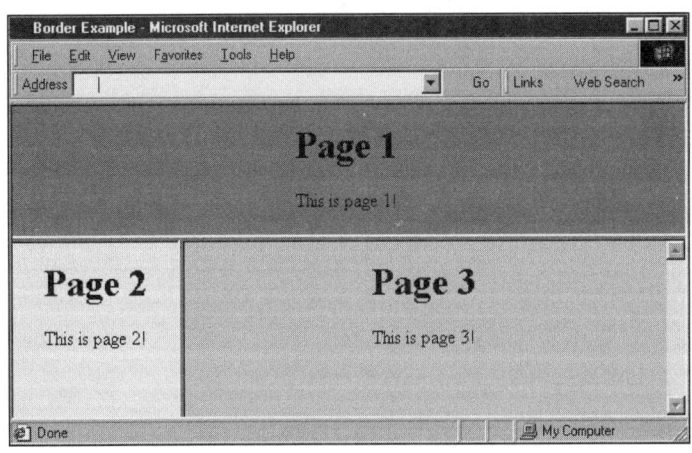

Figure 7.16 Using frame colors.

<iframe>—Creating Inline or Floating Frames

Purpose: Creates an inline or floating frame.

When used as HTML: Start tag/End tag: Required/Required

Supported: [1.0T, 1.0F, 4, IE3, IE4, IE5]

Attributes:

- **align**—Specifies alignment of text following on the screen, much as you align text with images. Possible values: **left**, **right**, **top**, **middle**, and **bottom**. [1.0T, 1.0F, 4, IE4, IE5]
- **class**—Class of the element (used for rendering). [1.0T, 1.0F, 4, IE4, IE5]
- **datafld**—Name of the column of the data-source object that supplies the bound data. Set to alphanumeric characters. [IE4, IE5]
- **datasrc**—Gives the URL or ID of the data-source object supplying data bound to this element. The World Wide Web Consortium (W3C) says this should be a URL; IE says it should be a data-source ID. [IE4, IE5]
- **dir**—Gives the direction of directionally neutral text (text that doesn't have an inherent direction in which you should read it). Possible values: **ltr**, left-to-right text or table; and **rtl**, right-to-left text or table. [1.0T, 1.0F]
- **frameborder**—Specifies whether or not borders surround the frame. For Netscape Navigator, set to **yes** (the default) or **no**; for Internet Explorer lists, set to **1** (the default) or **0** (no border). [1.0T, 1.0F, 4, IE3, IE4, IE5]
- **height**—Sets the height of the frame in pixels. As with images, you can set aside the appropriate space for the frame in the page by using the **height** and **width** properties. Set to positive integers. [1.0T, 1.0F, 4]
- **hspace**—Specifies horizontal spacing, in pixels, around the frame. Set to positive integers. [IE3, IE4, IE5]
- **id**—Unique alphanumeric identifier for the tag; use the ID to refer to the tag. [1.0T, 1.0F, 4, IE4, IE5]
- **lang**—Base language used for the tag. [1.0T, 1.0F, IE4, IE5]
- **language**—Scripting language used for the tag. [IE4, IE5]
- **longdesc**—Indicates the URL for a longer description of the frame contents. Set to a URL. [1.0T, 1.0F, 4]
- **marginheight**—Sets the size of the top and bottom margins used in the frame. Set to a pixel value. [1.0T, 1.0F, 4, IE3, IE4, IE5]
- **marginwidth**—Sets the size of the right and left margins used in the frame. Set to a pixel value. [1.0T, 1.0F, 4, IE3, IE4, IE5]

- **name**—Sets the name of the frame. You can use named frames as target destinations for **<a>**, **<area>**, **<base>**, and **<form>** elements. Set to a text string. [1.0T, 1.0F, 4, IE3, IE4, IE5]

- **scrolling**—Determines scrollbar action. Possible values: **auto** (the default; lets the browser decide when to display scrollbars), **yes** (always show a scrollbar), or **no** (never show a scrollbar). [1.0T, 1.0F, 4, IE3, IE4, IE5]

- **src**—Specifies the URL of the frame document. If you don't specify a URL, the frame will appear blank. Set to a URL. Required. [1.0T, 1.0F, 4, IE3, IE4, IE5]

- **style**—Inline style indicating how to render the element. [1.0T, 1.0F, 4, IE4, IE5]

- **title**—Holds additional information (which might be displayed in tool tips). [1.0T, 1.0F, 4, IE4, IE5]

- **vspace**—Specifies the vertical spacing, in pixels, around the frame. Set to positive integers. [IE3, IE4, IE5]

- **width**—Sets the width of the frame in pixels. As with images, you can set aside the appropriate space for the frame in the page by using the **height** and **width** properties. Set to positive integers. [1.0T, 1.0F, 4]

- **xml:lang**—Holds the base language for the element when the document is interpreted as an XML document. [1.0T, 1.0F]

XHTML events: None

The novice programmer wants to know, "Why do frames have to be right up against the edge of the browser window? Can't they be in the middle?" "In the middle?" asks the Web-page design czar, "What an idea!" You say, "It's possible."

Internet Explorer supports *inline frames*, which are also called *floating frames*. Inline frames can appear wherever you want them, including in the middle of the page. All you have to do is specify the height and width of the frame and specify the XHTML page to load into it, and you're set. Inline frames are supported with the **<iframe>** element, which in many ways is Internet Explorer's answer to Netscape Navigator's **<layer>** element. You can use inline frames to display a number of pages in one, and if you turn the borders off (see the next section), the result can be much like using the **<layer>** element.

Here's an example showing how to create two inline frames; note that because both the XHTML 1.0 Transitional and Frameset DTDs support **<iframe>**, I can use the Transitional DTD here:

Immediate Solutions

```
<?xml version="1.0"?>
<!DOCTYPE html PUBLIC "-//W3C//DTD XHTML 1.0 Transitional//EN"
    "http://www.w3.org/tr/xhtml1/DTD/xhtml1-transitional.dtd">
<html xmlns="http://www.w3.org/1999/xhtml" xml:lang="en" lang="en">
    <head>
        <title>
            Inline Frames!
        </title>
    </head>

    <body bgcolor="black">

        <center>
            <br />
            <br />

            <iframe width = "50%" height = "25%" id = "frame1"
                name = "frame1" src="frame1.htm">
            </iframe>


            <iframe width = "50%" height = "25%" id = "frame2"
                name = "frame2" src="frame2.htm">
            </iframe>


            <br />
            <br />

        </center>

    </body>

</html>
```

You can see the results in Figure 7.17. Note that it's up to the browser to place these frames, much like other elements, such as images.

NOTE: *Some versions of Internet Explorer, prior to the late beta versions of Internet Explorer 3, used extensions to the <frame> element to create inline frames, so it's possible you might run into this.*

TIP: *Internet Explorer lists a **border** attribute for the <iframe> element, but it actually appears to add padding (like **hspace** and **vspace**) around the frames, not an actual border.*

Chapter 7 Working with Frames

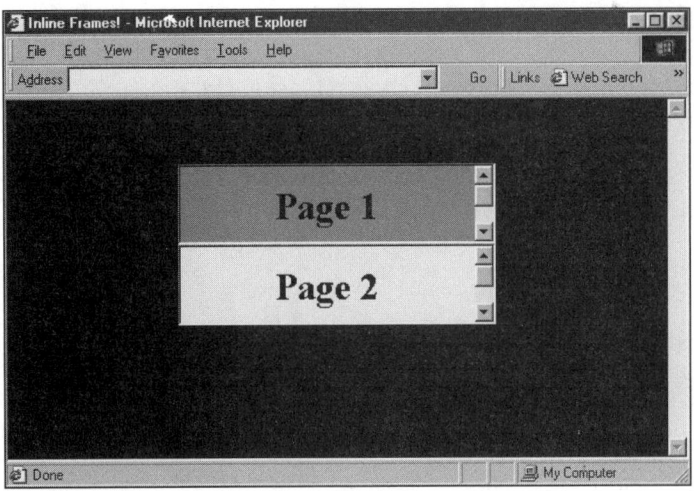

Figure 7.17 Using inline frames.

Creating Borderless Inline Frames

You can make inline frames borderless, and you do so just as you would with standard frames. Use the **frameborder** attribute to make the frame border invisible (by setting this attribute to **0**), and use the **scrolling** attribute to turn off the scrollbars (by setting this attribute to "**no**").

Here's an example showing how to display borderless inline frames:

```
<?xml version="1.0"?>
<!DOCTYPE html PUBLIC "-//W3C//DTD XHTML 1.0 Transitional//EN"
    "http://www.w3.org/tr/xhtml1/DTD/xhtml1-transitional.dtd">
<html xmlns="http://www.w3.org/1999/xhtml" xml:lang="en" lang="en">
    <head>
        <title>
            Inline Frames!
        </title>
    </head>

    <body bgcolor="black">

        <center>
            <br />
            <br />
```

```
            <iframe width = "50%" height = "25%" id = "frame1"
                name = "frame1" src="frame1.htm" frameborder="0"
                scrolling="no">
            </iframe>

            <iframe width = "50%" height = "25%" id = "frame2"
                name = "frame2" src="frame2.htm" frameborder="0"
                scrolling="no">
            </iframe>

        <br />
        <br />

    </center>

</body>

</html>
```

The results of this XHTML appear in Figure 7.18, where you can see that each inline frame is now borderless.

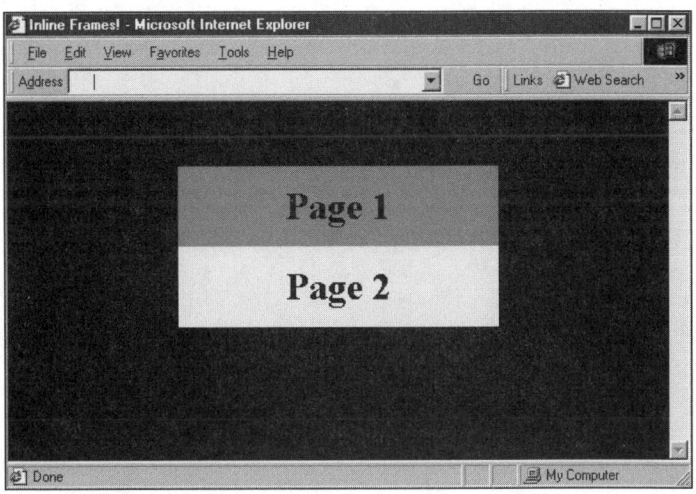

Figure 7.18 Borderless inline frames.

Chapter 8

Working with Multimedia

If you need an immediate solution to:	See page:
Creating Links to External Multimedia Files	470
What MIME Types Are Available?	471
<bgsound>—Adding Background Sounds	477
<embed>—Embedding Multimedia and Plug-Ins in a Web Page	479
<noembed>—Handling Browsers That Don't Handle Embedding	481
Creating Inline Sounds	482
<object> and <param>—Placing an Object into a Web Page	484
Creating Inline Video	494
Displaying Loading Images for Inline Video	496
Using Scrolling Marquees	498
Using Internet Explorer's Multimedia Controls	499

Chapter 8 Working with Multimedia

In Depth

There are plenty of multimedia sources out there in the world—CDs, video players, televisions, DVD players, and more. If the Web is going to compete with all of these media, it has to provide the same kind of multimedia support and even improve on it. As you know, the Web is reacting to this challenge. You now find Web pages with inline video, sound, and Shockwave presentations everywhere, and there's more coming all the time. I'll take a look at how multimedia has been developing on the Web and in Web browsers in this chapter. Much of this chapter has to do with what's available in the popular browsers today, so we'll see a number of browser-specific elements here that are not standard XHTML (and so strictly speaking, the pages that use those elements are not standard XHTML either).

There are two main ways of handling multimedia in a Web browser—as inline or external data, similar to working with images. *Inline multimedia* refers to files and data that are handled as part of the page and that play when the page is visible. You can embed video and sound in pages in many ways. You can also link to external files by using hyperlinks. For example, when the user clicks a hyperlink, the browser asks if it should download the corresponding file, and when it does download the file, it *launches* (that is, starts playing) that file with an external application, such as the Windows Media Player.

How does the browser know which application can handle the multimedia data? It can check the file extension—such as .jpg or .gif or .avi—if there is one. If the browser can match the extension with an application (which might be the Web browser itself), it can open the file. Also, when data is sent from the Web server, the server notifies the browser of the type of data by sending the data's Multipurpose Internet Mail Extension (MIME) type. There are a variety of MIME types, and I'll list them in this chapter; see the "Immediate Solutions" section "What MIME Types Are Available?"

NOTE: *You don't usually have to worry about MIME types unless you're doing something like sending binary data streams from programs on your Web server, as you can with Perl scripts. You will also need to be familiar with MIME types if you're using the* **<object>** *element or if your Web server can't handle the format of data you want to transfer through it because it doesn't know that data's MIME type.*

Netscape Navigator can handle multimedia in various formats with plug-ins. A *plug-in* is an application that fits smoothly into Netscape Navigator and handles data that the browser itself doesn't, often displaying multimedia inline in the Web page. If a plug-in that you don't have is needed, Netscape Navigator will ask you if the plug-in, which it can usually find from **netscape.com**, should be installed. You can find a complete list of available plug-ins at **http://home.netscape.com/plugins/index.html**. Here are some of the more popular plug-ins:

- *Crescendo*—Displays a CD-like control panel to let you stream Musical Instrument Digital Interface (MIDI) music. Written by LiveUpdate; see **www.liveupdate.com/crescendo.html**.

- *Flash Player*—Lets you stream animations directly to the browser (as does Shockwave). Streaming is useful because your browser can play the animations as it gets data without having to wait for all the data to be downloaded. For more information, see Macromedia's site, **www.macromedia.com**.

- *mBED*—Lets you display animations, sounds, interactive video, and RealAudio. Written by mBED Software; see **www.mbed.com**.

- *Shockwave*—Handles Macromedia Director movies. Macromedia Director is very popular among multimedia CD developers, and many multimedia presentations and games are written in it. Because of the power of Macromedia Director in creating terrific animations, Shockwave has become very popular. For more about Macromedia Director, see **www.macromedia.com**.

- *Sizzler*—Lets you view and interact with Web pages and supports animation streaming. Written by Totally Hip Software; see **www.totallyhip.com/Products/Products.html**.

TIP: *Some plug-ins, such as the Shockwave plug-in, come with Netscape Navigator (although you can elect not to install them when you install Netscape Navigator), but others do not. When you rely on a plug-in, it's often a good idea to be sure that the users of your page have the plug-in they'll need. (You can do that in JavaScript by checking the special Netscape Navigator **plugins** collection.)*

As of version 3, Internet Explorer also supports the **<embed>** element. Microsoft's preference, however, is to use ActiveX controls, which you embed with the **<object>** element to handle data in various multimedia formats. (ActiveX controls are often stored in Windows systems in the \Windows\System directory, in files with the extension .ocx.)

If Internet Explorer needs an ActiveX control that's not already installed on your machine, it will ask you before downloading and installing it. (You can specify the location of the ActiveX control with a URL in the **<object>** element's **codebase** attribute.) Internet Explorer has good multimedia support built into it, as we'll see throughout this chapter, but you can augment that support with ActiveX controls.

I'll take a look at that here as well; see the "Immediate Solutions" section, "<object> and <param>—Placing an Object into a Web Page."

I'll start digging into the details of handling multimedia in the next section. There are two main multimedia categories: sound and video. I'll concentrate on both and take a look at 3D multimedia as well.

Multimedia Sound

Using sound is one of the most popular uses of multimedia on the Web today because most computers are equipped to play sound. In fact, you can even add background music to Web pages, although that's becoming less and less popular as Web authors seem to realize how annoying it can be. I've seen page after page add and then remove background sounds. On the other hand, sound that you actually ask to hear is getting more and more popular. This includes *streaming* sound formats—such as RealAudio (also called *Web radio*)—which let you play sounds in real time as they're downloaded.

To convert sounds to digital files, computers take *samples* of those sounds. Each sample records the current amplitude of the sound wave. The more frequently you sample the sound wave, the better the reproduction of the sound. What's actually stored in the sound file are the sample measurements, usually compressed to take up less space. The software that plays back the sound uses those measurements to reproduce the sound wave.

NOTE: *Typical sampling rates today are 11kHz, 22kHz, and 44kHz. Samples are typically stored in 8-bit or 16-bit format, which is why you see ads for software that can handle 16-bit sound.*

There are a number of sound formats available, each with plusses and minuses. I'll take a look at the popular ones in the following sections.

μ-Law (AU) Sound Format

Probably the most popular sound format is the μ-Law, or AU, format (the μ is the Greek letter mu) because of its cross-platform capabilities. (Even the European version, called A-law, is in the same format.) Sun Microsystems and NeXT Computer Corporation use this sound format as their standard. When you see the extension .au on a sound file, you'll know you're dealing with a μ-Law sound file.

The sampling rate of the μ-Law sound format is quite low: only 8kHz (although there are some versions with nonstandard higher sampling rates). In addition, this sound is monophonic, not stereo, and it stores samples in 8-bit format only.

The upshot to using this sound format is that you'll be pretty sure users will be able to play it.

AIFF Sound Format

Audio Interchange File Format (AIFF) was developed by Apple Computer and is used mostly on the Macintosh. This format has built-in compression, 8-bit or 16-bit sampling, and mono or stereo sound. The extensions on files in this format are .aiff or .aif.

The compression algorithm used with AIFF is called Macintosh Audio Compression/Expansion (MACE), which comes in two versions: 3 to 1 compression, MACE3; and 6 to 1 compression, MACE6. Both compression schemes lose some sound fidelity.

Although AIFF is a good format, it is usually limited to the Macintosh.

Macintosh SND Sound Format

The SND (short for *sound*) format is the basic Macintosh sound-recording format. It is used for internal files on the Macintosh. Because these files are usually Macintosh-only and relatively low fidelity, you won't find them on the Web very often. However, this format easily converts into other formats.

Windows WAV Sound Format

The WAV format (short for *waveform*) was developed by Microsoft and IBM, and because it was part of Windows 3.1, it became a popular format. WAV files are quite flexible; they can use various compression schemes, and they can handle samples of just about any size, rate, and number of channels. You'll often find .wav files on the Web and in Usenet, but it's not truly a cross-platform format.

MPEG Audio Sound Format

The Moving Pictures Experts Group (MPEG) format has become popular for sound files, especially with the introduction of the MP2 and MP3 formats. The MPEG format was originally developed for video. Because video usually includes sound tracks, MPEG handles sound, too, and with good fidelity.

Although the sound and sampling rates are very good for MPEG audio, the chief attraction to this format is that these files remain well-compressed while reproducing quality sound. The upshot of using this format is that it provides small files that sound terrific. MPEG audio players are widespread and will probably be built into browsers one day.

RealAudio Sound Format

A relatively new, but exciting, sound format called RealAudio lets you stream audio to the browser in real time. You need a 14.4K modem, at least, or a 28.8K modem for better sound. Although RealAudio files are usually smaller than other formats, the sound quality is not as good.

MIDI Sound Format

MIDI is another popular sound format (see **www.midi.org**). The files compressed in this format have the extension .midi or .mid. The MIDI format is becoming increasingly cross-platform, and it is very flexible, offering a range of sampling rates, sampling sizes, and sound fidelity.

So how can you find some free sounds to add to your pages? Just search the Web. For example, a search for "MIDI" turns up more than three million matches; this seems overwhelming, but if you scan the Web-page titles, you'll see endless listings containing MIDI archives, collections, libraries, and more. Just check the copyrights to make sure they're okay to use.

Multimedia Video

Video is even more popular than multimedia sound. Several video formats are available, but these are currently the big four:

- MPEG video format
- QuickTime video format
- Shockwave video format
- Video For Windows format

MPEG Video Format

The MPEG video standard may be the most popular format used today. Actually, there are three MPEG standards: MPEG video (pictures only), MPEG audio, and MPEG systems (audio and video). It's expensive to encode MPEG files, and decompressing them is a slow process. It's so slow that there are many hardware boards you can buy to assist with the decompression process. However, picture quality is good. Although MPEG hardware encoders are very expensive, you can usually find companies that will do the work for you. The files in MPEG format use the extensions .mpg or .mpeg.

QuickTime Video Format

QuickTime was created by Apple Computer for the Macintosh, but it's become a fairly cross-platform format with QuickTime players standard in Windows as well.

On the Macintosh, QuickTime plays in MoviePlayer or SimplePlayer. On the PC, QuickTime plays in the QuickTime for Windows application. The QuickTime format supports many types of encoding and is quite flexible. Files in QuickTime format have the extension .qt or .mov.

TIP: *QuickTime movies made for the Macintosh must be specially prepared for other platforms through a process called flattening, so you can't assume that if it plays on the Macintosh it'll also play on the PC.*

Shockwave Video Format

As mentioned earlier, the Shockwave format brings Macromedia's Director to the Web. Director is a famous authoring product for multimedia presentations on CD-ROMs. Courseware, games, and interactive presentations of all kinds have been created with Director. Shockwave is available as a plug-in for Netscape Navigator and as an ActiveX control for Internet Explorer.

Video for Windows (AVI) Format

Video For Windows was created by Microsoft and has become popular for Windows platforms. These files are also called Audio Video Interleave (AVI) files because they use the .avi extension. Although AVI is popular in the Windows world, there is relatively little cross-platform support for other operating systems.

TIP: *Don't need all the power of full video? See how to create animated GIFs in Chapter 4.*

Multimedia 3D

Also available is Virtual Reality Modeling Language (VRML), which is a text-based language that lets you model and display 3D interactive graphics. Since its introduction in 1994, VRML has become more and more popular, although it has yet to take the Web by storm.

You can use VRML to model 3D images, but you'll need a VRML-enabled browser to view them. ActiveX controls that display VRML are now also available for Internet Explorer and for plug-ins for Netscape Navigator. Both browsers will load the ActiveX control or plug-in automatically when you start working with pages that include VRML.

For VRML resources, search the Web to find VRML examples and browsers (a search of the Web using the term "VRML" turns up nearly one million matches). Also check out **www.vrml.org** and the VRML repository at **www.web3d.org/vrml/vrml.htm**.

Creating Your Own Multimedia

So far, I've just looked at the consumer side of multimedia, but in case you actually want to produce your own multimedia for the Web, it's worth taking a look at the producer side, too. It's no secret that creating multimedia for the Web can be a very, very costly affair, although prices are coming down. The software alone can cost tens of thousands of dollars, and that's not counting hardware boards you might have to buy to connect video cameras to your computer.

Here's a sampler of sites and software available to help you produce your own multimedia projects:

- *3DSite (www.3dsite.com)*—Lists lots of resources for 3D Web design. Also includes online resources, mostly for the Macintosh.
- *Asymetrix Multimedia Toolbook (www.asymetrix.com)*—Provides tools usually used for training and education. Lets you create interactive courseware, 3D images, and digital videos. Expensive.
- *Autodesk/Kinetix's 3D Studio Max (www.ktx.com)*—Lets you create studio-quality 3D animations and videos. Photo-realistic animations with many tools and aids are also available. Expensive, but very powerful.
- *GoldWave (www.goldwave.com)*—Provides a shareware sound recorder and editor for Windows.
- *Macromedia (www.macromedia.com)*—Provides the famous Shockwave, which brings Macromedia Director, the basis of so many commercial CD multimedia products, to the Web. Here you'll find Director Multimedia Studio, Authorware Interactive Studio, as well as many other products, some with free trials. Expensive, but if you have the resources, it's hard to beat.
- *MacWorld (www.macworld.com)*—Provides a number of multimedia authoring software products for the Macintosh, some of which are reviewed on the site.
- *Movie Cleaner Pro (www.terran-int.com)*—Compresses and cleans videos for the best results. For the Macintosh.
- *Noteworthy Composer (www.ntworthy.com)*—Lets you compose your own MIDI files. A Windows product.
- *PCWorld (www.pcworld.com)*—Offers a lot of software for the PC, including multimedia authoring products. Similar to the MacWorld site for the Macintosh.
- *Personal AVI Editor (www.flickerfree.com)*—Provides a Windows editor for AVI files.
- *RealAudio and RealVideo (www.realaudio.com)*—Support what amounts to Web radio and (slow-scan) TV. Free and commercial plug-ins are available.

You can also pick up their server package here, which, although expensive, can put you in the RealAudio and RealVideo business.

- *Sound Forge (**www.sfoundry.com**)*—Provides a sound editor that is a high-end tool for assembling your own sound tracks. Also available in a less costly edition.
- *ZDNet's Hotfiles Software Library (**www.hotfiles.com/graphics.html**)*—Provides a large collection of reviewed shareware and trial software. Cross-platform selection.

TIP: *On Windows systems, you can create your own sound recordings by using a microphone, a sound card, and the Windows utility called Sound Recorder. The Macintosh can also record sounds, using its Sound utility in the control panel. Of course, there's a great deal of software out there to help you record and process sounds—in fact, sound cards often come with software applications, so you might want to check out your sound card's CD.*

As mentioned earlier, there are two ways of presenting multimedia in your Web pages: inline and as external files. I'll discuss external files in the next section.

Connecting to External Multimedia Files

Multimedia files can be very large, so most of the time you won't want to include them in a Web page directly. You really don't want users who don't want to see them to have to wait for them to download. Instead, you can link to the multimedia files and allow users to download these files by clicking the appropriate link when they want to.

These hyperlinks will link to the actual multimedia file, such as mozart.mid, which you'll see in the next example. When the hyperlink is clicked, the browser determines what type of file to download by checking its MIME type (as sent by the Web server) or file extension. If the browser finds an application (perhaps the browser itself) that handles that type of multimedia on the user's system, such as Windows Media Player, the browser opens the file in that application. If the type of data is unfamiliar to the browser, it'll ask users if they want to download and store the file on disk.

In this example, I'm creating a page with links to two sound files and one video file:

```
<?xml version="1.0"?>
<!DOCTYPE html PUBLIC "-//W3C//DTD XHTML 1.0 Transitional//EN"
    "http://www.w3.org/tr/xhtml1/DTD/xhtml1-transitional.dtd">
<html xmlns="http://www.w3.org/1999/xhtml" xml:lang="en" lang="en">
    <head>
        <title>
            Linking To External Multimedia Files
```

Chapter 8 Working with Multimedia

```
        </title>
    </head>

    <body>

        <h1>
            Linking To External Multimedia Files
        </h1>

        <table border = "1" cellpadding = "8" width = "90%">

            <tr align = "center">
                <th rowspan = "3">
                    <h2>High<br />culture<br />on<br />demand</h2>
                </th>
                <td>
                    Listen to some of <a href = "mozart.mid">
                    Mozart's music</a> (127K)
                </td>
            </tr>

            <tr align = "center">
                <td>
                    Listen to some <i>more</i> of
                    <a href = "mozart2.wav"> Mozart's music</a> (122K)
                </td>
            </tr>

            <tr align = "center">
                <td>
                    See a <a href=
                    "http://www.starpowder.com/steve/chaplin.avi">
                    Charlie Chaplin short movie</a> (173K)
                </td>
            </tr>
        </table>
    </body>
</html>
```

You can see the results of this page in Figure 8.1.

In Figure 8.2, I've downloaded a sound file, and Netscape Navigator has opened it in a sound player. Netscape calls such applications *helper applications*. To find out which helper application Navigator uses for different file types, select Edit|Preferences; then open the Navigator node in the Category box and click the Applications entry.

In Depth

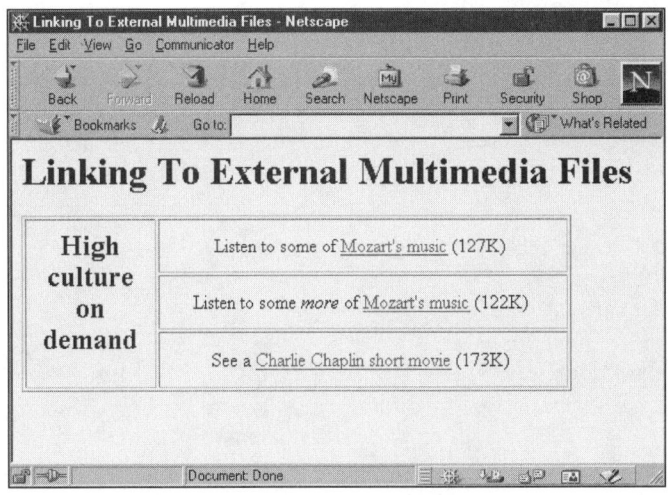

Figure 8.1   Linking to external multimedia files.

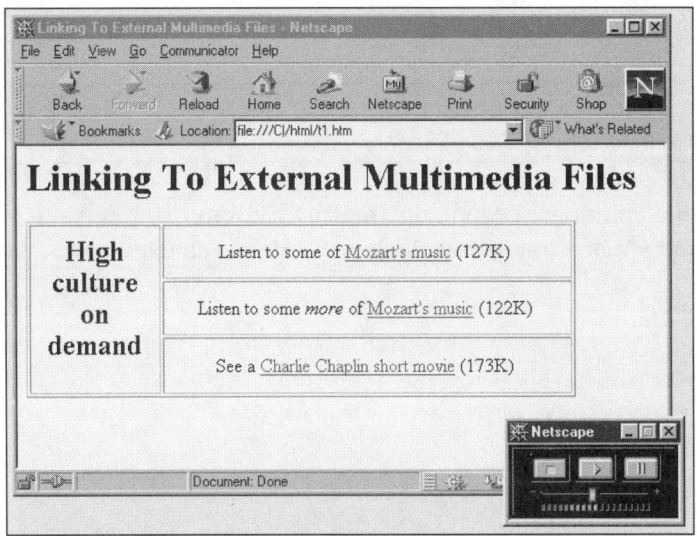

Figure 8.2   Netscape Navigator using a helper application.

Creating Inline Sound

You can also present multimedia inline as part of a page. For example, Internet Explorer includes the **<bgsound>** element, which lets you set background music for a page. Here's an example showing how to use this element:

```
<?xml version="1.0"?>
<!DOCTYPE html PUBLIC "-//W3C//DTD XHTML 1.0 Transitional//EN"
"http://www.w3.org/tr/xhtml1/DTD/xhtml1-transitional.dtd">
```

```
<html xmlns="http://www.w3.org/1999/xhtml" xml:lang="en" lang="en">
    <head>
        <title>
            Using Background Music
        </title>
    </head>

    <body>
        <h1>
            Playing Background Music
        </h1>
        <bgsound src="morzart.wav" loop="infinite" />
    </body>
</html>
```

On the other hand, background music can be annoying. You can turn it off or use the **<bgsound>** element's **volume** attribute to make the music softer. A better choice might be to use a helper application that lets the user control the volume of the music.

TIP: *To turn off sounds in Internet Explorer, select Tools|Internet Options; click the Advanced tab; then deselect the Play Sounds option under the Multimedia heading in the Settings box.*

Using the **<embed>** element, you can make Internet Explorer or Netscape Navigator display a sound application in your Web page. Here's an example:

```
<?xml version="1.0"?>
<!DOCTYPE html PUBLIC "-//W3C//DTD XHTML 1.0 Transitional//EN"
"http://www.w3.org/tr/xhtml1/DTD/xhtml1-transitional.dtd">
<html xmlns="http://www.w3.org/1999/xhtml" xml:lang="en" lang="en">
    <head>
        <title>
            Creating Inline Sound
        </title>
    </head>

    <body>
        <center>
            <h1>
                Creating Inline Sound
            </h1>
            <embed src="mozart.wav" width="145" height="60"></embed>
        </center>
    </body>
</html>
```

In Depth

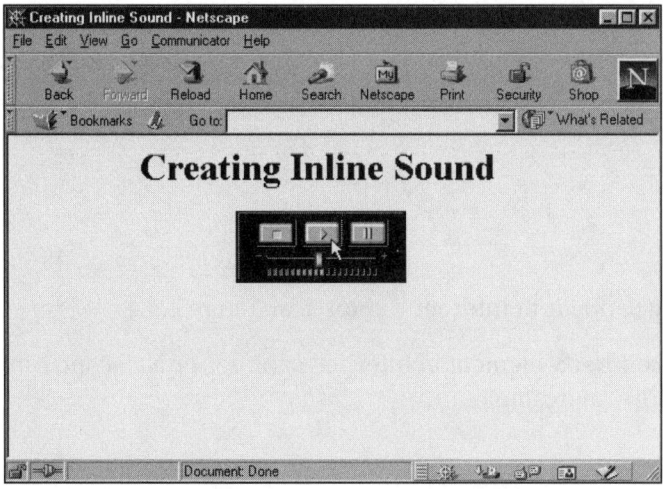

Figure 8.3   Playing sounds.

The results of this page appear in Figure 8.3, where you can see a control panel that the user can use to control the sound playback.

TIP: You can also use the <object> element to play sounds and videos, as we'll see in "<object> and <param>—Placing an Object into a Web Page" in the "Immediate Solutions" section.

Creating Inline Video

You can also include videos in your Web pages. One way to do this in Internet Explorer is to use the **<img>** element if you include the **dynsrc** attribute. Here, I'm adding a Charlie Chaplin movie to a Web page:

```
<?xml version="1.0"?>
<!DOCTYPE html PUBLIC "-//W3C//DTD XHTML 1.0 Transitional//EN"
"http://www.w3.org/tr/xhtml1/DTD/xhtml1-transitional.dtd">
<html xmlns="http://www.w3.org/1999/xhtml" xml:lang="en" lang="en">
    <head>
        <title>
            Video With the &lt;img&gt; Element
        </title>
    </head>

    <body>
        <center>
            <h1>
                Video With the &lt;img&gt; Element
            </h1>
```

```
            <br />
            <br />
            <img dynsrc="chaplin.avi" align="top" />
            <br />
            <br />
        </center>
    </body>
</html>
```

The results of this page appear in Internet Explorer in Figure 8.4.

You can also use the **<embed>** element in Internet Explorer or Netscape Navigator to play videos. Here's an example:

```
<?xml version="1.0"?>
<!DOCTYPE html PUBLIC "-//W3C//DTD XHTML 1.0 Transitional//EN"
    "http://www.w3.org/tr/xhtml1/DTD/xhtml1-transitional.dtd">
<html xmlns="http://www.w3.org/1999/xhtml" xml:lang="en" lang="en">
    <head>
        <title>
            Video With the &lt;embed&gt; Element
        </title>
    </head>

    <body>

        <center>
            <h1>
                Video With the &lt;embed&gt; Element
            </h1>
            <embed src="chaplin.avi"></embed>
        </center>
    </body>
</html>
```

The results of this page appear in Figure 8.5. As you can see, the short movie is playing.

TIP: *You can also use the **<object>** element to play sounds and videos, as we'll see in "**<object>** and **<param>**—Placing an Object into a Web Page" in the "Immediate Solutions" section.*

That's it for the introduction. We've gotten a good start with multimedia, and it's time to turn to the "Immediate Solutions" for more details and more topics.

In Depth

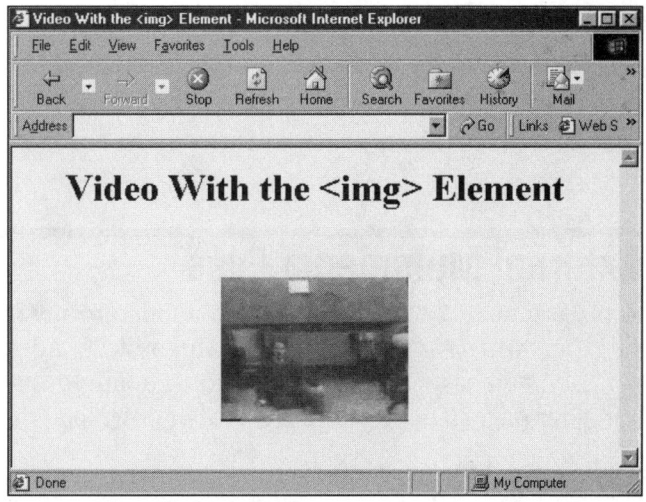

Figure 8.4   Using the **<img>** element to include video in Internet Explorer.

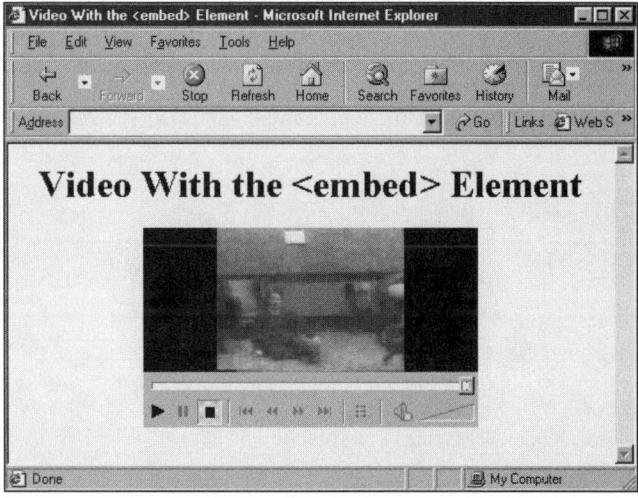

Figure 8.5   Using the **<embed>** element to include video.

Chapter 8 Working with Multimedia

Immediate Solutions

Creating Links to External Multimedia Files

"Darn," says the novice programmer; "ever since I added a video to my home page, everyone hates it." "Hm," you say, "how long is the video file?" "About 12 megabytes," says the NP. "Ah," you say; "how about providing a link to that file instead of embedding it in your page? That would save a lot of download time."

To avoid long download times for large multimedia files, you can treat them as external files in your Web page and include a hyperlink to them. We saw an example of this in the beginning of this chapter:

```
<?xml version="1.0"?>
<!DOCTYPE html PUBLIC "-//W3C//DTD XHTML 1.0 Transitional//EN"
"http://www.w3.org/tr/xhtml1/DTD/xhtml1-transitional.dtd">
<html xmlns="http://www.w3.org/1999/xhtml" xml:lang="en" lang="en">
    <head>
        <title>
            Linking To External Multimedia Files
        </title>
    </head>

    <body>

        <h1>
            Linking To External Multimedia Files
        </h1>

        <table border = "1" cellpadding = "8" width = "90%">

            <tr align = "center">
                <th rowspan = "3">
                    <h2>High<br />culture<br />on<br />demand</h2>
                </th>
                <td>
                    Listen to some of <a href = "mozart.mid">
                    Mozart's music</a> (127K)
                </td>
            </tr>
```

```
            <tr align = "center">
                <td>
                    Listen to some <i>more</i> of
                    <a href = "mozart2.wav"> Mozart's music</a> (122K)
                </td>
            </tr>

            <tr align = "center">
                <td>
                    See a <a href=
                    "http://www.starpowder.com/steve/chaplin.avi">
                    Charlie Chaplin short movie</a> (173K)
                </td>
            </tr>
        </table>
    </body>
</html>
```

You can see the results of this page in Figure 8.1. Note in particular that I list the size of each multimedia file so the user will have an idea of how long it will take to download. When I download a sound file, Netscape Navigator opens it in a helper application, as you see in Figure 8.2.

As discussed in the "In Depth" section of this chapter, it's up to the browser to handle files it downloads. If it can find a helper application (which might actually be the browser itself if it's registered to handle the type of file you're downloading), it'll open the file in the application. Otherwise, the browser will usually ask users if they want to store the file on disk or, if it's an executable file, if they want to open and run it.

How does the browser know what type of file it is downloading? It can check the file's extension, if there is one, or the MIME information from the Web server. For more on MIME types, see the next section.

What MIME Types Are Available?

There are many data types on the Web, and each recognized data format is given its own MIME type. If your Web server doesn't know how to handle some data's MIME type, the server will typically convert the data to text. Browsers use the data's MIME type to figure out how to handle data and to figure out which helper application to use with it. You specify the data's MIME type in certain elements, such as the **<object>** element.

So what MIME types are available? There are many types, such as image/gif (for GIF files) or text/html (for XHTML Web pages). You'll find a long list of all MIME media types, as assigned by the Internet Assigned Number Authority (IANA), in Table 8.1. To create a MIME type matching the type of data you want, separate the type from the subtype by using a forward slash (/), as in **text/plain**. Even though this is a long list, you'll likely find yourself referring to this table as your Web expertise grows.

Table 8.1 MIME media types assigned by the IANA.

Type	Subtype	Subtype
application	activemessage	mathematica
	andrew-inset	msword
	applefile	news-message-id
	atomicmail	news-transmission
	batch-SMTP	ocsp-request
	cals-1840	ocsp-response
	commonground	octet-stream
	cybercash	oda
	dca-rft	pdf
	dec-dx	pgp-encrypted
	EDI-Consent	pgp-keys
	EDIFACT	pgp-signature
	EDI-X12	pkcs7-mime
	eshop	pkcs7-signature
	http	pkcs10
	hyperstudio	pkix-cert
	iges	pkixcmp
	index	pkix-crl
	index.cmd	postscript
	index.obj	prs.alvestrand.titrax-sheet
	index.response	prs.cww
	index.vnd	prs.nprend
	ipp	remote-printing
	mac-binhex40	riscos
	macwriteii	rtf
	marc	sdp

(continued)

Table 8.1 MIME media types assigned by the IANA *(continued).*

Type	Subtype	Subtype
application	set-payment	vnd.ecowin.seriesupdate
	set-payment-initiation	vnd.enliven
	set-registration	vnd.epson.msf
	set-registration-initiation	vnd.epson.quickanime
	sgml	vnd.epson.salt
	sgml-open-catalog	vnd.epson.ssf
	slate	vnd.fdf
	vemmi	vnd.ffsns
	vnd.$commerce_battelle	vnd.FloGraphIt
	vnd.3M.Post-it-Notes	vnd.framemaker
	vnd.accpac.simply.aso	vnd.fujitsu.oasys
	vnd.accpac.simply.imp	vnd.fujitsu.oasys2
	vnd.acucobol	vnd.fujitsu.oasys3
	vnd.anser-web-certificate-issue-initiation	vnd.fujitsu.oasysgp
	vnd.anser-web-funds-transfer-initiation	vnd.fujitsu.oasysprs
	vnd.audiograph	vnd.fujixerox.docuworks
	vnd.businessobjects	vnd.fut-misnet
	vnd.claymore	vnd.hp-HPGL
	vnd.commonspace	vnd.hp-hpid
	vnd.comsocaller	vnd.hp-hps
	vnd.cups-postscript	vnd.hp-PCL
	vnd.cups-raster	vnd.hp-PCLXL
	vnd.cups-raw	vnd.ibm.MiniPay
	vnd.cybank	vnd.ibm.modcap
	vnd.dna	vnd.intercon.formnet
	vnd.dpgraph	vnd.intertrust.digibox
	vnd.dxr	vnd.intertrust.nncp
	vnd.ecdis update	vnd.intu.qbo
	vnd.ecowin.chart	vnd.intu.qfx
	vnd.ecowin.filerequest	vnd.is-xpr
	vnd.ecowin.fileupdate	vnd.japannet-directory-service
	vnd.ecowin.series	vnd.japannet-jpnstore-wakeup
	vnd.ecowin.seriesrequest	vnd.japannet-payment-wakeup

(continued)

Table 8.1 MIME media types assigned by the IANA *(continued)*.

Type	Subtype	Subtype
application	vnd.japannet-registration	vnd.ms-powerpoint
	vnd.japannet-registration-wakeup	vnd.ms-project
	vnd.japannet-setstore-wakeup	vnd.ms-tnef
	vnd.japannet-verification	vnd.ms-works
	vnd.japannet-verification-wakeup	vnd.musician
	vnd.koan	vnd.music-niff
	vnd.lotus-1-2-3	vnd.netfpx
	vnd.lotus-approach	vnd.noblenet-directory
	vnd.lotus-freelance	vnd.noblenet-sealer
	vnd.lotus-notes	vnd.noblenet-web
	vnd.lotus-organizer	vnd.novadigm.EDM
	vnd.lotus-screencam	vnd.novadigm.EDX
	vnd.lotus-wordpro	vnd.novadigm.EXT
	vnd.mediastation.cdkey	vnd.osa.netdeploy
	vnd.meridian-slingshot	vnd.pg.format
	vnd.mif	vnd.pg.osasli
	vnd.minisoft-hp3000-save	vnd.powerbuilder6
	vnd.mitsubishi.misty-guard.trustweb	vnd.powerbuilder6-s
	vnd.Mobius.DAF	vnd.powerbuilder7
	vnd.Mobius.DIS	vnd.powerbuilder7-s
	vnd.Mobius.MSL	vnd.powerbuilder75
	vnd.Mobius.PLC	vnd.powerbuilder75-s
	vnd.Mobius.TXF	vnd.previewsystems.box
	vnd.motorola.flexsuite	vnd.publishare-delta-tree
	vnd.motorola.flexsuite.adsi	vnd.rapid
	vnd.motorola.flexsuite.fis	vnd.seemail
	vnd.motorola.flexsuite.gotap	vnd.shana.informed.formdata
	vnd.motorola.flexsuite.kmr	vnd.shana.informed.formtemplate
	vnd.motorola.flexsuite.ttc	vnd.shana.informed.interchange
	vnd.motorola.flexsuite.wem	vnd.shana.informed.package
	vnd.ms-artgalry	vnd.street-stream
	vnd.ms-asf	vnd.svd
	vnd.ms-excel	vnd.swiftview-ics

(continued)

Table 8.1 MIME media types assigned by the IANA *(continued)*.

Type	Subtype	Subtype
application	vnd.triscape.mxs	vnd.vcx
	vnd.truedoc	vnd.visio
	vnd.ufdl	vnd.wap.wbxml
	vnd.uplanet.alert	vnd.wap.wmlc
	vnd.uplanet.alert-wbxml	vnd.wap.wmlscriptc
	vnd.uplanet.bearer-choice	vnd.webturbo
	vnd.uplanet.bearer-choice-wbxml	vnd.wrq-hp3000-labelled
	vnd.uplanet.cacheop	vnd.wt.stf
	vnd.uplanet.cacheop-wbmxl	vnd.xara
	vnd.uplanet.channel	vnd.xfdl
	vnd.uplanet.channel-wbxml	vnd.yellowriver-custom-menu
	vnd.uplanet.list	wita
	vnd.uplanet.list-wbxml	wordperfect5.1
	vnd.uplanet.listcmd	x400-bp
	vnd.uplanet.listcmd-wbxml	xml
	vnd.uplanet.signal	zip
audio	32kadpcm	vnd.lucent.voice
	basic	vnd.nortel.vbk
	L16	vnd.octel.sbc
	vnd.cns.anp1	vnd.qcelp
	vnd.cns.inf1	vnd.rhetorex.32kadpcm
	vnd.digital-winds	vnd.vmx.cvsd
image	cgm	vnd.cns.inf2
	g3fax	vnd.dwg
	gif	vnd.dxf
	ief	vnd.fastbidsheet
	jpeg	vnd.fpx
	naplps	vnd.mix
	png	vnd.net-fpx
	prs.btif	vnd.svf
	prs.pti	vnd.wap.wbmp
	tiff	vnd.xiff

(continued)

Table 8.1 MIME media types assigned by the IANA *(continued)*.

Type	Subtype	Subtype
message	delivery-status	news
	disposition-notification	partial
	external-body	s-http
	http	
model	iges	vnd.flatland.3dml
	mesh	vnd.gtw
	vnd.dwf	vrml
multipart	alternative	mixed
	appledouble	parallel
	byteranges	related
	digest	report
	encrypted	signed
	form-data	voice-message
	header-set	
text	calendar	uri-list
	css	vnd.abc
	directory	vnd.fly
	enriched	vnd.fmi.flexstor
	html	vnd.in3d.3dml
	plain	vnd.in3d.spot
	prs.lines.tag	vnd.latex-z
	rfc822-headers	vnd.motorola.reflex
	richtext	vnd.wap.wml
	rtf	vnd.wap.wmlscript
	sgml	xml
	tab-separated-values	
video	mpeg	vnd.motorola.videop
	quicktime	vnd.vivo
	vnd.motorola.video	

<bgsound>—Adding Background Sounds

Purpose: Plays background sound from AU, MIDI, or WAV files while the user is viewing a page. This element contains no content.

When used as HTML: Start tag/End tag: Required/Omitted

Supported: [IE3, IE4, IE5]

Attributes:

- **balance**—Sets the stereophonic balance. Setting this attribute to –10,000 creates left-only balance, and setting it to 10,000 creates right-only balance. Setting it to 0 (the default) results in balanced output between the two stereo output devices. [IE4, IE5]

- **id**—Unique alphanumeric identifier for the tag; use the ID to refer to the tag. [IE4, IE5]

- **loop**—Sets the number of times the sound should play. Set to positive integers or to –1, which means that the sound will play continuously until either the page is unloaded or sound is turned off in the browser. [IE3, IE4, IE5]

- **src**—Indicates the URL of the audio file to play; can be WAV, AU, or MIDI format. [IE3, IE4, IE5]

- **volume**—Sets the volume of the output device. Setting this to 0 (the default) results in full volume; –10,000 results in zero volume. [IE4, IE5]

XHTML events: None

The novice programmer appears with a dented hat and says, "The big boss didn't appreciate the change I made to the company Web page." "What was it?" you ask. "Well," the NP says, "I made it play 'Row, Row, Row Your Boat' at full volume continuously."

We saw how to use the **<bgsound>** element in the "In Depth" section of this chapter. Here's the example in which I'm playing a sound file over and over:

```
<?xml version="1.0"?>
<!DOCTYPE html PUBLIC "-//W3C//DTD XHTML 1.0 Transitional//EN"
"http://www.w3.org/tr/xhtml1/DTD/xhtml1-transitional.dtd">
<html xmlns="http://www.w3.org/1999/xhtml" xml:lang="en" lang="en">
    <head>
        <title>
            Using Background Music
        </title>
    </head>
```

```
<body>
    <h1>
        Playing Background Music
    </h1>

    <bgsound src="mozart.wav" loop="-1" />
</body>
</html>
```

In Internet Explorer, you can also do the same thing with the **<embed>** element by setting the **hidden** attribute to "**true**" to hide the sound player. (See "**<embed>**—Embedding Multimedia and Plug-ins in a Web Page" later in this chapter.) Here's an example:

```
<?xml version="1.0"?>
<!DOCTYPE html PUBLIC "-//W3C//DTD XHTML 1.0 Transitional//EN"
"http://www.w3.org/tr/xhtml1/DTD/xhtml1-transitional.dtd">
<html xmlns="http://www.w3.org/1999/xhtml" xml:lang="en" lang="en">
    <head>
        <title>
            Using Background Music
        </title>
    </head>

    <body>

        <h1>
            Playing Background Music
        </h1>
        <embed src="mozart.wav" width="145" height="60" hidden="true">
        </embed>
    </body>
</html>
```

Note that playing background sounds can be annoying, and the practice is on the decline.

---

*TIP: You can also use the **<object>** element to play sounds and videos, as we'll see in "**<object>** and **<param>**—Placing an Object into a Web Page" in the "Immediate Solutions" section.*

<embed>—Embedding Multimedia and Plug-Ins in a Web Page

Purpose: Lets you embed a plug-in in a Web page to play multimedia inline or to do anything else a plug-in can do. There are three required attributes: **height**, **width**, and **src**.

When used as HTML: Start tag/End tag: Required/Optional

Supported: [IE3, IE4, IE5, NS2, NS3, NS4]

Attributes:

- **accesskey**—Sets the access key for the embedded component. Users can use the access key with a platform-specific key, such as the Alt key in Windows, to give the component the focus. [IE5]
- **align**—Sets the text alignment around the embedded component. Possible values for Internet Explorer: **absbottom**, **absmiddle**, **baseline**, **bottom**, **left**, **middle**, **right**, **texttop**, or **top**. Possible values for Netscape Navigator: **left**, **right**, **top**, and **bottom**. [IE4, IE5, NS2, NS3, NS4]
- **border**—Sets the border width; set to positive pixel values. [NS2, NS3, NS4]
- **class**—Class of the element (used for rendering). [IE4, IE5]
- **dir**—Gives the direction of directionally neutral text (text that doesn't have an inherent direction in which you should read it). Possible values: **ltr**, left-to-right text or table; and **rtl**, right-to-left text or table. [IE5]
- **frameborder**—Sets the border. [NS2, NS3, NS4]
- **height**—Gives the height of the embedded component in the page. Set to a pixel measurement or a percentage of the available display height. Required. [IE3, IE4, IE5, NS2, NS3, NS4]
- **hidden**—Indicates whether the embedded component should be visible or not. Set to **true** (the default) or **false**. [NS2, NS3, NS4]
- **id**—Unique alphanumeric identifier for the tag; use the ID to refer to the tag. [IE4, IE5]
- **lang**—Base language used for the tag. [IE4, IE5]
- **language**—Scripting language used for the tag. [IE4, IE5]
- **name**—Sets the element's name. [NS2, NS3, NS4]
- **palette**—Sets the color palette to use in the component; set to **foreground** or **background**. [NS2, NS3, NS4]

- **pluginspage**—Provides the URL for the associated plug-in. [IE3, IE4, IE5, NS2, NS3, NS4]
- **pluginurl**—Provides the URL for the associated plug-in. [NS4]
- **src**—Sets the URL of the multimedia file. Required. [IE3, IE4, IE5, NS2, NS3, NS4]
- **style**—Inline style indicating how to render the element. [IE4, IE5]
- **title**—Sets the element's title [IE4, IE5]
- **type**—Sets the MIME type for the component. [NS2, NS3, NS4]
- **units**—Sets the height and width units of the component. [IE3, IE4, IE5, NS2, NS3, NS4]
- **width**—Gives the width of the embedded component in the page. Set to a pixel measurement or a percentage of the available display width. Required. [IE3, IE4, IE5, NS2, NS3, NS4]

XHTML events: None

The **<embed>** element lets you embed a plug-in in a page. Although the World Wide Web Consortium (W3C) has said that this element should be replaced with the **<object>** element, in more recent times the future of the **<object>** element itself has come into some doubt, and there's no doubt that **<embed>** will be around for some time.

There are all types of plug-ins available (you can find a complete list of available plug-ins at **http://home.netscape.com/plugins/index.html**), and many come with Netscape Navigator. If the browser needs a plug-in you don't have, the browser will ask you before downloading and installing the plug-in.

Here's an example of using the **<embed>** element from the beginning of this chapter; here, I'm playing a sound with that element:

```
<?xml version="1.0"?>
<!DOCTYPE html PUBLIC "-//W3C//DTD XHTML 1.0 Transitional//EN"
    "http://www.w3.org/tr/xhtml1/DTD/xhtml1-transitional.dtd">
<html xmlns="http://www.w3.org/1999/xhtml" xml:lang="en" lang="en">
    <head>
        <title>
            Creating Inline Sound
        </title>
    </head>

    <body>
        <center>
```

```
            <h1>
                Creating Inline Sound
            </h1>

            <embed src="mozart.wav" width="145" height="60">
            </embed>
        </center>
    </body>
</html>
```

TIP: You can also use the **<object>** element to play sounds and videos, as we'll see in "**<object>** and **<param>**—Placing an Object into a Web Page" in the "Immediate Solutions" section.

You can see the results of this page in Figure 8.3. If you're using a plug-in available on the Web, you can specify the plug-in's URL as well as the data's URL, like this:

```
<embed pluginurl="url" src="dataurl" width="pixelsx" height="pixelsy">
</embed>
```

<noembed>—Handling Browsers That Don't Handle Embedding

Purpose: Displays text (including hyperlinks) or XHTML that doesn't use embedded components. For browsers that don't handle the **<embed>** element.

When used as HTML: Start tag/End tag: Required/Required

Supported: [IE3, IE4, IE5, NS2, NS3, NS4]

Attributes: None

XHTML events: None

You use the **<noembed>** element to display text, hyperlinks, and nonembedded XHTML if a browser doesn't support the **<embed>** element.

Here's an example showing how to use this element:

```
<?xml version="1.0"?>
<!DOCTYPE html PUBLIC "-//W3C//DTD XHTML 1.0 Transitional//EN"
 "http://www.w3.org/tr/xhtml1/DTD/xhtml1-transitional.dtd">
<html xmlns="http://www.w3.org/1999/xhtml" xml:lang="en" lang="en">
```

```
        <head>
            <title>
                Creating Inline Sound
            </title>
        </head>

        <body>
            <center>

                <h1>
                    Creating Inline Sound
                </h1>

                <embed src="mozart.wav" width="145" height="60">
                    <noembed>
                        Sorry, your browser doesn't handle embeds!
                    </noembed>
                </embed>

            </center>
        </body>

</html>
```

Creating Inline Sounds

"I've finally got my favorite song in a MIDI file!" the novice programmer exults. "But how can I add it to my Web page?" "Well," you say, "you can use the **<embed>** element. There are other elements that you can use, like the **<object>** element, but **<embed>** is probably easier." "Just what I'm looking for!" says the NP.

Using the **<embed>** element you can embed inline sounds in your Web pages, complete with a console to let the user play those sounds. Here's an example from the beginning of this chapter using the **<embed>** element:

```
<?xml version="1.0"?>
<!DOCTYPE html PUBLIC "-//W3C//DTD XHTML 1.0 Transitional//EN"
"http://www.w3.org/tr/xhtml1/DTD/xhtml1-transitional.dtd">
<html xmlns="http://www.w3.org/1999/xhtml" xml:lang="en" lang="en">
    <head>
        <title>
```

```
                Creating Inline Sound
            </title>
        </head>

        <body>
            <center>

                <h1>
                    Creating Inline Sound
                </h1>

                <embed src="mozart.wav" width="145" height="60"></embed>
            </center>
        </body>
</html>
```

You can see the results of this page in Figure 8.3. If you prefer, you can hide the console by setting the **<embed>** element's **hidden** attribute to "**true**".

In the next example, I'm creating some inline sound with the **<object>** element:

```
<?xml version="1.0"?>
<!DOCTYPE html PUBLIC "-//W3C//DTD XHTML 1.0 Transitional//EN"
"http://www.w3.org/tr/xhtml1/DTD/xhtml1-transitional.dtd">
<html xmlns="http://www.w3.org/1999/xhtml" xml:lang="en" lang="en">
    <head>
        <title>
            Creating Inline Sound
        </title>
    </head>

    <body>
        <center>
            <h1>
                Creating Inline Sound
            </h1>

                <object data="mozart.mid" type="audio/midi"></object>
        </center>
    </body>
</html>
```

<object> and <param>—Placing an Object into a Web Page

<object>

Purpose: Embeds objects, such as ActiveX controls, in Web pages. Can also handle the tasks of the **<applet>**, **<embed>**, **<bgsound>**, **<sound>**, and **<img>** elements.

When used as HTML: Start tag/End tag: Required/Required

Supported: [1.0S, 1.0T, 1.0F, 4, IE3, IE4, IE5]

Attributes:

- **accesskey**—Sets the access key for the embedded component. Users can use the access key with a platform-specific key, such as the Alt key in Windows, to give the component the focus. [IE5]

- **align**—Sets the text alignment around the embedded component. Possible values for Internet Explorer: **absbottom**, **absmiddle**, **baseline**, **bottom**, **left**, **middle**, **right**, **texttop**, or **top**. Possible values for Netscape Navigator: **left**, **right**, **top**, and **bottom**. [1.0T, 1.0F, 4, IE4, IE5, NS2, NS3, NS4]

- **archive**—Archives information. Set to a space-separated list of Uniform Resource Identifiers (URIs). [1.0S, 1.0T, 1.0F]

- **border**—Sets a border width. Set to pixel values. [1.0T, 1.0F]

- **class**—Class of the element (used for rendering). [1.0S, 1.0T, 1.0F, 4, IE4, IE5]

- **classid**—Set to the class ID for the object. Set to a class ID value as set in the Windows Registry or a URL. [1.0S, 1.0T, 1.0F, 4, IE3, IE4, IE5, NS4]

- **code**—Holds a URL pointing to the object's code or class. [4, IE3, IE4, IE5]

- **codebase**—Specifies where to find the code for the object. [1.0S, 1.0T, 1.0F, 4, IE3, IE4, IE5, NS4]

- **codetype**—Indicates the MIME type of the code referred to by the **classid** attribute. Set to an alphanumeric MIME type. [1.0S, 1.0T, 1.0F, 4, IE3, IE4, IE5]

- **data**—Specifies the URL of the object's data. If you didn't specify a value for the **classid** attribute, the MIME type of the data sets a default value for the **classid** attribute. [1.0S, 1.0T, 1.0F, 4, IE3, IE4, IE5, NS4]

- **datafld**—Name of the column of the data-source object that supplies the bound data. Set to alphanumeric characters. [IE4, IE5]

- **datasrc**—Gives the URL or ID of the data-source object supplying data bound to this element. W3C says this should be a URL; Internet Explorer says it should be a data-source ID. [IE4, IE5]

- **declare**—Indicates that the object should not be created or instantiated until needed (this technique is called *late binding*). Standalone attribute. [1.0S, 1.0T, 1.0F, 4]
- **dir**—Gives the direction of directionally neutral text (text that doesn't have an inherent direction in which you should read it). Possible values: **ltr**, left-to-right text or table; and **rtl**, right-to-left text or table. [1.0S, 1.0T, 1.0F, IE5]
- **height**—Specifies the object's height in pixels. [1.0S, 1.0T, 1.0F, 4, IE3, IE4, IE5, NS4]
- **hspace**—Sets the horizontal spacing around objects. Set to pixel values. [1.0T, 1.0F, 4, IE3, IE4, IE5]
- **id**—Unique alphanumeric identifier for the tag; use the ID to refer to the tag. [1.0S, 1.0T, 1.0F, 4, IE4, IE5, NS4]
- **lang**—Base language used for the tag. [1.0S, 1.0T, 1.0F, IE4, IE5]
- **language**—Scripting language used for the tag. [IE4, IE5]
- **name**—Gives the object a name so you can use it with forms and scripts. [1.0S, 1.0T, 1.0F, 4, IE3, IE4, IE5]
- **standby**—Sets a text string for the browser to display while it loads the object. Set to alphanumeric characters. [1.0S, 1.0T, 1.0F, 4, IE3, IE4, IE5]
- **style**—Inline style indicating how to render the element. [1.0S, 1.0T, 1.0F, 4, IE4, IE5]
- **tabindex**—Sets the tab index of the object. Using the Tab key, the user can tab around the elements of the Web page. Set to positive or negative integers. [1.0S, 1.0T, 1.0F, 4, IE4, IE5]
- **title**—Holds additional information (which might be displayed in tool tips). [1.0S, 1.0T, 1.0F, 4, IE4, IE5]
- **type**—Specifies the MIME type of the data referred to in the **data** attribute. [1.0S, 1.0T, 1.0F, 4, IE3, IE4, IE5, NS4]
- **usemap**—Specifies the URL; usually in the same document of a client-side image map to be used with the object. [1.0S, 1.0T, 1.0F, 4, IE3, IE4, IE5]
- **vspace**—Specifies the vertical spacing around objects (top and bottom padding). Measured in pixels. Values: Positive integers. [1.0T, 1.0F, 4, IE3, IE4, IE5]
- **width**—Sets the object's width in pixels. [1.0S, 1.0T, 1.0F, 4, IE3, IE4, IE5, NS4]
- **xml:lang**—Holds the base language for the element when the document is interpreted as an XML document. [1.0S, 1.0T, 1.0F]

XHTML events: onclick, ondblclick, onmousedown, onmouseup, onmouseover, onmousemove, onmouseout, onkeypress, onkeydown, onkeyup

<param>

Purpose: Supplies parameters to the object specified by the enclosing **<object>** or **<applet>** element. The **<param>** element contains no content.

When used as HTML: Start tag/End tag: Required/Omitted

Supported: [1.0S, 1.0T, 1.0F, 1.1, 3.2, 4, IE3, IE4, IE5, NS2, NS3, NS4]

Attributes:

- **datafld**—Name of the column of the data-source object that supplies the bound data. Set to alphanumeric characters. [IE4, IE5]

- **dataformatas**—Specifies whether bound data is plain text or XHTML. Set to **html**, **plaintext**, or **text**. [IE4, IE5]

- **datasrc**—Gives the URL or ID of the data-source object supplying data bound to this element. W3C says this should be a URL; Internet Explorer says it should be a data-source ID. [IE4, IE5]

- **id**—Unique alphanumeric identifier for the tag; use the ID to refer to the tag. [1.0S, 1.0T, 1.0F, 1.1, 4]

- **name**—Specifies the name of the parameter. Set to an alphanumeric string. Required. [1.0S, 1.0T, 1.0F, 1.1, 3.2, 4, IE3, IE4, IE5, NS2, NS3, NS4]

- **type**—Sets the MIME type of the parameter. [1.0S, 1.0T, 1.0F, 1.1, 4]

- **value**—Specifies the value of the parameter. Set to alphanumeric values. [1.0S, 1.0T, 1.0F, 1.1, 3.2, 4, IE3, IE4, IE5, NS2, NS3, NS4]

- **valuetype**—Sets the MIME type of the value. [1.0S, 1.0T, 1.0F, 1.1, 4]

XHTML events: None

The **<object>** element, originally introduced by Microsoft in Internet Explorer 3 and now adopted by W3C in HTML 4, is designed to handle all inline elements. Created to embed ActiveX controls in Web pages, the **<object>** element can now handle the tasks of the **<applet>**, **<embed>**, **<bgsound>**, **<sound>**, and **<img>** elements. Note that the **<object>** element is not supported in XHTML 1.1—as yet, anyway.

NOTE: *If you're looking for coverage of the **<sound>** element in this chapter, you won't find it. This element is the same as the **<bgsound>** element, but it's supported only by the NCSA Mosaic browser, which has not been supported since 1997, and it's not a part of the XHTML specification.*

You can use the **<object>** element to display videos in Internet Explorer, like this:

```
<?xml version="1.0"?>
<!DOCTYPE html PUBLIC "-//W3C//DTD XHTML 1.0 Transitional//EN"
"http://www.w3.org/tr/xhtml1/DTD/xhtml1-transitional.dtd">
<html xmlns="http://www.w3.org/1999/xhtml" xml:lang="en" lang="en">

    <head>
        <title>
            Videos With the &lt;object&gt; Element
        </title>
    </head>

    <body>
        <center>
            <h1>
                Videos With the &lt;object&gt; Element
            </h1>
            <br />
            <br />
            <object data="chaplin.avi" type="video/msvideo"
                width="120"
                height="160">
            </object>
            <br />
            <br />
        </center>
    </body>
</html>
```

In this example, I'm creating some inline sound with the **<object>** element in Internet Explorer:

```
<?xml version="1.0"?>
<!DOCTYPE html PUBLIC "-//W3C//DTD XHTML 1.0 Transitional//EN"
"http://www.w3.org/tr/xhtml1/DTD/xhtml1-transitional.dtd">
<html xmlns="http://www.w3.org/1999/xhtml" xml:lang="en" lang="en">
    <head>
        <title>
            Creating Inline Sound
        </title>
    </head>

    <body>
        <center>
            <h1>
                Creating Inline Sound
            </h1>
```

Chapter 8 Working with Multimedia

```
            <object data="mozart.mid" type="audio/midi">
            </object>

        </center>
    </body>
</html>
```

Here's how you use the **<object>** element to display simple graphics files in Internet Explorer:

```
<?xml version="1.0"?>
<!DOCTYPE html PUBLIC "-//W3C//DTD XHTML 1.0 Transitional//EN"
"http://www.w3.org/tr/xhtml1/DTD/xhtml1-transitional.dtd">
<html xmlns="http://www.w3.org/1999/xhtml" xml:lang="en" lang="en">
    <head>
        <title>
            Images With the &lt;object&gt; Element
        </title>
    </head>

    <body>

        <center>
            <h1>
                Images With the &lt;object&gt; Element
            </h1>
            <br />
            <br />
            <object data="image.gif" type="image/gif"
                width="200"
                height="360">
            </object>
            <br />
            <br />
        </center>
    </body>
</html>
```

TIP: *To see what MIME types you can use in the **<object>** element, see "What MIME Types Are Available?" at the beginning of the "Immediate Solutions" section in this chapter. You can also use nested **<object>** elements to handle browsers that might not recognize your preferred data format. For example, if the browser can't handle the QuickTime file format in an **<object>** element, the browser will ignore the tag, and you might have a nested **<object>** element inside that element with another format, such as AVI, which the browser will be able to handle.*

In the past, the W3C has said that the **<object>** element was intended to supersede elements like **<embed>** and **<applet>**, which you use to embed Java applets. (We'll discuss Java applets in Chapter 19.) Executable applet files have the extension .class, and you can now set the **<object>** element's **classid** attribute like this: **<object classid="java:*filename.class*">**. W3C also suggests providing the appropriate MIME type for the applet, like this: **<object classid="java:*filename.class*" codetype="application/octet-stream">**. If your applet is in another location, you can specify that location with the **codebase** attribute, like this: **<object classid="java:*filename.class*" codetype="application/octet-stream" codebase="*url*">**. At this point, however, it's unclear what's going to happen with the **<object>** element—it's not part of the XHTML 1.1 specification, although the **<applet>** element is.

In this example, I'm using the **<object>** element to load a Java applet named button.class into a Web page:

```
<?xml version="1.0"?>
<!DOCTYPE html PUBLIC "-//W3C//DTD XHTML 1.0 Transitional//EN"
"http://www.w3.org/tr/xhtml1/DTD/xhtml1-transitional.dtd">
<html xmlns="http://www.w3.org/1999/xhtml" xml:lang="en" lang="en">
    <head>
        <title>
            Java Applets With the &lt;object&gt; Element
        </title>
    </head>

    <body>
        <center>
            <h1>
                Java Applets With the &lt;object&gt; Element
            </h1>
            <br />
            <br />
            <object codetype="application/octet-stream"
                classid="java:button.class"
                width="200" height="200" >
                Your browser does not handle Java...
            </object>
            <br />
            <br />
        </center>
    </body>
</html>
```

You can see the results of this page in Figure 8.6.

Chapter 8 Working with Multimedia

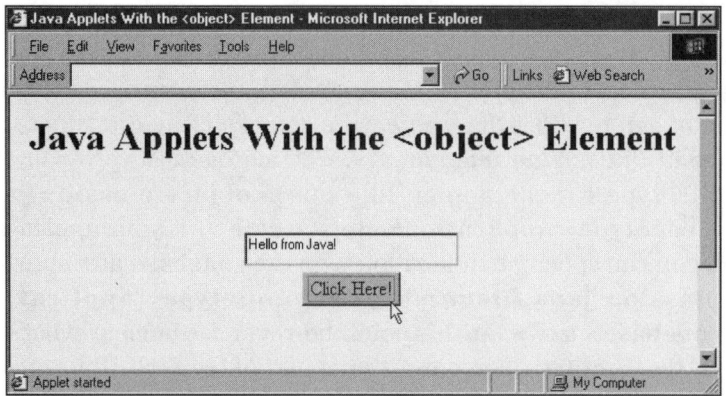

Figure 8.6 Using the <object> element to display an applet.

There are a great many ActiveX controls that you can use to create multimedia with the **<object>** element. For example, one ActiveX control that comes with Internet Explorer is the Structured Graphics control, and to use it, you must supply its *class ID* in the **<object>** element.

NOTE: *Each ActiveX control has its own class ID, which you can find in its documentation. You can also find it in the Windows Registry if you use a tool such as RegEdit, the Registry Editor (usually stored as c:\windows\regedit.exe).*

The Structured Graphics control needs you to tell it what to draw. You do this with **<param>** elements in the **<object>** element; the **<param>** elements pass parameter names and values to the control (and also to Java applets). Here's how that looks in an example:

```
<?xml version="1.0"?>
<!DOCTYPE html PUBLIC "-//W3C//DTD XHTML 1.0 Transitional//EN"
    "http://www.w3.org/tr/xhtml1/DTD/xhtml1-transitional.dtd">
<html xmlns="http://www.w3.org/1999/xhtml" xml:lang="en" lang="en">
    <head>
        <title>
            Creating Structured Graphics
        </title>
    </head>

    <body>
        <center>
            <h1>
                Creating Structured Graphics
            </h1>
```

```
            <object id="graphics"
                    classid="CLSID:369303C2-D7AC-11d0-89D5-00A0C90833E6"
                    style="width:150; height:150">
                <param name="Line0001" value="SetLineColor(255, 0, 0)" />
                <param name="Line0002" value="SetFillColor(0, 0, 255)" />
                <param name="Line0003" value="SetFillStyle(1)" />
                <param name="Line0004" value="Oval(-75, -75, 80, 80, 0)" />
                <param name="Line0005" value="SetFillColor(255, 0, 0)" />
                <param name="Line0006" value="Pie(-75, -75, 80, 80, 0,
                    90, 0)" />
                <param name="Line0007" value="Pie(-75, -75, 80, 80, 0,
                    90, 180)" />
            </object>
        </center>
    </body>
</html>
```

This code tells the structured graphics control to draw the image you see in Figure 8.7.

You can get as elaborate and complex as you like with objects in Web pages. The next example uses JavaScript (discussed in Chapters 10 and 11) with Internet Explorer's DirectAnimation control to draw a shape that moves and twists around on top of the content of a Web page. Here's the code:

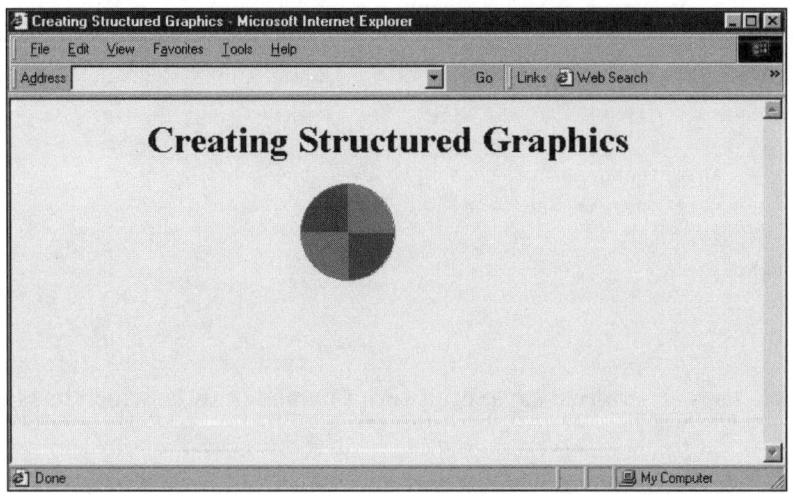

Figure 8.7   Using the **<object>** element to display structured graphics.

```
<?xml version="1.0"?>
<!DOCTYPE html PUBLIC "-//W3C//DTD XHTML 1.0 Transitional//EN"
    "http://www.w3.org/tr/xhtml1/DTD/xhtml1-transitional.dtd">
<html xmlns="http://www.w3.org/1999/xhtml" xml:lang="en" lang="en">
    <head>
        <title>
            Using DirectAnimation
        </title>
        <script type = "text/javascript"
            language = "JavaScript" src="draw.js"></script>
    </head>

    <body>
        <center>
            <h1>
                Using DirectAnimation
            </h1>

            <object id="DirectAnimationControl"
              style =
              "position:absolute; left:10%; top:150; width:90%; height:80%"
              classid="CLSID:B6FFC24C-7E13-11D0-9B47-00C04FC2F51D">
            </object>

            <br />
            <br />
            <br />
            <br />
            <br />
            <h2>
                Animated graphics that move over the
                text in your Web page!
            </h2>
        </center>
    </body>
</html>
```

This example uses an external JavaScript script named draw.js, which has these contents:

```
document.write("<center>")
document.write("<form name = form2>")
document.write(
    "<input type = ,button' value = " +
    ",Click here for a little animation!'" +
    " onClick = ,animate()'>"
```

```
    )
    document.write("</form>")
    document.write("</center>")

    function animate()
    {
        var MeterLibrary = DirectAnimationControl.MeterLibrary
        var surface = MeterLibrary.NewDrawingSurface()

        surface.FillColor(MeterLibrary.ColorRgb(1, 0, 0))
        surface.FillPath(MeterLibrary.Polyline(Array(0, 0, 400, 0,
            400, 400, 0, 400, 0, 0)))

        surface.FillColor(MeterLibrary.ColorRgb(1, 0, 0))
        surface.FillPath(MeterLibrary.Polyline(Array(200, 0, 0, 400,
            400, 400, 200, 0)))

        surface.FillColor(MeterLibrary.ColorRgb(1, 0, 0))
        surface.FillPath(MeterLibrary.Polyline(Array(0, 0, -400, 0,
            -400, -400, 0, -400, 0, 0)))

        surface.FillColor(MeterLibrary.ColorRgb(1, 0, 0))
        surface.FillPath(MeterLibrary.Polyline(Array(-200, -400, -400,
            0, 0, 0, -200, -400)))

        var axis = MeterLibrary.Vector3(20, 20, 20)
        var start = MeterLibrary.Point2(-2000, 0)
        var end = MeterLibrary.Point2(4000, 0)

       var Sweep = MeterLibrary.FollowPath(MeterLibrary.Line(start, end),
            10)

        var Twist = MeterLibrary.Rotate3RateDegrees(axis,
            180).Duration(10).ParallelTransform2()

        DirectAnimationControl.Image =
            surface.Image.Transform(Twist).Transform(Sweep)
            .Transform(MeterLibrary.Scale2(1./30000., 1./30000.))

        DirectAnimationControl.Start()
    }
```

You can see the results of this page in Figure 8.8. When you click the button, a red figure appears and twists over the text in the Web page while moving to the right.

Chapter 8 Working with Multimedia

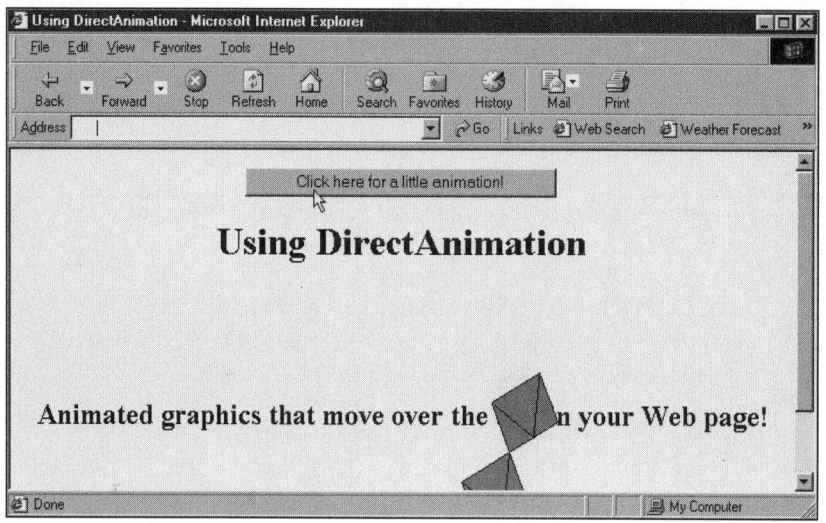

Figure 8.8   Using DirectAnimation and an **<object>** element.

Creating Inline Video

The big boss appears and says, "We need to add some video to our Web page; all the competitors are doing it." "What kind of video would you like?" you ask. "Why," the BB says, startled, "a video of me, of course."

Earlier in this chapter, we saw how to use the **<img>** element and the **<embed>** element to produce inline video. You can use the **<img>** element's **dynsrc** attribute in Internet Explorer to display videos. Here's the example we saw in the beginning of this chapter:

```
<?xml version="1.0"?>
<!DOCTYPE html PUBLIC "-//W3C//DTD XHTML 1.0 Transitional//EN"
"http://www.w3.org/tr/xhtml1/DTD/xhtml1-transitional.dtd">
<html xmlns="http://www.w3.org/1999/xhtml" xml:lang="en" lang="en">
    <head>
        <title>
            Video With the &lt;img&gt; Element
        </title>
    </head>

    <body>
        <center>
```

```
            <h1>
                Video With the &lt;img&gt; Element
            </h1>
            <br />
            <br />
            <img dynsrc="chaplin.avi" align="top" width="160"
                height="120" />
            <br />
            <br />
        </center>
    </body>
</html>
```

You can see the results of this page, which plays a Charlie Chaplin video, in Figure 8.4. In addition to using the **<img>** element's **dynsrc** attribute in Internet Explorer, you can use the **<embed>** element in either Internet Explorer or Netscape Navigator to display inline video, like this:

```
<?xml version="1.0"?>
<!DOCTYPE html PUBLIC "-//W3C//DTD XHTML 1.0 Transitional//EN"
"http://www.w3.org/tr/xhtml1/DTD/xhtml1-transitional.dtd">
<html xmlns="http://www.w3.org/1999/xhtml" xml:lang="en" lang="en">
    <head>
        <title>
            Video With the &lt;embed&gt; Element
        </title>
    </head>

    <body>
        <center>
            <h1>
                Video With the &lt;embed&gt; Element
            </h1>

            <embed src="chaplin.avi" border="0" autostart="true"
                loop="true" width="160" height="120"></embed>
        </center>
    </body>
</html>
```

You can see the results of this page in Figure 8.5. According to W3C, **<embed>** may be superseded by **<object>**, so you can use the **<object>** element to display inline videos, like this:

```
<?xml version="1.0"?>
<!DOCTYPE html PUBLIC "-//W3C//DTD XHTML 1.0 Transitional//EN"
    "http://www.w3.org/tr/xhtml1/DTD/xhtml1-transitional.dtd">
<html xmlns="http://www.w3.org/1999/xhtml" xml:lang="en" lang="en">
    <head>
        <title>
            Videos With the &lt;object&gt; Element
        </title>
    </head>

    <body>

        <center>
            <h1>
                Videos With the &lt;object&gt; Element
            </h1>
            <br />
            <br />
            <object data="chaplin.avi" type="video/msvideo"
                width="120"
                height="160">
            </object>
            <br />
            <br />
        </center>
    </body>
</html>
```

For more details, see "**<object>** and **<param>**—Placing an Object into a Web Page" in the "Immediate Solutions" section of this chapter.

Displaying Loading Images for Inline Video

Sometimes it takes a long time to download video files. In Internet Explorer, you can display an image containing a message to inform the user that the video is in the process of being downloaded. You do this with the **<img>** element's **src** attribute, which holds the image to display while the video is loading. Here's an example:

```
<?xml version="1.0"?>
<!DOCTYPE html PUBLIC "-//W3C//DTD XHTML 1.0 Transitional//EN"
"http://www.w3.org/tr/xhtml1/DTD/xhtml1-transitional.dtd">
<html xmlns="http://www.w3.org/1999/xhtml" xml:lang="en" lang="en">
    <head>
        <title>
            Displaying A Wait Image
        </title>
    </head>

    <body>
        <center>
            <h1>
                Displaying A Wait Image
            </h1>
            <br />
            <br />
            <img dynsrc="chaplin.avi" src="wait.gif" align = "top" />
            <br />
            <br />
        </center>
    </body>
</html>
```

You can see the image that this page displays in Figure 8.9.

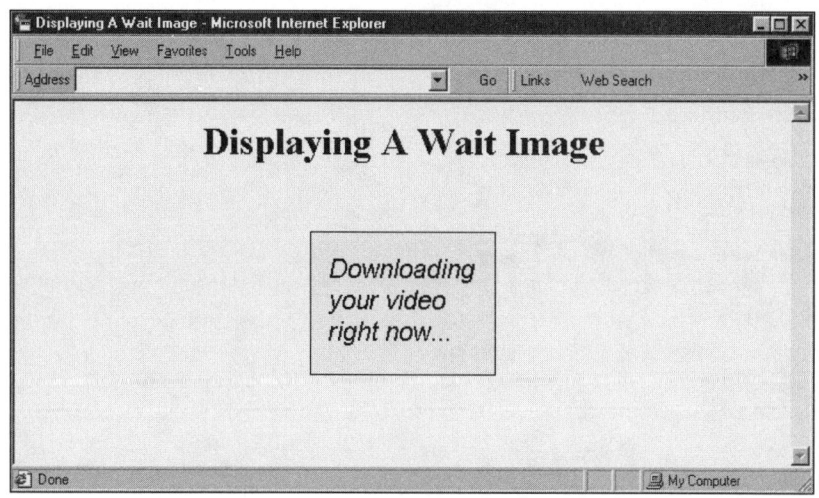

Figure 8.9   Displaying an image while downloading a video.

Using Scrolling Marquees

In Chapter 3, we discussed the use of scrolling marquees in Internet Explorer to display moving text. (For the details, see "**<marquee>**—Displaying Text in a Scrolling Marquee" in Chapter 3.)

Here's an example showing the various **<marquee>** options at work:

```
<?xml version="1.0"?>
<!DOCTYPE html PUBLIC "-//W3C//DTD XHTML 1.0 Transitional//EN"
"http://www.w3.org/tr/xhtml1/DTD/xhtml1-transitional.dtd">
<html xmlns="http://www.w3.org/1999/xhtml" xml:lang="en" lang="en">
    <head>
        <title>
            Using the &lt;marquee&gt; tag
        </title>
    </head>

    <body>

        <marquee align = "top" loop="infinite" behavior="bounce"
            bgcolor="#00ff00" direction="right">
            <h2>
                Here's a marquee!
            </h2>
        </marquee>

        <center>
            <h1>
                Using Marquees
            </h1>
        </center>

        <marquee align="left" loop="infinite" behavior="scroll"
            bgcolor="#ff0000" height="40" width="300" direction="down">
            <h2>
                Here's another marquee!
            </h2>
        </marquee>

        <marquee align = "top" loop="infinite" behavior="slide"
            bgcolor="#00ffff" width="100%" direction="right">
            <h2>
```

```
                                 And one more!
                        </h2>
                </marquee>

    </body>
</html>
```

The results of this page appear in Figure 8.10.

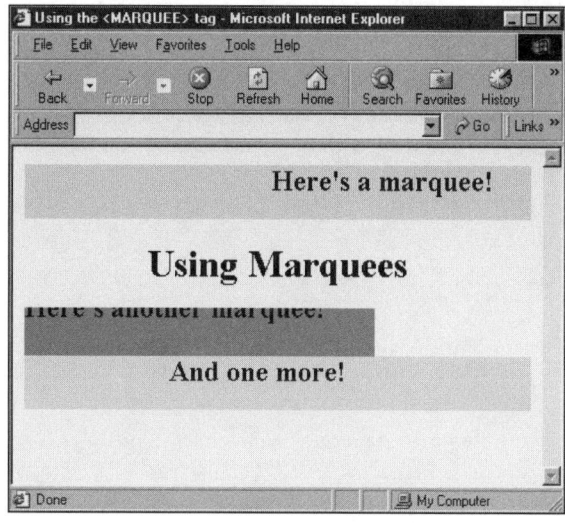

Figure 8.10   Using the <marquee> tag.

Using Internet Explorer's Multimedia Controls

As of version 4, Internet Explorer comes with a number of controls that Microsoft calls the multimedia controls. I'll cover these more when discussing dynamic XHTML in Chapter 16, but here's a short overview of these controls and their functions:

- *Behaviors*—Creates special behaviors for elements in the page.
- *Effects*—Lets you apply graphics filters to the page.
- *Hot Spot*—Converts regions of the screen into "clickable" regions.
- *Mixer*—Mixes WAV files.
- *Path*—Moves elements along a path, creating animation.
- *Sequencer*—Provides control for timing events.

- *Sprite*—Creates sprite-based animations.
- *Sprite Buttons*—Creates sprite-based animated buttons.
- *Structured Graphics*—Creates powerful graphics.

You can find an example of the Structured Graphics control in "**<object>** and **<param>**—Placing an Object into a Web Page" in the "Immediate Solutions" section of this chapter. Here's an example of using the Effects control to show how to apply a shadow filter to text:

```
<?xml version="1.0"?>
<!DOCTYPE html PUBLIC "-//W3C//DTD XHTML 1.0 Transitional//EN"
"http://www.w3.org/tr/xhtml1/DTD/xhtml1-transitional.dtd">
<html xmlns="http://www.w3.org/1999/xhtml" xml:lang="en" lang="en">
    <head>
        <title>
            Using Filters
        </title>
    </head>

    <body>
        <center>
            <h1>
                Using Filters
            </h1>

            <input value="Click Me" type="button"
                onclick="Div1.style.filter =
                'shadow(color=#550055, direction=300, enabled=1)'" />

            <p>
            <div id="Div1" style =
            "width:95%;font-size:24pt;font-family:verdana;font-style:bold">
            Here's some text showing what the shadow filter does.
            </div>
            </p>
        </center>
    </body>
</html>
```

You can see the results of this page in Figure 8.11, where you see a shadow applied to the text in that figure.

Immediate Solutions

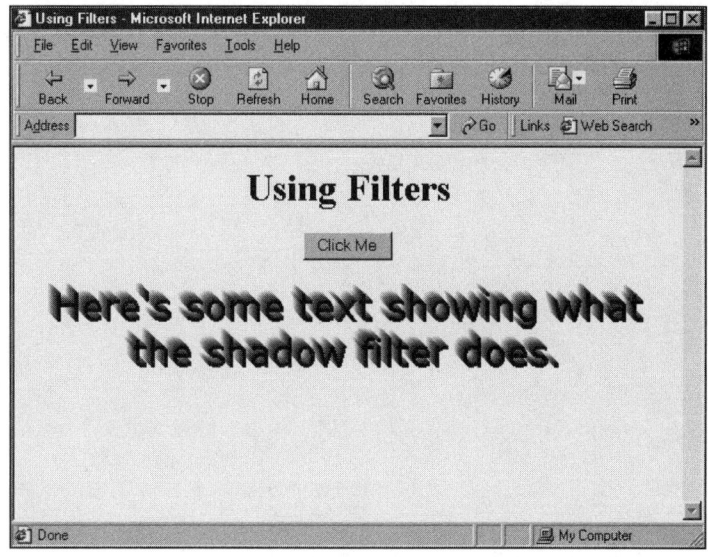

Figure 8.11   Using the Effects multimedia control.

Chapter 9

Cascading Style Sheets

If you need an immediate solution to:	See page:
Using External Style Sheets	522
`<style>`—Using Embedded Style Sheets	524
Using Inline Styles	525
Creating and Using Style Classes	527
Specifying Styles by Element ID	529
What Background and Color Properties Are Available?	530
What Positioning and Block Properties Are Available?	533
What XHTML Element Box Properties Are Available?	535
What Font Properties Are Available?	541
What List Properties Are Available?	543
What Text Properties Are Available?	545
What Table Properties Are Available?	548
What Visual Effects Properties Are Available?	550
Using `<span>` to Apply Styles	551
Using `<div>` to Apply Styles	552
Applying Styles to Text: Bold, Italic, and Underlined	553
Applying Styles to Fonts: Font, Font Size, Font Weight, Font Style	554
Setting Colors and Backgrounds	558
Applying Styles to Margins, Indentations, and Alignments	561
Applying Styles to Hyperlinks	562
Applying Styles to Lists	563
Using Styles to Position Elements: Absolute Positioning	565
Using Styles to Position Elements: Relative Positioning	567

In Depth

As you know, part of the onward and upward march of HTML has involved replacing style tags and attributes with cascading style sheets. In this chapter, I'm going to cover the details of how cascading style sheets work in XHTML. Using style sheets is particularly important in XHTML because you can create your own elements, and, using style sheets, you can specify how to display those new elements, as we'll see in Chapter 15.

One thing you should know is that many people find working with style sheets somewhat involved and difficult. I'll try to make the subject as clear as possible, but there's a fair bit of syntax to learn when you're applying styles, and there are three ways to apply styles in Web pages. The upshot is that this topic takes some patience and investment of time to master. In fact, it's a huge topic and entire books have been devoted to it.

What Are Style Sheets All About?

Style sheets represent the World Wide Web Consortium's (W3C's) effort to improve on the tag- and attribute-based method of formatting. The idea is that style sheets provide a way of customizing whole pages at once and in much more detail than is possible with the simple use of tags and attributes. For that reason, most style attributes (such as **align**) and many style tags (such as **<u>** for underlined text) have been deprecated. Instead, you can specify the style for a page's elements all at once. In this next example, I'm assigning styles for the **<body>**, **<a>**, and **<h1>** elements in the **<style>** element, which goes in a page's head:

```
<?xml version="1.0"?>
<!DOCTYPE html PUBLIC "-//W3C//DTD XHTML 1.0 Transitional//EN"
    "http://www.w3.org/tr/xhtml1/DTD/xhtml1-transitional.dtd">
<html xmlns="http://www.w3.org/1999/xhtml" xml:lang="en" lang="en">
    <head>
        <title>
            Welcome
        </title>
        <style type="text/css">
            body {background: white; color: black}
            a:link {color: red}
            a:visited {color: blue}
```

```
            a:active {color: green}
            h1 {font-size: 36pt}
        </style>

    </head>

    <body>
        Welcome to my page!
        If you don't like it, you can go to
        <a href="http://www.w3c.org">W3C</a>.
    </body>
</html>
```

Now the **<body>**, **<a>**, and **<h1>** elements will appear as we have styled them throughout the page. An expression like **h1 {font-size: 36pt}** is called a *rule*, and in this case, it sets the font size of **<h1>** elements to 36 points. An expression like **font-size** is called a *property*. This is the way style sheets work—you set a certain style, such as the size of a font, by assigning a value to the corresponding property and enclosing the assignment in curly braces. (Use a colon, not an equal sign, to assign that value to the property.) There are hundreds of properties to choose from—you'll find lists of them throughout this chapter. You assign values to properties in style rules. Style sheets themselves are just lists of rules.

You can create styles in three ways:

- *External style sheets*—These are useful when you want all the pages on your Web site to adhere to the same set of styles.

- *Embedded style sheets*—Styles are specified in the **<style>** element, like the one in the previous example.

- *Inline styles*—The **style** attribute of the tags you want to style is used, instead of the **<style>** element.

We'll use all three techniques in this chapter.

NOTE: *XML parsers, like the ones in XHTML browsers, are allowed to read and interpret every part of your document, so if your style sheet includes the characters < or & or]]> or —, you should make your style sheet external. Also, XML parsers, like the ones at the heart of XHTML browsers, are allowed to remove comments, so the practice of "hiding" style sheets inside comments—as Web authors sometimes did to make documents backward compatible—will probably not work as expected in XHTML.*

Style sheets themselves are implemented with the Cascading Style Sheets (CSS) specification, which is now in its second version. The first CSS specification is known as CSS1, and the second as CSS2. CSS2 implements CSS1 and adds a great deal to it. CSS3 is now under development, and you can follow its progress at **www.w3.org/Style/CSS/current-work**.

TIP: *There are more styles in CSS2—such as aural style sheets—than I can possibly include in this chapter. See* **www.w3.org/tr/REC-CSS2/** *for all the details.*

So what should you learn, CSS1 or the expanded and improved version CSS2? It all depends on your browser because most browsers have implemented only part of each specification. (These specifications are so large that one can easily imagine the browser programming teams being overwhelmed.) I can't stress this enough—test your code in as many browsers as you can. It is the most important thing you can do because style-sheet implementation varies a great deal from browser to browser.

If you're new to CSS, here are a few valuable resources:

- The W3C CSS validator is at **http://jigsaw.w3.org/css-validator/**, and it'll check the CSS in your pages for you.
- The TIDY program discussed in Chapter 1 can convert styles to CSS for you. You can find TIDY at **www.w3.org/People/Raggett/tidy**.
- There are dozens of CSS resources available at the W3C "Learning CSS" page, **www.w3.org/Style/CSS/**. If you're going to be using CSS a good deal, this is the online resource to check out.

As I mentioned, to some extent, styles are implemented in different ways in different browsers. In this example, I'll take a look at the same page in Internet Explorer and Netscape Navigator. Here's the XHTML:

```
<?xml version="1.0"?>
<!DOCTYPE html PUBLIC "-//W3C//DTD XHTML 1.0 Transitional//EN"
    "http://www.w3.org/tr/xhtml1/DTD/xhtml1-transitional.dtd">
<html xmlns="http://www.w3.org/1999/xhtml" xml:lang="en" lang="en">
    <head>
        <title>
            Style Differences
        </title>
    </head>

    <body>

        <center>
            <h1>Style Differences</h1>
        </center>

        <span style="letter-spacing: 20px">letter-spacing: 20px</span>
        <br />
        vertical-align:<span style="vertical-align: super">super</span>
        <br />
```

```
            <span style="text-decoration: underline">
                text-decoration: underline
            </span>
            <br />
            <span style="margin-left: 20%">margin-left: 20%</span>
            <br />
            <span style="text-indent: 20px">text-indent: 20px</span>
            <br />
            <span style="text-decoration: overline">
                text-decoration: overline
            </span>

    </body>

</html>
```

You can see the results of this XHTML in the two browsers in Figures 9.1 and 9.2. As you can see, there's quite a difference. Of course, I'm emphasizing the difference by choosing styles that these browsers implement differently, but the point is an important one—browsers do indeed implement styles in ways that can differ significantly.

Much of this chapter will list the properties that you use to set styles, discuss what elements those properties apply to, and show their possible settings because that's what you need to know before working with style sheets. However, before we get to those details, there's more information we should cover. For

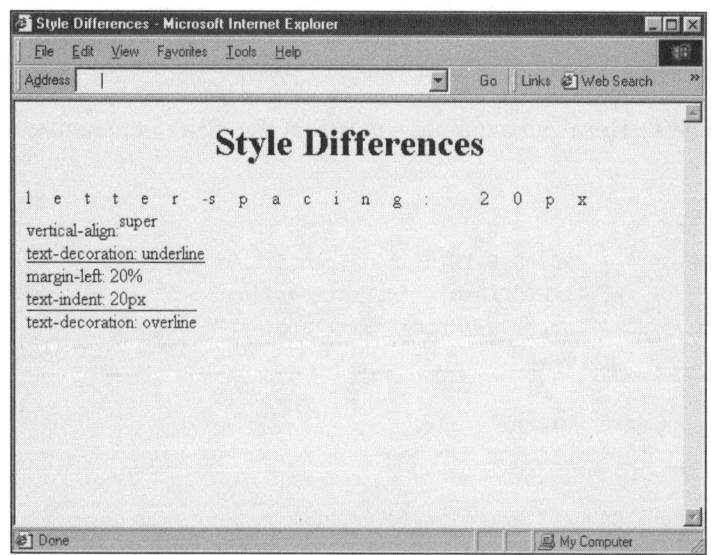

Figure 9.1   A styled page in Internet Explorer.

Chapter 9 Cascading Style Sheets

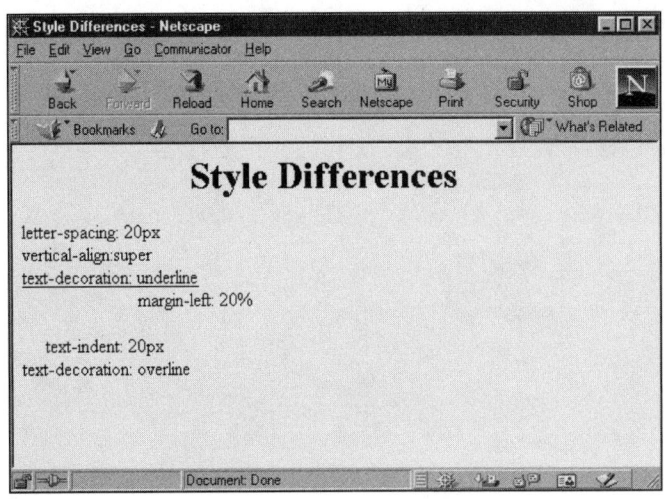

Figure 9.2 A styled page in Netscape Navigator.

example, I said that there are three ways to implement styles—external style sheets, embedded style sheets, and inline styles—so now I'll take a look at how those work.

External Style Sheets

External style sheets are just that—style sheets that are stored separately from your Web page. These are useful if you're setting the styles for an entire Web site (all the pages in the site). When you change the styles in an external style sheet, you change the styles of all the pages that use it. To specify that your page uses an external style sheet, you use the **<link>** element introduced in Chapter 5, setting its **href** attribute to the name of the style sheet (which has the extension .css for cascading style sheets). Here's an example—note that the **<link>** element goes in the page's head:

```
<?xml version="1.0"?>
<!DOCTYPE html PUBLIC "-//W3C//DTD XHTML 1.0 Transitional//EN"
"http://www.w3.org/tr/xhtml1/DTD/xhtml1-transitional.dtd">
<html xmlns="http://www.w3.org/1999/xhtml" xml:lang="en" lang="en">
    <head>
        <title>
            Using An External Style Sheet
        </title>

        <link rel="stylesheet" href="style.css" />

    </head>
```

```
    <body>

        <center>

            <h1>
                Using An External Style Sheet
            </h1>

            <p>
            This page uses an external style sheet.
            </p>

        </center>

    </body>
</html>
```

The style sheet itself simply contains CSS rules, one per line. Here's an example of style.css, which is a plain text file with the following contents:

```
body {background-color: #ffffcc; font-family: arial}
a:link {color: #0000ff}
a:visited {color: #ffff00}
a:hover {color: #00ff00}
a:active {color: #ff0000}
p {font-style: italic}
```

In the previous example, I'm setting the background color of the Web page by setting the background color property of the **<body>** element as well as setting the font it uses. In addition, I'm setting the colors used for the **<a>** element, setting the colors used for the hyperlinks, and making sure that paragraph text in the **<p>** element appears in italics. You can see the results in Figure 9.3.

As you can see from this example, working with styles is largely a matter of knowing which properties are available and what kinds of values they can take, which is why a large part of this chapter is arranged in a reference style, listing properties and values for easier access.

NOTE: *When you're setting the styles of hyperlinks, visited hyperlinks, hyperlinks with the mouse hovering over them, and active hyperlinks (those being clicked), you use a slight variation in syntax. You need to follow the* **<a>** *element with a colon (:) and one of the following terms:* **link**, **visited**, **hover**, *or* **active**. *See "Applying Styles to Hyperlinks" in the "Immediate Solutions" section of this chapter.*

Using **<link>** is an HTML technique, but note that XHTML documents can be treated as either HTML or XML. When you deliver an XHTML document as XML,

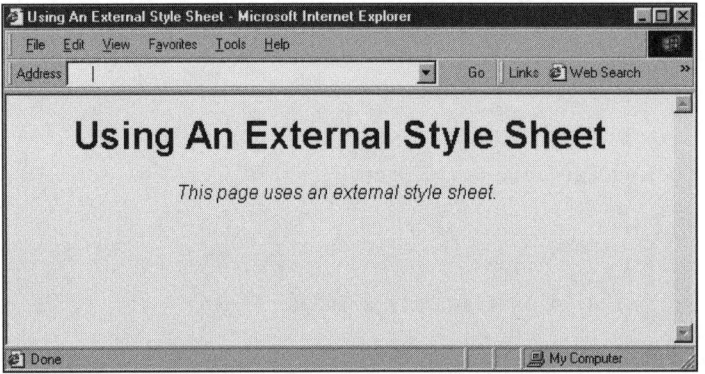

Figure 9.3 A result of using an external style sheet.

you use an XML processing instruction, **<?xml-stylesheet?>**, to indicate the style sheet you want to use. (You can't embed style sheets in straight XML documents; instead, you usually use external style sheets.) Here's how the previous XHTML document would look if you wanted to treat it as XML in an XML browser:

```
<?xml version="1.0"?>
<?xml-stylesheet type="text/css" href="style.css"?>
<!DOCTYPE html PUBLIC "-//W3C//DTD XHTML 1.0 Transitional//EN"
"http://www.w3.org/tr/xhtml1/DTD/xhtml1-transitional.dtd">
<html xmlns="http://www.w3.org/1999/xhtml" xml:lang="en" lang="en">
    <head>
        <title>
            Using An External Style Sheet
        </title>
    </head>

    <body>

        <center>

            <h1>
                Using An External Style Sheet
            </h1>

            <p>
            This page uses an external style sheet.
            </p>

        </center>

    </body>
</html>
```

> **NOTE:** The style type in the previous example is specified as text/css, but this is often not necessary because browsers will default to that type. Using this specification does serve to distinguish this style sheet from JavaScript style sheets, whose type is text/javascript, or XSL style sheets, whose type is text/xsl.

We'll see more about adding styles to XML documents in Chapter 15.

Embedded Style Sheets

Embedded style sheets are part of a Web page itself. They're useful because they collect the styles applied throughout the page and put them into one place—the **<style>** element in the page's head.

Here's an example—notice that the rules look just as they do in external style sheets and that the **<style>** element appears in the page's head:

```
<?xml version="1.0"?>
<!DOCTYPE html PUBLIC "-//W3C//DTD XHTML 1.0 Transitional//EN"
"http://www.w3.org/tr/xhtml1/DTD/xhtml1-transitional.dtd">
<html xmlns="http://www.w3.org/1999/xhtml" xml:lang="en" lang="en">
    <head>
        <title>
            This is a Web page!
        </title>

        <style type="text/css">
            body {background: white; color: black}
            a:link {color: red}
            a:visited {color: blue}
            a:active {color: green}
            p {font-style: italic}
        </style>

    </head>

    <body>
        Welcome to my page!
        <p>
            If you don't like it, you can go to
            <a href="http://www.w3c.org">W3C</a>.
        </p>
    </body>
</html>
```

You can see the results of this XHTML in Figure 9.4.

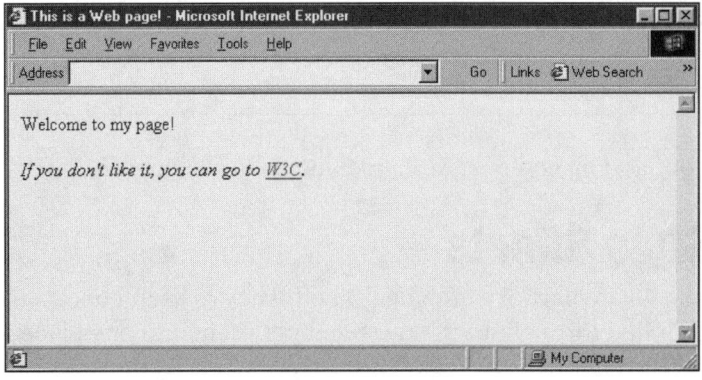

Figure 9.4   Using an embedded style sheet.

Using embedded style sheets is one of the most common ways of working with style sheets, but there is another way—using inline styles.

Inline Styles

One gets the strong feeling that style sheet purists would like to confine all styles to well-defined style sheets. This idea creates a problem, however—what if you want to deviate briefly from those styles, such as making a word italic? To handle such cases, XHTML tags include a **style** attribute (which is different from the **style** tag), which you can use to set styles for the corresponding element. Almost all XHTML elements that display something in a Web page support the **style** attribute.

Here's an example that we first saw in Chapter 6. In this case, I'm setting the colors of table cells one by one:

```
<table border="2">
    <tr>
        <th style="background-color: rgb(255, 0, 0)">Tic</th>
        <th style="background-color: rgb(255, 0, 0)">Tac</th>
        <th style="background-color: rgb(255, 0, 0)">Toe</th>
    </tr>
    <tr>
        <td style="background-color: rgb(255, 255, 255)">X</td>
        <td style="background-color: rgb(0, 0, 0); color:
            rgb(255, 255, 255)">
            O
        </td>
        <td style="background-color: rgb(255, 255, 255)">X</td>
    </tr>
```

```
        <tr>
            <td style="background-color: rgb(0, 0, 0); color:
                rgb(255, 255, 255)">
                0
            </td>
            <td style="background-color: rgb(255, 255, 255)">X</td>
            <td style="background-color: rgb(0, 0, 0); color:
                rgb(255, 255, 255)">
                0
            </td>
        </tr>
        <tr>
            <td style="background-color: rgb(255, 255, 255)">X</td>
            <td style="background-color: rgb(0, 0, 0); color:
                rgb(255, 255, 255)">
                0
            </td>
            <td style="background-color: rgb(255, 255, 255)">X</td>
        </tr>
</table>
```

You can see the results of this XHTML in Figure 9.5.

So, as you can see, there are three ways to apply styles: using external style sheets, using embedded style sheets with the **<style>** element, and using inline styles with the **style** attribute. What happens if they conflict? There's a well-defined precedence for documents treated as HTML: external styles can be overridden by embedded styles, and embedded styles can be overridden by inline styles.

In view of the fact that style purists have had to accept the **style** attribute and the resulting decentralization of style definitions, the CSS specification introduced style *classes* to ease the situation.

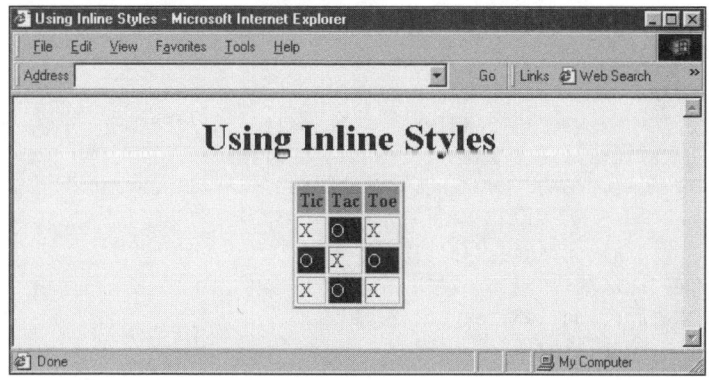

Figure 9.5   Using inline styles.

Creating Style Classes

A *style class* is a new style that you can apply to various elements throughout your page. When you create a class, you centralize the class's style definition with the rest of the styles in the **<style>** element or external style sheet.

In this next example, I'm creating a class named **big**, which can be applied only to **<p>** elements, and a style named **red**, which can be applied to any element. Note the syntax: To make sure you can use **big** only with **<p>** elements, you define it as **p.big**. To let the **red** class be used with any element that can display foreground colors, you define it as **.red** (the dot in front indicates that you're creating a universally applicable class). Here's the XHTML:

```
<?xml version="1.0"?>
<!DOCTYPE html PUBLIC "-//W3C//DTD XHTML 1.0 Transitional//EN"
"http://www.w3.org/tr/xhtml1/DTD/xhtml1-transitional.dtd">
<html xmlns="http://www.w3.org/1999/xhtml" xml:lang="en" lang="en">
    <head>
        <title>Using Style Classes</title>
        <style type="text/css">
            body {background: white; color: black}
            a:link {color: red}
            a:visited {color: blue}
            a:active {color: green}
            p.big {font-size: 18pt}
            .red {color: red}
        </style>
    </head>
    .
    .
    .
```

Now I apply these classes to various elements by using the **class** attribute that most displayable tags have. Here's how the example continues:

```
<?xml version="1.0"?>
<!DOCTYPE html PUBLIC "-//W3C//DTD XHTML 1.0 Transitional//EN"
"http://www.w3.org/tr/xhtml1/DTD/xhtml1-transitional.dtd">
<html xmlns="http://www.w3.org/1999/xhtml" xml:lang="en" lang="en">
    <head>
        <title>Using Style Classes</title>
        <style type="text/css">
            body {background: white; color: black}
            a:link {color: red}
            a:visited {color: blue}
```

```
            a:active {color: green}
            p.big {font-size: 18pt}
            .red {color: red}
        </style>
    </head>

    <body>
        <center>
            <h1>
                Using Style Classes
            </h1>
        </center>

        Welcome to my page!
        If you don't like it, you can go to
        <a href="http://www.w3c.org">W3C</a>.

        <p>
        Here's some normal paragraph text.
        </p>

        <p class="big">
        Here's some bigger paragraph text.
        </p>

        <p>
        Here's some <span class="red">text in red</span>.
        </p>
    </body>
</html>
```

Note that I use the **<span>** element to mark the text to which I want to apply the **red** class. That's what **<span>** is really for—to mark small sections of your page and apply a style. The results of this XHTML appear in Figure 9.6. The **<div>** element works much the same way, except that you use **<div>** to mark whole text blocks, not individual words.

The idea behind classes is that you can put all the style definitions in the same place and then just use classes in various elements as needed. This technique can be more useful than using the **style** attribute if the style you're applying is long and involved.

TIP: *You can also specify styles targeted to the ID you give to an element. See "Specifying Styles by Element ID" in the "Immediate Solutions" section of this chapter for the details.*

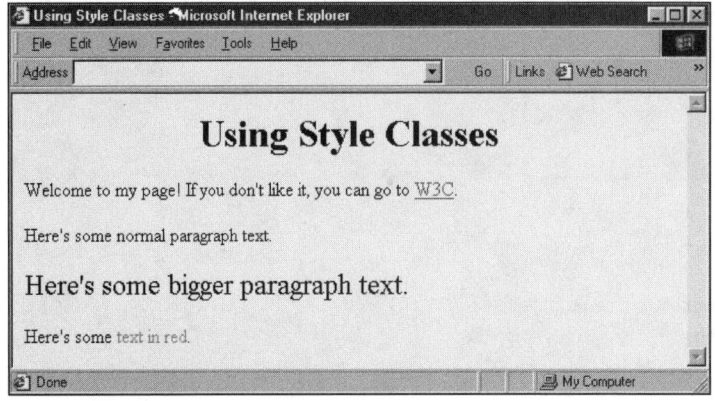

Figure 9.6 Using style classes.

There are still a few more points to clarify before moving to the "Immediate Solutions" section for details. For example, XHTML styles are called *cascading styles*. What does that mean? We'll discuss cascading styles in the next section.

Cascading Styles

Cascading styles are called cascading because a child element (that is, an element enclosed in another element) can inherit the styles of its parent. In this example, I'm applying a style (setting indentation and font size) to a **<div>** element. Another **<div>** element inside the first **<div>** element will inherit those styles:

```
<?xml version="1.0"?>
<!DOCTYPE html PUBLIC "-//W3C//DTD XHTML 1.0 Transitional//EN"
"http://www.w3.org/tr/xhtml1/DTD/xhtml1-transitional.dtd">
<html xmlns="http://www.w3.org/1999/xhtml" xml:lang="en" lang="en">
    <head>
        <title>
            Using Style Inheritance
        </title>

        <style type="text/css">
            div.indentlarge {font-size: 24pt; margin-left: 10%}
        </style>
    </head>

    <body>

        <center>
            <h1>Using Style Inheritance</h1>
        </center>
```

```
        <div class="indentlarge">
            This is the outer &lt;div&gt;.
        <br />
        <br />

        <div>
            This is the inner &lt;div&gt;, which
            has inherited its style from the outer &lt;div&gt;.
        </div>

        </div>

    </body>

</html>
```

Notice how this works—I'm applying the style to the outer **<div>** element only, not to the inner one, but the inner **<div>** element inherits the style from its parent. You can see the results of this XHTML in Figure 9.7.

Organizing Styles

As you become more familiar with working with styles, you'll appreciate the fact that style rules can take on various shortcut forms. For example, you can collapse all these rules:

```
h4 {font-weight: bold}
h4 {font-size: 12pt}
h4 {font-family: Arial}
h4 {font-style: normal}
```

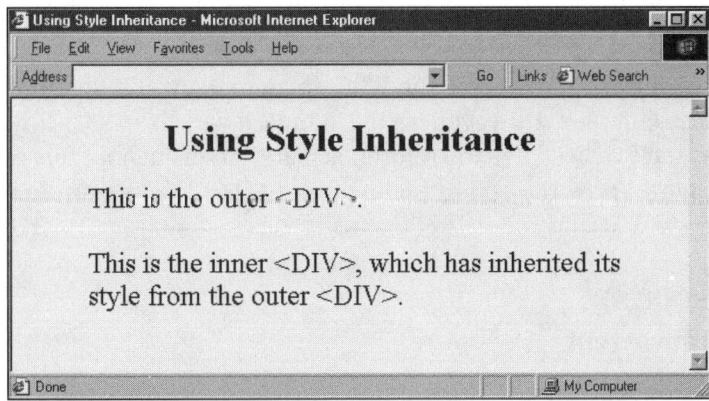

Figure 9.7   Using style inheritance.

into one, like this (note that you separate each property assignment with a semicolon):

```
h4 {
  font-weight: bold;
  font-size: 12pt;
  font-family: Arial;
  font-style: normal
}
```

You can specify that a style applies to more than one element in this way:

```
h1, h2, h3, h4 {
  font-weight: bold;
  font-size: 12pt;
  font-family: Arial;
  font-style: normal
}
```

You can also use *shorthand* properties. As you'll see in the reference material in the "Immediate Solutions" section, using some properties, such as the **font** property, allows you to handle assignments for a number of other properties at the same time, such as **font-family**, **font-size**, and **font-weight**. Here's an example. This rule:

```
body {font-family: arial, helvetica; font-size: 10pt; font-weight: bold}
```

is the same as this rule:

```
body {font: bold 10pt arial, helvetica}
```

Understanding Style Specifications

If you look at the style specifications in the W3C documents, you'll find that the syntax used is a little complex. However, it's the standard way to specify the syntax used for styles, and I've used it in the reference material throughout this chapter. For example, here's how the style specification for the **background-color** property looks:

background-color

CSS1: <color>|transparent

CSS2: inherit

Initial: transparent

Applies to: All elements

Inherited: No

Supported: [IE4, IE5, NS4]

This syntax is worth getting to know—or at least it's worth knowing that you can refer to the following list if things get confusing. Here is how the various syntax elements of this chapter's style specifications work:

- Terms in angle brackets (<) and (>) indicate units for values (see Table 9.1) or properties.
- Values separated with a pipe (|) character indicate alternatives, only one of which can be used.
- Values separated with a double pipe (||) indicate options, one or more of which must be used, in any order.
- Brackets ([) and (]) group statements that are evaluated much like mathematical statements.
- An asterisk (*) means that the preceding term occurs zero or more times.
- A plus sign (+) means that the preceding term occurs one or more times.
- A question mark (?) means that the preceding term is optional.
- Curly braces ({) and (}) surround pairs of numbers, giving the minimum and maximum number of times a term can occur (for example, {1, 4}).

Using this list, you can decipher the **background-color** property specification. Next, I'm listing the values that this style can take in the CSS1 specification, **<color>** or **transparent**, and then the values that CSS2 adds, which in this case is just the value **inherit**.

background-color

CSS1: <color>|transparent

CSS2: inherit

Initial: transparent

Applies to: All elements

Inherited: No

Supported: [IE4, IE5, NS4]

Although you can use the terms **transparent** and **inherit** directly—like this: {background-color: transparent}—expressions in angle brackets, like **<color>**, use a specific format. You'll find these formats in Table 9.1. There you'll see that

\<color\> can be set to a Red, Green, Blue (RGB) triplet value or a predefined color, which means that you can assign a color to the **background-color** property like this: **{background-color: "#ffff00"}**.

Note that in the specification of all properties, I indicate whether the property can inherit values from its parent element, which elements the property applies to, and the initial setting of the property. I also indicate which version of which browser supports each property. (Note, however, that although a browser might

Table 9.1 Predefined units in the CSS2 specification.

Unit Measurement	Description
\<absolute-size\>	Absolute font sizes; can be **xx-small**, **x-small**, **small**, **medium**, **large**, **x-large**, **xx-large**.
\<angle\>	Angles; can be **deg**, **grad**, or **rad**.
\<border-style\>	Border of box; can be **none**, **dotted**, **dashed**, **solid**, **double**, **groove**, **ridge**, **inset**, or **outset**.
\<border-width\>	Width of a border; can be **thin**, **medium**, **thick**, or an explicit length.
\<color\>	Color; can be specified with a predefined color value or an RGB triplet color value.
\<family-name\>	Name of a font family, such as Arial, Times New Roman, or Courier.
\<frequency\>	Frequency values; units may be Hz or kHz.
\<generic-family\>	Generic names for fonts that you use as a last resort if the browser can't find a specific font. Examples are **serif** (browser should choose a serif font), **sans-serif** (browser should choose a sans serif font), and **monospace** (browser should choose a monospace font).
\<generic-voice\>	Aural voices; can be male, female, or child.
\<integer\>	Standard integer values.
\<length\>	Length; can start with a **+** or **-** followed by a number, which may include a decimal point followed by a unit identifier. The unit identifier can be **em** (font size of the relevant font), **ex** (the x-height of the font), **px** (pixels as specified relative to the viewing device), **pt** (points, 1/72 of an inch), **in** (inches), **cm** (centimeters), **mm** (millimeters), or **pc** (picas, 1/6 of an inch).
\<number\>	Number; can include a sign and a decimal point.
\<percentage\>	Number; can include a sign followed by a percent sign (%).
\<relative-size\>	Font size relative to the parent element; can be either larger or smaller.
\<shape\>	Rectangle only, like this: **rect** (\<top\> \<right\> \<bottom\> \<left\>).
\<time\>	Time units specified as a number followed immediately by **ms** (for milliseconds) or **s** (for seconds).
\<uri\>	Uniform Resource Indicator (URI): the Web address of a page element, such as an image.

support a property, it might not support all possible values listed for that property.) Here is a specification:

background-color

CSS1: <color>|transparent

CSS2: inherit

Initial: transparent

Applies to: All elements

Inherited: No

Supported: [IE4, IE5, NS4]

Before we start going into more details in the "Immediate Solutions" section, you should know about two property values: **auto** and the new CSS2 value **inherit**. Assigning the **auto** value to a property means that the browser should set the property (the actual setting usually depends on context, such as the color of surrounding text). Assigning the **inherit** value to a property means that it should inherit this setting from its parent element, if there is one.

You should also know one more term—*box*. As far as style sheets are concerned, each element in your page is rendered in its own box. For that reason, many of the style specifications refer to the element's box, which is the invisible rectangle that surrounds the element. Boxes have borders, padding, and margins surrounding their content.

That's how style specifications work. Now it's time to start listing them and putting them to work. As I mentioned earlier in this chapter, learning to work with styles means knowing which properties are available for which elements and knowing which values they can take.

NOTE: *The style specifications I'll refer to in the "Immediate Solutions" section come from the official CSS2 specification—bear in mind that the way your browser uses these styles may differ.*

Immediate Solutions

Using External Style Sheets

The novice programmer says, "I've got two hundred Web pages that I want to format in the same way—what a job!" "Not really," you say; "just use external style sheets and apply the same style sheet to each page."

As mentioned in the "In Depth" section of this chapter, you can specify styles by using external style sheets. You connect external style sheets to a page by using the **<link>** element, like this:

```
<?xml version="1.0"?>
<!DOCTYPE html PUBLIC "-//W3C//DTD XHTML 1.0 Transitional//EN"
"http://www.w3.org/tr/xhtml1/DTD/xhtml1-transitional.dtd">
<html xmlns="http://www.w3.org/1999/xhtml" xml:lang="en" lang="en">
    <head>
        <title>
            Using An External Style Sheet
        </title>

        <link rel="stylesheet" href="style.css" />

    </head>

    <body>

        <center>

            <h1>
                Using An External Style Sheet
            </h1>

            <p>
            This page uses an external style sheet.
            </p>

        </center>

    </body>
</html>
```

This XHTML links the Web page to an external style sheet named style.css. Here's how that style sheet looks:

```
body {background-color: #FFFFCC; font-family: Arial}
a:link {color: #0000FF}
a:visited {color: #FFFF00}
a:hover {color: #00FF00}
a:active {color: #FF0000}
p {font-style: italic}
```

Note the syntax here, as discussed in the "In Depth" section of this chapter. You create style rules for the various elements you're styling. In this case, I'm creating a style for the **<body>** and **<p>** elements, as well as setting the colors for hyperlinks, visited hyperlinks, hyperlinks when the mouse is over them, and hyperlinks as they're being clicked. You can see the results of this XHTML in Figure 9.3.

Using **<link>** is an HTML technique, but XHTML documents can be treated as either HTML or XML. When you treat an XHTML document as XML, you use an XML processing instruction, **<?xml-stylesheet?>**, to indicate which style sheet you want to use. (You can't embed style sheets in straight XML documents; instead, you usually use external style sheets.) Here's how the previous XHTML document would look if you wanted to treat it as XML in an XML browser:

```
<?xml version="1.0"?>
<!DOCTYPE html PUBLIC "-//W3C//DTD XHTML 1.0 Transitional//EN"
    "http://www.w3.org/tr/xhtml1/DTD/xhtml1-transitional.dtd">
<?xml-stylesheet type="text/css" href="style.css"?>
<html xmlns="http://www.w3.org/1999/xhtml" xml:lang="en" lang="en">
    <head>
        <title>
            Using An External Style Sheet
        </title>
    </head>

    <body>

        <center>

            <h1>
                Using An External Style Sheet
            </h1>

            <p>
```

```
                    This page uses an external style sheet.
                </p>

            </center>

        </body>
</html>
```

\<style\>—Using Embedded Style Sheets

Purpose: Creates styles.

When used as HTML: Start tag/End tag: Required/Required

Supported: [1.0S, 1.0T, 1.0F, 1.1, 3, 3.2, 4, IE3, IE4, IE5, NS4]

Attributes:

- **dir**—Gives the direction of directionally neutral text (text that doesn't have an inherent direction in which you should read it). Possible values: **ltr**, left-to-right text or table; and **rtl**, right-to-left text or table. [1.0S, 1.0T, 1.0F, 1.1, 4]

- **disabled**—Specifies that the styles should not be applied initially. Standalone attribute in HTML. [IE4, IE5]

- **lang**—Base language used for the tag. [1.0S, 1.0T, 1.0F, 1.1, 4]

- **media**—Sets the media for style-sheet definitions (multiple destinations are delimited by commas). Possible values: **screen** (the default), **print**, **projection**, **braille**, **speech**, **all**. [1.0S, 1.0T, 1.0F, 1.1, 4, IE4, IE5]

- **title**—Allows the browser to build a menu of alternative style sheets. Set to alphanumeric values. [1.0S, 1.0T, 1.0F, 1.1, 4]

- **type**—Indicates the MIME type of the **\<style\>** element content. Set to **text/css** or **text/javascript**. Required. [1.0S, 1.0T, 1.0F, 1.1, 4, IE4, IE5, NS4]

- **xml:lang**—Holds the base language for the element when the document is interpreted as an XML document. [1.0S, 1.0T, 1.0F, 1.1]

- **xml:space**—Set to **preserve** to preserve spacing. [1.0S, 1.0T, 1.0F, 1.1]

XHTML events: None

The novice programmer says, "I don't want to have to fuss with external style sheets—can't I put everything into the same Web page?" "You certainly can," you say, "and that's exactly what the **\<style\>** element is for." "Yes?" the NP asks.

As discussed in the "In Depth" section of this chapter, you can use the **\<style\>** element to set styles for an entire Web page. This element goes in a Web page's head, as shown in this next example, which we saw in the beginning of the chapter:

```xml
<?xml version="1.0"?>
<!DOCTYPE html PUBLIC "-//W3C//DTD XHTML 1.0 Transitional//EN"
"http://www.w3.org/tr/xhtml1/DTD/xhtml1-transitional.dtd">
<html xmlns="http://www.w3.org/1999/xhtml" xml:lang="en" lang="en">
    <head>
        <title>This is a Web page!</title>
        <style type="text/css">
            body {background: white; color: black}
            a:link {color: red}
            a:visited {color: blue}
            a:active {color: green}
            p {font-style: italic}
        </style>
    </head>

    <body>
        Welcome to my page!
        <p>
            If you don't like it, you can go to
            <a href="http://www.w3c.org">W3C</a>.
        </p>
    </body>
</html>
```

As with other style sheets, I'm applying the various styles here to Web page elements by listing the style rules, such as **body {background: white; color: black}**. You can see the results of this XHTML in Figure 9.4.

NOTE: *XML parsers, like the ones in XHTML browsers, are allowed to read and interpret every part of your document, so if your style sheet includes the characters < or & or]]> or —, you should make your style sheet external. Also, XML parsers, like the ones at the heart of XHTML browsers, are allowed to remove comments, so the practice of "hiding" style sheets inside comments—as Web authors sometimes did to make documents backward compatible—will probably not work as expected in XHTML.*

Using Inline Styles

"Uh oh," says the novice programmer, "now I've got a problem. I want to apply a style to just a single word, making it italic. How can I do that with a style sheet?" "There are two ways," you say; "you can use style classes, or you can use inline styles."

As discussed in the "In Depth" section of this chapter, you can create inline styles, where you apply styles to one XHTML element only. You create inline styles with the **style** attribute that most XHTML elements have. Here's an example that we saw in the beginning of this chapter:

```
<table border="2">
    <tr>
        <th style="background-color: rgb(255, 0, 0)">Tic</th>
        <th style="background-color: rgb(255, 0, 0)">Tac</th>
        <th style="background-color: rgb(255, 0, 0)">Toe</th>
    </tr>
    <tr>
        <td style="background-color: rgb(255, 255, 255)">X</td>
        <td style="background-color: rgb(0, 0, 0); color:
            rgb(255, 255, 255)">
            0
        </td>
        <td style="background-color: rgb(255, 255, 255)">X</td>
    </tr>
    <tr>
        <td style="background-color: rgb(0, 0, 0); color:
            rgb(255, 255, 255)">
            0
        </td>
        <td style="background-color: rgb(255, 255, 255)">X</td>
        <td style="background-color: rgb(0, 0, 0); color:
            rgb(255, 255, 255)">
            0
        </td>
    </tr>
    <tr>
        <td style="background-color: rgb(255, 255, 255)">X</td>
        <td style="background-color: rgb(0, 0, 0); color:
            rgb(255, 255, 255)">
            0
        </td>
        <td style="background-color: rgb(255, 255, 255)">X</td>
    </tr>
</table>
```

The results of this XHTML appear in Figure 9.5.

TIP: *Inline styles are best used for short applications—for instance, when you italicize a single word. For more lengthy applications, it's a good idea to use style classes. See the next section, "Creating and Using Style Classes."*

> **NOTE:** XML parsers, like the ones in XHTML browsers, are allowed to read and interpret every part of your document, so if your style sheet includes the characters < or & or]]> or —, you should make your style sheet external. Also, XML parsers, like the ones at the heart of XHTML browsers, are allowed to remove comments, so the practice of "hiding" style sheets inside comments—as Web authors sometimes did to make documents backward compatible—will probably not work as expected in XHTML.

Creating and Using Style Classes

"Uh oh," says the novice programmer, "my styles are getting really long now, and it's hard to use them as inline styles because they're doubling the size of my Web page's XHTML." "Hm," you say, "how about using style classes?"

As discussed in the "In Depth" section of this chapter, you can create style classes and apply the styles in those classes to XHTML elements by using the **class** attribute of those elements. Following is an example that we saw at the beginning of this chapter. In this case, I'm creating a class named **big**, for use with **<p>** elements only, which displays larger text, and I'm creating a class named **red**, for use with any element, which changes the foreground color to red. (The dot in front of **red** indicates that **red** is a class, not an XHTML element.) Here's the code:

```
<?xml version="1.0"?>
<!DOCTYPE html PUBLIC "-//W3C//DTD XHTML 1.0 Transitional//EN"
"http://www.w3.org/tr/xhtml1/DTD/xhtml1-transitional.dtd">
<html xmlns="http://www.w3.org/1999/xhtml" xml:lang="en" lang="en">
    <head>
        <title>This is a Web page!</title>
        <style type="text/css">
            body {background: white; color: black}
            a:link {color: red}
            a:visited {color: blue}
            a:active {color: green}
            p.big {font-size: 18pt}
            .red {color: red}
        </style>
    </head>

    <body>
        Welcome to my page!
        If you don't like it, you can go to
        <a href="http://www.w3c.org">W3C</a>.
        <p>
        Here's some normal paragraph text.
        </p>
```

```
        <p class="big">
        Here's some bigger paragraph text.
        </p>
        <p>
        Here's some <span class="red">text in red</span>.
        </p>
    </body>
</html>
```

You can see the results of this XHTML in Figure 9.6.

In the next example, I'm creating a new class named **underlinedText**, which uses the **text-decoration** property to underline text:

```
<?xml version="1.0"?>
<!DOCTYPE html PUBLIC "-//W3C//DTD XHTML 1.0 Transitional//EN"
"http://www.w3.org/tr/xhtml1/DTD/xhtml1-transitional.dtd">
<html xmlns="http://www.w3.org/1999/xhtml" xml:lang="en" lang="en">
    <head>
        <title>
            Using Style Classes
        </title>
        <style type="text/css">
            .underlinedText {text-decoration: underline}
        </style>
    </head>

    <body>
        <center>
            <h1>
                Using Style Classes
            </h1>

            <br />

            <h1 class="underlinedText">
                This text is underlined.
            </h1>

        </center>

    </body>

</html>
```

You can see the results of this XHTML in Figure 9.8.

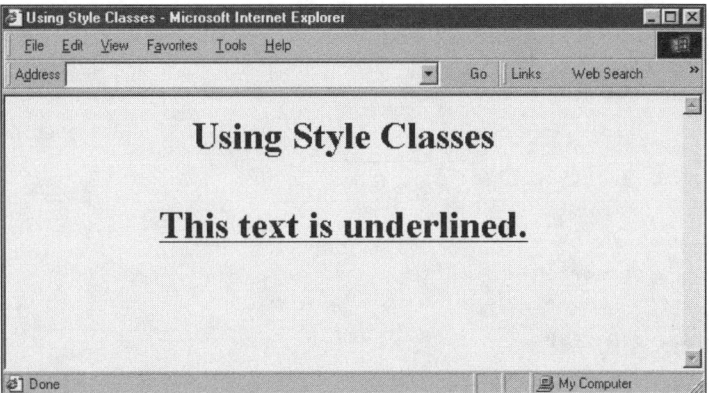

Figure 9.8 Using style classes to underline text.

Specifying Styles by Element ID

If you want to create a number of styles for a certain XHTML element, such as a paragraph, it won't work to list a style simply for the **<p>** element because you can create only one style for the **<p>** element that way. Classes—see the previous section—give you a way around this by allowing you to use different classes for different paragraphs in the document. There's also another way. You can set styles by element ID. To do this, you give an element an ID by using its **ID** attribute, and then you refer to that ID in the style sheet by prefacing it with a pound sign (**#**).

Here's an example in which I'm styling the paragraph with the **id para2** to be different from the other paragraphs in the document:

```
<?xml version="1.0"?>
<!DOCTYPE html PUBLIC "-//W3C//DTD XHTML 1.0 Transitional//EN"
"http://www.w3.org/tr/xhtml1/DTD/xhtml1-transitional.dtd">
<html xmlns="http://www.w3.org/1999/xhtml" xml:lang="en" lang="en">
    <head>
        <title>
            Using IDs To Style Elements
        </title>

        <style type="text/css">
            body {background: white; color: black}
            a:link {color: red}
            a:visited {color: blue}
            a:active {color: green}
            p {font-style: italic}
            #para2 {font-style: normal; color: red}
```

```
            </style>
        </head>

        <body>
            <h1>
                Using IDs To Style Elements
            </h1>
            <p>
                Here's a paragraph.
            <p id="para2">
                Here's a paragraph.
        </body>
</html>
```

What Background and Color Properties Are Available?

There are a huge number of style properties available. What follows are the background and color properties in CSS1 and CSS2.

background

CSS1: [<background-color>||<background-image>||<background-repeat> ||<background-attachment>||<background-position>]

CSS2: inherit

Initial: Not defined

Applies to: All elements

Inherited: No

Supported: [IE3, IE4, IE5]

Sets the specific background properties (such as **background-color**, **background-image**, **background-repeat**, **background-attachment**, and **background-position**) at the same time, which means this property is a shorthand property.

background-attachment

CSS1: scroll|fixed

CSS2: inherit

Initial: scroll

Immediate Solutions

Applies to: All elements

Inherited: No

Supported: [IE4, IE5]

Sets whether a background image is fixed or scrolls when the user scrolls the rest of the page.

background-color

CSS1: <color>|transparent

CSS2: inherit

Initial: transparent

Applies to: All elements

Inherited: No

Supported: [IE4, IE5, NS4]

Specifies the background color of an element by using either a **<color>** value or the keyword **transparent**, which makes the underlying color shine through.

background-image

CSS1: <uri>|none

CSS2: inherit

Initial: None

Applies to: All elements

Inherited: No

Supported: [IE4, IE5, NS4]

Specifies the background image of an element.

TIP: When you're setting a background image, you should also specify a background color that will be used when the image is unavailable.

---

background-position

CSS1: [[<percentage>|<length>]{1,2}|[[top|center|bottom]||[left|center|right]]]

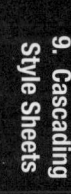

CSS2: inherit

Initial: 0% 0%

Applies to: Block-level and replaced elements

Inherited: No

Supported: [IE4, IE5]

Specifies a background image's initial position.

background-repeat
CSS1: repeat|repeat-x|repeat-y|no-repeat

CSS2: inherit

Initial: repeat

Applies to: All elements

Inherited: No

Supported: [IE4, IE5]

Specifies whether the background image is tiled (repeated), and if so, how.

color
CSS1: <color>

CSS2: inherit

Initial: Browser dependent

Applies to: All elements

Inherited: Yes

Supported: [IE3, IE4, IE5, NS4]

Sets the foreground color of elements that display text.

TIP: *You'll find a complete listing of the CSS1 specification at **www.w3.org/tr/REC-CSS1** and a complete listing of the CSS2 specification at **www.w3.org/tr/REC-CSS2/**. You can even take a look at the current work on CSS3 at **www.w3.org/Style/CSS/current-work**.*

What Positioning and Block Properties Are Available?

One of the major uses for style sheets is to set the position of elements in a Web page. (See the "Immediate Solutions" sections "Using Styles to Position Elements: Absolute Positioning" and "Using Styles to Position Elements: Relative Positioning.") You'll find that these specifications refer to the terms *box* and *block* quite a bit. An element's box is the rectangle it is drawn in. A block simply refers to a block of elements as marked with a **<div>** or other enclosing element.

What follows are the positioning and block properties in CSS1 and CSS2.

bottom, top, left, right
CSS2: <length>|<percentage>|auto|inherit

Initial: auto

Applies to: All elements

Inherited: No

Supported: [IE5, NS4]

Indicate how far a box's bottom, top, left, or right content edges should be offset from the corresponding edges of the box's containing area. These are the properties that position the box.

direction
CSS1: ltr|rtl

CSS2: inherit

Initial: ltr

Applies to: All elements

Inherited: Yes

Supported: [IE5]

Indicates the base writing direction of XHTML blocks as well as the direction of embeddings and overrides for the Unicode bidirectional algorithm.

display
CSS1: inline|block|list-item

CSS2: run-in|compact|marker|table|inline-table|table-row-group|table-header-group|table-footer-group|table-row|table-column-group|table-column|table-cell|table-caption|none|inherit

Initial: inline

Applies to: All elements

Inherited: No

Supported: [IE4, IE5]

Specifies how the contents of a block should be created.

float
CSS1: left|right|none

CSS2: inherit

Initial: None

Applies to: All but positioned elements

Inherited: No

Supported: [IE4, IE5, NS4]

Indicates whether a box should float to the left, to the right, or not at all.

position
CSS2: static|relative|absolute|fixed|inherit

Initial: static

Applies to: All elements, but not generated content

Inherited: No

Supported: [IE4, IE5, NS4]

Specifies which positioning algorithm to use; this makes a difference when you specify properties such as **left** and **right**.

unicode-bidi
CSS2: normal|embed|bidi-override|inherit

Initial: normal

Applies to: All elements

Inherited: No

Supported: [IE5]

Handles embedded elements with reversed Unicode order.

z-index
CSS2: auto|<integer>|inherit

Initial: auto

Applies to: Positioned elements

Inherited: No

Supported: [IE4, IE5, NS4]

Specifies the stacking level of the box in the stacking order for positioned boxes.

---

*TIP: You'll find a complete listing of the CSS1 specification at **www.w3.org/tr/REC-CSS1** and a complete listing of the CSS2 specification at **www.w3.org/tr/REC-CSS2/**. You can even take a look at the current work on CSS3 at **www.w3.org/Style/CSS/current-work**.*

What XHTML Element Box Properties Are Available?

An element's box is the rectangle it is drawn in; boxes have borders, margins, padding, and content. You can affect those parts of a box with the styles listed here.

border
CSS1: [<border-width>||<border-style>||<color>]

CSS2: inherit

Initial: Varies

Applies to: All elements

Inherited: No

Supported: [IE4, IE5]

Sets the width, style, and color for all four borders of a box at once. This **border** property is a shorthand property.

border-top, border-right, border-bottom, border-left

CSS1: [<border-top/right/bottom/left-width>||<border-style>||<color>]

CSS2: inherit

Initial: Varies

Applies to: All elements

Inherited: No

Supported: [IE4, IE5]

Set the width, style, and color of the top, right, bottom, and left borders of a box.

border-color

CSS1: <color>{1,4}|transparent

CSS2: inherit

Initial: Varies

Applies to: All elements

Inherited: No

Supported: [IE4, IE5, NS4]

Sets the color of the four borders of a box.

border-top-color, border-right-color, border-bottom-color, border-left-color

CSS1: <color>

CSS2: inherit

Initial: Varies

Applies to: All elements

Inherited: No

Supported: [IE4, IE5]

Set the color of specific borders of a box.

border-style

CSS1: <border-style>{1,4}

CSS2: inherit

Initial: Varies

Applies to: All elements

Inherited: No

Supported: [IE4, IE5, NS4]

Specifies the style of the four borders of a box. Can have from one to four values (the values will be set on the different sides of the box).

border-top-style, border-right-style, border-bottom-style, border-left-style

CSS1: <border-style>

CSS2: inherit

Initial: None

Applies to: All elements

Inherited: No

Supported: [IE4, IE5]

Set the style of specific borders of a box.

border-width

CSS1: <border-width>{1,4}

CSS2: inherit

Initial: Not defined

Applies to: All elements

Inherited: No

Supported: [IE4, IE5, NS4]

Sets the **border-top-width**, **border-right-width**, **border-bottom-width**, and **border-left-width** properties at the same time. This **border-width** property is a shorthand property.

border-top-width, border-right-width, border-bottom-width, border-left-width

CSS1: <border-width>

CSS2: inherit

Initial: medium

Applies to: All elements

Inherited: No

Supported: [IE4, IE5, NS4]

Set the border widths of a box's various sides.

clear

CSS1: None|left|right|both

CSS2: inherit

Initial: None

Applies to: Block-level elements

Inherited: No

Supported: [IE4, IE5, NS4]

Specifies that the sides of an element's boxes cannot be adjacent to an earlier floating box.

height, width

CSS1: <length>|<percentage>|auto

CSS2: inherit

Initial: auto

Applies to: All elements except inline elements, table columns, and column groups

Inherited: No

Supported: [IE4, IE5, NS4]

Give the content height and width of boxes.

margin

CSS1: <margin-width>{1,4}

CSS2: inherit

Initial: Not defined

Applies to: All elements

Inherited: No

Supported: [IE3, IE4, IE5, NS4]

Sets the **margin-top**, **margin-right**, **margin-bottom**, and **margin-left** properties at the same time. This **margin** property is a shorthand property.

margin-top, margin-right, margin-bottom, margin-left

CSS1: <margin-width>

CSS2: inherit

Initial: 0

Applies to: All elements

Inherited: No

Supported: [IE3, IE4, IE5, NS4]

Set the top, right, bottom, and left margins of a box.

max-height, max-width

CSS2: <length>|<percentage>|none|**inherit**

Initial: None

Applies to: All elements except nonreplaced inline elements and table elements

Inherited: No

Supported: None

Lets you constrain box heights to a certain range.

min-height

CSS2: <length>|<percentage>|inherit

Initial: 0

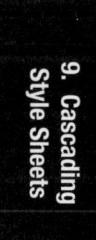

Applies to: All elements except nonreplaced inline elements and table elements

Inherited: No

Supported: [None]

Lets you constrain box heights and widths to a certain range.

min-width
CSS2: <length>|<percentage>inherit

Initial: 0

Applies to: All elements except non-replaced inline elements and table elements

Inherited: No

Supported: [None]

Lets you constrain box heights and widths to a certain range.

padding
CSS1: <length>|<percentage>

CSS2: inherit

Initial: Not defined

Applies to: All elements

Inherited: No

Supported: [IE4, IE5, NS4]

Sets the **padding-top**, **padding-right**, **padding-bottom**, and **padding-left** properties at the same time. This **padding** property is a shorthand property.

padding-top, padding-right, padding-bottom, padding-left
CSS1: length>|<percentage>

CSS2: inherit

Initial: 0

Applies to: All elements

Inherited: No

Supported: [IE4, IE5, NS4]

Specify the top, right, bottom, and left padding of a box.

TIP: *You'll find a complete listing of the CSS1 specification at **www.w3.org/tr/REC-CSS1** and a complete listing of the CSS2 specification at **www.w3.org/tr/REC-CSS2/**. You can even take a look at the current work on CSS3 at **www.w3.org/Style/CSS/current-work**.*

What Font Properties Are Available?

The font properties in CSS1 and CSS2 are listed here.

font

CSS1: [[<font-style>||<font-variant>||<font-weight>]?<font-size>[/<line-height>]?<font-family>

CSS2: caption|icon|menu|message-box|small-caption|status-bar|inherit

Initial: Varies

Applies to: All elements

Inherited: Yes

Supported: [IE4, IE5]

Simultaneously sets **font-style**, **font-variant**, **font-weight**, **font-size**, **line-height**, and **font-family** properties (in that order and without commas between them, except between font families). This **font** property is a shorthand property.

font-family

CSS1: [[<family-name>|<generic-family>],]*[<family-name>|<generic-family>]

CSS2: inherit

Initial: Depends on the browser

Applies to: All elements

Inherited: Yes

Supported: [IE3, IE4, IE5, NS4]

Indicates a list of font family names and/or generic family names. Because not all fonts are available on all systems, this property allows you to specify a list of fonts. The browser will use the first one it can find, starting with the first item in the list. Generic families refer to font characteristics that the browser should try to match, such as serif or monospace.

font-size
CSS1: <absolute-size>|<relative-size>|<length>|<percentage>

CSS2: inherit

Initial: medium

Applies to: All elements

Inherited: Yes

Supported: [IE3, IE4, IE5, NS4]

Specifies the size of a font.

font-stretch
CSS2: normal|wider|narrower|ultra-condensed|extra-condensed| condensed|semi-condensed|semi-expanded|expanded|extra-expanded| ultra-expanded|inherit

Initial: normal

Applies to: All elements

Inherited: Yes

Supported: [None]

Specifies a normal, condensed, or extended font face.

font-style
CSS1: normal|italic|oblique

CSS2: inherit

Initial: normal

Applies to: All elements

Inherited: Yes

Supported: [IE3, IE4, IE5, NS4]

Specifies normal (also called Roman or upright), italic, and oblique font faces.

Immediate Solutions

font-variant
CSS1: normal|small-caps

CSS2: inherit

Initial: normal

Applies to: All elements

Inherited: Yes

Supported: [IE4, IE5]

Specifies whether or not a font is a small-caps font.

font-weight
CSS1: normal|bold|bolder|lighter|100|200|300|400|500|600|700|800|900

CSS2: inherit

Initial: normal

Applies to: All elements

Inherited: Yes

Supported: [IE3, IE4, IE5, NS4]

Specifies the weight of a font, such as normal or bold.

TIP: *You'll find a complete listing of the CSS1 specification at **www.w3.org/tr/REC-CSS1** and a complete listing of the CSS2 specification at **www.w3.org/tr/REC-CSS2/**. You can even take a look at the current work on CSS3 at **www.w3.org/Style/CSS/current-work**.*

What List Properties Are Available?

Many style properties are available. Following are the properties that you use with lists in CSS1 and CSS2.

list-style
CSS1: [<list-style-type>||<list-style-position>||<list-style-image>]

CSS2: inherit

Initial: Not defined

Applies to: List items

Inherited: Yes

Supported: [IE4, IE5]

Sets the **list-style-type**, **list-style-image**, and **list-style-position** properties at the same time. This **list-style** property is a shorthand property.

list-style-image
CSS1: <uri>| none

CSS2: inherit

Initial: None

Applies to: List items

Inherited: Yes

Supported: [IE4, IE5]

Sets the image that will be used as the list item marker.

list-style-position
CSS1: inside|outside

CSS2: inherit

Initial: outside

Applies to: List items

Inherited: Yes

Supported: [IE4, IE5]

Specifies the position of the list item marker.

list-style-type
CSS1: disc|circle|square|decimal|decimal-leading-zero|lower-roman| upper-roman|lower-alpha|upper-alpha|none

CSS2: lower-greek|lower-latin|upper-latin|hebrew|armenian|georgian| cjk-ideographic|hiragana|katakana|hiragana-iroha|katakana-iroha|inherit

Initial: Disc

Applies to: List items

Inherited: Yes

Supported: [IE4, IE5, NS4]

Specifies the appearance of the list item marker if the **list-style-image** property has the value **none** (the default) or if the image pointed to by the URI in that property cannot be displayed.

---

*TIP: You'll find a complete listing of the CSS1 specification at **www.w3.org/tr/REC-CSS1** and a complete listing of the CSS2 specification at **www.w3.org/tr/REC-CSS2/**. You can even take a look at the current work on CSS3 at **www.w3.org/Style/CSS/current-work**.*

What Text Properties Are Available?

One of the main reasons people use styles is to format text. There are a number of style properties available for text, and they are listed here.

letter-spacing

CSS1: normal|<length>

CSS2: inherit

Initial: normal

Applies to: All elements

Inherited: Yes

Supported: [IE4, IE5]

Sets the spacing behavior between text characters.

line-height

CSS1: normal|<number>|<length>|<percentage>

CSS2: inherit

Initial: normal

Applies to: All elements

Inherited: Yes

Supported: [IE4, IE5, NS4]

Specifies the minimal height of the element's box.

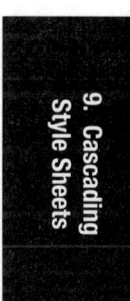

text-align
CSS1: left|right|center|justify

CSS2: <string>|inherit

Initial: Varies

Applies to: Block-level elements

Inherited: Yes

Supported: [IE3, IE4, IE5, NS4]

Specifies how the content of a block is aligned: left, right, center, or justified. In CSS2, you can specify a string on which to align the text.

text-decoration
CSS1: None|[underline||overline||line-through||blink]

CSS2: inherit

Initial: None

Applies to: All elements

Inherited: No

Supported: [IE3, IE4, IE5, NS4]

Specifies the decorations that are added to the text of an element, such as underlining, overlining, and line-through (that is, strike-through).

text-indent
CSS1: <length>|<percentage>

CSS2: inherit

Initial: 0

Applies to: Block-level elements

Inherited: Yes

Supported: [IE4, IE5, NS4]

Sets the indentation of the first line of text in a block.

text-shadow
CSS2: None|[<color>||<length><length><length>?,]*[<color>||<length><length><length>?]|inherit

Initial: None

Applies to: All elements

Inherited: No

Supported: [IE5]

Specifies a comma-separated list of shadow effects that should be applied to text in the element.

vertical-align
CSS1: baseline|sub|super|top|text-top|middle|bottom|text-bottom|<percentage>|<length>

CSS2: inherit

Initial: baseline

Applies to: Inline-level and table-cell elements

Inherited: No

Supported: [IE4, IE5]

Sets the vertical positioning of text in the element.

white-space
CSS1: normal|pre|nowrap

CSS2: inherit

Initial: normal

Applies to: Block-level elements

Inherited: Yes

Supported: [NS4]

Specifies how white space inside the element is handled.

word-spacing
CSS1: normal|<length>

CSS2: inherit

Initial: normal

Applies to: All elements

Inherited: Yes

Supported: [None]

Sets the spacing behavior between words.

---

*TIP: You'll find a complete listing of the CSS1 specification at **www.w3.org/tr/REC-CSS1** and a complete listing of the CSS2 specification at **www.w3.org/tr/REC-CSS2/**. You can even take a look at the current work on CSS3 at **www.w3.org/Style/CSS/current-work**.*

What Table Properties Are Available?

You can apply CSS styles to tables as of CSS2. The table properties follow.

border-collapse
CSS2: collapse|separate|inherit

Initial: collapse

Applies to: Table and inline table elements

Inherited: Yes

Supported: [IE5]

Sets a table's border model.

border-spacing
CSS2: <length><length>?|inherit

Initial: 0

Applies to: Table and inline table elements

Inherited: Yes

Supported: [None]

Sets the distance that separates adjacent cell borders.

column-span, row-span
CSS2: <integer>|inherit

Initial: 1

Applies to: Table cells, table columns, and table-column-group elements

Inherited: No

Supported: [None]

Sets the number of columns or rows spanned by a cell.

empty-cells
CSS2: show|hide|inherit

Initial: show

Applies to: Table cell elements

Inherited: Yes

Supported: [None]

Controls the drawing of borders around cells that have no visible content.

table-layout
CSS2: auto|fixed|inherit

Initial: auto

Applies to: Table and inline table elements

Inherited: No

Supported: [IE5]

Sets the algorithm used to lay out table cells, rows, and columns.

TIP: *You'll find a complete listing of the CSS1 specification at **www.w3.org/tr/REC-CSS1** and a complete listing of the CSS2 specification at **www.w3.org/tr/REC-CSS2/**. You can even take a look at the current work on CSS3 at **www.w3.org/Style/CSS/current-work**.*

What Visual Effects Properties Are Available?

Visual effects, which are new in CSS2, describe how elements are drawn. The visual-effects properties in CSS2 are listed here.

clip
CSS2: <shape>|auto|inherit

Initial: auto

Applies to: Block-level and replaced elements

Inherited: No

Supported: [IE5]

Sets the clipping region of an element (the clipping region specifies which part of an element is visible).

overflow
CSS2: visible|hidden|scroll|auto|inherit

Initial: visible

Applies to: Block-level and replaced elements

Inherited: No

Supported: [IE5]

Specifies whether the content of a block-level element is clipped when it overflows the element's box.

visibility
CSS2: visible|hidden|collapse|inherit

Initial: inherit

Applies to: All elements

Inherited: No

Supported: [IE5]

Specifies whether the element is displayed.

TIP: *You'll find a complete listing of the CSS1 specification at **www.w3.org/tr/REC-CSS1** and a complete listing of the CSS2 specification at **www.w3.org/tr/REC-CSS2/**. You can even take a look at the current work on CSS3 at **www.w3.org/Style/CSS/current-work**.*

Using <span> to Apply Styles

Often you want to apply styles not to whole blocks, like paragraphs, but rather to just a word or a few words. To mark an inline part of the page to apply styles to, you can use the **<span>** element (introduced in Chapter 3); this element supports both the **style** and **class** attributes. Here's an example showing how to use **<span>**:

```
<?xml version="1.0"?>
<!DOCTYPE html PUBLIC "-//W3C//DTD XHTML 1.0 Transitional//EN"
 "http://www.w3.org/tr/xhtml1/DTD/xhtml1-transitional.dtd">
<html xmlns="http://www.w3.org/1999/xhtml" xml:lang="en" lang="en">
    <head>
        <title>
            Styling Text
        </title>

        <style type="text/css">
            p {font-size: 18pt; font-style: italic; font-family:
                Arial, Helvetica; text-align: center}
        </style>
    </head>

    <body>
        <center>
            <h1>
                Styling Text
            </h1>
        </center>
        <p>
            Here is some text displayed in italics and
            <span style="font-weight: bold">bold</span>,
            as well as
            <span style="text-decoration: underline">
            underlined</span>, in Arial font.
        </p>
    </body>
</html>
```

See the next section to see how to use the **<div>** element to select XHTML blocks (as opposed to the inline selections you use with **<span>**).

Using <div> to Apply Styles

You can use **<span>** to mark smaller, inline sections of XHTML (see the previous section), but for longer blocks of XHTML, you usually use **<div>** (introduced in Chapter 3). The **<div>** element supports the **style** and **class** attributes you need for styles; here's an example showing how to use **<div>**:

```
<?xml version="1.0"?>
<!DOCTYPE html PUBLIC "-//W3C//DTD XHTML 1.0 Transitional//EN"
"http://www.w3.org/tr/xhtml1/DTD/xhtml1-transitional.dtd">
<html xmlns="http://www.w3.org/1999/xhtml" xml:lang="en" lang="en">
    <head>
        <title>
            Using the &lt;div&gt; tag
        </title>
    </head>

    <body>

        <div align="left">
            Manager
            <br />
            SlowPoke Products, Inc.
            <br />
            Languid, TX
        </div>

        <p>
            Dear You:
            <div align="center" style="color: red; font-style: italic">
                When are you going to ship my order?
            </div>

            <div align="right">
                <p>
                    President
                </p>
                <br />
                NeedItNow, Inc.
                <br />
                Speedy, CO
            </div>
        </p>
    </body>
</html>
```

Applying Styles to Text: Bold, Italic, and Underlined

"Arrgh," says the novice programmer, "I just can't get my text displayed in bold! You use the **font-style** property to do that, don't you?" "Sorry," you say; "use the **font-weight** property." "Well, then," the NP says, "underlining—you use **font-style** for underlining, right?" "Sorry," you say; "use **text-decoration**." "Arrgh!" says the NP.

Setting text styles is one of the more important aspects of cascading style sheets, but the process is not straightforward. For instance, in the following example, you'll notice that you use:

- **font-family**—To set the font face.
- **font-size**—To set the font size.
- **font-style**—To make text italic.
- **font-weight**—To make text bold.
- **text-align**—To center the text.
- **text-decoration**—To underline the text.

Here's what the example looks like:

```
<?xml version="1.0"?>
<!DOCTYPE html PUBLIC "-//W3C//DTD XHTML 1.0 Transitional//EN"
    "http://www.w3.org/tr/xhtml1/DTD/xhtml1-transitional.dtd">
<html xmlns="http://www.w3.org/1999/xhtml" xml:lang="en" lang="en">
    <head>
        <title>
            Styling Text
        </title>

        <style type="text/css">
            p {font-size: 18pt; font-style: italic; font-family:
                Arial, Helvetica; text-align: center}
        </style>
    </head>

    <body>
        <center>
            <h1>
                Styling Text
            </h1>
        </center>
        <p>
```

553

```
                        Here is some text displayed in italics and
                        <span style="font-weight: bold">bold</span>,
                        as well as
                        <span style="text-decoration: underline">
                        underlined</span>, in Arial font.
            </p>
    </body>
</html>
```

You can see the results of this XHTML in Figure 9.9.

TIP: *By the way, if you don't like underlined hyperlinks, just set* **text-decoration** *to* **none**.

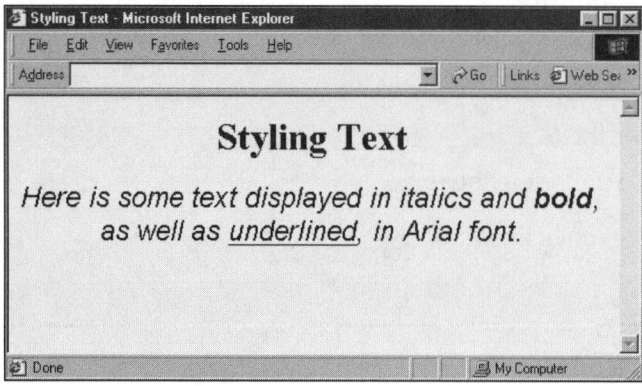

Figure 9.9 Applying styles to text.

Applying Styles to Fonts: Font, Font Size, Font Weight, Font Style

"Hm," says the novice programmer, "I just can't get this business about setting font properties right. How do you do it?" "Better pull up a chair," you say, "and get some coffee." "Uh oh," says the NP.

Here are the properties you use with fonts:

- **font-family**—Specifies the actual font, such as Arial or Helvetica. If you want to list alternative fonts in case the target computer is missing your first choice, specify them in a comma-separated list (for example, **{font-family: Arial, Helvetica}**).
- **font-size**—Refers to the size of the font.

- **font-stretch**—Indicates the desired amount of condensing or expansion in the letters used to draw the text.
- **font-style**—Specifies whether the text will be rendered using a normal, italic, or oblique face.
- **font-variant**— Specifies whether the text will be rendered using the normal letters for lowercase characters or rendered using small-cap letters for lowercase characters.
- **font-weight**—Refers to the boldness or lightness of the text, relative to other fonts in the same font family.
- **line-height**—Indicates the height given to each line.

Here's an example of putting font properties to work:

```
<?xml version="1.0"?>
<!DOCTYPE html PUBLIC "-//W3C//DTD XHTML 1.0 Transitional//EN"
"http://www.w3.org/tr/xhtml1/DTD/xhtml1-transitional.dtd">
<html xmlns="http://www.w3.org/1999/xhtml" xml:lang="en" lang="en">
    <head>
        <title>
            Setting Font Styles
        </title>
        <style type="text/css">
            body {font-style: italic; font-variant: normal;
            font-weight: bold; font-size: 12pt;
            line-height: 10pt; font-family: arial, helvetica;
            text-align: center}
        </style>
    </head>

    <body>
        <h1>Setting Font Styles</h1>
        <br />
        This text has been styled!
    </body>
</html>
```

The results of this XHTML appear in Figure 9.10.

There's a shortcut property you can use to set the **font-style, font-variant, font-weight, font-size, line-height,** and **font-family** properties all at once—the **font** property. You just specify values for all of these properties in this order, separating the **font-size** and **line-height** values with a forward slash (/) and listing all values without commas (except between font family names if you list more than one). Here's how the previous example looks using the **font** shorthand property:

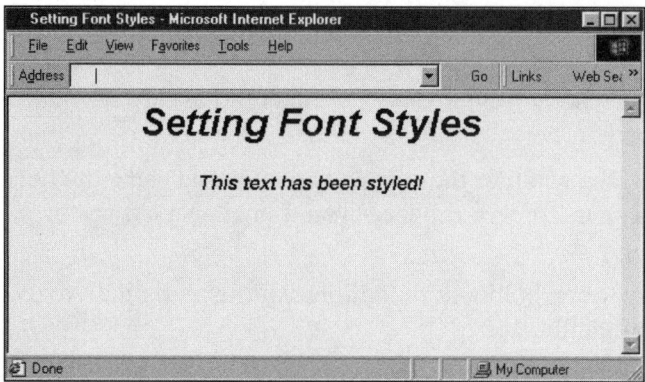

Figure 9.10 Applying styles to fonts.

```
<?xml version="1.0"?>
<!DOCTYPE html PUBLIC "-//W3C//DTD XHTML 1.0 Transitional//EN"
"http://www.w3.org/tr/xhtml1/DTD/xhtml1-transitional.dtd">
<html xmlns="http://www.w3.org/1999/xhtml" xml:lang="en" lang="en">
    <head>
        <title>
            Setting Font Styles
        </title>
        <style type="text/css">
            body {font: italic normal bold 12pt/10pt arial,
            helvetica; text-align: center}
        </style>
    </head>

    <body>
        <h1>Setting Font Styles</h1>
        <br />
        This text has been styled!
    </body>
</html>
```

You don't have to specify all values because the **font** property will leave the defaults intact for those properties you don't assign. Most browsers can also tolerate the list of values out of order. For example, this XHTML:

```
<?xml version="1.0"?>
<!DOCTYPE html PUBLIC "-//W3C//DTD XHTML 1.0 Transitional//EN"
"http://www.w3.org/tr/xhtml1/DTD/xhtml1-transitional.dtd">
<html xmlns="http://www.w3.org/1999/xhtml" xml:lang="en" lang="en">
    <head>
```

```
        <title>
            Setting Font Styles
        </title>
        <style type="text/css">
            body {font-family: arial, helvetica;
            font-size: 10pt; font-weight: bold}
        </style>
    </head>

    <body>
        <h1>Setting Font Styles</h1>
        <br />
        This text has been styled!
    </body>
</html>
```

gives the same result as this XHTML:

```
<?xml version="1.0"?>
<!DOCTYPE html PUBLIC "-//W3C//DTD XHTML 1.0 Transitional//EN"
"http://www.w3.org/tr/xhtml1/DTD/xhtml1-transitional.dtd">
<html xmlns="http://www.w3.org/1999/xhtml" xml:lang="en" lang="en">
    <head>
        <title>
            Setting Font Styles
        </title>
        <style type="text/css">
            body {font: bold 10pt arial, helvetica}
        </style>
    </head>

    <body>
        <h1>Setting Font Styles</h1>
        <br />
        This text has been styled!
    </body>
</html>
```

TIP: *As a last resort, you can assign a generic font family to **font-family** to use in case the user's computer doesn't have the one you specified. The browser will select a font family that's similar. Generic font families include serif, sans serif, cursive, fantasy, and monospace.*

Setting Colors and Backgrounds

"Darn," says the novice programmer, "all I want to do is create headings that are white on black instead of black on white. How can I do it?" "It's not hard," you say; "sit down and we'll go through it."

Here are the properties you use to set color and backgrounds:

- **color**—Sets the foreground color.
- **background-color**—Sets the background color.
- **background-image**—Sets the background image.
- **background-repeat**—Specifies whether the background image should be tiled.
- **background-attachment**—Specifies whether the background scrolls with the rest of the document.
- **background-position**—Sets the initial position of the background.

In this next example, I'm styling both the background and the foreground of a document:

```
<?xml version="1.0"?>
<!DOCTYPE html PUBLIC "-//W3C//DTD XHTML 1.0 Transitional//EN"
"http://www.w3.org/tr/xhtml1/DTD/xhtml1-transitional.dtd">
<html xmlns="http://www.w3.org/1999/xhtml" xml:lang="en" lang="en">
    <head>
        <title>
            Using the &lt;div&gt; tag
        </title>
    </head>

    <body style="background-color: #aaffff">

        <div align="left">
            Manager
            <br />
            SlowPoke Products, Inc.
            <br />
            Languid, TX
        </div>

        <p>
            Dear You:
            <div align="center" style="color: red; font-style: italic">
                When are you going to ship my order?
            </div>
```

```
            <div align="right">
                <p>
                    President
                </p>
                <br />
                NeedItNow, Inc.
                <br />
                Speedy, CO
            </div>
        </p>
    </body>
</html>
```

Here's another example that we saw in the beginning of this chapter:

```
<table border="2">
    <tr>
        <th style="background-color: rgb(255, 0, 0)">Tic</th>
        <th style="background-color: rgb(255, 0, 0)">Tac</th>
        <th style="background-color: rgb(255, 0, 0)">Toe</th>
    </tr>
    <tr>
        <td style="background-color: rgb(255, 255, 255)">X</td>
        <td style="background-color: rgb(0, 0, 0); color:
            rgb(255, 255, 255)">
            O
        </td>
        <td style="background-color: rgb(255, 255, 255)">X</td>
    </tr>
    <tr>
        <td style="background-color: rgb(0, 0, 0); color:
            rgb(255, 255, 255)">
            O
        </td>
        <td style="background-color: rgb(255, 255, 255)">X</td>
        <td style="background-color: rgb(0, 0, 0); color:
            rgb(255, 255, 255)">
            O
        </td>
    </tr>
    <tr>
        <td style="background-color: rgb(255, 255, 255)">X</td>
        <td style="background-color: rgb(0, 0, 0); color:
            rgb(255, 255, 255)">
```

```
                0
            </td>
            <td style="background-color: rgb(255, 255, 255)">X</td>
        </tr>
</table>
```

You can see the results of this XHTML in Figure 9.5.

Here's another example. In this case, I'm styling **<h1>** elements to have a white foreground and a black background:

```
<?xml version="1.0"?>
<!DOCTYPE html PUBLIC "-//W3C//DTD XHTML 1.0 Transitional//EN"
"http://www.w3.org/tr/xhtml1/DTD/xhtml1-transitional.dtd">
<html xmlns="http://www.w3.org/1999/xhtml" xml:lang="en" lang="en">
    <head>
        <title>
            Setting Colors And Backgrounds
        </title>
        <style type="text/css">
            h1 {background: black; color: white; text-align: center}
        </style>
    </head>

    <body>
        <h1>Setting Colors And Backgrounds</h1>
    </body>
</html>
```

You can see the results in Figure 9.11, which shows the box for the **<h1>** element quite clearly.

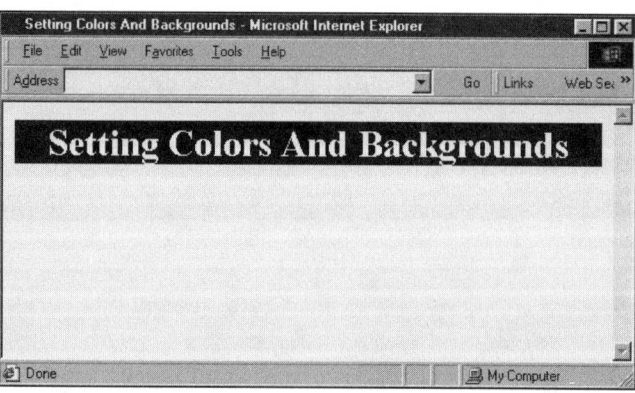

Figure 9.11 Applying background styles to text.

Applying Styles to Margins, Indentations, and Alignments

"Jeez," says the novice programmer, "I just can't get this text indented. How do I do it?" "With properties like **margin-left**," you say, "and a few others."

Here are the properties you use to work with margins, indentations, and alignments:

- **margin-left**—Sets the left margin.
- **margin-right**—Sets the right margin.
- **margin-top**—Sets the top margin.
- **text-indent**—Sets the indentation of text.
- **text-align**—Sets the alignment of text.

And here's an example showing how to put some of these properties to work:

```xml
<?xml version="1.0"?>
<!DOCTYPE html PUBLIC "-//W3C//DTD XHTML 1.0 Transitional//EN"
"http://www.w3.org/tr/xhtml1/DTD/xhtml1-transitional.dtd">
<html xmlns="http://www.w3.org/1999/xhtml" xml:lang="en" lang="en">
    <head>
        <title>
            Setting Margins And Alignments
        </title>

        <style type="text/css">
            body {margin-left: 10px}
            h1 {text-align: center}
            p {text-indent: 40px}
        </style>

    </head>

    <body>
        <h1>Setting Margins And Alignments</h1>
        <p>
            This text has been indented!
        </p>
    </body>
</html>
```

You can see the result of this XHTML in Figure 9.12.

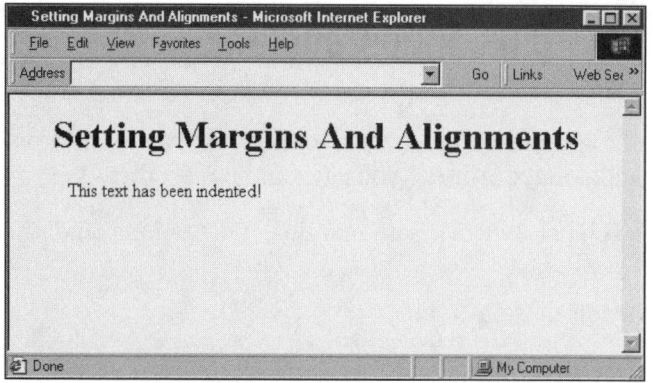

Figure 9.12 Applying alignment and indentation styles to text.

Applying Styles to Hyperlinks

"What about hyperlinks?" the novice programmer asks. "How can you style them? You can't just style the **<a>** element with one entry, can you? What about visited links, what about active links? It's impossible!" "Take it easy, NP," you say. "There's a way; you just use properties like **a:link** and **a:visited**."

You can specify styles for hyperlinks by using these terms:

- **a:link**—Hyperlinks as they originally appear.
- **a:visited**—Hyperlinks that have been visited.
- **a:hover**—Hyperlinks that have the mouse over them (Internet Explorer only).
- **a:active**—Hyperlinks that are active, that is, being clicked.

Here's an example. In this case, I'm setting the color of hyperlinks to red, visited links to blue, links with the mouse over them to yellow, and active links to green:

```
<?xml version="1.0"?>
<!DOCTYPE html PUBLIC "-//W3C//DTD XHTML 1.0 Transitional//EN"
"http://www.w3.org/tr/xhtml1/DTD/xhtml1-transitional.dtd">
<html xmlns="http://www.w3.org/1999/xhtml" xml:lang="en" lang="en">
    <head>
        <title>This is a Web page!</title>
        <style type="text/css">
            body {background: white; color: black}
            a:link {color: red}
            a:visited {color: blue}
```

```
                a:hover {color: yellow}
                a:active {color: green}
            </style>
        </head>

        <body>
            Welcome to my page!
            If you don't like it, you can go to
            <a href="http://www.w3c.org">W3C</a>.
        </body>
    </html>
```

Applying Styles to Lists

Here are the properties you typically use with lists:

- **list-style-image**—Sets the image that will be used as the list item marker (Internet Explorer only).

- **list-style-type**—Sets the appearance of the list item marker, such as disc, circle, square, decimal, lowercase Roman, uppercase Roman, and others.

In this example, I'm using **list-style-type** to set the marker in front of each list item in an unordered list to a square:

```
<?xml version="1.0"?>
<!DOCTYPE html PUBLIC "-//W3C//DTD XHTML 1.0 Transitional//EN"
    "http://www.w3.org/tr/xhtml1/DTD/xhtml1-transitional.dtd">
<html xmlns="http://www.w3.org/1999/xhtml" xml:lang="en" lang="en">
    <head>
        <title>
            Setting List Styles
        </title>

        <style type="text/css">
            li {list-style-type: square}
        </style>
    </head>

    <body>
        <h1 align="center">
            Setting List Styles
        </h1>
```

```
            Here are some items to consider when buying a computer:
            <ul>
                <li>Speed</li>
                <li>Cost</li>
                <li>RAM</li>
                <li>Disk space</li>
                <li>CD ROM speed</li>
            </ul>
        </body>
</html>
```

You can see the results of this XHTML in Figure 9.13.

Here's another example; this time, I'm using **list-style-type** to make an ordered list using uppercase letters:

```
<?xml version="1.0"?>
<!DOCTYPE html PUBLIC "-//W3C//DTD XHTML 1.0 Transitional//EN"
"http://www.w3.org/tr/xhtml1/DTD/xhtml1-transitional.dtd">
<html xmlns="http://www.w3.org/1999/xhtml" xml:lang="en" lang="en">
    <head>
        <title>
            Setting Ordered List Styles
        </title>

        <style type="text/css">
            li {list-style-type: upper-alpha}
        </style>
    </head>

    <body>
```

Figure 9.13 Setting an unordered list style.

Immediate Solutions

```
            <h1 align="center">
                Setting Ordered List Styles
            </h1>

            Here are some items to consider when buying a computer:
            <ol>
                <li>Speed</li>
                <li>Cost</li>
                <li>RAM</li>
                <li>Disk space</li>
                <li>CD ROM speed</li>
            </ol>
        </body>
</html>
```

You can see the results of this XHTML in Figure 9.14.

Figure 9.14   Setting an ordered list style.

Using Styles to Position Elements: Absolute Positioning

The novice programmer is back and asks, "I understand you can set the actual position of elements in a Web page by using styles—how does that work?" "There are two main ways," you say knowingly; "you can use absolute positioning or relative positioning."

You can use the **position** property to set the position of elements in a Web page. I'll take a look at positioning items absolutely in this section and relatively in the next section. Here are the properties you usually use when you're working with positioning:

- **position**—Holds values such as **absolute** and **relative**.
- **top**—Specifies the offset of the top of the element's box.
- **bottom**—Specifies the offset of the bottom of the element's box.
- **left**—Specifies the offset of the left edge of the element's box.
- **right**—Specifies the offset of the right edge of the element's box.

In this example, I set **position** to **absolute** and then specify the **top** and **left** properties for three **<div>** elements, each of which has an image and text:

```
<?xml version="1.0"?>
<!DOCTYPE html PUBLIC "-//W3C//DTD XHTML 1.0 Transitional//EN"
"http://www.w3.org/tr/xhtml1/DTD/xhtml1-transitional.dtd">
<html xmlns="http://www.w3.org/1999/xhtml" xml:lang="en" lang="en">
    <head>
        <title>
            Absolute Positioning
        </title>
    </head>

    <body>

        <h1 align="center">
            Absolute Positioning
        </h1>

        <div style=
            "position:absolute; left:50; top:60; border-width: thick">
            <img src="flower1.jpg" width="85" height="129" />
            <br />
            Flower 1
        </div>

        <div style=
            "position:absolute; left:200; top:90; border-width: thick">
            <img src="flower2.jpg" width="85" height="129" />
            <br />
            Flower 2
        </div>

        <div style="position:absolute; left:350; top:120;
            border-width: thick">
            <img src="flower3.jpg" width="85" height="129" />
            <br />
```

```
            Flower 3
        </div>

    </body>

</html>
```

You can see the results of this XHTML in Figure 9.15. As you can see, I've positioned the **<div>** elements and given them borders. You can also position elements in a relative way—see the next section.

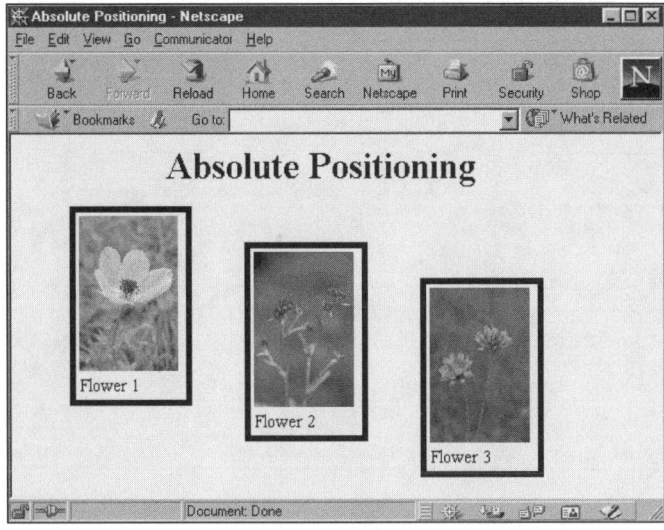

Figure 9.15   Setting absolute element positions.

Using Styles to Position Elements: Relative Positioning

In addition to absolute positioning—see the previous section—you can also use relative positioning. When you use relative positioning, elements are positioned relative to the location they would have had in the normal flow of elements in the Web browser.

Here are the properties you usually use when you're working with positioning:

- **position**—Holds values such as **absolute** and **relative**.
- **top**—Specifies the offset of the top of the element's box.
- **bottom**—Specifies the offset of the bottom of the element's box.
- **left**—Specifies the offset of the left edge of the element's box.
- **right**—Specifies the offset of the right edge of the element's box.

To position items in a relative way, you set **position** to **relative**. You can also set the other properties to indicate the new relative position. In this example, I'm moving some text up five pixels and other text down five pixels from the normal position at which the browser would place this text:

```
<?xml version="1.0"?>
<!DOCTYPE html PUBLIC "-//W3C//DTD XHTML 1.0 Transitional//EN"
"http://www.w3.org/tr/xhtml1/DTD/xhtml1-transitional.dtd">
<html xmlns="http://www.w3.org/1999/xhtml" xml:lang="en" lang="en">
    <head>
        <title>
            Relative Positioning
        </title>
    </head>

    <body>
        <h1 align="center">
            Relative Positioning
        </h1>
        This text goes
        <span style="position: relative; top: -5">up</span> and
        <span style="position: relative; top: 5">down</span>,
        as you can see.

    </body>
</html>
```

You can see the results of this XHTML in Figure 9.16, where some of the text is positioned higher and some lower than the rest, just as we designed it.

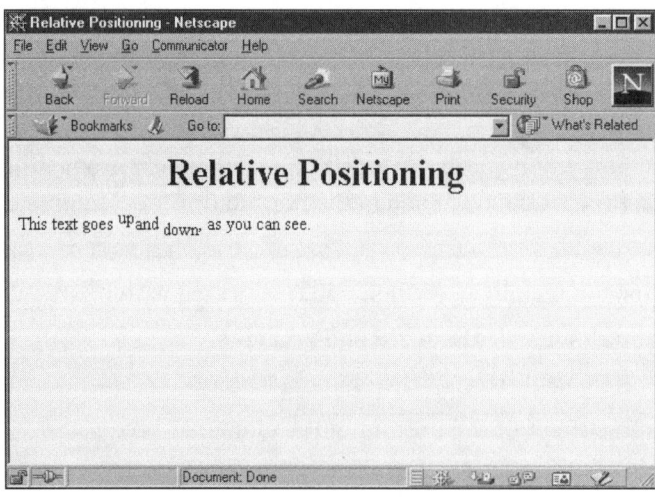

Figure 9.16   Setting relative element positions.

Chapter 10

Essential JavaScript

If you need an immediate solution to:	See page:
<script>—Creating a Script	589
<noscript>—Handling Browsers that Don't Handle JavaScript	591
<server>—Running Server-Side JavaScript Scripts	593
Commenting Your JavaScript	594
Working with Data in JavaScript	594
Working with JavaScript Operators	597
Creating **if** Statements	600
Creating **if...else** Statements	602
Creating **switch** Statements	604
Creating **for** Loop Statements	605
Creating **while** Loop Statements	609
Creating **do...while** Loop Statements	610
Creating Functions	611
Passing Arguments to Functions	613
Creating JavaScript Objects	616
Using JavaScript **String** Objects	617
Creating Arrays with the **Array** Class	620
Handling Events in Browsers	623
Event Handling: Mouse Events	628

In Depth

These days, knowing how to use JavaScript is becoming more and more necessary for Web programmers, especially those using dynamic XHTML, which relies on it. This chapter and Chapter 11 are all about JavaScript and using it to make your Web pages come alive.

What Is JavaScript?

JavaScript, originally supported by Netscape Navigator, is the most popular Web scripting language today. JavaScript lets you embed programs right in your Web pages and run these programs using the Web browser. You place these programs in a **<script>** element, usually within the **<head>** element. If you want the script to write directly to the Web page, you should place it in the **<body>** element.

In this example, I'm writing the text "Welcome to JavaScript!" directly into a Web page when that Web page is first displayed by the browser (we'll discuss how this works in Chapter 11):

```
<?xml version="1.0"?>
<!DOCTYPE html PUBLIC "-//W3C//DTD XHTML 1.0 Transitional//EN"
    "http://www.w3.org/tr/xhtml1/DTD/xhtml1-transitional.dtd">
<html xmlns="http://www.w3.org/1999/xhtml" xml:lang="en" lang="en">
    <head>
        <title>
            Welcome To JavaScript
        </title>
    </head>

    <body>
        <script type = "text/javascript" language="javascript">
            document.writeln("Welcome to JavaScript!")
        </script>

        <center>
            <h1>
                Welcome To JavaScript!
            </h1>
        </center>
    </body>
</html>
```

Figure 10.1   Our first JavaScript example.

You can see the results of this XHTML in Figure 10.1. The JavaScript program wrote the text you see in the upper-left corner. As you can see, one thing JavaScript lets you do is write your Web pages on the fly, which is a powerful feature.

So what's going on in the previous example? First, I use the **<script>** element to embed the JavaScript program into the page. Note that I set the **<script>** element's **language** attribute to "**javascript**" to tell the browser which scripting language I'm using and the **type** attribute to "text/javascript":

```
<?xml version="1.0"?>
<!DOCTYPE html PUBLIC "-//W3C//DTD XHTML 1.0 Transitional//EN"
"http://www.w3.org/tr/xhtml1/DTD/xhtml1-transitional.dtd">
<html xmlns="http://www.w3.org/1999/xhtml" xml:lang="en" lang="en">
    <head>
        <title>
            Welcome To JavaScript
        </title>

    </head>

    <body>

        <script type = "text/javascript" language="javascript">
            .
            .
            .
        </script>

        <center>
            <h1>
```

```
                Welcome To JavaScript!
            </h1>
        </center>

    </body>

</html>
```

In HTML programming, you used to enclose the actual JavaScript in an HTML comment, like this:

```
<?xml version="1.0"?>
<!DOCTYPE html PUBLIC "-//W3C//DTD XHTML 1.0 Transitional//EN"
"http://www.w3.org/tr/xhtml1/DTD/xhtml1-transitional.dtd">
<html xmlns="http://www.w3.org/1999/xhtml" xml:lang="en" lang="en">
    <head>
        <title>
            Welcome To JavaScript
        </title>

    </head>

    <body>

        <script type = "text/javascript" language="javascript">
            <!--
            .
            .
            .
            //-->
        </script>

        <center>
            <h1>
                Welcome To JavaScript!
            </h1>
        </center>
    </body>
</html>
```

NOTE: *I ended the HTML comment in this example with **//-->**. The double forward slash (**//**) is used to create a JavaScript comment. Had I omitted **//**, HTML browsers would have treated the enclosed JavaScript as an HTML comment and ignored it.*

Why was enclosing the JavaScript in an HTML comment a good idea? Recall that browsers that can't handle an HTML element just display the contents of the element as plain text in a Web page. If a browser can't handle JavaScript, it'll display the JavaScript code directly in the Web page. To avoid this, you used to place the actual JavaScript in the **<script>** element in an HTML comment. In XHTML, however, that's no longer a good idea because XML parsers are allowed to simply remove comments from XML pages without evaluating the content of the comment. For that reason, W3C now recommends that you avoid the practice of surrounding your script code in a comment, and in fact, that's no longer a problem with any major browser.

Now I'm ready to add the actual JavaScript. In this case, I'll use the JavaScript expression **document.writeln** to write the text "Welcome to JavaScript!" to the Web page:

```
<?xml version="1.0"?>
<!DOCTYPE html PUBLIC "-//W3C//DTD XHTML 1.0 Transitional//EN"
    "http://www.w3.org/tr/xhtml1/DTD/xhtml1-transitional.dtd">
<html xmlns="http://www.w3.org/1999/xhtml" xml:lang="en" lang="en">
    <head>
        <title>
            Welcome To JavaScript
        </title>
    </head>

    <body>
        <script type = "text/javascript" language="javascript">
            document.writeln("Welcome to JavaScript!")
        </script>

        <center>
            <h1>
                Welcome To JavaScript!
            </h1>
        </center>
    </body>
</html>
```

And that's all it takes. That's our first line of JavaScript: **document.writeln("Welcome to JavaScript!")**. As you can see, JavaScript is just embedded text in the Web page—the Web browser reads, interprets, and runs that script.

NOTE: *Following the lead of languages such as Java, the standard for JavaScript is to end each statement with a semicolon (;), so this JavaScript example technically should be* **document.writeln("Welcome to JavaScript!");**. *However, it's so easy to forget the semicolon that browsers no longer require it. Because the majority of JavaScript I see on the Internet these days omits the semicolon, I'll do the same here to follow popular usage.*

There's one more point to consider. The contents of **<script>** and **<style>** elements in XHTML are declared as *parsed character data* (defined as PCDATA in XML) in XHTML, which means that an XHTML browser can read and parse the code itself. That's a problem if your code contains any characters that look like XHTML (specifically, < or & or]]> or --) because an XHTML browser might try to interpret those characters as markup. As a solution to this problem, W3C suggests changing the type of **<script>** or **<style>** element content to standard (nonparsed) character data (CDATA in XML) if your script includes sensitive characters, like this:

```
<?xml version="1.0"?>
<!DOCTYPE html PUBLIC "-//W3C//DTD XHTML 1.0 Transitional//EN"
"http://www.w3.org/tr/xhtml1/DTD/xhtml1-transitional.dtd">
<html xmlns="http://www.w3.org/1999/xhtml" xml:lang="en" lang="en">
    <head>
        <title>
            Welcome To JavaScript
        </title>
    </head>

    <body>
        <script type = "text/javascript" language="javascript">
            <![CDATA[
                document.writeln("Welcome to JavaScript!")
            ]]>
        </script>

        <center>
            <h1>
                Welcome To JavaScript!
            </h1>
        </center>
    </body>
</html>
```

Unfortunately, this solution totally flummoxes both Netscape Navigator and Internet Explorer. A better solution is to use external scripts and style sheets. To include an external script in your page, you use the **src** attribute of the **<script>**

element. In the following example, I'm including a script stored in a file named script.js (you can use any name for the script file, but the extension .js is standard for JavaScript code):

```
<?xml version="1.0"?>
<!DOCTYPE html PUBLIC "-//W3C//DTD XHTML 1.0 Transitional//EN"
"http://www.w3.org/tr/xhtml1/DTD/xhtml1-transitional.dtd">
<html xmlns="http://www.w3.org/1999/xhtml" xml:lang="en" lang="en">
    <head>
        <title>
            Welcome To JavaScript
        </title>
    </head>

    <body>
        <script type = "text/javascript" language="javascript"
            src="script.js">
        </script>

        <center>
            <h1>
                Welcome To JavaScript!
            </h1>
        </center>
    </body>
</html>
```

In this case, script.js, stored in the same directory as the Web page, contains only this one line:

```
document.writeln("Welcome to JavaScript!")
```

The upshot, then, is that in XHTML, you should use external scripts if your script uses the characters < or & or]]> or -- because an XHTML browser might interpret those characters as markup.

The Main JavaScript Implementations

Despite its name, JavaScript is different from Java both in syntax and in use. Java is a separate language, and you compile Java programs to create *bytecode* files, and those files, which the browser can run, are stored separately from Web pages. JavaScript, on the other hand, is stored directly as text in the Web page, making it very easy to work with. In this chapter and Chapter 11, we're going to see how to write JavaScript in Web pages.

Because JavaScript is implemented in Web browsers, you might expect that the implementation of JavaScript might differ in Netscape Navigator and Internet Explorer, and you'd be quite right. Netscape Navigator's implementation of JavaScript is a pure one, and you can find documentation about Netscape Navigator's JavaScript at **http://developer.netscape.com/tech/javascript/index.html**. In fact, Netscape Communications is helping to pioneer server-side JavaScript, which runs on the server, not in the client Web browser. You can find Netscape's documentation for server-side JavaScript at **http://docs.iplanet.com/docs/manuals/ssjs.html**.

Microsoft's implementation of JavaScript differs slightly and extends the Netscape standards. In fact, Internet Explorer's implementation of JavaScript is called *JScript*. You can find the documentation for JScript at **http://msdn.microsoft.com/scripting/default.htm?/scripting/jscript/techinfo/jsdocs.htm**.

NOTE: *Microsoft also has a competing scripting language, VBScript, which runs in Web browsers and is based on Microsoft's Visual Basic language. However, VBScript hasn't gained much popularity over the years, at least not yet. JavaScript rules in the Web arena. You can find more information about VBScript, which is supported only in Internet Explorer, at **www.microsoft.com/vbscript/us/techinfo/vbsdocs.htm**.*

Isn't there a JavaScript standard that will settle the dispute between browsers? Actually, there is, and the European Computer Manufacturers Association (ECMA) in Geneva, Switzerland, created it. In fact, many people treat the official name of JavaScript as ECMAScript, but that name hasn't quite caught on. Netscape Navigator's version of JavaScript is ECMA-compliant.

As you might expect, JavaScript resources on the Web are abundant—just search for the word "JavaScript" and you'll be deluged with information. Here's a set of resources to get you started:

- **http://home.netscape.com/eng/mozilla/3.0/handbook/javascript/index.html**—Netscape's guide to JavaScript
- **http://javascript.internet.com**—Cut-and-paste scripts
- **www.infohiway.com/javascript/**—Ready-to-use scripts
- **www.jsworld.com**—Examples and archives of JavaScript
- **www.webteacher.com/javascript/**—Tutorial for JavaScript

Before we dig into JavaScript programming, it's a good idea to get an overview of where we're going, so I'll take a look at the bigger picture now.

JavaScript Objects

JavaScript is an object-oriented language. The term *object-oriented* might make you nervous, but using objects makes JavaScript programming tremendously easy. As far as we're concerned here, an object just refers to some aspect of the Web browser, which gives us access to that aspect.

JavaScript comes with a number of predefined objects, such as the **document** object that we saw in the first example in this chapter. The **document** object refers to the body of the current page in the browser, giving you an easy way to access the XHTML in that page. In fact, I used the **writeln** (write line) method of that object to write the text "Welcome to JavaScript" to the current Web page, like this:

```
<script type = "text/javascript" language="javascript">
    document.writeln("Welcome to JavaScript!")
</script>
```

You use a *method* of an object to perform some *action* with that object. In the previous example, I'm writing a line of text to the document. Other methods let you display message boxes, navigate to new pages, and submit data to the Web server.

So which objects are available for use in JavaScript and what do they stand for? Here's a list of some JavaScript objects you have access to in your code:

- **document**—Corresponds to the current Web page's body. Using this object, you have access to the XHTML of the page itself, including all the links, images, and anchors in it.
- **form**—Holds information about forms in the current page; forms can contain buttons, text fields, and all kinds of other XHTML elements. I'll look at these in Chapter 12.
- **frame**—Refers to a frame in the browser window.
- **history**—Holds the record of the sites that the Web browser has visited before reaching the current page. Gives you access to methods that let you move back to previous pages.
- **location**—Holds information about the location of the current Web page, such as its URL, the domain name, path, server port, and more.
- **navigator**—Refers to the browser itself, letting you determine which browser the user has.
- **window**—Refers to the current browser window.

TIP: *There are more JavaScript objects, and you can create your own objects as well. There's far more to JavaScript than we can cover in two chapters—for all the details, check out a few good JavaScript books.*

These objects come ready for you to use, but you can also create other objects by using JavaScript's predefined classes. A *class* is like a cookie cutter for an object—it defines the object's type. (We'll see how to use the **new** operator to create objects from JavaScript classes in the "Immediate Solutions" section "Creating JavaScript Objects.") There are many other utility classes, such as the **Date** and **Math** classes, in which you have to create your own objects before you can use them. (We'll see how that works in the "Immediate Solutions" section "Creating JavaScript Objects.")

To get anywhere in JavaScript, you need to know about two aspects of objects—methods, which we've already seen, and properties.

Object Properties and Methods

We've seen that the **document** object refers to the current page, but how do you actually *use* such an object? Well, we've already seen one way, which is to use object methods, such as the **writeln** method to write text to the Web page. You use an object's method by giving the object's name a dot (.) followed by the method name, such as **document.writeln**. Here are a few examples of methods:

- **document.write**—Writes text to the current Web page.
- **document.writeln**—Writes text to the current Web page and adds a line.
- **history.go**—Navigates the Web browser to a location in the browser's history.
- **window.alert**—Displays an alert dialog box.
- **window.open**—Opens a new browser window.

As you can see, these methods provide a lot of ready-made power that helps you work with the browser interactively. Besides using methods to perform actions with objects, you can also use properties to read and change settings in those objects. A *property* holds some setting of an object. For example, the **document.linkcolor** property holds the color of unvisited hyperlinks in the current Web page, and by changing the **document.linkcolor** property, you can change that color. Here are some example properties and the objects they belong to:

- **document.bgcolor**—Background color of the current page
- **document.fgcolor**—Foreground color of the current page
- **document.lastmodified**—Date the page was last modified
- **document.title**—Title of the current page

- **location.hostname**—Name of the Internet Service Provider (ISP) host
- **navigator.appName**—Name of the browser, which you can use to determine which browser the user has

Object properties and methods give you access to what's going on in the browser, letting you change just about everything under programmatic control. In this chapter, we're going to master the basics of JavaScript programming, and in Chapter 11, we'll work with the built-in objects.

Besides properties and methods, there is one more very important concept in JavaScript: *events*, and that's the next topic in our JavaScript survey.

JavaScript Events

Dynamic XHTML makes your Web pages come alive and allows you to respond to the user's actions. But how do you know when such an action has occurred? For example, what if you want to change the color of a Web page when the user clicks that page? To inform you when something's happened, JavaScript uses events, such as mouse clicks. When the user clicks the page, a *mouse down* event occurs. To handle that event, many XHTML tags now support events. You use the **onmousedown** event attribute when the mouse is clicked in a Web page's body.

Here's an example showing one way of responding to such events. In this case, I'll change the document's background color to red when the mouse is clicked in Internet Explorer (the code is slightly different in Netscape Navigator):

```
<?xml version="1.0"?>
<!DOCTYPE html PUBLIC "-//W3C//DTD XHTML 1.0 Transitional//EN"
"http://www.w3.org/tr/xhtml1/DTD/xhtml1-transitional.dtd">
<html xmlns="http://www.w3.org/1999/xhtml" xml:lang="en" lang="en">
    <head>
        <title>
            JavaScript Event Example
        </title>
    </head>

    <body onmousedown="document.bgColor='red'">
        <center>
            <h1>
                Click this page to turn it red!
            </h1>
        </center>
    </body>
</html>
```

I've indicated that I want to assign the predefined color red to **document.bgcolor** when the user clicks the mouse, and I do that with the JavaScript assignment **document.bgcolor='red'**. The equal sign in the assignment means that I want to set **document.bgcolor** to **'red'** (much like the way we've assigned values to attributes throughout the book). The results of this page, as they appear in Internet Explorer, are shown in Figure 10.2.

TIP: *The previous example is a particularly simple one because the actual JavaScript code is in the* **<body>** *element itself. For code longer than one line, you'll usually store the code in the* **<script>** *element instead, and* call *that code from elements such as* **<body>**. *We'll see how that works in the "Immediate Solutions" section "Creating Functions."*

What event attributes are available? Here are the common ones—note that support for these attributes varies by browser and by tag:

- **onabort**—Occurs when an action is aborted.
- **onblur**—Occurs when an element loses the input focus.
- **onchange**—Occurs when data in a control, such as a text field, changes.
- **onclick**—Occurs when an element is clicked.
- **ondblclick**—Occurs when an element is double-clicked.
- **ondragdrop**—Occurs when a drag-and-drop operation is undertaken.
- **onerror**—Occurs when there's been a JavaScript error.
- **onfocus**—Occurs when an element gets the focus.
- **onkeydown**—Occurs when a key goes down.
- **onkeypress**—Occurs when a key is pressed and the key code is available.
- **onkeyup**—Occurs when a key goes up.
- **onload**—Occurs when the page loads.

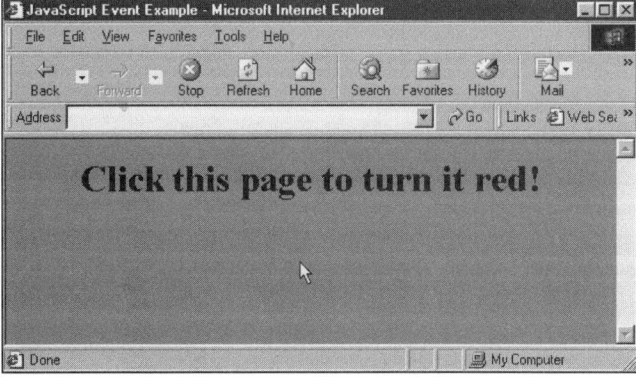

Figure 10.2   Using an event in JavaScript.

- **onmousedown**—Occurs when a mouse button goes down.
- **onmousemove**—Occurs when the mouse moves.
- **onmouseout**—Occurs when the mouse leaves an element.
- **onmouseover**—Occurs when the mouse moves over an element.
- **onmouseup**—Occurs when a mouse button goes up.
- **onmove**—Occurs when an element is moved.
- **onreset**—Occurs when the user clicks the Reset button.
- **onresize**—Occurs when an element or page is resized.
- **onselect**—Occurs when a selection takes place.
- **onsubmit**—Occurs when the user clicks the Submit button.
- **onunload**—Occurs when a page is unloaded.

You can find out which XHTML tags support which event attributes in Table 10.1 for Internet Explorer and Table 10.2 for Netscape Navigator.

We'll see how to handle events like these when we deal with dynamic XHTML in Chapter 13; for now, we'll just concentrate on the basics.

Table 10.1 Event attributes of Internet Explorer elements.

Element	Event Attributes
<a>	onbeforecopy, onbeforecut, onbeforeeditfocus, onbeforefocusenter, onbeforefocusleave, onbeforepaste, onblur, onclick, oncontextmenu, oncontrolselect, oncopy, oncut, ondblclick, ondrag, ondragend, ondragenter, ondragleave, ondragover, ondragstart, ondrop, onfocus, onfocusenter, onfocusleave, onhelp, onkeydown, onkeypress, onkeyup, onlosecapture, onmousedown, onmouseenter, onmouseleave, onmousemove, onmouseout, onmouseover, onmouseup, onpaste, onpropertychange, onreadystatechange, onresize, onresizeend, onresizestart, onselectstart
<body>	onafterprint, onbeforecut, onbeforefocusenter, onbeforefocusleave, onbeforepaste, onbeforeprint, onbeforeunload, onclick, oncontextmenu, oncontrolselect, oncut, ondblclick, ondrag, ondragend, ondragenter, ondragleave, ondragover, ondragstart, ondrop

(continued)

Table 10.1 Event attributes of Internet Explorer elements *(continued)*.

Element	Event Attributes
`<button>`	onbeforecut, onbeforeeditfocus, onbeforefocusenter, onbeforefocusleave, onbeforepaste, onblur, onclick, oncontextmenu, oncontrolselect, oncut, ondblclick, ondragenter, ondragleave, ondragover, ondrop, onfilterchange, onfocus, onfocusenter, onfocusleave, onhelp, onkeydown, onkeypress, onkeyup, onlosecapture, onmousedown, onmouseenter, onmouseleave, onmousemove, onmouseout, onmouseover, onmouseup, onpaste, onpropertychange, onreadystatechange, onresize, onresizeend, onresizestart, onselectstart
`<div>`	onbeforecopy, onbeforecut, onbeforeeditfocus, onbeforefocusenter, onbeforefocusleave, onbeforepaste, onblur, onclick, oncontextmenu, oncontrolselect, oncopy, oncut, ondblclick, ondrag, ondragend, ondragenter, ondragleave, ondragover, ondragstart, ondrop, onfilterchange, onfocus, onfocusenter, onfocusleave, onhelp, onkeydown, onkeypress, onkeyup, onlayoutcomplete, onlosecapture, onmousedown, onmouseenter, onmouseleave, onmousemove, onmouseout, onmouseover, onmouseup, onpaste, onpropertychange, onreadystatechange, onresize, onresizeend, onresizestart, onscroll, onselectstart
`<form>`	onbeforecopy, onbeforecut, onbeforefocusenter, onbeforefocusleave, onbeforepaste, onblur, onclick, oncontextmenu, oncontrolselect, oncopy, oncut, ondblclick, ondrag, ondragend, ondragenter, ondragleave, ondragover, ondragstart, ondrop, onfocus, onfocusenter, onfocusleave, onhelp, onkeydown, onkeypress, onkeyup, onlosecapture, onmousedown, onmouseenter, onmouseleave, onmousemove, onmouseout, onmouseover, onmouseup, onpaste, onpropertychange, onreadystatechange, onreset, onresize, onresizeend, onresizestart, onselectstart, onsubmit
`<frame>`	onbeforefocusenter, onbeforefocusleave, onblur, oncontrolselect, onfocus, onfocusenter, onfocusleave, onresize, onresizeend, onresizestart
`<iframe>`	onbeforefocusenter, onbeforefocusleave, onblur, oncontrolselect, onfocus, onfocusenter, onfocusleave, onresizeend, onresizestart

(continued)

In Depth

Table 10.1 Event attributes of Internet Explorer elements *(continued)*.

Element	Event Attributes
`<img>`	onabort, onbeforecopy, onbeforecut, onbeforefocusenter, onbeforefocusleave, onbeforepaste, onblur, onclick, oncontextmenu, oncontrolselect, oncopy, oncut, ondblclick, ondrag, ondragend, ondragenter, ondragleave, ondragover, ondragstart, ondrop, onerror, onfilterchange, onfocus, onfocusenter, onfocusleave, onhelp, onload, onlosecapture, onmousedown, onmouseenter, onmouseleave, onmousemove, onmouseout, onmouseover, onmouseup, onpaste, onpropertychange, onreadystatechange, onresize, onresizeend, onresizestart, onselectstart
`<input>` (button)	onbeforecut, onbeforeeditfocus, onbeforefocusenter, onbeforefocusleave, onbeforepaste, onblur, onclick, oncontextmenu, oncontrolselect, oncut, ondblclick, ondrag, ondragend, ondragenter, ondragleave, ondragover, ondragstart, ondrop, onfilterchange, onfocus, onfocusenter, onfocusleave, onhelp, onkeydown, onkeypress, onkeyup, onlosecapture, onmousedown, onmouseenter, onmouseleave, onmousemove, onmouseout, onmouseover, onmouseup, onpaste, onpropertychange, onreadystatechange, onresize, onresizeend, onresizestart, onselectstart
`<input>` (checkbox)	onbeforecut, onbeforeeditfocus, onbeforefocusenter onbeforefocusleave, onbeforepaste, onblur, onclick, oncontextmenu, oncontrolselect, oncut, ondblclick, ondrag, ondragend, ondragenter, ondragleave, ondragover, ondragstart, ondrop, onfilterchange, onfocus, onfocusenter, onfocusleave, onhelp, onkeydown, onkeypress, onkeyup, onlosecapture, onmousedown, onmouseenter, onmouseleave, onmousemove, onmouseout, onmouseover, onmouseup, onpaste, onpropertychange, onreadystatechange, onresizeend, onresizestart, onselectstart
`<input>` (radio button)	onbeforecut, onbeforeeditfocus, onbeforefocusenter, onbeforefocusleave, onbeforepaste, onblur, onclick, oncontextmenu, oncontrolselect, oncut, ondblclick, ondrag, ondragend, ondragenter, ondragleave, ondragover, ondragstart, ondrop, onfilterchange, onfocus, onfocusenter, onfocusleave, onhelp, onkeydown, onkeypress, onkeyup, onlosecapture, onmousedown, onmouseenter, onmouseleave, onmousemove, onmouseout, onmouseover, onmouseup, onpaste, onpropertychange, onreadystatechange, onresizeend, onresizestart, onselectstart

(continued)

Table 10.1 Event attributes of Internet Explorer elements *(continued)*.

Element	Event Attributes
`<input>` (Submit button)	onbeforecut, onbeforeeditfocus, onbeforefocusenter, onbeforefocusleave, onbeforepaste, onblur, onclick, oncontextmenu, oncontrolselect, oncut, ondblclick, ondrag, ondragend, ondragenter, ondragleave, ondragover, ondragstart, ondrop, onfilterchange, onfocus, onfocusenter, onfocusleave, onhelp, onkeydown, onkeypress, onkeyup, onlosecapture, onmousedown, onmouseenter, onmouseleave, onmousemove, onmouseout, onmouseover, onmouseup, onpaste, onpropertychange, onreadystatechange, onresize, onresizeend, onresizestart, onselectstart
`<input>` (text field)	onafterupdate, onbeforecut, onbeforeeditfocus, onbeforefocusenter, onbeforefocusleave, onbeforepaste, onbeforeupdate, onblur, onchange, onclick, oncontextmenu, oncontrolselect, oncut, ondblclick, ondrag, ondragend, ondragenter, ondragleave, ondragover, ondragstart, ondrop, onerrorupdate, onfilterchange, onfocus, onfocusenter, onfocusleave, onhelp, onkeydown, onkeypress, onkeyup, onlosecapture, onmousedown, onmouseenter, onmouseleave, onmousemove, onmouseout, onmouseover, onmouseup, onpaste, onpropertychange, onreadystatechange, onresize, onresizeend, onresizestart, onselect, onselectstart
`<li>`	onbeforecopy, onbeforecut, onbeforefocusenter, onbeforefocusleave, onbeforepaste, onblur, onclick, oncontextmenu, oncontrolselect, oncopy, oncut, ondblclick, ondrag, ondragend, ondragenter, ondragleave, ondragover, ondragstart, ondrop, onfocus, onfocusenter, onfocusleave, onhelp, onkeydown, onkeypress, onkeyup, onlayoutcomplete, onlosecapture, onmousedown, onmouseenter, object. , onmouseleave, onmousemove, onmouseout, onmouseover, onmouseup, onpaste, onpropertychange, onreadystatechange, onresize, onresizeend, onresizestart, onselectstart
`<marquee>`	onbeforecut, onbeforeeditfocus, onbeforefocusenter, onbeforefocusleave, onbeforepaste, onblur, onbounce, oncontextmenu, oncontrolselect, oncut, ondblclick, ondrag, ondragend, ondragenter, ondragleave, ondragover, ondragstart, ondrop, onfilterchange, onfinish, onfocus, onfocusenter, onfocusleave, onhelp, onkeydown, onkeypress, onkeyup, onlosecapture, onmousedown, onmouseenter, onmouseleave, onmousemove, onmouseout, onmouseover, onmouseup, onpaste, onpropertychange, onreadystatechange, onresize, onresizeend, onresizestart, onscroll, onselectstart, onstart

(continued)

Table 10.1 Event attributes of Internet Explorer elements *(continued)*.

Element	Event Attributes
`<object>`	onbeforeeditfocus, onbeforefocusenter, onbeforefocusleave, onblur, oncellchange, onclick, oncontrolselect, ondataavailable, ondatasetchanged, ondatasetcomplete, ondblclick, ondrag, ondragend, ondragenter, ondragleave, ondragover, ondragstart, ondrop, onerror, onfocus, onfocusenter, onfocusleave, onkeydown, onkeypress, onkeyup, onlosecapture, onpropertychange, onreadystatechange, onresize, onresizeend, onresizestart, onrowenter, onrowexit, onrowsdelete, onrowsinserted, onscroll, onselectstart
`<p>`	onbeforecopy, onbeforecut, onbeforefocusenter, onbeforefocusleave, onbeforepaste, onblur, onclick, oncontextmenu, oncontrolselect, oncopy, oncut, ondblclick, ondrag, ondragend, ondragenter, ondragleave, ondragover, ondragstart
`<pre>`	onbeforecopy, onbeforecut, onbeforefocusenter, onbeforefocusleave, onbeforepaste, onblur, onclick, oncontextmenu, oncontrolselect, oncopy, oncut, ondblclick, ondrag, ondragend, ondragenter, ondragleave, ondragover, ondragstart, ondrop, onfocus, onfocusenter, onfocusleave, onhelp, onkeydown, onkeypress, onkeyup, onlosecapture, onmousedown, onmouseenter, onmouseleave, onmousemove, onmouseout, onmouseover, onmouseup, onpaste, onpropertychange, onreadystatechange, onresize, onresizeend, onresizestart, onselectstart
`<select>`	onbeforecut, onbeforeeditfocus, onbeforefocusenter, onbeforefocusleave, onbeforepaste, onblur, onchange, onclick, oncontextmenu, oncontrolselect, oncut, ondblclick, ondragenter, ondragleave, ondragover, ondrop, onfocus, onfocusenter, onfocusleave, onhelp, onkeydown, onkeypress, onkeyup, onlosecapture, onmousedown, onmouseenter, onmouseleave, onmousemove, onmouseout, onmouseover, onmouseup, onpaste, onpropertychange, onreadystatechange, onresize, onresizeend, onresizestart, onscroll, onselectstart
`<span>`	onbeforecopy, onbeforecut, onbeforeeditfocus, onbeforefocusenter, onbeforefocusleave, onbeforepaste, onblur, onclick, oncontextmenu, oncontrolselect, oncopy, oncut, ondblclick, ondrag, ondragend, ondragenter, ondragleave, ondragover, ondragstart, ondrop, onfilterchange, onfocus, onfocusenter, onfocusleave, onhelp, onkeydown, onkeypress, onkeyup, onlosecapture, onmousedown, onmouseenter, onmouseleave, onmousemove, onmouseout

(continued)

Table 10.1 Event attributes of Internet Explorer elements *(continued)*.

Element	Event Attributes
`<table>`	onbeforecut, onbeforeeditfocus, onbeforefocusenter, onbeforefocusleave, onbeforepaste, onblur, onclick, oncontextmenu, oncontrolselect, oncut, ondblclick, ondrag, ondragend, ondragenter, ondragleave, ondragover, ondragstart, ondrop, onfilterchange, onfocus, onfocusenter, onfocusleave, onhelp, onkeydown, onkeypress, onkeyup, onlosecapture, onmousedown, onmouseenter, onmouseleave, onmousemove, onmouseout, onmouseover, onmouseup, onpaste, onpropertychange, onreadystatechange, onresize, onresizeend, onresizestart, onscroll, onselectstart
`<td>`	onbeforecopy, onbeforecut, onbeforeeditfocus, onbeforefocusenter, onbeforefocusleave, onbeforepaste, onblur, onclick, oncontextmenu, oncontrolselect, oncopy, oncut, ondblclick, ondrag, ondragend, ondragenter, ondragleave, ondragover, ondragstart, ondrop, onfilterchange, onfocus, onfocusenter, onfocusleave, onhelp, onkeydown, onkeypress, onkeyup, onlosecapture, onmousedown, onmouseenter, onmouseleave, onmousemove, onmouseout, onmouseover, onmouseup, onpaste, onpropertychange, onreadystatechange, onresizeend, onresizestart, onselectstart
`<textarea>`	onafterupdate, onbeforecopy, onbeforecut, onbeforeeditfocus, onbeforefocusenter, onbeforefocusleave, onbeforepaste, onbeforeupdate, onblur, onchange, onclick, oncontextmenu, oncontrolselect, oncut, ondblclick, ondrag, operation., ondragend, ondragenter, ondragleave, ondragover, ondragstart, ondrop, onerrorupdate, onfilterchange, onfocus, onfocusenter, onfocusleave, onhelp, onkeydown, onkeypress, onkeyup, onlosecapture, onmousedown, onmouseenter, onmouseleave, onmousemove, onmouseout, onmouseover, onmouseup, onpaste, onpropertychange, onreadystatechange, onresize, onresizeend, onresizestart, onscroll, onselect, onselectstart

Table 10.2 Event attributes of Netscape Navigator elements.

Element	Event Attributes
`<a>`	**onclick, onmouseout, onmouseover**
`<body>`	**onload, onunload, onblur, onfocus**
`<div>`	None
`<embed>`	None
`<form>`	**onreset, onsubmit**
`<frame>`	None
`<ilayer>`	None
`<img>`	**onabort, onerror, onload**
`<input>` (button)	**onclick**
`<input>` (checkbox)	**onclick**
`<input>` (radio button)	**onclick**
`<input>` (submit button)	**onclick**

JavaScript Programming

Our overview of JavaScript has given us a hint of the power available in its use. However, we'll need a good foundation to work from, so the remainder of this chapter is all about JavaScript programming basics.

In this chapter, I'll concentrate on what you need to write JavaScript itself. In Chapter 11, we'll boost the power of JavaScript by using the built-in objects we've already seen. In Chapter 12, we'll see how to work with XHTML *controls*, such as buttons, text fields (which you type text into), radio buttons, and more. After that, we'll launch directly into working with XHTML forms and dynamic XHTML.

At this point, let's look at essential JavaScript programming. For example, one of the most important parts of programming is to make decisions based on your data—in JavaScript, you can use the **if** statement to do so. In this next example, I'm using the **if** statement to compare the numbers 5 and 3. If 5 is greater than 3, the code will display the message "Yes, 5 is greater than 3!" in a Web page:

```
<?xml version="1.0"?>
<!DOCTYPE html PUBLIC "-//W3C//DTD XHTML 1.0 Transitional//EN"
  "http://www.w3.org/tr/xhtml1/DTD/xhtml1-transitional.dtd">
<html xmlns="http://www.w3.org/1999/xhtml" xml:lang="en" lang="en">
    <head>
        <title>
```

```
            Using The if Statement
        </title>

    </head>

    <body>

        <script type = "text/javascript" language="javascript">
            if(5 > 3){
                document.writeln("Yes, 5 is greater than 3!")
            }
        </script>

        <center>
            <h1>
                Using The if Statement
            </h1>
        </center>
    </body>
</html>
```

You can see the results in Figure 10.3, where we find that 5 is indeed greater than 3.

TIP: *If you make a mistake while developing your JavaScript code, Internet Explorer will display a dialog box indicating what the problem is, but Netscape Navigator will not run your code. To see what the problem with the code is in Netscape Navigator, type "javascript:" in the Location box and press Enter; the browser will open a new window telling you what's wrong with the code.*

We'll see how to use statements like **if** in the "Immediate Solutions" section "Creating **if...else** Statements" in this chapter—and put them to work in Chapter 11. It's time to start the "Immediate Solutions" section, so I'll do that right now.

Figure 10.3   Using the JavaScript **if** statement.

Immediate Solutions

<script>—Creating a Script

Purpose: Embeds a script, such as scripts written in JavaScript, JScript, or VBScript, in a Web page. This element is usually included in a page's head, except when the script writes to the Web page, in which case it should go into the page's body.

When used as HTML: Start tag/End tag: Required/Required

Supported: [1.0S, 1.0T, 1.0F, 1.1, 3.2, 4, IE3, IE4, IE5, NS1, NS2, NS3, NS4]

Attributes:

- **charset**—Specifies the character encoding of the script contents. Set to a Request for Comments (RFC) 2045 language character set string (the default is ISO-8859-1). [1.0S, 1.0T, 1.0F, 1.1, 4]

- **class**—Class of the element (used for rendering). [IE4, IE5]

- **defer**—Tells the browser that the script is not going to generate any document content (so the browser can continue parsing and drawing the page). Standalone attribute in HTML. [1.0S, 1.0T, 1.0F, 1.1, 4, IE4, IE5]

- **event**—Specifies the event for which the script is written. Set to an event name. [IE4, IE5]

- **for**—Indicates which element is bound to the script. Set to an XHTML element or element ID. [IE4, IE5]

- **id**—Unique alphanumeric identifier for the tag; use the ID to refer to the tag. [IE4, IE5]

- **language**—Sets the scripting language. This attribute is required if the **src** attribute is not set and is optional otherwise. Set to the name of a scripting language, such as JavaScript or VBScript. [1.0S, 1.0T, 1.0F, 4, IE3, IE4, IE5, NS3, NS4]

- **src**—Gives an external source for the script code. Set to a URL. [1.0S, 1.0T, 1.0F, 1.1, 4, IE3, IE4, IE5, NS3, NS4]

- **title**—Holds additional information (which might be displayed in tool tips). [IE4, IE5]

- **type**—Required. Indicates the Multipurpose Internet Mail Extension (MIME) type of the scripting code. Set to an alphanumeric MIME type. [1.0S, 1.0T, 1.0F, 1.1, 4, IE4, IE5]

- **xml:space**—Set to **preserve** to preserve spacing. [1.0S, 1.0T, 1.0F, 1.1]

XHTML events: None

The novice programmer says, "This is great! I can actually control what goes in my Web page, using JavaScript. Where do I start?" You smile and say, "Probably with the **<script>** element."

You embed JavaScript in Web pages by using the **<script>** element. You usually place this element in the **<head>** element, unless the script writes directly to the Web page, in which case you place it in the body of the document. In the "In Depth" section of this chapter, we already saw this example, which writes "Welcome to JavaScript!" to the current page:

```
<?xml version="1.0"?>
<!DOCTYPE html PUBLIC "-//W3C//DTD XHTML 1.0 Transitional//EN"
"http://www.w3.org/tr/xhtml1/DTD/xhtml1-transitional.dtd">
<html xmlns="http://www.w3.org/1999/xhtml" xml:lang="en" lang="en">
    <head>
        <title>
            Welcome To JavaScript
        </title>

    </head>

    <body>

        <script type = "text/javascript" language="javascript">
            document.writeln("Welcome to JavaScript!")
        </script>

        <center>
            <h1>
                Welcome To JavaScript!
            </h1>
        </center>
    </body>
</html>
```

You can see the results of this XHTML in Figure 10.1. Note that I'm using the **<script>** element's **language** attribute to specify the type of language as

JavaScript. Browsers are usually smart enough to figure out what scripting language you're using, but it's good practice to assign the actual name, **"javascript"**, to the **language** attribute.

You can also use external scripts, as explained in the "In Depth" section "What Is JavaScript?" at the beginning of this chapter. In fact, that's what you should do, as also explained in that section, if your script contains the characters < or & or]]> or --, which might be interpreted by an XHTML browser as markup.

Although the **<script>** element can contain JavaScript, what about browsers that don't handle JavaScript? See the next section.

<noscript>—Handling Browsers that Don't Handle JavaScript

Purpose: Used to add XHTML for browsers that don't use JavaScript or other scripting languages.

When used as HTML: Start tag/End tag: Required/Required

Supported: [1.0S, 1.0T, 1.0F, 1.1, 4, IE4, IE5, NS3, NS4]

Attributes:

- **class**—Class of the element (used for rendering). [1.0S, 1.0T, 1.0F, 1.1, 4]
- **dir**—Gives the direction of directionally neutral text (text that doesn't have an inherent direction in which you should read it). Possible values: **ltr**, left-to-right text or table; and **rtl**, right-to-left text or table. [1.0S, 1.0T, 1.0F, 1.1, 4]
- **id**—Unique alphanumeric identifier for the tag; use the ID to refer to the tag. [1.0S, 1.0T, 1.0F, 1.1, 4, IE4, IE5]
- **lang**—Base language used for the tag. [1.0S, 1.0T, 1.0F, 1.1, 4]
- **style**—Inline style indicating how to render the element. [1.0S, 1.0T, 1.0F, 1.1, 4]
- **title**—Holds additional information (which might be displayed in tool tips). [1.0S, 1.0T, 1.0F, 1.1, 4]
- **xml:lang**—Holds the base language for the element when the document is interpreted as an XML document. [1.0S, 1.0T, 1.0F, 1.1]

XHTML events: None

Chapter 10 Essential JavaScript

The novice programmer says, "I'm using my favorite Web browser, SuperDuperWebProKing 5.3, patch level 97, and it has a problem with JavaScript—all my scripting code appears in the page itself! My browser may be a little non-standard." "I'll say," you reply; "looks like your browser doesn't handle JavaScript."

What if you want to indicate to users that their browsers can't run JavaScript and they're missing something? You use the **<noscript>** element. JavaScript-enabled browsers will ignore this element, but the text in it will be displayed in browsers that can't handle JavaScript. Here's how you use it:

```
<?xml version="1.0"?>
<!DOCTYPE html PUBLIC "-//W3C//DTD XHTML 1.0 Transitional//EN"
"http://www.w3.org/tr/xhtml1/DTD/xhtml1-transitional.dtd">
<html xmlns="http://www.w3.org/1999/xhtml" xml:lang="en" lang="en">
    <head>
        <title>
            Welcome To JavaScript
        </title>
    </head>

    <body>
        <script type = "text/javascript" language="javascript">
            document.writeln("Welcome to JavaScript!")
        </script>

        <noscript>
            Sorry, your browser doesn't support JavaScript!
        </noscript>

        <center>
            <h1>
                Welcome To JavaScript!
            </h1>
        </center>
    </body>
</html>
```

TIP: It's a good idea to include a hyperlink to a non-JavaScript version of the page in the **<noscript>** element. In fact, it's an even better idea to include the entire non-JavaScript version of the page itself in the **<noscript>** element. Also, some browsers might not display text from elements in the **<head>** element, so you might want to place **<noscript>** outside the **<head>** element.

<server>—Running Server-Side JavaScript Scripts

Purpose: Embeds server-side scripts in a Web page. You use this element instead of **<script>** for server-side scripts.

When used as HTML: Start tag/End tag: Required/Required

Supported: Not applicable

Attributes: None

XHTML events: None

This element holds server-side JavaScript code, which is code that runs on the server. You can find Netscape's documentation for server-side JavaScript at **http://docs.iplanet.com/docs/manuals/ssjs.html**.

I'm going to stick to client-side JavaScript in this chapter, but here's a server-side example:

```
<?xml version="1.0"?>
<!DOCTYPE html PUBLIC "-//W3C//DTD XHTML 1.0 Transitional//EN"
    "http://www.w3.org/tr/xhtml1/DTD/xhtml1-transitional.dtd">
<html xmlns="http://www.w3.org/1999/xhtml" xml:lang="en" lang="en">
    <head>
        <title>
            Server-Side JavaScript
        </title>

    </head>

    <body>
        Hello - your server's IP address is
        <server>
            write(request.ip)
        </server>

        <center>
            <h1>
                Using Server-Side JavaScript
            </h1>
        </center>
    </body>
</html>
```

Commenting Your JavaScript

As with XHTML, you can add comments to JavaScript code by using the double forward slash (//) notation. The JavaScript interpreter in your browser will stop reading anything on a line past //, so you can comment your code like this:

```
<?xml version="1.0"?>
<!DOCTYPE html PUBLIC "-//W3C//DTD XHTML 1.0 Transitional//EN"
"http://www.w3.org/tr/xhtml1/DTD/xhtml1-transitional.dtd">
<html xmlns="http://www.w3.org/1999/xhtml" xml:lang="en" lang="en">
    <head>
        <title>
            Welcome To JavaScript
        </title>
    </head>

    <body>
        <script type = "text/javascript" language="javascript">
            //Write "Welcome to JavaScript!" in the page.
            document.writeln("Welcome to JavaScript!")
        </script>

        <noscript>
            Sorry, your browser doesn't support JavaScript!
        </noscript>

        <center>
            <h1>
                Welcome To JavaScript!
            </h1>
        </center>
    </body>
</html>
```

Working with Data in JavaScript

"OK," says the novice programmer, "I've gotten JavaScript to display a welcome message, but that's not too powerful. How can I start storing some data?" "Pull up a chair," you say, "and we'll go through it."

JavaScript recognizes five types of data: numbers, Boolean values, text strings, functions, and objects. Boolean data holds values of true or false. We'll discuss functions in the "Immediate Solutions" section "Creating Functions," and we've already seen objects. JScript recognizes six types of data: numbers, Boolean values, text strings, objects, null, and undefined. The null type simply holds a value of 0, and the undefined type indicates that the data has not been assigned a value.

So how do you store data values in JavaScript? As with other programming languages, you use *variables*. A variable is simply the name of a memory location in which you can store data and access it later. To create a variable in JavaScript, you use the **var** statement. After you've created the variable, you can store data in that variable.

In this example, I'm creating a variable named **number** with the **var** statement. Next, I'm assigning that variable the value of 366 with the *assignment* operator (=). Now when I use the name **number**, JavaScript will replace it with the value in that variable, so I can display the number of days in the year 2000, like this:

```
<?xml version="1.0"?>
<!DOCTYPE html PUBLIC "-//W3C//DTD XHTML 1.0 Transitional//EN"
    "http://www.w3.org/tr/xhtml1/DTD/xhtml1-transitional.dtd">
<html xmlns="http://www.w3.org/1999/xhtml" xml:lang="en" lang="en">
    <head>
        <title>
            Creating Variables In JavaScript
        </title>
    </head>

    <body>
        <script type = "text/javascript" language="javascript">
            var number
            number = 366
            document.writeln("There are " + number +
                " days in the year 2000.")
        </script>

        <center>
            <h1>
                Creating Variables In JavaScript
            </h1>
        </center>
    </body>
</html>
```

I'm using the *addition* JavaScript operator (**+**) to add the value in **number** into the middle of a text string (see "Working With JavaScript Operators" in the "Immediate Solutions" section of this chapter). You can see the results of this code in Figure 10.4, and as you see, 366 was indeed stored in the variable.

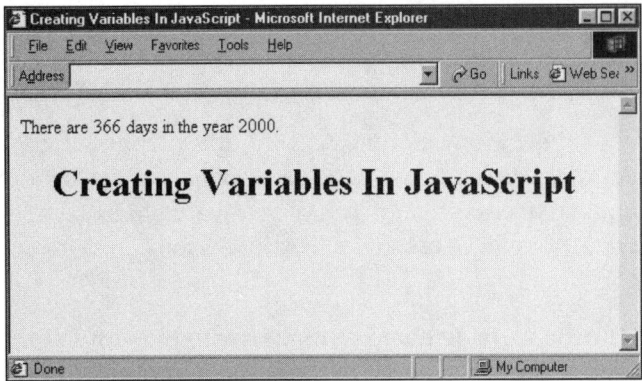

Figure 10.4 Using a variable in JavaScript.

There's a shorthand technique you should know about. You can also create a variable and assign a value to it at the same time, as in this next example:

```
var number = 366
document.writeln("There are " + number +
    " days in the year 2000.")
```

You can also store other types of data that JavaScript recognizes in variables. For example, you can store text strings in variables (just make sure the text string is enclosed in quotation marks). Here's an example in which I'm setting the variable **greeting** to "Welcome to JavaScript!":

```
<?xml version="1.0"?>
<!DOCTYPE html PUBLIC "-//W3C//DTD XHTML 1.0 Transitional//EN"
"http://www.w3.org/tr/xhtml1/DTD/xhtml1-transitional.dtd">
<html xmlns="http://www.w3.org/1999/xhtml" xml:lang="en" lang="en">
    <head>
        <title>
            Welcome To JavaScript
        </title>

    </head>

    <body>

        <script type = "text/javascript" language="javascript">
            var greeting
            greeting = "Welcome to JavaScript!"
            document.writeln(greeting)
        </script>
```

```
            <center>
                <h1>
                    Welcome To JavaScript!
                </h1>
            </center>

        </body>

</html>
```

This code produces the same display shown in Figure 10.1.

The JavaScript convention is to use lowercase letters for variable names if they are single words, like **counter** or **index**. However, if you form a variable name by putting more than one word together, the JavaScript convention is to capitalize the first letter of each word after the first word, as in **theNumber**, **countLeftUntilCompletion**, **numberOfImages**, or **aReallyReallyReallyLongVariableName**.

Working with JavaScript Operators

"Now that I can store data in variables," the novice programmer says, "how can I work with that data? I want to do something!" You smile and say, "A good place to start is with the JavaScript operators."

Say that you wanted to add two numbers, 2 plus 2. How could you do that in JavaScript? You can use the *addition* operator (+). Here's an example showing how this works:

```
<?xml version="1.0"?>
<!DOCTYPE html PUBLIC "-//W3C//DTD XHTML 1.0 Transitional//EN"
"http://www.w3.org/tr/xhtml1/DTD/xhtml1-transitional.dtd">
<html xmlns="http://www.w3.org/1999/xhtml" xml:lang="en" lang="en">
    <head>
        <title>
            Using Operators In JavaScript
        </title>
    </head>

    <body>
        <script type = "text/javascript" language="javascript">
            var number
            number = 2 + 2
```

```
            document.writeln("2 + 2 = " + number)
        </script>

        <center>
            <h1>
                Using Operators In JavaScript
            </h1>
        </center>
    </body>
</html>
```

You can see the results of this code in Figure 10.5.

Besides the addition operator, many other operators are available in JavaScript. For instance, the increment operator (**++**) adds one to the value in a variable. For example, if **number** holds 100, then after you've applied the increment operator to **number**—like this: **number++**—**number** will hold 101.

Here's the list of JavaScript operators—we'll be seeing these operators throughout this and the next few chapters:

- *Addition* (+)—Sums two numbers or concatenates two strings.
- *Assignment* (=)—Assigns a value to a variable.
- *Bitwise AND* (&)—Performs a bitwise AND on two expressions.
- *Bitwise left shift* (<<)—Shifts the bits of an expression to the left.
- *Bitwise NOT* (~)—Performs a bitwise NOT (negation) on an expression.
- *Bitwise OR* (|)—Performs a bitwise OR on two expressions.
- *Bitwise right shift* (>>)—Shifts the bits of an expression to the right, maintaining sign.

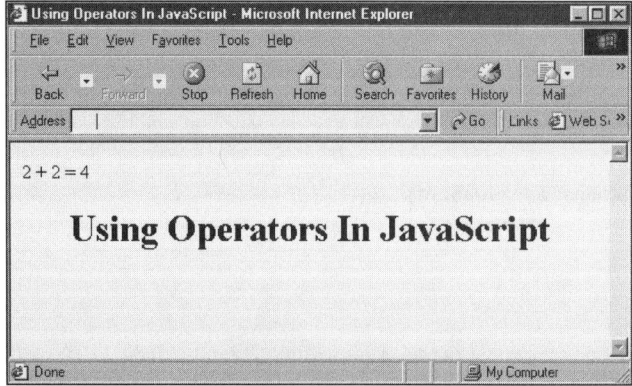

Figure 10.5   Using operators in JavaScript.

- *Bitwise XOR* (^)—Performs a bitwise exclusive OR on two expressions.
- *Comma* (,)—Causes two expressions to be executed sequentially.
- *Conditional (trinary)* (?:)—Executes one of two expressions depending on a condition.
- *Decrement* (--)—Decreases a variable by one.
- *Division* (/)—Divides two numbers and returns a numeric result.
- *Equality* (==)—Compares two expressions to determine if they are equal.
- *Greater than* (>)—Compares two expressions to determine if one is greater than the other.
- *Greater than or equal to* (>=)—Compares two expressions to determine if one is greater than or equal to the other.
- *Identity* (===)—Compares two expressions to determine if they are equal in value and of the same data type.
- *Increment* (++)—Increases a variable by one.
- *Inequality* (!=)—Compares two expressions to determine if they are unequal.
- *Less than* (<)—Compares two expressions to determine if one is less than the other.
- *Less than or equal to* (<=)—Compares two expressions to determine if one is less than or equal to the other.
- *Logical AND* (&&)—Performs a logical conjunction on two expressions.
- *Logical NOT* (!)—Performs a logical negation on an expression.
- *Logical OR* (||)—Performs a logical disjunction on two expressions.
- *Modulus* (%)—Divides two numbers and returns the remainder.
- *Multiplication* (*)—Multiplies two numbers.
- *New* (**new**)—Creates a new object.
- *Nonidentity* (!==)—Compares two expressions to determine if they are not equal in value or of the same data type.
- *Subtraction* (-)—Performs subtraction of two expressions.
- *Typeof* (**typeof**)—Returns a string that identifies the data type of an expression.
- *Unary negation* (-)—Indicates the negative value of a numeric expression.
- *Unsigned right shift* (>>>)—Performs an unsigned right shift of the bits in an expression.

There are also a number of combination assignment operators that combine assignment with another operation, such as +=, which adds a value and then assigns the result to the original value. For example, **variable1 += 2** adds 2 to the value in **variable1**. These operators are: +=, -=, *=, /=, %=, &=, |=, ^=, <<=, >>=, and >>>=.

A number of important operators are the *comparison operators*, such as equality (==) and greater than (>). These operators let you compare values and make decisions based on the results. How does this work? Take a look at the next section for some examples.

Creating if Statements

The big boss appears and says, "I need a secret Web page, which I can use to check to see if the budget is still in the black." "OK," you say, "I'll use the JavaScript **if** statement." "Just make sure we're solvent," says the BB.

You use the **if** statement in JavaScript to construct a test, executing the code in the statement only if the test turns out to be true. Here's the syntax of the **if** statement:

```
if (condition) {
    code
}
```

In this statement, **condition** is a situation that you want to check, and **code** is the code you want to execute if the condition is true. Note that you must enclose the code to execute in curly braces, { and }.

So how do you create a condition to check? You use the comparison operators, such as < (less than), > (greater than), == (equal to), <= (less than or equal to), or >= (greater than or equal to). Here's an example showing how to check if the value in a variable named **budget** is greater than 0:

```
<?xml version="1.0"?>
<!DOCTYPE html PUBLIC "-//W3C//DTD XHTML 1.0 Transitional//EN"
 "http://www.w3.org/tr/xhtml1/DTD/xhtml1-transitional.dtd">
<html xmlns="http://www.w3.org/1999/xhtml" xml:lang="en" lang="en">
    <head>
        <title>
            Using The if Statement In JavaScript
        </title>
```

```
        </head>

        <body>
            <script type = "text/javascript" language="javascript">
                var budget
                budget = 52.16
                if (budget > 0) {
                    document.writeln("The value in budget > 0, so the " +
                        "budget is still in the black")
                }
            </script>

            <center>
                <h1>
                    Using The if Statement In JavaScript
                </h1>
            </center>
        </body>
</html>
```

You can see the results of this code in Figure 10.6.

Here are some other examples of **if** statements:

```
if (number == 5) {
    document.writeln("The number is equal to 5.")
}

if (price > 2000.00) {
    document.writeln("WARNING: Price is over $2000.00.")
}
```

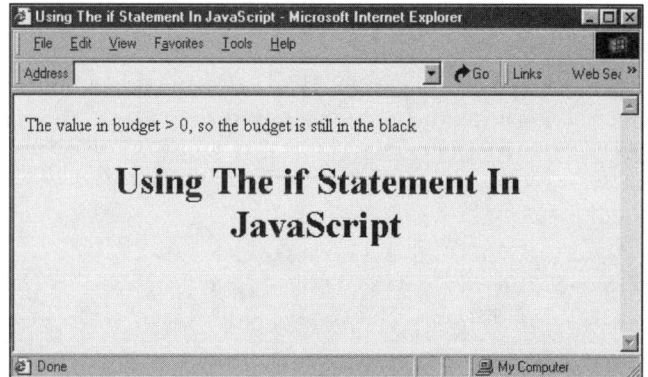

Figure 10.6 Using the **if** statement in JavaScript.

You can also use the AND operator (&&) and OR operator (||) to combine conditions. Here's an example:

```
if (day == 29 && month == "February") {
    document.writeln("Happy Leap Year!")
}
```

In the previous case, because I'm using the AND operator (&&), *both* **day == 29** *and* **month == "February"** must be true for the code in the **if** statement to be executed. On the other hand, take a look at this example:

```
if (hour < 8 || hour > 17) {
    document.writeln("Sorry, we're closed.")
}
```

Here, I'm using the OR operator. If the value in **hour** is less than 8 *or* greater than 17 (using a 24-hour clock), this code displays the message "Sorry, we're closed."

Creating if...else Statements

You can expand **if** statements to include an **else** clause, and the code in the **else** statement will be executed if the condition in the **if** statement is *false*, not true. Here's the syntax of the **if...else** statement:

```
if (condition) {
    code executed if condition is true
}
else {
    code executed if condition is true
}
```

In this next example, I'm checking the value in a variable named **budget**; if it's greater than zero, the code displays the message, "The value in budget > 0, so the budget is still in the black". Otherwise, the code displays the message, "The value in budget is below 0. Uh oh!" Here's the code:

```
<?xml version="1.0"?>
<!DOCTYPE html PUBLIC "-//W3C//DTD XHTML 1.0 Transitional//EN"
"http://www.w3.org/tr/xhtml1/DTD/xhtml1-transitional.dtd">
<html xmlns="http://www.w3.org/1999/xhtml" xml:lang="en" lang="en">
    <head>
```

```
            <title>
                Using The if...else Statement In JavaScript
            </title>

        </head>

        <body>
            <script type = "text/javascript" language="javascript">
                var budget
                budget = -200000.03
                if (budget > 0) {
                    document.writeln("The value in budget > 0, so the " +
                        "budget is still in the black")
                }
                else {
                    document.writeln("The value in budget is below 0. Uh oh!")
                }
            </script>

            <center>
                <h1>
                    Using The if...else Statement In JavaScript
                </h1>
            </center>
        </body>
</html>
```

You can see the results of this code in Figure 10.7.

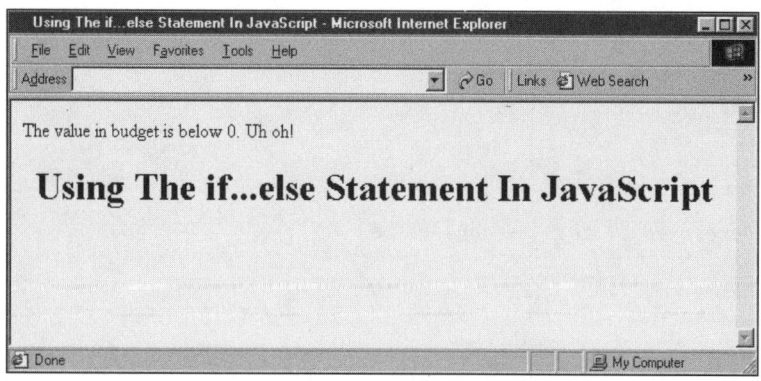

Figure 10.7   Using the **if...else** statement in JavaScript.

Creating switch Statements

"Jeez," says the novice programmer, "I have so many nested **if...else** statements in my code just to test for one value that I hardly know what's going on anymore." "What you need," you say, "is a **switch** statement."

The JavaScript **switch** statement is a powerful one, and it's appropriate if you have a lot of test cases and don't want to construct a long ladder of **if...else** statements. The **switch** statement lets you compare a test expression to a number of values, and if one of those values matches, the corresponding code is executed until it finds a statement named **break**. Here's what this statement looks like:

```
switch(test){
    case value1:
        .
        .
        .
        code executed if test matches value1
        .
        .
        .
        break;
    case value2:
        .
        .
        .
        code executed if test matches value2
        .
        .
        .
        break;
    case value3:
        .
        .
        .
        code executed if test matches value3
        .
        .
        .
        break;
    default:
        .
        .
        .
```

```
            code executed if test doesn't matches any case
            .
            .
            .
        break;
    }
```

Note that you list each possible value by using the **case** statement. There's also a **default** statement that always matches the value you're testing; you can use this statement to ensure that you've handled all possible test expressions.

In this next example, I'm checking a user-typed string—which is stored in the variable **userResponse**—against various possible strings, and then displaying an appropriate response:

```
switch(userResponse){
    case "GO":
        document.writeln("Do you want to navigate to a new URL?")
        break;
    case "PANIC!":
        document.writeln("Do not panic, just reboot your computer.")
        break;
    case "QUIT":
        document.writeln("Are you sure you want to quit?")
        break;
    default:
        document.writeln("Sorry, did not understand your response!")
        break;
}
```

TIP: *If you omit a **break** statement, program execution will continue with the code in the next **case** statement. This is usually undesirable, but at times it's useful to create a cascading effect, allowing each case to fall through to the code in the cases following it.*

Creating for Loop Statements

The novice programmer appears and says, "Help! The big boss wants a table of factorials quickly!" "OK," you say, "you can use JavaScript to create one." "Great," says the NP, "what's a factorial?"

A *factorial* is the product of all the positive integers from 1 to a number you specify. For example, 6 factorial, which is written as 6!, is $6 \times 5 \times 4 \times 3 \times 2 \times 1 = 720$.

To create a table of factorials, we'll have to perform many successive multiplication operations, a feat for which the **for** loop statement is renowned. Here's what this statement looks like:

```
for (initialization; test; increment) {
    code
}
```

Using loops, you can execute code as many times as you want. Here's how it works. Place a statement in the *initialization* part of the **for** loop (the initialization part, also called a *loop index variable*, typically initializes a variable to 0). Then test a condition in the *test* part of the loop each time the code in the loop has been executed. If the condition is false, the loop ends (typically you're checking to see if the value in the loop index exceeds a specified value). If the condition is true, the body of the loop is executed and the code in the *increment* part of the loop is executed to get the loop ready for the next iteration (typically by incrementing the loop index).

Here's an example to make this clear. In this case, I'm just setting a loop index variable, **loopIndex**, to 1, displaying "Hello from JavaScript
" on the Web page, and then testing to make sure that the value in **loopIndex** is less than or equal to 10. If it is, that value increments by one, using the handy JavaScript increment operator (**++**), which adds one to the value in the variable you apply it to. Because I'll use the <= operator in the code, I'll place that code in an external script so an XHTML browser will not interpret it as markup (see the "In Depth" section "What Is JavaScript?" for more details.) Here's what the page looks like:

```
<?xml version="1.0"?>
<!DOCTYPE html PUBLIC "-//W3C//DTD XHTML 1.0 Transitional//EN"
"http://www.w3.org/tr/xhtml1/DTD/xhtml1-transitional.dtd">
<html xmlns="http://www.w3.org/1999/xhtml" xml:lang="en" lang="en">
    <head>
        <title>
            Using The for Statement
        </title>
    </head>

    <body>
        <script type = "text/javascript"
            language = "javascript" src="script.js">
        </script>

        <center>
            <h1>
```

```
            Using The for Statement
         </h1>
      </center>
   </body>
</html>
```

Here's the external script, as stored in script.js:

```
for(var loopIndex = 1; loopIndex <= 10; loopIndex++){
    document.writeln("Hello from JavaScript!<br />")
}
```

Because **loopIndex** is a variable in this code, I have to declare it, so I'm using a JavaScript shortcut declaring **loopIndex** with a **var** statement right inside the initialization part of the **for** loop. This is a common practice, and I'm including it here because you'll see it often. The results of this code, which displays "Hello from JavaScript" ten times in the Web page, appear in Figure 10.8.

Here's the example that the big boss wanted; this code displays a table of factorials. It's easy to understand if you bear in mind that **loopIndex**, the loop index variable, is just another variable in the code; you have access to the value in it just by referring to it by name:

```
<?xml version="1.0"?>
<!DOCTYPE html PUBLIC "-//W3C//DTD XHTML 1.0 Transitional//EN"
"http://www.w3.org/tr/xhtml1/DTD/xhtml1-transitional.dtd">
<html xmlns="http://www.w3.org/1999/xhtml" xml:lang="en" lang="en">
    <head>
        <title>
            Using The for Statement
        </title>
    </head>

    <body>
        <script type = "text/javascript"
            language = "javascript" src="script.js">
        </script>

        <center>
            <h1>
                Using The for Statement
            </h1>
        </center>
    </body>
</html>
```

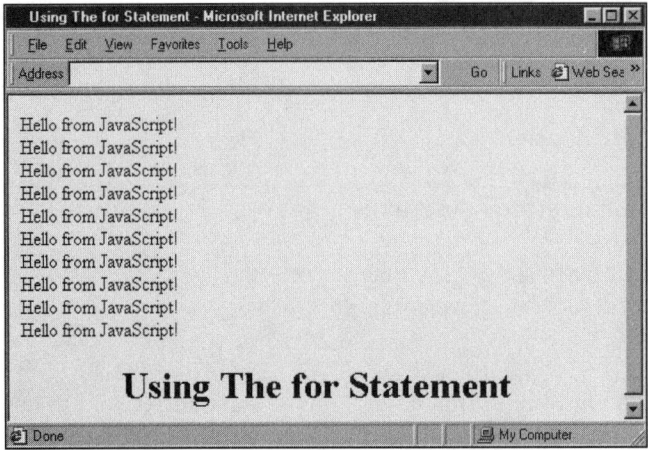

Figure 10.8   Using the **for** statement in JavaScript.

Here's the code in the external script, script.js:

```
var factorial = 1

for(var loopIndex = 1; loopIndex <= 10; loopIndex++){
    factorial = factorial * loopIndex
    document.writeln(loopIndex + "! = " + factorial + "<br />")
}
```

You can see the results of this code in Figure 10.9.

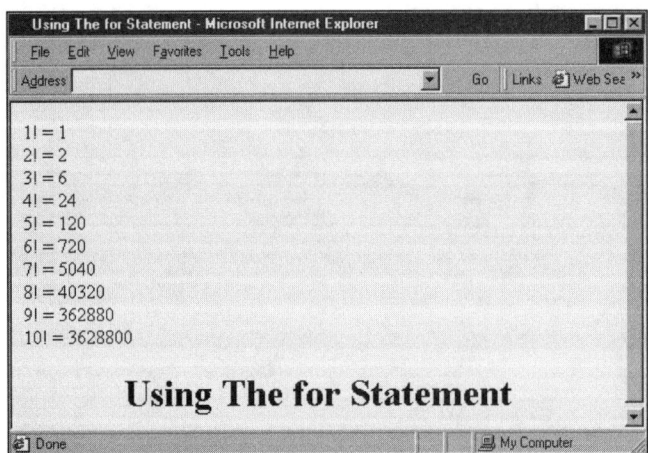

Figure 10.9   Using a **for** statement to compute factorials.

Creating while Loop Statements

In addition to the **for** loop, another powerful loop in JavaScript is the **while** loop. This loop tests a logical condition and, while the condition is true, executes the code in the statement. Here's the syntax of the **while** statement:

```
while (condition){
    code
}
```

In this next example, I use a **while** loop to store the value 2,001 in a variable, and I do it the hard way—by incrementing the value in the number, starting from 0:

```
var number = 0

while(number <= 2001){
    number++
}
```

Here's an example that converts the **for** loop in the previous section to a **while** loop:

```
<?xml version="1.0"?>
<!DOCTYPE html PUBLIC "-//W3C//DTD XHTML 1.0 Transitional//EN"
"http://www.w3.org/tr/xhtml1/DTD/xhtml1-transitional.dtd">
<html xmlns="http://www.w3.org/1999/xhtml" xml:lang="en" lang="en">
    <head>
        <title>
            Using The while Statement
        </title>
    </head>

    <body>
        <script type = "text/javascript"
            language = "javascript" src="script.js">
        </script>

        <center>
            <h1>
                Using The while Statement
            </h1>
        </center>
    </body>
</html>
```

Here's the external code in the file script.js:

```
var factorial = 1
var loopIndex = 1

while(loopIndex <= 10){
    factorial = factorial * loopIndex
    document.writeln(loopIndex + "! = " + factorial + "<br />")
    loopIndex++
}
```

You can see the results of this code in Figure 10.10.

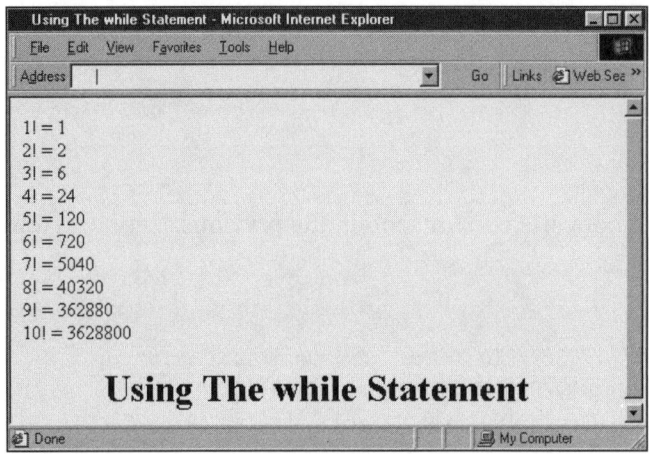

Figure 10.10   Using a **while** statement to compute factorials.

Creating do...while Loop Statements

A variation of the **while** loop is the **do...while** loop. They're actually the same loop except that the **while** loop tests its condition at the beginning of the loop and the **do...while** loop tests its condition at the end of the loop. Here's the syntax of the **do...while** loop statement:

```
do {
    code
} while (condition)
```

Testing the condition at the beginning or the end makes a difference because, unlike the **while** loop, the code in a **do...while** loop is always executed at least once. Look at this next portion of code—whether or not the value in *condition* is "**RED**", this code will always display "**PANIC!
**" at least once (and probably make the user somewhat uncomfortable):

```
do {
    document.writeln("PANIC!<br />")
} while (condition = "RED")
```

A better choice would be to use the **while** loop, which won't display "**PANIC!
" unless the value in condition is actually "RED**":

```
while (condition = "RED") {
    document.writeln("PANIC!<br />")
}
```

On the other hand, if you need to execute the body of the loop before testing to see if the loop should continue, using the **do...while** loop is the best solution.

Creating Functions

"Hm," says the novice programmer, "I need to determine the time of day in many places in my script. I guess that means I'll have to duplicate a lot of code, once for each place." "Not at all," you say; "just create a new function."

Functions are very important in Java programming. You can wrap code into a discrete programming construct called a *function*, and you can *call* that function to execute the code in it. You create functions with the **function** statement, which has the following syntax:

```
function functionname([argument1 [, argument2 [, ...argumentn]]])
{
    code
}
```

To return a value from a function, you use the **return** statement. To see how this works, I'll create a function named **getCurrentTime** in the next example. Note the syntax of the **function** statement, and note that I place an empty pair of parentheses after the name of the function (I do this because the function takes no arguments—see the next section for more details):

```
function getCurrentTime()
{
    var time = new Date
    var returnValue = "The current time is " +
        time.getHours() + ":" + time.getMinutes()
    return(returnValue)
}
```

I'm using the built-in JavaScript **Date** class to find the time. You create an object of this class with the **new** operator (see "Creating JavaScript Objects" in the "Immediate Solutions" section of this chapter), and then you can use the object's **getHours** and **getMinutes** methods to obtain the current time. After I get the current time and place it in a text string in the variable named **returnValue**, I return that value from the **getCurrentTime** function by using the **return** statement. You can now call this function from other parts of your script; JavaScript will run the code in the function and substitute the returned value for the name of the function.

In this next example, I'm calling **getCurrentTime** to get a string with the current time and display that time in a Web page. (If you place code in a **<script>** element, but not inside a function, that code is run automatically when the page is loaded; however, code inside a function is *not* run until that function is called.) Here's the code:

```
<?xml version="1.0"?>
<!DOCTYPE html PUBLIC "-//W3C//DTD XHTML 1.0 Transitional//EN"
    "http://www.w3.org/tr/xhtml1/DTD/xhtml1-transitional.dtd">
<html xmlns="http://www.w3.org/1999/xhtml" xml:lang="en" lang="en">
    <head>
        <title>
            Using Functions In JavaScript
        </title>
    </head>

    <body>

        <script type = "text/javascript" language = "javascript">
            document.writeln(getCurrentTime())

            function getCurrentTime()
            {
                var time = new Date
                var returnValue = "The current time is " +
                    time.getHours() + ":" + time.getMinutes()
                return(returnValue)
            }
        </script>

        <center>
            <h1>
                Using Functions In JavaScript
            </h1>
        </center>
    </body>
</html>
```

Immediate Solutions

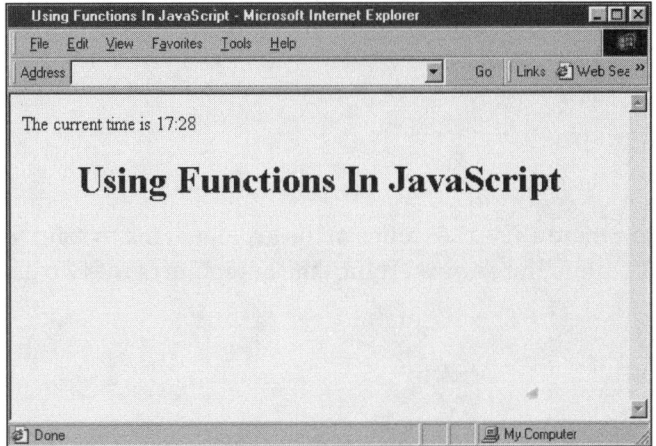

Figure 10.11   Creating and calling functions.

The result of this code appears in Figure 10.11. The current time is calculated in the **getCurrentTime** function, returned from that function, and displayed in the page.

You might also notice that I've included an empty pair of parentheses after the name of the function when calling the function. These parentheses are empty because I'm not passing any *arguments* to this function. However, if you want to pass data to the function, you can do so by passing that data as arguments—see the next section for details.

TIP: Methods in JavaScript are just functions that are built into objects.

Passing Arguments to Functions

"Arggh!" says the novice programmer, "I need to determine the minimum of two numbers in about a million places in my script, so I have to duplicate the code to find the minimum in all those places." "Not at all," you say; "just write a function, *pass* the two numbers to the function, and return the minimum. Then all you have to do is call the function each time you need it." "Oh," says the NP.

You can pass data as *arguments* to a function, and that data will become available inside the function. When you create a function, you use an argument list to indicate which arguments will be passed to the function. You place the argument list in parentheses, like this:

613

```
function min(value1, value2)
{
    .
    .
    .
}
```

Inside the function, you can now use the values in the argument list to refer to the values passed to your function. Here's how I return the minimum of the two passed values:

```
function min(value1, value2)
{
    if (value1 < value2) {
        return(value1)
    }
    else {
        return(value2)
    }
}
```

TIP: *The built-in JavaScript **Math** object has a **min** method. Using the **min** method would eliminate the need for the previous code.*

To pass values to the **min** function, you enclose them in parentheses following the function name when you call that function. Here's a page in which I'll call the **min** function with two values, 1 and 2:

```
<?xml version="1.0"?>
<!DOCTYPE html PUBLIC "-//W3C//DTD XHTML 1.0 Transitional//EN"
"http://www.w3.org/tr/xhtml1/DTD/xhtml1-transitional.dtd">
<html xmlns="http://www.w3.org/1999/xhtml" xml:lang="en" lang="en">
    <head>
        <title>
            Using Function Arguments In JavaScript
        </title>
    </head>

    <body>
        <script type = "text/javascript"
            language = "javascript" src="script.js">
        </script>
```

```
        <center>
            <h1>
                Using Function Arguments In JavaScript
            </h1>

        </center>
    </body>
</html>
```

Here's the code from the external script script.js:

```
document.writeln("The minimum of 1 and 2 is " +  min(1, 2))

function min(value1, value2)
{
    if (value1 < value2) {
        return(value1)
    }
    else {
        return(value2)
    }
}
```

You can see the results of this code in Figure 10.12. The values 1 and 2 were passed to the **min** function, which determined which of the two values was the minimum value and then returned that value to be displayed in the Web page.

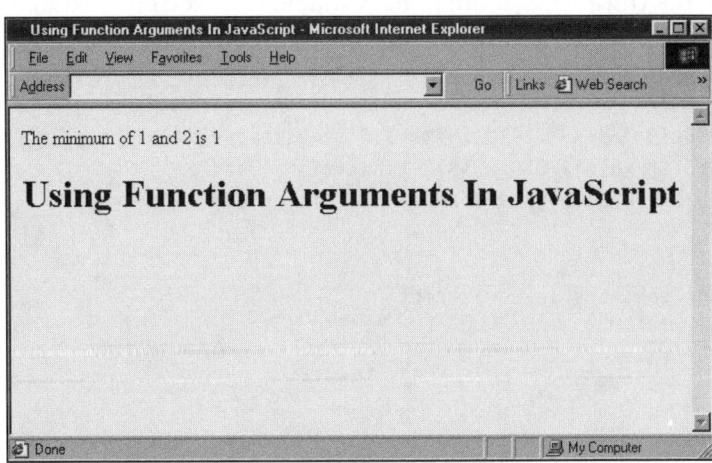

Figure 10.12 Passing arguments to functions.

TIP: *You can actually call a function with fewer arguments than you've used to declare the function. This is okay as long as you don't try to read values from arguments that were not passed. You can also pass more arguments to a function than the function is set up to take. To read such arguments, you can use the* arguments array, *which is available in every function. (We'll see how arrays work later in the "Immediate Solutions" section "Creating Arrays with the **Array** Class.") The first argument passed to the function is the first entry in the arguments array, and you refer to it as* **functionName.arguments[0]**; *the second argument is referred to as* **functionName.arguments[1]**; *and so on. (Using square brackets this way is how you use arrays.)*

NOTE: *By default in JavaScript, the items that are really passed to functions are* copies *of the arguments you pass, not the arguments themselves. This is referred to as* calling by value.

Creating JavaScript Objects

JavaScript comes with some ready-to-use objects, such as the **document**, **location**, **navigator**, and **history** objects. JavaScript also comes with many utility classes, such as the **Date** and **Math** classes, that you can use to create objects. Obviously, these objects aren't available until you create them.

As I mentioned in the "In Depth" section of this chapter, a *class* is like a cookie cutter for an object; you can think of a class as an object's *type*. Using a class, you can create an object with the **new** operator. In fact, we've already seen one example, which used the **Date** class. In this next example, I create a new JavaScript **Date** object from the **Date** class, store it in a variable named **time**, and then use the **getHours** and **getMinutes** methods of that object, like this:

```
<?xml version="1.0"?>
<!DOCTYPE html PUBLIC "-//W3C//DTD XHTML 1.0 Transitional//EN"
"http://www.w3.org/tr/xhtml1/DTD/xhtml1-transitional.dtd">
<html xmlns="http://www.w3.org/1999/xhtml" xml:lang="en" lang="en">
    <head>
        <title>
            Using Functions In JavaScript
        </title>
    </head>

    <body>
        <script type = "text/javascript" language = "javascript">
            document.writeln(getCurrentTime())

            function getCurrentTime()
            {
```

```
            var time = new Date
            var returnValue = "The current time is " +
                time.getHours() + ":" + time.getMinutes()
            return(returnValue)
        }
    </script>

    <center>
        <h1>
            Using Functions In JavaScript
        </h1>
    </center>
    </body>
</html>
```

To create objects, you use the **new** operator, as we've seen with the **Date** class:

```
var time = new Date
```

In this example, the **new** operator uses the **Date** class's *constructor*, which is a special method of the class that creates objects of that class. In the previous example, I didn't pass any arguments to the **Date** class's constructor, so the **Date** object created will correspond to the current time. On the other hand, you can pass a specified date to the **Date** class's constructor to create a **Date** object for that time, like this:

```
var time = new Date("9/2/2000")
```

The kind of data you can pass to class constructors in JavaScript varies by class—see the JavaScript documentation for details. You can also find another example of using constructors in the next section, where I'm working with the JavaScript **String** object.

Using JavaScript **String** Objects

The JavaScript **String** class is designed to hold text strings and let you work on them. You'll find the JavaScript methods of this class in Table 10.3 and the JScript methods of this class in Table 10.4.

In this next example, I'm creating an object of the JavaScript **String** class, using that object's **bold** method to make the string bold, and then using its **length** property to determine its length:

Table 10.3 Methods of the JavaScript **String** class.

Methods			
anchor	big	blink	bold
charAt	charCodeAt	concat	fixed
fontcolor	fontsize	indexOf	italics
lastIndexOf	link	match	replace
search	slice	small	split
strike	sub	substr	substring
sup	toLowerCase	toSource	toUpperCase
toString	valueOf		

Table 10.4 Methods of the JScript **String** class.

Methods			
anchor	big	blink	bold
charAt	charCodeAt	concat	fixed
fontcolor	fontsize	fromCharCode	indexOf
italics	lastIndexOf	link	match
replace	search	slice	small
split	strike	sub	substr
substring	sup	toLowerCase	toString
toUpperCase	valueOf		

```
<?xml version="1.0"?>
<!DOCTYPE html PUBLIC "-//W3C//DTD XHTML 1.0 Transitional//EN"
"http://www.w3.org/tr/xhtml1/DTD/xhtml1-transitional.dtd">
<html xmlns="http://www.w3.org/1999/xhtml" xml:lang="en" lang="en">
    <head>
        <title>
            Using The JavaScript String Class
        </title>
    </head>

    <body>
        <script type = "text/javascript" language = "javascript">
            var newString = new String("This is a JavaScript string")

            document.writeln("This string, " + newString.bold() +
            ", is exactly " + newString.length + " characters long.")
        </script>
```

```
            <center>
                <h1>
                    Using The JavaScript String Class
                </h1>
            </center>
        </body>
</html>
```

Note that I pass the text for the string in parentheses after the word **String** in this code. I do this because I'm passing that text as an argument to the **String** class's constructor, which is a special method with the same name as the class (which is **String** here) that creates objects. The results of this code appear in Figure 10.13.

It's worth mentioning that JavaScript treats the **String** class in a special way, allowing you to create objects of this class without the **new** operator because it's such a common thing to do. Here's an example that creates a new **String** object when you simply enclose text in quotation marks:

```
<?xml version="1.0"?>
<!DOCTYPE html PUBLIC "-//W3C//DTD XHTML 1.0 Transitional//EN"
"http://www.w3.org/tr/xhtml1/DTD/xhtml1-transitional.dtd">
<html xmlns="http://www.w3.org/1999/xhtml" xml:lang="en" lang="en">
    <head>
        <title>
            Using The JavaScript String Class
        </title>
    </head>

    <body>
        <script type = "text/javascript" language = "javascript">
            var newString = "This is a JavaScript string"

            document.writeln("This string, " + newString.bold() +
            ", is exactly " + newString.length + " characters long.")
        </script>

        <center>
            <h1>
                Using The JavaScript String Class
            </h1>
        </center>
    </body>
</html>
```

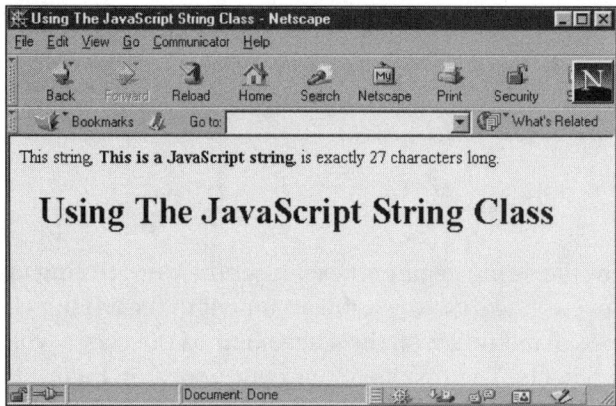

Figure 10.13 Creating JavaScript **String** objects.

Creating Arrays with the **Array** Class

"Hm," says the novice programmer, "I want to work with a whole set of data at once, and a **for** loop would be great. But how should I store the data?" "Sounds like you need an array," you say. "Let's try the JavaScript **Array** class."

Arrays can hold whole sets of data, allowing you to access each data item by specifying a numeric index. Arrays are perfect for working with loops because you can use the loop index to successively iterate through each item in the array. To create arrays in JavaScript, you use the JavaScript **Array** class. You can find the methods of this class in Table 10.5 and the methods of the JScript **Array** class in Table 10.6.

Here's an example in which I create an array, place data into the array, and then use a **for** loop to find the average value of that data. I start by creating the new array named **data** and a variable I'll use to hold the total of all the data items in the array:

Table 10.5 Methods of the JavaScript **Array** class.

concat	join	pop	push	reverse
shift	slice	splicesort	toSource	toString
unshift	valueOf			

Table 10.6 Methods of the JScript **Array** class.

concat	join	reverse	slice	sort
toString	valueOf			

```
var data = new Array
var total = 0
        .
        .
        .
```

Now I'm free to store data in the array, arranging it by using a numeric index. Arrays in JavaScript start with an index of 0 (although they didn't in earlier versions). You refer to a data item in an array like this: **data[1]**. This notation refers to the second item in the array named **data** (**data[0]** is the first element). To fill the new array with data, I execute this code:

```
var data = new Array
var total = 0

data[0] = 1
data[1] = 2
data[2] = 3
data[3] = 4
data[4] = 5
data[5] = 6
data[6] = 7
        .
        .
        .
```

All I need to do now is loop over this array with a **for** loop, adding all the data items together and then dividing the result by the total number of elements in the array. There's an easy way to find the number of elements in an array—use its **length** property. Here's the final Web page:

```
<?xml version="1.0"?>
<!DOCTYPE html PUBLIC "-//W3C//DTD XHTML 1.0 Transitional//EN"
"http://www.w3.org/tr/xhtml1/DTD/xhtml1-transitional.dtd">
<html xmlns="http://www.w3.org/1999/xhtml" xml:lang="en" lang="en">
    <head>
        <title>
            An Array Example
        </title>
    </head>

    <body>
        <script type = "text/javascript"
            language = "javascript" src="script.js">
        </script>
```

```
            <center>
                <h1>
                    Using JavaScript Arrays
                </h1>
            </center>
        </body>
</html>
```

And here's the code in the external script file, script.js:

```
var data = new Array
var total = 0

data[0] = 1
data[1] = 2
data[2] = 3
data[3] = 4
data[4] = 5
data[5] = 6
data[6] = 7

for(var loopIndex = 0; loopIndex < data.length; loopIndex++){
    total = total + data[loopIndex]
}

document.write("The average value of your data is " +
    total / data.length)
```

The results of this code appear in Figure 10.14, where you can see that the average value of the items in the array is 4.

Figure 10.14   The result of creating JavaScript **Array** objects.

Handling Events in Browsers

As I discussed in the "In Depth" section of this chapter, much of dynamic XHTML has to do with using JavaScript for handling events, such as mouse clicks or key presses. Here are the common events that JavaScript can handle. Each one is an event attribute that you can use in an XHTML tag:

- **onabort**—Occurs when an action is aborted.
- **onblur**—Occurs when an element loses the input focus.
- **onchange**—Occurs when data in a control, such as a text field, changes.
- **onclick**—Occurs when an element is clicked.
- **ondblclick**—Occurs when an element is double-clicked.
- **ondragdrop**—Occurs when a drag-and-drop operation is undertaken.
- **onerror**—Occurs when there's been a JavaScript error.
- **onfocus**—Occurs when an element gets the focus.
- **onkeydown**—Occurs when a key goes down.
- **onkeypress**—Occurs when a key is pressed and the key code is available.
- **onkeyup**—Occurs when a key goes up.
- **onload**—Occurs when the page loads.
- **onmousedown**—Occurs when a mouse button goes down.
- **onmousemove**—Occurs when the mouse moves.
- **onmouseout**—Occurs when the mouse leaves an element.
- **onmouseover**—Occurs when the mouse moves over an element.
- **onmouseup**—Occurs when a mouse button goes up.
- **onmove**—Occurs when an element is moved.
- **onreset**—Occurs when the user clicks the Reset button.
- **onresize**—Occurs when an element or page is resized.
- **onselect**—Occurs when a selection takes place.
- **onsubmit**—Occurs when the user clicks the Submit button.
- **onunload**—Occurs when a page is unloaded.

These event attributes have been added to many XHTML elements, and you can assign a JavaScript function to be called to one of these event attributes. You'll find the official XHTML events listed along with every XHTML tag when that tag is first introduced in this book. In addition, Table 10.1 lists event attributes for many XHTML elements as supported in Internet Explorer. Table 10.2 lists event attributes for many XHTML elements as supported in Netscape Navigator.

Here's an example of using two XHTML controls that we'll see in Chapter 12—text fields and buttons. You create these controls with the **<input>** element, setting the **type** attribute to **"text"** to create a text field and to **"button"** to create a button. When the user clicks the button, the code will display a message in the text field. As you'll see in the code, the **<input>** element must be used inside an XHTML **<form>** element. Technically in XHTML, this element must have an action attribute that gives a URL to send the form's data to, but we're not sending this form's data anywhere, so I'll set this attribute simply to "action". Here's how I create the text field and button (the **value** attribute of the button sets the button's caption):

```
<form name = "form1" action = "action">
    <h1>
        Handling JavaScript Events
    </h1>
    <br />
    <h2>
        Click the button!
    </h2>
    <br />
    <input type = "text" name = "Text" size = "60" />
    <br />
    <br />
    <input type="button" value="Click Me" />
</form>
```

To connect the button to a JavaScript function named **clickHandler**, so that **clickHandler** is called when the button is clicked, I set the button's **onclick** event attribute to "**clickHandler()**":

```
<form name = "form1"  action = "action">
    <h1>
        Handling JavaScript Events
    </h1>
    <br />
    <h2>
        Click the button!
    </h2>
    <br />
    <input type = "text" name = "Text" size = "60" />
    <br />
    <br />
    <input type="button" value="Click Me"
        onclick="clickHandler()" />
</form>
```

Now I create a JavaScript function named **clickHandler** that places the message "You clicked the button!" in the text field. As we'll see in Chapter 12, I can access the text field, which I've named **Text**, by using the document object called **document.form1.Text**. Here's what the code looks like:

```
<?xml version="1.0"?>
<!DOCTYPE html PUBLIC "-//W3C//DTD XHTML 1.0 Transitional//EN"
"http://www.w3.org/tr/xhtml1/DTD/xhtml1-transitional.dtd">
<html xmlns="http://www.w3.org/1999/xhtml" xml:lang="en" lang="en">
    <head>
        <title>
            Handling JavaScript Events
        </title>

        <script type = "text/javascript" language= "javascript">
            function clickHandler(e)
            {
                document.form1.Text.value = "You clicked the button!"
            }
        </script>
    </head>

    <body>
        <center>
            <form name = "form1"  action = "action">
                <h1>
                    Handling JavaScript Events
                </h1>
                <br />
                <h2>
                    Click the button!
                </h2>
                <br />
                <input type = "text" name = "Text" size = "60" />
                <br />
                <br />
                <input type="button" value="Click Me"
                    onclick="clickHandler()" />
            </form>
        </center>
    </body>
</html>
```

That's all it takes—now when the user clicks the button, the message is displayed in the text field, as you can see in Figure 10.15.

Figure 10.15 Handling events with JavaScript.

Why did I declare the event handler **clickHandler** as **clickHandler(e)** in the code in the previous example? I did so because when an event occurs, an object of the **event** class (which I'm naming **e** here) is passed to event handlers in Netscape Navigator. You'll find the properties of this event for Netscape Navigator in Table 10.7.

No object is passed to event handlers in Internet Explorer. (JavaScript is flexible enough, however, that you can still declare **clickHandler** as though it does take one argument, **clickHandler(e)**, so the same function works with both browsers.) Instead, you use the **window.event** object, which is accessible at any point in your code, to get data about the event. You'll find the properties of the **window.event** object for Internet Explorer in Table 10.8.

For an example that uses the event objects in Tables 10.7 and 10.8, see the next section.

Table 10.7 Netscape Navigator's **event** object properties.

Property	Description
data	Array of strings containing the URLs of the dropped objects; used with the **dragdrop** event
height	Height associated with the event
layerX	Cursor's horizontal position, relative to the layer in which the event occurred
layerY	Cursor's vertical position in pixels, relative to the layer in which the event occurred
modifiers	Modifier keys associated with a mouse or key event. Possible values: **ALT_MASK**, **CONTROL_MASK**, **SHIFT_MASK**, and **META_MASK**

(continued)

Table 10.7 Netscape Navigator's **event** object properties *(continued)*.

Property	Description
pageX	Cursor's horizontal position in pixels, relative to the page
pageY	Cursor's vertical position in pixels, relative to the page
screenX	Cursor's horizontal position in pixels, relative to the screen
screenY	Cursor's vertical position in pixels, relative to the screen
target	Target object of the event
type	Type of event
which	Mouse button that was pressed or the ASCII value of a pressed key
width	Width associated with the event
x	X location of the event
y	Y location of the event

Table 10.8 Internet Explorer's **window.event** object properties.

Property	Description
altKey	True if the Alt key is down
altLeft	True if the left Alt key is down
button	Specifies which mouse button, if any, is pressed
cancelBubble	Indicates whether this event should move up the event hierarchy
clientX	x-coordinate with respect to the client area
clientY	y-coordinate with respect to the client area
ctrlKey	True if the Ctrl key is down
ctrlLeft	True if the left Ctrl key is down
fromElement	Specifies the element being moved
keyCode	Code of the struck key
offsetX	Container-relative x position
offsetY	Container-relative y position
reason	Disposition of data transfer
returnValue	Specifies the return value from the event
screenX	x-coordinate relative to physical screen size
screenY	y-coordinate relative to physical screen size
shiftKey	True if the Shift key is down
shiftLeft	True if the left Shift key is down
srcElement	Element that caused the event

(continued)

Table 10.8 Internet Explorer's **window.event** object properties *(continued).*

Property	Description
srcFilter	Filter event if this is a **filterChange** event
toElement	Specifies the element being moved to
type	Returns the event type as a string
x	x position of the event in context
y	y position of the event in context

Event Handling: Mouse Events

In this section, I'm going to put the JavaScript mouse events to work so you can see a full-scale JavaScript program handling events. Here are the JavaScript events this program will use:

- **onmousedown**—Occurs when a mouse button goes down in the page.
- **onmouseout**—Occurs when the mouse leaves a hyperlink in the page.
- **onmouseover**—Occurs when the mouse moves over a hyperlink in a page.
- **onmouseup**—Occurs when a mouse button goes up in the page.

You can use the mouse in the Web page itself, and the code will report the mouse's location when an event occurs and whether the Ctrl, Shift, or Alt keys are down. I'll add a hyperlink to the page to show how the **onmouseover** and **onmouseout** events work.

You get event data in different ways for the two major browsers, so I'll need to write the code to handle both Internet Explorer and Netscape Navigator. I'll determine which browser the user has with a technique (discussed in Chapter 11) that checks the **navigator** object's **appName** property to determine the name of the browser.

There's one more point that should be mentioned. You would normally connect event handlers for **onmousedown** and **onmouseup** to the Web page by using the **<body>** element, like this:

```
<body onmousedown = "mouseDownFunction()" onmouseup = "mouseUpFunction()">
```

However, in Netscape Navigator, the **<body>** element does not support the **onmousedown** and **onmouseup** event attributes. Instead, you assign the name of the event-handler functions you want to use to the **document** object's **onmousedown** and **onmouseup** properties, like this, in the **<script>** element:

Immediate Solutions

```
<script type = "text/javascript" language= "javascript">

//Added for Netscape Navigator
    document.onmousedown = mouseDownFunction
    document.onmouseup = mouseUpFunction
        .
        .
        .
```

The remainder of the code follows what we've already accomplished in this chapter. You can see this example at work in Figure 10.16. The entire page, mouse.html, is shown in Listing 10.1, and the script that page uses, script.js, appears in Listing 10.2. Take a look at the code if you're so inclined—it's a pretty good example of event handling in the two browsers.

Listing 10.1   mouse.html displays information about mouse events.

```
<?xml version="1.0"?>
<!DOCTYPE html PUBLIC "-//W3C//DTD XHTML 1.0 Transitional//EN"
"http://www.w3.org/tr/xhtml1/DTD/xhtml1-transitional.dtd">
<html xmlns="http://www.w3.org/1999/xhtml" xml:lang="en" lang="en">
    <head>
        <title>
            Using The Mouse In JavaScript
        </title>
```

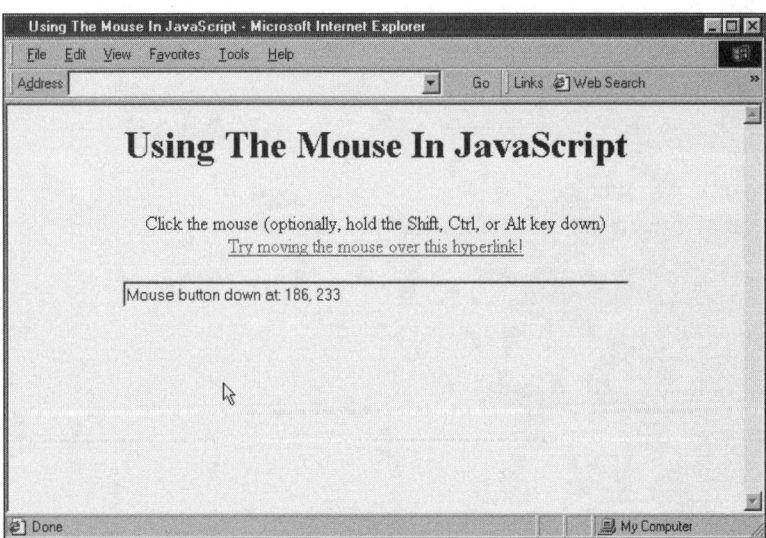

Figure 10.16   Handling mouse events with JavaScript.

```html
            <script type = "text/javascript"
                language= "javascript" src="script.js">
            </script>
    </head>

    <body onmousedown = "mouseDownFunction()" onmouseup =
        "mouseUpFunction()">
        <center>
            <form name = "form1"  action = "action">

            <h1>
                Using The Mouse In JavaScript
            </h1>

            <br />
                Click the mouse (optionally, hold the Shift, Ctrl, or Alt
                key down)
            <br />

            <a href="mouse.htm" name="mouseLink"
                onmouseover="mouseOverFunction()"
                onmouseout="mouseOutFunction()">
                Try moving the mouse over this hyperlink!
            </a>
            <br />
            <br />
            <input type = "text" name = "Textbox" size = "60" />
            </form>
        </center>
    </body>
</html>
```

Listing 10.2   script.js holds the code for mouse.html.

```javascript
//Added for Netscape Navigator
document.onmousedown = mouseDownFunction
document.onmouseup = mouseUpFunction

function mouseOverFunction(e)
{
    if (navigator.appName == "Microsoft Internet Explorer") {

        if(window.event.shiftKey && window.event.ctrlKey){
            document.form1.Textbox.value =
            "Shift and Ctrl keys down and mouse over at: " +
            window.event.x + ", " + window.event.y
            return
        }
```

```
            if(window.event.shiftKey)
            {
                document.form1.Textbox.value =
                "Shift key down and mouse over at: " +
                window.event.x + ", " + window.event.y
                return
            }

            if(window.event.ctrlKey)
            {
                document.form1.Textbox.value =
                "Ctrl key down and mouse over at: " +
                window.event.x + ", " + window.event.y
                return
            }

            if(window.event.altKey)
            {
                document.form1.Textbox.value =
                "Alt key down and mouse over at: " +
                window.event.x + ", " + window.event.y
                return
            }

            document.form1.Textbox.value = "Mouse over at: " +
                window.event.x + ", " + window.event.y
        }

        if(navigator.appName == "Netscape") {

            document.form1.Textbox.value = "Mouse over"
        }
    }

    function mouseOutFunction(e)
    {
        if (navigator.appName == "Microsoft Internet Explorer") {

            if(window.event.shiftKey && window.event.ctrlKey){
                document.form1.Textbox.value =
                "Shift and Ctrl keys down and mouse out at: " +
                window.event.x + ", " + window.event.y
                return
            }
```

```javascript
            if(window.event.shiftKey)
            {
                document.form1.Textbox.value =
                "Shift key down and mouse out at: " +
                window.event.x + ", " + window.event.y
                return
            }

            if(window.event.ctrlKey)
            {
                document.form1.Textbox.value =
                "Ctrl key down and mouse out at: " +
                window.event.x + ", " + window.event.y
                return
            }

            if(window.event.altKey)
            {
                document.form1.Textbox.value =
                "Alt key down and mouse out at: " +
                window.event.x + ", " + window.event.y
                return
            }

            document.form1.Textbox.value = "Mouse out at: " +
                window.event.x + ", " + window.event.y
        }

        if(navigator.appName == "Netscape") {
            document.form1.Textbox.value = "Mouse out"
        }

    }
    function mouseDownFunction(e)
    {
        if (navigator.appName == "Microsoft Internet Explorer") {

            if(window.event.shiftKey && window.event.ctrlKey){
                document.form1.Textbox.value =
                "Shift and Ctrl keys down and mouse button down at: " +
                window.event.x + ", " + window.event.y
                return
            }
```

```javascript
        if(window.event.shiftKey)
        {
            document.form1.Textbox.value =
            "Shift key down and mouse button down at: " +
            window.event.x + ", " + window.event.y
            return
        }

        if(window.event.ctrlKey)
        {
            document.form1.Textbox.value =
            "Ctrl key down and mouse button down at: " +
            window.event.x + ", " + window.event.y
            return
        }

        if(window.event.altKey)
        {
            document.form1.Textbox.value =
            "Alt key down and mouse button down at: " +
            window.event.x + ", " + window.event.y
            return
        }

        document.form1.Textbox.value = "Mouse button down at: " +
            window.event.x + ", " + window.event.y
    }

    if(navigator.appName == "Netscape") {

        switch(e.modifiers){
            case 0:
                document.form1.Textbox.value = "Mouse button down at: "
                    + e.pageX + ", " + e.pageY
                break
            case 2:
                document.form1.Textbox.value =
                "Ctrl key down and mouse button down at: " +
                e.pageX + ", " + e.pageY
                break
            case 4:
                document.form1.Textbox.value =
                "Shift key down and mouse button down at: " +
                e.pageX + ", " + e.pageY
                break
```

```
                case 6:
                    document.form1.Textbox.value =
                        "Shift and Ctrl keys down and mouse button down "
                        + "at: " +
                        e.pageX + ", " + e.pageY
                    break
                case 1:
                    document.form1.Textbox.value =
                    "Alt key down and mouse button down at: " +
                    e.pageX + ", " + e.pageY
                    break
            }
        }
    }

    function mouseUpFunction(e)
    {
        if (navigator.appName == "Microsoft Internet Explorer") {

            if(window.event.shiftKey && window.event.ctrlKey){
                document.form1.Textbox.value =
                "Shift and Ctrl keys down and mouse button up at: " +
                window.event.x + ", " + window.event.y
                return
            }

            if(window.event.shiftKey)
            {
                document.form1.Textbox.value =
                "Shift key down and mouse button up at: " +
                window.event.x + ", " + window.event.y
                return
            }

            if(window.event.ctrlKey)
            {
                document.form1.Textbox.value =
                "Ctrl key down and mouse button up at: " +
                window.event.x + ", " + window.event.y
                return
            }
```

```javascript
        if(window.event.altKey)
        {
            document.form1.Textbox.value =
            "Alt key down and mouse button up at: " +
            window.event.x + ", " + window.event.y
            return
        }

        document.form1.Textbox.value = "Mouse button up at: " +
            window.event.x + ", " + window.event.y
    }

    if(navigator.appName == "Netscape") {
        switch(e.modifiers){
            case 0:
                document.form1.Textbox.value = "Mouse button up at: "
                    + e.pageX + ", " + e.pageY
                break
            case 2:
                document.form1.Textbox.value =
                "Ctrl key down and mouse button up at: " +
                e.pageX + ", " + e.pageY
                break
            case 4:
                document.form1.Textbox.value =
                "Shift key down and mouse button up at: " +
                e.pageX + ", " + e.pageY
                break
            case 6:
                document.form1.Textbox.value =
                "Shift and Ctrl keys down " +
                "and mouse button up at: " + e.pageX + ", " + e.pageY
                break
            case 1:
                document.form1.Textbox.value =
                "Alt key down and mouse button up at: " +
                e.pageX + ", " + e.pageY
                break
        }
    }
}
```

Chapter 11

Putting JavaScript to Work

If you need an immediate solution to:	See page:
Determining Browser Type in Code	658
Creating a Self-Modifying Web Page	660
Setting a Page's Background Color	665
Reloading Images at Runtime	666
Opening a New Browser Window	667
Configuring and Writing to a New Window	672
Creating Alert Dialog Boxes	675
Creating Confirmation Dialog Boxes	676
Creating Prompt Dialog Boxes	678
Writing to the Browser's Status Bar	680
Navigating with the **location** Object	681
Navigating with the **history** Object	684
Creating JavaScript URLs: Improving Image Maps	686
Creating Cookies with JavaScript	688

In Depth

In the previous chapter, we worked through a lot of JavaScript syntax. In this chapter, it's time to put it to work by creating self-modifying Web pages, displaying Alert dialog boxes, writing to the status bar, navigating to past pages, and creating cookies.

After getting a good foundation in JavaScript syntax, you'll find that most JavaScript programming revolves around the predefined objects available to you in the browser. This chapter is about working with the principal objects: the **document**, **window**, **location**, and **history** objects. To put these objects in perspective, I'll start with an overview of which objects are available, and which objects contain which other objects, in Internet Explorer and Netscape Navigator.

JavaScript Objects in Overview

Before you even start working in JavaScript, the Web browser has created many objects for you to work with. These objects can also contain other objects. For example, in the previous chapter, we saw that the **window** object contains an **event** object in Internet Explorer. To access the **event** object inside the **window** object, you refer to it as **window.event**. In this way, you can access a whole hierarchy of objects. Here's what that hierarchy looks like for objects in Internet Explorer (not all objects are represented here because the list would be very long):

```
window
    |
    |--event
    |
    |--frames
    |
    |--history
    |--location
    |
    |--navigator
    |
     --document
            |
```

```
|--links
|
|--anchors
|
|--images
|
|--forms
|
|--applets
|
|--embeds
|
|--frames
|
|--scripts
|
|--all
|
|--selection
|
|--body
|
|--anchor
|
|--applet
|
|--image
|
|--link
|
 --form
     |
     |--elements
     |
     |--button
     |
     |--checkbox
     |
     |--fileUpload
     |
     |--hidden
     |
     |--option
     |
     |--password
     |
```

```
            |--radio
            |
            |--select
            |
            |--submit
            |
            |--text
            |
             --textarea
```

Here's the corresponding object hierarchy in Netscape Navigator (again, not all objects are listed):

```
       |
       |--navigator
       |     |
       |      --plugins
       |
        --window
              |
              |--location
              |
              |--history
              |
              |--frame
              |
              |--frames
              |
               --document
                     |
                     |--links
                     |
                     |--anchors
                     |
                     |--images
                     |
                     |--forms
                     |
                     |--applets
                     |
                     |--embeds
                     |
                     |--layers
                     |
                     |--anchor
                     |
```

```
|--applet
|
|--image
|
|--link
|
|--plugin
|
 --form
    |
    |--button
    |
    |--checkbox
    |
    |--fileUpload
    |
    |--hidden
    |
    |--option
    |
    |--password
    |
    |--radio
    |
    |--select
    |
    |--submit
    |
    |--text
    |
     --textarea
```

In this chapter, I'm going to put four of these objects—the most popular ones—to work:

- **document**—This object corresponds to a Web page, and you can use it to gain access to all elements in the page. You can also use it to write in a Web page and to use cookies.

- **window**—This object corresponds to the Web browser window, and you can use it to display all kinds of dialog boxes, among other things.

- **location**—This object holds or sets the current location, and you can use it to navigate to a new URL.

- **history**—This object records where the user has been and lets the user navigate back there.

These are the main objects used in JavaScript, and I'll look at each of these important objects in more detail in the next few sections. For reference, I'm going to list the properties, methods, and events of these objects. It's worth taking a moment to read the corresponding tables to see what's available.

The document Object

The **document** object has been available in Netscape Navigator since version 2 and in Internet Explorer since version 3. This object corresponds to a Web page; using this object, you can access all of the page's elements, such as its hyperlinks, images, and forms. For example, in "Reloading Images at Runtime" in the "Immediate Solutions" section of this chapter, I'll create a form named **form1** with an **<img>** element named **img1** in it. I can then access the **src** attribute of that element like this:

```
function reloadImage()
{
    document.form1.img1.src = "gif/image2.gif"
}
```

We'll see more about working with the elements in a page when we discuss dynamic XHTML in Chapter 13. As we've seen in Chapter 10, you can also use the **document** object's **writeln** method to write to a Web page as it's being loaded. Furthermore, you can use this object to create and read cookies, as we'll see at the end of this chapter.

As with any other object, the **document** object is full of properties, methods, and events. You can study this object by using JavaScript itself; you can find the setting of a property by using the expression **document.[*propertyname*]**, where ***propertyname*** is the name of the property you want to check. In fact, JavaScript can help out even more here with its **for...in** construct, which loops automatically over all the members of an object. Here's an example showing how this works. I'm listing all the properties of the **document** object and their settings:

```
<?xml version="1.0"?>
<!DOCTYPE html PUBLIC "-//W3C//DTD XHTML 1.0 Transitional//EN"
    "http://www.w3.org/tr/xhtml1/DTD/xhtml1-transitional.dtd">
<html xmlns="http://www.w3.org/1999/xhtml" xml:lang="en" lang="en">
    <head>
        <title>
            Document Object Properties
        </title>
    </head>
```

```
        <body>
            <script type = "text/javascript"
                language = "javascript" src = "script.js">
            </script>

            <center>
                <h1>
                    Document Object Properties
                </h1>
            </center>
        </body>
</html>
```

Here's the script, script.js, that does the work:

```
document.writeln(
    "<h1>Here are the properties of the document object:</h1>"
)

for(var property in document){
    document.writeln(property +
    " = " + document[property] + "<br />")
}
```

You can see the results of this code in Figure 11.1. As you can see, there are many properties in this object—many more than can fit into the browser window. What

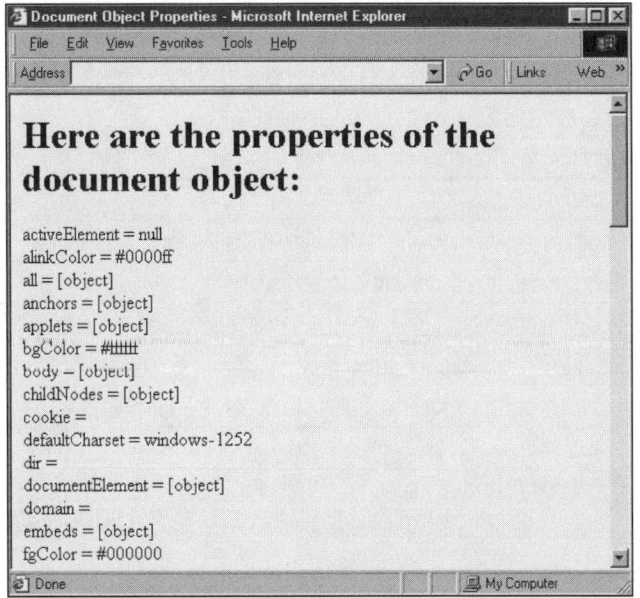

Figure 11.1 Examining **document** object properties.

are all these properties and what do they mean? You'll find Internet Explorer's **document** object properties in Table 11.1. In addition, you'll find the methods of this object in Table 11.2 and its events in Table 11.3. Internet Explorer's **document** object also has a number of *collections*, which are arrays of other objects; you'll find collections listed in Table 11.4.

Netscape Navigator's **document** object properties appear in Table 11.5, its methods in Table 11.6, and its events in Table 11.7.

As you can see, there's a lot to the **document** object—even though it differs radically by browser. We'll put this object to work in this chapter.

Table 11.1 Properties of the document object in Internet Explorer.

Property	Description
activeElement	Gets the object that has the current focus.
aLinkColor	Specifies or retrieves the color of all active links.
bgColor	Specifies or retrieves the background color for the **document** object.
body	Marks the beginning and end of the body of the document.
contentEditable	Indicates whether the user can edit the content of the object.
cookie	Holds the string corresponding to a cookie.
defaultCharset	Specifies or retrieves the default character set of the document.
designMode	Indicates whether the document can be edited.
documentElement	Holds a reference to the root node.
domain	Specifies or retrieves a security domain for the document.
expando	Indicates whether variables can be created in the **document** object.
fgColor	Specifies or retrieves the foreground color for the document.
fileCreatedDate	Gets the date the document was created.
fileModifiedDate	Gets the date the document was last modified.
fileSize	Gets the file size.
hideFocus	Specifies whether the object visibly indicates the focus.
lastModified	Gets the date the document was last modified.
linkColor	Specifies or retrieves the color of the document links.
location	Has the location of the current URL.
media	Indicates the type of media needed to display a document.
parentWindow	Gets a reference to the container of the window.
protocol	Specifies or retrieves the protocol part of a URL.

(continued)

Table 11.1 Properties of the **document** object in Internet Explorer *(continued)*.

Property	Description
readyState	Gets the current state of the **document** object while it is being downloaded.
referrer	Holds the URL that referred the browser to this page.
selection	Specifies the active selection in the document.
title	Holds the title of the document.
uniqueID	Gets a unique identifier that specifies the **document** object.
URL	Specifies or retrieves the URL of this document.
vlinkColor	Specifies or retrieves the color of links that the browser has already visited.

Table 11.2 Methods of the **document** object in Internet Explorer.

Method	Description
attachEvent	Binds a function to an event occurring in the **document** object.
clear	Clears the document.
clearAttributes	Clears the **document** object of all attributes and values.
close	Closes a stream of output.
createElement	Creates an element object for the given tag.
createEventObject	Creates an event object for handling event-context information in the **fireEvent** method.
createStyleSheet	Gets a style sheet.
createTextNode	Gets a text string.
detachEvent	Detaches the given function from an event.
elementFromPoint	Gets the element for the given coordinates.
execCommand	Executes a command.
focus	Makes a control receive the focus.
getElementById	Gets a reference to the object with the given **id**.
getElementsByName	Gets a collection of objects as specified by name.
getElementsByTagName	Gets a collection of objects as specified by tag name.
hasFocus	Indicates whether the object has the focus.
mergeAttributes	Copies attributes to the indicated element.
open	Opens a document.
queryCommandEnabled	Indicates whether the command can be executed with **execCommand**.
queryCommandIndeterm	Indicates whether the given command is indeterminate.

(continued)

Table 11.2 Methods of the document object in Internet Explorer *(continued)*.

Method	Description
queryCommandState	Indicates the state of the specified command.
queryCommandValue	Gets the value of the given command.
recalc	Recalculates all properties in the document.
releaseCapture	Releases mouse capture.
setActive	Sets the indicated object as the active object.
write	Writes XHTML to a document in the given window.
writeln	Writes XHTML and then a carriage return to a document in the given window.

Table 11.3 Events of the document object in Internet Explorer.

Event	Description
onbeforecut	Happens before the selection is deleted.
onbeforeeditfocus	Happens before the edit focus event.
onbeforefocusenter	Happens before the object gets the focus.
onbeforefocusleave	Happens before the object loses the focus.
onbeforepaste	Happens before the selection is pasted into the document.
onclick	Happens when the user clicks the mouse.
oncontextmenu	Happens when the right mouse button is clicked to open a context menu.
oncontrolselect	Happens when the user selects a control.
oncut	Happens when the selection is cut.
ondblclick	Happens when the user double-clicks.
ondrag	Happens during a mouse drag operation.
ondragend	Happens when a drag operation ends.
ondragenter	Happens when the user drags the document into a drop target.
ondragleave	Happens when the mouse moves out of a drop target.
ondragover	Happens while the document is dragged over a drop target.
ondragstart	Happens when a drag operation starts.
ondrop	Happens when the mouse button is released, dropping a dragged object.
onfocusenter	Happens when the object gets the focus.
onfocusleave	Happens when the object loses the focus.
onhelp	Happens when the F1 key is pressed.
onkeydown	Happens when a key is pressed.

(continued)

Table 11.3 Events of the document object in Internet Explorer (continued).

Event	Description
onkeypress	Happens when an alphanumeric key is pressed.
onkeyup	Happens when a key is released.
onmousedown	Happens when a mouse button is pressed.
onmousemove	Happens when the mouse is moved.
onmouseout	Happens when the mouse is moved out of the **document** object.
onmouseover	Happens when the mouse is moved over the **document** object.
onmouseup	Happens when a mouse button is released.
onpaste	Happens when data is pasted.
onpropertychange	Happens when a property changes.
onreadystatechange	Happens when the state of the **document** object changes.
onresizeend	Happens when a resize operation ends.
onresizestart	Happens when a resize operation starts.
onselectiontypechange	Happens when the type of a selection changes.
onstop	Happens when the Stop button is clicked.

Table 11.4 Collections of the document object in Internet Explorer.

Collection	Description
all	Gets the collection of elements in a **document** object.
anchors	Contains all **a** objects that have a **name** and/or **id** property.
applets	Contains all **applet** objects in the document.
childNodes	Contains all descendent elements of the **document** object.
children	Contains all descendent elements of the **document** object.
embeds	Contains all **embed** objects in the document.
forms	Contains all **form** objects in the document.
frames	Contains all frames in the document.
images	Contains the **img** objects in the document.
links	Contains the **a** objects with an **href** property, as well as all **area** objects.
namespaces	Contains the **namespace** objects.
scripts	Contains the **script** objects in the document.
styleSheets	Contains the **styleSheet** objects for each **link** or **style** object.

Table 11.5 Properties of the document object in Netscape Navigator.

Property	Description
alinkColor	Specifies the **alink** attribute.
anchors	Refers to an array holding the anchors in the document.
applets	Refers to an array holding the applets in the document.
bgColor	Specifies the **bgcolor** attribute.
classes	Creates **style** objects with a given **class** attribute.
cookie	Holds a cookie.
domain	Specifies the domain name of the document.
embeds	Refers to an array holding all plug-ins in the document.
fgColor	Indicates the **text** attribute.
formName	Refers to each form in the document.
forms	Refers to an array containing each form in the document.
height	Refers to the height of the document in pixels.
ids	Creates a **style** object to hold the style of XHTML tags.
images	Refers to an array holding all images.
lastModified	Indicates the last modified date of the document.
layers	Refers to an array holding all layers in the document.
linkColor	Indicates the **link** attribute.
links	Indicates the array holding all links.
plugins	Indicates the array holding all plug-ins.
referrer	Indicates the URL of the referring document.
tags	Creates a **style** object to specify XHTML tags.
title	Indicates the contents of the **title** tag.
URL	Indicates the complete URL of the document.
vlinkColor	Indicates the **vlink** attribute.
width	Refers to the width of the document in pixels.

Table 11.6 Methods of the document object in Netscape Navigator.

Method	Description
close	Closes an output stream.
open	Opens a stream for the **write** or **writeln** methods.
write	Writes XHTML to a document.
writeln	Writes XHTML, followed with a **newline** character, to a document.

Table 11.7 Events of the **document** object in Netscape Navigator.

Event	Description
onClick	Click event.
onDblClick	Double-click event.
onKeyDown	Key went down.
onKeyPress	Key was interpreted.
onKeyUp	Key went up.
onMouseDown	Mouse button went down.
onMouseUp	Mouse button went up.

The window Object

The **window** object has been available in Netscape Navigator since version 2 and in Internet Explorer since version 3. This object corresponds to the current browser window, which may contain a page or a number of pages in frames. The **document** object is a part of the **window** object, so the proper name of the **document** object is **window.document** (although you can omit the "window" part here and JavaScript will still know that you want to access the **window.document** object). The **window** object is the top object in Internet Explorer's hierarchy and nearly the top object in Netscape Navigator.

So what's available in the **window** object? The **document** object is the most-often-used browser object in JavaScript programming, but there's plenty of power in the **window** object as well. You'll find Internet Explorer's **window** object properties in Table 11.8, its methods in Table 11.9, its events in Table 11.10, and its collections in Table 11.11.

You'll find Netscape Navigator's **window** object properties in Table 11.12, its methods in Table 11.13, and its events in Table 11.14.

As you can see, the **window** object is another big one in JavaScript, and we'll put it to work in this chapter.

Table 11.8 Properties of the **window** object in Internet Explorer.

Property	Description
clipboardData	Returns clipboard formats.
closed	Indicates whether the window is closed.
defaultStatus	Holds the message in the status bar.
dialogArguments	Gets arguments passed to a modal dialog window.

(continued)

Table 11.8 Properties of the window object in Internet Explorer *(continued)*.

Property	Description
dialogHeight	Specifies or retrieves the height of the dialog window.
dialogLeft	Specifies or retrieves the left coordinate of the dialog window.
dialogTop	Specifies or retrieves the top coordinate of the dialog window.
dialogWidth	Specifies or retrieves the width of the dialog window.
document	Indicates the document in the browser.
event	Indicates the state of an event.
frameElement	Gets the **frame** or **iframe** object hosting the window.
hideFocus	Indicates whether the object shows the focus.
history	Holds the URLs visited.
length	Gets the number of objects in a collection.
location	Holds the location and additional information about the current URL.
name	Specifies or retrieves the name of the window or frame.
navigator	Indicates the object referring to the Web browser.
offscreenBuffering	Indicates whether objects are drawn off screen before being drawn on the screen.
opener	Specifies or retrieves the window that created the current window.
parent	Gets the parent of the current window.
returnValue	Specifies or retrieves the return value of the dialog window.
screen	Holds data about the client's screen capabilities.
screenLeft	Gets the x-coordinate of the upper-left corner of the client area of the browser.
screenTop	Gets the y-coordinate of the top corner of the client area of the browser.
self	Gets the current window or the current frame.
status	Specifies or retrieves the text in the status bar.
top	Gets the topmost window.

Table 11.9 Methods of the window object in Internet Explorer.

Method	Description
alert	Shows an Alert dialog box displaying a message.
attachEvent	Attaches a function to an event that occurs in the **window** object.
blur	Makes an object lose the focus.
clearInterval	Clears the interval started with the **setInterval** method.
clearTimeout	Clears a time-out set with the earlier **setTimeout** method.
close	Closes the browser window.

(continued)

Table 11.9 Methods of the **window** object in Internet Explorer *(continued)*.

Method	Description
confirm	Shows a Confirmation dialog box.
createPopup	Creates a popup.
detachEvent	Detaches the given function from an event.
execScript	Executes a script.
focus	Makes a control receive the focus.
moveBy	Moves the window by the specified x and y values.
moveTo	Moves the upper-left corner of the window.
navigate	Navigates to the indicated URL.
open	Opens a window.
print	Prints the document.
prompt	Displays a Prompt dialog box.
resizeBy	Resizes the window.
resizeTo	Resizes the window to the indicated width and length.
scroll	Scrolls the window.
scrollBy	Scrolls the window relative to the current position.
scrollTo	Scrolls the window to an x- and y-offset.
setActive	Makes the current object the active object.
setInterval	Sets a timer interval.
setTimeout	Evaluates an expression after a timer interval has elapsed.
showHelp	Shows a Help file.
showModalDialog	Shows a dialog box.
showModelessDialog	Shows a modeless dialog box.

Table 11.10 Events of the **window** object in Internet Explorer.

Event	Description
onafterprint	Happens after the document is printed.
onbeforefocusenter	Happens before the object gets the focus.
onbeforefocusleave	Happens before the object loses the focus.
onbeforeprint	Happens before the document is printed.
onbeforeunload	Happens before a page is unloaded.
onblur	Happens when the **window** object loses the focus.
oncontrolselect	Happens when a control is selected.
onerror	Happens when there's an error while a **window** object is loading.

(continued)

Table 11.10 Events of the **window** object in Internet Explorer *(continued)*.

Event	Description
onfocus	Happens when the **window** object gets the focus.
onfocusenter	Happens when the object gets the focus.
onfocusleave	Happens when the object loses the focus.
onhelp	Happens when the F1 key is pressed.
onload	Happens after the browser loads a **window** object.
onresize	Happens when the **window** object is resized.
onresizeend	Happens when a resize operation ends.
onresizestart	Happens when a resize operation starts.
onunload	Happens before the **window** object is unloaded.

Table 11.11 Collections of the **window** object in Internet Explorer.

Collection	Description
frames	Holds all **window** objects in the frames of the document.

Table 11.12 Properties of the **window** object in Netscape Navigator.

Property	Description
closed	Indicates whether a window was closed.
crypto	Provides access to Navigator's encryption capabilities.
defaultStatus	Holds the default message in the status bar.
document	Holds data about the current document; makes methods for displaying XHTML accessible.
frames	Refers to an array holding the frames in the window.
history	Holds data about the URLs the client has visited.
innerHeight	Gives the height of the window's content area in pixels.
innerWidth	Gives the width of the window's content area in pixels.
length	Refers to the number of frames in the window.
location	Holds data specifying the current URL.
locationbar	Refers to the object corresponding to the location bar.
menubar	Refers to the object corresponding to the menu bar.
name	Refers to the name of this window.
offscreenBuffering	Specifies whether rendering updates are performed off screen.
opener	Specifies the name of the calling document.

(continued)

Table 11.12 Properties of the window object in Netscape Navigator *(continued)*.

Property	Description
outerHeight	Gives the height of the window in pixels.
outerWidth	Gives the width of the window in pixels.
pageXOffset	Gives the x-position of a window's page in pixels.
pageYOffset	Gives the y-position of a window's page in pixels.
parent	Refers to the window (or frame) that contains the current frame.
personalbar	Corresponds to the browser window's personal bar.
screenX	Gives the x-coordinate of the window's left edge.
screenY	Gives the y-coordinate of the window's top edge.
scrollbars	Corresponds to the window's scrollbars.
self	Corresponds to the current window.
status	Holds a message in the status bar.
statusbar	Corresponds to the window's status bar.
toolbar	Corresponds to the window's toolbar.
top	Refers to the topmost browser window.
window	Corresponds to the current window.

Table 11.13 Methods of the window object in Netscape Navigator.

Method	Description
alert	Shows an Alert dialog box.
atob	Decodes string data encoded with Base64 encoding.
back	Moves back one history step.
blur	Releases the focus.
btoa	Codes a string using Base64 encoding.
captureEvents	Captures all events of the specified type.
clearInterval	Clears a time-out set earlier with the **setInterval** method.
clearTimeout	Clears a time-out set earlier with the **setTimeout** method.
close	Closes a window.
confirm	Shows a Confirmation dialog box.
crypto.random	Returns a pseudo-random text string.
crypto.signText	Returns an encoded text string corresponding to a signed object.
disableExternalCapture	Disables external event capturing.
enableExternalCapture	Enables external event capturing.
find	Locates the specified text string in a window.

(continued)

Table 11.13 Methods of the **window** object in Netscape Navigator *(continued)*.

Method	Description
focus	Assigns the focus to the specified object.
forward	Moves forward in the history list.
handleEvent	Calls an event handler.
home	Navigates to the user's home page.
moveBy	Moves the window.
moveTo	Moves the top-left corner of the window.
open	Opens a new browser window.
print	Prints the window or frame.
prompt	Shows a Prompt dialog box.
releaseEvents	Releases an event capture.
resizeBy	Resizes a window.
resizeTo	Resizes a window to the specified width and height.
routeEvent	Sends an event to the event hierarchy.
scroll	Scrolls a window.
scrollBy	Scrolls a window by the amount indicated.
scrollTo	Scrolls a window to the coordinates indicated.
setHotKeys	Enables or disables hot keys if the window does not support menus.
setInterval	Evaluates code every specified interval.
setResizable	Specifies whether a window can be resized.
setTimeout	Sets the number of milliseconds between calls to specified code.
setZOptions	Returns a window's z-order behavior.
stop	Ends a download.

Table 11.14 Events of the **window** object in Netscape Navigator.

Event	Description
onBlur	Lost focus.
onDragDrop	Occurrence of a drag-and-drop operation.
onError	Occurrence of an error.
onFocus	Gained focus.
onLoad	Loaded page.
onMove	Moved window.
onResize	Resized window.
onUnload	Unloaded page.

The location Object

The **location** object has been available in Netscape Navigator since version 2 and in Internet Explorer since version 3. This object is part of the **window** object (its full name is **window.location**), and it represents the complete URL of the page in the current window. By setting this object to a new URL, you can navigate to that URL. Here's an example; when you call this function, the Web browser will navigate to the World Wide Web Consortium (W3C) site:

```
function goW3C()
{
    window.location = "http://www.W3C.org"
}
```

So what's available in the **location** object? You'll find Internet Explorer's **location** object properties in Table 11.15 and its methods in Table 11.16 (it has no events or collections). As you can see in these tables, you can easily determine the current browser's location by using this object.

You'll find Netscape Navigator's **location** object properties in Table 11.17 and its methods in Table 11.18.

The last object I'll discuss in this chapter is the **history** object.

Table 11.15   Properties of the **location** object in Internet Explorer.

Property	Description
hash	Holds the part of the **href** property following the # mark.
host	Specifies or retrieves the hostname and port of the current URL.
hostname	Specifies or retrieves the hostname.
href	Specifies or retrieves the URL, returned as a string.
pathname	Specifies or retrieves the file name corresponding to the **location** object.
port	Specifies or retrieves the URL's port number
protocol	Specifies or retrieves the URL's protocol.
search	Specifies or retrieves the part of the URL following the question mark.

Table 11.16   Methods of the **location** object in Internet Explorer.

Method	Description
assign	Navigates to a new document.
reload	Reloads a page.
replace	Loads a new document, replacing the current one.

Table 11.17   Properties of the location object in Netscape Navigator.

Property	Description
hash	Refers to an anchor name as extracted from the URL.
host	Refers to the network host's name and domain name (or IP address).
hostname	Refers to the hostname and port of the current URL.
href	Refers to the URL.
pathname	Refers to the path part of the URL.
port	Refers to the server's port.
protocol	Refers to the protocol of the URL.
search	Refers to a query.

Table 11.18   Methods of the location object in Netscape Navigator.

Method	Description
reload	Reloads the current document in the window.
replace	Replaces the current document with a new one.

The history Object

The **history** object has been available in Netscape Navigator since version 2 and in Internet Explorer since version 3. Anyone familiar with the Back button in browsers knows about browser history. The history corresponds to an ordered list of the URLs the user has visited before the current page (and possibly after the current page if the user has already clicked the Back button to move back to the current page).

You can use the **forward**, **back**, and **go** methods of the **window.history** object to navigate around the browser's history list. The **forward** method navigates the browser forward one page in the history list, the **back** method navigates back one page, and the **go** method lets you specify how many pages to move.

What's in the **history** object? You'll find Internet Explorer's **history** object properties in Table 11.19 and its methods in Table 11.20 (it has no events or collections).

You'll find Netscape Navigator's **history** object properties in Table 11.21 and its methods in Table 11.22.

In Depth

Table 11.19 Properties of the history object in Internet Explorer.

Property	Description
length	Indicates how many objects exist in a collection.

Table 11.20 Methods of the history object in Internet Explorer.

Method	Description
back	Moves back in the **history** list.
forward	Moves forward in the **history** list.
go	Goes to a URL in the **history** list.

Table 11.21 Properties of the history object in Netscape Navigator.

Property	Description
current	Refers to the **history** object's current URL.
length	Refers to the number of items in the history list.
next	Refers to the next URL in the history list.
previous	Refers to the previous URL in the history list.

Table 11.22 Methods of the history object in Netscape Navigator.

Method	Description
back	Goes back one entry in the history list.
forward	Goes forward in the history list.
go	Goes to a URL in the history list.

As you've seen from all the tables in this chapter, there's a great deal of material here. In the "Immediate Solutions" section of this chapter, I'm going to look at the best of what these objects have to offer. In fact, I'm going to start with an entirely different object—the **navigator** object—because that object can tell you which browser, and which browser version, you're working with. (The **navigator** object is part of the **window** object in Internet Explorer but is a top-level object in Netscape Navigator.) A glance at the tables in this chapter can tell you how important it is because the implementation of JavaScript and the scripting object model is very different in the two browsers.

Immediate Solutions

Determining Browser Type in Code

"Darn," says the novice programmer, "I want to use Netscape layers, but they're not available in Internet Explorer." "That's why they're called Netscape layers," you say. "So how can I tell if someone is using Netscape Navigator or not?" the NP asks. "You can check the **navigator.appName** property," you say.

So much XHTML work differs by browser that it's sometimes very important to know which browser you're working with. To determine the browser application, check the **navigator.appName** property in your script. If it's "Microsoft Internet Explorer," you're working with Internet Explorer; if it's "Netscape," your script is executing in Netscape Navigator. You can also check the version of the browser with the **navigator.appVersion** property.

*TIP: In Internet Explorer, the **navigator** object is part of the **window** object, so its real name is **window.navigator**, but in Netscape Navigator, it's a top-level object, so its name is just **navigator**. However, JavaScript is usually very tolerant if you omit the beginning of the full name of a browser object, as long as it can uniquely identify the object you want. This means that you can refer to the **navigator** object simply by using this name in JavaScript in both browsers.*

Here's an example that will tell you which of the two browsers you're running, and what version:

```
<?xml version="1.0"?>
<!DOCTYPE html PUBLIC "-//W3C//DTD XHTML 1.0 Transitional//EN"
"http://www.w3.org/tr/xhtml1/DTD/xhtml1-transitional.dtd">
<html xmlns="http://www.w3.org/1999/xhtml" xml:lang="en" lang="en">
    <head>
        <title>
            Checking Your Browser Type
        </title>

    </head>

    <body>
        <script type = "text/javascript"
            language = "javascript" src = "script.js">
        </script>
```

```
            <center>
                <h1>
                    Checking Your Browser Type
                </h1>
            </center>
        </body>
</html>
```

Here's the code that does the work, script.js:

```
if (navigator.appName == "Microsoft Internet Explorer") {
    document.write("<center><b>")
    document.write("You have Microsoft Internet Explorer " +
        navigator.appVersion)
    document.write("</b></center>")
}

if(navigator.appName == "Netscape") {
    document.write("<center><b>")
    document.write("You have Netscape Navigator " +
        navigator.appVersion)
    document.write("</b></center>")
}
```

The results of this code appear in Figure 11.2, where you can see the browser application and version.

NOTE: Notice how useful this is—not only can you use different JavaScript code for each browser now, but, using **document.writeln**, you can also write entirely different Web pages, with each page suited to the browser it appears in.

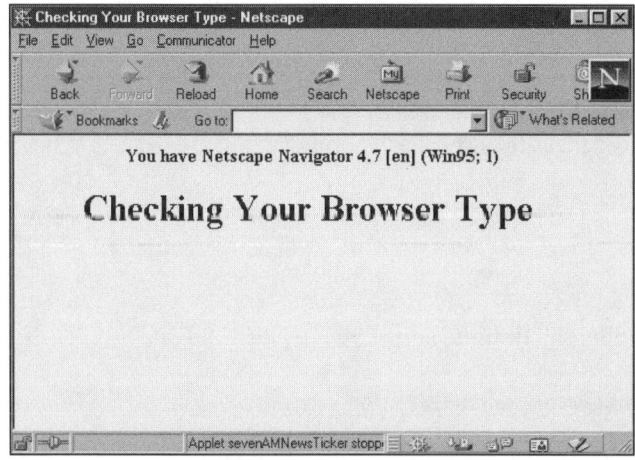

Figure 11.2   Checking the browser application.

Creating a Self-Modifying Web Page

"Jeez," says the novice programmer, "People are avoiding my Web page just because I have an image in it that's 1,024 × 1,024 pixels in 16.7 million colors. Of course, it can take about ten minutes to download." "Hm," you say, "why not *ask* the users if they want to download huge images before doing so?" "How do you mean?" the NP asks.

Using the document object's **write** and **writeln** (write line) methods, you can modify Web pages. In this next example, I'm using a Confirmation dialog box from JavaScript (see "Creating Confirmation Dialog Boxes" later in this chapter) to ask users if they want to download the large graphics image. This dialog box displays the message "View graphics intensive page?", and if a user clicks the OK button, the code writes an **<img>** element to download the large graphics file. However, if the user clicks the Cancel button, the code downloads a smaller version of the file. Here's what the code looks like:

```
<?xml version="1.0"?>
<!DOCTYPE html PUBLIC "-//W3C//DTD XHTML 1.0 Transitional//EN"
"http://www.w3.org/tr/xhtml1/DTD/xhtml1-transitional.dtd">
<html xmlns="http://www.w3.org/1999/xhtml" xml:lang="en" lang="en">
    <head>
        <title>
            Creating A Self-Modifying Web Page
        </title>
    </head>

    <body>
        <center>
            <h1>
                Creating A Self-Modifying Web Page
            </h1>

            <script type = "text/javascript"
                    language="javascript" src="script.js">
            </script>
        </center>
    </body>
</html>
```

Here's the code that handles the details, script.js:

```
if(confirm("View graphics intensive page?")) {
    document.write("<br /><img width='1024' height='1024' " +
        "src='gif/image1.gif' alt='image'/>")
```

```
}
else {
    document.write("<br /><img width='120' height='120' " +
        "src='gif/image1small.gif' alt='image'/>");
}
```

You can see the results in Figure 11.3, which shows the Confirmation dialog box.

Here's an important note—you often use **document.write** or **document.writeln** only when a page is first loaded (to write the page as it's loading). But you can also rewrite the page after it's been loaded. Take a look at this next example; when the user clicks the page, the whole page is replaced by the text "This is a new page!" (this example will work only in Internet Explorer):

```
<?xml version="1.0"?>
<!DOCTYPE html PUBLIC "-//W3C//DTD XHTML 1.0 Transitional//EN"
"http://www.w3.org/tr/xhtml1/DTD/xhtml1-transitional.dtd">
<html xmlns="http://www.w3.org/1999/xhtml" xml:lang="en" lang="en">
    <head>
        <title>
            Using document.writeln
        </title>

        <script type = "text/javascript">
            function rewrite()
            {
                document.writeln("This is a new page!")
            }
        </script>
    </head>
```

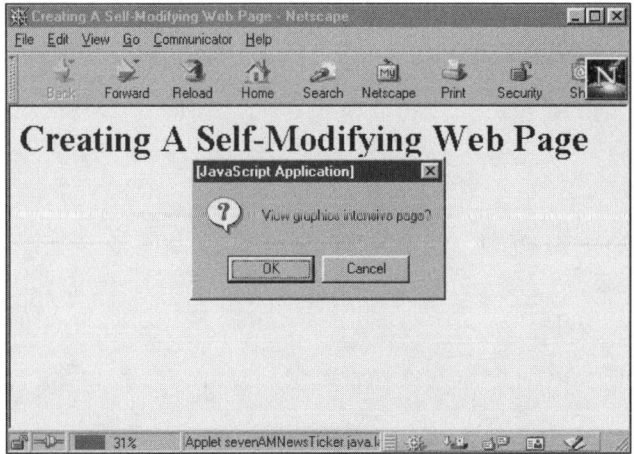

Figure 11.3   Creating a self-modifying Web page.

```
    <body onmousedown="rewrite()">
        <center>
            <h1>
                Click this page to rewrite it!
            </h1>
        </center>
    </body>
</html>
```

In Netscape Navigator, you need to open the document for writing and then close it as well. Note that you also need the line **document.onmousedown = rewrite** to connect the **rewrite** function to the **mousedown** event in the document in Netscape Navigator. Here's how it looks:

```
<?xml version="1.0"?>
<!DOCTYPE html PUBLIC "-//W3C//DTD XHTML 1.0 Transitional//EN"
"http://www.w3.org/tr/xhtml1/DTD/xhtml1-transitional.dtd">
<html xmlns="http://www.w3.org/1999/xhtml" xml:lang="en" lang="en">
    <head>
        <title>
            Using document.writeln
        </title>
    </head>

    <body onmousedown="rewrite()">
        <script type = "text/javascript">
            document.onmousedown = rewrite

            function rewrite()
            {
                document.open()
                document.writeln("This is a new page!")
                document.close()
            }
        </script>

        <center>
            <h1>
                Click this page to rewrite it!
            </h1>
        </center>
    </body>
</html>
```

TIP: We'll see other ways of rewriting Web pages when we discuss dynamic XHTML in Chapter 13.

Here's another example. This page presents a menu displaying the breakfast, lunch, or dinner menus automatically, based on the time of day (which is found using the JavaScript **Date** object):

```xml
<?xml version="1.0"?>
<!DOCTYPE html PUBLIC "-//W3C//DTD XHTML 1.0 Transitional//EN"
    "http://www.w3.org/tr/xhtml1/DTD/xhtml1-transitional.dtd">
<html xmlns="http://www.w3.org/1999/xhtml" xml:lang="en" lang="en">
    <head>
        <title>
            The JavaScript Menu Example
        </title>
    </head>

    <body>
        <script type = "text/javascript"
            language="javascript" src="script.js">
        </script>
    </body>
</html>
```

Here's the associated script, script.js:

```javascript
var dateNow = new Date()
var hourNow = dateNow.getHours()
document.write( "<center>")
document.write( "<h1>")
document.write( "Welcome To Our Restaurant")
document.write( "</h1>")
document.write( "</center>")

if (hourNow < 5 || hourNow > 23){
    document.write( "<center>")
    document.write( "<h1>")
    document.write( "Sorry, We Are Closed." )
    document.write( "</h1>")
    document.write( "</center>")
}

if (hourNow > 6 && hourNow < 12 ) {
    document.write( "<center>")
    document.write( "<table border='1'>")
    document.write(
        "<tr><th colspan = '2'>Breakfast</th></tr>")
    document.write(
        "<tr><td>Pancakes</td><td>$2.00</td></tr>")
```

Chapter 11 Putting JavaScript to Work

```
            document.write(
                "<tr><td>Eggs</td><td>$2.50</td></tr>")
            document.write(
                "<tr><td>Waffles</td><td>$1.50</td></tr>")
            document.write(
                "<tr><td>Oatmeal</td><td>$1.00</td></tr>")
            document.write( "</table>")
            document.write( "</center>")
        }

        if ( hourNow >= 12 && hourNow < 17 ) {
            document.write( "<center>")
            document.write( "<table border='1'>")
            document.write(
                "<tr><th colspan = '2'>Lunch</th></tr>")
            document.write(
                "<tr><td>Ham Sandwich</td><td>$3.50</td></tr>")
            document.write(
                "<tr><td>Chicken Sandwich</td><td>$3.50</td></tr>")
            document.write(
                "<tr><td>Cheese Sandwich</td><td>$3.00</td></tr>")
            document.write(
                "<tr><td>Lobster Nuggets</td><td>$5.00</td></tr>")
            document.write(
                "<tr><td>Peacock</td><td>$4.50</td></tr>")
            document.write(
                "<tr><td>Chili</td><td>$2.00</td></tr>")
            document.write(
                "<tr><td>Chicken Soup</td><td>$1.50</td></tr>")
            document.write( "</table>")
            document.write( "</center>")
        }

        if ( hourNow >= 17 && hourNow < 22 ) {
            document.write( "<center>")
            document.write( "<table border = '1'>")
            document.write(
                "<tr><th colspan = '2'>Dinner</th></tr>")
            document.write(
                "<tr><td>Lobster</td><td>$7.50</td></tr>")
            document.write(
                "<tr><td>Filet Mignon</td><td>$8.00</td></tr>")
            document.write(
                "<tr><td>Flank Steak</td><td>$7.00</td></tr>")
            document.write(
                "<tr><td>Tube Steak</td><td>$3.50</td></tr>")
```

```
document.write(
    "<tr><td>Salad</td><td>$2.50</td></tr>")
document.write(
    "<tr><td>Potato</td><td>$1.50</td></tr>")
document.write(
    "<tr><td>Eggplant</td><td>$1.50</td></tr>")
document.write( "</table>")
document.write( "</center>")
}
```

You can see the results of this code in Figure 11.4.

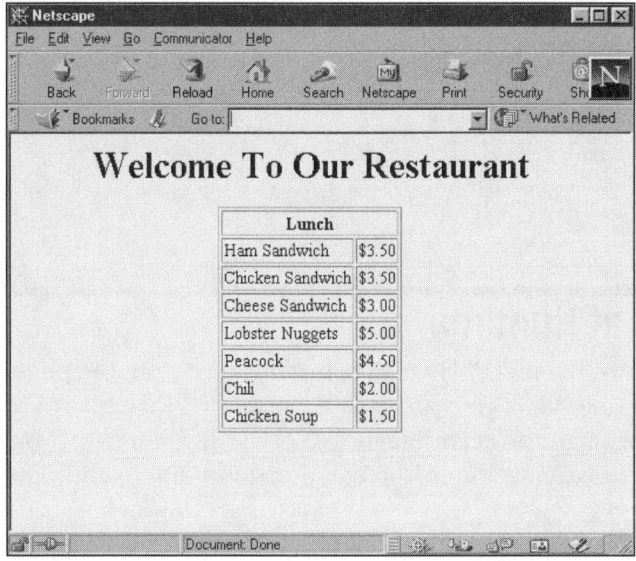

Figure 11.4　Example of a self-modifying Web page based on the time of day.

Setting a Page's Background Color

Here are some useful **document** object properties:

- **document.bgcolor**—Background color of the current page.
- **document.fgcolor**—Foreground color of the current page.
- **document.lastmodified**—Date the page was last modified.
- **document.title**—Title of the current page.

You can set these properties at runtime. Here's an example page that turns red when you click it in Internet Explorer:

```
<?xml version="1.0"?>
<!DOCTYPE html PUBLIC "-//W3C//DTD XHTML 1.0 Transitional//EN"
"http://www.w3.org/tr/xhtml1/DTD/xhtml1-transitional.dtd">
<html xmlns="http://www.w3.org/1999/xhtml" xml:lang="en" lang="en">
    <head>
        <title>
            Setting Background Color With JavaScript
        </title>
    </head>

    <body onmousedown="document.bgColor='red'">
        <center>
            <h1>
                Click this page to turn it red!
            </h1>
        </center>
    </body>
</html>
```

Reloading Images at Runtime

"Hm," says the novice programmer. "The big boss wants me to put the photos of the company picnic online, but there are two thousand of them. Am I going to have to create a new page for each image?" "Not at all," you say; "you can use JavaScript to load new images into the same page interactively." The NP says, "Huh?"

You can use the **document** object to reach the elements in a Web page if you name those elements. In the next example, I'm going to reload an image in an **<img>** element when the user clicks a button. I'll give the **<img>** element the name **img1**, and it will be in the same XHTML form as the button (we'll cover forms in Chapter 12). The form's name is **"form1"**, and it's an element in the document, so I can reach it as **document.form1**. I can then refer to the **<img>** element as **document.form1.img1** and refer to the actual **src** attribute of that image element as **document.form1.img1.src**. This means I can reload the image by resetting the **src** attribute of the **<img>** element, like this:

```
<?xml version="1.0"?>
<!DOCTYPE html PUBLIC "-//W3C//DTD XHTML 1.0 Transitional//EN"
"http://www.w3.org/tr/xhtml1/DTD/xhtml1-transitional.dtd">
<html xmlns="http://www.w3.org/1999/xhtml" xml:lang="en" lang="en">
    <head>
```

```
        <title>
            Reloading Images At Run Time
        </title>

        <script type = "text/javascript" language = "javascript">
            function reloadImage()
            {
                document.form1.img1.src = "gif/image2.gif"
            }
        </script>
    </head>

    <body>
        <center>
            <form name = "form1" action = "action">
                <img name = "img1" src = "gif/image1.gif"
                    width = "236" height = "118" alt = "image"/>
                <br />
                <br />
                <input type = "button" value = "Load new image"
                    onclick = "reloadImage()" />
            </form>
        </center>
    </body>
</html>
```

That's it; when the user clicks the button in this example, the Web browser loads a new image, replacing the old one.

Opening a New Browser Window

The novice programmer has a problem and says, "I want to let people who read my online novel open a glossary defining various terms—how do I open a new window when the user clicks a button?" "No problem," you say; "just use the **window** object's **open** method."

You can use the **window** object's **open** method to open new browser windows and to configure those windows. Here's how to use **window.open** in Netscape Navigator (optional arguments appear in brackets, **[** and **]**):

newWindow = window.open(*URL, Name* [, *Features*])

The **URL** argument is the URL of the new page to open, the **Name** argument is the name you want to give the new window, and the **Features** argument lets you configure the window, including hiding toolbars and status bars. The possible settings for the **Features** argument appear in Table 11.23. You place the features you want in a comma-separated list, enclose that list in quotes (like this: "height=200,width=400,status=no,toolbar=no,menubar=no,location=no"), and pass that string as the **Features** argument.

NOTE: Do not include spaces in the list in the **Features** string. Internet Explorer doesn't have a problem if you do, but Netscape Navigator won't understand what you want if you include spaces.

In Internet Explorer, you use **window.open** like this:

```
newWindow = window.open([URL] [, Name] [, Features] [, Replace])
```

As before, the **URL** argument is the URL of the new page to open, the **Name** argument is the name you want to give the new window, and the **Features** argument lets you configure the window. The possible settings for the **Features** argument appear in Table 11.24. The **Replace** argument specifies whether the URL that is loaded into the new page should create a new entry in the window's browsing history or replace the current entry in the browsing history. If this argument is set to **true**, no new history entry is created for the new page.

Table 11.23 Window features in Netscape Navigator.

Feature	Description
alwaysLowered	Set to **yes** to create a new window below other windows.
alwaysRaised	Set to **yes** to create a new window on top of other windows.
dependent	Set to **yes** to create a new window, a child of the current window.
directories	Set to **yes** to create the standard browser directory buttons.
height	Refers to the height of the window, as measured in pixels.
hotkeys	Set to **no** or **0** to disable most hotkeys in new windows that have no menu bar.
innerHeight	Refers to the height of the window's content area, as measured in pixels.
innerWidth	Refers to the width of the window's content area, as measured in pixels. When you want to create a window smaller than 100×100 pixels, use this feature.
location	Set to **yes** to create a **location** entry field.
menubar	Set to **yes** to create a menu bar at the top of the window.
outerHeight	Refers to the height, in pixels, of the outside edge of the window.
personalbar	Set to **yes** to create the Personal Toolbar.

(continued)

Table 11.23 Window features in Netscape Navigator *(continued)*.

Feature	Description
resizable	Set to **yes** to allow a user to resize the window.
screenX	Refers to the distance a new window should be set from the left side of the screen.
screenY	Refers to the distance a new window should be set from the top of the screen.
scrollbars	Set to **yes** to create horizontal and vertical scrollbars that appear when needed.
status	Set to **yes** to create a status bar, which is displayed at the bottom of the window.
titlebar	Set to **yes** to create a title bar.
toolbar	Set to **yes** to create the standard browser toolbar.
width	Refers to the width of the window, as measured in pixels.
z-lock	Set to **yes** to create a window that does not move above other windows when becoming active.

Table 11.24 Window features in Internet Explorer.

Feature	Description
channelmode	Specifies whether the window should be displayed in theater mode. By default, set to **no**. Can be **yes**, **no**, **1** (=yes), or **0** (=no).
directories	Specifies whether to display directory buttons. By default, set to **yes**. Can be **yes**, **no**, **1**, or **0**.
fullscreen	Specifies whether to display the browser in a full-screen or normal window. By default, set to **no** (which displays the browser as a normal window). Can be **yes**, **no**, **1**, or **0**.
height	Specifies the height of the window, as measured in pixels. The minimum possible value is 100 pixels.
left	Specifies the left location of the window in pixels.
location	Specifies whether to show the location box in the browser. By default, set to **yes**. Can be **yes**, **no**, **1**, or **0**.
menubar	Specifies whether the menu bar should be visible. By default, set to **yes**. Can be **yes**, **no**, **1**, or **0**.
resizable	Specifies whether to let the new window be resizable. By default, set to **yes**. Can be **yes**, **no**, **1**, or **0**.
scrollbars	Specifies whether the new window should display horizontal and vertical scrollbars. By default, set to **yes**. Can be **yes**, **no**, **1**, or **0**.

(continued)

Table 11.24 Window features in Internet Explorer *(continued).*

Feature	Description
status	Specifies whether the new window should display a status bar. By default, set to **yes**. Can be **yes**, **no**, **1**, or **0**.
titlebar	Specifies whether the new window should display a title bar. By default, set to **yes**. Can be **yes**, **no**, **1**, or **0**.
toolbar	Specifies whether the new window should display a browser toolbar. By default, set to **yes**. Can be **yes**, **no**, **1**, or **0**.
top	Specifies the top location of the window in pixels.
width	Specifies the width of the new window, as measured in pixels. The minimum possible value is 100.

TIP: *Although you can open a browser in full-screen mode, be careful. Because this mode hides the browser's title bar and menus, you should always provide a button to help the user close the window. Note that Alt+F4 also closes the new window.*

In the following example, I'm opening a glossary page, glossary.htm, when the user clicks a button:

```
<?xml version="1.0"?>
<!DOCTYPE html PUBLIC "-//W3C//DTD XHTML 1.0 Transitional//EN"
"http://www.w3.org/tr/xhtml1/DTD/xhtml1-transitional.dtd">
<html xmlns="http://www.w3.org/1999/xhtml" xml:lang="en" lang="en">
    <head>
        <title>
            Opening A New Window With JavaScript
        </title>

        <script type = "text/javascript" language = "javascript">
            function showGlossary()
            {
                window.open("glossary.htm")
            }
        </script>
    </head>

    <body>
        <form>
            <center>
                <br />
```

```
            <h1>
                Opening A New Window With JavaScript
            </h1>
            <br />
            <br />
            <input type = "button" value = "See Glossary"
            onclick = "showGlossary()" />
        </center>
    </form>
</body>
</html>
```

Here's the page I use for the glossary, glossary.htm:

```
<?xml version="1.0"?>
<!DOCTYPE html PUBLIC "-//W3C//DTD XHTML 1.0 Transitional//EN"
"http://www.w3.org/tr/xhtml1/DTD/xhtml1-transitional.dtd">
<html xmlns="http://www.w3.org/1999/xhtml" xml:lang="en" lang="en">
    <head>
        <title>
            Glossary
        </title>
    </head>

    <body>
        <center>
            <br />
            <h1>
                Glossary
            </h1>
        </center>
        <br />
        <ul>
            <li>HTML: HyperText Markup Language</li>
            <li>JavaScript: a fun scripting language</li>
            <li>W3C: The World Wide Web Consortium</li>
        </ul>
    </body>
</html>
```

The results of this code appear in Figure 11.5. For a more involved example showing how to use **window.open** to configure and write in a new window, see the next section.

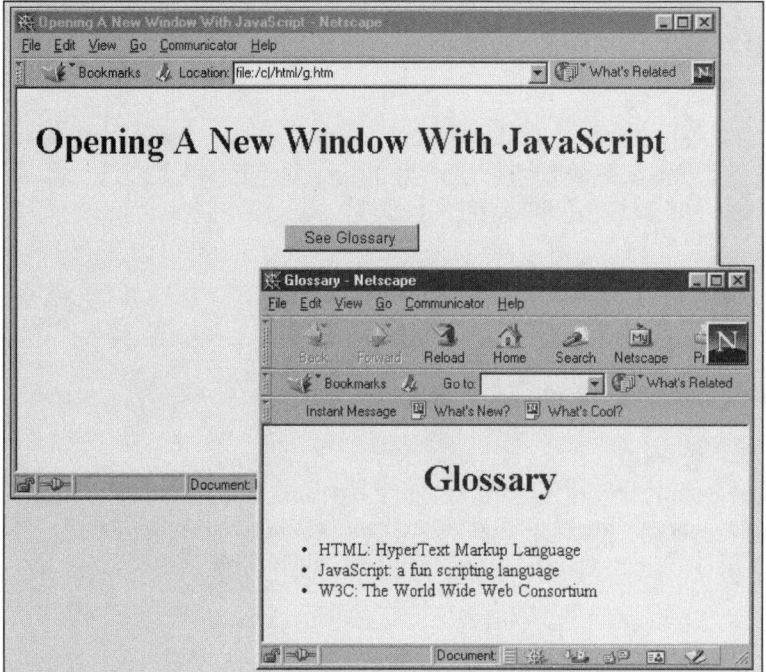

Figure 11.5   Opening a new window.

Configuring and Writing to a New Window

The big boss appears and says, "When someone navigates to our site, can we open a new browser window, without toolbars or status bars, to display advertising?" "You can," you say, "but that's kind of cheesy." "But will it bring in more sales?" the BB wants to know. You say, "It'll probably bring in more complaints than sales."

Using the **window.open** method (see the previous section), you can configure new windows as you open them. In this example, I'll create a window of a certain size without any toolbars or status bars. To do this, I just use the **window.open** method, specifying the way I want the new window to work, and then I use the **document.write** method to write to the new window, like this:

```
<?xml version="1.0"?>
<!DOCTYPE html PUBLIC "-//W3C//DTD XHTML 1.0 Transitional//EN"
    "http://www.w3.org/tr/xhtml1/DTD/xhtml1-transitional.dtd">
<html xmlns="http://www.w3.org/1999/xhtml" xml:lang="en" lang="en">
```

```
        <head>
            <title>
                Creating A New Window
            </title>

            <script type = "text/javascript"
                language = "javascript" src = "script.js">
            </script>
        </head>

        <body>
            <center>
                <br />
                <h1>
                    Creating A New Window
                </h1>
                <br />
                <br />
                <form action = "action">
                    <input type = "button" value = "Create New Window"
                        onclick = "createNewWindow()" />
                </form>
            </center>
        </body>
</html>
```

Here's the script, script.js:

```
function createNewWindow()
{
    var newWindow = window.open
    (
        "window.htm", null,
        "height=200,width=400,status=no," +
        "toolbar=no,menubar=no,location=no"
    )

    newWindow.document.write
    (
        "<br /><br /><center><h1>This window " +
        "has just been created!</h1></center>"
    )
}
```

Here's the page I use for the opened window, window.htm:

```
<?xml version="1.0"?>
<!DOCTYPE html PUBLIC "-//W3C//DTD XHTML 1.0 Transitional//EN"
"http://www.w3.org/tr/xhtml1/DTD/xhtml1-transitional.dtd">
<html xmlns="http://www.w3.org/1999/xhtml" xml:lang="en" lang="en">
    <head>
        <title>
            This Is A New Window
        </title>
    </head>

    <body>
    </body>
</html>
```

And that's all it takes—the results of this code appear in Figure 11.6. Now you know how to remove toolbars and status bars from a browser window.

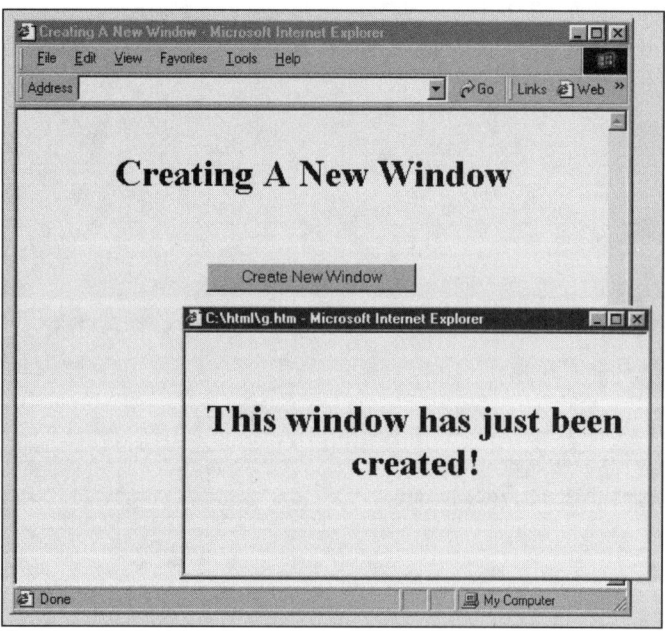

Figure 11.6   The result of opening and configuring a new window.

Creating Alert Dialog Boxes

The novice programmer says, "I need some way of strongly warning users. I need some way of grabbing their attention. I need some way of—" "Alert dialog boxes," you say; "what you need is an Alert dialog box."

When you want to bring a strong message to the attention of users and make sure they notice it before continuing, you can use the **window** object's Alert dialog box. This dialog box displays a message and an OK button; users must click the OK button before they can continue browsing.

Here's an example. In this case, I'm using the **location** object's **href** property to check the URL of a Web page. If the page is not where it should be, the code will display an Alert box with the message "Hey! You copied my page without permission!"—like this:

```
<?xml version="1.0"?>
<!DOCTYPE html PUBLIC "-//W3C//DTD XHTML 1.0 Transitional//EN"
    "http://www.w3.org/tr/xhtml1/DTD/xhtml1-transitional.dtd">
<html xmlns="http://www.w3.org/1999/xhtml" xml:lang="en" lang="en">
    <head>
        <title>
            Using An Alert Dialog Box
        </title>
    </head>

    <body>
        <script type = "text/javascript" language = "javascript">

            if (location.href !=
                "http://www.starpowder.com/steve/index.html") {
                window.alert("Hey! You copied my page without permission!")
            }
            else {
                document.writeln("Welcome to my Web page!")
            }
        </script>
    </body>
</html>
```

You can see the results of this XHTML in Figure 11.7; this page works in both Internet Explorer and Netscape Navigator.

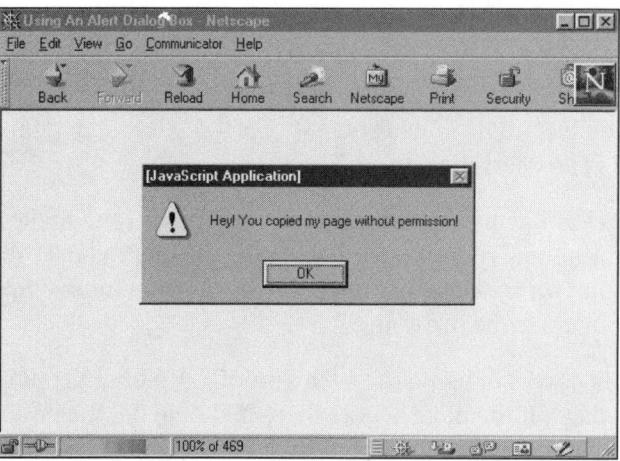

Figure 11.7   Using an Alert dialog box.

Creating Confirmation Dialog Boxes

"Hm," says the novice programmer. "Alert dialog boxes are nice, but I want an actual response from the user before continuing. Is there some way to get that?" "Well," you say, "you can try a Confirmation dialog box."

The **window** object's **confirm** method displays a Confirmation dialog box with two buttons: OK and Cancel. This method returns a Boolean value of **true** if users click the OK button or **false** if they click Cancel.

Here's an example putting **window.confirm** to work. In this case, the code displays a message saying "Your total comes to $34.23. Click OK to complete the order." If the user clicks OK, the page continues with the message "Thanks for your purchase." If the user clicks Cancel, the page displays "Would you like to order something else?" This page works in both Internet Explorer and Netscape Navigator:

```
<?xml version="1.0"?>
<!DOCTYPE html PUBLIC "-//W3C//DTD XHTML 1.0 Transitional//EN"
"http://www.w3.org/tr/xhtml1/DTD/xhtml1-transitional.dtd">
<html xmlns="http://www.w3.org/1999/xhtml" xml:lang="en" lang="en">
    <head>
        <title>
            Using A Confirmation Dialog Box
        </title>
    </head>
```

```
<body>
    <center>
        <h1>
            Using A Confirmation Dialog Box
        </h1>

        <script type = "text/javascript"
            language="javascript" src="script.js">
        </script>
    </center>
</body>
</html>
```

Here's the script for this example, script.js:

```
if(confirm("Your total comes to $34.23. Click OK to complete the order.")){
    document.write("<br />Thanks for your purchase.")
}
else {
    document.write("<br />Would you like to order something else?")
}
```

You can see the results of this code in Figure 11.8.

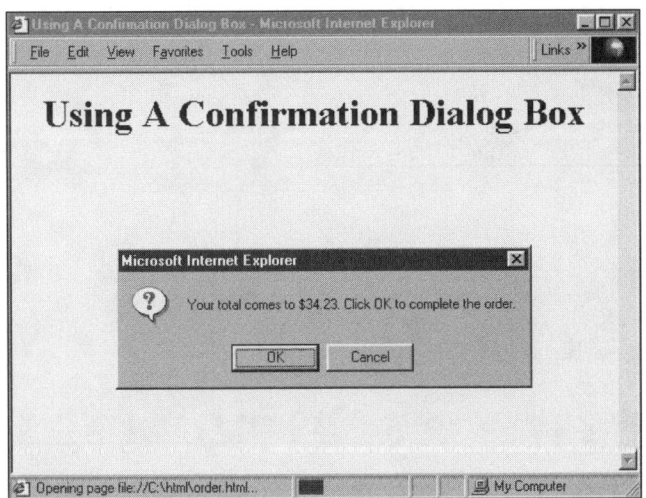

Figure 11.8   Using a Confirmation dialog box.

Creating Prompt Dialog Boxes

The novice programmer is perplexed and says, "I really need to have the user type something in, which means I can't use Alert or Confirmation dialog boxes. Am I stuck?" "By no means," you say suavely; "just use a Prompt dialog box."

You can use the **window** object's **prompt** method to display a dialog box that will display a prompt to the user and accept a typed string. The return value of this method will be the typed string.

In this next example, I'm using a Prompt dialog box to let the user type text directly into a Web page. You can specify two arguments to **window.prompt**—the prompt to display, and some default text, which will appear in the text field in the Prompt dialog box. Here, I'm setting the prompt to "Enter the text you want in this page," and I'm setting the default text to "Hi there!":

```
<?xml version="1.0"?>
<!DOCTYPE html PUBLIC "-//W3C//DTD XHTML 1.0 Transitional//EN"
"http://www.w3.org/tr/xhtml1/DTD/xhtml1-transitional.dtd">
<html xmlns="http://www.w3.org/1999/xhtml" xml:lang="en" lang="en">
    <head>
        <title>
            Creating A Prompt Dialog Box
        </title>
    </head>

    <body>
        <script type = "text/javascript"
            language = "javascript" src="script.js">
        </script>
    </body>
</html>
```

Here's the script, script.js, that makes this page work:

```
var text = prompt("Enter the text you want in this page", "Hi there! ")

if (text == "") {
    alert("You didn't enter anything.")
}
else {
    document.writeln("<center><h1>" + text + "</h1></center>")
}
```

You can see the results of this code in Figure 11.9. As you can see, the Prompt dialog box is displaying its prompt, and I've entered the text "Greetings!" in the text field. When I click the OK button, the Prompt dialog box disappears and "Greetings!" appears in the Web page, which you can see in Figure 11.10. It's a nice effect—users get the impression they've written directly to the XHTML of your Web page, and in fact, that is exactly what's happened.

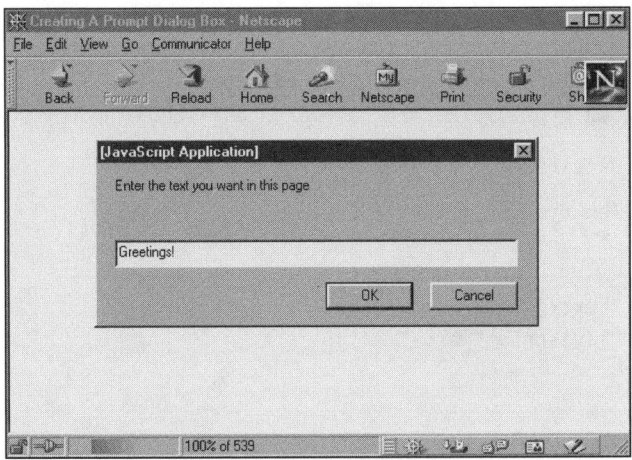

Figure 11.9   Creating a Prompt dialog box.

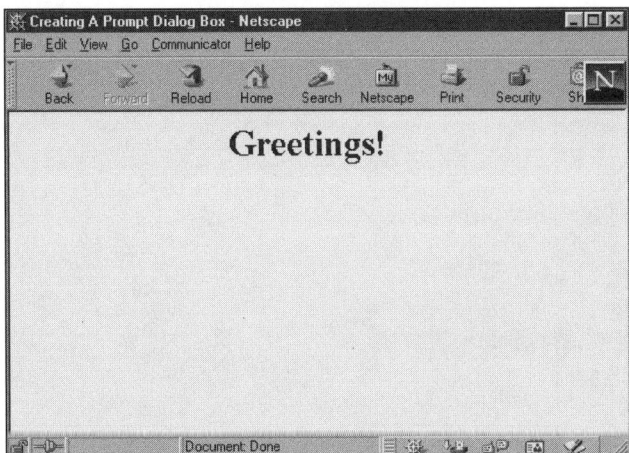

Figure 11.10   Writing a Web page at load time.

Writing to the Browser's Status Bar

You can use the **window** object's **defaultStatus** property to display text in the Web browser's status bar. In this example, I'm using a JavaScript **timer** event to call a function named **showMessage** once every two tenths of a second, allowing the code to scroll a message ("Welcome!") around in the status bar:

```
<?xml version="1.0"?>
<!DOCTYPE html PUBLIC "-//W3C//DTD XHTML 1.0 Transitional//EN"
"http://www.w3.org/tr/xhtml1/DTD/xhtml1-transitional.dtd">
<html xmlns="http://www.w3.org/1999/xhtml" xml:lang="en" lang="en">
    <head>
        <title>
            Writing To The Browser's Status Bar
        </title>

        <script type = "text/javascript"
            language = "javascript" src="script.js">
        </script>
    </head>

    <body>
        <center>
            <h1>
                Writing To The Browser's Status Bar
            </h1>
        </center>
    </body>
</html>
```

Here's the script for this page, script.js:

```
var position = 0
var message = "Welcome!"
timerID = setInterval('showMessage()', 200)

function showMessage()
{
    if (position > 20){
        position = 0
    }

    var text = " "
    for (var loopIndex = 0; loopIndex <= position;
        loopIndex++) {
```

```
        text = text + " "
   }

   text = text + message
   window.defaultStatus = text
   position++
}
```

Note how the **setInterval** method works—you pass it the JavaScript you want executed periodically and the interval between calls. In the previous example, I'm just calling the **showMessage** function every 200 milliseconds, and that function will display the message as needed. The results appear in Figure 11.11. This is a common effect seen in JavaScript-enabled Web pages: scrolling text in the status bar. It can be fun, but it can also look a little cutesy.

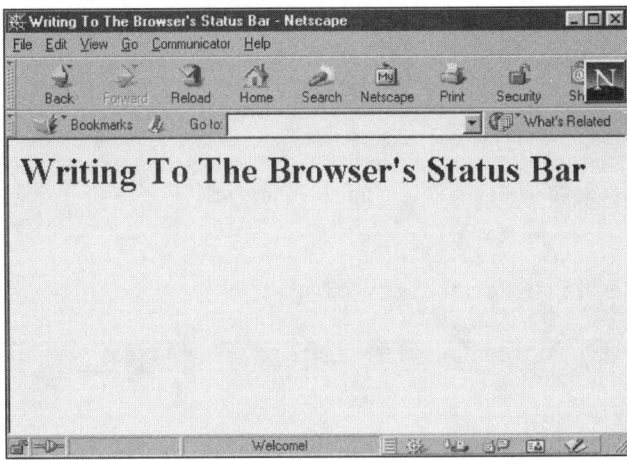

Figure 11.11   Writing to the browser's status bar.

Navigating with the location Object

"Well," the big boss says, "why can't we take control of what happens when users browse around our site? Let's send them directly to the page with the big photo of me." "Well," you say, "I can use the **location** object to do that, but…" "Great," says the BB, "do it."

When you set **window.location** to a new URL, the browser will navigate to that URL. In this example, I'm letting users enter a new URL in a text field and click a button marked "Navigate." When they do, the browser navigates to the new URL. Here's the example:

```xml
<?xml version="1.0"?>
<!DOCTYPE html PUBLIC "-//W3C//DTD XHTML 1.0 Transitional//EN"
"http://www.w3.org/tr/xhtml1/DTD/xhtml1-transitional.dtd">
<html xmlns="http://www.w3.org/1999/xhtml" xml:lang="en" lang="en">
    <head>
        <title>
            Navigating To A New URL Using JavaScript
        </title>

        <script type = "text/javascript"
            language = "javascript">
            function goTo()
            {
                window.location = document.form1.Textbox.value
            }
        </script>
    </head>

    <body>
        <center>
            <h1>
                Navigating To A New URL Using JavaScript
            </h1>

            <form name = "form1" action = "action">
                <br />
                <input type = "text" name = "Textbox" size = "60" />
                <br />
                <br />
                <input type = "button" value = "Navigate"
                    onclick = "goTo()" />
            </form>
        </center>
    </body>
</html>
```

You can see the results of this code in Figure 11.12. When the user enters a URL and clicks the Navigate button, the browser navigates to that URL.

In fact, you can redirect a browser to a new page immediately by using this technique, saving you the trouble of writing an http redirection header. This technique is commonly used when you've created a new Web page and want to direct people from the old URL to the new one. Here's an example that redirects users to the W3C Web site as soon as they open this page:

Immediate Solutions

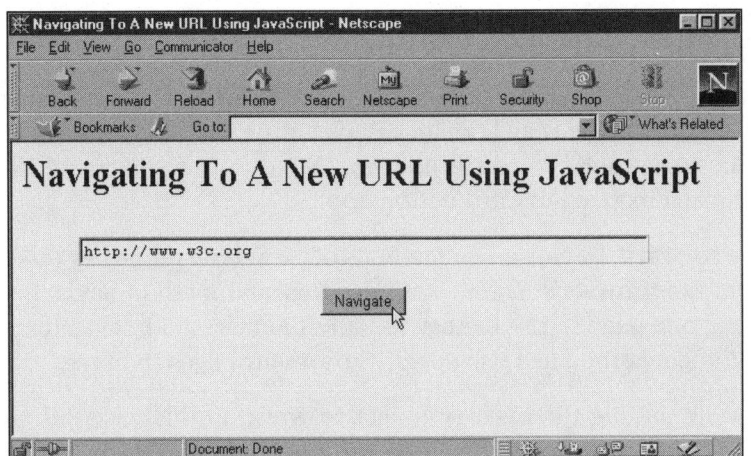

Figure 11.12 Using the **location** object to navigate.

```
<?xml version="1.0"?>
<!DOCTYPE html PUBLIC "-//W3C//DTD XHTML 1.0 Transitional//EN"
"http://www.w3.org/tr/xhtml1/DTD/xhtml1-transitional.dtd">
<html xmlns="http://www.w3.org/1999/xhtml" xml:lang="en" lang="en">
    <head>
        <title>
            Navigating To A New URL Using JavaScript
        </title>

        <script type = "text/javascript" language = "javascript">
            window.location = "http://www.W3C.org"
        </script>
    </head>

    <body>
        <center>
            <h1>
                Redirecting To A New URL Using JavaScript
            </h1>
            My page is down right now. Redirecting you now...
        </center>
    </body>
</html>
```

Navigating with the history Object

"Hmm," says the novice programmer. "Using the **location** object, I can navigate to a new URL, but it's too bad I can't create a Back button in a Web page—I'd have a browser within a browser!" You smile and say, "Not only can you create a Back button, but you can create a Forward button, too!"

You can use the **forward**, **back**, and **go** methods of the **window.history** object to navigate around the browser's history list. The **forward** method navigates the browser forward one page in the history list, the **back** method navigates back one page, and the **go** method lets you specify how many pages to move.

Here's an example putting the **history** object to work. In this case, I'll create Forward and Back buttons, along with Forward Two Pages and Back Two Pages buttons:

```
<?xml version="1.0"?>
<!DOCTYPE html PUBLIC "-//W3C//DTD XHTML 1.0 Transitional//EN"
"http://www.w3.org/tr/xhtml1/DTD/xhtml1-transitional.dtd">
<html xmlns="http://www.w3.org/1999/xhtml" xml:lang="en" lang="en">
    <head>
        <title>
            Using The history Object
        </title>

        <script type = "text/javascript" language = "javascript">
            function goBack()
            {
                window.history.back()
            }

            function goForward()
            {
                window.history.forward()
            }

            function goBackTwo()
            {
                window.history.go(-2)
            }

            function goForwardTwo()
            {
                window.history.go(2)
            }
        </script>
    </head>
```

Immediate Solutions

```
<body>
    <center>
        <h1>
            Using The history Object
        </h1>

        <form action = "action">
            <br />
            Navigate using the history object!
            <br />
            <br />
            <input type = "button" value = "< Back One Page"
                onclick = "goBack()" />
            <input type = "button" value = "Forward One Page >"
                onclick = "goForward()" />
            <br />
            <br />
            <input type = "button" value = "<< Back Two Pages"
                onclick = "goBackTwo()" />
            <input type = "button" value = "Forward Two Pages >>"
                onclick = "goForwardTwo()" />
        </form>
    </center>
</body>
</html>
```

You can see the results in Figure 11.13. The user can click the buttons in that page to move forward or back by one or two pages. You don't need buttons to navigate, of course; you can do it directly from code.

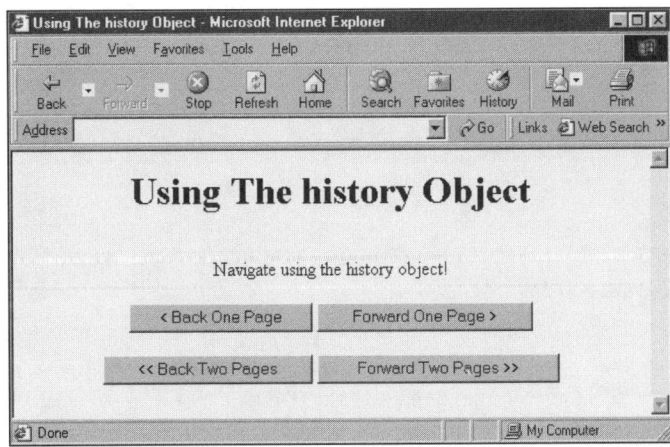

Figure 11.13   Using the **history** object to navigate.

Creating JavaScript URLs: Improving Image Maps

The Web-page design czar is worried and says, "Our image maps lack pizzazz. They should do something." "They *do* do something," you say, "but I could make them do more with a little JavaScript." The WPDC says, "Now you're talking!"

You can create JavaScript URLs that don't jump to a new page—instead, they jump to a JavaScript function. To do that, you use the **javascript:** protocol instead of the **http:** protocol, and you provide the name of a JavaScript function, not a URL. Here's an example. When the user clicks this link, the JavaScript function **displayWarning** is called; this function might display a Confirmation dialog box, and if users click OK, they navigate onto the appropriate URL:

```
If you dare, you can go to my
<a href="javascript:displayWarning()">dangerous page</a>!
```

Here's another example, modifying the image-map example from Chapter 5. In this case, I'll assume that the guest-book part of the Web site is down, so when the user clicks the guest-book region in the image map, I'll display an Alert dialog box with a message indicating that the guest book is not working:

```
<?xml version="1.0"?>
<!DOCTYPE html PUBLIC "-//W3C//DTD XHTML 1.0 Transitional//EN"
"http://www.w3.org/tr/xhtml1/DTD/xhtml1-transitional.dtd">
<html xmlns="http://www.w3.org/1999/xhtml" xml:lang="en" lang="en">
    <head>
        <title>
            Using A Client Side Image Map
        </title>

        <script type = "text/javascript" language="javascript">
            function sorry()
            {
                alert("Sorry, the guestbook is not working right now.")
            }
        </script>
    </head>

    <body bgcolor="black">
        <center>
            <img width="528" height="137" src="mainmenu.jpg"
                border="0" alt="Image Map" usemap="#imap" />
            <map name="imap" id = "map1">
                <area name="link1" shape="rect" coords="16,39 127,61"
                    id="link1" href="http://www.reuters.com" alt="News" />
```

```
            <area name="link2" shape="rect" coords="62,71 173,93"
                href="http://www.starpowder.com/steve/search.html"
                id="link2" alt="Web search" />
            <area name="link3" shape="rect" coords="98,104 209,126"
                id="link3"
                href="http://www.nnic.noaa.gov" alt="Weather" />
            <area name="link4" shape="rect" coords="411,35 522,57"
                id="link4" href="javascript:sorry()"
                alt="Guest book" />
            <area name="link5" shape="rect" coords="360,67 471,89"
                href="http://www.yahoo.com/Guides_and_Tutorials/"
                id="link5" alt="Create a Web page" />
            <area name="link6" shape="rect" coords="328,98 439,120"
                href="http://www.web21.com/services/hot100/index.html"
                id="link6" alt="Hottest 100 sites" />
            <area name="default" shape="default"
                href=
                "http://www.starpowder.com/steve/index.html#mainmenu"
                alt="Image map" />
        </map>
    </center>
  </body>
</html>
```

You can see the results in Figure 11.14. When the user clicks the guest-book URL, the Alert dialog box appears with the message that the guest book is out of commission. As you can imagine, this technique need not be applied only to image maps; you can create a graphical interface for nearly any purpose, including games, and tie it to JavaScript this way.

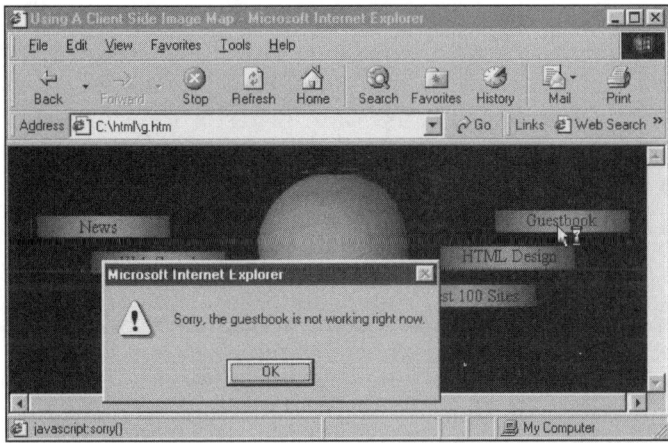

Figure 11.14 Adding a JavaScript URL to an image map.

Creating Cookies with JavaScript

The novice programmer races up and asks breathlessly, "Is it true? Can I really create cookies with JavaScript?" "Sure is," you say, "and it's easy." "Wow," cries the NP, "tell me how!"

Cookies are both loved and hated (so be careful before using them), and you can indeed set them by using JavaScript. A *cookie* is text that the browser stores on the local machine and that you can access at a later date. A common use of cookies is to store shopping-cart information—that is, a user's purchases—while he or she browses around a commercial site. If you're experienced with the Web, you know about cookies.

TIP: You should be aware that cookies really annoy some people (I almost count myself among them), so be judicious in using them if you have to. Also, you should know that most browsers set limits on the maximum number of cookies they'll store, such as 200, so don't set too many. I wish all Web authors were so considerate—I've seen a single page attempt to set nearly 100 cookies.

The **cookie** property of a page's **document** object holds the actual cookie text. Unless you make special preparations, you'll see only the cookie text that was stored for the current Web page or for other pages stored in the same directory on the server. I'll create an example here that creates a cookie when the user clicks a button and retrieves the cookie's text when the user clicks another button. (Of course, you can retrieve the cookie later by reloading this example and clicking the Retrieve button again.) In this case, I'll set the cookie to expire in one day.

Creating a Cookie

To create a cookie, all you need to do is set **document.cookie** to a string containing keyword/value pairs, separated by semicolons. For instance, I'll call the cookie in this example "greatCookie" and give it the text "This is the cookie text." To make the cookie expire on September 2, 2000 (that is, set a date for when the browser will delete the cookie), I'll use the **expires** keyword and set **document.cookie** to "**greatCookie=This is the cookie text.;expires=MON, 02-Sep-00 12:00:00 GMT**".

Here are the possible keywords you can use in **document.cookie** (all of them are optional):

- **domain=*domainname*** —This makes the cookie accessible to other pages at the same site.

- **expires=*date*** —This is the date on which the cookie expires; it must end with GMT for Netscape Navigator (here's the format: MON, 02-Sep-00 12:00:00 GMT).

- **name=*cookiename*** — This is the name of the cookie, which you use to refer to it.
- **path=*pathname*** — This is the directory to use for the cookie; pages with cookies in the same directory can read each other's cookies.
- **secure** — This cookie must be used with only a secure (https:) server.

*TIP: In a very early version of Netscape Navigator, version 1.1, you must set the **PATH** attribute to something—at least a forward slash (/)—if you set an **expires** keyword, or the cookie will not be stored.*

To create the cookie in this example, I'll write a function named **setCookie**. In this function, I'll create a new **Date** object to set the time this cookie expires. I want to make the cookie expire in one day, so I'll use the **Date** object's **getTime** method, which returns the time in milliseconds, and add 24 × 60 × 60 × 1000 milliseconds to that time. Then I'll convert the new date to GMT by using the JavaScript **toGMTString** function, display an Alert dialog box announcing that the cookie was created, and so create the new cookie, like this:

```
function setCookie()
{
    var cookieDate = new Date()
    cookieDate.setTime(cookieDate.getTime() + 24 * 60 * 60 *
        1000)

    document.cookie =
        "greatCookie=This is the cookie text.;expires="
        + cookieDate.toGMTString()

    window.alert("Cookie created!")
}
```

Now it's time to retrieve the newly set cookie.

Retrieving a Cookie

To read the cookie, you search the text in **document.cookie** (which is automatically loaded) for the beginning of the cookie text. In this case, the cookie text begins with "**greatCookie=**", so I'll search for that by using the JavaScript **String** class's **indexOf** method, which returns the location at which "**greatCookie=**" appears in the text. Next, I'll use the **String** class's **substring** method to retrieve the actual cookie text in a function named **getCookie**. (Note that if you have more than one cookie set, you should also search for the end of the cookie you're looking for because cookies are all stored in one long string.) The following code will return everything after the location at which "**greatCookie=**" appears:

```
function getCookie()
{
    var cookieData = new String(document.cookie)
    var cookieHeader = "greatCookie="

    var cookieStart = cookieData.indexOf(cookieHeader)

    if (cookieStart != -1){

        document.form1.Text.value =
            cookieData.substring(cookieStart
            + cookieHeader.length)
    }
    else{
        document.form1.Text.value = "Did not find the cookie."
    }
}
```

If the cookie is found, I display the text of the cookie in a text field. (This text is what you'd use in your code if you were using the cookie to store data, such as shopping-cart purchases.) Here's the whole example in place in a Web page:

```
<?xml version="1.0"?>
<!DOCTYPE html PUBLIC "-//W3C//DTD XHTML 1.0 Transitional//EN"
"http://www.w3.org/tr/xhtml1/DTD/xhtml1-transitional.dtd">
<html xmlns="http://www.w3.org/1999/xhtml" xml:lang="en" lang="en">
    <head>
        <title>
            Working With Cookies
        </title>

        <script type = "text/javascript" language="javascript">
            function setCookie()
            {
                var cookieDate = new Date()
                cookieDate.setTime(cookieDate.getTime() + 24 * 60 * 60 *
                    1000)

                document.cookie =
                    "greatCookie=This is the cookie text.;expires="
                    + cookieDate.toGMTString()

                window.alert("Cookie created!")
            }
```

```
            function getCookie()
            {
                var cookieData = new String(document.cookie)
                var cookieHeader = "greatCookie="

                var cookieStart = cookieData.indexOf(cookieHeader)

                if (cookieStart != -1){
                    document.form1.text.value =
                        cookieData.substring(cookieStart
                        + cookieHeader.length)
                }
                else{
                    document.form1.text.value = "Did not find the cookie."
                }
            }
        </script>
    </head>

    <body>
        <center>
            <h1>
                Working With Cookies In JavaScript
            </h1>
        </center>

        <form name = "form1" action = "action">
            <center>
                <input type="text" name="text" size="30" />
                <br />
                <br />
                <input type = "button" value = "Create the cookie"
                    onclick = "setCookie()" />
                <br />
                <br />
                <input type = "button" value = "Retrieve the cookie"
                    onclick = "getCookie()" />
            </center>
        </form>
    </body>
</html>
```

You can see the results in Figure 11.15. When the user clicks the Create The Cookie button, the cookie is created and stored. When the user clicks the Retrieve The Cookie button (or reloads the page within one day and clicks this

Chapter 11   Putting JavaScript to Work

Figure 11.15   Buttons for creating and retrieving a cookie.

button), the cookie text is retrieved and displayed. That's it—now you're working with cookies.

NOTE: *No one I know knows for sure why cookies are called cookies. Some people say it's because of the Unix fortune program, which displays a fortune-cookie message when you run it. My own preference is to believe that the name comes from the infamous cookie program I remember from the MIT Artificial Intelligence Lab. When you ran this program, it would startle someone by printing on their screen, "Please give me a cookie." If the person ignored it, the program would become more and more insistent over time, finally printing out the message "I WANT A COOKIE!" in letters one screen high. All you had to do was type "cookie" and the program would thank you politely and quit.*

Chapter 12

Creating XHTML Forms and XHTML Controls

If you need an immediate solution to:	See page:
<form>—Creating XHTML Forms	709
<input type="button">—Creating Buttons	713
<input type="checkbox">—Creating Checkboxes	716
<input type="file">—Creating File Input for a Form	721
<input type="hidden">—Creating Hidden Data	725
<input type="image">—Creating Image Submit Buttons	728
<input type="password">—Creating Password Controls	731
<input type="radio">—Creating Radio Buttons	735
<input type="reset">—Creating Reset Buttons	739
<input type="submit">—Creating Submit Buttons	741
<input type="text">—Creating Text Fields	745
<textarea>—Creating Text Areas	748
<button>—Creating a Customizable Button	751
<select>, **<option>**, and **<optgroup>**—Creating a Select Control	754
<fieldset>, **<legend>**, and **<label>**—Grouping and Labeling Form Elements	761
<isindex>—Using an Index	766
<keygen>—Processing Secure Transactions	767

In Depth

In the previous two chapters, we worked through a lot of JavaScript syntax. In this chapter, we'll put it to work with the original and still primary way of making your Web pages interactive—XHTML *forms*. Using forms, we'll be able to handle XHTML *controls*, such as buttons, checkboxes, radio buttons, select controls, and text areas.

What's a Form?

There's no denying the popularity of buttons, checkboxes, text fields, and other controls in Web pages. Everywhere you look, it seems that some Web page is asking you to enter your email address (be wary) or your credit card number (be even warier). Other pages are studded with buttons and checkboxes that let you work with them much as you'd work with a program on your own computer. To use XHTML controls like these, you must enclose them in XHTML forms.

Why do you need to enclose controls in forms before you can use them? Forms were originally intended to let the user send data back to the server. For instance, you type your email address into a text field (called a *text box* in other markup and programming languages) and click a Submit button to subscribe to an email list. When you click the Submit button in a form, all the data in the form's controls is collected and sent to the server. You can use code on the server to decipher that data and act on what the user has sent you. In this way, a form packages all the data from a group of controls, and all the data is then sent to the server.

TIP: *Although you need to enclose controls in a form in Netscape Navigator (or they won't appear), you don't need to enclose them in a form in Internet Explorer. However, if you want to send data from a particular set of controls back to a program on the server, you must enclose them in a form, even in Internet Explorer.*

We'll learn more about how to handle data sent to a Web server from a form when we discuss Common Gateway Interface (CGI) programming later in this book (and a little in this chapter). However, it's becoming more and more common not to send anything back to the server at all, but instead, to use controls in a Web page to make that page come alive. That's a large part of what dynamic XHTML is all about (which we'll work with starting in Chapter 13). For example, you might let the user customize the appearance of a page interactively by using buttons and text fields in a page. (You can even store the new settings by using a JavaScript cookie.) To work with dynamic XHTML, you need be able to handle XHTML controls, and to handle these controls, you need to work with forms.

Despite their name, forms are not visible objects on the screen—they are purely logical inventions that you create with the **<form>** element to group controls together. In fact, you can have multiple forms on a page (although it's not legal to nest forms—at least not yet).

Here are some online resources that can help you learn more about creating and using forms:

- **http://developer.netscape.com/docs/manuals/htmlguid/tags10.htm**— Netscape Navigator documentation on forms

- **http://dir.yahoo.com/Computers_and_Internet/Internet/ World_Wide_Web/Programming/Forms/**—Yahoo's forms pages

- **http://ecco.bsee.swin.edu.au/text/form-tut/ft.1.html**—Carlos's forms tutorial

- **www.utoronto.ca/webdocs/HTMLdocs/NewHTML/forms.html**—The Information Commons introduction to forms

- **www.webcom.com/~webcom/html/tutor/forms/**—Webcom's tutorial on forms

People use forms to display XHTML controls, and that raises the question: Just what controls are available to us? I'll take a look at that now.

What Controls Are Available?

There are plenty of controls available in XHTML, and, as you might expect, we'll look at all of them in this chapter. Following is a list of the XHTML controls and the XHTML element you use to create them. Note that many XHTML controls are created with the **<input>** element, but you use a different value for the **type** attribute to create the various controls. The current XHTML controls and corresponding elements are as follows:

- *Button (**<input type="button">**)*—Used to create the standard clickable buttons you see on so many Web pages these days.

- *Checkbox (**<input type="checkbox">**)*—Used to create checkboxes, which are usually displayed as small boxes containing checkmarks. The user can toggle the checkmark on or off by clicking the checkbox.

- *Customizable button (**<button>**)*—Used to display images and other XHTML inside itself. A relatively new element.

- *File-uploading control (<input type="file">)*—Allows the user to upload files to the server.

- *Hidden control (<input type="hidden">)*—Stores data that is not visible to users (unless they view the Web page's XHTML source).

- *Image control (<input type="image">)*—Used to create images that users can click and that work like Submit buttons. The actual location that the user clicks in the image is sent to the server with the rest of the data from the form.

- *Password control (<input type="password">)*—Used to create text fields that are masked; that is, this control masks each typed character by displaying an asterisk (*) instead of the character itself. This control is valuable for creating password fields for users because no one can read the password on the screen.

- *Radio button (<input type="radio">)*—Used to create radio buttons, which are usually displayed as circles; a selected radio button displays a dot in the middle of the circle. These controls act much like checkboxes except that they work in mutually exclusive groups in which only one radio button can be selected at a time.

- *Reset button (<input type="reset">)*—Allows users to clear all the data they've entered and start over. When users click the Reset button, all the controls in the form are returned to their original states, displaying the data they had when they first appeared. Great for complex forms.

- *Selection list (<select>)*—Used to create drop-down list boxes. Also called *select controls*.

- *Submit button (<input type="submit">)*—Used to be the most important control in forms because when you clicked the Submit button, all the data in the form (that is, all the data in the form's controls) was sent to a Web server for more processing. However, more and more forms are appearing that handle all the processing they need without sending anything back to a Web server, and the Submit button is omitted.

- *Text area (<textarea>)*—Used to create a multiline text field. Text areas can also support text wrapping.

- *Text field (<input type="text">)*—Allows the user to enter and edit a line of text. Called *text boxes* in other markup and programming languages.

So just how do you create a form and add controls to it? I'll explain how this works now.

Creating a Form and Adding XHTML Controls

To create a form, you use the **<form>** element. After you've created a form, you can fill it with controls and make those controls active with JavaScript or another scripting language.

Here's how it works. In this example, I'll add a button and a text field to a Web page; when the user clicks the button, the code will display the message "Hello from XHTML!" in the text field. To use controls like this in a Web page, I'll start with a form in the page (the **<form>** element lists the **action** attribute as required, but we won't really use that attribute, which specifies the target URL for the data in a form you send to a server, until Chapter 19, so I'm just setting it to a dummy value here):

```
<?xml version="1.0"?>
<!DOCTYPE html PUBLIC "-//W3C//DTD XHTML 1.0 Transitional//EN"
"http://www.w3.org/tr/xhtml1/DTD/xhtml1-transitional.dtd">
<html xmlns="http://www.w3.org/1999/xhtml" xml:lang="en" lang="en">
    <head>
        <title>
            Creating XHTML Forms
        </title>
    </head>

    <body>
        <center>
            <h1>Creating XHTML Forms</h1>

            <form name = "form1" action = "action">
                    .
                    .
                    .
            </form>
        </center>
    </body>
</html>
```

Note that I've given this new form a name, **form1**. I've done that because we'll need to refer to the form when we're working with the controls in it from JavaScript. (Note also that if you have a number of forms in the same page, you should name them to keep them straight.)

Next, I'll add two controls: a text field and a button. I'll start by creating the text field, which you do with the **<input>** element. In fact, you create nearly all XHTML controls by using the **<input>** element. (Now, however, the World Wide Web Consortium, W3C, is breaking away from the exclusive use of this element to create controls and is supporting other elements to create controls.)

You create controls—such as buttons, text fields, checkboxes, and radio buttons—with the **<input>** element's **type** attribute. To create a text field, you set **type** to **text**. In this example, I'll give the text field a width of 25 characters by using the **size** attribute, and I'll name it "**textfield**" by using the **name** attribute. Note that the **<input>** element is empty, so I end it with the standard XML shortcut **/>**. Here's the code:

```
<?xml version="1.0"?>
<!DOCTYPE html PUBLIC "-//W3C//DTD XHTML 1.0 Transitional//EN"
"http://www.w3.org/tr/xhtml1/DTD/xhtml1-transitional.dtd">
<html xmlns="http://www.w3.org/1999/xhtml" xml:lang="en" lang="en">
    <head>
        <title>
            Creating XHTML Forms
        </title>
    </head>

    <body>
        <center>
            <h1>Creating XHTML Forms</h1>
            <form name = "form1" action = "action">
                <input type = "text" name = "textfield" size = "25" />
                    .
                    .
                    .
            </form>
        </center>
    </body>
</html>
```

Now I'll create the button we'll need. To create a normal XHTML button, you use the **<input>** element with the **type** attribute set to **button**. In this case, the code will display its message in the text field when the user clicks this button, so I also add the caption "Display Message" to the button by using the **<input>** element's **value** attribute. Here's how it looks in XHTML:

```
<?xml version="1.0"?>
<!DOCTYPE html PUBLIC "-//W3C//DTD XHTML 1.0 Transitional//EN"
"http://www.w3.org/tr/xhtml1/DTD/xhtml1-transitional.dtd">
<html xmlns="http://www.w3.org/1999/xhtml" xml:lang="en" lang="en">
```

```
        <head>
            <title>
                Creating XHTML Forms
            </title>
        </head>

        <body>
            <center>
                <h1>Creating XHTML Forms</h1>
                <form name = "form1" action = "action">
                    <input type = "text" name = "textfield" size = "25" />
                    <br />
                    <br />
                    <input type = "button" value = "Display Message" />
                </form>
            </center>
        </body>
</html>
```

TIP: *The* **<input>** *element's* **value** *attribute has different meanings for different controls. For example, although it sets the caption of buttons, it also sets the default text contents of text fields. Refer to the "Immediate Solutions" section of this chapter for details.*

So far we've just displayed a text field and a button—and nothing happens when the user clicks the button. To make the button active, you use its events, just as with the other XHTML elements in the previous two chapters. In this case, all I need to do is connect the button's **onclick** event to the JavaScript code that will display the message in the text field. I'll place that code in a JavaScript function named **displayMessage** and connect that function to the button's **onclick** event:

```
<?xml version="1.0"?>
<!DOCTYPE html PUBLIC "-//W3C//DTD XHTML 1.0 Transitional//EN"
"http://www.w3.org/tr/xhtml1/DTD/xhtml1-transitional.dtd">
<html xmlns="http://www.w3.org/1999/xhtml" xml:lang="en" lang="en">
    <head>
        <title>
            Creating XHTML Forms
        </title>
    </head>

    <body>
        <center>
            <h1>Creating XHTML Forms</h1>
```

```
                <form name = "form1" action = "action">
                    <input type = "text" name = "textfield" size = "25" />
                    <br />
                    <br />
                    <input type = "button" value = "Display Message"
                        onclick = "displayMessage()" />
                </form>
            </center>
        </body>
</html>
```

All that remains is to write the JavaScript **displayMessage** function, which is called when the user clicks the button:

```
<?xml version="1.0"?>
<!DOCTYPE html PUBLIC "-//W3C//DTD XHTML 1.0 Transitional//EN"
"http://www.w3.org/tr/xhtml1/DTD/xhtml1-transitional.dtd">
<html xmlns="http://www.w3.org/1999/xhtml" xml:lang="en" lang="en">
    <head>
        <title>
            Creating XHTML Forms
        </title>

        <script language = "javascript" type = "text/javascript">
            function displayMessage()
            {
                    .
                    .
                    .
            }
        </script>
    </head>

    <body>
        <center>
            <h1>Creating XHTML Forms</h1>
            <form name = "form1" action = "action">
                <input type = "text" name = "textfield" size = "25" />
                <br />
                <br />
                <input type = "button" value = "Display Message"
                    onclick = "displayMessage()" />
            </form>
        </center>
    </body>
</html>
```

The code in the function **displayMessage** must be able to place the message "Hello from XHTML!" in the text field that we've named **textfield**. How do you access that text field? Recall that the **document** object represents the current Web page, and you can access all elements in the page by using that object. Because the text field is in the form we've named **form1**, we call it **document.form1.textfield**. To display text in this text field, you need to set its **value** attribute, which you can do by working with its **value** property in JavaScript as **document.form1.textfield.value**. Here's what the final XHTML looks like:

```xhtml
<?xml version="1.0"?>
<!DOCTYPE html PUBLIC "-//W3C//DTD XHTML 1.0 Transitional//EN"
"http://www.w3.org/tr/xhtml1/DTD/xhtml1-transitional.dtd">
<html xmlns="http://www.w3.org/1999/xhtml" xml:lang="en" lang="en">
    <head>
        <title>
            Creating XHTML Forms
        </title>

        <script language = "javascript" type = "text/javascript">
            function displayMessage()
            {
                document.form1.textfield.value = "Hello from XHTML!"
            }
        </script>
    </head>

    <body>
        <center>
            <h1>Creating XHTML Forms</h1>
            <form name = "form1" action = "action">
                <input type = "text" name = "textfield" size = "25" />
                <br />
                <br />
                <input type = "button" value = "Display Message"
                    onclick = "displayMessage()" />
            </form>
        </center>
    </body>
</html>
```

That's all it takes. You can see the results of this XHTML in Figure 12.1. When the user clicks the button, the message is displayed in the text field.

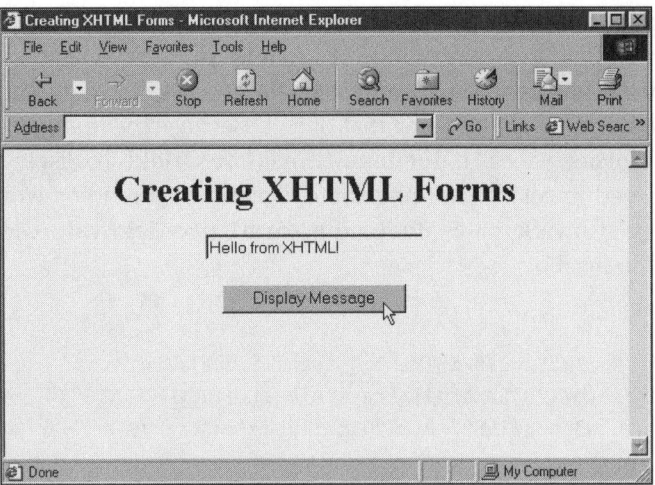

Figure 12.1   Using XHTML forms and controls.

Element Attributes Become JavaScript Properties

Using the JavaScript **value** property of the text field brings up an important point—most XHTML element attributes are accessible from JavaScript as JavaScript properties. For example, the **value** attribute is accessible as the **value** property. As we'll see in this chapter, the **checked** attribute of checkboxes and radio buttons is accessible as the **checked** property. In the previous chapter, we saw that you can use an image element's **src** property to set its **src** attribute, and in Chapter 13, we'll see that the **style** attribute is accessible as the **style** property. By making most attributes available as properties, JavaScript lets you interact immediately with the elements in a Web page. When you decide which attribute you want to work with, you automatically know the property that you need to work with in JavaScript because the property has the same name.

TIP: Although XHTML attributes usually have the same name as JavaScript properties, translating certain XHTML attributes to the corresponding JavaScript properties can be unpredictable; for example, the XHTML style **font-size** becomes the JavaScript property **fontSize**. You can find all the details about which properties are available for which elements in the documentation for Netscape Navigator's JavaScript at **http://developer.netscape.com/tech/javascript/index.html**. You can find the documentation for Microsoft's JScript at **http://msdn.microsoft.com/scripting/default.htm?/scripting/jscript/techinfo/jsdocs.htm**.

Referring to Controls in a Form in Code

Another thing to bear in mind—in the previous code, I refer to controls in a form from code as **document.formname.control**. That is, the **document** object contains all other objects, including the form you want to use, and the form contains the control you want to reach, so to refer to a control from code, you supply its full name: **document.formname.control**.

To set an attribute of a control, then, you set the corresponding JavaScript property like this: **document.formname.control.property**. To call a JavaScript method of the control, you use this syntax: **document.formname.control.method(*arguments*)**. As you can see in the previous example, I set the **value** property of a text field, which holds the text in the text field, like this: **document.form1.textfield.value = "Hello from XHTML!"**.

Submitting Data from Forms

In the previous section, we saw how you can use JavaScript to make something happen when you use controls in a page without sending anything to the server. However, I've mentioned sending data from a form back to the server, which was originally what forms were designed to do. The details will have to wait until we discuss CGI programming in Chapter 19, but I'll look at an example now.

There are two ways for forms to send data to code on a Web server: using the **get** method and using the **post** method.

NOTE: *When you send data by using the **get** method, a question mark **(?)** and the form data are appended to the target URL of the code on the server; this URL can point to a CGI file. For example, say that the URL of the CGI file that handles the data from your form is **http://www.starpowder.com/steve/cgi/cgidata.cgi**. If you had one text field named **name** and another one named **id**, the data from these text fields would be appended to the URL like this (spaces will be converted to plus signs [+]): **http://www.starpowder.com/steve/cgicgidata.cgi?name= Steve+Holzner&id=1000**. When you send data by using the **post** method, data from the form is sent as environment variables that are accessible to the CGI script.*

I'll use the **post** method in the next example. I'll create a form that accepts the user's name and then echoes it back from a CGI script. To use the **post** method, you set the **method** attribute of the **<form>** element to **post**. In addition, you set the **action** attribute of the form to the URL that you want the data to be sent to, so I'll use the URL **http://www.starpowder.com/steve/cgi/cgidata.cgi**. Here's what the form looks like—note that I'm including a Submit button. When the user clicks this button, the data in the text field will be posted to the URL in the **action** attribute:

```
<?xml version="1.0"?>
<!DOCTYPE html PUBLIC "-//W3C//DTD XHTML 1.0 Transitional//EN"
    "http://www.w3.org/tr/xhtml1/DTD/xhtml1-transitional.dtd">
<html xmlns="http://www.w3.org/1999/xhtml" xml:lang="en" lang="en">
    <head>
```

```
        <title>
            CGI Example
        </title>
    </head>

    <body>
        <form method="post"
            action="http://www.starpowder.com/steve/cgi/cgidata.cgi">

            Please enter your name:
            <input type="text" name="text" value="" />
            <p>
                <center>
                    <input type="submit" name="Submit" value="Submit" />
                    <input type="reset" />
                </center>
            </p>
        </form>
    </body>
</html>
```

The results of this XHTML appear in Figure 12.2. All you have to do is enter your name and click the Submit button to send it to the waiting CGI script, which will echo back what you typed.

What does the CGI script look like? I'll use the most popular CGI scripting language—Perl (although C++ and now server-side JavaScript are becoming popular). Here's a sneak peek at what the Perl code for this example looks like:

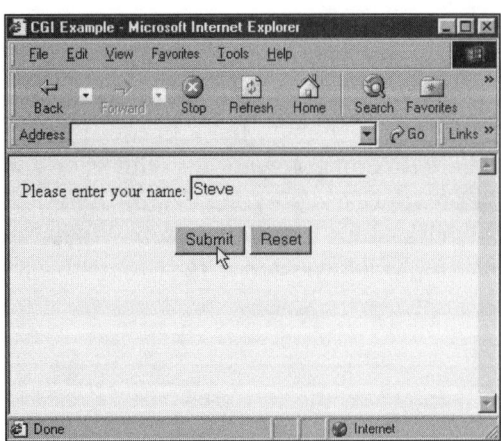

Figure 12.2 An XHTML form that will post data.

```perl
#!/usr/local/bin/perl

use CGI;

$co = new CGI;

print $co->header,

$co->start_html(
    -title=>'CGI Example',
    -author=>'Steve',
    -meta=>{'keywords'=>'CGI Perl'},
),

$co->hr;

if ($co->param()) {
    print
        "Your name is: ",$co->em($co->param('text')), ".";
}

print $co->hr;

print $co->end_html;
```

This CGI script is installed on the server, as we'll see in Chapter 19. When the name the user has typed into the text field in Figure 12.2 is sent, the script immediately creates a Web page and sends it back to the browser. This new page displays the name that was typed, which is what you see in Figure 12.3.

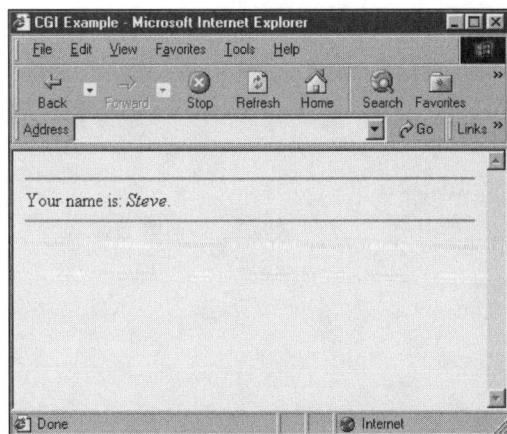

Figure 12.3 The result of using a CGI script to echo data sent to it.

There's another topic to discuss in this overview—using **<fieldset>**, **<legend>**, and **<label>**.

Using <fieldset>, <legend>, and <label>

The **<fieldset>**, **<legend>**, and **<label>** elements—which are relatively new— let you group controls in a form visually. You use the **<fieldset>** element to group elements in a form together in a box. (Although the actual rendering is left to the browser, this element is supported only in Internet Explorer, as far as I know, and this element comes up as a box.) You use the **<legend>** element to add a caption to the box, and use the **<label>** element to label the elements in the form. Here's an example in XHTML:

```
<?xml version="1.0"?>
<!DOCTYPE html PUBLIC "-//W3C//DTD XHTML 1.0 Transitional//EN"
"http://www.w3.org/tr/xhtml1/DTD/xhtml1-transitional.dtd">
<html xmlns="http://www.w3.org/1999/xhtml" xml:lang="en" lang="en">
    <head>
        <title>
            Using &lt;fieldset&gt;, &lt;legend&gt;, And &lt;label&gt;
        </title>
    </head>

    <body>
        <center>
            <h1>Using &lt;fieldset&gt;, &lt;legend&gt;, And
                &lt;label&gt;</h1>
            <form name = "form1" action = "action">
                <fieldset>
                    <legend accesskey="C">Color</legend>
                    <label accesskey="Y">
                        <input type="radio" name="color" value="yellow" />
                        Yellow
                    </label>
                    <br />
                    <label accesskey="W">
                        <input type="radio" name="color" value="orange" />
                        Orange
                    </label>
                </fieldset>
            </form>
        </center>
    </body>
</html>
```

In Depth

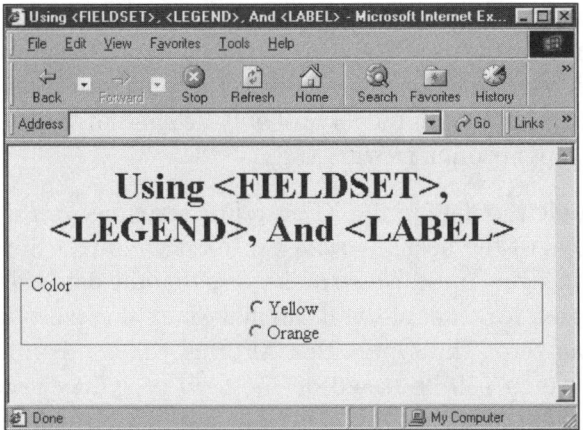

Figure 12.4 Using **<fieldset>**, **<legend>**, and **<label>**.

You can see the results in Figure 12.4. As you can see, the controls in the **<fieldset>** element are wrapped in a box, which has the caption we've given it with the **<legend>** element, and the controls have the captions we've given them with the **<label>** element.

XForms

W3C is working on a new version of forms—XForms, specifically designed to work with languages such as XHTML and XML. XForms are now in the early working-draft stage and are not implemented in any browser yet. In fact, as of this writing, no one knows what the actual implementation details will be.

In many ways, you can think of XForms as smart forms. Forms collect data and send that data back to the server, but these days, many programmers don't consider that enough. XForms allow you to check the data being entered and even change the appearance of the XForm as data is being entered (as when you want to display the data being entered in a table). In other words, XForms can be thought of as mini-applications that can do a great deal of data handling before sending that data to the server.

XForms work by splitting forms into three layers—a *presentation* layer, a *data* layer, and a *logic* layer. This separation follows the current vogue for separating data from programming logic.

The presentation layer displays the data in the XForm. You can tailor the presentation layer to specific browsers or environments, such as television-based Web clients or hand-held PCs or PDAs. You can also tailor the presentation layer for specific user preferences.

The data layer holds the data in the form—both the data stored as the XForm is initialized and the data entered by the user. You can use the data types that will be built in or create your own. Most of the data types now being considered are built using XML schemas (see Chapter 13), but they'll probably be simplified because not all Web authors will be super-proficient with XML.

The logic layer lets you handle the data in the XForm. For example, you might want to create a running total of the user's purchases; that total might then be displayed by the presentation layer. You can also make sure that the data entered falls within allowed boundaries; for example, you can make sure that cash transfer amounts are greater than zero. The syntax that XForms will use is a lightweight expression syntax, which will be based on the kind of syntax used in spreadsheets and existing forms packages. Although XForms probably won't support script code directly, you will still be able to call scripts when needed.

Here are some online XForms resources for further details:

- XForms overview—**www.w3.org/MarkUp/Forms/**
- An XForm sample built using JavaScript—**www.w3.org/MarkUp/Forms/Sample/acme.html**
- The W3C XForm working draft—**www.w3.org/tr/xhtml-forms-req**

That's all the introduction to forms and controls we need—it's time to dig into the details now.

Immediate Solutions

<form>—Creating XHTML Forms

Purpose: Creates an XHTML form; used to enclose XHTML controls, such as buttons and text fields.

When used as HTML: Start tag/End tag: Required/Required

Supported: [1.0S, 1.0T, 1.0F, 1.1, 2, 3, 3.2, 4, IE1, IE2, IE3, IE4, IE5, NS1, NS2, NS3, NS4]

Attributes:

- **accept**—Specifies a comma-separated list of content types that a server processing this form will handle correctly. [1.0S, 1.0T, 1.0F, 1.1, 4]

- **accept-charset**—Indicates a list of possible language character sets for the form data. Set to a space-separated or comma-separated list of language character sets. [1.0S, 1.0T, 1.0F, 1.1, 4]

- **action**—Gives the URL that will handle the form data. Required. Set to a URL. [1.0S, 1.0T, 1.0F, 1.1, 2, 3, 3.2, 4, IE1, IE2, IE3, IE4, IE5, NS1, NS2, NS3, NS4]

- **autocomplete**—Set to **true** (the default) if you want Internet Explorer to automatically complete data in controls based on what the user has entered before. [IE5]

- **class**—Class of the element. [1.0S, 1.0T, 1.0F, 1.1, 4, IE4, IE5]

- **contenteditable**—Set to **true** if users can edit the content of the form. [IE5]

- **dir**—Gives the direction of directionally neutral text (text that doesn't have an inherent direction in which you should read it). Possible values: **ltr**, left-to-right text or table; and **rtl**, right-to-left text or table. [1.0S, 1.0T, 1.0F, 1.1, 4, IE5]

- **disabled**—Set to **true** if the form should be disabled. [IE5]

- **enctype**—Sets the Multipurpose Internet Mail Extension (MIME) type used to encode the name/value pairs when sent to the action URL. The default is "**application/x-www-form-urlencoded**", but you can also use "**multipart/form-data**", which is for **<input type="file">** elements. [1.0S, 1.0T, 1.0F, 1.1, 2, 3, 3.2, 4, IE1, IE2, IE3, IE4, IE5, NS1, NS2, NS3, NS4]

- **id**—Unique alphanumeric identifier for the tag; use the ID to refer to the tag. [1.0S, 1.0T, 1.0F, 1.1, 4, IE4, IE5]

- **lang**—Base language used for the tag. [1.0S, 1.0T, 1.0F, 1.1, 3, 4, IE4, IE5]

- **language**—Scripting language used for the tag. [IE4, IE5]

- **method**—Indicates a method or protocol for sending data to the target action URL. The **get** method is the default. This method sends all form names and values in a URL that looks like: *URL?name=value&name=value&name=value*. When the **post** method is used, the contents of the form are encoded, as with the **get** method, but are sent in environment variables. Set to **get** (the default) or **post**. [1.0S, 1.0T, 1.0F, 1.1, 2, 3, 3.2, 4, IE1, IE2, IE3, IE4, IE5, NS1, NS2, NS3, NS4]

- **name**—Gives a name to the form so you can refer to it in code. Set to an alphanumeric string. [1.0T, 1.0F, 4, IE3, IE4, IE5, NS2, NS3, NS4]

- **style**—Inline style indicating how to render the element. [1.0S, 1.0T, 1.0F, 1.1, 4, IE4, IE5]

- **tabindex**—Sets a tab index for the form in the page. [IE5]

- **target**—Indicates a named frame in which the browser will display the form results. [1.0T, 1.0F, 4, IE3, IE4, IE5, NS2, NS3, NS4]

- **title**—Holds additional information (which might be displayed in tool tips). [1.0S, 1.0T, 1.0F, 1.1, 4, IE4, IE5]

- **xml:lang**—Holds the base language for the element when the document is interpreted as an XML document. [1.0S, 1.0T, 1.0F, 1.1]

XHTML events: onclick, ondblclick, onmousedown, onmouseup, onmouseover, onmousemove, onmouseout, onkeypress, onkeydown, onkeyup, onsubmit, onreset

- *Internet Explorer only*—**onbeforecopy, onbeforecut, onbeforefocusenter, onbeforefocusleave, onbeforepaste, onblur, onclick, oncontextmenu, oncontrolselect, oncopy, oncut, ondblclick, ondrag, ondragend, ondragenter, ondragleave, ondragover, ondragstart, ondrop, onfocus, onfocusenter, onfocusleave, onhelp, onkeydown, onkeypress, onkeyup, onlosecapture, onmousedown, onmouseenter, onmouseleave, onmousemove, onmouseout, onmouseover, onmouseup, onpaste, onpropertychange, onreadystatechange, onreset, onresize, onresizeend, onresizestart, onselectstart, onsubmit**

- *Netscape Navigator only*—**onsubmit, onreset**

The novice programmer enters breathlessly and cries, "I want to use XHTML controls in my Web page!" "Hold on there," you say, laughing; "you need to start by creating an XHTML form first." "I knew there would be a catch," the NP says. "It's no catch," you say, "and besides, it's easy."

To use controls in a Web page, you should enclose them in an XHTML form. Netscape Navigator insists that you use a form to display controls, and although Internet Explorer does not, you must still use forms if you want to collect and send data back to the Web server. We already saw this example of using a form in the "In Depth" section of this chapter:

```xhtml
<?xml version="1.0"?>
<!DOCTYPE html PUBLIC "-//W3C//DTD XHTML 1.0 Transitional//EN"
"http://www.w3.org/tr/xhtml1/DTD/xhtml1-transitional.dtd">
<html xmlns="http://www.w3.org/1999/xhtml" xml:lang="en" lang="en">
    <head>
        <title>
            Creating XHTML Forms
        </title>

        <script language = "javascript" type = "text/javascript">
            function displayMessage()
            {
                document.form1.textfield.value = "Hello from XHTML!"
            }
        </script>
    </head>

    <body>
        <center>
            <h1>Creating XHTML Forms</h1>
            <form name = "form1" action = "action">
                <input type = "text" name = "textfield" size = "25" />
                <br />
                <br />
                <input type = "button" value = "Display Message"
                    onclick = "displayMessage()" />
            </form>
        </center>
    </body>
</html>
```

You can see the results of this XHTML in Figure 12.1. This Web page is self-contained and sends nothing back to the server, but of course, you can also use forms to send data back to code on the server. There are two ways for forms to send data to code on a Web server—the **get** method and the **post** method.

When you send data by using the **get** method, a question mark (?) and the form data are added to the target URL of the code on the server; this URL points to a CGI file. Say that the URL of the CGI file that handles the data from your form is **http://www.starpowder.com/steve/cgi/cgidata.cgi**. If you had a text field named **name** and one named **id**, the data from these text fields would be appended to the URL like this (spaces would be converted to plus signs [+]): **http://www.starpowder.com/steve/cgi/cgidata.cgi?name=Steve+Holzner&id=1000**. When you send data by using the **post** method, data from the form is sent as environment variables, which are accessible to the CGI script.

I'll use the **post** method in an example. I'll create a form that accepts the user's name and then echoes it back from a CGI script (more on this in Chapter 19). To use the **post** method, you set the **method** attribute of the **<form>** element to **post**. In addition, you set the **action** attribute of the form to the URL that you want the data to be sent to, so I'll use the URL **http://www.starpowder.com/steve/cgi/cgidata.cgi** here.

In the following code for the form, note that I'm including a Submit button, so when the user clicks the button, the data in the text field will be posted to the URL in the **action** attribute. Note also that unless you use the **value** attribute to supply a caption for the Submit button, most browsers, including Netscape Navigator and Internet Explorer, will give the button a caption of Submit Query. Here's the code:

```
<?xml version="1.0"?>
<!DOCTYPE html PUBLIC "-//W3C//DTD XHTML 1.0 Transitional//EN"
"http://www.w3.org/tr/xhtml1/DTD/xhtml1-transitional.dtd">
<html xmlns="http://www.w3.org/1999/xhtml" xml:lang="en" lang="en">
    <head>
        <title>
            CGI Example
        </title>
    </head>

    <body>
        <form method="post"
            action="http://www.starpowder.com/steve/cgi/cgidata.cgi">

            Please enter your name:
            <input type="text" name="text" value="" />
            <center>
```

```
            <p>
                <input type="submit" name="Submit" value="Submit" />
                <input type="reset" />
            </p>
            </center>
        </form>
    </body>
</html>
```

In the "In Depth" section of this chapter, we saw the CGI script that will handle data from this form; the results appear in Figures 12.2 and 12.3.

TIP: You have to be careful with forms and the <layer> and <ilayer> elements. If a <layer> or <ilayer> element is nested inside a <form> element, and any controls for the form are inside the layer, they will not be drawn.

<input type="button">—Creating Buttons

Purpose: Creates an XHTML button in a form. This element takes no content.

When used as HTML: Start tag/End tag: Required/Omitted

Supported: [1.0S, 1.0T, 1.0F, 1.1, 4, IE3, IE4, IE5, NS1, NS2, NS3, NS4]

Attributes:

- **accesskey**—Keyboard shortcut key; a single character is used as the value of this attribute. The user can type a platform-dependent key (such as Alt) with the **accesskey** character to trigger the active field. Set to an alphanumeric character. [1.0S, 1.0T, 1.0F, 1.1, 4, IE4, IE5]

- **class**—Class of the element. [1.0S, 1.0T, 1.0F, 1.1, 4, IE4, IE5]

- **datafld**—Name of the column of the data-source object that supplies the bound data. Set to alphanumeric characters. [IE4, IE5]

- **dataformatas**—Specifies whether bound data is plain text or XHTML. Set to **HTML**, **plaintext**, or **text**. [IE4, IE5]

- **datasrc**—Gives the URL or ID of the data-source object supplying data bound to this element. W3C says this should be a URL; Internet Explorer says it should be a data-source ID. [IE4, IE5]

- **dir**—Gives the direction of directionally neutral text (text that doesn't have an inherent direction in which you should read it). Possible values: **ltr**, left-to-right text or table; and **rtl**, right-to-left text or table. [1.0S, 1.0T, 1.0F, 1.1, 4, IE5]

- **disabled**—Specifies that the element is disabled when first displayed. Standalone attribute in HTML. [1.0S, 1.0T, 1.0F, 1.1, 4, IE4, IE5]
- **id**—Unique alphanumeric identifier for the tag; use the ID to refer to the tag. [1.0S, 1.0T, 1.0F, 1.1, 4, IE4, IE5]
- **lang**—Base language used for the tag. [1.0S, 1.0T, 1.0F, 1.1, 4, IE4, IE5]
- **language**—Scripting language used for the tag. [IE4, IE5]
- **name**—Gives the element a name. Set to alphanumeric characters. Required. [1.0S, 1.0T, 1.0F, 1.1, 4, IE3, IE4, IE5, NS1, NS2, NS3, NS4]
- **size**—Sets the size. [1.0S, 1.0T, 1.0F, 1.1, 4, IE3, IE4, IE5]
- **style**—Inline style indicating how to render the element. [1.0S, 1.0T, 1.0F, 1.1, 4, IE4, IE5]
- **tabindex**—Sets the tab index of the element. This locates it in the tab order of the form, allowing the user to press the Tab key to navigate from element to element. Set to positive or negative integers. [1.0S, 1.0T, 1.0F, 1.1, 4, IE4, IE5]
- **title**—Holds additional information (which might be displayed in tool tips). [1.0S, 1.0T, 1.0F, 1.1, 4, IE4, IE5]
- **type**—Specifies the type of the element. [1.0S, 1.0T, 1.0F, 1.1, 4, IE3, IE4, IE5, NS1, NS2, NS3, NS4]
- **value**—Specifies the caption of the element. Set to alphanumeric characters. [1.0S, 1.0T, 1.0F, 1.1, 4, IE3, IE4, IE5, NS1, NS2, NS3, NS4]
- **xml:lang**—Holds the base language for the element when the document is interpreted as an XML document. [1.0S, 1.0T, 1.0F, 1.1]

XHTML events: onclick, ondblclick, onmousedown, onmouseup, onmouseover, onmousemove, onmouseout, onkeypress, onkeydown, onkeyup, onfocus, onblur, onselect, onchange

- *Internet Explorer*—**onbeforecut, onbeforeeditfocus, onbeforefocusenter, onbeforefocusleave, onbeforepaste, onblur, onclick, oncontextmenu, oncontrolselect, oncut, ondblclick, ondrag, ondragend, ondragenter, ondragleave, ondragover, ondragstart, ondrop, onfilterchange, onfocus, onfocusenter, onfocusleave, onhelp, onkeydown, onkeypress, onkeyup, onlosecapture, onmousedown, onmouseenter, onmouseleave, onmousemove, onmouseout, onmouseover, onmouseup, onpaste, onpropertychange, onreadystatechange, onresize, onresizeend, onresizestart, onselectstart**
- *Netscape Navigator*—**onclick**

"OK," says the novice programmer, "I've created a form. Now how do I add a button to it?" "One way," you say, "is with the **<input>** element, setting the **type** attribute to **button**."

There are now two ways to create buttons in XHTML—with the **<input type="button">** element and with the **<button>** element. I'll look at the first way in this section. In the "In Depth" section of this chapter, we already saw an example showing how to use **<input type="button">**—you use the **value** attribute to set the caption of the button and connect its **onclick** event to code:

```xhtml
<?xml version="1.0"?>
<!DOCTYPE html PUBLIC "-//W3C//DTD XHTML 1.0 Transitional//EN"
"http://www.w3.org/tr/xhtml1/DTD/xhtml1-transitional.dtd">
<html xmlns="http://www.w3.org/1999/xhtml" xml:lang="en" lang="en">
    <head>
        <title>
            Creating XHTML Forms
        </title>

        <script language = "javascript" type = "text/javascript">
            function displayMessage()
            {
                document.form1.textfield.value = "Hello from XHTML!"
            }
        </script>
    </head>

    <body>
        <center>
            <h1>Creating XHTML Forms</h1>
            <form name = "form1" action = "action">
                <input type = "text" name = "textfield" size = "25" />
                <br />
                <br />
                <input type = "button" value = "Display Message"
                    onclick = "displayMessage()" />
            </form>
        </center>
    </body>
</html>
```

You can see the results of this code in Figure 12.1.

Here's another example. I'm creating a button that will reload the current Web page, just as the Reload button in the browser would. To reload the page, I use the **reload** method of the **location** object:

```
<?xml version="1.0"?>
<!DOCTYPE html PUBLIC "-//W3C//DTD XHTML 1.0 Transitional//EN"
"http://www.w3.org/tr/xhtml1/DTD/xhtml1-transitional.dtd">
<html xmlns="http://www.w3.org/1999/xhtml" xml:lang="en" lang="en">
    <head>
        <title>
            Reloading A Web Page
        </title>
    </head>

    <body>
        <center>
            <form name = "form1" action = "action">
                <br />
                <input type = "button" value = "Reload this page"
                    onclick = "location.reload()" />
            </form>
        </center>
    </body>
</html>
```

Supplying a Reload button can be useful if you have many images in your page and the user's browser times out before loading them all. Just have the user click the Reload button, and the browser will download only the remaining images that aren't already in its cache.

TIP: *Internet Explorer 4.x and 5.x use all the white space and carriage returns that you place in the **value** attribute for this element. Note, however, that other browsers (and earlier Internet Explorer versions) do not.*

<input type="checkbox">—Creating Checkboxes

Purpose: Creates a checkbox in a form. This element takes no content.

When used as HTML: Start tag/End tag: Required/Omitted

Supported: [1.0S, 1.0T, 1.0F, 1.1, 2, 3, 3.2, 4, IE1, IE2, IE3, IE4, IE5, NS1, NS2, NS3, NS4]

Attributes:

- **accesskey**—Keyboard shortcut key; a single character is used as the value of this attribute. The user can type a platform-dependent key (such as Alt) with the **accesskey** character to trigger the active field. Set to an alphanumeric character. [1.0S, 1.0T, 1.0F, 1.1, 4, IE4, IE5]

- **checked**—Indicates whether or not the checkbox should appear checked initially. Standalone attribute in HTML. [1.0S, 1.0T, 1.0F, 1.1, 2, 3, 3.2, 4, IE1, IE2, IE3, IE4, IE5, NS1, NS2, NS3, NS4]
- **class**—Class of the element. [1.0S, 1.0T, 1.0F, 1.1, 3, 4, IE4, IE5]
- **datafld**—Name of the column of the data-source object that supplies the bound data. Set to alphanumeric characters. [IE4, IE5]
- **datasrc**—Gives the URL or ID of the data-source object supplying data bound to this element. W3C says this should be a URL; Internet Explorer says it should be a data-source ID. [IE4, IE5]
- **dir**—Gives the direction of directionally neutral text (text that doesn't have an inherent direction in which you should read it). Possible values: **ltr**, left-to-right text or table; and **rtl**, right-to-left text or table. [1.0S, 1.0T, 1.0F, 1.1, 4, IE5]
- **disabled**—Specifies that the element is disabled when first displayed. Standalone attribute in HTML. [1.0S, 1.0T, 1.0F, 1.1, 3, 4, IE4, IE5]
- **id**—Unique alphanumeric identifier for the tag; use the ID to refer to the tag. [1.0S, 1.0T, 1.0F, 1.1, 3, 4, IE4, IE5]
- **lang**—Base language used for the tag. [1.0S, 1.0T, 1.0F, 1.1, 3, 4, IE4, IE5]
- **language**—Scripting language used for the tag. [IE4, IE5]
- **name**—Gives the element a name. Set to alphanumeric characters. Required. [1.0S, 1.0T, 1.0F, 1.1, 2, 3, 3.2, 4, IE1, IE2, IE3, IE4, IE5, NS1, NS2, NS3, NS4]
- **size**—Sets the size. [1.0S, 1.0T, 1.0F, 1.1, 4, IE3, IE4, IE5]
- **style**—Inline style indicating how to render the element. [1.0S, 1.0T, 1.0F, 1.1, 4, IE4, IE5]
- **tabindex**—Sets the tab index of the element. This locates it in the tab order of the form, allowing the user to press the Tab key and navigate from element to element. Set to positive or negative integers. [1.0S, 1.0T, 1.0F, 1.1, 4, IE4, IE5]
- **title**—Holds additional information (which might be displayed in tool tips). [1.0S, 1.0T, 1.0F, 1.1, 2, 3, 4, IE4, IE5]
- **type**—Specifies the type of the element. [1.0S, 1.0T, 1.0F, 1.1, 2, 3, 3.2, 4, IE1, IE2, IE3, IE4, IE5, NS1, NS2, NS3, NS4]
- **value**—Represents the result of the checkbox when clicked, which is passed to the form's action URL. Set to alphanumeric characters. Required. [1.0S, 1.0T, 1.0F, 1.1, 2, 3, 3.2, 4, IE1, IE2, IE3, IE4, IE5, NS1, NS2, NS3, NS4]
- **xml:lang**—Holds the base language for the element when the document is interpreted as an XML document. [1.0S, 1.0T, 1.0F, 1.1]

XHTML events: onclick, ondblclick, onmousedown, onmouseup, onmouseover, onmousemove, onmouseout, onkeypress, onkeydown, onkeyup, onfocus, onblur, onselect, onchange

- *Internet Explorer*—**onbeforecut, onbeforeeditfocus, onbeforefocusenter, onbeforefocusleave, onbeforepaste, onblur, onclick, oncontextmenu, oncontrolselect, oncut, ondblclick, ondrag, ondragend, ondragenter, ondragleave, ondragover, ondragstart, ondrop, onfilterchange, onfocus, onfocusenter, onfocusleave, onhelp, onkeydown, onkeypress, onkeyup, onlosecapture, onmousedown, onmouseenter, onmouseleave, onmousemove, onmouseout, onmouseover, onmouseup, onpaste, onpropertychange, onreadystatechange, onresizeend, onresizestart, onselectstart**

- *Netscape Navigator*—**onclick**

"Darn," says the novice programmer, "I wish there was a button that, when clicked, would *stay* clicked. I'm trying to let the user select options like spell-checking in my Web page." "You can use a checkbox," you say, "and by the way, how does your Web page do spell-checking?" "I haven't got that part worked out yet," admits the NP.

A checkbox is much like a button; when clicked, it stays clicked. Checkboxes are usually drawn as small squares (although this is platform dependent). When a checkbox is clicked, a checkmark appears in the box; when a checkbox is clicked again, the checkmark disappears.

You create checkboxes with the **<input type = "checkbox">** element. As with XHTML buttons, checkboxes have an **onclick** event. Here's an example displaying five checkboxes and indicating which one was clicked:

```
<?xml version="1.0"?>
<!DOCTYPE html PUBLIC "-//W3C//DTD XHTML 1.0 Transitional//EN"
"http://www.w3.org/tr/xhtml1/DTD/xhtml1-transitional.dtd">
<html xmlns="http://www.w3.org/1999/xhtml" xml:lang="en" lang="en">
    <head>
        <title>
            Using Check Boxes
        </title>

        <script language = "javascript" type = "text/javascript">
            function check1Clicked()
            {
                document.form1.textfield.value = "You clicked check box 1."
            }
```

```
        function check2Clicked()
        {
            document.form1.textfield.value = "You clicked check box 2."
        }

        function check3Clicked()
        {
            document.form1.textfield.value = "You clicked check box 3."
        }

        function check4Clicked()
        {
            document.form1.textfield.value = "You clicked check box 4."
        }

        function check5Clicked()
        {
            document.form1.textfield.value = "You clicked check box 5."
        }
    </script>
</head>

<body>
    <center>
        <h1>
            Using Check Boxes
        </h1>

        <form name = "form1" action = "action">
            <table border = "1" bgcolor = "cyan" width = "200">
            <tr><td>
            <input type = "checkbox" name = "check1" onclick =
                "check1Clicked()" />Check 1
            </td></tr>
            <tr><td>
                <input type = "checkbox" name = "check2" onclick =
                    "check2Clicked()" />Check 2
            </td></tr>
            <tr><td>
                <input type = "checkbox" name = "check3" onclick =
                    "check3Clicked()" />Check 3
            </td></tr>
            <tr><td>
                <input type = "checkbox" name = "check4" onclick =
```

```
                            "check4Clicked()" />Check 4
                    </td></tr>
                    <tr><td>
                        <input type = "checkbox" name = "check5" onclick =
                            "check5Clicked()" />Check 5
                    </td></tr>
                    </table>
                    <br />
                        <input type = "text" name = "textfield" size = "25" />
                </form>
            </center>
        </body>
</html>
```

The result of this XHTML appears in Figure 12.5. When the user clicks a checkbox, the code indicates which one was checked.

The code in this example is longer than it needs to be. Rather than having a separate function for each checkbox, you can use the same function for all checkboxes and examine each checkbox's **checked** property (for example, **document.form1.check1.checked**) to see if the checkbox is displaying a checkmark. You can also set this property to **true** or **false** to select or clear the checkbox.

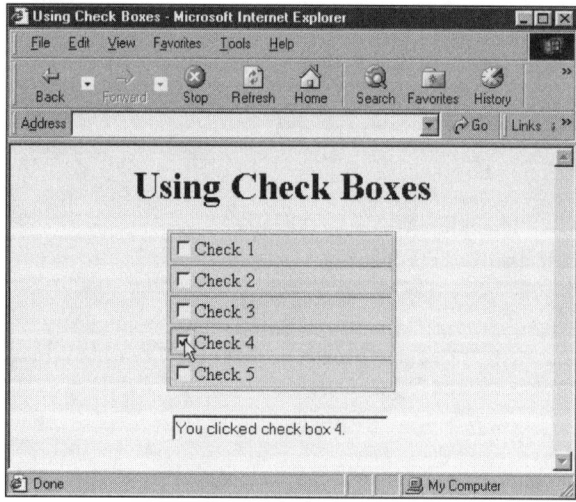

Figure 12.5   Using checkboxes.

<input type="file">—Creating File Input for a Form

Purpose: Lets the user upload files. This element takes no content.

When used as HTML: Start tag/End tag: Required/Omitted

Supported: [1.0S, 1.0T, 1.0F, 1.1, 3, 3.2, 4, IE4, IE5, NS2, NS3, NS4]

Attributes:

- **accept**—Sets the MIME type of the file transfer. Set to a MIME type or to a space-separated or comma-separated list of MIME types. [1.0S, 1.0T, 1.0F, 1.1, 4]
- **accesskey**—Keyboard shortcut key; a single character is used as the value of this attribute. The user can type a platform-dependent key (such as Alt) with the **accesskey** character to trigger the active field. Set to an alphanumeric character. [1.0S, 1.0T, 1.0F, 1.1, 4, IE4, IE5]
- **class**—Class of the element. [1.0S, 1.0T, 1.0F, 1.1, 4, IE4, IE5]
- **datafld**—Name of the column of the data-source object that supplies the bound data. Set to alphanumeric characters. [IE4, IE5]
- **datasrc**—Gives the URL or ID of the data-source object supplying data bound to this element. W3C says this should be a URL; Internet Explorer says it should be a data-source ID. [IE4, IE5]
- **dir**—Gives the direction of directionally neutral text (text that doesn't have an inherent direction in which you should read it). Possible values: **ltr**, left-to-right text or table; and **rtl**, right-to-left text or table. [1.0S, 1.0T, 1.0F, 1.1, 4, IE5]
- **disabled**—Specifies that the element is disabled when first displayed. Standalone attribute in HTML. [1.0S, 1.0T, 1.0F, 1.1, 3, 4, IE4, IE5]
- **id**—Unique alphanumeric identifier for the tag; use the ID to refer to the tag. [1.0S, 1.0T, 1.0F, 1.1, 4, IE4, IE5]
- **lang**—Base language used for the tag. [1.0S, 1.0T, 1.0F, 1.1, 4, IE4, IE5]
- **language**—Scripting language used for the tag. [IE4, IE5]
- **name**—Gives the element a name. Set to alphanumeric characters. Required. [1.0S, 1.0T, 1.0F, 1.1, 4, IE3, IE4, IE5, NS2, NS3, NS4]
- **size**—Sets the size. [1.0S, 1.0T, 1.0F, 1.1, 4, IE3, IE4, IE5]
- **style**—Inline style indicating how to render the element. [1.0S, 1.0T, 1.0F, 1.1, 4, IE4, IE5]
- **tabindex**—Sets the tab index of the element. This locates it in the tab order of the form, allowing the user to press the Tab key to navigate from

element to element. Set to positive or negative integers. [1.0S, 1.0T, 1.0F, 1.1, 4, IE4, IE5]

- **title**—Holds additional information (which might be displayed in tool tips). [1.0S, 1.0T, 1.0F, 1.1, 4, IE4, IE5]

- **type**—Specifies the type of the element. [1.0S, 1.0T, 1.0F, 1.1, 3, 3.2, 4, IE4, IE5, NS2, NS3, NS4]

- **xml:lang**—Holds the base language for the element when the document is interpreted as an XML document. [1.0S, 1.0T, 1.0F, 1.1]

XHTML events: onclick, ondblclick, onmousedown, onmouseup, onmouseover, onmousemove, onmouseout, onkeypress, onkeydown, onkeyup, onfocus, onblur, onselect, onchange

- *Internet Explorer*—**onbeforecut, onbeforeeditfocus, onbeforefocusenter, onbeforefocusleave, onbeforepaste, onblur, onclick, oncontextmenu, oncontrolselect, oncut, ondblclick, ondrag, ondragend, ondragenter, ondragleave, ondragover, ondragstart, ondrop, onfilterchange, onfocus, onfocusenter, onfocusleave, onhelp, onkeydown, onkeypress, onkeyup, onlosecapture, onmousedown, onmouseenter, onmouseleave, onmousemove, onmouseout, onmouseover, onmouseup, onpaste, onpropertychange, onreadystatechange, onresize, onresizeend, onresizestart, onselectstart**

- *Netscape Navigator*—None

The big boss appears and says, "We need to automate things now that we're displaying advertising on our Web site. What I want is one page that lets our operators enter the number of paid hits for each ad banner and that uploads the banner image itself." "No problem," you say. "I'll just use **<input type="file">**." "Whatever," says the BB.

You can upload files with the **<input type="file">** element. You need to add code on the server to handle any file that's been uploaded, so I'll do this with a CGI script. (To decipher what's going on here, see Chapter 19 on Perl.) One item to note is that if you use **<input type="file">**, you also need to set the **<form>** element's **enctype** attribute to **"multipart/form-data"**.

In this case, I'll create a Web page that will upload files and display their contents. I'll use a file named, originally enough, file.txt, which has this content:

```
Here is some text!
```

Here's the Perl CGI script that will create the file-upload control:

```perl
#!/usr/local/bin/perl

use CGI;

$co = new CGI;

if (!$co->param())
{
    print $co->header,
        $co->start_html('CGI File Upload Example'),
        $co->center(
        $co->br,
        $co->center($co->h1('CGI File Upload Example')),
        $co->start_multipart_form,
        $co->filefield(-name=>'filename', -size=>30),
        $co->br,
        $co->submit(-value=>'Upload'),
        $co->reset,
        $co->end_form
    ),
    $co->hr;

} else {
    print
        $co->header,
        $co->start_html('CGI File Upload Example'),
        $co->center($co->h1('CGI File Upload Example'));

    $file = $co->param('filename');

    @data = <$file>;

    foreach (@data) {
        s/\n/<br>/g;
    }

    print
        $co->center($co->h2("Here's the contents of $file...")),
        "@data";
}

print $co->end_html;
```

This CGI script uses the Perl CGI.pm module, which creates HTML (not XHTML yet). In the following code, note that I haven't added an **action** attribute to the **<form>** element, so data is sent back to the same CGI script when the user clicks the Submit button or, in this case, the Upload button. Here's the HTML created by this CGI script:

```
<html>
    <head>
        <title>
            CGI File Upload Example
        </title>
    </head>

    <body>
        <center>
            <br>
            <h1>
                CGI File Upload Example
            </h1>

            <form method="post"  enctype="multipart/form-data">
                <input type="file" name="filename" value="" size=30>
                <br>
                <input type="submit" name="submit" value="upload">
                <input type="reset">
            </form>
        </center>
        <hr>
    </body>
</html>
```

You can see this page in Figure 12.6. The file-upload control is actually two controls—a text field and a Browse button. If users click the Browse button, they can

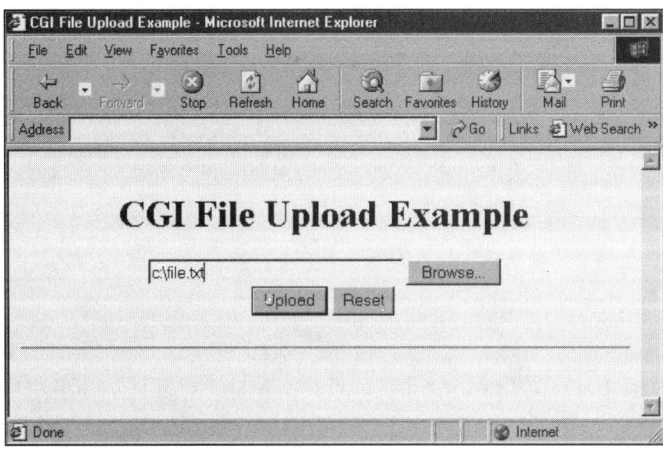

Figure 12.6   Uploading a file.

browse their disks to find the file to upload. In this case, I've just entered that file's path and name directly into the text field.

When the user clicks the Upload button (which is just a Submit button with the caption "Upload"), the contents of the file are sent to the CGI script. This script then displays the contents in a Web page, as you see in Figure 12.7.

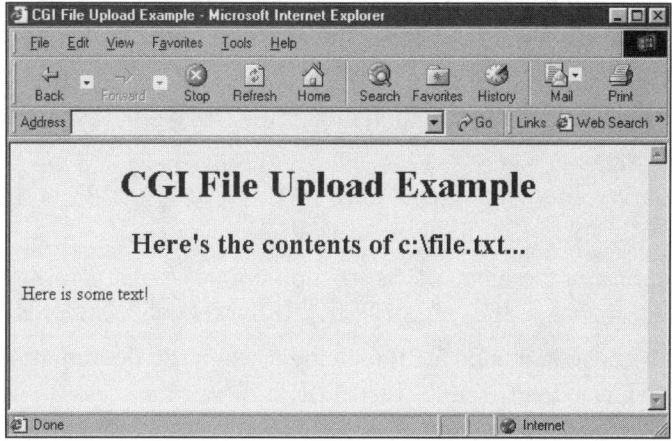

Figure 12.7   Displaying the contents of the uploaded file.

<input type="hidden">—Creating Hidden Data

Purpose: Stores hidden data; data is not visible to users unless they view the page source. This element takes no content.

When used as HTML: Start tag/End tag: Required/Omitted

Supported: [1.0S, 1.0T, 1.0F, 1.1, 2, 3, 3.2, 4, IE1, IE2, IE3, IE4, IE5, NS1, NS2, NS3, NS4]

Attributes:

- **class**—Class of the element. [1.0S, 1.0T, 1.0F, 1.1, 4, IE4, IE5]

- **datafld**—Name of the column of the data-source object that supplies the bound data. Set to alphanumeric characters. [IE4, IE5]

- **datasrc**—Gives the URL or ID of the data-source object supplying data bound to this element. W3C says this should be a URL; Internet Explorer says it should be a data-source ID. [IE4, IE5]

- **dir**—Gives the direction of directionally neutral text (text that doesn't have an inherent direction in which you should read it). Possible values: **ltr**, left-to-right text or table; and **rtl**, right-to-left text or table. [1.0S, 1.0T, 1.0F, 1.1, 4]

- **id**—Unique alphanumeric identifier for the tag; use the ID to refer to the tag. [1.0S, 1.0T, 1.0F, 1.1, 4, IE4, IE5]
- **lang**—Base language used for the tag. [1.0S, 1.0T, 1.0F, 1.1, 4, IE4, IE5]
- **language**—Scripting language used for the tag. [IE4, IE5]
- **name**—Gives the element a name. Set to alphanumeric characters. Required. [1.0S, 1.0T, 1.0F, 1.1, 4, IE3, IE4, IE5, NS1, NS2, NS3, NS4]
- **style**—Inline style indicating how to render the element. [1.0S, 1.0T, 1.0F, 1.1, 4, IE4, IE5]
- **title**—Holds additional information (which might be displayed in tool tips). [1.0S, 1.0T, 1.0F, 1.1, 4]
- **type**—Specifies the type of the element. [1.0S, 1.0T, 1.0F, 1.1, 2, 3, 3.2, 4, IE1, IE2, IE3, IE4, IE5, NS1, NS2, NS3, NS4]
- **value**—Sets the caption of the element. Set to alphanumeric characters. [1.0S, 1.0T, 1.0F, 1.1, 2, 3, 3.2, 4, IE1, IE2, IE3, IE4, IE5, NS1, NS2, NS3, NS4]
- **xml:lang**—Holds the base language for the element when the document is interpreted as an XML document. [1.0S, 1.0T, 1.0F, 1.1]

XHTML events: onclick, ondblclick, onmousedown, onmouseup, onmouseover, onmousemove, onmouseout, onkeypress, onkeydown, onkeyup, onfocus, onblur, onselect, onchange

- *Internet Explorer*—**onbeforeeditfocus, onbeforefocusenter, onbeforefocusleave, oncontrolselect, onfocus, onfocusenter, onfocusleave, onlosecapture, onpropertychange, onreadystatechange, onresizeend, onresizestart**
- *Netscape Navigator*—None

"I'm creating a Web word game," the novice programmer says, "and I don't want to have to keep track of the secret word on the server. Is there any way to store the secret word in the Web page that users see, but make sure they can't see that word?" "Sure," you say; "use an **<input type="hidden">** control. The control holds hidden text that users won't see in the Web page. Problem solved."

You can store invisible text in a hidden control in a Web page; you create this hidden control with the **<input type="hidden">** element. Hidden controls store text that you can read later and can be very useful by providing, for example, an alternative to cookies.

In this next example, I'll display the text "Hello from XHTML!" in a text field and store it in a hidden control. The user can edit the text in the text field, and then restore it from the hidden control just by clicking a button. Here's the XHTML:

```
<?xml version="1.0"?>
<!DOCTYPE html PUBLIC "-//W3C//DTD XHTML 1.0 Transitional//EN"
"http://www.w3.org/tr/xhtml1/DTD/xhtml1-transitional.dtd">
<html xmlns="http://www.w3.org/1999/xhtml" xml:lang="en" lang="en">
    <head>
        <title>
            Using Hidden Controls
        </title>
        <script language = "javascript" type = "text/javascript">
            function restoreText()
            {
                document.form1.Textbox.value = document.form1.backup.value
            }
        </script>
    </head>

    <body>
        <center>
            <h1>
                Edit the text, then click the "Restore text" button
                to restore it.
            </h1>

            <br />

            <form name = "form1" action = "action">
                <input type = "text" value="Hello from XHTML!"
                    name = "Textbox" size = "25" />
                <br />
                <br />
                <input type = "button" value = "Restore text"
                    onclick = "restoreText()" />
                <input type = "hidden" name = "backup" value =
                    "Hello from XHTML!" />
            </form>
        </center>
    </body>
</html>
```

You can see the results of this XHTML in Figure 12.8. When the user edits the text and then clicks the "Restore text" button, the original text is restored from the hidden control to the text field.

TIP: *If you're worried about security, you should know that storing text in a hidden control is not secure. The user can always view what's in the hidden control simply by viewing the source XHTML in the browser.*

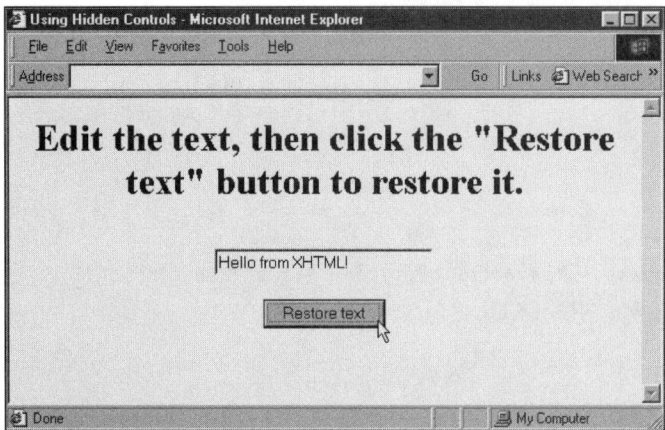

Figure 12.8   Restoring data from a hidden control.

<input type="image">—Creating Image Submit Buttons

Purpose: Specifies an image that users can click, much as they would a Submit button. The mouse coordinates in the image are also passed to the form's action URL. This element takes no content.

When used as HTML: Start tag/End tag: Required/Omitted

Supported: [1.0S, 1.0T, 1.0F, 1.1, 2, 3, 3.2, 4, IE1, IE2, IE3, IE4, IE5, NS1, NS2, NS3, NS4]

Attributes:

- **accesskey**—Keyboard shortcut key; a single character is used as the value of this attribute. The user can type a platform-dependent key (such as Alt) with the **accesskey** character to trigger the active field. Set to an alphanumeric character. [1.0S, 1.0T, 1.0F, 1.1, 4, IE4, IE5]

- **align**—Sets the alignment of text following the image. Set to **left**, **right**, **top** (the default), **texttop**, **middle**, **absmiddle**, **baseline**, **bottom**, or **absbottom**. [1.0T, 1.0F, 2, 3, 3.2, 4, IE1, IE2, IE3, IE4, IE5, NS1, NS2, NS3, NS4]

- **alt**—Sets the text that should be displayed for browsers that cannot handle images. Set to an alphanumeric string. [1.0S, 1.0T, 1.0F, 1.1, 4]

- **class**—Class of the element. [1.0S, 1.0T, 1.0F, 1.1, 3, 4, IE4, IE5]

- **datafld**—Name of the column of the data-source object that supplies the bound data. Set to alphanumeric characters. [IE4, IE5]

- **datasrc**—Gives the URL or ID of the data-source object supplying data bound to this element. W3C says this should be a URL; Internet Explorer says it should be a data-source ID. [IE4, IE5]

- **dir**—Gives the direction of directionally neutral text (text that doesn't have an inherent direction in which you should read it). Possible values: **ltr**, left-to-right text or table; and **rtl**, right-to-left text or table. [1.0S, 1.0T, 1.0F, 1.1, 4, IE5]

- **disabled**—Specifies that the element is disabled when first displayed. Standalone attribute in HTML. [1.0S, 1.0T, 1.0F, 1.1, 3, 4, IE4, IE5]

- **id**—Unique alphanumeric identifier for the tag; use the ID to refer to the tag. [1.0S, 1.0T, 1.0F, 1.1, 3, 4, IE4, IE5]

- **lang**—Base language used for the tag. [1.0S, 1.0T, 1.0F, 1.1, 3, 4, IE4, IE5]

- **language**—Scripting language used for the tag. [IE4, IE5]

- **name**—Gives the element a name. Set to alphanumeric characters. Required. [1.0S, 1.0T, 1.0F, 1.1, 2, 3, 3.2, 4, IE1, IE2, IE3, IE4, IE5, NS1, NS2, NS3, NS4]

- **src**—Specifies the URL of the image. Set to a URL. [1.0S, 1.0T, 1.0F, 1.1, 2, 3, 3.2, 4, IE1, IE2, IE3, IE4, IE5, NS1, NS2, NS3, NS4]

- **size**—Sets the size. [1.0S, 1.0T, 1.0F, 1.1, 4, IE3, IE4, IE5]

- **style**—Inline style indicating how to render the element. [1.0S, 1.0T, 1.0F, 1.1, 4, IE4, IE5]

- **tabindex**—Sets the tab index of the element. This locates it in the tab order of the form, allowing the user to press the Tab key to navigate from element to element. Set to positive or negative integers. [1.0S, 1.0T, 1.0F, 1.1, 4, IE4, IE5]

- **title**—Holds additional information (which might be displayed in tool tips). [1.0S, 1.0T, 1.0F, 1.1, 3, 4, IE4, IE5]

- **type**—Specifies the type of the element. [1.0S, 1.0T, 1.0F, 1.1, 2, 3, 3.2, 4, IE1, IE2, IE3, IE4, IE5, NS1, NS2, NS3, NS4]

- **value**—Indicates the symbolic result of the field that is passed to the form-processing script. [1.0S, 1.0T, 1.0F, 1.1, 2, 3, 3.2, 4 IE5, NS1, NS2, NS3, NS4]

- **xml:lang**—Holds the base language for the element when the document is interpreted as an XML document. [1.0S, 1.0T, 1.0F, 1.1]

XHTML events: onclick, ondblclick, onmousedown, onmouseup, onmouseover, onmousemove, onmouseout, onkeypress, onkeydown, onkeyup, onfocus, onblur, onselect, onchange

- *Internet Explorer*—**onbeforecut, onbeforeeditfocus, onbeforefocusenter, onbeforefocusleave, onbeforepaste, onblur, onclick, oncontextmenu, oncontrolselect, oncut, ondblclick, ondrag, ondragend, ondragenter,**

ondragleave, ondragover, ondragstart, ondrop, onfilterchange, onfocus, onfocusenter, onfocusleave, onhelp, onkeydown, onkeypress, onkeyup, onlosecapture, onmousedown, onmouseenter, onmouseleave, onmousemove, onmouseout, onmouseover, onmouseup, onpaste, onpropertychange, onreadystatechange, onresize, onresizeend, onresizestart, onselectstart

- *Netscape Navigator*—None

There's an easy way to use an image as a Submit button in a form—just use the **<input type="image">** element. To indicate what image to use, you set the **src** attribute.

Here's an example of using an image, submit.gif, as a Submit button:

```
<?xml version="1.0"?>
<!DOCTYPE html PUBLIC "-//W3C//DTD XHTML 1.0 Transitional//EN"
"http://www.w3.org/tr/xhtml1/DTD/xhtml1-transitional.dtd">
<html xmlns="http://www.w3.org/1999/xhtml" xml:lang="en" lang="en">
    <head>
        <title>
            CGI Example
        </title>
    </head>

    <body>
        <center>
            <h1>
                Using An Image Control
            </h1>
            <form method="post"
                action="http://www.starpowder.com/steve/cgi/cgidata.cgi">
                    Please enter your name:
                    <input type="text" name="text" />
                    <p>
                        <input type="image" src="submit.gif"
                        name="Submit" value="Submit" />
                    </p>
            </form>
        </center>
    </body>
</html>
```

You can see the results of this XHTML in Figure 12.9.

Figure 12.9   Using an image Submit button.

<input type="password">—Creating Password Controls

Purpose: Creates a password text field, which masks typed input. This element takes no content.

When used as HTML: Start tag/End tag: Required/Omitted

Supported: [1.0S, 1.0T, 1.0F, 1.1, 2, 3, 3.2, 4, IE1, IE2, IE3, IE4, IE5, NS1, NS2, NS3, NS4]

Attributes:

- **accesskey**—Keyboard shortcut key; a single character is used as the value of this attribute. The user can type a platform-dependent key (such as Alt) with the **accesskey** character to trigger the active field. Set to an alphanumeric character. [1.0S, 1.0T, 1.0F, 1.1, 4, IE4, IE5]

- **autocomplete**—Set to **true** (the default) if you want Internet Explorer to automatically complete data typed into the control based on what the user has entered before. [IE5]

- **class**—Class of the element. [1.0S, 1.0T, 1.0F, 1.1, 3, 4, IE4, IE5]

- **datafld**—Name of the column of the data-source object that supplies the bound data. Set to alphanumeric characters. [IE4, IE5]

- **datasrc**—Gives the URL or ID of the data-source object supplying data bound to this element. W3C says this should be a URL; Internet Explorer says it should be a data-source ID. [IE4, IE5]

- **dir**—Gives the direction of directionally neutral text (text that doesn't have an inherent direction in which you should read it). Possible values: **ltr**, left-to-right text or table; and **rtl**, right-to-left text or table. [1.0S, 1.0T, 1.0F, 1.1, 4, IE5]

- **disabled**—Specifies that the element is disabled when first displayed. Standalone attribute in HTML. [1.0S, 1.0T, 1.0F, 1.1, 3, 4, IE4, IE5]

- **id**—Unique alphanumeric identifier for the tag; use the ID to refer to the tag. [1.0S, 1.0T, 1.0F, 1.1, 3, 4, IE4, IE5]

- **lang**—Base language used for the tag. [1.0S, 1.0T, 1.0F, 1.1, 3, 4, IE4, IE5]

- **language**—Scripting language used for the tag. [IE4, IE5]

- **maxlength**—Sets the maximum length of the data in the control, in characters. [NS2, NS3, NS4, IE3, IE4, IE5]

- **name**—Gives the element a name. Set to alphanumeric characters. Required. [1.0S, 1.0T, 1.0F, 1.1, 2, 3, 3.2, 4, IE1, IE2, IE3, IE4, IE5, NS1, NS2, NS3, NS4]

- **readonly**—Set to **true** if you want the control to be read-only. [IE4, IE5]

- **size**—Specifies the size. [1.0S, 1.0T, 1.0F, 1.1, 4, IE3, IE4, IE5]

- **style**—Inline style indicating how to render the element. [1.0S, 1.0T, 1.0F, 1.1, 4, IE4, IE5]

- **tabindex**—Sets the tab index of the element. This locates it in the tab order of the form, allowing the user to press the Tab key to navigate from element to element. Set to positive or negative integers. [1.0S, 1.0T, 1.0F, 1.1, 4, IE4, IE5]

- **title**—Holds additional information (which might be displayed in tool tips). [1.0S, 1.0T, 1.0F, 1.1, 2, 3, 4, IE4, IE5]

- **type**—Specifies the type of the element. [1.0S, 1.0T, 1.0F, 1.1, 2, 3, 3.2, 4, IE1, IE2, IE3, IE4, IE5, NS1, NS2, NS3, NS4]

- **value**—Sets the default contents of the element. Set to an alphanumeric string. [1.0S, 1.0T, 1.0F, 1.1, 2, 3, 3.2, 4, IE1, IE2, IE3, IE4, IE5, NS1, NS2, NS3, NS4]

- **xml:lang**—Holds the base language for the element when the document is interpreted as an XML document. [1.0S, 1.0T, 1.0F, 1.1]

XHTML events: onclick, ondblclick, onmousedown, onmouseup, onmouseover, onmousemove, onmouseout, onkeypress, onkeydown, onkeyup, onfocus, onblur, onselect, onchange

- *Internet Explorer*—**onbeforecut, onbeforeeditfocus, onbeforefocusenter, onbeforefocusleave, onbeforepaste, onblur, onclick, oncontextmenu, oncontrolselect, oncut, ondblclick, ondrag, ondragend, ondragenter, ondragleave, ondragover, ondragstart, ondrop, onfilterchange, onfocus, onfocusenter, onfocusleave, onhelp, onkeydown, onkeypress, onkeyup, onlosecapture, onmousedown, onmouseenter, onmouseleave, onmousemove, onmouseout, onmouseover, onmouseup, onpaste, onpropertychange, onreadystatechange, onresize, onresizeend, onresizestart, onselectstart**

- *Netscape Navigator*—**onselect**

"Uh oh," says the novice programmer. "That darn Johnson was looking over my shoulder as I entered my password. Now what?" "Well," you say, "the first thing to do is to use a password control in your Web page from now on." "Thanks a lot," says the NP.

Password controls are just like text fields except that each character you enter appears as an asterisk (*), not as the character you typed. For example, the password "open sesame!" will be displayed as "************". In script, you can get the actual value of the password just by using the control's **value** property.

Here's an example. The user enters a password in a password control, and when the button is clicked, the actual text in the password control appears in a text field:

```
<?xml version="1.0"?>
<!DOCTYPE html PUBLIC "-//W3C//DTD XHTML 1.0 Transitional//EN"
"http://www.w3.org/tr/xhtml1/DTD/xhtml1-transitional.dtd">
<html xmlns="http://www.w3.org/1999/xhtml" xml:lang="en" lang="en">
    <head>
        <title>
            Using Password Controls
        </title>

        <script language = "javascript" type = "text/javascript">
            function showPassword()
            {
                document.form1.textfield.value = "Password:" +
                    document.form1.password.value
            }
        </script>
    </head>
```

```
<body>
    <center>
        <h1>
            Enter a password in the password field and click the button.
        </h1>

        <form name = "form1" action = "action">
            <input type = "password" name = "password" size = "25" />
            <br />
            <br />
            <input type = "text" name = "textfield" size = "25" />
            <br />
            <br />
            <input type = "button" value = "Show Password"
                onclick = "showPassword()" />
        </form>
    </center>
</body>
</html>
```

The results of this XHTML appear in Figure 12.10. Entering a password results in a string of asterisks, but you can access the actual password in your script.

TIP: *Would-be hackers might try to select the text in the password control and paste it into another control to see what that text is, but you don't have to worry. When you copy text from a password control (as when you press Ctrl+C in Windows), all you get is a series of asterisks.*

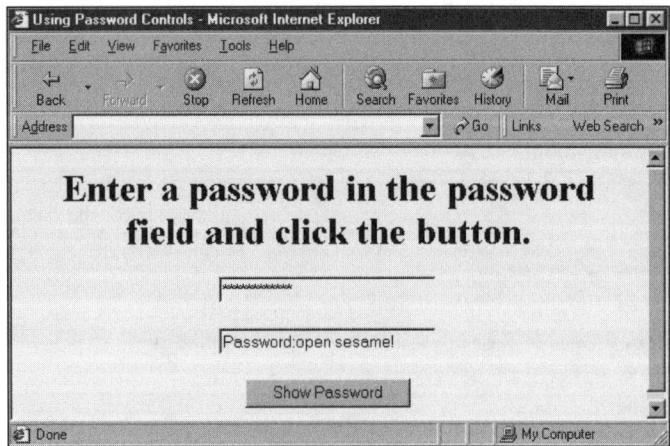

Figure 12.10   Using a password control.

<input type="radio">—Creating Radio Buttons

Purpose: Creates a radio button in a form. This element takes no content.

When used as HTML: Start tag/End tag: Required/Omitted

Supported: [1.0S, 1.0T, 1.0F, 1.1, 2, 3, 3.2, 4, IE1, IE2, IE3, IE4, IE5, NS1, NS2, NS3, NS4]

Attributes:

- **accesskey**—Keyboard shortcut key; a single character is used as the value of this attribute. The user can type a platform-dependent key (such as Alt) with the **accesskey** character to trigger the active field. Set to an alphanumeric character. [1.0S, 1.0T, 1.0F, 1.1, 4, IE4, IE5]

- **checked**—Indicates whether or not the radio button should appear checked initially. Standalone attribute in HTML. [1.0S, 1.0T, 1.0F, 1.1, 2, 3, 3.2, 4, IE1, IE2, IE3, IE4, IE5, NS1, NS2, NS3, NS4]

- **class**—Class of the element. [1.0S, 1.0T, 1.0F, 1.1, 3, 4, IE4, IE5]

- **datafld**—Name of the column of the data-source object that supplies the bound data. Set to alphanumeric characters. [IE4, IE5]

- **datasrc**—Gives the URL or ID of the data-source object supplying data bound to this element. W3C says this should be a URL; Internet Explorer says it should be a data-source ID. [IE4, IE5]

- **dir**—Gives the direction of directionally neutral text (text that doesn't have an inherent direction in which you should read it). Possible values: **ltr**, left-to-right text or table; and **rtl**, right-to-left text or table. [1.0S, 1.0T, 1.0F, 1.1, 4, IE5]

- **disabled**—Specifies that the element is disabled when first displayed. Standalone attribute in HTML. [1.0S, 1.0T, 1.0F, 1.1, 4, IE4, IE5]

- **id**—Unique alphanumeric identifier for the tag; use the ID to refer to the tag. [1.0S, 1.0T, 1.0F, 1.1, 3, 4, IE4, IE5]

- **lang**—Base language used for the tag. [1.0S, 1.0T, 1.0F, 1.1, 3, 4, IE4, IE5]

- **language**—Scripting language used for the tag. [IE4, IE5]

- **name**—Gives the element a name. Set to alphanumeric characters. Required. [1.0S, 1.0T, 1.0F, 1.1, 2, 3, 3.2, 4, IE1, IE2, IE3, IE4, IE5, NS1, NS2, NS3, NS4]

- **style**—Inline style indicating how to render the element. [1.0S, 1.0T, 1.0F, 1.1, 4, IE4, IE5]

- **size**—Sets the control's size. [1.0S, 1.0T, 1.0F, 1.1, 4, IE3, IE4, IE5]

- **tabindex**—Sets the tab index of the element. This locates it in the tab order of the form, allowing the user to press the Tab key to navigate from element to element. Set to positive or negative integers. [1.0S, 1.0T, 1.0F, 1.1, 4, IE4, IE5]

- **title**—Holds additional information (which might be displayed in tool tips). [1.0S, 1.0T, 1.0F, 1.1, 2, 3, 4, IE4, IE5]

- **type**—Specifies the type of the element. [1.0S, 1.0T, 1.0F, 1.1, 2, 3, 3.2, 4, IE1, IE2, IE3, IE4, IE5, NS1, NS2, NS3, NS4]

- **value**—Represents the result of the radio button when clicked; the result is passed to the form's action URL. Set to alphanumeric characters. Required. [1.0S, 1.0T, 1.0F, 1.1, 2, 3, 3.2, 4, IE1, IE2, IE3, IE4, IE5, NS1, NS2, NS3, NS4]

- **xml:lang**—Holds the base language for the element when the document is interpreted as an XML document. [1.0S, 1.0T, 1.0F, 1.1]

XHTML events: onclick, ondblclick, onmousedown, onmouseup, onmouseover, onmousemove, onmouseout, onkeypress, onkeydown, onkeyup, onfocus, onblur, onselect, onchange

- *Internet Explorer*—**onbeforecut, onbeforeeditfocus, onbeforefocusenter, onbeforefocusleave, onbeforepaste, onblur, onclick, oncontextmenu, oncontrolselect, oncut, ondblclick, ondrag, ondragend, ondragenter, ondragleave, ondragover, ondragstart, ondrop, onfilterchange, onfocus, onfocusenter, onfocusleave, onhelp, onkeydown, onkeypress, onkeyup, onlosecapture, onmousedown, onmouseenter, onmouseleave, onmousemove, onmouseout, onmouseover, onmouseup, onpaste, onpropertychange, onreadystatechange, onresizeend, onresizestart, onselectstart**

- *Netscape Navigator*—**onclick**

"Uh oh," says the novice programmer, "I have a problem. Users are supposed to enter the day of the week by clicking a checkbox, but sometimes they leave two checkboxes clicked, and my code gets all messed up." "That's an easy one," you say; "just use radio buttons instead of checkboxes."

Radio buttons can be selected and unselected just as checkboxes can, but you can *group* radio buttons together so that only one radio button in the group can be selected at one time. (If the user clicks a new radio button, the previously selected one is automatically deselected.)

Like checkboxes, radio buttons have an **onclick** event that you can use to connect them to code. To create a group of mutually exclusive radio buttons, you give them all the same name by using the **name** attribute. (You can have multiple groups of radio buttons in the same page.) Here's an example that displays five radio buttons in a group and indicates which one the user clicked:

```xml
<?xml version="1.0"?>
<!DOCTYPE html PUBLIC "-//W3C//DTD XHTML 1.0 Transitional//EN"
"http://www.w3.org/tr/xhtml1/DTD/xhtml1-transitional.dtd">
<html xmlns="http://www.w3.org/1999/xhtml" xml:lang="en" lang="en">
    <head>
        <title>
            Using Radio Buttons
        </title>

        <script language = "javascript" type = "text/javascript">
            function radio1Clicked()
            {
                document.form1.TextBox.value =
                    "You clicked radio button 1."
            }

            function radio2Clicked()
            {
                document.form1.TextBox.value =
                    "You clicked radio button 2."
            }

            function radio3Clicked()
            {
                document.form1.TextBox.value =
                    "You clicked radio button 3."
            }

            function radio4Clicked()
            {
                document.form1.TextBox.value =
                    "You clicked radio button 4."
            }

            function radio5Clicked()
            {
                document.form1.TextBox.value =
                    "You clicked radio button 5."
            }
        </script>

    </head>
```

```
<body>
    <form name = "form1" action = "action">
        <center>
            <h1>
                Using Radio Buttons
            </h1>

            <table border="1" bgcolor = "cyan" width = "200">
            <tr><td>
            <input type = "radio" name = "RadioButtons"
                onclick = "radio1Clicked()" />Radio 1
            </td></tr>
            <tr><td>
            <input type = "radio" name = "RadioButtons"
                onclick = "radio2Clicked()" />Radio 2
            </td></tr>
            <tr><td>
            <input type = "radio" name = "RadioButtons"
                onclick = "radio3Clicked()" />Radio 3
            </td></tr>
            <tr><td>
            <input type = "radio" name = "RadioButtons"
                onclick = "radio4Clicked()" />Radio 4
            </td></tr>
            <tr><td>
            <input type = "radio" name = "RadioButtons"
                onclick = "radio5Clicked()" />Radio 5
            </td></tr>
            </table>
            <br />
            <input type = "text" name = "TextBox" size = "35" />
        </center>
    </form>
</body>
</html>
```

You can see the results in Figure 12.11. When the user clicks one radio button, it's selected and all the others are deselected. Radio buttons are a good idea when you want to let the user select from a set of mutually exclusive options, such as days of the week.

The code in this example is longer than it needs to be. Rather than having a separate function for each radio button, you can use the same function for all radio buttons and examine each radio button's **checked** property (for example, **document.form1.radio1**) to see if the radio button is selected. You can also set this property to **true** or **false** to select or deselect the radio button.

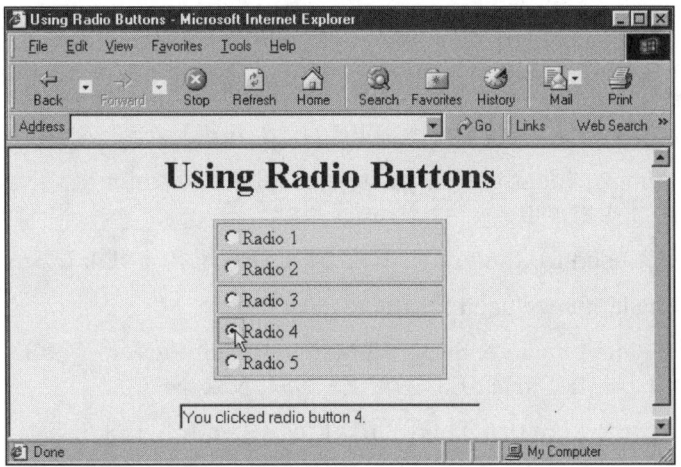

Figure 12.11   Using radio buttons.

<input type="reset">—Creating Reset Buttons

Purpose: In a form, creates a Reset button that resets all fields to their original values. This element takes no content.

When used as HTML: Start tag/End tag: Required/Omitted

Supported: [1.0S, 1.0T, 1.0F, 1.1, 2, 3, 3.2, 4, IE1, IE2, IE3, IE4, IE5, NS1, NS2, NS3, NS4]

Attributes:

- **accesskey**—Keyboard shortcut key; a single character is used as the value of this attribute. The user can type a platform-dependent key (such as Alt) with the **accesskey** character to trigger the active field. Set to an alphanumeric character. [1.0S, 1.0T, 1.0F, 1.1, 4, IE4, IE5]
- **class**—Class of the element. [1.0S, 1.0T, 1.0F, 1.1, 3, 4, IE4, IE5]
- **datafld**—Name of the column of the data-source object that supplies the bound data. Set to alphanumeric characters. [IE4, IE5]
- **datasrc**—Gives the URL or ID of the data-source object supplying data bound to this element. W3C says this should be a URL; Internet Explorer says it should be a data-source ID. [IE4, IE5]
- **dir**—Gives the direction of directionally neutral text (text that doesn't have an inherent direction in which you should read it). Possible values: **ltr**,

left-to-right text or table; and **rtl**, right-to-left text or table. [1.0S, 1.0T, 1.0F, 1.1, 4, IE5]

- **disabled**—Specifies that the element is disabled when first displayed. Standalone attribute in HTML. [1.0S, 1.0T, 1.0F, 1.1, 3, 4, IE4, IE5]
- **id**—Unique alphanumeric identifier for the tag; use the ID to refer to the tag. [1.0S, 1.0T, 1.0F, 1.1, 3, 4, IE4, IE5]
- **lang**—Base language used for the tag. [1.0S, 1.0T, 1.0F, 1.1, 3, 4, IE4, IE5]
- **language**—Scripting language used for the tag. [IE4, IE5]
- **name**—Gives the element a name. Set to alphanumeric characters. [1.0S, 1.0T, 1.0F, 1.1, 2, 3, 3.2, 4, IE1, IE2, IE3, IE4, IE5, NS1, NS2, NS3, NS4]
- **size**—Sets the size for the control. [1.0S, 1.0T, 1.0F, 1.1, 4, IE3, IE4, IE5]
- **style**—Inline style indicating how to render the element. [1.0S, 1.0T, 1.0F, 1.1, 4, IE4, IE5]
- **tabindex**—Sets the tab index of the element. This locates it in the tab order of the form, allowing the user to press the Tab key to navigate from element to element. Set to positive or negative integers. [1.0S, 1.0T, 1.0F, 1.1, 4, IE4, IE5]
- **title**—Holds additional information (which might be displayed in tool tips). [1.0S, 1.0T, 1.0F, 1.1, 2, 3, 4, IE4, IE5]
- **type**—Specifies the type of the element. [1.0S, 1.0T, 1.0F, 1.1, 2, 3, 3.2, 4, IE1, IE2, IE3, IE4, IE5, NS1, NS2, NS3, NS4]
- **value**—Gives this button another label besides the default, Reset. Set to alphanumeric characters. [1.0S, 1.0T, 1.0F, 1.1, 2, 3, 3.2, 4, IE1, IE2, IE3, IE4, IE5, NS1, NS2, NS3, NS4]
- **xml:lang**—Holds the base language for the element when the document is interpreted as an XML document. [1.0S, 1.0T, 1.0F, 1.1]

XHTML events: onclick, ondblclick, onmousedown, onmouseup, onmouseover, onmousemove, onmouseout, onkeypress, onkeydown, onkeyup, onfocus, onblur, onselect, onchange

- *Internet Explorer*—**onbeforecut, onbeforeeditfocus, onbeforefocusenter, onbeforefocusleave, onbeforepaste, onblur, onclick, oncontextmenu, oncontrolselect, oncut, ondblclick, ondrag, ondragend, ondragenter, ondragleave, ondragover, ondragstart, ondrop, onfilterchange, onfocus, onfocusenter, onfocusleave, onhelp, onkeydown, onkeypress, onkeyup, onlosecapture, onmousedown, onmouseenter, onmouseleave,**

onmousemove, onmouseout, onmouseover, onmouseup, onpaste, onpropertychange, onreadystatechange, onresize, onresizeend, onresizestart, onselectstart

- *Netscape Navigator*—**onclick**

A Reset button clears all the controls in a form, restoring them to the contents they displayed when they first appeared. Using a Reset button is useful when you have a complex form and users are likely to decide at some point that they want to start over. You'll find an example of using this element in the next section.

TIP: *Internet Explorer 4.x and 5.x use all the white space and carriage returns that you place in the **value** attribute for this element. Note, however, that other browsers (and earlier Internet Explorer versions) do not.*

<input type="submit">—Creating Submit Buttons

Purpose: Creates a Submit button that the user can click to send data in the form back to the Web server. This element takes no content.

When used as HTML: Start tag/End tag: Required/Omitted

Supported: [1.0S, 1.0T, 1.0F, 1.1, 2, 3, 3.2, 4, IE1, IE2, IE3, IE4, IE5, NS1, NS2, NS3, NS4]

Attributes:

- **accesskey**—Keyboard shortcut key; a single character is used as the value of this attribute. The user can type a platform-dependent key (such as Alt) with the **accesskey** character to trigger the active field. Set to an alphanumeric character. [1.0S, 1.0T, 1.0F, 1.1, 4, IE4, IE5]

- **class**—Class of the element. [1.0S, 1.0T, 1.0F, 1.1, 3, 4, IE4, IE5]

- **datafld**—Name of the column of the data-source object that supplies the bound data. Set to alphanumeric characters. [IE4, IE5]

- **datasrc**—Gives the URL or ID of the data-source object supplying data bound to this element. W3C says this should be a URL; Internet Explorer says it should be a data-source ID. [IE4, IE5]

- **dir**—Gives the direction of directionally neutral text (text that doesn't have an inherent direction in which you should read it). Possible values: **ltr**, left-to-right text or table; and **rtl**, right-to-left text or table. [1.0S, 1.0T, 1.0F, 1.1, 4, IE5]

- **disabled**—Specifies that the element is disabled when first displayed. Standalone attribute in HTML. [1.0S, 1.0T, 1.0F, 1.1, 3, 4, IE4, IE5]
- **id**—Unique alphanumeric identifier for the tag; use the ID to refer to the tag. [1.0S, 1.0T, 1.0F, 1.1, 3, 4, IE4, IE5]
- **lang**—Base language used for the tag. [1.0S, 1.0T, 1.0F, 1.1, 3, 4, IE4, IE5]
- **language**—Scripting language used for the tag. [IE4, IE5]
- **name**—Gives the element a name. Set to alphanumeric characters. [1.0S, 1.0T, 1.0F, 1.1, 2, 3, 3.2, 4, IE1, IE2, IE3, IE4, IE5, NS1, NS2, NS3, NS4]
- **size**—Specifies a size for the control. [1.0S, 1.0T, 1.0F, 1.1, 4, IE3, IE4, IE5]
- **style**—Inline style indicating how to render the element. [1.0S, 1.0T, 1.0F, 1.1, 4, IE4, IE5]
- **tabindex**—Sets the tab index of the element. This locates it in the tab order of the form, allowing the user to press the Tab key to navigate from element to element. Set to positive or negative integers. [1.0S, 1.0T, 1.0F, 1.1, 4, IE4, IE5]
- **title**—Holds additional information (which might be displayed in tool tips). [1.0S, 1.0T, 1.0F, 1.1, 2, 3, 4, IE4, IE5]
- **type**—Specifies the type of the element. [1.0S, 1.0T, 1.0F, 1.1, 2, 3, 3.2, 4, IE1, IE2, IE3, IE4, IE5, NS1, NS2, NS3, NS4]
- **value**—Gives this button another label besides the default, Submit Query. Set to alphanumeric characters. [1.0S, 1.0T, 1.0F, 1.1, 2, 3, 3.2, 4, IE1, IE2, IE3, IE4, IE5, NS1, NS2, NS3, NS4]
- **xml:lang**—Holds the base language for the element when the document is interpreted as an XML document. [1.0S, 1.0T, 1.0F, 1.1]

XHTML events: onclick, ondblclick, onmousedown, onmouseup, onmouseover, onmousemove, onmouseout, onkeypress, onkeydown, onkeyup, onfocus, onblur, onselect, onchange

- *Internet Explorer*—**onbeforecut, onbeforeeditfocus, onbeforefocusenter, onbeforefocusleave, onbeforepaste, onblur, onclick, oncontextmenu, oncontrolselect, oncut, ondblclick, ondrag, ondragend, ondragenter, ondragleave, ondragover, ondragstart, ondrop, onfilterchange, onfocus, onfocusenter, onfocusleave, onhelp, onkeydown, onkeypress, onkeyup, onlosecapture, onmousedown, onmouseenter, onmouseleave, onmousemove, onmouseout, onmouseover, onmouseup, onpaste, onpropertychange, onreadystatechange, onresize, onresizeend, onresizestart, onselectstart**
- *Netscape Navigator*—None

"OK," says the novice programmer, "my form is all set. Now how do I send its data back to the server?" "That's an easy one," you say; "just add a Submit button."

When the user clicks the Submit button in a form, the data in the form's controls is sent to the URL given by the form's **action** attribute. In other words, if you're sending data back to the server, the Submit button will be valuable to you. For an example showing how to send data to the server, see the "In Depth" section of this chapter.

TIP: *Unless you use the **value** attribute to supply a caption for the Submit button, most browsers, including Netscape Navigator and Internet Explorer, will give that button a caption of Submit Query.*

There's a very useful event you can use with the Submit button—**onsubmit**, which is an event of the **<form>** element. Code executed in this event's handler function can check the form and return a value of **true** if the data should be sent to the server, and **false** otherwise, in which case the data is not sent to the server. Here's an example. If the user doesn't enter a name when asked, the code displays an alert box and refuses to send the data from the form to the server:

```
<?xml version="1.0"?>
<!DOCTYPE html PUBLIC "-//W3C//DTD XHTML 1.0 Transitional//EN"
"http://www.w3.org/tr/xhtml1/DTD/xhtml1-transitional.dtd">
<html xmlns="http://www.w3.org/1999/xhtml" xml:lang="en" lang="en">
    <head>
        <title>
            Using Submit And Reset Buttons
        </title>

        <script language = "javascript" type = "text/javascript">
            function checkData()
            {
                if (document.form1.name.value == ""){
                    alert("Enter your name, please.")
                    return false
                }
                else{
                    return true
                }
            }
        </script>
    </head>
```

```
<body>
    <center>
        <h1>
            Using Submit And Reset Buttons
        </h1>

        <table border = "1" cellpadding = "6">
        <tr align = "center">
        <td bgcolor = "cyan">
            Sign the guestbook!
            <br />
            <form name = "form1" onsubmit = "return checkData()"
                method = "post" action=
                "http://www.starpowder.com/guestbook.cgi">
                Name: <input type="text" name="name" size="30"
                maxlength="30" />
                <p>
                    Email: <input type="text" name="address" size="30"
                        maxlength="30" />
                </p>
                <p>
                    <textarea rows="5" cols="60" name="body">
                    </textarea>
                    <br />
                    <br />
                </p>
                <input type="submit" value="Submit" />
                <input type="reset" value="Reset" />
            </form>
        </td>
        </tr>
        </table>
    </center>
</body>
</html>
```

You can see the result of this XHTML in Figure 12.12. If users don't enter anything in the Name field and then click Submit, the code will ask them to provide a name. They can enter a name and click Submit again to submit the data to the server.

TIP: *Internet Explorer 4.x and 5.x use all the white space and carriage returns that you place in the **value** attribute for this element. Note, however, that other browsers (and earlier Internet Explorer versions) do not.*

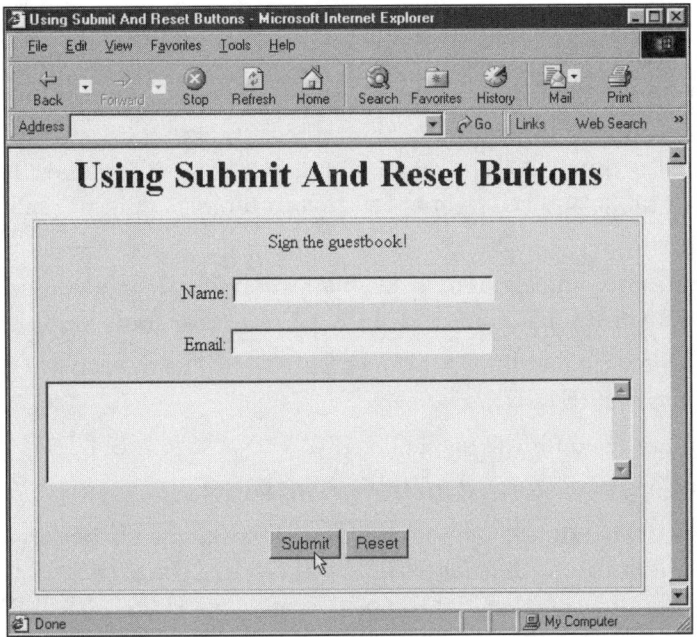

Figure 12.12 Using a Submit button.

<input type="text">—Creating Text Fields

Purpose: Creates a text field that the user can enter or edit text in. This element takes no content.

When used as HTML: Start tag/End tag: Required/Omitted

Supported: [1.0S, 1.0T, 1.0F, 1.1, 2, 3, 3.2, 4, IE1, IE2, IE3, IE4, IE5, NS1, NS2, NS3, NS4]

Attributes:

- **accesskey**—Keyboard shortcut key; a single character is used as the value of this attribute. The user can type a platform-dependent key (such as Alt) with the **accesskey** character to trigger the active field. Set to an alphanumeric character. [1.0S, 1.0T, 1.0F, 1.1, 4, IE4, IE5]

- **autocomplete**—Completes text in the control based on previously entered text. [IE5]

- **class**—Class of the element. [1.0S, 1.0T, 1.0F, 1.1, 3, 4, IE4, IE5]

- **datafld**—Name of the column of the data-source object that supplies the bound data. Set to alphanumeric characters. [IE4, IE5]

- **datasrc**—Gives the URL or ID of the data-source object supplying data bound to this element. W3C says this should be a URL; Internet Explorer says it should be a data-source ID. [IE4, IE5]

- **dir**—Gives the direction of directionally neutral text (text that doesn't have an inherent direction in which you should read it). Possible values: **ltr**, left-to-right text or table; and **rtl**, right-to-left text or table. [1.0S, 1.0T, 1.0F, 1.1, 4, IE5]

- **disabled**—Specifies that the element is disabled when first displayed. Standalone attribute in HTML. [1.0S, 1.0T, 1.0F, 1.1, 3, 4, IE4, IE5]

- **id**—Unique alphanumeric identifier for the tag; use the ID to refer to the tag. [1.0S, 1.0T, 1.0F, 1.1, 3, 4, IE4, IE5]

- **lang**—Base language used for the tag. [1.0S, 1.0T, 1.0F, 1.1, 3, 4, IE4, IE5]

- **language**—Scripting language used for the tag. [IE4, IE5]

- **maxlength**—Sets the maximum number of characters that can be entered into the text field. If **maxlength** is larger than the value of the **size** attribute, the text field will scroll as needed. Set to positive integers. [1.0S, 1.0T, 1.0F, 1.1, 2, 3, 3.2, 4, IE1, IE2, IE3, IE4, IE5, NS1, NS2, NS3, NS4]

- **name**—Gives the element a name. Set to alphanumeric characters. Required. [1.0S, 1.0T, 1.0F, 1.1, 2, 3, 3.2, 4, IE1, IE2, IE3, IE4, IE5, NS1, NS2, NS3, NS4]

- **readonly**—Indicates that the content of the text field cannot be modified. Standalone attribute in HTML. [1.0S, 1.0T, 1.0F, 1.1, 4, IE4, IE5]

- **size**—Sets the size of the text field in characters. Set to positive integers. [1.0S, 1.0T, 1.0F, 1.1, 2, 3, 3.2, 4, IE1, IE2, IE3, IE4, IE5, NS1, NS2, NS3, NS4]

- **style**—Inline style indicating how to render the element. [1.0S, 1.0T, 1.0F, 1.1, 4, IE4, IE5]

- **tabindex**—Sets the tab index of the element. This locates it in the tab order of the form, allowing the user to press the Tab key to navigate from element to element. Set to positive or negative integers. [1.0S, 1.0T, 1.0F, 1.1, 4, IE4, IE5]

- **title**—Holds additional information (which might be displayed in tool tips). [1.0S, 1.0T, 1.0F, 1.1, 2, 3, 4, IE4, IE5]

- **type**—Specifies the type of the element. [1.0S, 1.0T, 1.0F, 1.1, 2, 3, 3.2, 4, IE1, IE2, IE3, IE4, IE5, NS1, NS2, NS3, NS4]

- **value**—Holds the initial text in the text field. Set to alphanumeric characters. [1.0S, 1.0T, 1.0F, 1.1, 2, 3, 3.2, 4, IE1, IE2, IE3, IE4, IE5, NS1, NS2, NS3, NS4]

- **xml:lang**—Holds the base language for the element when the document is interpreted as an XML document. [1.0S, 1.0T, 1.0F, 1.1]

XHTML events: onclick, ondblclick, onmousedown, onmouseup, onmouseover, onmousemove, onmouseout, onkeypress, onkeydown, onkeyup, onfocus, onblur, onselect, onchange

- *Internet Explorer*—**onafterupdate, onbeforecut, onbeforeeditfocus, onbeforefocusenter, onbeforefocusleave, onbeforepaste, onbeforeupdate, onblur, onchange, onclick, oncontextmenu, oncontrolselect, oncut, ondblclick, ondrag, ondragend, ondragenter, ondragleave, ondragover, ondragstart, ondrop, onerrorupdate, onfilterchange, onfocus, onfocusenter, onfocusleave, onhelp, onkeydown, onkeypress, onkeyup, onlosecapture, onmousedown, onmouseenter, onmouseleave, onmousemove, onmouseout, onmouseover, onmouseup, onpaste, onpropertychange, onreadystatechange, onresize, onresizeend, onresizestart, onselect, onselectstart**

- *Netscape Navigator*—**onblur, onchange, onfocus, onselect**

"Say," asks the novice programmer, "just how do I create text fields? There's no **<textfield>** element." "You just use **<input type="text">**," you say; "no problem."

You can create a text field (referred to as a *text box* in other programming environments) with the **<input type="text">** element. You can set the size of the text field in characters with the **size** attribute and set the maximum length of text with the **maxlength** attribute. (The text field will scroll if the maximum length is greater than its size.) Here's an example:

```
<?xml version="1.0"?>
<!DOCTYPE html PUBLIC "-//W3C//DTD XHTML 1.0 Transitional//EN"
"http://www.w3.org/tr/xhtml1/DTD/xhtml1-transitional.dtd">
<html xmlns="http://www.w3.org/1999/xhtml" xml:lang="en" lang="en">
    <head>
        <title>Using Text Fields</title>
    </head>

    <body>
        <form name="form1" action = "action">
            <center>
                <br />
                <h1>Using Text Fields</h1>
                <br />
                <br />
                <input type = "text" name = "textfield" size = "40"
                    maxlength="60" />
```

```
            </center>
        </form>
    </body>
</html>
```

You can see the text field in Figure 12.13. From a programming point of view, you can refer to the text in a text field by using the JavaScript **value** property like this: **document.form1.textfield.value="Hello from XHTML!"**. See the examples in the "In Depth" section of this chapter for more information.

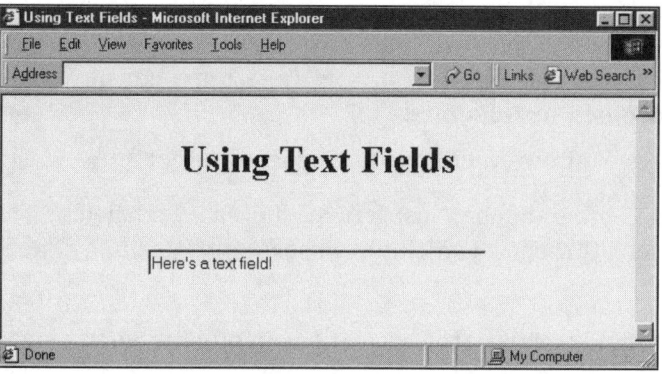

Figure 12.13   A text field.

<textarea>—Creating Text Areas

Purpose: Creates a text area, much like a multiline text field.

When used as HTML: Start tag/End tag: Required/Required

Supported: [1.0S, 1.0T, 1.0F, 1.1, 2, 3, 3.2, 4, IE1, IE2, IE3, IE4, IE5, NS1, NS2, NS3, NS4]

Attributes:

- **accesskey**—Keyboard shortcut key; a single character is used as the value of this attribute. The user can type a platform-dependent key (such as Alt) with the **accesskey** character to trigger the active field. Set to an alphanumeric character. [1.0S, 1.0T, 1.0F, 1.1, 4, IE4, IE5]

- **cols**—Specifies the number of columns visible in the control. Set to a positive integer. Required. [1.0S, 1.0T, 1.0F, 1.1, 2, 3, 3.2, 4, IE1, IE2, IE3, IE4, IE5, NS1, NS2, NS3, NS4]

- **class**—Class of the element. [1.0S, 1.0T, 1.0F, 1.1, 3, 4, IE4, IE5]

- **datafld**—Name of the column of the data-source object that supplies the bound data. Set to alphanumeric characters. [IE4, IE5]
- **datasrc**—Gives the URL or ID of the data-source object supplying data bound to this element. W3C says this should be a URL; Internet Explorer says it should be a data-source ID. [IE4, IE5]
- **dir**—Gives the direction of directionally neutral text (text that doesn't have an inherent direction in which you should read it). Possible values: **ltr**, left-to-right text or table; and **rtl**, right-to-left text or table. [1.0S, 1.0T, 1.0F, 1.1, 4, IE5]
- **disabled**—Specifies that the element is disabled when first displayed. Standalone attribute in HTML. [1.0S, 1.0T, 1.0F, 1.1, 3, 4, IE4, IE5]
- **id**—Unique alphanumeric identifier for the tag; use the ID to refer to the tag. [1.0S, 1.0T, 1.0F, 1.1, 3, 4, IE4, IE5]
- **lang**—Base language used for the tag. [1.0S, 1.0T, 1.0F, 1.1, 3, 4, IE4, IE5]
- **language**—Scripting language used for the tag. [IE4, IE5]
- **name**—Gives the element a name. Set to alphanumeric characters. [1.0S, 1.0T, 1.0F, 1.1, 2, 3, 3.2, 4, IE1, IE2, IE3, IE4, IE5, NS1, NS2, NS3, NS4]
- **readonly**—Indicates that the content of the text field cannot be modified. Standalone attribute in HTML. [1.0S, 1.0T, 1.0F, 1.1, 4, IE4, IE5]
- **rows**—Specifies the number of rows in the control. Set to positive integers. Required. [1.0S, 1.0T, 1.0F, 1.1, 2, 3, 3.2, 4, IE1, IE2, IE3, IE4, IE5, NS1, NS2, NS3, NS4]
- **style**—Inline style indicating how to render the element. [1.0S, 1.0T, 1.0F, 1.1, 4, IE4, IE5]
- **tabindex**—Sets the tab index of the element. This locates it in the tab order of the form, allowing the user to press the Tab key to navigate from element to element. Set to positive or negative integers. [1.0S, 1.0T, 1.0F, 1.1, 4, IE4, IE5]
- **title**—Holds additional information (which might be displayed in tool tips). [1.0S, 1.0T, 1.0F, 1.1, 2, 3, 4, IE4, IE5]
- **wrap**—Determines the word-wrap behavior for the control. Set to **off** (no word wrapping, the default), **soft** (text is wrapped, but the wrapping is not transmitted back to the server as return or linefeed characters), or **hard** (text is wrapped, and the wrapping is preserved when the data is submitted to the server). [IE4, IE5, NS2, NS3, NS4]
- **xml:lang**—Holds the base language for the element when the document is interpreted as an XML document. [1.0S, 1.0T, 1.0F, 1.1]

XHTML events: onclick, **ondblclick**, **onmousedown**, **onmouseup**, **onmouseover**, **onmousemove**, **onmouseout**, **onkeypress**, **onkeydown**, **onkeyup**, **onfocus**, **onblur**, **onselect**, **onchange**

- *Internet Explorer*—**onafterupdate**, **onbeforecopy**, **onbeforecut**, **onbeforeeditfocus**, **onbeforefocusenter**, **onbeforefocusleave**, **onbeforepaste**, **onbeforeupdate**, **onblur**, **onchange**, **onclick**, **oncontextmenu**, **oncontrolselect**, **oncut**, **ondblclick**, **ondrag**, **ondragend**, **ondragenter**, **ondragleave**, **ondragover**, **ondragstart**, **ondrop**, **onerrorupdate**, **onfilterchange**, **onfocus**, **onfocusenter**, **onfocusleave**, **onhelp**, **onkeydown**, **onkeypress**, **onkeyup**, **onlosecapture**, **onmousedown**, **onmouseenter**, **onmouseleave**, **onmousemove**, **onmouseout**, **onmouseover**, **onmouseup**, **onpaste**, **onpropertychange**, **onreadystatechange**, **onresize**, **onresizeend**, **onresizestart**, **onscroll**, **onselect**, **onselectstart**

- *Netscape Navigator*—**onblur**, **onchange**, **onfocus**, **onselect**

"I can't fit all I want to say in the Suggestions box in your Web page," the big boss says. "Well," you say, "I can use a text area there instead of a text field, I suppose." The BB hurries off to enter more suggestions on how you can improve yourself. You think, "Great."

Text areas are like multiline text fields, and you create them with the **<textarea>** element, not the **<input>** element. One reason there is a separate **<textarea>** element is that any text you enter in this element appears in the text area. (Unlike the **<input>** element, the **<textarea>** element requires a closing **</textarea>** tag.) You must set the number of rows and columns that you want in the text area by using the **rows** and **cols** attributes. Here's an example:

```
<?xml version="1.0"?>
<!DOCTYPE html PUBLIC "-//W3C//DTD XHTML 1.0 Transitional//EN"
"http://www.w3.org/tr/xhtml1/DTD/xhtml1-transitional.dtd">
<html xmlns="http://www.w3.org/1999/xhtml" xml:lang="en" lang="en">
    <head>
        <title>
            Using Text Areas
        </title>
    </head>

    <body>
        <form name="form1" action = "action">
            <center>
                <br />
                <h1>Using Text Areas</h1>
                <br />
```

```
                <textarea name = "textarea" rows = "10"
                    cols = "30">Hello from XHTML!
                </textarea>
            </center>
        </form>
    </body>
</html>
```

You can see the results of this XHTML in Figure 12.14. The text "Hello from XHTML!" is displayed in the text area.

TIP: *You can turn text wrapping on and off with the **wrap** attribute in Internet Explorer and Netscape Navigator.*

From a programming point of view, you can refer to the text in a text area by using the JavaScript **value** property like this: **document.form1.textarea.value= "Hello from XHTML!"**, just as you would with a text field. See the examples in the "In Depth" section of this chapter for more information.

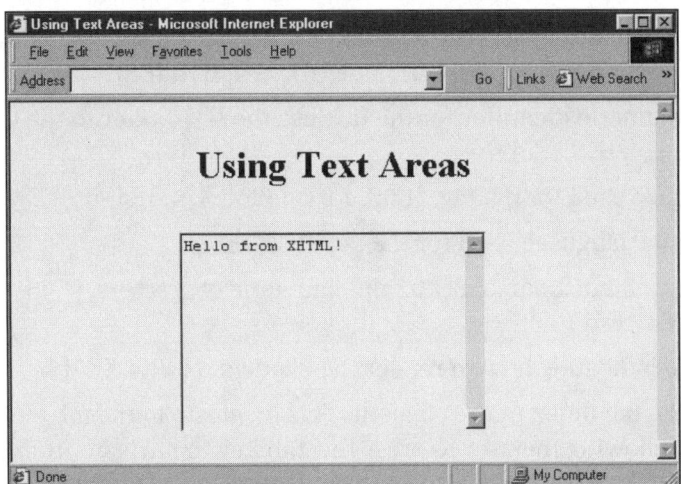

Figure 12.14   A text area.

\<button\>—Creating a Customizable Button

Purpose: Creates a customizable button.

When used as HTML: Start tag/End tag: Required/Required

Supported: [1.0S, 1.0T, 1.0F, 1.1, 4, IE4, IE5]

Attributes:

- **accesskey**—Keyboard shortcut key; a single character is used as the value of this attribute. The user can type a platform-dependent key (such as Alt) with the **accesskey** character to trigger the active field. Set to an alphanumeric character. [1.0S, 1.0T, 1.0F, 1.1, 4, IE4, IE5]
- **class**—Class of the element. [1.0S, 1.0T, 1.0F, 1.1, 4, IE4, IE5]
- **datafld**—Name of the column of the data-source object that supplies the bound data. Set to alphanumeric characters. [IE4, IE5]
- **dataformatas**—Specifies whether bound data is plain text or **XHTML**. Set to **HTML**, **plaintext**, or **text**. [IE4, IE5]
- **datasrc**—Gives the URL or ID of the data-source object supplying data bound to this element. W3C says this should be a URL; Internet Explorer says it should be a data-source ID. [IE4, IE5]
- **dir**—Gives the direction of directionally neutral text (text that doesn't have an inherent direction in which you should read it). Possible values: **ltr**, left-to-right text or table; and **rtl**, right-to-left text or table. [1.0S, 1.0T, 1.0F, 1.1, 4, IE5]
- **disabled**—Specifies that the element is disabled when first displayed. Standalone attribute in HTML. [1.0S, 1.0T, 1.0F, 1.1, 3, 4, IE4, IE5]
- **id**—Unique alphanumeric identifier for the tag; use the ID to refer to the tag. [1.0S, 1.0T, 1.0F, 1.1, 4, IE4, IE5]
- **lang**—Base language used for the tag. [1.0S, 1.0T, 1.0F, 1.1, 4, IE4, IE5]
- **language**—Scripting language used for the tag. [IE4, IE5]
- **name**—Gives the element a name. Set to alphanumeric characters. [1.0S, 1.0T, 1.0F, 1.1, 4, IE4, IE5]
- **style**—Inline style indicating how to render the element. [4, IE4, IE5]
- **tabindex**—Sets the tab index of the element. This locates it in the tab order of the form, allowing the user to press the Tab key to navigate from element to element. Set to positive or negative integers. [1.0S, 1.0T, 1.0F, 1.1, 4, IE4, IE5]
- **title**—Holds additional information (which might be displayed in tool tips). [1.0S, 1.0T, 1.0F, 1.1, 4, IE4, IE5]
- **type**—Specifies the purpose that the button will fulfill—that of the traditional Submit, Reset, or multipurpose button. Set to **submit**, **reset**, or **button**. [1.0S, 1.0T, 1.0F, 1.1, 4, IE4, IE5]
- **value**—Represents the result of the button when clicked. Set to alphanumeric characters. [1.0S, 1.0T, 1.0F, 1.1, 4, IE4, IE5]
- **xml:lang**—Holds the base language for the element when the document is interpreted as an XML document. [1.0S, 1.0T, 1.0F, 1.1]

XHTML events: onclick, ondblclick, onmousedown, onmouseup, onmouseover, onmousemove, onmouseout, onkeypress, onkeydown, onkeyup, onfocus, onblur

- *Internet Explorer*—**onbeforecut, onbeforeeditfocus, onbeforefocusenter, onbeforefocusleave, onbeforepaste, onblur, onclick, oncontextmenu, oncontrolselect, oncut, ondblclick, ondragenter, ondragleave, ondragover, ondrop, onfilterchange, onfocus, onfocusenter, onfocusleave, onhelp, onkeydown, onkeypress, onkeyup, onlosecapture, onmousedown, onmouseenter, onmouseleave, onmousemove, onmouseout, onmouseover, onmouseup, onpaste, onpropertychange, onreadystatechange, onresize, onresizeend, onresizestart, onselectstart**

- *Netscape Navigator*—Not applicable

"Wow," says the novice programmer, "I have a great idea. You know how you can display XHTML in Web pages? Well, what if you could do the same thing for the caption of a button? I'm going to patent this idea." "Too late," you say; "it already exists—as the **<button>** element."

You can customize the appearance of buttons in the caption of a **<button>** control. This capability has been supported in Internet Explorer since version 4 (but not in Netscape Navigator). You can use this control as a Submit, Reset, or standard button—just set the **type** attribute to **submit**, **reset**, or **button**. Here's an example showing how to use **<button>**:

```
<?xml version="1.0"?>
<!DOCTYPE html PUBLIC "-//W3C//DTD XHTML 1.0 Transitional//EN"
    "http://www.w3.org/tr/xhtml1/DTD/xhtml1-transitional.dtd">
<html xmlns="http://www.w3.org/1999/xhtml" xml:lang="en" lang="en">
    <head>
        <title>
            Using &lt;button&gt;
        </title>
    </head>

    <body>
        <center>
            <h1>
                Using &lt;button&gt;
            </h1>
            <form method="post"
                action="http://www.starpowder.com/steve/cgi/cgidata.cgi">
                Please enter your name:
                <input type="text" name="text" value="" />
                <p>
```

```
                    <button type="submit" name="helpbutton">
                        <img src="submit.gif" align="middle" /> Click
                        <strong>here</strong> to send the data.
                    </button>
                </p>
            </form>
        </center>
    </body>
</html>
```

You can see the results of this XHTML in Figure 12.15.

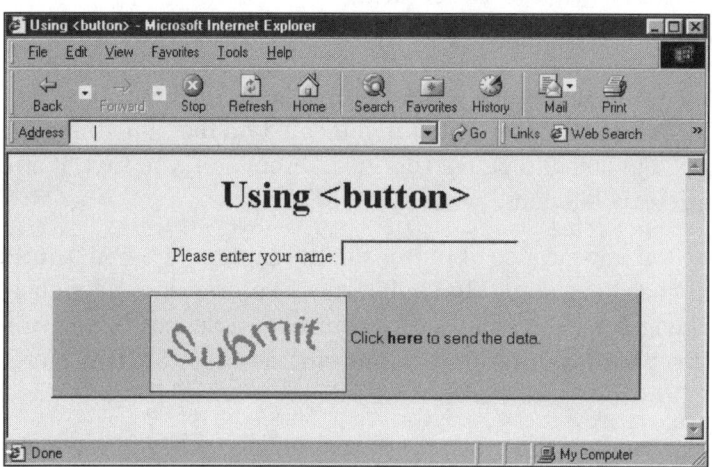

Figure 12.15 A **<button>** control.

<select>, <option>, and <optgroup>— Creating a Select Control

<select>

Purpose: Displays a select control, which is like a drop-down list box.

When used as HTML: Start tag/End tag: Required/Required

Supported: [1.0S, 1.0T, 1.0F, 1.1, 2, 3, 3.2, 4, IE1, IE2, IE3, IE4, IE5, NS1, NS2, NS3, NS4]

Attributes:

- **accesskey**—Keyboard shortcut key; a single character is used as the value of this attribute. The user can type a platform-dependent key (such as Alt) with the **accesskey** character to trigger the active field. Set to an alphanumeric character. [1.0S, 1.0T, 1.0F, 1.1, 4, IE4, IE5]

- **align**—Gives the alignment of the contents of the **select** control. Set to **left**, **right**, **top**, **middle**, or **bottom**. [IE4, IE5]

- **class**—Class of the element. [1.0S, 1.0T, 1.0F, 1.1, 3, 4, IE4, IE5]

- **datafld**—Name of the column of the data-source object that supplies the bound data. Set to alphanumeric characters. [IE4, IE5]

- **datasrc**—Gives the URL or ID of the data-source object supplying data bound to this element. W3C says this should be a URL; Internet Explorer says it should be a data-source ID. [IE4, IE5]

- **dir**—Gives the direction of directionally neutral text (text that doesn't have an inherent direction in which you should read it). Possible values: **ltr**, left-to-right text or table; and **rtl**, right-to-left text or table. [1.0S, 1.0T, 1.0F, 1.1, 4, IE5]

- **disabled**—Specifies that the element is disabled when first displayed. Standalone attribute in HTML. [1.0S, 1.0T, 1.0F, 1.1, 3, 4, IE4, IE5]

- **id**—Unique alphanumeric identifier for the tag; use the ID to refer to the tag. [1.0S, 1.0T, 1.0F, 1.1, 3, 4, IE4, IE5]

- **lang**—Base language used for the tag. [1.0S, 1.0T, 1.0F, 1.1, 3, 4, IE4, IE5]

- **language**—Scripting language used for the tag. [IE4, IE5]

- **multiple**—Indicates that more than one option can be selected at a time. Standalone attribute in HTML. [1.0S, 1.0T, 1.0F, 1.1, 2, 3, 3.2, 4, IE1, IE2, IE3, IE4, IE5, NS1, NS2, NS3, NS4]

- **name**—Gives the element a name. Set to alphanumeric characters. [1.0S, 1.0T, 1.0F, 1.1, 2, 3, 3.2, 4, IE1, IE2, IE3, IE4, IE5, NS1, NS2, NS3, NS4]

- **size**—Gives the number of items visible in the list. Set to a positive integer. [1.0S, 1.0T, 1.0F, 1.1, 2, 3.2, 4, IE1, IE2, IE3, IE4, IE5, NS1, NS2, NS3, NS4]

- **style**—Inline style indicating how to render the element. [1.0S, 1.0T, 1.0F, 1.1, 4, IE4, IE5]

- **tabindex**—Sets the tab index of the element. This locates it in the tab order of the form, allowing the user to press the Tab key to navigate from element to element. Set to positive or negative integers. [1.0S, 1.0T, 1.0F, 1.1, 4, IE4, IE5]

- **title**—Holds additional information (which might be displayed in tool tips). [1.0S, 1.0T, 1.0F, 1.1, 2, 3, 4]

- **xml:lang**—Holds the base language for the element when the document is interpreted as an XML document. [1.0S, 1.0T, 1.0F, 1.1]

XHTML events: onclick, ondblclick, onmousedown, onmouseup, onmouseover, onmousemove, onmouseout, onkeypress, onkeydown, onkeyup, onfocus, onblur, onchange

- *Internet Explorer*—**onbeforecut, onbeforeeditfocus, onbeforefocusenter, onbeforefocusleave, onbeforepaste, onblur, onchange, onclick, oncontextmenu, oncontrolselect, oncut, ondblclick, ondragenter, ondragleave, ondragover, ondrop, onfocus, onfocusenter, onfocusleave, onhelp, onkeydown, onkeypress, onkeyup, onlosecapture, onmousedown, onmouseenter, onmouseleave, onmousemove, onmouseout, onmouseover, onmouseup, onpaste, onpropertychange, onreadystatechange, onresize, onresizeend, onresizestart, onscroll, onselectstart**

- *Netscape Navigator*—**onblur, onchange, onclick, onfocus**

<option>

Purpose: Specifies a list item in the list of a **select** control.

When used as HTML: Start tag/End tag: Required/Optional

Supported: [1.0S, 1.0T, 1.0F, 1.1, 2, 3, 3.2, 4, IE1, IE2, IE3, IE4, IE5, NS1, NS2, NS3, NS4]

Attributes:

- **class**—Class of the element. [1.0S, 1.0T, 1.0F, 1.1, 3, 4, IE4, IE5]

- **dir**—Gives the direction of directionally neutral text (text that doesn't have an inherent direction in which you should read it). Possible values: **ltr**, left-to-right text or table; and **rtl**, right-to-left text or table. [1.0S, 1.0T, 1.0F, 1.1, 4, IE5]

- **disabled**—Specifies that the element is disabled when first displayed. Standalone attribute in HTML. [1.0S, 1.0T, 1.0F, 1.1, 3, 4, IE5]

- **id**—Unique alphanumeric identifier for the tag; use the ID to refer to the tag. [1.0S, 1.0T, 1.0F, 1.1, 3, 4, IE4, IE5]

- **label**—Holds a short label that should be used when you're using **optgroup** elements to create a hierarchy of list values. Set to alphanumeric characters. [1.0S, 1.0T, 1.0F, 1.1, 4]

- **lang**—Base language used for the tag. [1.0S, 1.0T, 1.0F, 1.1, 3, 4, IE4, IE5]

- **language**—Scripting language used for the tag. [IE4, IE5]

- **selected**—Indicates that the item should appear selected at first. Standalone attribute in HTML. [1.0S, 1.0T, 1.0F, 1.1, 2, 3, 3.2, 4, IE1, IE2, IE3, IE4, IE5, NS1, NS2, NS3, NS4]
- **style**—Inline style indicating how to render the element. [1.0S, 1.0T, 1.0F, 1.1, 4]
- **tabindex**—Sets the tab index of the element. This locates it in the tab order of the form, allowing the user to press the Tab key to navigate from element to element. Set to positive or negative integers. [1.0S, 1.0T, 1.0F, 1.1, 4]
- **value**—Holds the value to be sent to the server if the item is chosen. The default is the content of the **option** element. Set to an alphanumeric string. [1.0S, 1.0T, 1.0F, 1.1, 2, 3, 3.2, 4, IE1, IE2, IE3, IE4, IE5, NS1, NS2, NS3, NS4]
- **xml:lang**—Holds the base language for the element when the document is interpreted as an XML document. [1.0S, 1.0T, 1.0F, 1.1]

XHTML events:

- *Internet Explorer*—**onlayoutcomplete**, **onlosecapture**, **onpropertychange**, **onreadystatechange**, **onselectstart**
- *Netscape Navigator*—None

<optgroup>

Purpose: Groups selection list choices into a hierarchy.

When used as HTML: Start tag/End tag: Required/Required

Supported: [1.0S, 1.0T, 1.0F, 1.1, 4]

Attributes:

- **class**—Class of the element. [1.0S, 1.0T, 1.0F, 1.1, 4]
- **dir**—Gives the direction of directionally neutral text (text that doesn't have an inherent direction in which you should read it). Possible values: **ltr**, left-to-right text or table; and **rtl**, right-to-left text or table. [1.0S, 1.0T, 1.0F, 1.1, 4]
- **disabled**—Specifies that the element is disabled when first displayed. Standalone attribute in HTML. [1.0S, 1.0T, 1.0F, 1.1, 4]
- **Id**—Unique alphanumeric identifier for the tag; use the ID to refer to the tag. [1.0S, 1.0T, 1.0F, 1.1, 4]
- **label**—Required. Holds a short label that should be used when you're using **optgroup** elements to create a hierarchy of list values. Set to alphanumeric characters. [1.0S, 1.0T, 1.0F, 1.1, 4]
- **lang**—Base language used for the tag. [1.0S, 1.0T, 1.0F, 1.1, 4]

- **style**—Inline style indicating how to render the element. [1.0S, 1.0T, 1.0F, 1.1, 4]
- **xml:lang**—Holds the base language for the element when the document is interpreted as an XML document. [1.0S, 1.0T, 1.0F, 1.1]

XHTML events: onclick, ondblclick, onmousedown, onmouseup, onmouseover, onmousemove, onmouseout, onkeypress, onkeydown, onkeyup

You can use **select** controls to display a drop-down list in a Web page. You create a **select** control with the **<select>** element, and you create each of the items in the drop-down list with the **<option>** element. Here's an example in which I'm adding five items to a **select** control—note that I'm adding code to the **onchange** event to display the user's selections:

```
<?xml version="1.0"?>
<!DOCTYPE html PUBLIC "-//W3C//DTD XHTML 1.0 Transitional//EN"
"http://www.w3.org/tr/xhtml1/DTD/xhtml1-transitional.dtd">
<html xmlns="http://www.w3.org/1999/xhtml" xml:lang="en" lang="en">
    <head>
        <title>
            Using Select Controls
        </title>

        <script language = "javascript" type = "text/javascript">
            function reportSelection()
            {
                document.form1.textfield.value = "You chose item " +
                    (document.form1.select1.selectedIndex + 1)
            }
        </script>
    </head>

    <body>
        <form name = "form1" action = "action">
            <center>
                <h1>
                    Using Select Controls
                </h1>
                <input name = "textfield" type = "text" size = "20" />
                <br />
                <br />
                <select name = "select1" onchange = "reportSelection()">
                    <option>Item 1</option>
                    <option>Item 2</option>
                    <option>Item 3</option>
```

```
                    <option>Item 4</option>
                    <option>Item 5</option>
                </select>
            </center>
        </form>
    </body>
</html>
```

You can see the results of this XHTML in Figure 12.16. When the user makes a selection, that selection is reported in the text field.

You can also support multiple selections in a **select** control if you use the **multiple** attribute. Here's an example that allows you to do just that—you hold down the Ctrl key to select a number of items or hold down the Shift key to select a range of items. (The key you use is platform dependent.) Here's the XHTML (the **with** JavaScript statement is a shortcut statement that sets the default object for the code in the code block that follows):

```
<?xml version="1.0"?>
<!DOCTYPE html PUBLIC "-//W3C//DTD XHTML 1.0 Transitional//EN"
"http://www.w3.org/tr/xhtml1/DTD/xhtml1-transitional.dtd">
<html xmlns="http://www.w3.org/1999/xhtml" xml:lang="en" lang="en">
    <head>
        <title>
            Multiple Selection Example
        </title>

        <script language = "javascript" type = "text/javascript"
            src = "script.js">
        </script>
    </head>
```

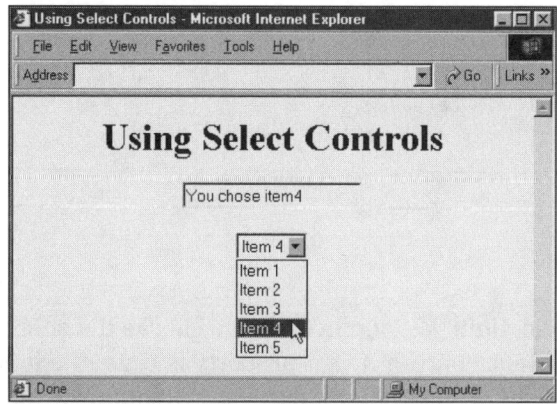

Figure 12.16   A **select** control.

```
<body>
    <center>
        <h1>
            Multiple Selection Example
        </h1>
        <br />
        <form name = "form1" action = "action">
            <textarea name = "textarea" cols = "20" rows = "5">
            </textarea>
            <br />
            <br />
            <select name = "select1" onchange = "reportSelection()"
                multiple = "multiple">
                <option>Item 1</option>
                <option>Item 2</option>
                <option>Item 3</option>
                <option>Item 4</option>
                <option>Item 5</option>
            </select>
        </form>
    </center>
</body>
</html>
```

Here's the script, script.js, that this page uses:

```
function reportSelection()
{
    document.form1.textarea.value = ""

    with(document.form1.select1){
        for(var loopIndex = 0; loopIndex < length;
            loopIndex++){
            if (options[loopIndex].selected){
                document.form1.textarea.value =
                    document.form1.textarea.value
                    + options[loopIndex].text + "\r\n"
            }
        }
    }
}
```

Every time the user makes a selection, the loop in the code checks the **selected** property of each item in the **select** control. If that property is **true**, the item is selected, and the code reports it as selected in the Web page's text area. You can see this code at work in Figure 12.17.

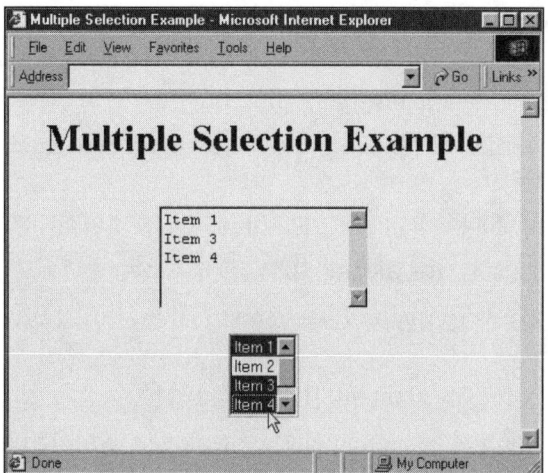

Figure 12.17   Making multiple selections in a **select** control.

The **<optgroup>** element lets you group selection choices into a hierarchy. Browsers might implement this as a collapsible hierarchy list—as yet, no major browser implements this element.

<fieldset>, <legend>, and <label>—Grouping and Labeling Form Elements

<fieldset>

Purpose: Groups elements in an XHTML form.

When used as HTML: Start tag/End tag: Required/Required

Supported: [1.0S, 1.0T, 1.0F, 1.1, 4, IE4, IE5]

Attributes:

- **accesskey**—Sets the access key for the element. [IE5]
- **align**—Gives the alignment of the contents of the **fieldset** control. Set to **left**, **center**, or **right**. [IE4, IE5]
- **class**—Class of the element. [1.0S, 1.0T, 1.0F, 1.1, 4, IE4, IE5]
- **contenteditable**—Set to **true** if users can edit the content. [IE5]
- **dir**—Gives the direction of directionally neutral text (text that doesn't have an inherent direction in which you should read it). Possible values: **ltr**,

left-to-right text or table; and **rtl**, right-to-left text or table. [1.0S, 1.0T, 1.0F, 1.1, 4, IE5]

- **disabled**—Set to **true** if the element is disabled. [IE4, IE5]
- **id**—Unique alphanumeric identifier for the tag; use the ID to refer to the tag. [1.0S, 1.0T, 1.0F, 1.1, 4, IE4, IE5]
- **lang**—Base language used for the tag. [1.0S, 1.0T, 1.0F, 1.1, 4, IE4, IE5]
- **language**—Scripting language used for the tag. [IE4, IE5]
- **style**—Inline style indicating how to render the element. [1.0S, 1.0T, 1.0F, 1.1, 4, IE4, IE5]
- **tabindex**—Sets the tab index for the element. [IE3, IE4, IE5]
- **title**—Holds additional information (which might be displayed in tool tips). [1.0S, 1.0T, 1.0F, 1.1, 4, IE4, IE5]
- **xml:lang**—Holds the base language for the element when the document is interpreted as an XML document. [1.0S, 1.0T, 1.0F, 1.1]

XHTML events: onclick, ondblclick, onmousedown, onmouseup, onmouseover, onmousemove, onmouseout, onkeypress, onkeydown, onkeyup

- *Internet Explorer*—**onbeforecopy, onbeforecut, onbeforeeditfocus, onbeforefocusenter, onbeforefocusleave, onbeforepaste, onblur, onclick, oncontextmenu, oncontrolselect, oncopy, oncut, ondblclick, ondrag, ondragend, ondragenter, ondragleave, ondragover, ondragstart, ondrop, onfilterchange, onfocus, onfocusenter, onfocusleave, onhelp, onkeydown, onkeypress, onkeyup, onlosecapture, onmousedown, onmouseenter, onmouseleave, onmousemove, onmouseout, onmouseover, onmouseup, onpaste, onpropertychange, onreadystatechange, onresize, onresizeend, onresizestart, onselectstart**
- *Netscape Navigator*—Not applicable

<legend>

Purpose: Adds a legend to a **fieldset**.

When used as HTML: Start tag/End tag: Required/Required

Supported: [1.0S, 1.0T, 1.0F, 1.1, 4, IE4, IE5]

Attributes:

- **accesskey**—Keyboard shortcut key; a single character is used as the value of this attribute. The user can type a platform-dependent key (such as Alt) with the **accesskey** character to trigger the active field. Set to an alphanumeric character. [1.0S, 1.0T, 1.0F, 1.1, 4, IE4, IE5]

- **align**—Gives the alignment of the contents of the **fieldset** control. Set to **left**, **center**, or **right**. [1.0S, 1.0T, 1.0F, 4, IE4, IE5]
- **class**—Class of the element. [1.0S, 1.0T, 1.0F, 1.1, 4, IE4, IE5]
- **contenteditable**—Set to **true** if users can edit the content. [IE4, IE5]
- **dir**—Gives the direction of directionally neutral text (text that doesn't have an inherent direction in which you should read it). Possible values: **ltr**, left-to-right text or table; and **rtl**, right-to-left text or table. [1.0S, 1.0T, 1.0F, 1.1, 4, IE5]
- **disabled**—Indicates whether the element is disabled. [IE4, IE5]
- **id**—Unique alphanumeric identifier for the tag; use the ID to refer to the tag. [1.0S, 1.0T, 1.0S, 1.1, 4, IE4, IE5]
- **lang**—Base language used for the tag. [1.0S, 1.0T, 1.0F, 1.1, 4, IE4, IE5]
- **language**—Scripting language used for the tag. [IE4, IE5]
- **style**—Inline style indicating how to render the element. [1.0S, 1.0T, 1.0F, 1.1, 4, IE4, IE5]
- **tabindex**—Holds the tab index for the element. [IE4, IE5]
- **title**—Holds additional information (which might be displayed in tool tips). [1.0S, 1.0T, 1.0F, 1.1, 4, IE4, IE5]
- **xml:lang**—Holds the base language for the element when the document is interpreted as an XML document. [1.0S, 1.0T, 1.0F, 1.1]

XHTML events: onclick, ondblclick, onmousedown, onmouseup, onmouseover, onmousemove, onmouseout, onkeypress, onkeydown, onkeyup

- *Internet Explorer*—**onbeforecopy, onbeforecut, onbeforefocusenter, onbeforefocusleave, onbeforepaste, onblur, onclick, oncontextmenu, oncontrolselect, oncopy, oncut, ondblclick, onfocus, onfocusenter, onfocusleave, onhelp, onkeydown, onkeypress, onkeyup, onlosecapture, onmousedown, onmouseenter, onmouseleave, onmousemove, onmouseout, onmouseover, onmouseup, onpaste, onpropertychange, onreadystatechange, onresize, onresizeend, onresizestart**
- *Netscape Navigator*—Not applicable

<label>

Purpose: Adds a label to an element in a **fieldset**.

When used as HTML: Start tag/End tag: Required/Required

Supported: [1.0S, 1.0T, 1.0F, 1.1, 4, IE4, IE5]

Attributes:

- **accesskey**—Keyboard shortcut key; a single character is used as the value of this attribute. The user can type a platform-dependent key (such as Alt) with the **accesskey** character to trigger the active field. Set to an alphanumeric character. [1.0S, 1.0T, 1.0F, 1.1, 4, IE4, IE5]

- **class**—Class of the element. [1.0S, 1.0T, 1.0F, 1.1, 4, IE4, IE5]

- **contenteditable**—Set to **true** if users can edit the content. [IE5]

- **dir**—Gives the direction of directionally neutral text (text that doesn't have an inherent direction in which you should read it). Possible values: **ltr**, left-to-right text or table; and **rtl**, right-to-left text or table. [1.0S, 1.0T, 1.0F, 1.1, 4, IE5]

- **disabled**—Indicates whether the element is disabled. [IE5]

- **for**—Indicates which form element the **label** is for. If you don't use this attribute, the label is associated with its contents. Set to an ID of a form element. [1.0S, 1.0T, 1.0F, 1.1, 4]

- **id**—Unique alphanumeric identifier for the tag; use the ID to refer to the tag. [1.0S, 1.0T, 1.0F, 1.1, 4, IE4, IE5]

- **lang**—Base language used for the tag. [1.0S, 1.0T, 1.0F, 1.1, 4, IE4, IE5]

- **language**—Scripting language used for the tag. [IE4, IE5]

- **style**—Inline style indicating how to render the element. [1.0S, 1.0T, 1.0F, 1.1, 4, IE4, IE5]

- **tabindex**—Holds the element's tab index. [IE5]

- **title**—Holds additional information (which might be displayed in tool tips). [1.0S, 1.0T, 1.0F, 1.1, 4, IE4, IE5]

- **xml:lang**—Holds the base language for the element when the document is interpreted as an XML document. [1.0S, 1.0T, 1.0F, 1.1]

XHTML events: onclick, ondblclick, onmousedown, onmouseup, onmouseover, onmousemove, onmouseout, onkeypress, onkeydown, onkeyup, onfocus, onblur

- *Internet Explorer*—**onbeforecopy, onbeforecut, onbeforefocusenter, onbeforefocusleave, onbeforepaste, onblur, onclick, oncontextmenu, oncontrolselect, oncut, ondblclick, ondrag, ondragend, ondragenter, ondragleave, ondragover, ondragstart, ondrop, onfocus, onfocusenter, onfocusleave, onhelp, onkeydown, onkeypress, onkeyup, onlosecapture, onmousedown, onmouseenter, onmouseleave, onmousemove, onmouseout, onmouseover, onmouseup, onpaste, onpropertychange, onreadystatechange, onresize, onresizeend, onresizestart, onselectstart**

- *Netscape Navigator*—Not applicable

"Darn," says the novice programmer. "The form in my Web page is becoming pretty confusing—I've got 73 groups of radio buttons, and even I can't keep things straight anymore." "Well," you smile, "why not break them up into visual groups with the **<fieldset>** element?" "How does that work?" the NP wants to know.

You use the **<fieldset>** element to group elements in a form together in a box. (Although the actual rendering is left to the browser, this element is supported only in Internet Explorer so far, and it uses boxes.) You use the **<legend>** element to add a caption to the box, and use the **<label>** element to label the elements in the form. Here's the example we saw in the "In Depth" section at the beginning of this chapter:

```
<?xml version="1.0"?>
<!DOCTYPE html PUBLIC "-//W3C//DTD XHTML 1.0 Transitional//EN"
"http://www.w3.org/tr/xhtml1/DTD/xhtml1-transitional.dtd">
<html xmlns="http://www.w3.org/1999/xhtml" xml:lang="en" lang="en">
    <head>
        <title>
            Using &lt;fieldset&gt;, &lt;legend&gt;, And &lt;label&gt;
        </title>
    </head>

    <body>
        <center>
            <h1>Using &lt;fieldset&gt;, &lt;legend&gt;, And
                &lt;label&gt;</h1>
            <form name = "form1" action = "action">
                <fieldset>
                    <legend accesskey="C">Color</legend>
                    <label accesskey="Y">
                        <input type="radio" name="color" value="yellow" />
                        Yellow
                    </label>
                    <br />
                    <label accesskey="W">
                        <input type="radio" name="color" value="orange" />
                        Orange
                    </label>
                </fieldset>
            </form>
        </center>
    </body>
</html>
```

You can see the results in Figure 12.4. As you can see, grouping elements visually like this can be a great aid for organizing your page.

<isindex>—Using an Index

Purpose: Indicates that the browser should let the user search an index by entering keywords. This element takes no content. This element is deprecated.

When used as HTML: Start tag/End tag: Required/Omitted

Supported: [1.0T, 1.0F, 2, 3, 3.2, 4, IE1, IE2, IE3, IE4, IE5, NS1, NS2, NS3, NS4]

Attributes:

- **action**—Gives the URL of code to process the **isindex** data. Set to a URL. [IE1, IE2, IE3, IE4, IE5]
- **accesskey**—Sets an access key. [IE5]
- **class**—Class of the element. [1.0T, 1.0F, 4, IE4, IE5]
- **contenteditable**—Set to **true** if users can edit the content. [IE5]
- **dir**—Gives the direction of directionally neutral text (text that doesn't have an inherent direction in which you should read it). Possible values: **ltr**, left-to-right text or table; and **rtl**, right-to-left text or table. [1.0T, 1.0F, 4]
- **disabled**—Set to **true** to disable the index. [IE4, IE5]
- **id**—Unique alphanumeric identifier for the tag; use the ID to refer to the tag. [1.0T, 1.0F, 4, IE4, IE5]
- **lang**—Base language used for the tag. [1.0T, 1.0F, 4, IE4, IE5]
- **language**—Scripting language used for the tag. [IE4, IE5]
- **prompt**—Specifies an alternate string that should be used to query the user. Set to alphanumeric text. [1.0T, 1.0F, 3, 3.2, 4, IE1, IE2, IE3, IE4, IE5, NS1, NS2, NS3, NS4]
- **style**—Sets the style for this element. [IE4, IE5]
- **tabindex**—Sets the tab index for this element. [IE4, IE5]
- **xml:lang**—Holds the base language for the element when the document is interpreted as an XML document. [1.0T, 1.0F]

XHTML events: None

The **<isindex>** element was an early form of a text input field and was used to let users search an index by entering keywords. However, this element is now deprecated; I'm including it here only for completeness. This element is usually found in the **<head>** section of a page:

```
<?xml version="1.0"?>
<!DOCTYPE html PUBLIC "-//W3C//DTD XHTML 1.0 Transitional//EN"
"http://www.w3.org/tr/xhtml1/DTD/xhtml1-transitional.dtd">
```

```
<html xmlns="http://www.w3.org/1999/xhtml" xml:lang="en" lang="en">
    <head>
        <title>
            Using &lt;isindex&gt;
        </title>

        <isindex prompt="Enter your name: " />
    </head>

    <body>
        <center>
            <h1>
                Using &lt;isindex&gt;
            </h1>
            <br />
        </center>
    </body>
</html>
```

You can see the results of this XHTML in Figure 12.18.

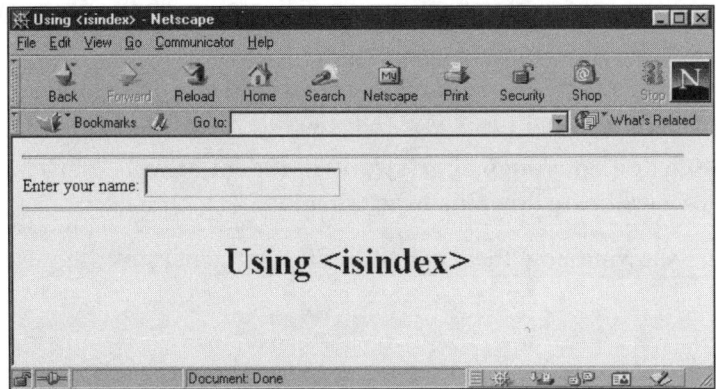

Figure 12.18   Using **<isindex>**.

<keygen>—Processing Secure Transactions

Purpose: Processes secure transactions in Netscape Navigator. This element takes no content.

When used as HTML: Start tag/End tag: Required/Omitted

Supported: [NS3, NS4]

Attributes:

- **challenge**—Specifies the challenge string that will be packaged with the public key for verification of the form submission. Set to alphanumeric characters. [NS3, NS4]

- **name**—Paired with the challenge string. Set to alphanumeric characters. Required. [NS3, NS4]

The **<keygen>** element—available only in Netscape Navigator so it is *not* true XHTML—is used to handle security transactions with Web-based certificate management systems. It's an advanced element that is used in an XHTML form to construct a certificate request, which involves generating a key and submitting a public key. The transaction results in a signed certificate, which the form can use to generate a challenge string paired with the **<keygen>** element's **name** attribute.

The **<keygen>** element displays a menu of choices from which the user can select a key size. When the form contents are submitted, the browser generates a key of the specified size. If you are a developer and want to dig deeper into this element, here are some resources you can explore:

- **http://developer.netscape.com/docs/manuals/htmlguid/tags10.htm#1615503**—Netscape Communications' documentation on the **<keygen>** element

- **http://home.netscape.com/eng/security/cert-exts.html**—Developer-oriented documentation about **<keygen>** interaction with servers

- **http://home.netscape.com/eng/security/downloadcert.html**—Netscape Communications' certificate download specification.

Here's an example showing how the **<keygen>** element generates the menu of key sizes:

```
<?xml version="1.0"?>
<!DOCTYPE html PUBLIC "-//W3C//DTD XHTML 1.0 Transitional//EN"
"http://www.w3.org/tr/xhtml1/DTD/xhtml1-transitional.dtd">
<html xmlns="http://www.w3.org/1999/xhtml" xml:lang="en" lang="en">
    <head>
        <title>
            Using &lt;keygen&gt;
        </title>

    </head>

    <body>
        <center>
```

```
            <h1>
                Using &lt;keygen&gt;
            </h1>
            <br />
            <form method="post"
                action="http://www.starpowder/cgi/secure.cgi"
                enctype="application/x-www-form-urlencoded">
                <keygen name="securekey" challenge="12345678" />
                <input type="text" value="Data" />
                <input type="submit" value="Submit" />
            </form>
        </center>
    </body>
</html>
```

You can see the results of this page in Figure 12.19.

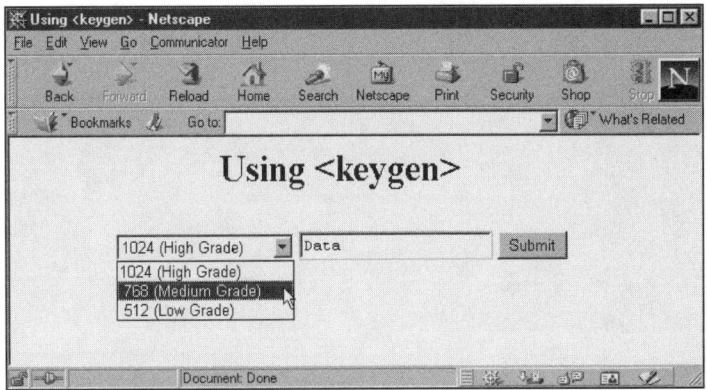

Figure 12.19 Using **<keygen>**.

Chapter 13

Dynamic XHTML: Changing Web Pages on the Fly

If you need an immediate solution to:	See page:
Using Dynamic Styles	784
Toggling Style Sheets On and Off	787
Dynamic Content: **document.write**	791
Dynamic Content: The **insertAdjacentHTML** and **insertAdjacentText** Methods	795
Dynamic Content: The **innerText**, **outerText**, **innerHTML**, and **outerHTML** Properties	797
Dynamic Content: Using Text Ranges	800
Dynamic Content: Using the **createElement** Method	802
Dynamic Content: Creating Dynamic Tables	804
Dynamic Content: Using Conditional Comments to Set Content on the Fly	807
Creating Amazing **mouseover** Effects	808
Positioning Elements by Using Styles	813
Creating Animation	815
Creating Animation with Layers	817
Using Vector Markup Language (VML)	819
Setting Element Visibility	821
Printing Web Pages	824
Using Dynamic Fonts	825
Visual Effects: Filters	827
Visual Effects: Transitions	831
Visual Effects: Transitions Using Layers	835

In Depth

In this chapter, I'll start looking at a huge topic, which I'm going to call—dynamic XHTML. It's a good thing we've gotten JavaScript under our belts in the previous few chapters because we'll need it here. As you've seen in Chapter 12, you can use a scripting language like JavaScript to make the controls in your Web page, such as buttons and checkboxes, come alive. With dynamic XHTML, there are no limits, and just about every element in a Web page can come alive in the same way by being scripted to handle events.

Note that there is no official term "dynamic XHTML" yet—I'm using that term for our purposes to indicate the natural progression from dynamic HTML to XHTML. Dynamic HTML is hugely popular with Web authors, so it's one we should cover in depth, but please note that much of this chapter's material is *not* true XHTML as W3C defines it. For this and the next chapter, the term "dynamic XHTML" means the same with respect to XHTML as "dynamic HTML" meant to HTML—that is, it refers to browser-supported augmentations of the W3C standard. It's important to realize that the term "dynamic XHTML" as we'll use it means extending XHTML to handle what various browsers call dynamic HTML today; it's not a W3C term.

NOTE: *You can always tell what's true XHTML and what's not by checking whether or not a tag or attribute is supported by XHTML, as listed in this book. For example, some of this chapter uses the <layer> element to support dragging and dropping in the Netscape Navigator, but as you know, the <layer> element is Netscape-specific, and not a part of official XHTML. When in doubt, just check to see if the element or attribute you want to use is supported in official XHTML by checking the reference material for the element in this book.*

Here's an example we saw in Chapter 11 when we were working with the **document** object. In that example, I used the **<body>** element's **bgColor** property to change the background color of a Web page to red:

```
<?xml version="1.0"?>
<!DOCTYPE html PUBLIC "-//W3C//DTD XHTML 1.0 Transitional//EN"
 "http://www.w3.org/tr/xhtml1/DTD/xhtml1-transitional.dtd">
<html xmlns="http://www.w3.org/1999/xhtml" xml:lang="en" lang="en">
    <head>
        <title>
            Setting Background Color With JavaScript
```

```
        </title>
    </head>

    <body onmousedown="document.bgColor='red'">
        <center>
            <h1>
                Click this page to turn it red!
            </h1>
        </center>
    </body>
</html>
```

When you click this page, it changes to red before your very eyes—in Internet Explorer, anyway. As it stands, this code won't work in Netscape Navigator, raising a very big issue when it comes to dynamic XHTML—it means different things in different browsers. Isn't there some standard? What does the World Wide Web Consortium (W3C) have to say on the issue? Let's take a look, starting with dynamic HTML and then continuing on to dynamic XHTML.

W3C and Dynamic HTML

You can find W3C's comments on this topic at **www.w3.org/DOM**, and here's an excerpt:

"'Dynamic HTML' is a term used by some vendors to describe the combination of HTML, style sheets, and scripts that allows documents to be animated. W3C has received several submissions from members' companies on the way in which the object model of HTML documents should be exposed to scripts. These submissions do not propose any new HTML tags or style sheet technology. The W3C DOM WG is working hard to make sure interoperable and scripting-language neutral solutions are agreed upon."

Unfortunately, that's as far as W3C has gotten, which means that the browser companies have been free to develop in different directions. And they have. It must be said that the dynamic HTML support in Internet Explorer is far more comprehensive than what you'll find in Netscape Navigator. I'll take a look at what dynamic HTML means in Internet Explorer first and then take a look at what it means in Netscape Navigator.

Dynamic HTML in Internet Explorer

You can find information about Microsoft's dynamic HTML at **www.msdn.microsoft.com/workshop/c-frame.htm#/workshop/author/default.asp**. Dynamic HTML in Internet Explorer is extensive, virtually turning Web pages into entire applications that run in the browser without any round-trips to the server.

> **TIP:** In fact, Microsoft has invested heavily in the idea that Web pages can indeed be applications that run in your browser. You can develop applications with packages—such as Microsoft Visual Basic—that include executable files that run in the browser as active documents. You can also use Visual Basic's built-in editor to create extensive dynamic HTML pages that will run in Internet Explorer. Making Web pages into applications allows a unique form of distributed computing in which, for example, agents in the field can open the latest form of the software they need simply by navigating to a URL.

The following list describes the key features of dynamic HTML in Internet Explorer:

- *Absolute positioning*—Using cascading-style-sheet positioning, you can change the location of elements in a page to create animated effects.
- *Behaviors*—Represent Microsoft's attempt to separate code from data in Web pages and let you specify how elements in your Web page work. We'll learn more about behaviors in Chapter 14.
- *Data binding*—Writes Web pages that display, sort, filter, and update data in a database from the browser.
- *Document Object Model (DOM)*—Using Microsoft's dynamic HTML, all page elements are represented as objects. From the Web author's point of view, this means that page elements can be manipulated easily in code.
- *Dynamic content*—Using dynamic HTML, you can add, delete, or change Web page content on the fly. For example, a Web page can display a headline that's updated without refreshing the page from the server.
- *Dynamic styles*—Change the style of elements, such as color and font, without a server round-trip. For instance, text can change color or size when a mouse pointer passes over it.
- *Scriptlets*—Refers to scripts that function as components in Web applications.
- *Special ActiveX controls*—Support many visual effects, such as animation, filtering, and visual transitions, that appear when you move to a new page.

As you can see, the support for dynamic HTML is extensive in Internet Explorer. I'll take a look at what's available in Netscape Navigator next.

Dynamic HTML in Netscape Navigator

Netscape's implementation of dynamic HTML is more limited than Microsoft's. You can find information about it at **http://developer.netscape.com/docs/manuals/communicator/dynhtml/index.htm**.

The following list describes the key elements of Netscape Communications' version of dynamic HTML:

- *Absolute positioning*—You can update cascading-style-sheet positioning coordinates in a page at any time to create animated effects, and you can use layers to do the same thing.
- *DOM*—Netscape's dynamic HTML provides an object model for HTML, just as Microsoft's does. However, as we've seen in previous chapters, Netscape's DOM is more limited.
- *Downloadable fonts*—You can download fonts from the Internet and install them in your Web pages.
- *Dynamic content*—You can change the content of a page in Netscape Navigator at any time, adding or deleting items.

As you can see, Netscape's implementation of dynamic HTML is more restricted than Microsoft's. For us, this means that nearly all the topics in this chapter and Chapter 14 will apply to Internet Explorer only, although I'll try to mimic Internet Explorer's dynamic HTML effects in Netscape Navigator when I can.

TIP: *Because dynamic XHTML varies so much by browser, it's crucial to know which browser your page is being viewed in. See Chapter 11 to learn how to make that determination.*

All the dynamic HTML I've mentioned so far is supported as dynamic XHTML as well, so let's start talking in terms of XHTML. It's worth taking a look at some of the most popular aspects of dynamic XHTML now in overview before digging into the details, and I'll do that now.

Dynamic Styles: Setting Styles on the Fly

Because you can now set attributes on the fly in Internet Explorer, you can set the styles of elements dynamically. Here's an example in which I set the font size of some displayed text to 48 points when the mouse moves over it—note the JavaScript keyword **this**, which refers to the current element:

```
<?xml version="1.0"?>
<!DOCTYPE html PUBLIC "-//W3C//DTD XHTML 1.0 Transitional//EN"
    "http://www.w3.org/tr/xhtml1/DTD/xhtml1-transitional.dtd">
<html xmlns="http://www.w3.org/1999/xhtml" xml:lang="en" lang="en">
    <head>
        <title>
            Using Dynamic Styles
        </title>
    </head>

    <body>
        <center>
```

```
            <h1>
                Using Dynamic Styles.
            </h1>
            <span onmouseover="this.style.fontSize = '48'">
                This text gets bigger when you move the mouse over it!
            </span>
        </center>
    </body>
</html>
```

You can see the results in Figure 13.1. When the mouse moves over the text in the page, its style changes to 48-point text. Dynamically changing styles open the door to many possibilities—now your Web page can react to users as they move the mouse around.

Another feature of dynamic XHTML in Internet Explorer is that by using the **document** object's **styleSheets** collection, you can now toggle style sheets on and off, selecting which style sheet you want to apply on the fly. See the Immediate Solutions section "Toggling Style Sheets On and Off" for the details.

Dynamic Content: Changing Web Pages on the Fly

The usual way of changing a Web page on the fly is to use the **document.write** method. Here's an example that rewrites a Web page as it's being loaded, depending on which button the user clicks in a confirmation dialog box. If the user so

Figure 13.1 Using dynamic styles.

directs, the code writes code to display a large image in the page; otherwise, it writes code to display a small image:

```
<?xml version="1.0"?>
<!DOCTYPE html PUBLIC "-//W3C//DTD XHTML 1.0 Transitional//EN"
"http://www.w3.org/tr/xhtml1/DTD/xhtml1-transitional.dtd">
<html xmlns="http://www.w3.org/1999/xhtml" xml:lang="en" lang="en">
    <head>
        <title>
            Creating A Self-Modifying Web Page
        </title>
    </head>

    <body>
        <center>
            <h1>
                Creating A Self-Modifying Web Page
            </h1>

            <script type = "text/javascript"
                language = "javascript" src = "script.js">
            </script>
        </center>
    </body>
</html>
```

Here's the JavaScript code for this page, script.js:

```
if(confirm("View graphics intensive page?")) {
    document.write("<br /><img width='1024' height='1024' " +
    "alt='image' src='gif/image1.gif' />")
}
else {
    document.write("<br /><img width='120' height='120' " +
    "alt='image' src='gif/image1small.gif' />")
}
```

Because this code writes the Web page as it's being loaded, the code works with both Netscape Navigator and Internet Explorer. However, you can also modify a Web page by using the **document.write** method *after* a Web page has been loaded. Here's another example. In this case, the code rewrites the entire page (to just the text "This is a new page!") in Internet Explorer when the user clicks the page (note that the page as rewritten here is not conforming XHTML):

```
<?xml version="1.0"?>
<!DOCTYPE html PUBLIC "-//W3C//DTD XHTML 1.0 Transitional//EN"
```

```
            "http://www.w3.org/tr/xhtml1/DTD/xhtml1-transitional.dtd">
<html xmlns="http://www.w3.org/1999/xhtml" xml:lang="en" lang="en">
    <head>
        <title>
            Using document.writeln
        </title>

        <script type = "text/javascript">
            function rewrite()
            {
                document.writeln("This is a new page!")
            }
        </script>
    </head>

    <body onmousedown="rewrite()">
        <center>
            <h1>
                Click this page to rewrite it!
            </h1>
        </center>
    </body>
</html>
```

In Netscape Navigator, you can do the same thing, but you have to connect the **mousedown** event to the code, as well as explicitly opening and closing the document (this page will also work in Internet Explorer):

```
<?xml version="1.0"?>
<!DOCTYPE html PUBLIC "-//W3C//DTD XHTML 1.0 Transitional//EN"
"http://www.w3.org/tr/xhtml1/DTD/xhtml1-transitional.dtd">
<html xmlns="http://www.w3.org/1999/xhtml" xml:lang="en" lang="en">
    <head>
        <title>
            Using document.writeln
        </title>

        <script type = "text/javascript">
            document.onmousedown = rewrite

            function rewrite()
            {
                document.open()
                document.writeln("This is a new page!")
                document.close()
            }
```

```
        </script>
    </head>

    <body onmousedown="rewrite()">
        <center>
            <h1>
                Click this page to rewrite it!
            </h1>
        </center>
    </body>
</html>
```

There's often more than one way to do things in Internet Explorer, and in addition to **document.write**, you can rewrite a Web page on the fly by using the following methods:

- **innerHTML**—Changes the contents of the element between the start and end tags; can include XHTML.
- **innerText**—Lets you change the text between the start and end tags of an element.
- **insertAdjacentHTML**—Lets you insert new XHTML (which the browser will read and handle as XHTML) into a page.
- **insertAdjacentText**—Lets you insert new text into a page.
- **outerHTML**—Contains the contents of an element, including start and end tags; treats text as XHTML.
- **outerText**—Lets you change all the element's text, including the start and end tags.
- **pasteHTML**—Used with text ranges to paste XHTML into a document.

These methods are more precise than **document.write** because they let you work with specific parts of a Web page, not the whole thing at once. Here's an example of using the **outerHTML** property. I'll use the **outerHTML** method of an **<h1>** element to rewrite that element entirely as a **<marquee>** element when the user clicks the element (the **<marquee>** element is specific to the Internet Explorer, so note that this document is not conforming XHTML):

```
<?xml version="1.0"?>
<!DOCTYPE html PUBLIC "-//W3C//DTD XHTML 1.0 Transitional//EN"
"http://www.w3.org/tr/xhtml1/DTD/xhtml1-transitional.dtd">
<html xmlns="http://www.w3.org/1999/xhtml" xml:lang="en" lang="en">
    <head>
        <title>
            Changing XHTML on the fly
        </title>
```

Chapter 13   Dynamic XHTML: Changing Web Pages on the Fly

```
        <script type = "text/javascript"
            language = "javascript" src = "script.js">
        </script>
    </head>

    <body>
        <center>
            <h1 id = "header" onclick = "changeHeader()">Dynamic XHTML</h1>
            Click the above header to change it....
        </center>
    </body>
</html>
```

Here's the script, script.js, that this page uses:

```
function changeHeader()
{
    header.outerHTML =
        "<marquee style='font-size: 54;'>" +
        "This marquee was just created!</marquee>"
}
```

Figure 13.2 shows the results after the user has clicked the **<h1>** element. The browser has rewritten just a single element in a Web page, changing the content of the Web page dynamically.

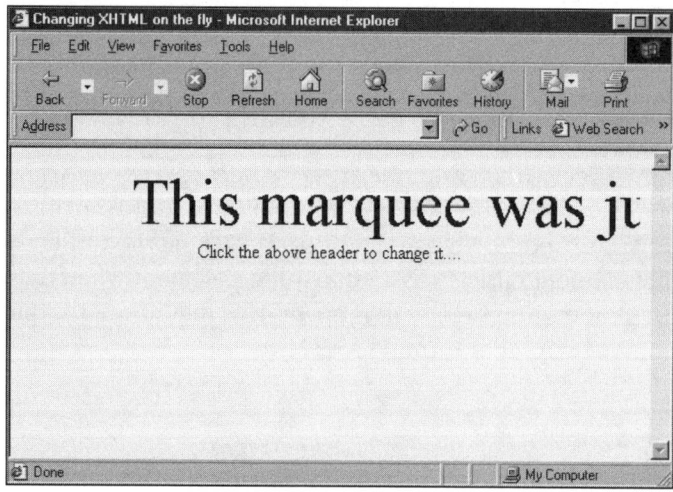

Figure 13.2   Rewriting an element.

Creating mouseover Effects

Undoubtedly the most common use for dynamic HTML is for **mouseover** effects. You've probably seen these effects—when you move the mouse, a hyperlink or other text changes when the mouse is over it. The change can involve making text larger, displaying a new image, or any of dozens of other effects. There are many ways to implement such effects in Internet Explorer, some simple and some complex, and I'll take a look at them in the Immediate Solutions section of this chapter. Here's an example of using the **mouseover** and **mouseout** events in Internet Explorer. This example changes the color of a header from black to red when the mouse is over it and changes it back to black when the mouse moves away (the **this** keyword in JavaScript refers to the current element):

```xml
<?xml version="1.0"?>
<!DOCTYPE html PUBLIC "-//W3C//DTD XHTML 1.0 Transitional//EN"
"http://www.w3.org/tr/xhtml1/DTD/xhtml1-transitional.dtd">
<html xmlns="http://www.w3.org/1999/xhtml" xml:lang="en" lang="en">
    <head>
        <title>
            Using Dynamic Styles
        </title>
    </head>

    <body>
        <center>
            <h1 onmouseover="this.style.color = 'red';"
                onmouseout="this.style.color = 'black';">
                Turn me red with the mouse.
            </h1>
        </center>
    </body>
</html>
```

In this next example, I'll swap images when the mouse moves over an image. The second image is the same as the first, but lighter in color, so it appears that the image is highlighted when the mouse is over it (again, this won't work in Netscape Navigator):

```xml
<?xml version="1.0"?>
<!DOCTYPE html PUBLIC "-//W3C//DTD XHTML 1.0 Transitional//EN"
"http://www.w3.org/tr/xhtml1/DTD/xhtml1-transitional.dtd">
<html xmlns="http://www.w3.org/1999/xhtml" xml:lang="en" lang="en">
    <head>
        <title>
            Mouseover Image Handling
```

```
            </title>
        </head>

        <body>
            <center>
                <h1>
                    Mouseover Image Handling
                </h1>

                <img src="flower.jpg" alt='image'
                    onmouseover="this.src='flower2.jpg'"
                    onmouseout="this.src='flower.jpg'" />
            </center>
        </body>
</html>
```

You can see the results in Figure 13.3. When the user moves the mouse over the image, a lighter version of the same image is displayed, making the image appear to be highlighted.

Here's an example of creating **mouseover** effects by using layers in Netscape Navigator. I set the background of the text to cyan when the mouse is over it (note that the **<layer>** element is specific to the Netscape Navigator, so this example is not conforming XHTML):

```
<?xml version="1.0"?>
<!DOCTYPE html PUBLIC "-//W3C//DTD XHTML 1.0 Transitional//EN"
"http://www.w3.org/tr/xhtml1/DTD/xhtml1-transitional.dtd">
```

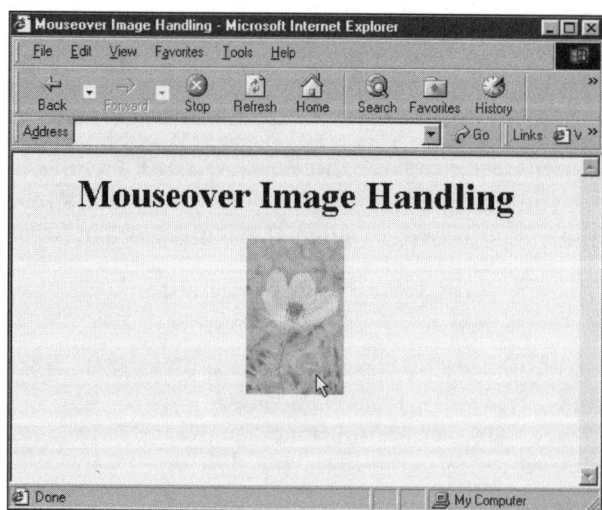

Figure 13.3   Highlighting an image when the mouse is over it.

```
<html xmlns="http://www.w3.org/1999/xhtml" xml:lang="en" lang="en">
    <head>
        <title>
            Mouseover Effects Using Layers
        </title>
    </head>

    <body>
        <layer bgcolor="white" top="40" left="40"
            onmouseover="setcolor('cyan')" onmouseout="setcolor('white')" >
            <script type = "text/javascript" language="javascript">
                function setcolor(color)
                {
                    bgColor=color
                }
            </script>
            <h1>
                Mouseover Effects Using Layers
            </h1>
        </layer>
    </body>
</html>
```

The results appear in Figure 13.4. When the user moves the mouse over the text in the Web page, a box appears behind it, highlighting it.

We'll also learn how to handle animation, downloadable fonts, visual filters and transitions, and more, coming up next.

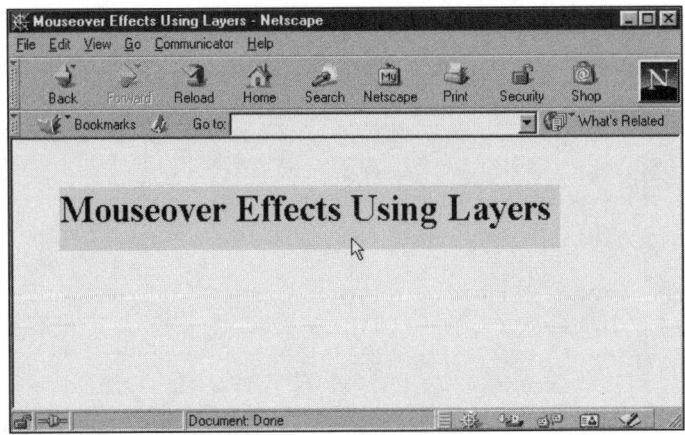

Figure 13.4 Using layers for **mouseover** effects.

Immediate Solutions

Using Dynamic Styles

The novice programmer wants to know, "Where's a good place to start with dynamic XHTML?" "Well," you say, "one good way to make your Web pages come alive is to make your styles dynamic, modifying how things appear in response to user actions." "Give me an example," the NP says. You say, "I can give you several."

You can change styles on the fly in Internet Explorer (but not in Netscape Navigator) in several ways. Here's an example from the "In Depth" section of this chapter. I'm changing the color of text from black to red and then back to black when the mouse moves over it—note the JavaScript keyword **this**, which refers to the current element:

```
<?xml version="1.0"?>
<!DOCTYPE html PUBLIC "-//W3C//DTD XHIML 1.0 Transitional//EN"
"http://www.w3.org/tr/xhtml1/DTD/xhtml1-transitional.dtd">
<html xmlns="http://www.w3.org/1999/xhtml" xml:lang="en" lang="en">
    <head>
        <title>
            Using Dynamic Styles
        </title>
    </head>

    <body>
        <center>
            <h1 onmouseover="this.style.color = 'red';"
                onmouseout="this.style.color = 'black';">
                Turn me red with the mouse.
            </h1>
        </center>
    </body>
</html>
```

Here's another example, also from the "In Depth" section of this chapter. Here, I'm changing the font size of text when you move the mouse over it:

```
<?xml version="1.0"?>
<!DOCTYPE html PUBLIC "-//W3C//DTD XHTML 1.0 Transitional//EN"
"http://www.w3.org/tr/xhtml1/DTD/xhtml1-transitional.dtd">
<html xmlns="http://www.w3.org/1999/xhtml" xml:lang="en" lang="en">
    <head>
        <title>
            Using Dynamic Styles
        </title>
    </head>

    <body>
        <center>
            <h1>
                Using Dynamic Styles.
            </h1>
            <span onmouseover = "this.style.fontSize = '48'">
                This text gets bigger when you move the mouse over it!
            </span>
        </center>
    </body>
</html>
```

You can see the results of this page in Figure 13.1. Here's another example, using Internet Explorer. This time I'm changing the mouse cursor from an arrow to a hand when the mouse is over a header, and then back to an arrow when the mouse moves away. To do this, I set the **cursor** style:

```
<?xml version="1.0"?>
<!DOCTYPE html PUBLIC "-//W3C//DTD XHTML 1.0 Transitional//EN"
"http://www.w3.org/tr/xhtml1/DTD/xhtml1-transitional.dtd">
<html xmlns="http://www.w3.org/1999/xhtml" xml:lang="en" lang="en">
    <head>
        <title>
            Using Dynamic Styles
        </title>
    </head>

    <body>
        <center>
            <h1 onmouseover="this.style.cursor = 'hand';"
                onmouseout="this.style.cursor = 'default';">
                Change the cursor with the mouse.
            </h1>
        </center>
    </body>
</html>
```

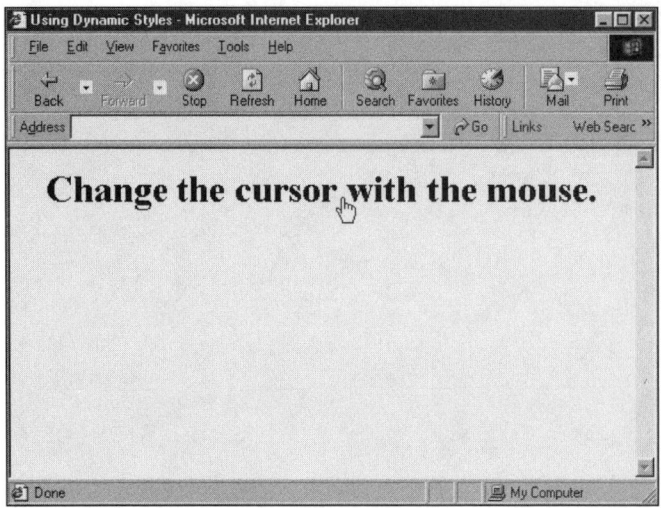

Figure 13.5   Setting the mouse cursor in response to mouse location.

You can see the results of this document in Figure 13.5. When the mouse cursor is over the header, the cursor changes to a hand. This is useful to show the user what's clickable in your page and what's not.

Here's another example in which I'm using classes to change styles dynamically. I'm assigning a whole new class to an element in response to mouse movements:

```
<?xml version="1.0"?>
<!DOCTYPE html PUBLIC "-//W3C//DTD XHTML 1.0 Transitional//EN"
"http://www.w3.org/tr/xhtml1/DTD/xhtml1-transitional.dtd">
<html xmlns="http://www.w3.org/1999/xhtml" xml:lang="en" lang="en">
    <head>
        <title>
            Dynamic Styles Using Classes
        </title>
        <style type="text/css">
            .red {color:red}
            .blue {color:blue}
        </style>
    </head>

    <body>
        <center>
            <h1 class="blue" onmouseover="this.className='red'"
                onmouseout="this.className='blue'">
```

```
                    Move the mouse here to change colors.
                </h1>
            </center>
        </body>
</html>
```

You can see the results in Figure 13.6. When the mouse is moved over the header in the page, the code switches the style class, and as a result the text appears in red, not blue.

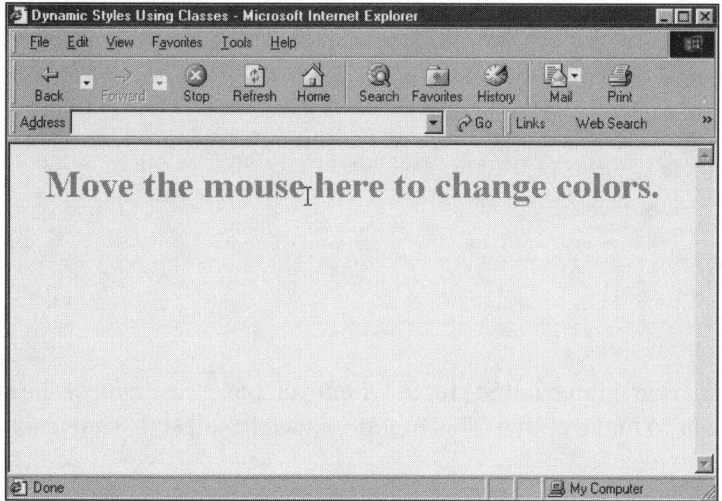

Figure 13.6   Using dynamic style classes.

Toggling Style Sheets On and Off

"It's no use," the novice programmer says. "I just can't decide. Should I use my normal style sheet or the dramatic one in my Web page?" "Why not let the user decide?" you ask. The NP says, "Huh?"

You can now determine which style sheet to apply to a page in Internet Explorer when the page is being viewed. To do that, you use the **styleSheets** collection of the **document** object. To select which style sheet applies to the page, you simply disable all other style sheets, setting their **disabled** property to **true**.

Here's an example. I'll add two style sheets to a Web page, giving them the names **normal** and **dramatic** (note that **disabled** is an attribute of the **<style>** element only in Internet Explorer, so this example is not conforming XHTML):

Chapter 13 Dynamic XHTML: Changing Web Pages on the Fly

```
<?xml version="1.0"?>
<!DOCTYPE html PUBLIC "-//W3C//DTD XHTML 1.0 Transitional//EN"
"http://www.w3.org/tr/xhtml1/DTD/xhtml1-transitional.dtd">
<html xmlns="http://www.w3.org/1999/xhtml" xml:lang="en" lang="en">
    <head>
        <title>
            Toggling Style Sheets
        </title>

        <style type="text/css" id = "dramatic">
            body
                {font-family: verdana; color: white; background-color: black}
        </style>

        <style type="text/css" "id = normal" disabled = "true">
            body {font-family: 'times new roman'; color: black;
                background-color: white}
        </style>
            .
            .
            .
```

Next, I'll add a function named **setStyle**, to which you pass the name of the style sheet that you want to make active. This function disables all style sheets except the one you want to use:

```
<?xml version="1.0"?>
<!DOCTYPE html PUBLIC "-//W3C//DTD XHTML 1.0 Transitional//EN"
"http://www.w3.org/tr/xhtml1/DTD/xhtml1-transitional.dtd">
<html xmlns="http://www.w3.org/1999/xhtml" xml:lang="en" lang="en">
    <head>
        <title>
            Toggling Style Sheets
        </title>

        <style type="text/css" id = "dramatic">
            body
                {font-family: verdana; color: white; background-color: black}
        </style>

        <style type="text/css" id = "normal" disabled = "true">
            body {font-family: 'times new roman'; color: black;
                background-color: white}
        </style>
```

```
        <script type = "text/javascript"
            language = "javascript" src = "script.js">
        </script>
    </head>
         .
         .
         .
```

Here's the script file used, script.js:

```
function setStyle(styleName)
{
    var sheet
    for (var loopIndex = 0; loopIndex <
        document.styleSheets.length; loopIndex++) {
        sheet = document.styleSheets[loopIndex]
        sheet.disabled = true
        if (sheet.id == styleName) {
            sheet.disabled = false
        }
    }
}
```

All that's left to do is add two buttons to let users decide which style sheet they want to use:

```
<?xml version="1.0"?>
<!DOCTYPE html PUBLIC "-//W3C//DTD XHTML 1.0 Transitional//EN"
"http://www.w3.org/tr/xhtml1/DTD/xhtml1-transitional.dtd">
<html xmlns="http://www.w3.org/1999/xhtml" xml:lang="en" lang="en">
    <head>
        <title>
            Toggling Style Sheets
        </title>

        <style type="text/css" id = "dramatic">
            body
                {font-family: verdana; color: white; background-color: black}
        </style>

        <style type="text/css" id = "normal" disabled = "true">
            body {font-family: 'times new roman'; color: black;
                background-color: white}
        </style>
```

```
        <script type = "text/javascript"
            language = "javascript" src = "script.js">
        </script>
    </head>

    <body>
        <h1>
            Toggling Style Sheets
        </h1>

        <center>
            <input type = "button" value = "Normal Style"
                onclick="setStyle('normal')" />
            <input type = "button" value = "Dramatic Style"
                onclick="setStyle('dramatic')" />
        </center>
        <p>
            You can set the style sheet for the entire document just
            by clicking a button.
        </p>
    </body>
</html>
```

That's it. The results appear in Figure 13.7. When the user clicks the Normal Style button, the **normal** style sheet is used in the page; when the user clicks the Dramatic Style button, the **dramatic** style sheet is used. In this way, you can change style sheets on the fly, producing some cool effects.

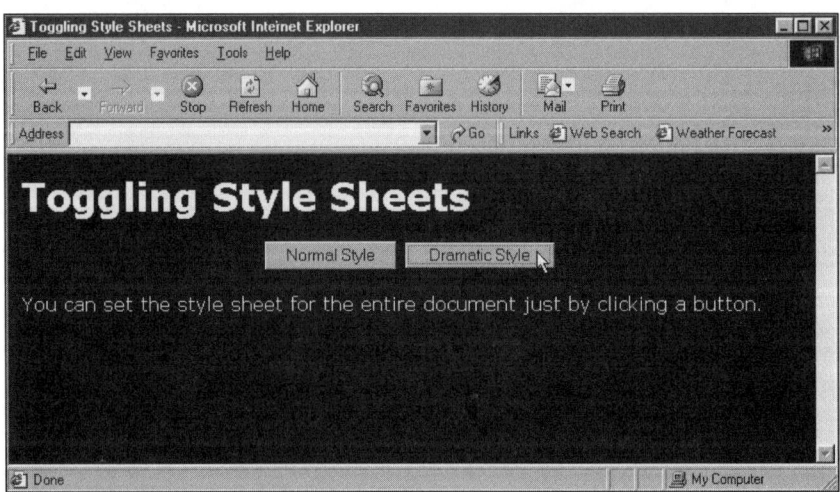

Figure 13.7   Toggling style sheets.

Dynamic Content: document.write

Using the **document** object's **write** and **writeln** (write line) methods, you can modify Web pages on the fly. We discussed **document.write** in Chapter 11, but I'll review it here.

Here's an example in which I'm using a Confirmation dialog box from JavaScript to ask users if they want to download the large image. This dialog box will display the message "View graphics intensive page?"; if users click OK, the code will write an **<img>** element to download the large graphics file. If users click Cancel, the code will download a smaller version of the file. Here's what the code looks like:

```xml
<?xml version="1.0"?>
<!DOCTYPE html PUBLIC "-//W3C//DTD XHTML 1.0 Transitional//EN"
"http://www.w3.org/tr/xhtml1/DTD/xhtml1-transitional.dtd">
<html xmlns="http://www.w3.org/1999/xhtml" xml:lang="en" lang="en">
    <head>
        <title>
            Creating A Self-Modifying Web Page
        </title>
    </head>

    <body>
        <center>
            <h1>
                Creating A Self-Modifying Web Page
            </h1>

            <script type = "text/javascript"
                language = "javascript" src = "script.js">
            </script>
        </center>
    </body>
</html>
```

Here's the script, script.js, used by this page:

```javascript
if(confirm("View graphics intensive page?")) {
    document.write("<br /><img width='1024' height='1024' "
    + "alt='image' src='gif/image1.gif' />")
}
else {
    document.write("<br /><img width='120' height='120' " +
    "alt='image' src='gif/image1small.gif' />")
}
```

You can see the results in Chapter 11, in Figure 11.3, where the Confirmation dialog box is visible.

Take a look at this next example from the "In Depth" section of this chapter. When the user clicks the page, the whole page is replaced by the text "This is a new page!" (note that the page as rewritten is no longer compliant XHTML in this case):

```
<?xml version="1.0"?>
<!DOCTYPE html PUBLIC "-//W3C//DTD XHTML 1.0 Transitional//EN"
"http://www.w3.org/tr/xhtml1/DTD/xhtml1-transitional.dtd">
<html xmlns="http://www.w3.org/1999/xhtml" xml:lang="en" lang="en">
    <head>
        <title>
            Using document.writeln
        </title>

        <script type = "text/javascript">
            function rewrite()
            {
                document.writeln("This is a new page!")
            }
        </script>
    </head>

    <body onmousedown="rewrite()">
        <center>
            <h1>
                Click this page to rewrite it!
            </h1>
        </center>
    </body>
</html>
```

In Netscape Navigator, you can do the same thing, but you have to connect the **mousedown** event to the code, as well as explicitly opening and closing the document (this page will also work in Internet Explorer):

```
<?xml version="1.0"?>
<!DOCTYPE html PUBLIC "-//W3C//DTD XHTML 1.0 Transitional//EN"
"http://www.w3.org/tr/xhtml1/DTD/xhtml1-transitional.dtd">
<html xmlns="http://www.w3.org/1999/xhtml" xml:lang="en" lang="en">
    <head>
        <title>
            Using document.writeln
        </title>
```

```
        <script type = "text/javascript">
            document.onmousedown = rewrite

            function rewrite()
            {
                document.open()
                document.writeln("This is a new page!")
                document.close()
            }
        </script>
    </head>

    <body onmousedown="rewrite()">
        <center>
            <h1>
                Click this page to rewrite it!
            </h1>
        </center>
    </body>
</html>
```

Using **document.write**, you can tailor your Web pages to the time of day. Here's an example in which the page presents a menu to the user, and the page displays the breakfast, lunch, or dinner menu automatically, based on the time of day:

```
<?xml version="1.0"?>
<!DOCTYPE html PUBLIC "-//W3C//DTD XHTML 1.0 Transitional//EN"
 "http://www.w3.org/tr/xhtml1/DTD/xhtml1-transitional.dtd">
<html xmlns="http://www.w3.org/1999/xhtml" xml:lang="en" lang="en">
    <head>
        <title>
            Welcome to our restaurant
        </title>
    </head>

    <body>
        <script type = "text/javascript"
            language = "javascript" src = "script.js">
        </script>
    </body>
</html>
```

Here's the script that does all the work, script.js:

```
var dateNow = new Date()
var hourNow = dateNow.getHours()
document.write( "<center>")
```

```
document.write( "<h1>")
document.write( "Welcome To Our Restaurant")
document.write( "</h1>")
document.write( "</center>")

if (hourNow < 5 || hourNow > 23){
    document.write( "<center>")
    document.write( "<h1>")
    document.write( "Sorry, We Are Closed." )
    document.write( "</h1>")
    document.write( "</center>")
}

if (hourNow > 6 && hourNow < 12 ) {
    document.write( "<center>")
    document.write( "<table border='1'>")
    document.write(
        "<tr><th colspan = '2'>Breakfast</th></tr>")
    document.write(
        "<tr><td>Pancakes</td><td>$2.00</td></tr>")
    document.write(
        "<tr><td>Eggs</td><td>$2.50</td></tr>")
    document.write(
        "<tr><td>Waffles</td><td>$1.50</td></tr>")
    document.write(
        "<tr><td>Oatmeal</td><td>$1.00</td></tr>")
    document.write( "</table>")
    document.write( "</center>")
}

if ( hourNow >= 12 && hourNow < 17 ) {
    document.write( "<center>")
    document.write( "<table border='1'>")
    document.write(
        "<tr><th colspan = '2'>Lunch</th></tr>")
    document.write(
        "<tr><td>Ham Sandwich</td><td>$3.50</td></tr>")
    document.write(
        "<tr><td>Chicken Sandwich</td><td>$3.50</td></tr>")
    document.write(
        "<tr><td>Cheese Sandwich</td><td>$3.00</td></tr>")
    document.write(
        "<tr><td>Lobster Nuggets</td><td>$5.00</td></tr>")
    document.write(
        "<tr><td>Peacock</td><td>$4.50</td></tr>")
    document.write(
        "<tr><td>Chili</td><td>$2.00</td></tr>")
```

```
        document.write(
            "<tr><td>Chicken Soup</td><td>$1.50</td></tr>")
        document.write( "</table>")
        document.write( "</center>")
    }

    if ( hourNow >= 17 && hourNow < 22 ) {
        document.write( "<center>")
        document.write( "<table border = '1'>")
        document.write(
            "<tr><th colspan = '2'>Dinner</th></tr>")
        document.write(
            "<tr><td>Lobster</td><td>$7.50</td></tr>")
        document.write(
            "<tr><td>Filet Mignon</td><td>$8.00</td></tr>")
        document.write(
            "<tr><td>Flank Steak</td><td>$7.00</td></tr>")
        document.write(
            "<tr><td>Tube Steak</td><td>$3.50</td></tr>")
        document.write(
            "<tr><td>Salad</td><td>$2.50</td></tr>")
        document.write(
            "<tr><td>Potato</td><td>$1.50</td></tr>")
        document.write(
            "<tr><td>Eggplant</td><td>$1.50</td></tr>")
        document.write( "</table>")
        document.write( "</center>")
    }
```

You can see the results of this code in Chapter 11, in Figure 11.4.

Dynamic Content: The insertAdjacentHTML and insertAdjacentText Methods

"Hey," says the novice programmer, "I don't want to rewrite a whole Web page with **document.write**; I just want to insert a new control when the user wants one. How do I do that?" "There are a couple of ways," you say, "and one of the best ways is to use the **insertAdjacentHTML** and **insertAdjacentText** methods."

Compared to **document.write**, the **insertAdjacentHTML** and **insertAdjacentText** methods give you finer control over the placement of inserted markup and text in pages in Internet Explorer. The **insertAdjacentHTML** method lets you insert markup and text next to an element that already exists, and the

insertAdjacentText method lets you insert text (which will not be parsed as XHTML by the browser) in the same way. You can determine where the new text or markup will go with respect to the existing element by passing the constants **BeforeBegin**, **AfterBegin**, **BeforeEnd**, or **AfterEnd** to **insertAdjacentHTML** and **insertAdjacentText**.

In this next example, I'll write code using **insertAdjacentHTML** to insert a new text field after a **<div>** element when the user clicks a button. Here's what the code looks like:

```xml
<?xml version="1.0"?>
<!DOCTYPE html PUBLIC "-//W3C//DTD XHTML 1.0 Transitional//EN"
"http://www.w3.org/tr/xhtml1/DTD/xhtml1-transitional.dtd">
<html xmlns="http://www.w3.org/1999/xhtml" xml:lang="en" lang="en">
    <head>
        <title>
            Using insertAdjacentHTML
        </title>

        <script type = "text/javascript"
            language = "javascript" src = "script.js">
        </script>
    </head>

    <body>
        <center>
            <h1>
                Using insertAdjacentHTML
            </h1>
        </center>

        <div id="div1">
            <input type = "button" value="Click Me!" onclick="showMore()" />
        </div>
    </body>
</html>
```

And here's the script, script.js, that does all the work:

```javascript
function showMore()
{
    div1.insertAdjacentHTML("AfterEnd", "<p>A new text field: " +
        "<input type='text' value='Hello!' /></p>");
}
```

Now when the user clicks the button, the code in the page adds a new text field right after the **<div>** element. Clicking the button several times adds several text fields, as you can see in Figure 13.8.

TIP: *There's another way to add elements to a Web page; see the "Immediate Solutions" section "Dynamic Content: Using the **createElement** Method."*

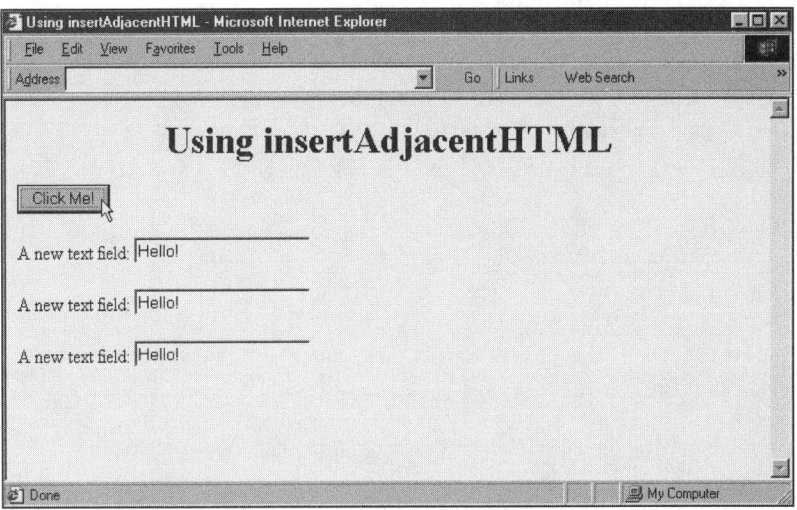

Figure 13.8 Using **insertAdjacentHTML**.

Dynamic Content: The **innerText**, **outerText**, **innerHMTL**, and **outerHTML** Properties

"OK," says the novice programmer, "I can insert new markup and text into a Web page with the **insertAdjacentHTML** method, but isn't there a way to modify elements that already exist in a Web page?" "There sure is," you say; "you can use the **innerText**, **outerText**, **innerHTML**, and **outerHTML** properties of virtually every element in Internet Explorer." "To do what?" the NP wants to know.

You can modify existing elements in a Web page in Internet Explorer by using the **innerText**, **outerText**, **innerHTML**, and **outerHTML** properties of almost every element. The following list describes these properties:

- **innerText**—Lets you change the text between the start and end tags.

- **outerText**—Lets you change all of the element's text, including the start and end tags.

- **innerHTML**—Changes contents of elements between the start and end tags; treats text as XHTML.
- **outerHTML**—Changes contents of an element, including the start and end tags; treats text as XHTML.

Here's an example of using the **innerText** property. This property lets you change the text content of an element. I'll change the text in a header from "Dynamic XHTML" to "This is the new header":

```
<?xml version="1.0"?>
<!DOCTYPE html PUBLIC "-//W3C//DTD XHTML 1.0 Transitional//EN"
"http://www.w3.org/tr/xhtml1/DTD/xhtml1-transitional.dtd">
<html xmlns="http://www.w3.org/1999/xhtml" xml:lang="en" lang="en">
    <head>
        <title>
            Changing XHTML on the fly
        </title>

        <script type = "text/javascript" language = "javascript">
            function changeHeader()
            {
                header.innerText = "This is the new header"
            }
        </script>
    </head>

    <body>
        <center>
            <h1 id = "header" onclick = "changeHeader()">Dynamic XHTML</h1>

            Click the above header to change it....
        </center>
    </body>
</html>
```

Figure 13.9 shows the results of this code after the user has clicked the header. When the header is clicked, the text changes to what you see in the figure.

If I used the **innerHTML** property, I could change the text content of the header to something that the browser will interpret as XHTML. For example, I can change the original text "Dynamic XHTML" in the **<h1>** header to a **<marquee>** element. Because I'm using **innerHTML**, the outer **<h1>** tag is preserved, so the text in the marquee is styled by the enclosing **<h1>** header (note that the **<marquee>** element is specific to Internet Explorer and so is not official XHTML):

Immediate Solutions

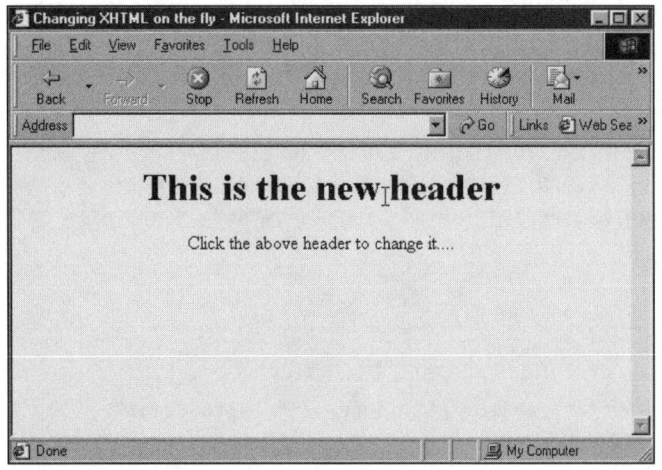

Figure 13.9 Using the **innerText** property.

```
<?xml version="1.0"?>
<!DOCTYPE html PUBLIC "-//W3C//DTD XHTML 1.0 Transitional//EN"
"http://www.w3.org/tr/xhtml1/DTD/xhtml1-transitional.dtd">
<html xmlns="http://www.w3.org/1999/xhtml" xml:lang="en" lang="en">
    <head>
        <title>
            Changing XHTML on the fly
        </title>

        <script type = "text/javascript" language = "javascript">

            function changeHeader()
            {
                header.innerHTML =
                    "<marquee>This marquee was just created!</marquee>"
            }
        </script>
    </head>

    <body>
        <center>
            <h1 id = "header" onclick = "changeHeader()">Dynamic XHTML</h1>

            Click the above header to change it....
        </center>
    </body>
</html>
```

If you want to replace the element entirely, including the surrounding **<h1>** tag, you can use the **outerHTML** property:

```
<?xml version="1.0"?>
<!DOCTYPE html PUBLIC "-//W3C//DTD XHTML 1.0 Transitional//EN"
    "http://www.w3.org/tr/xhtml1/DTD/xhtml1-transitional.dtd">
<html xmlns="http://www.w3.org/1999/xhtml" xml:lang="en" lang="en">
    <head>
        <title>
            Changing XHTML on the fly
        </title>

        <script type = "text/javascript" language = "javascript">
            function changeHeader()
            {
                header.outerHTML =
                    "<marquee style = 'font-size: 54;'>" +
                    "This marquee was just created!</marquee>"
            }
        </script>
    </head>

    <body>
        <center>
            <h1 id = "header" onclick = "changeHeader()">Dynamic XHTML</h1>

            Click the above header to change it....
        </center>
    </body>
</html>
```

Now when the user clicks the header, the entire header is rewritten as a marquee with 54-point text. You can see the results in Figure 13.2.

Dynamic Content: Using Text Ranges

Another way to modify a Web page on the fly in Internet Explorer is to use a **TextRange** object. Using text ranges, you can select, copy, and replace text in a Web page in a general way.

Here's an example in which I create a text range with the **createTextRange** method, select the text of an element with the **moveToElementText** method, and replace that text with the **pasteHTML** method:

Immediate Solutions

```xml
<?xml version="1.0"?>
<!DOCTYPE html PUBLIC "-//W3C//DTD XHTML 1.0 Transitional//EN"
"http://www.w3.org/tr/xhtml1/DTD/xhtml1-transitional.dtd">
<html xmlns="http://www.w3.org/1999/xhtml" xml:lang="en" lang="en">
    <head>
        <title>
            Using the TextRange Object
        </title>

        <script type = "text/javascript" language = "JavaScript">
            function replaceText()
            {
                var range = document.body.createTextRange()
                range.moveToElementText(text1)
                range.pasteHTML("Here is the new text.")
            }
        </script>
    </head>

    <body>
        <center>
            <h1>
                Using the TextRange Object
            </h1>
        </center>

        <input type = "button" value="Click Me" onclick="replaceText()" />

        <br />
        <br />

        <div id = "text1" style =
            "font-family:Arial, sans-serif; font-weight:bold">
            Click the button to replace all this text at once.
        </div>
    </body>
</html>
```

When you display this page in Internet Explorer, you see the text "Click the button to replace all this text at once." When you do click the button, that text is selected and replaced by the text "Here is the new text.", as you can see in Figure 13.10.

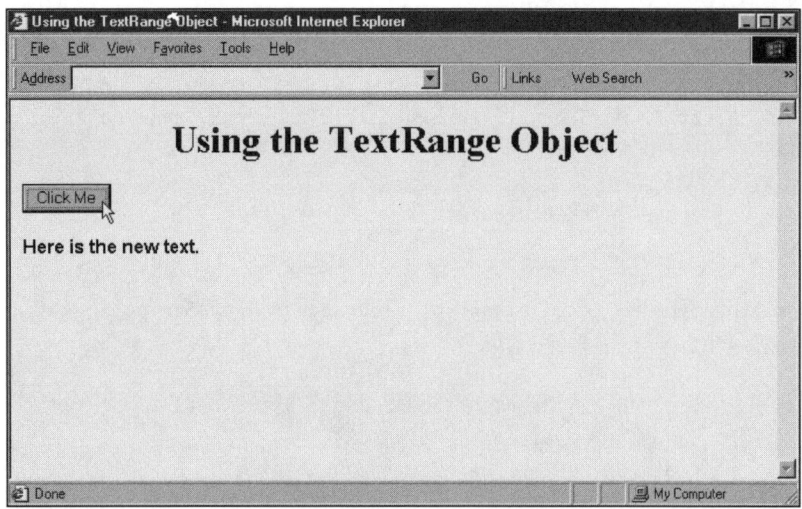

Figure 13.10 Using the **TextRange** object to modify a Web page on the fly.

Dynamic Content: Using the createElement Method

The novice programmer says, "I can rewrite elements in a Web page in Internet Explorer by using various properties and methods, but isn't there a way that is dedicated only to creating new Web page elements?" "Yes," you say, "there is. You can use the **createElement** method." "Tell me how!" the NP says.

As of Internet Explorer 5, you can use the **createElement** method to create new Web page elements, and you can use methods such as **insertBefore** and **insertAfter** to insert those elements into a Web page. In this example, I'm mimicking the example shown earlier (in "Dynamic Content: The **insertAdjacentHTML** and **insertAdjacentText** Methods"), where I added text fields to a Web page. However, this time I'm using **createElement** to create the new elements and using **insertBefore** to insert them into a Web page. I'm also using the **createTextNode** method to create new text in the Web page. Here's what the example looks like:

```
<?xml version="1.0"?>
<!DOCTYPE html PUBLIC "-//W3C//DTD XHTML 1.0 Transitional//EN"
"http://www.w3.org/tr/xhtml1/DTD/xhtml1-transitional.dtd">
<html xmlns="http://www.w3.org/1999/xhtml" xml:lang="en" lang="en">
    <head>
```

```
        <title>
            Using createElement To Create New Elements
        </title>

        <script type = "text/javascript" language = "javascript">
            function showMore()
            {
                var newDiv, newTextfield, newText;

                newDiv = document.createElement("div");
                newDiv.id = "Newdiv";

                newTextfield = document.createElement("input");
                newTextfield.type = "text";
                newTextfield.value = "Hello!"

                newText = document.createTextNode("A new text field: ");

                newDiv.insertBefore(newText, null);
                newDiv.insertBefore(newTextfield, null);

                document.body.insertBefore(newDiv, null);
            }
        </script>
    </head>

    <body>
        <center>
            <h1>
                Using createElement To Create New Elements
            </h1>
        </center>

        <div id="initialdiv">
            <input type = "button" value="Click Me" onclick="showMore()" />
        </div>
    </body>
</html>
```

You can see the results of this code in Figure 13.11. When the user clicks the button, the code uses the **createElement** method to create new elements and insert them in the Web page on the fly.

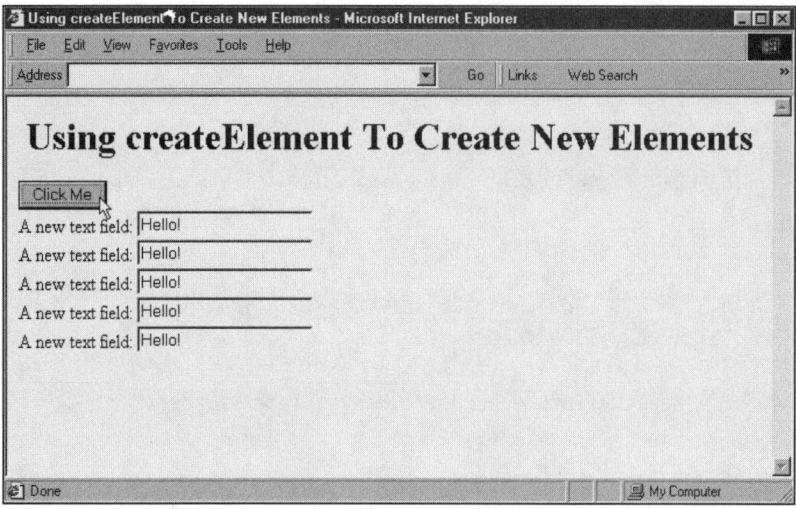

Figure 13.11   Using **createElement** to create new elements.

Dynamic Content: Creating Dynamic Tables

"Say," says the novice programmer, "I'm having some trouble making tables dynamic. I can rewrite the whole table, but I can't seem to access just one cell at a time." "Tables are special unto themselves in Internet Explorer," you say, "and there's special methods to deal with them to make them dynamic." "It figures," says the NP.

The **<table>** and **<tr>** elements have their own set of methods to make them dynamic in Internet Explorer. The following list describes the methods for the **<table>** element:

- **object.deleteRow(index)**—Deletes a row. The **index** value indicates the row index of the row to delete.
- **object.insertRow(index)**—Inserts a new row. Returns the inserted **<tr>** element (which will be empty) or **null** for failure. If **index** isn't supplied, the **<tr>** element will be inserted at the end.
- **object.rows(index)**—Returns a collection (array) of the rows in the table.

And the following list describes the methods for **<tr>** elements:

- **object.cells(index)**—Returns a collection (array) of the cells in the row.
- **object.deleteCell(index)**—Deletes a cell. The **index** value indicates the position in the cell collection to delete.

- **object.insertCell(index)**—Inserts a new cell and returns the inserted **<td>** element (which will be empty) or **null** for failure. If **index** isn't supplied, the **<td>** element will be inserted at the end of the row.

- **object.rowIndex**—Returns the row index of the row. Useful for inserting and deleting rows.

Here's an example showing how to create a dynamic table in Internet Explorer. I'll insert a new row in a table with the **insertRow** method, insert three cells into the new row with the **insertCell** method, and set the contents of the cell with the **innerText** property. Here's the code:

```
<?xml version="1.0"?>
<!DOCTYPE html PUBLIC "-//W3C//DTD XHTML 1.0 Transitional//EN"
"http://www.w3.org/tr/xhtml1/DTD/xhtml1-transitional.dtd">
<html xmlns="http://www.w3.org/1999/xhtml" xml:lang="en" lang="en">
    <head>
        <title>
            Creating Dynamic Tables
        </title>

        <script type = "text/javascript" language = "javascript">
            function addem()
            {
                var newRow = table1.insertRow(3)
                var newCell = newRow.insertCell(0)
                newCell.innerText = "X"
                newCell = newRow.insertCell(1)
                newCell.innerText = "O"
                newCell = newRow.insertCell(2)
                newCell.innerText = "X"
            }
        </script>
    </head>

    <body>
        <center>
            <h1>
                Creating Dynamic Tables
            </h1>

            <table id="table1" border="2">
                <tr>
                    <th>Tic</th>
                    <th>Tac</th>
```

```
                    <th>Toe</th>
                </tr>
                <tr>
                    <td>X</td>
                    <td>O</td>
                    <td>X</td>
                </tr>
                <tr>
                    <td>O</td>
                    <td>X</td>
                    <td>O</td>
                </tr>
                <tr>
                    <td>X</td>
                    <td>O</td>
                    <td>X</td>
                </tr>
            </table>

            <input type="button" value="Add Row" onclick="addem()" />
        </center>
    </body>
</html>
```

This Web page appears in Figure 13.12. When the user clicks the button, a new row, complete with Xs and Os, appears in the table.

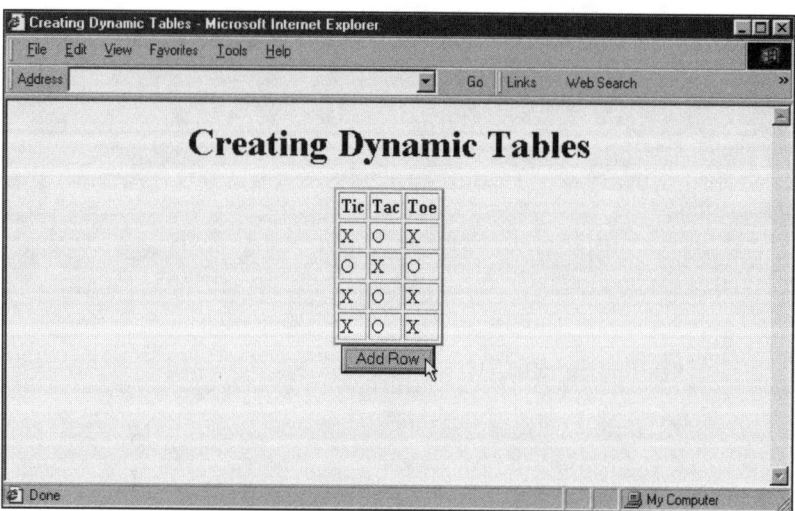

Figure 13.12   Creating a dynamic table.

Dynamic Content: Using Conditional Comments to Set Content on the Fly

There's one additional way to set Web page content on the fly—using conditional comments. In Internet Explorer, conditional comments take the form **<!--[***condition***]>**, where ***condition*** is a logical condition. For example, the condition could be the comment **<!--[if IE 5]>**, which checks if the browser is Internet Explorer 5, or the comment **<!--[if IE]>**, which checks if the browser is Internet Explorer. Here's an example targeted to Internet Explorer:

```
<?xml version="1.0"?>
<!DOCTYPE html PUBLIC "-//W3C//DTD XHTML 1.0 Transitional//EN"
    "http://www.w3.org/tr/xhtml1/DTD/xhtml1-transitional.dtd">
<html xmlns="http://www.w3.org/1999/xhtml" xml:lang="en" lang="en">
    <head>
        <title>
            Using Conditional Comments
        </title>
    </head>

    <body>
        <center>
            <h1>
                Using Conditional Comments
            </h1>

            <!--[if IE ]>
                Welcome to Internet Explorer.
            <![endif]>

            <!--[if IE 5]>
                In fact, welcome to Internet Explorer 5!
            <![endif]>

            <!--[if ! IE 5]>
                Please upgrade to Internet Explorer 5.
            <![endif]>
    </body>
</html>
```

You can see the results of this code in Figure 13.13. (Unfortunately, these conditional elements are not valid XHTML and will not pass the W3C XHTML validator.)

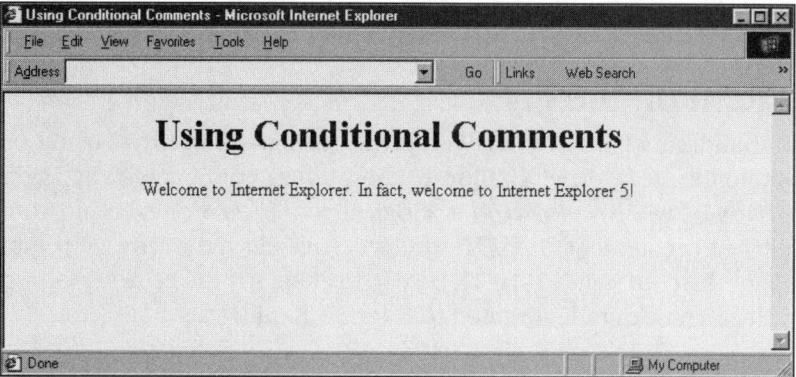

Figure 13.13 Using conditional comments in Internet Explorer.

Creating Amazing mouseover Effects

The novice programmer appears and says, "I wonder if I can use dynamic XHTML to make my Web page respond when the user moves the mouse over it." You laugh and say, "No problem whatsoever."

There are many ways to use dynamic XHTML to let a Web page react as the user moves the mouse over it—and most of these require using Internet Explorer. In this section, I'll discuss these ways as well as one way of working with layers in Netscape Navigator to create **mouseover** effects.

One easy way to create **mouseover** effects using hyperlinks in Internet Explorer is to use the **hover** attribute, which was created for just this purpose. Here's an example in which I'm setting the style of hyperlinks to bold, red, and a large font size when the mouse hovers over them:

```
<?xml version="1.0"?>
<!DOCTYPE html PUBLIC "-//W3C//DTD XHTML 1.0 Transitional//EN"
"http://www.w3.org/tr/xhtml1/DTD/xhtml1-transitional.dtd">
<html xmlns="http://www.w3.org/1999/xhtml" xml:lang="en" lang="en">
    <head>
        <title>
            Using The hover Attribute
        </title>
        <style type="text/css">
            a {font-family: verdana; font-weight: normal; color: blue}
            a:hover {font-weight: bold; color: red; font-size: 24}
            a:active {font-weight: bold; color: red;
            background-color: darkgray}
```

```
                a:visited {font-weight: bold; color: gray;
                background-color: darkgray}
        </style>
</head>

<body>
    <center>
        <h1>
            Using The hover Attribute
        </h1>
    </center>
            <a href="http://www.starpowder.com">
                Move the mouse over me
            </a>
            <a href="http://www.starpowder.com">
                Now over me!
            </a>
</body>
</html>
```

You can see the results of this code in Figure 13.14. When the user moves the mouse over a hyperlink, the new style takes effect, as you can see in the figure, and when the mouse moves away, the original hyperlink style is restored.

Here's another example in Internet Explorer. This time I'm changing the style of a header to red when the mouse is over it and back to black when the mouse moves away:

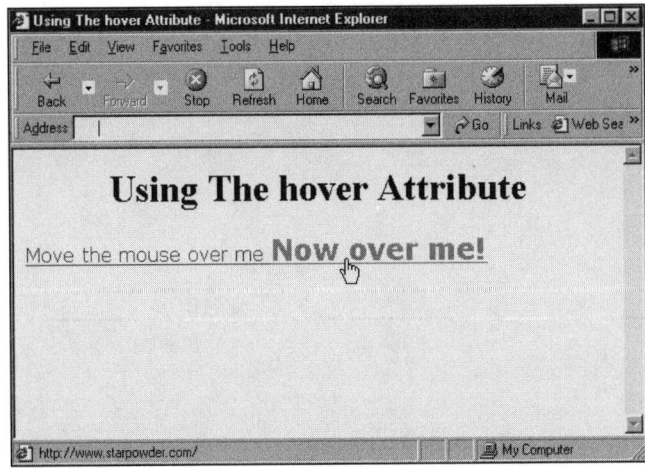

Figure 13.14 Using the **hover** attribute for **mouseover** effects.

```xml
<?xml version="1.0"?>
<!DOCTYPE html PUBLIC "-//W3C//DTD XHTML 1.0 Transitional//EN"
"http://www.w3.org/tr/xhtml1/DTD/xhtml1-transitional.dtd">
<html xmlns="http://www.w3.org/1999/xhtml" xml:lang="en" lang="en">
    <head>
        <title>
            Using Dynamic Styles
        </title>
    </head>

    <body>
        <center>
            <h1 onmouseover="this.style.color = 'red';"
                onmouseout="this.style.color = 'black';">
                Turn me red with the mouse.
            </h1>
        </center>
    </body>
</html>
```

Here's another example (from the "In Depth" section of this chapter), which uses dynamic styles to create **mouseover** effects:

```xml
<?xml version="1.0"?>
<!DOCTYPE html PUBLIC "-//W3C//DTD XHTML 1.0 Transitional//EN"
"http://www.w3.org/tr/xhtml1/DTD/xhtml1-transitional.dtd">
<html xmlns="http://www.w3.org/1999/xhtml" xml:lang="en" lang="en">
    <head>
        <title>
            Using Dynamic Styles
        </title>
    </head>

    <body>
        <center>
            <h1>
                Using Dynamic Styles.
            </h1>
            <span onmouseover = "this.style.fontSize = '48'">
                This text gets bigger when you move the mouse over it!
            </span>
        </center>
    </body>
</html>
```

You can see the results of this code in Figure 13.1. Here's another example, which we saw in the Immediate Solutions section "Using Dynamic Styles." In this case, I'm changing the cursor to a hand shape when the cursor moves over a header—note the use of the JavaScript term **this**, which refers to the current element:

```xml
<?xml version="1.0"?>
<!DOCTYPE html PUBLIC "-//W3C//DTD XHTML 1.0 Transitional//EN"
"http://www.w3.org/tr/xhtml1/DTD/xhtml1-transitional.dtd">
<html xmlns="http://www.w3.org/1999/xhtml" xml:lang="en" lang="en">
    <head>
        <title>
            Using Dynamic Styles
        </title>
    </head>

    <body>

        <center>
            <h1 onmouseover = "this.style.cursor = 'hand';"
                onmouseout = "this.style.cursor = 'default';">
                Change the cursor with the mouse.
            </h1>
        </center>
    </body>
</html>
```

You can see the results of this code in Figure 13.5. Here's another example; this time I'm using style classes to change text from blue to red when the mouse moves over it:

```xml
<?xml version="1.0"?>
<!DOCTYPE html PUBLIC "-//W3C//DTD XHTML 1.0 Transitional//EN"
"http://www.w3.org/tr/xhtml1/DTD/xhtml1-transitional.dtd">
<html xmlns="http://www.w3.org/1999/xhtml" xml:lang="en" lang="en">
    <head>
        <title>
            Dynamic Styles Using Classes
        </title>
        <style type="text/css">
            .red {color:red}
            .blue {color:blue}
        </style>
    </head>
```

```
        <body>
            <center>
                <h1 class = "blue" onmouseover = "this.className='red'"
                    onmouseout = "this.className='blue'">
                    Move the mouse here to change colors.
                </h1>
            </center>
        </body>
</html>
```

Here's an example (from earlier in this chapter) that uses layers in Netscape Navigator to create a **mouseover** effect. In this case, I set the background color of the layer when the mouse moves over it, creating a **mouseover** effect much like that in Internet Explorer (recall that because the **<layer>** element is Netscape-specific, this document is not conforming XHTML):

```
<?xml version="1.0"?>
<!DOCTYPE html PUBLIC "-//W3C//DTD XHTML 1.0 Transitional//EN"
"http://www.w3.org/tr/xhtml1/DTD/xhtml1-transitional.dtd">
<html xmlns="http://www.w3.org/1999/xhtml" xml:lang="en" lang="en">
    <head>
        <title>
            Mouseover Effects Using Layers
        </title>

    </head>

    <body>
        <layer bgcolor = "white" top = "40" left = "40"
            onmouseover = "setcolor('cyan')" onmouseout =
                "setcolor('white')" >
            <script type = "text/javascript" language = "javascript">
                function setcolor(color)
                {
                    bgColor = color
                }
            </script>
            <h1>
                Mouseover Effects Using Layers
            </h1>
        </layer>
    </body>
</html>
```

You can see the results of this code in Figure 13.4. Here's another example for Internet Explorer. In this case, I'll use the **src** attribute of an image to display a new image when the mouse moves over it. The new image is the same as the original image except that it's lighter, giving the impression that moving the mouse over the image selects it:

```
<?xml version="1.0"?>
<!DOCTYPE html PUBLIC "-//W3C//DTD XHTML 1.0 Transitional//EN"
"http://www.w3.org/tr/xhtml1/DTD/xhtml1-transitional.dtd">
<html xmlns="http://www.w3.org/1999/xhtml" xml:lang="en" lang="en">
    <head>
        <title>
            Mouseover Image Handling
        </title>
    </head>

    <body>
        <center>
            <h1>
                Mouseover Image Handling
            </h1>

            <img src = "flower.jpg" alt="image"
                onmouseover = "this.src = 'flower2.jpg'"
                onmouseout = "this.src = 'flower.jpg'" />
        </center>
    </body>
</html>
```

You can see the results of this code in Figure 13.3.

Positioning Elements by Using Styles

One more aspect of dynamic XHTML is to position elements in a Web page. We first saw this in Chapter 9; I'll take another look at it here.

You use the **position** style property to set the position of elements in a Web page. The following list describes the properties you usually use when you work with positioning:

- **position**—Can hold values such as **absolute** and **relative**.
- **top**—Offset of the top of the element's box.
- **bottom**—Offset of the bottom of the element's box.
- **left**—Offset of the left edge of the element's box.
- **right**—Offset of the right edge of the element's box.

In this next example, I set **position** to **absolute** and then specify the **top** and **left** properties for three **<div>** elements, each of which has an image and text:

```
<?xml version="1.0"?>
<!DOCTYPE html PUBLIC "-//W3C//DTD XHTML 1.0 Transitional//EN"
"http://www.w3.org/tr/xhtml1/DTD/xhtml1-transitional.dtd">
<html xmlns="http://www.w3.org/1999/xhtml" xml:lang="en" lang="en">
    <head>
        <title>
            Absolute Positioning
        </title>
    </head>

    <body>
        <h1 align="center">
            Absolute Positioning
        </h1>

        <div style=
            "position:absolute; left:50; top:60; border-width: thick">
            <img alt="image" src="flower1.jpg" width = "85"
                height = "129" />
            <br />
            Flower 1
        </div>

        <div style=
            "position:absolute; left:200; top:90; border-width: thick">
            <img alt="image" src="flower2.jpg" width = "85"
                height = "129" />
            <br />
            Flower 2
        </div>

        <div style="position:absolute; left:350; top:120;
            border-width: thick">
            <img alt="image" src="flower3.jpg" width = "85"
                height = "129" />
            <br />
            Flower 3
        </div>

    </body>
</html>
```

In addition to absolute positioning, you can use relative positioning. What are elements positioned relative *to*? They're positioned relative to the location they would have had in the normal flow of elements in the Web browser.

To position items in a relative way, you set **position** to **relative** and then set the other properties to indicate the new relative position. In this example, I'm moving some text up five pixels and other text down five pixels from the normal position at which the browser would place that text:

```
<?xml version="1.0"?>
<!DOCTYPE html PUBLIC "-//W3C//DTD XHTML 1.0 Transitional//EN"
"http://www.w3.org/tr/xhtml1/DTD/xhtml1-transitional.dtd">
<html xmlns="http://www.w3.org/1999/xhtml" xml:lang="en" lang="en">
    <head>
        <title>
            Relative Positioning
        </title>
    </head>

    <body>
        <h1 align="center">
            Relative Positioning
        </h1>
        This text goes
        <span style="position: relative; top: -5">up</span> and
        <span style="position: relative; top: 5">down</span>,
        as you can see.
    </body>
</html>
```

I'll apply this idea of element positioning in the next section.

Creating Animation

The novice programmer appears and says, "I thought dynamic XHTML would be dynamic. What about creating animation in a Web page?" "No sooner said than done," you say.

You can reset the position of Web page elements by using dynamic styles—see the previous section for more details. You can set the location of elements by using the JavaScript style properties **posLeft** and **posTop**. Here's an example in which I'm moving three **<div>** elements around the page by using JavaScript. I'm relating the location of the second and third **<div>** elements to the position of the first **<div>** element with the **expression** keyword, which lets you calculate an expression in the **style** attribute:

```xml
<?xml version="1.0"?>
<!DOCTYPE html PUBLIC "-//W3C//DTD XHTML 1.0 Transitional//EN"
    "http://www.w3.org/tr/xhtml1/DTD/xhtml1-transitional.dtd">
<html xmlns="http://www.w3.org/1999/xhtml" xml:lang="en" lang="en">
    <head>
        <title>
            Animation Using Dynamic Properties
        </title>
        <script type = "text/javascript"
            language = "javascript" src = "script.js">
        </script>
    </head>

    <body>
        <center>
            <h1>
                Animation Using Dynamic Properties
            </h1>
        </center>

        <div id = "text1" style =
            "position: absolute; top: 80; left: 0; height: 30;
            width: 100; background: cyan; font-size: 16">
            Hello from dynamic XHTML!
        </div>

        <div id = "text2" style =
            "position: absolute; top: 140; left:
            expression(text1.style.posLeft * 0.75); height: 30;
            width: 100; background: pink; font-size: 16">
            Hello again from dynamic XHTML!
        </div>

        <div id = "text3" style =
            "position: absolute; top: 200; left:
            expression(text1.style.posLeft * 0.5); height: 30;
            width: 100; background: yellow; font-size: 16">
            Hello once again from dynamic XHTML!
        </div>
    </body>
</html>
```

Here's the script, script.js, used by this page:

```
var increment = 1;
function setPosition()
{
    text1.style.posLeft = text1.style.posLeft + increment;
    if (text1.style.posLeft >= 600 || text1.style.posLeft < 0)
    {
        increment = -1 * increment;
    }
}
setInterval ("setPosition()", 50)
```

You can see the results of this code in Figure 13.15. In this page, the three **<div>** elements move from left to right and back again. The second **<div>** element moves three-quarters as fast as the top **<div>** element, and the third element moves only half as fast.

Note that you cannot use dynamic styles in Netscape Navigator yet; however, you can use layers to support animation—see the next section.

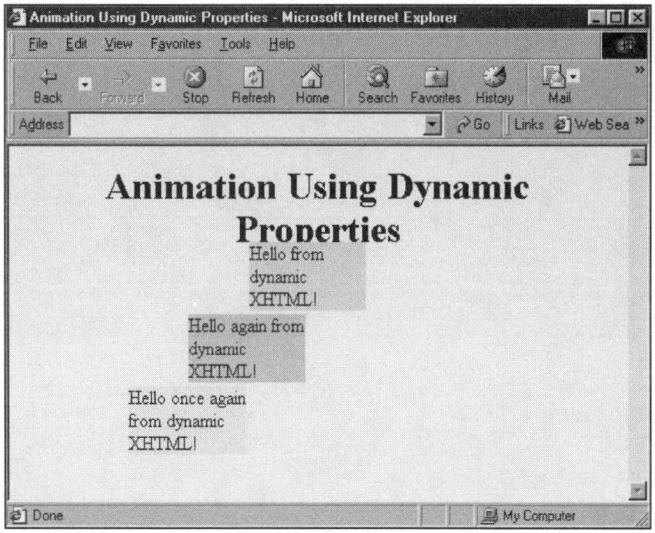

Figure 13.15   Animation using dynamic styles.

Creating Animation with Layers

The novice programmer stomps in and says, "I'm using Netscape Navigator. How can I create animation in a Web page using this browser?" "With layers," you say. "Ah," says the NP, "of course."

You can move layers around in Netscape Navigator by using the **left** and **top** properties. Here's an example in which I display one layer on top of another and then move one layer over to the left, uncovering the other layer steadily (recall that because the **<layer>** element is Netscape-specific, this document is not strictly conforming XHTML):

```xml
<?xml version="1.0"?>
<!DOCTYPE html PUBLIC "-//W3C//DTD XHTML 1.0 Transitional//EN"
"http://www.w3.org/tr/xhtml1/DTD/xhtml1-transitional.dtd">
<html xmlns="http://www.w3.org/1999/xhtml" xml:lang="en" lang="en">
    <head>
        <title>
            Animation With Layers
        </title>

        <script type = "text/javascript" language = "javascript">
            function handleTransition()
            {
                document.layers['layer1'].left =
                    document.layers['layer1'].left - 5

                if (document.layers['layer1'].left > -256) {
                    setTimeout('handleTransition()',50)
                }
            }
        </script>
    </head>

    <body>
        <center>
            <h1>
                Animation Using Layers
            </h1>
        </center>

        <div style="position:absolute;top:60;left:0">
            <img alt="image" src="image1.jpg" />
        </div>

        <layer name="layer1" left="0" top = "60">
            <img alt="image" src="image2.jpg" />
        </layer>
```

```
            <div style="position:absolute;top:340;left:40">
                <form action = "action">
                <input type="button" name="startTrans" value="Start Transition"
                    onclick="handleTransition()" />
                </form>
            </div>
        </body>
</html>
```

You can see the results of this code in Figure 13.16. When the user clicks the button in this page, the animation begins, and the top layer slides off to the right.

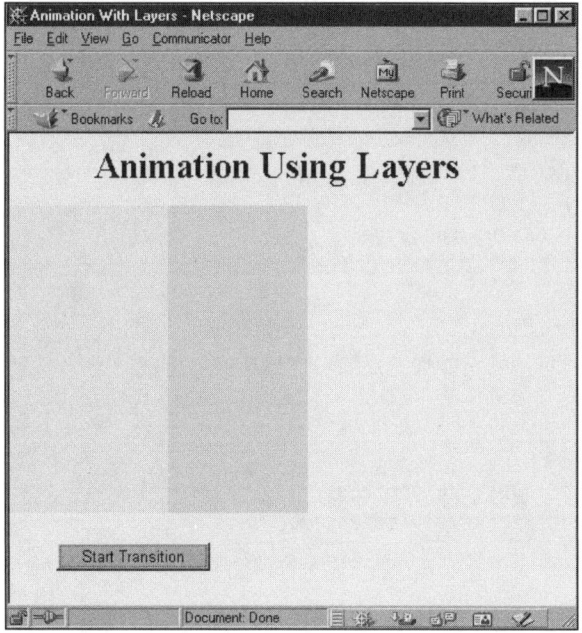

Figure 13.16   Creating animation by using layers.

Using Vector Markup Language (VML)

There's a way to draw figures in Internet Explorer that's worth mentioning—Vector Markup Language (VML). VML is implemented as a *behavior* in Internet Explorer, and we'll see how behaviors work in Chapter 14. Here's an example showing how to draw ovals, rectangles, and polylines with VML. I'm adding an XML namespace named **v** for VML to the default namespace created for XHTML:

```
<?xml version="1.0"?>
<!DOCTYPE html PUBLIC "-//W3C//DTD XHTML 1.0 Transitional//EN"
"http://www.w3.org/tr/xhtml1/DTD/xhtml1-transitional.dtd">
<html xmlns="http://www.w3.org/1999/xhtml"
    xmlns:v="urn:schemas-microsoft-com:vml"
    xml:lang="en" lang="en">
    <head>
        <title>
            Using Vector Markup Language
        </title>

        <style type="text/css">
        v\:* {behavior: url(#default#VML);}
        </style>
    </head>

    <body>
        <center>
            <h1>
                Using Vector Markup Language
            </h1>
        </center>
        <p>
        <v:oval style='width:100pt; height:75pt' fillcolor="yellow">
        </v:oval>
        </p>
        <p>
        <v:rect style='width:100pt; height:75pt' fillcolor="blue"
            strokecolor="red" strokeweight="2pt"/>
        </p>
        <p>
        <v:polyline points="20pt,55pt,100pt,-10pt,180pt,65pt,260pt,25pt"
            strokecolor="red" strokeweight="2pt"/>
        </p>
    </body>
</html>
```

The result of this code appears in Figure 13.17.

TIP: *To learn more about VML, see* **http://msdn.microsoft.com/standards/vml/ref/**.

Immediate Solutions

Figure 13.17   Using VML in Internet Explorer.

Setting Element Visibility

"Now I've got another problem," the novice programmer says, "because I want to make some controls in my Web page visible at times and invisible at others. What can I do?" "There are a few ways to handle that in Internet Explorer," you say. "Great!" says the NP.

In Internet Explorer, you can make elements visible or invisible by using two style properties: **visibility** and **display**. Here's an example of using the **visibility** property, which you can set to either **hidden** or **visible**. In this case, when the user clicks a button, previously hidden text is displayed.

```
<?xml version="1.0"?>
<!DOCTYPE html PUBLIC "-//W3C//DTD XHTML 1.0 Transitional//EN"
"http://www.w3.org/tr/xhtml1/DTD/xhtml1-transitional.dtd">
<html xmlns="http://www.w3.org/1999/xhtml" xml:lang="en" lang="en">
```

```
        <head>
            <title>
                Making Elements Visible With The visibility Property
            </title>

            <script type = "text/javascript" language = "javascript">
                function showMore()
                {
                    div1.style.visibility = "visible"
                }
            </script>
        </head>

        <body>
            <center>
                <h1>
                    Making Elements Visible With The visibility Property
                </h1>
            </center>

            <input type = "button" value="Click Me" onclick="showMore()" />
            <p>
                <div id = "div1" style = "visibility:hidden">
                    Here's some newly-visible text!
                </div>
            </p>
        </body>
</html>
```

You can see the results after the user clicks the button, and the text has been made visible, in Figure 13.18.

Here's the same example rewritten to use the **display** property, which you can set to an empty string to display the element or set to **none** to hide the element:

```
<?xml version="1.0"?>
<!DOCTYPE html PUBLIC "-//W3C//DTD XHTML 1.0 Transitional//EN"
"http://www.w3.org/tr/xhtml1/DTD/xhtml1-transitional.dtd">
<html xmlns="http://www.w3.org/1999/xhtml" xml:lang="en" lang="en">
    <head>
        <title>
            Making Elements Visible With The display Property
        </title>
```

Immediate Solutions

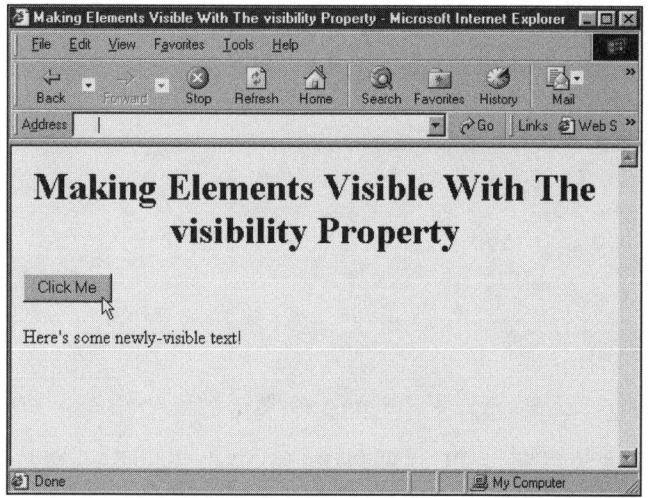

Figure 13.18 Making elements visible with the **visibility** property in Internet Explorer.

```
        <script type = "text/javascript" language = "javascript">
            function showMore()
            {
                div1.style.display = ""
            }
        </script>
    </head>

    <body>
        <center>
            <h1>
                Making Elements Visible With The display Property
            </h1>
        </center>

        <input type = "button" value = "Click Me" onclick = "showMore()" />
        <p>
            <div id="div1" style="display: none">
                Here's some newly-visible text!
            </div>
        </p>
    </body>
</html>
```

The results of this code appear in Figure 13.19.

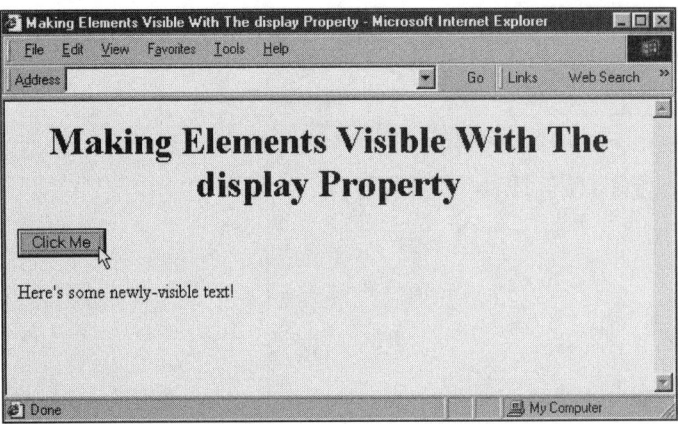

Figure 13.19 Making elements visible with the **display** property in Internet Explorer.

Printing Web Pages

The big boss is upset and says, "What if users want a hard copy of the Web page that has my picture on it? How can we do that?" "No problem," you say. "As of Internet Explorer 5, I can use the **window.print** method to print the page at the click of a button." "Hm," says the BB, "better make the printing automatic so it prints as soon as the page appears."

As of Internet Explorer 5, you can use the **window.print** method to print a Web page. In fact, you can control the placement of page breaks in your documents by using the **page-break-before** and **page-break-after** style properties. These properties indicate when to break to a new page when printing the document.

Here's an example. When the user clicks the button, the page is printed. I've also set up the page so a page break occurs before the **<p>** element:

```
<?xml version="1.0"?>
<!DOCTYPE html PUBLIC "-//W3C//DTD XHTML 1.0 Transitional//EN"
"http://www.w3.org/tr/xhtml1/DTD/xhtml1-transitional.dtd">
<html xmlns="http://www.w3.org/1999/xhtml" xml:lang="en" lang="en">
    <head>
        <title>
            Printing Web Pages
        </title>

        <script type = "text/javascript" language = "javascript">
            function showMore()
            {
```

```
                window.print()
            }
        </script>

        <style type="text/css">
            p {page-break-before: always}
        </style>

    </head>

    <body>
        <center>
            <h1>
                Printing Web Pages
            </h1>
        </center>

        <input type = "button" value = "Print Page" onclick="showMore()" />
        <p>
            Here's some text!
        </p>
    </body>
</html>
```

When the user clicks the Print Page button, a Print dialog box opens. If the user wants to print, the page is printed with a page break before the **<p>** element.

Using Dynamic Fonts

One aspect of dynamic XHTML in Netscape Navigator is using dynamic fonts, which you can download from the Internet. To indicate that you want to download a font, you use the **<link>** element, setting the **rel** attribute to **fontDEF** and setting the **src** attribute to the URL of the dynamic font (note that in official W3C XHTML, the **<link>** element does not support the **src** attribute, so this is not conforming XHTML):

```
<link rel = "fontdef" src = "font.pfr">
```

Here's an example in which I'll download the Chianti font from Bitstream, Inc., and use it in a Web page. To find out more about the dynamic fonts that Bitstream, Inc., offers, see **www.truedoc.com/webpages/intro/**.

Here's the code:

```xhtml
<?xml version="1.0"?>
<!DOCTYPE html PUBLIC "-//W3C//DTD XHTML 1.0 Transitional//EN"
"http://www.w3.org/tr/xhtml1/DTD/xhtml1-transitional.dtd">
<html xmlns="http://www.w3.org/1999/xhtml" xml:lang="en" lang="en">
    <head>
        <title>
            Using Dynamic Fonts
        </title>

        <link rel = "fontdef"
            src = "http://www.truedoc.com/webpages/chianti.pfr" />
    </head>

    <body>
        <center>
            <h1>
                Using Dynamic Fonts
            </h1>
        </center>

        <p>
            <font face = "Chianti BT" size = "5" color = "#000000">
                Chianti ROMAN
            </font>
        </p>
        <p>
            <font face = "Chianti It BT" size = "5" color = "#000000">
                Chianti ITALIC
            </font>
        </p>
        <p>
            <font face = "Chianti BT" size = "5" color = "#000000">
                <b>Chianti BOLD</b>
            </font>
        </p>
        <p>
            <font face = "Chianti BdIt BT" size = "5" color = "#000000">
                Chianti BOLD ITALIC
            </font>
        </p>
        <p>
            <font face = "Chianti XBd BT" size = "5" color = "#000000">
                Chianti EXTRA BOLD
            </font>
        </p>
    </body>
</html>
```

Immediate Solutions

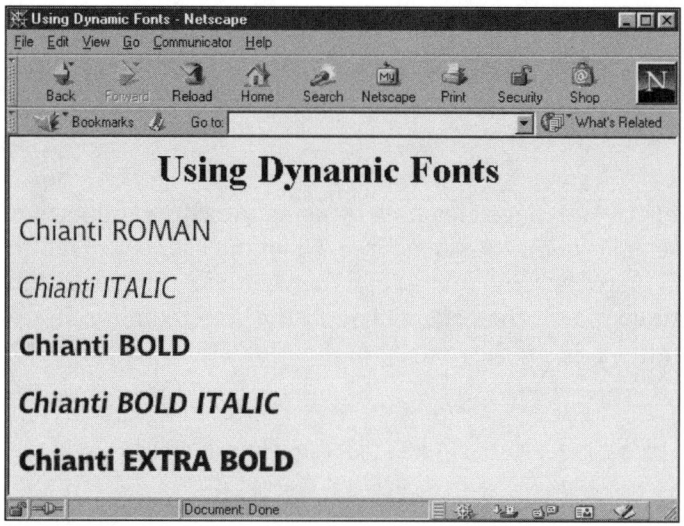

Figure 13.20 Using dynamic fonts.

You can see the results of this code in Figure 13.20, where you can see the dynamic font loaded and in use.

Visual Effects: Filters

"I've heard that you can use visual filters in Internet Explorer," says the novice programmer. "How does that work?" "It's easy," you say; "just pull up a chair and we'll go through it."

Internet Explorer lets you apply the following visual filters to elements:

- Alpha (sets opacity; 0 percent equals transparent, and 100 percent equals opaque)
- Blur
- Chroma
- Drop shadow
- Flip horizontal
- Flip vertical
- Glow
- Gray
- Invert

- Mask
- Shadow
- Wave
- XRay

You apply these filters to Web page elements by using the **filter** property of the **style** object of an element. In this next example, I'll let the user select a filter for a **<div>** element that displays some text. When the user clicks a button that displays the caption "Apply Filter," the code will apply the selected filter. Here's the code—note that I let the user set the opacity of the Alpha filter with a text field:

```
<?xml version="1.0"?>
<!DOCTYPE html PUBLIC "-//W3C//DTD XHTML 1.0 Transitional//EN"
"http://www.w3.org/tr/xhtml1/DTD/xhtml1-transitional.dtd">
<html xmlns="http://www.w3.org/1999/xhtml" xml:lang="en" lang="en">
    <head>
        <title>
            Using Visual Filters
        </title>

        <script type = "text/javascript" language = "javascript">

            function useFilter()
            {
                div1.style.filter=""

                if (radio01.checked)
                    div1.style.filter = "fliph(enabled=1)"
                if (radio02.checked)
                    div1.style.filter = "flipv(enabled=1)"
                if (radio03.checked)
                    div1.style.filter = "gray(enabled=1)"
                if (radio04.checked)
                    div1.style.filter = "invert(enabled=1)"
                if (radio05.checked)
                    div1.style.filter = "xray(enabled=1)"
                if (radio06.checked){
                    var newOpacity
                    newOpacity = Opacity.value
                    div1.style.filter = "alpha(opacity=" + newOpacity +
                        ", enabled=1)"
                }
```

```
                if (radio07.checked)
                    div1.style.filter =
                        "blur(direction=45, strength=15, add=0, enabled=1)"
                if (radio08.checked)
                    div1.style.filter = "chroma(color=#FFFF00, enabled=1)"
                if (radio09.checked)
                    div1.style.filter = "dropshadow(offx=5, offy=9, " +
                        "color=#008fff, enabled=1)"
                if (radio10.checked)
                    div1.style.filter = "glow(strength=5, color=#ffff00, "
                    + "enabled=1) "
                if (radio11.checked)
                    div1.style.filter = "mask(color=#FF0000 ,enabled=1)"
                if (radio12.checked)
                    div1.style.filter =
                    "shadow(color=#FF0088,direction=315,enabled=1)"
                if (radio13.checked)
                    div1.style.filter = "wave(freq=2, strength=6, phase=0,"
                    + " lightstrength=0, add=0, enabled=1)"
            }
        </script>
    </head>

    <body>
        <center>
            <h1>
                Using Filters
            </h1>
            <input type="radio" name="radios" id="radio01" />
                Flip Horizontal
            <input type="radio" name="radios" id="radio02" />Flip Vertical
            <input type="radio" name="radios" id="radio03" />Gray
            <input type="radio" name="radios" id="radio04" />Invert
            <input type="radio" name="radios" id="radio05" />XRay
            <br />
            <br />
            <input type="radio" name="radios" id="radio07" />Blur
            <input type="radio" name="radios" id="radio08" />Chroma
            <input type="radio" name="radios" id="radio09" />Drop Shadow
            <input type="radio" name="radios" id="radio10" />Glow
            <input type="radio" name="radios" id="radio11" />Mask
            <br />
            <br />
            <input type="radio" name="radios" id="radio12" />Shadow
            <input type="radio" name="radios" id="radio13" />Wave
```

```
                <input type="radio" name="radios"
                    id="radio06" />
                Alpha   Opacity: 
                <input type="text" id="Opacity" value="50" size="3"
                    maxlength="3" />
                <p>
                    <input type="submit" name="startFilter"
                        value="Apply Filter" onclick="useFilter()" />
                </p>
            </center>

            <div id="div1" style="position:absolute; width:300; height:80;
                top:250; left:30%; font-size:24pt;font-family:verdana;
                font-style:bold; color:blue;">
                Filter this text!
            </div>
        </body>
</html>
```

You can see the result of this code in Figure 13.21, where I've applied the shadow filter to the text in the **<div>** element. To get a feeling for the various filters, you can play around with this page—all it takes is two clicks per filter and you see the results immediately.

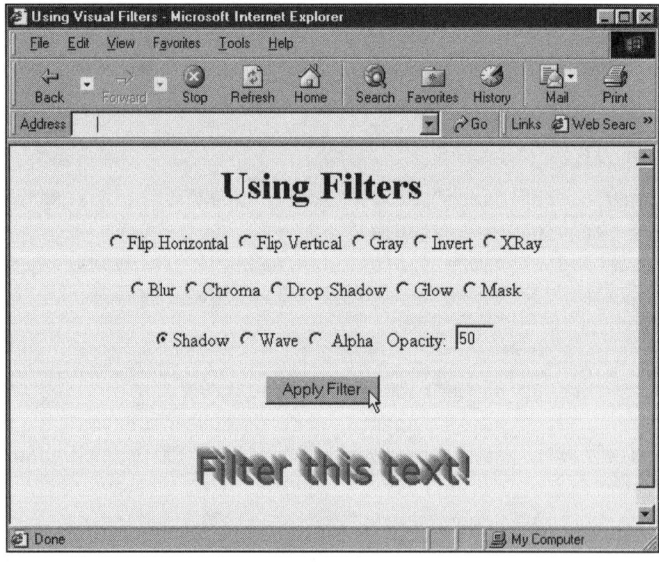

Figure 13.21   Using visual filters.

Visual Effects: Transitions

"Visual filters are nice," says the novice programmer, "but what about *transitions*? Can't you use all kinds of transitions when you're showing or hiding elements in Internet Explorer?" "You sure can," you say; "get some coffee and we'll take a look."

There are all kinds of visual transitions you can use when you're showing or hiding an element in Internet Explorer. The following list contains the possible transitions:

- Box in
- Box out
- Checkerboard across
- Checkerboard down
- Circle in
- Circle out
- Horizontal blinds
- Random
- Random bars horizontal
- Random bars vertical
- Random dissolve
- Split horizontal in
- Split horizontal out
- Strips left down
- Strips left up
- Strips right down
- Strips right up
- Split vertical in
- Split vertical out
- Vertical blinds
- Wipe down
- Wipe left
- Wipe right
- Wipe up

Transitions happen when you switch an element's **visibility** property from **hidden** to **visible**. You select a transition with the **Transition** property and make it occur with the **play** method. Here's an example to show how this works. The user can select which transition to make with a **select** control, and then click a button with the caption "Start Transition" to make the transition happen. Here, I'll add yellow and cyan images in a **<div>** element. To show how elements appear and disappear in transitions, I'll make one image disappear when the other is appearing and vice versa. Here's the code (note that in W3C XHTML, elements like **<div>** do not support the **onfilterchange** attribute, so this example is not strictly conforming XHTML):

```
<?xml version="1.0"?>
<!DOCTYPE html PUBLIC "-//W3C//DTD XHTML 1.0 Transitional//EN"
"http://www.w3.org/tr/xhtml1/DTD/xhtml1-transitional.dtd">
<html xmlns="http://www.w3.org/1999/xhtml" xml:lang="en" lang="en">
    <head>
        <title>
            Using Visual Transitions
        </title>

        <script type = "text/javascript" language = "javascript">
            var transitionDuration
            var transitionDirection
            var transitionHappening

            transitionDirection = 0
            transitionDuration = 3

            function filterChange()
            {
                transitionHappening = false
            }

            function handleTransition()
            {
                if (transitionHappening)
                    return

                div1.filters.item(0).apply()

                if (transitionDirection == 1){
                    transitionDirection = 2
                    Image2.style.visibility = "visible"
                    Image1.style.visibility = "hidden"
                }
```

```
            else {
                transitionDirection = 1
                Image1.style.visibility = "visible"
                Image2.style.visibility = "hidden"
            }
            div1.filters.item(0).Transition = select1.selectedIndex
            div1.filters(0).play(transitionDuration)
            transitionHappening = true
        }

    </script>
</head>

<body>
    <center>
        <h1>
            Using Visual Transitions
        </h1>
    </center>

    <div style="position:absolute;top:270;left:25%">
        <select id="select1">
            <option>Box In Transition</option>
            <option>Box Out Transition</option>
            <option>Circle In Transition</option>
            <option>Circle Out Transition</option>
            <option>Wipe Up Transition</option>
            <option>Wipe Down Transition</option>
            <option>Wipe Right Transition</option>
            <option>Wipe Left Transition</option>
            <option>Vertical Blinds Transition</option>
            <option>Horizontal Blinds Transition</option>
            <option>Checker Board Across Transition</option>
            <option>Checker Board Down Transition</option>
            <option>Random Dissolve Transition</option>
            <option>Split Vertical In Transition</option>
            <option>Split Vertical Out Transition</option>
            <option>Split Horizontal In Transition</option>
            <option>Split Horizontal Out Transition</option>
            <option>Strips Left Down Transition</option>
            <option>Strips Left Up Transition</option>
            <option>Strips Right Down Transition</option>
            <option>Strips Right Up Transition</option>
            <option>Random Bars Horizontal Transition</option>
```

```
            <option>Random Bars Vertical Transition</option>
            <option>Random Transition</option>
        </select>

        <input type="submit" name="startTrans" value="Start Transition"
            onclick="handleTransition()" />
    </div>

    <div id="div1" style="position:absolute; width:450; height:210;
        top:60; left:15%; FILTER:revealTrans(Duration=1.0,
        Transition=1)"
            onfilterchange="filterChange()">
        <img id="Image1" alt="image" style=
            "Position:absolute;Width:200;height:200;visibility:hidden"
            src="image1.jpg" width="256" height="256" />
        <img id="Image2" alt="image" style=
            "Position:absolute;Width:200;height:200;left:210"
            src="image2.jpg" width="256" height="256" />
    </div>
    </body>
</html>
```

You can see the results of this code in Figure 13.22. When the user selects a transition in the **select** control and clicks the Start Transition button, the transition begins. For example, you can see the circle in transition occurring in Figure 13.22. The cyan image on the left is appearing as the transition circle becomes smaller

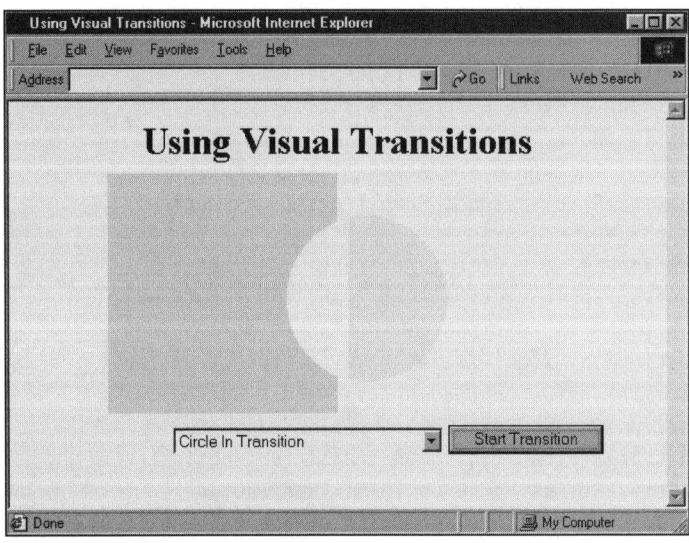

Figure 13.22 Using visual transitions.

and smaller, and the yellow image on the right is disappearing at the same time. If you click the button again, the cyan image will disappear and the yellow image will appear.

Using transitions in Web pages can add a touch of professionalism to your Web pages—give it a try.

Visual Effects: Transitions Using Layers

You can't use transition effects by using filters in Netscape Navigator, but you can use layers instead. We saw this example in the "Immediate Solutions" section "Creating Animation with Layers" (recall that since the **<layer>** element is specific to Netscape Navigator, this example is not strictly conforming XHTML):

```
<?xml version="1.0"?>
<!DOCTYPE html PUBLIC "-//W3C//DTD XHTML 1.0 Transitional//EN"
"http://www.w3.org/tr/xhtml1/DTD/xhtml1-transitional.dtd">
<html xmlns="http://www.w3.org/1999/xhtml" xml:lang="en" lang="en">
    <head>
        <title>
            Visual Transitions With Layers
        </title>

        <script type = "text/javascript" language = "javascript">
            function handleTransition()
            {
                document.layers['layer1'].left =
                    document.layers['layer1'].left - 5

                if (document.layers['layer1'].left > -256) {
                    setTimeout('handleTransition()',50)
                }
            }
        </script>
    </head>

    <body>
        <center>
            <h1>
                Visual Transitions With Layers
            </h1>
        </center>
```

```
            <div style="position:absolute;top:60;left:0">
                <img alt="image" src="image1.jpg" />
            </div>

            <layer name = "layer1" left = "0" top = "60">
                <img alt="image" src="image2.jpg" />
            </layer>

            <div style="position:absolute;top:340;left:40">
                <form action="action">

                <input type="button" name="startTrans" value="Start Transition"
                    onclick="handleTransition()" />
                </form>
            </div>
        </body>
</html>
```

This code displays one layer on top of another and, when the user clicks the button, slides the top layer off to the right. You can see the results of this code in Figure 13.16.

Chapter 14

Dynamic XHTML: Drag and Drop, Data Binding, and Behaviors

If you need an immediate solution to:	See page:
Dragging and Dropping	851
Dragging and Dropping Data	853
Dragging and Dropping by Using Layers	856
Using the MSHTML Data Source Control	859
Creating Tables with the MSHTML Control	865
Using the Tabular Data Control	867
Creating Tables with the TDC	871
Using the XML Data Source Control	873
Creating Tables with the XML Data Source Control	877
Using the RDS Control	879
Creating Tables with the RDS Control	885
Behaviors: Attaching to Events	887
Behaviors: Creating Properties	889
Behaviors: Creating Methods	895
Behaviors: Creating Events	897
Behaviors: Using Default Behaviors	898

In Depth

In this chapter, I'm going to take a look at some advanced topics in dynamic XHTML: dragging and dropping, data binding, and behaviors. Netscape Navigator does not support these techniques, unfortunately, except for dragging and dropping, and, of course, you implement that differently than you would in Internet Explorer. The upshot is that this chapter is almost exclusively an Internet Explorer chapter, except where I use layers to implement dragging and dropping. Much of the material in this chapter goes beyond the XHTML specification and is browser specific—for example, behaviors are exclusively implemented by the Internet Explorer, and layers by Netscape Navigator. However, there's so much going on in this area that it's impossible to ignore, especially for a book like this one, which is intended to be a complete Web authoring resource, giving you as much authoring power as possible.

Dragging and Dropping

There are two ways to implement dragging and dropping in Internet Explorer—simple dragging and dropping by using absolute positioning with styles, and dragging and dropping data. Simple dragging and dropping involves using the mouse and setting an element's position to match mouse movements. Dragging and dropping data, on the other hand, involves specialized data transfer; you can even drag and drop data across applications. In Netscape Navigator, you use layers to implement dragging and dropping. It's not as easy as it sounds because you have to make sure that the layer captures mouse events correctly (see the "Immediate Solutions" section "Dragging and Dropping by Using Layers" in this chapter).

To get us started, I'll discuss how to implement simple dragging and dropping in Internet Explorer. In Figure 14.1, a Web page displays two images, both of which you can drag around by using the mouse. Just press the mouse button when the mouse cursor is over an image, and drag that image around while holding the mouse button down.

The dragging operation begins when the mouse button is pressed when the mouse is over an image. Because there are two images in this example, the code needs to determine which one is being dragged, and I do that with the **event** object's **srcElement** property. Before allowing the element to be dragged, I also check to make sure that it is indeed an image. Then I store the dragged image's ID in a variable named **draggingID**:

In Depth

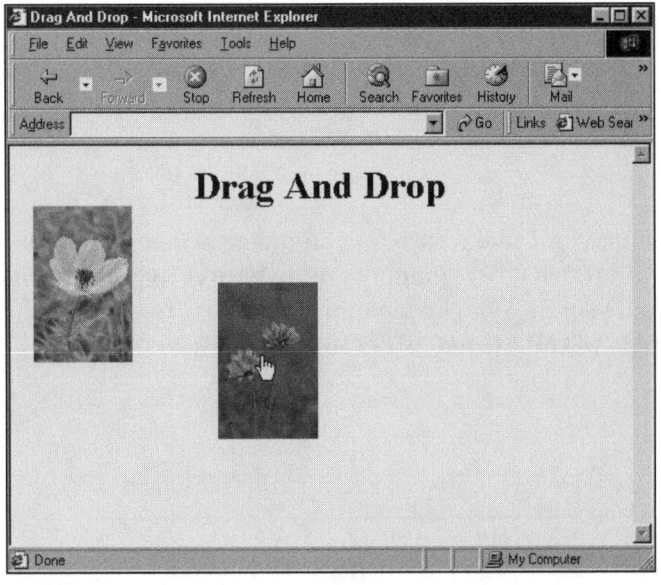

Figure 14.1 Dragging and dropping in Internet Explorer.

```
function mouseDownEvent()
{
    if (event.srcElement.tagName == "IMG"){

        draggingID = event.srcElement.id
            .
            .
            .
    }
}
```

Note that because there are two images, I have to set their *z order*—that is, their stacking order—so the image that's being dragged will ride over the stationary image like this:

```
function mouseDownEvent()
{
    if (event.srcElement.tagName == "IMG"){

        draggingID = event.srcElement.id

        if (draggingID == "img1"){
            document.all["img1"].style.zIndex = 1
            document.all["img2"].style.zIndex = 0
        }
```

```
        else {
            document.all["img1"].style.zIndex = 0
            document.all["img2"].style.zIndex = 1
        }
    }
}
```

Next, when the mouse moves, I make sure that an image is being dragged; I do this by checking **draggingID** in a new function, **mouseMoveEvent**. If an image is indeed being dragged, I set the image's location to the new mouse location by using the style properties **pixelLeft** and **pixelTop**, like this:

```
function mouseMoveEvent()
{
    if (draggingID != null && event.srcElement.tagName == "IMG"){
        document.all[draggingID].style.pixelLeft = event.x -
            document.all[draggingID].width/2
        document.all[draggingID].style.pixelTop = event.y -
            document.all[draggingID].height/2

        event.returnValue = false
    }
}
```

At the end of this code, I set the return value of the **event** object to **false** to indicate that we've handled the event.

TIP: You can support events in hierarchies of elements in Internet Explorer. In Internet Explorer, events bubble, which means that if one element doesn't handle the event, it propagates up to the element's parent element to see if that element can handle the event. In the previous example, events would bubble from the images to their parent, the **document** object itself. The idea is that you can provide one event handler for the parent element instead of separate event handlers for each child element. If you want to prevent event bubbling from happening, you can set the event object's **cancelBubble** property to **true (event.cancelBubble = true)**.

When the mouse button is released, I place the image in its final position, set the **draggingID** variable to **null**, and set the event object's return value to **false** to indicate that we've handled the event in one final function, **mouseUpEvent**:

```
function mouseUpEvent()
{
    if (draggingID != null  && event.srcElement.tagName == "IMG"){
        document.all[draggingID].style.pixelLeft = event.x -
            document.all[draggingID].width/2
```

```
            document.all[draggingID].style.pixelTop = event.y -
                document.all[draggingID].height/2

        draggingID = null
        event.returnValue = false
    }
}
```

That's what the JavaScript for this example looks like. You'll find the full Web page in the "Immediate Solutions" section "Dragging and Dropping." You can see the results in Figure 14.1.

Data Binding

Another important aspect of dynamic XHTML in Internet Explorer is *data binding*. Using data binding, you can connect elements in a Web page to a data source. There are two aspects to this process—using data source objects (DSOs) and binding to elements.

TIP: *You can find information about data binding in Internet Explorer at* ***http://msdn.microsoft.com/workshop/c-frame.htm#/workshop/author/default.asp.***

Data Source Objects

Internet Explorer has a variety of DSOs, including the Microsoft HTML (MSHTML) DSO, the Tabular Data Control (TDC) DSO, and the XML data source object. I'll look at all of them in this chapter. I'll also look at the more complex Remote Data Service (RDS) DSO, which you use to connect to database applications on Web servers. In this chapter, I'll use RDS to connect to the Microsoft SQL Server on a Web server.

DSOs are invisible in the Web page, but you can bind them to elements and control their behavior with buttons and other controls. Using the MSHTML control makes this process easy. For example, say that you have a Web page with data about various employees. This page, employee.htm, looks like the following example, in which a **<span>** element is used to identify the fields of your database—**name**, **id**, **hire_date**, and **department**. Each group of such elements forms a *record*.

```
<?xml version="1.0"?>
<!DOCTYPE html PUBLIC "-//W3C//DTD XHTML 1.0 Transitional//EN"
    "http://www.w3.org/tr/xhtml1/DTD/xhtml1-transitional.dtd">
<html xmlns="http://www.w3.org/1999/xhtml" xml:lang="en" lang="en">
    <head>
```

```xhtml
        <title>
            Data Page
        </title>
    </head>

    <body>
        <h1>
            This page holds data.
        </h1>
        Name: <span id="name">Tony</span><br />
        id: <span id="id">1234</span><br />
        Hire Date: <span id="hire_date">
            4-1-2001</span><br />
        Department: <span id="department">
            Shipping</span><br />
        Title: <span id="title">Packer</span><br />
        Name: <span id="name">Ed</span><br />
        id: <span id="id">1235</span><br />
        Hire Date: <span id="hire_date">
            4-1-2001</span><br />
        Department: <span id="department">
            Programming</span><br />
        Title: <span id="title">Programmer</span><br />
        Name: <span id="name">Francis</span><br />
        id: <span id="id">1236</span><br />
        Hire Date: <span id="hire_date">
            4-1-2001</span><br />
        Department: <span id="department">
            Shipping</span><br />
        Title: <span id="title">Packer</span><br />
        Name: <span id="name">Linda</span><br />
        id: <span id="id">1237</span><br />
        Hire Date: <span id="hire_date">
            4-1-2001</span><br />
        Department: <span id="department">
            Shipping</span><br />
        Title: <span id="title">Packer</span><br />
        Name: <span id="name">Louise</span><br />
        id: <span id="id">1238</span><br />
        Hire Date: <span id="hire_date">
            4-1-2001</span><br />
        Department: <span id="department">
            Shipping</span><br />
        Title: <span id="title">Packer</span><br />
    </body>
</html>
```

The MSHTML control can read this document and assemble it into an internal database, called a *record set*, which you can bind to elements. Here's how you would create an MSHTML control with the name **dsoEmployees** and a connection to employee.htm:

```
<object id="dsoEmployees" data="employee.htm" height="0" width="0">
</object>
```

You can use the DSO's **Recordset** property to access methods and properties of the record set, and I'll do that throughout this chapter. Some common methods are **MoveFirst**, **MoveLast**, **MoveNext**, and **MovePrevious**, which let you navigate from record to record in the record set. I'll put those methods to work throughout this chapter. To actually display the data from this DSO, you can bind it to elements.

Bound Tags

Many tags in Internet Explorer now support properties that you can bind to data sources; to bind these tags to a data source, you use their **datasrc** and **datafld** attributes. The **datasrc** attribute points to the DSO, and the **datafld** attribute points to the field (such as **name** or **id** in this example) in the database you want to bind to. The element then displays the data supplied by the DSO. For example, if the current record in a DSO is the first record in employee.htm, and you have a text field bound to the **name** field, the text field will display the word "Tony." When you make the DSO move to the next record, the text field will display the word "Ed."

The following is a list of tags showing which property is actually bound when you use the **datasrc** and **datafld** attributes:

- **a**—Binds to the **href** property; does not update data.
- **applet**—Binds to the **param** property; updates data.
- **button**—Binds to the **value** property; does not update data.
- **div**—Binds to the **innerText** and **innerHTML** properties; does not update data.
- **frame**—Binds to the **src** property; does not update data.
- **iframe**—Binds to the **src** property; does not update data.
- **img**—Binds to the **src** property; does not update data.
- **input type=button**—Binds to the **value** property; does not update data.
- **input type=checkbox**—Binds to the **checked** property; updates data.
- **input type=hidden**—Binds to the **value** property; updates data.

- **input type=password**—Binds to the **value** property; updates data.
- **input type=radio**—Binds to the **checked** property; updates data.
- **input type=text**—Binds to the **value** property; updates data.
- **label**—Binds to the **value** property; does not update data.
- **marquee**—Binds to the **innerText** and **innerHTML** properties; does not update data.
- **object**—Binds to the **objects** property; updates data.
- **param**—Binds to the **param** property; updates data.
- **select**—Binds to the **text** property of an option; updates data.
- **span**—Binds to the **innerText** and **innerHTML** properties; does not update data.
- **table**—Constructs an entire table; does not update data.
- **textarea**—Binds to the **value** property; updates data.

In addition, tags have certain events that you use with data bindings. These events are:

- **onafterupdate**—Occurs after the data in the tag is sent to the DSO.
- **onbeforeunload**—Occurs before the page is unloaded.
- **onbeforeupdate**—Occurs when the data in the tag is sent to the DSO.
- **onerrorupdate**—Occurs if there is an error that stops data from being sent to the DSO.

Here's how you put the MSHTML DSO and text fields to work. I'll use the **datasrc** and **datafld** attributes of the text fields to connect to the **dsoEmployees** DSO and to connect the **MoveFirst**, **MoveLast**, **MoveNext**, and **MovePrevious** methods to buttons to let users navigate around the record set. (For details on how this code works, see the "Immediate Solutions" section "Using the MSHTML Data Source Control" in this chapter.) Here's the code:

```
<?xml version="1.0"?>
<!DOCTYPE html PUBLIC "-//W3C//DTD XHTML 1.0 Transitional//EN"
    "http://www.w3.org/tr/xhtml1/DTD/xhtml1-transitional.dtd">
<html xmlns="http://www.w3.org/1999/xhtml" xml:lang="en" lang="en">
    <head>
        <title>
            Using The MSHTML Control
        </title>
    </head>
```

```html
<body>
    <center>
        <h1>
            Using The MSHTML Control
        </h1>

        <object id="dsoEmployees" data="employee.htm"
            height = "0" width = "0">
        </object>

        Name: <input type="text" datasrc="#dsoEmployees"
            datafld="name" size = "10" />
        <p>
        id: <input type="text" datasrc="#dsoEmployees"
            datafld="id" size="5" />
        </p>
        <p>
        Hire date: <span datasrc="#dsoEmployees"
            datafld="hire_date"></span>
        </p>
        <p>
        Title: <span datasrc="#dsoEmployees" datafld="title">
        </span>
        </p>
        <p>
        Department: <select datasrc="#dsoEmployees"
            datafld="department" size=1>
            <option value="Shipping">Shipping
            <option value="Programming">Programming
            <option value="Editing">Editing
            <option value="Writing">Writing
        </select>
        </p>
        <p>
        <button onclick=
            "dsoEmployees.recordset.MoveFirst()" >&lt;&lt;</button>
        <button onclick="if (!dsoEmployees.recordset.BOF)
            dsoEmployees.recordset.MovePrevious()" >&lt;</button>
        <button onclick="if (!dsoEmployees.recordset.EOF)
            dsoEmployees.recordset.MoveNext()" >&gt;</button>
        <button onclick=
            "dsoEmployees.recordset.MoveLast()">&gt;&gt;</button>
        </p>
    </center>
</body>
</html>
```

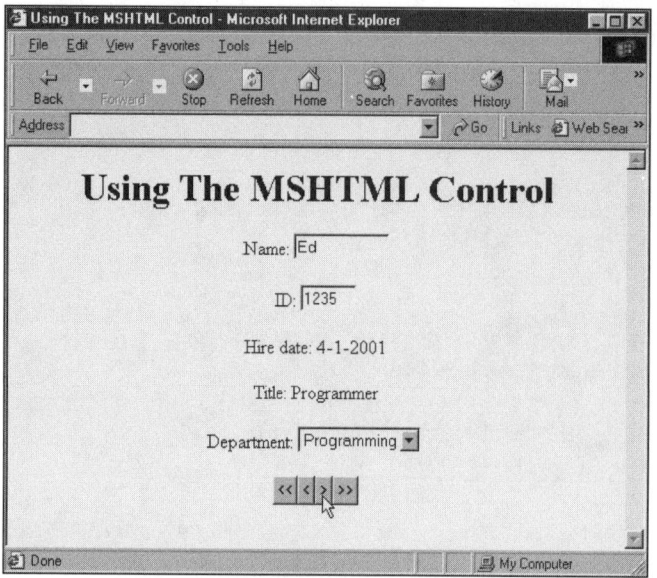

Figure 14.2   Using the MSHTML data source object.

The results of this page appear in Figure 14.2, where you can see one record from the record set displayed in the text fields of the Web page. The user can navigate from record to record by simply clicking the buttons in the page.

You can do a lot with HTML bound tags. For example, you can bind a DSO to a table and see all the data in the database at once or even connect to a SQL database on a server using the RDS. I'll take a look at these topics later in this chapter; see the "Immediate Solutions" section "Using the RDS Control" for more details.

Internet Explorer Behaviors

As of Internet Explorer 5, dynamic XHTML supports *behaviors*. As the name indicates, behaviors set the actions of elements. For example, you can create a behavior that applies a different filter to elements each time the behavior is invoked. You can think of behaviors much like styles, which you can code using JavaScript or other scripting languages.

*TIP: You can find information about behaviors in Internet Explorer at **http://msdn.microsoft.com/workshop/c-frame.htm#/workshop/author/default.asp**.*

To create a behavior, you write an HTML *component* (HTC), which is a separate HTML file that holds the script for the behavior. Microsoft's motivation in creating HTCs was to separate code from data. This separation has become a big movement in HTML coding these days (and it's one of the reasons the World Wide Web Consortium wouldn't make the **<layer>** element an official element).

An HTC file is nothing but an HTML file saved with the extension .htc; this file contains scripts and a set of HTC-specific custom elements that expose properties, methods, and events that define the component. As an HTML file, an HTC provides the same access as dynamic XHTML to all elements on the page. In other words, within an HTC, all HTC elements are accessible from scripts as objects using those elements' **id** attributes. This accessibility allows you to use scripts to manipulate all attributes and methods of HTC elements as properties and methods of objects.

You can use HTCs to implement behaviors that do the following:

- *Access the containing page's Dynamic XHTML Object Model*—You can use the **element** object in HTCs to access the element that has the behavior attached. Using this object, you can access properties, methods, and events of the containing document.
- *Expose custom events*—You can create events with the **event** element. These events will be sent to the containing page with the element's **fire** method.
- *Expose properties and methods*—You can create properties and methods with the **property** and **method** elements, respectively.
- *Receive notifications*—You can use the **attach** element to make sure that the browser will pass on standard events to the HTC.

Here's an example. In this case, I'll create an HTC, called glow.htc, that will make elements glow (using the glow filter we saw in Chapter 13) when the mouse is over them, as you see in Figure 14.3.

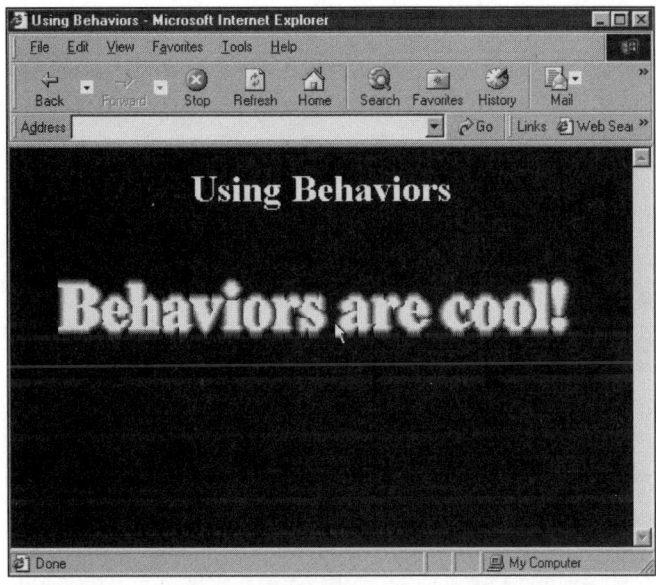

Figure 14.3   Using a behavior in Internet Explorer.

Chapter 14   Dynamic XHTML: Drag and Drop, Data Binding, and Behaviors

To apply a behavior, you can create a style—I'll call that style *glow* here—and use the **behavior** keyword to provide the URL of the associated HTC, like this:

```
<?xml version="1.0"?>
<!DOCTYPE html PUBLIC "-//W3C//DTD XHTML 1.0 Transitional//EN"
"http://www.w3.org/tr/xhtml1/DTD/xhtml1-transitional.dtd">
<html xmlns="http://www.w3.org/1999/xhtml" xml:lang="en" lang="en">
    <head>
        <title>
            Using Behaviors
        </title>

        <style>
            .glow {font-size:40pt; font-weight:bold;
            color:white; position:absolute; cursor:default;
            filter:glow(color=yellow, strength=6, enabled=0);
            behavior:url(glow.htc);}
        </style>
    </head>
    .
    .
    .
```

Now I'll apply the glow style to a **<div>** element, like this:

```
<?xml version="1.0"?>
<!DOCTYPE html PUBLIC "-//W3C//DTD XHTML 1.0 Transitional//EN"
"http://www.w3.org/tr/xhtml1/DTD/xhtml1-transitional.dtd">
<html xmlns="http://www.w3.org/1999/xhtml" xml:lang="en" lang="en">
    <head>
        <title>
            Using Behaviors
        </title>

        <style>
            .glow {font-size:40pt; font-weight:bold;
            color:white; position:absolute; cursor:default;
            filter:glow(color=yellow, strength=6, enabled=0);
            behavior:url(glow.htc);}
        </style>
    </head>

    <body style="background-color: black">
        <center>
            <h1 style="color: white;">
                Using Behaviors
```

```
            </h1>
        </center>
        <div class="glow" style="top:100; left:40">
            Behaviors are cool!
        </div>
    </body>
</html>
```

The next step is to create glow.htc, which makes elements glow when the mouse passes over them. HTCs start with the **<public:component>** element. To attach this behavior to the **onmouseover** and **onmouseout** events for an event, you use the **<attach>** element, which is an empty element. (Because the root element is **<public:component>**, not **<html>**, HTCs are written in Microsoft's own format, not conforming XHMTL.) Here's how this works:

```
<public:component>
    <attach event="onmouseover" for="element" handler="showGlow" />
    <attach event="onmouseout" for="element" handler="hideGlow" />
         .
         .
         .
```

Now, I've tied the function **showGlow** to the **onmouseover** event of elements that use this behavior, and I've tied the function **hideGlow** to their **onmouseout** events. To complete the HTC, I just implement those functions like this (you can refer to the element to which the behavior is connected simply as **element** in the HTC):

```
<public:component>
    <attach event="onmouseover" for="element" handler="showGlow" />
    <attach event="onmouseout" for="element" handler="hideGlow" />

    <script language="javascript">
        function showGlow()
        {
                element.filters.glow.color = (65536 * 255) + (256 * 255)
                element.filters.glow.enabled = true;
        }

        function hideGlow()
        {
                element.filters.glow.enabled = false;
        }
    </script>
</public:component>
```

And that's all there is to it. Now the new behavior is connected to the element you specified, and the results appear in Figure 14.3.

Besides attaching behaviors to events, you can also create properties, methods, and custom events with behaviors. I'll do that throughout this chapter. In fact, it's time to turn to the "Immediate Solutions" section of the chapter now and dig into the details.

Dragging and Dropping

"Drag and drop, drag and drop," the novice programmer says, "all I hear about is drag and drop. So how can I implement it in a Web page?" "There are several ways," you say, "and the simplest involves just setting an element's absolute position to match the mouse."

You can implement dragging and dropping of Web-page elements by setting those elements' absolute position when the mouse moves. Because you can't set absolute positions in Netscape Navigator after a page has fully loaded, this example is for Internet Explorer only. We worked through the JavaScript for this example in the "In Depth" section of this chapter, and here's the full page (I'm setting the mouse cursor to a hand when it's over a draggable image):

```
<?xml version="1.0"?>
<!DOCTYPE html PUBLIC "-//W3C//DTD XHTML 1.0 Transitional//EN"
"http://www.w3.org/tr/xhtml1/DTD/xhtml1-transitional.dtd">
<html xmlns="http://www.w3.org/1999/xhtml" xml:lang="en" lang="en">
    <head>
        <title>
            Drag And Drop
        </title>

        <script type = "text/javascript" language = "javascript">
            var draggingID = null;

            function mouseDownEvent()
            {
                if (event.srcElement.tagName == "IMG"){

                    draggingID = event.srcElement.id

                    if (draggingID == "img1"){
                        document.all["img1"].style.zIndex = 1
                        document.all["img2"].style.zIndex = 0
                    }
```

```
                    else {
                        document.all["img1"].style.zIndex = 0
                        document.all["img2"].style.zIndex = 1
                    }
                }
            }

            function mouseMoveEvent()
            {
                if (draggingID != null && event.srcElement.tagName ==
                    "IMG"){
                    document.all[draggingID].style.pixelLeft = event.x -
                        document.all[draggingID].width/2
                    document.all[draggingID].style.pixelTop = event.y -
                        document.all[draggingID].height/2

                    event.returnValue = false
                }
            }

            function mouseUpEvent()
            {
                if (draggingID != null  && event.srcElement.tagName ==
                    "IMG"){
                    document.all[draggingID].style.pixelLeft = event.x -
                        document.all[draggingID].width/2
                    document.all[draggingID].style.pixelTop = event.y -
                        document.all[draggingID].height/2

                    draggingID = null
                    event.returnValue = false
                }
            }

            document.onmousedown=mouseDownEvent
            document.onmousemove=mouseMoveEvent
            document.onmouseup=mouseUpEvent
        </script>
    </head>

    <body>
        <center>
            <h1>
                Drag And Drop
            </h1>
        </center>
```

```
            <img id="img1" src="flower.jpg" alt="image 1"
                style="position:absolute; top=50; left=20; width=85; height=130;
                zindex: 0" onmouseover="this.style.cursor = 'hand';"
                onmouseout="this.style.cursor = 'default';" />
            <img id="img2" src="flower3.jpg" alt="image 2"
                style="position:absolute; top=50; left=220; width=85; height=130;
                zindex: 0" onmouseover="this.style.cursor = 'hand';"
                onmouseout="this.style.cursor = 'default';" />
    </body>
</html>
```

You can see the results of this page in Figure 14.1. This certainly implements drag-and-drop operations in the way most people think of them, allowing you to use the mouse to drag and drop elements in a Web page. However, there's also a more complex version of dragging and dropping that Internet Explorer supports—dragging and dropping data.

Dragging and Dropping Data

You can use the **dataTransfer** object of the **event** object in Internet Explorer to implement drag-and-drop operations that also transfer data. Following is an example showing how this works. In this case, I'll let the user drag and drop the same image I used in the example in the previous section, but this time I'll add some data to the drag-and-drop operation.

When the dragging operation starts, the code will call a function named **startDrag**—which contains the **dataTransfer** object's **setData** method—to add the text, "The data reached the target!" to the drag operation. The code will also call the **effectAllowed** property to indicate that the drag-and-drop operation should copy the item being dragged:

```
function startDrag()
{
    event.dataTransfer.setData("Text",
        "The data reached the target!");
    event.dataTransfer.effectAllowed = "copy"
}
```

Now when users drag the image, they can drag it to another application, such as Microsoft Word or WordPad, and drop it into that application. To actually retrieve the text associated with the image, however, we'll need to add a little more code. To show how this works, I'll add a **<div>** element to the Web page and make it into a *drop target*, giving it the ID **droptarget**:

```
<div id = "droptarget"
    style="background:cyan; width:300; height:100;">
    Drop the image here!
</div>
```

To allow items to be dropped into the **<div>** element, I'll connect that element's **ondrop** event to the function **endDrag**, which looks like this:

```
function endDrag()
{
    event.returnValue = false
    event.dataTransfer.dropEffect = "copy"
    droptarget.innerHTML =
        event.dataTransfer.getData("Text")
}
```

In this case, I'm indicating that the **<div>** element can act as a drop target, and by using the **getData** method to get the text associated with the dropped image, display it in the **<div>** element. When the user drags the image, the mouse cursor changes to a circle with a slash through it—unless the cursor is over a drop target, in which case it'll turn into an arrow with a plus sign (**+**) next to it, indicating that you can drop the dragged item there. To indicate that the **<div>** element can handle drops, I connect its **ondragenter** and **ondragover** events to the **dragOver** function:

```
function dragOver()
{
    event.returnValue = false
    event.dataTransfer.dropEffect = "copy"
}
```

All that's left to do is connect the **<div>** element itself to the functions we've defined. You do that with the **ondragenter**, **ondrop**, and **ondragover** event attributes, like this:

```
<div id = "droptarget"
    style="background:cyan; width:300; height:100;"
    ondragenter="dragOver()" ondrop="endDrag()"
    ondragover="dragOver()">
    Drop the image here!
</div>
```

And that's all we need. Here's the whole page:

```
<?xml version="1.0"?>
<!DOCTYPE html PUBLIC "-//W3C//DTD XHTML 1.0 Transitional//EN"
"http://www.w3.org/tr/xhtml1/DTD/xhtml1-transitional.dtd">
<html xmlns="http://www.w3.org/1999/xhtml" xml:lang="en" lang="en">
    <head>
        <title>
            Dragging And Dropping Data
        </title>

        <script>

            function startDrag()
            {
                event.dataTransfer.setData("Text",
                    "The data reached the target!");
                event.dataTransfer.effectAllowed = "copy"
            }

            function endDrag()
            {
                event.returnValue = false
                event.dataTransfer.dropEffect = "copy"
                droptarget.innerHTML =
                    event.dataTransfer.getData("Text")
            }

            function dragOver()
            {
                event.returnValue = false
                event.dataTransfer.dropEffect = "copy"
            }

        </script>
    </head>

    <body>
        <center>
            <h1>
                Dragging And Dropping Data
            </h1>
            <img id="img1" src="flower.jpg" ondragstart="startDrag()" />
            <div id = "droptarget"
                style="background:cyan; width:300; height:100;"
                ondragenter="dragOver()" ondrop="endDrag()"
                ondragover="dragOver()">
                Drop the image here!
```

```
            </div>
        </center>
    </body>
</html>
```

The results of this page—after the user has dropped the image into the **<div>** element—appear in Figure 14.4. As you can see, the **<div>** element's text has changed to the data that was dropped—"The data reached the target!"

Figure 14.4   Dragging and dropping data.

Dragging and Dropping by Using Layers

"Ugh," says the novice programmer, "I'd like to implement dragging and dropping, but I'm using Netscape Navigator and can't use absolute positioning after the page has loaded. What can I do?" "Well," you say, "you can use layers instead." "Hm," says the NP, "that's an idea."

You can indeed use layers to implement dragging and dropping in Netscape Navigator. To show how this works, I'll let users drag around the same image they dragged around in the previous two sections. I start by creating a layer in JavaScript when the page first loads, placing the image in that layer, assigning that layer to a variable (**draglayer**), and making sure that layer captures the **mousedown** event with the **captureEvents** method. I also connect the **mousedown** event to the **mouseDown** function:

```
var draglayer

document.write("<layer name='layer1' left='100' top='100'>" +
    "<img src='flower.jpg' /></layer>")
draglayer=document.layers.layer1
draglayer.captureEvents(Event.MOUSEDOWN);
draglayer.onmousedown=mouseDown
    .
    .
    .
```

In the **mouseDown** function, I capture the **mousemove** and **mouseup** events and connect the **mouseDrag** and **mouseUp** functions to them:

```
function mouseDown(e)
{
    draglayer.offX=e.pageX-draglayer.pageX
    draglayer.offY=e.pageY-draglayer.pageY
    window.captureEvents(Event.MOUSEMOVE|Event.MOUSEUP)
    window.onmousemove=mouseDrag
    window.onmouseup=mouseUp
    return false
}
```

In the **mouseDrag** function, called when the user wants to drag the layer, I set the position of the dragged layer to the new mouse position:

```
function mouseDrag(e)
{
    draglayer.pageX=e.pageX-draglayer.offX
    draglayer.pageY=e.pageY-draglayer.offY
    return false
}
```

Finally, in the **mouseUp** function, all I have to do is release the **mousemove** and **mouseup** events, like this:

```
function mouseUp ()
{
    window.releaseEvents(Event.MOUSEMOVE | Event.MOUSEUP)
    return false
}
```

And that's it. Here's the full page:

```
<?xml version="1.0"?>
<!DOCTYPE html PUBLIC "-//W3C//DTD XHTML 1.0 Transitional//EN"
"http://www.w3.org/tr/xhtml1/DTD/xhtml1-transitional.dtd">
<html xmlns="http://www.w3.org/1999/xhtml" xml:lang="en" lang="en">
    <head>
        <title>
            Drag And Drop With Layers
        </title>

        <script language = "javascript">

            var draglayer

            document.write("<layer name='layer1' left='100' top='100'>" +
                "<img src='flower.jpg' /></layer>")
            draglayer=document.layers.layer1
            draglayer.captureEvents(Event.MOUSEDOWN);
            draglayer.onmousedown=mouseDown

            function mouseDown(e)
            {
                draglayer.offX=e.pageX-draglayer.pageX
                draglayer.offY=e.pageY-draglayer.pageY
                window.captureEvents(Event.MOUSEMOVE|Event.MOUSEUP)
                window.onmousemove=mouseDrag
                window.onmouseup=mouseUp
                return false
            }

            function mouseDrag(e)
            {
                draglayer.pageX=e.pageX-draglayer.offX
                draglayer.pageY=e.pageY-draglayer.offY
                return false
            }

            function mouseUp ()
            {
                window.releaseEvents(Event.MOUSEMOVE | Event.MOUSEUP)
                return false
            }
        </script>
    </head>
```

```
        <body>
            <center>
                <h1>
                    Drag And Drop With Layers
                </h1>
            </center>
        </body>
</html>
```

You can see the results of this page in Figure 14.5, where I'm using layers in Netscape Navigator to drag around the image.

Figure 14.5   Dragging and dropping by using layers.

Using the MSHTML Data Source Control

The big boss appears and says, "All of our agents in the field need the latest pricing information. What's the easiest way of getting it to them?" "Well," you say, "we can put a database on the Web server and display its data in Web pages. When do you need it?" "Is it done yet?" the BB asks.

As discussed in the "In Depth" section of this chapter, you can use DSOs in Internet Explorer (as of version 4) to connect Web pages to databases, and you can bind elements to DSOs to display the data in the database.

The first DSO I'll take a look at is the MSHTML data source control. Using this control as a DSO is easy. You use the **<object>** element in a Web page, giving the

MSHTML DSO the ID you want to use to refer to it in the rest of the page, designating the height and width as zero, and setting the tag's **data** attribute to the page you want to use as the source of the data. Here's the code:

```
<object id="dsoEmployees" data="employee.htm" height="0" width="0">
</object>
```

The following list contains the events of this DSO:

- **onDataAvailable**—Occurs each time a batch of data is downloaded.
- **onDatasetChanged**—Occurs when the data set is changed.
- **onDatasetComplete**—Occurs when the data is downloaded and ready for use.
- **onReadyStateChange**—Occurs when the **ReadyState** property changes.
- **onRowEnter**—Occurs when a new record becomes the current one.
- **onRowExit**—Occurs just before the current record is exited.

To use the MSHTML DSO, I'll start by constructing the database. You can construct this Web page in a free-form way, using all kinds of tags, as long as the type of tag you use has both an opening tag and a closing tag (for example, **<h1>** and **</h1>**) as well as an **id** attribute. The MSHTML control will open and read the data page, treating the **id** attribute values as fields and treating successive groupings of fields as records. You can then treat the values you set for the **id** attributes as fields in a database and bind them to other tags by using the **datafld** attribute.

Following is an example of setting up a small database of employee records. In this case, I'm using the **<span>** element to define fields in records. The MSHTML control ignores tags that do not have their **id** attribute set, so you can add other tags to the page as you like. Here's the code:

```
<?xml version="1.0"?>
<!DOCTYPE html PUBLIC "-//W3C//DTD XHTML 1.0 Transitional//EN"
"http://www.w3.org/tr/xhtml1/DTD/xhtml1-transitional.dtd">
<html xmlns="http://www.w3.org/1999/xhtml" xml:lang="en" lang="en">
    <head>
        <title>
            Data Page
        </title>
    </head>

    <body>
        <h1>
            This page holds data.
        </h1>
```

```
            Name: <span id="name">Tony</span><br />
            id: <span id="id">1234</span><br />
            Hire Date: <span id="hire_date">
                4-1-2001</span><br />
            Department: <span id="department">
                Shipping</span><br />
            Title: <span id="title">Packer</span><br />
            Name: <span id="name">Ed</span><br />
            id: <span id="id">1235</span><br />
            Hire Date: <span id="hire_date">
                4-1-2001</span><br />
            Department: <span id="department">
                Programming</span><br />
            Title: <span id="title">Programmer</span><br />
            Name: <span id="name">Francis</span><br />
            id: <span id="id">1236</span><br />
            Hire Date: <span id="hire_date">
                4-1-2001</span><br />
            Department: <span id="department">
                Shipping</span><br />
            Title: <span id="title">Packer</span><br />
            Name: <span id="name">Linda</span><br />
            id: <span id="id">1237</span><br />
            Hire Date: <span id="hire_date">
                4-1-2001</span><br />
            Department: <span id="department">
                Shipping</span><br />
            Title: <span id="title">Packer</span><br />
            Name: <span id="name">Louise</span><br />
            id: <span id="id">1238</span><br />
            Hire Date: <span id="hire_date">
                4-1-2001</span><br />
            Department: <span id="department">
                Shipping</span><br />
            Title: <span id="title">Packer</span><br />
        </body>
</html>
```

I'll call this database page employee.htm. Now that we have a database, I'll put it to work with the MSHTML control. Because the MSHTML control is built into Internet Explorer, we can put it to work without any additional preparation, connecting it to the employee.htm data page. I'll start by using the **<object>** element to point the MSHTML control to the data page, employee.htm, and name this new DSO **dsoEmployees**:

```xml
<?xml version="1.0"?>
<!DOCTYPE html PUBLIC "-//W3C//DTD XHTML 1.0 Transitional//EN"
"http://www.w3.org/tr/xhtml1/DTD/xhtml1-transitional.dtd">
<html xmlns="http://www.w3.org/1999/xhtml" xml:lang="en" lang="en">
    <head>
        <title>
            Using The MSHTML Control
        </title>
    </head>

    <body>

        <center>
            <h1>
                Using The MSHTML Control
            </h1>

            <object id="dsoEmployees" data="employee.htm"
                height="0" width="0">
            </object>
            .
            .
            .
```

To display the data in the database, I can connect text fields to the new DSO by setting their **datasrc** attribute to **#dsoEmployees** and setting their **datafld** attribute to the field I want to display (such as **name** or **id**):

```xml
<?xml version="1.0"?>
<!DOCTYPE html PUBLIC "-//W3C//DTD XHTML 1.0 Transitional//EN"
"http://www.w3.org/tr/xhtml1/DTD/xhtml1-transitional.dtd">
<html xmlns="http://www.w3.org/1999/xhtml" xml:lang="en" lang="en">
    <head>
        <title>
            Using The MSHTML Control
        </title>
    </head>

    <body>
        <center>
            <h1>
                Using The MSHTML Control
            </h1>

            <object id="dsoEmployees" data="employee.htm"
                height="0" width="0">
            </object>
```

```
            Name: <input type="text" datasrc="#dsoEmployees"
                datafld="name" size="10" />
        <p>
        id: <input type="text" datasrc="#dsoEmployees"
                dataflд="id" size="5" />
        </p>
        <p>
        Hire date: <span datasrc="#dsoEmployees"
                datafld="hire_date"></span>
        </p>
        <p>
        Title: <span datasrc="#dsoEmployees" datafld="title">
        </span>
        </p>
        <p>
        Department: <select datasrc="#dsoEmployees"
                datafld="department" size=1>
                <option value="Shipping">Shipping</option>
                <option value="Programming">Programming</option>
                <option value="Editing">Editing</option>
                <option value="Writing">Writing</option>
        </select>
        </p>
        <p>
            .
            .
            .
```

Finally, as discussed in the "In Depth" section of this chapter, I'll use the **MoveFirst**, **MoveLast**, **MoveNext**, and **MovePrevious** methods of the DSO's **Recordset** object to let the user navigate through the record set. These methods are methods of the DSO's **Recordset** object. I can also check the **Recordset** object's **BOF** (Beginning Of File) and **EOF** (End Of File) properties to see if we've reached the beginning or end of the record set, respectively:

```
<?xml version="1.0"?>
<!DOCTYPE html PUBLIC "-//W3C//DTD XHTML 1.0 Transitional//EN"
"http://www.w3.org/tr/xhtml1/DTD/xhtml1-transitional.dtd">
<html xmlns="http://www.w3.org/1999/xhtml" xml:lang="en" lang="en">
    <head>
        <title>
            Using The MSHTML Control
        </title>
    </head>
```

```xhtml
<body>
    <center>
        <h1>
            Using The MSHTML Control
        </h1>

        <object id="dsoEmployees" data="employee.htm"
            height="0" width="0">
        </object>

        Name: <input type="text" datasrc="#dsoEmployees"
            datafld="name" size="10" />
        <p>
        id: <input type="text" datasrc="#dsoEmployees"
            datafld="id" size="5" />
        </p>
        <p>
        Hire date: <span datasrc="#dsoEmployees"
            datafld="hire_date"></span>
        </p>
        <p>
        Title: <span datasrc="#dsoEmployees" datafld="title">
        </span>
        </p>
        <p>
        Department: <select datasrc="#dsoEmployees"
            datafld="department" size="1">
            <option value="Shipping">Shipping</option>
            <option value="Programming">Programming</option>
            <option value="Editing">Editing</option>
            <option value="Writing">Writing</option>
        </select>
        </p>
        <p>
        <button onclick=
            "dsoEmployees.recordset.MoveFirst()" >&lt;&lt;</button>
        <button onclick="if (!dsoEmployees.recordset.BOF)
            dsoEmployees.recordset.MovePrevious()" >&lt;</button>
        <button onclick="if (!dsoEmployees.recordset.EOF)
            dsoEmployees.recordset.MoveNext()" >&gt;</button>
        <button onclick=
            "dsoEmployees.recordset.MoveLast()">&gt;&gt;</button>
        </p>
    </center>
</body>
</html>
```

And that's it. You can see the results of this page in Figure 14.2. The user can navigate through the database with the buttons in that Web page, and the text fields in the page display the data from each record.

Besides using buttons to navigate through the record set, you can also use tables to display all the data in a record set at once. I'll take a look at this in the next section.

Creating Tables with the MSHTML Control

The big boss appears and says, "I don't like the way you've set up the data in the company's Web page. I want to see it all at once." "No problem," you say, "I'll just bind a DSO to a table." The BB asks, "Huh?"

To show how to display a whole database table at once, I'll create a new page that will use the MSHTML control to display the data in employee.htm in a table. To do this, I include the MSHTML DSO as in the previous section. Next, I create a **<table>** element, setting its **datasrc** attribute to the DSO, setting the **datafld** attribute of each cell to the corresponding field in the database, and setting the **dataformatas** attribute of each cell to HTML, like this:

```
<?xml version="1.0"?>
<!DOCTYPE html PUBLIC "-//W3C//DTD XHTML 1.0 Transitional//EN"
    "http://www.w3.org/tr/xhtml1/DTD/xhtml1-transitional.dtd">
<html xmlns="http://www.w3.org/1999/xhtml" xml:lang="en" lang="en">
    <head>
        <title>
            Using The MSHTML Control And Tables
        </title>
    </head>

    <body>
        <center>
            <h1>
                Using The MSHTML Control And Tables
            </h1>

            <object id="dsoEmployees" data="employee.htm"
                height="0" width="0"></object>

            <table datasrc="#dsoEmployees" cellspacing = "10">
                <thead>
                    <tr>
```

```
                <th>Name</th>
                <th>id</th>
                <th>Hire Date</th>
                <th>Department</th>
            </tr>
        </thead>
        <tbody>
            <tr>
                <td><span datafld="name"
                    dataformatas="HTML"></span></td>
                <td><span datafld="id" dataformatas="HTML"></span></td>
                <td><span datafld="hire_date"
                    dataformatas="HTML"></span></td>
                <td><span datafld="department"
                    dataformatas="HTML"></span></td>
            </tr>
        </tbody>
    </table>
</center>
</body>
</html>
```

The table will be filled with data from the database automatically; the results appear in Figure 14.6. As you can see, using tables like this makes life very easy—all the data in the record set is displayed for viewing.

Besides the MSHTML control, another control comes with Internet Explorer, and I'll take a look at it in the next section.

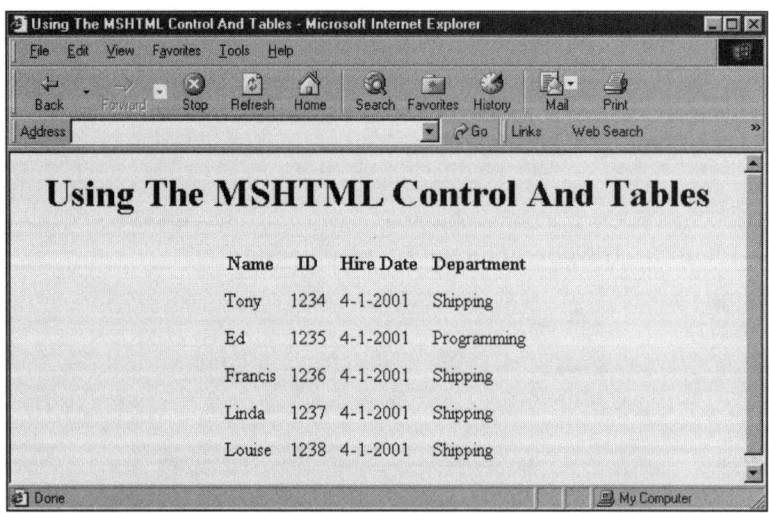

Figure 14.6 Using the MSHTML control to display a table of data.

Using the Tabular Data Control

"I understand that you can use the MSHTML data source object to bind databases to elements," the novice programmer says, "but my database isn't in XHTML format; it's in text format. Guess I'll have to spend a few days converting it." "Not at all," you say; "you can use the Tabular Data Control." "The what?" the NP asks.

The MSHTML control is great when you want to work with data stored in a Web page, but you can also use the Tabular Data Control (TDC) to work with data stored in text files. You can use this control to work with delimited text files. (These are text files in which the fields are separated with a certain character, such as a comma or a semicolon. A common format used for exchanging data between database formats is called the comma-separated value, or CSV, format.)

Here's how you use the **<object>** element to place the TDC in a Web page. (The TDC is registered on your system when you install Internet Explorer.) Here's the code:

```
<object
    classid="clsid:333C7BC4-460F-11D0-BC04-0080C7055A83"
    id="dsoEmployees" width="0" height="0">
    <param name="DataURL" value="employees.csv" />
</object>
```

Note that I'm using an element that we'll see in Chapter 15, the **<param>** element. This element passes parameter data to Web-page objects and applets, as we saw in Chapter 8. In this case, the **DataURL** parameter is a property specific to the TDC; you use this property to specify the data that should get loaded along with the page. The following list contains the names of the **<param>** elements you can use with the TDC:

- **AppendData**—Determines whether new data is appended or replaces existing data.
- **CaseSensitive**—Indicates whether the TDC distinguishes characters in the data set based upon their case.
- **CharSet**—Identifies the character set of the data file.
- **DataURL**—Specifies the location of the data file.
- **EscapeChar**—Specifies the character used to escape special characters.
- **FieldDelim**—Specifies the character used to mark the end of data fields.
- **Filter**—Specifies the criteria to use for filtering the data.
- **Language**—Specifies the language of the data file, including numerical and date formats.

- **Recordset**—Retrieves the record set if the object is a data provider.
- **RowDelim**—Specifies the character used to mark the end of each row.
- **Sort**—Identifies the columns to be sorted in ascending or descending sort order.
- **TextQualifier**—Specifies the optional character that surrounds a field.
- **UseHeader**—Specifies whether the first line of the data file contains header information.

The TDC has one method, called **Reset**, which causes the control to filter or sort its data based on new settings.

The TDC also supports these events:

- **onDataAvailable**—Occurs each time a batch of data is downloaded.
- **onDatasetChanged**—Occurs when the data set is changed.
- **onDatasetComplete**—Occurs when the data is downloaded and ready for use.
- **onReadyStateChange**—Occurs when the **ReadyState** property changes.
- **onRowEnter**—Occurs when the new record becomes the current one.
- **onRowExit**—Occurs just before the current record is exited.

I'll look at an example now to make this more concrete. In this case, I'll store the employee data from employee.htm, which we saw in the "In Depth" section of this chapter, in a text file called employee.txt. Note the format here; I start with a header line naming each field and giving its type (**String**, **Int** for integer, or **Date** for a date), and then supply one line of text for each record:

```
name:String;id:Int;hire_date:Date;department:String;title:String
Tony;1234;4-1-2001;Shipping;Packer
Ed;1235;4-1-2001;Programming;Programmer
Francis;1236;4-1-2001;Shipping;Packer
Linda;1237;4-1-2001;Shipping;Packer
Louise;1238;4-1-2001;Shipping;Packer
```

Now I can use the TDC to read this database, similar to the way I used the MSHTML control earlier in this chapter—the only difference is that I have to use the **<object>** element differently. In this case, I'll use the parameter **DataURL** to indicate the URL of the database text file, the parameter **FieldDelim** to indicate the delimited character between fields in the database (in this case, a semicolon), the parameter **UseHeader** to indicate that the database file has a one-line header, and the parameter **Sort** to indicate that the database should be sorted:

```xhtml
<?xml version="1.0"?>
<!DOCTYPE html PUBLIC "-//W3C//DTD XHTML 1.0 Transitional//EN"
"http://www.w3.org/tr/xhtml1/DTD/xhtml1-transitional.dtd">
<html xmlns="http://www.w3.org/1999/xhtml" xml:lang="en" lang="en">
    <head>
        <title>
            Using The Tabular Data Control
        </title>
    </head>

    <body>
        <center>
            <h1>
                Using the Tabular Data Control
            </h1>

            <object classid="clsid:333C7BC4-460F-11D0-BC04-0080C7055A83"
                id="dsoEmployees" width="0" height="0">
                <param name="DataURL" value="employee.txt" />
                <param name="FieldDelim" value=";" />
                <param name="UseHeader" value="True" />
                <param name="Sort" value="id" />
            </object>

            Name: <input type="text" datasrc="#dsoEmployees"
                datafld="name" size="10" />
            <p>
            id: <input type="text" datasrc="#dsoEmployees"
                datafld="id" size="5" />
            </p>
            <p>
            Department: <select datasrc="#dsoEmployees"
                datafld="department" size="1">
                <option value="Shipping">Shipping</option>
                <option value="Programming">Programming</option>
                <option value="Editing">Editing</option>
                <option value="Writing">Writing</option>
            </select>
            </p>
            <p>
            Hire date: <span datasrc="#dsoEmployees"
                datafld="hire_date"></span>
            </p>
            <p>
            Title: <span datasrc="#dsoEmployees" datafld="title"></span>
            </p>
```

```
            <p>
            <button onclick="dsoEmployees.recordset.MoveFirst()" >
                &lt;&lt;
            </button>
            <button onclick="if (!dsoEmployees.recordset.BOF)
                dsoEmployees.recordset.MovePrevious()" >
                &lt;
            </button>
            <button onclick="if (!dsoEmployees.recordset.EOF)
                dsoEmployees.recordset.MoveNext()" >
                &gt;
            </button>
            <button onclick="dsoEmployees.recordset.MoveLast()">
                &gt;&gt;
            </button>
            </p>
        </center>
    </body>
</html>
```

You can see the results in Figure 14.7. As with the MSHTML control, the user can navigate through the record set by using the buttons that appear in the page.

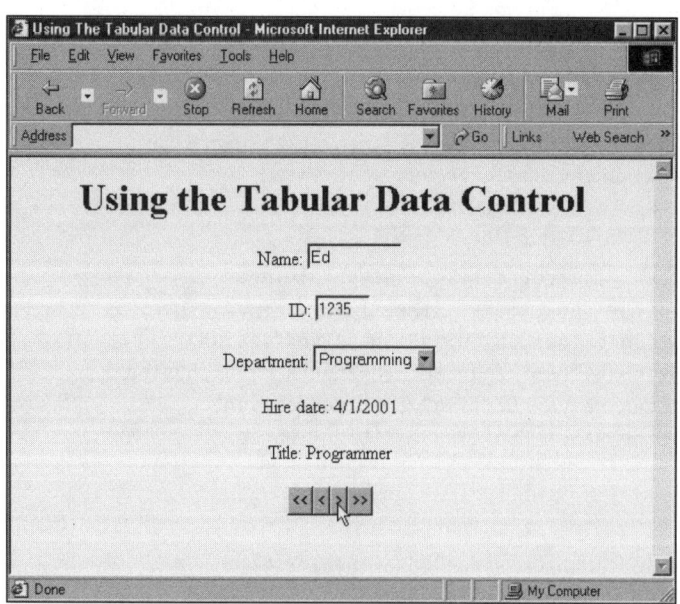

Figure 14.7 Using the TDC control to display a table of data.

Creating Tables with the TDC

In the previous section, we saw how to connect the TDC to elements such as text fields in a Web page. You can also use the TDC to present data in a table. To do this, you just bind the TDC to a table (see the "Immediate Solutions" section "Creating Tables with the MSHTML Control" earlier in this chapter). Here's an example showing how this works; I just add a TDC to a Web page and bind it to a table, like this:

```xml
<?xml version="1.0"?>
<!DOCTYPE html PUBLIC "-//W3C//DTD XHTML 1.0 Transitional//EN"
"http://www.w3.org/tr/xhtml1/DTD/xhtml1-transitional.dtd">
<html xmlns="http://www.w3.org/1999/xhtml" xml:lang="en" lang="en">
    <head>
        <title>
            Using the Tabular Data Control With Tables
        </title>
    </head>

    <body>
        <center>
            <h1>
                Using the Tabular Data Control With Tables
            </h1>

            <object classid="clsid:333C7BC4-460F-11D0-BC04-0080C7055A83"
                id="dsoEmployees" width="0" height="0">
                <param name="DataURL" value="employee.txt" />
                <param name="FieldDelim" value=";" />
                <param name="UseHeader" value="True" />
                <param name="Sort" value="id" />
            </object>

            <table datasrc="#dsoEmployees" cellspacing = "10">
                <thead>
                    <tr>
                        <th>Name</th>
                        <th>id</th>
                        <th>Hire Date</th>
                        <th>Department</th>
                    </tr>
                </thead>
```

```
                    <tbody>
                        <tr>
                            <td><span datafld="name" dataformatas="HTML">
                            </span></td>
                            <td><span datafld="id" dataformatas="HTML">
                            </span></td>
                            <td><span datafld="hire_date"
                                dataformatas="HTML">
                            </span></td>
                            <td><span datafld="department"
                                dataformatas="HTML"></span></td>
                        </tr>
                    </tbody>
                </table>
            </center>
        </body>
</html>
```

That's all it takes. The results appear in Figure 14.8. You can bind the TDC to tables just as easily as binding tables to the MSHTML control.

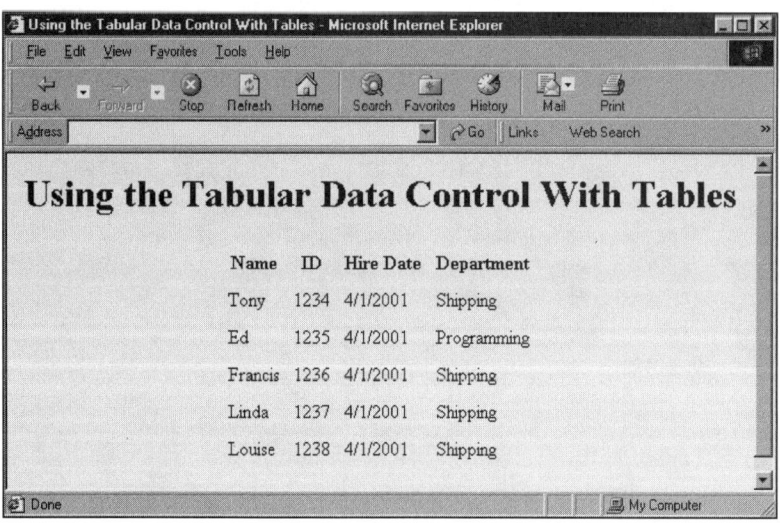

Figure 14.8   Using the TDC control to display a table of data.

Using the XML Data Source Control

"Uh oh," says the novice programmer, "now the big boss wants me to format my database in XML of all things. How can I display it in a browser?" "Well," you say, "one way is to use the XML DSO and data binding." "That will work?" asks the NP.

As we'll see in Chapters 15 and 16, you can use Extensible Markup language (XML) to describe data in a structured way on the Web. XML DSOs have an advantage over other DSOs because you can use XML to structure your data many levels deep. As of Internet Explorer 4, an applet that comes with the browser lets you create an XML DSO, like this:

```
<applet
    code="com.ms.xml.dso.XMLDSO.class"
    id="dsoEmployees"
    width="0"
    height="0"
    mayscript="true">
    <param name="URL" value="employee.xml" />
</applet>
```

In this case, you use the **URL** parameter to pass the XML page that holds the data. The XML data source control supports the usual DSO events:

- **onDataAvailable**—Fires each time a batch of data is downloaded.
- **onDatasetChanged**—Fires when the data set is changed.
- **onDatasetComplete**—Fires when the data is downloaded and ready for use.
- **onReadyStateChange**—Fires when the **ReadyState** property changes.
- **onRowEnter**—Fires when a new record becomes the current one.
- **onRowExit**—Fires just before the current record is exited.

Internet Explorer 5 goes one step further and integrates XML support directly by using XML *data islands*. You can use XML data islands to embed data in XML format in a page. We'll learn more about data islands in Chapters 15 and 16; I'll take a look at the XML DSO here. In this case, I'll translate the employee database, employee.htm, into an XML page, employee.xml. I'll start by giving the XML version:

```
<?xml version="1.0"?>
```

Next, I'll create a new XML tag named **<employees>**:

```
<?xml version="1.0"?>
<employees>
    .
    .
    .
```

I'll give each employee's record **<name>**, **<id>**, **<hire_date>**, **<department>**, and **<title>** elements, like this:

```
<?xml version="1.0"?>
<employees>
    <item>
        <name>Tony</name>
        <id>1234</id>
        <hire_date>4-1-2001</hire_date>
        <department>Shipping</department>
        <title>Packer</title>
    </item>
    <item>
        <name>Ed</name>
        <id>1235</id>
        <hire_date>4-1-2001</hire_date>
        <department>Programming</department>
        <title>Programmer</title>
    </item>
    <item>
        <name>Francis</name>
        <id>1236</id>
        <hire_date>4-1-2001</hire_date>
        <department>Shipping</department>
        <title>Packer</title>
    </item>
    <item>
        <name>Linda</name>
        <id>1237</id>
        <hire_date>4-1-2001</hire_date>
        <department>Shipping</department>
    <title>Packer</title>
    </item>
    <item>
        <name>Louise</name>
        <id>1238</id>
        <hire_date>4-1-2001</hire_date>
```

```
            <department>Shipping</department>
            <title>Packer</title>
        </item>
</employees>
```

That completes employee.xml. In this example, I'll use the XML data source control to bind the data to the employee.xml file, presenting the user with a set of navigation buttons. I start by adding the XML data source control to a Web page:

```
<?xml version="1.0"?>
<!DOCTYPE html PUBLIC "-//W3C//DTD XHTML 1.0 Transitional//EN"
"http://www.w3.org/tr/xhtml1/DTD/xhtml1-transitional.dtd">
<html xmlns="http://www.w3.org/1999/xhtml" xml:lang="en" lang="en">
    <head>
        <title>
            Using the XML Data Source Control
        </title>
    </head>

    <body>
        <center>
            <h1>
                Using the XML Data Source Control
            </h1>
            <applet code="com.ms.xml.dso.XMLDSO.class"
                id="dsoEmployees" width="0" height="0" mayscript="true">
                <param name="URL" value="employee.xml" />
            </applet>
            .
            .
            .
```

Then I bind this DSO to elements, as we've done before in this chapter (see "Using the MSHTML Data Source Control"):

```
<?xml version="1.0"?>
<!DOCTYPE html PUBLIC "-//W3C//DTD XHTML 1.0 Transitional//EN"
"http://www.w3.org/tr/xhtml1/DTD/xhtml1-transitional.dtd">
<html xmlns="http://www.w3.org/1999/xhtml" xml:lang="en" lang="en">
    <head>
        <title>
            Using the XML Data Source Control
        </title>
    </head>
```

```xhtml
<body>
    <center>
        <h1>
            Using the XML Data Source Control
        </h1>

        <applet code="com.ms.xml.dso.XMLDSO.class"
            id="dsoEmployees" width="0" height="0" mayscript="true">
            <param name="URL" value="employee.xml" />
        </applet>

        Name: <input type="text" datasrc="#dsoEmployees"
            datafld="name" size = "10" />
        <p>
        id: <input type="text" datasrc="#dsoEmployees"
            datafld="id" size = "5" />
        </p>
        <p>
        Department: <select datasrc="#dsoEmployees"
            datafld="department" size="1">
            <option value="Shipping">Shipping</option>
            <option value="Programming">Programming</option>
            <option value="Editing">Editing</option>
            <option value="Writing">Writing</option>
        </select>
        </p>
        <p>
        Hire date: <span datasrc="#dsoEmployees"
            datafld="hire_date"></span>
        </p>
        <p>
        Title: <span datasrc="#dsoEmployees" datafld="title"></span>
        </p>
        <p>
        <button onclick="dsoEmployees.recordset.MoveFirst()" >
            &lt;&lt;
        </button>
        <button onclick="if (!dsoEmployees.recordset.BOF)
            dsoEmployees.recordset.MovePrevious()" >
            &lt;
        </button>
        <button onclick="if (!dsoEmployees.recordset.EOF)
            dsoEmployees.recordset.MoveNext()" >
            &gt;
        </button>
```

```
            <button onclick="dsoEmployees.recordset.MoveLast()">
                &gt;&gt;
            </button>
        </p>
    </center>
    </body>
</html>
```

That's all it takes; the results appear in Figure 14.9. As you can see, the XML data source control can function just like other DSOs. You can also connect the XML DSO to tables—see the next section for the details.

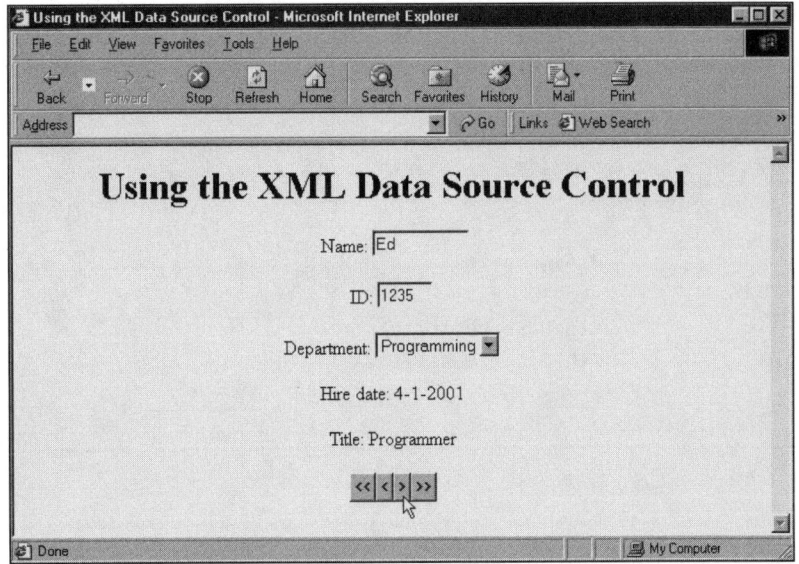

Figure 14.9   Using the XML data source control.

Creating Tables with the XML Data Source Control

In the previous section, we saw that you can use the XML data source control with buttons to navigate through a record set. You can also use the XML data source control with tables, binding it to tables, as we've done already in this chapter (see "Creating Tables with the MSHTML Control"). Here's an example showing how this works:

```
<?xml version="1.0"?>
<!DOCTYPE html PUBLIC "-//W3C//DTD XHTML 1.0 Transitional//EN"
    "http://www.w3.org/tr/xhtml1/DTD/xhtml1-transitional.dtd">
<html xmlns="http://www.w3.org/1999/xhtml" xml:lang="en" lang="en">
```

```
<head>
    <title>
        Using the XML Data Source Control With Tables
    </title>
</head>

<body>
    <center>
        <h1>
            Using the XML Data Source Control With Tables
        </h1>

        <applet code="com.ms.xml.dso.XMLDSO.class"
            id="dsoEmployees" width="0" height="0" mayscript="true">
            <param name="URL" value="employee.xml" />
        </applet>

        <table datasrc="#dsoEmployees" cellspacing = "10">
            <thead>
                <tr>
                    <th>Name</th>
                    <th>Id</th>
                    <th>Hire Date</th>
                    <th>Department</th>
                </tr>
            </thead>

            <tbody>
                <tr>
                    <td><span datafld="name" dataformatas="HTML">
                        </span></td>
                    <td><span datafld="id" dataformatas="HTML">
                        </span></td>
                    <td><span datafld="hire_date"
                        dataformatas="HTML">
                        </span></td>
                    <td><span datafld="department"
                        dataformatas="HTML"></span></td>
                </tr>
            </tbody>
        </table>
    </center>
</body>
</html>
```

The results of this page appear in Figure 14.10.

Immediate Solutions

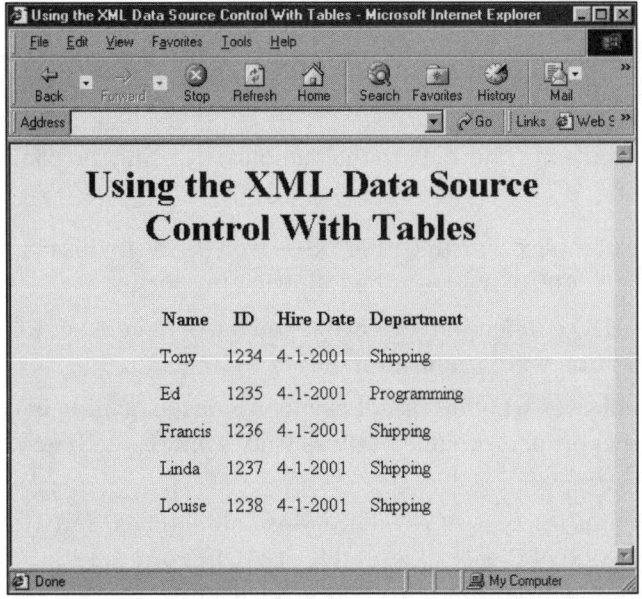

Figure 14.10   Using the XML data source control with tables.

Using the RDS Control

The big boss appears, agitated, and says, "Our competitors are using RDS on their Web site. What is that?" "It's a way of accessing databases on Web sites using Microsoft SQL Server and other database programs." "We need it," the BB says. "Add it to our server right away."

You can use the RDS data control to connect to a database application on a Web server, and then bind tags in the Web page to that data control's internal record set. This record set is a special kind of simplified Microsoft ActiveX Data Object (ADO) record set, called an ADO Reduced (ADOR) record set. Here's how you use the RDS data control in a Web page:

```
<object
    classid="clsid:BD96C556-65A3-11D0-983A-00C04FC29E33"
    id="dsoRDSControl">
    <param name="Connect" value="connection string" />
    <param name="Server" value="http://server" />
    <param name="SQL" value="SQL text" />
</object>
```

To use the RDS data control, you need to set only the **SQL**, **Connect**, and **Server** properties by using **<param>** elements, which will automatically create a client-side record set. Usually, you will bind elements to an RDS data control, and then add, edit, and delete records in the client-side record set. After you update the client-side data, you can save the new data to the database by using the control's **SubmitChanges** method.

The RDS control is more complex than the other DSOs we've seen in this chapter. To configure the RDS data control, you use the following properties:

- **Connect**—Holds the ADO connection string that you'd use to connect to the database if your application were running on the server.

- **ExecuteOptions**—Indicates whether or not asynchronous execution is enabled. You can set this property to one of these values: **adcExecSync = 1** or **adcExecAsync = 2** (default).

- **FetchOptions**—Indicates the type of asynchronous data fetches. You can set this property to one of these values: **adcFetchUpFront = 1**, **adcFetchBackground = 2**, or **adcFetchAsync = 3** (default).

- **FilterColumn**—Specifies the column on which to evaluate the filter criteria. You set this property to a string holding the name of the column on which to filter; you set the actual filtering criterion with the **FilterCriterion** property. To perform the filtering operation, you call the **Reset** method.

- **FilterCriterion**—Specifies the operator to use for a filter; can be <, <=, >, >=, =, or <>.

- **FilterValue**—Sets the data value with which to filter records. You use this property with the **FilterColumn** and **FilterCriterion** properties. To perform the filtering operation, you call the **Reset** method.

- **InternetTimeout**—Holds the number of milliseconds to wait before a request times out.

- **ReadyState**—Holds the progress of the control as it fetches data into its **Recordset** object. Possible values are **adcReadyStateLoaded = 2**, **adcReadyStateInteractive = 3**, and **adcReadyStateComplete = 4**. You use the **onReadyStateChange** event method to monitor changes in the **ReadyStateChange** property during an asynchronous query operation.

- **Recordset** and **SourceRecordset**—The **Recordset** property holds the RDS data control's internal ADOR record-set object that it has fetched from the Web. You can set the **SourceRecordset** property to specify the record set that the control will use. The **Recordset** property is read-only, and the **SourceRecordset** property is write-only.

- **Server**—Sets the name of the server you want to use with the RDS data control. The following are some of the ways you can set this property: **<param name="Server" value="http://servername" />**, **<param name="Server" value="http://servername:port" />**, or **<param name="Server" value="https://servername" />**.

- **SortColumn**—Sets the name of the column you want to use for sorting a record set.

- **SortDirection**—Determines whether sorts are made in ascending or descending order. This property has two possible values: **True** sorts in ascending order; **False** sorts in descending order. To perform the sort, you call the **Reset** method.

- **SQL**—Sets the SQL query string used to retrieve the **Recordset** object. This is the SQL that the database system on the server will execute.

- **URL**—Refers to the associated URL.

The RDS data control has the following methods:

- **Cancel**—Cancels the current asynchronous execution or fetch operation. You use it without any parameters, like this: **RDSDataControl.Cancel**.

- **CancelUpdate**—Discards all the pending changes in its **Recordset** object, so it restores the values since the last **Refresh** method call. This method takes no parameters.

- **CreateRecordset**—Creates a new, empty, disconnected **Recordset** object in the RDS data control.

- **MoveFirst**, **MoveLast**, **MoveNext**, and **MovePrevious**—Move to the first, last, next, or previous record in the current record set; they take no parameters.

- **Refresh**—Requeries the data source given by the **Connect** property and updates the **Recordset** object in the RDS data control. This method takes no parameters.

- **Reset**—Executes a sort or filter operator on a record set based on the specified sorting and filtering properties. Here's how you use this method: **RDSDataControl.Reset** *value*. The *value* parameter is **true** (the default) if you want to filter the current "filtered" record set or **false** if you want to filter the original data.

- **SubmitChanges**—Submits any pending changes of the locally cached, updatable **Recordset** object to the data source specified in the **Connect** property. This method takes no parameters.

The RDS data control has the following events:

- **onDataAvailable**—Occurs each time a batch of data is downloaded.
- **onDatasetChanged**—Occurs when the data set is changed.
- **onDatasetComplete**—Occurs when the data is downloaded and ready for use.
- **onError**—Occurs when an error occurs during some operation.
- **onReadyStateChange**—Occurs when the value of the **ReadyState** property changes. You can add code to this event handler when you want to watch the progress of asynchronous operations.
- **onRowEnter**—Occurs when a new record becomes the current one.
- **onRowExit**—Occurs just before the current record is exited.

Following is an example using the RDS data control. I'll use an RDS data control to connect to the Microsoft SQL Server on a Web server (I'll use the Microsoft Personal Web Server). I'll use SQL Server to connect to the Nwind.mdb database (which comes with the Microsoft Visual Studio suite as an example database) on the Web server. I'll use the RDS data control to work with a table named "Employees" in the Nwind.mdb database. (Note that the **Connect** parameter is just the usual ADO connection string you'd use to connect to that database, and the SQL parameter selects the **Employees** table.) Here's how I use the RDS control to connect to that table:

```
<?xml version="1.0"?>
<!DOCTYPE html PUBLIC "-//W3C//DTD XHTML 1.0 Transitional//EN"
 "http://www.w3.org/tr/xhtml1/DTD/xhtml1-transitional.dtd">
<html xmlns="http://www.w3.org/1999/xhtml" xml:lang="en" lang="en">
    <head>
        <title>
            Using The Remote Data Service
        </title>
    </head>

    <body>
        <center>
            <h1>
                Using The Remote Data Service
            </h1>

            <object classid="clsid:BD96C556-65A3-11D0-983A-00C04FC29E33"
                id="dsoEmployees" height="0" width="0">
                <param name="Server" value="http://default" />
```

```
            <param name="Connect" value="Provider=SQLOLEDB.1;Persist
            Security Info=False;User id=sa;Initial
            Catalog=Northwind" />
            <param name="SQL" value="select * FROM Employees" />
        </object>
            .
            .
            .
```

After you set up the RDS control, you can bind elements to it, as we've already done throughout this chapter:

```
<?xml version="1.0"?>
<!DOCTYPE html PUBLIC "-//W3C//DTD XHTML 1.0 Transitional//EN"
"http://www.w3.org/tr/xhtml1/DTD/xhtml1-transitional.dtd">
<html xmlns="http://www.w3.org/1999/xhtml" xml:lang="en" lang="en">
    <head>
        <title>
            Using The Remote Data Service
        </title>
    </head>

    <body>
        <center>
            <h1>
                Using The Remote Data Service
            </h1>

            <object classid="clsid:BD96C556-65A3-11D0-983A-00C04FC29E33"
                id="dsoEmployees" height = "0" width = "0">
                <param name="Server" value="http://default" />
                <param name="Connect" value="Provider=SQLOLEDB.1;Persist
                Security Info=False;User id=sa;Initial
                Catalog=Northwind" />
                <param name="SQL" value="select * FROM Employees" />
            </object>

            First Name:
            <input type="text" datasrc="#dsoEmployees"
                datafld="FirstName" size = "20" />
            <p>
            Last Name:
            <input type="text" datasrc="#dsoEmployees"
                datafld="LastName" size = "20" />
            </p>
```

```
                <p>
                <button onclick="dsoEmployees.recordset.MoveFirst()" >
                    &lt;&lt;
                </button>
                <button onclick="if (!dsoEmployees.recordset.BOF)
                    dsoEmployees.recordset.MovePrevious()" >
                    &lt;
                </button>
                <button onclick="if (!dsoEmployees.recordset.EOF)
                    dsoEmployees.recordset.MoveNext()" >
                    &gt;
                </button>
                <button onclick="dsoEmployees.recordset.MoveLast()">
                    &gt;&gt;
                </button>
                </p>
            </center>
        </body>
</html>
```

That's all it takes. The results of this code appear in Figure 14.11. As you can see, we've been able to open a table from a record set on a Web server.

As with the other DSOs discussed in this chapter, you can also bind the RDS data control to tables, and I'll do that in the next section.

Figure 14.11   Using the RDS DSO.

Creating Tables with the RDS Control

In the previous example, we saw how to use the RDS control in a Web page. This next example uses the RDS data control to populate a table with the **First Name** and **Last Name** fields from the **Employees** table of the Nwind database on the Web server. I start by adding an RDS data control to a Web page:

```
<?xml version="1.0"?>
<!DOCTYPE html PUBLIC "-//W3C//DTD XHTML 1.0 Transitional//EN"
"http://www.w3.org/tr/xhtml1/DTD/xhtml1-transitional.dtd">
<html xmlns="http://www.w3.org/1999/xhtml" xml:lang="en" lang="en">
    <head>
        <title>
            Using The Remote Data Service With Tables
        </title>
    </head>

    <body>
        <center>
            <h1>
                Using The Remote Data Service With Tables
            </h1>
            <object classid="clsid:BD96C556-65A3-11D0-983A-00C04FC29E33"
                id="dsoEmployees" height = "0" width = "0">
                <param name="Server" value="http://default" />
                <param name="Connect" value="Provider=SQLOLEDB.1;Persist
                Security Info=False;User id=sa;Initial Catalog=Northwind"
                />
                <param name="SQL" value="select * FROM Employees" />
            </object>
            .
            .
            .
```

Now you can bind that DSO to a table, as we have throughout this chapter, by using the **datasrc** and **datafld** attributes:

```
<?xml version="1.0"?>
<!DOCTYPE html PUBLIC "-//W3C//DTD XHTML 1.0 Transitional//EN"
"http://www.w3.org/tr/xhtml1/DTD/xhtml1-transitional.dtd">
<html xmlns="http://www.w3.org/1999/xhtml" xml:lang="en" lang="en">
    <head>
```

```xhtml
            <title>
                Using The Remote Data Service With Tables
            </title>
        </head>

        <body>
            <center>
                <h1>
                    Using The Remote Data Service With Tables
                </h1>

                <object classid="clsid:BD96C556-65A3-11D0-983A-00C04FC29E33"
                id="dsoEmployees" height = "0" width = "0">
                    <param name="Server" value="http://default" />
                    <param name="Connect" value="Provider=SQLOLEDB.1;Persist
                    Security Info=False;User id=sa;Initial Catalog=Northwind"
                    />
                    <param name="SQL" value="select * FROM Employees" />
                </object>

                <table datasrc="#dsoEmployees" border = "1">
                    <thead>
                        <tr>
                            <th>First Name</th>
                            <th>Last Name</th>
                        </tr>
                    </thead>
                    <tbody>
                        <tr>
                            <td><span datafld="FirstName"></span></td>
                            <td><span datafld="LastName"></span></td>
                        </tr>
                    </tbody>
                </table>
            </center>
        </body>
</html>
```

The results of this page appear in Figure 14.12. The RDS data control has connected to the **DataFactory** object on the server and filled the table with data.

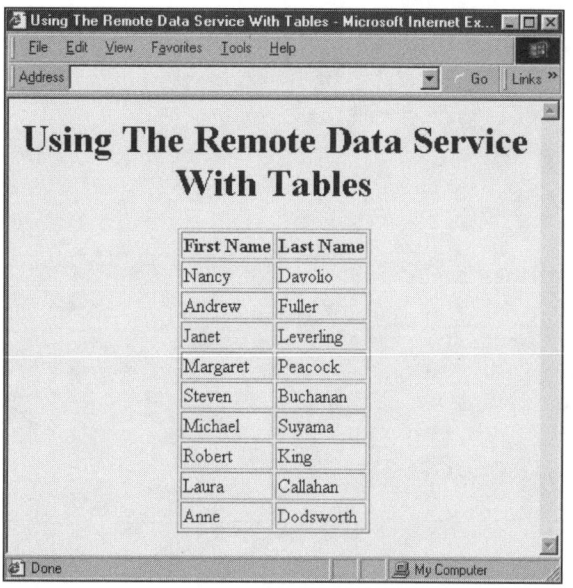

Figure 14.12 Using the RDS DSO with tables.

Behaviors: Attaching to Events

"I keep hearing about Internet Explorer *behaviors*," says the novice programmer. "What do they do for you?" "Well," you say, "you can think of them as you would styles that include scripting." "Can you give me an example?" the NP asks. "Sure," you say, "pull up a chair."

As we saw in the "In Depth" section of this chapter, the idea behind behaviors is that you can separate code from data by creating HTCs. When you've created a behavior, you can use styles to apply it to elements. The example we saw in the beginning of the chapter, glow.htc, made elements glow when the mouse passed over them. To apply this behavior to the text in a **<div>** element, I create a style named "glow" which uses the **behavior** keyword, specify the URL of glow.htc, and apply it to the **<div>** like this:

```
<?xml version="1.0"?>
<!DOCTYPE html PUBLIC "-//W3C//DTD XHTML 1.0 Transitional//EN"
    "http://www.w3.org/tr/xhtml1/DTD/xhtml1-transitional.dtd">
<html xmlns="http://www.w3.org/1999/xhtml" xml:lang="en" lang="en">
    <head>
        <title>
            Using Behaviors
        </title>
```

```
        <style>
            .glow {font-size:40pt; font-weight:bold;
                color:white; position:absolute; cursor:default;
                filter:glow(color=yellow, strength=6, enabled=0);
                behavior:url(glow.htc);}
        </style>
    </head>

    <body style="background-color: black">
        <center>
            <h1 style="color: white;">
                Using Behaviors
            </h1>
        </center>
        <div class="glow" style="top:100; left:40">
            Behaviors are cool!
        </div>
    </body>
</html>
```

I also created glow.htc in the "In Depth" section of this chapter. In this file, I create the HTC with the **<public:component>**. Next, I use the **<attach>** element to attach functions named **showGlow** and **hideGlow** to the **onmouseover** and **onmouseout** events of the element to which this behavior will be applied:

```
<public:component>
    <attach event="onmouseover" for="element" handler="showGlow" />
    <attach event="onmouseout" for="element" handler="hideGlow" />
      .
      .
      .
```

All that is left is to implement the **showGlow** and **hideGlow** functions:

```
<public:component>
    <attach event="onmouseover" for="element" handler="showGlow" />
    <attach event="onmouseout" for="element" handler="hideGlow" />
    <script language="javascript">
        function showGlow()
        {
                element.filters.glow.color = (65536 * 255) + (256 * 255)
                element.filters.glow.enabled = true;
        }

        function hideGlow()
        {
```

```
                element.filters.glow.enabled = false;
            }
        </script>
</public:component>
```

And that's it. You can see the results of this page in Figure 14.3.

However, there's more to behaviors than just attaching them to events—you can create new properties, methods, and events for the elements you apply behaviors to. I'll take a look at how this works in the remaining sections in this chapter.

Behaviors: Creating Properties

The novice programmer appears and says, "I'm hearing all kinds of good things about behaviors. How far can you go with them?" "Pretty far," you say. "You can use **<public:property>** to create properties for the elements you assign the behavior to, use **<public:method>** to create methods, use **<public:event>** to create events, and—" The NP holds up a hand and says, "Sorry I asked."

In this and the next two sections, I'll create a behavior with an HTC, behav.htc, that supports properties, methods, and events. Using this behavior, you can display text that changes colors as you watch.

You can see how this behavior works in Figure 14.13, in which the color-changing text appears at the bottom of the page. To make this example work, you enter the

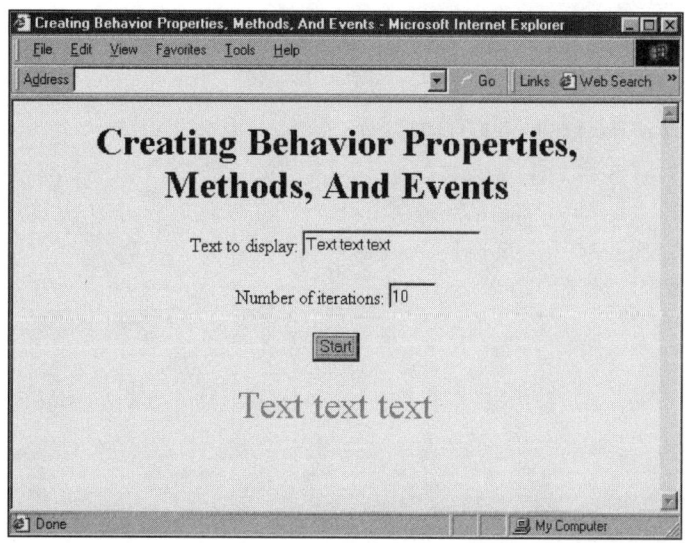

Figure 14.13 Creating a behavior with properties, methods, and events.

text you want displayed in the top text field, and you enter the number of color changes you want in the other text field. Then you click the Start button to start the color changing. When the text is done changing colors, the Web page displays the message "Finished!", which you see in Figure 14.14.

Here's what happens behind the scenes: the text is displayed in a **<div>** element with the behav.htc behavior applied to it. This behavior has two properties: **text**, which holds the text to display; and **iterations**, which holds the number of color changes you want. When you click the Start button, the JavaScript in the page assigns the two values in the text fields to the two properties; it then calls the behavior's **go** method repeatedly to display the color changes. (There's one color change for each call to the **go** method.) When the number of color changes that you've specified has occurred, a custom event, **oncomplete**, takes place, and the Web page stops calling the **go** method and displays the message "Finished!" in a **<div>** element.

For reference, here's the Web page you see in Figures 14.13 and 14.14:

```
<?xml version="1.0"?>
<!DOCTYPE html PUBLIC "-//W3C//DTD XHTML 1.0 Transitional//EN"
"http://www.w3.org/tr/xhtml1/DTD/xhtml1-transitional.dtd">
<html xmlns="http://www.w3.org/1999/xhtml" xml:lang="en" lang="en">
    <head>
        <title>
            Creating Behavior Properties, Methods, And Events
        </title>
```

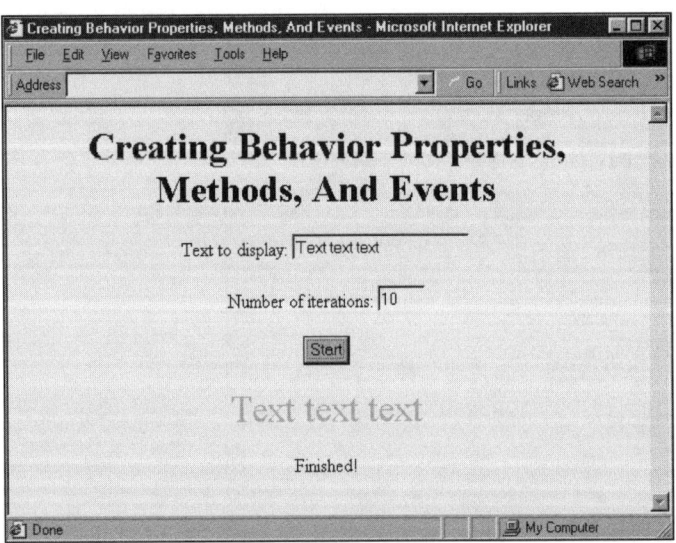

Figure 14.14 Displaying the message "Finished!" after the behavior has been completed.

```
        <style>
            .display {font-size:24pt; behavior:url(behav.htc);}
        </style>

        <script language="javascript">
            var timer1
            var object1

            function startDisplay()
            {
                object1 = document.all("displaydiv")
                object1.text = document.all("displayText").value
                object1.iterations =
                document.all("displayIterations").value
                timer1 = setInterval("object1.go()", 200)
            }

            function finished()
            {
                clearInterval(timer1)
                document.all("messagediv").innerText = "Finished!"
            }
        </script>
    </head>

    <body>
        <center>
            <h1>
                Creating Behavior Properties, Methods, And Events
            </h1>

            Text to display:
            <input type="text" id="displayText" value="Text text text" />
            <p>
                Number of iterations:
                <input type="text" id="displayIterations" value="10"
                size="4" />
            </p>
            <p>
                <input type = "button" value="Start"
                onclick="startDisplay()" />
            </p>
            <p>
                <div class="display" id="displaydiv"
                oncomplete="finished()">
                </div>
            </p>
```

```
            <p>
                <div id="messagediv">
                </div>
            </p>
        </center>
    </body>
</html>
```

Here's the HTC, behav.htc, that implements the properties, methods, and events:

```
<public:component>
<public:property name="text" put="setText"/>
<public:property name="iterations" put="setIterations"/>
<public:method name="go"/>
<public:event name="oncomplete" id="completeEvent"/>

<script language = "javascript">
    var loopIndex
    var loopMax
    var text

    function setText(data)
    {
        text = data
    }

    function setIterations(data)
    {
        loopIndex = 0
        loopMax = data
    }

    function go()
    {
        if (loopIndex < loopMax)
        {
            loopIndex++
            element.innerHTML = text
            var newRed = (Math.round(Math.random() * 155) + 100) * 65536
            var newGreen = (Math.round(Math.random() * 155) + 100) * 256
            var newBlue = Math.round(Math.random() * 155) + 100
            var newColor = newRed + newGreen + newBlue

            element.style.color = newColor
        }
```

```
        else {
            raiseEvent()
        }
    }

    function raiseEvent()
    {
        var event1 = createEventObject()
        completeEvent.fire(event1)
    }
</script>
</public:component>
```

I'll go through this code in this section and the next two sections. Here I'll take a look at creating properties for behaviors (the **text** and **iterations** properties). In the next two sections I'll create the custom method (the **go** method) and the event (**oncomplete**).

When you create a public property for a behavior, you use the **<public:property>** element. This element has two attributes: **put** and **get**. You use the **put** attribute to specify the name of a function that should be called when a new value is assigned to the property. You use the **get** attribute to specify the name of a function that should be called when you want to retrieve the value of the property.

The two properties in this example, **text** and **iterations**, store the values for the text to be displayed and the number of times it should change color. I'll store the values assigned to these properties in internal variables. I'll also set a loop index to zero, which will keep track of the number of iterations that have already occurred:

```
<public:component>
<public:property name="text" put="setText" />
<public:property name="iterations" put="setIterations" />

<script language = "javascript">
    var loopIndex
    var loopMax
    var text

    function setText(data)
    {
        text = data
    }
```

```
function setIterations(data)
{
    loopIndex = 0
    loopMax = data
}
        .
        .
        .
</script>
</public:component>
```

In the main Web page, the **<div>** element that holds the text to be displayed is called **displaydiv**:

```
<div class="display" id="displaydiv">
</div>
```

This **<div>** element has the style class **display** applied to it, and this class uses the behavior we're defining:

```
<style>
    .display {font-size:24pt; behavior:url(behav.htc);}
</style>
```

When the user clicks the Start button, the **startDisplay** function is called. In that function, I create an object from **displaydiv** and then set the object's **text** and **iterations** properties from the values that the user typed in the text fields. I also use the **setInterval** function to make JavaScript call the object's **go** method every 200 milliseconds:

```
function startDisplay()
{
    object1 = document.all("displaydiv")
    object1.text = document.all("displayText").value
    object1.iterations = document.all("displayIterations").value
    timer1 = setInterval("object1.go()", 200)
}
```

Every time the **go** method is called, the behavior changes the color of the text. I'll take a look at how to create this method in the next section.

Behaviors: Creating Methods

In this section, I'll add the **go** method to the behavior we developed in the previous section. To add a public method to a behavior, you use the **<public:method>** element, like this:

```
<public:component>
<public:property name="text" put="setText"/>
<public:property name="iterations" put="setIterations"/>
<public:method name="go"/>
    .
    .
    .
```

This method changes the color of the text in the element to which the behavior is applied, using a new random color. I can use the keyword **element** to refer to the element to which the behavior is applied, so I can change its color with the expression **element.style.color**. We also need to keep track of the number of color changes that have occurred to make sure that we don't exceed the number of iterations the user has requested. That number is in the variable **loopMax**, and the current number of iterations that have occurred is in **loopIndex**. Here's what the **go** function looks like:

```
<public:component>
<public:property name="text" put="setText"/>
<public:property name="iterations" put="setIterations"/>
<public:method name="go"/>
    .
    .
    .
    function go()
    {
        if (loopIndex < loopMax)
        {
            loopIndex++
            element.innerHTML = text
            var newRed = (Math.round(Math.random() * 155) + 100) * 65536
            var newGreen = (Math.round(Math.random() * 155) + 100) * 256
            var newBlue = Math.round(Math.random() * 155) + 100
            var newColor = newRed + newGreen + newBlue

            element.style.color = newColor
        }
```

```
            .
            .
            .
    }
```

What if we've already executed as many iterations as we should? In that case, we can make the custom event, **oncomplete**, occur; this is called *raising* an event. To raise that event, I call a new function, **raiseEvent**:

```
<public:component>
<public:property name="text" put="setText"/>
<public:property name="iterations" put="setIterations"/>
<public:method name="go"/>

<script language = "javascript">
    var loopIndex
    var loopMax
    var text

    function setText(data)
    {
        text = data
    }

    function setIterations(data)
    {
        loopIndex = 0
        loopMax = data
    }

    function go()
    {
        if (loopIndex < loopMax)
        {
            loopIndex++
            element.innerHTML = text
            var newRed = (Math.round(Math.random() * 155) + 100) * 65536
            var newGreen = (Math.round(Math.random() * 155) + 100) * 256
            var newBlue = Math.round(Math.random() * 155) + 100
            var newColor = newRed + newGreen + newBlue

            element.style.color = newColor
        }
```

```
        else {
            raiseEvent()
        }
    }
</script>
</public:component>
```

In the main page, the **<div>** element that displays the color-changing text indicates that the function **finished** should be called when the **oncomplete** event occurs:

```
<div class="display" id="displaydiv" oncomplete="finished()">
</div>
```

In the **finished** function in the main Web page, the code turns off the timer so the color changes stop and the page displays the word "Finished!":

```
function finished()
{
    timer1 = null
    document.all("messagediv").innerText = "Finished!"
}
```

I'll implement the **oncomplete** event in the next section by writing the **raiseEvent** function.

Behaviors: Creating Events

In this section, I'll create the **raiseEvent** function that will raise the **oncomplete** event for the behavior we've been developing over the last two sections. To create a public event for a behavior, you use the **<public:event>** element. In this case, the name of the event is **oncomplete**, and I'll give it the ID **completeEvent**:

```
<public:component>
<public:property name="text" put="setText"/>
<public:property name="iterations" put="setIterations"/>
<public:method name="go"/>
<public:event name="oncomplete" id="completeEvent"/>
       .
       .
       .
```

This event is raised in the function **raiseEvent** (called when all the iterations have been completed). In that function, I create an **event** object with the **createEventObject** method, then pass that event to the **completeEvent** object, like this:

```
<public:component>
<public:property name="text" put="setText"/>
<public:property name="iterations" put="setIterations"/>
<public:method name="go"/>
<public:event name="oncomplete" id="completeEvent"/>

<script language = "javascript">
    function raiseEvent()
    {
        event1 = createEventObject()
        completeEvent.fire(event1)
    }
</script>
</public:component>
```

As we saw in the previous section, when this event occurs, the code in the main page turns off the timer that's been calling the **go** method repeatedly and displays the word "Finished!" in the page, as you see in Figure 14.14.

Behaviors: Using Default Behaviors

The following list contains a number of default behaviors that come with Internet Explorer:

- **anchor**—Enables the browser to navigate to a folder view.
- **anim**—Defines an instance of the Microsoft DirectAnimation viewer in a document to render DirectAnimation objects and play DirectAnimation sounds.
- **animation**—Defines a timed animation element in a document.
- **audio**—Defines a timed audio element in a document.
- **clientCaps**—Provides information about features supported by Microsoft Internet Explorer as well as a way to install browser components on demand.
- **download**—Downloads a file and notifies a specified callback function when the download is complete.

- **event**—Defines a custom event to be fired at a specified time.
- **excl**—Defines a time container that allows only one child element to play at any given time.
- **homePage**—Contains information about a user's home page.
- **httpFolder**—Contains scripting features that enable browser navigation to a folder view.
- **img**—Defines a timed image element in a document.
- **media**—Defines a generic, timed media element in a document.
- **par**—Defines a new timeline container in a document for independently timed elements.
- **saveFavorite**—Enables the object to persist data in a Favorites folder.
- **saveHistory**—Enables the object to persist data in the browser history.
- **saveSnapshot**—Enables the object to persist data when a Web page is saved.
- **seq**—Defines a new timeline container in a document for sequentially timed elements.
- **time**—Provides an active timeline for an element.
- **time2**—Provides an active timeline for an element or group of elements.
- **userdata**—Enables the object to persist data in user data.
- **video**—Defines a timed video element in a document.

To use a default behavior, you specify a URL of the form **#default#*behaviorName*** for the HTC. You also have to know how to use each default behavior before adding it to a Web page. You can find the reference for default behaviors at **http://msdn.microsoft.com/workshop/author/behaviors/reference/reference.asp**.

Here's an example that uses the **userdata** default behavior. I'll use this behavior to save data from a Web page that can be restored at any time, even in a new browser session (such data is called *persisted*). I begin by creating a new style class named **saveable**:

```
<?xml version="1.0"?>
<!DOCTYPE html PUBLIC "-//W3C//DTD XHTML 1.0 Transitional//EN"
"http://www.w3.org/tr/xhtml1/DTD/xhtml1-transitional.dtd">
<html xmlns="http://www.w3.org/1999/xhtml" xml:lang="en" lang="en">
    <head>
        <title>
            Using The userdata Default Behavior
        </title>
```

```
<style>
    .saveable {behavior:url(#default#userdata);}
</style>
```
.
.
.

I apply this class to a text field that will hold the text to be saved, connect the function **saveData** to one button, and connect the function **loadData** to another button:

```
<input class="saveable" type="text" id="text1"
    value="Data Data Data" />
<p>
    <input type = "button" value="Save Data" onclick="saveData()" />
    <input type = "button" value="Load Data" onclick="loadData()" />
</p>
```

In the **saveData** function, I get an object corresponding to the text field, create an attribute I'll name **PersistedValue**, then use the **save** method to invoke the behavior and store the data with the key **"SavedData"**:

```
function saveData()
{
    var object1 = document.all("text1");
    object1.setAttribute("PersistedValue", object1.value);
    object1.save("SavedData");
}
```

In the **loadData** function, I want to restore the data to the text field. I do that by getting an object corresponding to the text field, loading the data, and restoring it to the text field:

```
function loadData()
{
    var object1 = document.all("text1");
    object1.load("SavedData");
    object1.value = object1.getAttribute("PersistedValue")
}
```

Here's what the whole Web page looks like:

```
<?xml version="1.0"?>
<!DOCTYPE html PUBLIC "-//W3C//DTD XHTML 1.0 Transitional//EN"
"http://www.w3.org/tr/xhtml1/DTD/xhtml1-transitional.dtd">
<html xmlns="http://www.w3.org/1999/xhtml" xml:lang="en" lang="en">
    <head>
        <title>
            Using The userdata Default Behavior
        </title>

        <style>
            .saveable {behavior:url(#default#userdata);}
        </style>

        <script language = "javascript">
            function saveData()
            {
                var object1 = document.all("text1");
                object1.setAttribute("PersistedValue", object1.value);
                object1.save("SavedData");
            }

            function loadData()
            {
                var object1 = document.all("text1");
                object1.load("SavedData");
                object1.value = object1.getAttribute("PersistedValue")
            }
        </script>
    </head>

    <body>
        <center>
            <h1>
                Using The userdata Default Behavior
            </h1>

            <input class="saveable" type="text" id="text1"
                value="Data Data Data" />
            <p>
            <input type="button" value="Save Data" onclick="saveData()" />
            <input type="button" value="Load Data" onclick="loadData()" />
            </p>
        </center>
    </body>
</html>
```

You can see the results in Figure 14.15. The text entered into the text field is stored when the user clicks the Save Data button and restored to the text field when the user clicks the Load Data button. That's it; we've put one default behavior to use. These behaviors can be very useful because they're already built into Internet Explorer.

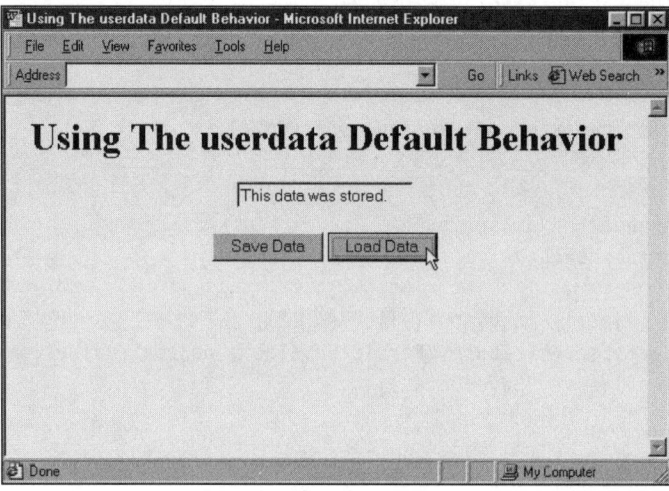

Figure 14.15 Using a default behavior.

Chapter 15
XML and Extending XHTML

If you need an immediate solution to:	See page:
Creating XML Documents	926
Creating XML Documents with DTDs	927
Specifying Attributes in DTDs	931
Creating XML Documents with Schemas	934
Accessing XML Data by Loading XML Documents	936
<xml>—Accessing XML Data with an XML Data Island	939
Getting Attribute Values from XML Elements	943
Parsing XML Documents in Code	946
Parsing XML to Get Element Content	948
Parsing XML to Get Attribute Values	952
Handling Events while Loading XML Documents	956
Extending XHTML by Adding New Attributes	958
Extending XHTML 1.0 by Adding New Elements	959
Understanding XHTML 1.1 Modules	961
Extending XHTML 1.1 by Adding New Elements	966
Customizing XHTML 1.1 by Removing Modules	967
Using XHTML with Other Namespaces	968

In Depth

As you know, Extensible Markup Language (XML) is the base language of XHTML. To be able to extend XHTML with new elements and attributes, we're going to dig into XML in this chapter, seeing how it works and then using it to extend XHTML. I'll begin with a solid foundation of XML.

XML is a markup language that you use to describe data, and it allows far more precise structuring of that data than is possible with HTML. In XML, you create your own tags and syntax for those tags, so you can let the document structure follow the data structure. Using a scripting language like JavaScript, you can access the various elements of an XML page and make use of your data. In this chapter, I'll start by discussing how to create an XML document and how to work with it using JavaScript. In the next chapter, I'll take a look at the data-binding uses for XML.

The following list contains some resources you can use to learn more about XML:

- **http://msdn.microsoft.com/workshop/xml/index.asp**—Microsoft's discussion of XML.

- **http://msdn.microsoft.com/xml/tutorial/default.asp**—Microsoft's XML tutorial.

- **www.projectcool.com/developer/xmlz/index.html**—Project Cool's in-depth tutorial.

- **www.w3.org/TR/REC-xml**—The latest XML specification. The World Wide Web Consortium (W3C) is in charge of the specification of XML. W3C sets the rules on how to create Document Type Definitions (DTDs) and other elements that we'll see throughout this chapter.

What Does XML Look Like?

I'll create an XML page that holds the purchasing records of several customers, showing how easy it is to create data structures in XML. As you might expect, to start an XML page, you begin with the XML processing instruction **<?xml version = "1.0"?>**, which tells the browser that this document is XML.

Here's the necessary first line of an XML document, just as in XHTML:

```
<?xml version = "1.0"?>
    .
    .
    .
```

You can name your own tags in XML, and I'll do that here. The body of the XML document should be enclosed in one XML element, which I'll call **<DOCUMENT>**:

```
<?xml version = "1.0"?>
<DOCUMENT>
    .
    .
    .
</DOCUMENT>
```

Now I'll start storing purchasing data by customer. To store a customer's data, I'll create a new element, **<CUSTOMER>**, which goes inside the **<DOCUMENT>** element:

```
<?xml version = "1.0"?>
<DOCUMENT>
    <CUSTOMER>
        .
        .
        .
    </CUSTOMER>
</DOCUMENT>
```

I can also store the customer's name by creating a new **<NAME>** element, which itself contains two elements—**<LAST_NAME>** and **<FIRST_NAME>**:

```
<?xml version = "1.0"?>
<DOCUMENT>
    <CUSTOMER>
        <NAME>
            <LAST_NAME>Thomson</LAST_NAME>
            <FIRST_NAME>Susan</FIRST_NAME>
        </NAMF>
        .
        .
        .
    </CUSTOMER>
</DOCUMENT>
```

Additionally, I store the date of the record and the customer orders in an **<ORDERS>** element, where I place all the items the customer bought:

```
<?xml version = "1.0"?>
<DOCUMENT>
    <CUSTOMER>
        <NAME>
            <LAST_NAME>Thomson</LAST_NAME>
            <FIRST_NAME>Susan</FIRST_NAME>
        </NAME>
        <DATE>September 1, 2001</DATE>
        <ORDERS>
            <ITEM>
                <PRODUCT>Video tape</PRODUCT>
                <NUMBER>5</NUMBER>
                <PRICE>$1.25</PRICE>
            </ITEM>
            <ITEM>
                <PRODUCT>Shovel</PRODUCT>
                <NUMBER>2</NUMBER>
                <PRICE>$4.98</PRICE>
            </ITEM>
        </ORDERS>
    </CUSTOMER>
       .
       .
       .
</DOCUMENT>
```

I can store the records of as many customers as I want in this XML page. Here's how I add a new customer's record:

```
<?xml version = "1.0"?>
<DOCUMENT>
    <CUSTOMER>
        <NAME>
            <LAST_NAME>Thomson</LAST_NAME>
            <FIRST_NAME>Susan</FIRST_NAME>
        </NAME>
        <DATE>September 1, 2001</DATE>
        <ORDERS>
            <ITEM>
                <PRODUCT>Video tape</PRODUCT>
                <NUMBER>5</NUMBER>
                <PRICE>$1.25</PRICE>
            </ITEM>
            <ITEM>
                <PRODUCT>Shovel</PRODUCT>
```

```
            <NUMBER>2</NUMBER>
            <PRICE>$4.98</PRICE>
        </ITEM>
    </ORDERS>
</CUSTOMER>
<CUSTOMER>
    <NAME>
        <LAST_NAME>Smithson</LAST_NAME>
        <FIRST_NAME>Nancy</FIRST_NAME>
    </NAME>
    <DATE>September 2, 2001</DATE>
    <ORDERS>
        <ITEM>
            <PRODUCT>Ribbon</PRODUCT>
            <NUMBER>12</NUMBER>
            <PRICE>$2.95</PRICE>
        </ITEM>
        <ITEM>
            <PRODUCT>Goldfish</PRODUCT>
            <NUMBER>6</NUMBER>
            <PRICE>$1.50</PRICE>
        </ITEM>
    </ORDERS>
</CUSTOMER>
</DOCUMENT>
```

As you can see, XML provides you with a way of creating and structuring your data in a manner that fits that data. You might be wondering how browsers deal with such free-form data. For example, how will a browser know how you want the **<CUSTOMER>** element displayed? This points out a fundamental difference between XML and HTML; XML provides a way of structuring your data, not a method to display it as HTML does. (However, you can use Cascading Style Sheets [CSS] or the Extensible Stylesheet Language [XSL] to do just that.) Although HTML can indicate which text should be bold and which text italic, XML has no such formatting built-in.

Internet Explorer provides you with access to the elements in an XML page, as we'll see throughout this chapter, in which I'll use JavaScript to access the data in XML pages. It's up to you to interpret the data in the document itself—Internet Explorer only makes it available to you through an object model with properties and methods.

Internet Explorer can display an XML document directly, and you can see the page we've just created in Figure 15.1. (You must give the file the extension .xml to documents you want to view as XML documents.)

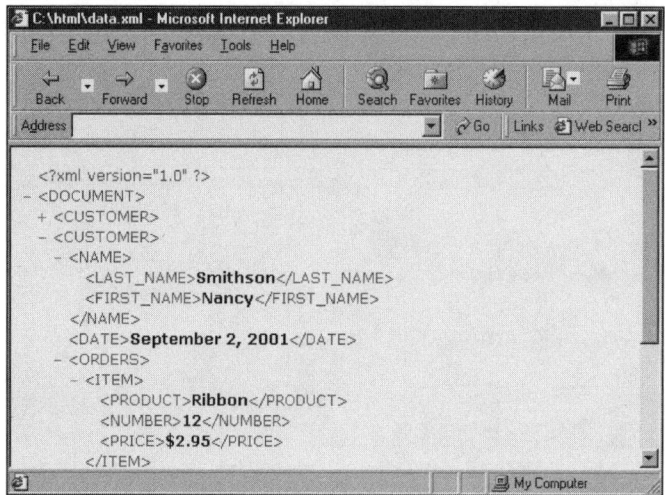

Figure 15.1   An XML document in Internet Explorer.

You can click the plus (+) and minus (–) signs to expand and collapse XML elements. As you see in the figure, I've collapsed the first **<CUSTOMER>** element and expanded the second.

XML browsers can do even more—they can check the XML page's syntax. You provide the elements in the page and specify what syntax is legal and what is not. For example, you indicate which elements may contain other elements, exactly which elements an element can contain, how many elements it can contain, and so on. There are two ways of specifying syntax for an XML page—using a Document Type Definition (DTD), as we've seen with XHTML, or using an XML *schema*. An XML schema is a Microsoft innovation that serves the same purpose as a DTD, although the schema is supposed to be easier to create and allow you more control. I'll take a look at creating both DTDs and schemas in this chapter.

The latest technique in Web pages is separating the user interface from data, and XML enables you to do this. (The lack of such a separation is the reason W3C didn't adopt Netscape's **<LAYER>** element as official.) On its Microsoft Developer Network (MSDN) Web site, Microsoft says, "XML separates the data from the presentation and the process, enabling you to display and process the data as you wish by applying different style sheets and applications." In practice, what this means is that the real XML processing takes place in code, and you're responsible for writing that code. As the XML tags you use become standardized in your group or corporation, you can exchange XML pages with others. The JavaScript you write can extract the data from the XML page and work with it, even displaying that data to your specification. We'll see quite a few examples of this in this chapter.

From Microsoft's point of view, you can use XML to create:

- An ordinary document
- A structured record, such as an appointment record or purchase order
- An object with data and methods, such as the persistent form of a Java object or ActiveX control
- A data record, such as the result set of a query
- Metacontent about a Web site, such as Channel Definition Format (CDF) data
- A graphical presentation, such as an application's user interface
- XML schemas and types

We've seen how to create a basic XML document, but there's more to the process. Ideally, XML documents—and therefore XHTML documents—should also be *valid* and *well-formed*, and I'll discuss what this means before getting into the details of working with an XML document's data.

Valid and Well-Formed XML Documents

An XML document is considered *valid* if there is a DTD or an XML schema associated with it and if the document complies with the DTD or schema. That's all there is to making a document valid.

TIP: *To check the validity of an XML page, you can open it in Internet Explorer, which will tell you if the document does not comply with the DTD or the schema. Also, you might want to check out the Microsoft XML validator page at* **http://msdn.microsoft.com/downloads/samples/internet/xml/xml_validator/default.asp**. *You can download and run the Microsoft validator to test XML documents, or enter the URL of an XML document to check it online.*

An XML document is considered *well formed* if it contains one or more elements, if there is precisely one element (the *root* or *document* element) for which neither the start nor the end tag is inside any other element, and if all other tags nest within each other correctly. In addition, all elements used in the document must be predefined in XML, a DTD, or an XML schema.

TIP: *Note in particular the requirement that the entire XML document be enclosed in one element, the root element. This fact will be important when we start working with the contents of XML documents in code because we'll get access to the root element first, and then move to other elements as required. Take a look at the previous XML example, in which the root element is* **<DOCUMENT>**. *In XHTML documents, the root element is* **<html>**.

Here's an example. I'll add a DTD to the XML document we created in the beginning of the chapter to make it both valid and well formed:

```xml
<?xml version = "1.0" ?>
<!DOCTYPE DOCUMENT [
<!ELEMENT DOCUMENT (CUSTOMER)*>
<!ELEMENT CUSTOMER (NAME,DATE,ORDERS)>
<!ELEMENT NAME (LAST_NAME,FIRST_NAME)>
<!ELEMENT LAST_NAME (#PCDATA)>
<!ELEMENT FIRST_NAME (#PCDATA)>
<!ELEMENT DATE (#PCDATA)>
<!ELEMENT ORDERS (ITEM)*>
<!ELEMENT ITEM (PRODUCT,NUMBER,PRICE)>
<!ELEMENT PRODUCT (#PCDATA)>
<!ELEMENT NUMBER (#PCDATA)>
<!ELEMENT PRICE (#PCDATA)>
]>
<DOCUMENT>
    <CUSTOMER>
        <NAME>
            <LAST_NAME>Thomson</LAST_NAME>
            <FIRST_NAME>Susan</FIRST_NAME>
        </NAME>
        <DATE>September 1, 2001</DATE>
        <ORDERS>
            <ITEM>
                <PRODUCT>Video tape</PRODUCT>
                <NUMBER>5</NUMBER>
                <PRICE>$1.25</PRICE>
            </ITEM>
            <ITEM>
                <PRODUCT>Shovel</PRODUCT>
                <NUMBER>2</NUMBER>
                <PRICE>$4.98</PRICE>
            </ITEM>
        </ORDERS>
    </CUSTOMER>
    <CUSTOMER>
        <NAME>
            <LAST_NAME>Smithson</LAST_NAME>
            <FIRST_NAME>Nancy</FIRST_NAME>
        </NAME>
        <DATE>September 2, 2001</DATE>
        <ORDERS>
            <ITEM>
                <PRODUCT>Ribbon</PRODUCT>
                <NUMBER>12</NUMBER>
                <PRICE>$2.95</PRICE>
            </ITEM>
            <ITEM>
```

```
                <PRODUCT>Goldfish</PRODUCT>
                <NUMBER>6</NUMBER>
                <PRICE>$1.50</PRICE>
            </ITEM>
        </ORDERS>
    </CUSTOMER>
</DOCUMENT>
```

Here's a document that is well formed but not valid (because there is no DTD or schema):

```
<?xml version="1.0"?>
<DOCUMENT>
    <TITLE>
        A Noisy Noise Annoys An Oyster
    </TITLE>
</DOCUMENT>
```

Here is a document that contains a nesting error and no DTD, so it is neither valid nor well formed:

```
<?xml version="1.0"?>
    <TITLE>
        A Noisy Noise Annoys An Oyster
    <HEADING>
    </TITLE>
        A Study Of Shellfish And Audio Disturbances
    </HEADING>
```

Most XML parsers, like the one in Internet Explorer, require XML documents to be well formed but not necessarily valid. (Most XML parsers do not require a DTD, but if there is one, the parser will use it to check the XML document.) The formal specification recommends that your XML documents be both valid and well formed.

To make an XML document valid, you must check it against a DTD or schema. In the following sections, I'll briefly discuss how to create both of these items and what they look like. (Note also that neither a DTD nor a schema is necessary before Internet Explorer will work with an XML document.)

XML Document Type Definitions

We've already seen how easy it is to create XML documents. In fact, if you want to make sure your documents are valid (that is, adhere to the syntax rules you set), you'll need a DTD or a schema. Creating these items is more complex than creating XML documents. I'll take a look at DTDs first.

You can use internal or external DTDs with XML documents. Here's an example of an internal DTD. Note that you enclose the DTD in a **<!DOCTYPE>** element, providing the name of the root element of the document (which is **THESIS** here) in the **<!DOCTYPE>** element:

```
<?xml version="1.0"?>
<!DOCTYPE THESIS [
    <!ELEMENT THESIS (P*)>
    <!ELEMENT P (#PCDATA)>
]>
<THESIS>
    <P>
        This is my Ph.D. thesis.
    </P>
    <P>
        Do you like it?
    </P>
    <P>
        If so, please give me my Ph.D.
    </P>
</THESIS>
```

The DTD indicates how the syntax works for the XML elements you're creating. For example, which elements can be inside which other elements? This DTD follows the W3C syntax conventions, which means that you specify each element with **<!ELEMENT>**. You can also specify that the contents of an element be parsed character data (**#PCDATA**), other elements that you've created, or both. In this example, I'm indicating that the **<THESIS>** element must contain only **<P>** elements, but it can contain zero or more occurrences of the **<P>** element (which is what the asterisk [*] after **P** in **<!ELEMENT THESIS (P*)>** means). The following list contains the symbols that you can use when defining the syntax of an element:

- **a b**—**a** followed by **b**.
- **a | b**—**a** or **b** but not both.
- **a - b**—The set of strings represented by **a** but not represented by **b**.
- **a?**—**a** or nothing.
- **a+**—One or more occurrences of **a**.
- **a***—Zero or more occurrences of **a**.
- *(expression)*—Surrounding an expression with parentheses means that it is treated as a unit and can carry the suffix operator ?, *, or +.

In addition to defining the **<THESIS>** element, I define the **<P>** element so that it can hold only text, that is, parsed character data, with the keyword **#PCDATA**:

```
<?xml version="1.0"?>
<!DOCTYPE THESIS [
    <!ELEMENT THESIS (P*)>
    <!ELEMENT P (#PCDATA)>
]>
<THESIS>
    <P>
        This is my Ph.D. thesis.
    </P>
    <P>
        Do you like it?
    </P>
    <P>
        If so, please give me my Ph.D.
    </P>
</THESIS>
```

In this way, I've specified the syntax of these two elements, **<THESIS>** and **<P>**. We'll learn how to create DTDs, and we'll review an extensive example in the section "Creating XML Documents with DTDs" in the "Immediate Solutions" section.

You can also specify an *external* DTD with the **SYSTEM** keyword in the **<!DOCTYPE>** element. (The **SYSTEM** keyword is primarily for private DTDs; as we'll see in the "Immediate Solutions" section "Creating Public Extended XHTML DTDs," you can also use the **PUBLIC** keyword to create public DTDs.) Here's an example of an external DTD:

```
<?xml version="1.0"?>
<!DOCTYPE DOCUMENT SYSTEM "dtdthesis.dtd">
<DOCUMENT>
    <P>
        This is my Ph.D. thesis.
    </P>
    <P>
        Do you like it?
    </P>
    <P>
        If so, please give me my Ph.D.
    </P>
</DOCUMENT>
```

The file dtdthesis.dtd just contains the **<!ELEMENT>** elements, like this:

```
<!ELEMENT THESIS (P*)>
<!ELEMENT P (#PCDATA)>
```

And that's all it takes to create an external DTD. Besides specifying the syntax of XML elements, you can also specify which attributes elements can have, as we'll see in "Specifying Attributes in DTDs" in the "Immediate Solutions" section. In the meantime, I'll take a look at creating XML schemas now.

XML Schemas

XML schemas are an alternative to DTDs, and are supported in some measure by Microsoft. If you want to create valid XML documents for use with Internet Explorer, you can use either a DTD or a schema.

NOTE: *The XML Schema implementation that ships with Internet Explorer 5 is based on the XML-Data Note (**www.w3.org/TR/1998/NOTE-XML-data-0105/**) posted by the W3C in January 1998 and on the Document Content Description (DCD) Note (**www.w3.org/TR/NOTE-dcd**). It's out of date with the current W3C XML Schema working draft, which you can find at **www.w3.org/TR/xmlschema-0**.*

Here's an example in which I'm creating an XML document with the root element **<TASKFORCE>**. To specify the name of a schema that resides in a separate file, you use the **xmlns** (XML namespace) attribute in an XML document, like this:

```
<?xml version="1.0" ?>
<TASKFORCE xmlns="x-schema:schema1.xml">
    <EMPLOYEE>George Patton</EMPLOYEE>
    <EMPLOYEE>Douglas MacArthur</EMPLOYEE>
    <DESCRIPTION>XML Programming Taskforce</DESCRIPTION>
</TASKFORCE>
```

In this case, I'm indicating that the schema for this XML document is schema1.xml. In schema1.xml, you start with the **<SCHEMA>** element like this:

```
<SCHEMA NAME="schema1">
    .
    .
    .
</SCHEMA>
```

To use schemas, you must include the following two lines, which create two XML namespaces with the **xmlns** keyword, which you set to the Uniform Resource Names (URNs) for the Microsoft definitions for use in schemas:

```
<SCHEMA NAME="schema1"
    xmlns="urn:schemas-microsoft-com:xml-data"
    xmlns:dt="urn:schemas-microsoft-com:datatypes">
        .
        .
        .
</SCHEMA>
```

The **xmlns** attribute defines an XML namespace, and we've been using **xmlns** all along in XHTML documents to define the approved XHTML namespace, **http://www.w3.org/1999/xhtml**:

```
<?xml version="1.0"?>
<!DOCTYPE html PUBLIC "-//W3C//DTD XHTML 1.0 Transitional//EN"
"http://www.w3.org/tr/xhtml1/DTD/xhtml1-transitional.dtd">
<html xmlns="http://www.w3.org/1999/xhtml" xml:lang="en" lang="en">
    <head>
        <title>
        .
        .
        .
```

Namespaces were introduced to avoid element and attribute name clashes. For example, the code snippet just before the previous one defines a namespace called **dt**, for data type, which includes an attribute named **type**. You might have already defined an attribute named **type**, so to avoid clashes with Microsoft's attribute with the same name, you qualify the Microsoft attributes with the **dt** namespace prefix, like this: **dt:type="int"**. You can also qualify element names with namespaces in the same way, such as **<coriolis:document>**, which creates a **<document>** element as defined in the **coriolis** namespace. Namespaces become important when you're importing someone else's XML element and attribute definitions, which you do when you're creating a Microsoft XML schema. (I'll cover how to use namespaces in schemas in "Creating XML Documents with Schemas" in the "Immediate Solutions" section.)

To specify the syntax of an element in a schema, you use the **<ELEMENTTYPE>** element, as in this next example. I'm specifying that the **<EMPLOYEE>** and **<DESCRIPTION>** elements can contain only text and that their specifications are *closed*, which means that they cannot accept any content other than what is listed. (If you leave the specifications open, the element can contain content other than what you list.) Here's the code:

```
<SCHEMA NAME="schema1"
    xmlns="urn:schemas-microsoft-com:xml-data"
    xmlns:dt="urn:schemas-microsoft-com:datatypes">
```

```
<ELEMENTTYPE name="EMPLOYEE" content="textOnly" model="closed"/>
<ELEMENTTYPE name="DESCRIPTION" content="textOnly" model="closed"/>
   .
   .
   .
</SCHEMA>
```

Here's how I define the **<TASKFORCE>** element, which can contain both **<EMPLOYEE>** and **<DESCRIPTION>** elements—but can contain *only* elements (not text). You specify this condition with the **eltOnly** keyword. I'm also specifying that the **<EMPLOYEE>** element must occur at least once, and the **<DESCRIPTION>** element must occur once, but only once, in the **<TASKFORCE>** element:

```
<SCHEMA NAME="schema1"
    xmlns="urn:schemas-microsoft-com:xml-data"
    xmlns:dt="urn:schemas-microsoft-com:datatypes">

    <ELEMENTTYPE name="EMPLOYEE" content="textOnly" model="closed"/>
    <ELEMENTTYPE name="DESCRIPTION" content="textOnly" model="closed"/>

    <ELEMENTTYPE name="TASKFORCE" content="eltOnly" model="closed">
        <ELEMENT type="EMPLOYEE" minOccurs="1" maxOccurs="*"/>
        <ELEMENT type="DESCRIPTION" minOccurs="1" maxOccurs="1"/>
    </ELEMENTTYPE>
</SCHEMA>
```

That completes our overview of XML DTDs and schemas; I'll discuss how to work with XML documents in Internet Explorer 5 next.

XML in Internet Explorer 5

The support for XML in Internet Explorer 5 is fairly substantial. Here's an overview:

- *Direct viewing of XML*—The Microsoft XML implementation lets users view XML directly. You can also view XML using XSL or CSS in Internet Explorer.

- *Extensible Stylesheet Language (XSL) support*—The Microsoft XSL processor, which is based on the latest W3C Working Draft, allows developers to apply style sheets to XML data and to display the data in a dynamic and flexible way that can be customized.

- *High-performance, validating XML engine*—The Internet Explorer's XML engine has been enhanced. It fully supports W3C XML 1 and XML namespaces, which let you qualify element names uniquely on the Web and thus avoid conflicts between elements with the same name.

- *XML Document Object Model (DOM)*—The XML DOM is a standard object application programming interface that gives developers control of XML document content, structure, and formats. The Microsoft XML implementation includes support for the W3C XML DOM recommendation and is accessible from Web page scripts, Visual Basic, C++, and other languages.
- *XML schemas*—Schemas define the rules of an XML document, including element names and data types, which elements can appear in combination, and which attributes are available for each element.

At last, it's time to start working with the actual data in an XML document.

Loading XML Documents

To work with an XML document in Internet Explorer 5, you can load it in two ways. To show both ways in action, I'll use the XML document, school.xml, which records a school class on XML, including the names of students in the class:

```
<?xml version="1.0"?>
<SCHOOL>
    <CLASS type="seminar">
        <CLASS_TITLE>XML In Theory And Practice</CLASS_TITLE>
        <CLASS_NUMBER>10.306</CLASS_NUMBER>
        <SUBJECT>XML</SUBJECT>
        <START_DATE>1/1/2001</START_DATE>
        <STUDENTS>
            <STUDENT status="attending">
                <FIRST_NAME>Mark</FIRST_NAME>
                <LAST_NAME>Swansburg</LAST_NAME>
            </STUDENT>
            <STUDENT status="withdrawn">
                <FIRST_NAME>Thomas</FIRST_NAME>
                <LAST_NAME>Preston</LAST_NAME>
            </STUDENT>
        </STUDENTS>
    </CLASS>
</SCHOOL>
```

The first way of working with school.xml is to load it in with the **Microsoft.XMLDOM** object, creating a new ActiveX object. To see how this works, I'll read in school.xml and retrieve the name of the second student. After creating a new ActiveX object, I use the **load** method to load in school.xml with JavaScript:

```
<?xml version="1.0"?>
<!DOCTYPE html PUBLIC "-//W3C//DTD XHTML 1.0 Transitional//EN"
"http://www.w3.org/tr/xhtml1/DTD/xhtml1-transitional.dtd">
<html xmlns="http://www.w3.org/1999/xhtml" xml:lang="en" lang="en">
```

```
<head>
    <title>
        Finding Element Values in an XML Document
    </title>

    <script type="text/javascript" language="javascript">
        function getStudentData()
        {
            var xmldoc;
            xmldoc = new ActiveXObject("Microsoft.XMLDOM");
            xmldoc.load("school.xml");
            .
            .
            .
        }
    </head>
</html>
```

Now I get the root element of the XML document (which contains all the other elements), using the **documentElement** property of this new object. I'm now free to navigate around the XML document by using the **firstChild**, **nextChild**, **previousChild**, and **lastChild** methods, which let you access the child elements of an element, and the **firstSibling**, **nextSibling**, **previousSibling**, and **lastSibling** methods, which let you access elements on the same level. To get the root element of the XML document, you start with the **documentElement** method; then navigate to the second student element and create objects corresponding to the student's first and last names:

```
<?xml version="1.0"?>
<!DOCTYPE html PUBLIC "-//W3C//DTD XHTML 1.0 Transitional//EN"
"http://www.w3.org/tr/xhtml1/DTD/xhtml1-transitional.dtd">
<html xmlns="http://www.w3.org/1999/xhtml" xml:lang="en" lang="en">
    <head>
        <title>
            Finding Element Values in an XML Document
        </title>

        <script type="text/javascript" language="javascript">
            function getStudentData()
            {
                var xmldoc;
                xmldoc = new ActiveXObject("Microsoft.XMLDOM");
                xmldoc.load("school.xml");
```

```
                nodeSchool = xmldoc.documentElement;
                nodeClass = nodeSchool.firstChild;
                nodeStudents = nodeClass.lastChild;
                nodeStudent = nodeStudents.lastChild;
                nodeFirstName = nodeStudent.firstChild;
                nodeLastName = nodeFirstName.nextSibling;
                    .
                    .
                    .
    </head>
</html>
```

To recover the data from the XML document—that is, the content of an element—you use the **nodeValue** property. Here's how I retrieve the name of the second student in school.xml and display it in a **<DIV>** element in the document's body:

```
<?xml version="1.0"?>
<!DOCTYPE html PUBLIC "-//W3C//DTD XHTML 1.0 Transitional//EN"
"http://www.w3.org/tr/xhtml1/DTD/xhtml1-transitional.dtd">
<html xmlns="http://www.w3.org/1999/xhtml" xml:lang="en" lang="en">
    <head>
        <title>
            Finding Element Values in an XML Document
        </title>

        <script type="text/javascript" language="javascript">
            function getStudentData()
            {
                var xmldoc;
                xmldoc = new ActiveXObject("Microsoft.XMLDOM");
                xmldoc.load("school.xml");

                nodeSchool = xmldoc.documentElement;
                nodeClass = nodeSchool.firstChild;
                nodeStudents = nodeClass.lastChild;
                nodeStudent = nodeStudents.lastChild;
                nodeFirstName = nodeStudent.firstChild;
                nodeLastName = nodeFirstName.nextSibling;

                outputMessage = "Name: " +
                    nodeFirstName.firstChild.nodeValue + ' '
                    + nodeLastName.firstChild.nodeValue;
                message.innerHTML=outputMessage;
            }
        </script>
    </head>
```

```
<body>
    <center>
        <h1>
            Finding Element Values in an XML Document
        </h1>

        <div id="message"></div>
        <p>
        <input type="button" value="Get Second Student's Name"
            onclick="getStudentData()" />
        </p>
    </center>
</body>
</html>
```

Note also that I'm adding a button to the Web page to run the JavaScript that will read the second name. You can see the results in Figure 15.2. When the user clicks the button, the browser reads in school.xml and displays the name of the second student. We've made some progress.

Using Data Islands

Starting with Internet Explorer 5, you can also use *data islands* to handle XML. Data islands enclose XML inside a standard HTML (or XHTML) document. You create a data island with the **<xml>** element, enclosing the XML you want to use in the **<xml>** element:

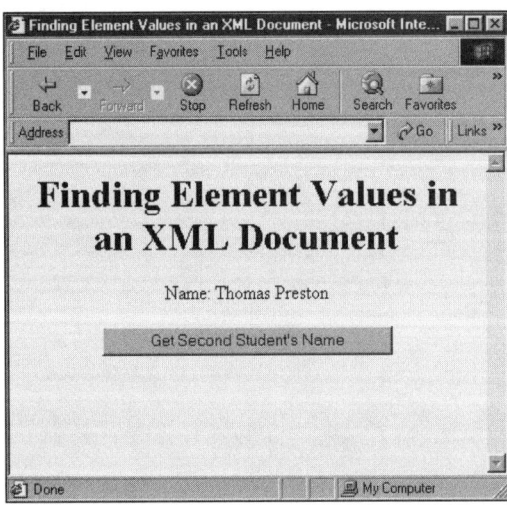

Figure 15.2 Accessing data in an XML document in Internet Explorer.

```
<xml id="xmlid">
    <xmldata>
        <data>Here's some data!</data>
    </xmldata>
</xml>
```

The **<xmldata>** and **<data>** elements are XML elements, so I could have named them anything. Using the **<xml>** element's ID, you can access the XML in the element. By using the **<xml>** element's **src** attribute, you can also use a data island to handle an external XML document. To get the root element of the XML document, you use the **XMLDocument** property. Here's how I convert the previous example to use a data island instead of the **Microsoft.XMLDOM** object (note that since the **<xml>** element is specific to Internet Explorer, this document is not strictly conforming XHTML):

```
<?xml version="1.0"?>
<!DOCTYPE html PUBLIC "-//W3C//DTD XHTML 1.0 Transitional//EN"
"http://www.w3.org/tr/xhtml1/DTD/xhtml1-transitional.dtd">
<html xmlns="http://www.w3.org/1999/xhtml" xml:lang="en" lang="en">
    <head>
        <title>
            Finding Element Values in an XML Document Using Data Islands
        </title>

        <xml id="schoolXML" src="school.xml"></xml>

        <script type="text/javascript" language="javascript">
            function getStudentData()
            {
                xmldoc= document.all("schoolXML").XMLDocument;

                nodeSchool = xmldoc.documentElement;
                nodeClass = nodeSchool.firstChild;
                nodeStudents = nodeClass.lastChild;
                nodeStudent = nodeStudents.lastChild;
                nodeFirstName = nodeStudent.firstChild;
                nodeLastName = nodeFirstName.nextSibling;

                outputMessage = "Name: " +
                    nodeFirstName.firstChild.nodeValue + ' '
                    + nodeLastName.firstChild.nodeValue;
                message.innerHTML=outputMessage;
            }
        </script>
    </head>
```

```
<body>
    <center>
        <h1>
            Finding Element Values in an XML Document Using
            Data Islands
        </h1>

        <div id="message"></div>
        <p>
        <input type="button" value="Get Second Student's Name"
            onclick="getStudentData()" />
        </p>
    </center>
</body>
</html>
```

This example works as the previous example did, as you see in Figure 15.3. Now we've seen two ways of working with an XML document in Internet Explorer—by loading the document in explicitly and by using a data island. I'll use both approaches in this chapter but will use data islands the most because it's the most common technique.

Extending XHTML

One of the attractive aspects of XHTML is that because it's based on XML, you can extend it with your own elements and attributes. I'll take a look at an example here, and elaborate the process in this chapter.

Figure 15.3 Accessing data with data islands in an XML document in Internet Explorer.

In Depth

> **NOTE:** Note that the material on extending XHTML is only in the working draft stage, and will probably change. You can find more information at **www.w3.org/TR/xhtml-building/**.

For example, standard XHTML documents have a **<head>** and **<body>**; I'll add a new element, **<foot>**, to hold a footer for the document. To add this element, I'll create a new DTD named extend.dtd, which defines this new element. I'll also give this new element an attribute, footattribute, to show how that works. To create an attribute, you use the **<!ATTLIST>** element (see the Immediate Solutions section "Specifying Attributes in DTDs"). Here's another important point; W3C says that new XHTML elements should have their own namespace, and I'll give them the namespace **doc** here, like this:

```
<!ELEMENT doc:foot (#PCDATA) >
<!ATTLIST doc:foot
    footattribute    CDATA    #IMPLIED
>
    .
    .
    .
```

You also have to specify how the new element fits in with the other elements in XHTML to make sure the documents you create are valid. The **<doc:foot>** element is a child element of the **<html>** element, so you have to indicate that. In the XHTML 1.0 Transitional DTD, the **<html>** element is defined this way:

```
<!ELEMENT html (head, body)>
```

I'll augment the **<html>** element's content model to include the **<doc:foot>** element this way:

```
<!ELEMENT doc:foot (#PCDATA) >
<!ATTLIST doc:foot
    footattribute    CDATA    #IMPLIED
>

<!ELEMENT html (head, body, doc:foot)>
    .
    .
    .
```

When you redefine an element like this, the new definition takes precedence over the old one (although browsers like Internet Explorer are not yet up to redefining elements this way). Having redefined the **<html>** element to contain the **<doc:foot>** element, I can include the rest of the XHTML 1.0 Transitional DTD with a *parameter entity*. You use parameter entities in DTDs to include resources in exactly this way, and I'll define a parameter entity named **xhtml10T.dtd** to stand for the entire XHTML 1.0 Transitional DTD. I can then include that DTD with the parameter entity *reference* **%xhtml10T.dtd;** this way:

```
<!ELEMENT doc:foot (#PCDATA) >
<!ATTLIST doc:foot
     footattribute    CDATA    #IMPLIED
>

<!ELEMENT html (head, body, doc:foot)>

<!ENTITY % xhtml10T.dtd PUBLIC "-//W3C//DTD XHTML 1.0 Transitional//EN"
     "http://www.w3.org/TR/xhtml1/DTD/xhtml1-transitional.dtd">
%xhtml10T.dtd;
```

That completes the new DTD, extend.dtd. You can indicate how you want text in the new element displayed in a style sheet, which I'll call extend.css; here are the contents of that style sheet:

```
doc:foot {font-size: 8pt; color: #FF0000}
p (color: #FF0000}
```

The following code shows how you can use the new DTD in a new XHTML page using the **<doc:foot>** element, along with the style sheet extend.css. Note that I'm now declaring the **doc** namespace and making the XHTML namespace the default namespace:

```
<!DOCTYPE html PUBLIC "-//Extender//DTD XHTML-Extensions 1.0//EN"
"http://www.starpowder.com/steve/extend.dtd" >
<html xmlns="http://www.w3.org/1999/xhtml" xmlns:doc="http://
www.starpowder.com/steve/extend.dtd">
    <head>
        <title>
            Extending XHTML
        </title>

        <link rel="stylesheet" href="extend.css" />
    </head>
```

```
    <body>
        <p>
            Here is some text.
        </p>
    </body>

    <doc:foot>
        This is the page's foot.
    </doc:foot>
</html>
```

That's just one way to extend XHTML—we'll see others as well. For example, now that we're into the details of XML and extending XHTML, I'll also discuss how XHTML 1.1 modules work, so you can see how to get into the heart of those modules and incorporate entirely new elements into existing XHTML 1.1 elements.

Immediate Solutions

Creating XML Documents

"OK," says the novice programmer, "I'm ready to work with XML. Where do I start?" "By creating an XML document," you say. "Lead on," says the NP, "and I'll follow." "It'll be $100 for the first lesson," you say. The NP says, "Uh oh."

In the "In Depth" section of this chapter, we saw that you can create XML elements in a relatively free-form way, defining your own elements. Here's the example I discussed earlier (note that you must start an XML document with the **<?xml version = "1.0"?>** processing instruction, and you must have one element that contains all others):

```
<?xml version = "1.0"?>
<DOCUMENT>
    <CUSTOMER>
        <NAME>
            <LAST_NAME>Thomson</LAST_NAME>
            <FIRST_NAME>Susan</FIRST_NAME>
        </NAME>
        <DATE>September 1, 2001</DATE>
        <ORDERS>
            <ITEM>
                <PRODUCT>Video tape</PRODUCT>
                <NUMBER>5</NUMBER>
                <PRICE>$1.25</PRICE>
            </ITEM>
            <ITEM>
                <PRODUCT>Shovel</PRODUCT>
                <NUMBER>2</NUMBER>
                <PRICE>$4.98</PRICE>
            </ITEM>
        </ORDERS>
    </CUSTOMER>
    <CUSTOMER>
        <NAME>
            <LAST_NAME>Smithson</LAST_NAME>
            <FIRST_NAME>Nancy</FIRST_NAME>
        </NAME>
        <DATE>September 2, 2001</DATE>
```

```
            <ORDERS>
                <ITEM>
                    <PRODUCT>Ribbon</PRODUCT>
                    <NUMBER>12</NUMBER>
                    <PRICE>$2.95</PRICE>
                </ITEM>
                <ITEM>
                    <PRODUCT>Goldfish</PRODUCT>
                    <NUMBER>6</NUMBER>
                    <PRICE>$1.50</PRICE>
                </ITEM>
            </ORDERS>
        </CUSTOMER>
</DOCUMENT>
```

See the "In Depth" section of this chapter for the step-by-step construction of this example. You can see this XML document in Internet Explorer in Figure 15.1. Note that although Internet Explorer can deal with XML documents like this, you can also include a DTD or a schema to make sure its syntax is acceptable. See the next few sections for the details on DTDs and schemas.

Creating XML Documents with DTDs

"Hey," says the novice programmer, "there are problems with the data in my XML document!" "Could be a syntax problem," you say. "Why not let Internet Explorer use a DTD to check the syntax of your document?" "Good idea," says the NP.

You use a DTD to let the browser check your XML document's syntax. DTDs aren't required but can be a good idea to ensure data integrity. You can create internal or external DTDs.

Creating DTDs can be somewhat complex, so I'll work through a second example in this section (there's an example in the beginning of this chapter). Here's the XML document I'll create; the DTD is enclosed in the **<!DOCTYPE>** element:

```
<?xml version="1.0"?>
<!DOCTYPE DOCUMENT [
    <!ELEMENT p (#PCDATA)>
    <!ELEMENT DOCUMENT    (TITLE,SUBTITLE?,PREFACE?,(SECTION | PART)+)>
    <!ELEMENT TITLE       (TITLE2)*>
    <!ELEMENT TITLE2      (#PCDATA)>
    <!ELEMENT SUBTITLE    (p)+>
    <!ELEMENT PREFACE     (HEADING, p+)+>
    <!ELEMENT PART        (HEADING, CHAPTER+)>
```

```
        <!ELEMENT SECTION       (HEADING, p+)>
        <!ELEMENT HEADING       (#PCDATA)>
        <!ELEMENT CHAPTER       (CHAPTERTITLE, p+)>
        <!ELEMENT CHAPTERTITLE  (#PCDATA)>
]>
<DOCUMENT>
    <TITLE>
        <TITLE2>
            My Novel
        </TITLE2>
    </TITLE>
    <PART>
        <HEADING>Ice Cream Consumption</HEADING>
        <CHAPTER>
            <CHAPTERTITLE>CHAPTER 1</CHAPTERTITLE>
            <p>I enjoy fishing.</p>
            <p>And I enjoy travel.</p>
            <p>How about you?</p>
        </CHAPTER>
    </PART>
</DOCUMENT>
```

This code contains several elements: **<DOCUMENT>**, **<TITLE>**, **<PART>**, **<HEADING>**, and so on. I'll start the DTD by declaring the **<P>** element, which I want to hold text only—that is, "parsed character data," as far as XML is concerned. You specify this condition with the keyword **#PCDATA**:

```
<!ELEMENT p             (#PCDATA)>
           .
           .
           .
```

Next, I declare the root element, **<DOCUMENT>**. I'll set up the **<DOCUMENT>** element to contain a **<TITLE>** tag, possibly a **<SUBTITLE>** tag (by placing a question mark after the **SUBTITLE** declaration) or a **<PREFACE>** tag, and one or more sections or parts declared with the **<SECTION>** and **<PART>** tags. The pipe character [|] used in the following example means "or." (For details about the syntax allowed in a DTD, see the "In Depth" section of this chapter.) Here's the code:

```
<!ELEMENT p             (#PCDATA)>
<!ELEMENT DOCUMENT      (TITLE,SUBTITLE?,PREFACE?,(SECTION | PART)+)>
           .
           .
           .
```

Next, I declare a **<TITLE>** tag that contains zero or more occurrences of subtitle tags. I'll call it **<TITLE2>**:

```
<!ELEMENT p              (#PCDATA)>
<!ELEMENT DOCUMENT       (TITLE,SUBTITLE?,PREFACE?,(SECTION | PART)+)>
<!ELEMENT TITLE          (TITLE2)*>
    .
    .
    .
```

The **<TITLE2>** element, in turn, can contain character data:

```
<!ELEMENT p              (#PCDATA)>
<!ELEMENT DOCUMENT       (TITLE,SUBTITLE?,PREFACE?,(SECTION | PART)+)>
<!ELEMENT TITLE          (TITLE2)*>
<!ELEMENT TITLE2         (#PCDATA)>
    .
    .
    .
```

Next, I declare the **<SUBTITLE>** element, which must contain one or more paragraphs:

```
<!ELEMENT p              (#PCDATA)>
<!ELEMENT DOCUMENT       (TITLE,SUBTITLE?,PREFACE?,(SECTION | PART)+)>
<!ELEMENT TITLE          (TITLE2)*>
<!ELEMENT TITLE2         (#PCDATA)>
<!ELEMENT SUBTITLE       (p)+>
    .
    .
    .
```

The **<PREFACE>** element must contain one or more **<P>** elements and can contain **<HEADING>** elements:

```
<!ELEMENT p              (#PCDATA)>
<!ELEMENT DOCUMENT       (TITLE,SUBTITLE?,PREFACE?,(SECTION | PART)+)>
<!ELEMENT TITLE          (TITLE2)*>
<!ELEMENT TITLE2         (#PCDATA)>
<!ELEMENT SUBTITLE       (p)+>
<!ELEMENT PREFACE        (HEADING, p+)+>
    .
    .
    .
```

And I'll specify that the **<PART>** element can be empty, or it can contain **<HEADING>** or **<CHAPTER>** elements:

```
<!ELEMENT p              (#PCDATA)>
<!ELEMENT DOCUMENT       (TITLE,SUBTITLE?,PREFACE?,(SECTION | PART)+)>
<!ELEMENT TITLE          (TITLE2)*>
<!ELEMENT TITLE2         (#PCDATA)>
<!ELEMENT SUBTITLE       (p)+>
<!ELEMENT PREFACE        (HEADING, p+)+>
<!ELEMENT PART           (HEADING, CHAPTER+)>
    .
    .
    .
```

In addition, I'll specify that the **<CHAPTER>** element can be empty, or it can contain **<CHAPTERTITLE>** and **<P>** elements:

```
<!ELEMENT p              (#PCDATA)>
<!ELEMENT DOCUMENT       (TITLE,SUBTITLE?,PREFACE?,(SECTION | PART)+)>
<!ELEMENT TITLE          (TITLE2)*>
<!ELEMENT TITLE2         (#PCDATA)>
<!ELEMENT SUBTITLE       (p)+>
<!ELEMENT PREFACE        (HEADING, p+)+>
<!ELEMENT PART           (HEADING, CHAPTER+)>
<!ELEMENT SECTION        (HEADING, p+)>
<!ELEMENT HEADING        (#PCDATA)>
<!ELEMENT CHAPTER        (CHAPTERTITLE, p+)>
    .
    .
    .
```

Finally, the **<CHAPTERTITLE>** element contains parsed character data:

```
<!ELEMENT p              (#PCDATA)>
<!ELEMENT DOCUMENT       (TITLE,SUBTITLE?,PREFACE?,(SECTION | PART)+)>
<!ELEMENT TITLE          (TITLE2)*>
<!ELEMENT TITLE2         (#PCDATA)>
<!ELEMENT SUBTITLE       (p)+>
<!ELEMENT PREFACE        (HEADING, p+)+>
<!ELEMENT PART           (HEADING, CHAPTER+)>
<!ELEMENT SECTION        (HEADING, p+)>
<!ELEMENT HEADING        (#PCDATA)>
<!ELEMENT CHAPTER        (CHAPTERTITLE, p+)>
<!ELEMENT CHAPTERTITLE   (#PCDATA)>
```

When you enclose everything in the **<!DOCTYPE>** element, the DTD is complete:

```
<?xml version="1.0"?>
<!DOCTYPE DOCUMENT [
    <!ELEMENT p (#PCDATA)>
    <!ELEMENT DOCUMENT     (TITLE,SUBTITLE?,PREFACE?,(SECTION | PART)+)>
    <!ELEMENT TITLE        (TITLE2)*>
    <!ELEMENT TITLE2       (#PCDATA)>
    <!ELEMENT SUBTITLE     (p)+>
    <!ELEMENT PREFACE      (HEADING, p+)+>
    <!ELEMENT PART         (HEADING, CHAPTER+)>
    <!ELEMENT SECTION      (HEADING, p+)>
    <!ELEMENT HEADING      (#PCDATA)>
    <!ELEMENT CHAPTER      (CHAPTERTITLE, p+)>
    <!ELEMENT CHAPTERTITLE (#PCDATA)>
]>
<DOCUMENT>
    <TITLE>My Novel</TITLE>
    <PART>
        <HEADING>Ice Cream Consumption</HEADING>
        <CHAPTER>
            <CHAPTERTITLE>CHAPTER 1</CHAPTERTITLE>
            <p>I enjoy fishing.</p>
            <p>And I enjoy travel.</p>
            <p>How about you?</p>
        </CHAPTER>
    </PART>
</DOCUMENT>
```

In this case, I defined several elements but no attributes. For information on specifying attributes as well as elements, see the next section.

Specifying Attributes in DTDs

"Hey," asks the novice programmer, "how do you specify element attributes in a DTD? I know how to specify elements but not their attributes." "To specify attributes," you say, "you can use the **<!ATTLIST>** element." "How does that work?" the NP wants to know.

You use the **<!ATTLIST>** element to specify the attributes of the elements in a DTD. In the **<!ATTLIST>** element, you list another element's attributes, one after the other. You can specify default values for attributes as well as whether or not an attribute is required. Here's how you can use the **<!ATTLIST>** element to create attributes for the XML element whose name is **ELEMENT_NAME**. I'll indicate the three ways to declare attributes here. In practice, your **<!ATTLIST>** element may have more or fewer lines:

```
<!ATTLIST ELEMENT_NAME
    ATTRIBUTE_NAME TYPE DEFAULT_VALUE
    ATTRIBUTE_NAME TYPE #IMPLIED
    ATTRIBUTE_NAME TYPE #REQUIRED>
```

The first line with **ATTRIBUTE_NAME** in it indicates one way to declare an attribute. In this case, I'm specifying an attribute name, its type, and its default value. If no value is supplied for the attribute, the default value is used. The usual **TYPE** you use for attributes is unparsed character data, **CDATA**. However, instead of the **CDATA** type, you can also use *tokenized types*—which are defined by W3C as **ID**, **IDREF**, **IDREFS**, **ENTITY**, **ENTITIES**, **NMTOKEN** (name token), or **NMTOKENS**—to indicate the purpose of the attribute if it fits one of these descriptions. Here's how W3C defines these terms:

- **CDATA**—Character data
- **ID**—A document-unique identifier
- **IDREF**—A reference to a document-unique identifier
- **NAME**—A name with the same character constraints as ID
- **NMTOKEN**—A name composed of CDATA characters but no white space
- **NMTOKENS**—Multiple names composed of CDATA characters separated by white space
- **PCDATA**—Parsed character data (text which does not contain any markup)

You can also set up and use *enumerated* attribute types, which means that the attribute can be set to only those values in a list that you define (such as "Monday," "Tuesday," "Wednesday," "Thursday," or "Friday").

The next line in this example specifies another way to declare an attribute: making it *implied*. This means that it doesn't need to be used in the XML element.

The last line specifies a *required* attribute, which means that Internet Explorer will report an error if you omit it.

Here's an example that creates attributes. I'll create a DTD for the sample XML document that I created in the "In Depth" section of this chapter. Here, I'm adding attributes to the **<CUSTOMER>** element—in particular, an attribute named **CITIZENSHIP** that has a default value of "US", an implied **AGE** attribute, and a required **TYPE** attribute. (Again, your **<!ATTLIST>** element may have more or fewer lines, depending on how many attributes you want to define for the XML element involved.) Here's the code:

```
<?xml version = "1.0"?>
<!DOCTYPE DOCUMENT [
<!ELEMENT DOCUMENT (CUSTOMER)*>
<!ELEMENT CUSTOMER (NAME,DATE,ORDERS)>
<!ELEMENT NAME (LAST_NAME,FIRST_NAME)>
<!ELEMENT LAST_NAME (#PCDATA)>
<!ELEMENT FIRST_NAME (#PCDATA)>
<!ELEMENT DATE (#PCDATA)>
<!ELEMENT ORDERS (ITEM)*>
<!ELEMENT ITEM (PRODUCT,NUMBER,PRICE)>
<!ELEMENT PRODUCT (#PCDATA)>
<!ELEMENT NUMBER (#PCDATA)>
<!ELEMENT PRICE (#PCDATA)>
<!ATTLIST CUSTOMER
    CITIZENSHIP CDATA "US"
    AGE CDATA #IMPLIED
    TYPE CDATA #REQUIRED>
]>
<DOCUMENT>
    <CUSTOMER TYPE="Insolvent">
        <NAME>
            <LAST_NAME>Thomson</LAST_NAME>
            <FIRST_NAME>Susan</FIRST_NAME>
        </NAME>
        <DATE>September 1, 2001</DATE>
        <ORDERS>
            <ITEM>
                <PRODUCT>Video tape</PRODUCT>
                <NUMBER>5</NUMBER>
                <PRICE>$1.25</PRICE>
            </ITEM>
            <ITEM>
                <PRODUCT>Shovel</PRODUCT>
                <NUMBER>2</NUMBER>
                <PRICE>$4.98</PRICE>
            </ITEM>
        </ORDERS>
    </CUSTOMER>
    <CUSTOMER TYPE="Solvent">
        <NAME>
            <LAST_NAME>Smithson</LAST_NAME>
            <FIRST_NAME>Nancy</FIRST_NAME>
        </NAME>
        <DATE>September 2, 2001</DATE>
        <ORDERS>
```

```
            <ITEM>
                <PRODUCT>Ribbon</PRODUCT>
                <NUMBER>12</NUMBER>
                <PRICE>$2.95</PRICE>
            </ITEM>
            <ITEM>
                <PRODUCT>Goldfish</PRODUCT>
                <NUMBER>6</NUMBER>
                <PRICE>$1.50</PRICE>
            </ITEM>
        </ORDERS>
    </CUSTOMER>
</DOCUMENT>
```

Creating XML Documents with Schemas

"Writing DTDs isn't easy," says the novice programmer. "I've heard that you can use Microsoft schemas to do the same thing. How does that work?" "Some people don't find schemas that much easier," you say, "but pull up a chair and let's take a look." The NP rushes off to get coffee.

As we saw in the "In Depth" section of this chapter, XML schemas are Microsoft's alternative to DTDs. If you want to create valid XML documents for use with Internet Explorer, you can use either a DTD or a schema.

*TIP: For Microsoft XML references and information on how to create schemas, see **http://msdn.microsoft.com/workshop/xml/index.asp**.*

Here's the example I presented in the "In Depth" section of this chapter. This XML document uses a schema named schema1.xml:

```
<?xml version="1.0" ?>
<TASKFORCE xmlns="x-schema:schema1.xml">
    <EMPLOYEE>George Patton</EMPLOYEE>
    <EMPLOYEE>Douglas MacArthur</EMPLOYEE>
    <DESCRIPTION>XML Programming Taskforce</DESCRIPTION>
</TASKFORCE>
```

And here's the schema, schema1.xml, we also developed in the "In Depth" section:

```
<SCHEMA NAME="schema1"
    xmlns="urn:schemas-microsoft-com:xml-data"
    xmlns:dt="urn:schemas-microsoft-com:datatypes">
```

```
        <ELEMENTTYPE name="EMPLOYEE" content="textOnly" model="closed"/>
        <ELEMENTTYPE name="DESCRIPTION" content="textOnly" model="closed"/>

        <ELEMENTTYPE name="TASKFORCE" content="eltOnly" model="closed">
            <ELEMENT type="EMPLOYEE" minOccurs="1" maxOccurs="*"/>
            <ELEMENT type="DESCRIPTION" minOccurs="1" maxOccurs="1"/>
    </ELEMENTTYPE>
</SCHEMA>
```

Schemas can get vastly more complex than this, of course. For example, you can use the **dt:type** attribute to specify the data type of elements (assuming that you create a namespace named **dt** for Microsoft's XML data types, as I have in the immediately preceding code). Here's an example in which I'm specifying that an element can hold integer content:

```
<ElementType name="count" dt:type="int"/>
```

You can also use the **<datatype>** element to do the same thing explicitly:

```
<ElementType name="count">
    <datatype dt:type= "int"/>
</ElementType>
```

The following list contains the possible data types:

- *bin.base64*—Multipurpose Internet Mail Extension (MIME)-style Base64 encoded binary object.
- *bin.hex*—Hexadecimal digits.
- *boolean*—0 or 1; 0 means false and 1 means true.
- *char*—String; one character long.
- *date*—Date with a subset ISO 8601 format that does not contain time data. For example: "2001-09-02".
- *dateTime*—Date with a subset ISO 8601 format that contains optional time data but not optional zone data. Fractional seconds can be as exact as nanoseconds. For example, "2001-04-07T22:00:07".
- *dateTime.tz*—Date with a subset ISO 8601 format that contains both optional time and optional zone data. Fractional seconds can be as precise as nanoseconds. For example: "2001-04-07T22:00:07-08:00".
- *fixed.14.4*—Same as "number" except that there can be no more than 14 digits to the left of the decimal point and no more than 4 to the right.
- *float*—Real number with no digit limitation; can have leading sign, fractional digits, and optionally, exponent. Values range from 1.7976931348623157E+308 through 2.2250738585072014E-308.

- *int*—Integer with optional sign but without fractions or exponent.
- *number*—Number with no digit limitation; potentially can have leading sign, fractional digits, and optionally, exponent. Precision has a range of 1.7976931348623157E+308 through 2.2250738585072014E-308.
- *time*—Time with a subset ISO 8601 format that does not contain date or time zone. For example: "09:03:54".
- *time.tz*—Time with a subset ISO 8601 format that does not contain date but does contain optional time zone. For example: "09:03:54-07:00".
- *i1*—Integer denoted in one byte. A number with optional sign but without fractions or exponent. For example: "7, 119, -123".
- *i2*—Integer denoted in one word. A number with optional sign but without fractions or exponent. For example: "7, 225, -32000".
- *i4*—Integer denoted in four bytes. A number with optional sign but without fractions or exponent. For example: "1, -32000, 278911".
- *r4*—Real number having seven-digit precision; can contain leading sign, fractional digits, and optionally, exponent. Values range from 3.40282347E+38F through 1.17549435E-38F.
- *r8*—Real number having 15-digit precision; potentially can contain leading sign, fractional digits, and optionally, exponent. Values range from 1.7976931348623157E+308 through 2.2250738585072014E-308.
- *ui1*—Unsigned integer. A number, unsigned, with no fractions or exponent. For example: "231, 6".
- *ui2*—Unsigned integer, two bytes. A number, unsigned, with no fractions or exponent. For example: "18, 211, 56789".
- *ui4*—Unsigned integer, four bytes. A number, unsigned, no with fractions or exponent. For example: "5, 209, 1234500000".
- *uri*—Universal Resource Identifier (URI).
- *uuid*—Hexadecimal digits denoting octets; optional embedded hyphens are ignored. For example: "195D6A3F-358B4E1D-A439-553A351AAC91".

For more information on schemas, look at the Microsoft XML site.

Accessing XML Data by Loading XML Documents

"Hm," says the novice programmer, "now I can create an XML document, and even view it in Internet Explorer. But how can I, um, access the data in it?" You smile and say, "There are two ways—you create an ActiveX object and load an

XML page into it, or you can create a data island." "Let's see the first way first," says the NP.

To load an XML document into Internet Explorer, you can use the **Microsoft.XMLDOM** object to create an ActiveX object, and then use the **load** method to load the XML document. After the document is loaded, you can use the ActiveX object's **documentElement** property to reach the root element of the XML document. After you have the root element, you can navigate around the XML document by using the **firstChild**, **nextChild**, **previousChild**, and **lastChild** methods, which let you access the child elements of an element, and the **firstSibling**, **nextSibling**, **previousSibling**, and **lastSibling** methods, which let you access elements on the same level.

Let's look at an example, from the "In Depth" section of this chapter, using the XML document, school.xml:

```
<?xml version="1.0"?>
<SCHOOL>
    <CLASS type="seminar">
        <CLASS_TITLE>XML In Theory And Practice</CLASS_TITLE>
        <CLASS_NUMBER>10.306</CLASS_NUMBER>
        <SUBJECT>XML</SUBJECT>
        <START_DATE>1/1/2001</START_DATE>
        <STUDENTS>
            <STUDENT status="attending">
                <FIRST_NAME>Mark</FIRST_NAME>
                <LAST_NAME>Swansburg</LAST_NAME>
            </STUDENT>
            <STUDENT status="withdrawn">
                <FIRST_NAME>Thomas</FIRST_NAME>
                <LAST_NAME>Preston</LAST_NAME>
            </STUDENT>
        </STUDENTS>
    </CLASS>
</SCHOOL>
```

The Web page I developed in the "In Depth" section of this chapter read in this XML document and, by using the navigation methods already discussed, moved to the second student's record. To access the data in that record, I use the **nodeValue** property:

```
<?xml version="1.0"?>
<!DOCTYPE html PUBLIC "-//W3C//DTD XHTML 1.0 Transitional//EN"
"http://www.w3.org/tr/xhtml1/DTD/xhtml1-transitional.dtd">
<html xmlns="http://www.w3.org/1999/xhtml" xml:lang="en" lang="en">
```

```
<head>
    <title>
        Finding Element Values in an XML Document
    </title>

    <script type="text/javascript" language="javascript">
        function getStudentData()
        {
            var xmldoc;
            xmldoc = new ActiveXObject("Microsoft.XMLDOM");
            xmldoc.load("school.xml");

            nodeSchool = xmldoc.documentElement;
            nodeClass = nodeSchool.firstChild;
            nodeStudents = nodeClass.lastChild;
            nodeStudent = nodeStudents.lastChild;
            nodeFirstName = nodeStudent.firstChild;
            nodeLastName = nodeFirstName.nextSibling;

            outputMessage = "Name: " +
                nodeFirstName.firstChild.nodeValue + ' '
                + nodeLastName.firstChild.nodeValue;
            message.innerHTML=outputMessage;
        }
    </script>
</head>

<body>
    <center>
        <h1>
            Finding Element Values in an XML Document
        </h1>

        <div id="message"></div>
        <p>
        <input type="button" value="Get Second Student's Name"
            onclick="getStudentData()" />
        </p>
    </center>
</body>
</html>
```

You can see the results of this HTML and XML in Figure 15.2. Loading an XML document with the **load** method is one way of accessing it; the other is to use data islands.

<xml>—Accessing XML Data with an XML Data Island

Purpose: Creates an XML data island in Internet Explorer and embeds an XML document in a Web page.

When used as HTML: Start tag/End tag: Required/Required

Supported: [IE5]

Attributes:

- **disabled**—Indicates whether the element is disabled. [IE5]
- **id**—Unique alphanumeric identifier for the tag; use the ID to refer to the tag. [IE5]
- **src**—Specifies the source for the XML document. Set to a URL. [IE5]

XHTML events: None

"Hm," says the novice programmer, "loading in an XML element is OK, but didn't you say something about data islands?" "Yes," you say, "I sure did. You create data islands with the **<xml>** element, and you can mix XHTML and XML in this way."

You use Internet Explorer's HTML **<xml>** element to enclose XML data in a Web page, creating a data island. Here's an example in which I'm embedding school.xml, an XML document that contains student records, in a data island (note that since the **<xml>** element is specific to Internet Explorer, this example is not strictly conforming XHTML):

```
<?xml version="1.0"?>
<!DOCTYPE html PUBLIC "-//W3C//DTD XHTML 1.0 Transitional//EN"
    "http://www.w3.org/tr/xhtml1/DTD/xhtml1-transitional.dtd">
<html xmlns="http://www.w3.org/1999/xhtml" xml:lang="en" lang="en">
    <head>
        <title>
            Creating An XML Data Island
        </title>

            <xml id="schoolXML">
                <SCHOOL>
                    <CLASS type="seminar">
                        <CLASS_TITLE>XML In Theory And Practice</CLASS_TITLE>
                        <CLASS_NUMBER>10.306</CLASS_NUMBER>
                        <SUBJECT>XML</SUBJECT>
                        <START_DATE>1/1/2001</START_DATE>
                        <STUDENTS>
                            <STUDENT status="attending">
                                <FIRST_NAME>Mark</FIRST_NAME>
```

```
                        <LAST_NAME>Swansburg</LAST_NAME>
                    </STUDENT>
                    <STUDENT status="withdrawn">
                        <FIRST_NAME>Thomas</FIRST_NAME>
                        <LAST_NAME>Preston</LAST_NAME>
                    </STUDENT>
                </STUDENTS>
            </CLASS>
        </SCHOOL>
    </xml>
</head>

<body>
    <center>
        <h1>
            Creating An XML Data Island
        </h1>
    </center>
</body>
</html>
```

You don't need to embed the whole XML document in the data island, however; you can simply use the **SRC** attribute to point to the XML document:

```
<?xml version="1.0"?>
<!DOCTYPE html PUBLIC "-//W3C//DTD XHTML 1.0 Transitional//EN"
"http://www.w3.org/tr/xhtml1/DTD/xhtml1-transitional.dtd">
<html xmlns="http://www.w3.org/1999/xhtml" xml:lang="en" lang="en">
    <head>
        <title>
            Creating An XML Data Island
        </title>

        <xml id="schoolXML" src="school.xml"></xml>
    </head>

    <body>
        <center>
            <h1>
                Creating An XML Data Island
            </h1>
        </center>
    </body>
</html>
```

Here's the file school.xml:

```xml
<?xml version="1.0"?>
<SCHOOL>
    <CLASS type="seminar">
        <CLASS_TITLE>XML In Theory And Practice</CLASS_TITLE>
        <CLASS_NUMBER>10.306</CLASS_NUMBER>
        <SUBJECT>XML</SUBJECT>
        <START_DATE>1/1/2001</START_DATE>
        <STUDENTS>
            <STUDENT status="attending">
                <FIRST_NAME>Mark</FIRST_NAME>
                <LAST_NAME>Swansburg</LAST_NAME>
            </STUDENT>
            <STUDENT status="withdrawn">
                <FIRST_NAME>Thomas</FIRST_NAME>
                <LAST_NAME>Preston</LAST_NAME>
            </STUDENT>
        </STUDENTS>
    </CLASS>
</SCHOOL>
```

In an example from the "In Depth" section of this chapter, I demonstrated how to use the navigation methods to get to the second student's record and display that student's name. You navigate around the XML document by using the **firstChild**, **nextChild**, **previousChild**, and **lastChild** methods, which let you access the child elements of an element, and the **firstSibling**, **nextSibling**, **previousSibling**, and **lastSibling** methods, which let you access elements on the same level. To get the content of an element, I use the **nodeValue** property. Here's the JavaScript that we developed:

```xml
<?xml version="1.0"?>
<!DOCTYPE html PUBLIC "-//W3C//DTD XHTML 1.0 Transitional//EN"
"http://www.w3.org/tr/xhtml1/DTD/xhtml1-transitional.dtd">
<html xmlns="http://www.w3.org/1999/xhtml" xml:lang="en" lang="en">
    <head>
        <title>
            Finding Element Values in an XML Document Using Data Islands
        </title>

        <xml id="schoolXML" src="school.xml"></xml>

        <script type="text/javascript" language="javascript">
            function getStudentData()
            {
                xmldoc= document.all("schoolXML").XMLDocument;
```

```
                    nodeSchool = xmldoc.documentElement;
                    nodeClass = nodeSchool.firstChild;
                    nodeStudents = nodeClass.lastChild;
                    nodeStudent = nodeStudents.lastChild;
                    nodeFirstName = nodeStudent.firstChild;
                    nodeLastName = nodeFirstName.nextSibling;

                    outputMessage = "Name: " +
                        nodeFirstName.firstChild.nodeValue + ' '
                        + nodeLastName.firstChild.nodeValue;
                    message.innerHTML=outputMessage;
                }
            </script>
        </head>

        <body>
            <center>
                <h1>
                    Finding Element Values in an XML Document Using
                    Data Islands
                </h1>

                <div id="message"></div>
                <p>
                <input type="button" value="Get Second Student's Name"
                    onclick="getStudentData()" />
            </center>
        </body>
</html>
```

You can see the results in Figure 15.3.

In this case, I used the **XMLDocument** property to get an object corresponding to the HTML document, and then used the **documentElement** property of that object to get the root element of the document. However, there's a shortcut for this process. You can simply use the **documentElement** property of the data island to get the root element of the XML document:

```
<?xml version="1.0"?>
<!DOCTYPE html PUBLIC "-//W3C//DTD XHTML 1.0 Transitional//EN"
"http://www.w3.org/tr/xhtml1/DTD/xhtml1-transitional.dtd">
<html xmlns="http://www.w3.org/1999/xhtml" xml:lang="en" lang="en">
    <head>
        <title>
            Finding Element Values in an XML Document
        </title>
```

```
        <xml id="schoolXML" src="school.xml"></xml>

        <script type="text/javascript" language="javascript">
            function getStudentData()
            {
                var xmldoc;

                nodeSchool = schoolXML.documentElement;
                nodeClass = nodeSchool.firstChild;
                nodeStudents = nodeClass.lastChild;
                nodeStudent = nodeStudents.lastChild;
                nodeFirstName = nodeStudent.firstChild;
                nodeLastName = nodeFirstName.nextSibling;
                    .
                    .
                    .
</html>
```

Note that these examples extract the values of XML elements from an XML document, but not their attributes. To extract attribute values as well, see the next section.

Getting Attribute Values from XML Elements

"One problem," says the novice programmer. "I know I can use the **nodeValue** property to get the content of XML elements, but what about getting the values of *attributes*?" "No problem," you say; "just use the **attributes** property."

Say that you have an XML document named school.xml, in which the **<STUDENT>** element has one attribute, **STATUS**:

```
<?xml version="1.0"?>
<SCHOOL>
    <CLASS type="seminar">
        <CLASS_TITLE>XML In Theory And Practice</CLASS_TITLE>
        <CLASS_NUMBER>10.306</CLASS_NUMBER>
        <SUBJECT>XML</SUBJECT>
        <START_DATE>1/1/2001</START_DATE>
        <STUDENTS>
            <STUDENT status="attending">
                <FIRST_NAME>Mark</FIRST_NAME>
                <LAST_NAME>Swansburg</LAST_NAME>
            </STUDENT>
```

```
            <STUDENT status="withdrawn">
                <FIRST_NAME>Thomas</FIRST_NAME>
                <LAST_NAME>Preston</LAST_NAME>
            </STUDENT>
        </STUDENTS>
    </CLASS>
</SCHOOL>
```

How can you recover these attribute values? Here's an example showing how it's done. In this case, I'm reading the value of the **status** attribute of the second student's record. I use the **attributes** property to get that record's attributes. Then I use the **getNamedItem** method to get the value of the **status** attribute, like this: **statusStudent = attributes.getNamedItem("status");**. I then use **statusStudent.value** to get the text that the attribute was set to. Here's what the JavaScript looks like:

```
<?xml version="1.0"?>
<!DOCTYPE html PUBLIC "-//W3C//DTD XHTML 1.0 Transitional//EN"
"http://www.w3.org/tr/xhtml1/DTD/xhtml1-transitional.dtd">
<html xmlns="http://www.w3.org/1999/xhtml" xml:lang="en" lang="en">
    <head>
        <title>
            Finding Attribute Values in an XML Document
        </title>

        <xml id="schoolXML" src="school.xml"></xml>

        <script type="text/javascript" language="javascript">
            function getStudentData()
            {
                xmldoc= document.all("schoolXML").XMLDocument;

                nodeSchool = xmldoc.documentElement;
                nodeClass = nodeSchool.firstChild;
                nodeStudents = nodeClass.lastChild;
                nodeStudent = nodeStudents.lastChild;
                nodeFirstName = nodeStudent.firstChild;
                nodeLastName = nodeFirstName.nextSibling;
                attributes = nodeStudent.attributes;
                statusStudent = attributes.getNamedItem("status");
                outputMessage = "Name: " +
                    nodeFirstName.firstChild.nodeValue + ' '
                    + nodeLastName.firstChild.nodeValue + " Status: " +
                    statusStudent.value;
```

```
            message.innerHTML=outputMessage;
        }
    </script>
</head>

<body>
    <center>
        <h1>
            Finding Attribute Values in an XML Document
        </h1>

        <div id="message"></div>
        <p>
        <input type="button" value="Get Second Student's Status"
            onclick="getStudentData()" />
        </p>
    </center>
</body>
</html>
```

And that's all it takes. In Figure 15.4, you see that the status of the second student is "**withdrawn**".

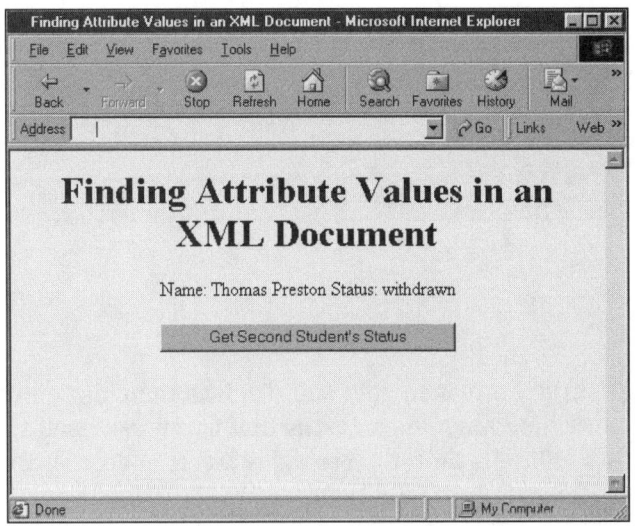

Figure 15.4 Accessing attribute values in an XML document.

Parsing XML Documents in Code

So far in this chapter I've used navigation methods such as **nextSibling** and **nextChild** to navigate through XML documents. However, I knew just what element I was after and wrote the code accordingly. Usually (that is, when you don't know the exact contents of the files the user is asking you to read), you should parse XML documents, working through the entire document and unpacking the data in it.

One way of parsing an XML document is to use the **childNodes** property, which tells you whether an element has any children. In this example, I'll work through the entire XML document, school.xml, displaying all its elements in an XHTML Web page:

```xml
<?xml version="1.0"?>
<SCHOOL>
    <CLASS type="seminar">
        <CLASS_TITLE>XML In Theory And Practice</CLASS_TITLE>
        <CLASS_NUMBER>10.306</CLASS_NUMBER>
        <SUBJECT>XML</SUBJECT>
        <START_DATE>1/1/2001</START_DATE>
        <STUDENTS>
            <STUDENT status="attending">
                <FIRST_NAME>Mark</FIRST_NAME>
                <LAST_NAME>Swansburg</LAST_NAME>
            </STUDENT>
            <STUDENT status="withdrawn">
                <FIRST_NAME>Thomas</FIRST_NAME>
                <LAST_NAME>Preston</LAST_NAME>
            </STUDENT>
        </STUDENTS>
    </CLASS>
</SCHOOL>
```

I'll create a function, **getChildren**, which gets and displays the children of an element. (This is a *recursive* function, which means that it can call itself to get the children of an element's children, and so on to many levels in depth). To display the current element's name, I use the **nodeName** property. To start parsing the whole page then, I just have to call **getChildren** on the root node of the whole document. I do that in a function named **parseXML**, which I connect to a button in this Web page:

```
<?xml version="1.0"?>
<!DOCTYPE html PUBLIC "-//W3C//DTD XHTML 1.0 Transitional//EN"
```

```
                        "http://www.w3.org/tr/xhtml1/DTD/xhtml1-transitional.dtd">
                    <html xmlns="http://www.w3.org/1999/xhtml" xml:lang="en" lang="en">
                        <head>
                            <title>
                                Parsing an XML Document with Recursion
                            </title>

                            <xml id="schoolXML" src="school.xml"></xml>

                            <script type="text/javascript" language="javascript"
                                src="script.js">
                            </script>
                        </head>

                        <body>
                            <center>
                                <h1>
                                    Parsing an XML Document
                                </h1>
                            </center>

                            <div id="divResults"></div>

                            <center>
                                <input type="button" value="Parse the XML Document"
                                    onclick="parseXML()" />
                            </center>
                        </body>
                    </html>
```

Here's the script used by this page, script.js:

```
function parseXML()
{
    documentXML = document.all("schoolXML").XMLDocument;
    divResults.innerHTML = getChildren(documentXML, "");
}

function getChildren(nodeXML, indent)
{
    var text = indent + nodeXML.nodeName + "<br />";

    if (nodeXML.childNodes.length > 0) {
        for (var loopIndex = 0; loopIndex <
            nodeXML.childNodes.length; loopIndex++) {
```

```
            text += getChildren(nodeXML.childNodes(loopIndex),
            indent + "    ");
        }
    }
    return text;
}
```

When you click the button in this page, it will read school.xml and display its structure, as you see in Figure 15.5. In this way, you can loop over every element in an XML document. There's one detail to note—Internet Explorer considers more than just elements in the document to be nodes; processing instructions, the text content of elements, the root element, and more are all nodes (see the next section for more information). Usually, you'll just look for specific elements and want to read their data content—the next section discusses how to do this.

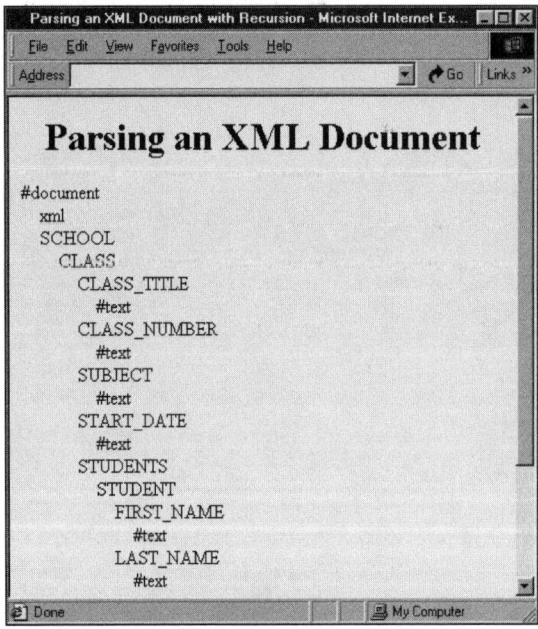

Figure 15.5 Parsing an XML document.

Parsing XML to Get Element Content

In the previous section, we saw how to parse an entire XML document, school.xml, by "walking" through it recursively. However, that example just listed the structure of the XML document. Here, I'll elaborate on that code by also displaying each node's type and content. I do that by checking the **nodeType** property to get the node's type and checking the **nodeValue** property to get the node's value. In this example, note the different types of items that Internet Explorer considers to be nodes in XML documents: processing instructions, the text content of an element, comments, and even the document (root) element itself. Here's the new code:

```
<?xml version="1.0"?>
<!DOCTYPE html PUBLIC "-//W3C//DTD XHTML 1.0 Transitional//EN"
"http://www.w3.org/tr/xhtml1/DTD/xhtml1-transitional.dtd">
<html xmlns="http://www.w3.org/1999/xhtml" xml:lang="en" lang="en">
    <head>
        <title>
            Parsing an XML Document To Get Element Content
        </title>

        <xml id="schoolXML" src="school.xml"></xml>

        <script type="text/javascript" language="javascript"
            src="script.js">
        </script>
    </head>

    <body>
        <center>
            <h1>
                Parsing an XML Document To Get Element Content
            </h1>
        </center>

        <div id="divResults"></div>

        <center>
            <input type="button" value="Parse the XML Document"
                onclick="parseXML()" />
        </center>
    </body>
</html>
```

Here's the script, script.js, used by this page:

```
function parseXML()
{
    documentXML = document.all("schoolXML").XMLDocument;
    divResults.innerHTML = getChildren(documentXML, "");
}
```

```
function getChildren(nodeXML, indent)
{
    var typeXML;

    switch (nodeXML.nodeType) {
        case 1:
            typeXML = "element";
            break;
        case 2:
            typeXML = "attribute";
            break;
        case 3:
            typeXML = "text";
            break;
        case 4:
            typeXML = "CDATA section";
            break;
        case 5:
            typeXML = "entity reference";
            break;
        case 6:
            typeXML = "entity";
            break;
        case 7:
            typeXML = "processing instruction";
            break;
        case 8:
            typeXML = "comment";
            break;
        case 9:
            typeXML = "document";
            break;
        case 10:
            typeXML = "document type";
            break;
        case 11:
            typeXML = "document fragment";
            break;
        case 12:
            typeXML = "notation";
    }

    var text = indent + nodeXML.nodeName
        + (nodeXML.nodeValue ?
```

```
            "  = " + nodeXML.nodeValue
        + "  (Type: " + typeXML
        + ")<br />" :
            "  (Type: " + typeXML
        + ")<br />");

    if (nodeXML.childNodes.length > 0) {
        for (var loopIndex = 0; loopIndex <
            nodeXML.childNodes.length; loopIndex++) {
            text += getChildren(nodeXML.childNodes(loopIndex),
            indent + "    ");
        }
    }
    return text;
}
```

You can see the results of this HTML and XML in Figure 15.6. The code displays not only the type of each node but also the content if the node is a text node.

Some of the elements in school.xml have attributes—so how can we list them, too? See the next section.

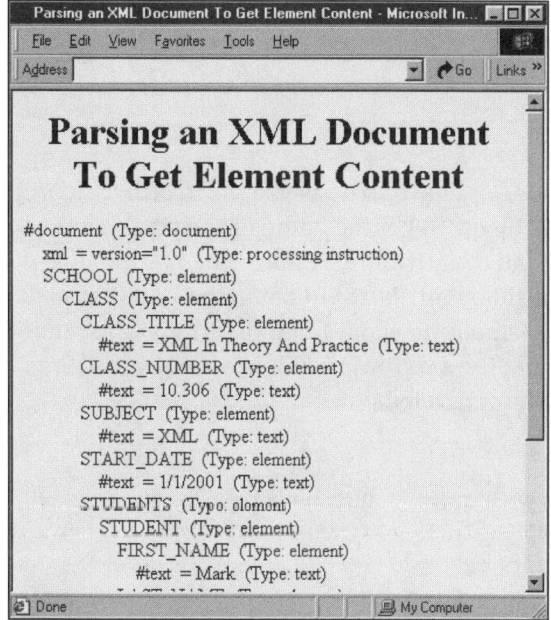

Figure 15.6 Parsing an XML document to get element content.

Parsing XML to Get Attribute Values

In the previous two sections, we developed JavaScript code to display the full structure of an XML document, school.xml, and to display its node types and data. But so far we haven't displayed any attribute values, even though some of the elements in school.xml have attributes:

```
<?xml version="1.0"?>
<SCHOOL>
    <CLASS type="seminar">
        <CLASS_TITLE>XML In Theory And Practice</CLASS_TITLE>
        <CLASS_NUMBER>10.306</CLASS_NUMBER>
        <SUBJECT>XML</SUBJECT>
        <START_DATE>1/1/2001</START_DATE>
        <STUDENTS>
            <STUDENT status="attending">
                <FIRST_NAME>Mark</FIRST_NAME>
                <LAST_NAME>Swansburg</LAST_NAME>
            </STUDENT>
            <STUDENT status="withdrawn">
                <FIRST_NAME>Thomas</FIRST_NAME>
                <LAST_NAME>Preston</LAST_NAME>
            </STUDENT>
        </STUDENTS>
    </CLASS>
</SCHOOL>
```

To access the attributes of a node, all I have to do is use the **attributes** property to get access to the **attributes** object. To get the name of the attribute, I can use the **nodeName** property, and to get the attribute's value, I can use the **nodeValue** property. (Internet Explorer considers attributes to be nodes.) All that's left is to loop over all the attributes an element has, and I can determine the number of attributes to loop over by checking the **attributes** object's **length** property. Here is how I list all the attributes of an XML element:

```
<?xml version="1.0"?>
<!DOCTYPE html PUBLIC "-//W3C//DTD XHTML 1.0 Transitional//EN"
"http://www.w3.org/tr/xhtml1/DTD/xhtml1-transitional.dtd">
<html xmlns="http://www.w3.org/1999/xhtml" xml:lang="en" lang="en">
    <head>
        <title>
            Parsing an XML Document To Get Element And Attribute Content
        </title>
```

Immediate Solutions

```
        <xml id="schoolXML" src="school.xml"></xml>

        <script type="text/javascript"
            language="javascript" src="script.js">
        </script>
    </head>

    <body>
        <center>
            <h1>
                Parsing an XML Document To Get Element And Attribute Content
            </h1>
        </center>

        <div id="divResults"></div>

        <center>
            <input type="button" value="Parse the XML Document"
                onclick="parseXML()" />
        </center>
    </body>
</html>
```

Here's the script, script.js, used by this page:

```
function parseXML()
{
    documentXML = document.all("schoolXML").XMLDocument;
    divResults.innerHTML = getChildren(documentXML, "");
}

function getChildren(nodeXML, indent)
{
    var typeXML;

    switch (nodeXML.nodeType) {
        case 1:
            typeXML = "element";
            break;
        case 2:
            typeXML = "attribute";
            break;
        case 3:
            typeXML = "text";
            break;
```

```
            case 4:
                typeXML = "CDATA section";
                break;
            case 5:
                typeXML = "entity reference";
                break;
            case 6:
                typeXML = "entity";
                break;
            case 7:
                typeXML = "processing instruction";
                break;
            case 8:
                typeXML = "comment";
                break;
            case 9:
                typeXML = "document";
                break;
            case 10:
                typeXML = "document type";
                break;
            case 11:
                typeXML = "document fragment";
                break;
            case 12:
                typeXML = "notation";
        }

        var text = indent + nodeXML.nodeName
            + (nodeXML.nodeValue ?
            "  = " + nodeXML.nodeValue
            + "  (Type: " + typeXML
            + ")" :
            "  (Type: " + typeXML
            + ")");

        if (nodeXML.attributes != null) {
            if (nodeXML.attributes.length > 0) {
                for (var loopIndex = 0; loopIndex <
                    nodeXML.attributes.length; loopIndex++) {
                    text += " (Attribute: " +
                        nodeXML.attributes(loopIndex).nodeName +
                        " = " +
                        nodeXML.attributes(loopIndex).nodeValue
                        + ")";
```

```
                    }
                }
            }

        text += "<br />";

        if (nodeXML.childNodes.length > 0) {
            for (var loopIndex = 0; loopIndex <
                nodeXML.childNodes.length; loopIndex++) {
                text += getChildren(nodeXML.childNodes(loopIndex),
                    indent + "    ");
            }
        }
        return text;
}
```

The result of this HTML and XML appears in Figure 15.7, where you can see the names and values of attributes as well as the names and values of the XML elements.

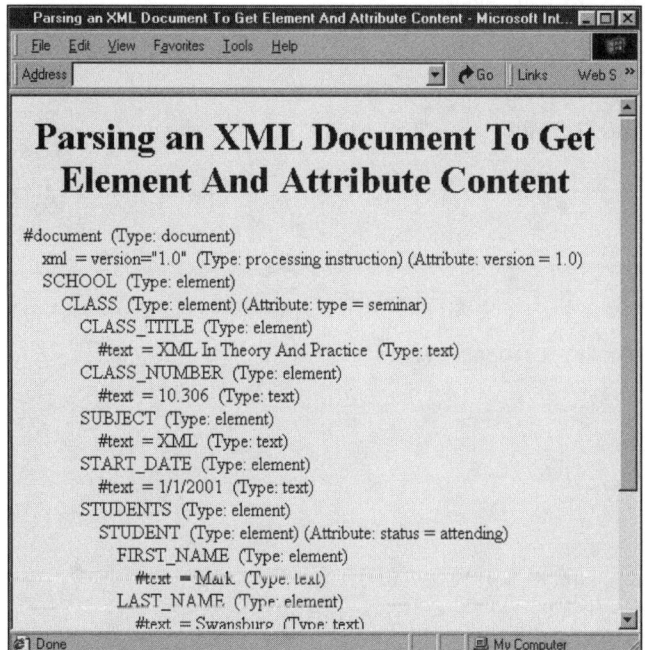

Figure 15.7   Parsing an XML document to get element and attribute content.

Handling Events while Loading XML Documents

"One more question," the novice programmer says. "My XML document is coming in from the Internet and it takes half an hour to load. How can I make sure the document is fully loaded before I use it?" "No idea," you say. The NP says, "Huh?" "Just kidding," you smile and say. "You can use the **ondataavailable** event."

You can use the **onreadystatechange** and **ondataavailable** events to monitor the progress of loading XML documents. You can also check the **readyState** property in the **onreadystatechange** event to determine the status of the document. Here's an example that monitors and displays the progress of loading an XML document:

```
<?xml version="1.0"?>
<!DOCTYPE html PUBLIC "-//W3C//DTD XHTML 1.0 Transitional//EN"
"http://www.w3.org/tr/xhtml1/DTD/xhtml1-transitional.dtd">
<html xmlns="http://www.w3.org/1999/xhtml" xml:lang="en" lang="en">
    <head>
        <title>
            Handling XML Loading Events
        </title>

        <script type="text/javascript"
            language="javascript" src="script.js">
        </script>
    </head>

    <body>
        <center>
            <h1>
                Handling XML Loading Events
            </h1>
        </center>

        <div id="div1"></div>

        <center>
            <input type="button" value="Load the XML file"
                onclick="loadFile()" />
        </center>
    </body>
</html>
```

Here's the script, script.js, used by this page:

```
    var xmldoc;

    function loadFile()
    {
        xmldoc = new ActiveXObject("microsoft.XMLDOM");

        xmldoc.onreadystatechange = dataChange;
        xmldoc.ondataavailable = dataAvailable;

        xmldoc.load('school.xml');
    }

    function dataChange()
    {
        switch (xmldoc.readyState)
        {
            case 1:
                div1.innerHTML += "Data is uninitialized.<br />";
                break;
            case 2:
                div1.innerHTML += "Data is loading.<br />";
                break;
            case 3:
                div1.innerHTML += "Data has been loaded.<br />";
                break;
            case 4:
                div1.innerHTML += "Data loading is complete.<br />";
                if (xmldoc.parseError.errorCode != 0) {
                    div1.innerHTML += "An error occurred.<br />";
                }
                else {
                    div1.innerHTML += "File loaded OK.<br />";
                }
                break;
        }
    }

    function dataAvailable()
    {
        div1.innerHTML += 'Data is available.<br />';
    }
```

You can see the results of this HTML and XML in Figure 15.8, which reports each step of the loading process.

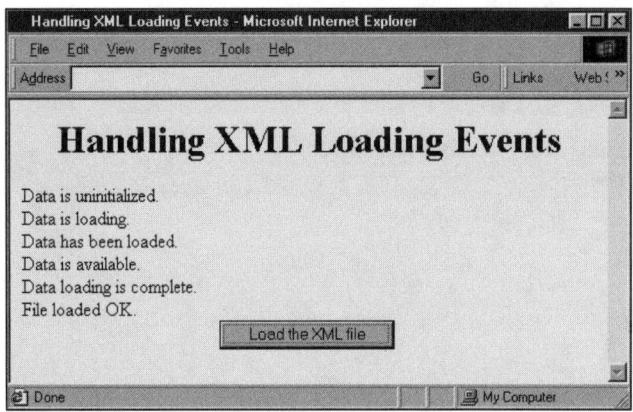

Figure 15.8   Handling XML loading events.

Extending XHTML by Adding New Attributes

It turns out to be easy to add new attributes to XHTML elements, because you can use an **<!ATTLIST>** element anywhere to add attributes to existing ones. Here's an example; in this case, I'm creating a new DTD, extend.dtd, to add a date attribute to the **<p>** element; note that after using the **<!ATTLIST>** element, I include the entire XHTML 1.0 Transitional DTD with a parameter entity as we did in the beginning of the chapter:

```
<!ATTLIST p
    date    CDATA    #IMPLIED
>

<!ENTITY % xhtml10T.dtd PUBLIC "-//W3C//DTD XHTML 1.0 Transitional//EN"
    "http://www.w3.org/TR/xhtml1/DTD/xhtml1-transitional.dtd">
%xhtml10T.dtd;
```

Now when you use this new DTD, you can use the **date** attribute in the **<p>** element:

```
<!DOCTYPE html PUBLIC "-//Extender//DTD XHTML-Extensions 1.0//EN" "http://
www.starpowder.com/steve/extend.dtd" >
<html xmlns="http://www.w3.org/1999/xhtml" xmlns:doc="http://
www.starpowder.com/steve/extend.dtd">
    <head>
        <title>
            Extending XHTML
        </title>
```

```
            <link rel="stylesheet" href="extend.css" />
        </head>

        <body>
            <p date="10-15-2001">
                Here is some text.
            </p>
        </body>
</html>
```

Extending XHTML 1.0 by Adding New Elements

"Say," says the novice programmer, "I want to create a new XHTML element and have Web browsers know what I mean. What are the chances?" You say, "You'll do better when true XHTML browsers appear. But you can come close right now."

As we saw in the beginning of this chapter, you can extend XHTML just as you can XML. In our example, I'm creating a new element named **<doc:foot>** in a new DTD named extend.dtd. Note that I'm also indicating that this new element is a child element of the **<html>** element, and including the entire XHTML 1.0 Transitional DTD with a parameter entity, as discussed in the "In Depth" section of this chapter:

```
<!ELEMENT doc:foot (#PCDATA) >
<!ATTLIST doc:foot
     footattribute    CDATA    #IMPLIED
>

<!ELEMENT html (head, body, doc:foot)>

<!ENTITY % xhtml10T.dtd PUBLIC "-//W3C//DTD XHTML 1.0 Transitional//EN"
     "http://www.w3.org/TR/xhtml1/DTD/xhtml1-transitional.dtd">
%xhtml10T.dtd;
```

Here's an XHTML page, extend.html, that uses this new element; note that I'm creating a formal public identifier (FPI) for the new DTD ("-//Extender//DTD XHTML-Extensions 1.0//EN"), setting the default namespace to the XHTML namespace, and also defining the **doc** namespace for the **<doc:foot>** element:

```
<!DOCTYPE html PUBLIC "-//Extender//DTD XHTML-Extensions 1.0//EN"
"http://www.starpowder.com/steve/extend.dtd" >
<html xmlns="http://www.w3.org/1999/xhtml" xmlns:doc="http://
www.starpowder.com/steve/extend.dtd">
```

```
            <head>
                <title>
                    Extending XHTML
                </title>

                <link rel="stylesheet" href="extend.css" />
            </head>

            <body>
                <p>
                    Here is some text.
                </p>
            </body>

            <doc:foot>
                    This is the page's foot.
            </doc:foot>
</html>
```

Here are specific rules for creating FPIs:

- In an FPI, fields must be separated by a double slash (//).

- The first field in an FPI indicates the relationship of your DTD to a formal standard. For DTDs you're defining yourself, this field must be "-". For formal standards, this field is a reference to the standard itself (such as **ISO/IEC 13449:2000**).

- The second field must hold the name of the group or person that will maintain the DTD. Here, you should use a name that is unique and that identifies your group easily (for example, W3C simply uses **W3C**).

- The third field must be **ELEMENTS XHTML-** followed by a unique identifier of some kind (such as **Custom Version 1.0**). This part should include a version number that you'll update.

- The fourth field specifies the language your DTD uses (for example, for English you use **EN**).

So far, I've only extended XHTML 1.0, but you can do the same for XHTML 1.1. However, doing so means that you have to understand how to modify the content models for elements in XHTML 1.1—which means you have to understand how to work with XHTML 1.1 modules. Take a look at the next section for the details.

Understanding XHTML 1.1 Modules

XHTML 1.1 is the module-based version of XHTML. Now that we've gained experience with XML, we can understand what this means. In particular, the XHTML 1.1 DTD consists of a master driver DTD that includes the parts of XHTML 1.1 as modules. What's a module? A module has two parts—an abstract part that specifies what the module does, and the module's code itself, which is just a DTD fragment that contains element types, a set of attribute list declarations, and a set of content model declarations.

You can find the XHTML 1.1 driver DTD at **http://www.w3.org/TR/xhtml11/xhtml11_dtd.html#a_xhtml11_driver**, and you can find the implementation of the XHTML 1.1 modules at **http://www.w3.org/TR/xhtml-modularization/dtd_module_defs.html#a_xhtml11_modules**. (There are modules for forms, text, images, and so on.) You'll find the XHTML 1.1 modules listed in Table 15.1.

As I mentioned, modules have two parts, and I'll take a look at them both here.

Table 15.1 The XHTML 1.1 modules.

Module	Contents
xhtml-applet.module	Java applet element module
xhtml-base.module	Base element module
xhtml-bdo.module	BIDI-override module
xhtml-csismap.module	Client-side image-map module
xhtml-edit.module	Edit module
xhtml-events.module	Events module
xhtml-form.module	Forms module
xhtml-framework.module	Modular framework module
xhtml-hypertext.module	Hypertext module
xhtml-image.module	Image module
xhtml-link.module	Link element module
xhtml-list.module	Lists module
xhtml-meta.module	Document meta-information module
xhtml-param.module	<Param> element module
xhtml-postfw-redecl.module	Post-framework redeclaration module
xhtml-prefw-redecl.module	Pre-framework redeclaration module
xhtml-pres.module	Presentation module
xhtml-ruby.module	Ruby module

(continued)

Table 15.1 The XHTML 1.1 modules *(continued)*.

Module	Contents
xhtml-script.module	Scripting module
xhtml-ssismap.module	Server-side image-map module
xhtml-struct.module	Document structure module
xhtml-style.module	Style sheets module
xhtml-table.module	Tables module
xhtml-text.module	Basic text module

Table 15.2 The img abstract module.

Elements	Attributes	Minimal Content Model
<img>	**common**, **alt**, **height**, **longdesc**, **src**, **width**	EMPTY

Abstract Modules

Each XHTML 1.1 module has an abstract definition that specifies what's available in the module. This abstract part is just for people to read so they can know what's going on in the module. As an example, the abstract module for the **<img>** element appears in Table 15.2.

The Common attributes referred to in Table 15.2 are: **class**, **id**, **title**, **dir**, **xml:lang**, **onclick**, **ondblclick**, **onmousedown**, **onmouseup**, **onmouseover**, **onmousemove**, **onmouseout**, **onkeypress**, **onkeydown**, **onkeyup**, and **style**. You can find the abstract versions of the modules in XHTML 1.1 at **http://www.w3.org/TR/xhtml-modularization/xhtml_modules.html#s_xhtmlmodules**.

Module Implementations

So what's in an actual module? A module is a DTD fragment that can hold element types, attribute list declarations, and content model declarations. (A content model declaration is the part of the DTD that indicates what content, such as other elements, an element can hold.) In other words, a module is really just part of a DTD.

As an example, here's the XHTML 1.1 images module, xhtml11-image-1.mod, which you'll find at **www.w3.org/TR/xhtml-modularization/xhtml_modules.html#s_imagemodule**:

```
<!--
.............................................................
-->
<!-- XHTML 1.1 Images Module
```

Immediate Solutions

```
..........................................  -->
<!-- file: xhtml11-image-1.mod

     This is XHTML 1.1, a modular variant of XHTML 1.0.
     Copyright 1998-2000 W3C (MIT, INRIA, Keio), All Rights Reserved.
     Revision: $Id: dtd_module_defs.html,v 1.2 2000/01/05 20:58:33
shane Exp $ SMI

     This DTD module is identified by the PUBLIC and SYSTEM
identifiers:

     PUBLIC "-//W3C//ELEMENTS XHTML 1.1 Images 1.0//EN"
     SYSTEM "xhtml11-image-1.mod"

     Revisions:
     (none)
     ..........................................
-->

<!-- Images

        img

     This module provides markup to support basic image embedding.
-->

<!-- To avoid problems with text-only UAs as well as to make
     image content understandable and navigable to users of
     non-visual UAs, you need to provide a description with
     the 'alt' attribute, and avoid server-side image maps.
-->

<!ENTITY % Img.element    "INCLUDE" >
<![%Img.element;[
<!ENTITY % Img.content    "EMPTY" >
<!ELEMENT img  %Img.content; >
<!-- end of Img.element -->]]>

<!ENTITY % Img.attlist    "INCLUDE" >
<![%Img.attlist;[
<!ATTLIST img
     %Common.attrib;
     src          %URI.datatype;         #REQUIRED
     alt          %Text.datatype;        #REQUIRED
     longdesc     %URI.datatype;         #IMPLIED
```

```
            height          %Length.datatype;          #IMPLIED
            width           %Length.datatype;          #IMPLIED
>
<!-- end of Img.attlist -->]]>

<!-- end of xhtml11-image-1.mod -->
```

> **NOTE:** The name and trademarks of copyright holders may NOT be used in advertising or publicity pertaining to this document or its contents without specific, written prior permission. Title to copyright in this document will at all times remain with copyright holders.

Here's how that module is included into the XHTML 1.1 driver DTD:

```
<!-- Image Module ............................................. -->
<!ENTITY % xhtml-image.module "INCLUDE" >
<![%xhtml-image.module;[
<!ENTITY % xhtml-image.mod
     PUBLIC "-//W3C//ELEMENTS XHTML 1.1 Images 1.0//EN" "xhtml11-image-1.mod" >
%xhtml-image.mod;]]>
```

Note the parameter entity **xhtml-image.module**, which is set to **INCLUDE** by default. Using parameters like this, you can customize XHTML 1.1 by setting a parameter to **IGNORE** to exclude a module. Customization of XHTML 1.1 is driven by parameters like this (this is why W3C says the XHTML 1.1 DTD is "fully parameterized"). This means that you usually don't have to edit the XHTML 1.1 driver DTD to customize XHTML 1.1. See the section "Customizing XHTML 1.1 by Removing Modules" later in this chapter.

Note also the parameter name **xhtml-image.mod** as used in the XHTML 1.1 driver DTD. Parameter entities in the XHTML 1.1 driver DTD use specific suffixes to mean various things. Here are the suffixes you'll see in that DTD:

- **.mod**—Parameter entities with this suffix are used to represent a DTD module.

- **.module**—Parameter entities with this suffix are used to control the inclusion of a DTD module, and you can set them to **INCLUDE** (the default) or **IGNORE**.

- **.content**—Parameter entities with this suffix are used to specify the content model of an element. You specify what elements go inside what other elements with the content model (like this for the **<object>** element: **<!ENTITY % Object.content "(% Flow.mix | param | myelement)*">**).

- **.class**—Parameter entities with this suffix are used to specify elements of the same class.

Document Notice for xhtml11-image-1.mod

Copyright © 1994-2000 World Wide Web Consortium, (Massachusetts Institute of Technology, Institut National de Recherche en Informatique et en Automatique, Keio University). All Rights Reserved.

http://www.w3.org/Consortium/Legal/

Public documents on the W3C site are provided by the copyright holders under the following license. The software or Document Type Definitions (DTDs) associated with W3C specifications are governed by the Software Notice. By using and/or copying this document, or the W3C document from which this statement is linked, you (the licensee) agree that you have read, understood, and will comply with the following terms and conditions:

Permission to use, copy, and distribute the contents of this document, or the W3C document from which this statement is linked, in any medium for any purpose and without fee or royalty is hereby granted, provided that you include the following on ALL copies of the document, or portions thereof, that you use:

A link or URL to the original W3C document.

The pre-existing copyright notice of the original author, or if it doesn't exist, a notice of the form: "Copyright © 2000 World Wide Web Consortium, (Massachusetts Institute of Technology, Institut National de Recherche en Informatique et en Automatique, Keio University). All Rights Reserved. **http://www.w3.org/Consortium/Legal/**" (Hypertext is preferred, but a textual representation is permitted.)

If it exists, the STATUS of the W3C document.

When space permits, inclusion of the full text of this NOTICE should be provided. We request that authorship attribution be provided in any software, documents, or other items or products that you create pursuant to the implementation of the contents of this document, or any portion thereof.

No right to create modifications or derivatives of W3C documents is granted pursuant to this license. However, if additional requirements (documented in the Copyright FAQ) are satisfied, the right to create modifications or derivatives is sometimes granted by the W3C to individuals complying with those requirements.

THIS DOCUMENT IS PROVIDED "AS IS," AND COPYRIGHT HOLDERS MAKE NO REPRESENTATIONS OR WARRANTIES, EXPRESS OR IMPLIED, INCLUDING, BUT NOT LIMITED TO, WARRANTIES OF MERCHANTABILITY, FITNESS FOR A PARTICULAR PURPOSE, NON-INFRINGEMENT, OR TITLE; THAT THE CONTENTS OF THE DOCUMENT ARE SUITABLE FOR ANY PURPOSE; NOR THAT THE IMPLEMENTATION OF SUCH CONTENTS WILL NOT INFRINGE ANY THIRD PARTY PATENTS, COPYRIGHTS, TRADEMARKS OR OTHER RIGHTS.

COPYRIGHT HOLDERS WILL NOT BE LIABLE FOR ANY DIRECT, INDIRECT, SPECIAL OR CONSEQUENTIAL DAMAGES ARISING OUT OF ANY USE OF THE DOCUMENT OR THE PERFORMANCE OR IMPLEMENTATION OF THE CONTENTS THEREOF.

- **.mix**—Parameter entities with this suffix are used to specify a collection of elements from different classes.
- **.attrib**—Parameter entities with this suffix are used to specify a group of tokens that indicate one or more attribute specifications in an **ATTLIST** declaration.

Extending XHTML 1.1 by Adding New Elements

Extending XHTML 1.1 works much like extending XHTML 1.0, except that you have to indicate how the new element fits in with the rest of the XHTML 1.1 elements, which means understanding how the XHTML 1.1 modules work. For example, here's how the content of the **<html>** element is defined in XHTML 1.1:

```
<!ENTITY % Html.content "( head, body )" >
```

That means I can modify the extend.dtd DTD I developed in the beginning of this chapter to work with XHTML 1.1 by modifying the **<html>** element's content model to add **<doc:foot>** and including the entire XHTML 1.1 DTD this way:

```
<!ELEMENT doc:foot (#PCDATA) >
<!ATTLIST doc:foot
    footattribute    CDATA    #IMPLIED
>

<!ENTITY % Html.content "( head, body, doc:foot )" >

<!ENTITY % xhtml11.dtd PUBLIC "-//W3C//DTD XHTML 1.1//EN"
"http://www.w3.org/TR/xhtml11/DTD/xhtml11.dtd"> %xhtml11.dtd;
```

Now I can use this new DTD as we've used the XHTML 1.0 version of extend.dtd:

```
<!DOCTYPE html PUBLIC "-//Extender//DTD XHTML-Extensions
1.0//EN" "http://www.starpowder.com/steve/extend.dtd" >
<html xmlns="http://www.w3.org/1999/xhtml"
xmlns:doc="http://www.starpowder.com/steve/extend.dtd">
    <head>
        <title>
            Extending XHTML
        </title>

        <link rel="stylesheet" href="extend.css" />
    </head>
```

```
    <body>
        <p>
            Here is some text.
        </p>
    </body>

    <doc:foot>
            This is the page's foot.
    </doc:foot>
</html>
```

Customizing XHTML 1.1 by Removing Modules

"Hey," says the big boss, "our new hand-held device doesn't support all of XHTML 1.1. What can we do?" "I can customize XHTML 1.1 for the new device by removing some modules," you say; "what support don't we have?" "Well," says the BB, "images, hyperlinks, sounds, fonts, multimedia, colors—" "Hm," you say.

Each XHTML 1.1 module is included in the XHTML 1.1 driver DTD with a parameter entity corresponding to the module's name. For the module that handles forms, **xhtml-form.module**, the parameter entity looks like this:

```
<!ENTITY % xhtml-form.module "INCLUDE" >
<![%xhtml-form.module;[ <!ENTITY % xhtml-form.mod PUBLIC "-//W3C//ELEMENTS
XHTML 1.1 Forms 1.0//EN" "xhtml11-form-1.mod" > %xhtml-form.mod;]]>
```

By default, most of these parameter entities are set to **INCLUDE**, but by setting them to **IGNORE**, you can omit those modules. For example, say you have a device that doesn't handle forms or hypertext; you can create a new custom XHTML 1.1. DTD that omits those modules. (You'll find the XHTML 1.1 modules listed in Table 15.1.) Here's the code:

```
<!ENTITY % XHTML1.ns "http://www.starpowder.com/DTDs/extend.dtd" >

<!ENTITY % XHTML1-form.module "IGNORE" >
<!ENTITY % XHIML1-xhtml-hypertext.module "IGNORE" >

<!ENTITY % XHTML11new.dtd PUBLIC "-//W3C//DTD XHTML 1.1//EN"
     "http://www.w3.org/TR/xhtml11/DTD/xhtml11.dtd">
%XHTML11new.dtd;
```

TIP: *Some modules are required and may not be omitted. These are the basic text, hypertext, lists, and document structure modules.*

Using XHTML with Other Namespaces

You can use XHTML in XML documents if you're careful to avoid conflicts between elements, and one way to ensure that is to use different namespaces. Here's an example showing how to use an XML language, MathML (defined at **http://www.w3.org/Math/**), inside an XHTML document:

```
<html xmlns="http://www.w3.org/1999/xhtml" xml:lang="en" lang="en">
    <head>
        <title>
            Using MathML inside XHTML
        </title>
    </head>

    <body>
        <math xmlns="http://www.w3.org/1998/Math/MathML">
            <apply>
                <plus/>
                <apply>
                    <power/>
                    <ci>y</ci>
                    <cn>6</cn>
                </apply>
            </apply>
        </math>
    </body>
</html>
```

You can also go the other way and embed XHTML in another XML document:

```
<?xml version="1.0">
<class xmlns = "http://www.starpowder.com/class"
    xml:lang="en" lang="en">
    <title>
        Introductory XHTML
    </title>
    <schedule>
        1:00 MWF
    </schedule>
    <p xmlns = "http://www.w3.org/1999/xhtml">
        <b>CAUTION</b> You must be on time!
    </p>
</class>
```

As you might recall from Chapter 13, you can also assign a token to a namespace, and use that token as a prefix for elements from then on. Following is an example showing how to draw ovals, rectangles, and polylines with Vector Markup Language (VML). In this case, I'm adding a namespace named v for VML to the default namespace created for XHTML:

```
<?xml version="1.0"?>
<!DOCTYPE html PUBLIC "-//W3C//DTD XHTML 1.0 Transitional//EN"
"http://www.w3.org/tr/xhtml1/DTD/xhtml1-transitional.dtd">
<html xmlns="http://www.w3.org/1999/xhtml"
    xmlns:v="urn:schemas-microsoft-com:vml"
    xml:lang="en" lang="en">
    <head>
        <title>
            Using Vector Markup Language
        </title>

        <style type="text/css">
        v\:* {behavior: url(#default#VML);}
        </style>
    </head>

    <body>
        <center>
            <h1>
                Using Vector Markup Language
            </h1>
        </center>
        <p>
        <v:oval style='width:100pt; height:75pt' fillcolor="yellow" />
        </p>
        <p>
        <v:rect style='width:100pt; height:75pt' fillcolor="blue"
            strokecolor="red" strokeweight="2pt" />
        </p>
        <p>
        <v:polyline points="20pt,55pt,100pt,-10pt,180pt,65pt,260pt,25pt"
            strokecolor="red" strokeweight="2pt" />
        </p>
    </body>
</html>
```

You can see the result of this XHTML in Chapter 13, in Figure 13.17.

Chapter 16

Essential Java

If you need an immediate solution to:	See page:
Getting and Installing the Java SDK	982
Writing Code: Creating Code Files	983
Writing Code: Creating an Application	983
Compiling Code	986
Running Code	987
Basic Skills: Commenting Your Code	988
Basic Skills: Importing Java Packages and Classes	990
Creating Variables	993
Creating Arrays	995
Creating Strings	998
Using Operators	999
Using Conditional Statements: **if**, **if...else**, **switch**	1001
Using Loops: **for**, **while**, **do...while**	1002
Declaring and Creating Objects	1004

In Depth

Even if you haven't programmed in Java, you've probably heard about it—it's a programming language that lets you create applets, which you can display in Web pages. *Applets* are small programs that take over a section of a Web page to display text, images, and controls, and applets work much like any other program on your computer. For example, you can see a Java applet at work in Figure 16.1. I wrote this applet a few years ago. It's a word-unscrambling game in which users try to unscramble the mixed-up word that the applet displays. Users can click one of the checkboxes at the top of the page to make the applet display the unscrambled word, as you see in the figure. Users can also click the rotating animated box on the right to get a new mixed-up word to work on.

TIP: *If you noticed that all the aspects of this applet can be handled by dynamic XHTML today, you'd be right. However, Java runs in nearly all browsers, and dynamic XHTML differs radically between browsers, so many developers prefer Java.*

In this chapter, I'm going to work through the mechanics of creating Java programs, including installation issues, writing Java code, making sure that your Java program can find what it needs, and displaying simple output. You can use these skills when we start writing applets in Chapter 16, in which we'll learn how to

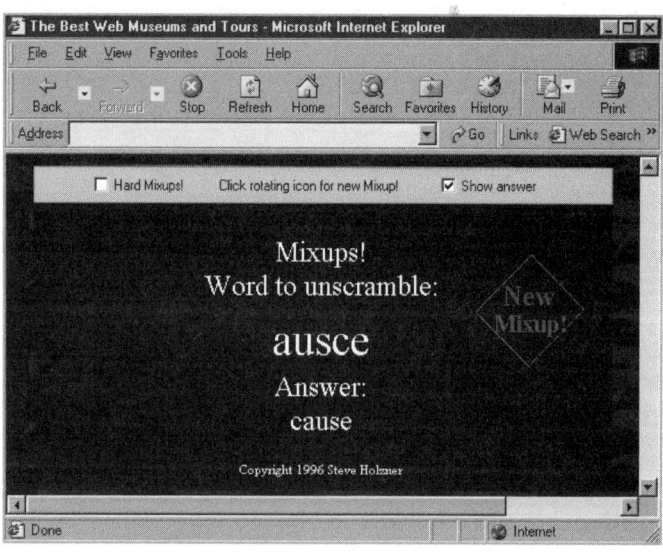

Figure 16.1   An applet at work.

handle controls like buttons and checkboxes in applets, and work with images, text, and more. In fact, we already have a substantial amount of JavaScript under our belts, so we've got a leg up on Java—JavaScript and Java are not the same, but they're both modeled on C++.

Java is a product of Sun Microsystems. The following list of Web sites contains some Java resources that you can use online, most of them at Sun:

- **http://developer.netscape.com/tech/java/**—Netscape Communications' "Java Developer Central"
- **http://java.sun.com**—The main Java site; packed with information
- **http://java.sun.com/docs/**—The Java documentation
- **http://java.sun.com/jdk/**—The current Java Software Development Kit (SDK)
- **http://java.sun.com/jdk/demos/**—The Sun applet demonstrations
- **http://java.sun.com/products/jdk/1.2/**—Version 1.2 (officially called Java 2, version 1.2) of the Java software development kit
- **http://java.sun.com/j2se/1.3/**—Version 1.3, the latest version of the Java software development kit.
- **www.javaworld.com**—Lots of Java resources and discussion

This next list contains some free online tutorials that you can use to develop your Java skills:

- **http://java.sun.com/docs/books/tutorial/index.html**—Sun's Java tutorial
- **http://stars.com/Authoring/Java/Intro/**—Tutorial on developing your first applet
- **www.gamelan.com/javaprogramming/javanotes/**—Gamelan's Java tutorial
- **www.javacoffeebreak.com**—Online Java tutorial
- **www-4.ibm.com/software/developer/education/buildapplet/**—IBM's Java tutorial with some cool features

Note that programming Java is not for everyone, and as you'll see in this chapter and the next chapter, there's a lot to learn (these chapters provide only an introduction to Java). Many people prefer to obtain free applets from the Internet instead of writing them from scratch, so here's a starter list of resources for applets you can use in your Web pages (as with other resources, make sure the applets you use are really free before putting them in your own pages):

- **http://freewarejava.com**—This site had no less than 637 free applets last time I checked.
- **http://java.sun.com/applets/index.html**—Sun's collection of free applets.

- **http://java.wiwi.uni-frankfurt.de/**—"The Java Repository," with lots of applets and code.
- **http://javaboutique.internet.com**—A large selection of applets and a nice site.
- **www.ericharshbarger.org/java/**—"The Applet Depot," which had 45 free applets at last count.
- **www.gamelan.com/downloads/freeware/dir.java1.html**—Applets and other free downloads.
- **www.jars.com/jars_resources_java.html**—A large selection of applets.
- **www.javapowered.com/werks.html**—Also a large selection of applets.

Writing Java Programs

As you know, your browser already runs Java applets—but how do you create them? That's where Java programming comes in. You write applets as Java code and then compile them with the Java Software Development Kit (the Java SDK; before Java 2, the SDK was called the Java Development Kit [JDK], and some people still call it that). To download the Java SDK (it's free), see the "Immediate Solutions" section "Getting and Installing the Java SDK." There's a lot to learn to become proficient with the Java SDK, but the results are worth it.

Java programs come in two main types: applications and applets (I'll use the term *program* to refer to both applets and applications). As we've seen, applets are Java programs that you can download and run in your Web browser, and they're what have made Java so popular.

NOTE: *The major Web browsers have sometimes been slow to implement the most recent versions of Java, so Sun has taken charge and created a Java plug-in for Netscape Navigator and Microsoft Internet Explorer. The plug-in implements all the latest features of Java as a Netscape plug-in and an Internet Explorer ActiveX control. We'll discuss this in Chapter 17.*

You can see another applet at work in Figure 16.2, which shows an applet running in Microsoft Internet Explorer and displaying a greeting (I'll create this applet step-by-step later in this chapter).

The Java SDK also comes with an applet viewer, which you can use to look at applets. In Figure 16.3 you see the same applet as in Figure 16.2, but this time in Sun's Java Applet Viewer.

Besides downloadable applets, Java also supports *applications* that are designed to be run on the local machine. Java applications work like other computer applications—you can install and run them on your computer. Because they are

In Depth

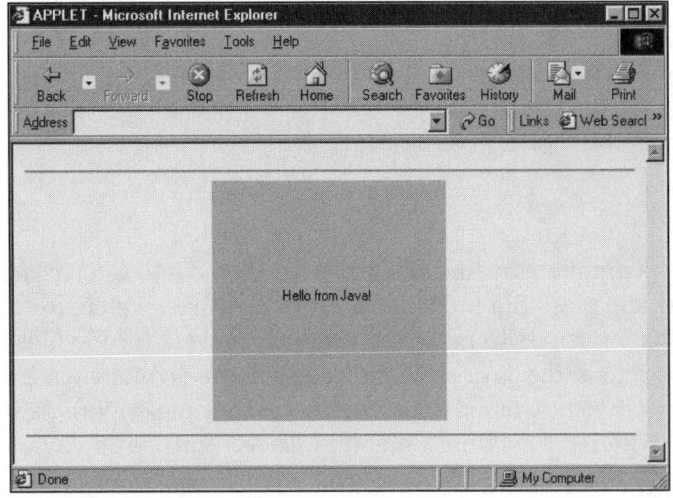

Figure 16.2 Another applet at work.

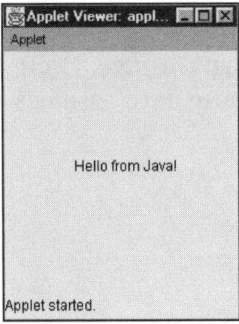

Figure 16.3 An applet at work in the Java Applet Viewer.

installed on your computer rather than just downloaded with a Web page, applications have more privileges than applets do by default. For example, applications have the capability to read and write files (applets can do that too, but only after you use the Java security tool to grant them higher security access).

You need less code for applications than for applets, so while we're learning Java in this chapter, I'll create Java applications. The applications I'll use will be the simplest type of Java applications—*console* applications. These are text-based applications that you run from the command line (in Windows, this means from the DOS window); they can read and display text. For example, say you have a Java application named **app** that prints the message "Hello from Java!" as the applet we've just seen does. In this case, the application will display that message in the console. For example, here's how to create an application named **app**, which is stored in a file named app.java (details will be covered later in this chapter):

```java
public class app
{
    public static void main(String[] args)
    {
        System.out.println("Hello from Java!");
    }
}
```

When you use the Java compiler, the file app.java is translated into a *bytecode* file named app.class. The app.class file holds these bytecode files, which are what Java actually reads and interprets to make the program run. (Bytecode files can be much more compact than the Java code they came from—which means that Java applets can be faster to download than lengthy JavaScript scripts). As we'll see in the "Immediate Solutions" section "Compiling Code," you use the Java compiler **javac** to create the bytecode file for app.java:

```
C:\>javac app.java
```

As we'll see in the "Immediate Solutions" section "Running Code," you use the file app.class when you run the application, using the tool named **java**. (Note that you omit the .class part of the app.class file name because Java assumes that you'll be running a .class file). Here's the code:

```
C:\>javac app.java
C:\>java app
Hello from Java!
```

You run the application with the **java** command (which runs java.exe, which comes with the Java SDK), passing it the name of the application you want to run. In Unix, the command might look like this, where a percent sign (%) is the command prompt:

```
%java app
Hello from Java!
```

In Windows, it might look like this:

```
C:\>java app
Hello from Java!
```

That's what a Java application looks like. One item that's reassuring—Java code is much like JavaScript code, so the material on JavaScript in Chapters 10 and 11 will help you in this chapter. However, there are some differences; for example, you use the **var** statement in JavaScript to create a variable like this:

```
var counter = 0
```

In Java, variables are *typed*, so you'll have to specify which type of variable you want to create. Here's how to create an integer variable in Java by using the **int** statement (see the "Immediate Solutions" section "Creating Variables" for details):

```
int counter = 0;
```

Another important difference is that Java is much more *object-oriented* than JavaScript is.

Java Is Object-Oriented

Java code is *object-oriented*, and it's important to understand what that means before you begin writing code. Object-oriented programming is really just another technique to let you implement that famous programming dictum: divide and conquer. The idea is that you encapsulate data and functions into objects, making each object semiautonomous, enclosing private (that is, purely internal) data and functions in a way that stops them from cluttering up the program in general. The object can then interact with the rest of the program through a well-defined interface defined by its public (that is, externally accessible) functions.

Object-oriented programming was first created to handle large programs by separating them into functional units. It takes the idea of breaking a program into functions one step further because objects can have both multiple subroutines and data inside them. The result of encapsulating parts of your program into an object is easily conceptualized and prevents you from having to deal with all the components that make up the object internally.

Imagine how your kitchen would look filled with pipes, pumps, a compressor, and all kinds of switches that you would need to keep food cold. Every time the temperature of the food got too high, you'd turn on the compressor, open valves, and start cranking the pumps manually. Now wrap all that functionality into an *object*—a refrigerator—in which all those operations are handled internally with the appropriate feedback between the internal parts and handled automatically inside the object.

That's the idea behind encapsulation—taking a complex system that demands a lot of attention and turning it into an object that handles all its own work internally. It can be easily conceptualized, much like a refrigerator. If the first dictum of object-oriented programming is "divide and conquer," the second is surely "out of sight, out of mind."

In Java, object-oriented programming revolves around a few key concepts: classes, data members, inheritance, methods, and objects. The following list defines these terms:

- *Class*—A template from which you can create objects. The definition of the class includes the formal specifications for the class and any data and methods in it.

- *Data members*—The variables that are part of an object; they're used to store the data used by the object.

- *Inheritance*—The process of deriving one class, called the *derived* class, from another, the *base* class, and being able to use the base class's methods in the derived class.

- *Method*—A function built into an object. In JavaScript, they're called functions, but in Java, they're methods.

- *Object*—An *instance* of a class. You can think of a class as the *type* of an object, just as **int** is the *type* of the variable named **counter** in this statement: **int counter = 0;**. If a class is a cookie cutter, the objects are the cookies.

All these constructs are important to object-oriented programming, and we'll get more details on each of them in the next section.

Classes and Objects

In object-oriented programming, classes provide a sort of template for objects. You can consider a class an object's *type*—just as **int** is the *type* of the variable named **counter** in this statement: **int counter = 0;**.

To create an object, you call a class's *constructor*, which is a method with the same name as the class itself. This constructor creates a new object of the class. When you create a new object, you have to use the Java **new** operator. For example, Java comes with a built-in class named **String** (see the "Immediate Solutions" section "Creating Strings"). You can create a new **String** object named **greeting**, which holds the text **"Hello from Java!"**, by passing that text to the **String** class's constructor:

```
public class app
{
    public static void main(String[] args)
    {
        String greeting = new String("Hello from Java!");
            .
            .
            .
    }
}
```

Notice how you specify **String** as the type of this new object, similar to the way you would use **int** as the type of an integer variable:

```
public class app
{
    public static void main(String[] args)
    {
        int counter = 0;
           .
           .
           .
    }
}
```

After creating the new **String** object, you can print the data in it:

```
public class app
{
    public static void main(String[] args)
    {
        String greeting = new String("Hello from Java!");

        System.out.println(greeting);
    }
}
```

Running this application in Windows gives you this:

```
C:\>java app
Hello from Java!
```

So far, it's not very different from treating the **greeting** object as a variable that just holds data. However, objects can also have built-in *methods*. The **String** class has a built-in method named **toUpperCase**, which is a function that converts the string's text to uppercase. Here's how I apply this method to the text in the **greeting** object (similar to the way we apply methods to XHTML objects):

```
public class app
{
    public static void main(String[] args)
    {
        String greeting = new String("Hello from Java!");
        System.out.println(greeting.toUpperCase());
    }
}
```

And here's the new result:

```
C:\>java app
HELLO FROM JAVA!
```

Besides built-in methods, objects can also hold data in *data members* (also called *fields*). The data members of an object are the variables inside the object. Data members can be accessible outside an object, or you can make them internal to the object for the private use of the methods inside the object. They're much like the properties of the XHTML objects we've already seen in this book.

Here's an example showing how you might use an object's data member. Say you have a class named **Data_Class**, and you create an object of this class named **data_object**:

```
Data_Class data_object = new Data_class("Hello from Java!");
    .
    .
    .
```

If **Data_Class** defines a publicly accessible data member named, say, **data**, you can refer to the **data** member of **data_object** by using the **dot** operator (.), like this: **data_object.data**. You can print the data in **data_object**:

```
Data_Class data_object = new Data_Class("Hello from Java!");
```

```
System.out.println(data_object.data);
```

In this way, you can refer to an object's data members that the object makes publicly accessible.

There's one more object-oriented concept to master before we get to the code—inheritance.

Inheritance

Inheritance is one of the formally defining aspects of object-oriented programming. Using inheritance, you can *derive* a new class from an old class, and the new class will *inherit* all the methods and member data of the old class. The new class is called the *derived* class, and the original class is called the *base* class. The idea behind inheritance is that you add what you want to the new class to give it more customized functionality than the base class.

For example, if you had a class named **vehicle**, you might derive from it a new class named **car** and add a new method, **horn**, which, when called, prints "beep."

In this way, you've created a new class from a base class and augmented that class with an additional method.

Inheritance is an important topic in Java because you can use the huge class libraries available in Java by deriving your own classes from them. We'll learn how to use inheritance in Chapter 17.

And that's all the introduction to Java concepts we'll need before digging into the code—which I'll do now.

Immediate Solutions

Getting and Installing the Java SDK

The big boss gives you a call at the last minute—as usual. You have twenty minutes to write a new Web page that will give users an overview of your company's products. What are you going to do? Knowing how well Java works in cases like this, you select Java as the language of choice to get the task done. Of course, you've got to make sure you have it before you can use it to write applets.

It's time to download and install the Java SDK, so you can create your own applets. You can find it at **http://java.sun.com/jdk/**. After downloading the Java SDK, usually as one executable package that installs itself, follow the installation instructions on the **http://java.sun.com** site.

I'd love to be able to provide the actual installation instructions here, but these instructions change frequently. For this reason, the best thing you can do is to see how Sun wants you to install the Java SDK, so please refer to the installation instructions as posted on the Java site. The installation process has been getting easier with every new version of Java, and now typically just involves running the file you've downloaded.

As indicated in the Sun installation instructions, make sure that your machine can find the Java tools, including the Java compiler. To do this, make sure that the Java bin subdirectory is in your computer's path. For example, in Windows, if the Java bin subdirectory is at c:\jdk\bin, you can add a line like the following to autoexec.bat:

```
SET PATH=%PATH%;C:\JDK\BIN
```

You must reboot your computer to make these changes take effect. When the bin directory is in the path, you'll be able to use the Java tools directly from the command line instead of having to preface them with a path name each time you want to use them at the command line.

Immediate Solutions

Writing Code: Creating Code Files

The design team coordinator calls to congratulate you on getting Java installed. You accept the accolades gracefully. "So, what programs have you been writing?" the DTC asks. Hm, you think—*programs*?

Java programs are plain text files made up of Java statements and declarations. We'll start investigating these in the next section. To create a Java program, you should have a text editor or word processor that can save files in plain text format, just as you would XHTML pages.

In addition, your programs should be stored in files that have the extension .java. For example, if you are writing an application named **app**, you should store the actual Java program in a file named app.java. You pass this file to the Java compiler to create the actual bytecode file, as we'll see in a few pages.

So far so good—we've got the selection of editor or word processor down. Now how about writing some code?

Writing Code: Creating an Application

The big boss arrives and says, "So now you can write Java? Give me a demonstration!" You turn to your terminal and immediately your mind goes blank. What will you write?

Here's a sample Java application that I'll develop through the compiling and running stages over the next few sections. Place this code in a file named app.java:

```java
public class app
{
    public static void main(String[] args)
    {
        System.out.println("Hello from Java!");
    }
}
```

This application will print the text "Hello from Java!" when you run it. For example, here's how things would look in a DOS window in Windows:

```
c:\>java app
Hello from Java!
```

Not the most significant of programs, but a good one to get us started. I'll take this program apart line by line now.

public class app

Here's the first line in app.java:

```
public class app
{
    .
    .
    .
}
```

This line indicates that I'm creating a new Java class named **app**. After I translate this class into bytecode files, Java will be able to create objects of this class and run them.

Note the keyword **public** in the previous code. This keyword is an *access specifier*. The **public** access specifier indicates that this class is available anywhere in a program that makes use of it. If you make a class public, Java insists that you name the file after it. That is, you can have only one public class in a .java file. The reason for this is that the Java compiler will translate the .java file into a bytecode file with the extension .class, which means that app.java will be translated into app.class, and if Java needs the **app** class, it'll know to look in the app.class file. Because Java uses the name of the file to determine which public classes are in the file, you can have only one public class in a file. For this reason, the code for the **app** class must be in a file named app.java. Note that Java is particular about this and capitalization counts.

The actual implementation of the class we're defining will go between the curly braces, { and }:

```
public class app
{
    .
    .
    .
}
```

Java always encloses blocks of code within curly braces. I'll continue building this application by proceeding to the next line of code.

public static void main(String[] args)

The next line of code in our application is as follows:

```
public class app
{
    public static void main(String[] args)
    {
        .
        .
        .
    }
}
```

In this line, I'm creating a method in the **app** class. A *method* in object-oriented programming is like a function in standard programming—a block of code that you can pass control to and that can return a value. Methods provide handy ways of wrapping code into a single functional unit; when you call a method, the code in the method is executed by Java.

The method, named **main**, is the method that Java will look for when it starts an application (applets do not have a **main** method). When it finds the **main** method, Java passes control to it. We'll place the code we want to execute in this method's code block.

*TIP: You may be wondering about the details of the **main** method. The **main** method must be declared with the **public** access specifier, which means that it can be called outside its class. The **main** method must also be declared **static** (technically, this means that **main** is a class method, not an instance method; Java doesn't need to create an object of the **app** class before calling **main**). The **main** method must not return a value when it's finished executing—the reason I use the keyword **void** in the previous code. (A return value of type **void** means that there is no return value.) Finally, note the argument in the parentheses following **main: String[] args**. You place an argument list in the parentheses of a method declaration to indicate which values are passed to the method and can be used by the code in the method. In this case, I'm indicating that **main** is passed an array (see the "Immediate Solutions" section "Creating Arrays") of string values, which I'm calling **args**. These string values hold the values passed from the command line when you start the application; for example, if you typed **java app Hello there**, then "Hello" and "there" would be the two strings in the **args** array. Because I won't use any command-line arguments in this application, I won't use **args** in the code for the **main** method.*

This line of code starts the **main** method. The purpose of this method is to print the text "Hello from Java!", and I'll do that in the next line of code.

System.out.println("Hello from Java!");

The **main** method has one line of code in it:

```java
public class app
{
    public static void main(String[] args)
    {
        System.out.println("Hello from Java!");
    }
}
```

This is the line of code that does all the work. In this case, I'm using some of the code that the programmers at Sun have already created to display the text "Hello from Java!" In particular, I'm using the **java.lang** package's **System** class here. Libraries of classes are called *packages* in Java, and the **java.lang** package is built into every Java program, so you don't have to take special steps to use it, as you do with other Java packages. The **java.lang** package's **System** class includes a data member named **out**; this is an object itself, and it has a method named **println** that displays text.

Note that this line of code ends with a semicolon. This end-of-statement convention is something that Java has inherited from C and C++ (in fact, it's inherited a lot from C and C++). You end nearly all statements in Java with a semicolon. Although JavaScript, as implemented in the major browsers, lets you drop the semicolons at the end of each statement, Java insists that they be there, so we can't skip them here.

That's that. You've created your new application and stored it in a file named app.java. What's the next step? How do you get it to actually *run*? See the next section.

Compiling Code

The big boss, while chomping on a cigar and standing right behind you as you enter your new Java application into a file, says, "Hm," clearly not impressed. "What's next?" "Now," you say, "I have to compile the program and then I can run it." "OK," the big boss says, "amaze me."

To translate a Java program into a bytecode file, you use the Java compiler called javac (on Windows machines, this program is called javac.exe and is located in the bin subdirectory). Here's the syntax for using **javac**:

```
javac [options] [sourcefiles] [@files]
```

Here are the arguments for javac:

- *options*—Command-line options
- *sourcefiles*—One or more source files to be compiled (such as app.java)
- *@files*—One or more files that list source files

To compile app.java, I'll use this command (which assumes that app.java is in the C:\ directory—change to the appropriate directory as needed):

```
C:\>javac app.java
```

Assuming that there are no errors, the Java compiler, javac, compiles the file app.java, translating it and creating a new file named app.class. If there are errors, the Java compiler will tell you what they are, including what line of code is wrong. In this case, I've forgotten the **println** method and tried to use one called **printline**:

```
C:\>javac app.java
app.java:5: Method printline(java.lang.String) not found in class
java.io.PrintStream.
        System.out.printline("Hello from Java!");
                      ^
1 error
```

When app.java is successfully compiled to bytecode files, the new file app.class contains all that Java will need to create objects from the **app** class. So now that we've created app.class—how do we run it? See the next section.

Running Code

The big boss is getting impatient. You've written a new application and compiled it without errors the first time (which you can feel proud of), but nothing has really happened that the BB can see. It's time to run the new application.

You run Java applications with the program named *java* (in Windows, this is the java.exe file in the bin subdirectory). The java program, called the java *tool*, is what actually runs the Java environment. For example, to run the application named **app**, located in the file app.class, I can execute this command at the command line (note that you omit the .class part of app.class):

```
C:\>java app
```

The result appears immediately:

```
C:\>java app
Hello from Java!
```

Figure 16.4 shows you how this works in a DOS window in Windows.

That's all it takes—now you've written, compiled, and run your first Java application. Congratulations! (Note that if your application isn't responding, or you want to stop it for some reason, you can press Ctrl+C. If that doesn't work, try the Escape key.)

While we're on the topic of compiling and running code, there is another detail that we should cover—commenting your Java code.

Figure 16.4   Running an application in a DOS window.

Basic Skills: Commenting Your Code

The programming correctness czar comes in and looks at you reprovingly. "What's wrong, PCC?" you ask. "It's your code," the PCC says; "I can't make heads or tails of what's going on in it." "I guess I forgot to comment it," you say. "I guess you did," the PCC says; "fix it."

Sometimes code can be very cryptic. For this reason, Java, like JavaScript, lets you place descriptive comments in your code to let you explain to anyone who reads that code how the program works and what it does. As an example, I'll add comments to the application we developed in the previous section.

You can surround a comment of any length with the characters /* and */:

```
/* This application prints out "Hello from Java!" */

public class app
{
    public static void main(String[] args)
    {
        System.out.println("Hello from Java!");
    }
}
```

The Java compiler will ignore all the text between the /* and */ markers. You can split comments between /* and */ across multiple lines:

```
/* This application prints out "Hello from Java!"
   Created by: G. Whiz, 1/1/00                    */

public class app
{
    public static void main(String[] args)
    {
        System.out.println("Hello from Java!");
    }
}
```

Like JavaScript, Java also supports a one-line comment using a double slash (//). The Java compiler will ignore everything on a line after the // marker, so you can create whole lines that are comments, or just add a comment to an individual line:

```
/* This application prints out "Hello from Java!" */

public class app    //Create the app class
{
    //Create main(), the entry point for the application.
    public static void main(String[] args)
    {
        //Print out the message with
        System.out.println("Hello from Java!");
    }
}
```

Commenting your code can be invaluable in team environments where you share your code source files with others, or when someone else is going to take over a project after you.

Basic Skills: Importing Java Packages and Classes

"Hm," says the novice programmer, "I've got a problem. The design team coordinator told me to use the **Date** class to print the current date in my application, but Java doesn't seem to have ever heard of the **Date** class—I get an error every time I try to use it." "That's because the **Date** class is part of the Java **util** package, and you have to import that package before you can use it." The NP asks, "Import it?"

The ready-to-use classes created by Sun Microsystems are stored in class libraries called *packages*. To make a class in a package available to your code, you have to import the package, which means that the compiler will search that package for classes. You can also import individual classes that are not part of a package. By default, only the basic Java statements—that is, the statements in the core **java.lang** Java package—are available to you in an application. The compiler automatically imports the **java.lang** package for you, but to use the rest of the classes that come with Java, you'll have to do your own importing with the **import** statement. Here's the syntax for that statement:

```
import [package1[.package2...].](classname|*);
```

Note that you put a dot (.) between package and class names to keep them separate. The standard Java packages themselves are stored in a large package called **java**, so the **util** package is really called the **java.util** package. (There are other large packages like the **java** package available; for example, the extensive **swing** package is stored in the **javax** package.) I can refer to the **Date** class in **java.util** as **java.util.Date**, so here's how I import that class into a program:

```
import java.util.Date;

public class app
{
    .
    .
    .
```

If you're going to use **import** statements to import classes in a program, the **import** statements should be at the top of the code. Now I'm free to create an object from the **Date** class by using the Java **new** operator:

```
import java.util.Date;

public class app
{
    public static void main(String[] args)
    {
        System.out.println("Today = " + new Date());
    }
}
```

When you run this application, you'll see the current date displayed:

```
C:\>java app
Today = Mon Aug 02 12:15:13 EDT 2001
```

As you can see by studying the syntax of the **import** statement in the previous code, there's also a shorthand that will load in all the classes in a package. You can use an asterisk (*) as a wildcard to represent all the classes in a particular package. Here's how that looks if I want to import all the classes in the **java.util** package at once:

```
import java.util.*;

public class app
{
    public static void main(String[] args)
    {
        System.out.println("Today = " + new Date());
    }
}
```

TIP: *Importing packages and classes only tells the compiler where to look for the code it needs—it does not increase the size of your code. For this reason, the bytecode file app.class will be the same size whether you use **import java.util.Date;** or **import java.util.*;**.*

Importing classes like this is fine if you stick with importing the Sun-provided classes because Java knows where to look for the classes it was installed with. But what if you want to import your own classes or ones provided by a third party?

Here's an example. Say that you have a class named **printer** in a file named printer.java, and that class has one method named **print**:

```
public class printer
{
    public void print()
    {
        System.out.println("Hello from Java!");
    }
}
```

You might want to use the **print** method in other classes. In this case, I'm using the **new** operator to create a new object of the **printer** class and using that object's **print** method in an application named **app**:

```
public class app
{
    public static void main(String[] args)
    {
        (new printer()).print();
    }
}
```

To do this, you can import the **printer** class:

```
import printer;

public class app
{
    public static void main(String[] args)
    {
        (new printer()).print();
    }
}
```

This works just as it should—congratulations, you've imported a class into a program!

TIP: *This technique works well if printer.class is in the same directory in which you're compiling the application because the Java compiler will search the current directory by default. However, say that you want to store all your classes in a directory named c:\classes. How will the Java compiler find printer.class there? In this case, you'll have to add the directory c:\classes to the Java variable named* **CLASSPATH**—*see the Java documentation for more details.*

Creating Variables

"I'm ready to store data in variables," the novice programmer says, "so I should use **var** as I did in JavaScript, right?" "Wrong," you say; "it's a little more involved than that."

As with JavaScript, variables serve as placeholders in memory for data. Unlike JavaScript, however, Java variables come in different *types*. The types vary according to which format the data is stored in and how much memory is set aside to hold that data. For example, an integer variable type, the **int** type, is made up of 4 bytes or 32 bits, and you use it to store integer values. This format gives the data in the **int** type a range of possible values between –2,147,483,648 and 2,147,483,647. Java provides many variable types, such as integers, floating-point numbers, and individual characters.

Before you use a variable in Java, you must *declare* it, specifying its data type. Here's how you declare variables in Java:

```
type name [= value][, name [= value]...];
```

Here's an example showing how to declare a variable of the **int** type, which means that I'll store an integer in it. This variable is named **days**:

```
public class app
{
    public static void main(String[] args)
    {
        int days;
            .
            .
            .
    }
}
```

This code allocates 32 bits of storage in memory and labels the location of that storage, as far as the Java compiler is concerned, as **days**, so you can now refer to that name in code. Here's how I store a numeric value of 365 in **days** by using the Java assignment operator (=):

```
public class app
{
    public static void main(String[] args)
    {
        int days;
```

```
            days = 365;
            .
            .
            .
    }
}
```

To verify that **days** now holds 365, I can print it on the console:

```
public class app
{
    public static void main(String[] args)
    {
        int days;

        days = 365;

        System.out.println("Number of days = " + days);
    }
}
```

Here's the result of this code:

```
C:\>java app
Number of days = 365
```

As you can see, we've created a variable, stored data in it, and retrieved that data to print it on the screen. That's how it works.

As with JavaScript, there's also a convenient shortcut that lets you initialize a variable when you declare it. Here, I'm declaring **days** and initializing it to **365** in one step:

```
public class app
{
    public static void main(String[] args)
    {
        int days = 365;

        System.out.println("Number of days = " + days);
    }
}
```

The **int** type is only one kind of simple variable that you can use. Following are a few others:

- *Boolean*—Holds only two types of values: **true** and **false**.
- *Character*—Holds representations of characters such as letters and numbers.
- *Floating-point number*—Refers to **float** and **double** (for double precision), which hold signed floating-point numbers.
- *Integer*—Refers to **byte** (one byte), **short** (usually two bytes), **int** (usually four bytes), and **long** (usually eight bytes), which hold signed, whole-value numbers.

Java puts considerable emphasis on its data types. It's a strongly *typed* language; it insists that the simple variables you declare and use must fit into one of the types in the preceding list. Every variable must have a type, and Java is very particular about maintaining the integrity of those types, especially if you try to assign a value of one type to a variable of another type. In fact, Java is more strongly typed than a language like C++. In C++, for example, you can assign a floating-point number to an integer and C++ will handle the type conversion for you, but you can't do this in Java—in Java, you have to perform the conversion explicitly.

Creating Arrays

Simple data types, of the kind we saw in the previous section, are fine for storing single data items, but data is often more complex. Say, for example, that you want to start a new bank, the Java Programming Bank, and need to keep track of the amount of money in every account indexed by an account number. A method of working with compound data is best, and that's what arrays provide.

Using an array, you can group simple data types into a more compound data structure and refer to that new data structure by name. What's more important, you can refer to the array's individual data items by numeric index. This is important because computers excel at performing millions of operations very quickly, so if your data is referred to by a numeric index, you can work through a whole set of data very quickly by incrementing the array index and accessing all the items in the array.

Here's an example. I'll start the Java Programming Bank with 100 new accounts, and each one will have its own entry in an array named **accounts[]**. The square brackets at the end of **accounts[]** indicate that it's an array, and in these brackets, you place the index number of the array item that you want to access. Here's how I create the **accounts[]** array, making each entry in it the floating-point type double for extra precision. First, I declare the array; then I create it with the **new** operator, which is what Java uses to allocate memory:

```
public class app
{
    public static void main(String[] args)
    {
        double accounts[];

        accounts = new double[100];
        .
        .
        .
```

Now that I've created an array with 100 items, I can refer to those items numerically. Here I'm storing $43.95 in Account 3 and printing that amount:

```
public class app
{
    public static void main(String[] args)
    {
        double accounts[];

        accounts = new double[100];

        accounts[3] = 43.95;

        System.out.println("Account 3 has $" + accounts[3]);
    }
}
```

Here's the results of this program:

```
C:\>java app
Account 3 has $43.95
```

As you can see, you can now refer to the items in the array by using a numeric index, which organizes them in an easy way. In Java, the lower bound of an array you declare this way is **0**, so the statement **accounts = new double[100]** creates an array with a first item of **accounts[0]** and a last item of **accounts[99]**.

You can combine the declaration and creation steps into one step:

```
public class app
{
    public static void main(String[] args)
    {
        double accounts[] = new double[100];
```

```
            accounts[3] = 43.95;

            System.out.println("Account 3 has $" + accounts[3]);
    }
}
```

You can also initialize an array with values when you declare the array if you enclose the list of values you want to use in curly braces (see the "Immediate Solutions" section "Creating Arrays"). For example, this code creates four accounts and stores 43.95 in **accounts[3]**:

```
public class app
{
    public static void main(String[] args)
    {
        double accounts[] = {0, 0, 0, 43.95};

        System.out.println("Account 3 has $" + accounts[3]);
    }
}
```

Now, let's say that some of the customers in the Java Programming Bank are unhappy; they want a checking account in addition to a savings account. How will you handle that and still keep things indexed by account number?

The **accounts[]** array is a one-dimensional array; you can think of it as a single list of numbers that you can index with one number. However, arrays can be multiply dimensioned in Java, meaning that you can have multiple array indexes. In this next example, I'll extend **accounts[]** into a two-dimensional array, **accounts[][]**, to handle both a savings and a checking account. The first index of **accounts[][]** will be **0** for savings accounts and **1** for checking accounts, and the second index will be the account number. Here's how this works in code:

```
public class app
{
    public static void main(String[] args)
    {
        double accounts[][] = new double[2][100];

        accounts[0][3] = 43.95;
        accounts[1][3] = 2385489382.06;

        System.out.println("Savings account 3 has $" + accounts[0][3]);
        System.out.println("Checking account 3 has $" + accounts[1][3]);
    }
}
```

Now that **accounts[][]** is a two-dimensional array, each item in it is referred to using two index values; for example, the savings balance for Account 3 is now **accounts[0][3]**, and the checking balance is **accounts[0][3]**. Here are the results when you run this application:

```
C:\>java app
Savings account 3 has $43.95
Checking account 3 has $2.38548938206E9
```

Note that I've given Account 3 a checking balance of $2,385,489,382.06 (wishful thinking) and that Java has printed 2.38548938206E9. This is Java's shorthand for $2.38548938206 \times 10^9$, not an inconsiderable bank balance by any means.

Creating Strings

As with JavaScript, I've been using the plus (+) operator to create the text to print in the examples in this chapter:

```
public class app
{
    public static void main(String[] args)
    {
        double accounts[][] = new double[2][100];

        accounts[0][3] = 43.95;
        accounts[1][3] = 2385489382.06;

        System.out.println("Savings account 3 has $" + accounts[0][3]);
        System.out.println("Checking account 3 has $" + accounts[1][3]);
    }
}
```

That's because text strings are supported by their own class in Java, the **String** class. You can think of the **String** class as defining a new data type. For example, here's how I create a string named **greeting**, which holds the text **"Hello from Java!"**:

```
public class app
{
    public static void main(String[] args)
    {
```

```
        String greeting = "Hello from Java!";
            .
            .
            .
```

Now I can treat this string as I would other types of variables, including printing it:

```
public class app
{
    public static void main(String[] args)
    {
        String greeting = "Hello from Java!";

        System.out.println(greeting);
    }
}
```

Here's the result of this application:

```
C:\>java app
Hello from Java!
```

There are actually two string classes in Java: **String** and **StringBuffer**. You use the **String** class to create text strings that cannot change and use **StringBuffer** to create strings that you can modify. As you can see in the previous code, you can use strings as you would any simple data type in Java, even using operators like + and - on them. You'll find all the Java operators in the next section.

Using Operators

"OK," sighs the novice programmer, "I want to multiply two numbers together in Java. In JavaScript, I'd use the multiplication operator, but I suppose it's different in Java?" "Nope," you say, "same thing."

The most basic way to work with the data in a Java program is with the built-in Java operators. For example, say you have stored a value of 46 in one variable and a value of 4 in another. You can multiply those two values with the Java multiplication operator (*), as seen in this code:

```
public class app
{
    public static void main(String[] args)
```

```
    {
        int operand1 = 46, operand2 = 4, product;

        product = operand1 * operand2;

        System.out.println(operand1 + " * " + operand2 +
            " = " + product);
    }
}
```

Here are the results of this code:

```
C:\>java app
46 * 4 = 184
```

So what operators are available in Java? Table 16.1 contains all of them—note that nearly all of them are shared by JavaScript as well.

Table 16.1 Java operators.

Operator	Operation Performed	Operator	Operation Performed
++	Increment	--	Decrement
=	Assignment	==	Equal to
+	Addition	+=	Addition assignment
-	Subtraction	-=	Subtraction assignment
*	Multiplication	*=	Multiplication assignment
/	Division	/=	Division assignment
<	Less than	<=	Less than or equal to
<<	Shift left	<<=	Shift left assignment
>	Greater than	>=	Greater than or equal to
>>	Shift right	>>=	Shift right assignment
>>>	Shift right with zero fill	>>>=	Shift right zero fill assignment
^	Logical XOR	^=	Bitwise XOR assignment
|	Logical OR	||	Short-circuit OR
|=	Bitwise OR assignment	~	Bitwise unary NOT
!	Logical unary NOT	!=	Not equal to
&	Logical AND	&&	Short-circuit AND
&=	Bitwise AND assignment	?:	Ternary if-then-else
%	Modulus	%=	Modulus assignment

Using Conditional Statements: **if**, **if...else**, **switch**

The novice programmer appears and says, "How do you create a conditional statement in Java? In JavaScript, I'd use an **if** statement." "With the Java **if** statement," you say. "OK," the NP asks, "but what about a **switch** statement?" "With the Java **switch** statement," you say. The NP says, "This is too easy!"

The next step up from using simple operators is to use *conditional statements*, also called *branching statements*, in your code. You use conditional statements to make decisions based on the value of your data and make the flow of the program go in different directions accordingly. Java supports the same kind of conditional statements as JavaScript: **if**, **if...else**, and **switch**.

TIP: *For more details on these statements, see Chapter 10.*

For example, say that you want to report on the weather, and if it's under 80 degrees Fahrenheit, you want a Java program to print the message "It's not too hot." You can do that by checking the current temperature as stored in the program with a Java **if** statement, which compares the value in the variable **temperature** to 80, and if that value is under 80, prints the message:

```
public class app
{
    public static void main(String[] args)
    {
        int temperature = 73;

        if (temperature < 80) {
            System.out.println("It is not too hot.");
        }
    }
}
```

The **if** statement tests whether its condition, the part that appears in parentheses (in this case, **temperature < 80**), is true. Because I've set the value to **73**, the **if** statement's condition is true, so the code in the body of the **if** statement will be executed. Here are the results of this code:

```
C:\>java app
It is not too hot.
```

You can make **if** statements more complex by adding **else** clauses, which must follow an **if** statement and are executed when the **if** statement's condition is false. Here's an example:

```java
public class app
{
    public static void main(String[] args)
    {
        int temperature = 73;

        if (temperature < 80) {
            System.out.println("It\'s not too hot.");
        }
        else {
            System.out.println("It\'s too hot!");
        }
    }
}
```

Using Loops: **for, while, do...while**

The novice programmer is back and is still excited about making the move from JavaScript to Java. The NP asks, "Does Java have a **for** loop with the same syntax as the JavaScript **for** loop?" "Yep," you say. "And does it also have a **while** loop?" "Yep," you say. "And a **do...while** loop?" "Yes, yes, yes," you say. "Wow!" says the NP.

Loops are fundamental programming constructs that let you handle tasks by executing specific code repeatedly. Like JavaScript, Java has a **for** loop, a **while** loop, and a **do...while** loop.

TIP: For more details on these statements, see Chapter 10.

For example, you might want to handle the items in a set of data by working with each item in succession, or you might want to keep performing a task until a particular condition becomes true. The basic **loop** statement is the **for** statement, which lets you execute a block of code using a *loop index*. Each time the code goes through the loop, the loop index will have a different value, and you can use the loop index to specify a different data item in your data set, as when you use the loop index as an index for an array.

Following is the syntax for the Java **for** loop. Note that the statement that makes up the body of the **for** loop can be a compound statement; it can be made up of several single statements enclosed in curly braces:

```
for (initialization_expression; end_conditon; iteration_expression) {
    statement
}
```

You can initialize a loop index in the initialization expression (in fact, you can use multiple loop indexes in a **for** loop). You can also provide a test condition for ending the loop when that test condition becomes false in the end condition, and add some way of changing, usually by incrementing, the loop index in the iteration expression.

Here's an example to make this clear. I'll use a **for** loop to total the grades of six students in an array and compute the average grade. Here's how this looks in code—note that I am declaring and initializing the loop index to **0** in the initialization expression of the **for** loop:

```
public class app
{
    public static void main(String[] args)
    {
        double grades[] = {88, 99, 73, 56, 87, 64};
        double sum, average;

        sum = 0;

        for (int loop_index = 0; loop_index < grades.length;
                loop_index++) {
            sum += grades[loop_index];
        }

        average = sum / grades.length;

        System.out.println("Average grade = " + average);
    }
}
```

This code loops over all items in the **grades** array and adds them, leaving the result in the variable named **sum**. This result is then divided by the total number of entries in the array to find the average value. I loop over all elements by using a loop index that starts at **0** and is steadily incremented each time through the loop, up to the last item in the array. Here are the results of this code:

```
C:\>java app
Average grade = 77.83333333333333
```

Declaring and Creating Objects

The novice programmer appears, ready to discuss object-oriented programming. "I know all about objects now," the NP says, "only..." "Only what?" you ask. "Only, how do I actually *create* an object?"

You need to declare an object before you can use it. You can declare objects the same way that you declare variables of the simple data types: using the class as the object's type. And you can use the **new** operator to create objects in Java. Let's look at an example of using the Java **String** class. To start, I'll declare a new object of the **String** class, **s1**:

```
public class app
{
    public static void main(String[] args)
    {
        String s1;
        .
        .
        .
}
```

Although declaring a simple variable creates that variable, declaring an object doesn't create it. To actually create the object, I can use the **new** operator. Using this general form, I'm passing parameters to the class's constructor:

```
object = new class([parameter1 [, parameter2...]]);
```

The **String** class has several constructors, and you can pass quoted strings to one of the **String** class's constructors, so I can create the new object, **s1**:

```
public class app
{
    public static void main(String[] args)
    {
        String s1;
        s1 = new String("Hello from Java!");
        .
        .
        .
}
```

Now the new object, **s1**, exists, and is ready for use. For example, to convert all the characters in **s1** to lowercase, you can use the **String** class's **toLowerCase** method: **s1.toLowerCase();**.

You can also combine the declaration and creation steps into one step. In this case, I'm declaring a new **String** object, **s2**, and creating it with the **new** operator all in one line:

```
public class app
{
    public static void main(String[] args)
    {
        String s1;
        s1 = new String("Hello from Java!");

        String s2 = new String("Hello from Java!");
        .
        .
        .
}
```

Classes often have several different constructors, each of which can take a different argument list—that is, different argument types and numbers of arguments. From the types and number of arguments you use, the Java compiler knows which constructor you want to use. In object-oriented terms, these constructors are *overloaded*. For example, the **String** class's constructor is overloaded to take character arrays as well as text strings, so I can create a new object, **s3**, by using a character array:

```
public class app
{
    public static void main(String[] args)
    {
        String s1;
        s1 = new String("Hello from Java!");

        String s2 = new String("Hello from Java!");

        char c1[] = {'H', 'i', ' ', 't', 'h', 'e', 'r', 'e'};
        String s3 = new String(c1);
        .
        .
        .
}
```

Sometimes classes will have methods that return objects, which means that they'll use the **new** operator internally and you don't have to. Here's an example of using a method of the **String** class, **valueOf**; here, I convert the number in a **double** variable into text in a **String** object:

```java
public class app
{
    public static void main(String[] args)
    {
        String s1;
        s1 = new String("Hello from Java!");

        String s2 = new String("Hello from Java!");

        char c1[] = {'H', 'i', ' ', 't', 'h', 'e', 'r', 'e'};
        String s3 = new String(c1);

        double double1 = 1.23456789;
        String s4 = String.valueOf(double1);
        .
        .
        .
}
```

In addition, you can assign one object to another, as I've done here:

```java
public class app
{
    public static void main(String[] args)
    {
        String s1;
        s1 = new String("Hello from Java!");

        String s2 = new String("Hello from Java!");

        char c1[] = {'H', 'i', ' ', 't', 'h', 'e', 'r', 'e'};
        String s3 = new String(c1);

        double double1 = 1.23456789;
        String s4 = String.valueOf(double1);

        String s5;
        s5 = s1;

        System.out.println(s1);
        System.out.println(s2);
        System.out.println(s3);
        System.out.println(s4);
        System.out.println(s5);
    }
}
```

Internally, what's really happening here is that a reference to **s1** is copied to **s5**. What this means in practice is that **s1** and **s5** refer to the *same* object. That's important to know because if you change the instance data in **s1**, you also change the instance data in **s5**, and vice versa. If two variables refer to the same object, be careful—multiple references to the same object can create bugs that are extremely hard to find, especially when you think you're really dealing with different objects.

At the end of the previous code, I print all the strings I've created, and here's what appears when you run the program:

```
C:\>java app
Hello from Java!
Hello from Java!
Hi there
1.23456789
Hello from Java!
```

That's how you declare and create objects. It's similar to the way you declare and create simple variables, with the added power of configuring objects by passing data to a class's constructor.

Chapter 17

Creating Java Applets

If you need an immediate solution to:	See page:
Creating Applets	1020
<applet>—Embedding Applets in Web Pages	1021
Handling Non-Java Browsers	1025
Using the **init**, **start**, **stop**, **destroy**, **paint**, and **update** Methods—and Setting Applet Color	1025
Using the Java Browser Plug-in	1027
Reading Parameters in Applets	1028
Using Java Consoles in Browsers	1029
Creating Text Fields	1030
Creating Buttons	1032
Handling Events	1033
Creating Labels	1038
Creating Checkboxes	1039
Creating Radio Buttons	1042
Using Fonts	1044
Handling Images	1047
Drawing Graphics	1049

In Depth

In the previous chapter, we worked through a lot of Java syntax, and in this chapter, we'll put it to work by creating Java applets. We're going to learn how to use the Java Abstract Windowing Toolkit (AWT) to create applets that you can embed in your Web pages.

NOTE: *Java 2 also includes the new Java Swing visual components, but I'll stick to the AWT due to space constraints. It takes considerable work to understand the handling of **javax** packages and to understand the various applet panes.*

TIP: *There's a lot of depth to Java programming, and of course only some of that depth will fit into this chapter. If you find yourself needing or wanting more details, take a look at my* Java Black Book *(The Coriolis Group, ©2000).*

The Abstract Windowing Toolkit

It's no exaggeration to say that the Abstract Windowing Toolkit (AWT) was the driving force behind Java's popularity. Using the AWT, you can create and display buttons, labels, menus, combo boxes, text fields, and other user-interface controls that users expect in windowed programs. The following list contains an overview of the most popular AWT classes:

- **Applet**—Creates an applet.
- **Button**—Creates a button.
- **Canvas**—Creates a canvas you can draw in.
- **Checkbox**—Creates a checkbox.
- **Choice**—Creates a choice control.
- **ComboBox**—Creates a combo box.
- **Dialog**—Creates a dialog box.
- **Frame**—Creates a frame for windowed applications.
- **Label**—Creates a label.
- **List**—Creates a list control.
- **Menu**—Creates a menu.
- **Panel**—Creates a panel that can contain other controls.
- **PopupMenu**—Creates a popup menu.

- **CheckboxGroup**—Creates a radio button.
- **Scrollbar**—Creates a scrollbar.
- **ScrollPane**—Creates a scrollable surface.
- **TextArea**—Creates a two-dimensional text control.
- **TextField**—Creates a one-dimensional text field (called a *text box* in other languages).
- **Window**—Creates a free-standing window.

The AWT **Applet** class is what you base AWT applets on, and I'll take a look at this class first.

Creating Applets

It's time to build an applet. AWT applets are built on the **Applet** class, which is in the **java.applet** package, so I'll start by importing that class into a new Java source-code file, which I'll call applet.java:

```
import java.applet.Applet;
        .
        .
        .
```

The **java.applet.Applet** class is the class that forms the base of standard applets. You *derive* your own applet classes from that class by using the **extends** keyword:

```
import java.applet.Applet;

public class applet extends Applet
{
        .
        .
        .
}
```

Deriving a class like this means that our new class is going to *inherit* all the functionality of the **java.applet.Applet** class, including all the built-in functions we'll use (see the discussion of inheritance in Chapter 16).

So far, so good. Now it's time to add code to this new applet. Applets don't have a **main** method like applications do—in fact, that's the chief code difference between applets and applications. So how can you display text directly in an applet?

The actual drawing of an applet is accomplished in its **paint** method, which Java calls when it's time to display the applet. The **java.applet.Applet** class has its own **paint** method, but we can *override* (an object-oriented programming term that means "redefine") that method by defining our own **paint** method:

```
import java.applet.Applet;
import java.awt.*;

public class applet extends Applet
{
    public void paint(Graphics g)
    {
        .
        .
        .
    }
}
```

The **paint** method is actually a part of the Java AWT. Because we'll be using the AWT a great deal here, I've imported the AWT classes with the statement **import java.awt.***. Here's how this method works: The **paint** method is passed a Java object of the **Graphics** class, and I'm naming this object **g** in this code. You can use this object's **drawString** method to actually draw the text. In this case, I'll draw the text "Hello from Java!" at location (60, 100) in the applet. Coordinates like (60, 100) are measured in pixels from the upper-left corner of the applet, so this position is 60 pixels from the left border of the applet and 100 pixels from the top. Here's what the code looks like:

```
import java.applet.Applet;
import java.awt.*;

public class applet extends Applet
{
    public void paint(Graphics g)
    {
        g.drawString("Hello from Java!", 60, 100);
    }
}
```

That's all it takes. Now, compile applet.java to applet.class by using the **javac** tool, as we did in the previous chapter. It looks like this in Windows:

```
C:\>javac applet.java
```

We're almost done. There's just one more step—creating and using a Web page to display the applet in, and I'll take a look at this next.

Running Applets

To display an applet, you can use a Web page with an **<applet>** element in it. Originally, the **<applet>** element was officially deprecated by the World Wide Web Consortium (W3C) in favor of the **<object>** element, but that seems to have changed in XHTML 1.1—the **<object>** element doesn't appear in XHTML 1.1, but the **<applet>** element does. That's good as far as applets go, because no browser, except Internet Explorer, lets you handle applets with the **<object>** element yet. I'll stick with the **<applet>** element in this chapter.

TIP: *To see how to use* **<object>** *in place of* **<applet>**, *see the section "***<applet>***—Embedding Applets in Web Pages" in the "Immediate Solutions" section of this chapter.*

The following Web page, applet.html, will display the applet we've developed (note that I specify the bytecode file for the applet, applet.class, in the **<applet>** element):

```
<?xml version="1.0"?>
<!DOCTYPE html PUBLIC "-//W3C//DTD XHTML 1.0 Transitional//EN"
"http://www.w3.org/tr/xhtml1/DTD/xhtml1-transitional.dtd">
<html xmlns="http://www.w3.org/1999/xhtml" xml:lang="en" lang="en">
    <head>
        <title>
            Applet Example
        </title>
    </head>

    <body>
        <hr />
        <center>
            <applet
                code="applet.class"
                width="200"
                height="200" >
            </applet>
        </center>
        <hr />
    </body>
</html>
```

Chapter 17 Creating Java Applets

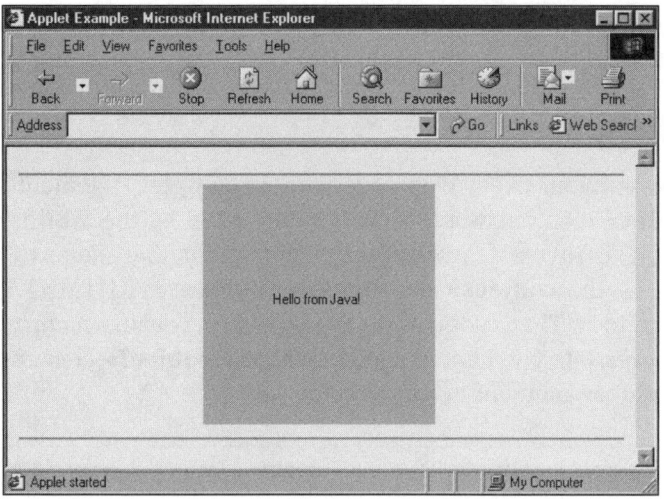

Figure 17.1   Running an applet in Internet Explorer.

You can open this Web page in a Web browser. Figure 17.1 shows the opened applet in Microsoft Internet Explorer.

There's a handy shortcut you can use with the Java Applet Viewer (appletviewer.exe) that comes with the Java Software Development Kit (SDK). You can embed the **<applet>** element right into the Java source code if you put the element into a Java comment:

```
import java.applet.Applet;
import java.awt.*;

/*
<applet
    code = "applet.class"
    width = "200"
    height = "200" >
</applet>
*/

public class applet extends Applet
{
    public void paint(Graphics g)
    {
        g.drawString("Hello from Java!", 60, 100);
    }
}
```

In Depth

The java compiler, javac, will ignore the **<applet>** element, but you can use the Java Applet Viewer with this file directly, so you don't have to create a separate HTML Web page while developing your applet, as here in Windows:

```
C:\>appletviewer applet.java
```

You can see the results in Figure 17.2; I'll use this technique often in this chapter.

Uploading Applets

You've run the applet you saw in Figures 17.1 and 17.2 on your local computer—but how do you install them on your Web server? You first compile an applet into a bytecode .class file. When you have your .class file, you upload it to your Internet Service Provider (ISP) by using a File Transfer Protocol (FTP) program. Some ISPs have Web pages that let you upload files. Contact your ISP's technical staff to determine how to upload files.

You can give the applet the same protection you would give a Web page, making sure that anyone can read the applet .class file. (For example, in Unix, you might give the applet the permission setting 644, which lets anyone read the file; this is the default protection that many FTP programs give to uploaded files on Unix systems.)

TIP: *Unix file permissions consist of three octal digits corresponding to, in order, the file owner's permission, the permission of others in the same user group, and the permission of all others. In each octal digit, a value of 4 indicates read permission, a value of 2 indicates write permission, and a value of 1 indicates execute permission. You add these values together to set the individual digits in a permission setting—for example, a permission of 600 means that the file's owner, and only the file's owner, can both read and write the file.*

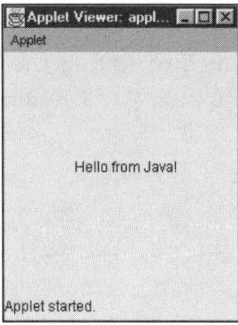

Figure 17.2 Running an applet in the Java Applet Viewer.

Although you're reading the applet from the Web now, you can still embed the new applet in a Web page with the **<applet>** element. You do this by indicating the name of the .class file for the applet and by telling the Web browser how much space (in pixels) to leave for the applet:

```
<?xml version="1.0"?>
<!DOCTYPE html PUBLIC "-//W3C//DTD XHTML 1.0 Transitional//EN"
"http://www.w3.org/tr/xhtml1/DTD/xhtml1-transitional.dtd">
<html xmlns="http://www.w3.org/1999/xhtml" xml:lang="en" lang="en">
    <head>
        <title>
            Applet Example
        </title>
    </head>

    <body>

        <center>
            <applet
                code = "applet.class"
                width = "300"
                height = "200"
            >
            </applet>
        </center>
    </body>
</html>
```

In this case, I've set up a centered 300×200 pixel space in a Web page in which to display the applet, and I've told the Web browser to download the applet.class file and run it.

This example is okay if the applet's .class file is in the same directory as the Web page. But if you want to specify a different URL for the applet, you can use the **codebase** attribute of the **<applet>** element:

```
<?xml version="1.0"?>
<!DOCTYPE html PUBLIC "-//W3C//DTD XHTML 1.0 Transitional//EN"
"http://www.w3.org/tr/xhtml1/DTD/xhtml1-transitional.dtd">
<html xmlns="http://www.w3.org/1999/xhtml" xml:lang="en" lang="en">
    <head>
        <title>
            Applet Example
        </title>
    </head>
```

```
            <body>
                <hr />
                <center>
                    <applet
                        code = "applet.class"
                        codebase="http://www.starpowder.com/steve"
                        width= "300"
                        height = "200" >
                    </applet>
                </center>
                <hr />
            </body>
</html>
```

See the section "**<applet>**—Embedding Applets in Web Pages" in the "Immediate Solutions" section for more details about the attributes of the **<applet>** element.

Controls in Applets

So far, this applet doesn't actually do anything very useful, like respond to the user. But we can change that. One of the biggest features of applets is letting the user interact with the program, and you do that with *events*. When the user performs some action—clicking a button, closing a window, selecting an item in a list, or using the mouse, for example—Java, like JavaScript, considers each of these an event. (See "Handling Events" later in this chapter.)

You use events with controls such as text fields, buttons, checkboxes, and so on. Just like HTML, Java supports these controls, and they work similarly to the way they do in HTML. In the following sections, I'll briefly look at the controls we'll see in this chapter.

Text Fields

As in HTML, text fields are the basic text-handling components of the AWT. These components handle a one-dimensional string of text that lets you display text, lets the user enter text, allows you to take passwords by masking typed text, reads the text the user has entered, and more. These components and buttons are the most fundamental AWT components.

Buttons

Buttons provide the user with a quick way to start some action—all users have to do is to click them. Every user is familiar with buttons, and we've already taken a look at buttons in HTML. You can give buttons a label, and when the user clicks the button, your code is notified of the event.

Checkboxes

Checkboxes are much like buttons except that they are *dual state*, which means that they can appear as selected or unselected. When selected, they display a visual indication of some kind, such as a checkmark or an X. (The indicator varies by operating system in AWT programming, which is one of the reasons Sun Microsystems introduced Swing; Swing can display components with the same appearance across many operating systems.)

The user can click a checkbox to select options, such as choosing items in a sandwich, enabling automatic spelling checking, or enabling background printing. You use checkboxes to let the user select nonexclusive options; for example, both automatic spelling checking and background printing may be enabled at the same time. Radio buttons, however, are a different story.

Radio Buttons

As in HTML, you let the user select one of a set of mutually exclusive options by using radio buttons. Only one of a set of option buttons can be selected at one time; for example, using radio buttons, you can let the user select a printing color or the day of the week. In the AWT, radio buttons are actually a type of checkbox, and when selected, they display a round dot, a clicked square, or some other indicator (again, the visual indicator depends on the operating system). You use radio buttons in groups, and we'll see how this works in the "Immediate Solutions" section "Creating Radio Buttons."

Graphics in Applets

The final topic I'll take a look at in this chapter is graphics, an important topic in Java. The following list contains some of the AWT graphics methods:

- **draw3DRect**—Draws a 3D rectangle.
- **drawArc**—Draws an arc.
- **drawBytes**—Draws text, given a byte array.
- **drawChars**—Draws text, given a character array.
- **drawImage**—Draws an image.
- **drawLine**—Draws a line.
- **drawOval**—Draws an oval, including circles.
- **drawPolygon**—Draws a polygon.
- **drawPolyline**—Draws a line with multiple segments.
- **drawRect**—Draws a rectangle.
- **drawRoundRect**—Draws a rounded rectangle.

- **drawString**—Draws a string of text.
- **paint**—Called when the applet is to be redrawn.
- **repaint**—Called to force the applet to be painted.
- **setBackground**—Sets the background color.
- **setForeground**—Sets the foreground (drawing) color.

Two methods that are particularly worth noting are the **paint** method, in which you paint the applet, and the **repaint** method, which forces the **paint** method to be called to redraw the applet (for instance, when it's been updated).

Immediate Solutions

Creating Applets

"Finally!" says the novice programmer. "At last I'm ready to create an applet." "That's right," you say; "now which one would you like to create?" "Hm," says the NP.

You base standard applets on the **java.applet.Applet** class, which is itself subclassed from the **jawa.awt.Container** class:

```
java.lang.Object
|____java.awt.Component
     |____java.awt.Container
          |____java.awt.Panel
               |____java.applet.Applet
```

Let's see an example. Here, I'll create the applet that we saw earlier in this chapter; the applet displayed the text "Hello from Java!" in the file applet.java. I start by deriving a new class, **applet**, from the **java.applet.Applet** class:

```
import java.applet.Applet;

public class applet extends Applet
{
        .
        .
        .
}
```

To display the message in the applet, I'll use the **paint** method, which the applet inherits from the **Container** class. When an applet is displayed, its **paint** method is called, and in that method you can place the code you want to draw in the applet. The **paint** method is passed an object of the **Graphics** class, which is the basis of graphical work in applets. This object supports a method named **drawString**, which I'll use to draw a string of text in the applet. The **Graphics** class is an AWT class, so I'll import the AWT classes when I override the default **Applet paint** method:

```
import java.applet.Applet;
import java.awt.*;

public class applet extends Applet
{
    public void paint(Graphics g)
    {
        .
        .
        .
    }
}
```

Now I customize the overridden **paint** method to draw the text "Hello from Java!" at location (60, 100) in the applet. Applet coordinates are in pixels, so (60, 100) is 60 pixels from the left edge of the applet and 100 pixels below the top of the applet. Here's the code:

```
import java.applet.Applet;
import java.awt.*;

public class applet extends Applet
{
    public void paint(Graphics g)
    {
        g.drawString("Hello from Java!", 60, 100);
    }
}
```

This new **paint** method draws directly on the surface of the applet. Note that you also can place controls such as buttons and text fields directly on the surface of the applet. We'll see how this works in "Immediate Solutions" sections such as "Creating Text Fields" and "Creating Buttons."

You can compile applet.java into applet.class by using javac. Now you've created an applet. It's time to get a look at the applet at work—see the next section.

<applet>—Embedding Applets in Web Pages

Purpose: Embeds applets in Web pages. This is the big tag as far as applets go.

When used as HTML: Start tag/End tag: Required/Required

Supported: [1.0T, 1.0F, 1.1, 3.2, 4, IE3, IE4, IE5, NS2, NS3, NS4]

Attributes:

- **accesskey**—Sets the access key for the element. [IE5]
- **align**—Specifies the alignment of text following or next to the applet. Set to: **left**, **right**, **top**, **bottom**, **middle**, **baseline**, **texttop**, **absmiddle**, or **absbottom**. [1.0T, 1.0F, 3.2, 4, IE3, IE4, IE5, NS2, NS3, NS4]
- **alt**—Text to be displayed if a browser supports applets but cannot run this one for some reason. Set to alphanumeric characters. [1.0T, 1.0F, 3.2, 4, IE3, IE4, IE5, NS2, NS3, NS4]
- **archive**—Used when you've stored the applet in a Java Archive (JAR) or ZIP file to reduce download time. Set to a URL. [1.0T, 1.0F, 4, NS3, NS4]
- **class**—Class of the element (used for rendering). [1.0T, 1.0F, 4, IE4, IE5]
- **code**—Indicates a URL pointing to the applet's class. Set to a URL. [1.0T, 1.0F, 3.2, 4, IE3, IE4, IE5, NS2, NS3, NS4]
- **codebase**—Specifies the base URL of the applet if the **code** attribute is relative. And if the **codebase** URL is relative, it is treated as such in relation to the current document URL or the **base href** element. Set to a URL. [1.0T, 1.0F, 3.2, 4, IE3, IE4, IE5, NS2, NS3, NS4]
- **contenteditable**—Set to **true** if the content can be edited. [IE5]
- **datafld**—Name of the column of the data-source object that supplies the bound data. Set to alphanumeric characters. [IE4, IE5]
- **datasrc**—Gives the URL or ID of the data-source object supplying data bound to this element. W3C says this should be a URL; Internet Explorer says it should be a data-source ID. [IE4, IE5]
- **disabled**—Indicates whether the element is disabled. [IE5]
- **height**—Specifies the height of the space reserved for the applet in the Web page. Set to positive pixel values. Required. [1.0T, 1.0F, 3.2, 4, IE3, IE4, IE5, NS2, NS3, NS4]
- **hspace**—Specifies the padding space allocated to the right and left of the applet. Set to pixel values. [1.0T, 1.0F, 3.2, 4, IE3, IE4, IE5, NS2, NS3, NS4]
- **id**—Unique alphanumeric identifier for the tag; use the ID to refer to the tag. [1.0T, 1.0F, 4, IE3, IE4, IE5]
- **lang**—Base language used for the tag. [1.0T, 1.0F, IE4, IE5]
- **language**—Scripting language used for the tag. [IE4, IE5]
- **mayscript**—Gives the applet access to JavaScript in a page. Standalone attribute. [NS3, NS4]

- **name**—Name of the applet in the Web browser; applets must be given names if you want other applets or scripts to find and interact with them. Set to alphanumeric characters. [1.0T, 1.0F, 3.2, 4, IE3, IE4, IE5, NS2, NS3, NS4]

- **object**—Gives the name of the resource that contains a serialized representation of an applet (the applet will be deserialized by the browser). Set to alphanumeric characters. [1.0T, 1.0F, 4]

- **src**—Specifies a URL reference to an applet (similar to the **code** and **codebase** attributes). Set to a URL. [IE4, IE5]

- **style**—Inline style indicating how to render the element. [1.0T, 1.0F, 4, IE4, IE5]

- **tabindex**—Holds the tab index for the element. [IE4, IE5]

- **title**—Holds additional information (which might be displayed in tool tips). [1.0T, 1.0F, 3, 4, IE4, IE5]

- **vspace**—Specifies the padding space allocated above and below the applet. Set to pixel values. [1.0T, 1.0F, 3.2, 4, IE3, IE4, IE5, NS2, NS3, NS4]

- **width**—Specifies the width of the space reserved for the applet in the Web page. Set to positive pixel values. Required. [1.0T, 1.0F, 3.2, 4, IE3, IE4, IE5, NS2, NS3, NS4]

- **xml:lang**—Holds the base language for the element when the document is interpreted as an XML document. [1.0S, 1.0T, 1.0F]

XHTML events: onclick, **ondblclick**, **onmousedown**, **onmouseup**, **onmouseover**, **onmousemove**, **onmouseout**, **onkeypress**, **onkeydown**, **onkeyup**

"OK," says the novice programmer, "I've created an applet and compiled it into a .class file. How do I actually *look* at it?" "You can use the HTML **<applet>** element," you say.

When you've created an applet's .class file, you can upload the applet to an ISP (or view it on your own machine) and set its protection (see the "In Depth" section of this chapter) so it can be read. Next, you can create a Web page using the **<applet>** element to display the applet.

The Web page, applet.html, displays the applet we created in the previous section. Note that in XHTML, the only required attributes are the **width** and **height** attributes:

```
<?xml version="1.0"?>
<!DOCTYPE html PUBLIC "-//W3C//DTD XHTML 1.0 Transitional//EN"
 "http://www.w3.org/tr/xhtml1/DTD/xhtml1-transitional.dtd">
<html xmlns="http://www.w3.org/1999/xhtml" xml:lang="en" lang="en">
```

```
<head>
    <title>
        Applet Example
    </title>
</head>

<body>

    <center>
        <applet
            code = "applet.class"
            width = "200"
            height = "300"
        >
        </applet>
    </center>
</body>
</html>
```

In this case, I'm not specifying a code base, so I place applet.class in the same directory as applet.html. This Web page, opened in Internet Explorer, appears in Figure 17.1. You can also use the Java Applet Viewer to view applets, opening the Web page in Windows:

```
C:\>appletviewer applet.html
```

The results appear in Figure 17.2.

TIP: *The Java Applet Viewer that comes in the Java SDK always supports the latest version of Java, so if your Web browser doesn't, and you don't want to install the Java plug-in, you can always use the Java Applet Viewer to test your applets.*

Originally, the **<object>** element was intended to supersede the **<applet>** element, but now **<object>** is missing from XHTML 1.1, and **<applet>** is supported. Nonetheless, there is some support for applets in the Internet Explorer using **<object>** element (in addition to **<applet>**). Here's how it works: you can set the **<object>** element's **classid** attribute like this: **<object classid= "java:*filename.class*">**. You should also provide the appropriate Multipurpose Internet Mail Extension (MIME) type for the applet, like this: **<object classid="java:*filename.class*" codetype="application/octet-stream">**. If your applet is in another location, you can specify that location with the **codebase** attribute, like this: **<object classid="java:*filename.class*" codetype= "application/octet-stream" codebase="*URL*">**.

Handling Non-Java Browsers

"Uh oh," says the novice programmer, "There's a problem. Some users are using a slightly nonstandard Web browser named *SuperWildcat14b*—" "That does sound slightly nonstandard," you say. "And," the NP continues, "it doesn't support Java. Is there any way to inform those users that they're missing something?" "There sure is," you say. "Pull up a chair and we'll go through it."

If you enclose text inside an **<applet>** element, that text will be displayed if the Web browser does not support Java. For example, here's how you might alert users that they're missing your applet:

```
<applet code = "applet.class" width = "100" height = "100">
    Sorry, you don't have Java, so you can't see my beautiful applet.
</applet>
```

Using the init, start, stop, destroy, paint, and update Methods—and Setting Applet Color

The novice programmer is back and says, "My browser has gone all wacky—it draws my applets in gray!" "That's the default for many Web browsers," you say. "But you can change that by using the **init** method to add some initialization code to your applet."

Your applet will inherit several important applet methods from the **java.applet.Applet** class. These include:

- **destroy**—Called when the applet is about to be removed from memory. You can perform cleanup here.
- **init**—Called first; called only once. You initialize the applet here.
- **paint**—Called when the applet is to be redrawn. This method is passed an object of the **Graphics** class, and you can use that object's methods to draw in the applet.
- **start**—Called after **init**. The **start** method is called each time an applet appears again on the screen. That is, if the user moves to another page and then comes back, the **start** method is called again.
- **stop**—Called when the browser moves to another page. You can use this method to stop additional execution threads that your applet might have started.
- **update**—Called when a portion of the applet is to be redrawn. The default version fills the applet with the background color before redrawing the

applet. This can lead to flickering when the applet is performing animation, so you often override this method in that case.

You can override (that is, redefine) these methods to customize them as you like. I've already overridden the **paint** method to draw a string of text in the "In Depth" section of this chapter. Here I override the **init** method to change the background of the applet to white; I'm using the applet **setBackground** method and passing it the **white** property of the Java **Color** class. This applet also provides a skeletal implementation of the other methods listed previously:

```java
import java.applet.Applet;
import java.awt.*;

/*
<applet
    code = "applet.class"
    width = "200"
    height = "200" >
</applet>
*/

public class applet extends Applet
{
    public void init()
    {
        setBackground(Color.white);
    }

    public void start()
    {
    }

    public void paint(Graphics g)
    {
        g.drawString("Hello from Java!", 60, 100);
    }

    public void stop()
    {
    }

    public void destroy()
    {
    }
}
```

The **init** method is a very useful one, and it's commonly overridden because it lets you initialize your applet. In this case, I've changed the background color from the default gray in many browsers to white. Applets excel at graphics, and I'll take a brief look at handling graphics in applets at the end of this chapter; see the section "Drawing Graphics."

TIP: *You can specify colors as **Color.white**, **Color.black**, **Color.cyan**, **Color.magenta**, **Color.pink**, and others. However, you can also create your own colors by using color triplets, just as in a Web page. For example, to create a new color, you can specify red, green, and blue values (in the 0 through 255 range) for the **Color** class's constructor: **Color c = new Color(red, green, blue);**.*

Using the Java Browser Plug-in

"Hey," says the novice programmer, "there's a problem. I'm using the big two Web browsers, but they don't support the latest Java features. What can I do?" "There's an easy solution," you say. "Use the Java plug-in."

The Java plug-in lets you run the latest version of Java applets in Netscape Navigator and Internet Explorer by implementing the Java runtime environment as a plug-in for Netscape and an ActiveX control for Internet Explorer. You can download the plug-in from **http://java.sun.com/products/plugin/**. It's also installed automatically when you install the Java SDK.

To use Web pages with the plug-in, you need to convert their HTML first by using the Sun HTML Converter, which you can also get at **http://java.sun.com/products/plugin/**. The HTML Converter is a Java .class file that you run on HTML pages to convert the **<applet>** element to use the plug-in.

To convert a Web page to use the plug-in, you select an HTML file or files in the HTML Converter and click the Convert button. The Converter will change an **<applet>** tag like this:

```
<applet code=adder.class width=200 height=200></applet>
```

into something like this:

```
<!--"CONVERTED_applet"-->
<!-- CONVERTER VERSION 1.0 -->
<OBJECT classid="clsid:8AD9C840-044E-11D1-B3E9-00805F499D93"
width = 200 height = 200
codebase="http://java.sun.com/products/plugin/1.2/jinstall-12-
```

```
                win32.cab#Version=1,2,0,0">
                <param NAME = code VALUE = adder.class >

                <param NAME="type" VALUE="application/x-java-applet;version=1.2">
                <COMMENT>
                <EMBED type="application/x-java-applet;version=1.2" java_code =
                adder.class width = 200 height = 200
                pluginspage="http://java.sun.com/products/plugin/1.2/plugin-
                install.html"><NOEMBED></COMMENT>

                </NOEMBED></EMBED>
                </object>

                <!--
                <applet  code = adder.class width = 200 height = 200 >


                </applet>
                -->
                <!--"END_CONVERTED_applet"-->
```

The new HTML file will use the Java plug-in instead of the browser's default.

Reading Parameters in Applets

The big boss appears, chomping on a cigar, and says, "We need to personalize the greeting in our applet by customer." "But there are thousands of customers," you say. "We can't recompile the applet for each one and store each new version on the Web site." "What do you suggest?" the BB asks. What will you say?

You can pass parameters to applets in the **<applet>** element, and the applet code can read the value of those parameters; this means that to customize the applet, you only need to supply different parameters in the **<applet>** element. To actually get the value of a parameter, you use the **Applet** class's **getParameter** method, passing it the name of the parameter as specified in the **<param>** element (which we first saw in Chapter 8). The **getParameter** method will return the value of the parameter that was set in the **<param>** element.

Here's an example in which I pass a parameter named **string** to an applet; the value of this parameter is the text that the applet should display. Here's how this looks in code:

```
import java.applet.Applet;
import java.awt.*;
```

```
/*
<applet
    code = "applet.class"
    width = "200"
    height = "200" >
    <param name = "string" value = "Hello from Java!">
</applet>
*/

public class applet extends Applet
{
    public void paint(Graphics g)
    {
        g.drawString(getParameter("string"), 60, 100);
    }
}
```

Using Java Consoles in Browsers

"All this **drawString** stuff is OK," the novice programmer says, "But what about the Java console? What if I use **System.out.println**, which you use for text output in Java applications, in an applet?" "That depends," you say, "on your browser."

Here's an applet that displays a message and uses **System.out.println** to print to the console:

```
import java.applet.Applet;
import java.awt.*;

/*
<applet
    code = "applet.class"
    width = "200"
    height = "200" >
</applet>
*/

public class applet extends Applet
{
    public void paint(Graphics g)
    {
        g.drawString("Hello from Java!", 60, 100);
        System.out.println("Hello from Java!");
    }
}
```

If you run this applet with the Java Applet Viewer, the applet will open in a separate window and you'll see "Hello from Java!" in the console window.

Web browsers often have a Java console as well, although you often have to enable them before using them. The way to enable the Java console differs, unfortunately, not only from browser to browser, but also from version to version. Currently, you enable the Java console in Internet Explorer by selecting Tools|Internet Options, clicking the Advanced tab, and selecting the Java Console Enabled checkbox. Figure 17.3 shows the result of the previous applet as it appears in Internet Explorer's Java console, which pops up when you print to it.

In Netscape Navigator, you can open the Java console by selecting Communicator|Tools|Java Console.

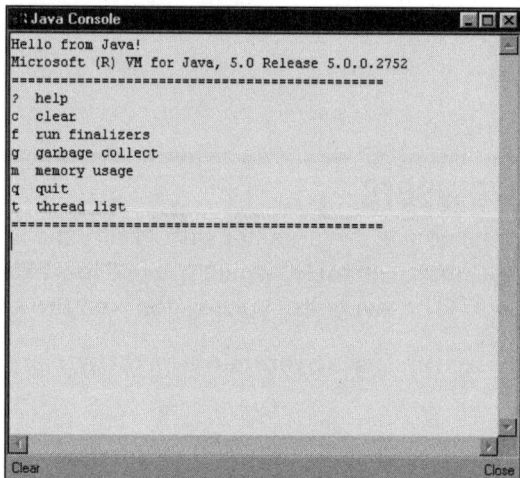

Figure 17.3 Using Internet Explorer's Java console.

Creating Text Fields

"OK," says the novice programmer, "I can draw text in an applet now. But what if I want to let the user *enter* some text?" "For that," you say, "you can use all kinds of text controls, such as text fields."

In Java, text fields are supported with the **TextField** class. Here is the inheritance diagram for the **TextField** class:

```
java.lang.Object
   |____java.awt.Component
         |____java.awt.TextComponent
               |____java.awt.TextField
```

Text fields are the most basic controls you can use in the AWT, so they provide a good starting point. A text field displays and lets the user edit text as displayed on a single line. Here's a text field example. In this case, I'm creating a text field 20 characters wide in an applet's **init** method; note also that I'm importing the AWT classes to be able to use text fields:

```
import java.applet.Applet;
import java.awt.*;

/*
<applet
    code = "applet.class"
    width = "200"
    height = "200" >
</applet>
*/

public class applet extends Applet
{
    public TextField text1;

    public void init()
    {
        text1 = new TextField(20);
        .
        .
        .
    }
}
```

After creating a new control, you must *add* it to the applet so it's displayed:

```
    public void init()
    {
        text1 = new TextField(20);
        add(text1);
        .
        .
        .
    }
```

The **add** method adds the control to the current *layout manager*, which decides where the control should be placed. Java comes with a number of layout managers; here, I'll just use the default flow layout manager, which arranges controls like a word processor arranges words, across the first line and then down to the next line and so on. Now that the text field has been added to the applet, I can place the text "Hello from Java!" in the text field with the **setText** method:

```
public void init()
{
    text1 = new TextField(20);
    add(text1);
    text1.setText("Hello from Java!");
}
```

The results of this code appear in Figure 17.4, where you can see the text field with the message we've put into it. The user can also edit that text.

Another basic control is the AWT button control; I'll use buttons and text fields to discuss event handling, so I'll introduce the button control in the next section.

Figure 17.4   Adding a text field to an applet.

Creating Buttons

"I'm ready for the next step," the novice programmer reports; "I've added text fields to my applets; what's next?" "Buttons," you say; "pull up a chair and let's talk about them."

Every user of a graphical user interface (GUI) is familiar with buttons—those elementary controls that you click to signal a program to start some action. For example, you might let the user click a button to change the background color of an application. Buttons are supported in the **java.awt.Button** class, and here is the lineage of that class:

```
java.lang.Object
|____java.awt.Component
     |____java.awt.Button
```

Users can click buttons in your applet to signal that they want to perform some action; for example, you might have a button labeled "Change Color," which, when clicked, changes the background color of the applet by using the **setBackground** method. It's easy enough to add a button to an applet; you can do this in much the same way as adding a text field to an applet. In this case, I'm creating and adding a button with the label "Click Here!":

```
public class applet extends Applet
{
    TextField text1;
    Button button1;

    public void init()
    {
        text1 = new TextField(20);
        add(text1);
        button1 = new Button("Click Here!");
        add(button1);
        .
        .
        .
    }
}
```

The real trick is to get something to happen when you click the button, and for that, we'll have to look at event handling; see the next section.

Handling Events

"Hey," says the novice programmer, "I've put a button into my applet, but when I click it, nothing happens. What gives?" "What gives," you say, "is that you have to implement event handling."

Event handling—the process of responding to button clicks, mouse movements, and so on—has become a complex topic in Java. Starting with Java 1.1, event handling changed significantly; the current model is called *delegated event handling*. In this model of event handling, you must specifically *register* with Java if you want to handle a particular event, like a button click. (The idea is that performance is improved if only the code that handles specific events is informed of those events, and not the rest of your code.)

You register for events by using an *event listener interface*. The following list contains the available event listeners and the kinds of events they handle:

- **ActionListener**—Handles action events, such as button clicks.
- **AdjustmentListener**—Handles adjustment events, such as scrollbar movements.
- **AWTEventListener**—Handles AWT events.
- **ComponentListener**—Handles cases in which a component is hidden, moved, resized, or shown.
- **ContainerListener**—Handles the cases in which a component is added to or removed from a container.
- **FocusListener**—Handles the cases in which a component gains or loses the focus.
- **InputMethodListener**—Handles **input** method events.
- **ItemListener**—Handles the case in which the state of an item changes.
- **KeyListener**—Listens for keyboard events.
- **MouseListener**—Listens for the cases in which the mouse is clicked, enters a component, exits a component, or is pressed.
- **MouseMotionListener**—Listens for the case in which the mouse is dragged or moved.
- **TextListener**—Listens for text value changes.
- **WindowListener**—Handles the cases in which a window is activated, closed, deactivated, deiconified, iconified, opened, or quit.

Each listener is a Java interface, and it's up to you to implement the methods of the interface (that is, add those methods to your code, even if you leave them empty). An *interface* is much like a Java class except that you use the **implements** keyword when you're inheriting from it instead of from the **extends** keyword. Like classes, interfaces can have methods, and each of those methods is passed a type of event object that corresponds to the kind of event. Following is a list of the types of event objects:

- **ActionEvent**—Handles buttons, list controls, double-clicks, and menu-item clicks.
- **AdjustmentEvent**—Handles scrollbar movements.
- **ComponentEvent**—Handles the cases in which a component is hidden, moved, resized, or shown.
- **ContainerEvent**—Indicates a change in a container's contents when a component is added or removed. A low-level event.
- **FocusEvent**—Handles the cases in which a component gains or loses the focus.

- **InputEvent**—Handles checkbox or list-item clicks when a choice control selection is made or a checkable menu item is clicked.
- **InputMethodEvent**—Holds information about text that is being composed using an **input** method.
- **InvocationEvent**—Executes the **run** method when dispatched by the AWT event dispatcher thread.
- **KeyEvent**—Handles input from the keyboard.
- **MouseEvent**—Handles the cases in which the mouse is dragged, moved, clicked, pressed, or released, or the mouse enters or exits a component.
- **PaintEvent**—Occurs when an element is painted.
- **TextEvent**—Occurs when the value of a text field or text area is changed.
- **WindowEvent**—Handles the cases in which a window is activated, closed, deactivated, deiconified, opened, or quit.

It's time to put some of this knowledge to work. I'll start by adding a new button with the text "Click Me!" to an applet and adding an action listener, which will be notified when the button is clicked. To add an action listener to the button, you use the button's **addActionListener** method, passing it an object that implements the methods of the **ActionListener** interface. This object can be an object of the applet's **main** class, which means that we'll have to implement the methods of the interface in that class.

*TIP: You can also unregister an event listener by using the **removeListener** method.*

Here's how I add an action listener to a button with **addActionListener(this)**. As in JavaScript, the **this** keyword refers to the current object, so here I'm passing the current applet object to **addActionListener**. The result is that Java will send event notifications to the current applet object—note also that I indicate that the **Applet** class now implements the **ActionListener** interface with the **implements** keyword:

```
import java.applet.Applet;
import java.awt.*;
import java.awt.event.*;

/*
<applet
    code = "applet.class"
    width = "200"
    height = "200" >
</applet>
*/
```

```java
public class applet extends Applet implements ActionListener
{
    TextField text1;
    Button button1;

    public void init()
    {
        text1 = new TextField(20);
        add(text1);
        button1 = new Button("Click Here!");
        add(button1);
        button1.addActionListener(this);
    }
}
   .
   .
   .
```

Because action listener events will now be passed to the main **applet** object, I have to implement the methods of the **ActionListener** interface in that object. This interface has only one method, **actionPerformed**, which is passed an object of the **ActionEvent** class when the button is clicked:

```
void actionPerformed(ActionEvent e)
```

TIP: *The documentation that comes with Java, as well as the* Java Black Book *(The Coriolis Group, ©2000), lists every method an interface has, which objects are passed to them, and the methods of those objects.*

ActionEvent objects inherit a method named **getSource** from the **EventObject** class, and this method returns the object that caused the event. This means that I can check whether this event was caused by the button, **button1**, and if so, place the text "Hello from Java!" into the text field, **text1**, in the **actionPerformed** method that's called when the button is clicked:

```java
import java.applet.Applet;
import java.awt.*;
import java.awt.event.*;

/*
<applet
    code = "applet.class"
    width = "200"
```

```
        height = "200" >
</applet>
*/

public class applet extends Applet implements ActionListener
{
    TextField text1;
    Button button1;

    public void init()
    {
        text1 = new TextField(20);
        add(text1);
        button1 = new Button("Click Here!");
        add(button1);
        button1.addActionListener(this);
    }

    public void actionPerformed(ActionEvent event)
    {
        String msg = new String ("Hello from Java!");
        if(event.getSource() == button1){
            text1.setText(msg);
        }
    }
}
```

This applet appears in Figure 17.5. When you click the button, the text "Hello from Java!" appears in the text field.

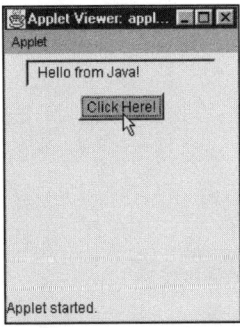

Figure 17.5   Supporting button clicks.

Creating Labels

AWT labels are much like AWT text fields except that the user can't edit the text in the labels. You can use labels to present noneditable text or, as their name implies, to label other components. Here is the inheritance diagram for the **Label** class:

```
java.lang.Object
|____java.awt.Component
     |____java.awt.Label
```

You can justify the text in a label by passing the fields **Label.LEFT**, **Label.CENTER**, and **Label.RIGHT** to the label's constructor. Here's an example that creates three labels with the various possible text justifications in an example named label.java:

```java
import java.applet.Applet;
import java.awt.*;

/*
<applet
    code=label.class
    width = "200"
    height = "200" >
</applet>
*/

public class label extends Applet
{
    Label label1;
    Label label2;
    Label label3;

    public void init()
    {
        label1 = new Label("Hello from Java!", Label.LEFT);
        add(label1);
        label2 = new Label("Hello from Java!", Label.CENTER);
        add(label2);
        label3 = new Label("Hello from Java!", Label.RIGHT);
        add(label3);
    }
}
```

The results of this applet appear in Figure 17.6.

Figure 17.6   Aligning text in a label.

Creating Checkboxes

"Now there's another problem," the novice programmer says; "I want to let users select what they want on a pizza, so I'd like a button, when clicked, to stay clicked so users knows what they've already selected." "No problem at all," you say. "Don't use buttons." "No?" the NP asks. "No," you say; "use checkboxes."

A checkbox allows the user to select options; when the user clicks a checkbox, a visual indication, such as a checkmark, appears to indicate that the option is selected. (The indicator varies for each operating system when you're using the AWT.) Clicking the checkbox again deselects the checkbox. In AWT, checkboxes are supported with the **java.awt.Checkbox** class, which has this inheritance diagram:

```
java.lang.Object
|____java.awt.Component
      |____java.awt.Checkbox
```

Note in particular that you can set the state of checkboxes with **setState** and get the state with **getState**.

Here's an example. I'll add four checkboxes to an applet and, when the user clicks a checkbox, indicate in a text field which checkbox was clicked. Note that checkboxes do not use **ActionListeners** as buttons do; instead, they use **ItemListeners**, which are set up to handle components that can be selected or deselected. The **ItemListener** interface has only one method, **itemStateChanged**, which is passed a parameter of class **ItemEvent**:

```
void itemStateChanged(ItemEvent e)
```

Here's how I add the checkboxes to an applet and add an **ItemListener** to each one in an example named checks.java:

```
import java.applet.Applet;
import java.awt.*;
import java.awt.event.*;
```

```java
/*
<applet
    code=checks.class
    width = "200"
    height = "200" >
</applet>
*/

public class checks extends Applet implements ItemListener {
    Checkbox checkbox1, checkbox2, checkbox3, checkbox4;
    TextField text1;

    public void init()
    {
        checkbox1 = new Checkbox("1");
        add(checkbox1);
        checkbox1.addItemListener(this);
        checkbox2 = new Checkbox("2");
        add(checkbox2);
        checkbox2.addItemListener(this);
        checkbox3 = new Checkbox("3");
        add(checkbox3);
        checkbox3.addItemListener(this);
        checkbox4 = new Checkbox("4");
        add(checkbox4);
        checkbox4.addItemListener(this);
        text1 = new TextField(20);
        add(text1);
    }
```

Now I override the **itemStateChanged** method, determining which checkbox was clicked by using the **ItemEvent** object's **getItemSelectable** method:

```java
    public void itemStateChanged(ItemEvent e)
    {
        if(e.getItemSelectable() == checkbox1){
            text1.setText("Check box 1 clicked!");
        } else if(e.getItemSelectable() == checkbox2){
            text1.setText("Check box 2 clicked!");
        } else if(e.getItemSelectable() == checkbox3){
            text1.setText("Check box 3 clicked!");
        } else if(e.getItemSelectable() == checkbox4){
            text1.setText("Check box 4 clicked!");
        }
    }
}
```

You can also use the **ItemEvent** object's **getStateChanged** method to determine whether the checkbox was selected or deselected; this method returns **Checkbox.SELECTED** or **Checkbox.DESELECTED**. And, of course, you can use the checkbox's **getState** method to make the same determination. You can also set the state of the checkbox with the **setState** method.

The results of this applet appear in Figure 17.7.

It's tedious to have so many **if** statements in the if-else ladder in the previous code, so in an example named checks2.java, I can display the clicked checkbox by getting its label directly:

```
import java.applet.Applet;
import java.awt.*;
import java.awt.event.*;

/*
<applet
    code=checks2.class
    width = "200"
    height = "200" >
</applet>
*/

public class checks2 extends Applet implements ItemListener {
    Checkbox checkbox1, checkbox2, checkbox3, checkbox4;
    TextField text1;

    public void init()
    {
        checkbox1 = new Checkbox("1");
        add(checkbox1);
```

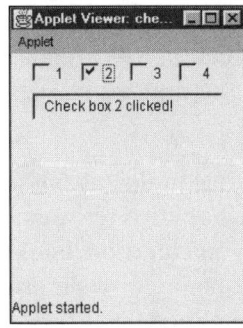

Figure 17.7 Handling checkbox clicks.

Chapter 17 Creating Java Applets

```java
            checkbox1.addItemListener(this);
            checkbox2 = new Checkbox("2");
            add(checkbox2);
            checkbox2.addItemListener(this);
            checkbox3 = new Checkbox("3");
            add(checkbox3);
            checkbox3.addItemListener(this);
            checkbox4 = new Checkbox("4");
            add(checkbox4);
            checkbox4.addItemListener(this);
            text1 = new TextField(20);
            add(text1);
        }

        public void itemStateChanged(ItemEvent e)
        {
            text1.setText("Check box " +
                ((Checkbox) e.getItemSelectable()).getLabel() + " clicked!");
        }
    }
```

There's another kind of checkbox you can use—radio buttons—and I'll take a look at these in the next section.

Creating Radio Buttons

"Uh oh," says the novice programmer; "there's another problem. I put some checkboxes in my program so the user could select the day of the week, but one user selected Wednesday *and* Friday." "Well," you say, "you should use radio buttons to display exclusive options like days of the week, not checkboxes."

In AWT programming, radio buttons are a special kind of checkbox; you use radio buttons in groups. Only one radio button in a group can be selected at one time. When the user selects one radio button in a group, the others in the group are automatically deselected.

When you add checkboxes to a checkbox group, they become radio buttons automatically. The AWT supports checkbox groups with the **CheckboxGroup** class. Note that because radio buttons are really checkboxes, you can use **Checkbox** methods such as **getState** and **setState** with them. For example, to determine which radio button is selected in a group, use the **CheckboxGroup** classes **getSelectedCheckbox** method, and to set which one is selected, use the **setSelectedCheckbox** method.

Here's an example. I'll create a checkbox group named **radios** and add four radio buttons to that group. You add a radio button to a checkbox group by adding the group as a parameter in a checkbox's constructor, which turns it into a radio button. Here's what this looks like in an example named radios.java:

```java
import java.applet.Applet;
import java.awt.*;
import java.awt.event.*;

/*
<applet
    code=radios.class
    width = "200"
    height = "200" >
</applet>
*/

public class radios extends Applet implements ItemListener {
    CheckboxGroup radios;
    Checkbox radio1, radio2, radio3, radio4;
    TextField text1;

    public void init()
    {
        radios = new CheckboxGroup();

        radio1 = new Checkbox("1", false, radios);
        add(radio1);
        radio1.addItemListener(this);

        radio2 = new Checkbox("2", false, radios);
        add(radio2);
        radio2.addItemListener(this);

        radio3 = new Checkbox("3", false, radios);
        add(radio3);
        radio3.addItemListener(this);

        radio4 = new Checkbox("4", false, radios);
        add(radio4);
        radio4.addItemListener(this);

        text1 = new TextField(20);
        add(text1);
    }
```

Note that I've added an **ItemListener** to each radio button so I can implement the **ItemListener** interface and the **itemStateChanged** method to indicate which radio button was clicked:

```
public void itemStateChanged(ItemEvent e)
{
    text1.setText("Radio button " +
        ((Checkbox) e.getItemSelectable()).getLabel() + " clicked!");
}
}
```

The results of this code appear in Figure 17.8.

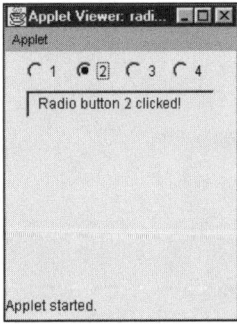

Figure 17.8 Handling radio-button clicks.

Using Fonts

"The banner you created for the Company Pride Picnic was good," the big boss says, "but it didn't seem to be bursting with pride." "Why not?" you ask. "Well, for one thing," the BB says, "it was only a quarter of an inch tall." "Hm," you say, "guess I better use a bigger font."

*TIP: You can select the type and style of fonts with the **Font** class. Using this class, you can select a font (such as Helvetica, Arial, or Courier), set its size, and specify its typestyle (boldface, italics, and so on).*

Let's see an example showing how to use fonts in Java. I'll let the user type characters and display them in Courier text. I'll center them in an applet by determining the screen size of the text by using the Java **FontMetrics** class's **stringWidth** and **getHeight** methods and determining the width and height of the applet with the applet's **getSize** method. I'll also let the user specify the size of the text as well as whether or not it should be italic or bold, and set a **Font** object accordingly. To

Immediate Solutions

actually install the font so that when you print text it appears in that font, you use a **Graphics** object's **setFont** method.

Note that I'll also read keystrokes, so I implement the **KeyListener** interface, which has three methods that we have to add to the code: **keyPressed(KeyEvent e)**, **keyReleased(KeyEvent e)**, and **keyTyped(KeyEvent e)**. To get the actual key that was typed in the **keyTyped** method, I use the **KeyEvent** object's **getKeyChar** method. I also use the **repaint** method to force Java to call the **paint** method and repaint the applet (as discussed in the "In Depth" section of this chapter). Here's what the applet, fonts.java, looks like:

```java
import java.awt.*;
import java.awt.event.*;
import java.applet.Applet;

/*
  <applet
      code=fonts.class
      width=600
      height = "200" >
  </applet>
*/

public class fonts extends Applet implements ActionListener, KeyListener
{
    String text = "";

    Button boldbutton, italicbutton, largebutton;
    boolean bold = false;
    boolean italic = false;
    boolean large = false;

    public void init()
    {
        boldbutton = new Button("Bold font");
        italicbutton = new Button("Italic font");
        largebutton = new Button("Large font");

        boldbutton.addActionListener(this);
        italicbutton.addActionListener(this);
        largebutton.addActionListener(this);

        add(boldbutton);
        add(italicbutton);
        add(largebutton);
```

17. Creating Java Applets

1045

Chapter 17 Creating Java Applets

```java
            addKeyListener(this);
            requestFocus();
        }

        public void actionPerformed(ActionEvent event)
        {
            if(event.getSource() == boldbutton) bold = !bold;
            if(event.getSource() == italicbutton) italic = !italic;
            if(event.getSource() == largebutton) large = !large;
            requestFocus();
            repaint();
        }

        public void paint(Graphics g)
        {
            String fontname = "Courier";
            int type = Font.PLAIN;
            int size = 36;
            Font font;
            FontMetrics fm;

            if(bold) type = type | Font.BOLD;
            if(italic) type = type | Font.ITALIC;
            if(large) size = 72;

            font = new Font(fontname, type, size);
            g.setFont(font);

            fm = getFontMetrics(font);
            int xloc = (getSize().width - fm.stringWidth(text)) / 2;
            int yloc = (getSize().height + fm.getHeight()) / 2;

            g.drawString(text, xloc, yloc);
        }

        public void keyTyped(KeyEvent e)
        {
            text = text + e.getKeyChar();
            repaint();
        }

        public void keyPressed(KeyEvent e) {}
        public void keyReleased(KeyEvent e) {}
    }
```

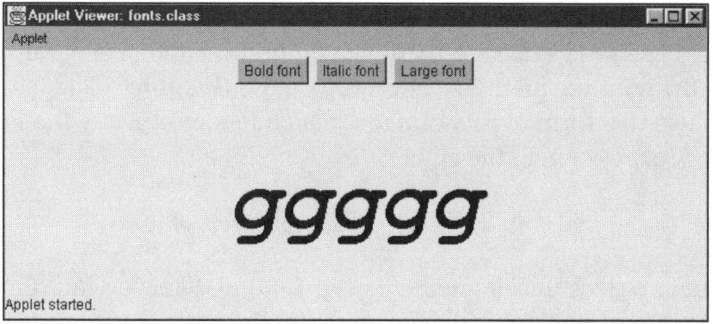

Figure 17.9   Using fonts.

You can see the results in Figure 17.9. When users type text, the text appears centered in the applet, and when they use the Bold Font, Italic Font, and Large Font buttons, the text appears with the corresponding attributes.

Now it's time to move on to working with images—see the next section.

Handling Images

The big boss says, "About this photo essay you wrote for the company newspaper..." "Yes?" you ask. "Where are the photos?" the BB asks. "Hm," you say, "this looks like a job for the **Image** class."

You can support images in the AWT with the **Image** class, which is derived directly from the **java.lang.Object**:

```
java.lang.Object
|____java.awt.Image
```

To load an image into an applet, you can use the **Applet** class's **getImage** method, which has two forms. (Java recognizes which form you're using by the types and number of the arguments you pass.) The forms are:

```
Image getImage(URL url)
Image getImage(URL url, String name)
```

You can use the **URL** class to specify the URL of the image file that you want to read. You can create a **URL** object by using the **URL** class's constructor like this: **URL("http://java.sun.com/products/jdk/1.2/")**. As far as this chapter is concerned, however, I'll use the **Applet** class's **getCodeBase** and **getDocumentBase** methods to get the URL for the applet itself and use that URL to find the image file.

Here's a short example that just reads in an image, image.jpg, and displays it. To read in the image, I use the **getImage** method, and to draw the image, I use the **Graphics** class's **drawImage** method. (For more on the **Graphics** class, see the next section.) I'll use this form of **drawImage**, which lets me specify the image object to draw and its position in the applet:

```
boolean drawImage(Image img, int x, int y, ImageObserver observer)
```

You have to pass an object that implements the **ImageObserver** interface to **drawImage**. **ImageObserver** objects let you monitor the progress of image loading operations. There's a default implementation of this interface in the **Applet** class, so you can just use a **this** keyword as the **ImageObserver** object, as in this example, image.java:

```
import java.awt.*;
import java.applet.*;

/*
  <applet
      code=image.class
      width=500
      height=150 >
  </applet>
*/

public class image extends Applet
{
    Image image;

    public void init()
    {
        image = getImage(getDocumentBase(), "image.jpg");
    }

    public void paint(Graphics g)
    {
        g.drawImage(image, 10, 10, this);
    }
}
```

The results appear in Figure 17.10, where you can see the loaded image.

Immediate Solutions

Figure 17.10   Displaying an image.

Drawing Graphics

The big boss appears in a puff of cigar smoke and says, "The design team has come up with a winning program that I want you to write." "What does it do?" you ask. "Lets the user draw lines, rectangles, ovals, or freehand with the mouse," the BB says. "Real cutting-edge stuff," you say.

The real core of AWT graphics is the huge AWT **Graphics** class, which is derived directly from **java.lang.Object**. I'm going to put the **Graphics** class to work here by creating a graphics program that lets the user draw lines, ovals, rectangles, rounded rectangles, and freehand with the mouse, as you see in Figure 17.11.

Here's how this program, draw.class, works: Users click a button indicating what kind of figure they want to draw; this sets a Boolean flag inside the program. When users press the mouse in the drawing area, I store that location as **start**, using a Java **Point** object (which has two data members: **x** and **y**). When users release the mouse in a new location, I store that location as **end**. Releasing the mouse also repaints the program, and I can select which figure to draw—a line, oval, rectangle, or rounded rectangle—between **start** and **end** based on the Boolean flags set by clicking the buttons.

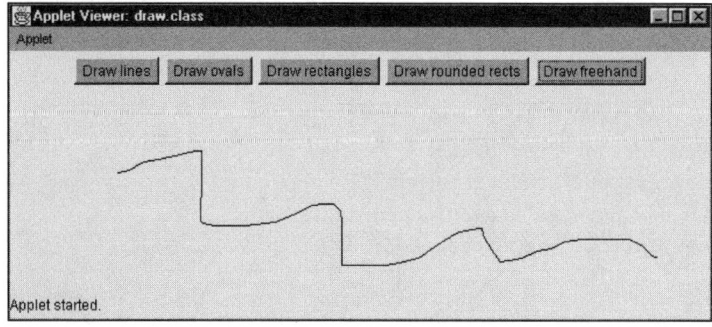

Figure 17.11   Drawing freehand with the mouse.

Drawing freehand with the mouse is a little different, though. In this case, I store up to 1,000 points that the mouse moves over, and when it's time to draw the program, I just connect the dots with lines. (A mouse event is not generated for each pixel the mouse moves over, so I need to draw lines between the mouse locations that Java does report.) Here's what draw.java looks like; I'll discuss the drawing sections in detail in the following pages:

```java
import java.awt.*;
import java.lang.Math;
import java.awt.event.*;
import java.awt.Graphics;
import java.applet.Applet;

/*
  <applet
      code=draw.class
      width=600
      height = "200" >
  </applet>
*/

public class draw extends Applet implements ActionListener,
    MouseListener, MouseMotionListener {
    Button bDraw, bLine, bOval, bRect, bRounded;
    Point dot[] = new Point[1000];
    Point start, end;
    int dots = 0;

    boolean mouseUp = false;
    boolean draw = false;
    boolean line = false;
    boolean oval = false;
    boolean rectangle = false;
    boolean rounded = false;

    public void init()
    {
        bLine = new Button("Draw lines");
        bOval = new Button("Draw ovals");
        bRect = new Button("Draw rectangles");
        bRounded = new Button("Draw rounded rects");
        bDraw = new Button("Draw freehand");

        add(bLine);
        add(bOval);
        add(bRect);
```

```java
        add(bRounded);
        add(bDraw);

        bLine.addActionListener(this);
        bOval.addActionListener(this);
        bRect.addActionListener(this);
        bRounded.addActionListener(this);
        bDraw.addActionListener(this);

        addMouseListener(this);
        addMouseMotionListener(this);
    }

    public void mousePressed(MouseEvent e)
    {
        mouseUp = false;
        start = new Point(e.getX(), e.getY());
    }

    public void mouseReleased(MouseEvent e)
    {
        if(line){
            end = new Point(e.getX(), e.getY());
        } else {
            end = new Point(Math.max(e.getX(), start.x),
                Math.max(e.getY(), start.y));
            start = new Point(Math.min(e.getX(), start.x),
                Math.min(e.getY(), start.y));
        }
        mouseUp = true;
        repaint();
    }

    public void mouseDragged(MouseEvent e)
    {
        if(draw){
            dot[dots] = new Point(e.getX(), e.getY());
            dots++;
            repaint();
        }
    }

    public void mouseClicked(MouseEvent e){}
    public void mouseEntered(MouseEvent e){}
    public void mouseExited(MouseEvent e){}
    public void mouseMoved(MouseEvent e){}
```

```java
    public void paint (Graphics g)
    {
        if (mouseUp) {
            int width = end.x - start.x;
            int height = end.y - start.y;

            if(line){
                g.drawLine(start.x, start.y, end.x, end.y);
            }
            else if(oval){
                g.drawOval(start.x, start.y, width, height);
            }
            else if(rectangle){
                g.drawRect(start.x, start.y, width, height);
            }
            else if(rounded){
                g.drawRoundRect(start.x, start.y, width, height, 10, 10);
            }
            else if(draw){
                for(int loop_index = 0; loop_index < dots - 1;
                    loop_index++){
                    g.drawLine(dot[loop_index].x, dot[loop_index].y,
                        dot[loop_index + 1].x, dot[loop_index + 1].y);
                }
            }
        }
    }

    public void actionPerformed(ActionEvent e)
    {
        setFlagsFalse();
        if(e.getSource() == bDraw)draw = true;
        if(e.getSource() == bLine)line = true;
        if(e.getSource() == bOval)oval = true;
        if(e.getSource() == bRect)rectangle = true;
        if(e.getSource() == bRounded)rounded = true;
    }

    void setFlagsFalse()
    {
        rounded = false;
        line = false;
        oval = false;
        rectangle = false;
        draw = false;
    }
}
```

That's what draw.java looks like, and in this section, I'll take a look at some of its drawing functions. All of these drawing functions, except freehand drawing, will draw a figure between the locations **start** and **end**, which the user indicates by dragging the mouse. Note that to create this program, we'll need to be able to handle the mouse, so I'll start with that.

Using the Mouse

You can work with the mouse by using two AWT interfaces—**MouseListener**, which handles mouse clicks, presses, and releases, and cases in which the mouse enters a component and leaves it; and **MouseMotionListener**, which handles mouse movements and drag operations. The following list contains the methods of the **MouseListener** interface, all of which you'll have to implement to use this interface:

- **void mouseClicked(MouseEvent e)**—Called when the mouse has been clicked on a component.
- **void mouseEntered(MouseEvent e)**—Called when the mouse enters a component.
- **void mouseExited(MouseEvent e)**—Called when the mouse exits a component.
- **void mousePressed(MouseEvent e)**—Called when a mouse button has been pressed on a component.
- **void mouseReleased(MouseEvent e)**—Called when a mouse button has been released on a component.

The following are the methods of the **MouseMotionListener** interface, both of which you'll have to implement to use this interface:

- **void mouseDragged(MouseEvent e)**—Called when a mouse button is pressed on a component and then dragged.
- **void mouseMoved(MouseEvent e)**—Called when the mouse button has been moved on a component (with no buttons held down).

Each of the mouse interface methods is passed an object of class **MouseEvent**, and the inheritance diagram for that class looks like this:

```
java.lang.Objcct
|____java.util.EventObject
     |____java.awt.AWTEvent
          |____java.awt.event.ComponentEvent
               |____java.awt.event.InputEvent
                    |____java.awt..event.MouseEvent
```

Let's see a quick example. This applet, mouse.java, will display most of what the mouse can do. To catch particular mouse actions, you just override the corresponding mouse listener method. To get the current location of the mouse from a **MouseEvent** object, you can use the **getX** and **getY** methods. To determine which button was pressed, you can use the **MouseEvent** class's **getModifiers** method, applying **AND** to the result with these fields from the **InputEvent** class's fields: **ALT_GRAPH_MASK**, **ALT_MASK**, **BUTTON1_MASK**, **BUTTON2_MASK**, **BUTTON3_MASK**, **CTRL_MASK**, **META_MASK**, and **SHIFT_MASK**. Here's what the mouse.java applet looks like, putting all this to work:

```java
import java.applet.Applet;
import java.awt.*;
import java.awt.event.*;

/*
<applet
    code=mouse.class
    width=300
    height = "200" >
</applet>
*/

public class mouse extends Applet implements MouseListener,
    MouseMotionListener
{
    TextField text1;

    public void init(){
        text1 = new TextField(30);
        add(text1);
        addMouseListener(this);
        addMouseMotionListener(this);
    }

    public void mousePressed(MouseEvent e)
    {
        if((e.getModifiers() & InputEvent.BUTTON1_MASK) ==
            InputEvent.BUTTON1_MASK){
            text1.setText("Left mouse button down at " + e.getX() + "," +
                e.getY());
        }
        else{
            text1.setText("Right mouse button down at " + e.getX() + "," +
                e.getY());
        }
    }
```

```java
    public void mouseClicked(MouseEvent e)
    {
        text1.setText("You clicked the mouse at " + e.getX() + "," +
            e.getY());
    }

    public void mouseReleased(MouseEvent e)
    {
        text1.setText("The mouse button went up.");
    }

    public void mouseEntered(MouseEvent e)
    {
        text1.setText("The mouse entered.");
    }

    public void mouseExited(MouseEvent e)
    {
        text1.setText("The mouse exited.");
    }

    public void mouseDragged(MouseEvent e)
    {
        text1.setText("The mouse was dragged.");
    }

    public void mouseMoved(MouseEvent e)
    {
        text1.setText("The mouse was moved.");
    }
}
```

You can see this applet at work in Figure 17.12. When you move the mouse or use a mouse button, the applet lets you know what's going on.

That gets us up to speed on using the mouse in Java—now it's time to turn to the drawing part of draw.java.

Drawing Lines

Using a **Graphics** object, you can draw a line between the points (*x1*, *y1*) and (*x2*, *y2*) with the **drawLine** method:

```
drawLine(int x1, int y1, int x2, int y2);
```

Chapter 17 Creating Java Applets

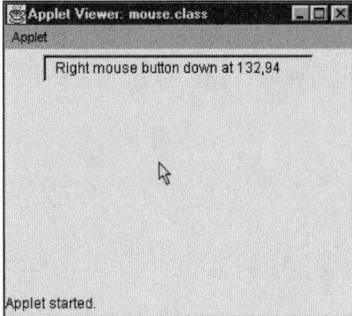

Figure 17.12 Using the mouse.

Here's how this looks in draw.java:

```
g.drawLine(start.x, start.y, end.x, end.y);
```

You can see the results in draw.java in Figure 17.13.

Drawing Ovals

Ellipses, including circles, are called *ovals* in the AWT, and you can draw them with the **Graphics** class's **drawOval** method:

```
drawOval(int x, int y, int width, int height);
```

Here's how I draw ovals as specified by the user when running draw.java:

```
int width = end.x - start.x;
int height = end.y - start.y;
g.drawOval(start.x, start.y, width, height);
```

You can see the results in draw.java in Figure 17.14.

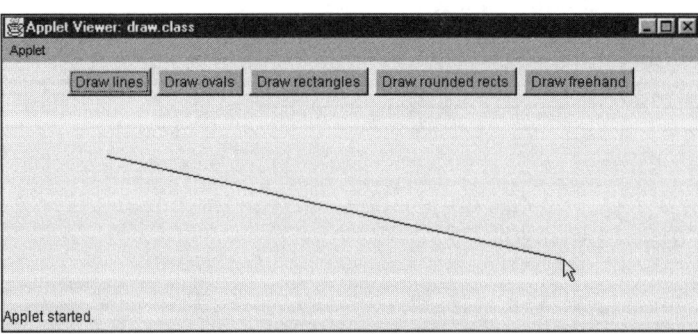

Figure 17.13 Drawing a line with the mouse.

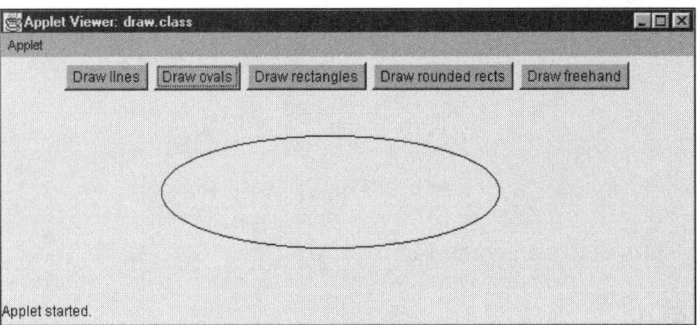

Figure 17.14 Drawing ovals with the mouse.

Drawing Rectangles

You can draw rectangles by using the **Graphics** class's **drawRect** method:

```
drawRect(int x, int y, int width, int height);
```

Here's how I do this in draw.java:

```
int width = end.x - start.x;
int height = end.y - start.y;
g.drawRect(start.x, start.y, width, height);
```

You can see the results in draw.java in Figure 17.15.

Drawing Rounded Rectangles

You can draw rounded rectangles—rectangles with rounded corners, that is—using the **Graphics** class's **drawRoundRect** method:

```
drawRoundRect(int x, int y, int width, int height, int arcWidth, int
    arcHeight);
```

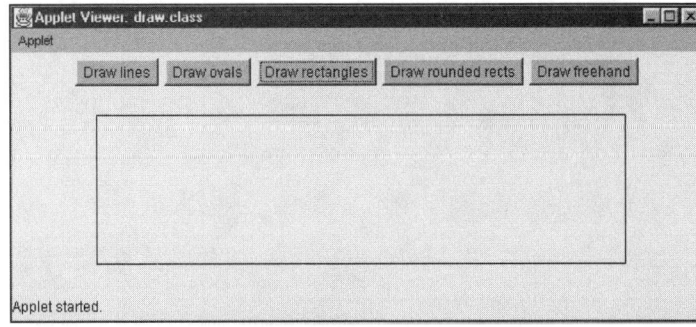

Figure 17.15 Drawing a rectangle with the mouse.

You specify the arc width and height in pixels, and this specifies the rounding of the corners. Here's how I draw a rounded rectangle in draw.java:

```
int width = end.x - start.x;
int height = end.y - start.y;
g.drawRoundRect(start.x, start.y, width, height, 10, 10);
```

You can see the results in draw.java in Figure 17.16.

Drawing Freehand

Using the AWT **Graphics** class, you can let the user draw freehand with the mouse, but we'll have to support it ourselves in code. Here's how I do this in draw.java in the **mouseDragged** method. After making sure that the **draw** flag is true to determine that the user is drawing freehand, I save all the mouse locations as the mouse is dragged in an array named **dot[ ]**:

```
public void mouseDragged(MouseEvent e)
{
    if(draw){
        dot[dots] = new Point(e.getX(), e.getY());
        dots++;
        repaint();
    }
}
```

Then, when it's time to draw the figure, I just connect the dots with lines:

```
for(int loop_index = 0; loop_index < dots - 1; loop_index++){
    g.drawLine(dot[loop_index].x, dot[loop_index].y,
        dot[loop_index + 1].x, dot[loop_index + 1].y);
}
```

You can see the results in Figure 17.11.

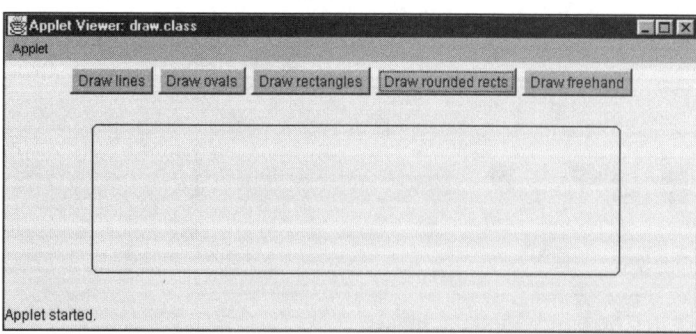

Figure 17.16   Drawing rounded rectangles with the mouse.

Chapter 18

Essential Perl

If you need an immediate solution to:	See page:
Writing Code: Creating Code Files	1073
Writing Code: Statements and Declarations	1074
Writing Code: Finding the Perl Interpreter	1074
Running Perl Code	1076
Basic Skills: Text Input and Output	1077
Basic Skills: Using the **print** Function	1077
Basic Skills: Commenting Your Code	1078
Basic Skills: Reading Typed Input	1079
Basic Skills: Using the Default Variable **$_**	1080
Basic Skills: Cleaning up Typed Input	1081
Basic Skills: Avoiding Immediate Script Closings in Windows	1082
Creating Scalar Variables	1084
Using Assignment Operators on Scalars	1085
Using Numbers in Scalar Variables	1086
Handling Truth Values in Perl	1087
Using Strings in Scalar Variables	1087
Using Variable Interpolation	1088
Defining a List	1089
Assigning Lists to Other Lists	1090
Joining a List into a String	1091
Creating Arrays	1092
Using Arrays	1094
Creating Hashes	1095
Using Hashes	1098

(continued)

If you need an immediate solution to:	See page:
Using Perl Operators	1100
Using Relational (Comparison) Operators	1100
Using Equality Operators	1101
Using the **if** Statement	1102
Looping with the **for** Loop	1104
Looping with the **foreach** Loop	1106
Looping with the **while** Loop	1107
Using the **die** Statement	1108
Creating Objects	1108

In Depth

In this chapter, I'll discuss creating Common Gateway Interface (CGI) scripts, which enable you to create Web pages on the server. This is a great method to use for interacting with users, including letting users click checkboxes and radio buttons, enter text for guest books, and participate in multiuser chat. CGI scripts can also be used for Web hit counters and sending data back to a script on the server. CGI also supports server push actions, cookies, server-based databases, games, shopping carts, site searches, redirection of browsers to new Web sites, file uploads, and much more. To create CGI scripts that run on the Web server and send Web pages to browsers, I'll use the most popular CGI scripting language, Perl (Practical Extraction and Reporting Language).

The officially recognized method of creating Web pages with Perl is to use the Perl module CGI.pm. Currently, however, the Perl methods in CGI.pm create *HTML* Web pages, not XHTML Web pages. There's no doubt that Perl will be updated one day, but in the meantime, in this and the following chapter, we'll be working with what's available now which means working with HTML pages. (If you simply want to print an XHTML Web page verbatim, you can do that in Perl without using the HTML methods in the CGI.pm module, and I'll discuss that in the next chapter.)

There's a great deal more to Perl than we can cover in one or two chapters, so for more details, you might want to check out a good book on Perl. There are many books on Perl, including my *Perl Black Book* (The Coriolis Group, ©1999), which examines all the topics mentioned in the previous paragraph and much more.

In this chapter, I'll work through the basics of Perl programming. In Chapter 19, I'll put them to work creating a Web page that can interpret buttons, radio buttons, checkboxes, scrolling lists, password fields, text fields, and more. The user can use these controls to enter data and then click the Submit button; the CGI script on the server will summarize the user-supplied data and display it in a new Web page in the browser.

TIP: *Because this is only an introduction to Perl, keep in mind that the Perl coverage in this chapter unavoidably skips a great deal of Perl programming, including such topics as writing data to and reading data from files (for example, when you want to store user comments in a guest book on your Web server). For details, refer to the* Perl Black Book *(The Coriolis Group, ©1999).*

Following is a sample Perl script that you can install on your server. When opened in a Web browser, this script will display a text area with the text "Welcome To Perl!" in it:

```perl
#!/usr/local/bin/perl

use CGI;

$co = new CGI;

print $co->header,

$co->start_html(-title=>'CGI Example'),

$co->center($co->h1('Welcome To Perl!')),

$co->start_form(),

$co->textarea
(
    -name=>'textarea',
    -default=>'Welcome To Perl!',
    -rows->'10',
    -columns=>'60'
),

$co->end_form(),

$co->end_html;
```

You can see the results of this CGI script in Figure 18.1. We'll learn how to create scripts like this in Chapter 19. In this chapter, we'll build the foundation of Perl programming.

Many, many Web pages on Perl are available for additional study (a random Web search turns up a mere 1,527,903 pages mentioning Perl). The following is a list of some good ones.

- The Perl homepage is at **www.perl.com**. You can find source code and Perl ports for various operating systems, documentation, modules, bug reports, and a Perl "frequently asked questions" (FAQ) list. (The FAQ is located at **www.perl.com/perl/faq**).

- To get Perl, Perl modules, Perl extensions, and tons of other Perl items, look at the Comprehensive Perl Archive Network (CPAN) at **www.cpan.org**. This is the most comprehensive source for information about Perl. If you browse

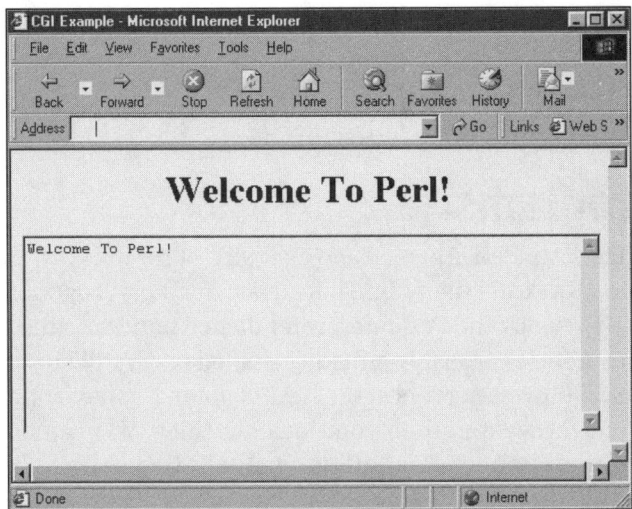

Figure 18.1   A text area created by a Perl script.

through CPAN, you're sure to see lots of valuable code, ranging from Perl language extensions to image handling and from Internet modules to database interfaces.

- The Perl Mongers at **www.pm.org** is a nonprofit organization that works to establish Perl user groups. See the Perl Mongers site for lists of groups.

- The online Perl documentation is located at **www.cpan.org/doc/manual/ html/pod/perl.html**. This is the official Perl documentation.

Many other sites for special Perl interests—such as security, CGI programming, and more—are available; just search the Web if you want to be overwhelmed.

The following list contains a number of Usenet groups for Perl programmers:

- **comp.lang.perl.announce**—A low-traffic group.

- **comp.lang.perl.misc**—A high-traffic site that also posts a Perl FAQ.

- **comp.lang.perl.modules**—A group about creating modules and reusing your own or someone else's code.

- **comp.lang.perl.tk**—A group about the connection between Perl and the Tcl language's Tk toolkit. The Tk toolkit supports many visual controls—such as buttons, menus, and so on—that you can use with Perl, and it's become pretty popular.

If you're interested in CGI programming, take a look at **comp.infosystems.www. authoring.cgi**—it doesn't have Perl in the name, but it's a good place to talk with others about Perl CGI programming.

In the next section, we'll begin to create Perl programs. Fortunately, we have some knowledge of creating Perl programs because, like JavaScript and Java, Perl is based on C++. We are familiar with many constructs used in Perl, such as **if** and **while** statements.

Creating Perl Programs

Like JavaScript, and unlike Java, Perl is parsed and executed at runtime instead of being compiled into binary form and then run. This means that Perl programs are actually scripts, and they're run by the Perl interpreter named *perl* (note the lowercase "p"). The Perl interpreter is probably already installed on your Web server, and we'll learn how to use it on Web servers in the next chapter. For development purposes, however, you might want Perl on your local machine. You can download the latest version from **www.perl.com/pub/language/info/software.html**. (A very good version for Windows is the ActiveState Perl implementation.)

TIP: *When you're creating your own Perl programs, a good asset to have is the Perl documentation, which comes with Perl. You can also view it online at **www.cpan.org/doc/manual/html/pod/perl.html**.*

Creating Perl scripts can be very easy. All you have to do is save a plain text file with the Perl code you want in it. In the "Immediate Solutions" section "Writing Code: Creating Code Files," I'll run scripts locally and give such files the extension .pl. In Chapter 19, we'll create CGI scripts and use the extension .cgi. For example, say you have a file named hello.pl with the following Perl statement in it, which is designed to print the message "Hello from Perl!":

```
print "Hello from Perl!\n";
```

Note that the **\n** character set represents a newline character, which makes the output skip to the next line. Like Java, Perl insists that each statement ends with a semicolon (;). If you have Perl installed on your computer and you're using Windows, you can run this script in an MS-DOS session:

```
C:\>perl hello.pl
```

When you do, the message "Hello from Perl!" is displayed at once:

```
C:\>perl hello.pl

Hello from Perl!
```

This gives us our start with Perl scripts—I'll press on to explain how to work with data.

Handling Data in Perl

In this chapter, I'll discuss how Perl handles two types of data: scalar variables and lists. *Scalar variables* hold a single data item, and *lists* hold multiple data items. From the outset, it's important to understand the difference between scalar variables and lists. Although scalar variables are actual data types—that is, you can allocate storage for them—there is no list data type in Perl. The difference between scalar variables and lists is one of *context*, not data types—Perl knows whether you're working in what it calls *scalar context* or *list context*. Many Perl functions and operators are sensitive to context, so if your code uses such a function or operator in list context—for example, you might assign its return value to a list—that's a signal to Perl that you expect a list of data items. If the function is used in scalar context, Perl knows you expect a scalar variable.

Scalar Variables

Scalar variables are what many programming languages refer to as *simple variables* (and in Perl, they're often just called *scalars*); they hold a single data item, such as a number or a string. Scalars are called scalars to differentiate them from constructs, such as arrays, that can hold more than one item. (In scientific terms, a scalar is a simple numeric value, whereas vectors can have multiple values; in fact, one-dimensional arrays are often called *vectors* in programming.)

You preface a scalar variable's name with a dollar sign ($). In Perl terms, $ is the *prefix dereferencer* for scalars. Using it for scalars means that Perl will know how to treat your scalar—and that none of your scalar variable names will conflict with reserved words in Perl (i.e., the words built into the Perl language). You don't need to declare variables in Perl before using them, as you do in Java (Perl has no **var**, **int**, or **float** statements).

TIP: *There is a different type of prefix dereferencer for each data format in Perl: $ for scalars, @ for arrays, and % for hashes.*

There are two main types of scalars: numbers and strings. You assign values to a scalar variable with the assignment operator (=):

```
$scalar1 = 5;
$scalar2 = "Hello there!";
```

You can also use Perl operators and functions with scalars. The operators and functions you use usually depend on whether the data in the scalar is a number or a string. Keep in mind that scalar variables represent actual memory locations that store a single item of data—a string or a number. They're the fundamental unit of data storage in Perl.

Lists

As you can gather from their name, lists are just that: lists of data elements. Unlike scalars, which are a data type, there is no specific list data type, but the concept of lists in Perl is very important. A list is a construct that associates data elements, and you can specify a list by enclosing those elements in parentheses and separating them with commas. In the following code, I'm printing the elements in the list ("H", "e", "l", "l", "o") with the **print** function, which is designed to take a list argument:

```
print ("H", "e", "l", "l", "o");

Hello
```

In this case, I did not assign the list ("H", "e", "l", "l", "o") to a variable before printing it because there is no explicit list variable type in Perl.

When you're working with lists, you can also omit the parentheses if you don't need them to indicate that you want to work in list context and if there's no possibility of confusion. That's the case here, where I pass "H", "e", "l", "l", "o" to the **print** function:

```
print "H", "e", "l", "l", "o";

Hello
```

The functions built into Perl are divided into two groups: those that expect scalar arguments and those that expect lists (although many functions are written to take either).

Scalar Context and List Context

How does Perl know when to treat data as a scalar and when to treat data as a list? Perl makes its decision based on the context. There are two main contexts: scalar context and list context. (These in turn have categories; for example, numeric context and text string context are both scalar contexts.)

If Perl is expecting a list (for instance, when you use a function that takes only a list), it treats your data as a list. If Perl is expecting a scalar, it treats your data as a scalar. In other words, the way the data is treated is *implicit* in Perl programming, based on the context in which you use that data, and not explicitly set in code. If you're working with functions that take or return list arguments, for example, those arguments are automatically treated as lists.

After scalars and lists, the next step in data organization is to use an array.

Arrays

Arrays let you organize a list of items by numeric index and let you refer to those items by using that index. Being able to access data items by index is often invaluable in code because you can increment or decrement that index and work through the entire array under programmatic control.

You can create an array by assigning a list to an array variable, which starts with an @ sign in Perl (@ is the array prefix dereferencer):

```
@array = (1, 2, 3);
```

You refer to the individual elements of a simple array by indicating the index of the element inside brackets, [and], and by substituting $ for @—note that array indices are zero-based in Perl:

```
print $array[0];
```

1

TIP: It's often confusing to novice Perl programmers that you use $ as the prefix dereferencer, instead of @, when referring to individual array elements. But when you consider that Perl uses the prefix dereferencer to determine the type of variable, it makes sense, because an individual element in a simple array is a scalar, whose prefix dereferencer is $.

Besides standard arrays, Perl supports another type of array—*associative arrays*, also called *hashes*.

Hashes

Novice programmers often start using Perl with no idea of what a hash is, but a little programming experience makes them an expert on the topic because they're ubiquitous in Perl. Hashes are also called *associative arrays*, and they work very much like arrays except that you use *text string keys*—not numeric indices—to organize data in a hash. Hashes are useful for data that you want to refer to with a name, such as "title," instead of by number as you would with a standard array. (In this way, working with hashes can be considered one step closer to true database programming than is working with standard arrays.)

When you create a hash, you associate a value, such as **apple**, with a key, such as **fruit**:

```
$hash{'fruit'} = 'apple';
```

Note the similarity to working with standard arrays. The main difference is that with hashes you use curly braces, { and }, when referring to a specific item, not straight brackets, [and], as with standard arrays. Also, you index values with a text string key—such as **fruit**—not a numeric index. Note also that, as with arrays, when you refer to single values in a hash, you use the $ prefix dereferencer.

You can refer to the new value in the hash to print it:

```
$hash{'fruit'} = 'apple';
print "$hash{'fruit'}\n";
```

apple

The prefix dereferencer for hashes is %, and, as with arrays, you can create hashes with list assignments. When you do so, you can associate the values stored in the hash with text keys by using *key/value pairs*:

```
%hash = (
    'fruit'    , 'apple',
    'sandwich' , 'hamburger',
    'drink'    , 'bubbly',
);
```

Now you can refer to the values in the hash by key:

```
%hash = (
    'fruit'    , 'apple',
    'sandwich' , 'hamburger',
    'drink'    , 'bubbly',
);

print "$hash{'fruit'}\n";
```

apple

Like JavaScript and Java, Perl has operators based on C++ (although with a number of additions). I'll provide an overview of them next.

Operators

Using operators, you can manipulate your data. For example, you can use a simple addition function by using the addition operator (+) in this way:

```
print 2 + 2;
```

4

The Perl operators appear in Table 18.1 in descending order of precedence (i.e., the first line has highest precedence and so is evaluated first). The column labeled "Associativity" indicates which direction the operator looks for its arguments: to the right or to the left.

Conditional Statements

As in JavaScript and Java, conditional statements let you direct code execution depending on logical tests that you make. In other words, conditional statements let you make decisions in code and act on them.

Table 18.1 Operator precedence in Perl.

Operators	Associativity
Terms and leftward list operators	Left
->	Left
++ --	N/A
**	Right
! ~ \ and unary + and -	Right
=~ !~	Left
* / % x	Left
+ - .	Left
<< >>	Left
Named unary operators and file text operators	N/A
< > <= >= lt gt le ge	N/A
== != <=> eq ne cmp	N/A
&	Left
	^	Left
&&	Left
||	Left
.. ...	N/a
?:	Right
= += -= *= etc.	Right
, =>	Left
Rightward list operators	N/A
not	Right
and	Left
or xor	Left

You use conditional statements to perform tests on data and take the appropriate actions. For example, I might want to test the value in **$variable** to see if it's equal to 5. I can use an **if** statement to do that. If the value is 5, the code will display the string, "Yes, it's five."; otherwise, the code displays the string, "No, it's not five.":

```
$variable = 5;

if ($variable == 5) {
    print "Yes, it's five.\n";
} else {
    print "No, it's not five.\n";
}
```

Yes, it's five.

The **if** statement is a compound statement, which means that you use curly braces to delimit the code block(s) in it. Note that because Perl skips white space, including new lines, you can write the previous code like this:

```
$variable = 5;

if ($variable == 5) {
    print "Yes, it's five.\n";
}
else {
    print "No, it's not five.\n";
}
```

However, you *cannot* use the JavaScript-style **if** statement syntax, which makes the curly braces optional if a code block includes only one line. Note that I'm creating a Perl comment here by prefacing the comment text with a pound sign (#):

```
$variable = 5;

if ($variable == 5)                    #wrong!
    print "Yes, it's five.\n";
else
    print "No, it's not five.\n";
```

Perl also includes loop statements.

Loop Statements

Here's an example Perl **for** loop, which calculates a factorial value. The loop index is a variable called **$loop_index**. Note how much this looks like the corresponding JavaScript or Java **for** loop:

```
$factorial = 1;

for ($loop_index = 1; $loop_index <= 6; $loop_index++) {
    $factorial *= $loop_index;
}
print "6! = $factorial\n";

6! = 720
```

Using a loop index, you can index the values in a data set, working through that data value by value, as in this case, where I iterate through an array. Perl fills the expression **$#*arrayname*** with the index value of the last element in the array named **@*arrayname***:

```
@array = ("one", "two", "three");
for ($loop_index = 0; $loop_index <= $#array; $loop_index++)
{
    print $array[$loop_index] . " ";
}

one two three
```

That's it. Conditional statements let you make decisions in code, and loop statements let you handle repetitive operations on your data. There are two more skills we'll need to discuss before we can start writing CGI scripts in Chapter 19: using Perl modules and creating objects in Perl.

Using Perl Modules

Java comes with many classes already created for you, as well as packages of classes, and you can add them to your programs with the **import** statement. Similarly, there are hundreds of Perl *modules* available, some of which come with Perl and some of which you can obtain from the CPAN site. In the next chapter, we'll use the CGI.pm module to create CGI scripts. To add a module to your script, you can add a **use** statement to your code. Here's an example in which I'm using the Perl **integer** module, which adds support for integer math:

```
use integer;
print 5/3;
```

Integer math discards the remainders of division operations, so the result of this division is 1:

```
use integer;
print 5/3;
```

```
1
```

We'll need one more skill for the next chapter—creating objects.

Creating Objects

In Chapter 19, we'll use the CGI module to create CGI scripts. Like much of modern Perl, the CGI module is object-oriented. To create a Web page to send back to a Web browser, I include the CGI module and use the **new** operator to create an object named **$co** of the CGI class:

```
use CGI;
$co = new CGI;
```

The variable **$co** really contains a *reference* to a new CGI object (for more on Perl references, see the *Perl Black Book* [The Coriolis Group, ©1999]). You can access its data members and methods by using the arrow operator (->), like this, where I'm calling the new CGI object's **header** method:

```
use CGI;
$co = new CGI;
print $co->header;
```

The **header** method returns the header text of a Web page (such as the **Content-Type: text/html** text that tells the browser what kind of document is being sent to it). When the script runs as a CGI script, the **print** function will send that header back to the browser.

And that brings us up to speed—it's time to turn to the details of Perl programming.

Immediate Solutions

Writing Code: Creating Code Files

The design team coordinator calls to congratulate you on getting Perl installed. You accept the accolades gracefully. "So what scripts have you been writing?" he asks. "Hm," you say. "Scripts?"

Perl scripts are just plain text files made up of Perl statements as needed. To create a Perl script, you should have a text editor or word processor that can save files in plain text format.

As you already know if you edit your own XHTML pages, saving text in plain text format is a simple achievement that seems to be difficult in some word processors. However, in Microsoft Word, you can save plain text files by using the File|Save As dialog box. The general rule is, if you can type the file at the command line (for example, in DOS on both DOS- and Windows-based computers) and not see any odd, nonalphanumeric characters, it's a plain text file. The real test, of course, is if Perl can read and interpret your script.

NOTE: *One big difference between text files in Unix and MS-DOS/Windows is that Unix files use a single character at the end of each line, and MS-DOS/Windows files use two characters (i.e., a carriage return and a line feed). This can be a problem when you move scripts from one operating system to another because Perl, on the target system, may have problems with scripts written on the source system. (Note that many FTP programs now automatically convert line endings to the correct version for the target system.)*

You can name your Perl code files just about any way you want to—no special extension is necessary. However, the very popular Windows port—Win32 ActiveState Perl—associates the extension .pl with Perl scripts, so you can run them just by double-clicking them. In fact, file extensions can be useful when you come back to long lists of files three years from now and wonder what kind they are. For these reasons, I'll use the extension .pl for scripts in this chapter. Just bear in mind that you don't have to use this extension or any other (including the other popular Perl script extension, .p).

So far so good—we've finished our discussion on the selection of an editor or a word processor. Now how about writing some code?

Writing Code: Statements and Declarations

The big boss is looking over your shoulder. You've got your editor open and are about to start impressing the BB with your Perl expertise. The BB is waiting—what will you type?

Perl statements come in two forms: simple and compound. A *simple statement* is an expression that performs some specific action. In code, a simple statement ends with a semicolon (;), as you can see in the following code line. We'll use the **print** function to display the string "Hello!", followed by a newline character, **\n**, which skips to the next line:

```
print "Hello!\n";
```

Compound statements are composed of expressions and blocks. In Perl, blocks are delimited with curly braces, { and }, and can hold multiple simple statements. You do not place a semicolon after the curly braces. Here's an example in which I use a block to create a compound **for** loop statement, which is the most basic of the Perl loops:

```
for ($loop_index = 1; $loop_index <=5; $loop_index++) {
    print "Hello ";
    print "there!\n";
}
```

If you enter either of the previous scripts into a file, such as hello.pl, you've created a Perl script. The next step is making sure you can connect that script and the Perl interpreter to get the script to run.

Writing Code: Finding the Perl Interpreter

The big boss is still looking over your shoulder as you type at your workstation. You've created your first lines of Perl script. The BB is mighty impressed. But how do you make sure that the script can find the Perl interpreter? The BB says, "I'm waiting...."

There are two principal ways to make sure that a Perl script can find the Perl interpreter: explicitly and implicitly. I'll look at them both in the following sections.

Finding Perl Explicitly

You can find Perl by passing your script to perl, the Perl interpreter, explicitly from the command line:

```
C:\>perl hello.pl
```

This assumes, of course, that Perl has been installed correctly on your machine, which means that Perl is in your command path. If it isn't, you'll find yourself having to use the fully qualified path to the Perl executable, like this in MS-DOS:

```
D:\>c:\perl\bin\perl hello.pl
```

I don't recommend using the fully qualified path and suggest that you add Perl to your path if it's not already there. (It should be in your command path if Perl was installed properly.)

Finding Perl Implicitly

Besides passing your script to Perl explicitly, you can also make sure that your script can find Perl by itself. This means that you can run your scripts more like standalone commands, like this in Unix (where the % is the command prompt):

```
%hello.pl
```

Or, if you have named the Perl script's file without an extension, like this:

```
%hello
```

This looks more like a system command, which is the idea. Making sure that your script can find Perl by itself differs by operating system, and I'll explain how to do it in Unix here because most Web servers that support Perl run Unix.

You can let Unix know that your file is a Perl script by making the following line the first line of your script (you don't need this line if you invoke the Perl interpreter explicitly):

```
#!/usr/local/bin/perl
```

If you use the special #! syntax, it must be the very first line in your script. This line refers to the standard location of Perl on most Unix systems. Note that Perl might be at a different location on your machine, such as /usr/bin/perl (on many machines, the paths /usr/bin/perl and /usr/local/bin/perl are aliased to be the same).

To specify that you want to use Perl 5, you might have to use a line like this on many systems:

```
#!/usr/local/bin/perl5
```

Now it's time to actually run your script; see the next section.

Running Perl Code

You've finished writing your Perl script, and the big boss is watching over your shoulder. The company's future hinges on your new script. "OK," says the BB. "It's the big moment. How do you get all this to run?"

Assume that you have a short file named hello.pl, containing this Perl script:

```
#!/usr/local/bin/perl

print "hello\n";
```

Getting scripts like this to run is a basic Perl step. There are many variations, and I'll take a look at them in some detail in the following sections.

If Your Script Can Find Perl

If your script can find Perl, you can run the script easily. In Unix, this means that you've included a line such as **#!/usr/local/bin/perl** as the first line in your script. In Unix, you make the script an executable file with **chmod**, like this: **chmod +x hello.pl**. Also, make sure that the script is in your path (e.g., check your .login file and look for **set path** commands). Then you just run the script at the command line:

```
%hello.pl
```

In Windows and on the Macintosh, just double-click the script file to run it. (Make sure you've given the script file the extension .pl in Windows, which is the extension that the ActiveState software connects to the Perl interpreter.)

You can also invoke Perl from the command line explicitly, and I'll take a look at this next.

If You Want to Use Perl from the Command Line

To run a script explicitly with the Perl interpreter, make sure that perl is in your path and use the **perl** command. You can place your script in a file and pass that file's name to the Perl interpreter. For example, if the following code line is the content of the file hello.pl (I'm omitting the #! line because I'm running the Perl interpreter explicitly):

```
print "Hello!\n";
```

then you could run that script this way, specifying that file name:

```
C:\>perl hello.pl

Hello!
```

TIP: *To end a Perl script while it's running—for example, while it's waiting for input from you, but you want to quit—you press Ctrl+C.*

Basic Skills: Text Input and Output

Perl treats input and output as *channels*, and you work with these channels by using file handles. A *file handle* is just a value that represents a file to Perl. You get a file handle for a file when you open that file.

There are three predefined file handles that you can use with text: **STDIN**, **STDOUT**, and **STDERR**. **STDIN** is the normal input channel for your script, **STDOUT** is the normal output channel, and **STDERR** is the normal output channel for errors. By default, **STDIN** corresponds to the keyboard, and **STDOUT** and **STDERR** correspond to the screen. I'll use predefined file handles throughout this chapter; for instance, see the next section, where I use **STDOUT** to display text.

Basic Skills: Using the print Function

The programming team coordinator is mighty pleased with your new script, which handles no end of data and does no end of data crunching. The script finally ends and you turn triumphantly to the PTC. "But," the PTC asks, "where's the output?" You think: *output*? "Try the **print** function," the PTC says.

To print text to a file, including to **STDOUT**, you use the **print** function. It may be the most commonly used function in Perl. We've already seen the **print** function in this chapter, but I'll take a more systematic look at it now. The **print** function has these forms:

```
print FILEHANDLE LIST
print LIST
print
```

If you don't specify a file handle, **STDOUT** is used. If you don't specify a list of items to print (such a list can be made up of only one item), the **print** function prints whatever is in the special Perl variable $_ to the output channel. The variable $_ is the default variable that holds input from the input channel (see "Basic Skills: Using the Default Variable $_" in the "Immediate Solutions" section).

Here's an example where I just print "Hello!" and a newline character to the output channel:

```
print "Hello!\n";
```

Hello!

The **print** function is really a list function that takes a list of items. This means that you can pass a list of items to print, separating the list items with commas:

```
print "Hello ", "there!\n";
```

Hello there!

Basic Skills: Commenting Your Code

Your new script is so popular that the home office has distributed it to all the field offices. But now you're getting calls and emails from all over asking what line 14 does, if you really meant to do that in line 28, if line 42 is really legal code, and what about line 56—surely that's an error? As you hang up the phone wearily, you wonder if there is a better way to let other programmers know just how your programs work. There is—you can comment your code.

When you create complicated scripts, you may want to add comments—that is, reminders or explanatory text ignored by Perl—to make the structure and workings of these scripts easier to understand. In Perl, you preface comments with a # symbol because Perl will ignore all the text on a line after the # symbol. Here's an example:

```
#!/usr/bin/perl -w     # Use Perl with warnings
my $count = 0;         # $count used to match {}, (), etc.
my $statement = "";    # $statement holds multi-line statements
local $SIG{__WARN__} = sub {}; # Suppress error reporting

while (<>) {           # Accept input from the keyboard

    chomp;             # Clean up input
    while (/{|\(|\[/g) {$count++};    # Watch for {, (, etc.
    while (/}|\)|\]/g) {$count--};    # Pair with }, ), etc.
```

```perl
    $statement .= $_ . " ";     # Append input to current statement

    if (!$count) {              # Only evaluate if {, ( matches }, ) etc.

        eval $statement; # Evaluate the Perl statement
        if($@) {print "Syntax error.\n"};  # Notify of error
        $statement = ""; # Clear the current statement
        $count = 0       # Clear the multi-line {, ( etc. count

    }
}
```

Comments can help programmers reading your code at a later date to understand what's going on. Keep in mind that the programmer you help might be yourself.

Basic Skills: Reading Typed Input

Well, your new Perl calculator is a terrific success—it adds 7 + 7 and prints 14 every time. The big boss is very happy with it. "Let me try it," the BB says. "How do you enter the numbers to add?" You say, "Enter them? You can't do that—the calculator only adds 7 + 7 and that's it." "No good," says the BB. "You've got to let users type in their own numbers to add." So how do you do that?

As we've seen earlier, you can use the **print** function to display output—but how do you accept input? You can read input from the **STDIN** file handle by using angle brackets, < and >. For example, here's how to use a **while** loop (just like the JavaScript or Java **while** loop) to read each line the user types, storing those lines in a variable named **$temp**, and printing each line:

```perl
while ($temp = <STDIN>) {
    print $temp;
}
```

When you run this script and type, for example, "Hello!", the script echoes what you've typed:

```perl
while ($temp = <STDIN>) {
    print $temp;
}

Hello!
```

In fact, as is often the case in Perl, there's a short way to do this—see the next section.

Basic Skills: Using the Default Variable $_

When you use the construct **<STDIN>** without assigning its return value to a variable, Perl automatically assigns that return value to a special variable named **$_**. This variable, called the *default variable,* is a special variable that many Perl functions use as a default if you don't specify another. This means that you can use the **print** function without specifying a variable to print the contents of **$_**. (There are plenty of other special variables, too, like **$!**, which holds the current error if there is one.)

You can omit the **STDIN** altogether if you just use the angle brackets < and > alone without specifying any file handle—**STDIN** is used by default. (Perl is full of defaults like this, which can make things easier for experts but opaque for novices. That may explain why the experts like it.) Here's how the code from the previous section looks after you use these shortcuts:

```
while(<>) {
    print;
}
```

This is really a short version of the following code:

```
while($_ = <STDIN>) {
    print $_;
}
```

Some stylists have objected to the overuse of **$_** because its implicit, behind-the-scenes nature can be very hard to keep track of over many pages of code. That is, if you have five pages of code to look over, you might miss some operation that implicitly sets **$_** on page three and think that the **$_** used on page five holds the same value as in the code on page one. However, Perl scripts are typically rather short, and even if they're not, the operations that use **$_** are typically localized and not spread over many pages.

Note that there's no way to provide a set of simple rules to make it clear when you can use **$_** and when you can't—because some of the Perl functions use **$_** and some don't. This means that you have to make this determination on a function-by-function basis.

When you're used to working with **$_**, it usually makes programming much easier, even if it's more confusing to the uninitiated. Here's an example in which every statement uses **$_** implicitly:

```
while (<>) {
    for (split) {
        s/m/y/g;
        print;
    }
}
```

What does this script do? It breaks the line you type into words, loops over those words, converts all **m** characters to **y** characters, and prints the result. Here, I've typed "them" and gotten back "they":

%perl mtoy.pl

them
they

So how does this code look if you put the **$_** default variable back in explicitly? It looks like this—note how much cleaner the previous code is without the explicit **$_** symbol:

```
while ($_ = <>) {
    for $_ (split / /, $_) {
        $_ =~ s/m/y/g;
        print $_;
    }
}
```

Using **$_** is a learned skill in Perl. You can use it with some loops, functions, and constructs, but not with others. It's one of the things that can increase the learning curve. But when you know what you're doing, you'll use **$_** implicitly all the time—it becomes second nature. We'll see which loops, functions, and constructs use **$_** in this and the next chapter.

Basic Skills: Cleaning up Typed Input

Program Quality Control is on the phone with a complaint about the code you wrote, which was supposed to take simple "yes" or "no" responses from the users. But the actual strings that are showing up when the program is run all have a newline character appended to them: "yes\n" and "no\n". What's going on?

Input read from **STDIN** includes everything the user has typed, including the newline character at the end. To get rid of that newline character, you can use the **chop** or **chomp** functions. Here's how you use **chop**:

```
chop VARIABLE
chop LIST
chop
```

This function chops off the last character of a string and returns the character chopped. If **VARIABLE** is omitted, **chop** removes the default variable **$_**. For example, look at this script:

```
while (<>) {
    print;
}
```

When the script prints each line of input, you'll see that each line is followed by a newline character (to end a script like this, press Ctrl+C). However, if you chop the input, there will be no newline character when the scripts prints each line:

```
while (<>) {
    chop;
    print;
}
```

Besides using **chop**, you can also use **chomp**:

```
chomp VARIABLE
chomp LIST
chomp
```

The **chomp** function is a safer version of **chop**. It removes any line ending that corresponds to the current value of $/, which is the special Perl variable holding the input record separator (and defaults to a newline). This function returns the total number of characters removed. It's usually used to remove the newline character from the end of an input record. If **VARIABLE** is omitted, it chomps $_.

Basic Skills: Avoiding Immediate Script Closings in Windows

Program Quality Control is on the phone again—there's a problem with your script when it runs in Windows. The user is very patiently double-clicking your script to run it and is watching as something flickers on the screen—that's all that happens. Can you fix it?

Immediate Solutions

Here's what's happening if you're using Perl for Windows. When you double-click a file with the extension .pl, an MS-DOS window appears, the script executes, and then the MS-DOS window closes immediately without giving you the chance to see the script's output.

You can fix this if you make the script wait for keyboard input after executing. Just add these two lines to the end of your script:

```
print "Hello!\n";

print "Press <Enter> to continue...";
<STDIN>
```

The result appears in Figure 18.2. The script executes and then waits until you press the Enter key.

You can make the previous two lines of code even shorter because **<>** is the same as **<STDIN>**:

```
print "Hello!\n";

print "Press <Enter> to continue...";
<>
```

Figure 18.2   Holding a Perl script open in an MS-DOS window.

Creating Scalar Variables

The novice programmer says, "OK, I can get a Perl script to print something, but what about handling data?" "Good question," you say. "Let's start with scalar variables."

As we saw in the "In Depth" section of this chapter, scalar variables can hold simple data items, such as numbers and strings. Following is an example—note that to add strings together, you use the dot operator (.). (See "Using Strings in Scalar Variables" in the "Immediate Solutions" section of this chapter.) Here's the code:

```
$count = 1;
print "The current count is " . $count;

The current count is 1
```

The name you use for a scalar variable can contain letters, numbers, and underscores. Such a name must start with the $ symbol, which stops it from conflicting with reserved words in Perl. A scalar variable's name can be long—although the length is platform-dependent, a variable's name can be at least 255 characters long.

TIP: *Scalar variable names can also contain single quotes, although that practice is now deprecated.*

Because scalar variable names begin with a $ and don't conflict with Perl reserved words, you can write them in lowercase, which most programmers do. (Almost all Perl reserved words are lowercase, except for file handles like **STDIN** or implicitly called functions like the **BEGIN** block in a package.)

Note in particular that scalar variable names are case sensitive—**$variable1** is not the same as **$Variable1**—which is something to bear in mind if your operating system is not otherwise case sensitive (such as MS-DOS).

After the initial $, you can start a variable name with any letter or an underscore. You can even use a number as the first character after the $, but if you start a variable name with a number, the name must be made up of all numbers. You can use nonalphanumeric and nonunderscore characters in a variable name, but if you do, that variable name can be made up of only two characters: the $ and one character after the $ (just like the built-in Perl special variables, such as $_).

The $ symbol that starts all scalar variables is called a "funny character" in Perl. As mentioned earlier in this chapter, it's called a *prefix dereferencer*. The following are the data prefix dereferencers in Perl and their uses:

- **$**—Scalar variables
- **%**—Hash variables (associative arrays)
- **@**—Arrays

Unlike many other programming languages, you don't need to declare scalar variables in Perl to use them. The first time you use a scalar, Perl will create it if it doesn't already exist.

NOTE: Watch out for spelling errors—you might inadvertently misspell a variable and consequently create a new, uninitialized one. Perl does not consider this an error, and it's very hard to find when you're trying to debug your code.

However, the scalars you create this way are available to code throughout the current package; therefore, if you don't divide your code into packages, it's available anywhere in the script. Such scalars are called *global* and have global scope. The *scope* of a variable consists of all the code in which you can access it.

*TIP: It's often desirable to limit the scope of variables, however, and it will become a consideration if you start dividing code into blocks when you're creating subroutines. There are two ways to declare variables with restricted scope—you use the **my** or **local** keywords. See the Perl Black Book (The Coriolis Group, 1999) for more information.*

Using Assignment Operators on Scalars

The programming team coordinator is going through your code. "All these new scalars are very fine," the PTC says, "but you never seem to assign any data to them." "Well," you say, "how do you do that?" "Use scalar assignment," the PTC says.

How do you place data in a scalar variable? You use the assignment operator, as in this case where I place the value **5** in a variable named **$variable1**:

```perl
$variable1 = 5;
```

String assignments work much the same way:

```perl
$variable1 = "Hello there!";
```

Besides single assignments, you can perform multiple assignments in the same statement:

```perl
$x = $y = $z = 1;
```

In this case, each scalar is set to the same value, **1**, as you see by printing them (I'll use the **join** list function later in this chapter):

```
$x = $y = $z = 1;
print join (", ", $x, $y, $z);
```

```
1, 1, 1
```

You can use many operators besides assignments on scalars, of course. You can perform addition, subtraction, multiplication, and so on:

```
$x = $x + 2;
$x = $x - 2;
$x = $x * 5;
```

Using Numbers in Scalar Variables

So what kinds of numbers can you work with in Perl? Perl supports a variety of numeric formats, which are listed in Table 18.2.

Note in particular the underlined numeric format, which lets you format digits in a number in groups of three for easy recognition of numbers, as in 1,234,567. (Perl will generate an error if the underscores bind groups of anything but three digits.) Here's how you use that format:

```
$variable1 = 1_234_567;
```

TIP: *There's one more sticky point here: numeric precision. Because Perl is a cross-platform language, and because the precision of stored numeric values differs by machine (there's no way to list the kind of numeric precision you can expect), you might get different results using the same code on different machines. It's something to watch out for.*

Table 18.2 Perl numeric data types.

Type	Example
Floating	1.23
Hex	0x123
Integer	123
Octal	0123
Scientific	1.23E4
Underlines	1_234_567

Handling Truth Values in Perl

You've explained to the novice programmer that scalars can hold numbers and strings in Perl. The novice programmer nods, impressed, and asks, "What about the values true and false; how does Perl store those?" "Pull up a chair," you say, "and I'll go over it."

There are two ways to use scalars to store true and false values, and those ways correspond to the two scalar contexts, numeric and string. Here's the rule to remember: in numeric context, **0** is false and *any* other value is true; in string context, the empty string, "", is false and *any* other value is true.

The fact that any nonzero value represents true is especially useful in constructs like loops. For example, it keeps this **while** loop going because **<>** always returns something even if the user enters a blank line (in which case, **<>** returns a newline character because it always appends a newline character to what the user enters):

```perl
while(<>) {
    print;
}
```

Programmers often rely on the fact that any nonzero or nonempty string is true. You'll find it frequently in Perl code, as in this example, where I'm checking the value of the divisor to avoid dividing by zero. (This is not the greatest programming practice—for clarity I should check **$bottom** against **0** explicitly, but this example is just to give you an indication of a common programming practice.) Here's the example:

```perl
if ($bottom) {
    $result = $top / $bottom;
}
else {
    $result = 0;
}
```

Using Strings in Scalar Variables

You're writing in your new Perl text editor and have to decide how to save that text. If you were writing your program in C, you'd be working with awkward character arrays. Can Perl do any better? It sure can. Besides numbers, scalar variables can also hold strings:

```perl
$variable1 = "Hello!";
```

Perl allocates space to match the length of your strings, so theoretically, they can grow very large. As far as Perl is concerned, the difference between strings and numbers is one of context—if you use a scalar in numerical context (which you can force by adding **0** to a scalar), Perl treats the scalar's value as a number. If you treat the scalar as a string, Perl does, too. For example, Perl has two sets of comparison operators: one for use on scalars when you're treating them as strings, and one for use on scalars when you're treating them as numbers.

To place a double quote in your text, you can use the \" escape character this way:

```
print "I said, \"Hello\".";

I said, "Hello".
```

And note that you use the dot operator (.) to add two strings together:

```
$count = 1;
print "The current count is " . $count;

The current count is 1
```

Using Variable Interpolation

The programming team coordinator is looking over your code again. "What are all these dots in code like **print "The value at " . $index . " is " . $value**?" "Just the Perl string concatenation operator," you say, "which adds two strings together." "Use string interpolation," the PTC says, "because the code will be cleaner."

When you enclose a string that includes variable names in double quotes, Perl automatically substitutes the value stored in that variable into the string. For example, if you have a variable named **$text** that holds the word "Hello":

```
$text = "Hello";
```

then you can use that variable by name in double quotes, and Perl will substitute the contents of that variable—the string "Hello"—for the variable:

```
$text = "Hello";
print "Perl says: $text!\n";

Perl says: Hello!
```

This process is called *interpolation*. In particular, Perl has interpolated the value in the variable **$text** into the string enclosed in double quotes.

However, if you use single quotes, not double quotes, Perl will not perform interpolation:

```
$text = "Hello";
print 'Perl says: $text!\n';
```

Perl says: $text!\n

This means that you use single quotes when you don't want Perl to try to evaluate the enclosed expression.

You can also use a backtick—the backward leaning single quote (`)—to cause Perl to pass a command to the underlying operating system. For example, in Unix, you can execute the **uptime** command (which shows how long the host computer has been up) this way:

```
$uptime = `uptime`;
print $uptime;
```

4:29pm   up 18 days, 21:22,   13 users,   load average: 0.30, 0.39, 0.42

Programmers often use interpolation to concatenate strings, as in this example:

```
$a = "Hello";
$b = "there";
$c = "$a $b\n";
print $c;
```

Hello there

Defining a List

Now that you're a Perl professional, technical support has sent over some code for you to check. Everything is going well until you get to the line **($name, $id, $unit) = ("Sam", 1332, "Sales");**. What the heck is going on here? You call technical support to report an error in the code. "That's not an error," the technical support specialist says. "That's a list assignment."

As discussed in the "In Depth" section of this chapter, Perl allows you to assemble scalar variables (and other types, such as hashes and arrays) into *lists*. A list represents a number of items that you can work with as a whole. Lists are very important in Perl, and the built-in functions in Perl are divided into two groups: those that can handle scalars and those that can handle lists (although some functions can handle both).

There is no specific list data type in Perl because using lists is really a coding technique, and it doesn't represent a data storage format. However, there is a list operator, which is a pair of parentheses, and you can create a list by using commas to separate elements inside a pair of parentheses. For example, the expression (1, 2, 3) returns a list with three elements: 1, 2, and 3.

The **print** function is a list function, and if you pass it a list, it will concatenate (join) the elements in the list into one string. For example, if you pass it the list **(1, 2, 3)**:

```
print (1, 2, 3);
```

then **print** will display **123**:

```
print (1, 2, 3);
123
```

In fact, you can even omit the parentheses:

```
print 1, 2, 3;
123
```

You can also add a comma after the last list element if you like; this makes it easy to add future elements. (You'll often see this in Perl code, and I mention it here so you won't have to wonder what's going on when you see it.) Here's an example:

```
print (1, 2, 3,);
123
```

Assigning Lists to Other Lists

You can assign one list to another by using the assignment operator (=). For example, here's how you assign the elements in the list **($c, $d)** to the respective elements in the list **($a, $b)**:

```
($a, $b) = ($c, $d);
```

In this way, you can treat lists as assignable entities. The two lists can even contain some or all of the same variables. For example, here I swap the contents of two variables, **$a** and **$b**, by using list assignments without using a temporary variable:

```
($a, $b) = ($b, $a);
```

The lists you assign to each other can even be of different sizes. In this example, **$a** and **$b** receive the first two elements, respectively, of the longer list:

```
($a, $b) = (1, 2, 3);
print $a;

1
print $b;

2
```

When you work with a list in your code, you're working in list context. As we'll see when handling arrays, you can create an array, which has the prefix dereferencer @, by passing it a list of data, because the array recognizes list context:

```
@a = (2, 4, 6);
print @a;

246
```

Joining a List into a String

You're getting kind of tired of the **print** function concatenating all the items in the list you pass it. For example, **print ("Now", "is", "the", "time")** displays **Nowisthetime**, which looks a little less than professional when it comes up on the client's screen. Is there any way to format a list into a string that makes sense?

There is. To concatenate—that is, join—the elements of a list into a string, you can use the Perl **join** function, which has this syntax:

```
join EXPR, LIST
```

This function surrounds the strings in **LIST** with the value in **EXPR** and joins them into a single string, returning that resulting string. For example, here's how to handle the list **("Now", "is", "the", "time")** a little better by separating the elements with spaces:

```
print join(" ", ("Now", "is", "the", "time"));
```

Now is the time

EXPR can be more than one character. For example, you can also use commas and spaces together—which is great for printing a list:

```
print join(", ", ("Nancy", "Claire", "Linda", "Sara"));
```

Nancy, Claire, Linda, Sara

Here's another example showing how you can join the elements in the list **("12", "00", "00")** with a colon between fields to create the string **12:00:00**:

```
print join (":", "12", "00", "00");
```

12:00:00

Of course, you don't need to specify any characters to use when you're joining list elements. In this case, I pass the empty string, "", to join **H, e, l, l, o**, which results in output just as **print** would have displayed it:

```
print join ("", H, e, l, l, o);
```

Hello

Creating Arrays

The programming correctness czar wants to know why you're using 40,000 separate variables in the company's payroll program to hold the names of employees. "Well," you say, "we have 40,000 employees, and...." The PCC says, "Use an array and index it by employee ID." So how do you create arrays?

Array variables start with an @; otherwise, the same naming convention that scalars use applies. In Perl, a standard array is one-dimensional and it holds its elements, one after the other, in a single row, like this: **1, 2, 3**. The power of arrays is that you can refer to each element in the array by index—the first element is element **0**, the next element is element **1**, and so on. Using array indices and a loop, you can iterate over all the data in the array.

You can create an array by assigning a list to an array variable:

```
@array = (1, 2, 3);
```

To see the data in the new array, you can print it (note that **print** treats the array as a list and concatenates the elements as "123"):

```
@array = (1, 2, 3);
print @array;
```

123

As with scalars, Perl creates arrays when you first refer to them, and the arrays created have global scope—that is, they are universally accessible. You can refer to individual array elements by index by using [and] and the $ prefix dereferencer. You use $ because the individual element of a standard array is a scalar:

```
@array = (1, 2, 3);
print $array[0];
```

1

Besides numbers, of course, you can store other types of scalars, such as strings, in an array:

```
@array = ("one", "two", "three");
print @array;
```

onetwothree

Because Perl skips over white space (including new lines) when handling lists, you can set up your array assignment this way (as usual with lists, the final comma in the list is optional):

```
@array = (
    "one", "two", "three",
    "four", "five", "six",
);

print @array;
```

onetwothreefourfivesix

You can use the x repetition operator, as in this case, where I create an array of 100 zeroes:

```
@array = (0) x 100;
```

You can use the .. notation (called the *range operator*) as well. This example fills **@array** with the numbers 1 through 10:

```
@array = (1 .. 10);
```

When you refer to an array element that doesn't exist yet, Perl creates it automatically:

```
@array = (1, 2, 3);
$array[5] = "Here is a new element!";
print "$array[5]\n";
```

```
Here is a new element!
```

Programmers that use other languages often wonder if you can allocate resources for arrays before using them in Perl. In fact, you can extend arrays to an arbitrary length after you've created them using the previous technique—just refer to an element that doesn't exist yet. If you "grow" an array to the size you want to use this way, you save some time over constructing an array element by element.

Using Arrays

You've been able to create a new array and add elements, impressing the programming correctness czar. In fact, you've been able to store the names of all 40,000 employees in a single array. "OK," the PCC says. "Now how are you going to access the data in that array." You think, *access* it?

After creating an array, you can refer to the individual elements of an array as scalars by prefacing the array name with $ and using a numeric index in square brackets:

```
@array = ("one", "two", "three");
print $array[1];
```

```
two
```

In other words, you can treat a standard array as an indexed collection of scalars simply by enclosing that index in square brackets. You can also work with the elements in an array *en masse*, as here, where I copy one array to another:

```
@a1 = ("one", "two", "three");
@a2 = @a1;

print $a2[1];

two
```

Because you use an index to access array elements, arrays can function as lookup tables. In this example, I translate a decimal value the user types (0–15) into a hexadecimal digit:

```
while(<>) {
    @array = ('0' .. '9', 'a' .. 'f');
    $hex = $array[$_];
    print "$hex\n";
}
```

Creating Hashes

The novice programmer is in trouble again. "I just can't get used to thinking of everything in terms of numbers," the NP says. "I've stored all my data in an array, but I always get mixed up: Is the index of the day of the week 491 or 419?" "Well, NP," you say, "you should use a hash. With a hash, you can index your data with text string keys like 'weekday.' Problem solved."

Hashes are also called *associative arrays*, which might be a more descriptive name. Instead of using a numeric index to retrieve a value, you use a *key* (a text string) that is associated with that value.

Because you refer to the values in a hash with keys, not numbers, it's often more intuitive to store your data in a hash rather than in an array. However, it can be more difficult to set up loops over the data in a hash because you can't directly index data in a hash with a numeric loop index.

You preface a hash variable's name with %, as in this example where I set up an empty hash:

```
%hash = ();
```

As with arrays, you use the $ prefix dereferencer when working with individual hash elements. For example, here's how I place a few items in our new hash ("fruit" is the first key in the hash, and it corresponds to the value "apple"; "sandwich" is the second key and corresponds to the value "hamburger", and so on):

```
%hash = ();
```

```
$hash{fruit} = apple;
$hash{sandwich} = hamburger;
$hash{drink} = bubbly;
```

Note that you use curly braces, { and }, to denote a hash element, not square brackets, [and], as you do with arrays.

At this point, you can refer to individual elements in the hash by key value:

```
%hash = ();

$hash{fruit} = apple;
$hash{sandwich} = hamburger;
$hash{drink} = bubbly;

print $hash{sandwich};
```

hamburger

In this way, we've created a hash with keys and values associated with those keys.

You do not need to create an empty hash in order to start filling it. If you start working with a hash that does not yet exist, Perl creates it automatically. This means that this code works just as well as the previous code:

```
$hash{fruit} = apple;
$hash{sandwich} = hamburger;
$hash{drink} = bubbly;

print $hash{sandwich};
```

hamburger

You may recall that Perl ignores white space when reading a new array's elements, making constructs like this convenient if you have lots of array elements:

```
@array = (
    "one", "two", "three",
    "four", "five", "six",
);
```

In the same way, you can create a hash like this, specifying the key/value pairs that you want to fill the hash with:

```
%hash = (
    'fruit'    , 'apple',
    'sandwich' , 'hamburger',
    'drink'    , 'bubbly',
);

print "$hash{'fruit'}\n";
```

apple

In fact, there's a synonym for a comma (**=>**). Using this operator makes the relationship between keys and values clearer, so programmers often write hash creation statements like this:

```
%hash = (
    fruit    => apple,
    sandwich => hamburger,
    drink    => bubbly,
);
print "$hash{fruit}\n";
```

apple

Note that the **=>** operator is not doing anything special—it really is just the same as a comma operator except for one thing: It forces any word to the left of it to be interpreted as a string. For example, this statement:

```
print "x"=>"y"=>"z";
```

xyz

is the same as this one:

```
print "x", "y", "z";
```

xyz

You can use keys with spaces in them, as in this case, where I'm creating a hash element with the key "ice cream":

```
$hash2{cake} = chocolate;
$hash2{pie} = blueberry;
$hash2{'ice cream'} = pecan;
```

You can refer to this item in the way you'd expect:

```perl
$hash2{cake} = chocolate;
$hash2{pie} = blueberry;
$hash2{'ice cream'} = pecan;

print "$hash{'ice cream'}\n";
```

pecan

You can also use double-quote interpolation to create hash keys, or use variables directly:

```perl
$value = $hash{$key};
```

Hashes provide a powerful technique for storing your data, but keep in mind that you can't refer to the values in a hash directly with a numeric index.

Using Hashes

"OK," says the novice programmer, "I've created my new hash and loaded it up with data. I'm all set to go. There's only one problem: How do I get that data out of the hash again?" "No problem," you say. "Just use the keys you've set up."

After you've created a hash, you can use it by addressing the values in the hash by key:

```perl
$value = $hash{$key};
```

In addition, you can place elements in the hash simply by using the assignment operator, as in this example from the previous topic:

```perl
$hash{fruit} = apple;
$hash{sandwich} = hamburger;
$hash{drink} = bubbly;

print $hash{sandwich};
```

hamburger

If you use a hash in a list context, it interpolates all the key/value pairs into the list:

```perl
$hash{fruit} = apple;
$hash{sandwich} = hamburger;
```

```perl
$hash{drink} = bubbly;

print join(" ", %hash);
```

drink bubbly sandwich hamburger fruit apple

This example illustrates an important point: The items in a hash are *not* stored in the order in which you inserted them. Perl stores them in its own order for efficiency because it assumes that you'll be retrieving those items by using a key and not relying on the order in which they're stored.

If you use a hash in a scalar context, it returns a value of **true** if there are any key/value pairs in the hash.

Hashes are not quite as convenient to use in loops as arrays are because you don't use an easily incremented numeric index with a hash. However, Perl supplies various ways of improving this situation. One such way is the **each** function, which returns successive key/value pairs:

```perl
$hash{fruit} = apple;
$hash{sandwich} = hamburger;
$hash{drink} = bubbly;

while(($key, $value) = each(%hash)) {
    print "$key => $value\n";
}
```

drink => bubbly
sandwich => hamburger
fruit => apple

Another way to work with hashes in loops is the **keys** function, which returns a list of the keys in a hash, making those keys almost as easy to handle as a numeric index:

```perl
$hash{fruit} = apple;
$hash{sandwich} = hamburger;
$hash{drink} = bubbly;

foreach $key (keys %hash) {
    print $hash{$key} . "\n";
}
```

bubbly
hamburger
apple

Using Perl Operators

The operators in Perl are much the same as in JavaScript or Java, with a few additions. You can find the Perl operators listed in Table 18.1. The Perl operators are generally like the ones we've seen in JavaScript or Java, but the relational and equality operators are worth a closer look; see the next two sections.

Using Relational (Comparison) Operators

"Look," says the novice programmer, "I'm alphabetizing a list of strings with this comparison code: **if ($a < $b)**...." "Hold on right there," you say. "There's a problem. You're using the wrong comparison operator."

Perl relational operators are binary operators that perform comparisons, returning **1** for **true** and **false** otherwise. The relational operators, such as greater-than-or-equal-to, less-than-or-equal-to, and so on, appear in Table 18.3.

Note in particular that you use one set of operators for numeric comparisons and another set for string comparisons (the string comparisons are done using ASCII values). The relational operators are listed in Table 18.3. Also note that the greater-than-or-equal-to operator is **>=**, not **=>**, which is the comma synonym operator.

Here's an example in which I check the user's input numerically, displaying an error message if that input is greater than 100:

```
while (<>) {
    if ($_ > 100) {
        print "Too big!\n";
    }
}
```

Table 18.3 Relational operators.

Operator	Data Type	Returns
<	Numeric	True if the left operand is less than the right operand.
<=	Numeric	True if the left operand is less than or equal to the right operand.
>	Numeric	True if the left operand is greater than the right operand.
>=	Numeric	True if the left operand is greater than or equal to the right operand.
ge	String	True if the left operand is greater than or equal to the right operand.
gt	String	True if the left operand is greater than the right operand.
le	String	True if the left operand is less than or equal to the right operand.
lt	String	True if the left operand is less than the right operand.

You can also use the logical operators, such as && and ||, or their low-precedence cousins, the **and** operator and the **or** operator, to connect logical clauses together. In this example, I require user input to be a letter between **k** and **m**:

```
print "Please enter letters from k to m\n";
while (<>) {
    chop;
    if ($_ lt 'k' or $_ gt 'm') {
        print "Please enter letters from k to m\n";
    } else {
        print "Thank you - let's have another!\n";
    }
}
```

Using Equality Operators

Perl supports the equality operators listed in Table 18.4. Note that, like the relational operators, there are separate sets of operators to use on numbers and on strings. Also note the very useful != operator, which tests for inequality.

Here's an example in which I ask users to type the character **y** and keep displaying an error message until they do:

```
print "Please type the letter y\n";
while (<>) {
    chop;
    if ($_ ne 'y') {
        print "Please type the letter y\n";
    } else {
        print "Do you always do what you're told?\n";
        exit;
    }
}
```

Here's the output the user might get from this code:

```
Please type the letter y
a
Please type the letter y
b
Please type the letter y
c
Please type the letter y
y
Do you always do what you're told?
```

Table 18.4 Equality operators.

Operator	Type	Returns
!=	Numeric	True if the left operand is not equal to the right operand.
<=>	Numeric	–1, 0, or 1, depending on whether the left operand is numerically less than, equal to, or greater than the right operand.
==	Numeric	True if the left operand is equal to the right operand.
cmp	String	–1, 0, or 1, depending on whether the left operand is less than, equal to, or greater than the right operand.
eq	String	True if the left operand is equal to the right operand.
ne	String	True if the left operand is not equal to the right operand.

Using the if Statement

"I've got a decision to make," the novice programmer says. "What is it?" you ask. The NP says, "The question is, is the value of **$budget** greater than or less than zero?" You ask, "What's the difference?" The NP says, "If **$budget** is less than zero, I'm fired." "OK," you say. "Better check it with an **if** statement."

As in JavaScript and Java, the **if** statement is the core conditional statement in Perl. This statement checks a condition specified in parentheses. If that condition evaluates to true (i.e., nonzero or not an empty string), the statement executes the code in the associated block.

You can also use an **else** clause to hold code that is executed if the statement's condition is false, and you can use **elsif** (not *else if* or *elseif* as in other languages) clauses to perform additional tests on other conditions. Here's the syntax of the **if** statement:

```
if (EXPR) BLOCK
if (EXPR) BLOCK else BLOCK
if (EXPR) BLOCK elsif (EXPR) BLOCK ... else BLOCK
```

Note the expression **EXPR**. That is the expression that determines the program flow in this statement; if **EXPR** evaluates to true, the code in the succeeding block is executed. If **EXPR** evaluates to false, the code in the succeeding block is not executed—instead, the code in the following **else** block, if there is one, is executed.

If there is no **else** statement, Perl looks for an **elsif** statement, which is an **else** statement combined with a new **if** statement, so it includes a new condition to be tested. If the condition in an **elsif** statement evaluates to true, the code in its block is executed; if it evaluates to false, Perl looks for a following **elsif** statement, and the test begins again.

Note that you can have only one **else** statement following an **if** statement, but you can have many **elsif** statements, each with its own condition. And the **else** statement must follow any **elsif** statements.

That's how **if** statements work. Let's look at an example. In this case, I'm using the equality operator (**==**) to check if a variable equals 5, and if so, indicate that result to the user with a message:

```
$variable = 5;

if ($variable == 5) {
    print "Yes, it's five.\n";
}

Yes, it's five.
```

Note the expression in the parentheses. That expression is a logical expression, which evaluates to true or false. (Because any nonzero or nonempty string is regarded as true, you can get pretty creative with the **if** statement's condition.) If the result is true, the code in the block following the **if** statement is executed.

You can use multiple logic clauses in the **if** statement's condition by tying them together with operators such as && and || (or the **and** operator and the **or** operator):

```
use integer;

$variable = 5;

if ($variable < 6 && $variable > 4) {
    print "Yes, it's five.\n";
}

Yes, it's five.
```

You can also include code in an **else** clause, which is executed if the preceding **if** statement's condition evaluates to false:

```perl
$variable = 6;

if ($variable == 5) {
    print "Yes, it's five.\n";
} else {
    print "No, it's not five.\n";
}
```

No, it's not five.

You can also add **elsif** clauses to perform an arbitrary number of tests. In this case, if the first condition is false, the second is tested; if the second condition is false, the next is tested, and so on. If none of the conditions are true, the code in the **else** clause is executed:

```perl
$variable = 2;

if ($variable == 1) {
    print "Yes, it's one.\n";
} elsif ($variable == 2) {
    print "Yes, it's two.\n";
} elsif ($variable == 3) {
    print "Yes, it's three.\n";
} elsif ($variable == 4) {
    print "Yes, it's four.\n";
} elsif ($variable == 5) {
    print "Yes, it's five.\n";
} else {
    print "Sorry, can't match it!\n";
}
```

Yes, it's two.

Looping with the for Loop

"I'm fed up with this," the novice programmer declares. "With what?" you ask. "Adding all these values one by one," the NP says. "I must have two dozen addition statements in my code." "Get rid of them," you say, "and use a **for** loop."

As in JavaScript and Java, you use the **for** loop to iterate over the statement(s) in the loop body, usually by using a loop index. Here's the syntax of the **for** loop:

LABEL for (*EXPR1*; *EXPR2*; *EXPR3*) *BLOCK*

The first expression, **EXPR1**, is executed before the body (**BLOCK**) of the loop is executed The first expression is where you do any initialization, such as setting the initial value of a loop index, which counts how many times the loop has executed.

The second expression, **EXPR2**, is tested before each loop iteration (i.e., each time before the body of the loop is executed). If the result is false, it terminates the loop. (The body of the loop might not even be executed once if the condition turns out to be false when the loop starts.) This is how you specify when the loop is to end. For example, you might check the value of the loop index, if you're using one, and terminate the loop if the loop index has reached a certain value.

The third expression, **EXPR3**, is executed after each loop iteration. You can use this expression to get ready for the next iteration of the loop by, for example, incrementing a loop index if you're using one.

The actual code executed each time through the loop—that is, the body of the loop—is in **BLOCK**.

There are a number of ways to use this loop. The classic way is with a simple loop index like this, where I use a loop variable named **$loop_index** to print "Hello!" (with a new line) ten times:

```
for ($loop_index = 1; $loop_index <= 10; $loop_index++) {
    print "Hello!\n";
}

Hello!
Hello!
Hello!
Hello!
Hello!
Hello!
Hello!
Hello!
Hello!
Hello!
```

Note how this works: The first expression in the **for** loop initializes the loop index, the next expression is the test that must evaluate to true for the loop to continue looping, and the third expression, executed after each loop iteration, increments the loop index. Using a loop index like this is one way to make sure that the **for** loop executes only a certain number of times.

Looping with the foreach Loop

Technical support is on the phone asking for your help. "The code loops over a list with a **while** loop, and—" "Stop right there," you say, "I see the problem. When you're looping over a list, you should use a **foreach** loop if you can. Problem solved."

Although it's actually the same loop as **for** (see the previous section), programmers often use **foreach** when using a variable to iterate through a list. (That is, you can read the loop as "for each element in....") Here's how you (usually) use **foreach**:

```
LABEL foreach VAR (LIST) BLOCK
```

This loop iterates over a list, setting the variable *VAR* to be each successive element of the list, and executes the code in *BLOCK*. You can refer to *VAR* in the code in *BLOCK* so your code can work on each successive element in the list.

The **foreach** loop is specifically designed to let you work with a list of elements without needing to use an index to iterate over the elements in the list. Instead of iterating a loop index, a loop variable is automatically filled with a new element from the list after every iteration. You don't have to worry about ending the loop when you reach the end of the list because it's done automatically.

Here's an example using **foreach** on a list. In this case, I sum the values in an array without using an array index:

```perl
@array = (1, 2, 3);
$running_sum = 0;

foreach $element (@array) {
    $running_sum += $element;
}

print "Total = $running_sum";
```

```
Total = 6
```

If you don't supply a loop variable name, **foreach** uses **$_** as the loop variable; this can be convenient if you're using functions that use **$_** by default, like **print**. Here's an example in which I print the elements of an array while relying on the default variable **$_**:

```perl
@array = ("Hello ", "there.\n");

foreach (@array) {print;}
```

Hello there.

Looping with the **while** Loop

The novice programmer is in trouble again. "My code," the NP says, "reads in lines from a file using a **for** loop, but I don't know when to terminate the loop." "Well," you say, "how many lines are there in the file?" "That's just it," the novice programmer says. "I have no idea." "The solution is clear," you say. "Use a **while** loop."

The **while** loop is a significant one in Perl because you can use it to execute code over and over while a condition that you specify remains true. Here's the syntax of the **while** loop:

```
LABEL while (EXPR) BLOCK
LABEL while (EXPR) BLOCK continue BLOCK
```

This loop executes the code in ***BLOCK*** as long as ***EXPR*** is true. The code in a **while** loop's **continue** block, if there is one, is executed every time the loop executes fully, or if you use a loop command that explicitly goes to the next iteration of the loop.

The **while** loop is an easy one to use. Here's an example in which I keep adding the users' savings until they've made a million dollars:

```perl
$savings = 0;
while ($savings < 1_000_000) {
    print "Enter the amount you earned today: ";
    $savings += <>;
}

print "Congratulations, millionaire!\n";
```

Using the die Statement

What if there's a problem and you want to display an error message when you end the program? You can use the **die** function, which has this syntax:

```
die LIST
```

This function prints the value of *LIST* to **STDERR** and stops the program. Here's an example in which I try to open a nonexistent file (you'll invariably see a **die** statement tacked onto the end of an **open** statement this way in Perl):

```
$filename = "nonexist.pl";
open FileHandle, $filename or die "Cannot open $filename\n";
```

This script ends with this error message:

```
Cannot open nonexist.pl
```

Creating Objects

In Chapter 19, we'll use the CGI module to create CGI scripts. The CGI module is object-oriented (for more on object-oriented programming, see Chapter 14). To create a Web page to send back to a Web browser, I include the CGI module and use the **new** operator to create an object named **$co** of the CGI class:

```
use CGI;
$co = new CGI;
```

The variable **$co** really contains a *reference* to a new CGI object. You can access its data members and methods by using the arrow operator, ->, as in this example, where I'm calling the new CGI object's **header** method:

```
use CGI;
$co = new CGI;
print $co->header;
```

The **header** method returns the header text of a Web page. When the script runs as a CGI script, the **print** function will send that header back to the browser, as we'll see in the next chapter.

Chapter 19

CGI Scripting with Perl

If you need an immediate solution to:	See page:
Starting a Document	1128
Displaying Images	1128
Creating Headings	1129
Centering Elements	1130
Creating a Bulleted List	1130
Creating a Hyperlink	1131
Creating Horizontal Rules	1132
Creating a Form	1132
Working with Text Fields	1133
Reading Data from Controls	1134
Working with Text Areas	1135
Working with Checkboxes	1136
Working with Scrolling Lists	1137
Working with Radio Buttons	1139
Working with Password Fields	1140
Working with Pop-up Menus	1141
Working with Hidden Data Fields	1142
Creating Submit and Reset Buttons to Upload Data from an HTML Form	1143
Ending a Form	1144
Ending a Document	1145
Calling a CGI Script from an XHTML Page	1146

In Depth

In this chapter, we'll learn about Web programming using Common Gateway Interface (CGI) scripts. CGI programming is all about creating and using CGI scripts. In Perl programming, a CGI script is just a Perl program in a file that (typically) has the extension .cgi. You place CGI scripts on your Web server, and the scripts will use Perl code to create Web pages dynamically, responding to user actions. From now on, we'll be sending output to Web browsers, not to the console.

Creating Web pages on the fly can make your Web pages come alive. Using CGI scripts, you can place buttons, scrolling lists, popup menus, and more in your Web pages. Scripts can enable users to interact with your Web pages, access databases, run programs, play games, and even make purchases on the Web. Perl is the power behind interactive Web pages for tens of thousands of programmers.

The beauty of CGI programming in Perl is that you use code to create the Web page you want, responding dynamically to the user. Perl CGI programming is the same kind of programming used in the previous chapter except that your code runs on a Web server. Also, the **STDIN**, **STDOUT**, and **STDERR** file handles are not tied to the console. Other than that, it's just Perl, so the skills you've already developed are applicable in this chapter. The only change is the I/O (input/output), and it isn't terribly different.

When you run a Perl CGI script, the standard I/O file handles are different from those in programs you write to work with the console. The following list describes how **STDIN**, **STDOUT**, and **STDERR** are set up for CGI scripts:

- **STDIN**—Sends the input to your script from controls such as buttons, text fields, and scrolling lists. This information is encoded, and to parse this information, you use a Perl module such as CGI.pm to fill variables with the data from a Web page.

- **STDOUT**—Goes back to the user's Web browser. To create a new Web page, either you print that Web page's text directly to **STDOUT**, or you use the methods of modules such as CGI.pm to create the HTML you want and then send that to **STDOUT**. (CGI.pm doesn't create XHTML yet.)

- **STDERR**—Goes to the Web server's error log. This is not very useful for the majority of CGI programmers because they don't have easy access to their ISPs' server logs.

CGI Programming with CGI.pm

In this chapter, we're going to master the essentials of CGI script programming with CGI.pm, the CGI module that comes with Perl. As I mentioned in Chapter 18, CGI.pm prints HTML, not XHTML yet, so we'll be dealing mostly with HTML pages here. Therefore, as created by the methods of CGI.pm, some elements won't have closing tags (as is normal in HTML); all element and attribute names will be in capital letters; attribute values won't necessarily be enclosed in quotes; and attributes can be standalone (that is, appear in an element without being assigned a value). All this will be fixed one day when CGI.pm is upgraded to create true XHTML.

In this chapter, I'll create two CGI scripts. The first is cgi1.cgi, which creates a Web page full of controls (buttons, scrolling lists, radio buttons, popup menus, and so on). When the user clicks the Submit button in that Web page, the Web browser will send the data in those controls to a second CGI script, cgi2.cgi. That script will read and report that data back to the user. Using this approach, you'll learn how to use all the common controls in CGI scripts.

Before we begin, I'll assume that you have an ISP hosting your Web site and that you can upload your Web pages to that site. (Uploading is usually a simple matter of using an FTP program or using an ISP Web page that can upload files.) I'll also assume that your ISP runs Unix, which is the usual operating system for Web servers that can run Perl.

You'll also need to be able to run CGI scripts on your ISP's Web server; some ISPs do not allow this, usually for security reasons. Some ISPs restrict your CGI scripts to a directory—named cgi-bin or just cgi—in your account, and that directory must have special permissions assigned before you can execute any scripts. There can be other restrictions as well; for example, some Web servers will not allow your CGI script to execute system commands using the backticks operator because it's a big source of security leaks.

Assuming that you can run CGI scripts, you must remember to set any pertinent permission levels for those files (without compromising your security or your system's security). Unix file permissions consist of three octal digits corresponding to, in order, the file owner's permission, the permission of others in the same user group, and the permission of all others. In each octal digit, a value of 4 indicates read permission, a value of 2 indicates write permission, and a value of 1 indicates execute permission. You add these values together to set the individual digits in a permission setting. For example, a permission of 600 means that the file's owner, and only the file's owner, can both read and write the file.

On a Unix machine, you can use the **chmod** command to set permissions, like this: **chmod 755 script.cgi**. The number 755 is a common permission setting for CGI scripts because it gives the file's owner read, write, and execute permission, and it gives everyone else read and execute permission, which they'll need to use your CGI script.

Increasingly, ISPs are not allowing users to have shell access to the Web areas of the ISPs' servers for security reasons. However, many modern FTP programs allow you to set file permissions as well as upload files, so it's becoming more common to set CGI script permissions instead of using the **chmod** command directly in a shell. If your FTP program doesn't let you set file permissions using octal values like 755, give your CGI script read and execute permissions for all three levels of users, and give the owner level write permission as well.

NOTE: For more information on the uploading process for your ISP, check with your technical support specialists.

So how do you create a CGI script? Theoretically, it's easy: Your CGI program just executes normal Perl code like any Perl program when it's called by a Web browser (i.e., when a Web browser navigates to your CGI file's URL). Anything you print to the standard output channel is sent to the Web browser.

Because you can't invoke Perl on a CGI script directly (by typing its name at the command prompt), you must use a line like **#!/usr/local/bin/perl** as the first line of your CGI script; this means that the scripts have to find Perl by themselves. See Chapter 18 for more details.

If your CGI script executes the command to **print "Hello!"**, that text is sent back to the browser and "Hello!" appears in the Web page. But that's a very rudimentary use of a CGI script. What if you want to read input from controls in a Web page? What if you want to use a script to create those controls? To perform these functions and more, I'll use the CGI.pm package that comes with Perl. If you have Perl installed on your system, you should have CGI.pm.

When a user calls your CGI script—either directly by its URL or through a Web page—and clicks the Submit button, data from that page (such as the data in controls) is encoded and sent to your script. That data is usually appended as text to the end of the URL of your script. To read that data, most programmers use a module such as CGI.pm to decode the data and store it in variables.

To start using CGI.pm, you use its **new** method to get a CGI object, then call its various methods. There's a method corresponding to every major HTML tag, and calling a method generates the tag using the attributes you pass. You can also get the data sent to your CGI script from a Web page by using the **param** method. I'll take a look at programming with CGI.pm in more detail now.

CGI.pm methods can take *named parameters*, which means that you can pass the name of the attribute you're setting and the value to which you're setting it as a key/value pair. Following is an example in which I use a CGI object to create a Web page, and I use that object's methods to create tags. I am passing named parameters to the CGI.pm **textarea** method to create a text-area control (a *text area* is like a two-dimensional text box), to name it ('**textarea**'), and to specify a size (10 rows and 60 columns). In a named parameter, the hyphen before the attribute name is optional, so you can write **-name=>'textarea'** as **name=> 'textarea'** if you prefer:

```
#!/usr/local/bin/perl
use CGI;

$co = new CGI;
print $co->header,
$co->start_html(-title=>'CGI Example'),
$co->center($co->h1('Welcome to CGI!')),
$co->start_form(),
$co->textarea
(
    -name=>'textarea',
    -rows=>'10',
    -columns=>'60'
),
$co->end_form(),
$co->end_html;
```

The CGI.pm methods, such as **textarea**, return only HTML. To get that HTML into a Web page, you use the **print** function to send it to **STDOUT**. In fact, scripts that use CGI.pm can simply be one long **print** statement, as in the previous code. The following code creates a complete Web page containing a text-area control (because this is HTML and not XHTML, all tag names are in capital letters):

```
<!DOCTYPE HTML PUBLIC "-//IETF//DTD HTML//EN">
<HTML>
<HEAD>
<TITLE>CGI Example</TITLE>
</HEAD>

<BODY>
<CENTER>
<H1>Welcome to CGI!</H1>
```

```
</CENTER>
<FORM METHOD="post"  ENCTYPE="application/x-www-form-urlencoded">

<TEXTAREA NAME="textarea" ROWS="10" COLS="60">
</TEXTAREA>

</FORM>
</BODY>
</HTML>
```

I only used the attributes of the **<TEXTAREA>** element to set up that element as you see here: **<TEXTAREA NAME="textarea" ROWS="10" COLS="60">**. But what if I wanted to enclose some content between the opening and closing tags? For example, what if I wanted to enclose the text "Welcome to CGI!" between HTML **<P>** and **</P>** tags, like this: **<P>Welcome to CGI!</P>**?

In this case, the text "Welcome to CGI!" is the content of the element, not an attribute. If you're going to pass the content of an element as well as attributes to CGI.pm, you enclose the attributes in a hash to tell CGI.pm that they're attributes. Then you pass the actual content as the argument(s) following that hash:

```
#!/usr/local/bin/perl

use CGI;

$co = new CGI;

print $co->header,
$co->start_html(-title=>'CGI Example'),
$co->center($co->h1('Welcome to CGI!')),
$co->start_form(),
$co->textarea
(
    -name=>'textarea',
    -rows=>10,
    -columns=>60
),
$co->end_form(),
$co->p({-align=>center}, 'Welcome to CGI!'),
$co->end_html;
```

The following code produces this HTML page:

```
<!DOCTYPE HTML PUBLIC "-//IETF//DTD HTML//EN">
<HTML>
<HEAD>
<TITLE>CGI Example</TITLE>
</HEAD>

<BODY>
<CENTER>
<H1>Welcome to CGI!</H1>
</CENTER>
<FORM METHOD="post"  ENCTYPE="application/x-www-form-urlencoded">
<TEXTAREA NAME="textarea" ROWS="10" COLS="60">
</TEXTAREA>
</FORM>
<P ALIGN="center">
Welcome to CGI!
</P>
</BODY>
</HTML>
```

The curly braces create a hash and let CGI.pm distinguish between tag attributes and tag contents; the attributes go in the hash.

Methods that create HTML tags in CGI.pm are called *shortcuts*. You'll find the available shortcut methods in Table 19.1; note that they have the same name as the tags they create. These methods are called shortcuts because they let you create HTML easily. (If you prefer, you can simply print HTML or XHTML directly to **STDOUT** without using CGI.pm shortcuts—and sometimes that's easier than using shortcuts.)

If you want to specify the attributes of an element that you create with one of these shortcut methods, you need to pass those attributes in a hash, even if you're not giving the element any content. You also have to provide a key/value pair for each attribute. If the attribute does not have a value, pass an empty string, "". On the other hand, if you're just passing text that you want to use as the tag's content and not any attributes, you can pass the text directly as an argument to the shortcut. Here are some CGI shortcut examples and the HTML they create:

Table 19.1   CGI pm shortcuts.

a	address	applet	b	base	basefont	big	blink	body	br	caption	center
cite	code	dd	dfn	div	dl	dt	em	font	form	frame	frameset	h1	h2	h3
h4	h5	h6	head	html	hr	i	img	input	kbd	li	ol	p	pre	samp	select
small	strong	sup	table	td	th	title	tr	tt	ul	var	

```
p();                              ----> <P>
p('Hello there');                 ----> <P>Hello there</P>
p('Hello', 'there');              ----> <P>Hello there</P>
p({-align=>right});               ----> <P ALIGN="RIGHT">
p({-align=>right}, 'text');       ----> <P ALIGN="RIGHT">text</P>
p({-align=>right}, 'text');       ----> <P ALIGN="RIGHT">text</P>
p({-align=>right}, ['text1', 'text2']);  ----> <P ALIGN="RIGHT">text1</P>
                                         <P ALIGN="RIGHT">text2</P>
```

Notice the last example; I'm passing a hash of attributes and an *array* of element contents. When you pass an array of content arguments, an element with the given attributes is created for *each* item in the array.

The names of controls, like the **textarea** control, do not appear among the list of shortcut methods because the default text in a control is placed in the content of the element. For example, the default text in the **textarea** control is placed in the content of the **<TEXTAREA>** element, as in the following code, where the default text in this text area is "Hello!":

```
<!DOCTYPE HTML PUBLIC "-//IETF//DTD HTML//EN">
<HTML>
<HEAD>
<TITLE>CGI Example</TITLE>
</HEAD>

<BODY>
<CENTER>
<H1>Welcome to CGI!</H1>
</CENTER>
<FORM METHOD="post" ENCTYPE="application/x-www-form-urlencoded">
<TEXTAREA NAME="textarea" ROWS="10" COLS="60">
Hello!
</TEXTAREA>
</FORM>
<P ALIGN="center">
Welcome to CGI!
</P>
</BODY>
</HTML>
```

However, CGI.pm creates controls with shortcuts, so you use attributes to set up controls. In this case, you use the **-value** attribute to set the default text in the text area:

```perl
#!/usr/local/bin/perl
use CGI;

$co = new CGI;
print $co->header,
$co->start_html(-title=>'CGI Example'),
$co->center($co->h1('Welcome to CGI!')),
$co->start_form(),
$co->textarea
(
    -name=>'textarea',
    -value=>'Hello!',
    -rows=>'10',
    -columns=>'60'
),
$co->end_form(),
$co->p({-align=>center}, 'Welcome to CGI!'),
$co->end_html;
```

This code produces the preceding HTML, in which the **<TEXTAREA>** element has both content text and attributes.

Note that I pass the attributes to the **textarea** method in a simple list, not in a hash. Until version 2.38 of CGI.pm, you always passed attributes in a list to control-creation methods such as **textarea**. But in more recent versions of CGI.pm, you can pass attributes in a hash if you prefer; this is more consistent with the way you pass attributes to HTML shortcuts.

*TIP: If you call control-creation methods, such as **textarea**, with just one argument (like **$co->textarea('text1')**), not one or more pairs of arguments (like **$co->(-name => 'textarea', -value=>'Hello!')**), then that single argument is taken to be the control's name.*

Creating HTML Controls in cgi1.cgi

To show you how CGI.pm works, and to create some code you can use in your own CGI scripts, I'll write two scripts in this chapter: one that creates a Web page full of controls, such as text fields, checkboxes, and radio buttons; and another script that reads the data the user has entered into that Web page. Both CGI scripts consist of little more than one long **print** statement, which I use to create a Web page by sending text to **STDOUT** (i.e., to the Web browser).

The first CGI script is cgi1.cgi. For the sake of reference, it appears in Listing 19.1 at the end of the "In Depth" section. How do you run this script? You just navigate to it in a Web browser. When the user opens this CGI script in his or her Web browser, the script returns a Web page containing HTML controls and text, including a sample Web page survey that the user can fill out. This survey appears in Netscape Navigator in Figures 19.1, 19.2, and 19.3.

As you see in Figure 19.1, the Web page welcomes users with an image and suggests that if they don't want to fill out the survey, they can jump to the CPAN site with a hyperlink.

Scrolling down the page (see Figure 19.2), the survey asks for the user's name with a text field and asks for the user's opinions with a text area.

Scrolling farther down the page (see Figure 19.3), you see even more controls in the survey page: checkboxes, radio buttons, scrolling lists, popup menus, a password control, and Submit and Reset buttons. These controls are there to accept more survey data from the user. We'll learn how to create these controls from a CGI script throughout this chapter.

When the user clicks the Submit button at the bottom of the survey, the Web browser collects all the data from the controls in the Web page and sends that data to another CGI script, cgi2.cgi.

The cgi2.cgi script reads the data sent to it and produces a summary of that data in a new Web page. For reference, cgi2.cgi appears in Listing 19.2 at the end of the "In Depth" section, and the results of that script appear in Figure 19.4, where you can see the summary of the data the user has entered in the survey Web page.

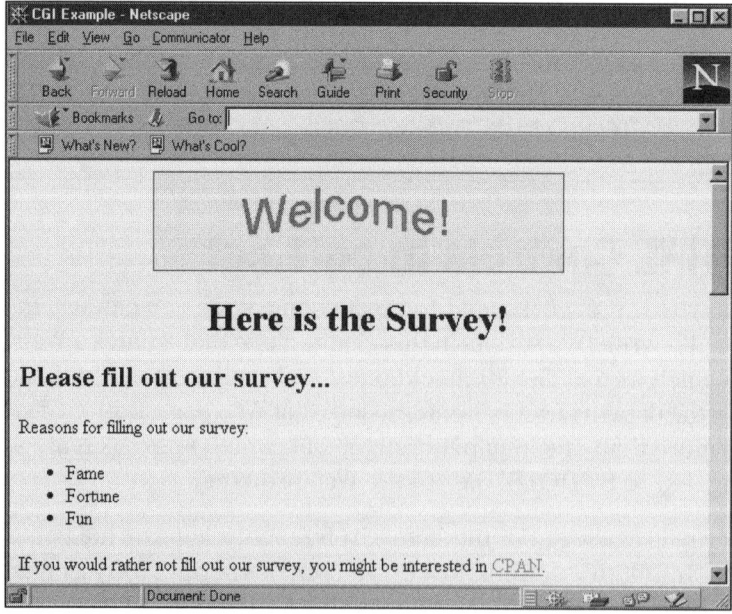

Figure 19.1   Text, a bulleted list, and a hyperlink.

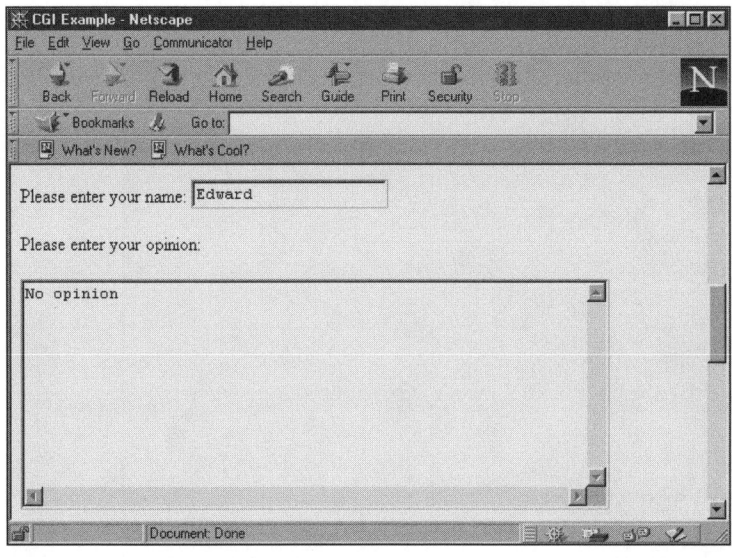

Figure 19.2   A text field and text area.

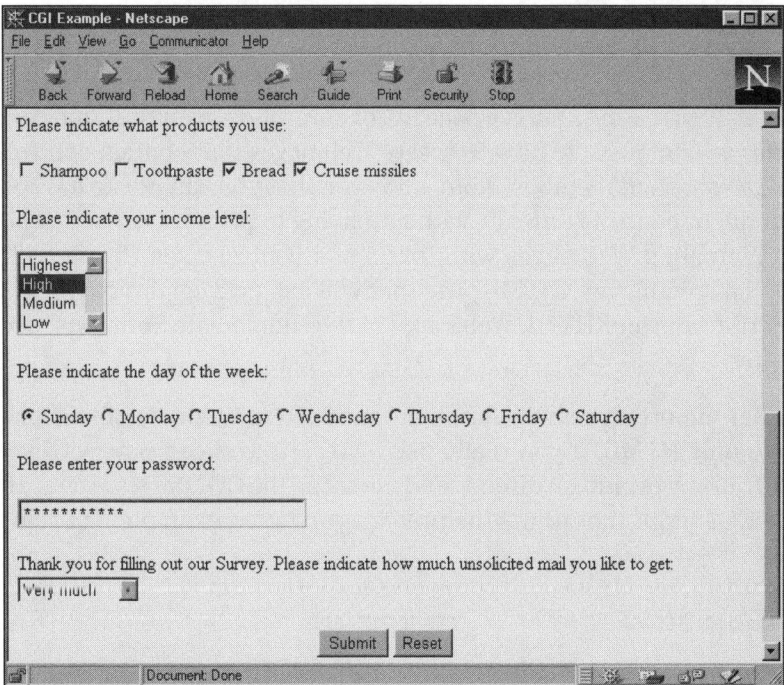

Figure 19.3   Web page controls.

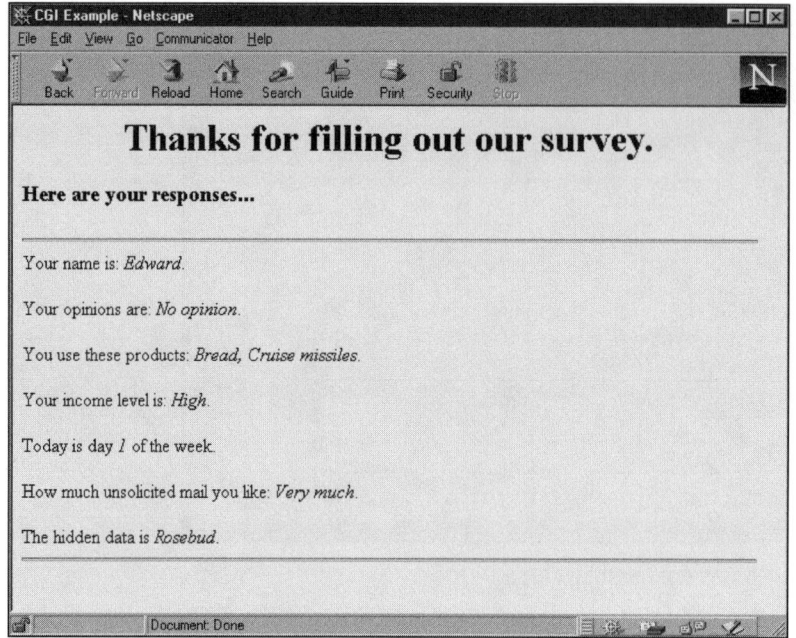

Figure 19.4 The cgi2.cgi script shows the survey results.

In this chapter, I'm creating a survey page full of controls by using a script, cgi1.cgi. I'm doing this to demonstrate how to create Web pages that contain controls using the CGI.pm shortcut methods. Note, however, that you can create a Web page with a form full of controls directly, without having to print it from a CGI script. For more on creating Web pages with forms and controls, see Chapter 12. For information on creating an XHTML page that will call cgi2.cgi directly, see "Calling a CGI Script from an XHTML Web Page" in the "Immediate Solutions" section of this chapter.

Here's another important point—although the shortcut methods of CGI.pm currently create only HTML, if you really need XHTML, you can have CGI scripts print XHTML just by printing it directly and not using the CGI.pm shortcuts. Here's an example CGI script that prints the previous text-area example, but this time in XHTML:

```perl
#!/usr/local/bin/perl
use CGI;
$co = new CGI;

print $co->header,
"<?xml version='1.0'?>",
"<!DOCTYPE html PUBLIC \"-//W3C//DTD XHTML 1.0 Transitional//EN\"",
```

```
"\"http://www.w3.org/tr/xhtml1/DTD/xhtml1-transitional.dtd\">",
"<html xmlns=\"http://www.w3.org/1999/xhtml\" xml:lang=\"en\" lang=\"en\">",
"<head>",
"<title>CGI Example</title>",
"</head>",
"<body>",
"<center>",
"<h1>Welcome to CGI!</h1>",
"</center>",
"<form method=\"post\"  enctype=\"application/x-www-form-urlencoded\">",
"<textarea name='textarea' rows='10' cols='60'>",
"Hello!",
"</textarea>",
"</form>",
"<p align='center'>",
"Welcome to CGI!",
"</p>",
"</body>",
"</html>";
```

How does the survey Web page know where to send the survey data? All the controls in that page are in the same form. As we saw in Chapter 12, a form is not a visible Web page entity; it's simply a construct that contains a collection of controls. The form's **action** attribute holds the URL of cgi2.cgi. When the user clicks the Submit button, the Web browser sends the data from the controls in the form to that URL. In cgi2.cgi, the code reads and displays the data that the user has entered.

In the following example, I place a text field in a form along with Submit and Reset buttons. I also indicate that the text in the text field is to be sent to **http://www.starpowder.com/username/cgi/cgi2.cgi** when the user clicks the Submit button:

```
<form method="post" action=
    "http://www.starpowder.com/username/cgi/cgi2.cgi"
    enctype="application/x-www-form-urlencoded">
    <input type="text" name="text" value="" />
    <input type="submit" name="Submit" value="Submit" />
    <input type="reset" />
</form>
```

It's also possible to use a CGI script to create a Web page that has a form in it. If you're using CGI.pm, you use the **start_form** method to create a form in a Web page. You write the form in a CGI script and specify where to post that data, like this in cgi1.cgi:

```perl
#!/usr/local/bin/perl

use CGI;

$co = new CGI;
print $co->start_form
(
    -method=>'post',
    -action=>"http://www.yourserver.com/user/cgi/cgi2.cgi"
);
```

If you call **start_form** without any arguments, the Submit button will post (send) the form's data back to the same CGI script that created the Web page. This means that you can send data from a form back to the same script that generated that form. For example, the first time you call the script, it can generate one Web page; when you call it again with data from a form in that page, it can read and use the data to create a new page. After creating a form, you can add controls to that form, such as a text area:

```perl
#!/usr/local/bin/perl
use CGI;

$co = new CGI;
print $co->start_form
(
    -method=>'post',
    -action=>"http://www.yourserver.com/user/cgi/cgi2.cgi"
),
$co->textarea
(
    -name=>'textarea',
    -value=>'Hello!',
    -rows=>'10',
    -columns=>'60'
);
```

You can add a Submit button to the form with the **submit** method, add a Reset button with the **reset** method, and end the form with the **end_form** method:

```perl
#!/usr/local/bin/perl
use CGI;

$co = new CGI;
print $co->start_form
```

```
(
    -method=>'post',
    -action=>"http://www.yourserver.com/user/cgi/cgi2.cgi"
),
$co->textarea
(
    -name=>'textarea',
    -value=>'Hello!',
    -rows=>'10',
    -columns=>'60'
),
$co->submit('Submit'),
$co->reset,
$co->end_form;
```

Now when the user clicks the Submit button, the data from the controls in the form are sent to cgi2.cgi. The next step is to read that data.

Reading Data from HTML Controls in cgi2.cgi

When the user clicks the Submit button in an HTML form, the data from the controls in the form is posted to your CGI script. When the data arrives, you can use the CGI.pm module's **param** method to read it.

You call the **param** method with the name you've given to a control (you name a control with the **-name** attribute), and the return value is the data that is in the control. To see if any data is available, you can call the **param** method with no arguments; if it returns a value of **true**, there is some data from a form waiting for you.

Here's an example from cgi2.cgi. I'm reading the data that the user typed into a text field named "text" and a text area named "textarea," and I'm printing them in a new Web page. (The **em** method you see here just produces an HTML **<EM>** element for emphasized text, which is usually rendered in italics, as you see in Figure 19.4.) Here's the code:

```
#!/usr/local/bin/perl
use CGI;

$co = new CGI;
if ($co->param()) {
    print
        "Your name is: ",$co->em($co->param('text')), ".",
        $co->p,
```

```
            "Your opinions are: ",$co->em($co->param('textarea')), ".",
        $co->p,
            .
            .
            .
}
```

We'll learn more about how to read the data from controls in Perl throughout this chapter. That's it. We've discussed how to create pages that call CGI scripts and how to read the data they send. Now it's time to start writing some code.

Listing 19.1   The cgi1.cgi script.

```perl
#!/usr/local/bin/perl
use CGI;

$co = new CGI;
$labels{'1'} = 'Sunday';
$labels{'2'} = 'Monday';
$labels{'3'} = 'Tuesday';
$labels{'4'} = 'Wednesday';
$labels{'5'} = 'Thursday';
$labels{'6'} = 'Friday';
$labels{'7'} = 'Saturday';

print $co->header,
$co->start_html
(
    -title=>'CGI Example',
    -author=>'Steve',
    -meta=>{'keywords'=>'CGI Perl'},
    -bgcolor=>'white',
    -link=>'red'
),
$co->center($co->img({-src=>'welcome.gif'})),
$co->center($co->h1('Here is the Survey!')),
$co->h2('Please fill out our survey...'),
"Reasons for filling out our survey:",
$co->p,
$co->ul
(
    $co->li('Fame'),
    $co->li('Fortune'),
    $co->li('Fun'),
),
"If you would rather not fill out our survey, ",
"you might be interested in ",
```

```perl
    $co->a({href=>"http://www.cpan.org/"},"CPAN"), ".",
    $co->hr,
    $co->start_form
    (
        -method=>'post',
        -action=>"http://www.yourserver.com/username/cgi2.cgi"
    ),
    "Please enter your name: ",
    $co->textfield('text'), $co->p,
    "Please enter your opinion: ",
    $co->p,
    $co->textarea
    (
        -name=>'textarea',
        -default=>'No opinion',
        -rows=>10,
        -columns=>60
    ),
    $co->p,
    "Please indicate what products you use: ", $co->p,
    $co->checkbox_group
    (
        -name=>'checkboxes',
        -values=>['Shampoo','Toothpaste','Bread','Cruise missiles'],
        -defaults=>['Bread','Cruise missiles']
    ),
    $co->p,
    "Please indicate your income level: ",
    $co->p,
    $co->scrolling_list
    (
        'list',
        ['Highest','High','Medium','Low'],
        'High',
    ),
    $co->p,
    "Please indicate the day of the week: ",
    $co->p,
    $co->radio_group
    (
        -name=>'radios',
        -values=>['1','2','3', '4', '5', '6', '7'],
        -default=>'1',
        -labels=>\%labels
    ),
```

```perl
    $co->p,
    "Please enter your password: ", $co->p,
    $co->password_field
    (
        -name=>'password',
        -default=>'open sesame',
        -size=>30,
    ),
    $co->p,
    "Thank you for filling out our Survey. Please indicate how
    much unsolicited mail you like to get: ",
    $co->popup_menu
    (
        -name=>'popupmenu',
        -values=>['Very much','A lot','Not so much','None']
    ),
    $co->p,
    $co->hidden
    (
        -name=>'hiddendata',
        -default=>'Rosebud'
    ),
    $co->center
    (
        $co->submit('Submit'),
        $co->reset,
    ),
    $co->hr,
    $co->end_form,
    $co->end_html;
```

Listing 19.2 The cgi2.cgi script.

```perl
#!/usr/local/bin/perl
use CGI;
$co = new CGI;
print $co->header,
$co->start_html
(
    -title=>'CGI Example',
    -author=>'Steve',
    -meta=>{'keywords'=>'CGI Perl'},
    -bgcolor=>'white',
    -link=>'red'
),
```

```perl
        $co->center
        (
            $co->h1('Thanks for filling out our survey.')
        ),
        $co->h3
        (
            'Here are your responses...'
        ),
        $co->hr;
        if ($co->param()) {
            print
                "Your name is: ",$co->em($co->param('text')),
                ".",
                $co->p,
                "Your opinions are: ",$co->em($co->param('textarea')),
                ".",
                $co->p,
                "You use these products: ",$co->em(join(", ",
                $co->param('checkboxes'))), ".",
                $co->p,
                "Your income level is: ",$co->em($co->param('list')),
                ".",
                $co->p,
                "Today is day ", $co->em($co->param('radios')),
                " of the week.",
                $co->p,
                "Your password is: ",$co->em($co->param('password')),
                ".",
                $co->p,
                "How much unsolicited mail you like: ",
                $co->em($co->param('popupmenu')),
                ".",
                $co->p,
                "The hidden data is ",$co->em(join(", ",
                $co->param('hiddendata'))),
                ".";
        }
        print $co->hr;
        print $co->end_html;
```

Immediate Solutions

Starting a Document

"OK," says the novice programmer; "I'm ready to start creating CGI scripts with CGI.pm. Where do I start?" "You start," you say, "by creating an HTTP header."

To start an HTML document using CGI.pm, you create a CGI object and create an HTTP header with that object's **header** method. (I'll create a simple header here, although you can create more complex ones with cookies and other attributes.) You start the document with the **start_html** method. The **header** method just prints "Content-Type: text/html", which tells the browser what type of document is being sent.

The **start_html** method creates a **<head>** section for the Web page and allows you to specify various attributes for the **<body>** part, such as the background and link color. Here's how I start the survey Web page example in cgi1.cgi—note that to get the output from the header and **start_html** into the Web page, you use the Perl **print** function:

```perl
#!/usr/local/bin/perl
use CGI;
$co = new CGI;

print $co->header,
$co->start_html
(
    -title=>'CGI Example',
    -author=>'Steve',
    -meta=>{'keywords'=>'CGI Perl'},
    -bgcolor=>'white',
    -link=>'red'
)
```

Displaying Images

The novice programmer appears and says, "So how do I display an image in a Web page that I'm creating from a CGI script?" "No problem at all," you say; "use the **img** method."

The CGI.pm **img** method creates HTML **<IMG>** elements, which you use to display images. Here's an example from cgi1.cgi:

```
$co->center
(
    $co->img
        (
            {-src=>'welcome.gif'}
        )
)
```

In this case, I'm displaying the image welcome.gif in the survey Web page. You can see the results in Figure 19.1. Here is the HTML created:

```
<IMG SRC="welcome.gif">
```

The attributes you can set in the **img** method are **-align**, **-alt**, **-border**, **-height**, **-width**, **-hspace**, **-ismap**, **-src**, **-lowsrc**, **-vspace**, and **-usemap**.

Creating Headings

"Great," says the novice programmer. "I've put a welcome banner into my dynamically generated Web page. Now—what about creating headings?" "No problem at all," you say; "just use methods like **h1** and **h2**."

You can use CGI.pm methods such as **h1**, **h2**, **h3**, and so on to create headings corresponding to the HTML **<H1>**, **<H2>**, and **<H3>** elements.

For example, here's how I create two headings—an HTML **<H1>** heading and **<H2>** heading—welcoming the user to the survey. The headings appear at the top of the survey Web page created by cgi1.cgi:

```
#!/usr/local/bin/perl
use CGI;

$co = new CGI;
print
    .
    .
    .
$co->h1('Here is the Survey!'),
$co->h2('Please fill out our survey...')
```

And you can see the results in Figure 19.1. Here is the HTML created:

```
<H1>Here is the Survey!</H1>
<H2>Please fill out our survey...</H2>
```

The attributes you can set are **-align** and **-class**.

Centering Elements

"Hm," says the novice programmer, "I've put an HTML **<H1>** heading into my Web page, but it's aligned to the left of the Web page. How do I center elements?" You say, "You can often use the **-align** attribute in a tag, or, if you want to center a number of elements, use the **center** method."

You can center text by printing HTML **<CENTER>** elements with the CGI method **center**. Here's an example in which I center the **<H1>** element created in the last section:

```
#!/usr/local/bin/perl
use CGI;

$co = new CGI;

print
    .
    .
    .
$co->center($co->h1('Here is the Survey!')),
$co->h2('Please fill out our survey...')
```

You can see the results of this code in Figure 19.1.

Creating a Bulleted List

"I want to introduce my dynamically created Web page with a bulleted list of items," the novice programmer says. "How do I do that?" "That's no problem," you say. "You can use methods like **ul** and **li**."

You can create unordered bulleted lists with the **ul** and **li** CGI methods, which create HTML **<UL>** and **<LI>** elements. For example, here's how I display a bulleted list in the survey Web page in cgi1.cgi, indicating some good reasons to fill out the survey:

```perl
#!/usr/local/bin/perl
use CGI;

$co = new CGI;
print
    .
    .
    .
"Reasons for filling out our survey:",
$co->p,
$co->ul
(
    $co->li('Fame'),
    $co->li('Fortune'),
    $co->li('Fun'),
)
```

The results of this code appear in Figure 19.1. Here's the HTML created:

```
<UL>
<LI>Fame</LI>
<LI>Fortune</LI>
<LI>Fun</LI>
</UL>
```

You can use the **-compact** and **-type** attributes with **ul**, and use the **-type** and **-value** attributes with **li**.

Creating a Hyperlink

"OK," says the novice programmer, "I have another question. How do I create hyperlinks using CGI.pm?" "No trouble," you say; "just use the **a** method."

You can create a hyperlink with the **a** CGI method. In this example, I offer users another URL to jump to if they're not interested in filling out the cgi1.cgi survey:

```perl
#!/usr/local/bin/perl
use CGI;
$co = new CGI;

print
    .
    .
    .
```

```
"If you would rather not fill out our survey, ",
"you might be interested in ",
$co->a({href=>"http://www.cpan.org/"},"CPAN"), "."
```

The results of this code appear in Figure 19.1. Here's the HTML created:

```
If you would rather not fill out our survey, you might be interested in
<A HREF="http://www.cpan.org/">CPAN</A>.
```

You can use these attributes with the **a** method: **-href**, **-name**, **-onClick**, **-onMouseOver**, and **-target**.

Creating Horizontal Rules

"Hm," says the novice programmer, "I want to separate the content of my HTML page using horizontal rules. Is there an **hr** method?" "There sure is," you say, "and it creates HTML **<HR>** elements for you."

To create horizontal rules by using the HTML **<HR>** element, you just use the CGI **hr** method:

```
#!/usr/local/bin/perl
use CGI;
$co = new CGI;

print
    .
    .
    .
$co->hr
```

The horizontal rule created by this code appears at the bottom of Figure 19.1. The attributes you can use with **hr** are **-align**, **noshade**, **-size**, and **-width**.

Creating a Form

"OK," says the novice programmer, "I'm ready to start putting controls in my Web page. I want to use buttons and text fields and—" "Whoa," you say. "Before you start, you have to set up a form to hold those controls."

To use controls in a Web page, you must enclose them in a form. In the survey example cgi1.cgi, I used the CGI **start_form** method to create a form. When the user clicks the Submit button (which I'll add soon), the data from the controls in this form are sent to the script that will produce the data summary, cgi2.cgi. I target cgi2.cgi by placing its URL in the form's **action** attribute:

```
#!/usr/local/bin/perl
use CGI;

$co = new CGI;
print
    .
    .
    .
$co->start_form
(
    -method=>'post',
    -action=>"http://www.yourserver.com/user/cgi/cgi2.cgi"
)
```

Note that all the following controls, up to the section "Ending a Form," are enclosed in the form because executing **start_form** inserts an HTML **<FORM>** tag into the Web page. Here is the HTML created by the previous code:

```
<FORM METHOD="post"
ACTION="http://www.yourserver.com/username/cgi/cgi2.cgi"
ENCTYPE="application/x-www-form-urlencoded">
```

These are the attributes you can use with **start_form**: **-action**, **-enctype**, **-method**, **-name**, **-onSubmit**, and **-target**.

If you call **start_form** without any arguments, the Submit button will post (send) the form's data back to the same CGI script that created the Web page. For information on creating forms using XHTML directly, so you can call CGI scripts from Web pages that you write manually, see "Calling a CGI Script from an XHTML Web Page" in the "Immediate Solutions" section.

Working with Text Fields

"This is great," says the novice programmer. "Now I've created a form to put controls in. The first control I want to use is a text field. How do I create one?" "That's easy," you say. "You use the **textfield** method."

To create a text field by using CGI.pm, you use the CGI method **textfield**. Here's how I create and name a text field that will hold the user's name in cgi1.cgi:

```
#!/usr/local/bin/perl
use CGI;

$co = new CGI;
print
    .
    .
    .
"Please enter your name: ",
$co->textfield('text')
```

You can see the resulting text field at the top of Figure 19.2. Here's the HTML created:

```
Please enter your name:
<INPUT TYPE="text" NAME="text" VALUE="">
```

These are the attributes you can use with **textfield**: **-maxLength**, **-name**, **-onChange**, **-onFocus**, **-onBlur**, **-onSelect**, **-override**, **-force**, **-size**, **-value**, and **-default**.

How do you read the data in a text field after the user clicks the Submit button to send the form to you? See the next topic.

Reading Data from Controls

"Hm," says the novice programmer. "Now that I've added a text field to my Web page, how can I read the data in that text field when the user clicks the Submit button and sends that data to my CGI script?" "You can use the CGI.pm **param** method," you say. "Pull up a chair, and we'll take a look."

When the user clicks the Submit button in the survey example, the Web browser posts the data in the form to cgi2.cgi. In that script, I use the CGI method **param** to read the data in the text field.

To use **param**, I pass it the name I've given to the text field, **'text'** (see the previous topic). This is how I display the data the user entered in the text field (the **em** method creates an **<EM>** tag, which translates to italics in most browsers):

```perl
#!/usr/local/bin/perl
use CGI;

$co = new CGI;
print "Your name is: ",
    $co->em($co->param('text')),
    ".";
```

You can see the results in Figure 19.4. That's how to read the data in a control—just pass the name of the control to the **param** method. Note that if you call **param** without any arguments, it'll return **true** if there is any data waiting, and **false** otherwise.

Working with Text Areas

"I can't fit all the text I need into a text field," the novice programmer says. "Is there anything bigger?" You say, "Sure—text areas."

As we saw in Chapter 12, unlike a text field, a text area can hold several rows of text. Here's how I create a text area in cgi1.cgi to hold any opinions the user wants to enter. I give the text area 10 rows, 60 columns, some default text, and a name, **'textarea'**:

```perl
#!/usr/local/bin/perl
use CGI;

$co = new CGI;

print
    .
    .
    .
"Please enter your opinion: ",
$co->p,
$co->textarea
(
    -name=>'textarea',
    -default=>'No opinion',
    -rows=>'10',
    -columns=>'60'
)
```

You can see the results in Figure 19.2. Here's the HTML created:

```
Please enter your opinion:
<P>
<TEXTAREA NAME="textarea" ROWS="10" COLS="60">
No opinion
</TEXTAREA>
```

These are the attributes you can use with the **textarea** method: **-cols** (also **-columns**), **-name**, **-onChange**, **-onFocus**, **-onBlur**, **-onSelect**, **-rows**, **-override**, **-force**, **-value**, **-default**, and **-wrap**.

Here's how I use the CGI **param** method to read the text from the text area in cgi2.cgi, the CGI script that reports the survey data, which is shown in Figure 19.4:

```
print  "Your opinions are: ",
    $co->em($co->param('textarea'))
    , ".";
```

Working with Checkboxes

"This one's a little tougher," says the novice programmer. "How do I set up a group and checkbox controls and give them each a caption?" "Get some coffee," you say, "and we'll go over it."

You can create checkboxes in a group. You group checkboxes together so the names of all the boxes that are checked are reported in the same list.

In the following example, in cgi1.cgi, I use the CGI method **checkbox_group** to create a group of checkboxes that will let users indicate what commercial products they use. I name the checkbox group, pass an array of labels for the checkboxes, and list the default checkboxes that should be clicked when the Web page first appears. I do all this in another array:

```
#!/usr/local/bin/perl
use CGI;

$co = new CGI;
print
    .
    .
    .
```

```
"Please indicate what products you use: ",
$co->p,
$co->checkbox_group
(
    -name=>'checkboxes',
    -values=>['Shampoo','Toothpaste','Bread','Cruise missiles'],
    -defaults=>['Bread','Cruise missiles']
)
```

You can see the results in Figure 19.3. Here's the HTML created (the **CHECKED** attributes are standalone and have no values assigned to them):

```
Please indicate what products you use:
<P>
<INPUT TYPE="checkbox" NAME="checkboxes" VALUE="Shampoo">Shampoo
<INPUT TYPE="checkbox" NAME="checkboxes" VALUE="Toothpaste">Toothpaste
<INPUT TYPE="checkbox" NAME="checkboxes" VALUE="Bread" CHECKED>Bread
<INPUT TYPE="checkbox" NAME="checkboxes" VALUE="Cruise missiles" CHECKED>
Cruise missiles
```

Using this code in cgi2.cgi, I read and report the checkboxes that were checked; these results are shown in Figure 19.4. Note that **param** returns a list of checkbox names, and I use **join** to create a string from that list:

```
print "You use these products: ",
    $co->em(join(", ",
    $co->param('checkboxes'))),
    ".";
```

Working with Scrolling Lists

"How about scrolling lists?" the novice programmer asks. "Can I create them, too?" "Yes," you say, "if you use the **scrolling_list** method."

A scrolling list displays a list of items that can scroll if all the items cannot be displayed at once. You create a scrolling list with the CGI.pm **scrolling_list** method.

Here's how I create a scrolling list in cgi1.cgi to let users select the level of their income. I name it **'list'**, place the items **'Highest'**, **'High'**, **'Medium'**, and **'Low'** in it, and select **'High'** by default:

```perl
#!/usr/local/bin/perl
use CGI;

$co = new CGI;
print
    .
    .
    .
"Please indicate your income level: ",
$co->p,
$co->scrolling_list
(
    'list',
    ['Highest','High','Medium','Low'],
    'High',
)
```

You can see the results in Figure 19.3. Here's the HTML created:

```
Please indicate your income level:
<P>
<SELECT NAME="list" SIZE=4>
<OPTION  VALUE="Highest">
Highest
<OPTION SELECTED VALUE="High">
High
<OPTION  VALUE="Medium">
Medium
<OPTION  VALUE="Low">
Low
</SELECT>
```

These are the attributes you can set with the **scrolling_list** method: **-default**, **-defaults**, **-labels**, **-multiple**, **-name**, **-onBlur**, **-onChange**, **-onFocus**, **-override**, **-force**, **-size**, **-value**, and **-values**.

Here's how I read the selected items in cgi2.cgi, which is shown in Figure 19.4:

```perl
print "Your income level is: ",
    $co->em($co->param('list')),
    ".";
```

Working with Radio Buttons

"Now I can work with checkbox controls," says the novice programmer, "but the options I want to present are mutually exclusive—in fact, I want to let the user choose the day of the week—so I need to use a control where only one of a set can be selected at one time." "That," you say, "is the radio button control."

As we saw in Chapter 12, you can use radio buttons to let the user select one of a number of mutually exclusive options. For example, in cgi1.cgi, I use seven radio buttons to let the user indicate the day of the week.

In this case, I create a set of radio buttons that operate in a group named **'radios'** and give those radio buttons the values **'1'** through **'7'**. (The user can select only one radio button from the group.) I use a hash named **%labels** to hold the label of each radio button with the **radio_group** method:

```perl
#!/usr/local/bin/perl

$co = new CGI;

$labels{'1'} = 'Sunday';
$labels{'2'} = 'Monday';
$labels{'3'} = 'Tuesday';
$labels{'4'} = 'Wednesday';
$labels{'5'} = 'Thursday';
$labels{'6'} = 'Friday';
$labels{'7'} = 'Saturday';

print
    .
    .
    .
"Please indicate the day of the week: ",$co->p,
$co->radio_group
(
    -name=>'radios',
    -values=>['1','2','3','4','5','6','7'],
    default=>'1',
    -labels=>\%labels
)
```

You can see the results in Figure 19.3. Here's the HTML created:

```
<P>Please indicate the day of the week:
<P>
<INPUT TYPE="radio" NAME="radios" VALUE="1" CHECKED>Sunday
<INPUT TYPE="radio" NAME="radios" VALUE="2">Monday
<INPUT TYPE="radio" NAME="radios" VALUE="3">Tuesday
<INPUT TYPE="radio" NAME="radios" VALUE="4">Wednesday
<INPUT TYPE="radio" NAME="radios" VALUE="5">Thursday
<INPUT TYPE="radio" NAME="radios" VALUE="6">Friday
<INPUT TYPE="radio" NAME="radios" VALUE="7">Saturday
```

Now we've created radio buttons in a Web page from a CGI script. These are the attributes you can use with **radio_group**: **-cols** (or **-columns**), **-colheaders**, **-default**, **-labels**, **-linebreak**, **-name**, **-nolabels**, **-onClick**, **-override**, **-force**, **-rows**, **-rowheaders**, **-value**, and **-values**.

Here's how I read and report which radio button was selected in cgi2.cgi, which is shown in Figure 19.4:

```
print "Today is day ",
    $co->em($co->param('radios')), "
    of the week.";
```

Working with Password Fields

"Uh oh," says the novice programmer. "That darn Johnson was looking over my shoulder when I was typing my password into the page created by my CGI script." "Uh oh," you say. "You better use a password field control." The NP asks, "You can do that?"

You use a password field to let the user enter a password. A password field is just like a text field except that the user's entry appears as a series of asterisks, so no one can read what the user is typing. In fact, Web browsers protect password fields by not allowing you to copy the data in it and paste it elsewhere.

You create a password with the **password_field** method, as in this code from cgi1.cgi:

```
#!/usr/local/bin/perl
$co = new CGI;

print
    .
    .
    .
```

```
    "Please enter your password: ",
$co->p,
$co->password_field
(
    -name=>'password',
    -default=>'open sesame',
    -size=>'30',
)
```

You can see the results in Figure 19.3. Here's the HTML created:

```
Please enter your password:
<P>
<INPUT TYPE="password" NAME="password" VALUE="open sesame" SIZE="30">
```

These are the attributes you can use with **password_field**: **-maxLength**, **-name**, **-onChange**, **-onFocus**, **-onBlur**, **-onSelect**, **-override**, **-force**, **-size**, **-value**, and **-default**.

Here's how I read and report what the user typed into the password control in cgi2.cgi, which is shown in Figure 19.4:

```
print
    "Your password is: ",$co->em($co->param('password')),
    ".";
```

Working with Pop-up Menus

"Hm," says the novice programmer; "I've got a lot of choices to present to the user in the page my CGI script generates. How can I do that?" "Easy," you say, "just use a popup menu."

A popup menu—familiar to Windows users as a drop-down list box and discussed in Chapter 12 as a **<select>** control—presents a list of items that the user can open by clicking a button that usually displays a down arrow. The user can select an item in that menu, and you can determine which item the user has chosen.

Here's how I ask users how much unsolicited mail they want from the survey. I place items in an HTML **<SELECT>** control by using the CGI **popup_menu** method:

```perl
#!/usr/local/bin/perl
use CGI;

$co = new CGI;
print
"Thank you for filling out our Survey. Please indicate how
much unsolicited mail you like to get: ",
$co->popup_menu
(
    -name=>'popupmenu',
    -values=>['Very much','A lot','Not so much','None']
)
```

You can see the results in Figure 19.3. Here's the HTML created:

```
Thank you for filling out our Survey. Please indicate how
much unsolicited mail you like to get:
<SELECT NAME="popupmenu">
<OPTION   VALUE="Very much">Very much
<OPTION   VALUE="A lot">A lot
<OPTION   VALUE="Not so much">Not so much
<OPTION   VALUE="None">None
</SELECT>
```

These are the attributes you can set with the **popup_menu** method: **-default**, **-labels**, **-name**, **-onBlur**, **-onChange**, **-onFocus**, **-override**, **-force**, **-value**, and **-values**.

Here's how I read and display the user's selection in cgi2.cgi, which is shown in Figure 19.4:

```perl
print "How much unsolicited mail you like: ",
    $co->em($co->param('popupmenu')),
    ".";
```

Working with Hidden Data Fields

The novice programmer says, "Hm, I'm writing a game and want to hide the secret word in a Web page so I can read it in a CGI script. But when I store that word in a password field, it looks pretty amateurish." "I'll bet," you say. "You should use a hidden field instead."

You can store data in a hidden field in a Web page, and that field is invisible to the user. This technique is useful if you want to store data pertinent to a Web page that will be posted back to a script. To create a hidden field, you use the **hidden** method.

Here's how I store hidden data in the survey Web page created by cgi1.cgi:

```
#!/usr/local/bin/perl
use CGI;

$co = new CGI;
print
    .
    .
    .
$co->hidden(-name=>'hiddendata', -default=>'Rosebud');
```

Here's the HTML that's generated:

```
<INPUT TYPE="hidden" NAME="hiddendata" VALUE="Rosebud">
```

These are the attributes you can use with **hidden**: **-name**, **-override**, **-force**, **-value**, **-values**, **-default.**

Here's how I display the data in the hidden field in cgi2.cgi, which is shown in Figure 19.4:

```
print "The hidden data is ",$co->em(join(", ",
    $co->param('hiddendata'))),
    ".";
```

Creating Submit and Reset Buttons to Upload Data from an HTML Form

"OK," says the novice programmer, "I've added the controls to my form—now how can the user actually send the data in those controls to my CGI script?" "Easy," you say; "you use a Submit button in a form. When the user clicks that button, the data from the controls in your form is sent to the CGI script you designated when you created the form."

To upload the data in a form, the user must click a Submit button. You create a Submit button with the CGI.pm **submit** method. You can also create a Reset button by using the **reset** method, which clears the data in the form.

Here's how I add Submit and Reset buttons to the survey Web page created by cgi1.cgi:

```
#!/usr/local/bin/perl
use CGI;

$co = new CGI;
print
    .
    .
    .
$co->center
(
    $co->submit,
    $co->reset,
)
```

This code creates two buttons, one with the caption Submit and one with the caption Reset, shown in Figure 19.3. Here's the HTML created:

```
<CENTER>
<INPUT TYPE="submit" NAME="Submit" VALUE="Submit">
<INPUT TYPE="reset">
</CENTER>
```

You can set the caption used in this button with the **-value** attribute. When the user clicks the Submit button, the data in the form in cgi1.cgi is posted to cgi2.cgi for decoding and use. The attributes you can set with the **submit** method are **-name**, **-onClick**, **-value**, and **-label**.

Ending a Form

"OK," says the novice programmer, "I've added my controls to my Web page—I'm ready to go!" "Not so fast," you say; "don't forget to end the form with the **end_form** method."

All the controls we created in the previous topics are part of the same form in the survey page that we created in cgi1.cgi. I created that form with the **start_form** method, and to end the form, I use the **end_form** method:

```
#!/usr/local/bin/perl
use CGI;

$co = new CGI;

print
      .
      .
      .
$co->end_form
```

This method just returns the HTML **</FORM>** element, which I print to the Web page to end the form.

Ending a Document

"OK," says the novice programmer, "I've written my Web page and put a form in it—*now* I'm ready to go!" "Not so fast," you say; "don't forget to end the Web page with the **end_html** method."

To end an HTML document, use the CGI **end_html** method. This method returns "**</BODY></HTML>**", which should end an HTML Web page.

Here's how I end the survey Web page in cgi1.cgi:

```
#!/usr/local/bin/perl
use CGI;

$co = new CGI;
print
      .
      .
      .
$co->end_html;
```

That completes cgi1.cgi. When you navigate to this CGI script, you see the Web survey page that appears in Figures 19.1, 19.2, and 19.3. When the user enters data into that page and clicks the Submit button, the data in that page is sent to cgi2.cgi, which displays a summary of that data, shown in Figure 19.4.

By dissecting this example, you can see in detail how to create and read the data in most controls.

Calling a CGI Script from an XHTML Page

In this chapter, I've used a script, cgi1.cgi, to create a Web page that will call cgi2.cgi when the user clicks the Submit button. But the methods available in CGI.pm create only HTML, not XHTML. You can, however, use a CGI script to print XHTML directly with a simple **print** statement, as discussed in the "In Depth" section of this chapter, or you can call a CGI script directly from an XHTML Web page.

To call a CGI script from an XHTML Web page, you can create a form with a Submit button. In this case, I'm adding a text field to a form:

```
<form method="post"
action="http://www.yourserver.com/username/cgi/cgi2.cgi"
enctype="application/x-www-form-urlencoded">
Please enter your name:
    <input type="text" name="text" value="" />
    <input type="submit" name="Submit" value="Submit" />
    <input type="reset" />
</form>
```

When the user clicks the Submit button, the data in the text field is sent to cgi2.cgi. If the user clicks the Reset button, the text in the text field is cleared. Here's a complete Web page in XHTML that displays the survey you see in Figures 19.1, 19.2, and 19.3. When you click the Submit button, it sends its data to cgi2.cgi:

```
<?xml version="1.0"?>
<!DOCTYPE html PUBLIC "-//W3C//DTD XHTML 1.0 Transitional//EN"
"http://www.w3.org/tr/xhtml1/DTD/xhtml1-transitional.dtd">
<html xmlns="http://www.w3.org/1999/xhtml" xml:lang="en" lang="en">
    <head>
        <title>
            CGI Example
        </title>
    </head>

    <body bgcolor="white" link="red">
        <center>
            <img src="http://www.yourserver.com/username/cgi/welcome.gif"
                alt="image" />
        </center>
        <center>
            <h1>Here is the Survey!</h1>
        </center>

        <hr />
```

```
<form method="post"
    action="http://www.yourserver.com/username/cgi/cgi2.cgi"
    enctype="application/x-www-form-urlencoded">

    Please enter your name:
    <input type="text" name="text" value="" />
    <p>
        Please enter your opinion:
    </p>
    <p>
        <textarea name="textarea" rows="10" cols="60">
            No opinion
        </textarea>
    </p>
    <p>
        Please indicate what products you use:
    </p>
    <p>
        <input type="checkbox" name="checkboxes" value="Shampoo" />
            Shampoo
        <input type="checkbox" name="checkboxes"
            value="Toothpaste" />Toothpaste
        <input type="checkbox" name="checkboxes" value="Bread"
            checked="checked" />Bread
        <input type="checkbox" name="checkboxes" value="Cruise
            missiles" checked="checked" />Cruise missiles
    </p>
    <p>
        Please indicate your income level:
    </p>
    <p>
        <select name="list" SIZE="4">
            <option value="Highest">Highest</option>
            <option selected="selected" value="High">
                High</option>
            <option  value="Medium">
                Medium</option>
            <option  value="Low">
                Low</option>
        </select>
    </p>
    <p>Please indicate the day of the week:</p>
    <p>
        <input type="radio" name="radios" value="1"
            checked="checked" />Sunday
        <input type="radio" name="radios" value="2" />Monday
        <input type="radio" name="radios" value="3" />Tuesday
```

```
                <input type="radio" name="radios" value="4" />Wednesday
                <input type="radio" name="radios" value="5" />Thursday
                <input type="radio" name="radios" value="6" />Friday
                <input type="radio" name="radios" value="7" />Saturday
            </p>
            <p>
            Please enter your password:
            </p>
            <p>
            <input type="password" name="password"
                value="open sesame" size="30" />
            </p>
            <p>
                Thank you for filling out our Survey. Please indicate how
                much unsolicited mail you like to get:
            </p>
            <select name="popupmenu">
                <option    value="Very much">Very much</option>
                <option    value="A lot">A lot</option>
                <option    value="Not so much">Not so much</option>
                <option    value="None">None</option>
            </select>
            <center>
                <input type="hidden" name="hiddendata" value="Rosebud" />
                <p>
                    <input type="submit" name="Submit" value="Submit" />
                    <input type="reset" />
                </p>
            </center>
            <hr />
            <input type="hidden" name=".cgifields" value="radios" />
            <input type="hidden" name=".cgifields" value="list" />
            <input type="hidden" name=".cgifields" value="checkboxes" />
        </form>
    </body>
</html>
```

You can also have a CGI script print this XHTML page by using a single long **print** statement.

And that's it—we've finished our introduction to Perl, and we've finished the book. We've seen a great deal of XHTML here, from the basics on up to the advanced topics, such as using XML to extend XHTML. All that remains now is to put all this to work for yourself—happy programming.

Index

\#
  color values, 57
  Perl comment delimiter, 1078
  referencing anchors, 288
$, 1065, 1084
$_, 1080–1081
%, 1085, 1095
&, 23–24, 128
*
  defining frame dimensions, 409, 427
  element definitions, 912
  password controls, 733
  style specification syntax, 519
+
  element definitions, 912
  style specification syntax, 519
?
  element definitions, 912
  style specification syntax, 519
@, 1067, 1092
', 1089
|
  element definitions, 912
  style specification syntax, 519
||, 519
" ," 1088
( ), 912
-, 912
< >
  Perl scripts, 1080
  style specification syntax, 519
[ ]
  array notation, 621, 995, 1067
  style specification syntax, 519
{ }
  hash notation, 1068
  style specification syntax, 519
//, 594
/* */, 989
<!—>, 60–63
<!—[ ]>, 807–808
3D multimedia, 461
3D Studio Max, 462
3DSite, 462
M-law sound format, 458

A

<a>, 273–276, 581, 587
  applying styles to hyperlinks, 562–563
  data binding, 843
  text hyperlinks, 255–256
A-law sound format, 458
a method, 1131–1132
abbr, 360, 363
<abbr>, 109–110
Abbreviations, 109–110
above, 193, 197
Absolute positioning, 565–567, 814
Absolute URLs, 264
Abstract modules, 962
Abstract Windowing Toolkit (AWT), 1010–1011.
  See also Applets.
accept, 709, 721
accept-charset, 709
Access keys, 284
Access specifiers, 984
accesskey
  <a>, 273, 284
  <applet>, 1022
  <area>, 297
  <body>, 47
  <button>, 752
  <embed>, 479
  <fieldset>, 761
  <input type="button">, 713
  <input type="checkbox">, 716
  <input type="file">, 721
  <input type="image">, 728
  <input type="password">, 731
  <input type="radio">, 735
  <input type="reset">, 739
  <input type="submit">, 741
  <input type="text">, 745
  <isindex>, 766
  <label>, 764
  <legend>, 762
  <object>, 484
  <select>, 755
  <textarea>, 748

<acronym>, 110–111
action, 709, 712, 766, 1121
ActionEvent, 1034
ActionListener, 1034
active property, 562
ActiveX controls, 490–491
add method, 1031
<address>, 124–126
Addresses, 124–126
AdjustmentEvent, 1034
AdjustmentListener, 1034
Adobe Illustrator, 215
Adobe Photoshop, 215
AIFF sound format, 459
Alchemy Mindworks, 215, 223
Alert dialog boxes, 675–676
align
  <applet>, 1022
  <caption>, 366
  <col>, 382
  <colgroup>, 381, 384
  <div>, 179–182
  <embed>, 479
  <fieldset>, 761
  <h1>...<h6>, 81
  <hr>, 163
  <iframe>, 449
  <img>, 225, 235–236
  <input type="image">, 728
  <legend>, 763
  <object>, 484
  <p>, 160, 162
  <select>, 755
  <spacer>, 174
  <table>, 356, 374–375
  <td>, 338, 363, 375–376
  <th>, 360, 375–376
  <thead>, 388
  <tr>, 358, 375–376
Aligning table data, 338, 339, 375–376
Aligning tables, 374–375
Aligning text and images, 156–157, 236–239
alink, 47, 51, 276
Alis Technology, 32
alt
  <applet>, 1022
  <area>, 297
  <img>, 226, 228, 229–231
  <input type="image">, 728
Alternate text, displaying, 229–231
altKey property, 627
altLeft property, 627
Amaya, 32
&amp, 23–24
Ampersand (&), 23–24, 128
anchor behavior, 898

Anchors, 258, 288–290
anim behavior, 898
Animation
  animated GIF images, 223–224
  DirectAnimation control, 491–494
  moving elements, 815–817
  using layers, 817–819
animation behavior, 898
Annotating text, 201–206
Annotating Web pages, 60–61
<applet>, 843, 1013, 1021–1024
Applet class, 1010, 1020–1021
Applet Viewer, Java, 1014
Applets. *See also* Java.
  AWT classes, 1010–1011
  buttons, 1017, 1032–1033
  checkboxes, 1018, 1039–1042
  color specifications, 1027
  consoles, enabling, 1029–1030
  controls, 1017–1018, 1030–1033, 1038–1042
  creating, 1011–1012, 1020–1021
  drawing graphics, 1018–1019, 1049–1058
  drawing text, 1012
  embedding in Web pages, 1013, 1016, 1023–1024
  event handling, 1033–1037
  file permissions, 1111–1112
  fonts, 1044–1047
  free applets, 973–974
  images, 1047–1049
  Java plug-in, 1027–1028
  labels, 1038–1039
  mouse actions, 1053–1055
  non-Java-enabled browsers, 1025
  <object>, 489
  paint method, 1012, 1019, 1020–1021, 1025
  parameters, 1028–1029
  radio buttons, 1018, 1042–1044
  text fields, 1017, 1030–1032
  uploading, 1015–1017
  viewing, 1014–1015
Appletviewer.exe, 1014
Application MIME types (list), 472–475
Applications, 974, 983–986. *See also* Java.
archive, 484, 1022
<area>, 296–299
Arguments
  CGI scripts, 1113
  displaying in Web pages, 105–106
  passing to applets, 1028–1029
  passing to functions, 613–616
Arranging text. *See* Formatting text.
Arrays
  Java, 995–998
  JavaScript, 620–622
  Perl, 1067, 1092–1095

Associative arrays, 1067–1068, 1095–1099
Asymetrix Multimedia Toolbook, 462
<attach>, 849
<!ATTLIST>, 931–932, 958
Attribute minimization, 22
Attribute values, 21–22, 23–24
Attributes
   accessing using JavaScript, 702
   creating at runtime. *See* CGI scripts.
   defining for XHTML elements, 958–959
   event attributes, 581–587, 623
   retrieving from XML elements, 943, 952–955
   specifying in DTDs, 931–934
   standalone attributes, 22
   tag attributes, 6–7, 21–22, 23–24, 702
attributes property, 943–944, 952
AU sound format, 458
audio behavior, 898
Audio Interchange File Format sound format, 459
Audio multimedia. *See also* Multimedia.
   embedded audio, 465–467, 477–478, 482–483, 487–488
   MIME types (list), 475
   sound formats, 458–460
auto, 521
autocomplete
   <form>, 709
   <input type="password">, 731
   <input type="text">, 745
Autodesk/Kinetix, 462
AVI video format, 461
AWT classes, 1010–1011
AWTEventListener, 1034
axis, 360, 363

B

<b>, 83–84
background
   <body>, 47, 51, 243–245
   <ilayer>, 197
   <layer>, 194
   <table>, 356
   <td>, 363
   <th>, 360
background-attachment property, 530–531, 558
Background audio, 465–467, 477–478, 482–483, 487–488
Background color
   setting using JavaScript, 665–666
   setting using style sheets, 558–560
   in tables, 343–344, 372–374, 402–404

Background/color properties, 530–532, 558
background-color property, 531, 558
background-image property, 531, 558
Background images, 243–245, 558–560
background-position property, 531–532, 558
background property, 530
background-repeat property, 532, 558
balance, 477
Banners. *See* Marquees.
Barry's Clip Art Server, 216
<base>, 41, 279–280
Base classes, 980
Base fonts, 116–118
Base URLs, 279
<basefont>, 41, 116–118
<bdo>, 126–128
behavior, 176
Behaviors, Internet Explorer
   attaching to events, 849–850, 887–889
   creating events, 889–890, 897–898
   creating methods, 889–890, 895–897
   creating properties, 889–890, 893–894
   default behaviors, 898–902
   overview, 846–850
   VML, 819–821
Behaviors control, 499
below, 194, 197
bgcolor
   <body>, 47, 51
   <col>, 382
   <colgroup>, 381
   <ilayer>, 197
   <layer>, 194
   <marquee>, 176
   <table>, 343–344, 356
   <td>, 343–344, 363, 372
   <th>, 343–344, 361, 372
   <thead>, 388
   <tr>, 343–344, 359
bgproperties, 47
<bgsound>, 41, 465–466, 477–478
Bidirectional text, 126–128
<big>, 91–93
Binding data. *See* Data binding.
Bitmap graphics, 212
_blank, 436
<blink>, 119–120
Block properties, 533–535
Block quotes, 168–170
<blockquote>, 168–170
Blocks of text, 146–148, 179–182, 200–201
Bobby, 34
<body>, 39, 47–53, 64, 581, 587
</body>, 64
Bold text, 83–84

border
  <embed>, 479
  <frameset>, 425, 440
  <img>, 226, 232–233
  <object>, 484
  <table>, 334, 356, 367–368
border-bottom-color property, 536
border-bottom property, 536
border-bottom-style property, 537
border-bottom-width property, 538
border-collapse property, 548
border-color property, 536
border-left-color property, 536
border-left property, 536
border-left-style property, 537
border-left-width property, 538
border property, 535
border-right-color property, 536
border-right property, 536
border-right-style property, 537
border-right-width property, 538
border-spacing property, 548–549
border-style property, 537
border-top-color property, 536
border-top property, 536
border-top-style property, 537
border-top-width property, 538
border-width property, 537
bordercolor
  <frame>, 428, 447
  <frameset>, 425, 447
  <table>, 356
  <td>, 363
  <th>, 361
  <tr>, 359
Borderless frames, 439–440, 452–453
Borders
  frame borders, 439–440, 446–447, 447–448, 452–453
  image borders, 232–233
  row group borders, 393–396
  table borders, 334, 335, 367–368
bottom property, 533, 566, 567, 813
bottommargin, 47
Bouncing text. *See* Marquees.
Bound data. *See* Data binding.
Bower, Neil, 34
Box properties, 535–541
Boxes, 521

, 141–143, 154–157
Bradley, John, 215
break statement, 604
Breaks. *See* Line breaks.
Brightness, 217

Browsers
  browser type, determining, 658–659
  cached images, 229
  Java consoles, enabling, 1029–1030
  list of, 32–33
  navigating using JavaScript, 681–685
  non-embedding-enabled browsers, 481–482
  non-frame-enabled browsers, 412–414, 436–437
  non-Java-enabled browsers, 1025
  non-layer-enabled browsers, 196–197
  non-script-enabled browsers, 592
  opening browser windows, 667–671, 672–674
  opening frames in new windows, 422–424, 438–439
  redirecting, 682–683
  support for XHTML, 26–27, 32–33
  testing images, 224–225
  writing to status bar, 680–681
Bulleted lists, 1130–1131
Bullets, 314–315
<button>, 582, 695, 751–754, 843
Button class, 1010, 1032–1033
button property, 627
Buttons
  in applets, 1017, 1032–1033
  creating, 713–716
  customizable buttons, 695, 751–754
  data binding, 843
  image buttons, 696, 728–730
  reset buttons, 696, 739–741, 1143–1144
  submit buttons, 696, 728–731, 741–745, 753–754, 1121, 1143–1144
Bytecode files, 976

C

Cached images, 229
Calling CGI scripts from XHTML pages, 1146–1148
cancelBubble property, 627
Canvas class, 1010
<caption>, 365–367
Captions
  grouped controls, 765
  rubies, 201–206
  tables, 365–367
Cascading styles, 516–517. *See also* CSS; Style sheets.
Case sensitivity, 21
case statement, 605
CAST, 34
CDATA type, 574, 932

cellpadding, 334–336, 356, 369
cells method, 804
cellspacing, 334, 336–337, 369–370
<center>, 59–60, 166–167
center method, 1130
Centering text, 59–60, 166–167, 1130
CERN image-map processing, 302–304
Certificate-based transactions, 768
CGI scripts. *See also* Perl script programming.
   attributes, 1114–1115
   bulleted lists, 1130–1131
   calling from XHTML pages, 1146–1148
   centering elements, 1130
   checkboxes, 1136–1137
   controls, 1116–1123, 1133–1134, 1135–1143
   data, reading from controls, 1123, 1134–1135
   displaying images, 1128–1129
   element content, 1114–1115
   file handles, 1110
   file permissions, 1111–1112
   forms, 1121–1122, 1132–1133, 1133, 1144–1145
   headers, 1128
   headings, 1129–1130
   hidden data fields, 1142–1143
   horizontal rules, 1132
   HTML documents, 1128, 1145
   hyperlinks, 1131–1132
   images, 1129
   named parameters, 1113
   overview, 1110, 1111–1112
   password control, 731–734, 1140–1141
   popup menus, 1141–1142
   radio buttons, 1139–1140
   resetting forms, 1122, 1143–1144
   running CGI scripts, 1112
   scrolling lists, 1137–1138
   shortcuts, 1115
   submitting data to server, 703–705, 712, 743, 1121–1122, 1143–1144
   tags, 1113, 1115
   text areas, 1135–1136
   text fields, 1133–1134
   uploading files, 722–723
CGI.pm module. *See* CGI scripts.
challenge, 768
char
   <col>, 383
   <colgroup>, 381
   <td>, 363
   <th>, 361
   <thead>, 388
   <tr>, 359
Character encodings, 128–138
Characters
   bidirectional text, 126–128

character entities, 75, 128–138
character sets, 67–69
charoff
   <col>, 383
   <colgroup>, 381
   <td>, 363
   <th>, 361
   <thead>, 388
   <tr>, 359
charset
   <a>, 273
   <link>, 281
   <meta>, 68
   <script>, 589
Checkbox class, 1010, 1039–1042
Checkboxes
   applets, 1018, 1039–1042
   CGI scripts, 1136–1137
   XHTML forms, 695, 716–720
CheckboxGroup class, 1011, 1042–1044
checkbox_group method, 1136–1137
checked, 717, 720, 735, 738
Checking XHTML compliance, 33–34
childNodes property, 946
Choice class, 1010
chomp function, 1081–1082
chop function, 1081–1082
Circles, clickable areas, 298
Citations, 108–109
cite
   <blockquote>, 168–170
   <del>, 123
   <ins>, 121
<cite>, 108–109
class, 37, 514, 527–529
Classes
   derived classes, 980, 1011
   importing, 990–992
   inheritance, 980
   overview, 978–979
   style classes, 514, 527–529, 786
clear
   **
**, 154, 156–157, 239–241
   <dd>, 321
   <dl>, 319
   <dt>, 320
   <ol>, 313
   <ul>, 310
clear property, 538
Clickable footnotes, 291–292
Clickable regions, image maps, 296–299
Client-side image maps
   <area>, 296–299
   clickable regions, 296–299

clientCaps behavior

combining with server-side image maps, 305–307
creating, 299–301
<map>, 295–296
overview, 267–269
clientCaps behavior, 898
clientX, clientY properties, 627
clip, 194, 197
Clip art, 216
clip property, 550
CLIP! XML Editor, 28
Closing tags, 5, 21
code, 484, 1022
<code>, 101–102
codebase, 484, 1016, 1022
codetype, 484
<col>, 382–383, 386–387
<colgroup>, 381–382, 384–385
color
   <basefont>, 116
   <font>, 112
   <hr>, 163
Color properties, 530–532
color property, 532, 558
Colors
   background. *See* Background color.
   frame border color, 447–448
   GIF image format, 212
   HSB model, 217
   Java applets, 1027
   JPEG image format, 212
   predefined colors, 54–56
   RGB color values, 57–58, 217
   setting using style sheets, 53, 373–374, 558–560
   setting using tag attributes, 52, 372–373
   tables, 343–344, 372–374, 402–404
ColorWorks, 215
cols
   <frameset>, 409, 425, 426–427, 430–431
   <multicol>, 172
   <pre>, 170
   <table>, 357
   <textarea>, 748, 750
colspan, 340–341, 361, 363, 380
Column groups, 381–387
column-span property, 549
Columns in tables
   column width, 370–372
   grouping, 381–387
   spanning, 340–341, 380
Columns in text, 172–174
ComboBox class, 1010
Comments
   conditional comments, 807–808
   enclosing JavaScript in Web pages, 573

   HTML documents, 60–61
   Java, 988
   JavaScript, 594
   Perl, 1078–1079
compact
   <dir>, 325
   <dl>, 319
   <menu>, 325
   <ol>, 313
   <ul>, 310
Comparison operators, 599, 1100–1101
Compiling Java programs, 986–987
ComponentEvent, 1034
ComponentListener, 1034
Compound statements, Perl, 1074
Compression, 213, 214
Conditional comments, 807–808
Conditional statements
   Java, 1001–1002
   JavaScript, 600–603
   Perl, 1069–1070, 1102–1104
Confirmation dialog boxes, 676–677
Console applications, 975, 1029–1030. *See also* Java.
Constructors, 1004, 1005
ContainerEvent, 1034
ContainerListener, 1034
Content. *See also* **<body>**.
   creating dynamically, 776–781, 791–807
   creating in CGI scripts, 1114–1115
   missing, replacing with images, 246–247
   retrieving from XML elements, 948–951
   text, adding to Web pages, 58–59
content, 44
contenteditable
   <applet>, 1022
   <body>, 48
   <fieldset>, 761
   <form>, 709
   <isindex>, 766
   <label>, 764
   <legend>, 763
Controls. *See also* Forms.
   adding to forms, 697–699, 711, 1116–1123
   associating with events, 699–700
   buttons, 695, 713–716
   in CGI scripts, 1116–1123, 1133–1134, 1135–1143
   checkboxes, 695, 716–720, 1136–1137
   customizable buttons, 695, 751–754
   file-uploading control, 696, 721–725
   grouping in forms, 706–707, 761–765
   hidden control, 696, 725–728, 821–824
   hidden data fields, 1142–1143
   image buttons, 696, 728–730
   index search field, 766–767

list of available controls, 695–696
password control, 696, 731–734, 1140–1141
popup menus, 1141–1142
radio buttons, 696, 735–739, 1018, 1042–1044, 1139–1140
reading data from, 701, 1123, 1134–1135
referencing in forms, 702–703
reset buttons, 696, 739–741, 1143–1144
scrolling lists, 1137–1138
secure transaction processing, 768
selection list controls, 696
submit buttons, 696, 728–731, 741–745, 753–754, 1121, 1143–1144
text areas, 696, 1135–1136
text fields, 696, 745–748, 1133–1134
Converting HMTL to XHTML, 24–26
Cookies, 688–692
CoolText.com, 215–216
coords, 273, 297, 298
Copying text, 800
CorelDRAW!, 215
createElement method, 802–804
createTextRange method, 800–801
Crescendo, 457
CSE 3310 HTML Validator, 34
CSS. *See also* Style sheets; Styles.
   boxes, 521
   cascading styles, 516–517
   predefined property units, 520
   specifications, 505–506
   style specification syntax, 518–521
CSV files, 867
ctrkKey property, 627
ctrlLeft property, 627
Customizable buttons, 695, 751–754
CuteFTP, 31–32
CWSApps, 30

D

Data. *See also* Data binding.
   data islands, 920–922, 939–943
   dragging and dropping, 853–856
   hidden data, 696, 725–728, 821–824, 1142–1143
   reading from controls, 701, 1123, 1134–1135
   retrieving from XML documents, 919–922, 937–938, 939–945, 948–955
   submitting from forms, 703–706, 712, 743, 1143–1144
   table data, 338, 339, 363–365, 375–376
data, 484, 626, 860
Data binding
   bound tags, 843–846
   DSOs, 841–843
   events, 844
   MSHTML data source control, 859–866
   RDS data control, 879–887
   in tables, 865–866, 871–872, 877–879, 885–887
   Tabular Data Control, 867–872
   XML data source control, 873–879
Data islands, 920–922, 939–943
Data layer, XForms, 708
Data source objects. *See* DSOs.
Data types
   attribute definitions, 932
   element definitions, 935–936
   Java, 993–995
   JavaScript, 594–595
   Perl, 1065–1066, 1086
Databases. *See* Data binding.
datafld
   <applet>, 1021
   <body>, 48
   bound HTML tags, 841–843, 865
   <button>, 752
   <frame>, 428
   <img>, 226
   <input type="button">, 713
   <input type="checkbox">, 717
   <input type="file">, 721
   <input type="hidden">, 725
   <input type="image">, 728
   <input type="password">, 731
   <input type="radio">, 735
   <input type="reset">, 739
   <input type="submit">, 741
   <input type="text">, 745
   <object>, 484
   <param>, 486
   <select>, 755
   <textarea>, 749
dataformatas
   <body>, 48
   bound HTML tags, 865
   <button>, 752
   <input type="button">, 713
   <param>, 486
datapagesize, 357
datasrc
   <applet>, 1021
   <body>, 48
   bound HTML tags, 843, 865
   <button>, 752
   <frame>, 428
   <img>, 226
   <input type="button">, 713
   <input type="checkbox">, 717
   <input type="file">, 721
   <input type="hidden">, 725
   <input type="image">, 729
   <input type="password">, 731

<input type="radio">, 735
<input type="reset">, 739
<input type="submit">, 741
<input type="text">, 746
<object>, 484
<param>, 486
<select>, 755
<table>, 357
<textarea>, 749
dataTransfer object, 853
<**datatype**>, 935
datetime, 121, 123
<**dd**>, 321–322
DeBablizer, 215
declare, 485
Default behaviors, 898–902
default statement, 605
Default variable, Perl, 1080–1081
Default Web pages, 32
defer, 589
Definition lists
  creating, 319–323
  definition descriptions, 321–322
  definition terms, 319–320
  overview, 271–272
Definitions, 106–107
<**del**>, 122–124
Delegated event handling, 1033–1037
deleteCell method, 804
Deleted text, 122–124
deleteRow method, 804
Delimited data files, 867
Derived classes, 980, 1011
destroy method, 1025
<**dfn**>, 106–107
Dialog boxes
  alert dialog boxes, 675–676
  confirmation dialog boxes, 676–677
  prompt dialog boxes, 678–679
Dialog class, 1010
die statement, 1108
dir, 37, 126
<**dir**>, 325
DirectAnimation control, 491–494
direction, 176
direction property, 533
Directionality of languages, 127
Directory lists, 325
disabled
  <applet>, 1022
  <button>, 752
  <fieldset>, 762
  <form>, 709
  <input type="button">, 714
  <input type="checkbox">, 717
  <input type="file">, 721

<input type="image">, 729
<input type="password">, 732
<input type="radio">, 735
<input type="reset">, 740
<input type="submit">, 742
<input type="text">, 746
<label>, 764
<link>, 281
<optgroup>, 757
<option>, 756
<select>, 755
<style>, 524, 787
<textarea>, 749
<xml>, 939
display property, 533–534, 821, 822
Displaying elements, 821–824
Displaying Web pages, 32–33
<**div**>, 146–148, 179–182, 582, 587
  applying styles, 180–182, 552
  data binding, 843
  overlapping images, 251–252
  positioning text, 200–201
<**dl**>, 319–320
<**!DOCTYPE**>, 16, 36–37, 912, 927
document object, 577, 578–579, 641, 642–649
Document profiles, 20
document.bgcolor property, 578, 665
document.cookie property, 688–692
documentElement property, 918, 942
document.fgcolor property, 578, 665
document.lastmodified property, 578, 665
Documents, HTML
  body element, 39, 47–53, 64
  comments, 60–61
  creating using CGI scripts, 1128, 1145
  document object, 577, 578–579, 641, 642–649
  head element, 39, 40–41, 46–47
  linking to sections of documents, 257–261, 288–290
  relationships between documents, 281–283
  root element, 37–39, 64
  tracking document changes, 120–124
Documents, XML
  creating, 904–907, 926–927
  displaying document structure, 946–948
  event handling, 956–958
  loading, 917–918, 936–937, 956–958
  parsing, 946–955
  retrieving attribute values, 943–945
  retrieving data, 919–922, 937–938, 939–945, 948–955
  retrieving elements, 918, 937
document.title property, 578, 665
document.write method, 578, 660, 661, 776–779, 791–795

document.writeln method, 578, 660, 661, 791
do...while loop statements, 610–611
download behavior, 898
Download time, for images, 225
Downloading files, 294–295
Downloading fonts, 825–827
Dragging and dropping
    data, 853–856
    drop targets, 853, 854
    elements, 851–853
    overview, 838–841
    using layers, 856–859
draw3DRect method, 1018
drawArc method, 1018
drawBytes method, 1018
drawChars method, 1018
drawImage method, 1018, 1048
Drawing. *See also* Graphics; Images.
    freehand drawing, 1050, 1058
    graphics methods, 1018–1019, 1049
    lines, 1055–1056
    mouse actions, 1053–1055
    ovals, 1056
    rectangles, 1057
    rounded rectangles, 1057–1058
    Vector Markup Language (VML), 819–821
drawLine method, 1018, 1055
drawOval method, 1018, 1056
drawPolygon method, 1018
drawPolyline method, 1018
drawRect method, 1018, 1057
drawRoundRect method, 1018, 1057
drawString method, 1012, 1019
Drop-down list controls, 696, 754–761
Drop targets, 853, 854
DSOs
    MSHTML data source control, 859–866
    overview, 841–843
    RDS data control, 879–887
    XML data source control, 873–879
<dt>, 320–321
DTDs
    defining elements, 912–913, 928–931, 966–967
    external DTDs, 913–914
    FPIs, 959–960
    HTML 4, 9
    internal DTDs, 912–913, 927–931
    location of, 18–19
    parameter entities, 924, 964, 967
    specifying attributes, 931–934
    XHMTL, 18, 408
Dynamic HTML. *See also* Dynamic XHTML.
    in Internet Explorer, 773–774
    in Netscape Navigator, 774–775
    W3C and, 773

Dynamic XHTML. *See also* Dynamic HTML.
    animation, 815–819
    conditional comments, 807–808
    dynamic content, 776–781, 791–807
    dynamic elements, 797–800, 802–804
    dynamic fonts, 825–827
    dynamic style sheets, 787–790
    dynamic styles, 775–776, 784–787
    dynamic tables, 804–806
    filters, 827–830
    hidden elements, 821–824
    mouseover effects, 781–783, 808–813
    overview, 772–773
    positioning elements, 813–815
    printing Web pages, 824–825
    text ranges, 800–802
    transitions, 831–836
    visibility of elements, 821–824
    VML, 819–821
dynsrc, 226, 467, 494

E

each function, 1099
ECMAScript, 576
Editors, XHMTL, 28–29
Effects, visual
    animation, 223–224, 491–494, 815–819
    dynamic fonts, 825–827
    element visibility, 821–824
    filters, 827–830
    mouseover effects, 808–813
    positioning elements, 813–815
    properties, 550
    transitions, 831–836
    Vector Markup Language (VML), 819–821
Effects control, 499
<!ELEMENT>, 912, 959
Element box properties, 535–541, 565–567
Elements
    adding attributes, 958–959
    centering, 59–60, 166–167, 1130
    changing contents dynamically, 797–800
    creating at runtime. *See* CGI scripts.
    creating dynamically. *See* Dynamic HTML.
    defined, 4
    defining in DTDs, 912–913, 928–931
    defining in schemas, 915–916, 934–936
    defining XHTML elements, 922–925, 959–960, 966–967
    dragging and dropping, 838–841, 851–853
    empty elements, 22–23
    names, 666
    positioning using styles, 813–815

retrieving from XML documents, 918–919, 937, 948–951
specifying as drop targets, 854
visibility, 821–824
<ELEMENTTYPE>, 915
else clause, 602–603
eltOnly keyword, 916
<em>, 98–99
Email hyperlinks, 292–293
<embed>, 479–481, 587
Embedded audio, 465–467, 477–478, 482–483, 487–488
Embedded style sheets, 511–512, 524–525
Embedded video, 467–469, 486–487, 494–497
Emphasizing text, 98–100
empty-cells property, 549
Empty elements, 5, 22–23
Encapsulation, 977
encoding, 35, 67–68
Encodings, character, 128–138
enctype, 709, 722
End tags, 21
end_form method, 1122, 1144–1145
end_html method, 1145
Equality operators, 599, 1101–1102
Error messages, Perl scripts, 1108
event, 589, 626–627, 853
event behavior, 899
Event bubbling, 840
Event handlers, 624–626, 628–629
Event listener interfaces, 1033–1034, 1035–1036
Events, elements
attaching behaviors to, 849–850, 887–889
attaching HTC functions to, 849
creating using behaviors, 889–890, 897–898
loading XML documents, 956–958
raising, 896, 898
Events, Java, 1033–1037
Events, JavaScript
associating with controls, 699–700
event attributes, 581–586, 587, 623
event handlers, 624–626, 628–629
event object properties, 626–627
overview, 579–581
winodw.event object properties, 627, 628–629
excl behavior, 899
Exclusions, 23
extends keyword, 1011
Extensible Stylesheet Language, 916
External DTDs, 913–914
External images, 210
External multimedia files, 463–465, 470–471
External scripts, 574–575
External style sheets, 509–511, 522–524

F

face, 112, 116
<fieldset>, 706–707, 761–762, 765
File formats, 212–214, 458–459
File handles, 1077, 1110
File permissions, 1015, 1111–1112
File Transfer Protocol, 30–32
File-uploading control, 696, 721–725
File URL type, 265
Files, downloading, 294–295
filter property, 828
Filters, 827–830
firstChild method, 918, 937, 941
firstSibling method, 918, 937, 941
Fixed-width fonts. *See* Monospaced fonts.
Flash Player, 457
float property, 534
Floating frames, 449–453
Flowing text around images, 156–157, 237–239
FocusEvent, 1034
FocusListener, 1034
<font>, 76, 111–114
font-family property, 541, 553, 554
Font properties, 541–543
font property, 541, 555
font-size property, 542, 553, 554
font-stretch property, 542, 555
font-style property, 542, 553, 555
font-variant property, 543, 555
font-weight property, 543, 553, 555
FontMetrics class, 1044
Fonts. *See also* Text.
applying styles, 554–557
base font, 116–118
big fonts, 91–93
dynamic fonts, 825–827
point size, 115–116
small fonts, 93–94
specifying in applets, 1044–1047
specifying using **<font>**, 76, 111–116
Footnotes, clickable, 291–292
for, 589, 764
for loops, 605–608, 1002–1003, 1071, 1104–1105
foreach loops, Perl, 1106
<form>, 582, 587, 697, 709–713
form object, 577
Formal public identifiers, 959–960
Formatting text
abbreviations, 109–110
acronyms, 110–111
addresses, 124–126
base fonts, 116–118
bidirectional text, 126–128

big text, 91–93
blinking text, 119–120
blocks of text, 146–148, 179–182, 200–201
bold text, 83–84
centering text, 166–167
citations, 108–109
columns, 172–174
deleted text, 122–124
emphasizing text, 98–100
fonts, specifying, 111–118
headings, 76–78, 80–82, 140–141
horizontal rules, 150, 163–165, 1132
horizontal spacing, 174–176
inserted text, 120–122
italic text, 84–85
layers, 149–150, 193–196, 193–200
line breaks, 141–143, 154–163
marquees, 150, 176–179
multiple columns, 150, 172–174
overview, 144–146
paragraphs, 141–143, 160–163
plain text, 79–80, 153
point sizes, 115–116
positioning text, 200–201, 813–815
preformatted text, 150–152, 170–172
program code, 101–102
program variables and arguments, 105–106
quotations, 118–119, 168–170
rubies, 201–206
sample program output, 102–104
sections of text, 146–147, 148–149
setting fonts, 76
small text, 93–94
spacing, 174–176
strikethrough text, 89–91
subscripts, 94–96
superscripts, 96–98
"teletype" text, 85–87
term definitions, 106–107
text to be typed by user, 104–105
tracking document changes, 120–124
turning off automatic formatting, 171
underlined text, 87–89
using style sheets. *See* Style sheets.
using styles, 545–548, 561–562
using tables, 184–193, 390–404
using XHTML elements, 69
vertical spacing, 174–176
Forms. *See also* CGI scripts; Controls.
adding controls, 697–699, 711, 1116–1123, 1133–1134, 1135–1143
creating, 697, 709–713, 1132–1133
ending, 1144–1145
file input, 721–725
grouping controls, 706–707, 761–765
overview, 694–695
reading data from controls, 701, 1123, 1134–1135
referencing controls in forms, 702–703
resetting fields, 696, 739–741, 1143–1144
secure transaction processing, 768
submitting data, 703–706, 705, 712, 743, 1143–1144
XForms, 707–708
FPIs, 959–960
frame, 357, 393–394
<frame>, 408, 410, 427–429, 582, 587
data binding, 843
named frames, 419–421
Frame class, 1010
frame object, 577
frameborder
<embed>, 479
<frame>, 428, 440
<frameset>, 425, 440
<iframe>, 449, 452
Frames
border color, 447–448
border thickness, 446–447
borderless frames, 439–440, 452–453
creating, 408–412, 425–427, 429
horizontal frames, 414–415, 415–418, 431–432, 432–434
inline frames, 449–453
named frames, 419–421, 434–435
navigation bars, 441–444
nested frames, 415–418, 432–434
non-frame-enabled browsers, 412–414, 436–437
opening in new windows, 422–424, 438–439
overview, 406–407
pages, displaying, 410–412
predefined target names, 436
resizing, 446
scroll bars, 444–445
user dislike of, 407–408
vertical frames, 408–412, 415–418, 430–431, 432–434
<frameset>, 408, 409, 414, 415–416, 425–427
Frameset HTML 4 DTD, 9
Frameset XHTML 1 DTD, 18, 408
framespacing, 425, 440, 446
Freehand Graphics Studio, 215
fromElement property, 627
FTP, 30–32
FTP hyperlinks, 294–295
FTP URL type, 265
function statement, 611
Functions, 611–616

G

get, 893
get method, 712
getImage method, 1047
getNamedItem method, 944
getParameter method, 1028
GIF Construction Set, 215, 223–224
GIF images
    animated images, 223–224
    file format, 212–214
    interlaced images, 214, 221–222
    transparent images, 220–221
GIFTrans, 215
GIMP, 215
GoldWave, 462
Gopher URL type, 265
Graphical hyperlinks, 256–257, 285–286
Graphics. *See also* Drawing; Images.
    in applets, 1049–1058
    color, 216–217
    file formats, 212–214
    graphics programs (list), 215–216
    Vector Markup Language (VML), 819–821
Graphics class, 1049
Grouping columns, 381–387
Grouping controls, 706–707, 761–765
Grouping elements, 163–165, 1132
Grouping radio buttons, 736
Grouping rows, 388–396
gutter, 172

H

<h1>...<h6>, 76–78, 80–82, 1129–1130
h1...h6 methods, 1129–1130
Handling events, 624–626, 628–629
Hashes, 1067–1068, 1095–1099, 1114–1115
<head>, 39, 40–41
</head>, 46–47
header method, 1072, 1128
headers, 361, 364
Headings
    heading tags, 76–78, 80–82
    table headings, 360–362
    text headings, 140–141, 1129–1130
height
    <applet>, 1022
    <embed>, 479
    event object property, 626
    <iframe>, 449
    <ilayer>, 198
    <img>, 226, 231–232, 241–242

    <layer>, 194
    <marquee>, 176
    <object>, 485
    <spacer>, 174
    <table>, 357
    <td>, 364
    <th>, 361
height property, 538
hidden, 479
Hidden controls, 696, 725–728, 821–824
Hidden data, 696, 725–728
Hidden data fields, 1142–1143
Hidden elements, 821–824
hidden method, 1142–1143
history object, 577, 641, 656, 684–685
history.back, 684
history.forward, 684
history.go, 578, 684
homePage behavior, 899
Horizontal alignment
    table data, 338, 375–376
    text and images, 237–239
Horizontal rules, 150, 163–165, 1132
Horizontal spacing, 174–176
Hot Spot control, 499
Hotfiles Software Library, 463
HotJava, 32
Hotspots, 296
Hover color, 277
hover property, 562, 808–813
<hr>, 163–165
href
    <a>, 255, 273, 288
    <area>, 297
    <base>, 279
    <link>, 281
hreflang, 273, 281
HSB color values, 217
hspace
    <applet>, 1022
    <iframe>, 449
    <img>, 226, 234
    <marquee>, 176
    <table>, 357
HTCs, 846–847
HTML. *See also* XHTML.
    attributes, 6–7
    compared to XHTML, 21–24
    converting to XHTML, 24–26
    creating at runtime. *See* CGI scripts.
    documents. *See* HTML documents.
    forms. *See* Forms.
    HTML 4, 7–9
    overview, 2–5
<html>, 17, 37–39, 64

</html>, 64
HTML 4, 7–9
HTML components. *See* HTCs.
HTML converter, 1027
HTML documents
  body element, 39, 47–53, 64
  comments, 60–61
  creating using CGI scripts, 1128, 1145
  document object, 577, 578–579, 641, 642–649
  head element, 39, 40–41, 46–47
  linking to sections of documents, 257–261, 288–290
  relationships between documents, 281–283
  root element, 37–39, 64
  tracking document changes, 120–124
HTML exclusions, 23
HTML frameset 4 DTD, 9
HTML strict 4 DTD, 9
HTML transitional 4 DTD, 9
HTML validators, 34
http-equiv, 44
HTTP hyperlinks, 294
HTTP URL type, 265
httpFolder behavior, 899
HTTPS URL type, 265
Hue, 217
Hue, Saturation, Brightness color values, 217
Hyperlinks. *See also* Image maps.
  <a>, 273
  access keys, 284
  anchors, 258, 288–290
  applying styles, 562–563
  base URLs, 279
  colors, 276–278
  creating using CGI scripts, 1131–1132
  email hyperlinks, 292–293
  footnotes, clickable, 291–292
  FTP hyperlinks, 294–295
  graphical hyperlinks, 256–257, 278–279, 285–286
  HTTP hyperlinks, 294
  linking to external multimedia files, 463–465, 470–471
  linking to named frames, 419–421, 434–435
  linking to sections of documents, 257–261, 288–290
  mouseover effects, 781–783
  navigation bars, 286–288
  navigational aids, 261–263, 285–286
  opening in new browser windows, 422–424, 438–439
  predefined target names, 436
  relative hyperlinks, 280
  text hyperlinks, 255–256

I

<i>, 84–85
IBAND Clip Art Mega Site, 216
id, 37
  <a>, 258, 259, 274, 288
  <area>, 297
  bound HTML tags, 860
  <embed>, 479
  <frame>, 419, 428
  <frameset>, 425
  <html>, 37
  <iframe>, 449
  <map>, 295, 296
  <noframes>, 436
  <script>, 589
  specifying styles, 529–530
  <xml>, 939
ID type, 932
IDREF type, 932
if statements
  Java, 1001–1002
  JavaScript, 600–603
  Perl, 1069–1070, 1102–1104
<iframe>, 449–450, 582, 587, 843
<ilayer>, 197–200
Illustrator, 215
Image buttons, 696, 728–730
Image class, 1047
Image maps
  <area>, 296–299
  client-side, 267–269, 295–301
  combining client-side and server-side maps, 305–307
  image-map tools (list), 269
  jumping to JavaScript functions, 686–687
  <map>, 295
  <object>, 305
  server-side, 266–267, 301–304
Image MIME types (list), 475
ImageObserver, 1048
Images. *See also* Image maps.
  adding to Web pages, 208–212, 488
  aligning with text, 156–157, 235–239
  allocating space, 231–232
  alternate text, displaying, 229–231
  animated images, 223–224
  in applets, 1047–1049
  background images, 243–245
  borders, 232
  cached images, 229
  clip art, 216
  color, 216–217
  creating, 215–216, 218–219
  dimensions, 232

displaying using CGI scripts, 1128–1129
download time, 225
dragging and dropping, 838–841
external images, 210
GIF image format, 212–214
graphical hyperlinks, 256–257
graphics programs, 215–216
image buttons, 728–731
inline images, 210
inserting using **<object>**, 245–246, 488
interlaced images, 214, 221–222
JPEG image format, 214
low-resolution versions, 243
overlapping, 250–252
previewing, 243
reloading at runtime, 666–667
replacing missing content, 246–247
scaling, 241–242
scanning, 219
spacing between images, 234
in tables, 249–250, 377–378
testing in browsers, 224–225
tiling, 247–250
transparent images, 220–221
width, 224
Imaptool, 269
<img>, 225–229, 583, 587
   data binding, 843
   graphical hyperlinks, 256–257, 278–279
   inline video, 467–469, 494–497
img behavior, 899
img method, 1129
implements keyword, 1034
Implied attributes, 932
import statement, 990
Importing classes and packages, 990–992
Index search field, 766–767
inherit value, 521
Inheritance, 980–981
init method, 1025, 1026–1027
Inline audio, 465–467, 477–478, 482–483, 487–488
Inline frames, 449–453
Inline images, 210, 488
Inline layers, 197–200
Inline quotations, 118–119
Inline styles, 512–513, 525–527
Inline video, 467–469, 486–487, 494–497
innerHTML method, 779
innerHTML property, 798
innerText method, 779
innerText property, 797, 798
Input, accepting from users. *See also*
  Controls; Forms.
   password controls, 731–734
   Perl scripts, 1079, 1080–1083

<input>, 697–699
<input type="button">, 583, 587, 695, 713–716, 843
<input type="checkbox">, 583, 587, 695, 716–720, 843
<input type="file">, 695, 721–725
<input type="hidden">, 696, 725–728, 843
<input type="image">, 696, 728–731
<input type="password">, 696, 731–734, 844
<input type="radio">, 583, 587, 696, 735–739, 844
<input type="reset">, 696, 739–741
<input type="submit">, 584, 587, 696, 741–745
<input type="text">, 584, 696, 745–748, 844
InputEvent, 1035
InputMethodEvent, 1035
InputMethodListener, 1034
<ins>, 120–122
insertAdjacentHTML method, 779, 795–797
insertAdjacentText method, 779, 795–796
insertCell method, 805
Inserted text, 120–122
InsertRow method, 804, 805
Interfaces, event listener, 1033–1034, 1035–1036
Interlaced GIF images, 214, 221–222
Internal DTDs, 912–913, 927–931
Internet Explorer, 33
  behaviors. *See* Behaviors, Internet Explorer.
  dynamic HTML, 773–774
  events, JavaScript, 581–586
  JavaScript implementation, 576
  multimedia controls, 499–501
  predefined colors, 55
Interpolation, 1088–1089
Invisible text, 696, 726
InvocationEvent, 1035
<isindex>, 41, 766–767
ismap, 226, 301
Italic text, 84–85
ItemListener, 1034, 1039–1042

J

Java. *See also* JavaScript.
  access specifiers, 984
  applets. *See* Applets.
  applications, 974, 983–986
  arrays, 995–998
  AWT classes, 1010–1011
  bytecode files, 976
  classes, 978–980, 990–992
  commenting programs, 988

compiling programs, 986–987
conditional statements, 1001–1002
consoles, enabling in browsers, 1029–1030
controls, 1017–1018, 1030–1033, 1038–1042
drawing graphics, 1018–1019, 1049–1058
event listener interfaces, 1033–1034, 1035–1036
event objects, 1034–1035
file permissions, 1111–1112
free applets, 973–974
if statements, 1001
images, 1047–1049
inheritance, 980–981
installing, 982
Java plug-in, 1027–1028
loop statements, 1002–1003
methods, 979, 985
mouse actions, 1053–1055
non-Java-enabled browsers, 1025
object-oriented programming, 977–981
objects, 978–979, 1004–1007
operators, 999–1000
packages, 986, 990–992
parameters, 1028–1029
program files, 983
programs, 974–977
resources, 973
running programs, 976, 987–988
SDK, 982
strings, 998–1000
tutorials, 973
variables, 993–995
java, 987–988
Java Applet Viewer, 1014
javac, 986–987
java.lang package, 986
JavaScript. *See also* Java.
alert dialog boxes, 675–676
Array class, 620–622
browser type, determining, 658–659
calling functions from image maps, 686–687
commenting scripts, 594
conditional statements, 600–605
confirmation dialog boxes, 676–677
cookies, 688–692
data types, 594–595
ECMAScript, 576
enclosing script in comments, 573
events, 579–587, 623–629
functions, 611–613
informational resources, 576
loop statements, 605–611
Microsoft's implementation, 576
navigating using **history** object, 684–685
navigating using **location** object, 681–683
Netscape's implementation, 576
non-script-enabled browsers, 592
objects. *See* Objects, JavaScript.
opening browser windows, 667–671, 672–674
operators, 597–600
overview, 570–575, 587–588
PCDATA *vs.* CDATA, 574
prompt dialog boxes, 678–679
redirecting browsers, 682–683
reloading images at runtime, 666–667
self-modifying Web pages, 660–665
server-side scripts, 593
String class, 617–620
this keyword, 784
variables, 595–597
writing to status bar, 680–681
javascript: protocol, 686
join function, 1091–1092
JPEG image format, 214

K

<kbd>, 104–105
Keyboard shortcuts, 284
keyCode property, 627
KeyEvent, 1035
<keygen>, 767–769
KeyListener, 1034, 1045
keys function, 1099
Keywords for search engines, 44–45

L

label, 756, 757
<label>, 706–707, 763–764, 765, 844
Label class, 1010, 1038–1039
Labels, 1038–1039
lang, 17, 37
language, 48, 126, 589, 590–591
Languages, directionality of, 127
lastChild method, 918, 937, 941
lastSibling method, 918, 937, 941
<layer>, 193–196, 782, 835
Layers, Netscape Navigator
animation, 817–819
arranging text, 149–150, 193–196
dragging and dropping elements, 856–859
inline layers, 197–200
mouseover effects, 782, 812
non-layer-enabled browsers, 196–197
transitions, 835–836

layerX, **layerY** properties, 626
left, 194, 198
leftmargin, 48, 50
<legend>, 706–707, 762–763, 765
length property, 952
letter-spacing property, 545
Ley, Andreas, 215
<li>, 309, 584
li method, 1130–1131
Line art, 212
Line breaks
    arranging text, 141–143
    avoiding, 157–159
    inserting, 154–157
    paragraphs, 160–163
    word breaks, 159–160
line-height property, 545, 555
link, 48, 51, 276
<link>, 41, 281–283
    downloading fonts, 825–827
    external style sheets, 509, 522–523
link property, 562
Links. *See* Hyperlinks.
List class, 1010
List context, 1066
list-style-image property, 544, 563
list-style-position property, 544
list-style property, 543–544
list-style-type property, 544–545, 563, 564
Listener interfaces, 1033–1034
<listing>, 78
Lists
    applying styles, 563–565
    bulleted lists, 1130–1131
    bullets, 314–315
    creating, 310–312
    definition lists, 271–272, 319–323
    directory lists, 325
    drop-down list controls, 696, 754–761
    <li>, 309, 1130–1131
    list items, 309–310
    list properties, CSS, 543–545
    menu lists, 325–327
    nested lists, 323–324
    numbering systems, 316–319
    ordered lists, 270–271, 308, 312–314, 316–319
    overview, 269–270, 307
    Perl scripts. *See* Lists, Perl.
    scrolling lists, 1137–1138
    <ul>, 310, 1130–1131
    unordered lists, 269–270, 307, 310–312, 314–315
Lists, Perl
    assigning to other lists, 1090–1091
    defining, 1089–1090
    joining, 1091–1092
    list context, 1066
    overview, 1066
LiveImage, 269
load method, 917, 937
Loading images at runtime, 666–667
Loading XML documents, 917–918, 936–937, 956–958
location object
    methods, 655, 656
    navigating to new URLs, 681–683
    overview, 577, 641, 655
    properties, 655, 656
    redirecting browsers, 682–683
location.hostname, 579
location.reload, 715
Logic layer, XForms, 709
Logical operators, 599, 1101
Logical styles, 71, 72–76
longdesc
    <frame>, 428
    <iframe>, 449
    <img>, 226
loop, 177, 477
Loop statements
    Java, 1002–1003
    JavaScript, 605–611
    Perl, 1071, 1104–1107
Low-resolution images, 243
lowsrc, 226, 243
LView Pro, 215, 218–219
Lynx, 32

M

Macromedia Director, 462
Macromedia Freehand Graphics Studio, 215
MacWorld, 462
Mailto URL type, 266, 292–293
main method, 985
<map>, 295
Map files, 301–303
Mapedit, 269
margin-bottom property, 539
margin-left property, 539, 561
margin property, 539
margin-right property, 539, 561
margin-top property, 539, 561
marginheight
    <body>, 48
    <frame>, 428
    <iframe>, 449
marginwidth
    <body>, 48, 50–51

<frame>, 428
<iframe>, 449
<marquee>, 176–179, 498–499, 584
    data binding, 844
Marquees, 150, 176–179, 498–499
Masking typed input, 731–734
max-height property, 539
max-width property, 539
maxlength, 732, 746, 747
mayscript, 1022
mBED, 457
media, 281, 524
media behavior, 899
<**menu**>, 325–327
Menu class, 1010
Menu lists, 325–327
Message MIME types (list), 476
<**meta**>, 41, 43–46
Metadata, 43
method, 703, 709, 712
Methods
    creating using behaviors, 889–890, 895–897
    Java, 979, 985
    JavaScript, 578–579
methods, 274
Microsoft Internet Explorer, 33
Microsoft.XMLDOM object, 917
MIDI sound format, 460
MIME types, 471–477
min-height property, 539–540
min-width property, 540
Mixer control, 499
Model MIME types (list), 476
modifiers property, 626
Modifying Web pages at runtime, 660–665
Modules
    Perl, 1071–1072
    XHTML, 961–966, 967
Monospaced fonts
    program code, 101–102
    sample program output, 102–104
    "teletype" text, 85–87
    text to be typed by user, 104–105
Morphon XML Editor, 29
Mosaic, 33
Mosaics, 247–250
Mouse actions
    in applets, 1053–1055
    mouseover effects, 808–813
mouseClicked method, 1053
mouseDragged method, 1053
mouseEntered method, 1053
MouseEvent, 1035
mouseExited method, 1053
MouseListener, 1034, 1053

MouseMotionListener, 1034, 1053
mouseMoved method, 1053
mouseout event, 781
mouseover effects, 808–813
mouseover event, 781
mousePressed method, 1053
mouseReleased method, 1053
moveToElementText method, 800–801
Movie Cleaner Pro, 462
MPEG sound format, 459
MPEG video format, 460
MSHTML data source control, 859–866
<**multicol**>, 172–174
Multimedia
    3D multimedia, 461
    ActiveX controls, 457, 490–491
    audio formats, 458–460
    embedded audio, 465–467, 477–478, 482–483, 487–488
    embedded multimedia, 456–457, 480–481
    embedded video, 467–469, 486–487, 494–497
    external multimedia files, 463–465, 470–471
    MIME types, 471–477
    multimedia controls, 499–501
    multimedia creation software (list), 462–463
    non-embedding-enabled browsers, 481–482
    overview, 456–457
    plug-ins, 456–457, 480
    video formats, 460–461
Multipart MIME types (list), 476
multiple, 755, 759
Multiple columns, 150

N

name, 23
    <**a**>, 258, 259, 274
    <**applet**>, 1022
    <**button**>, 752
    <**form**>, 709
    <**frame**>, 419, 428
    <**img**>, 226
    <**input type="button"**>, 714
    <**input type="checkbox"**>, 717
    <**input type="file"**>, 721
    <**input type="hidden"**>, 726
    <**input type="image"**>, 729
    <**input type="password"**>, 732
    <**input type="radio"**>, 735, 736
    <**input type="reset"**>, 740
    <**input type="submit"**>, 742
    <**input type="text"**>, 746
    <**keygen**>, 768
    <**map**>, 295, 296

\<meta\>, 44
\<ruby\>, 202
\<select\>, 755
\<textarea\>, 749
NAME type, 932
Names
   element names, 666
   font names, 114
   JavaScript variable names, 597
   Perl variable names, 1084
Namespaces, 914–915, 968–969
Navigation bars, 286–288, 441–444
Navigational hyperlinks, 261–263, 285–286
Navigator, 33
navigator object, 577
navigator.appName property, 579, 658
navigator.appVersion property, 658
NCSA image-map processing, 302–304
NCSA Mosaic, 33
Nested lists, 323–324
Nesting tables, 378–379
Netscape Navigator, 33
   dynamic HTML, 774–775
   events, JavaScript, 587
   JavaScript implementation, 576
   layers. *See* Layers, Netscape Navigator.
   onmousedown, **onmouseup** events, 628–629
   plug ins, 456 457, 480
   predefined colors, 56
new operator
   Java, 1004
   JavaScript, 599, 616–617
   Perl, 1072, 1108
Newline character, 1081–1082
News URL type, 266
nextChild method, 918, 937, 941
\<**nextid**\>, 41
nextSibling method, 918, 937, 941
NMTOKEN type, 932
NMTOKENS type, 932
\<**nobr**\>, 157–159
nodeName property, 946, 952
nodeType property, 948–949
nodeValue property, 919, 937, 941, 949, 952
\<**noembed**\>, 481–482
\<**noframes**\>, 413, 436–437
nohref, 297
\<**nolayer**\>, 196–197
Non-embedding-enabled browsers, 481–482
Non-frame-enabled browsers, 412–414, 436–437
Non-Java-enabled browsers, 1025
Non-layer-enabled browsers, 196–197
Non-script-enabled browsers, 592
noresize, 428, 446
\<**noscript**\>, 41, 591–592

noshade, 163
Noteworthy Composer, 462
nowrap
   \<**body**\>, 48
   \<**td**\>, 364
   \<**th**\>, 361
Numbered lists, 308, 316–319

O

object, 1022
\<**object**\>, 484–485, 491–494, 585
   ActiveX controls, 490
   applets, 489
   data binding, 844, 859–860
   embedding applets, 1024
   image maps, 305
   images, 245–246, 488
   inline audio, 483, 487–488
   inline video, 486–487, 495–496
Object-oriented programming
   overview, 977–978
      classes, 978–980
      data members, 980
      inheritance, 980 981
      methods, 979
      objects, 978–979
Objects, Java, 978–979, 1004–1007
Objects, JavaScript. *See also* Names of specific objects.
   creating, 616–617
   methods, 578–579
   object hierarchy, Internet Explorer, 638–640
   object hierarchy, Netscape Navigator, 640–641
   overview, 577–578
   properties, 578–579
Objects, Perl, 1108
offsetX, **offsetY** properties, 627
\<**ol**\>, 312–313
onabort event, 580, 623
onafterupdate event, 844
onbeforeunload event, 844
onbeforeupdate event, 844
onblur event, 580, 623
onchange event, 580, 623
onclick event, 580, 623, 715, 718
onDataAvailable event, 860, 868, 873, 882
ondataavailable event, 956
onDatasetChanged event, 860, 868, 873, 882
onDatasetComplete event, 860, 868, 873, 882
ondblclick event, 580, 623
ondragdrop event, 580, 623
onerror event, 580, 623
onerrorupdate event, 844

onfocus event, 580, 623
onkeydown event, 580, 623
onkeypress event, 580, 623
onkeyup event, 580, 623
onload event, 580, 623
onmousedown event, 579, 581, 623, 628–629
onmousemove event, 581, 623
onmouseout event, 581, 623, 628–629
onmouseover event, 581, 623, 628–629
onmouseup event, 581, 623, 628–629
onmove event, 581, 623
onReadyStateChange event, 860, 868, 873, 882
onreadystatechange event, 956
onreset event, 581, 623
onresize event, 581, 623
onRowEnter event, 860, 868, 873, 882
onRowExit event, 860, 868, 873, 882
onselect event, 581, 623
onsubmit event, 581, 623, 743
onunload event, 581, 623
Opening Web pages, 32–33
Opera, 33
Operators
    Java, 999–1000
    JavaScript, 597–600
    Perl, 1068–1069, 1100–1105
<optgroup>, 757–758, 761
<option>, 756–760
Ordered lists
    creating, 312–314
    numbering systems, 316–319
    <ol>, 312–313
    overview, 270–271, 308
outerHTML method, 779
outerHTML property, 798, 800
outerText method, 779
outerText property, 797
Output, printing, 1077–1078
overflow property, 550
Overlapping images, 250–252

P

<p>, 59–60, 141–143, 160–163, 585
Packages, Java, 986, 990–992
padding-bottom property, 540
padding-left property, 540
padding property, 540
padding-right property, 540
Padding table cells, 334–336, 369
padding-top property, 540
page-break-after, 824
page-break-before, 824
Page breaks, 824–825

pagex, pagey, 194, 198
pageX, pageY properties, 627
paint method, 1012, 1019, 1020–1021, 1025
Paint program, Windows, 218–219
Paint Shop Pro, 215
PaintEvent, 1035
palette, 479
Palette reduction, 225
Panel class, 1010
par behavior, 899
Paragraphs, 59–60, 141–143, 160–163
<param>, 486, 490–491
    ActiveX controls, 490–491
    applet parameters, 1028
    data binding, 844, 867–868
param method, 1123, 1134–1135
Parameter entities, 924, 964, 967
Parameter pairs in URLs, 265
Parameters
    CGI scripts, 1113
    displaying in Web pages, 105–106
    passing to applets, 1028–1029
    passing to functions, 613–616
_parent, 436
Parsing XML documents
    displaying document structure, 946–948
    retrieving attribute values, 952–955
    retrieving element content, 948–951
Password control, 696, 731–734, 1140–1141
password_field method, 1140–1141
pasteHTML method, 779, 800–801
Path control, 499
PCDATA type, 574, 932
PCWorld, 462
Perl interpreter, 1074–1075, 1076
Perl script programming. *See also* CGI scripts.
    arrays, 1067, 1092–1095
    avoiding immediate script closings, 1082–1083
    CGI module. *See* CGI scripts.
    chomp function, 1081–1082
    chop function, 1081–1082
    commenting scripts, 1078–1079
    comparison operators, 1100–1101
    conditional statements, 1069–1070, 1102–1104
    creating scripts, 1064
    data types, 1065–1066, 1086
    default variable, 1080–1081
    die statement, 1108
    displaying output, 1077–1078
    each function, 1099
    equality operators, 1101–1102
    error messages, 1108
    file handles, 1077
    hashes, 1067–1068, 1095–1099
    header method, 1072

if statements, 1069–1070, 1102–1104
join function, 1091–1092
keys function, 1099
lists, 1066, 1089–1092
logical operators, 1101
loop statements, 1071, 1104–1107
modules, 1071–1072
new operator, 1072, 1108
newline character, 1081–1082
numeric formats, 1086
objects, 1072, 1108
online resources, 1062–1063
operators, 1068–1069, 1085–1086, 1100–1105
overview, 1061–1062
Perl interpreter, 1074–1075, 1076
print function, 1077–1078, 1090–1091
program files, 1073
reading user input, 1079, 1080–1083
running scripts, 1076
scalar context, 1066
scalar variables, 1065, 1084–1088
statements, 1074
stopping scripts, 1108
strings, 1087–1088
truth values, 1086
use statement, 1071
variable interpolation, 1088–1089
waiting for user input, 1082–1083
Permissions
   CGI scripts, 1111–1112
   Java applets, 1015
Personal AVI Editor, 462
PHOTO-PAINT, 215
Photoshop, 215
Physical styles, 71, 72
Plain text, 79–80, 153
<plaintext>, 78
play method, 832
Plug-ins, 456–457, 480, 1027–1028
pluginspage, 480
pluginurl, 480
point-size, 112, 115–116
Polygons, 298
Pop-up menus, 1141–1142
PopupMenu class, 1010
popup_menu method, 1141–1142
position property, 534, 566, 567–568, 813–815
Positioning/block properties, 533–535, 565–566, 567–568, 813–815
Positioning elements using styles, 813–815
posLeft property, 815
post method, 703–704, 712
posTop property, 815

<pre>, 151–152, 170–172, 585
Predefined colors, 54–56, 57–58
Predefined target names, 436
Predefined units, CSS properties, 520
Prefix dereferencers, Perl, 1065, 1067, 1084, 1085
Preformatted text, 150–152, 170–172
Presentation layer, XForms, 707
Previewing images, 243
previousChild method, 918, 937, 941
previousSibling method, 918, 937, 941
print function, 1077–1078, 1090–1091
Printing Web pages, 824–825
profile, 40, 41
Program code, 101–102
Program files, 983, 1073
prompt, 766
Prompt dialog boxes, 678–679
Properties, creating using behaviors, 889–890, 893–894
Properties, CSS
   background/color properties, 530–532
   element box properties, 535–541, 561–562, 565–567
   font properties, 541–543
   list properties, 543–545, 563–565
   overview, 505
   positioning/block properties, 533–535, 565–566, 567–568, 813–815
   predefined property units, 520
   shorthand properties, 518, 555–556
   style specification syntax, 518–521
   table properties, 548–559
   text properties, 545–548, 553–554, 561–562
   visual effects properties, 550
Properties, JavaScript, 578–579, 702
public keyword, 984
<public:component>, 849
<public:event>, 897–898
<public:method>, 895
<public:property>, 889, 893–894
put, 893

Q

<q>, 118–119
QuickTime video format, 461
Quotations
   block quotations, 168–170
   inline quotations, 118–119

R

Radio buttons
  applets, 1018, 1042–1044
  CGI scripts, 1139–1140
  XHTML forms, 696, 735–739
radio_group method, 1139–1140
Ragget, Dave, 24
Raster graphics, 212
<rb>, 204
<rbc>, 203
RDS data control, 879–887
Reading cookies, 689–692
Reading data from controls, 701, 1123, 1134–1135
readonly
  <input type="password">, 732
  <input type="text">, 746
  <textarea>, 749
readyState property, 956
RealAudio, 460, 462
RealVideo, 462–463
reason property, 627
Rectangles, 298
Redirecting browsers, 682–683
Referencing controls in forms, 702–703
rel, 274, 281, 282–283
Relational operators, 599, 1100–1101
Relationships between documents, 281–283
Relative hyperlinks, 280
Relative positioning, 567–568, 815
Relative URLs, 209, 264
Reload buttons, 715–716
Reloading images at runtime, 666–667
Removed tags, 78
Removing XHTML modules, 967
repaint method, 1019
Replacing text, 800
Required attributes, 932
Reset buttons, 696, 739–741, 753–754, 1143–1144
Reset method, 868
reset method, 1122, 1143–1144
Resizing frames, 446
Retrieving cookies, 689–692
returnValue property, 627
rev, 274, 281
RGB color values, 57–58, 217
right property, 533, 566, 567, 813
rightmargin, 48
Root element
  HTML documents, 37–39, 64
  specifying in DTDs, 912, 928
  XML documents, 909
Row groups, 388–396
row-span property, 549
rowIndex method, 805

Rows
  <frameset>, 414–415, 425, 426–427, 431–432
  <textarea>, 749, 750
Rows in tables, 342, 358–360, 380–381
rows method, 804
rowspan, 189–190, 342, 361, 364, 380–381
<rp>, 205
<rt>, 204–205, 206
<rtc>, 203–204
Rubies, 201–206
<ruby>, 202, 206
rules, 357, 394
Rules, CSS, 505
Running Java programs, 987–988

S

<s>, 89–91
<samp>, 102–104
Sample program output, 102–104
Saturation, 217
saveFavorite behavior, 899
saveHistory behavior, 899
saveSnapshot behavior, 899
Scalar context, 1066
Scalar variables, 1065, 1084–1088
Scaling images, 241–242
Scanning images, 219
<SCHEMA>, 914
Schemas, 914–916, 934–936
scheme, 44
scope
  <td>, 364
  <th>, 361
screenX, **screenY** properties, 627
<script>, 41, 573, 574, 589–591
Scripts
  CGI. *See* CGI scripts.
  enclosing in comments, 573
  external scripts, 574–575
  JavaScript. *See* JavaScript.
  Perl. *See* Perl.
  server-side scripts, 593
scroll, 48
Scroll bars, 444–445
scrollamount, 177
Scrollbar class, 1011
scrolldelay, 177
scrolling, 428, 444–445, 450, 452
Scrolling lists, 1137–1138
Scrolling marquees, 176–179, 498–499
scrolling_list method, 1137–1138
ScrollPane class, 1011
SDK, Java, 982

Search engines, keywords, 44–45
Secure transactions, processing, 768
<select>, 585, 754–756, 758–760, 844
Select controls, 696, 754–761, 1141–1142
selected, 757, 760
Selecting text, 800
Selection list controls, 696, 754–761
_self, 436
Self-Modifying Web pages, 660–665
Separating elements, 163–165, 1132
seq behavior, 899
Sequencer control, 499
<server>, 593
Server-side image maps, 266–267, 301–304, 305–307
Server Side Includes, 61–63
Server-side scripts, 593
setBackground method, 1019
setForeground method, 1019
shape, 274, 297, 298
shiftKey property, 627
shiftLeft property, 627
Shockwave, 457, 461
Shortcuts, CGI scripts, 1115
Shorthand properties, 518, 555–556
Simple statements, Perl, 1074
size
   <basefont>, 116
   <font>, 112
   <hr>, 163
   <input type="button">, 714
   <input type="checkbox">, 717
   <input type="file">, 721
   <input type="image">, 729
   <input type="radio">, 735
   <input type="text">, 746
   <select>, 755
   <spacer>, 174
Sizzler, 457
Sliding text. See Marquees.
<small>, 93–94
Small text, 93–94
SND sound format, 459
SoftQuad Software Inc., 29
Sound Forge, 463
<spacer>, 174–176
Spacers, 150
Spacing
   horizontal and vertical, 174–176
   between images, 234
   between table cells, 336–337, 369–370
span, 382, 383, 384
<span>, 182–184, 585
   applying styles, 148–149, 183–184, 551
   data binding, 844

Spanning columns, 340–341, 380
Spanning rows, 342, 380–381
Special characters, 128–138
SPG, 215
Sprite Buttons control, 500
Sprite control, 500
src
   <applet>, 1022
   <bgsound>, 477
   <embed>, 480
   <frame>, 410, 428
   <iframe>, 450
   <img>, 226, 228, 496–497
   <input type="image">, 729
   <layer>, 194
   <link>, 282
   <script>, 589
   <xml>, 939, 940
srcElement property, 627
srcFilter property, 628
Stacking images. See Layers, Netscape Navigator.
standalone, 35
Standalone attributes, 22
standby, 485
start, 313
start method, 1025
start_form method, 1121, 1133
start_html method, 1128
Statements, Perl, 1074
Status bars, 680–681
STDERR, 1077, 1110
STDIN, 1077, 1079, 1080–1081, 1110
STDOUT, 1077, 1110
stop method, 1025
Strict HTML 4 DTD, 9
Strict XHTML 1 DTD, 18, 408
<strike>, 89–91
Strikethrough text, 89–91
String class
   Java, 998–1000
   JavaScript, 617–620
String interpolation, 1088–1089
StringBuffer class, 999
Strings. See also Text.
   Java, 998–1000
   JavaScript, 617–620
   Perl, 1087–1088
<strong>, 99–100
Structured Graphics control, 490–491, 500
style
   <div>, 200–201
   dynamic styles, 775–776, 784–787
   inline styles, 512–513, 525–527

\<style\>, 41, 524–525
  embedded style sheets, 511
Style classes, 514–515, 527–529
Style sheets. *See also* Styles.
  applying dynamically, 787–790
  background/color properties, 530–532, 558–560
  boxes, 521
  cascading styles, 516–517
  CSS specifications, 505–506
  element box properties, 535–541, 561–562, 565–567
  embedded style sheets, 511–512, 524–525
  Extensible Stylesheet Language, 916
  external style sheets, 509–511, 522–524
  font properties, 541–543, 554–557
  formatting text, 70–71
  inline styles, 512–513, 525–527
  list properties, 543–545, 563–565
  organizing rules, 517–518
  overview, 504–508
  positioning/block properties, 533–535, 565–566, 567–568, 813–815
  predefined property units, 520
  properties. *See* Properties, CSS.
  resources, 506
  rules, 505, 517–518
  shorthand properties, 518, 555–556
  syntax, 518–521
  table properties, 548–559
  text properties, 545–548, 553–554, 561–562
  visual effects properties, 550
  in XML, 509–510, 523
Style specification syntax, 518–521
Style tags. *See also* Names of specific tags.
  logical styles, 71, 72–76
  physical styles, 71, 72
  text style tags, 69
Styles. *See also* Style sheets.
  applying to fonts, 554–557
  applying to hyperlinks, 562–563
  applying to lists, 563–565
  applying to text, 545–548, 553–554
  applying using **\<div\>**, 179–182, 552
  applying using **\<span\>**, 182–184, 551
  cascading styles, 516–517
  dynamic styles, 775–776, 784–787
  formatting text, 545–548, 561–562
  positioning elements, 533–535, 565–566, 567–568, 813–815
  predefined property units, 520
  setting backgrounds, 558–560
  setting colors, 558–560
  setting dynamically, 775–776
  specifying by element IDs, 529–530
  style classes, 514–515, 527–529
  style specification syntax, 518–521
  in XML documents, 509–510
\<sub\>, 94–96
Submit buttons
  CGI scripts, 1121, 1143–1144
  forms, 696, 728–731, 741–745, 753–754
submit method, 1122, 1143–1144
Submitting data from forms
  CGI scripts, 1121, 1143–1144
  Web pages, 703–706, 712, 743
Subscripts, 94–96
summary, 357
Sun HTML converter, 1027
\<sup\>, 96–98
Superscripts, 96–98
suppress, 228
switch statements, 604–605
Syntax, style specifications, 518–521
SYSTEM keyword, 913

T

tabindex
  \<a\>, 274
  \<applet\>, 1022
  \<area\>, 298
  \<body\>, 48
  \<button\>, 752
  \<fieldset\>, 762
  \<form\>, 709
  \<input type="button"\>, 714
  \<input type="checkbox"\>, 717
  \<input type="file"\>, 721
  \<input type="image"\>, 729
  \<input type="password"\>, 732
  \<input type="radio"\>, 736
  \<input type="reset"\>, 740
  \<input type="submit"\>, 742
  \<input type="text"\>, 746
  \<isindex\>, 766
  \<label\>, 764
  \<legend\>, 763
  \<object\>, 485
  \<option\>, 757
  \<select\>, 755
  \<textarea\>, 749
\<table\>, 184–189, 356–358, 586
  data binding, 844
  dynamic tables, 804, 805
table-layout property, 549
Tables
  aligning data, 338–340, 375–376
  aligning tables, 374–375

binding data to tables, 865–866, 871–872, 877–879, 885–887
borders, 334, 335, 367–368
captions, 365–367
cell padding, 334–336, 369
cell spacing, 336–337, 369–370
colors, 343–344, 372–374, 402–404
creating, 331–333, 356–358
data, 363–365
displaying images, 249–250, 377–378
dynamic tables, 804–806
formatting column groups, 382–383, 386–387
formatting text, 184–193, 396–404
grouping columns, 381–387
grouping rows, 388–396
headings, 360–362
nesting, 378–379
overview, 330–331
rows, 358–360
spanning columns, 340–341, 380
spanning rows, 342, 380–381
table properties, CSS, 548–559
tiling images, 249–250
width (columns), 370–372
width (tables), 370–372
Tabular Data Control, 867–872
Tag attributes, 6–7
Tags. *See also* Names of specific tags.
bound tags, 843–846
closing tags, 5, 21
creating at runtime, 1113, 1115
overview, 3–4, 21
removed tags, 78
tag attributes, 6–7, 21–22, 23–24, 702
Tango, 32
target
\<a\>, 274, 419, 435, 436, 438
\<area\>, 298, 436, 438
\<base\>, 279, 436, 438
\<form\>, 436, 438, 709
\<link\>, 282
Target frames. *See also* Frames.
named frames, 419–421, 434–435
opening in new windows, 422–424, 438–439
predefined target names, 436
target property, 627
\<tbody\>, 389
\<td\>, 332, 363–365, 586
TDC, 867–872
Techno2000, 28
"Teletype" text, 85–87
Term definitions, 106–107
Testing images in browsers, 224–225

Text. *See also* Fonts; Strings.
adding to Web pages, 58–59
aligning in table cells, 338–340, 375–376
aligning with images, 156–157, 235–239
alternate text, displaying, 229–231
applying styles, 553–557
character sets, 67–69
CSS properties, 545–548, 553–554, 561–562
drawing in applets, 1012
formatting. *See* Formatting text.
formatting in tables, 184–193, 396–404
formatting using style sheets, 70–71
formatting using styles, 545–548, 561–562
formatting using XHTML elements, 69
plain text, 79–80, 153
scrolling marquees, 498–499
selecting, 800
styles. *See* Text styles.
text areas, 696, 748–751, 1135–1136
text fields, 696, 745–748, 1133–1134
text ranges, 800–802
text, 48, 51
text-align property, 546, 553, 561
Text areas, 696, 748–751, 1135–1136
Text columns, 172–174
text-decoration property, 546, 553
Text fields
in applets, 1017, 1030–1032
in CGI scripts, 1133–1134
password control, 731–734, 1140–1141
XHTML forms, 696, 745–748
Text for user to type , 104–105
Text hyperlinks, 255–256
text-indent property, 546, 561
Text MIME types (list), 476
Text properties, CSS, 545–548, 553–554, 561–562
Text ranges, 800–802
text-shadow property, 547
Text style tags, 69
Text styles. *See also* Formatting text.
abbreviations, 109–110
acronyms, 110–111
addresses, 124–126
base fonts, 116–118
bidirectional text, 126–128
big text, 91–93
blinking text, 119–120
bold text, 83–84
citations, 108–109
deleted text, 122–124
emphasizing text, 98–100
fonts, specifying, 111–118
inserted text, 120–122
italic text, 84–85
point sizes, 115–116

program code, 101–102
program variables and arguments, 105–106
quotations, 118–119, 168–170
sample program output, 102–104
small text, 93–94
strikethrough text, 89–91
subscripts, 94–96
superscripts, 96–98
"teletype" text, 85–87
term definitions, 106–107
text to be typed by user, 104–105
tracking document changes, 120–124
underlined text, 87–89
<textarea>, 586, 696, 748–751, 844
TextArea class, 1011
textarea method, 1135–1136
TextEvent, 1035
TextField class, 1011, 1030–1032
textfield method, 1133–1134
TextListener, 1034
<tfoot>, 390
<th>, 332, 360–362
<thead>, 388
this keyword, 784
Tidy, 24–26
Tiling images, 247–250
time behavior, 899
time2 behavior, 899
title
   <a>, 274
   <acronym>, 114
   <body>, 49
   <style>, 524
<title>, 41, 42–43
toElement property, 628
Tool tips, 230
top, 194, 198
_top, 436
top property, 533, 566, 567, 813, 818
topmargin, 49
<tr>, 332, 358–360, 804–805
Tracking document changes, 120–124
Transition property, 832
Transitional HTML 4 DTD, 9
Transitional XHTML 1 DTD, 18, 408
Transitions
   Transition property, 831–835
   using layers, 835–836
Translating HMTL to XHTML, 24–26
Transparent GIF images, 220–221
truespeed, 177
Truth values, Perl, 1086
<tt>, 85–87
TUCOWS, 30
Tutorials, Java, 973

type
   <a>, 274
   <button>, 752, 753
   <embed>, 480
   <input>, 697–699
   <input type="button">, 714
   <input type="checkbox">, 717
   <input type="file">, 721
   <input type="hidden">, 726
   <input type="image">, 729
   <input type="radio">, 736
   <input type="reset">, 740
   <input type="submit">, 742
   <input type="text">, 746
   <li>, 309
   <link>, 282
   <object>, 485
   <ol>, 313, 316–317
   <param>, 486
   <script>, 589
   <spacer>, 174
   <style>, 524
   <ul>, 310, 314–315
type property, 627, 628
Typeof, 599
Types, Java variables, 993–995

U

<u>, 87–89
<ul>, 310
ul method, 1130–1131
Underlined text, 87–89
unicode-bidi property, 534–535
Uniform Resource Locators. *See* URLs.
Unisys, 213
units, 480
Unordered lists
   bullet types, 314–315
   creating, 310–312
   directory lists, 325
   menu lists, 325–327
   overview, 269–270, 307
   <ul>, 310
update method, 1025
Uploading applets, 1015–1017
Uploading files, 721–725
Uploading Web pages, 30–32
URLs , 29–30
   absolute URLs, 264
   base URLs, 279
   JavaScript URLs, 686–687
   location object, 655
   navigating using JavaScript, 681–685

parameter pairs, 265
relative URLs, 209, 264
types of URLs (list), 265–266
urn, 275
use statement, 1071
usemap, 226, 298, 485
userdata behavior, 899

V

Valid XML documents, 13
Validators
   HTML, 34
   XHTML, 33
valign
   <caption>, 366
   <col>, 383
   <colgroup>, 382
   <td>, 338, 364, 375–376
   <th>, 362, 375–376
   <thead>, 388
   <tr>, 359, 375–376
value
   <button>, 752
   <input type="button">, 714, 715
   <input type="checkbox">, 717
   <input type="hidden">, 726
   <input type="image">, 729
   <input type="password">, 732, 733
   <input type="radio">, 736
   <input type="reset">, 740
   <input type="submit">, 742
   <input type="text">, 746
   <li>, 309
   <option>, 757
   <param>, 486
valuetype, 486
var, 595
<var>, 105–106
Variable interpolation, 1088–1089
Variables
   displaying in Web pages, 105–106
   Java, 993–995
   JavaScript, 595–597
   Perl, 1065–1068
Vector graphics, 212
Vector Markup Language, 819–821
version, 35, 37
Version of browser, determining, 658
vertical-align property, 547
Vertical alignment
   table data, 338–339, 375–376
   text and images, 156–157, 236–237
Vertical spacing, 174–176

video behavior, 899
Video for Windows video format, 461
Video multimedia
   embedded video, 467–469, 486–487, 494–497
   MIME types (list), 476
   video formats, 460–461
Viewing Web pages, 32–33
Virtual Reality Modeling Language, 461
visibility, 194, 198
Visibility of elements, 821–824
visibility property, 550, 821, 832
visited property, 562
Visual effects
   animation, 223–224, 491–494, 815–819
   dynamic fonts, 825–827
   element visibility, 821–824
   filters, 827–830
   mouseover effects, 808–813
   positioning elements, 813–815
   properties, 550
   transitions, 831–836
   Vector Markup Language (VML), 819–821
Visual Markup, 29
vlink, 49, 51, 276
VML, 819–821
volume, 466, 477
VRML, 461
vspace
   <applet>, 1022
   <iframe>, 450
   <img>, 226, 234
   <marquee>, 177
   <object>, 485
   <table>, 357

W

Wagon Train Animated GIFs, 216
WAV sound format, 459
<wbr>, 159–160
Web HotSpots, 269
Web pages. *See also* HTML documents; XML documents.
   background color. *See* Background color.
   background images, 243–245
   body element, 47–53
   comments, 60–61
   creating, 27–29
   creating at runtime. *See* CGI scripts.
   default Web page, 32
   embedded audio, 465–467, 477–478, 482–483, 487–488
   embedded video, 467–469, 486–487, 494–497
   embedding applets, 1013, 1016

head element, 40–41
installing, 29, 30–32
modifying at run time. *See* Dynamic XHTML.
printing, 824–825
self-modifying Web pages, 660–665
structure, 39
text, adding, 58–59
uploading, 30–32
using Java plug-in, 1027
validating XHTML compliance, 33–34
viewing, 32–33
Weblint, 34
WebTechs Validation Service, 34
Well-formed XML documents, 14, 21
which, 627
While loops, 609–610, 1107
white-space property, 547
Width
    columns, 370–372
    tables, 370–372
width
    <applet>, 1022
    <col>, 383
    <colgroup>, 382
    <embed>, 480
    <hr>, 164
    <iframe>, 450
    <ilayer>, 198
    <img>, 226, 231–232, 241–242
    <layer>, 194
    <marquee>, 177
    <multicol>, 173
    <object>, 485
    <pre>, 171
    <spacer>, 174
    <table>, 357, 370–372
    <td>, 364, 370–372
    <th>, 362, 370–372
width property, 538, 627
Window class, 1011
window object, 577, 641, 649–654, 668–670
window.alert method, 578, 675–676
window.back method, 656
window.confirm method, 676–677
window.defaultStatus property, 680–681
window.document object. *See*
    Document object.
WindowEvent, 1035
window.event object, 627, 628–629
window.forward method, 656
window.go method, 656
window.history object. *See* **History** object.
WindowListener, 1034
window.location object. *See* **Location** object.
window.open method, 578, 667–671, 672–674

window.print method, 824–825
window.prompt method, 678–679
Windows
    opening using JavaScript, 667–671, 672–674
    window object, 577, 641, 649–654, 668–670
    writing to status bar, 680–681
Windows Paint program, 218–219
Word breaks, 159–160
word-spacing property, 548
wrap, 171, 749
Wrapping text
    around images, 156–157, 237–239, 239–241
    plain text, 153–154

X

x property, 627, 628
XForms, 707–708
XHTML. *See also* XML.
    browsers, 26–27
    calling CGI scripts, 1146–1148
    compared to HTML, 21–24
    converting from HTML, 24–26
    creating using CGI scripts, 1120
    defining attributes, 958–959
    defining XHTML elements, 922–925, 959–960, 966–967
    document profiles, 20
    DTDs, 18, 408
    editors, 28–29
    HTML exclusions, 23
    modules, 961–966, 967
    namespaces, 914–915, 968–969
    overview, 14–17
    style sheets, 509–510, 523
    true XHTML documents, 20
    validating, 33–34
    version 1, 18–19
    version 1.1. *See* XHTML 1.1.
XHTML 1.1
    adding elements, 966–967
    modules, 961–966, 967
    overview, 19–20
XHTML Basic, 20
XHTML frameset 1 DTD, 18, 408
XHTML strict 1 DTD, 18, 408
XHTML transitional 1 DTD, 18, 408
XMetal, 29
XML. *See also* XHTML; XML documents.
    data islands, 920–922, 939–943
    defining XHTML elements, 922–925, 959–960, 966–967
    defining XML elements, 912–913, 928–931
    DTDs. *See* DTDs.

<xml>

namespaces, 914–915, 968–969
online resources, 904
overview, 10, 13, 904–909
parameter entities, 924, 964, 967
parsing XML documents, 946–955
schemas, 914–916, 934–936
specifying attributes, 931–934
style sheets, 509–510, 523
support in Internet Explorer, 916–917
valid documents, 13, 909–911
well-formed documents, 14, 21, 909–911
in XHTML documents, 920–922

<xml>, 920–922, 939
<?xml?>, 15, 35–36, 67–68
XML data source control, 873–879
XML documents
creating, 904–907, 926–927
displaying document structure, 946–948
event handling, 956–958
loading, 917–918, 936–937, 956–958
parsing, 946–955
retrieving attribute values, 943–945
retrieving data, 919–922, 937–938, 939–945, 948–955
retrieving elements, 918, 937

XML DOM, 917
XML Spy, 28
<?xml-stylesheet?>, 510, 523
XMLDocument property, 921
xml:lang, 17, 37
xmlns, 17, 37, 914–915
xml:space, 524
XMLwriter, 28
<xmp>, 78
XOOM's Free Clip Art Library, 216
XSL, 916
XV Image Viewer, 215

Y

y property, 627, 628

Z

z-index, 194, 198
z-index property, 535
ZDNet, 463

Index of XHTML Tags

<!—>, 60
<!—[ ]>, 807
</head>, 46

A

<a>, 273
<abbr>, 109
<acronym>, 110
<address>, 124
<applet>, 1021
<area>, 296
<!ATTLIST>, 931

B

<b>, 83
<base>, 279
<basefont>, 116
<bdo>, 126
<bgsound>, 477
<big>, 91
<blink>, 119
<blockquote>, 168
<body>, 47

, 154
<button>, 751

C

<caption>, 365
<center>, 166
<cite>, 108
<code>, 101
<col>, 382
<colgroup>, 381

D

<datatype>, 935
<dd>, 321
<del>, 122
<dfn>, 106
<dir>, 325
<div>, 179
<dl>, 319
<!DOCTYPE>, 36
<dt>, 320

E

<em>, 98
<embed>, 479

F

<fieldset>, 761
<font>, 111
<form>, 709
<frame>, 427
<frameset>, 425

H

<h1>...<h6>, 80
<head>, 40
<hr>, 163
<html>, 37

I

<i>, 84
<iframe>, 449
<ilayer>, 197
<img>, 225

<input type="button">, 713
<input type="checkbox">, 716
<input type="file">, 721
<input type="hidden">, 725
<input type="image">, 728
<input type="password">, 731
<input type="radio">, 735
<input type="reset">, 739
<input type="submit">, 741
<input type="text">, 745
<ins>, 120
<isindex>, 766

K

<kbd>, 104
<keygen>, 767

L

<label>, 763
<layer>, 193
<legend>, 762
<li>, 309
<link>, 281

M

<map>, 295
<marquee>, 176
<menu>, 325
<meta>, 43
<multicol>, 172

N

<nobr>, 157
<noembed>, 481
<noframes>, 436
<nolayer>, 196
<noscript>, 591

O

<object>, 484
<ol>, 312
<optgroup>, 757
<option>, 756

P

<p>, 160
<param>, 486
<pre>, 170
<public:event>, 897
<public:method>, 895
<public:property>, 889

Q

<q>, 118

R

<rb>, 204
<rbc>, 203
<rp>, 205
<rt>, 204
<rtc>, 203
<ruby>, 202

S

<s>, 89
<samp>, 102
<script>, 589
<select>, 754
<server>, 593
<small>, 93
<spacer>, 174
<span>, 182
<strike>, 89
<strong>, 99
<sub>, 94
<sup>, 96

T

<table>, 356
<tbody>, 389
<td>, 363
<textarea>, 748
<tfoot>, 390
<th>, 360
<thead>, 388
<title>, 42
<tr>, 358
<tt>, 85

U

<u>, 87
<ul>, 310

V

<var>, 105

W

<wbr>, 159

X

<xml>, 939
<?xml?>, 35

What's on the CD-ROM

The *XHTML Black Book* companion CD-ROM contains elements specifically selected to enhance the usefulness of this book, including code for the book's projects as well as the following and much more:

PC Software:

- *Applet FX Freeware Edition*—A package of 20 high-quality Java effects.
- *AutoEye*—(Demo version.) AutoEye offers professional designers a new way to make their photographs look their best by reclaiming lost color an detail.
- *Coffee Cup HTML Editor++*—A full-featured HTML editor.
- *Edit Revolution*—Freeware HTML, Javascript, CSS, Perl, and text editor for Windows 95 and above.
- *Net Toob*—Easy to use and integrate software that works with multiple browsers. It plays *all* the digital video standards, as well as real-time MPEG-1 audio and video.
- *Page Submit*—Freeware software that guides you through the process of submitting your Web page to search engines.
- *Photo/Graphic Edges*—(Demo version.) Gives you incredible control over the edge effect to create unique feathered deckles, custom edges, and creative matte backgrounds.
- *Ulead Gif Animator Lite*—(Demo version.) The industry standard for GIF Animation.

Mac Software:

- *AutoEye*—(Demo version.) AutoEye offers professional designers a new way to make their photographs look their best by reclaiming lost color and detail.
- *HTML Gorm*—A powerful application for creating HTML forms.
- *HTML.edit*—An HTML editor for the Mac.
- *Net Toob*—Easy to use and integrate software that works with multiple browsers. It plays *all* the digital video standards, as well as real-time MPEG-1 audio and video.
- *Photo/Graphic Edges*—(Demo version.) Gives you incredible control over the edge effect to create unique feathered deckles, custom edges, and creative matte backgrounds.
- *Table Tool*—An application that makes the process of creating HTML tables easy.

System Requirements

Software

- Window 95/98/NT or Macintosh System 8 or higher
- Table Tool application for Macintosh requires HyperCard Player 2.1 or later

Hardware

- Intel (or equivalent) Pentium 100MHz processor is the minimum platform required; an Intel (or equivalent) Pentium 133MHz processor is recommended
- RAM: Windows 32MB required; Macintosh 32MB required
- CD-ROM drive